The Lost Tales

The Complete Oz

Volume 3

written by

Ruth Plumly Thompson & Jack Snow

Royal Historians of Oz

A Classics Compilation by

TRILOGUS BOOKS
www.trilogus.com

The Lost Tales
The Complete Oz:
Volume 3
written by Ruth Plumly Thompson and Jack Snow
Royal Historians of Oz

Copyright © 2008 by Trilogus Books

Published by Trilogus Books

ISBN-10:   1441404481
ISBN-13:   9781441404480

Trilogus Books Trade Publication / December 2008

Table of Contents

The Royal Book of Oz

by Ruth Plumly Thompson

Chapter 1 - Professor Wogglebug's Great Idea

"The very thing!" exclaimed Professor Wogglebug, bounding into the air and upsetting his gold inkwell. "The very next idea!"

"Who — me?" A round-faced little Munchkin boy stuck his head in the door and regarded Professor Wogglebug solemnly. He was working his way through the Professor's Athletic college, and one of his duties was to wait upon this eminent educator of Oz.

"Certainly not!" snapped Professor Wogglebug. "You're a nobody or a nothing. Stop gaping and fetch me my hat. I'm off to the Emerald City. And mind the pupils take their history pills regularly while I'm gone," he added, clapping his tall hat Zif held out to him on the back of his head.

"Yes, sir!" said the little Munchkin respectfully.

"Don't hurry back, sir!" This last remark the Professor did not hear, for he was already half way down the college steps.

"Ozma will be delighted with the idea. How clever I am!" he murmured, twirling his antennae and walking rapidly down the pleasant blue lane.

The Professor, whose College of Art and Athletic Perfection is in the southwestern part of the Munchkin country, is the biggest bug in Oz, or in anyplace else, for that matter. He has made education painless by substituting school pills for books. His students take Latin, history and spelling pills; they swallow knowledge of every kind with ease and pleasure and spend the rest of their time in sport. No wonder he is so well thought of in Oz! No wonder he thinks so well of himself!

Swinging his cane jauntily, the Professor hurried toward the yellow brick road that leads to the Emerald City, and by nightfall had reached the lovely capital of Oz.

Oz! — that marvelous country where no one grows old — where animals and birds talk as sensibly as people, and adventures happen every day. Indeed, of all fairylands in the world, Oz is the most delightful, and of all fairy cities, the Emerald City is the most beautiful. A soft green light shone for miles about, and the gemmed turrets and spires of the palace flashed more brightly than the stars. But its loveliness was familiar to Professor Wogglebug, and without a pause he proceeded to Ozma's palace and was at once admitted to the great hall.

A roar of merriment greeted his ears. Ozma, the lovely girl ruler of Oz, was having a party, and the room was full of most surprising people — surprising to some, that is, but old friends to most of us.

Jack, holding tightly to his pumpkin head, was running as fast as his wooden feet and wobbly legs would take him from Dorothy. A game of blind-man's-buff was in full swing, and Scraps and Tik-Tok, the Scarecrow and Nick Chopper, the Glass Cat and the Cowardly Lion, the Wizard of Oz and the wooden Sawhorse, Cap'n Bill and Betsy Bobbin, Billina and the Hungry Tiger were tumbling over each other in an effort to keep away from the blindfolded little girl.

But Dorothy was too quick for them. With a sudden whirl, she spun 'round and grasped a coatsleeve.

"The Scarecrow!" she laughed triumphantly. "I can tell by the way he skwoshes — and now he's it!"

"I'm always it!" chuckled the droll person. "But — hah! Behold the learned Professor standing so aloofly in our midst."

No one had noticed Professor Wogglebug, who had been quietly watching the game.

"I don't like to interrupt the party," he began, approaching Ozma's throne apologetically, "but I've just had a most brilliant idea!"

"What? Another?" murmured the Scarecrow, rolling up his eyes.

"Where did you lose it?" asked Jack Pumpkinhead, edging forward anxiously.

"Lose it! Who said I'd lost it?" snapped the Professor, glaring at poor Jack.

"Well, you said you'd had it, and had is the past tense, so —" Jack's voice trailed off uncertainly, and Ozma, seeing he was embarrassed, begged the Professor to explain.

"Your Highness!" began Professor Wogglebug, while the company settled down in a resigned circle on the floor, "As Oz is the most interesting and delightful country on the Continent of Imagination and its people the most unusual and talented, I am about to compile a Royal Book which will give the names and history of all our people. In other words, I am to be the Great, Grand Genealogist of Oz!"

"Whatever that is," the Scarecrow whispered in Dorothy's ear.

"And," the Professor frowned severely on the Scarecrow, "with your Majesty's permission, I shall start at once!"

"Please do," said the Scarecrow with a wave toward the door, "and we will go on with the party!"

Scraps, the Patchwork Girl, who had been staring fixedly at the Professor with her silver suspender-button eyes, now sprang to her feet:

"What is a genealogist? It's something no one here has missed; What puts such notions in your head? Turn out your toes — or go to bed!"

she shouted gaily, then, catching Ozma's disapproving glance, fell over backwards.

"I don't understand it at all," said Jack Pumpkinhead in a depressed voice. "I'm afraid my head's too ripe."

"Nor I," said Tik-Tok, the copper clockwork man. "Please wind me up a lit-tle tight-er Dor-o-thy, I want to think!"

Dorothy obligingly took a key suspended from a hook on his back and wound him up under his left arm. Everybody began to talk at once, and what with the Cowardly Lion's deep growl and Tik-Tok's squeaky voice and all the rest of the tin and meat and wooden voices, the confusion was terrible.

"Wait!" cried Ozma, clapping her hands.

Immediately the room grew so still that one could hear Tik-Tok's machinery whirring 'round.

"Now!" said Ozma, "One at a time, please, and let us hear from the Scarecrow first."

The Scarecrow rose. "I think, your Highness," he said modestly, "that anyone who has studied his Geozify already knows who we are and —"

"Who you are?" broke in the Wogglebug scornfully — "Of course they do — but I shall tell them who you were!"

"Who I were?" gasped the Scarecrow in a dazed voice, raising his cotton glove to his forehead. "Who I were? Well, who were I?"

"That's just the point," said Professor Wogglebug. "Who were you? Who were your ancestors? Where is your family? Where is your family tree? From what did you descend?"

At each question, the Scarecrow looked more embarrassed. He repeated the last one several times.

"From what did I descend? From what did I descend? Why, from a bean pole!" he cried.

This was perfectly true, for Dorothy, a little girl blown by a Kansas cyclone to the Kingdom of Oz, had discovered the Scarecrow in a farmer's cornfield and had lifted him down from his pole. Together they had made the journey to the Emerald City, where the Wizard of Oz had fitted him out with a fine set of brains. At one time, he had ruled Oz and was generally considered its cleverest citizen.

Before he could reply further, the Patchwork Girl, who was simply irrepressible, burst out:

"An ex-straw-ordinary man is he!

A bean pole for his family tree,

A Cornishman, upon my soul,

Descended from a tall, thin Pole!"

"Nonsense!" said Professor Wogglebug sharply, "Being stuffed with straw may make him extraordinary, but it is quite plain that the Scarecrow was nobody before he was himself. He has no ancestors, no family; only a bean pole for a family tree, and is therefore entitled to the merest mention in the Royal Book of Oz!"

"How about my brains?" asked the Scarecrow in a hurt voice. "Aren't they enough?"

"Brains have simply nothing to do with royalty!" Professor Wogglebug waved his fountain pen firmly. "Now —"

"But see here, wasn't I ruler of Oz?" put in the Scarecrow anxiously.

"A Ruler but never a royalty!" snapped out the Professor. "Now, if you will all answer my questions as I call your names, I'll get the necessary data and be off."

He took out a small memorandum book.

5

"Your Highness," he bowed to Ozma, "need not bother. I have already entered your name at the head of the list. Being descended as you are from a long line of fairies, your family tree is the oldest and most illustrious in Oz."

"Princess Dorothy!"

At the sound of her name, the little girl stood up.

"I know you are from Kansas and were created a Princess of Oz by our gracious Ruler, but can you tell me anything of your ancestors in America?" demanded the Professor, staring over the top of his thick glasses.

"You'll have to ask Uncle Henry and Aunt Em," said Dorothy rather sulkily. The Professor had hurt the feelings of her best friend, the Scarecrow, and ancestors did not interest her one little bit.

"Very well," said the Professor, writing industriously in his book. "I'll just enter you as 'Dorothy, Princess of Oz and sixth cousin to a President!' "

"I'm not!" Dorothy shook her head positively.

"Oh, everyone in America can claim that!" said the Professor easily.

"Nick Chopper!"

Now up rose our old friend the Tin Woodman, who had also been discovered by Dorothy on her first trip to the Fairyland of Oz.

"You were a man of meat at one time and a woodman by trade?" queried Professor Wogglebug, poising his pen in the air.

"I am a Tin Woodman, and you may enter me in your book under the name of Smith, for a tin Smith made me, and as Royal Emperor of the Winkies, I do not care to go back to my meat connections," said the Tin Woodman in a dignified voice.

The company applauded, and the Cowardly Lion thumped the floor with his tail.

"Smith is a very good name. I can work up a whole chapter on that," smiled the Professor. The Tin Woodman had once been a regular person, but a wicked witch enchanted his ax, and first it chopped off one leg, then the other, and next both arms and his head. After each accident, Nick went to a tinsmith for repairs, and finally was entirely made of tin. Nowhere but in Oz could such a thing happen. But no one can be killed in this marvelous country, and Nick, with his tin body, went gaily on living and was considered so distinguished that the Winkies had begged him to be their Emperor.

"Scraps!" called the Professor as Nick sat stiffly down beside Dorothy.

The Patchwork Girl pirouetted madly to the front. Putting one finger in her mouth, she sang:

"I'm made of patches, as you see.

A clothes tree is my family tree

But, pshaw! It's all the same to me!"

A clothes tree? Even Professor Wogglebug grinned. Who could help laughing at Scraps? Made of odd pieces of goods and brought to life by the powder of life, the comical girl was the jolliest person imaginable.

"Put me down as a man of me-tal!" drawled Tik-Tok the copper man as the laugh following Scraps' rhyme had subsided. Tik-Tok was still another of Dorothy's discoveries, and this marvelous machine man, guaranteed to last a thousand years, could think, walk, and talk when properly wound.

The Cowardly Lion was entered as a King in his own right. One after the other, the celebrities of Oz came forward to answer Professor Wogglebug's questions. The Professor wrote rapidly in his little book. Ozma listened attentively to each one, and they all seemed interested except the Scarecrow. Slumped down beside Dorothy, he stared morosely at the ceiling, his jolly face all wrinkled down on one side.

"If I only knew who I were!" he muttered over and over. "I must think!"

"Don't you mind." Dorothy patted his shoulder kindly. "Royalties are out of date, and I'll bet the Professor's family tree was a milkweed!"

But the Scarecrow refused to be comforted, and long after the company had retired he sat hunched sadly in his corner.

"I'll do it! I'll do it!" he exclaimed at last, rising unsteadily to his feet. Jellia Jamb, Ozma's little waiting maid, returning somewhat later to fetch a handkerchief her mistress had dropped, was surprised to see him running through the long hall.

"Why, where are you going?" asked Jellia.

"To find my family tree!" said the Scarecrow darkly, and drawing himself up to his full height, he fell through the doorway.

Chapter 2 - The Scarecrow's Family Tree

The moon shone brightly, but everyone in the Emerald City was fast asleep! Through the deserted streets hurried the Scarecrow. For the first time since his discovery by little Dorothy, he was really unhappy. Living as he did in a Fairyland, he had taken many things for granted and had rather prided himself on his unusual appearance. Indeed, not until Professor Wogglebug's rude remarks concerning his family had he given his past a thought.

"I am the only person in Oz without a family!" he reflected sorrowfully. "Even the Cowardly Lion has kingly parents and a palm tree! But I must keep thinking. My brains have never failed me yet. Who was I? Who were I? Who were I?"

Often he thought so hard that he forgot to look where he was going and ran headlong into fences, stumbled down gutters, and over stiles. But fortunately, the dear fellow could not hurt himself, and he would struggle up, pat his straw into shape, and walk straightway into something else. He made good time in between falls, however, and was soon well on his way down the yellow brick road that ran through the Munchkin Country. For he had determined to return to the Munchkin farm where Dorothy had first discovered him and try to find some traces of his family.

Now being stuffed with straw had many advantages, for requiring neither food nor sleep the Scarecrow could travel night and day without interruption. The stars winked out one by one, and by the time the cocks of the Munchkin farmers began to crow, he had come to the banks of a broad blue river!

The Scarecrow took off his hat and scratched his head thoughtfully. Crossing rivers is no easy matter in Oz, for there isn't a ferry in the Kingdom, and unless one is a good swimmer or equipped with some of the Wizard's magic it is mighty troublesome. Water does not agree with the Scarecrow at all, and as for swimming, he can no more swim than a bag of meal.

But he was too wise a person to give up merely because a thing appeared to be impossible. It was for just such emergencies that his excellent brains had been given to him.

"If Nick Chopper were here, he would build a raft in no time," murmured the Scarecrow, "but as he is not, I must think of another way!"

Turning his back on the river, which distracted his mind, he began to think with all his might. Before he could collect his thoughts, there was a tremendous crash, and next minute he was lying face down in the mud. Several little crashes followed, and a shower of water. Then a wet voice called out with a cheerful chuckle:

"Come on out, my dear Rattles. Not a bad place at all, and here's breakfast already waiting!"

"Breakfast!" The Scarecrow turned over cautiously. A huge and curious creature was slashing through the grass toward him. A smaller and still more curious one followed. Both were extremely damp and had evidently just come out of the river.

"Good morning!" quavered the Scarecrow, sitting up with a jerk and at the same time reaching for a stick that lay just behind him.

"I won't eat it if it talks — so there!" The smaller creature stopped and stared fixedly at the Scarecrow.

The Scarecrow, hearing this, tried to think of something else to say, but the appearance of the two was so amazing that, as he told Dorothy afterwards, he was struck dumb. The larger was at least two hundred feet long and made entirely of blocks of wood. On each block was a letter of the alphabet. The head was a huge square block with a serpent's face and long, curling, tape- measure tongue. The little one was very much smaller and seemed to consist of hundreds of rattles, wood, celluloid, and rubber, fastened together with wires. Every time it moved, the rattles tinkled. Its face, however, was not unpleasant, so the Scarecrow took heart and made a deep bow.

"And I'm not going to eat anything that squirms." This time it was the big serpent who spoke.

"Thank you!" said the Scarecrow, bowing several times more. "You relieve my mind. I've never been a breakfast yet, and I'd rather not begin. But if I cannot be your breakfast, let me be your friend!" He extended his arms impulsively.

There was something so jolly about the Scarecrow's smile that the two creatures became friendly at once, and moreover told him the story of their lives.

"As you have doubtless noted," began the larger creature, "I am an A-B-Sea Serpent. I am employed in the nursery of the Mer children to teach them their letters. My friend, here, is a Rattlesnake, and it is his business to amuse the Mer babies while the Mermaids are mer-marketing. Once a year, we take a vacation, and proceeding from the sea depths up a strange river, we came out upon this shore. Perhaps you, Sir, will be able to tell us where we are?"

"You are in the Munchkin Country of the Land of Oz," explained the Scarecrow politely. "It is a charming place for a vacation. I would show you about myself if I were not bound on an important mission." Here the Scarecrow sighed deeply.

"Have you a family?" he asked the A-B-Sea Serpent curiously.

"Yes, indeed," replied the monster, snapping its tape-measure tongue in and out, "I have five great-grandmothers, twenty-one grandnieces, seven brothers, and six sisters-in-law!"

"Ah!" murmured the Scarecrow, clasping his hands tragically, "How I envy you. I have no one — no aunts — no ancestors — no family — no family tree but a bean pole. I am, alas, a man without a past!" The Scarecrow looked so dejected that the Rattlesnake thought he was going to cry.

"Oh, cheer up!" it begged in a distressed voice. "Think of your presence — here — I give you permission to shake me!" The Scarecrow was so affected by this kind offer that he cheered up immediately.

"No past but a presence — I'll remember that!" He swelled out his straw chest complacently, and leaning over, stroked the Rattlesnake on the head.

"Are you good at riddles?" asked the Rattlesnake timidly.

"Well," answered the Scarecrow judiciously, "I have very good brains, given me by the famous Wizard of Oz."

"Then why is the A-B-Sea Serpent like a city?" asked the Rattlesnake promptly.

The Scarecrow thought hard for several seconds.

"Because it is made up of blocks!" he roared triumphantly. "That's easy; now it's my turn. Why is the A-B-Sea Serpent such a slow talker?"

"Give it up!" said the Rattlesnake after shaking himself several times.

"Because his tongue is a tape measure, and he has to measure his words!" cried the Scarecrow, snapping his clumsy fingers. "And that's a good one, if I did make it myself. I must remember to tell it to Dorothy!"

Then he sobered quite suddenly, for the thought of Dorothy brought back the purpose of his journey. Interrupting the Rattlesnake in the midst of a new riddle, he explained how anxious he was to return to the little farm where he had been discovered and try to find some traces of his family.

"And the real riddle," he sighed with a wave of his hand, "is how to cross this river."

"That's easy and no riddle at all," rumbled the A-B-Sea Serpent, who had been listening attentively to the Scarecrow's remarks. "I'll stretch across, and you can walk over." Suiting the action to the word, he began backing very cautiously toward the river so as not to shake the Scarecrow off his feet.

"Mind your P's and Q's!" called the Rattlesnake warn-ingly. It was well that he spoke, for the A-B-Sea Serpent had doubled the P and Q blocks under, and they were ready to snap off. Finally, however, he managed to make a bridge of himself, and the Scarecrow stepped easily over the blocks, the huge serpent holding himself rigid. Just as he reached Y, the unfortunate creature sneezed, and all the blocks rattled together. Up flew the Scarecrow and escaped falling into the stream only by the narrowest margin.

"Blockhead!" shrilled the Rattlesnake, who had taken a great fancy to the Scarecrow.

"I'm all right," cried the Scarecrow rather breathlessly. "Thank you very much!" He sprang nimbly up the bank. "Hope you have a pleasant vacation!"

"Can't, with a rattlepate like that." The A-B-Sea Serpent nodded glumly in the Rattlesnake's direction.

"Now don't quarrel," begged the Scarecrow. "You are both charming and unusual, and if you follow that Yellow Road, you will come to the Emerald City, and Ozma will be delighted to welcome you."

"The Emerald City! We must see that, my dear Rattles." Forgetting his momentary displeasure, the A-B-Sea Serpent pulled himself out of the river, and waving his X Y Z blocks in farewell to the Scarecrow, went clattering down the road, the little Rattlesnake rattling along behind him.

As for the Scarecrow, he continued his journey, and the day was so delightful and the country so pleasant that he almost forgot he had no family. He was treated everywhere with the greatest courtesy and had innumerable invitations from the hospitable Munchkins. He was anxious to reach his destination, however, so he refused them all, and traveling night and day came without further mishap or adventure late on the second evening to the little Munchkin farm where Dorothy had first discovered him. He was curious to know whether the pole on which he had been hoisted to scare away the crows still stood in the cornfield and whether the farmer who had made him could tell him anything further about his history.

"It is a shame to waken him," thought the kind Scarecrow. "I'll just take a look in the cornfield." The moon shone so brightly that he had no trouble finding his way about. With a little cry of pleasure, he pushed his way through the dry cornstalks. There in the center of the field stood a tall pole — the very identical bean pole from which he had descended.

"All the family or family tree I've got!" cried the Scarecrow, running toward it with emotion.

"What's that?" A window in the farmhouse was thrown up, and a sleepy Munchkin thrust out his head. "What are you doing?" he called crossly.

"Thinking!" said the Scarecrow, leaning heavily against the bean pole.

"Well, don't do it out loud," snapped the farmer. Then, catching a better view of the Scarecrow, he cried in surprise: "Why, it's you! — Come right in, my dear fellow, and give us the latest news from the Emerald City. I'll fetch a candle!"

The farmer was very proud of the Scarecrow. He had made him long ago by stuffing one of his old suits with straw, painting a jolly face on a sack, stuffing that, and fastening the two together. Red boots, a hat, and yellow gloves had finished his man — and nothing could have been jollier than the result. Later on, when the Scarecrow had run off with Dorothy and got his brains from the Wizard of Oz and become ruler of the Emerald City, the little farmer had felt highly gratified.

The Scarecrow, however, was not in a humor for conversation. He wanted to think in peace. "Don't bother!" he called up. "I'm going to spend the night here. I'll see you in the morning."

"All right! Take care of yourself," yawned the farmer, and drew in his head.

For a long time the Scarecrow stood perfectly still beside the bean pole — thinking. Then he got a spade from the shed and began clearing away the cornstalks and dried leaves from around the base of the pole. It was slow work, for his fingers were clumsy, but he persevered. Then a wonderful idea came to him.

"Perhaps if I dig down a bit, I may discover —" He got no further, for at the word "discover," he pushed the spade down with all his might. There was a loud crash. The bottom dropped out of things, and the Scarecrow fell through.

"Gr-eat cornstalks!" cried the Scarecrow, throwing up his arms. To his surprise, they came in contact with a stout pole, which he embraced. It was a lifesaver, for he was shooting down into the darkness at a great rate.

"Why!" he gasped as soon as he regained his breath, for he was falling at a terrific rate of speed, "Why, I believe I'm sliding down the bean pole!"

Chapter 3 - Down the Magic Bean Pole

Hugging the bean pole for dear life, the Scarecrow slid rapidly downward. Everything was dark, but at times a confused roaring sounded in his ears.

"Father, I hear something falling past!" shouted a gruff voice all at once.

"Then reach out and pull it in," growled a still deeper voice. There was a flash of light, a door opened suddenly, and a giant hand snatched the air just above the Scarecrow's head.

"It's a good thing I haven't a heart to fail me," murmured the Scarecrow, glancing up fearfully and clinging more tightly to the pole. "Though I fall, I shall not falter. But where under the earth am I falling to?" At that minute, a door opened far below, and someone called up:

"Who are you? Have out your toll and be ready to salute the Royal Ruler of the Middlings!"

The Scarecrow had learned in the course of his many and strange adventures that it was best to accede to every request that was reasonable or possible. Realizing that unless he answered at once he would fall past his strange questioners, he shouted amiably:

"I am the Scarecrow of Oz, sliding down my family tree!" The words echoed oddly in the narrow passageway, and by the time he reached the word "tree" the Scarecrow could make out two large brown men leaning from a door somewhere below. Next minute he came to a sharp stop. A board had shot out and closed off the passageway. So sudden was the stop that the Scarecrow was tossed violently upward. While he endeavored to regain his balance, the two Middlings eyed him curiously.

"So this is the kind of thing they grow on top," said one, holding a lantern close to the Scarecrow's head.

"Toll, Toll!" droned the other, holding out a horribly twisted hand.

"One moment, your Royal Middleness!" cried the Scarecrow, backing as far away from the lantern as he could, for with a straw stuffing one cannot be too careful of fire. He felt in his pocket for an emerald he had picked up in the Emerald City a few days before and handed it gingerly to the Muddy monarch.

"Why do you call me Middleness?" the King demanded angrily, taking the emerald.

"Is your kingdom not in the middle of the earth, and are you not royalty? What could be more proper than Royal Middleness?" asked the Scarecrow, flecking the dust from his hat.

Now that he had a better view, he saw that the two were entirely men of mud, and very roughly put together. Dried grass hair stood erect upon each head, and their faces were large and lumpy and had a disconcerting way of changing shape. Indeed, when the King leaned over to examine the Scarecrow, his features were so soft they seemed to run into his cheek, which hung down alarmingly, while his nose turned sideways and lengthened at least an inch!

Muddle pushed the King's nose back and began spreading his cheek into place. Instead of hands and feet, the Middlings had gnarled and twisted roots which curled up in a perfectly terrifying manner. Their teeth were gold, and their eyes shone like small electric lights. They wore stiff coats of dried mud, buttoned clumsily with lumps of coal, and the King had a tall mud crown. Altogether, the Scarecrow thought he had never seen more disagreeable looking creatures.

"What he needs," spluttered the King, fingering the jewel greedily, "is a coat of mud! Shall we pull him in, Muddle?"

"He's very poorly made, your Mudjesty. Can you work, Carescrow?" asked Muddle, thumping him rudely in the chest.

"Scarecrow, if you please!" The Scarecrow drew himself up and spoke with great difficulty. "I can work with my head!" he added proudly.

"Your head!" roared the King. "Did you hear that, Muddle? He works with his head. What's the matter with your hands?" Again the King lunged forward, and this time his face fell on the other side and had bulged enormously before Muddle could pat it into shape. They began whispering excitedly together, but the Scarecrow made no reply, for looking over their shoulder he glimpsed a dark, forbidding cavern lighted only by the flashing red eyes of thousands of Middlings. They appeared to be digging, and above the rattle of the shovels and picks came the hoarse voice of one of them singing the Middling National Air. Or so the Scarecrow gathered from the words:

"Oh, chop the brown clods as they fall with a thud!
Three croaks for the Middlings, who stick in the Mud.
Oh, mud, rich and wormy! Oh, mud, sweet and squirmy!
Oh what is so lovely as Mud! Oh what is so lovely as Mud!
Three croaks for the Middlings, who delve all the day
In their beautiful Kingdom of soft mud and clay!"

The croaks that came at the end of the song were so terrifying that the Scarecrow shivered in spite of himself.

"Ugh! Hardly a place for a pleasant visit!" he gasped, flattening himself against the wall of the passage. Feeling that matters had gone far enough, he repeated in a loud voice:

"I am the Scarecrow of Oz and desire to continue my fall. I have paid my toll and unless your Royal Middleness release me —"

"Might as well drop him — a useless creature!" whispered Muddle, and before the King had time to object, he jerked the board back. "Fall on!" he screeched maliciously, and the Scarecrow shot down into the darkness, the hoarse screams of the two Middlings echoing after him through the gloom.

No use trying to think! The poor Scarecrow bumped and banged from side to side of the passage. It was all he could do to keep hold of the bean pole, so swiftly was he falling.

"A good thing I'm not made of meat like little Dorothy," he wheezed breathlessly. His gloves were getting worn through from friction with the pole, and the rush of air past his ears was so confusing that he gave up all idea of thinking. Even magic brains refuse to work under such conditions. Down — down — down he plunged till he lost all count of time. Down — down - down — hours and hours! Would he never stop? Then suddenly it grew quite light, and he flashed through what appeared to be a hole in the roof of a huge silver palace, whirled down several stories and landed in a heap on the floor of a great hall. In one hand he clutched a small fan, and in the other a parasol that had snapped off the beanstalk just before he reached the palace roof.

Shaken and bent over double though he was, the Scarecrow could see that he had fallen into a company of great magnificence. He had a confused glimpse of silken clad courtiers, embroidered screens, inlaid floors, and flashing silver lanterns, when there was a thundering bang that hurled him halfway to the roof again. Falling to a sitting position and still clinging to the bean pole, he saw two giant kettle drums nearby, still vibrating from the terrible blows they had received.

The company were staring at him solemnly, and as he attempted to rise, they fell prostrate on their faces. Up flew the poor flimsy Scarecrow again, such was the draught, and this time landed on his face. He was beginning to feel terribly annoyed, but before he could open his mouth or stand up, a deep voice boomed:

"He has come!"

"He has come!" shrilled the rest of the company, thumping their heads on the stone floor. The language seemed strange to the Scarecrow, but oddly enough, he could understand it perfectly. Keeping a tight grasp on the bean pole, he gazed at the prostrate assemblage, too astonished to speak. They looked exactly like the pictures of some Chinamen he had seen in one of Dorothy's picture books back in Oz, but instead of being yellow, their skin was a curious gray, and the hair of old and young alike was silver and worn in long, stiff queues. Before he had time to observe any more, an old, old courtier hobbled forward and beckoned imperiously to a page at the door. The page immediately unfurled a huge silk umbrella and, running forward, held it over the Scarecrow's head.

"Welcome home, sublime and noble Ancestor! Welcome, honorable and exalted Sir." The old gentleman made several deep salaams.

"Welcome, immortal and illustrious Ancestor! Welcome, ancient and serene Father!" cried the others, banging their heads hard on the floor — so hard that their queues flew into the air.

"Ancestor! Father!" mumbled the Scarecrow in a puzzled voice. Then, collecting himself somewhat, he made a deep bow, and sweeping off his hat with a truly royal gesture began: "I am indeed honored —" But he got no farther. The silken clad courtiers sprang to their feet in a frenzy of joy. A dozen seized him bodily and carried him to a great silver throne room.

"The same beautiful voice!" cried the ancient gentleman, clasping his hands in an ecstasy of feeling.

"It is he! The Emperor! The Emperor has returned! Long live the Emperor!" shouted everyone at once. The confusion grew worse and worse.

"Ancestor! Father! Emperor!" The Scarecrow could scarcely believe his ears. "For a fallen man, I am rising like yeast!" he murmured to himself. Half a dozen courtiers had run outdoors to spread the wonderful news, and soon silver gongs and bells began ringing all over the kingdom, and cries of "The Emperor! The Emperor!" added to the general excitement. Holding fast to the sides of the throne and still grasping the little fan and parasol, the Scarecrow sat blinking with embarrassment.

"If they would just stop emperoring, I could ask them who I am," thought the poor Scarecrow. As if in answer to his thoughts, the tottery old nobleman raised his long arm, and at once the hall became absolutely silent.

"Now!" sighed the Scarecrow, leaning forward. "Now I shall hear something of interest."

Chapter 4 - Dorothy's Lonely Breakfast

Dorothy, who occupied one of the coziest apartments in Ozma's palace, wakened the morning after the party with a feeling of great uneasiness. At breakfast, the Scarecrow was missing. Although he, the Tin Woodman and Scraps did not require food, they always livened up the table with their conversation. Ordinarily Dorothy would have thought nothing of the Scarecrow's absence, but she could not forget his distressed expression when Professor Wogglebug had so rudely remarked on his family tree. The Professor himself had left before breakfast, and everybody but Dorothy had forgotten all about the Royal Book of Oz.

Already many of Ozma's guests who did not live in the palace were preparing to depart, but Dorothy could not get over her feeling of uneasiness. The Scarecrow was her very best friend, and it was not like him to go without saying goodbye. So she hunted through the gardens and in every room of the palace and questioned all the servants. Unfortunately, Jellia Jamb, who was the only one who had seen the Scarecrow go, was with her mistress. Ozma always breakfasted alone and spent the morning over state matters. Knowing how busy she was, Dorothy did not like to disturb her. Betsy Bobbin and Trot, real little girls like Dorothy, also lived in the Fairy palace, and Ozma was a great chum for them. But the Kingdom of Oz had to be governed in between times, and they all knew that unless Ozma had the mornings to herself, she could not play with them in the afternoons. So Dorothy searched by herself.

"Perhaps I didn't look hard enough," thought the little girl, and searched the palace all over again.

"Don't worry," advised the Tin Woodman, who was playing checkers with Scraps. "He's probably gone home."

"He is a man of brains; why worry Because he's left us in a hurry?"

chuckled Scraps with a careless wave of her hand, and Dorothy, laughing in spite of herself, ran out to have another look in the garden.

"That is just what he has done, and if I hurry, I may overtake him. Anyway, I believe I'll go and pay him a visit," thought Dorothy.

Trot and Betsy Bobbin were swinging in one of the royal hammocks, and when Dorothy invited them to go along, they explained that they were going on a picnic with the Tin Woodman. So without waiting to ask anyone else or even whistling for Toto, her little dog, Dorothy skipped out of the garden.

The Cowardly Lion, half asleep under a rose bush, caught a glimpse of her blue dress flashing by, and bounding to his feet thudded after her.

"Where are you going?" he asked, stifling a giant yawn.

"To visit the Scarecrow," explained Dorothy. "He looked so unhappy last night. I am afraid he is worrying about his family tree, and I thought p'raps I could cheer him up."

The Cowardly Lion stretched luxuriously. "I'll go too," he rumbled, giving himself a shake. "But it's the first time I ever heard of the Scarecrow worrying."

"But you see," Dorothy said gently, "Professor Wogglebug told him he had no family."

"Family! Family fiddlesticks! Hasn't he got us?" The Cowardly Lion stopped and waved his tail indignantly.

"Why, you dear old thing!" Dorothy threw her arms around his neck. "You've given me a lovely idea!" The Cowardly Lion tried not to look pleased.

"Well, as long as I've given it to you, you might tell me what it is," he suggested mildly.

"Why," said Dorothy, skipping along happily, "we'll let him adopt us and be his really relations. I'll be his sister, and you'll be —"

"His cousin — that is, if you think he wouldn't mind having a great coward like me for a cousin," finished the Cowardly Lion in an anxious voice.

"Do you still feel as cowardly as ever?" asked Dorothy sympathetically.

"More so!" sighed the great beast, glancing appre-hensively over his shoulder. This made Dorothy laugh, for although the lion trembled like a cup custard at the approach of danger, he always managed to fight with great valor, and the little girl felt safer with him than with the whole army of Oz, who never were frightened but who always ran away.

Now anyone who is at all familiar with his geozify knows that the Fairyland of Oz is divided into four parts, exactly like a parchesi board, with the Emerald City in the very center, the purple Gillikin Country to the north, the red Quadling Country to the south, the blue Munchkin Country to the east, and the yellow Country of the Winkies to the west. It was toward the west that Dorothy and the Cowardly Lion turned their steps, for it was in the Winkie Country that the Scarecrow had built his gorgeous golden tower in exactly the shape of a huge ear of corn.

Dorothy ran along beside the Cowardly Lion, chatting over their many adventures in Oz, and stopping now and then to pick buttercups and daisies that dotted the roadside. She tied a big bunch to the tip of her friend's tail and twined some more in his mane, so that he presented a very festive appearance indeed. Then, when she grew tired, she climbed on his big back, and swiftly they jogged through the pleasant land of the Winkies. The people waved to them from windows and fields, for everyone loved little Dorothy and the big lion, and as they passed a neat yellow cottage, a little Winkie Lady came running down the path with a cup of tea in one hand and a bucket in the other.

"I saw you coming and thought you might be thirsty," she called hospitably. Dorothy drank her cup without alighting.

"We're in an awful hurry; we're visiting the Scarecrow," she exclaimed apologetically. The lion drank his bucket of tea at one gulp. It was so hot that it made his eyes water.

"How I loathe tea! If I hadn't been such a coward, I'd have upset the bucket," groaned the lion as the little Winkie Lady went back into her house. "But no, I was afraid of hurting her feelings. Ugh, what a terrible thing it is to be a coward!"

"Nonsense!" said Dorothy, wiping her eyes with her handkerchief. "You're not a coward, you're just polite. But let's run very fast so we can reach the Scarecrow's in time for lunch."

So like the wind away raced the Cowardly Lion, Dorothy holding fast to his mane, with her curls blowing straight out behind, and in exactly two Oz hours and seventeen Winkie minutes they came to the dazzling corn-ear residence of their old friend. Hurrying through the cornfields that surrounded his singular mansion, Dorothy and the Cowardly Lion rushed through the open door.

"We've come for lunch," announced Dorothy.

"And I'm hungry enough to eat crow," rumbled the lion. Then both stopped in dismay, for the big reception room was empty. From a room above came a shuffling of feet, and Blink, the Scarecrow's gentlemanly housekeeper, came running down the stairs.

"Where's the Scarecrow?" asked Dorothy anxiously. "Isn't he here?"

"Here! Isn't he there? Isn't he in the Emerald City?" gasped the little Winkie, putting his specs on upside down.

"No — at least, I don't think so. Oh, dear, I just felt that something had happened to him!" wailed Dorothy, sinking into an ebony armchair and fanning herself with a silk sofa cushion.

"Now don't be alarmed." The Cowardly Lion rushed to Dorothy's side and knocked three vases and a clock off a little table, just to show how calm he was. "Think of his brains! The Scarecrow has never come to harm yet, and all we have to do is to return to the Emerald City and look in Ozma's Magic Picture. Then, when we know where he is, we can go and find him and tell him about our little adoption plan," he added, looking hopefully at Dorothy.

"The Scarecrow himself couldn't have spoken more sensi-bly," observed Blink with a great sigh of relief, and even Dorothy felt better.

In Ozma's palace, as many of you know, there is a Magic Picture, and when Ozma or Dorothy want to see any of their friends, they have merely to wish to see them, and instantly the picture shows the person wished for and exactly what he is doing at that certain time.

"Of course!" sighed Dorothy. "Why didn't I think of it myself?"

"Better have some lunch before you start back," suggested Blink, and bustling about had soon set out an appetizing repast. Dorothy was too busy worrying about the Scarecrow to have much appetite, but the Cowardly Lion swallowed seventeen roasts and a bucket of corn syrup.

"To give me courage!" he explained to Dorothy, licking his chops. "There's nothing that makes me so cowardly as an empty stomach!"

It was quite late in the afternoon before they could get away. Blink insisted on putting up a lunch, and it took some time to make enough sandwiches for the Cowardly Lion. But at last it was ready and packed into an old hat box belonging to Mops, the Scarecrow's cook. Then Dorothy, balancing the box carefully on her lap, climbed on the Cowardly Lion's back, and assuring Blink that they would return in a few days with his master, they bade him farewell. Blink almost spoiled things by bursting into tears, but he managed to restrain himself long enough to say goodbye, and Dorothy and the Cowardly Lion, feeling a little solemn themselves, started toward the Emerald City.

"My, but it's growing dark," said Dorothy after they had gone several miles. "I believe it's going to storm."

Scarcely had she finished speaking before there was a terrific crash of thunder. The Cowardly Lion promptly sat down. Off of his back bounced the sandwich box and into the sandwich box rolled Dorothy, head first.

"How terribly upsetting," coughed the Cowardly Lion.

"I should say it was!" Dorothy crawled indignantly out of the hat box and began wiping the butter from her nose. "You've simply ruined the supper!"

"It was my heart," explained the Cowardly Lion sorrowfully. "It jumped so hard that it upset me, but climb on my back again, and I'll run very fast to some place of shelter."

"But where are you?" Dorothy asked in real alarm, for it had grown absolutely dark.

"Here," quavered the Cowardly Lion, and guided by his voice, Dorothy stumbled over to him and climbed again on his back. One crash of thunder followed another, and at each crash the Cowardly Lion leapt forward a bit faster until they fairly flew through the dark.

"It won't take us long to reach the Emerald City at this rate!" called Dorothy, but the wind tossed the words far behind her, and seeing that conversation was impossible, she clung fast to the lion's mane and began thinking about the Scarecrow. The thunder continued at frequent intervals, but there was no rain, and after they had been running for what seemed to Dorothy hours and hours, a sudden terrific bump sent her flying over the lion's head into a bush. Too breathless to speak, she felt herself carefully all over. Then, finding that she was still in one piece, she called to the Cowardly Lion. She could hear him moaning and muttering about his heart.

"Any bones broken?" she asked anxiously.

"Only my head," groaned the lion dismally. Just then the darkness lifted as suddenly as it had fallen, and Dorothy saw him leaning against a tree with his eyes closed. There was a big bump on his head. With a little cry of sympathy, Dorothy hurried toward him, when all at once something strange about their surroundings struck her.

"Why, where are we?" cried the little girl, stopping short. The lion's eyes flew open, and forgetting all about his bump, he looked around in dismay. No sign of the Emerald City anywhere. Indeed, they were in a great, dim forest, and considering the number of trees, it is a wonder that they had not run into one long ago.

"I must have run the wrong way," faltered the Cowardly Lion in a distressed voice.

"You couldn't help that; anyone would lose his way in the dark," said Dorothy generously. "But I wish we hadn't fallen in the sandwiches. I'm hungry!"

"So am I. Do you think anyone lives in this forest, Dorothy?"

Dorothy did not answer, for just then she caught sight of a big sign nailed to one of the trees.

"Turn to the right," directed the sign.

"Oh, come on!" cried Dorothy, cheering up immediately. "I believe we're going to have another adventure."

"I'd rather have some supper," sighed the Cowardly Lion wistfully, "but unless we want to spend the night here, we might as well move along. I'm to be fed up on adventure, I suppose."

"Turn to the left," advised the next sign, and the two turned obediently and hurried on, trying to keep a straight course through the trees. In a Fairyland like Oz, where there are no trains or trolleys or even horses for traveling ('cepting Ozma's sawhorse), there are bound to be unexplored portions. And though Dorothy had been at one time or another in almost every part of Oz, the country through which they were now passing was totally unfamiliar to her. Night was coming on, and it was growing so dark that she could hardly read the third sign when they presently came upon it.

"Don't sing," directed the sign sternly.

13

"Sing!" snapped Dorothy indignantly, "Who wants to sing?"

"We might as well keep to the left," said the Cowardly Lion in a resigned voice, and they walked along for some time in silence. The trees were thinning out, and as they came to the edge of the forest, another sign confronted them.

"Slow down," read Dorothy with great difficulty. "What nonsense! If we slow down, how shall we ever get anywhere?"

"Wait a minute," mused the Cowardly Lion, half closing his eyes. "Aren't there two roads just ahead, one going up and one going down? We're to take the down road, I suppose. 'Slow down,' isn't that what it says?"

Slow down it surely was, for the road was so steep and full of stones that Dorothy and the Cowardly Lion had to pick their way with utmost care. But even bad roads must end somewhere, and coming suddenly to the edge of the woods, they saw a great city lying just below. A dim light burned over the main gate, and toward this the Cowardly Lion and Dorothy hurried as fast as they could. This was not very fast, for an unaccountable drowsiness was stealing over them.

Slowly and more slowly, the tired little girl and her great four-footed companion advanced toward the dimly lighted gate. They were so drowsy that they had ceased to talk. But they dragged on.

"Hah, hoh, hum!" yawned the Cowardly Lion. "What makes my feet so heavy?"

He stopped short and examined each of his four feet sleepily.

Dorothy swallowed a yawn and tried to run, but a walk was all she could manage.

"Hah, hoh, hum!" she gaped, stumbling along with her eyes closed.

By the time they had reached the gate, they were yawning so hard that the Cowardly Lion had nearly dislocated his jaw, and Dorothy was perfectly breathless. Holding to the lion's mane to steady herself, Dorothy blinked up uncertainly at the sign over the gate.

"Hah — here we are — Hoh!" She held her hand wearily before her mouth.

Then, with a great effort, she read the words of the sign.

"Um — Great — Grand and Mighty Slow Kingdom of Pokes! Uh-hah — Pokes! Do you hear? Hah, hoh, hu, uum!"

Dorothy looked about in alarm, despite her sleepiness.

"Do you hear?" she repeated anxiously as no answer came through the gloom.

The Cowardly Lion did not hear. He had fallen down and was fast asleep, and so in another minute was Dorothy, her head pillowed against his kind, comfortable, cowardly heart. Fast asleep at the gates of a strange gray city!

Chapter 5 - Sir Hokus of Pokes

It was long past sunup before Dorothy awoke. She rubbed her eyes, yawned once or twice, and then shook the Cowardly Lion. The gates of the city were open, and although it looked even grayer in the daytime than it looked at night, the travelers were too hungry to be particular. A large placard was posted just inside:

THIS IS POKES!

DON'T RUN!

DON'T SING!

TALK SLOWLY!

DON'T WHISTLE!

Order of the Chief Poker.

read Dorothy. "How cheerful! Hah, hoh, hum-mm!"

"Don't!" begged the Cowardly Lion with tears in his eyes. "If I yawn again, I'll swallow my tail, and if I don't have something to eat soon, I'll do it anyway. Let's hurry! There's something queer about this place, Dorothy! Ah, hah, hoh, hum-mm!"

Stifling their yawns, the two started down the long, narrow street. The houses were of gray stone, tall and stiff with tiny barred windows. It was absolutely quiet, and not a person was in sight. But when they turned the corner, they saw a crowd of queer-looking people creeping toward them. These singular individuals stopped between each step and stood perfectly still, and Dorothy was so surprised at their unusual appearance that she laughed right in the middle of a yawn.

In the first place, they never lifted their feet, but pushed them along like skates. The women were dressed in gray polka-dot dresses with huge poke bonnets that almost hid their fat, sleepy, wide-mouthed faces. Most of them had pet snails on strings, and so slowly did they move that it looked as though the snails were tugging them along.

The men were dressed like a party of congressmen, but instead of high hats wore large red nightcaps, and they were all as solemn as owls. It seemed impossible for them to keep both eyes open at the same time, and at first Dorothy thought they were winking at her. But as the whole company continued to stare fixedly with one open eye, she burst out laughing. At the unexpected sound (for no one had ever laughed in Pokes before), the women picked up their snails in a great fright, and the men clapped their fingers to their ears or to the places where their ears were under the red nightcaps.

"These must be the Slow Pokes," giggled Dorothy, nudging the Cowardly Lion. "Let's go to meet them, for they'll never reach us at the rate they are coming!"

"There's something wrong with my feet," rumbled the Cowardly Lion without looking up. "Hah, hoh, hum! What's the use of hurrying?" The fact of the matter was that they couldn't hurry if they tried. Indeed, they could hardly lift their feet at all.

"I wish the Scarecrow were with us," sighed the Cowardly Lion, shuffling along unhappily. "He never grows sleepy, and he always knows what to do."

"No use wishing," yawned Dorothy. "I only hope he's not as lost as we are."

By struggling hard, they just managed to keep moving, and by the time they came up with the Slow Pokes, they were completely worn out. A cross-looking Poke held up his arm threateningly, and Dorothy and the Cowardly Lion stopped.

"You —" said the Poke; then closed his mouth and stood staring vacantly for a whole minute.

"Are —" He brought out the word with a perfectly enormous yawn, and Dorothy began fanning the Cowardly Lion with her hat, for he showed signs of falling asleep again.

"What?" she asked crossly.

"Under —" sighed the Poke after a long pause, and Dorothy, seeing that there was no hurrying him, began counting to herself. Just as she reached sixty, the Poke pushed back his red nightcap and shouted:

"Arrest!"

"Arrest!" shouted all the other Pokes so loud that the Cowardly Lion roused himself with a start, and the pet snails stuck out their heads. "A rest? A rest is not what we want! We want breakfast!" growled the lion irritably and started to roar, but a yawn spoiled it. (One simply cannot look fierce by yawning.)

"You —" began the Poke. But Dorothy could not stand hearing the same slow speech again. Putting her fingers in her ears, she shouted back:

"What for?"

The Pokes regarded her sternly. Some even opened both eyes. Then the one who had first addressed the, covering a terrific gape with one hand, pointed with the other to a sign on a large post at the corner of the street.

"Speed limit 1/4 mile an hour" said the sign.

"We're arrested for speeding!" shouted Dorothy in the Cowardly Lion's ear.

"Did you say feeding?" asked the poor lion, waking up with a start. "If I go to sleep again before I'm fed, I'll starve to death!"

"Then keep awake," yawned Dorothy. By this time, the Pokes had surrounded them and were waving them imperiously ahead. They looked so threatening that Dorothy and the Cowardly Lion began to creep in the direction of a gloomy, gray castle. Of the journey neither of them remembered a thing, for with the gaping and yawning Pokes it was almost impossible to keep awake. But they must have walked in their sleep, for the next thing Dorothy knew, a harsh voice called slowly:

"Poke — him!"

Greatly alarmed, Dorothy opened her eyes. They were in a huge stone hall hung all over with rusty armor, and seated on a great stone chair, snoring so loudly that all the steel helmets rattled, was a Knight. The tallest and crossest of the Pokes rushed at him with a long poker, giving him such a shove that he sprawled to the floor.

"So —" yawned the Cowardly Lion, awakened by the clatter, "Knight has fallen!"

"Prisoners — Sir Hokus!" shouted the Chief Poker, lifting the Knight's plume and speaking into the helmet as if he were telephoning.

The Knight arose with great dignity, and after straightening his armor, let down his visor, and Dorothy saw a kind, timid face with melancholy blue eyes — not at all Pokish, as she explained to Ozma later.

*"What means this unwonted clamor?" asked Sir Hokus, peering curiously at the prisoners.

"We're sorry to waken you," said Dorothy politely, "but could you please give us some breakfast?"

"A lot!" added the Cowardly Lion, licking his chops.

"It's safer for me to sing," said the Knight mournfully, and throwing back his head, he roared in a high, hoarse voice:

"Don't yawn! Don't yawn!
We're out of breath —
Begone — BEGONE
Or die the death!"

The Cowardly Lion growled threateningly and began lashing his tail.

"If he weren't in a can, I'd eat him," he rumbled, "but I never could abide tinned meat."

"He's not in a can, he's in armor," explained Dorothy, too interested to pay much attention to the Cowardly Lion, for at the first note of the Knight's song, the Pokes began scowling horribly, and by the time he had finished they were backing out of the room faster than Dorothy ever imagined they could go.

"So that's why the sign said don't sing," thought Dorothy to herself. The air seemed clearer somehow, and she no longer felt sleepy.

When the last Poke had disappeared, the Knight sighed and climbed gravely back on his stone chair.

"My singing makes them very wroth. In faith, they cannot endure music; it wakens them," explained Sir Hokus. "But hold, 'twas food you asked of me. Breakfast, I believe you called it." With an uneasy glance at the Cowardly Lion, who was sniffing the air hungrily, the Knight banged on his steel armor ith his sword, and a fat, lazy Poke shuffled slowly into the hall.

"Pid, bring the stew," roared Sir Hokus as the Poke stood blinking at them dully.

"Stew, Pid!" he repeated loudly, and began to hum under his breath, at which Pid fairly ran out of the room, returning in a few minutes with a large yellow bowl. This he handed ungraciously to Dorothy. Then he brought a great copper tub of the stuff for the Cowardly Lion and retired sulkily.

Dorothy thought she had never tasted anything more delicious. The Cowardly Lion was gulping down his share with closed eyes, and both, I am very sorry to say, forgot even to thank Sir Hokus.

"Are you perchance a damsel in distress?"

Quite startled, Dorothy looked up from her bowl and saw the Knight regarding her wistfully.

"She's in Pokes, and that's the same thing," said the Cowardly Lion without opening his eyes.

"We're lost," began the little girl, "but —"

There was something so quaint and gentle about the Knight, that she soon found herself talking to him like an old friend. She told him all of their adventures since leaving the Emerald City and even told about the disappearance of the Scarecrow.

"Passing strange, yet how refreshing," murmured Sir Hokus. "And if I seem a little behind times, you must not blame me. For centuries, I have dozed in this gray castle, and it cometh over me that things have greatly changed. This beast now, he talks quite manfully, and this Kingdom that you mention, this Oz? Never heard of it!"

"Never heard of Oz?" gasped the little girl. "Why, you're a subject of Oz, and Pokes is in Oz, though I don't know just where."

Here Dorothy gave him a short history of the Fairy country, and of the many adventures she had had since she had come there. Sir Hokus listened with growing melancholy.

"To think," he sighed mournfully, "that I was prisoner here while all that was happening!"

"Are you a prisoner?" asked Dorothy in surprise. "I thought you were King of the Pokes!"

"Uds daggers!" thundered Sir Hokus so suddenly that Dorothy jumped. "I am a knight!"

Seeing her startled expression, he controlled himself. "I was a knight," he continued brokenly. "Long centuries ago, mounted on my goodly steed, I fared from my father's castle to offer my sword to a mighty king. His name?" Sir Hokus tapped his forehead uncertainly. "Go to, I have forgot."

"Could it have been King Arthur?" exclaimed Dorothy, wide-eyed with interest. "Why, just think of your being still alive!"

"That's just the point," choked the Knight. "I've been alive — still, so still that I've forgotten everything. Why, I can't even remember how I used to talk," he confessed miserably.

"But how did you get here?" rumbled the Cowardly Lion, who did not like being left out of the conversation.

16

"I had barely left my father's castle before I met a stranger," said Sir Hokus, sitting up very straight, "who challenged me to battle. I spurred my horse forward, our lances met, and the stranger was unseated. But by my faith, 'twas no mortal Knight." Sir Hokus sighed deeply and lapsed into silence.

"What happened?" asked Dorothy curiously, for Sir Hokus seemed to have forgotten them.

"The Knight," said he with another mighty sigh, "struck the ground with his lance and cried, 'Live Wretch, for centuries in the stupidest country out of the world,' and disappeared. And here — here I am!" With a despairing gesture, Sir Hokus arose, big tears splashing down his armor.

"I feel that I am brave, very brave, but how am I to know until I have encountered danger? Ah, friends, behold in me a Knight who has never had a real adventure, never killed a dragon, nor championed a Lady, nor gone on a Quest!"

Dropping on his knees before the little girl, Sir Hokus took her hand. "Let me go with you on this Quest for the valiant Scarecrow. Let me be your good Night!" he begged eagerly.

"Good night," coughed the Cowardly Lion, who, to tell the truth, was feeling a bit jealous. But Dorothy was thrilled, and as Sir Hokus continued to look at her pleadingly, she took off her hair ribbon and bound it 'round his arm.

"You shall be my own true Knight, and I your Lady Fair!" she announced solemnly, and exactly as she had read in books.

At this interesting juncture the Cowardly Lion gave a tremendous yawn, and Sir Hokus with an exclamation of alarm jumped to his feet. The Pokes had returned to the hall, and Dorothy felt herself falling asleep again.

"Up, up, my lieges and away!
We take the field again —
For Ladies fair we fight today
And KING! Up, up, my merry men!"

shrilled the Knight as if he were leading an army to battle. The Pokes opened both eyes, but did not immediately retire. Sir Hokus bravely swallowed a yawn and hastily clearing his throat shouted another song, which he evidently made up on the spur of the moment:

Avaunt! Be off! Be gone - Methinks
We'll be asleep in forty winks!

This time the Pokes left sullenly, but the effect of their presence had thrown Dorothy, the Cowardly Lion, and the Knight into a violent fit of the gapes.

"If I fall asleep, nothing can save you," said Sir Hokus in an agitated voice. "Hah, hoh, hum! Hah —!"

The Knight's eyes closed.

"Don't do it, don't do it!" begged Dorothy, shaking him violently. "Can't we run away?"

"I've been trying for five centuries," wailed the Knight in a discouraged voice, "but I always fall asleep before I reach the gate, and they bring me back here. They're rather fond of me in their slow way," he added apologetically.

"Couldn't you keep singing?" asked the Cowardly Lion anxiously, for the prospect of a five-century stay in Pokes was more than he could bear.

"Couldn't we all sing?" suggested Dorothy. "Surely all three of us won't fall asleep at once."

"I'm not much of a singer," groaned the Cowardly Lion, beginning to tremble, "but I'm willing to do my share!"

"I like you," said Sir Hokus, going over and thumping the Cowardly Lion approvingly on the back. "You ought to be knighted!"

The lion blinked his eyes, for Sir Hokus' iron fist bruised him severely, but knowing it was kindly meant, he bore it bravely.

"I am henceforth a beknighted lion," he whispered to Dorothy while Sir Hokus was straightening his armor. Next the Knight took down an iron poker, which he handed to Dorothy.

"To wake us up with," he explained. "And now, Lady Dorothy, if you are ready, we will start on the Quest for the honorable Scarecrow, and remember, everybody sing — Sing for your life!"

Chapter 6 - Singing their Way Out of Pokes

Taking a deep breath, Sir Hokus, the Cowardly Lion and Dorothy burst out of the hall singing at the top of their voices.

"Three blind mice —!" sang Dorothy.

"Across the plain!" shouted Sir Hokus.

"I am the Cowardly Lion of Oz!" roared the lion.

The Pokes were so taken aback at the horrid sounds that they ran scurrying right and left. In another minute the three were out of the castle and singing their way through the gloomy garden. Dorothy stuck to the Three Blind Mice. Sir Hokus sang verse after verse of an old English ballad, and the Cowardly Lion roared and gurgled a song of his own making, which, considering it was a first attempt, was not so bad:

"I am the Cowardly Lion of Oz!
Be good! Begone! Beware! Becoz
When I am scared full fierce I be;
Br—rah—grr—ruff, look out for me!"

The Pokes stumbled this way and that, and all went well until they rushed into a company of Pokes who were playing croquet. The slowness with which they raised their mallets fascinated Dorothy, and she stopped to watch them in spite of herself.

"Don't stop! Sing!" growled the Cowardly Lion in the middle of a line. To make up for lost time, Dorothy closed her eyes and sang harder than ever, but alas! next instant she fell over a wicket, which so deprived her of breath that she could barely scramble up, let alone sing. As soon as she stopped singing, the Pokes paused in their flight, and as soon as they paused Dorothy began to gape. Singing for dear life, Sir Hokus jerked Dorothy by the arm, and the Cowardly Lion roared so loud that the Pokes covered their ears and began backing away.

"There was a Knight! Come on, come on!" sang Sir Hokus, and Dorothy came, and in a few minutes was able to take up the "Three Blind Mice" again. But running and singing at the same time is not an easy task. And running through Pokes is like trying to run through water. (You know how hard that is?)

"Three Blind Mice — uh — hah — Three Blind — Mice — uh-hah — I can't sing another note! Thu — ree—!" gasped poor Dorothy, stumbling along, while the Cowardly Lion was puffing like an engine. The Pokes in the garden had recovered from their first alarm and were following at a safe distance. The gates of the city were only a short distance off, but it seemed to Dorothy that she could not go another step.

A large group of Pokes had gathered at the gates, and unless they could sing their way through, they would fall asleep and be carried ignominiously back to the castle.

"Now!" wheezed Sir Hokus, "Remember, it is for the Scarecrow!" All of them swallowed, took a deep breath, and put their last remaining strength into their voices. But a wily Poke who had stuffed some cotton in his ears now approached pushing a little cart.

"Take —!" he drawled, and before Dorothy realized what she was doing, she had accepted a cone from the Poke.

"Hah, hoh, hum! Why, it's hokey pokey!" spluttered Dorothy, and with a deep sigh of delight she took a large bite of the pink ice cream. How cool it felt on her dry throat! She opened her mouth for a second taste, yawned terrifically, and fell with a thud to the stone pavement.

"Dorothy!" wailed Sir Hokus, stopping short in his song and bending over the little girl. The poor Cowardly Lion gave a gulp of despair and began running around the two, roaring and singing in a choked voice. The Pokes nodded to each other in a pleased fashion, and the Chief Poker started cautiously toward them with a long, thick rope. The Cowardly Lion redoubled his efforts. Then, seeing Sir Hokus about to fall, he jumped on the Knight with all his strength. Down crashed Sir Hokus, his armor clanging against the stones that paved the gateway.

"Sing!" roared the Cowardly Lion, glaring at him fiercely. The fall wakened the poor Knight, but he had not the strength to rise. Sitting on the hard stones and looking reproachfully at the Cowardly Lion, he began his ballad in a half-hearted fashion. The Cowardly Lion's heart was like to burst between lack of breath and fear, but making one last tremendous effort and still roaring his song, he bounded at the Chief Poker, seized the rope, and was back before the stupid creature had time to yawn.

"Tie it around your waist; take Dorothy in your arms!" gasped the Cowardly Lion out of the corner of his mouth. Sir Hokus, though completely dazed, had just enough presence of mind to obey, and the next minute the Cowardly Lion, growling between his teeth like a good fellow, was dashing through the group of Pokes, the other end of the rope in his mouth.

Bumpety bump — bump — bump! Bangety-bang-bang! went Sir Hokus over the cobbles, holding his helmet with one hand and Dorothy fast in the other arm. The Pokes fell this way and that, and such was the determination of the Cowardly Lion that he never stopped till he was out of the gate and halfway up the rough road they had so recently traveled. Then with a mighty sigh, he dropped the rope, rolled over and over down the hill, and lay panting with exhaustion at the bottom.

The bumping over the cobbles had wakened Sir Hokus thoroughly. Indeed, the poor Knight was black and blue, and his armor dented and scraped frightfully in important places.

Dorothy, considerably shaken, opened her eyes and began feebly singing "Three Blind Mice."

"No need," puffed Sir Hokus, lifting her off his lap and rising stiffly.

"Yon noble beast has rescued us."

"Won't the Pokes come up here?" asked Dorothy, staring around a bit dizzily.

"They cannot live out of the kingdom," said the Knight, and Dorothy drew a big sigh of relief. Sir Hokus, however, was looking very grave.

"I have failed on my first adventure. Had it not been for the Cowardly Lion, we would now be prisoners in Pokes," he murmured sadly. Then he unfastened the plume from his helmet. "It beseemeth me not to wear it," sighed the Knight mournfully, and though Dorothy tried her best to comfort him, he refused to put it back. Finally, she fastened the plume to her dress, and they went down to the Cowardly Lion.

There was a little spring nearby, and after they had poured six helmets of water over his head, the lion opened his eyes. "Been in a good many fights," gasped the lion, "but I never fought one like this. Singing, bah!"

"Noble Sir, how can I ever repay you?" faltered the Knight. "Alas, that I have failed in the hour of trial!"

"Why, it wasn't a question of courage at all," rumbled the Cowardly Lion, greatly embarrassed. "I had the loudest voice and the most breath, that's all! You got the rough end of it." Sir Hokus looked ruefully at his armor. The back was entirely squashed.

"Never mind!" said the Knight bravely. "It is the front one presents to the foe."

"Now you're talking like a real Knight," said Dorothy. "A while ago you said, 'Yon' and 'beseemeth,' and first thing you know the talk will all come back to you." Sir Hokus' honest face shone with pleasure.

"Odds bludgeons and truncheons! The little maid is right!" he exclaimed, striking an attitude. "And once it does, the rest will be easy."

"Don't say rest to me," begged the Cowardly Lion, getting slowly to his feet. "Hah, hoh, hum! Just to think of it makes me yawn. Now don't you think we had better start off?"

"If you're rested," began Dorothy. The Cowardly Lion put his paw over his ear and looked so comical that both Dorothy and Sir Hokus laughed heartily.

"If you're ready," amended Dorothy, and the three adventurers started up the steep road. "The first thing to do," said the little girl, "is to get back to the Emerald City as quickly as we can."

At this very minute Glinda, the Good Sorceress of Oz, in her palace in the Quadling Country, was puzzling over an entry in the Magic Record Book. This book tells everything that is happening in the world and out, and while it does not give details, it is a very useful possession.

"The Emperor of the Silver Islands," read Glinda, "has returned to his people."

"Now who is the Emperor of the Silver Islands?" she asked herself. She puzzled about it for a long while, and then, deciding that it had nothing to do with the Fairy Kingdom of Oz, she closed the book and went for a walk in the palace garden.

Dorothy and Sir Hokus and the Cowardly Lion had meanwhile reached the first sign in the dim forest, the sign directing travelers to Pokes. Two roads branched out through the forest, and after much debating they took the wider.

"Do you 'spose this leads to the Emerald City?" asked Cowardly Lion dubiously.

"Time will tell, time will tell," said Sir Hokus cheerfully.

"Yes," murmured the Cowardly Lion, "time will tell. But what?"

Chapter 7 - The Scarecrow is Hailed as Emperor!

Leaning forward on the great throne, the Scarecrow waited impatiently for the ancient gentleman to speak. The gray-skinned courtiers were eyeing him expectantly, and just as the suspense became almost unendurable, the old man threw up his arms and cried sharply:

"The prophecy of the magic beanstalk has been fulfilled. In this radiant and sublime Scarecrowcus, the spirit of Chang Wang Woe, the mighty, has returned. And I, the Grand Chew Chew of the realm, prostrate myself before this wonderful Scarecrowcus, Emperor of the Silver Islands." So, likewise, did all the company present, and the Scarecrow, taken unawares, flew up several feet and landed in a heap on the steps leading to the throne. He climbed back hurriedly, picking up the fan and parasol that he had plucked from the beanstalk.

"I wish Professor Wogglebug could hear this," said the Scarecrow, settling himself complacently. "But I must watch out, and remember to hold on."

The Grand Chew Chew was the first to rise, and folding his arms, he asked solemnly:

"What are your commands, Ancient and Honorable Scarecrowcus?"

"If you'd just omit the Cus," begged the Scarecrow in an embarrassed voice, "I believe I could think better. Am I in China, or where? Are you Chinamen, or what?"

"We are Silvermen," said the Grand Chew Chew impressively, "and a much older race than our Chinese cousins. They are people of the sun. We are people of the stars. Has your Highness so soon forgotten?"

"I am afraid," said the Scarecrow, rubbing his chin reflectively, "that I have." He gazed slowly around the great throne room. Ozma's palace itself was not more dazzling. The floor of dull silver blocks was covered with rich blue rugs. Furniture, chairs, screens and everything were made of silver inlaid with precious stones. Filigreed silver lanterns hung from the high ceilings, and tall silver vases filled with pink and blue blossoms filled the rooms with their perfume. Blue flags embroidered with silver stars fluttered from the walls and the tips of the pikebearers' spears, and silver seemed to be so plentiful that even shoes were fashioned of it. Faintly through the windows came the sweet tones of a hundred silver chimes, and altogether the Scarecrow was quite dazed by his apparent good fortune. Surely they had called him Emperor, but how could that be? He turned to address the Grand Chew Chew; then as he saw out of the corner of his eye that the assemblage were making ready to fall upon their faces, he exclaimed in a hoarse whisper:

"May I speak to you alone?" The Grand Chew Chew waved his hand imperiously, and the courtiers with a great crackling of silver brocade backed from the hall.

"Very kind of them to bow, but I wish they wouldn't," sighed the Scarecrow, sinking back on the great throne. "It blows one about so. I declare, if another person falls at my feet, I'll have nervous prostration."

Again he took a long survey of the hall, then turned to the Grand Chew Chew. "Would you mind," he asked simply, "telling me again who I am and how?"

"Who and how? Who — You are, illustrious Sir, the Emperor Chang Wang Woe, or to be more exact, his spirit!"

"I have always been a spirited person," observed the Scarecrow dubiously, "but never a spirit without a person. I must insist on being a person."

"How?" the Grand Chew Chew proceeded without noticing the Scarecrow's remarks. "Fifty years ago — after your Extreme Highness had defeated in battle the King of the Golden Islands — a magician entered the realm. This magician, in the employ of this wicked king, entered a room in the palace where your Highness lay sleeping and by an act of necromancy changed you to a crocus!"

"Ouch!" exclaimed the Scarecrow, shuddering involun-tarily.

"And had it not been for the Empress, your faithful wife, you would have been lost forever to the Empire."

"Wife?" gasped the Scarecrow faintly. "Have I a wife?"

"If your Highness will permit me to finish," begged the Grand Chew Chew with great dignity. The Scarecrow nodded. "Your wife, Tsing Tsing, the beautiful, took the crocus, which was fading rapidly, and planted it in a silver bowl in the center of this very hall and for three days kept it fresh with her tears. Waking on the third morning, the Empress was amazed to see in place of the crocus a giant bean pole that extended to the roof of the palace and disappeared among the clouds."

"Ah!" murmured the Scarecrow, looking up, "My family tree!"

"Beside the bean pole lay a crumpled parchment." The Grand Chew Chew felt in the sleeve of his kimono and brought out a bit of crumpled silver paper, and adjusting his horn spectacles, read slowly.

"Into the first being who touches this magic pole — on the other side of the world — the spirit of Emperor Chang Wang Woe will enter. And fifty years from this day, he will return — to save his people."

The Grand Chew Chew took off his specs and folded up the paper. "The day has come! You have come down the bean pole, and are undoubtedly that being who has gone from Emperor to crocus to Scarecrowcus. I have ruled the Islands these fifty years; have seen to the education of your sons and grandsons. And now, gracious and exalted Master, as I am an old man I ask you to relieve me from the cares of state."

"Sons! Grandsons!" choked the Scarecrow, beginning to feel very much alarmed indeed. "How old am I?"

"Your Highness," said the Grand Chew Chew with a deep salaam, "is as old as I. In other words, you are in the ripe and glorious eighty-fifth year of your Majesty's illustrious and useful age."

"Eigh-ty five!" gasped the Scarecrow, staring in dismay at the gray, wrinkled face of the old Silverman. "Now see here, Chew Chew, are you sure of that?"

"Quite sure, Immortal and Honored Master!"

The Scarecrow could not help but be convinced of the truth of the Grand Chew Chew's story. The pole in the Munchkin farmer's cornfield was none other than the magic beanstalk, and he, thrust on the pole by the farmer to scare away the crows, had received the spirit of the Emperor Chang Wang Woe. "Which accounts for my cleverness," he thought gloomily. Now, surely he should have been pleased, for he had come in search of a family, but the acquisition of an empire, sons and grandsons, and old age, all in a trice, fairly took his breath away.

"Does the prophecy say anything about restoring my imperial person?" he asked anxiously, for the thought of looking like Chew Chew was not a cheerful one.

"Alas, no!" sighed the Grand Chew Chew sorrowfully. "But we have very clever wizards on the Island, and I shall set them at work on the problem at once."

"Now don't be in such a rush," begged the Scarecrow, secretly determined to lock up the wizards at the first opportunity. "I'm rather fond of this shape. You see, it requires no food and never grows tired — or old!"

"The royal robes will in a measure conceal it," murmured the Grand Chew Chew politely, and clapped his hands. A little servitor bounced into the hall.

"A royal robe, Quick Silver, for his Radiant Highness," snapped the Grand Chew Chew. In a moment Quick Silver had returned with a magnificent purple satin robe embroidered in silver threads and heavy with jewels, and a hat of silver cloth with upturned brim. The Scarecrow wrapped himself in the purple robe, took off his old Munchkin hat, and substituted the Imperial headpiece.

"How do I look, Chew?" he asked anxiously.

"Quite like your old Imperial Self, except —" The old Prime Minister ran unsteadily out of the room. There was a muffled scream from the hall, and the next instant he returned with a long, shiny, silver queue which he had evidently clipped from the head of one of the servants. Removing the Scarecrow's hat, he pinned the queue to the back, set it on the Scarecrow's head, and stood regarding him with great satisfaction. "Ah, if the Empress could only see you!" he murmured rapturously.

"Where — where is she?" asked the Scarecrow, looking around nervously. His long, care-free life in Oz had somewhat unfitted him, he reflected, for family life.

"Alas!" sighed the Grand Chew Chew, wiping his eyes on the sleeve of his kimono, "She has returned to her silver ancestors."

"Then show me her picture," commanded the Scarecrow, visibly affected. The Grand Chew Chew stepped to a side wall, and pulling on a silken cord, disclosed the picture of a large, gray lady with curiously small eyes and a curiously large nose.

"Is she not beautiful?" asked the Grand Chew Chew, bowing his head.

"Beautiful — er — er, beautiful!" gulped the Scarecrow. He thought of lovely little Ozma and dear little Dorothy, and all at once felt terribly upset and homesick. He had no recollection of the Silver Island or his life here whatever. Who was he, anyway — the Scarecrow of Oz or Emperor Chang Wang Woe? He couldn't be both.

"Ah!" whispered the Grand Chew Chew, seeing his agitation. "You remember her?" The Scarecrow shook his head, with an inward shudder.

"Now show me myself, Chew," he asked curiously. Pulling the cord of a portrait beside the Empress, Chew Chew revealed the picture of Chang Wang Woe as he had been fifty years ago. His face was bland and jolly, and to be perfectly truthful, quite like the Scarecrow's in shape and expression. "I am beside myself," murmured the Scarecrow dazedly — which in truth he was.

"You were — er — are a very royal and handsome person," stammered the Grand Chew Chew.

The Scarecrow, stepping off the throne to examine himself more closely, dropped the little fan and parasol. He had really not had time to examine them since they snapped off the beanstalk, and now, looking at them carefully, he found them extremely pretty.

"Dorothy will like these," thought the Scarecrow, slipping them into a large inside pocket of his robe. Already, in the back of his head, was a queer notion that he would at some time or other return to Oz. He started to give the Grand Chew Chew a spirited description of that wonderful country, but the ancient gentleman yawned and, waving his hands toward the door, interrupted him with:

"Would not your Supreme Highness care to inspect your present dominions?"

"I suppose I may as well!" With a deep sigh, the Scarecrow took the Grand Chew Chew's arm and, holding up his royal kimono (which was rather long) with the other hand, walked unsteadily down the great salon. They were about to pass into the garden when a little fat Silverman slid around the door, a huge silver drumstick upraised in his right hand and a great drum hung about his neck.

The drummer beamed on the Scarecrow.

"Chang Wang Woe, the Beautiful,
The Beautiful has come!
Sublime and silver Scarecrow,
Let sound the royal drum!"

chanted the little man in a high, thin voice, and started to bring the drumstick down upon the huge head of his noisy instrument.

"No you don't!" cried the Scarecrow, leaping forward and catching his arm.

"I positively forbid it!"

"Then I shall have no work!" screamed the drummer, falling on his face. "Ah, Gracious Master, don't you remember me?"

"Yes," said the Scarecrow kindly, "who are you?"

"Oh, don't you remember little Happy Toko?" wheezed the little man, the tears rolling down his cheeks. "I was only a boy, but you used to be fond of me."

"Why, of course, my dear Tappy," said the Scarecrow, not liking to hurt the little fellow's feelings. "But why do you beat the drum?"

"It is customary to sound the drum at the approach of your Royal Highness," put in the Grand Chew Chew importantly.

"Was customary," said the Scarecrow firmly. "My dear Tappy Oko, never sound it in my presence again; it is too upsetting." Which was true enough, for one blow of the drum sent the flimsy Scarecrow flying into the air.

"You're dismissed, Happy," snapped the Grand Chew Chew. At this, the little Silver Islander began weeping and roaring with distress.

"Stop! What else can you do besides beat a drum?" asked the Scarecrow kindly.

"I can sing, stand on my head, and tell jokes," sniffed Happy Toko, shuffling from one foot to the other.

"Very good," said the Scarecrow. "You are henceforth Imperial Punster to my Person. Come along, we're going to look over the Island."

The Grand Chew Chew frowned so terribly that Happy Toko's knees shook with terror.

"It is not fitting for a slave to accompany the Grand Chew Chew and the Emperor," he hissed angrily.

The Scarecrow looked surprised, for the Kingdom of Oz is quite democratic, and no one is considered better than another. But seeing this was not the time to argue, he winked broadly behind the Grand Chew Chew's back.

"I'll see you again, Tappy my boy," he called genially, and passed out into the garden, where a magnificent silver palanquin, surrounded by pikemen and shieldbearers, awaited him.

Chapter 8 - The Scarecrow Studies the Silver Island

Two days had passed since the Scarecrow had fallen into his Kingdom. He was not finding his royal duties as pleasant as he had anticipated. The country was beautiful enough, but being Emperor of the Silver Islands was not the simple affair that ruling Oz had been. The pigtail on the back of his hat was terribly distracting, and he was always tripping over his kimono, to which he could not seem to accustom himself. His subjects were extremely quarrelsome, always pulling one another's queues or stealing fruit, umbrellas, and silver polish. His ministers, the Grand Chew Chew, the Chief Chow Chow, and General Mugwump, were no better, and keeping peace in the palace took all the Scarecrow's cleverness.

In the daytime he tried culprits in the royal court, interviewed his seventeen secretaries, rode out in the royal palanquin, and made speeches to visiting princes. At night he sat in the great silver salon and by the light of the lanterns studied the Book of Ceremonies. His etiquette, the Grand Chew Chew informed him, was shocking. He was always doing something wrong, dodging the Imperial Umbrella, speaking kindly to a palace servant, or walking unattended in the gardens.

The royal palace itself was richly furnished, and the Scarecrow had more than five hundred robes of state. The gardens, with their sparkling waterfalls, glowing orange trees, silver temples, towers and bridges, were too lovely for words. Poppies, roses, lotus and other lilies perfumed the air, and at night a thousand silver lanterns turned them to a veritable fairyland.

The grass and trees were green as in other lands, but the sky as always full of tiny silver clouds, the waters surrounding the island were of a lovely liquid silver, and as all the houses and towers were of this gleaming metal, the effect was bewil-dering and beautiful.

But the Silver Islanders themselves were too stupid to appreciate this beauty. "And what use is it all when I have no one to enjoy it with me," sighed the Scarecrow. "And no time to play!"

In Oz no one thought it queer if Ozma, the little Queen, jumped rope with Dorothy or Betsy Bobbin, or had a quiet game of croquet with the palace cook. But here, alas, everything was different. If the Scarecrow so much as ventured a game of ball with the gardener's boy, the whole court was thrown into an uproar. At first, the Scarecrow tried to please everybody, but finding that nothing pleased the people in the palace, he decided to please himself.

"I don't care a kinkajou if I am the Emperor, I'm going to talk to whom I please!" he exclaimed on the second night, and shaking his glove at a bronze statue, he threw the Book of Ceremonies into the fountain. The next morning, therefore, he ascended the throne with great firmness. Immediately, the courtiers prostrated themselves, and the Scarecrow's arms and legs blew about wildly.

"Stand up at once," puffed the Scarecrow when he had regained his balance.

"You are giving me nervous prostration. Chew, kindly issue an edict forbidding prostrations. Anyone caught bowing in my presence again shall lose —" the courtiers looked alarmed "— his pigtail!" finished the Scarecrow.

"And now, Chew, you will take my place, please. I am going for a walk with Tappy Oko."

The Grand Chew Chew's mouth fell open with surprise, but seeing the Scarecrow's determined expression, he dared not disobey, and he immediately began making strange marks on a long, red parchment. Happy Toko trembled as the Scarecrow Emperor took his arm, and the courtiers stared at one another in dismay as the two walked quietly out into the garden.

Nothing happened, however, and Tappy, regaining his composure, took out a little silver flute and started a lively tune.

"I had to take matters into my own hands, Tappy," said the Scarecrow, listening to the music with a pleased expression. "Are there any words to that song?"

"Yes, illustrious and Supreme Sir!"

"Two spoons went down a Por-ce-Lane,

To meet a China saucer,

A 'talking China in a way

To break a white man's jaw, Sir!"

sang Happy, and finished by standing gravely on his head.

"Your Majesty used to be very fond of this song," spluttered Happy. (It is difficult to speak while upside down, and if you don't think so, try it!)

"Ah!" said the Scarecrow, beginning to feel more cheerful, "Tell me something about myself and my family, Tappy Oko."

"Happy Toko, if it pleases your Supreme Amiability," corrected the little silver man, somersaulting to a standstill beside the Scarecrow.

"It does and it doesn't," murmured the Scarecrow. "There is something about you that reminds me of a pudding, and you tapped the drum, didn't you? I believe I shall call you Tappy Oko, if you don't mind!"

The Scarecrow seated himself on a silver bench and motioned for the Imperial Punster to sit down beside him. Tappy Oko sat down fearfully, first making sure that he was not observed.

"Saving your Imperial Presence, this is not permitted," said Tappy uneasily.

"Never mind about my Imperial Presence," chuckled the Scarecrow. "Tell me about my Imperial Past."

"Ah!" said Tappy Oko, rolling up his eyes, "You were one of the most magnificent and magnanimous of monarchs."

"Was I?" asked the Scarecrow in a pleased voice.

"You distributed rice among the poor, and advice among the rich, and fought many glorious battles," continued the little man. "I composed a little song about you. Perhaps you would like to hear it?"

The Scarecrow nodded, and Tappy, throwing back his head, chanted with a will:

Chang Wang Woe did draw the bow -

And twist the queues of a thousand foe!

"In Oz," murmured the Scarecrow reflectively as Tappy finished, "I twisted the necks of a flock of wild crows — that was before I had my excellent brains, too. Oh, I'm a fighting man, there's no doubt about it. But tell me, Tappy, where did I meet my wife?"

"In the water!" chuckled Tappy Oko, screwing up his eyes.

"Never!" The Scarecrow looked out over the harbor and then down at his lumpy figure.

"Your Majesty forgets you were then a man like me — er — not stuffed with straw, I mean," exclaimed Happy, looking embarrassed. "She was fishing," continued the little Punster, "when a huge silver fish became entangled in her line. She stood up, the fish gave a mighty leap and pulled her out of the boat. Your Majesty, having seen the whole affair from the bank, plunged bravely into the water and, swimming out, rescued her, freed the fish, and in due time made her your bride. I've made a song about that, also."

"Let's hear it," said the Scarecrow. And this is what Happy sung:

"Tsing Tsing, a Silver Fisher's daughter,

Was fishing in the silver water.

The moon shone on her silver hair
And there were fishes everywhere!
Then came a mighty silver fish,
It seized her line and with a swish
Of silver fins upset her boat.
Tsing Tsing could neither swim nor float.
She raised her silver voice in fear
And who her call of help should hear
But Chang Wang Woe, the Emperor,
Who saved and married her, what's more!"

"Did I really?" asked the Scarecrow, feeling quite flattered by Happy's song.

"Yes," said Happy positively, "and invited me to the wedding, though I was only a small boy."

"Was Chew Chew there?" The Scarecrow couldn't help wondering how the old Nobleman had taken his marriage with a poor fisherman's daughter.

Happy chuckled at the memory. "He had a Princess all picked out for you," he confided merrily:
And there he stood in awful pride
And scorned the father of the bride!

"Hoh!" roared the Scarecrow, falling off the bench. "That's the Ozziest thing I've heard since I landed in the Silver Islands. Tappy, my boy, I believe we are going to be friends! But let's forget the past and think of the present!"

The Scarecrow embraced his Imperial Punster on the spot. "Let's find something jolly to do," he suggested.

"Would your Extreme Highness care for kites?" asked Happy. 'Tis a favorite sport here!"

"Would I! But wait, I will disguise myself." Hiding his royal hat under the bench, he put on Happy Toko's broad-rimmed (sic) peasant hat. It turned down all 'round and almost hid his face. Then he turned his robe inside out and declared himself ready.

They passed through a small silver town before they reached the field where the kites were to be flown, and the Scarecrow was delighted with its picturesque and quaint appearance. The streets were narrow and full of queer shops. Silver lanterns and little pennants hung from each door, the merchants and maidens in their gay sedans and the people afoot made a bright and lively picture.

"If I could just live here instead of in the palace," mused the Scarecrow, pausing before a modest rice shop. It is dangerous to stop in the narrow streets, and Happy jerked his master aside just in time to prevent his being trodden on by a huge camel. It sniffed at the Scarecrow suspiciously, and they were forced to flatten themselves against a wall to let it pass. Happy anxiously hurried the Emperor through the town, and they soon arrived at the kite flying field. A great throng had gathered to watch the exhibition, and there were more kites than one would see in a lifetime here. Huge fish, silver paper dragons, birds — every sort and shape of kite was tugging at its string, and hundreds of Silver Islanders — boys, girls and grown-ups — were looking on.

"How interesting," said the Scarecrow, fascinated by a huge dragon that floated just over his head. "I wish Dorothy could see this, I do indeed!"

But the dragon kite seemed almost alive, and horrors! Just as it swooped down, a hook in the tail caught in the Scarecrow's collar, and before Happy Toko could even wink, the Emperor of the Silver Islands was sailing towards the clouds. The Scarecrow, as you must know, weighs almost nothing, and the people shouted with glee, for they thought him a dummy man and part of the performance. But Happy Toko ran after the kite as fast as his fat little legs would carry him.

"Alas, alas, I shall lose my position!" wailed Happy Toko, quite convinced that the Scarecrow would be dashed to pieces on the rocks. "Oh, putty head that I am to set myself against the Grand Chew Chew!"

The Scarecrow, however, after recovering from the first shock, began to enjoy himself. Holding fast to the dragon's tail, he looked down with great interest upon his dominions. Rocks, mountains, tall silver pagodas, drooping willow trees, flashed beneath him. Truly a beautiful island! His gaze strayed over the silver waters surrounding the island, and he was astonished to see a great fleet sailing into the harbor — a great fleet of singular vessels with silken sails.

"What's this?" thought the Scarecrow. But just then the dragon kite became suddenly possessed. It jerked him up, it jerked him down, and shook him this way and that. His hat flew off, his arms and legs whirled wildly, and pieces of straw began to float downward. Then the hook ripped and tore through his coat and, making a terrible slit in his back, came out. Down, down, down flashed the Scarecrow and landed in a heap on the rocks. Poor Happy Toko rushed toward him with streaming eyes.

"Oh radiant and immortal Scarecrowcus, what have they done to you?" he moaned, dropping on his knees beside the flimsy shape of the Emperor.

"Merely knocked out my honorable stuffing," mumbled the Scarecrow. "Now Tappy, my dear fellow, will you just turn me over? There's a rock in my eye that keeps me from thinking."

Happy Toko, at the sound of a voice from the rumpled heap of clothing, gave a great leap.

"Is there any straw about?" asked the Scarecrow anxiously. "Why don't you turn me over?"

"It's his ghost," moaned Happy Toko, and because he dared not disobey a royal ghost, he turned the Scarecrow over with trembling hands.

"Don't be alarmed," said the Scarecrow, smiling reassuringly. "I'm not breakable like you meat people. A little straw will make me good as new. A little straw — straw, do you hear?" For Happy's pigtail was still on end, and he was shaking so that his silver shoes clattered on the rocks.

"I command you to fetch straw!" cried the Scarecrow at last, in an angry voice. Happy dashed away.

When he returned with an arm full of straw, the Scarecrow managed to convince him that he was quite alive. "It is impossible to kill a person from Oz," he explained proudly, "and that is why my present figure is so much more satisfactory than yours. I do not have to eat or sleep and can always be repaired. Have you some safety pins?" Happy produced several and under the Scarecrow's direction stuffed out his chest and pinned up his rents.

"Let us return," said the Scarecrow. "I've had enough pleasure for one day, and can't you sing something, Tappy?" Running and fright had somewhat affected Happy's voice, but he squeaked out a funny little song, and the two, keeping time to the tune, came without further mishap to the Imperial gardens. Happy had just set the royal hat upon the Scarecrow's head and brushed off his robes when a company of courtiers dashed out of the palace door and came running toward them.

"Great Cornstarch!" exclaimed the Scarecrow, sitting heavily down on the silver bench. "What's the matter now? Here are all the Pig-heads on the Island, and look how old Chew Chew is puffing!"

"One would expect a Chew Chew to puff," observed Happy slyly. "One would —" But he got no further, for the whole company was upon them.

"Save us! Save us!" wailed the courtiers, forgetting the royal edict and falling on their faces.

"What from?" asked the Scarecrow, holding fast to the silver bench.

"The King — the King of the Golden Islands!" shrieked the Grand Chew Chew.

"Ah yes!" murmured the Scarecrow, frowning thoughtfully. "Was that his fleet coming into the harbor?"

The Grand Chew Chew jumped up in astonishment. "How could your Highness see the fleet from here?" he stuttered.

"Not from here — there," said the Scarecrow, pointing upward and winking at Happy Toko. "My Highness goes very high, you see!"

"Your Majesty does not seem to realize the seriousness of the matter," choked the Grand Chew Chew. "He will set fire to the island and make us all slaves." At this, the courtiers began banging their heads distractedly on the grass.

"Set fire to the island!" exclaimed the Scarecrow, jumping to his feet. "Then peace to my ashes! Tappy, will you see that they are sent back to Oz?"

"Save us! Save us!" screamed the frightened Silvermen.

"The prophecy of the beanstalk has promised that you would save us. You are the Emperor Chang Wang Woe," persisted the Grand Chew Chew, waving his long arms.

"Woe is me," murmured the Scarecrow, clasping his yellow gloves. "But let me think."

Chapter 9 - "Save Us with your Magic, Exalted One!"

For several minutes, the Scarecrow sat perfectly still while the company stood shaking in their shoes. Then he asked loudly, "Where is the Imperial Army?"

"It has retired to the caves at the end of the Island," quavered the Grand Chew Chew.

"I thought as much," said the Scarecrow. "But never mind, there are quite a lot of us."

"Us!" spluttered a tall Silverman indignantly. "We are not common soldiers."

"No, very uncommon ones, but you have hard heads and long nails, and I dare say will manage somehow. Come on, let's go. Chew, you may take the lead."

"Go!" shrieked the Grand Chew Chew. "Us?" The Courtiers began backing away in alarm. "Where — er — what — are your Highness' plans?"

"Why, just to conquer the King of the Golden Islands and send him back home," said the Scarecrow, smiling engagingly. "That's what you wanted, isn't it?"

"But it is not honorable for noblemen to fight. It —"

"Oh, of course, if you prefer burning —" The Scarecrow rose unsteadily and started for the garden gates. Not a person stirred. The Scarecrow looked back, and his reproachful face was too much for Happy Toko.

"I'll come, exalted and radiant Scarecrowcus! Wait, hon-orable and valiant Sir!"

"Bring a watering can, if you love me," called the Scarecrow over his shoulder, and Happy, snatching one from a frightened gardener, dashed after his Master.

"If things get too hot, I'd like to know that you can put me out," said the Scarecrow, his voice quivering with emotion. "You shall be rewarded for this, my brave Tappy."

Happy did not answer, for his teeth were chattering so he could not speak.

The harbor lay just below the Imperial Palace, and the Scarecrow and Happy hurried on through the crowds of fleeing Silvermen, their household goods packed upon their heads. Some cheered faintly for Chang Wang Woe, but none offered to follow, save the faithful Happy.

"Is this king old?" asked the Scarecrow, looking anxiously at the small boats full of warriors that were putting out from the fleet.

"He is the son of the King whom your Majesty conquered fifty years ago," gulped Happy. "Ha— has your Imperial Highness any — plan?"

"Not yet," said the Scarecrow cheerfully, "but I'm thinking very hard."

"Then, goodbye to Silver Island!" choked Happy Toko, dropping the watering can with a crash.

"Never mind," said the Scarecrow kindly. "If they shoot me and I catch fire, I'll jump in the water and you must fish me out, Tappy. Now please don't talk any more. I must think!"

Poor Happy Toko had nothing else to say, for he considered his day finished. The first of the invaders were already landing on the beach, and standing up in a small boat, encased in glittering gold armor, was the King of the Golden Islands, himself. The sun was quite hot, and there was a smell of gunpowder in the air.

Now the Scarecrow had encountered many dangers in Oz and had usually thought his way out of them, but as they came nearer and nearer to the shore and no idea presented itself, he began to feel extremely nervous. A bullet fired from the king's boat tore through his hat, and the smoke made him more anxious than ever about his straw stuffing. He felt hurriedly in his pocket, and his clumsy fingers closed over the little fan he had plucked from the bean pole.

Partly from agitation and partly because he did not know what else to do, the Scarecrow flipped the fan open. At that minute, a mighty roar went up from the enemy, for at the first motion of the fan they had been jerked fifty feet into the air, and there they hung suspended over their ships, kicking and squealing for dear life. The Scarecrow was as surprised as they, and as for Happy Toko, he fell straightway on his nose!

"Magic!" exclaimed the Scarecrow. "Someone is helping us," and he began fanning himself gently with the little fan, waiting to see what would happen next. At each wave of the fan, the King of the Golden Islands and his men flew higher until at last not one of them could be seen from the shore.

"The fan. The magic is in the fan!" gasped Happy Toko, jumping up and embracing the Scarecrow.

"Why, what do you mean?" asked the Scarecrow, closing the fan with a snap. Happy's answer was drowned in a huge splash. As soon as the fan was closed, down whirled the king's army into the sea, and each man struck the water with such force that the spray rose high as a skyscraper. And not till then did the Scarecrow realize the power of the little fan he had been saving for Dorothy.

"Saved!" screamed Happy Toko, dancing up and down. "Hurrah for the Emperor!"

The Emperor, without a plan,

Has won the victory with a fan.

The Silver Islanders had paused in their flight at the queer noises coming from the harbor, and now all of them, hearing Tappy Oko's cries, came crowding down to the shore and were soon cheering themselves hoarse. No wonder! The drenched soldiers of the king were climbing swiftly back into their boats, and when they were all aboard, the Scarecrow waved his fan sidewise (he did not want to blow them up again), and the ships swept out of the harbor so fast that the water churned to silver suds behind them, and they soon were out of sight.

"Ah!" cried the Grand Chew Chew, arriving breathlessly at this point, "We have won the day!"

"So we have!" chuckled the Scarecrow, putting his arm around Happy Toko. "Call the brave army and decorate the generals!"

"It shall be done," said the Grand Chew Chew, frowning at Happy. "There shall be a great celebration, a feast, and fireworks."

"Fireworks," quavered the Scarecrow, clutching his Imperial Punster. By this time, the Silver Islanders were crowding around the Emperor, shouting and squealing for joy, and before he could prevent it, they had placed him on their shoulders and carried him in triumph to the palace. He managed to signal Happy, and Happy nodded reassuringly and ran off as fast as his fat little legs could patter. He arrived at the palace almost as soon as the Scarecrow, lugging a giant silver watering can, and, sitting calmly on the steps of the throne, fanned himself with his hat. The Scarecrow eyed the watering can with satisfaction.

"Now let them have their old fireworks," he muttered under his breath, and settled himself comfortably. The Grand Chew Chew was hopping about like a ditched kite, arranging for the celebration. The courtiers were shaking hands with themselves and forming in a long line. A great table was being set in the hall.

"What a fuss they are making over nothing," said the Scarecrow to Happy Toko. "Now in Oz when we win a victory, we all play some jolly game and sit down to dinner with Ozma. Why, they haven't even set a place for you, Happy!"

"I'd rather sit here, amiable Master," sighed Happy Toko happily. "Is the little fan safely closed?"

The Scarecrow felt in his pocket to make sure, then leaned forward in surprise. The Royal Silver Army were marching stiffly into the hall, and the courtiers were bobbing and bowing and cheering like mad.

The General came straight to the great silver throne, clicked his silver heels, bowed, and stood at attention.

"Well," said the Scarecrow, surveying this splendid person curiously, "what is it?"

"They have come for their decorations," announced the Grand Chew Chew, stepping up with a large silver platter full of medals.

"But I thought Tappy Oko and I saved the Island," chuckled the Scarecrow, nudging the Imperial Punster.

"Had the Imperial Army not retired and left the field to you, there would have been no victory," faltered the General in a timid voice. "Therefore, in a way we are responsible for the victory. A great general always knows when to retire."

"There's something in that," admitted the Scarecrow, scratching his head thoughtfully. "Go ahead and decorate 'em, Chew Chew!"

This the Grand Chew Chew proceeded to do, making such a long speech to each soldier that half of the Court fell asleep and the Scarecrow fidgeted uncomfortably.

"They remind me of the Army of Oz," he confided to Happy Toko, "but we never have long speeches in Oz. I declare, I wish I could go to sleep, too, and that's something I have never seen any use in before."

"They've just begun," yawned Happy Toko, nearly rolling down the steps of the throne, and Happy was not far wrong, for all afternoon one after the other of the courtiers arose and droned about the great victory, and as they all addressed themselves to the Scarecrow, he was forced to listen politely. When the speeches were over, there was still the grand banquet to be got through, and as the Silver Islanders ate much the same fare as their Chinese cousins, you can imagine the poor Scarecrow's feelings.

"Ugh!" shivered the Scarecrow as the strange dishes appeared, "I'm glad none of my friends are here. How fortunate that I'm stuffed with straw!" The broiled mice, the stewed shark fins and the bird nest soup made him stare. He had ordered Happy Toko to be placed at his side, and to watch him happily at work with his silver chopsticks and porcelain spoon was the only satisfaction he got out of the feast.

"And what is that?" he asked, pointing to a steaming bowl that had just been placed before Happy.

"Minced cat, your Highness," replied Happy, sprinkling it generously with silver polish.

"Cat?" shrieked the Scarecrow, pouncing to his feet in horror. "Do you mean to tell me you are eating a poor, innocent, little cat?"

"Not a poor one at all. A very rich one, I should say," replied Happy Toko with his mouth full. "Ah, had your Highness only your old body, how you would enjoy this!"

"Never!" shouted the Scarecrow so loudly that all of the Courtiers looked up in surprise. "How dare you eat innocent cats?" Indignantly he thought of Dorothy's pet kitten back in Oz. Oz — why had he ever left that wonderful country?

"Your Highness has eaten hundreds," announced the Grand Chew Chew calmly. "Hundreds!"

The Scarecrow dropped back into his chair, too shocked for speech. He, the Scarecrow of Oz, had eaten hundreds of cats! What would Dorothy say to that? Ugh! This was his first experience with Silver Island fare. He had always spent the dinner hours in the garden. He sighed, and looked wistfully at the bean pole in the center of the hall. Every minute he was feeling less and less like the Emperor of the Silver Island and more and more like the plain Scarecrow of Oz.

"Your Majesty seems out of spirits," said Happy Toko as he placed himself and the huge watering can beside the Emperor's bench in the garden later in the evening.

"I wish I were," said the Scarecrow. "To have an Emperor's spirit wished on you is no joke, my dear Tappy. It's a blinking bore!" At that moment, the fireworks commenced. The garden, ablaze with many shaped silver lanterns, looked more like Fairyland than ever. But each rocket made the Scarecrow wince. Showers of stars and butterflies fell 'round his head, fiery dragons leaped over the trees, and in all the Fourth of July celebrations you could imagine there were never such marvelous fireworks as these. No wonder Happy Toko, gazing in delight, forgot his promises to his Royal Master.

Soon the Scarecrow's fears were realized, and his straw stuffing began to smoke.

"Put me out! Put me out!" cried the Scarecrow, as a shower of sparks settled in his lap. The royal band made such a din and the courtiers such a clatter that Happy did not hear.

All of the Silver Islanders were intent on the display, and they forgot all about their unhappy and smoking Emperor.

"Help! Water! Water! Fire!" screamed the Scarecrow, jumping off his throne and knocking Happy head over heels. Thus brought to his senses, Happy hurriedly seized the watering can and sprinkled its contents on the smoking Emperor.

"Am I out?" gasped the Emperor anxiously. "A fine way to celebrate a victory, lighting me up like a Roman candle!"

"Yes, dear Master," said the repentant Happy, helping the dripping Scarecrow to his feet, "it only scorched your royal robe. And it's all over, anyway. Let us go in."

The dripping Emperor was quite ready to follow his Imperial Punster's advice.

"Now that I am put out, let us by all means go in," said the Scarecrow gloomily, and the two slipped off without anyone noticing their departure.

"I'm afraid I'll have to have some new stuffing tomorrow," observed the Scarecrow, sinking dejectedly on his throne. "Tappy, my dear boy, after this never leave me alone, do you hear?" Happy Toko made no reply. He had fallen asleep beside the Imperial Throne.

The Scarecrow might have called his court, but he was in no mood for more of the Silver Islanders' idea of a good time. He longed for the dear friends of his loved Land of Oz.

One by one the lights winked out in the gardens, and the noisy company dispersed, and soon no one in the palace was awake but the Scarecrow. His straw was wet and soggy, and even his excellent brains felt damp and dull.

"If it weren't for Tappy Oko, how lonely I should be." He stared through the long, dim, empty hall with its shimmering silver screens and vases. "I wonder what little Dorothy is doing," sighed the Scarecrow wistfully.

Chapter 10 - Princess Ozma and Betsy Bobbin Talk it Over

"Dorothy must be having a lovely time at the Scarecrow's," remarked Betsy Bobbin to Ozma one afternoon as they sat reading in the Royal Gardens several days after Dorothy's departure from the Emerald City of Oz.

"One always has a jolly time at the Scarecrow's," laughed the little Queen of Oz. "I must look in my Magic Picture and see what they are doing. Too bad she missed the A-B-Sea Serpent and Rattlesnakes. Weren't they the funniest creatures?"

Both the little girls (for Ozma is really just a little girl) went off into a gale of laughter. The two queer creatures had followed the Scarecrow's advice and had spent their vacation in the Emerald City, and partly because they were so dazzled by their surroundings and partly because they have no sort of memories whatever, they never mentioned the Scarecrow himself or said anything about his plan to hunt his family tree. They talked incessantly of the Mer City and told innumerable A-B-Sea stories to Scraps and the Tin Woodman and the children of the Emerald City. When they were ready to go, the A-B-Sea Serpent snapped off its X block for Ozma. X, he said, meant almost everything, and pretty well expressed his gratitude to the lovely little ruler of Oz. Ozma in turn gave each of the visitors an emerald collar, and that very morning they had started back to the Munchkin River, and all the celebrities of Oz had gotten up to see them off.

"Maybe they'll come again some time," said Betsy Bobbin, swinging her feet. "But look, Ozma, here comes a messenger." A messenger it surely was, dressed in the quaint red costume of the Quadlings. It was from Glinda, the Good Sorceress, and caused the Princess to sigh with vexation.

"Tell Jack Pumpkinhead to harness the Sawhorse to the red wagon," said Ozma after glancing hastily at the little note. "The Horners and Hoppers are at war again. And tell the Wizard to make ready for a journey."

"May I come, too,?" asked Betsy. Ozma nodded with a troubled little frown, and Betsy bustled off importantly. Not many little girls are called upon to help settle wars and rule a country as wonderful as Oz.

The Horners and Hoppers are a quarrelsome and curious folk living in the Quadling mountains, and soon Ozma, Jack Pumpkinhead, Betsy and the Wizard of Oz were rattling off at the best speed the Sawhorse could manage. This was pretty fast, for the little horse, being made of wood and magically brought to life, never tires and could outrun anything on legs in the fairy Kingdom of Oz.

But the fact that interests us is that Ozma did not look in the Magic Picture or see what exciting adventures the Scarecrow and Dorothy really were having!

As for Professor Wogglebug, who had caused all the trouble, he was busily at work on the twelfth chapter of the Royal Book of Oz, which he had modestly headed:

H. M. WOGGLEBUG T.E., PRINCE OF BUGS,

Cultured and Eminent Educator

and also

Great Grand and General Genealogist of Oz.

Chapter 11 - Sir Hokus Overcometh The Giant

"I don't believe we'll ever find the way out of this forest."

Dorothy stopped with a discouraged little sigh and leaned against a tree. They had followed the road for several hours. First it had been fine and wide, but it had gradually dwindled to a crooked little path that wound crazily in and out through the trees. Although it was almost noonday, not a ray of sun penetrated through the dim green depths.

"Methinks," said Sir Hokus, peering into the gloom ahead, "that a great adventure is at hand."

The Cowardly Lion put back his ears. "What makes you methink so?" he rumbled anxiously.

"Hark thee!" said Sir Hokus, holding up his finger warningly. From a great way off sounded a curious thumping. It was coming nearer and nearer.

"Good gracious!" cried Dorothy, catching hold of the Cowardly Lion's mane.

"This is worse than Pokes!"

"Perchance it is a dragon," exulted the Knight, drawing his short sword. "Ah, how it would refresh me to slay a dragon!"

"I don't relish dragons myself. Scorched my tongue on one once," said the Cowardly Lion huskily. "But I'll fight with you, brother Hokus. Stand back, Dorothy dear."

As the thuds grew louder, the Knight fairly danced up and down with excitement. "Approach, villain!" he roared lustily.

"Approach till I impale thee on my lance. Ah, had I but a horse!"

"I'd let you ride on my back if it weren't for that hard tin suit," said the Cowardly Lion. "But cheer up, my dear Hokus, your voice is a little hoarse." Dorothy giggled nervously, then seized hold of a small tree, for the whole forest was rocking.

"How now!" gasped the Knight. There was a terrific quake that threw Sir Hokus on his face and sent every hair in the lion's mane on end, and then a great foot came crashing down through the treetops not three paces from the little party. Before they could even swallow, a giant hand flashed down-ward, jerked up a handful of trees by the roots, and disappeared, while a voice from somewhere way above shouted:

What are little humans for?   To feed the giant Bangladore.   Broiled or toasted, baked or roasted,   I smell three or maybe four!

"You hear that?" quavered the Cowardly Lion. Sir Hokus did not answer. His helmet had been jammed down by his fall, and he was tugging it upward with both hands. Frightened though Dorothy was, she ran to the Knight's assistance.

"Have at you!" cried Sir Hokus as soon as the opening in his helmet was opposite his eyes. "Forward!"

"My heart is beating a retreat," gulped the Cowardly Lion, but he bounded boldly after Sir Hokus.

"Varlet!" hissed the Knight, and raising his sword gave a mighty slash at the giant's ankle, which was broad as three tree trunks, while the Cowardly Lion gave a great spring and sank his teeth in the giant's huge leg.

"Ouch!" roared the giant in a voice that shook every leaf in the forest. "You stop, or I'll tell my father!" With that, he gave a hop that sent Sir Hokus flying into the treetops, stumbled over a huge rock, and came crashing to the earth,

29

smashing trees like grass blades. At the giant's first scream, Dorothy shut her eyes and, putting her hands over her ears, had run as far and as fast as she could. At the awful crash, she stopped short, opened her eyes, and stared 'round giddily.

The giant was flat on his back, but as he was stretched as far as four city blocks, only half of him was visible. The Cowardly Lion still clung to his leg, and he was gurgling and struggling in a way Dorothy could not understand.

She looked around in a panic for the Knight. Just then, Sir Hokus dropped from the branch of a tree.

"Uds daggers!" he puffed, looking ruefully at his sword, which had snapped off at the handle, " 'Tis a pretty rogue!"

"Don't you think we'd better run?" shiver Dorothy, thinking of the giant's song.

"Not while I wear these colors!" exclaimed Sir Hokus, proudly touching Dorothy's hair ribbon, which still adorned his arm. "Come, my good Lion, let us dispatch this braggart and saucy monster."

"Father!" screamed the giant, making no attempt to move.

"He seems to be frightened, himself," whispered Dorothy to the Knight. "But whatever is the matter with the Cowardly Lion?"

At that minute, the Cowardly Lion gave a great jerk and began backing with his four feet braced. The piece of giant leg that he had hold of stretched and stretched, and while Sir Hokus and Dorothy stared in amazement, it snapped off and the Cowardly Lion rolled head over paws.

"Taffy!" roared the Cowardly Lion, sitting up and trying to open his jaws, which were firmly stuck together.

"Taffy!" At this, Sir Hokus sprang nimbly on the giant's leg, ran up his chest, and perched bravely on his peppermint collar.

"Surrender, Knave!" he demanded threateningly. Dorothy, seeing she could do nothing to help the Cowardly Lion, followed. On her way up, she broke off a tiny piece of his coat and found it most delicious chocolate.

"Why, he's all made of candy!" she cried excitedly.

"Oh, hush!" sobbed the giant, rolling his great sourball eyes. "I'd be eaten in a minute if it were known."

"You were mighty anxious to eat us a while ago," said Dorothy, looking longingly at the giant's coat buttons. They seemed to be large marshmallows.

"Go away!" screamed the giant, shaking so that Dorothy slid into his vest pocket. "No one under forty feet is allowed in this forest!"

Dorothy climbed crossly out of the giant's pocket. "We didn't come because we wanted to," she assured him, wiping the chocolate off her nose.

"Odds bodikins! I cannot fight a great baby like this," sighed Sir Hokus, dodging just in time a great, sugary tear that had rolled down the giant's nose. "He's got to apologize for that song, though."

"Wait!" cried Dorothy suddenly. "I have an idea. If you set us down on the edge of the forest and give us all your vest buttons for lunch, we won't tell anyone you're made of candy. We'll let you go," she called loudly, for the giant had begun to sob again.

"Won't you? Will you?" sniffed the foolish giant.

"Never sing that song again!" commanded the Knight sternly.

"No, Sir," answered the giant meekly. "Did your dog chew much of my leg, Sir?" Then, before Dorothy or Sir Hokus had time to way a word, they were snatched up in sticky fingers and next minute were dropped with a thump in a large field of daisies.

"Oh!" spluttered Dorothy as the giant made off on his taffy legs. "Oh, we've forgotten the Cowardly Lion!" But at that minute, the giant reappeared, and the lion was dropped beside them.

"What's this? What's this?" growled the Cowardly Lion, looking around wildly.

"We got him to lift us out of the forest," explained Dorothy. "Have you swallowed the taffy?" The lion was still dizzy from his ride and only shook his head feebly.

Sir Hokus sighed and sat heavily down on a large rock. "There is no sort of honor, methinks, in overcoming a candy giant," he observed, looking wistfully at the plume still pinned to Dorothy's dress. "Ah, had it but been a proper fight!"

"You didn't know he was candy. I think you were just splendid." Jumping up, Dorothy fastened the plume in the Knight's helmet. "And you're talking just beautifully, more like a Knight every minute," she added with conviction. Sir Hokus tried not to look pleased.

"Give me a meat enemy! My teeth ache yet! First singing, then candy-leg pulling! Gr-ugh! What next?" growled the Cowardly Lion.

"Why, lunch, if you feel like eating," said Dorothy, beginning to give out the vest buttons which the giant had obediently ripped off and left for them. They were marshmallows, the size of pie plates, and Dorothy and Sir Hokus

30

found them quite delicious. The Cowardly Lion, however, after a doubtful sniff and sneeze from the powdered sugar, declined and went off to find something more to his taste.

"We had better take some of these along," said Dorothy when she and Sir Hokus had eaten several. "We may need them later."

"Everything is yellow, so we must be in the Winkie Country," announced the Cowardly Lion, who had just returned from his lunch. "There's a road, too."

"Mayhap it will take us to the jeweled city of your gracious Queen." Sir Hokus shaded his eyes and stared curiously at the long lane stretching invitingly ahead of them.

"Well, anyway, we're out of the forest and Pokes, and maybe we'll meet someone who will tell us about the Scarecrow. Come on!" cried Dorothy gaily. "I think we're on the right track this time."

Chapter 12 - Dorothy and Sir Hokus come to Fix City

The afternoon went pleasantly for the three travelers. The road was wide and shady and really seemed a bit familiar. Dorothy rode comfortably on the Cowardly Lion's back and to pass the time told Sir Hokus all about Oz. He was particularly interested in the Scarecrow.

"Grammercy! He should be knighted!" he exclaimed, slapping his knee, as Dorothy told how the clever straw man had helped outwit the Gnome King when that wicked little rascal had tried to keep them prisoners in his underground kingdom.

"But, go to! Where is the gallant man now?" The Knight sobered quickly. "Mayhap in need of a strong arm! Mayhap at the mercy of some terrible monster!"

"Oh, I hope not!" cried Dorothy, dismayed at so dark a picture. "Why, oh why, did he bother about his family tree?"

"Trust the Scarecrow to take care of himself," said the Cowardly Lion in a gruff voice. Nevertheless, he quickened his steps. "The sooner we reach the Emerald City, the sooner we'll know where he is!"

The country through which they were passing was beautiful, but quite deserted. About five o'clock, they came to a clear little stream, and after Dorothy and Sir Hokus had washed their faces and the Cowardly Lion had taken a little plunge, they all felt refreshed. Later they came to a fine pear orchard, and as no one was about they helped themselves generously.

The more Dorothy and the Cowardly Lion saw of Sir Hokus, the fonder of him they grew. He was so kind-hearted and so polite.

"He'll be great company for us back in the Emerald City," whispered the Cowardly Lion as the Knight went off to get Dorothy a drink from a little spring. "That is, if he forgets this grammercy, bludgeon stuff."

"I think it sounds lovely," said Dorothy, "and he's remembering more of it all the time. But I wonder why there are no people here. I do hope we meet some before night." But no person did they meet. As it grew darker, Sir Hokus' armor began to creak in a quite frightful manner. Armor is not meant for walking, and the poor Knight was stiff and tired, but he made no complaint.

"Need oiling, don't you?" asked the Cowardly Lion, peering anxiously at him through the gloom.

"Joints in my armor a bit rusty," puffed Sir Hokus, easing one foot and then the other. "Ah, had I my good horse!" He expressively waved a piece of the giant's button at which he had been nibbling.

"Better climb up behind Dorothy," advised the Cowardly Lion, but Sir Hokus shook his head, for he knew the lion was tired, too.

"I'll manage famously. This very night I may find me a steed!"

"How?" asked the lion with a yawn.

"If I sleep beneath these trees, I may have a Knight mare," chuckled Sir Hokus triumphantly.

"Br-rrr!" roared the Cowardly Lion while Dorothy clapped her hands. But they were not to sleep beneath the trees after all, for a sudden turn in the road brought them right to the gates of another city. They knew it must be a city because a huge, lighted sign hung over the gate.

"Fix City," read Dorothy. "What a funny name!"

"Maybe they can fix us up," rumbled the lion, winking at Sir Hokus.

"Perchance we shall hear news of the valiant Scarecrow!" cried the Knight, and limping forward he thumped on the gate with his mailed fist. Dorothy and the Cowardly Lion pressed close behind him and waited impatiently for someone to open the gate.

A bell rang loud back in the town. The next instant, the gates flew open so suddenly that the three adventurers were flung violently on their faces.

"Out upon them!" blustered Sir Hokus, getting up stiffly and running to help Dorothy. "What way is this to welcome strangers?" He pulled the little girl hastily to her feet, then they all ran forward, for the gates were swinging shut again.

It was almost as light as day, for lanterns were everywhere, but strangely enough they seemed to dart about like huge fireflies, and Dorothy ducked involuntarily as a red one bobbed down almost in her face. Then she gasped in real earnest and caught hold of Sir Hokus.

"Uds daggers!" wheezed the Knight. Two large bushes were running down the path, and right in front of Dorothy the larger caught the smaller and began pulling out its leaves.

"Leave off! Leave off!" screamed the little bush.

"That's what I'm doing," said the big bush savagely. "There won't be a leaf on when I get through with you."

"Unhand him, villain!" cried Sir Hokus, waving his sword at the large bush. The two bushes looked up in surprise, and when they saw Dorothy, the Cowardly Lion and Sir Hokus, they fell into each other's branches and burst into the most uproarious laughter.

"My dear Magnolia, this is rich! Oh, dear fellow, wait till Sit sees this; he will be convulsed!" Quite forgetting their furious quarrel, the two went rollicking down the path together, stopping every few minutes to look back and laugh at the three strangers.

"Is this usual?" asked Sir Hokus, looking quite dazed.

"I never heard of bushes talking or running around, but I confess I'm a few centuries behind times!"

"Neither did I!" exclaimed Dorothy. "But then — almost anything's likely to happen in Oz."

"If these lanterns don't look out something will happen. I'll break 'em to bits," growled the Cowardly Lion, who had been dodging half a dozen at once.

"How would we look — out?" sniffed one, flying at Dorothy.

"You could light out — or go out," giggled the little girl.

"We never go out unless we're put out," cried another, but as the Cowardly Lion made a few springs, they flew high into the air and began talking indignantly among themselves. By this time, the three had become accustomed to the changing lights.

"I wonder where the people are," said Dorothy, peering down a wide avenue. "There don't seem to be any houses. Oh, look!"

Three tables set for dinner with the most appetizing viands were walking jauntily down the street, talking fluent china.

"There must be people!" cried Dorothy.

"One dinner for each of us," rumbled the Cowardly Lion, licking his chops. "Come on!"

"Perchance they will invite us. If we follow the dinners, we'll come to the diners," said Sir Hokus mildly.

"Right — as usual." The Cowardly Lion looked embarrassed, for he had intended pouncing on the tables without further ceremony.

"Hush! Let's go quietly. If they hear us, they may run and upset the dishes," warned Dorothy. So the three walked softly after the dinner tables, their curiosity about the people of Fix growing keener at every step. Several chairs, a sofa and a clothes tree rushed past them, but as Dorothy said later to Ozma, after talking bushes, nothing surprised them. The tables turned the corner at the end of the avenue three abreast, and the sight that greeted Dorothy and her comrades was strange indeed. Down each side of a long street as far as they could see stood rows and rows of people. Each one was in the exact center of a chalked circle, and they were so still that Dorothy thought they must be statues.

But no sooner had the three tables made their appearance than bells began ringing furiously all up and down the street, and dinner tables and chairs came running from every direction. All the inhabitants of Fix City looked alike. They had large, round heads, broad placid faces, double chins, and no waists whatever. Their feet were flat and about three times as long as the longest you have ever seen. The women wore plain Mother Hubbard dresses and straw sailor hats, and the men gingham suits.

While the three friends were observing all this, the tables had been taking their places. One stopped before each Fix, and the chairs, after much bumping and quarreling, placed themselves properly. At a signal from the Fix in the center, the whole company sat down without so much as moving their feet. Dorothy, Sir Hokus and the Cowardly Lion had been too interested to speak, but at this minute a whole flock of the mischievous lanterns clustered over their heads, and at the sudden blare of light the whole street stopped eating and stared.

"Oh!" cried the Fix nearest them, pointing with his fork, "Look at the runabouts!"

"This way, please! This way, please! Don't bark your shins. Don't take any more steps than you can help!" boomed an important voice from the middle of the street. So down the center marched the three, feeling — as the Cowardly Lion put it — exactly like a circus.

"Stop! Names, please!" The Fix next to the center put up his knife commandingly. Sir Hokus stepped forward with a bow:

"Princess Dorothy of Oz, the Cowardly Lion of Oz."

"And Sir Hokus of Pokes," roared the Lion as the Knight modestly stepped back without announcing himself.

"Sir Pokus of Hoax, Howardly Kion of Boz, and Little Girl Beginning with D," bellowed the Fix, "meet His Royal Highness, King Fix It, and the noble Fixitives."

"Little Girl Beginning with D! That's too long," complained the King, who, with the exception of his crown, looked like all the rest of them, "I'll leave out the middle. What do you want, Little With D?"

"My name is Dorothy, and if your Highness could give us some dinner and tell us something about the Scarecrow and —"

"One thing at a time, please," said the King reprovingly. "What does Poker want, and Boz? Have they anything to spend?"

"Only the night, an' it please your Gracious Highness," said Sir Hokus with his best bow.

"It doesn't please me especially," said the King, taking a sip of water. "And there! You've brought up another question. How do you want to spend it?"

He folded his hands helplessly on the table and looked appealingly at the Fix next to him. "How am I to settle all these questions, Sticken? First they come running around like crazy chairs, and —"

"You might ring for a settle," suggested Sticken, looking curiously at Sir Hokus. The King leaned back with a sigh of relief, then touched a bell. There were at least twenty bells set on a high post at his right hand, and all of the Fixes seemed to have similar bell posts.

"He's talking perfect nonsense," said Dorothy angrily. The Cowardly Lion began to roll his eyes ominously.

"Let me handle this, my dear. I'm used to Kings," whispered Sir Hokus. "Most of 'em talk nonsense. But if he grows wroth, we'll have all the furniture in the place around our ears. Now just —"

Bump! Sir Hokus and Dorothy sat down quite suddenly. The settle had arrived and hit them smartly behind the knees. The Cowardly Lion dodged just in time and lay down with a growl beside it.

"Now that you're settled," began the King in a resigned voice, "we might try again. What is your motto?"

This took even Sir Hokus by surprise, but before he could answer, the King snapped out:

"Come late and stay early! How's that?"

"Very good," said Sir Hokus with a wink at Dorothy.

"Next time, don't come at all," mumbled Sticken Plaster, his mouth full of biscuit.

"And you wanted?" the King asked uneasily.

"Dinner for three," said the Knight promptly and with another bow.

"Now that's talking." The King looked admiringly at Sir Hokus. "This Little With D had matters all tangled up. One time at a thing! That's my motto!"

Leaning over, the King pressed another button. By this time, the Fixes had lost interest in the visitors and went calmly on with their dinners. Three tables came pattering up, and the settle drew itself up of its own accord. Dorothy placed the Cowardly Lion's dinner on the ground, and then she and Sir Hokus enjoyed the first good meal they had had since they left Pokes. They were gradually becoming used to their strange surroundings.

"You ask him about the Scarecrow," begged Dorothy. Everybody had finished, and the tables were withdrawing in orderly groups. The King was leaning sleepily back in his chair.

"Ahem," began the Knight, rising stiffly, "has your Majesty seen aught of a noble Scarecrow? And could your Supreme Fixity tell us aught —"

The King's eyes opened. "You're out of turn," he interrupted crossly. "We're only to the second question. How will you spend the night?"

"In sleep," answered Sir Hokus promptly, "if your Majesty permits."

"I do," said the King solemnly. "That gets me out of entertaining. Early to bed and late to rise, that's my motto. Next! It's your turn," he added irritably as Sir Hokus did not immediately answer.

"Have you seen aught of the noble Scarecrow?" asked Sir Hokus, and all of them waited anxiously for the King's reply.

"I don't know about the Scarecrow. I've seen a Scarecrow, and a sensible chap he was, hanging still like a reasonable person and letting chairs and tables chase themselves 'round."

"Where was he?" asked Sir Hokus in great agitation.

33

"In a picture," said the King. "Wait, I'll ring for it."

"No use," said the Knight in a disappointed voice. "We're looking for a man."

"Would you mind telling me why you are all so still, and why all your furniture runs around?" asked Dorothy, who was growing a little restless.

"You forget where you are, and you're out of turn. But I'll overlook it this once," said the King. "Have you ever noticed, Little With D, that furniture lasts longer than people?"

"Why, yes," admitted Dorothy.

"Well, there you are!" King Fix Sit folded his hands and regarded her complacently. "Here we manage things better. We stand still and let the furniture run around and wear itself out. How does it strike you?"

"It seem sensible," acknowledged Dorothy. "But don't you ever grow tired of standing still?"

"I've heard of growing hair and flowers and corn, but never of growing tired. What is it?" asked Sticken Plaster, leaning toward Dorothy.

"I think she's talked enough," said the King, closing his eyes.

Sir Hokus had been staring anxiously at the King for some time. Now he came close to the monarch's side, and standing on tiptoe whispered hoarsely: "Hast any dragons here?"

"Did you say wagons?" asked the King, opening his eyes with a terrible yawn.

"Dragons!" hissed the Knight.

"Never heard of 'em," said the King. The Cowardly Lion chuckled behind his whiskers, and Sir Hokus in great confusion stepped back.

"What time is it?" demanded the King suddenly. He touched a bell, and next minute a whole company of clocks came running down the street. The big ones pushed the little ones, and a grandfather clock ran so fast that it tripped over a cobblestone and fell on its face, which cracked all the way across.

"You've plenty of time; why don't you take it?" called the King angrily, while two clothes trees helped the clock to its feet.

"They're all different," giggled Dorothy, nudging the Cowardly Lion. Some pointed to eight o'clock, some to nine, and others to half past ten.

"Why shouldn't they be different?" asked Sticken haughtily. "Some run faster than others!"

"Pass the time, please," said the King, looking hard at Dorothy.

"The lazy lump!" growled the Cowardly Lion. But Dorothy picked up the nearest little clock and handed it to King Fix Sit.

"I thought so," yawned the King, pointing at the clock. At this, everybody began ringing bells till Dorothy was obliged to cover her ears. In an instant, the whole street was filled with beds, "rolling up just as if they were taxis," laughed Dorothy to Sir Hokus. The Knight smiled faintly, but as he had never seen a taxi, he could not appreciate Dorothy's remark.

"Here come your beds," said the King shortly. "Tell them to take you around the corner. I can't abide snoring."

"I don't snore, thank you," said Dorothy angrily, but the King had stepped into his bed and drawn the curtains tight.

"We might as well go to bed, I 'spose," said the little girl. "I'm so tired!"

The three beds were swaying restlessly in the middle of the street. They were tall, four-post affairs with heavy chintz hangings. Dorothy chose the blue one, and Sir Hokus lifted her up carefully and then went off to catch his bed, which had gotten into an argument with a lamppost. When he spoke to it sharply, it left off and came trotting over to him. The Cowardly Lion, contrary to his usual custom, leaped into his bed, and soon the three four-posters were walking quietly down the street, evidently following the King's instructions.

Dorothy slipped off her shoes and dress and nestled comfortably down among the soft covers. "Just like sleeping in a train," she thought drowsily. "What a lot I shall have to tell the Scarecrow and Ozma when I get home."

"Good night!" said the bed politely.

"Good night!" said Dorothy, too nearly asleep to even think it strange for a bed to talk. "Good night!"

Chapter 13 - Dancing Beds and the Roads that Unrolled

"It must be a shipwreck," thought Dorothy, sitting up in alarm. She seemed to be tossing about wildly.

"Time for little girls to get up," grumbled a harsh voice that seemed to come from the pillows.

Dorothy rubbed her eyes. One of the bedposts was addressing her, and the big four-poster itself was dancing a regular jig.

"Oh, stop!" cried Dorothy, holding on to the post to keep from bouncing out.

"Can't you see I'm awake?"

"Well, I go off duty now, and you'll have to hurry," said the bed sulkily. "I'm due at the lecture at nine."

"Lecture?" gasped Dorothy.

"What's so queer about that?" demanded the bed coldly. "I've got to keep well posted, haven't I? I belong to a polished set, I do. Hurry up, little girl, or I'll throw you out."

"I'm glad my bed doesn't talk to me in this impertinent fashion," thought Dorothy, slipping into her dress and combing her hair with her side comb. "Imagine being ordered about by a bed! I wonder if Sir Hokus is up." Parting the curtains, she jumped down, and the bed, without even saying goodbye, took itself off.

Sir Hokus was sitting on a stile, polishing his armor with a pillowslip he had taken from his bed, and the Cowardly Lion was lying beside him lazily thumping his tail and making fun of the passing furniture.

"Have you had breakfast?" asked Dorothy, joining her friends.

"We were waiting for your Ladyship," chuckled the Cowardly Lion. "Would you mind ordering two for me, Hokus? I find one quite insufficient."

Sir Hokus threw away the pillowslip, and talking cheerfully they walked toward King Fix Sit's circle. The beds had been replaced by breakfast tables, and the whole street was eating busily.

"Good morning, King," said Sir Hokus. "Four breakfasts, please."

The king rang a bell four times without looking up from his oatmeal. Seeing that he did not wish to be disturbed, the three waited quietly for their tables.

"In some ways," said Dorothy, contentedly munching a hot roll, "in some ways this is a very comfortable place."

"In sooth 'tis that," mumbled Sir Hokus, his mouth full of baked apple. As for the Cowardly Lion, he finished his two breakfasts in no time. "And now," said Sir Hokus as the tables walked off, "let us continue our quest. Could'st tell us the way to the Emerald City, my good King Fix?"

"If you go, go away. And if you stay, stay away. That's my motto," answered King Fix shortly. "I can't have people running around here like common furniture," he added in a grieved voice. All the Fix Its nodded vigorously.

"Let them take their stand or their departure," said Sticken Plaster firmly.

The King felt in his pocket and brought out three pieces of chalk. "Go to the end of the street. Choose a place and draw your circle. In five minutes you will find it impossible to move out of the circle, and you will be saved all this unnecessary motion."

"But we don't want to come to a standstill," objected Dorothy.

"No, by my good sword!" spluttered the Knight, glaring around nervously. Then, seeing the King looked displeased, he made a low bow. "If your Highness could graciously direct us out of the city —"

"Buy a piece of road and go where it takes you," snapped the King.

Seeing no more was to be got out of him, they started down the long street.

"I wonder what they do when it rains?" said Dorothy, looking curiously at the solemn rows of people.

"Call for roofs, silly!" snapped a Fix, staring at her rudely. "If you would spend your time thinking instead of walking, you'd know more."

"Go to, and swallow a gooseberry!" roared the Knight, waving his sword at the Fix, and Dorothy, fearing an encounter, begged him to come on, which he did — though with many backward glances.

Fix City seemed to consist of one long street, and they had soon come to the very end.

"Uds daggers!" gasped Sir Hokus.

"Great palm trees," roared the Cowardly Lion.

As for Dorothy, she could do nothing but stare. The street ended surely enough, and beyond there was nothing at all. That is, nothing but air.

"Well," said the Cowardly Lion, backing a few paces, "this is a pretty fix."

"Glad you like it," said a wheezy voice. The three travelers turned in surprise. A huge Fix was regarding them with interest. His circle, which was the last in the row, was about twenty times as large as the other circles, and on the edge stood a big sign:'

ROAD SHOP.

"Don't you remember, the King said something about buying a road," said Dorothy in an excited undertone to the Knight.

"Can'st direct us to a road, my good man?" asked Sir Hokus with a bow. The Fix jerked his thumb back at the sign. "What kind of a road to you want?" he asked hoarsely.

"A road that will take us back to the Emerald City, please," said Dorothy.

"I can't guarantee anything like that," declared the Fix, shaking his head.

"Our roads go where they please, and you'll have to go where they take you. Do you want to go on or off?"

"On," shivered the Cowardly Lion, looking with a shudder over the precipice at the end of the street.

"What kind of a road will you have? Make up your minds, please. I am busy."

"What kind of roads have you?" asked Dorothy timidly. It was her first experience at buying roads, and she felt a bit perplexed.

"Sunny, shady, straight, crooked, and cross-roads," snapped the Fix.

"We wouldn't want a cross one," said Dorothy positively. "Have you any with trees at both sides and water at the end?"

"How many yards?" asked the Fix, taking a pair of shears as large as himself off a long counter beside him.

"Five miles," said Sir Hokus as Dorothy looked confused. "That ought to take us somewhere!"

The Fix rang one of the bells in the counter. The next minute, a big trap door in the ground opened, and a perfectly huge roll bounced out at his feet.

"Get on," commanded the Fix in such a sharp tone that the three jumped to obey. Holding fast to Sir Hokus, Dorothy stepped on the piece of road that had already unrolled. The Cowardly Lion, looking very anxious, followed. No sooner had they done so than the road gave a terrific leap forward that stretched the three flat upon their backs and started unwinding from its spool at a terri- fying speed. As it unrolled, tall trees snapped erect on each side and began laughing derisively at the three travelers huddled together in the middle.

"G-g-glad we only took five miles," stuttered Dorothy to the Knight, whose armor was rattling like a Ford.

The Cowardly Lion had wound his tail around a tree and dug his claws into the road, for he had no intention of falling off into nothingness. As for the road, it snapped along at about a mile a minute, and before they had time to grow accustomed to this singular mode of travel, it gave a final jump that sent them circling into the air, and began rapidly winding itself up.

Down, down, down whirled Dorothy, falling with a resounding splash into a broad stream of water. Then down, down, down again, almost to the bottom.

"Help!" screamed Dorothy as her head rose above water, and she began striking out feebly. But the fall through the air had taken all her breath.

"What do you want?" A thin, neat little man was watching her anxiously from the bank, making careful notes in a book that he held in one hand.

"Help! Save me!" choked Dorothy, feeling herself going down in the muddy stream again.

"Wait! I'll look it up under the 'H's," called the little man, making a trumpet of his hands. "Are you an island? An island is a body of land entirely surrounded by water, but this seems to be a some-body," Dorothy heard him mutter as he whipped over several pages of his book. "Sorry," he called back, shaking his head slowly, "but this is the wrong day. I only save lives on Monday."

"Stand aside, Mem, you villain!" A second little man exactly like the first except that he was exceedingly untidy plunged into the stream.

"It's no use," thought Dorothy, closing her eyes, for he had jumped in far below the spot where she had fallen and was making no progress whatever. The waters rushed over her head the second time. Then she felt herself being dragged upward.

When she opened her eyes, the Cowardly Lion was standing over her. "Are you all right?" he rumbled anxiously. "I came as soon as I could. Fell in way upstream. Seen Hokus?"

"Oh, he'll drown," cried Dorothy, forgetting her own narrow escape. "He can't swim in that heavy armor!"

"Never fear, I'll get him," puffed the Cowardly Lion, and without waiting to catch his breath he plunged back into the stream. The little man who only saved lives on Monday now approached timidly. "I'd like to get a statement from you, if you don't mind. It might help me in the future."

"You might have helped me in the present," said Dorothy, wringing out her dress. "You ought to be ashamed of yourself."

"I'll make a note of that," said the little man earnestly. "But how did you feel when you went down?" He waited, his pencil poised over the little book.

"Go away," cried Dorothy in disgust.

"But my dear young lady —"

"I'm not your dear young lady. Oh, dear, why doesn't the Cowardly Lion come back?"

"Go away, Mem." The second little man, dripping wet, came up hurriedly.

"I was only trying to get a little information," grumbled Mem sulkily.

"I'm sorry I couldn't swim faster," said the wet little man, approaching Dorothy apologetically.

"Well, thank you for trying," said Dorothy. "Is he your brother? And could you tell me where you are? You're dressed in yellow, so I 'spose it must be somewhere in the Winkie Country."

"Right in both cases," chuckled the little fellow. "My name is Ran and his name is Memo." He jerked his thumb at the retiring twin. "Randum and Memo — see?"

"I think I do," said Dorothy, half closing her eyes. "Is that why he's always taking notes?"

"Exactly," said Ran. "I do everything at Random, and he does everything at memorandum."

"It must be rather confusing," said Dorothy. Then as she caught sight of the Cowardly Lion dragging Sir Hokus, she jumped up excitedly. Ran, however, took one look at the huge beast and then fled, calling for Mem at the top of his voice. And that is the last Dorothy saw of these singular twins.

The Lion dropped Sir Hokus in a limp heap. When Dorothy unfastened his armor, gallons of water rushed out.

"Sho good of — of — you," choked the poor Knight, trying to straighten up.

"Save your breath, old fellow," said the Cowardly Lion, regarding him affectionately.

"Oh, why did I ask for water on the end of the road?" sighed Dorothy. "But, anyway, we're in some part of the Winkie Country."

Sir Hokus, though still spluttering, was beginning to revive. "Yon noble bheast shall be knighted. Uds daggers! That's the shecond time he's shaved my life!" Rising unsteadily, he tottered over to the Lion and struck him a sharp blow on the shoulder. "Rishe, Shir Cowardly Lion," he cried hoarsely, and fell headlong, and before Dorothy or the lion had recovered from their surprise he was fast asleep, mumbling happily of dragons and bludgeons.

"We'll have to wait till he gets rested," said Dorothy. "And until I get dry." She began running up and down, then stopped suddenly before the Lion.

"And there's something else for Professor Wogglebug to put in his book, Sir Cowardly Lion."

"Oh, that!" mumbled the Cowardly Lion, looking terribly embarrassed. "Whoever heard of a Cowardly Knight? Nonsense!"

"No, it isn't nonsense," said Dorothy stoutly. "You're a knight from now on. Won't the Scarecrow be pleased?"

"If we ever find him," sighed the Lion, settling himself beside Sir Hokus.

"We will," said Dorothy gaily. "I just feel it."

Chapter 14 - Sons and Grandsons Greet the Scarecrow

Although the Scarecrow had been on Silver Island only a few days, he had already instituted many reforms, and thanks to his cleverness the people were more prosperous than ever before. Cheers greeted him wherever he went, and even old Chew Chew was more agreeable and no longer made bitter remarks to Happy Toko. The Scarecrow himself, however, had four new wrinkles and was exceedingly melancholy. He missed the carefree life in Oz, and every minute that he was not ruling the island he was thinking about his old home and dear, jolly comrades in the Emerald City.

"I almost hope they will look in the Magic Picture and wish me back again," he mused pensively. "But it is my duty to stay here. I have a family to support." So he resolved to put the best face he could on the matter, and Happy Toko did his utmost to cheer up his royal master. The second morning after the great victory, he came running into the silver throne room in a great state of excitement.

"The honorable Offspring have arriven!" (sic) announced Happy, turning a somersault. "Come, ancient and amiable Sir, and gaze upon your sons and grandsons!" The Scarecrow sprang joyously from his silver throne, upsetting a bowl of silver fish and three silver vases. At last a real family! Ever since his arrival, the three Princes and their fifteen little sons had been cruising on the royal pleasure barge, so that the Scarecrow had not caught a glimpse of them.

"This is the happiest moment of my life!" he exclaimed, clasping his yellow gloves and watching the door intently. Happy looked a little uneasy, for he knew the three Princes to be exceedingly haughty and overbearing, but he said nothing, and next minute the Scarecrow's family stepped solemnly into the royal presence.

"Children!" cried the Scarecrow, and with his usual impetuousness rushed forward and flung his arms around the first richly clad Prince.

"Take care! Take care, ancient and honorable papa!" cried the young Silverman, backing away. "Such excitement is not good for one of your advanced years." He drew himself away firmly and, adjusting a huge pair of silver spectacles, regarded the Scarecrow attentively. "Ah, how you have changed!"

"He looks very feeble, Too Fang, but may he live long to rule this flowery island and our humble selves!" said the second Prince, bowing stiffly.

"Do you not find the affairs of state fatiguing, darling papa?" inquired the third Prince, fingering a jeweled chain that hung around his neck.

"I, as your eldest son, shall be delighted to relieve you should you wish to retire. Get back ten paces, you!" he roared at Happy Toko.

The poor Scarecrow had been so taken aback by this cool reception that he just stared in disbelief.

"If the three honorable Princes will retire themselves, I will speak with my grandsons," he said dryly, bowing in his most royal manner. The three Princes exchanged startled glances. Then, with three low salaams, they retired backward from the hall.

"And now, my dears —!" The Scarecrow looked wistfully at his fifteen silken- clad little grandsons. Their silver hair, plaited tightly into little queues, stood out stiffly on each side of their heads and gave them a very curious appearance. At his first word, the fifteen fell dutifully on their noses. As soon as they were right side up, the Scarecrow, beginning at the end of the row, addressed a joking question to each in his most approved Oz style. But over they went again, and answered merely:

"Yes, gracious Grand-papapapah!" or "No honorable Grandpapapapah!" And the constant bobbing up and down and papahing so confused the poor Scarecrow that he nearly gave up the conversation.

"It's no use trying to talk to these children," he wailed in disgust, "they're so solemn. Don't you ever laugh?" he cried in exasperation, for he had told them stories that would have sent the Oz youngsters into hysterics.

"It is not permissible for a Prince to laugh at the remarks of his honorable grandparent," whispered Happy Toko, while the fifteen little Princes banged their heads solemnly on the floor.

"Honorable fiddlesticks!" exclaimed the Scarecrow, slumping back on his throne. "Bring cushions." Happy Toko ran off nimbly, and soon the fifteen little Princes were seated in a circle at the Scarecrow's feet. "To prevent prostrations," said the Scarecrow.

"Yes, old Grandpapapapapah!" chorused the Princes, bending over as far as they could.

"Wait!" said the Scarecrow hastily, "I'll tell you a story. Once upon a time, to a beautiful country called Oz, which is surrounded on all sides by a deadly desert, there came a little girl named Dorothy. A terrible gale — Well, what's the matter now?" The Scarecrow stopped short, for the oldest Prince had jerked a book out of his sleeve and was flipping over the pages industriously.

"It is not on the map, great Grand papapapah," he announced solemnly, and all of the other little Princes shook their heads and said dully, "Not on the map."

"Not on the map — Oz? Of course it's not. Do you suppose we want all the humans in creation coming there?" Calming down, the Scarecrow tried to continue his story, but every time he mentioned Oz, the little Princes shook their heads stubbornly and whispered, "Not on the map," till the usually good-tempered Scarecrow flew into perfect passion.

"Not on the map, you little villains!" he screamed, forgetting they were his grandsons. "What difference does that make? Are your heads solid silver?"

"We do not believe in Oz," announced the oldest Prince serenely. "There is no such place."

"No such place as Oz — Happy, do you hear that?" The Scarecrow's voice fairly crackled with indignation. "Why, I thought everybody believed in Oz!"

"Perhaps your Highness can convince them later," suggested the Imperial Punster. "This way, offspring." His Master, he felt, had had enough family for one day. So the fifteen little Princes, with fifteen stiff little bows, took themselves back to the royal nursery. As for the Scarecrow, he paced disconsolately up and down his magnificent throne room, tripping over his kimona at every other step.

"You're a good boy, Tappy," said the Scarecrow as Happy returned, "but I tell you being a grandparent is not what I thought it would be. Did you hear them tell me right to my face they did not believe in Oz? And my sons — ugh!"

"Fault of their bringing up," said Happy Toko comfortingly. "If your serene Highness would just tell me more of that illustrious country!" Happy knew that nothing cheered the Scarecrow like talking of Oz, and to tell the truth Happy himself never tired of the Scarecrow's marvelous stories. So the two slipped quietly into the palace gardens, and the Scarecrow related for the fourteenth time the story of his discovery by Dorothy and the story of Ozma, and almost forgot that he was an Emperor.

"Your Highness knows the history of Oz by heart," said Happy admiringly as the Scarecrow paused.

"I couldn't do that," said the Scarecrow gently, "for you see, Happy, I have no heart."

"Then I wish we all had none!" exclaimed Happy Toko, rolling up his eyes. The Scarecrow looked embarrassed, so the little Punster threw back his head and sang a song he had been making up while the Scarecrow had been telling his stories:

"The Scarecrow was standing alone in a field,
Inviting the crows to keep off,
When the straw in his chest began tickling his vest
And he couldn't resist a loud cough.
The noise that was heard so surprised ev'ry bird,
that the flock flew away in a fright,
But the Scarecrow looked pleased, and he said "If I'd sneezed
It wouldn't have been so polite."

"Ho!" roared the Scarecrow, "You're almost as good at making verses as Scraps, Write that down for me, Tappy. I'd like to show it to her."

"Hush!" whispered Happy, holding up his finger warningly. The Scarecrow turned so suddenly that the silver pigtail pinned to the back of his hat wound itself tightly around his neck. No wonder! On the other side of the hedge the three Princes were walking up and down, conversing in indignant whispers.

"What a horrible shape our honorable Papa has reappeared in. I hear that it never wears out," muttered one. "He may continue just as he is for years and years. How am I ever to succeed him, I'd like to know. Why, he may outlive us all!"

"We might throw him into the silver river," said the second hopefully.

"No use," choked the third. "I was just talking to the Imperial Soothsayer, and he tells me that no one from this miserable Kingdom of Oz can be destroyed. But I have a plan. Incline your Royal ears — listen." The voices dropped to such a low whisper that neither Happy nor the Scarecrow could hear one word.

"Treason!" spluttered Happy, making ready to spring through the hedge, but the Scarecrow seized him by the arm and drew him away.

"I don't believe they like their poor papa," exclaimed the Scarecrow when they were safely back in the throne room. "I'm feeling older than a Kinkajou. Ah, Happy Oko, why did I ever slide down my family tree? It has brought me nothing but unhappiness."

Chapter 15 - The Three Princes Plot to Undo the Emperor

"Let me help your Imperial Serenity!"

"Bring a cane!"

"Carefully, now!"

The three royal Princes, with every show of affection, were supporting the Scarecrow to the silver bench in the garden where he usually sat during luncheon.

"Are you quite comfortable?" asked the elder. "Here, Happy, you rogue, fetch a scarf for his Imperial Highness. You must be careful, dear Papa Scarecrow. At your age, drafts are dangerous." The rascally Prince wound the scarf about the Scarecrow's neck.

"What do you suppose they are up to?" asked the Scarecrow, staring after the three suspiciously. "Why this sudden devotion? It upsets my Imperial Serenity a lot."

"Trying to make you feel old," grumbled Happy. Several hours had passed since they had overheard the conversation in the garden. The Scarecrow had decided to watch his sons closely and fall in with any plan they suggested so they would suspect nothing. Then, when the time came, he would act. Just what he would do he did not know, but his excellent brains would not, he felt sure, desert him. Happy Toko sat as close to the Scarecrow as he could and scowled terribly whenever the Princes approached, which was every minute or so during the afternoon.

"How is the Scarecrow's celestial old head?"

"Does he suffer from honorable gout?"

"Should they fetch the Imperial Doctor?"

The Scarecrow, who had never thought of age in his whole straw life, became extremely nervous.

Was he really old? Did his head ache? When no one was looking, he felt himself carefully all over. Then something of his old time Oz spirit returned. Seizing the cushion that his eldest son was placing at his back, he hurled it over his head. Leaping from his throne, he began turning handsprings in a careless and sprightly manner.

"Don't you worry about your honorable old papa," chuckled the Scarecrow, winking at Happy Toko. "He's good for a couple of centuries!"

The three Princes stared sourly at this exhibition of youth.

"But your heart," objected the eldest Prince.

"Have none," laughed the Scarecrow. Snatching off the silver cord from around his waist, he began skipping rope up and down the hall. The Princes, tapping their foreheads significantly, retired, and the Scarecrow, throwing his arm around Happy Toko, began whispering in his ear. He had a plan himself. They would see!

*　*　*　*　*

Meanwhile, off in his dark cave in one of the silver mountains, the Grand Gheewizard of the Silver Island was stirring a huge kettle of magic. Every few moments he paused to read out of a great yellow book that he had propped up on the mantle. The fire in the huge grate leaped fiercely under the big, black pot, and the sputtering candles on each side of the book sent creepy shadows into the dark cave. Dark chests, books, bundles of herbs, and heaps of gold and silver were everywhere. Whenever the Gheewizard turned his back, a rheumatic silver-scaled old dragon would crawl toward the fire and swallow a mouthful of coals, until the old Gheewizard caught him in the act and chained him to a ring in the corner of the cave.

"Be patient, little joy of my heart! Our fortune is about to be made," hissed the wizened little man, waving a long iron spoon at the dragon. "You shall have a bucket of red-hot coals every hour and I a silver cap with a tassel. Have not the Royal Princes promised it?" The dragon shuffled about and finally went to sleep, smoking sulkily.

"Is it finished, son of a yellow dog?" Through the narrow opening of the cave, the youngest Prince stuck his head.

"I am working as fast as I can, Honorable Prince, but the elixir must boil yet one more night. Tomorrow, when the sun shines on the first bar of your celestial window, come, and all will be ready."

"Are you sure you have found it?" asked the Prince, withdrawing his head, for the smoking dragon and steam from the kettle made him cough.

"Quite sure," wheezed the Grand Gheewizard, and fell to stirring the kettle with all his might.

*　*　*　*　*

The Scarecrow, although busy with trials in the great courtroom of the palace, felt that something unusual was in the air. The Princes kept nodding to one another, and the Grand Chew Chew and General Mugwump had their heads together at every opportunity.

"Something's going to happen, Tappy. I feel it in my straw," whispered the Scarecrow as he finished trying the last case. At that very minute, the Grand Chew Chew arose and held up his hand for silence. Everybody paused in their way to the exits and looked with surprise at the old Silverman.

"I have to announce," said the Grand Chew Chew in a solemn voice, "that the Great and Imperial Chang Wang Woe will tomorrow be restored to his own rightful shape. The Grand Gheewizard of the realm has discovered a magic formula to break the enchantment and free him from this distressing Scarecrow body. Behold for the last the Scarecrow of Oz. Tomorrow he will be our old and glorious Emperor!"

"Old and glorious?" gasped the Scarecrow, nearly falling from his throne.

"Tappy! I forgot to lock up the wizards. Great Cornstarch! Tomorrow I will be eighty-five years old."

Such cheers greeted the Grand Chew Chew's announcement that no one even noticed the Scarecrow's distress.

"I, also, have an announcement!" cried the eldest Prince, standing up proudly. "To make the celebration of my royal Papa's restoration complete, we have chosen the lovely and charming Orange Blossom for his bride."

"Bride!" gulped the Scarecrow. "But I do not approve of second marriages. I refuse to —"

No one paid the slightest attention to the Scarecrow's remarks.

"Hold my hand, Tappy," sighed the Scarecrow weakly. "It may be your last chance." Then he sat up and stared in good earnest, for the Prince was leading forward a tall, richly clad lady.

"Orange Blossom!" muttered the Scarecrow under his breath. "He means Lemon Peel! Silver grandmother, Tappy!" Orange Blossom was a cross-looking Princess of seventy-five, at least.

"She is a sister of the King of the Golden Islands," whispered General Mugwump. "Of a richness surpassing your own. Let me felicitate your Highness."

"Fan me, Tappy! Fan me!" gasped the Scarecrow. Then he straightened himself suddenly. The time had come for action. He would say nothing to anyone, but that night he would escape and try to find his way back to Oz, family or no family! He bowed graciously to Princess Orange Blossom, to the Grand Chew Chew, and to his sons.

"Let everything be made ready for the ceremony, and may tomorrow indeed bring me to myself," he repeated solemnly. Nothing was talked of that evening but the Emperor's impending marriage and the Grand Gheewizard's discovery. The Scarecrow seemed the least excited person in the palace. Sitting on his throne, he pretended to read the Royal Silver Journal, but he was really waiting impatiently for the courtiers to retire. Finally, when the last one had bowed himself out and only Happy Toko remained in the throne room, the Scarecrow began making his plans.

"It's no use, Tappy," said he, tying up a few little trinkets for Dorothy in a silk handkerchief, "I'd rather be straw than meat. I'd rather be a plain Scarecrow in Oz than Emperor of the Earth! They may be my sons, but all they want is my death. I'm going back to my old friends. I'd rather —". He got no farther. A huge slave seized him suddenly from behind, while another caught Happy Toko around his fat little waist.

"Tie them fast," said the eldest Prince, smiling wickedly at the Scarecrow. "Here, tie him to the beanstalk. Merely a part of the Grand Gheewizard's formula," he exclaimed maliciously as the struggling Scarecrow was bound securely to his family tree. "Good night, dear papa Scarecrow. Tomorrow you will be your old self again, and in a few short years I will be Emperor of the Silver Islands!"

"This rather upsets our plans, eh Tappy?" wheezed the Scarecrow after a struggle with his bonds.

"Pigs! Weasels!" choked Tappy. "What are we to do?"

"Alas!" groaned the Scarecrow. "Tomorrow there will be no Scarecrow in Oz. What will Dorothy and Ozma think? And once I am changed into my old Imperial self, I can never make the journey to the Emerald City. Eighty-six is too old for traveling."

"Has your Majesty forgotten the wonderful brains given to you by the Wizard of Oz?"

"I had — for a moment," confessed the Scarecrow. "Be quiet, Tappy, while I think." Pressing his head against the magic beanpole, the Scarecrow thought and thought, harder than he had ever done in the course of his adventurous life, and in the great, silent hall Happy Toko struggled to set himself free.

Chapter 16 - Dorothy and her Guardians Meet New Friends

While all these exciting things were happening to the poor Scarecrow, Dorothy, Sir Hokus and the Cowardly Lion had been having adventures of their own. For three days, they had wandered through a deserted part of the Winkie Country, subsisting largely on berries, sleeping under trees, and looking in vain for a road to lead them back to the Emerald City. On the second day, they had encountered an ancient woodsman, too old and deaf to give them any information. He did, however, invite them into his hut and give them a good dinner and a dozen sandwiches to carry away with them.

"But, oh, for a good old pasty!" sighed Sir Hokus late on the third afternoon as they finished the last of the crumbly sandwiches.

"Do you know," said Dorothy, looking through the straggly fields and woods ahead, "I believe we've been going in the wrong direction again."

"Again!" choked the Cowardly Lion. "You mean still. I've been in a good many parts of Oz, but this — this is the worst."

"Not even one little dragon!" Sir Hokus shook his head mournfully. Then, seeing that Dorothy was tired and discouraged, he pretended to strum on a guitar and sang in his high-pitched voice:

> A rusty Knight in steel bedite
> And Lady Dot, so fair,
> Sir Lion bold, with mane of gold
> And might besides to spa—ha—hare!
> And might beside to spare!
> The dauntless three, a company
> Of wit and bravery are,
> Who seek the valiant Scarecrow man,
> Who seek him near and fa—har—har,
> Who seek him near and fa—har!

"Oh, I like that!" cried Dorothy, jumping up and giving Sir Hokus a little squeeze. "Only you should have said trusty Knight."

The Cowardly Lion shook his golden mane. "Let's do a little reconnoitering, Hokus," he said carelessly. He felt he must live up to the song somehow. "Perhaps we'll find a sign."

"I don't believe in signs anymore," laughed Dorothy, "but I'm coming too." Sir Hokus' song had cheered them all, and it wasn't the first time the Knight had helped make the best of a tiresome journey.

"The air seemeth to grow very hot," observed Sir Hokus after they had walked along silently for a time. "Hast noticed it, Sir Cowardly?"

"No, but I've swallowed some of it," coughed the Cowardly Lion, looking suspiciously through the trees.

"I'll just step forward and see what it is," said the Knight. As he disappeared, the truth dawned on Dorothy.

"Wait! Wait! Don't go! Please, please, Sir Hokus, come back, come back!" cried the little girl, running after him as fast as she could.

"What's the matter?" rumbled the Cowardly Lion, thudding behind her. Then both, coming suddenly out of the woods, gave a terrible scream, which so startled Sir Hokus that he fell over backwards. Just in time, too, for another step would have taken him straight on to the Deadly Desert, which destroys every living thing and keeps all intruders away from Oz.

"What befell?" puffed Sir Hokus, getting to his feet. Naturally, he knew nothing of the poisonous sands.

"You did," wheezed the Cowardly Lion in an agitated voice.

"Was it a dragon?" asked the Knight, limping toward them hopefully.

"Sit down!" The Cowardly Lion mopped his brow with his tail. "One step on that desert and it would have been one long goodnight."

"I should say it would!" shuddered Dorothy, and explained to Sir Hokus the deadly nature of the sands. "And do you know what this means?" Dorothy was nearer to tears than even I like to think about. "It means we've come in exactly the wrong direction and are farther away from the Emerald City than we were when we started."

"And seek him near and fa—hah—har," mumbled Sir Hokus with a very troubled light in his kindly blue eyes.

"And seek him near and far."

"Fah—har—har! I should say it was," said the Cowardly Lion bitterly. "But you needn't sing it."

"No, I s'pose not. Uds helmets and hauberks! I s'pose not!" The Knight lapsed into a discouraged silence, and all three sat and stared drearily at the stretch of desert before them and thought gloomily of the rough country behind.

"It's a caravan," wheezed a hoarse voice.

"I doubt that, Camy, I doubt it very much." The shrill nasal voices so startled the three travelers that they swung about in astonishment.

"Great dates and deserts!" burst out the Cowardly Lion, jumping up. And on the whole, this exclamation was entirely suitable, for ambling toward them were a long-legged camel and a wobbly-necked dromedary.

"At last! A steed!" cried the Knight, bounding to his feet.

"I doubt that." The dromedary stopped and looked at him coldly.

"Try me," said the camel amiably. "I'm more comfortable."

"I doubt that, too."

"The doubtful dromedary wept,
As o'er the desert sands he stept,
Association with the sphinx
Has made him doubtful, so he thinks!"

chortled the Knight with his head on one side.

"How did you know?" asked the Dromedary, opening his eyes wide.

"It just occurred to me," admitted Sir Hokus, clearing his throat modestly.

"I doubt that. Somebody told you," said the Doubtful Dromedary bitterly.

"Pon my honor," said Sir Hokus.

"I doubt it, I doubt it very much," persisted the Dromedary, wagging his head sorrowfully.

"You seem to doubt everything!" Dorothy laughed in spite of herself, and the Dromedary regarded her sulkily.

"He does," said the Camel. "It makes him very doubtful company. Now, I like to be comfortable and happy, and you can't be if you're always doubting things and people and places. Eh, my dear?"

"Where did you comfortable and doubtful parties come from?" asked the Cowardly Lion. "Strangers here?"

42

"Well, yes," admitted the Camel, nibbling the branch of a tree. "There was a terrific sandstorm, and after blowing and blowing and blowing, we found ourselves in this little wood. The odd part of it is that you talk in our language. Never knew a two-leg to understand a word of Camelia before."

"You're not talking Camelia, you're talking Ozish," laughed Dorothy. "All animals can talk here."

"Well, now, that's very comfortable, I must say," sighed the Camel, "and if you'd just tell me where to go, it would be more comfortable still."

"I doubt that," snapped the Dromedary. "They're no caravan."

"Where do you want to go?" asked the Cowardly Lion, ignoring the Doubtful Dromedary.

"Anywhere, just so we keep moving. We're used to being told when to start and stop, and life is mighty lonely without our Karwan Bashi," sighed the Comfortable Camel.

"Why, I didn't know you smoked!" exclaimed Dorothy in surprise. She thought the camel was referring to a brand of tobacco.

"He means his camel driver," whispered Sir Hokus, eyeing the soft, pillowed seat on the camel's back longingly. Besides the seat, great sacks and bales of goods hung from its sides. The Doubtful Dromedary was similarly loaded.

"Goodness!" exclaimed Dorothy. A sudden idea had struck her. "You haven't anything to eat in those sacks, have you?"

"Plenty, my child — plenty!" answered the Camel calmly.

"Three cheers for the Comfortable Camel!" roared the Cowardly Lion, while Sir Hokus, following the camel's directions, carefully unfastened a large, woven basket from one of the sacks on its side.

"You may be my Karwan Bashi," announced the Comfortable Camel judiciously as Sir Hokus paused for breath.

"Hear that, Lady Dot?" Sir Hokus swept the camel a bow and fairly beamed with pleasure. Dorothy, meanwhile, had set out an appetizing repast on a small, rocky ledge — a regular feast, it appeared to the hungry travelers. There were loaves of black bread, figs, dates, cheese, and a curious sort of dried meat which the Cowardly Lion swallowed in great quantities.

"Isn't this cozy?" said Dorothy, forgetting the long, weary way ahead. "My, I'm glad we met you!"

"Very comforting to us, too, my dear," said the Camel, swaying complacently. "Isn't it, Doubty?"

"There are some silk cushions in my right-hand saddle sack, but I doubt very much whether you'll like 'em," mumbled the Dromedary gruffly.

"Out with them!" cried Sir Hokus, pouncing on the Doubtful Dromedary, and in a minute each of the party had a cushion and was as snug as possible.

"Could anything have been more fortunate?" exulted the Knight. "We can now resume our journey properly mounted."

"I think I'll ride the Cowardly Lion," said Dorothy, looking uneasily at the high seat on the camel's back. "Let's start before it grows any darker."

They had eaten to heart's content, and now, packing up the remainder of the feast, the little party made ready to start.

Sir Hokus, using the Cowardly Lion as a footstool, mounted the camel, and then Dorothy climbed on her old friend's back, and the little caravan moved slowly through the forest.

"There's a tent in my left-hand saddle sack, but I doubt very much whether you can put it up," said the Doubtful Dromedary, falling in behind the Comfortable Camel. "I doubt it very much indeed."

"How now, what means this doubting?" called Sir Hokus from his perilous seat. "I'll pitch it when the time comes."

"Mind you don't pitch out when the Camel goes!" called the Cowardly Lion, who would have his little joke. Sir Hokus, to tell the truth, was feeling tossed about and dizzy, but he was too polite to mention the fact. As they proceeded, Dorothy told the Comfortable Camel all about the Scarecrow and Oz.

An occasional word jolted down from above told her that the Knight was singing. They had gone possibly a mile when Dorothy pointed in excitement to a road just ahead.

"We must have missed it before! Wait, I'll see what it's like." Jumping down from the Cowardly Lion's back, she peered curiously at the narrow, tree-lined path. "Why, here's a sign!"

"What of?" asked the Comfortable Camel, lurching forward eagerly and nearly unseating the Knight.

WISH WAY

read Dorothy in a puzzled voice.

"Looks like a pretty good road," said the Comfortable Camel, squinting up its eyes.

"I doubt it, Camy, I doubt it very much," said the Doubtful Dromedary tremulously.

"What does my dear Karwan Bashi think?" asked the Comfortable Camel, looking adoringly back at the Knight.

"It is unwise to go back when the journey lieth forward," said the Knight, and immediately returned to his song. So, single file, the little company turned in at the narrow path, the Comfortable Camel advancing with timid steps and the Doubtful Dromedary bobbing his head dubiously.

Chapter 17 - Doubty and Camy Vanish into Space

For a short time, everything went well. Then Dorothy, turning to see how Sir Hokus was getting along, discovered that the Doubtful Dromedary had disappeared.

"Why, where in the world?" exclaimed Dorothy. The Comfortable Camel craned his wobbly neck and, when he saw that his friend was gone, burst into tears. His sobs heaved Sir Hokus clear out of his seat and flung him, helmet first, into the dust.

"Go to!" exploded the Knight, sitting up. "If I were a bird, riding in yon nest would be easier." The last of his sentence ended in a hoarse croak. Sir Hokus vanished, and a great raven flopped down in the center of the road.

"Oh, where is my dear Karwan Bashi? Oh, where is Doubty?" screamed the Comfortable Camel, running around in frenzied circles. "I wish I'd never come on this path!"

"Magic!" gasped Dorothy, clutching the Cowardly Lion's mane. The Comfortable Camel had melted into air before their very eyes.

"I doubt it, I doubt it very much!" coughed a faint voice close to her ear. Dorothy ducked her head involuntarily as a big yellow butterfly settled on the Cowardly Lion's ear.

"Our doubtful friend," whispered the lion weakly. "Oh, be careful, Dorothy dear. We may turn into frogs or something worse any minute."

Dorothy and the Cowardly Lion had had experiences with magic transformations, and the little girl, pressing her fingers to her eyes, tried to think of something to do. The raven was making awkward attempts to fly and cawing "Go to, now!" every other second.

"Oh, I wish dear Sir Hokus were himself again," wailed Dorothy after trying in vain to recall some magic sentences. Presto! The Knight stood before them, a bit breathless from flying, but hearty as ever.

"I see! I see!" said the Cowardly Lion with a little prance. "Every wish you make on this road comes true. Remember the sign: 'Wish Way.' I wish the Comfortable Camel were back. I wish the Doubtful Dromedary were himself again," muttered the Cowardly Lion rapidly, and in an instant the two creatures were standing in the path.

"Uds bodikins! So I did wish myself a bird!" gasped the Knight, rubbing his gauntlets together excitedly.

"There you are! There you are!" cried the Comfortable Camel, stumbling toward him and resting his foolish head on his shoulder. "Dear, dear Karwan Bashi! And Doubty, old fellow, there you are too! Ah, how comfortable this all is."

"Not two — one," wheezed the Doubtful Dromedary. "And Camy, I doubt very much whether I'd care for butterflying. I just happened to wish myself one!"

"Don't make any more wishes," said the Cowardly Lion sternly.

"Methinks a proper wish might serve us well," observed Sir Hokus. He had been pacing up and down in great excitement. "Why not wish —"

"Oh, stop!" begged Dorothy. "Wait till we've thought it all out. Wishing's awfully particular work!"

"One person better speak for the party," said the Cowardly Lion. "Now, I suggest —"

"Oh, be careful!" screamed Dorothy again. "I wish you would all stop wishing!" Sir Hokus looked at her reproachfully. No wonder. At Dorothy's words, they all found themselves unable to speak. The Doubtful Dromedary's eyes grew rounder and rounder. For the first time in its life, it was unable to doubt anything.

"Now I'll have to do it all," thought Dorothy, and closing her eyes she tried to think of the very best wish for everybody concerned. It was night and growing darker. The Cowardly Lion, the Camel and Dromedary and Sir Hokus peered anxiously at the little girl, wondering what in the world was going to happen. Being wished around is no joke. For five minutes Dorothy thought and thought. Then, standing in the middle of the road, she made her wish in a clear, distinct voice. It was not a very long wish. To be exact, it had only eight words. Eight — short — little words! But stars! No sooner were they out of Dorothy's mouth than the earth opened with a splintering crash and swallowed up the whole company!

Chapter 18 - Dorothy Finds the Scarecrow!

The next thing Dorothy knew, she was sitting on the hard floor of a great, dark hall. One lantern burned feebly, and in the dim, silvery light she could just make out the Comfortable Camel scrambling awkwardly to his feet.

"I smell straw," sniffed the Camel softly.

"I doubt very much whether I am going to like this place." The voice of the Doubtful Dromedary came hesitatingly through the gloom.

"By sword and scepter!" gasped the Knight, "Are you there, Sir Cowardly?"

"Thank goodness, they are!" said Dorothy. Wishing other people about is a risky and responsible business. "They're all here, but I wonder where here is." She jumped up, but at a shuffle of feet drew back.

"Pigs! Weasels!" shrilled an angry voice, and a fat little man hurled himself at Sir Hokus, who happened to have fallen in the lead.

"Uds trudgeons and bludgeons and maugre thy head!" roared the Knight, shaking him off like a fly.

"Tappy, Tappy, my dear boy. Caution! What's all this?" At the sound of that dear, familiar voice Dorothy's heart gave a skip of joy, and without stopping to explain she rushed forward.

"Dorothy!" cried the Scarecrow, stepping on his kimona and falling off his silvery throne. "Lights, Tappy! More lights, at once!" But Tappy was too busy backing away from Sir Hokus of Pokes.

"Approach, vassal!" thundered the Knight, who under-stood not a word of Tappy's speech. "Approach! I think I've been insulted!" He drew his sword and glared angrily through the darkness, and Tappy, having backed as far as possible, fell heels over pigtail into the silver fountain. At the loud splash, Dorothy hastened to the rescue.

"They're friends, and we've found the Scarecrow, we've found the Scarecrow!" She seized Sir Hokus and shook him till his armor rattled.

"Tappy! Tappy!" called the Scarecrow. "Where in the world did he pagota?" That's exactly what he said, but to Dorothy it sounded like no language at all.

"Why," she cried in dismay, "it's the Scarecrow, but I can't understand a word he's saying!"

"I think he must be talking Turkey," droned the Comfortable Camel, "or donkey! I knew a donkey once, a very uncomfortable party, I —"

"I doubt it's donkey," put in the Dromedary importantly, but no one paid any attention to the two beasts. For Happy Toko had at last dragged himself out of the fountain and set fifteen lanterns glowing.

"Oh!" gasped Dorothy as the magnificent silver throne room was flooded with light, "Where are we?"

The Scarecrow had picked himself up, and with outstretched arms came running toward her talking a perfect Niagara of Silver Islandish.

"Have you forgotten your Ozish so soon?" rumbled the Cowardly Lion reproachfully as Dorothy flung her arms around the Scarecrow. The Scarecrow, seeing the Cowardly Lion for the first time, fairly fell upon his neck. Then he brushed his clumsy hand across his forehead.

"Wasn't I talking Ozish?" he asked in a puzzled voice.

"Oh, now you are!" exclaimed Dorothy. And sure enough, the Scarecrow was talking plain Ozish again. (Which I don't mind telling you is also plain English.)

The Knight had been watching this little reunion with hardly repressed emotion. Advancing hastily, he dropped on one knee.

"My good sword and lance are ever at thy service, my Lord Scarecrow!" he exclaimed feelingly.

"Who is this impulsive person?" gulped the Scarecrow, staring in undisguised astonishment at the kneeling figure of the (yes, the "the" is there) Sir Hokus of Pokes.

"He's my Knight Errant, and he's taken such good care of me," explained Dorothy eagerly.

"Splendid fellow," hissed the Cowardly Lion in the Scarecrow's other painted ear, "if he does talk odds and ends."

"Any friend of little Dorothy's is my friend," said the Scarecrow, shaking hands with Sir Hokus warmly. "But what I want to know is how you all got here."

"First tell us where we are," begged the little girl, for the Scarecrow's silver hat and queue filled her with alarm.

"You are on the Silver Island," said the Scarecrow slowly. "And I am the Emperor — or his good-for-nothing spirit — and tomorrow," the Scarecrow glared around wildly, "tomorrow I'll be eighty-five going on eighty-six." His voice broke and ended in a barely controlled sob.

"Doubt that," drawled the Doubtful Dromedary sleepily.

"Eighty-five years old!" gasped Dorothy. "Why, no one in Oz grows any older!"

"We are no longer in Oz." The Scarecrow shook his head sadly. Then, fixing the group with a puzzled stare, he exclaimed, "But how did you get here?"

"On a wish," said the Knight in a hollow voice.

"Yes," said Dorothy, "we've been hunting you all over Oz, and at last we came to Wish Way, and I said 'I wish we were all with the Scarecrow,' just like that — and next minute —"

"We fell and fell — and fell — and fell," wheezed the Comfortable Camel.

"And fell — and fell — and fell — and fell," droned the Dromedary, "And —"

"Here you are," finished the Scarecrow hastily, for the Dromedary showed signs of going on forever.

"Now tell us every single thing that has happened to you," demanded Dorothy eagerly.

Happy Toko had recognized Dorothy and the Cowardly Lion from the Scarecrow's description, and he now approached with an arm full of cushions. These he set in a circle on the floor, with one for the Scarecrow in the center, and with a warning finger on his lips placed himself behind his Master.

"Tappy is right!" exclaimed the Scarecrow. "We must be as quiet as possible, for a great danger hangs over me."

Without more ado, he told them of his amazing fall down the beanstalk; of his adventures on Silver Island; of his sons and grandsons and the Gheewizard's elixir which would turn him from a lively Scarecrow into an old, old Emperor. All that I have told you, he told Dorothy, up to the very point where his eldest son had bound him to the bean pole and tied up poor, faithful Happy Toko. Happy, it seems, had at last managed to free himself, and they were about to make their escape when Dorothy and her party had fallen into the throne room. The Comfortable Camel and Doubtful Dromedary lis-tened politely at first, but worn out by their exciting adventures, fell asleep in the middle of the story.

Nothing could have exceeded Dorothy's dismay to learn that the jolly Scarecrow of Oz, whom she had discovered herself, was in reality Chang Wang Woe, Emperor of Silver Island.

"Oh, this spoils everything!" wailed the little girl. (The thought of Oz without the Scarecrow was unthinkable.) "It spoils everything! We were going to adopt you and be your truly family. Weren't we?"

The Cowardly Lion nodded. "I was going to be your cousin," he mumbled in a choked voice, "but now that you have a family of your own —" The lion miserably slunk down beside Dorothy.

Sir Hokus looked fierce and rattled his sword, but he could think of nothing that would help them out of their trouble.

"To-morrow there won't be any Scarecrow in Oz!" wailed Dorothy. "Oh, dear! Oh, dear!" And the little girl began to cry as if her heart would break.

"Stop! Stop!" begged the Scarecrow, while Sir Hokus awkwardly patted Dorothy on the back. "I'd rather have you for my family any day. I don't care a Kinkajou for being Emperor, and as for my sons, they are unnatural villains who make my life miserable by telling me how old I am!"

"Just like a poem I once read," said Dorothy, brightening up:

"You are old, Father William," the young man said, "And your hair has become very white, And yet you incessantly stand on your head! Do you think, at your age, it is right?"

"That's it, that's it exactly!" exclaimed the Scarecrow as Dorothy finished repeating the verse. " 'You are old, Father Scarecrow!' That's all I hear. I did stand on my head, too. And Dorothy, I can't seem to get used to being a grandparent," added the Scarecrow in a melancholy voice. "It's turning my straws gray." He plucked several from his chest and held them out to her. "Why, those little villains don't even believe in Oz! 'It's not on the map, old Grandpapapapapah!' " he mumbled, imitating the tones of his little grandsons so cleverly that Dorothy laughed in spite of herself.

"This is what becomes of pride!" The Scarecrow extended his hands expressively. "Most people who hunt up their family trees are in for a fall, and I've had mine."

"But who do you want to be?" asked the Knight gravely. "A Scarecrow in Oz — or the — er — Emperor that you were?"

"I don't care who I were!" In his excitement, the Scarecrow lost his grammar completely. "I want to be who I am. I want to be myself."

"But which one?" asked the Cowardly Lion, who was still a bit confused.

"Why, my best self, of course," said the Scarecrow with a bright smile. The sight of his old friends had quite restored his cheerfulness. "I've been here long enough to know that I am a better Scarecrow than an Emperor."

"Why, how simple it is!" sighed Dorothy contentedly. "Professor Wogglebug was all wrong. It's not what you were, but what you are — it's being yourself that counts."

"By my Halidom, the little maid is right!" said Sir Hokus, slapping his knee in delight. "Let your Gheewizard but try his transformations! Out on him! But what says yon honest henchman?" Happy Toko, although he understood no word of the conversation, had been watching the discussion with great interest. He had been trying to attract the Scarecrow's attention for some time, but the Knight was the only one who had noticed him.

"What is it, Tappy?" asked the Scarecrow, dropping easily back into Silver Islandish.

"Honored Master, the dawn approaches and with it the Royal Princes and the Grand Gheewizard — and your bride!" Happy paused significantly. The Scarecrow shuddered.

"Let's go back to Oz!" said the Cowardly Lion uneasily.

The Scarecrow was feeling in the pocket of his old Munchkin suit which he always wore under his robes of state. "Here!" said he, giving a little pill to Happy Toko. "It's one of Professor Wogglebug's language pills," he exclaimed to Dorothy, "and will enable him to speak and understand Ozish." Happy swallowed the pill gravely.

"Greetings, honorable Ozites!" he said politely as soon as the pill was down. Dorothy clapped her hands in delight, for it was so comfortable to have him speak their own language.

"I could never have stood it here without Tappy Oko!" The Scarecrow looked fondly at his Imperial Punster.

"Queer name he has," rumbled the Cowardly Lion, looking at Happy Toko as if he had thoughts of eating him.

"Methinks he should be knighted," rumbled Sir Hokus, beaming on the little Silverman. "Rise, Sir Pudding!"

"The sun will do that in a minute or more, and then, then we shall all be thrown into prison!" wailed Happy Toko dismally.

"We were going to escape in a small boat," explained the Scarecrow, "but —" It was not necessary for him to finish. A boat large enough to hold Dorothy, the Cowardly Lion, the Scarecrow, Happy Toko, the camel and the dromedary could not very well be launched in secret.

"Oh, dear!" sighed Dorothy, "If I'd only wished you and all of us back in the Emerald City!"

"You wished very well, Lady Dot," said the Knight. "When I think of what I was going to wish for —"

"What were you going to wish, Hokus?" asked the Cowardly Lion curiously.

"For a dragon!" faltered the Knight, looking terribly ashamed.

"A dragon!" gasped Dorothy. "Why, what good would that have done us?"

"Wait!" interrupted the Scarecrow. "I have thought of something! Why not climb my family tree? It is a long, long way, but at the top lies Oz!"

"Grammercy, a pretty plan!" exclaimed Sir Hokus, peering up at the bean pole.

"Wouldn't that be social climbing?" chuckled Happy Toko, recovering his spirits with a bound. The Cowardly Lion said nothing, but heaved a mighty sigh which no one heard, for they were all running toward the bean pole. It was a good family tree to climb, sure enough, for there were handy little notches in the stalk.

"You go first!" Sir Hokus helped Dorothy up. When she had gone a few steps, the Scarecrow, holding his robes carefully, followed, then honest Happy Toko.

"I'll go last," said Sir Hokus bravely, and had just set his foot on the first notch when a hoarse scream rang through the hall.

Chapter 19 - Planning To Fly From The Silver Island

It was the Comfortable Camel. Waking suddenly, he found himself deserted. "Oh, where is my dear Karwan Bashi?" he roared dismally. "Come back! Come back!"

"Hush up, can't you?" rumbled the Cowardly Lion. "Do you want Dorothy and everybody to be thrown into prison on our account? We can't climb the bean pole and will have to wait here and face it out."

"But how uncomfortable," wailed the camel. He began to sob heavily. Dorothy, although highest up the bean pole, heard all of this distinctly. "Oh," she cried remorsefully, "we can't desert the Cowardly Lion like this. I never thought about him."

"Spoken like the dear little Maid you are," said the Knight. "The good beast never reminded us of it, either. There's bravery for you!"

"Let us descend at once, I'll not move a step without the Cowardly Lion!" In his agitation, the Scarecrow lost his balance and fell headlong to the ground, knocking Sir Hokus's helmet terribly askew as he passed. The others made haste to follow him and were soon gathered gravely at the foot of the beanstalk.

"I'll have to think of some other plan," said the Scarecrow, looking nervously at the sky, which showed, through the long windows, the first streaks of dawn. The Comfortable Camel controlled its sobs with difficulty and pressed as close to Sir Hokus as it could. The Doubtful Dromedary was still asleep.

"It would have been a terrible climb," mused the Scarecrow, thinking of his long, long fall down the pole. "Ah, I have it!"

"What?" asked Dorothy anxiously.

"I wonder I did not think of it before. Ah, my brains are working better! I will abdicate," exclaimed the Scarecrow triumphantly. "I will abdicate, make a farewell speech, and return with you to Oz!"

"What if they refuse to let your radiant Highness go?" put in Happy Toko tremulously. "What if the Gheewizard should work his magic before you finished your speech?"

"Then we'll make a dash for it!" said Sir Hokus, twirling his sword recklessly.

"I'm with you," said the Cowardly Lion huskily, "but you needn't have come back for me."

"All right!" said the Scarecrow cheerfully. "And now that everything's settled so nicely, we might as well enjoy the little time left. Put out the lights, Tappy. Dorothy and I will sit on the throne, and the rest of you come as close as possible."

Sir Hokus wakened the Doubtful Dromedary and pulled and tugged it across the hall, where it immediately fell down asleep again. The Comfortable Camel ambled about eating the flowers out of the vases. The Cowardly Lion had placed himself at Dorothy's feet, and Sir Hokus and Happy Toko seated themselves upon the first step of the gorgeous silver throne.

Then, while they waited for morning, Dorothy told the Scarecrow all about the Pokes and Fix City, and the Scarecrow told once again of his victory over the king of the Golden Islands.

"Where is the magic fan now?" asked Dorothy at the end of the story.

The Scarecrow smiled broadly, and feeling in a deep pocket brought out the little fan and also the parasol he had plucked from the beanstalk. "Do you know," he said smiling, "so much has happened I haven't thought of them since the battle. I was saving them for you, Dorothy."

"For me!" exclaimed the little girl in delight. "Let me see them!" The Scarecrow handed them over obligingly, but Happy Toko trembled so violently that he rolled down the steps of the throne.

"I beg of you!" He scrambled to his feet and held up his hands in terror. "I beg of you, don't open that fan!"

"She's used to magic, Tappy. You needn't worry," said the Scarecrow easily.

"Of course I am," said Dorothy with great dignity. "But this'll be mighty useful if anyone tries to conquer Oz again. We can just fan 'em away."

Dorothy pulled a hair from the Cowardly Lion's mane, and winding it around the little fan, put it carefully in the pocket of her dress. The parasol she hung by its ribbon to her arm.

"Perhaps Ozma will look in the Magic Picture and wish us all back again," said the little girl after they had sat for a time in silence.

"I doubt it." The Dromedary stirred and mumbled in its sleep.

"Singular beast, that!" ejaculated the Knight. "Doubting never gets one anywhere."

"Hush!" warned the Scarecrow. "I hear footsteps!"

"Come here." Sir Hokus called hoarsely to the camel, who was eating a paper lantern at the other end of the room. The beast ran awkwardly over to the throne, and swallowing the lantern with a convulsive gulp, settled down beside the dromedary.

"Whatever happens, we must stick together," said the Knight emphatically. "Ah —!"

Dorothy held fast to the Scarecrow with one hand and to the throne with the other. The sun had risen at last. There was a loud crash of drums and trumpets, a rush of feet, and into the hall marched the most splendid company Dorothy had seen in her whole life of adventures.

Chapter 20 - Dorothy Upsets the Ceremony of the Island

"A caravan!" whistled the Comfortable Camel, lurching to his feet. "How nice!"

"I doubt that!" The dromedary's eyes flew open, and he stared sleepily at the magnificent procession of Silver Islanders.

First came the musicians, playing their shining silver trumpets and flutes. The Grand Chew Chew and General Mugwump followed, attired in brilliant silk robes of state. Then came the three Princes, glittering with jeweled chains and medals, and the fifteen little Princes, like so many silver butterflies in their satin kimonas. Next appeared a palanquin bearing the veiled Princess Orange Blossom, followed by a whole company of splendid courtiers and after them as many of the everyday Silver Islanders as the hall would hold. There was a moment of silence. Then the whole assemblage, contrary to the Scarecrow's edict, fell upon their faces.

"My!" exclaimed Dorothy, impressed in spite of herself. "Are you sure you want to give up all this?"

"Great Emperor, beautiful as the sun, wise as the stars, and radiant as the clouds, the Ceremony of Restoration is about to begin!" quavered the Grand Chew Chew, rising slowly. Then he paused, for he was suddenly confused by the strange company around the Scarecrow's throne.

"Treachery!" hissed the eldest Prince to the others. "We left him tied to the bean pole. Ancient Papa Scarecrow needs watching! Who are these curious objects he has gathered about him, pray?"

Now by some magic which even I cannot explain, the people from Oz found they could understand all that was being said. When Dorothy heard herself called an object and saw the wicked faces of the three Princes and the stupid little grandsons, she no longer wondered at the Scarecrow's decision.

The Scarecrow himself bowed calmly. "First," said he cheerfully, "let me introduce my friends and visitors from Oz."

The Silver Islanders, who really loved the Scarecrow, bowed politely as he called out the names of Dorothy and the others. But the three Silver Princes scowled and whispered indignantly among themselves.

"I am growing very wroth!" choked Sir Hokus to the Cowardly Lion.

"Let the ceremony proceed!" called the eldest Prince harshly, before the Scarecrow had finished his introductions. "Let the proper body of his Serene Highness be immediately restored. Way for the Grand Gheewizard! Way for the Grand Gheewizard!"

"One moment," put in the Scarecrow in a dignified voice. "I have something to say." The Silver Islanders clapped loudly at this, and Dorothy felt a bit reassured. Perhaps they would listen to reason after all and let the Scarecrow depart peacefully. How they were ever to escape if they didn't, the little girl could not see.

"My dear children," began the Scarecrow in his jolly voice, "nothing could have been more wonderful than my return to this lovely island, but in the years I have been away from you I have changed very much, and I find I no longer care for being Emperor. So with your kind permission, I will keep the excellent body I now have and will abdicate in favor of my eldest son and return with my friends to Oz. For in Oz I really belong."

A dead silence followed the Scarecrow's speech — then perfect pandemonium.

"No! No! You are a good Emperor! We will not let you go!" shrieked the people. "You are our honorable little Father. The Prince shall be Emperor after you have peacefully returned to your ancestors, but not now. No! No! We will not have it!"

"I feared this!" quavered Happy Toko.

"It is not the Emperor, but the Scarecrow who speaks!" shrilled the Grand Chew Chew craftily. "He knows not what he says. But after the transformation — Ah, you shall see!"

The company calmed down at this. "Let the ceremony proceed! Way for the Grand Gheewizard!" they cried exultantly.

"Chew Chew," wailed the Scarecrow, "you're off the track!" But it was too late. No one would listen.

"I'll have to think of something else," muttered the Scarecrow, sinking dejectedly back on his throne.

"Oh!" shuddered Dorothy, clutching the Scarecrow, "Here he comes!"

"Way for the Grand Gheewizard! Way for the Grand Gheewizard!"

The crowd parted. Hobbling toward the throne came the ugly little Gheewizard of the Silver Island holding a large silver vase high above his head, and after him —!

When Sir Hokus caught a glimpse of what came after, he leaped clean over the Comfortable Camel.

"Uds daggers!" roared the Knight. "At last!" He rushed forward violently. There was a sharp thrust of his good sword, then an explosion like twenty giant firecrackers in one, and the room became quite black with smoke. Before anyone realized what had happened, Sir Hokus was back, dragging something after him and shouting exuberantly, "A dragon! I have slain a dragon! What happiness!"

Everyone was coughing and spluttering from the smoke, but as it cleared Dorothy saw that it was indeed a dragon Sir Hokus had slain, the rheumatic dragon of the old Gheewizard himself.

"Why didn't you get the wizard?" rumbled the Cowardly Lion angrily.

"Must have exploded," said the Comfortable Camel, sniffing the skin daintily.

"Treason!" yelled the three Princes, while the Grand Gheewizard flung himself on the stone floor and began tearing strand after strand from his silver pigtail.

"He has killed the little joy of my hearth!" screeched the old man. "I will turn him to a cat, a miserable yellow cat, and roast him for dinner!"

"Oh!" cried Dorothy, looking at Sir Hokus sorrowfully. "How could you?"

The slaying of the dragon had thrown the whole hall into utmost confusion. Sir Hokus turned a little pale under his armor, but faced the angry mob without flinching.

"Oh, my dear Karwan Bashi, this is so uncomfortable!" wheezed the camel, glancing back of him with frightened eyes.

"There's a shiny dagger in my left-hand saddlesack. I doubt very much whether they would like it," coughed the Doubtful Dromedary, pressing close to the Knight.

"On with the ceremony!" cried the eldest Prince, seeing that the excitement was giving the Scarecrow's friends too much time to think. "The son of an iron pot shall be punished later!"

"That's right!" cried a voice from the crowd. "Let the Emperor be restored!"

"I guess it's all over," gulped the Scarecrow. "Give my love to Ozma and tell her I tried to come back."

In helpless terror, the little company watched the Gheewizard approach. One could fight real enemies, but magic! Even Sir Hokus, brave as he was, felt that nothing could be done.

"One move and you shall be so many prunes," shrilled the angry old man, fixing the people from Oz with his wicked little eyes. The great room was so still you could have heard a pin drop. Even the Doubtful Dromedary had not the heart to doubt the wizard's power, but stood rigid as a statue.

The wizard advanced slowly, holding the sealed vase carefully over his head. The poor Scarecrow regarded it with gloomy fascination. One more moment and he would be an old, old Silverman. Better to be lost forever! He held convulsively to Dorothy.

As for Dorothy herself, she was trembling with fright and grief. When the Grand Gheewizard raised the vase higher and higher and made ready to hurl it at the Scarecrow, disregarding his dire threat she gave a shrill scream and threw up both hands.

"Great grandmothers!" gasped the Scarecrow, jumping to his feet. As Dorothy had thrown up her arms, the little parasol swinging at her wrist had jerked open. Up, up, up, and out through the broken skylight in the roof sailed the little Princess of Oz!

The Grand Gheewizard, startled as anyone, failed to throw the vase. Every neck was craned upward, and everyone was gasping with astonishment.

The oldest Prince, as usual, was the first to recover. "Don't stand staring like an idiot! Now's your chance!" he hissed angrily in the Gheewizard's ear.

"I didn't come here to be harried and hurried by foreigners," sobbed the little man. "How is one to work magic when interrupted every other minute? I want my little dragon."

"Oh, come on now, just throw it. I'll get you another dragon," begged the Prince, his hands trembling with excitement.

In the face of this new disaster, the Scarecrow had forgotten all about the Gheewizard. He and the Cowardly Lion and Sir Hokus were running distractedly around the great throne trying to think up a way to rescue Dorothy. As for the Doubtful Dromedary, he was doubting everything in a loud, bitter voice, while the Comfortable Camel fairly snorted with sorrow.

"There! Now's your chance," whispered the Prince. The Scarecrow, with his back to the crowd, was gesturing frantically.

Taking a firm hold on the neck of the vase and with a long incantation which there is no use at all in repeating, the Gheewizard flung the bottle straight at the Scarecrow's head. But scarcely had it left his hand before there was a flash and a flutter and down came Dorothy and the magic parasol right on top of the vase.

Zip! The vase flew in quite another direction, and next minute had burst over the luckless heads of the three plotting Princes, while Dorothy floated gently to earth.

Sir Hokus embraced the Scarecrow, and the Scarecrow hugged the Cowardly Lion, and I don't wonder at all. For no sooner had the magic elixir touched the Princes, than two of them became silver pigs and the eldest a weasel. They had been turned to their true shapes instead of the Scarecrow. And while the company hopped about in alarm, they ran squealing from the hall and disappeared in the gardens.

"Seize the Gheewizard and take him to his cave," ordered the Scarecrow, asserting his authority for the first time since the proceedings has started. He had noticed the old man making queer signs and passes toward Sir Hokus. A dozen took hold of the struggling Gheewizard and hurried him out of the hall.

Sir Hokus, at the request of the Scarecrow, clapped his iron gauntlets for silence.

"You will agree with me, I'm sure," said the Scarecrow in a slightly unsteady voice, "that magic is a serious matter to meddle with. If you will all return quietly to your homes, I will try to find a way out of our difficulties."

The Silver Islanders listened respectfully and after a little arguing among themselves backed out of the throne room. To tell the truth, they were anxious to spread abroad the tale of the morning's happenings.

Princess Orange Blossom, however, refused to depart. Magic or no magic, she had come to marry the Emperor, and she would not leave till the ceremony had been performed.

"But my dear old Lady, would you wish to marry a Scarecrow?" coaxed the Emperor.

"All men are Scarecrows," snapped the Princess sourly.

"Then why marry at all?" rumbled the Cowardly Lion, making a playful leap at her palanquin. This was too much. The Princess swooned on the spot, and the Scarecrow, taking advantage of her unconscious condition, ordered her chair bearers to carry her away as far and as fast as they could run.

"Now," said the Scarecrow when the last of the company had disappeared, "let us talk this over."

Chapter 21 - The Escape from the Silver Island

"Well!" gasped Dorothy, fanning herself with her hat, "I never was so s'prised in my life!"

"Nor I," exclaimed the Scarecrow. "The Grand Gheewizard will be suing you for parassault and battery. But how did it happen?"

"Well," began Dorothy, "as soon as the parasol opened, I flew up so fast that I could hardly breathe. Then, after I'd gone ever so far, it came to me that if the parasol went up when it was up, it would come down when it was down. I couldn't leave you all in such a fix — so I closed it, and —"

"Came down!" finished the Scarecrow with a wave of his hand. "You always do the right thing in the right place, my dear."

"It was lucky I hit the vase, wasn't it?" sighed Dorothy. "But I'm rather sorry about the Princes."

"Served 'em right," growled the Cowardly Lion. "They'll make very good pigs!"

"But who's to rule the island?" demanded Sir Hokus, turning his gaze reluctantly from the smoking dragonskin.

"This will require thought," said the Scarecrow pensively. "Let us all think."

"I doubt that I can ever think again." The Doubtful Dromedary wagged his head from side to side in a dazed fashion.

"Just leave it to our dear Karwan Bashi." The Comfortable Camel nodded complacently at the Knight and began plucking sly wisps from the Scarecrow's boot top. For a short time there was absolute silence.

Then Sir Hokus, who had been thinking tremendously with his elbows on his knees, burst out, "Why not Sir Pudding, here? Why not this honest Punster? Who but Happy Toko deserves the throne?"

"The very person!" cried the Scarecrow, clasping his yellow gloves, and taking off his silver hat, he set it impulsively upon the head of the fat little Silver Islander.

"He'll make a lovely Emperor," said Dorothy. "He's so kind-hearted and jolly. And now the Scarecrow can abdicate and come home to Oz."

They all looked triumphantly at the Imperial Punster, but Happy Toko, snatching off the royal hat, burst into tears.

"Don't leave me behind, amiable Master!" he sobbed disconsolately. "Oh, how I shall miss you!"

"But don't you see," coaxed Dorothy, "the Scarecrow needs you here more than anyplace, and think of all the fine clothes you will have and how rich you will be!"

"And Tappy, my dear boy," said the Scarecrow, putting his arm around Happy Toko, "you might not like Oz any more than I like Silver Island. Then think — if everything goes well, you can visit me — just as one Emperor visits another!"

"And you won't forget me?" sniffed Happy, beginning to like the idea of being Emperor.

"Never!" cried the Scarecrow with an impressive wave.

"And if anything goes wrong, will you help me out?" questioned Happy uncertainly.

"We'll look in the Magic Picture of Oz every month," declared Dorothy, "and if you need us we'll surely find some way to help you."

"An' you ever require a trusty sword, Odds Bodikins!" exclaimed Sir Hokus, pressing Tappy's hand, "I'm your man!"

"All right, dear Master!" Happy slowly picked up the Imperial hat and set it sideways on his head. "I'll do my best."

"I don't doubt it at all," said the Doubtful Dromedary to everyone's surprise.

"Three cheers for the Emperor! Long live the Emperor of the Silver Island," rumbled the Cowardly Lion, and everybody from Oz, even the camel and dromedary, fell upon their knees before Happy Toko.

"You may have my bride, too, Tappy," chuckled the Scarecrow with a wink at Dorothy. "And Tappy," he asked, sobering suddenly, "will you have my grandsons brought up like real children? Just as soon as I return, I shall send them all the Books of Oz."

Happy bowed, too confused and excited for speech.

"Now," said the Scarecrow, seizing Dorothy's hand, "I can return to Oz with an easy mind."

"Doubt that," said the Doubtful Dromedary.

"You needn't!" announced Dorothy. "I've thought it all out." In a few short sentences she outlined her plan.

"Bravo!" roared the Cowardly Lion, and now the little party began in real earnest the preparation for the journey back to Oz.

First, Happy brought them a delicious luncheon, with plenty of twigs and hay for the camel and dromedary and meat for the Cowardly Lion. The Scarecrow packed into the camel's sacks a few little souvenirs for the people of Oz. Then they dressed Happy Toko in the Scarecrow's most splendid robe and ordered him to sit upon the throne. Next, the Scarecrow rang for one of the palace servants and ordered the people of the Silver Islands to assemble in the hall.

Presently the Silvermen began to come trooping in, packing the great throne room until it could hold no more. Everyone was chattering excitedly.

It was quite a different company that greeted them. The Scarecrow, cheerful and witty in his old Munchkin suit, Dorothy and Sir Hokus smiling happily, and the three animal members of the party fairly blinking with contentment.

"This," said the Scarecrow pleasantly when everyone was quiet, "is your new Emperor, to whom I ask you to pledge allegiance." He waved proudly in the direction of Happy Toko, who, to tell the truth, presented a truly royal appearance. "It is not possible for me to remain with you, but I shall always watch over this delightful island and with the magic fan vanquish all its enemies and punish all offenders."

Happy Toko bowed to his subjects.

The Silver Islanders exchanged startled glances, then, as the Scarecrow carelessly lifted the fan, they fell prostrate to the earth.

"Ah!" said the Scarecrow with a broad wink at Happy. "This is delightful. You agree with me, I see. Now then, three cheers for Tappy Oko, Imperial Emperor of the Silver Island."

The cheers were given with a will, and Happy in acknowledgement made a speech that has since been written into the Royal Book of state as a masterpiece of eloquence.

Having arranged affairs so satisfactorily, the Scarecrow embraced Happy Toko with deep emotion. Dorothy and Sir Hokus shook hands with him and wished him every success and happiness. Then the little party from Oz walked deliberately to the bean pole in the center of the hall.

The Silver Islanders were still a bit dazed by the turn affairs had taken and stared in astonishment as the Scarecrow and Sir Hokus fastened thick ropes around the Cowardly Lion, the Doubtful Dromedary and the Comfortable Camel. Similar ropes they tied around their own waists and Dorothy's, and the ends of all were fastened securely to the handle of the magic parasol, which Dorothy held carefully.

"Goodbye, everybody!" called the little girl, suddenly opening the parasol.

"Goodbye!" cried the genial Scarecrow, waving his hand.

Too stupefied for speech, the assemblage gaped with amazement as the party floated gently upward. Up — up — and out of sight whirled the entire party.

Chapter 22 - The Flight Of The Parasol

Holding the handle of the parasol, Dorothy steered it with all the skill of an aviator, and in several minutes after their start the party had entered the deep, black passage down which the Scarecrow had fallen. Each one of the adventurers was fastened to the parasol with ropes of different length so that none of them bumped together, but even with all the care in the world it was not possible to keep them from bumping the sides of the tube. The Comfortable Camel grunted plaintively from time to time, and Dorothy could hear the Doubtful Dromedary complaining bitterly in the darkness. It was pitch dark, but by keeping one hand in touch with the bean pole, Dorothy managed to hold the parasol in the center.

"How long will it take?" she called breathlessly to the Scarecrow, who was dangling just below.

"Hours!" wheezed the Scarecrow, holding fast to his hat. "I hope none of the parties on this line hear us," he added nervously, thinking of the Middlings.

"What recks it?" blustered Sir Hokus. "Hast forgotten my trusty sword?" But his words were completely drowned in the rattle of his armor.

"Hush!" warned the Scarecrow, "Or we'll be pulled in." So for almost an hour, they flew up the dark, chimney-like tube with only an occasional groan as one or another scraped against the rough sides of the passage. Then, before they knew what was happening, the parasol crashed into something, half closed, and the whole party started to fall head over heels over helmets.

"O!" gasped Dorothy, turning a complete somersault, "catch hold of the bean pole, somebody!"

"Put up the parasol!" shrieked the Scarecrow. Just then Dorothy, finding herself right side up, grasped the pole herself and snapped the parasol wide open. Up, up, up they soared again, faster than ever!

"We're flying up much faster than I fell down. We must be at the top!" called the Scarecrow hoarsely, "and somebody has closed the opening!"

Chapter 23 - Safe at Last in the Land of Oz

"Must we keep bumping until we bump through?" panted Dorothy anxiously.

"No, by my hilts!" roared Sir Hokus, and setting his foot in a notch of the beanstalk, he cut with his sword the rope that bound him to the parasol. "Put the parasol down half way, and I'll climb ahead and cut an opening."

With great difficulty Dorothy partially lowered the parasol, and instantly their speed diminished. Indeed, they barely moved at all, and the Knight had soon passed them on his climb to the top.

"Are you there?" rumbled the Cowardly Lion anxiously. A great clod of earth landed on his head, filling his eyes and mouth with mud.

"Ugh!" roared the lion.

"It's getting light! It's getting light!" screamed Dorothy, and in her excitement snapped the parasol up.

Sir Hokus, having cut with his sword a large circular hole in the thin crust of earth covering the tube, was about to step out when the parasol, hurling up from below, caught him neatly on its top, and out burst the whole party and sailed up almost to the clouds!

"Welcome to Oz!" cried Dorothy, looking down happily on the dear familiar Munchkin landscape.

"Home at last!" exulted the Scarecrow, wafting a kiss downward.

"Let's get down to earth before we knock the sun into a cocked hat," gasped the Cowardly Lion, for Dorothy, in her excitement, had forgotten to lower the parasol.

Now the little girl lowered the parasol carefully at first, then faster and faster and finally shut it altogether.

Sir Hokus took a high dive from the top. Down tumbled the others, over and over. But fortunately for all, there was a great haystack below, and upon this they landed in a jumbled heap close to the magic bean pole. As it happened, there was no one in sight. Up they jumped in a trice, and while the Comfortable Camel and Doubtful Dromedary munched contentedly at the hay, Sir Hokus and the Scarecrow placed some loose boards over the opening around the bean pole and covered them with dirt and cornstalks.

"I will get Ozma to close it properly with the Magic Belt," said the Scarecrow gravely. "It wouldn't do to have people sliding down my family tree and scaring poor Tappy. As for me, I shall never leave Oz again!"

"I hope not," growled the Cowardly Lion, tenderly examining his scratched hide.

"But if you hadn't, I'd never have had such lovely adventures or found Sir Hokus and the Comfortable Camel and Doubtful Dromedary," said Dorothy. "And what a lot I have to tell Ozma! Let's go straight to the Emerald City."

"It's quite a journey," explained the Scarecrow to Sir Hokus, who was cleaning off his armor with a handful of straw.

"I go where Lady Dot goes," replied the Knight, smiling affectionately at the little girl and straightening the ragged hair ribbon which he still wore on his arm.

"Don't forget me, dear Karwan Bashi," wheezed the Comfortable Camel, putting his head on the Knight's shoulder.

"You're a sentimental dunce, Camy. I doubt whether they'll take us at all!" The Doubtful Dromedary looked wistfully at Dorothy.

"Go to, now!" cried Sir Hokus, putting an arm around each neck. "You're just like two of the family!"

"It will be very comfortable to go to now," sighed the camel.

"We're all a big, jolly family here," said the Scarecrow, smiling brightly, "and Oz is the friendliest country in the world."

"Right," said the Cowardly Lion, "but let's get started!" He stretched his tired muscles and began limping stiffly toward the yellow brick road.

"Wait," cried Dorothy, "have you forgotten the parasol?"

"I wish I could," groaned the Cowardly Lion, rolling his eyes.

Sir Hokus, with folded arms, was gazing regretfully at the bean pole. "It has been a brave quest," he sighed, "but now, I take it, our adventures are over!" Absently, the Knight felt in his boot-top and drawing out a small red bean popped it into his mouth. Just before reaching the top of the tube, he had pulled a handful of them from the beanstalk, but the others had fallen out when he dove into the hay.

"Shall we use the parasol again, Lady Dot?" he asked, still staring pensively at the bean pole. "Shall—?"

He got no farther, nor did Dorothy answer his question. Instead, she gave a loud scream and clutched the Scarecrow's arm. The Scarecrow, taken by surprise, fell over backward, and the Comfortable Camel, raising his head inquiringly, gave a bellow of terror. From the Knight's shoulders a green branch had sprung, and while the company gazed in round-eyed amazement it stretched toward the bean pole, attached itself firmly, and then shot straight up into the air, the Knight kicking and struggling on the end. In another second, he was out of sight.

"Come back! Come back!" screamed the Comfortable Camel, running around distractedly.

"I doubt we'll ever see him again!" groaned the Doubtful Dromedary, craning his neck upward.

"Do something! Do something!" begged Dorothy. At which the Scarecrow jumped up and dashed toward the little farmhouse.

"I'll get an ax," he called over his shoulder, "and chop down the bean pole."

"No, don't do that!" roared the Cowardly Lion, starting after him. "Do you want to break him to pieces?"

"Oh! Oh! Can't you think of something else?" cried Dorothy. "And hurry, or he'll be up to the moon!"

The Scarecrow put both hands to his head and stared around wildly. Then, with a triumphant wave of his hat, declared himself ready to act.

"The parasol!" cried the late Emperor of Silver Island. "Quick, Dorothy, put up the parasol!"

Snatching the parasol, which lay at the foot of the bean pole, Dorothy snapped it open, and the Scarecrow just had time to make a flying leap and seize the handle before it soared upward, and in a trice they, too, had disappeared.

"Doubty! Doubty!" wailed the Comfortable Camel, crowding up to his humpbacked friend, "we're having a pack of trouble. My knees are all a-tremble!"

"Now don't you worry," advised the Cowardly Lion, sitting down resignedly. "I'm frightened myself, but that's because I'm so cowardly. Queer things happen in Oz, but they usually turn out all right. Why, Hokus is just growing up with the country, that's all, just growing up with the country."

"Doubt that," sniffed the Doubtful Dromedary faintly. "He was grown up in the beginning."

"But think of the Scarecrow's brains. You leave things to the Scarecrow." But it was no use. Both beasts began to roar dismally.

"I don't want a plant. I want my Karwan Bashi," sobbed the Comfortable Camel broken-heartedly.

"Well, don't drown me," begged the Cowardly Lion, moving out of the way of the camel's tears. "Say, what's that draft?"

What indeed? In the trees overhead, a very cyclone whistled, and before the three had even time to catch their breath, they were blown high into the air and the next instant were hurtling toward the Emerald City like three furry cannonballs, faster and faster.

Chapter 24 - Homeward Bound to the Emerald City

Dorothy and the Scarecrow, clinging fast to the magic parasol, had followed the Knight almost to the clouds. At first, it looked as if they would never catch up with him, so swiftly was the branch growing, but it was not long before the little umbrella began to gain, and in several minutes more they were beside Sir Hokus himself.

"Beshrew me, now!" gasped the Knight, stretching out his hand toward Dorothy. "Can'st stop this reckless plant?"

"Give me your sword," commanded the Scarecrow, "and I'll cut you off."

Dorothy, with great difficulty, kept the parasol close to the Knight while the Scarecrow reached for the sword. But Sir Hokus backed away in alarm. "

'Tis part of me, an' you cut it off, I will be cut off, too. 'Tis rooted in my back," he puffed.

"What shall we do?" cried Dorothy in distress. "Maybe if we take hold of his hands we can keep him from going any higher."

The Scarecrow, jamming down his hat so it wouldn't blow off, nodded approvingly, and each holding the parasol with one hand gave the other to the Knight. And when Dorothy pointed the parasol down, to her great delight Sir Hokus came also, the thin green branch growing just about as fast as they moved.

Just then the little fan, which had been rolling around merrily in Dorothy's pocket, slipped out and fell straight down toward the three unsuspecting beasts below. Draft! No wonder!

But Dorothy never missed it, and quite unconscious of such a calamity anxiously talked over the Knight's predicament with the Scarecrow. They both decided that the best plan was to fly straight to the Emerald City and have Ozma release the Knight from the enchanted beanstalk.

"I'm sorry you got tangled up in my family tree, old fellow," said the Scarecrow after they had flown some time in silence, "but this makes us relations, doesn't it?" He winked broadly at the Knight.

"So it does," said Sir Hokus jovially. "I'm a branch of your family now. Yet methinks I should not have swallowed that bean."

"Bean?" questioned Dorothy. "What bean?" The Knight carefully explained how he had plucked a handful of red beans from the beanstalk just before reaching the top of the tube and how he had eaten one.

"So that's what started you growing!" exclaimed Dorothy in surprise.

"Alas, yes!" admitted the Knight. "I've never felt more grown-up in my life," he finished solemnly. "An adventurous country, this Oz!"

"I should say it was," chuckled the Scarecrow. "But isn't it almost time we were reaching the Emerald City, Dorothy?"

"I think I'm going in the right direction," answered the little girl, "but I'll fly a little lower to be sure."

"Not too fast! Not too fast!" warned Sir Hokus, looking nervously over his shoulder at his long, wriggling stem.

"There's Ozma's palace!" cried the Scarecrow all at once.

"And there's Ozma!" screamed Dorothy, peering down delightedly. "And Scraps and Tik-Tok and everybody!"

She pointed the parasol straight down, when a sharp tug from Sir Hokus jerked them all back. They were going faster than the poor Knight was growing, so Dorothy lowered the parasol half way, and slowly they floated toward the earth, landing gently in one of the flower beds of Ozma's lovely garden.

"Come along and meet the folks," said the Scarecrow as Dorothy closed the parasol. But Sir Hokus clutched him in alarm.

"Hold! Hold!" gasped the Knight. "I've stopped growing, but if you leave me I'll shoot up into the air again."

The Scarecrow and Dorothy looked at each other in dismay. Sure enough, the Knight had stopped growing, and it was all they could do to hold him down to earth, for the stubborn branch of beanstalk was trying to straighten up. They had fallen quite a distance from the palace itself, and all the people of Oz had their backs turned, so had not seen their singular arrival.

"Hello!" called the Scarecrow loudly. Then "Help! Help!" as the Knight jerked him twice into the air. But Ozma, Trot, Jack Pumpkinhead and all the rest were staring upward and talking so busily among themselves that they did not hear either Dorothy's or the Scarecrow's cries. First one, then the other was snatched off his feet, and although Sir Hokus, with tears in his eyes, begged them to leave him to his fate, they held on with all their might. Just as it looked as if they all three would fly into the air again, the little Wizard of Oz happened to turn around.

"Look! Look!" he cried, tugging Ozma's sleeve.

"Why, it's Dorothy!" gasped Ozma, rubbing her eyes. "It's Dorothy and —"

"Help! Help!" screamed the Scarecrow, waving one arm wildly. Without waiting another second, all the celebrities of Oz came running toward the three adventurers.

"Somebody heavy come take hold!" puffed Dorothy, out of breath with her efforts to keep Sir Hokus on the ground.

The Ozites, seeing that help was needed at once, suppressed their curiosity.

"I'm heavy," said Tik-Tok solemnly, clasping the Knight's arm. The Tin Woodman seized his other hand, and Dorothy sank down exhausted on the grass.

Princess Ozma pressed forward.

"What does it all mean? Where did you come from?" asked the little Queen of Oz, staring in amazement at the strange spectacle before her.

"And who is this medieval person?" asked Professor Wogglebug, pushing forward importantly. (He had returned to the palace to collect more data for the Royal Book of Oz.)

"He doesn't look evil to me," giggled Scraps, dancing up to Sir Hokus, her suspender button eyes snapping with fun.

"He isn't," said Dorothy indignantly, for Sir Hokus was too shaken about to answer. "He's my Knight Errant."

55

"Ah, I see," replied Professor Wogglebug. "A case of 'When Knighthood was in flower.'" And would you believe it — the beanstalk at that minute burst into a perfect shower of red blossoms that came tumbling down over everyone. Before they had recovered from their surprise, the branch snapped off close to the Knight's armor, and Tik-Tok, the Tin Woodman and Sir Hokus rolled over in a heap. The branch itself whistled through the air and disappeared.

"Oh," cried Dorothy, hugging the Knight impulsively, "I'm so glad."

"Are you all right?" asked the Scarecrow anxiously.

"Good as ever!" announced Sir Hokus, and indeed all traces of the magic stalk had disappeared from his shoulders.

"Dorothy!" cried Ozma again. "What does it all mean?"

"Merely that I slid down my family tree and that Dorothy and this Knight rescued me," said the Scarecrow calmly.

"And he's a real Royalty — so there!" cried Dorothy with a wave at the Scarecrow and making a little face at Professor Wogglebug. "Meet his Supreme Highness, Chang Wang Woe of Silver Island, who had abdicated his throne and returned to be a plain Scarecrow in Oz!"

Then, as the eminent Educator of Oz stood gaping at the Scarecrow, "Oh, Ozma, I've so much to tell you!"

"Begin! Begin!" cried the little Wizard. "For everything's mighty mysterious. First, the Cowardly Lion and two unknown beasts shoot through the air and stop just outside the third-story windows, and there they hang although I've tried all my magic to get them down. Then you and the Scarecrow drop in with a strange Knight!"

"Oh, the poor Cowardly Lion!" gasped Dorothy as the Wizard finished speaking. "The magic fan!" She felt hurriedly in her pocket. "It's gone!"

"It must have slipped out of your pocket and blown them here, and they'll never come down till that fan is closed," cried the Scarecrow in an agitated voice.

All of this was Greek to Ozma and the others, but when Dorothy begged the little Queen to send for her Magic Belt, she did it without question. This belt Dorothy had captured from the Gnome King, and it enabled the wearer to wish people and objects wherever one wanted them.

"I wish the magic fan to close and to come safely back to me," said Dorothy as soon as she had clasped the belt around her waist. No sooner were the words out before there was a loud crash and a series of roars and groans. Everybody started on a run for the palace, Sir Hokus ahead of all the rest. The fan had mysteriously returned to Dorothy's pocket.

The three animals had fallen into a huge cluster of rose bushes and, though badly scratched and frightened, were really unhurt.

"I doubt that I'll like Oz," quavered the Doubtful Dromedary, lurching toward Sir Hokus.

"You might have been more careful of that fan," growled the Cowardly Lion reproachfully, plucking thorns from his hide. The Comfortable Camel was so overjoyed to see the Knight that he rested his head on Sir Hokus's shoulder and began weeping down his armor.

And now that their adventures seemed really over, what explanations were to be made! Sitting on the top step of the palace with all of them around her, Dorothy told the whole wonderful story of the Scarecrow's family tree. When her breath gave out, the Scarecrow took up the tale himself, and as they all realized how nearly they had lost their jolly comrade, many of the party shed real tears. Indeed, Nick Chopper hugged the Scarecrow till there was not a whole straw in his body.

"Never leave us again," begged Ozma, and the Scarecrow, crossing Nick Chopper's heart (he had none of his own), promised that he never would.

And what a welcome they gave Sir Hokus, the Doubtful Dromedary and the Comfortable Camel! Only Professor Wogglebug seemed disturbed. During the strange recital, he had grown quieter and quieter and finally, with an embarrassed cough, had excused himself and hurried into the palace.

He went directly to the study, and seating himself at a desk opened a large book, none other than The Royal Book of Oz. Dipping an emerald pen in the ink, he began a new chapter headed thus:

HIS IMPERIAL MAJESTY, THE SCARECROW
Late Emperor and Imperial Sovereign of Silver Island

Then, flipping over several pages to a chapter headed "Princess Dorothy!", he wrote carefully at the end, "Dorothy, Princess and Royal Discoverer of Oz."

Meanwhile, below stairs, the Scarecrow was distributing his gifts. There were silver chains for everyone in the palace and shining silver slippers for Ozma, Betsy Bobbin, Trot and Dorothy, and a bottle of silver polish for Nick Chopper.

Dorothy presented Ozma with the magic fan and parasol, and they were safely put away by Jellia Jamb with the other magic treasures of Oz.

Next, because they were all curious to see the Scarecrow's wonderful Kingdom, they hurried upstairs to look in the Magic Picture.

"Show us the Emperor of Silver Island," commanded Ozma. Immediately the beautiful silver throne room appeared. Happy Toko had removed his imperial hat and was standing on his head to the great delight of the whole court, and a host of little Silver Islander boys were peeking in at the windows.

"Now doesn't that look cheerful?" asked the Scarecrow delightedly. "I knew he'd make a good Emperor."

"I wish we would hear what he's saying," said Dorothy. "Oh, do look at Chew Chew!" The Grand Chew Chew was standing beside the throne scowling horribly.

"I think I can arrange for you to hear," muttered the Wizard of Oz, and taking a queer magic instrument from his pocket, he whispered "Aohbeeobbuy."

Instantly they heard the jolly voice of Happy Toko singing:

Oh shine his shoes of silver,

And brush his silver queue,

For I am but an Emperor

And he's the Grand Chew Chew!

Ozma laughed heartily as the picture faded away, and so did the others. Indeed, there was so much to ask and wonder about that it seemed as if they never would finish talking.

"Let's have a party — an old-fashioned Oz party," proposed Ozma when the excitement had calmed down a bit. And an old-fashioned party it was, with places for everybody and a special table for the Cowardly Lion, the Hungry Tiger, Toto, the Glass Cat, the Comfortable Camel, the Doubtful Drome-dary and all the other dear creatures of that amazing Kingdom.

Sir Hokus insisted upon stirring up a huge pasty for the occasion, and there were songs, speeches and cheers for everyone, not forgetting the Doubtful Dromedary.

At the cheering he rose with an embarrassed jerk of his long neck. "In my left-hand saddle-sack," he said gruffly, "there is a quantity of silken shawls and jewels. I doubt whether they are good enough, but I would like Dorothy and Queen Ozma to have them."

"Hear! Hear!" cried the Scarecrow, pounding on the table with his knife. Then everything grew quiet as Ozma told how she, with the help of Glinda, the Good Sorceress, had stopped the war between the Horners and Hoppers.

When she had finished, Sir Hokus sprang up impulsively. "I prithee, lovely Lady, never trouble your royal head about wars again. From now on, I will do battle for you and little Dorothy and Oz, and I will be your good Knight every day." At this, the applause was tremendous.

Ye good Knight of Oz, full of courage and vim,

Will do battle for us, and we'll take care of him!

shouted Scraps, who was becoming more excited every minute.

"I'll lend you some of my polish for your armor, old fellow," said Nick Chopper as the Knight sat down, beaming with pleasure.

"Well," said Ozma with a smile when everyone had feasted and talked to heart's content, "is everybody happy?"

"I am!" cried the Comfortable Camel. "For here I am perfectly comfortable."

"I am!" cried Dorothy, putting her arm around the Scarecrow, who sat next to her. "For I have found my old friend and made some new ones."

"I'm happy!" cried the Scarecrow, waving his glass, "because there is no age in Oz, and I am still my old Ozish self."

"As for me," said the Knight, "I am happy, for I have served a Lady, gone on a Quest, and Slain a Dragon! Ozma, and Oz forever!

The End

Kabumpo in Oz

by Ruth Plumly Thompson

Dear children:

Do you like Elephants? Do you believe in Giants? And do you love all the jolly people of the Wonderful Land of Oz? Well then you'll want to hear about the latest happenings in that delightful Kingdom. All are set forth in true Oz fashion in "Kabumpo in Oz," the fifteenth Oz book. Kabumpo is an Elegant Elephant. He is very old and wise, and has a kindly heart, as have all the Oz folks. In the new book you'll meet Prince Pompa, and Peg Amy, a charming Wooden Doll. There are new countries, strange adventures and the most surprising Box of Magic you have ever heard of. Ruggedo , the wicked old Gnome King, does a lot of mischief with this before Princess Ozma can stop him. Of course Dorothy, the Scarecrow, Scraps, Glinda the Good, Tik-Tok, and other old friends all are alive and busy in the new book. I am just back from the Emerald City with the best of Oz wishes for everybody, but especially you.

Philadelphia
Spring of 1922

Ruth Plumly Thompson

This book is dedicated with all of my heart To Janet My littlest sister but biggest assistor

Ruth Plumly Thompson

Chapter 1 - The Exploding Birthday Cake

"The cake, you chattering Chittimong! Where is the cake? Stirem, Friem, Hashem, where is the cake?" cried Eejabo, chief footman in the palace of Pumperdink, bouncing into the royal pantry.

The Three cooks, too astonished for speech, and with staring eyes, pointed to the center table. The great gorgeous birthday cake was gone, though not two seconds before it had been placed on the table by Hashem himself.

"It was my m-m-asterpiece," sobbed Hashem, tearing off his cap and throwing his apron over his head.

"Help! Robbers! Thieves!" cried Friem, running to the window.

Here was a howdedo. The trumpets blowing for the celebration to begin and the best part of the celebration was gone!

"We'll all be dipped for this!" wailed Eejabo, flinging open the second best china closet so violently that three silver cups and a pewter mug tumbled out. Just then there was a scream from Hashem, who had removed the apron from his head. "Look!" he shrieked "There it is!"

Back to the table rushed the other three, Stirem and Friem rubbing their eyes and Eejabo his head where the cups had bumped him severely. Upon the table stood the royal cake, as pink and perfect as ever.

"It was there all the time, mince my eyebrows!" spluttered Hashem in an injured voice. "Called me a Chittimong, did you?" Grasping a big wooden spoon he ran angrily at Eejabo.

"Was it gone or wasn't it?" cried Eejabo, appealing to the others and hastily catching up a bread knife to defend himself. Instantly there arose a babble.

"It was!"

"It wasn't!"

"Was!" Rap, bang, clatter. In a minute they were in a furious argument, not only with words but with spoons, forks and bowls. And dear knows what would have become of the cake had not a bell rung loudly and the second footman poked his head through the door. "The cake! Where is the cake?" he wheezed importantly.

So Eejabo, dodging three cups and a salt cellar, seized the great silver platter and dashed into the great banquet hall. One pink coat tail was missing and his wig was somewhat elevated over the left ear from the lump raised by the pewter mug, but he summoned what dignity he could and joined the grand procession of footmen who were bearing gold and silver dishes filled with goodies for the birthday feast of Prince Pompadore of Pumperdink.

The royal guests were already assembled and just as Eejabo entered the pages blew a shrill blast upon their silver trumpets and the Prime Pumper stepped forward to announce their Majesties.

"Oyes! Oyez!" shouted the Prime Pumper, pounding on the floor with his silver staff, while the guests politely inclined their heads just as if they had not heard the same announcement dozens of times before:

"Oyez! Oyez!" "Pompus the Proud And Pozy Pink, King and Queen Of Pumperdink — Way for the King And clear the floor Way for our good Prince Pompadore. Way for the Elegant Elephant— Way For the King and The Queen and the Prince, I say!"

So everybody wayed, which is to say they bowed, and down the center of the room swept Pompus, very fat and gorgeous in his purple robes and jeweled crown, ermine cloak, and Prince Pompadore very straight and handsome! In fact, they looked exactly as a good old-fashioned royal family should.

But Kabumpo, who swayed along grandly after the Prince — few royal families could boast of so royal and elegant an elephant! He was huge and gray. On his head he wore jeweled bands and a jeweled court robe billowed out majestically as he walked. His little eyes twinkled merrily and his ears flapped so sociably, that just to look at him put one in a good humor. Kabumpo was the only elephant in Pumperdink, or in any Kingdom near Pumperdink, so no wonder he was a prime favorite at Court. He had been given to the King at Pompa's christening by a friendly stranger and since then had enjoyed every luxury and advantage. He was always addressed as Sir by all of the palace servants.

He lends an air of elegance to our Court," the King was fond of saying, and the Elegant Elephant he surely had become. Now an Elegant Elephant at Court might seem strange in a regular up-to-date country, but Pumperdink is not at all regular nor up to date. It is a cozy, old-fashioned Kingdom 'way up in the northern part of the Gilliken country of Oz; old-fashioned enough to wear knee breeches and have a King and cozy enough to still enjoy birthday parties and candy pulls.

If Pompus, the King was a bit proud who could blame him? His Queen was the loveliest, his son the most charming and his elephant the most elegant and unusual for twenty Kingdoms round about. And Pompus, for all his pride, had a very simple way of ruling. When the Pumperdinkians did right they were rewarded; when they did wrong they were dipped.

In the very center of the courtyard there is a great stone well with a huge stone bucket. Into this Pumperdink well all offenders and law breakers were lowered. Its waters were dark blue and as the color stuck to one for several days the inhabitants of Pumperdink were careful to behave well, so that the Chief Dipper, who often had days at a time with nothing to do. This time he spent in writing poetry and as Prince Pompadore took the place of honor at the head of the table the Chief Dipper rose from his humble place at the foot and with a moist flourish burst forth:

"Oh, Pompadore of Pumperdink, Of all perfection you're the pink; Your praises now I utter! Your eyes are clear as apple sauce, Your head the best I've come across; Your heart is soft as butter."

"Very good," said the of the King, and the Chief Dipper down, blushing with pride and confusion. Prince Pompadore bowed and the rest of the party clapped tremendously.

"Sounds like a dipper full of nonsense to me," wheezed Kabumpo, who stood directly back of Prince Pompadore's throne, leisurely consuming a bale of hay placed on the floor beside him. It may surprise you to know that all the animals in Oz can talk. but such is the case, and Pumperdink being in the fairy country of Oz, Kabumpo could talk as well as any man and better than most.

"Eyes like apple sauce—heart of butter! Ho-ho, kerumph!" The Elegant elephant laughed so hard he shook all over; then slyly reaching over the Prime Pumper's shoulder, he snatched his glass of Pink Lemonade and emptied it down his great throat, setting the tumbler back before the old fellow turned his head.

"Did you call, sir?" asked Eejabo, hurrying over. He had mistaken Kabumpo's laugh for a command.

"Yes; why did you not give his Excellency lemonade?" demanded the Elegant Elephant sternly.

"I did; he must have drunk it, Sir!" stuttered Eejabo.

"Drunk it!" cried the Prime Pumper, pounding on the table indignantly. "I never had any!"

"Fetch him a glass at once,: rumbled Kabumpo, waving his trunk, and Eejabo, too wise to argue with a member of the royal family, brought another glass of lemonade. But no sooner had he done so than the mischievous elephant stole that, next the Prime Pumper's plate and roll, and all so quickly, no one but Prince Pompadore knew what was happening and Poor Eejabo was kept running backwards and forwards till his wig stood on end with confusion and rage.

All of this was very amusing to the Prince, and helped him to listen pleasantly to the fifteen long birthday speeches addressed to him by members of the Royal Guard. But if the speeches were dull, the dinner was not. The fiddlers fiddled so merrily, and the chief cook Hashem had so outdone himself in the preparation of new and delicious dainties that by ice-cream-and-cake time everyone was in a high good humor.

"The cake, my good Eejabo! Fetch forth the cake!" commanded King Pompus, beaming fondly upon his son. Nervously Eejabo stepped to the side table and lighted the eighteen tall birthday candles. A cake that had disappeared once might easily do so again, and Eejabo was anxious to have it cut and out of the way—out of his way at least.

Hashem, looking through a tiny crack in the door, almost burst with pride as his gorgeous pink masterpiece was set down before the Prince.

"Many happy returns of your eighteenth birthday!" cried the Courtiers, jumping to their feet and waving their napkins enthusiastically.

"Thank you! Thank you!" chuckled Pompadore, bowing low. "I feel that this is but one of many more to come!" Which may sound strange, but Pumperdink being in Oz, one may have as many eighteenth birthdays as one cares to have. This was Pompa's tenth and while the courtiers drank his health the Prince made ready to blow out the birthday candles.

"That's right, blow 'em all out at once!" cried King. So Pompa puffed out his cheeks and blew like a porpoise; so did Queen Pozy and the Prime Pumper; so did everybody. They blew until every dish upon the table skipped and sank back exhausted in their chairs, but the candles burned as merrily as ever.

Then Kabumpo took a hand—or rather a trunk. He had been watching the proceedings with his twinkling little eyes. Now he took a tremendous breath, pointed his trunk straight at the cake and blew with all his strength. Every candle went out— but stars! As they did, the great pink cake exploded with such force that half the Courtiers were flung under the table and the rest knocked unconscious by flying fragments of icing tumblers and plates.

"Treason!" screamed Pompus, the first to recover from the shock. "Who dared put gunpowder in the cake?" Brushing the icing from his nose, he glared around angrily. The first person to catch his eye was Hashem, the cook who stood trembling in the door-way.

"Dip him!" shouted the King furiously. And the Chief dipper, only too glad of an excuse to escape, seized poor Hashem. "And him!" ordered the King, as Eejabo tried to sidle out of the room. "And them!" as all the other footmen started to run. Forming his victims in a line the Chief Dipper marched them sternly from the banquet hall.

"Oyez! Oyez Everybody shall be dipped!" mumbled the Prime Pumper, feebly raising his head.

"Oh, no! Oh, no! Nothing of the sort!" snapped the King, fanning poor Queen Pozy Pink with a plate. She had fainted dead away.

"What is the meaning of this outrage?" shouted Pompus, his anger rising again.

"How should I know?" wheezed Kabumpo, dragging Prince Pompadore from beneath the table and pouring a jug of cream over his head.

"Something hit me," moaned the Prince, opening his eyes.

"Of course it did!" said Kabumpo. "The cake hit you. Made a great hit with us all—that cake!" The Elegant Elephant looked ruefully at his silk robe of state, which was hopelessly smeared with icing; then put his trunk to his head, for something hard had struck him between the eyes. He felt about the floor and found a round shiny object which he was about to show the King when Pompus pounced upon a tall scroll sitting upright in his tumbler. In the confusion of the moment it had escaped his attention.

"Perhaps this will explain," spluttered the King breaking the seal. Queen Pozy Pink opened her eyes with a sigh and the Courtiers, crawling out from beneath the table, looked up anxiously, for everyone was still dazed from the tremendous explosion. Pompus read the scroll to himself with popping eyes and then began to dance up and down in a frenzy.

"What is it? What is it?" cried the Queen, trying to read over his shoulder. Then she gave a well-bred scream and fainted away in the arms of General Quakes, who had come up behind her?

By this time the Prime Pumper had recovered sufficiently to remember that reading scrolls and court papers was his business. Somewhat unsteadily he walked over and took the scroll from the King.

"Oyez! Oyez!" he faltered, pounding on the table. "Oh, never mind that!" rumbled Kabumpo, flapping his ears. "Let's hear what it says!" "Know ye, " began the old man in a high shaky voice, "know ye that unless ye Prince of ye

60

ancient and honorable Kingdom of Pumperdink wed ye Proper Fairy Princess in ye proper span of time ye Kingdom of Pumperdink shall disappear forever and even longer from ye Gilliken country of Oz. J.G."

"What?" screamed Pompadore, bounding to his feet. "Me? But I don't want to marry!"

"You'll have to," groaned the King, with a wave at the scroll. The Courtiers sat staring at one another in dazed disbelief. From the courtyard came the splash and splutter of the luckless footmen and the dismal creaking of the stone bucket.

"Oh!" wailed Pompa, throwing up his hands. "This is the worst eighteenth birthday I've ever had. I'll never have another as long as I live!"

Chapter 2 - Picking a Proper Princess

"What shall we do first?" groaned the King, holding his head with both hands. "Let me think!"

"Right," said Kabumpo. "Think by all means."

So the great hall was cleared and the King, with the mysterious scroll spread out before him, thought and thought and thought. But he did not make much headway, for, as he explained over and over to Queen Pozy, who—with Pompadore, the Elegant Elephant and the Prime-Pumper— had remained to help him, "How is one to know where to find the Proper Princess, and how is one to know the proper time for Pompa to wed her?"

Who was J.G.? How did the scroll get in the cake?

The more the King thought about these questions, the more wrinkled his forehead became.

"Why! We're liable to wake up any morning and find ourselves gone," he announced gloomily. "How does it feel to disappear, I wonder?"

"I suppose it would give one rather a gone feeling, but I don't believe it would hurt—much!" volunteered Kabumpo, glancing uneasily over his shoulder. "Perhaps not, but it would not get us anywhere. My idea is to marry the prince at once to a Proper Princess, "

"You're in a great hurry to marry me off, aren't you," said Pompadore sulkily. "For my part, I don't want to marry at all!"

"Well, that's very selfish of you Pompa," said the King in a grieved voice. "Do you want your poor old father to disappear?"

"Not only your poor old father," choked the Prime Pumper, rolling up his eyes. "How about me?"

Oh, you—you can disappear any time you want," said the Prince unfeelingly.

"It all started with that wretched cake," sighed the Queen. "I am positive the scroll flew out of the cake."

"Of course it did!" cried Pompus. "Let us send for the cook and question him."

So Hashem, very wet and blue from his dip, was brought before the King.

"A fine cook you are!" roared Pompus, "mixing gun powder and scrolls in a birthday cake."

"But I didn't " wailed Hashem, falling on his knees. "Only eggs, your Highness—very best eggs—sugar, flour, spice and—"

"Bombshells!" cried the King angrily.

"The cake disappeared before the party, your Majesty!" cried Eejabo.

Everyone jumped at the sudden interruption, and Eejabo, who had crept in unnoticed, stepped before the throne.

"Disappeared," continued Eejabo hoarsely, dripping blue water all over the royal rugs. "One minute there it was on the pantry table. Next minute—gone!" croaked Eejabo flinging up his hands and shrugging his shoulders.

"Then, before a fellow could turn around, it was back. 'Tween't our fault if magic got mixed into it, and here we have been dipped for nothing!"

"Well, why didn't you say so before!" asked the King in exasperation.

"Fine chance I had to say anything!" sniffed Eejabo, wringing out his lace ruffles.

"eh-rr-you may have the day off, my good man," said Pompus, with an apologetic cough— "And you also," with a wave at Hashem. Very stiffly the two walked to the door.

"It's an off day for us, all right," said Eejabo ungraciously, and without so much as a bow the two disappeared.

"I fear you were a bit hasty, my love," murmured Queen Pozy, looking after them with a troubled little frown.

"Well, who wouldn't be!" cried Pompus, ruffling up his hair. "Here we are liable to disappear any minute and all you do is to stand around and criticize me. Begone!" he puffed angrily, as a page stuck his head in the door.

"No use shouting at people to Begone," said the Elegant Elephant testily. "We'll all begone soon enough."

At this Queen Pozy began to weep into her silk handkerchief, which sight so affected Prince Pompadore that he rushed forward and embraced her tenderly.

"I'll marry!" cried the Prince impulsively. "I'll do anything! The trouble is there aren't any Fairy Princesses around here!"

"There must be," said the King.

"There is—There are!" screamed the Prime Pumper, bounceing up suddenly. "Oyez, Oyez! Has your Majesty forgotten Faleero, royal Princess. She must be the proper one!"

"Fa-leero!" trumpeted the Elegant Elephant, sitting down with a terrific thud. "That awful old creature? You ought to be ashamed of yourself!"

"Silence!" thundered the King.

"Nonsense!" trumpeted Kabumpo. "She's a thousand years old and as ugly as a stone Lukoogoo. Don't you marry her, Pompa."

"I command him to marry her!" cried the King opening his eyes very wide and bending forward.

"Faleero?" gasped the Prince, scarcely believing his ears. No wonder Pompadore was shocked. Faleero, although a Princess in her own right and of royal fairy descent, was so unattractive that in all her thousand years of life no one had wished to marry her. She lived in a small hut in the great forest kingdom next to Pumperdink and did nothing all day but gather faggots. Her face was long and lean, her hair thin and black and her nose so large that it made you think of a cauliflower. "Ugh!" groaned Prince Pompadore, falling back on Kabumpo for support.

"Well, she's a Princess and a fairy— the only one in any Kingdom. I don't see why you want to be so fussy!" said the King Fretfully.

"Shall I tell her Royal Highness of the great and good fortune that has befallen her?" asked the Prime Pumper, starting for the door.

"Do so at once," snapped Pompus. Just then he gave a scream of fright and pain, for a round shiny object had flown through the air and struck him in the head. "What was that?"

The Prime Pumper looked suspiciously at the Elegant Elephant. Kabumpo glared back.

"A-a warning!" stuttered the Prime Pumper, afraid to say that Kabumpo had flung the offending missile. "A warning, your Majesty!"

"It's nothing of the kind," said the King angrily.

"You're getting old, Pumper and stupid. It's—why it's a door knob! Who dares to hit me with a door knob?"

"It hit me once," mumbled Kabumpo, shifting uneasily from one foot to the other three. "How does it strike you?"

"As an outrageous piece of impertinence!" spluttered Pompus, turning red as a turkey cock.

"Perhaps it has something to do with the scroll," suggested Queen Pozy, taking it from the King. "See! It is gold and all the door knobs in the palace are ivory. And look! Here are some initials!"

Sure enough! It was gold and in the very center were the initials P.A.

Just at this interesting juncture the page, who had been poking his head in the door every few minutes, gathered his courage together and rushed up to the King.

"Pardon, most High Highness, but General Quakes bade me say that this mirror was found under the window," stuttered the page and before Pompus had an opportunity to cry "Begone!" or "Dip him!" the little fellow made a dash for the door and disappeared.

"It grows more puzzling every minute," wailed the King, looking from the door knob to the mirror from the mirror to the scroll.

"If you take my advice you'll have this marriage performed at once," said the Prime Pumper in a trembling voice.

"I believe I will!" sighed Pompus, rubbing the bump on his head. "Go and fetch the Princess Faleero and you, Pompa, prepare for your wedding."

"But Father!" began the Prince.

"Not another word or you'll be dipped!" rumbled the King of Pumperdink. "I'm not going to have my kingdom disappearing if I can help it!"

"You mean if I can help it," muttered Pompadore gloomily.

"This is ridiculous!" stormed the Elegant Elephant, as the Prime Pumper rushed importantly out of the room. "Don't you know that this country of ours is only a small part of the great Kingdom of Oz? there must be hundreds of Princesses for Pompadore to choose from. Why should he not wed Ozma, the princess of us all? Haven't you read any Oz history? Have you never heard of the wonderful Emerald City? Let Pompadore start out at once. I, myself, will accompany him, and if Ozma refuses to marry him well" the Elegant Elephant drew himself up "I will carry her off — that's all!"

"It's a long way to the Emerald City," mused Queen Pozy, "but still—"

"Yes, and what is to become of us in the meantime pray? While you are wandering all over Oz we can disappear I suppose! No Sir! Not one step do you go out of Pumperdink. Faleero is the Proper Princess and Pompadore shall marry her!" said Pompus.

"You're talking through your crown," wheezed Kabumpo. "How about the door knob and mirror? They came out of the cake as well as the scroll. What are you going to do about them? Let's have a look at that mirror."

"Just a common gold mirror," fumed Pompus, holding it up for the Elegant Elephant to see.

"What's the matter?" as Kabumpo gave a snort.

On the face of the mirror as Kabumpo looked in two words appeared: Elegant elephant.

And when Pompus snatched the mirror, above his reflection stood the words: Fat Old King

Then Queen Pozy peeped into the mirror, which promptly flashed: Lovely Queen.

"Why, it's telling the truth!" screamed Pompa, looking over his mother's shoulder. At this the words "Charming Prince" formed quickly in the glass.

The Prince grinned at his father, who was now quite beside himself with rage. "You think I'm fat and old, do you!" snorted the King flinging the gold mirror face down on the table. "this is a nice day, I must say! Scrolls, door knobs, mirrors and insults!"

"But what can P.A. stand for?" mused Queen Pozy thoughtfully. "Plain enough," chuckled Kabumpo, maliciously. "It stands for perfectly awful!"

"Who's perfectly awful?" asked Pompus suspiciously.

"Why, Faleero," sniffed the Elegant Elephant. "That's plain enough to everybody!"

"Dip him!" shrieked Pompus. "I've had enough of this!! Dip him—do you hear?"

"That," yawned Kabumpo, straightening his silk robe, "is impossible!" And, considering his size it was. But just that minute the Prime Pumper returned and in his interest to hear what the Princess Faleero had said the King forgot about dipping Kabumpo.

The courier from the Princess stepped forward. "Her Highness,"puffed the Prime Pumper, who had run all the way, "Her Highness accepts Prince Pompadore with pleasure and will marry him to-mor-ow morning."

Prince Pompadore gave a dismal groan.

"Fine!" cried the King, rubbing his hands together. "Let everything be made ready for the ceremony, and in the meantime"—Pompus glared about fiercely—"I forbid anyone's disappearing. I am still the King! Set a guard around the castle, Pumper, to watch for any signs of disappearance, and if so much as a fence paling disappears,"—he drew himself up—"notify me at once!" Then turning to the throne Pompus gave his arm to Queen Pozy and together they started for the garden.

"Do you mean to say you are going to pay no attention to the mirror or door knob?" cried Kabumpo, planting himself in the King's path.

"Go away," said Pompus crossly

"Oyes! Oyes! Way for their Majesties!" cried the Prime Pumper, running ahead with his silver staff, and the royal couple swept out of the banquet hall.

"Never mind, Kabumpo," said the Prince, flinging his arm affectionately around the Elegant Elephant's trunk, "I dare say Faleero has her good points—and we cannot let the old Kingdom disappear, you know!"

"Fiddlesticks!" choked Kabumpo. She'll make a door mat of you, Pompa—Prince Pompadormat—that's what you'll be! Let's run away" he proposed, his little eyes twinkling anxiously.

"I couldn't do that and let the Kingdom disappear, it wouldn't be right," sighed the Prince, and sadly he followed his parents into the royal gardens.

"The King's a Gooch!" gulped the Elegant Elephant unhappily. Then, all at once he flung up his trunk. "Somebody's going to disappear around here," he wheezed darkly, "that's certain!" With a mighty rustling of his silk robe, Kabumpo hurried off to his own royal quarters in the palace.

Left alone, Prince Pompa threw himself down at the foot of the throne, and gazed sadly into space.

Chapter 3 - Kabumpo and Pompa Disappear

Once in his own apartment, Kabumpo pulled the bell rope furiously.

"My pearls and my purple plush robe! Bring them at once!" he puffed when his personal attendant appeared in the doorway.

"Yes, Sir! Are you going out, Sir?" murmured the little Pumperdinkian, hastening to a great chest in the corner of the big marble room, to get out of the robe.

"Not unless disappearing is going out," said Kabumpo more mildly, for he was quite fond of this little man who waited on him. "But I'm liable to disappear any minute. So are you. So is everybody, and I, for my part, wish to do the thing well and disappear with as much elegance as possible. Have you heard about the magic scroll, Spezzle?"

"Yes Sir!" quavered Spezzle, mounting a ladder to adjust the Elegant Elephant's pearls and gorgeous robe of state. "Yes, Sir, and my head's going round and round like—"

"Like what?" asked Kabumpo, looking approvingly at his reflection in the long mirror.

"I can't rightly say, Sir," sighed Spezzle. "This disappearing has me that mixed up I don't know what I'm doing."

"Well, don't start by losing your head," chuckled Kabumpo. "there—that will do very well." He lifted the little man down from the ladder.

"Good-bye, Spezzle. If you should disappear before I should see you again, try to do it in style."

"Yes, Sir!" gulped Spezzle. Then taking out a bright red handkerchief he blew his nose violently and rushed out of the room.

Kabumpo walked up and down before the mirror, surveying himself from all angles. A very gorgeous appearance he presented, in his purple plush robe of state, all embroidered in silver, and his head bands of shining pearls. In the left side of his robe there was a deep pocket. Into this the Elegant Elephant slipped all the jewels he possessed, taking them from a drawer in the chest.

"I must get that gold door knob," he rumbled thoughtfully. "And the mirror." Noiselessly(for all his tremendous size, Kabumpo could move without a sound) he made his way back to the banquet hall and loomed up suddenly behind the Prime Pumper. The old fellow was staring with popping eyes into the gold mirror.

"Ho, Ho!" roared Kabumpo. "Ho, Ho! Kerumph!"

"No wonder! Above the shocked reflection of the foolish statesman stood the words "Old Goose!"

"A truthful mirror, indeed," wheezed the Elegant Elephant.

"Heh? What?" stuttered the Prime Pumper slapping the mirror down on the table in a hurry. "Where'd you come from? What are you all dressed up for?"

"For my disappearance," said Kabumpo, sweeping the door knob and mirror into his pocket. "I'm getting ready to disappear. How do I look?"

Before the Prime Pumper had time to answer, the elegant Elephant was gone.

Back in his own room, Kabumpo paced impatiently up and down waiting for night. "I do not see how she could refuse us," he mumbled every now and then to himself.

That was an anxious afternoon and evening in the palace of Pumperdink. Every few minutes the Courtiers felt themselves nervously to see if they were still there. The servants went about on tip-toe, looking fearfully over their shoulders for the first signs of disappearance. As it grew darker the gates and windows were securely barred and not a candle was lighted. "The less the castle shows, the less likely it is to disappear," reasoned the King.

The darkness suited Kabumpo. He waited until everyone in the palace had retired and a full hour longer. Then he stepped softly down the passage to the Prince's apartment. Pompadore, without undressing, had flung himself upon a couch and fallen into an uneasy slumber.

Without making a sound, Kabumpo took the Prince's crown from a dressing cabinet, slipped it carefully into the pocket of his robe, and then carefully lifted the sleeping Prince in his curling trunk and started cautiously down the great hall. Setting him gently on the floor as he reached the palace doors, he pushed back the golden bolts and stepped out into the garden.

The voices of the watchmen calling to each other from the great wall came faintly through the darkness, but the Elegant Elephant hurried to a secret unguarded entrance known only to himself and Pompadore and passed like a great shadow through the swinging gates. Once outside, he swung the sleeping Prince to his broad back and ran swiftly and silently through the night.

"What are we doing?" murmured the Prince drowsily in his sleep.

"Disappearing," chuckled Kabumpo under his breath. "Disappearing from Pumperdink, my lad."

Chapter 4 - The Curious Cottabus Appears

"Ouch!" Prince Pompadore stirred uneasily and rolled over. "Ouch!" he groaned again, giving his pillow a fretful thump. "Ouch!" This time his eyes flew wide open, for his knuckles were tingling with pain.

"A rock!" gasped the Prince sitting up indignantly.

"A rock under my head! No wonder it aches! Great Gilikens! Where am I?" He stared about wildly. There was not a familiar object in sight. Indeed he was in a dim, deep forest, and from the distance came the sound of someone sawing wood.

"Oh! Oh! I know!" muttered the Prince, rubbing his head miserably. "it's that wretched scroll. I've disappeared and this is the place I've disappeared to." Stiffly he got to his feet and started to walk in the direction of the sawing, but had only gone a few steps before he gave a cry of joy, for there, learning up against a tree, snoring like twenty wood-cutters at work, was Kabumpo.

"Wake up!" cried Pompadore, pounding him with all his might. "Wake up, Kabumpo. We've disappeared!"

"Have we?" yawned the Elegant Elephant, opening one eye. You don't say? Hah, Hoh, Hum!" with a tremendous yawn he opened the other eye and began to chuckle and shake all over.

"We stole a march on 'em, Pompa I'd like to see the King's face when he finds us gone. Old Pumper will be Oyezing all over the palace. He'll think we've disappeared by magic."

"Well, didn't we?" asked Pompadore in amazement.

"Not unless you call me magic. I carried you off in the night. Did you suppose old Kabumpo was going to stand quietly by while they married you to a fagotty old fairy like Faleero? Not much," wheezed the Elegant Elephant. "I have other plans for you, little one!"

"But this is terrible!" cried the Prince, catching hold of a tree. "Here you have left my poor old father, my lovely mother, and the whole Kingdom of Pumperdink to disappear. We'll have to go right straight back—right straight back to Pumperdink. Do you hear?"

"Do have a little sense!" Kabumpo shook himself crossly. "You can't save them by going back. The thing to do is to go forward, find the Proper Princess and marry her. No scroll magic takes effect for seven days, anyway!"

"How do you know?" asked Pompa anxiously.

"Read it in a witch book," answered Kabumpo promptly. "Now, that gives us plenty of time to go to the Emerald City and present ourselves to the lovely ruler of OZ. There's a Proper Princess for you, Pompa!"

"But suppose she refuses me," said the Prince uncertainly.

"You're very handsome, Pompa, my boy." The Elegant Elephant gave the Prince a playful poke with his trunk. "I've brought all my jewels as gifts and the magic mirror and door knob as well. If she refuses you and the worst comes to the worst"— Kabumpo cleared his throat gravely—"well—just leave it to me!"

After a bit more coaxing and after eating the breakfast Kabumpo had thoughtfully brought along, Pompa allowed the Elegant Elephant to lift him on his head and off they set at Kabumpo's best speed for the Emerald City of Oz.

Neither the Prince nor the Elegant Elephant had ever been out of Pumperdink, but Kabumpo had found an old map of Oz in the palace library. According to this map, the Emerald City lay directly to the South of their own country. "So all we have to do is to keep going South," chuckled Kabumpo softly. Pompadore nodded, but he was trying to recall the exact words of the mysterious scroll:

"Know Ye, that unless ye Prince of ye ancient and honorable Kingdom of Pumperdink shall wed ye Proper Fairy Princess in ye proper span of time ye Kingdom of Pumperdink shall disappear forever and even longer from ye Gilliken Country of Oz. J.G."

Pompadore repeated the words solemnly; then fell a-thinking of all he had heard of Ozma of Oz, the loveliest little fairy imaginable.

"She wouldn't want one of her Kingdom to disappear," reflected Pompadore sagely. Now, as it happened, Ozma did not even know of the existence of Pumperdink. Oz is so large and inhabited by so many strange and singular peoples that although fourteen books of history have been written about it only half the story has been told. There are no Oz railway or steamship lines and traveling is tedious and slow, owing to the magic nature of the land itself, its many mountains and fairy forests, so that Pumperdink, like many of the small Kingdoms on the outskirts of Oz, has never been explored by Ozma.

Oz itself is a huge oblong country divided into four parts, the North being the purple Gilliken country, the East the blue Munchkins country, the South the red lands of the Quadlings, and the West the pleasant yellow country of the Winkies. In the very center of Oz, as almost every boy and girl knows, is the wonderful Emerald City, and in its gorgeous green palace lives Ozma, the lovely little Fairy Princess, whom Kabumpo wanted Pompadore to marry.

"Do you know," mused the Prince, after they had traveled some time through the dim forest, "I believe that gold mirror has a lot to do with all this. I believe it was put in the cake to help me find the Proper Princess."

"Where would you find a more Proper Princess than Ozma?" puffed Kabumpo Indignantly. "Ozma is the one— depend upon it!"

"Just the same," said Pompa firmly, "I'm going to try every Princess we meet!"

65

"Do you expect to find 'em running wild in the woods?" snorted Kabumpo, who didn't like to be contradicted.

"You never can tell." The Prince of Pumperdink settled back comfortably. Now that they were really started, he was finding traveling extremely interesting. "I should have done this long ago," murmured the Prince to himself. "Every Prince should go on a journey of adventure."

"How long will it take us to reach the Emerald City?" he asked presently.

"Two days, if nothing happens," answered Kabumpo. "Say—what's that?" He stopped short and spread his ears till they looked like sails. The underbrush at the right was crackling from the springs of some large animal, and next minute a hoarse voice roared:

"I want to know The which and what, The where and how and why? A curious, luxurious Old Cottabus am I!

I want to know the When and who, The whatfor and whyso, Sir! So please attend, there is no end To things I want to know, Sir!"

"Aha!" exulted the voice triumphantly. "There you are!" And a great round head was thrust out, almost in Kabumpo's face. "Oh! I'm going to enjoy this. Don't move!"

Kabumpo was too astonished to move, and the next instant the Cottabus had flounced out of the bushes and settled itself directly in front of the two travelers. It was large as a pony, but shaped like a great overfed cat. Its eyes bulged unpleasantly and the end of its tail ended in a large fan.

"Well," grunted Kabumpo after the strange creature had regarded them for a full minute without blinking.

"Well," what?" it asked, beginning to fan itself sulkily. "You act as if you had never seen a Cottabus before."

"We never have," admitted Pompa, peering over Kabumpo's head and secretly wishing he had brought along his jeweled sword.

"Why haven't you?" asked the Cottabus, rolling up its eyes. "How frightfully ignorant!" It closed its fan tail with a snap and looked up at them disapprovingly. "Will you kindly tell me who you are, where you came from, when you came, what you are going for, how you are going to get it, why you are going and what you are going to do when you do get it!"

"I don't see why we should tell you all that," grumbled Kabumpo. "It's none of your affair."

"Wrong!" shrieked the creature hysterically. "It is the business of a Cottabus to find out everything. I live on other people's affairs, and unless"—here it paused, took a large handkerchief out of a pocket in its fur and began to wipe its eyes—"unless a Cottabus asks fifty questions a day it curls up in its porch rocker and d-d-dies, and this is my fifth questionless day."

"Curl up and die, then," said Kabumpo gruffly. But the kind-hearted Prince felt sorry for the foolish creature.

"If we answer your questions, will you answer ours?"

"I'll try," sniffed the Curious Cottabus, and leaning over it dragged a rocking chair out of the bushes and seated itself comfortably.

"Well, then," began Pompa, "this is the Elegant Elephant and I am a Prince. We came from Pumperdink because our Kingdom was threatened with disappearance unless I marry a Proper Princess."

"Yes," murmured the Cottabus, rocking violently. "Yes, yes!"

"And we are going to the Emerald City to ask princess Ozma for her hand," continued the Prince.

"How do you know she is the one? When did this happen? Who brought the message? What are you going to do if Ozma refuses you?" asked the Cottabus, leaning forward breathlessly.

"Are you going to stand talking to this ridiculous creature all day?" grumbled Kabumpo. But Pompadore, perhaps because he was so young, felt flattered that even a curious old Cottabus should take such an interest in his affairs. So beginning at the very beginning he told the whole story of his birthday party.

"Yes, yes," gulped the Cottabus wildly each time the Prince paused for breath. "Yes, yes," fluttering its fan excitedly. When Pompadore had finished the Cottabus leaned back, closed its eyes and put both paws on the arms of the rocker. "I never heard anything more curious in my life," said the curious one. "This will keep me amused for three days!"

"Of course—that's what we're here for—to amuse you!" said Kabumpo scornfully. "Let's be going, Pompa!"

"Perhaps the Curious Cottabus can tell us something of the country ahead. Are there any Princesses living 'round here?" the Prince asked eagerly.

"Never heard of any," said the Cottabus, opening its eyes. "Can you multiply—add—divide and subtract? Are you good at fractions, Prince?"

"Not very," admitted Pompadore, looking mystified.

"Then you won't make much headway," sighed the Cottabus, shaking its head solemnly. "Now, don't ask me why," it added lugubriously, dragging its rocker back into the brush, and while Kabumpo and Pompa stared in amazement it wriggled away into the bushes.

"Come on," cried Kabumpo with a contemptuous grunt, but he had only gone a few steps when the Curious Cottabus stuck its head out of an opening in the trees just ahead. "When are you coming back?" it asked, twitching its nose anxiously.

"Never!" trumpeted Kabumpo, increasing his speed. Again the Cottabus disappeared, only to reappear at the first turn in the road.

"Did you say the door knob hit you on the head?" it asked pleadingly.

Kabumpo gave a snort of anger and rushed along so fast that Pompa had to hang on for dear life.

"Guess we've left him behind this time," spluttered the Elegant Elephant, after he had run almost a mile.

But at that minute there was a wheeze from the underbrush and the head of the Cottabus was thrust out. Its tongue was hanging out and it was panting with exhaustion. "How old are you?" it gasped, rolling its eyes pitifully. "Who was your grandfather on your father's side, and was he bald?"

"Kerumberty Bumpus!" raged the Elegant Elephant, flouncing to the other side of the road.

"But why was the door knob in the cake?" gulped the Cottabus, two tears trickling off its nose.

"How should we know," said Pompa coldly.

"Then just tell me the date of your birth," wailed the Cottabus, two tears trickling off its nose.

"No! No!" screamed Kabumpo, and this time he ran so fast that the tearful voice of the Cottabus became fainter and fainter and finally died away altogether.

"Provokingest creature I've ever met," grumbled the Elegant Elephant, and this time Pompa agreed with him.

"Isn't it almost lunch time?" asked the Prince. He was beginning to feel terribly hungry.

"And aren't there any villages or cities between here and the Emerald City?" Pompa spoke again.

"Don't know," wheezed Kabumpo, swinging ahead.

"Oh! There's a flag!" cried Pompa suddenly. "It's flying above the tree tops just ahead."

And so it was— a huge, flapping black flag covered with hundreds of figures and signs.

"Hurry up, Kabumpo," urged the Prince. "This looks interesting."

Chapter 5 - In the City of The Figure Heads

"It reminds me of something disagreeable," answered Kabumpo, as he eyed the flag.
Nevertheless he quickened his steps and in a moment they came to a clearing in the forest, surrounded by a tall black picket fence. The only thing visible above the fence was the strange black flag, and as the forest on either side was too dense to penetrate and there seemed to be no way around, Kabumpo thumped loudly on the center gate.

It was flung open at once, so suddenly that Kabumpo, who had his head pressed against the bars fell on his knees and shot Pompadore clear over his head. Altogether it was a very undignified entrance.

"Oh! Oh! Now we shall have some fun!" screamed a high, thin voice, and immediately the cry was taken up by hundreds of other voices. A perfect swarm of strange creatures surrounded the two travelers. The Elegant Elephant took one look, put back his ears and snatched Pompa from the paving stones.

"Stop that!" he rumbled threateningly. "Who are you anyway?" The crowd paid no attention to the elegant Elephant's question, but continued to dance up and down and scream with glee. Clutching Kabumpo's ear, Pompa peered down with many misgivings. They were entirely surrounded by thin, spry little people, who had figures instead of heads, and the fours, eighths, sevens and ciphers hobbling up and down made it terribly confusing.

"Let's go!" said Pompa, who was growing dizzier every minute. But the Figure heads were wedged so closely around them Kabumpo could not move and they were shouting so lustily that the Elegant Elephant's voice was drowned in the hubbub. finally, Kabumpo's eyes began to snap angrily and, taking a deep breath, he threw up his trunk and trumpeted like fifty ferry-boat whistles. The effect was immediate and astonishing. Half of the Figure Heads fell on their faces, and the other half fell on their backs and stared vacantly up at the sky.

"Conduct us to your Ruler!" roared Kabumpo in the dead silence that followed. "How'd you know we had a Ruler?" asked a Seven, getting cautiously to its feet. "Most countries have," said the Elegant Elephant shortly. "He's got no right to order us around," said a Six, sitting up and jerking its thumb at Kabumpo.

"Yes—but!" Seven frowned at Six and put his hands over his ears. "This way," he said gruffly, and Kabumpo, stepping carefully, for many of the Figure Heads were still on their backs, followed Seven.

If the inhabitants of this strange city were queer, their city was even more so. The air was dry and choky and the houses were dull, oblong affairs, set in rows and rows with never a garden in sight. Each street had a large signpost on the corner, but they were not at all like the signs one usually sees in cities. For these were plus and minus signs with here and there a long division sign.

"I suppose everything in this street's divided up," mumbled Pompadore, looking up at a division sign curiously.

"Hope they don't subtract any of our belongings," whispered Kabumpo, as they turned into Minus Alley. "Look, Pompa, at the houses. Ever see anything like 'em before?"

"They remind me of something disagreeable," mused the Prince. "Why, they're books, Kabumpo, great big arithmetic books!" Pompa pointed at one.

"You mean they are shaped like books," said the Elegant Elephant. "I never saw books with windows and doors!"

"A lot you know!" said Seven, looking back scornfully, but Kabumpo was too interested to. care. Out of the windows of the big book houses leaped hundreds of the little Figure Heads, and they laughed and jeered at Pompa and Kabumpo. "Ho! Ho!" yelled one, leaning out so far it nearly fell on its Eight. "Wait till the Count sees 'em. He'll make an example of 'em!"

"What an awful country," whispered Pompadore, ducking just in time, as a Four snatched at his hair from an open window. But just then they turned a corner and entered a large gloomy court. Sitting on a square and solid wood throne, surrounded by a guard of Figure Heads, sat the Giant Ruler of this strange city. "What have you got there, seven?" roared the Ruler.

"I am the Elegant Elephant and this is the Prince of Pumperdink," announced Kabumpo before Seven could answer. Pompadore, him-self, could say nothing for he had never before been addressed by a wooden ruler in his life And that is exactly what the King of the Figure heads was—an ordinary school ruler, twice as large as a man, with arms and legs and a great square head set atop of his thin flat body.

"I don't care a rap who you are. I want to know what you are?" said the Ruler. "We are travelers," spoke up Pompa, swallowing hard—travelers in search of a Proper Princess."

"Well, you won't find any here," grunted the Ruler shortly. "We don't believe in 'em!"

"Would you mind telling me the name of your Kingdom," asked Pompa, somewhat cast down by these words.

"You have no heads," announced the Ruler calmly, "or you would have known that this is Rith Metic. I," he hammered himself upon the wooden chest— "I am its Ruler and every inch a King—King of the Figure Heads," he added, glancing around as if he expected someone to contradict him. "All right! All right!" wheezed Kabumpo, bowing his head twice. "I knew twelve inches made a foot rule, but I never knew they made a King Rule. But could you give us some luncheon and allow us to pass peaceably through your Kingdom?"

"Pass through!" exclaimed the King, standing up indignantly. "We don't pass anyone through here. You've got to work your way through. Pass through, indeed! And when you've worked your way through we'll put you in a problem and make an example of you."

"They'll make a very good example, your Majesty," said a tall thin individual standing next to the Ruler. He eyed the two cunningly.

"If a thin Prince sets out on a fat elephant to find a Proper Princess, how many yards of fringe will the elephant lose from his robe and how bald will the Prince be at the end of the journey? I don't believe anyone could figure "It might be done by subtraction," said the King, looking at the two critically.

"Great hay stacks!" rumbled Kabumpo, glaring over his shoulder to see if he had lost any fringe so far. "What have we gotten into?"

"Bald!" gulped Pompa, rubbing his head. "Do you mean to say you take poor innocent travelers and make them into arithmetic problems?"

"Why not?" said the thin one, who looked exactly like a giant lead pencil. "And please address me as Count, after this—Count It Up is my name. What's the matter with living in a problem, my boy? Life is a problem, after all, and you will get used to it in time. I'll try to assign you to a comfortable book and you'll find book-keeping a lot more simple than house-keeping. This way, please!"

"Please go," yawned the Ruler, waving his hand. "The Count will take you in charge now." And so dazed was the Elegant Elephant by all this strange reasoning that he tamely followed the lead pencil person.

"Good-bye!" shouted the Ruler hoarsely. "Start them on simple additions," he said as they moved off.

The street ahead was filled with Figure Heads and as Kabumpo paused they began forming themselves into sums. The first row sat down, the next knelt behind them, the third stood up, the fourth nimbly leaped upon the shoulders of the third, and so on, until a long addition confronted the travelers.

"Now," said Count It Up in his blunt way, as you haven't figures for heads, let us see if you have heads for figures." Kabumpo pushed back his pearl headdress and drops of perspiration began to run down his trunk. Prince Pompa, lying flat on Kabumpo's head, started to add up the first line of figures. "Eighty-three," he announced anxiously.

"Say three and eight to carry, snapped Count It Up. "Here, Three!" A Three stepped out of the crowd and placed itself under the line. "I've got to be carried!" cried Eight, looking sulkily at Pompa.

"Carried!" snorted Kabumpo, snatching Eight into the air. "Well, I'll attend to you. You do the adding, Pompa, and I'll do the carrying."

He landed the Eight head down at the bottom of the line of Figure Heads and swung his trunk carelessly while he waited for his next victim. So, slowly and painfully, Pompa counted up the long lines and Kabumpo carried and if they made the slightest mistake the Figure Heads shouted with scorn and danced about till the confusion was terrible. When an example was finished, the Figure Heads in it marched away but another would immediately form lines ahead so that it took them a whole hour to go two blocks.

"Oh!" groaned Pompa at last, "We'll never get through this, Kabumpo. Look at those awful fractions ahead! Can't I skip fractions?" he asked looking pleadingly at Count It Up.

"Certainly not!" said the pencilly man stroking his shiny hair, which was straight and black and grew up into a sharp point. "You shall skip nothing!"

"That gives me an idea," whispered Kabumpo huskily. "Why shouldn't we skip altogether? We're bigger than they are. Why—

"How are you getting on?" At the sound of that hoarse, familiar voice both the Prince and Kabumpo jumped.

"You don't mind me asking, I hope?" Clinging to the high picket fence and looking anxiously through the bars was the Curious Cottabus.

"Have you found the Greatest Common Divisor yet?"

"Who's he?" asked the Elegant Elephant suspiciously.

"Isn't there any way out of Rith Metic but this?" wailed Pompa, looking at the Cottabus pleadingly. He was too tired to mind being questioned.

The curious beast was delighted to have this new opportunity to talk to the travelers.

"Will you answer a few questions if I tell you?" asked the Cottabus, raising itself with great difficulty and looking over the palings.

"Yes—yes—anything," promised Pompa.

"Do you care for strawberry tarts?" asked the Cottabus, twitching its nose very rapidly.

"Of course," said the Prince. "Oh! Do hurry. Count It Up will be back in a moment!" He had run ahead to arrange a new problem and the rest of the Figure Heads paid no attention to the queer creature clinging to the palings.

"Are you going to invite the Scarecrow to your wedding?" gulped the Cottabus.

"I don't know any scarecrow," said Pompa, "so how could I?"

"Are you fond of that old elephant?" The Cottabus waved at Kabumpo, who stamped first one foot then another and fairly snorted with rage.

"All right," sighed the Curious Cottabus, "that makes my fifty questions."

Hanging on to the fence with one paw it waved the other backward and forward as it chanted:

"How many tics in Rith Metic? Tell me that and tell me quick! But if you can't it's not my fault, So simply turn a wintersault!"

The head of the Cottabus disappeared.

"Now isn't that provoking," gulped the Prince. "After it promised to help us, too!"

"I meant summersault," wheezed the Cottabus, reappearing suddenly—"And if you can't it's not your fault, So simply turn a summersault!"

it recited dolefully, and losing its balance fell off the fence and landed with a thud on the ground below.

"Here! Hurry along" scolded Count It Up, prodding Kabumpo with a sharp pencil. "The next is a nice little problem in fractions."

"I wonder if it meant anything?" mused Pompadore, as Kabumpo approached the new problem. " 'If you can't it's not your fault, so simply turn a summersault.' Anyway it wouldn't hurt to try. Stop a minute, Kabumpo!"

Sliding down the Elegant Elephant's trunk, the Prince put his head on the ground and very carefully and deliberately turned a somersault. At his first motion Count It Up gave a deafening scream, fell on his head and broke off his point, while the Figure Heads began to run in every direction.

"Do it again! Do it again!" cried Kabumpo joyfully. So Pompa turned another somersault and another, and another, and another, till not a Figure Head was in sight. Even the Figure Heads at the windows of the houses tumbled out and dashed madly around the corner. Before they could return, Kabumpo snatched up Pompa and tore through the deserted streets of Rith Metic till he came to the black iron gate at the other end of the city. Butting it open with his head, the Elegant Elephant dashed through and never stopped running till he was miles away from there.

"Have to rest a bit and eat some leaves," puffed Kabumpo, at last slowing down. "Whe-w!"

"Wish I could eat leaves," sighed the Prince, as Kabumpo began lunching off the tree tops. "But, never mind, we're out of Rith Metic! Wasn't it lucky that Cottabus followed us? I never would have thought of getting out of sums by somersaulting. Would you?"

"Only sensible thing it ever said, probably," answered the Elegant Elephant, with his mouth full of leaves. "There's a lot more to be learned by traveling than by studying, my boy. Somer-saults for sums—let's always remember that!"

Pompa did not answer. He slid down Kabumpo's trunk and began hunting anxiously around for something to eat. Not far away he found a large nut tree and, gathering a handful of nuts, he sat down and began to crack them on a white marble slab near by. Next instant Kabumpo heard a thud and a muffled cry.

The Prince of Pumperdink had vanished, as if by magic.

"Where are you?" screamed the Elegant Elephant, pounding through the brush. "Pompa! Pompa! He's disappeared," gasped Kabumpo, rushing over to the marble slab. There was not a sign of the Royal Prince of Pumperdink anywhere, but carved carefully on the white stone were these words:

Please Knock Before You Fall In.

"Fall in!" snorted Kabumpo, his eyes rolling wildly. "Great Gooch!"

Chapter 6 - Ruggedo's History in Six Rocks

On the same night that Prince Pompa and Kabumpo had disappeared from Pumperdink, a little gray gnome crouched in a deep chamber, tunneled under the Emerald City, laboriously carving letters on a big rock. It was Ruggedo, the old Gnome King, carving and grumbling and grumbling and carving, and pausing every few minutes to light his pipe with a hot coal which he kept in his pocket for that purpose. A big emerald lamp cast a glow over the strange cavern and made the gnome look like a bad green goblin, which he was.

"Wag!" screamed the gnome, suddenly throwing down the chisel, "Where are you, you long-eared villain?" There was a slight stir at the back of the cave and a rabbit, of about the same size as the gnome, shuffled slowly forward.

"What you want?" he asked, rubbing one eye with his paw.

"Bring me a cup of melted mud, idiot!" roared the gnome, pounding on the rock. "And serve it to me on my throne at once!"

"Now, see here," the rabbit twitched his nose rapidly, "I'll get you a cup of melted mud, but don't you call me an idiot. I don't mind working for one, nor digging for one and listening to his foolishness, but nobody can call me an idiot—not even a make—believe King!"

"Oh, you make me tired!" fumed the gnome. "Then go to sleep," advised the rabbit with a yawn. "What's the use of trying to pretend you're a King, Rug? Ho, ho! King over one wooden doll, six rocks and twenty-seven sofa cushions! You may have been a King once, but now you're just a plain gnome and nothing else, and if you go and sit quietly in your plain rocking chair I'll bring you a cup of plain mud."

With a chuckle, the rabbit retired, and Ruggedo, spluttering with fury, flounced into a doll's broken rocker that was set in the exact center of the cave.

"Here I give that rabbit everything I steal and he won't even allow me the little luxury of calling him an idiot or of pulling his ears. How can I pretend to be a King without an ear to pull?" grumbled the gnome.

"What are you grinning at?" Bouncing out of his chair, Ruggedo flew at a merry-faced wooden doll who sat propped up against the wall and shook her till her head turned round backwards and her arms and legs flew every which way. Then he hurled her violently into a corner. Quite out of breath he sank back in his chair and stared angrily about.

When Wag returned the gnome snatched the tin cup of melted mud and tossed it down with one gulp. Then, flinging the cup at the doll, he went back to work.

The rabbit shook his head mournfully and, picking up the wooden doll, straightened her out and placed her on a cushion. Then, yawning again, he lit a candle and started for the passage at the back of the cave.

"How are you getting on?" he asked, pausing to look over the gnome's shoulder with a grin.

"Fine!" answered Ruggedo, forgetting to scowl. "I'm up to the sixth rock and expect to finish to-night."

"Who do you think will read it?" asked the rabbit, putting back both ears and stroking his whiskers. Then he gave a great spring, just escaped the chisel Ruggedo had flung at his head, and pattered away into the darkness. For several minutes the gnome danced up and down with fury. Then, as there was no one to pinch or shake, he started to work harder than ever on the sixth rock of his history. There were six of the great Stones set in a row on one side of the cavern and the carving on them had taken the old gnome King the best part of two years. The letters were crooked and roughly chiseled, but quite readable. On the first rock he had carved:

History of Ruggedo in Six Rocks Ruggedo the Rough-King of the Gnomes One time Metal Monarch, at other times a Limoneag, a goose, a nut, and now a common gnome by order of Ozma of Oz.

The second rock told of Ruggedo's magnificent Kingdom under the mountains of Ev, of the thousands of gnomes he had ruled and the great treasure of precious gems he had possessed, in those good old days before he was banished from his dominions.

The third rock told of his transformation of the Queen of Ev and her children into ornaments for his palace and of their rescue by a party from Oz, through the cleverness of Billina, a yellow hen. It told of the loss of his Magic Belt which was captured at this same time by Dorothy, a little girl from Kansas.

The fourth rock related how Ruggedo had tried to conquer Oz and recovered his belt; how all of his plans failed and how he tumbled into the Fountain of Oblivion and forgot all about his campaign.

The fifth rock had taken Ruggedo the longest to carve, for it gave the story of his banishment by the Great Jinn Titihoochoo. You have probably read this story yourself. How Tik Tok, Betsy Bobbin, Shaggyman and Polychrome, trying to find Shaggy's brother, hidden in the Gnome King's metal forest, were thrown down a long tube to the other side of the world, and how the owner of the tube sent Quox, the dragon, to punish Ruggedo by banishment from his Kingdom and how Kaliko was made King of the Gnomes.

The sixth rock told of Ruggedo's last attempt to capture Oz. Meeting Kiki Aru, a Highup boy who knew a magic transformation word, Ruggedo suggested that they change themselves to Limoneags queer beasts with lion heads, monkey tails and eagle wings get all the beasts of Oz to help and march on the Emerald City. But this plan failed, too. Kiki lost his temper and changed Ruggedo to a goose, the Wizard of Oz discovered the magic word and changed both the conspirators to nuts. Later on they were changed back to their normal shapes, but again Ruggedo was plunged into the Fountain of Oblivion and again forgot his wicked plans. This ended the rock history, except for a short sentence stating that Ruggedo now lived in the Emerald City.

But the magic of the Fountain of Oblivion had soon worn off and it was not long before Ruggedo began to remember his past wicked-ness. That is why he decided to carve his life story in rock, so that it would be handy should he ever fall into the forgetful fountain again. And it had taken six rocks to tell all of his adventures. He had not carved these stories just as they had happened, nor ever called himself wicked, but he had told most of the facts, leaving out the parts most unflattering to himself. And now it was finished—his whole history in six rocks. Throwing down his chisel for the last time, Ruggedo straightened up and regarded his work with glowing pride.

"I don't believe there's another history like this in all Oz," puffed the gnome, tugging at his silver beard.

"It's a good thing," chuckled Wag, who had come back to eat a carrot. "Oz would not be a very happy place if there were many folks like you.

He seated himself quietly on the first rock of Ruggedo's history, and began nibbling his carrot.

"Get up! How dare you sit on my history?" Ruggedo stamped his foot and started threateningly toward Wag.

"All right," said the rabbit, "it's too hard, anyway."

"Of course it's hard," stormed Ruggedo. "I've had a hard life; hard as those rocks. Everybody's been against me from the very start, and all because I'm so little," he finished bitterly.

"No, because you are so wicked," said the rabbit calmly. "Now, don't throw your pipe at me, for you know it's the truth."

Ruggedo glared at the rabbit for a minute, then rushed over to the wooden doll, and began shaking her furiously. He always vented his rage on the wooden doll.

"Stop that," screamed Wag, "or I'll leave upon the spot. You ought to be ashamed of yourself. You old scrabble-scratch."

"She's not alive," snapped Ruggedo sulkily.

"How do you know?" retorted the rabbit. "Anyway, she's a jolly creature. I'm not going to have her banging around. Here you've taken her away from her little mother, and she hasn't even anyone to rock her to sleep."

"I'll rock her to sleep," screamed Ruggedo, maliciously. And flinging the doll on the floor he began hurling small rocks at the helpless little figure.

Scrambling to his feet, Wag rescued the wooden doll again, and Ruggedo, who really was afraid the rabbit would leave him, subsided into his rocking chair. Then reaching up to a small shelf over his head, he pulled down an accordion. At the first doleful wheeze Wag gave a great hop, dropped Peg and disappeared into his room in the farthest corner of the cave.

After his last attempt to capture Oz, the gnome had been given a small cottage to live in, just outside the Emerald City. But Ruggedo could not bear life above ground. The sunlight hurt his eyes, and the contented, happy faces of the people hurt his feelings, for he was exactly what Wag had called him—an old scrabble-scratch. So, while he pretended to live in the little cottage, according to Ozma's orders, he really spent most of his time in this deep, dark cave. He entered it by a secret passage, opening from his cellar.

Digging the long passage had been the hardest work Ruggedo had ever done in his bad little life. While toiling one day, he had bumped into the underground burrow of Wag, a wandering rabbit of Oz, and after a deal of bargaining, the rabbit had agreed to help him. Wag was to receive a ruby a month for his services, for the gnome still had a large bag of precious stones, which he had brought from the old Kingdom. After the bargain with Wag was made, the passage progressed rapidly, for the rabbit was an expert digger.

It was Ruggedo's idea to tunnel himself out a secret chamber, directly under Ozma's palace, and there establish a kingdom of his own. But when they had almost reached the spot, the earth began to crumble away, and a few strokes of Ruggedo's spade revealed a great dark cavern, already tunneled by someone else. It was huge and the exact shape of the royal palace. This Ruggedo discovered by careful measurement, and also that it was directly beneath the gorgeous green edifice, so that the footsteps of the servants could be heard faintly, pattering to and fro.

This dark, underground retreat suited the former Gnome King exactly and, without stopping to wonder to whom it had belonged, Ruggedo gleefully took possession. For almost two years he had lived here without anyone suspecting it, but so far his kingdom had not progressed very well. Wag had tried to coax some of his rabbit relations to serve the old gnome as subjects, but Ruggedo, besides his terrible temper, had a mean habit of pulling their ears, so that the whole crew had deserted the first week. He had pulled Wag's ears once, but the rabbit tore out a pawful of his whiskers, and bit him so severely in the leg that Ruggedo had never dared to try it again. Wag had stayed partly because Ruggedo amused him and partly because of the bribes, for every day, in fear of losing his only retainer, Ruggedo brought Wag something from the Emerald City—something he had stolen! In return, Wag waited on the bad little gnome and listened to his grumblings against everybody in Oz. All the furnishings of this strange cave had been stolen from various houses in the Emerald City. The twenty-seven brocade cushions had been taken, one at a time from the palace; the green emerald lamp also. Every day Ruggedo ran innocently about the city, pretending to visit this one and that, and every day cups, spoons, and candlesticks disappeared.

The doll's rocker, which Ruggedo insisted upon calling his throne, he had taken from Betsy Bobbin, a little girl who lived with Ozma in the palace. He had lugged it through the secret passage with great difficulty. The wooden doll had been stolen from Trot, another of Ozma's companions. She was Trot's favorite doll, for she had been carved out of wood by Captain Bill, an old one-legged sailor, who was one of the most celebrated characters in all Oz. He had carved her for Trot one day when they were on a picnic in the Winkie Country, from the wood of a small yellow tree, and as Captain Bill had old-fashioned notions, Peg was a very old-fashioned doll. But she had splendid joints and could sit down and stand up. Her face was painted and as pleasant as laughing blue eyes, a turned-up nose, and a smiling mouth could make it. Trot had dressed her in a funny, old-fashioned dress, with pantalettes, and then, thinking Peg too short a name, the little girl had added Amy, because she was so amiable, she confided laughingly to the old sailor. Captain Bill had wagged his head understandingly, and Peg Amy had straightway become the most popular doll in the palace; that is, until she disappeared, for Ruggedo had found her one day in the garden and, chuckling wickedly, had carried her off to his cave.

How Trot would have felt if she had seen her poor doll being shaken and scolded by the old Gnome King! But Trot never knew. She hunted and hunted for her doll, and finally gave up in despair. Fortunately, Peg was well made, or she would have been shaken to bits, but her joints held bravely, and nothing—not even the terrible scolding of the bad old gnome—could change her pleasant expression.

Being the sole subject of so wicked a King, however, was wearing even for a wooden doll, and Peg was beginning to show signs of wear. Her nose was badly chipped, one pantalette was missing, and both sleeves had been jerked from her dress by the furious old gnome. If the rabbit was around, Ruggedo did not shake Peg as hard as he wanted to, but when the rabbit was gone, he pretended she was his old steward, Kaliko, and scolded and flung her about to his heart's content.

When not carving his history or shaking Peg, Ruggedo had spent most of his time digging new tunnels and chambers, so that leading off from the main cavern was a perfect network of underground passages. In the back of Ruggedo's head was a notion that some day he would conquer the Emerald City, regain his magic powers and then, after changing all the inhabitants to mouldy muffins, return to his dominions and oust Kaliko from his throne. Just how this was to be done, he had not decided, but the secret passages would be useful. So meanwhile he dug secret passages.

Above ground the little rascal went about so meekly and pretended to be delighted with his life among the inhabitants of the Emerald City, that Ozma really thought he had reformed. Wag, to whom he confided his plans, would shake his head gloomily and often planned to leave the services of the wicked old gnome. There was no real harm in Wag, but the rabbit had a weakness for collecting, and the spoons, cups and odds and ends that Ruggedo brought him from the Emerald City filled him with delight. He felt that they were not gotten honestly, but his work for Ruggedo was

72

honest and hard, "and it's not my fault if the old scrabble-scratch steals 'em," Wag would mumble to himself. In his heart he knew that he was doing wrong to stay with Ruggedo, but like all foolish creatures he could not make up his mind to go. So this very night, while the old gnome sat playing the accordion and howling doleful snatches of the Gnome National Air, Wag was gloating over his treasures. They quite filled his little dug-out room. There were two emerald plates, a gold pencil, a dozen china cups and saucers, twenty thimbles stolen from the work baskets of the good dames of Oz, scraps of silk, pictures and almost everything you could imagine.

"I'll soon have enough to marry and go to housekeeping on," murmured the rabbit, clasping his paws and twitching his nose very fast. He picked up a pair of purple wool socks that had once belonged to a little girl's doll and regarded them rapturously. Out of all the articles Ruggedo had given him, Wag considered these purple socks the most valuable, perhaps because they exactly fitted him and were the only things he could really use. The squeaking of the accordion stopped at last and, supposing his wicked little master had retired for the night, Wag prepared to enjoy himself. Draping a green silk scarf over his shoulders, he strutted before the mirror, pretending he was a Courtier of Oz. Then, throwing down the scarf, he sat down on the floor and had just drawn on one of the socks when a loud shrill scream from Ruggedo made his ears stand straight on end in amazement.

"What now?" coughed the rabbit, seizing the candle. Ruggedo was on his knees before the rocking chair.

"As I was sitting here, playing and singing," spluttered the old gnome, "I noticed a little ring in one of the rocks on the floor!"

"Well, what of it?" sniffed Wag, leaning down to pull up his socks. "What of it?" shrieked the gnome.

"What of it, you poor, puny earth worm! Look!" leaning over Ruggedo's shoulder and dropping hot candle grease down the gnome's neck, Wag peered into a square opening on the floor. There lay a small gold box. Studded in gems on the lid were these words:

Glegg's Box of Mixed Magic.

"Mixed magic!" stuttered Wag, dropping the candle. "Oh, my socks and soup spoons!" Ruggedo said nothing, but his little red eyes blazed maliciously. Reaching down, he lifted out the box and, clasping it to his fat little stomach, shook his fist at the high domed ceiling of the cave.

"Now!" hissed Ruggedo triumphantly. "Now we shall see what mixed magic will do to the Emerald City of Oz!"

Chapter 7 - Sir Hokus and the Giants

"Oh!" sighed Sir Hokus of Pokes and Oz, stretching his armored legs to the fire. "How I yearn to slay a giant! How it would refresh me! Hast any real giants in Oz, Dorothy?"

"Don't you remember the candy giant?" laughed the little girl, looking up from the handkerchief she was making for Ozma.

"Not to my taste," said the Knight, "though his vest buttons were vastly nourishing."

"Well, there's Mr. Yoo he's a real blood-and-bone giant. There are plenty of giants, I guess, if we knew just where to find them!" said the little girl, biting off her thread.

"Find 'em—bind 'em, Get behind 'em! Hokus Pokus He don't mind 'em!"

screamed the Patch Work Girl, bounding out of her chair. "But why can't you stay peaceably at home, old Iron Sides, and be jolly like the rest of us?"

"You don't understand, Scraps," put in Dorothy gravely. "Sir Hokus is a Knight and it is a true Knight's duty to slay giants and dragons and go on quests!"

"That it is, my Lady Patches!" boomed Sir Hokus, puffing out his chest. "I've rusted here in idleness long enough. To-morrow, with Ozma's permission, I shall start on a giant quest."

"I'd go with you, only I've promised to help Ozma count the royal emeralds," said the Scarecrow, who had ridden over from his Corn-Ear residence to spend. a week with his old friends in the Emerald City.

"Giants, Sir, are bluff and rude And might mistake a man for food! Hokus Pokus, be discreet, Or you will soon be giant meat!"

chuckled the Patch Work Girl, crooking her finger under the Knight's nose,

"Nonsense!" blustered Sir Hokus, waving Scraps aside. Rising from his green arm chair, he strode up and down the room, his armor clanking at every step. Straightway the company began to tell about wild giants they had read of or known. Trot and Betsy Bobbin held hands as they sat together on the sofa, and Toto, Dorothy's small dog, crept closer to his little mistress, the bristles on his back rising higher as each story was finished, "Giant stories are all very well, but why tell 'em at night?" shivered Toto, peering nervously at the long shadows in the corners of the room.

It was the evening after Ruggedo's strange discovery of the mixed magic and in the royal palace Ozma and most of the Courtiers had retired. But a few of Princess Dorothy's special friends had gathered in the cozy sitting-room of her apartment to talk about old times. They were very unusual and interesting friends, not at all the sort one would expect to find in a royal palace, even in Fairyland. Dorothy, herself, before she had become a Princess of Oz, had been a little girl from Kansas but, after several visits to this delightful country, she had preferred to make Oz her home.

Trot and Betsy Bobbin also had come from the United States by way of shipwrecks, so to speak, and had been invited to remain by Ozma, the little fairy Princess who ruled Oz, and now each of these girls had a cozy little apartment in the royal palace. Toto had come with Dorothy, but the rest of the company were of more or less magic extraction.

The Scarecrow, a stuffed straw person, with a marvelous set of mixed brains given to him by the Wizard of Oz, was Dorothy's favorite. In fact she had discovered him herself upon a Munchkin farm, lifted him down from his bean pole and brought him to the Emerald City. Tik Tok was a wonderful man made entirely of copper, who could talk, think and act as well as the next fellow when properly wound. You would have been amazed to hear the giant story he was ticking off at this very minute. As for Scraps, she had been made by a magician's wife out of old pieces of patch-work and magically brought to life. Her bright patches, yarn hair and silver suspender button eyes gave Scraps so comical an expression that just to look at her tickled one's funny bone. Her head was full of nonsense rhymes and she was so amusing and cheerful that Ozma insisted upon her living with the rest of the celebrities in the Emerald City.

Sir Hokus of Pokes was a comparative newcomer in the capital city of Oz. Yet the Knight was so old that it would give me lumbago just to try to count up his birthdays. He dated back to King Arthur, in fact, and had been wished into the Land of Oz centuries before by an enemy sorcerer. Dorothy had found and rescued him, with the Cowardly Lion's help, from Pokes, the dullest Kingdom of Oz. As there were no other Knights in the Emerald City, Sir Hokus was much stared at and admired. Even the Soldier with the Green Whiskers, the one and only soldier and entire army of Oz—yes, even the soldier with the Green Whiskers saluted Sir Hokus when he passed. Ozma, herself, felt more secure since the Knight had come to live in the palace. He was well versed in adventure and always courageous and courteous, withal.

But, while I've been telling you all this, Tik Tok had finished his story of a three-legged giant who lived in Ev.

"And where is Ev?" puffed Sir Hokus, planting himself before Tik Tok.

"Ev," began Tik Tok in his precise fashion, "is to the north-west of here on the other side of the im— There was a whirr and a click and the copper man stood motionless and soundless, his round eyes fixed solemnly on the Knight.

"Pass-able desert," finished the Scarecrow, jumping up and kindly winding all of Tik Tok's keys as if nothing had happened.

"Pass-able desert," continued the Copper Man.

"That's where the old Gnome King used to live," piped Betsy Bobbin, bouncing up and down upon the sofa, "under the mountains of Ev, and he threw us down a tube and tried to melt you in a crucible, didn't he, Tok Tok?"

"He was a ve-ry bad per-son," said the Copper Man.

"Ruggedo was a wicked King, 'Tho' now he's good as pie, But none the less, I must confess, He has a wicked eye!"

burst out Scraps, who was tired of sitting still listening to giant Stories.

But Sir Hokus could not be got off the subject of giants. "To Ev!" thundered the Knight, raising his sword. "To-morrow I'm off to Ev to conquer this terrible monster. Large as a mountain, you say, Tik Tok? Well, what care I for mountains? I, Sir Hokus of Pokes, will slay him!"

"Hurrah for the giant killer!" giggled Scraps, turning a somersault and nearly falling in the fire.

"Let's go to bed!" said Dorothy uneasily. She had for the last few minutes been hearing strange rumbles. Of course it could not be giants; still the conversation, she concluded, had better be finished by sunlight.

But it never was, for at that moment there was a deafening crash. The lights went out; the whole castle shivered; furniture fell every which way. Down clattered Sir Hokus, falling with a terrible clangor on top of the Copper Man. Down rolled the little girls and the Scarecrow and Scraps. Down tumbled every-body.

"Cyclone!" gasped Dorothy, who had experienced several in Kansas.

"Giants!" stuttered Betsy Bobbin, clutching Trot.

The Wizard of Oz tried to reassure the agitated company. He told them there was no cause for alarm, and that they would soon find out what was the trouble. The soothing words of the Wizard were scarcely heard.

What the others said was lost in the noise that followed. Thumps-bangs-rashes-screams came from every room in the rocking palace.

"We're flying! The whole castle's flying up in the air!" screamed Dorothy. Then she subsided, as an emerald clock and three pictures came thumping down on her head.

What had happened? No one could say. Dorothy, Betsy Bobbin and Trot had fainted dead away. The Scarecrow and Sir Hokus were tangled up on the floor, clasped in each other's arms.

74

The confusion was terrific. Only the Wizard was still calm and smiling.

Chapter 8 - Woe in the Emerald City

The Soldier with the Green Whiskers finished his breakfast slowly, combed his beard, pinned on all of his medals and solemnly issued forth from his little house at the garden gates.

"Forward march!" snapped the soldier. He had to give himself orders, being the only man, general or private in the army. And forward march he did. It was his custom to report to Ozma every morning to receive his orders for the day. When he had gone through the little patch of trees that separated his cottage from the palace, the Soldier with the Green Whiskers gave a great leap.

"Halt! Break ranks!" roared the Grand Army of Oz, clutching his beard in terror. "Great Goulashes!" He rubbed his eyes and looked again. Yes, the gorgeous emerald-studded palace had disappeared, leaving not so much as a gold brick to tell where it had stood. Trembling in every knee, the Grand Army of Oz approached. A great black hole, the exact shape of the palace, yawned at his feet. He took one look down that awful cavity, then shot through the palace gardens like a green comet.

Like Paul Revere he had gone to give the alarm, and Paul Revere himself never made better time. He thumped on windows and banged on doors and dashed through the sleeping city like a whirlwind. In five minutes there was not a man, woman or child who did not know of the terrible calamity. They rushed to the palace gardens in a panic. Some stared up in the air; others peered down the dark hole; still others ran about wildly trying to discover some trace of the missing castle.

"What shall we do?" they wailed dismally. For to have their lovely little Queen and the Wizard and all the most important people in Oz disappear at once was simply terrifying. They were a gentle and kindly folk, used to obeying orders, and now there was no one to tell them what to do.

At last Unk Nunkie, an old Munchkin who had taken up residence in the Emerald City, pushed through the crowd. Unk was a man of few words, but a wise old chap for all that, so they made way for him respectfully. First Unk Nunkie stroked his beard; then pointing with his long lean finger toward the south he snapped out one word—GLINDA!"

Of course! They must tell Glinda. Why had they not thought of it themselves? Glinda would know just what to do and how to do it. Three cheers for Unk Nunkie! Glinda, you know, is the good Sorceress of Oz, who knows more magic than anyone in the Kingdom, but who only practices it for the people's good. Indeed, Glinda and the Wizard of Oz are the only ones permitted to practice magic, for so much harm had come of it that Ozma made a law forbidding sorcery in all of its branches. But even in a fairy country people do not always obey the laws and everyone felt that magic was at the bottom of this disaster.

So away to fetch Glinda dashed the Grand Army, his green whiskers streaming behind him. Fortunately the royal stables had not disappeared with the palace, so the gallant army. sprang upon the back of the Saw Horse, and without stopping to explain to the other royal beasts, bade it carry him to Glinda as fast as it could gallop. Being made of wood with gold shod feet and magically brought to life, the Saw Horse can run faster than any animal in Oz. It never tired or needed food and when it understood that the palace and its dear little Mistress had disappeared it fairly flew; for the Saw Horse loved Ozma with all its saw dust and was devoted as only a wooden beast can be.

In an hour they had reached Glinda's shining marble palace in the southern part of the Quadling country, and as soon as the lovely Sorceress had heard the soldier's story, she hurried to the magic Book of Records. This is the most valuable book in Oz and it is kept padlocked with many golden chains to a gold table, for in this great volume appear all the events happening in and out of the world.

Now, Glinda had been so occupied trying to discover the cause of frowns that she had not referred to the book for several days and naturally there were many pages to go over. There were hundreds of entries concerning automobile accidents in the United States and elsewhere. These Glinda passed over hurriedly, till she came to three sentences printed in red, for Oz news always appeared in the book in red letters. The first sentence did not seem important. It merely stated that the Prince of Pumperdink was journeying toward the Emerald City. The other two entries seemed serious.

"Glegg's box of Mixed Magic has been discovered," said the second, and "Ruggedo has something on his mind," stated the third. Glinda pored over the book for a long time to see whether any more information would be given but not another red sentence appeared. With a sigh, Glinda turned to the Soldier with the Green Whiskers.

"The old Gnome King must be mixed up in this," she said anxiously, "and as he was last seen in the Emerald City, I will return with you at once." So Glinda and the Soldier with the Green Whiskers flew back to the Emerald City drawn in Glinda's chariot by swift flying swans and the little Saw Horse trotted back by himself. When they reached the gardens a great crowd had gathered by the Fountain of Oblivion and a tall green grocer was speaking excitedly.

"What is it?" asked Glinda, shuddering as she passed the dreadful hole where Ozma's lovely palace had once stood. Everyone started explaining at once so that Glinda was obliged to clap her hands for silence.

"Foot print!" Unk Nunkie stood upon his tip toes and whispered it in Glinda's ear and when she looked where Unk pointed she saw a huge, shallow cave-in that crushed the flower beds for as far as she could see.

"Foot print!" gasped Glinda in amazement.

"Uh huh!" Unk Nunkie wagged his head determinedly and then, pulling his hat down over his eyes, spoke his last word on the subject: "GIANT!"

"A giant foot print! Why so it is!" cried Glinda.

"What shall we do?" cried the frightened inhabitants of the Emerald City, wringing their hands.

"First, find Ruggedo," ordered Glinda, suddenly remembering the mysterious entry in the Book of Records. So, away to the little cottage hurried the crowd. They searched it from cellar to garret, but of course found no trace of the wicked little gnome. As no one knew about the secret passage in Ruggedo's cellar, they never thought of searching underground.

Meanwhile Glinda sank down on one of the golden garden benches and tried to think. The Comfortable Camel stumbled broken-heartedly across the lawn and dropping on its knees begged the Sorceress in a tearful voice to save Sir Hokus of Pokes. The Camel and the Doubtful Dromedary had been discovered by the Knight on his last adventure and were deeply attached to him. Soon all the palace pets came and stood in a dejected row before Glinda—Betsy's mule, Hank, hee-hawing dismally and the Hungry Tiger threatening to eat everyone in sight if any harm came to the three little girls.

"I doubt if we'll ever see them again," groaned the Doubtful Dromedary, leaning up against a tree.

"Oh Doubty—how can you?" wailed the Camel, tears streaming down its nose.

"Please do be quiet," begged Glinda, "or I'll forget all the magic I know. Let me see, now—how does one catch a marauding giant who has run off with a castle?"

On her fingers Glinda counted up all the giants in the four countries of Oz. No! It could not be an Oz giant; there was none large enough. It must be a giant from some strange country.

When the crowd returned with the news that Ruggedo had disappeared Glinda felt more uneasy still. But hiding her anxiety she bade the people return to their homes and continue their work and play as usual. Then, promising to return that evening with a plan to save the castle, and charging the Soldier with the Green Whiskers to keep a strict watch in the garden, Glinda stepped into her chariot and flew back to the South. All that day, in her palace in the Quadling country, Glinda bent over her encyclopedia on giants, and far into the night the lights burned from her high turret-chamber, as she consulted book after book of magic.

Chapter 9 - Mixed Magic Makes Mischief

The Book of Records had been perfectly correct in stating that Ruggedo had something on his mind. He had! To understand the mysterious disappearance of Ozma's palace, we must go back to the old Ex-King of the Gnomes. The whole of the night after he had found Glegg's box of Mixed Magic, Ruggedo had spent trying to open the box. But pry and poke as he would it stubbornly refused to give up its secrets.

"Better come to bed," advised Wag, twitching his nose nervously. "Mixed Magic isn't safe, you know. It might explode."

"Idiot!" grumbled Ruggedo. "I don't know who Glegg is or was, but I'm going to open this box if it takes me a century."

"All right," quavered Wag, retiring backward and holding up his paw. "All right, but remember I warned you! Don't meddle with magic, that's my motto!"

"I don't care a harebell what your motto is," sneered the gnome, continuing to hammer on the gold lid.

When he reached his room, Wag shut the door and sank dejectedly upon the edge of the bed.

"There's no manner of use trying to stop him," sighed the rabbit, "so I've got to get out of here before he gets me into trouble. I'll go tomorrow!" resolved Wag, pulling his long ear nervously. With this good resolution, the little rabbit drooped off asleep.

Very cautiously he opened the door of his little rockroom next morning. Ruggedo was sound asleep on the floor, his head on the magic box, and Peg Amy, with her wooden arms and legs flung out in every direction, lay sprawled in a corner.

"Been shaking you again, the old scrabble-scratch!" whispered the rabbit indignantly, "just 'cause he couldn't open that box. Well, never mind, Peg, I'm leaving today and as surely as I've ears and whiskers you shall go too!" Picking up the poor wooden doll Wag tucked her under his arm. Was it imagination, or did the little wooden face break into a sunny smile? It seemed so to Wag and, with a real thrill of pleasure, he tip-toed back to his room and began tossing his treasures into one of the bed sheets. He seated Peg in his own small rocking chair and from time to time he nodded to her reassuringly.

"We'll soon be out now, my dear," he chuckled, quite as if Peg had been alive. She often did seem alive to Wag. "Then we'll see what Ozma has to say to this Mixed Magic," continued the bunny, wiggling his ears indignantly. And so occupied was he collecting his treasures that he did not hear Ruggedo's call and next minute the angry gnome himself stood in the doorway.

"What does this mean?" he cried furiously, pointing to the tied up sheet. Then he stamped his foot so hard that Peg Amy fell over sideways in the chair and all the ornaments in the room skipped as if alive.

The rabbit whirled 'round in a hurry.

"It means I'm leaving you for good, you wicked little monster!" shrilled Wag, his whiskers trembling with agitation and his ears sticking straight out behind. "Leaving do you hear?"

Then he snatched Peg Amy in one paw and his treasures in the other and tried to brush past Ruggedo. But the gnome was too quick for him. Springing out of the room, he slammed the door and locked it. Wag could hear him rolling up rocks for further security.

"Thought you'd steal a march on old Ruggedo; thought you'd tell Ozma all his plans and get a nice little reward! Well, think again!" shouted the gnome through the keyhole.

Wag had plenty of time to think, for Ruggedo never came near the rabbit's room all day. At every sound poor Wag leaped into the air, for he felt sure each blow could only mean the opening of the dreaded magic box. To reassure himself he held long conversations with the wooden doll and Peg's calm cheerfulness steadied him a lot.

"I might dig my way out but it would take so long! My ear tips! How provoking it is!" exclaimed Wag. "But perhaps he'll relent by nightfall!" Slowly the day dragged on but nothing came from the big rock room but thumps, grumbles and bangs.

"It is fortunate that you do not eat, Peg, dear," sighed the rabbit late in the afternoon, nibbling disconsolately on a stale biscuit he had found under his bureau. "Shall you care very much if I starve? I probably shall, you know. Of course no one in Oz can die, but starving forever is not comfortable either." At this the wooden doll seemed to shake her head, as much as to say: "You won't starve, Wag dear; just be patient a little longer." Not that she really said this, mind you, but Wag knew from her smile that this is what she was thinking.

It was hot and stuffy in the little rock chamber and the faint light that filtered down from the hole in the ceiling was far from cheerful. At last night came, and that was worse. Wag lit his only candle but it was already partly burned down and soon with a dismal sputter it went out and left the two sitting in the dark. Peg Amy stared cheerfully ahead but the rabbit, worn out by his long day of fright and worry, fell into a heavy slumber.

Meanwhile Ruggedo had worked on the magic box and every minute he became more impatient. All his poundings failed to make even a dent on the gold lid and even jumping on it brought no result. The little gnome had eaten nothing since morning and by nightfall he was stamping around the box in a perfect fury. His eyes snapped and twinkled like live coals and his wispy white hair fairly crackled with rage. Hidden in this box were magic secrets that would doubtless enable him to capture the whole of Oz but, klumping kaloogas, how was he to get at 'em? He finally gave the gold box such a vindictive kick that he almost crushed his curly toes; then holding onto one foot, he hopped about on the other till he fell over exhausted.

For several minutes he lay perfectly still; then jumping up he seized the box and flung it with all his gnome might against the rock wall.

"Take that!" screamed Ruggedo furiously. There was a bright flash; then the box righted itself slowly and sailed straight back into Ruggedo's hands and, more wonderful still, it was open' With his eyes almost popping from his head, the gnome sat down on the floor, the box in his lap.

In the first tray were four golden flasks and each one was carefully labeled. The first was marked, "Flying Fluid"; "Vanishing Cream" was in the second. The third flask held "Glegg's Instantaneous Expanding Extract," and in the fourth was "Spike's Hair Strengthener."

Ruggedo rubbed his hands gleefully and lifted out the top tray. In the next compartment was a tiny copper kettle, a lamp and a package marked "Triple Trick Tea." So anxious was Ruggedo to know what was in the last compartment that he scarcely glanced at Glegg's tea set. Quickly he peered into the bottom of the casket. There were two boxes. Taking up the first Ruggedo read, "Glegg's Question Box. Shake three times after each question."

"Great Grampus!" spluttered the gnome, "this is a find!" He was growing more excited every minute and his hands shook so he could hardly read the label on the last box. Finally he made it out: "Re-animating Rays, guaranteed to reawaken any person who has lost the power of life through sorcery, witchcraft or enchantment," said the label.

Well, did anyone ever hear anything more magic than that? Ruggedo glanced from one to the other of the little gold flasks and boxes. There were so many he hardly knew which to use first. "Flying Fluid and Vanishing Cream," mused the gnome. Well, they might help after he had captured Oz, but he felt it would take more powerful magic than Flying Fluid and Vanishing Cream to capture the fairy Kingdom. Next he picked up the bottle labeled "Spike's Hair Strengthener." Anything that strengthened would be helpful, so, with one eye on the last bottle, Ruggedo absently rubbed some of the hair strengthener on his head. He stopped rubbing in a hurry and put his finger in his mouth with a howl of pain. The he jumped up in alarm and ran to a small mirror hanging on the wall. Every hair on his head had become an iron spike and the result was so terrible that it frightened even the old gnome. He flung the bottle angrily on the ground. But stop! He could butt his enemies with the sharp spikes! Comforting himself with this cheerful thought, Ruggedo returned to the magic box.

"Instantaneous Expanding Extract," muttered the gnome, turning the bottle over carefully. "That ought to make me larger—and if I were larger—if I were larger!" He snapped his fingers and began hopping up and down. He was about to empty the bottle over his head when he suddenly reflected that it might be safer to try this powerful extract on someone else. But on whom?

Ruggedo glanced quickly around the cave and then remembered the wooden doll. He would try a little on Peg Amy and see how it worked. Turning the key he stepped softly into Wag's room. Without wakening the rabbit, Ruggedo dragged out the wooden doll. Propping her up against the wall, the gnome uncorked the bottle of expanding fluid and dropped two drops on Peg Amy's head. Peg was about ten inches high, but no sooner had the expanding fluid touched her than she shot up four feet and with such force that she lost her balance and came crashing down on top of Ruggedo, almost crushing him flat.

"Get off, you great log of wood!" screamed the gnome, struggling furiously. But this Peg Amy was powerless to do and it was only after a frightful struggle that Ruggedo managed to drag himself out. He started to shake Peg but as she was now four times his size he soon gave that up.

"Well, anyway it works," sighed the gnome, rubbing his nose and the middle of his back. "I wonder how it would act on a live person? I'll try a little on that silly rabbit," he concluded, tip-toeing back into Wag's room. Now Wag's apartment was about seven feet square—plenty large enough for a regular rabbit—but two drop's of the expanding fluid—and, stars! Wag was no longer a regular rabbit but a six-foot funny bunny, stretching from one end of the room to the other. He expanded without even waking up. Ruggedo had to squeeze past him in order to get out and, chuckling with satisfaction, the gnome hurried back to his box of magic. His mind was now made up. He would take Glegg's Mixed Magic under his arm, go above ground and with the Expanding Fluid change himself into a giant. Then conquering Oz would be a simple matter.

It was all going to be so easy and amusing that Ruggedo felt he had plenty of time to examine the rest of the bottles and boxes. He rubbed some of the Vanishing Cream on a sofa cushion and it instantly disappeared. The box of Re-animating Rays, guaranteed to reawaken anyone from enchantment, interested the old gnome immensely, but how could he try them when there was no bewitched person about—at least none that he knew of? Then his eye fell on the Question Box. Why not try that? So, "How shall I use the Re-animating Rays?" asked Ruggedo, shaking the box three times. Nothing happened at first. Then, by the light from his emerald lamp, the gnome saw a sentence forming on the lid.

"Try them on Peg," said the box shortly. Without thinking of consequences or wondering what the Question Box meant by suggesting Peg, the curious gnome opened the box of rays and held it over the huge wooden doll. For as long as it would take to count ten Peg lay perfectly still. Then, with a creak and jerk, she sprang to her feet.

"How perfectly pomiferous!" cried Peg Amy, with an awkward jump. "I'm alive! Why, I'm alive all over!" She moved one arm, then the other and turned her head stiffly from side to side. "I can walk!" cried Peg. "I can walk; I can skip; I can run!" Here Peg began running around the cave, her joints squeaking merrily at every step.

At Peg's first move Ruggedo had jumped back of a rock, his every spike standing on end. Too late he realized his mistake. This huge wooden creature clattering around the cave was positively dangerous. Why, she might easily pound him to bits. Why on earth had he meddled with the magic rays and why under the earth should a wooden doll come to life? He waited till Peg had run to the farthest end of the cave; then he dashed to the magic casket and scrambled the bottles, the Trick Tea Set and the flasks back into place and started for the door that led to the secret passage as fast as his crooked little legs would carry him.

But he was not fast enough, for Peg heard and in a flash was after him.

"Stop! Go away!" screamed Ruggedo.

"Why, it's the old gnome!" cried the Wooden Doll in surprise. "The wicked old gnome who used to shake me all the time. Why, how small he is! I could pick him up with one hand!" She made a snatch at Ruggedo.

"Go away!" shrieked Ruggedo, ducking behind a rock. "Go away—there's a dear girl," he added coaxingly. "I didn't shake you much—not too much, you know!"

Peg Amy put a wooden finger to her forehead and regarded him attentively.

"I remember," she murmured thoughtfully. "You found a magic box, and you're going to harm Ozma and try to conquer Oz. I must get that box!"

Reaching around the rock she seized Ruggedo by the arm.

In a panic, he jerked away. "Help! Help!" cried the gnome King, darting off toward the other end of the cave. "Help! Help!"

In his little rock room Wag stirred uneasily. Then, as Ruggedo's cries grew louder, he bounced erect and almost cracked his skull on the low ceiling. Hardly knowing what he was doing he rushed at the door only to knock himself almost senseless against the top, for of course he did not realize he had expanded into a giant rabbit. But as the cries from the other room became louder and louder he got up and rubbing his head in a dazed fashion he somehow crowded himself through the door and hopped into the cave. When he saw Peg Amy chasing Ruggedo, Wag fell back against the wall.

"My wocks and hoop soons!" stuttered the rabbit. "She is alive! And he's shrunk!"

Wag's voice rose triumphantly. "I'm going to pound his curly toes off!" he shouted. With this he joined merrily in the chase.

"I'll catch him!" he called, "I'll catch him, Peg, my dear, and make him pay for all the shakings he has given you. I'll pound his curly toes off!"

"Oh, Wag! Don't do that," cried the Wooden Doll, stopping short. "I didn't mind the shakings and gnomes don't know any better!"

"Neither do rabbits!" cried Wag stubbornly, bounding after Ruggedo. "I'll pound his curly toes off, I tell you!"

The old gnome was sputtering like a fire-cracker. What chance had he now with two after him? Then suddenly he had an idea. Without stopping, he fumbled in the box which he still clutched under one arm and pulled out the bottle of Expanding Fluid. Uncorking the bottle he poured its contents over his head—every single drop!

This is what happened: First he shot out sideways, till Peg and Wag were almost crushed against the wall. With a hoarse scream Wag dragged Peg Amy back into his room, which was now barely large enough to hold them. They were just in time, for Ruggedo was still spreading. Soon there was not an inch of space left to expand in. Then he shot up and grew up and grew and grew and groaned and grew till there wasn't any more room to grow in. So, he burst through the top of the cave, with a noise like fifty boilers exploding.

No wonder Dorothy thought it was a cyclone! For what was on the top of the cave but the royal palace of Oz? The next instant it was impaled fast on the spikes of Ruggedo's giant head and shooting up with him toward the clouds. And that wretched gnome never stopped growing till he was three-quarters of mile high!

If the people in the palace were frightened, Ruggedo was more frightened still. Being a giant was a new experience for him and having a castle jammed on his head was worse still. The first thing he tried to do, when he stopped growing, was to lift the castle off, but his spikes were driven fast into the foundations and it fitted closer than his scalp.

In a panic Ruggedo began to run, and when a giant runs he gets somewhere. Each step carried him a half mile and shook the country below like an earthquake and rattled the people in the castle above like pennies in a Christmas bank. Shaking with terror and hardly knowing why, the gnome made for his old Kingdom, and in an hour had reached the little country of Oogaboo, which is in the very northwestern corner of Oz, opposite his old dominions.

The Deadly Desert is so narrow at this point that with one jump Ruggedo was across and, puffing like a volcano about to erupt, he sank down on the highest mountain in Ev. Fortunately he had not stepped on any cities in his flight, although he had crushed several forests and about a hundred fences. "Oh, Oh, My head!" groaned Ruggedo, rocking to and fro. He seemed to have forgotten all about conquering Oz. He was full of twinges and growing pains. Ozma's castle was giving him a thundering headache, and there he sat, a fearsome figure in the bright moonlight, moaning and groaning instead of conquering.

The Book of Records had been right indeed when it stated that Ruggedo had something on his mind. Ozma's castle itself sat squarely upon that mischievous mind—and every moment it seemed to grow heavier.

No wonder there had been confusion in the castle! Every time Ruggedo shook his aching head Ozma and her guests were tossed about like leaves in a storm. Mixed magic had made mischief indeed.

Chapter 10 - Peg and Wag to the Rescue

For a long time after the terrific bang following Ruggedo's final expansion, Wag and Peg
Amy had been too stunned to even move. Crowded together in the little rock room, they lay perfectly breathless.

"Umpthing sappened," quavered the rabbit at last.

"That sounds rather queer, but I think I know what you mean," said Peg, sitting up cautiously.

"Something has happened. Ruggedo's been blown up, I guess."

"Mixed Magic!" groaned Wag gloomily. "I knew it would explode. Say, Peg, what makes this room so small?"

"I don't know," sighed the doll in a puzzled voice, for neither Peg nor Wag realized how much they had grown. "But let's go above ground and see what has become of Ruggedo." One at a time and with great difficulty they got through the door.

"Why, there are the stars!" cried Peg Amy, clasping her wooden hands rapturously. "Real stars!" The top of the cave had gone off with the old gnome King and the two stood looking up at the lovely skies of Oz.

"It doesn't seem so high as it used to," said the rabbit, looking at the walls. "Why, I believe I could jump out if I took a good run and carry you, too. Come ashort, Peg!"

"Aren't you mixed, Wag dear? Don't you mean come along?" asked Peg, smoothing down her torn dress.

"Well, now that you mention it, my head does feel queer," admitted the rabbit, twitching his nose, "bort of sackwards!"

"Sort of backwards," corrected Peg gently. "Well, never mind. I know what you mean. Peg and Wag to the Rescue But do let's try to find that awful box of magic.

You know Ruggedo brought me to life, Wag, with something in that box!"

"Only good thing he ever did," said Wag, shaking his head. "But I think you were alive before," he added solemnly. "You always seemed alive to me."

"I think so, too," whispered Peg excitedly. "I can't remember just how, or where, but Oh! Wag! I know I've been alive before. I remember dancing."

Peg took a few awkward steps and Wag looked on dubiously, too polite to criticize her efforts. He didn't even laugh when Peg Amy fell down. Peg laughed herself, however, as merrily as possible. "It's going to be such fun being alive," she said, picking herself up gaily, "such fun, Wag dear. Why, there's Glegg's box!" She pounced upon the little shining gold casket. "Ruggedo didn't take it after all!"

"Is it shut?" asked Wag, clapping both paws to his ears. "Look out for explosions, say I."

"No, but I'll soon close it," said Peg and, shutting Glegg's box, she slipped it into pocket of her dress. It was about half the size of this book you are reading and as Peg's pockets were big and old fashioned, it fitted quite nicely.

"Come ashort," said Wag again, looking uneasily, for he was anxious to get out of the gnome's cave. So Peg seated herself carefully on his back and clasped her wooden arms around his neck. Then Wag ran back a few steps, gave a great jump and sailed up, up and out of the cave.

"Ten penny tea cups!" shrieked the Soldier with the Green Whiskers, falling over backwards. "What next?" For Wag with Peg on his back had leaped straight over his head.

Picking himself up, and with every whisker in his beard prickling straight on end, the Grand Army of Oz backed toward the royal stable. When he had backed half the distance he turned and ran for his life. But he need not have been afraid.

"What a funny little man," chuckled Wag. "Why, he's no bigger than we are. He's n—!" Then suddenly Wag clutched his ears. "Oh!" he screamed, beginning to hop up and down, "I forgot all my treasures—my olden goop soons. Oh! Oh! My urple sool wocks! I've forgotten my urple sool wocks!"

"Your what?" cried Peg Amy, clutching him by the fur. "Now Wag, dear, you're all mixed up. Perhaps it's 'cause your ears are crossed. There, now, do stop wiggling your whiskers and turn out your toes!"

But Wag continued to wiggle his whiskers and turn in his toes and roar for his urple sool wocks.

"Stop!" screamed Peg at last, with both hands over her wooden ears. "I know what you mean! Your purple wool socks!"

"Yes," sobbed the rabbit, slumping down on a rock and holding his head in both paws.

"Well, don't you think—the Wooden Doll shook her head jerkily—Don't you think it's just as well? Ruggedo stole all those things and you wouldn't want stolen soup spoons, now would you?"

Wag took a long breath and regarded Peg uncertainly. Then something in her pleasant wooden face seemed to brace him up.

"No!" he sighed solemnly—I 'spose not. I ought to have left Rug long ago.

"But then you couldn't have helped me, said Peg brightly. "Let's don't think about it any more. You've been awfully good to me, Wag."

"Have I?" said Wag more cheerfully. "Well, you're a good sort, Peg—a regular Princess!" he finished, puffing out his chest, "and anything you say goes.

"Princess?" laughed the Wooden Doll, pleased nevertheless. "I'm a funny Princess, in this old dress. Did you ever hear of a wooden Princess, Wag?"

"You look like a Princess to me," said the rabbit stoutly. "Dresses don't matter."

This speech so tickled the Wooden Doll that she gave Wag a good hug and began dancing again. "Being alive is such fun!" she called gaily over her shoulder, "and you are so wonderful!"

Wag's chest expanded at least three inches and his whiskers trembled with emotion. "Hop on my back Peg and I'll take you anywhere you want to go," he puffed magnificently.

But the Wooden Doll had suddenly grown sober. "Wherever is the castle?" she cried anxiously. She remembered exactly where it had stood when she was an unalive doll and now not a tower or turret of the castle was to be seen."Oh!" groaned Peg Amy, "Ruggedo has done something dreadful with his Mixed Magic!"

Wag rubbed his eyes and looked all around. "Why, it's gone!" he cried, waving his paws. "What shall we do? If only we weren't so small!"

"We've got the magic box," said Peg hopefully, "and somehow I don't feel as small as I used to feel; do you?"

"Well, I feel pretty queer, myself," said the rabbit, twitching his nose. "Maybe it's because I'm hungry. There's a kitchen garden over there near the royal stables and I think if I had some carrots I'd feel better."

"Of course you would!" cried Peg, jumping up; "I forgot you had to eat." So, very cautiously they stole into the royal cook's garden. Wag had often helped himself to carrots from this garden before, but now sitting on his haunches he stared around in dazed surprise.

"Everything's different!" wailed the rabbit dismally. "You're the same and I'm the same but everything else is all mixed up. Look at this carrot. Why, it's no bigger than a blade of grass." Wag held up a carrot in disgust. "Why, it will take fifty of these to give me even a taste and the lettuce—look at it! Everything's shrunk, even the houses!" cried the big funny bunny, looking around. "My wocks and hoop soons, sheverything's hunk!"

Peg Amy had followed Wag's gaze and now she jumped up in great excitement. "I see it now!" cried Peg. "It's us, Wag. Everything's the same but we are different. Some of that Mixed Magic has made us grow. We're bigger and everything else is the same. I am as tall as the little girl who used to play with me and you are even bigger and I'm glad, because now we can help find the castle and Ruggedo and try to make everything right again."

Peg clasped her wooden hands. "Aren't you glad too, Wag?"

The rabbit shook his head. "It's going to take an awful lot to fill me up," he said doubtfully. "I'll have to eat about six times as much as I used to."

"Well, you're six times as large; isn't that any comfort?"

"My head doesn't feel right," insisted Wag. "As soon as I talk fast the words all come wrong.

"Maybe it didn't grow as fast as the rest of you," laughed the Wooden Doll. "But don't you care, Wag. I know what you mean and I think you're just splendid! Now hurry and finish your carrots so we can decide what to do.

"If Mixed Magic caused all this trouble," added Peg half to herself, "Mixed Magic's got to fix it. I'm going to look at that box." Wag, nibbling industriously, had not heard Peg's last speech or he would doubtless have taken to his heels.

Sitting unconcernedly in a cabbage bed, the Wooden Doll took the gold box from her pocket. Fortunately she had not snapped the magic snap and it opened quite easily. Her fingers were stiff and clumsy and the moon was the only light she had to see by, but it did not take Peg Amy long to realize the importance of Glegg's magic.

"I wonder if he rubbed this on the castle," she murmured, holding up the bottle of Vanishing Cream. "And how would one bring it back? Let me see, now. One after the other, she took out the bottles and boxes and the tiny tea set. The Re-animating Rays she passed over, without realizing they were responsible for bringing her to life, but the Question Box, Peg pounced upon with eager curiosity.

"Oh, if it only would answer questions!" fluttered Peg. Then, holding the box close to her mouth, she whispered, "Where is Ruggedo?"

"Who are you talking to?" asked Wag, looking up in alarm. "Now don't you get mixed up, Peg!"

"It's a Question Box," said the Wooden Doll,"but it's not working very well." She shook it vigorously and held it up so that the light streaming down from the stable window fell directly on it. In silver letters on the lid of the box was one word—Ev!

81

"Ev—Ruggedo's in Ev!" cried Peg Amy, rushing over to the rabbit. "Can you take me to Ev, Wag dear?"

"Of course," said Wag, nibbling faster and faster at his carrots. "I'll take you anywhere, Peg."

"Then it's going to be all right; I know it," chuckled the Wooden Doll, and putting all the magic appliances back into the box she closed the lid with a snap. And this time the magic catch caught.

"Is it far to Ev?" asked Peg Amy, looking thoughtfully at the place where the castle had once been.

"Quite a long journey," said Wag, "but we'll go a hopping. Ev is near Ruggedo's old home and it's across the Deadly Desert, but we'll get there somehow. Trust me. And when I do!" spluttered Wag, thumping his hind feet determinedly, "I'll pound his curly toes off—the wicked little monster!"

"Did you ask the Question Box where the castle was?" he inquired hastily, for he saw Peg was going to tell him he must not pound Ruggedo.

"Why, no! How silly of me!" Peg felt in her pocket and brought out the gold box. She tried to open it as she had done before but it was no use. She pulled and tugged and shook it. Then Wag tried.

"There's a secret to it," puffed the rabbit at last. "Took Rug a whole night and day to discover it, Can't you remember how you opened it before, Peg?"

The Wooden Doll shook her head sadly.

"Well, never mind," said Wag comfortingly. "Once we find Ruggedo we can make him tell. We'd better start right off, because if any of the people around here saw us they might try to capture us and put us in a circus. We are rather unusual, you know." The rabbit regarded Peg Amy complacently. "One doesn't see six-foot rabbits and live dolls every day, even in Oz."

"No," agreed Peg Amy slowly, "I s'pose not!" The moon, looking down on the strange pair, ducked behind a cloud to hide her smile, for the giant funny bunny, strutting about pompously, and old-fashioned wooden Peg, in her torn frock, were enough to make anyone smile.

"You think of everything," sighed Peg, looking affectionately at Wag.

"Who wouldn't for a girl like you? You're a Princess, Peg—a regular Princess." The rabbit said it with conviction and again Peg happily smoothed her dress.

"Hop on," chuckled Wag, "and then I'll hop off."

Seating herself on his back and holding tight to one of his long ears, Peg announced herself ready. Then away through the night shot the giant bunny—away toward the western country of the Winkies—and each hop carried him twelve feet forward, and sent up great spurts of dust behind.

Chapter 11 - The King of the Illumi Nation

While Ruggedo was working all this mischief in the Emerald City, Pompadore and the Elegant Elephant had fallen into strange company. After the Prince's disappearance, Kabumpo stared long and anxiously at the white marble stone with its mysterious inscription, "Knock before you fall in."

What would happen if he knocked, as the sign directed? Something upsetting, the Elegant Elephant was sure, else why had Pompa called for help?

Kabumpo groaned, for he was a luxurious beast and hated discomfort of any sort. As for falling in—the very thought of it made him shudder in every pound. But selfish and luxurious though he was, the Elegant Elephant loved Pompa with all his heart. After all, he had run off with the Prince and was responsible for his safety. If Pompa had fallen in he must fall in too. With a resigned sigh, Kabumpo felt in his pocket to see that his treasures were safe, straightened his robe and, taking one last long breath, rapped sharply on the marble stone with his trunk. Without a sound, the stone swung inward, and as Kabumpo was standing on it he shot headlong into a great black opening. There was a terrific rush of air and the slab swung back, catching as it did so the fluttering edge of the Elegant Elephant's robe of state. This halted his fall for about a second and then with a spluttering tear the silk fringe ripped loose and down plunged the Elegant Elephant, trunk over heels.

After the third somersault, Kabumpo, right side up, fortunately, struck a soft inclined slide, down which he shot like a scenic railway train.

"Great Grump!" coughed Kabumpo, holding his jeweled headpiece with his trunk. "Great— Before he reached the second grump, his head struck the top of the passage with terrific force, and that was the last he remembered about his fall. How long he lay in an unconscious state the Elegant Elephant never knew. After what seemed several ages he became aware of a confused murmur. Footsteps seemed to be pattering all around him, but he was still too stunned to be curious.

"Nothing will make me get up," thought Kabumpo dully. "I'm going to lie here forever and-ever-and ever-and— Just as he reached this drowsy conclusion, something red hot fell down his neck and a voice louder than all the rest shouted in his ear. "What are you?"

"Ouch!" screamed Kabumpo, now thoroughly aroused. He opened one eye and rolled over on his side. A tall, curious creature was bending over him. Its head was on fire and as Kabumpo blinked angrily another red hot shower spattered into his ear. With a trumpet of rage Kabumpo lunged to his feet. The hot-headed person fell over backwards and a crowd of similar creatures pattered off into the corner and regarded Kabumpo uneasily. They were as tall as Pompa but very thin and tube-like in shape and their heads appeared to be a mass of flickering flames.

"Like giant candles," reflected the Elegant Elephant, his curiosity getting the better of his anger. He glanced about hurriedly. He was in a huge white tiled chamber and the only lights came from the heads of its singular occupants. A little distance away Prince Pompadore sat rubbing first his knees and then his head.

"It's another faller," said one of the giant Candlemen to the other. "Two fallers in one day! This is exciting—an 'Ouch' it calls itself!"

"I don't care what it calls itself," answered the second Candleman crossly. "I call it mighty rude. How dare you blow out our king?" shouted the hot-headed fellow, shaking his fist at the Elegant Elephant. "Here, some of you, light him up!"

"Blow out your King?" gasped Kabumpo in amazement. Sure enough, he had. There at his feet lay the King of the Candles, stiff and lifeless and with never a head to bless himself with. While the Elegant Elephant stared at the long candlestick figure a fat little Candleman rushed forward and lit with his own head the small black wick sticking out of the King's collar.

Instantly the ruddy flame face of the King appeared, his eyes snapping dangerously. Jumping to his feet he advanced toward Pompadore. "Is this your Ouch?" spluttered the King, jerking his thumb at Kabumpo. "You must take him away at once. I never was so put out in my life. Me, the hand-dipped King of the whole Illumi Nation, to be blown out by a bumpy creature without any headlight. Where's your headlight?" he demanded fiercely, leaning over the Prince and dropping hot tallow down his neck.

Pompa jumped up in a hurry and backed toward Kabumpo. "Be careful how you talk to him," roared the Elegant Elephant, swaying backwards and forward like a big ship. "He's a Prince the Prince of Pumperdink!" Kabumpo tossed his trunk threateningly.

"A Prince?" spluttered the King, changing his tone instantly. "Well, that's different. A Prince can fall in on us any time and welcome but an Ouch! Why bring this great clumsy Ouch along?" He rolled his eyes mournfully at Kabumpo.

"He's not an Ouch," explained Pompa, who was gradually recovering from the shock of his fall. "He is Kabumpo, an Elegant Elephant, and he blew you out by mistake. Didn't you, Kabumpo?"

"Purely an accident—nothing intentional, I assure you," chuckled Kabumpo. He was beginning to enjoy himself. "If there's any more trouble I'll blow 'em all out," he reflected comfortably, "for they're nothing but great big candles."

Seeing their King in friendly conversation with the strangers, the other Candlemen came closer—too close for comfort, in fact. They were always leaning over and dropping hot tallow on a body and the heat from their flaming heads was simply suffocating.

"Sing the National Air for them," said the Candle King carelessly and the Candlemen, in their queer crackling voices, sang the following song, swaying rhythmically to the tune:

"Flicker, flicker, Candlemen, Cheer our King and cheer again! Neat as wax and always bright, Cheer's the King of candle light!

Kindle lightly windle slightly, Here we burn both day and nightly, Here we have good times to burn Till each one goes out in turn."

"Thank you," said Pompa, mopping his head with his silk handkerchief.

"Thank you very much," Kabumpo groaned plaintively, for the great elephant was nearly stifled.

"How is it you are so tall and thin?" asked Pompa after an awkward pause.

"How is it you are so short and lumpy and unevenly dipped?" responded King Cheer promptly. "If I were in your place," he gave Kabumpo a contemptuous glance, "I'd have myself redipped. Where are your wicks? And how can you walk about without being lighted?"

"We're not fireworks," puffed Kabumpo indignantly and then he gave a shrill scream. Ten Candlemen tottered and went out, falling to the ground with a great clatter. Then Pompa leaped several feet in the air and his scream put out five more.

"Stop!" cried King Cheer angrily. "Stand where you are!" But Kabumpo and Pompa neither stopped nor stood where they were. The Elegant Elephant rushed over to the Prince and threw his heavy robe over his head. And just in time, for Pompa's golden locks were a mass of flames. Then the Prince tore off his velvet jacket and clapped it to Kabumpo's tail, which also was blazing merrily.

"Great Grump!" rumbled the Elegant Elephant furiously, when he had extinguished Pompa and Pompa had extinguished him. "I'll put you all out for this!" He raised his trunk and pointed it straight at the Candlemen, who cowered in the far corner.

"I was only trying to light you up," wailed a little fellow, holding out his hands pleadingly. "I thought that was your wick." He pointed a trembling finger at Kabumpo's tail and another at Pompa's head.

"Wick!" snorted Kabumpo in a rage while the Prince ran his hand sorrowfully through his once luxuriant pompadour, of which nothing but a short stubble remained—Wick! What would we be doing with wicks?"

"I don't think he meant any harm," put in. Pompadore, whose kind heart was touched by the little Candleman's terror. "And it wouldn't help us any."

"Thought it was my wick," shrilled Kabumpo, glancing over his shoulder at his poor scorched tail. "He's a wicked little wretch. He's ruined your looks."

"I know!" Pompa sighed dismally. "No one will want to marry me now. It's all coming true, Kabumpo, just as Count It Up said. Remember? 'If a thin Prince sets out on a fat elephant to find a Proper Princess, how many yards of fringe will the elephant lose from his robe and how bald will the Prince be at the end of the journey?' And we've scarcely begun!"

"Great haystacks!" whistled Kabumpo, his little eyes twinkling. "So I have lost every bit of fringe from my robe and my tail and half the back of my robe besides. This is nice, I must say.

"We only tried to give you a warm welcome," said the King timidly.

"Warm welcome! Well I should think you did," sniffed Kabumpo. "How do we get out of here?"

"Oh, that's very simple," said the King, cheering up. "Tommy, go for the Snuffer."

Before Kabumpo or Pompa realized what this would mean a little Candleman named Tommy Tallow had returned with a tall black candle person. He stepped to the side wall, quickly jerked a rope and down over Kabumpo dropped a great brass snuffer and over the Prince another.

"That ought to put the cross old things out," Pompa heard the King say just before his snuffer reached the floor.

"This is terrible," fumed the poor Prince, thumping on the sides of the huge brass dome. "I might as well have stayed at home and disappeared comfortably. My poor old father and my mother! I wonder where they are now?"

Sunk in gloomy reflection, Pompadore leaned against the side of the snuffer. And one cannot blame him for feeling dismal. The fall down the deep passage, the shock of losing his hair and now imprisonment under a stifling brass dome were enough to extinguish the hopes of the stoutest hearted adventurer.

"I shall never find a Proper Princess!" wailed Pompa, tying and untying his handkerchief. But just then there was a creak from without and the great dome lifted as suddenly as it had fallen—so suddenly in fact that Pompa fell flat on his back. There stood Kabumpo winding up the long rope with his trunk and grumbling furiously all the while.

"Takes more than a snuffer to keep me down," wheezed the Elegant Elephant, hurrying over and jerking the Prince to his feet. "Three humps of my shoulders and off she goes! What makes it so dark?"

"The Candlemen have all gone," sighed Pompa, brushing his hand wearily across his forehead. "All except that one."

In a distant corner sat Tommy Tallow and the light from his head was the only light in the great chamber. He was reading a book with tin leaves and looked up in surprise when he saw the Elegant Elephant and Pompadore approaching. Then he started to sputter and ran toward a bell rope at the side of the chamber.

"Stop!" shouted Kabumpo, "or I'll blow off your head!" At that the little Candleman trembled so violently that his flame head almost went out.

"Now suppose you show us the way out," snapped the Elegant Elephant, stamping one big foot until the floor trembled.

"You could burn out!" gasped Tommy faintly. "That's what we do!"

"Don't say out," whispered Pompa anxiously. "We want to go away from here," he explained earnestly. "Back on the top of the ground, you know."

"Oh!" whistled Tommy Tallow, his face lighting up. "That's easy—this way, please!" He almost ran to a big door at one side of the room and tugging it open, waved them through.

"Goodbye!" he called, slamming the door quickly behind them.

Kabumpo and the Prince found themselves in a wide dim hallway. It slanted up gradually and there were tall candle guards stationed about a hundred yards apart all of the way.

"Are you going to a birthday party or a wedding?" asked the first guard, as they passed him.

"Wedding," sniffed Kabumpo. "Why?"

"Well, hardly any of the candles go out of here unless they're needed for a birthday or a wedding," explained the guard, shifting his big feet. "You're mighty poorly made though. What kind of candles do you call yourselves?"

"Roman," chuckled Kabumpo with a wink. "We roam around," he added ponderously.

"Do all the candles used above ground come from here?" asked Pompa curiously.

"Certainly," replied the guard. "All candles come from Illumi and they don't like to leave either because as soon as they strike the upper air they shrink down to ordinary cake and candlestick size. Distressing, isn't it?"

"I suppose it must be," smiled Pompadore. "Goodbye!" The guard touched his flame hat and Kabumpo quickened his pace.

"I want air," rumbled the great elephant, panting along as fast as he could go. "I've seen and felt about all I care to see and feel of the Illumi Nation."

"So have I!" The Prince of Pumperdink touched his scorched locks and sighed deeply. "I'm afraid Ozma will never marry me now, and Pumperdink will disappear forever!"

"Don't be a Gooch!" snapped the Elegant Elephant shortly. "Our adventures have only begun."

They passed the rest of the guards without further conversation, and after about two hours came to the end of the long tiled passageway and stepped upon firm ground again.

Kabumpo was terribly out of breath, for the whole way had been up hill. For a full minute he stood sniffing the fresh night air. Then, turning around, he looked for the opening through which they had come. Not a sign of the passage anywhere!

"That's curious," puffed the Elegant Elephant. "But never mind. We don't want to go back anyway.

"I should say not," gasped the Prince wearily. "Where are we now, Kabumpo?"

"Still in the Gilliken country, I think, but headed in the right direction. All we have to do is to keep going South," said the Elegant Elephant cheerfully.

"But we've had nothing to eat since morning," objected Pompadore.

"That's so," agreed Kabumpo, scratching his head thoughtfully, "and not a house in sight!"

"But I smell something cooking," insisted the Prince, sniffing hungrily.

"So do I," said the Elegant Elephant, lifting his trunk, "and it smells like soup. Let's follow our noses, Pompa, my boy."

"Yours is the longest," laughed the Prince, as Kabumpo swung him upon the elephant's back. So, guided by the fragrant whiffs that came floating toward them, Kabumpo set out through the trees.

Chapter 12 ‒ The Delicious Sea of Soup

Strange puffed Kabumpo, swinging along rapidly.

"I hear water," answered Pompa, peering out over Kabumpo's head, "and there it is!" Rippling silver under the rays of the moon, which shone brightly, lay a great inland sea.

The trees had thinned out, and a smooth, sandy beach stretched down to the shore. A slight mist hunt in the air and all around was the delicious fragrance of vegetable soup.

"Somebody's making soup," sighed the Prince, "but who, and where?"

"Never mind, Pompa," wheezed the Elegant Elephant, walking down to the water's edge, "perhaps you can catch some fish, and while you cook them I'll go back and eat some leaves."

With a jerk of his trunk, Kabumpo pulled a length of the heavy silver thread from his torn robe and handed it up to Pompa. Fastening a jeweled pin to one end, the Prince cast his line far out into the waves. At the first tug he drew it in. "What is it?" asked the Elegant Elephant, as Pompa pulled the dripping line over his trunk.

"Oh, how delicious! How wonderful!" ex-claimed the once fastidious Prince of Pumper-dink. Kabumpo could hear him munching away with relish.

"What is it?" he asked again.

"A carrot! A lovely, red, delightful, tender carrot!"

"Carrot! Who ever heard of a sea carrot?" grunted Kabumpo. "I'm afraid you're not yourself, my boy. Let me see it."

Snaps and crunches, as Pompa consumed his strange catch, were the only answer, and in real alarm the Elegant Elephant moved away from the shore, and in doing so bumped against a white sign, stuck in the sand.

"Please Don't Fall In," directed the sign politely. "It Spoils the Soup.

"Soup!" sputtered Kabumpo. Then another sign caught his eye: "Soup Sea—Salted To Taste—Help Yourself"

85

"Come down—come down here directly!" cried the Elegant Elephant, snatching the Prince from his back. "Here's the soup—a whole sea full. Now all you need is a bowl."

Swallowing convulsively the last bit of carrot, Pompa stood staring out over the tossing, smoking soup sea. Every now and then a bone or a vegetable would bob out of the waves, and the poor hungry Prince of Pumperdink thought he had never seen a more lovely sight in his life.

"We'll probably be awarded a china medal for this," chuckled the Elegant Elephant. "Won't old Pumper's eyes stick out when we tell him about it? But now for a bowl!"

Swinging his trunk gently, Kabumpo walked up the white beach, and had not gone more than a dozen steps before he came to a cluster of huge shells. He turned one over curiously. "Why, it's a soup bowl," whistled the Elegant Elephant. He rushed back with it to Pompadore, who still stood dreamily surveying the soup.

"I never thought I'd be so thrilled by a common soup bowl," thought Kabumpo, staring at the Prince in amusement. He stepped out on a rock and dipped up a bowl of the hot liquid.

"Here! Drink!" commanded the Elegant Elephant, handing the bowl to the Prince. "Drink to the Proper Princess and the future Queen of Pumperdink."

"Don't go," begged the Prince between gulps, "I shall want two—three—several!"

Kabumpo laughed good naturedly. "This is the pleasantest thing that has happened to us. Here! have another!"

Then both Pompa and the Elegant Elephant gasped, for out of the bubbling waves arose the most curious figure that they had ever seen—the most curious and the jolliest. He was made entirely of soup bones, and his head was a monster cabbage, with a soup bowl set jauntily on the side for a cap. For a cabbage head he sang very well and this was the song to which he kept time by waving a silver ladle:

"Ho! I am the King of the Soup Sea, Yes, I am the King of the Deep; My crown is a bowl and my scepter a ladle, I fell in the soup when I fell from the cradle, And find it exceedingly cheap!

I stir it up nightly, and pepper it rightly—A liquid perfection you'll find. And here is a roll, sirs, So fill up your bowl, sirs, And think of me after you've dined."

When he came to "dined," the Soup King gave a playful leap and disappeared backward into the waves.

Pompa rubbed his eyes and looked at Kabumpo to see whether he had been dreaming.

"Oh!" cried Kabumpo, his eyes as round as little saucers. Floating gently toward them were two large, crisp, buttered rolls.

"The most charming King I've ever met," chuckled Kabumpo, scooping up the rolls and handing them to Pompa.

Pompa, staring dreamily ahead, first took a drink of soup, then a nibble of roll, too happy for speech. Four times the Elegant Elephant refilled the bowl. Then, his stomach full for the first time since they had left Pumperdink, the Prince stretched himself out on the sands.

"Now," puffed the Elegant Elephant ceremoniously, "if you think you've had quite enough, I'll snatch a few bites myself." Chuckling softly he made his way back to some young trees, and dined luxuriously off their tops.

When he returned to the beach, Pompa was fast asleep, and for a few moments Kabumpo was inclined to sleep himself. "But then," he reflected, "Ozma may require a lot of coaxing before she consents to marry Pompa, and two of our precious seven days are gone. It is plainly my duty to save Pumperdink. Besides, when Pompa is married he will be King of Oz! Then I, the Elegant Elephant, will be the biggest figure at Court."

Kabumpo threw up his trunk and trumpeted softly to the stars. Then, giving himself a big shake and a little stretch, he lifted the sleeping Prince to his back and started on again. In about two hours he had circled the Soup Sea and, guiding himself by a particularly bright and twinkling star, ran swiftly and steadily toward the South.

As the first streaks of dawn appeared in the sky, Kabumpo passed through a quaint little Gilliken village. He snatched a bag of rolls from a doorstep and stuck them into his pocket, but he did not stop, and so fast asleep was the little village that except for a few wide-awake roosters, no one knew how important a person had passed through.

The sky grew pinker and pinker. You have no idea how pink the morning skies in Oz can be. Just as the sun got out of bed, the Elegant Elephant came to the wonderful Emerald City itself, shining and fairylike as a dream under the lovely colors of sunrise. Kabumpo paused and took a deep breath. Even he was impressed, and it took a good bit to impress him. He reached back and touched Pompa with his trunk.

"Wake up, my boy," whispered Kabumpo in a trembling voice. "Wake up and put on your crown, for we have come to the city of your Proper Princess."

Pompa sat up and rubbed his eyes in amazement. Without a word, he took the crown Kabumpo handed up to him, and set it on his scorched, golden head. Accustomed as Pompa was to grandeur, for Pumperdink is very magnificent in its funny old-fashioned way, he could not help but gasp at Ozma's fair city. The lovely green parks, and houses studded with countless emeralds, the shining marble streets, filled the Prince with wonder.

"I don't believe she'll ever marry me," he stuttered, beginning to feel quite frightened at his boldness.

"Nonsense," wheezed Kabumpo faintly. He was beginning to have misgivings himself. "Sit up now! Look your best, and I'll carry you straight into the palace gardens."

No one was awake. Even the Soldier with the Green Whiskers lay snoring against a tree, so that Kabumpo stole unobserved into the Royal Gardens.

"I don't see the palace," whispered Pompa anxiously. "Wouldn't it show above the trees?"

"It ought to," said Kabumpo, wrinkling up his forehead. "But look! Who is that?"

Pompa's heart almost stopped, and even Kabumpo's gave a queer jump. On a golden bench, just ahead, sat the loveliest person either had seen in all of their eighteenth birthdays.

"Ozma," gasped the Elegant Elephant, as soon as he had breath enough to whisper. "What luck! You must ask her at once.

"Not now," begged the Prince of Pumperdink, as Kabumpo unceremoniously helped him to the ground. His knees shook, his tongue stuck to the roof of his mouth. He had never proposed to a Fairy Princess before in his whole life. Then all at once he had an idea. Slipping his hand into the Elegant Elephant's pocket, he drew out the magic mirror. "I'll see if she's a princess," stuttered Pompa.

The elephant shook his head angrily but was afraid to speak again lest he disturb the quiet figure on the bench.

"And I'll not propose unless she is the one," said Pompa, tip-toeing toward the bench. Without making a sound he suddenly held the mirror before the startled and lovely lady.

"Glinda, good Sorceress of Oz," flashed the mirror promptly.

"Great gooseberries!" cried Glinda, springing to her feet in alarm and swinging around on Pompa. "Where did you come from?" After studying a whole day and night in her magic books, Glinda had returned to the Emerald City to try to perfect her plan for rescuing Ozma.

"From Pumperdink, your Highness," puffed Kabumpo, lunging forward anxiously. He, too, had seen the words in the mirror and the fear of offending a Sorceress made him quake in his skin—which was loose enough to quake in, dear knows!

"A thousand pardons!" cried the Prince, dropping on one knee and taking off his crown.

"We were seeking Princess Ozma, the Fairy Ruler of Oz."

Glinda looked from Kabumpo to the Prince and controlled a desire to laugh. The Elegant Elephant's torn and scorched robe hung in rags from his shoulders and his jeweled headpiece was dangling over one ear. Pompa's clothes were equally shabby and his almost bald head with a lock sticking up here and there gave him a singular and comical appearance.

"Pumperdink?" mused Glinda, tapping her foot thoughtfully. Then, like a flash she remembered the entry in the Book of Records—The Prince of Pumperdink is journeying toward the Emerald City."

"Why did you want to see Ozma?" asked Glinda anxiously. Perhaps these two strangers could throw some light on the mysterious disappearance of the Royal Palace.

"Our country was threatened with disappearance and I thought—

"He thought Ozma might help us," finished the Elegant Elephant breathlessly. He did not believe in telling strange Sorceresses about everything.

Now if Glinda had not been so occupied with the disappearance of the palace and all the dearest people in Oz, she might have been more curious about the disappearance of Pumperdink. As it was she just shook her head sadly. "I'm afraid Ozma cannot help you," she said, "for Ozma herself has disappeared—Ozma and everyone in the palace."

"Disappeared!" trumpeted the Elegant Elephant, sitting down with a thud. "Great Grump! The thing's getting to be a habit!"

What was to become of Pompa now? Would he never be King, nor he, Kabumpo, ever be known as the most Elegant Elephant in Oz? Had they made the long journey in vain?

"Where? When?" gasped Prince Pompadore.

"Night before last," explained Glinda. "I've been consulting my magic books ever since but have only been able to discover one fact."

"What is that?" asked Kabumpo faintly.

"That they are in Ev," said Glinda, "and that a giant carried them off. I came here early this morning to see whether I could discover anything new. Would you care to see where the castle stood?"

"Did he carry the castle off, too?" shuddered Pompa. Glinda nodded gloomily and led them over to the great hole in the center of the gardens.

For a minute she stood watching them. Then, glancing at a golden sun dial set in the center of a lovely flower bed, she murmured half to herself, "I must be off!" Next instant she clapped her hands and down swept a shining chariot drawn by white swans.

"Good-bye!" called Glinda, springing in lightly. "I'm off to Ev to try my magic against the giant's. Wait here and when I've helped Ozma perhaps I can help you!"

"Can't we help? Can't we go?" cried Pompa, running a few steps after the chariot, but Glinda, already high in the air, did not hear him and in the wink of an eye the chariot and its lovely occupant had melted into the pink morning clouds.

"Now what shall we do?" groaned the Prince, letting his arms drop heavily at his sides.

"Do!" snorted Kabumpo. "The thing for you to do is to act like a Prince instead of a Gooch! There are other ways of getting to Ev than by chariot."

The thought of Kabumpo in Glinda's chariot made Pompa smile in spite of himself.

"There! That's better," said the Elegant Elephant more pleasantly.

"Now, what's to hinder us from going to Ev and rescuing Princess Ozma? She couldn't help marrying you if you saved her from a giant, could she?"

"But could I save her—that's the question," muttered the Prince, looking uneasily at the yawning cavity where the castle had stood. "This giant must be a terrible fellow!"

"Pooh!" said Kabumpo airily. "Who's afraid of giants? I'll wind my trunk around his leg and pull him to earth. Then you can dispatch the villain. We must get you a sword, though," he added softly.

"All right! I'll do it!" cried the Prince, throwing out his chest. The very thought of killing a giant made him feel about ten feet high. "Do you know the way to Ev, Kabumpo? We'll have to hurry, because unless I marry Ozma before the seven days are up my poor old father and mother and all of Pumperdink will disappear forever."

You see, even Pompa had now got it into his head that Ozma was the Proper Princess mentioned in the scroll.

"We'll start at once," sighed the Elegant Elephant a bit ruefully. "I've had no sleep and precious little to eat but when you are King of Oz you can reward old Kabumpo as he deserves."

"Everything I have will be yours," cried the Prince, giving the elephant, or as much of him as he could grasp, a sudden hug. Then each took a long drink from one of the bubbling fountains and, munching the rolls Kabumpo had picked up in the Gilliken village, the two adventurers stole out of the gardens.

As they reached the gates, Kabumpo paused and his little eyes twinkled with delight. There lay the Soldier with the Green Whiskers, snoring tremendously and beside him was a long, sharp sword with an emerald handle. "Just what we need," chuckled Kabumpo, snatching it up in his trunk. Then out through the gates and swiftly through the still sleeping city swept the Elegant Elephant and the Prince of Pumperdink, off to rescue Princess Ozma, a prisoner in Ev!

Chapter 13 - On the Road to Ev

In their journey to Ev, Peg and Wag had a night's start of Kabumpo and Prince Pompadore, but towards morning Wag's ears began to droop with sleep.

"Gotta natch a sap, Peg," Wag muttered thickly, as they halted on a little hill.

"Natch a sap? What's that?" asked the Wooden Doll anxiously. Wag made no answer—just flopped on his side and in a minute was asleep and snoring tremendously.

"Oh!" whispered Peg, pulling herself gently from beneath the sleeping rabbit. "He meant snatch a nap.

She laughed softly and seated herself under a small tree. The birds were beginning to waken and their singing filled Peg Amy with delight. "How wonderful it all is," she murmured, gazing up at the little ruffly pink clouds. "How wonderful it is to be alive!"

"Hello! Mr. Robin!" she called gaily, as a bird flew to a low bush beside her. "Are your children quite well?"

The robin swung backward and forward on his swaying branch; then burst into his best morning song.

"Oh!" cried Peg Amy, clasping her wooden hands. "I've heard that before! But how could I?" she reasoned, "I'm only a Wooden Doll and this is the first morning I have been alive. But then, how did I know it was a robin?"

Peg rubbed her wooden forehead in perplexity, for it was all very puzzling indeed. Below their little hill stretched the lovely land of the Winkies, with its great green forests and little yellow villages. The wind sent the leaves dancing above Peg's head and the early sun-beams made lovely patterns on the grass.

"I've seen it before!" gasped the Wooden Doll breathlessly. "The trees, the birds, the houses and everything!" Springing to her feet she ran awkwardly from bush to tree, touching the leaves and bending over the flowers as if they were old friends. Had it not been for the squeaking of her wooden joints, Peg would almost have forgotten she was a Wooden Doll, for at the sight of the lovely green growing things something warm and sunny seemed to waken in her stiff wooden breast. "I've been alive before," said Peg Amy over and over.

Suddenly, through the still morning air, came a loud, shrill laugh. Peg, who had been standing with her cheek pressed closely against a small tree, swung around quickly—so quickly in fact that she fell over and lay in a ridiculously bent double position before the new-comers.

It was Kabumpo and the Prince of Pumper-dink. Traveling by the same road Wag had chosen but much more rapidly, the Elegant Elephant had come at sunrise to the little hill. He had been watching Peg for some time, and when he saw her dance awkwardly over to the tree, he could no longer restrain himself.

"Get out your mirror!" roared Kabumpo, shaking all over with mirth. "Here is your Proper Princess, Pompa, my boy—as royal a maiden as the country boasts. Ho, ho! Ker-umph!"

"Don't be ridiculous," snapped Pompa, looking down curiously at the comical figure of Peg Amy.

"But she's so funny!" gasped Kabumpo, the tears rolling down his big cheeks.

"Who's funny?" demanded an angry voice and Wag, who had been awakened by Kabumpo's loud roars, hopped up, his ears quivering with rage.

"I'll pull your long nose for you!" cried Wag, advancing threateningly. "Don't you dare make fun of Peg. What are you, anyway?"

"Great Grump!" choked Kabumpo, without answering Wag's inquiry. "What kind of a rabbit is this?"

"A clawing, chawing, scratching kind—as you'll soon find out!" Wag drew himself up into a ball and prepared to launch himself at Kabumpo's head, when Peg straightened up and caught him by the ear.

"Don't, Wag, please," she begged. "He couldn't help laughing. I am funny. You know I am!" she sighed a bit ruefully.

"You're not funny to me," blustered Wag, still glaring at Kabumpo. "Who does he think he is?"

"I?" sniffed Kabumpo, spreading out his ears complacently, "I am the Elegant Elephant of Pumperdink. Notice my pearls; gaze upon my robe."

"You don't look very elegant to me," snorted Wag. "You look more like a tramp. Says he's a lelegant nelephant from Dumperpink," he whispered scornfully to Peg.

"And what's that you've got on your back?" he called, with a wave of his paw at Pompa. "A dunce?"

"Dunce!" screamed Kabumpo furiously. "This is the Prince of Pumperdink, you good-for-nothing lettuce-eater! What do you mean by laughing at royalty?"

"Royalty! Oh, ha, ha, ha!" roared Wag, rolling over and over in the grass. "But he's so funny!" He paused to take another look at the Prince. At this Kabumpo lunged forward, his eyes snapping angrily.

"Stop!" begged the Prince, tugging Kabumpo by the ear. "You were rude to his friend that-er-doll, so you must expect him to be rude to me. It's all your fault," he added reproachfully.

"Are you a Prince?" asked Peg Amy, staring up at Pompa with her round, painted eyes.

"Of course he's a Prince. Didn't I say so before? Who is that hoppy creature?"

"That's Wag—such a dear fellow." Peg smiled confidently at Kabumpo and he was suddenly ashamed of himself for laughing at her.

"Well, he needn't get waggish with me," grumbled the Elegant Elephant in a lower voice.

"Oh, don't quarrel!" begged Peg. "It's such a lovely morning and you both look so interesting."

Kabumpo eyed the big Wooden Doll attentively. It was smart of her to think him interesting. He cleared his throat gruffly. "You're not as funny as you look," he admitted grandly, which was the nearest to an apology he had ever come. "But what are you doing here and why are you alive?"

"I don't know," explained Peg apologetically. "It just happened last night."

"It did? Well, where are you going?" Wag still looked cross and his nose was twitching violently, but Peg politely answered Kabumpo's question.

"We're on our way to Ev to try to help Ozma," said the Wooden Doll, folding her hands quaintly.

"Why so are we!" cried Pompa, sliding down Kabumpo's trunk in a hurry.

"How do you expect to help her?" grunted Kabumpo, looking at Wag and Peg contemptuously.

"Don't mind him," begged Pompa, running up to Peg Amy. "Tell me everything you know about Ozma. Is she pretty?"

"Beautiful," breathed Peg, looking up at the sky. "Beautiful and lovely and good. That's why I want to help her."

"Then I sha'n't mind marrying her at all," said Pompa, with a great sigh of relief.

"Gooch!" roared Kabumpo angrily—Telling everything you know!"

"Do you mean to say you think Ozma would marry you?" gasped Wag, sitting up with a jerk. "Oh, my wocks and hoop soons!" His ears crossed and uncrossed and with a final gurgle of disbelief Wag fell back on the grass.

"Well, is there anything so strange in that?" asked Pompa in a hurt voice. "I've got to marry her," he added, desperately appealing to Peg Amy. And while Kabumpo stood sulkily swinging his trunk the Prince told Peg the whole story of the magic scroll.

"I said you looked interesting," breathed Peg, as Pompa paused for breath. "Did you hear that, Wag? Unless he marries a Proper Princess in a proper time his whole Kingdom will disappear—his Kingdom and everyone in it!"

"But how do you know Ozma is the Proper Princess?" asked Wag, chewing a blade of grass. "The scroll didn't say Ozma, did it?"

"Kabumpo thinks Ozma is the Proper Princess," explained Pompadore, nodding toward the Elegant Elephant, "and he's usually right!"

"Humph!" sniffed Wag. "Well, maybe you are a Prince. You're not really bad looking if you had some fur on your head," he remarked more amiably. "What happened? Somebody pull it out?"

"Oh, Wag!" murmured Peg Amy, in a shocked voice.

"Burned off," sighed Pompa, and proceeded to tell of their fall into the Illumi Nation. He even told them about the Soup Sea and of their meeting with Glinda, the Good.

"Don't you care," said the big Wooden Doll, as Pompa mournfully rubbed his scorched head. "It will soon grow again and I don't see how Ozma could help loving you—you're so tall, and so polite." This kind little speech affected Pompa so deeply that he dropped on one knee and raised Peg's wooden hand to his lips.

"The creature has a lot of sense," mumbled Kabumpo, with his mouth full of leaves.

"Creature!" exclaimed Wag, sitting up straight and opening his eyes wide. "Her name is Peg Amy, Mr. Nelegant Lelephant."

"Oh, all right," sniffed Kabumpo hastily. "But you'll have to admit she's curious."

"Of course she is," said Wag complacently. "That's why I like her. She wasn't cut out to be a beauty, but to be companionable, and she is. When you've known Peg as long as I have—Wag paused impressively—you'll be proud to carry her on your back, Mr. Long Nose!"

"I've only known her a few minutes and I adore her!" said Pompa heartily. "Mistress Peg and I are good friends already." Peg curtseyed awkwardly. "I've done this before," she reflected curiously to herself.

"Shall we tell them about Ruggedo?" Peg asked aloud, turning to Wag.

"Yes, do!" begged Pompa. "Tell us something about yourselves. I never saw so large a rabbit in my life as Wag and as for you!—Pompa paused, for Wag was eyeing him resentfully—you are the largest, most delightful doll I have ever met, the only alive one, I might say. How did you know about Ozma's disappearance and how were you going to help her?"

"Mixed Magic!" whispered Wag, crossing his ears and his eyes as well. "Mixed Magic!"

"Magic?" gulped Kabumpo, swallowing a branch of sticky leaves whole. "Have you any magic?"

"A whole box full," sighed Peg Amy, patting her pocket softly.

"In that box is the magic that brought Peg to life!" shrilled Wag, pointing a trembling paw. In that box is the magic that made us grow. In that box is the magic that caused Ozma's castle to disappear—!"

"Great Grump!" whistled Kabumpo. "How fortunate we fell in with them, Pompa." He held out his trunk. "Give me the box, my good girl, and you shall be fittingly rewarded when Pompa is King of Oz."

"That's a long time to wait," chuckled Wag, tickled by Kabumpo's outrageous impudence. "No, Peg and I will just keep the box, thank you.

"Of course you will," said Prince Pompadore, frowning at Kabumpo. "But as we are both bound on the same errand, let us travel together. Kabumpo and I are going to kill the giant who ran off with the castle."

The Prince held up his long sword. "And if you can help us, I shall thank you from the bottom of my heart." Pompa stretched out his hand impulsively.

"Well, that's more like," said Wag, pulling his ear thoughtfully. "And four heads are better than two!"

"Of course we'll help you!" cried Peg Amy. "The trouble is, we don't know ourselves how to open the magic box, but we do know that Ruggedo is in Ev and when we get there we will make him open the box and undo all this mischief."

"You mentioned him before," said Kabumpo, holding up his trunk. "Who is Ruggedo and what has he to do with Ozma?"

"Ruggedo is a wicked little gnome," explained Peg Amy gravely. "He used to be King of the Gnomes but he was banished from his Kingdom and Ozma gave him a little cottage in the Emerald City. He pretended to live there, but instead he tunneled a cave right underneath the palace. Wag helped him dig." Peg waved her hand at the rabbit. "And he was the only one who would stay with him. Then Ruggedo stole me. I was only a small, unalive doll, belonging to Trot, a little girl who lives with Ozma. Ruggedo stole me just to shake," continued Peg shuddering.

90

"That's why I'm going to pound his curly toes off!" screamed Wag, beginning to hop about at the very thought of Ruggedo.

"But how did you come to be so large and alive?" asked Kabumpo, who was growing more interested.

"Well, one night—Peg dropped her voice to a whisper—One night Ruggedo found this box of Mixed Magic hidden in the cave and then—"

"Then," screamed Wag hoarsely, "in some way we don't understand, Peg and I grew big, Peg came alive, the top blew off the cave—and depend upon it, whatever's happened to Ozma and her palace happened from something in that box. It's all Ruggedo's fault. When I catch him"—Wag began to wiggle his nose and paw his whiskers—"my wocks and hoop soons! I'll pound his curly toes off!"

"And I'll help you!" cried Kabumpo heartily. He could not help but admire such spirit. "Come on—let's start. You may ride on my back with Pompa if you care to," finished the Elegant Elephant with a sidelong glance at Peg.

"Oh, thank you," smiled the Wooden Doll, "but Wag will carry me."

"I always carry Peg," said Wag jealously. "I've known her the longest."

"Oh, all right," sniffed Kabumpo, lifting Pompa up, "but if she ever wants to ride on my back she may."

"Humph!" grunted Wag, as the Wooden Doll settled herself on his shoulders. "Isn't he generous!"

Peg pulled down one of Wag's long ears. "It was kindly meant," whispered the Wooden Doll merrily.

"Ready?" puffed Kabumpo, backing Out into the road. "We've no time to lose, for if we lose time we lose our Kingdom too. Forward for Pumperdink!"

"All right!" cried Wag, giving a great leap. "Follow me." And off hopped the giant bunny so fast that Kabumpo had to stretch his legs even to keep him in sight.

Chapter 14 - Terror in Ozma's Palace

Meanwhile strange things had been happening in Ozma's palace. For the people inside it had been a very mean time indeed. During Ruggedo's run to the mountains of Ev, they had almost been shaken out of their wits and when he sat down upon the mountain top there was not a person nor piece of furniture standing in the whole palace. Courtiers and servants who were not knocked senseless lay shaking in their beds or huddled in corners and under sofas and chairs, just as they had fallen when the first terrible crash lifted the palace into the air.

Ozma's four poster bed had collapsed, pinning the little Fairy Princess under a mass of silk hangings and curtain poles. Being a fairy, Ozma was unhurt, but not being able to move, nor to reach her Magic Belt or even make herself heard, she was forced to lie perfectly still and wait for help.

In Dorothy's sitting room there was not a sound but the ticking of the Copper Man's machinery. Trot and Betsy Bobbin had knocked their heads together so smartly that they were unconscious. Sir Hokus had been hurled violently against Tik Tok and the poor Knight had known nothing since. Dorothy lay quietly beside him, an ugly bruise on her forehead, where the emerald clock had landed.

"Scraps!" called the Scarecrow, sometime after the rumble and tumble had ceased, "are you there?"

"No, here!" gasped the Patch Work Girl, sitting up cautiously. She had bounced all around the room and finally rolled into a corner quite close to the Scarecrow himself. She put out her cotton hand as she spoke and touched him.

"How fortunate we are unbreakable," said the Scarecrow, pressing her cotton fingers convulsively and trying to peer out through the intense blackness of the room. "What happened?"

"Earthquake!" shivered Scraps. "And maybe it's not over!"

"Must have knocked everybody silly," said the Scarecrow huskily.

"Except us," giggled the Patch Work Girl. "We couldn't be knocked silly 'cause we were silly in the first place."

"Now, don't make jokes, please," begged the Scarecrow. "This is serious. Besides, I want to think."

"All right," said Scraps cheerfully. "I don't—but I'm going to feel around and see if I can find the matches. There used to be some candles on the mantel and—" As she spoke, Scraps fell headlong over Sir Hokus of Pokes and as luck would have it her cotton fingers closed over a small gold match box. Picking herself up carefully, Scraps struck a match on Sir Hokus' armor and looked anxiously around the room.

"They need water," said the Patch Work Girl, wrinkling up her patchwork forehead.

"So will you if you don't blow out that match!" cried the Scarecrow in alarm, for Scraps continued to hold the match till it burned to the very end. He jumped up clumsily and puffed out the light just in time. Scraps promptly lit another and as she did so the Scarecrow saw a tall blue candle sticking out of the waste basket.

"Here," said the Straw Man nervously. "Light this and stand it on the mantel there." By the flickering candle light the Scarecrow and Scraps tried to set Dorothy's room to rights. They dragged the mattress from the bed-room and placed the little girls on it, side by side. Sir Hokus was too heavy to move, so they merely loosened his armor and put a sofa cushion under his head. Then, just as Scraps was going for some water, the room began to tremble again.

"I told you it wasn't over," cried Scraps, flinging both arms about the Scarecrow s neck. And as they rocked to and fro she shouted merrily:

"Shaker! Shaker! Who art thee, To shake a castle like a tree? Shaker! Shaker! Go away And come again some other day!"

"Now, Scraps," begged the Scarecrow, steadying the Patch Work Girl with one hand and catching hold of a table with the other, everything depends on us. Do try to keep your head!"

"Keep my head!" shrilled Scraps, as the room tilted over and slid all the furniture sideways. "I'll be lucky if I keep my feet. Whoopee! Here we go!" And go they did with a rush into the farthest corner. Slowly the room righted itself and everything grew quiet again.

"I know what I'm going to do," said the Scarecrow determinedly. "Before anything else happens I'm going to see what has happened already."

"How?" asked Scraps, bouncing to her feet.

"The Magic Picture," gasped the Scarecrow. "You bring the candle, Scraps, like a good girl. You're less liable to take fire than I am. Then we'll come back and help Dorothy and the others."

"Good idea," said Scraps, taking the candle from the mantel. Breathlessly the two tip-toed along the hall to Ozma's apartment. On the wall in one of Ozma's rooms hangs the most magic possession in Oz. It is a picture representing a country scene, but when you ask it where a certain person is, immediately he is shown in the picture and also what he is doing at the time.

"So," murmured the Scarecrow, as they gained the room in safety, "if it tells where other people are, it ought to tell us where we are ourselves."

Drawing aside the curtain that covered the picture the Scarecrow demanded loudly, "Where are we?"

Scraps held the candle so that its flickering rays fell directly on the picture. Then both jumped in earnest, for in a flash the face of Ruggedo, the wicked old gnome King, appeared, on his head a great, green towering sort of hat.

The Scarecrow seized the candle from Scraps and held it closer to the picture. He squinted up one eye and almost rubbed his painted nose off.

"Great Kinkajous!" spluttered the Straw Man distractedly. "That's a palace on his head—an Emerald palace— Ozma's palace!"

"But how?" asked Scraps, her suspender button eyes almost dropping out. "He's nothing but a gnome. He's—"

Before Scraps could finish her sentence the palace began to tilt forward and they both fell upon their faces. Then the picture jerked loose and fell with a clattering slam on their heads, followed by such ornaments as had not already tumbled down before. Through it all Scraps held the candle high in air and fortunately it did not go out, despite the turmoil.

In a few moments the palace stopped rocking and a muffled call from Ozma sent the Scarecrow and Scraps hurrying to her bedside. After some trouble, for they were both flimsily made, they managed to free the little Princess of Oz from the poles and bed curtains.

"Goodness!" sighed Ozma, looking around at the terrible confusion.

"Not goodness, but badness," said the Scare-crow, settling his hat firmly, "and Ruggedo is at the bottom of it and of us." He quickly explained to Ozma what he had seen in the Magic Picture.

Slipping on a silk robe, Ozma followed them into the next room. When the picture had been rehung, they all looked again. This time Ozma asked where the palace was. Immediately the old Gnome King appeared and there could be no mistake—the palace was set squarely on his head. The picture did not show the real size of Ruggedo nor of the palace, but it was enough.

"He must have sprung into a giant," gasped Ozma, scarcely believing her eyes. "Oh, what shall we do?"

"The first thing to do is to keep him quiet. Every time he shakes his head it tumbles us about so," complained the Scarecrow, plumping up the straw in his chest. "And we must look after Dorothy and Betsy and Trot."

"And Sir Hokus," added the Patch Work Girl, flinging out one hand. "He's yearning to slay a giant. 'Way for the Giant Killer!"

Without waiting for the others Scraps ran back to Dorothy's sitting room. Lighting another candle, for all the lights in the palace were out, Ozma and the Scarecrow followed.

"Odds Goblins!" gasped the Knight, as they entered. He was sitting up with one hand to his head.

"Not goblins—giants!" cried the Patch Work Girl, with a bounce, while Ozma ran for some water to restore her three little friends.

"Where?" puffed the Knight, lurching to his feet.

"Beneath you," said the Scarecrow, clutching at a wisp of straw that stuck out of his head. "Say! Some one wind up Tik Tok. There's a lot of thinking to be done here and his head works very well, even if it has wheels inside."

Sir Hokus, though still a bit dizzy, hastened to wind up all the Copper Man's keys.

"Thanks," said Tik Tok immediately. "Give me a lift up, Hokus." The Knight obligingly helped the Copper Man to his feet. Then both stared in amazement at the topsy turvy room. Even in the dim candle light they could see that something very serious had occurred.

Jack Pumpkinhead picked himself up out of a corner, looking very much dazed.

Just then Dorothy opened her eyes, and Betsy and Trot, spluttering from the water the Patch Work Girl was pouring on their heads, sat up and wanted to know what had happened. In a few words Ozma told them what the magic picture had revealed.

"Ruggedo to a giant's grown And set us on his head. We've made some headway, you'll admit, Since we have gone to bed!"—shouted Scraps, who was growing more and more excited.

"Rug-ge-do will never re-form," ticked the Copper Man sadly.

"But what are we going to do?" wailed Dorothy. "Suppose he leans over and spills us all out?"

"I shall take my sword," said Sir Hokus, speaking very determinedly, and backing toward the window as he spoke, "climb down, and slay the villain." He threw one leg over the sill.

"Come back!" cried Ozma. "Dear Sir Hokus, don't you realize that if you kill Ruggedo he will fall down and break us to pieces? Besides, wicked as he is, I could not have him killed."

"Yes, we should be all broken up if you did that," sighed the Scarecrow. "We must try something else."

Reluctantly, the Knight dropped back into the room. "Close the windows," ordered Ozma with a little shudder.

"I've thought of a plan," said Tik Tok, in his slow, painstaking way. "A ve-ry good plan."

"Tell us what it is," begged Dorothy. "And Oh, Tik Tok, hurry!"

"Eggs," said the Copper Man solemnly.

"Oh" gasped Dorothy, "I remember. Eggs are the only things in Oz that Ruggedo is afraid of; for if an egg touches a gnome he shrivels up and disappears."

"Then where are the eggs?" demanded Sir Hokus gloomily. "In faith, this sounds more like an omelet than a battle. But if we're to fight with eggs instead of swords, let us draw them at once.

"You mean throw them," corrected Dorothy. But Tik Tok shook his head violently.

"Not throw them," said the Copper Man slowly, "threat-en to throw them."

"But how can we threaten a giant so far below us?" asked Ozma.

"Print a sign," directed Tic Tok calmly, "and low-er it down to him."

"Tik Tok," cried the Scarecrow, rushing forward and embracing him impulsively, "your patent-action-double-guaranteed brains are marvels. I couldn't have thought up a better plan myself."

Now off ran Scraps to fetch a huge piece of cardboard, and the Scarecrow for a paint brush, and Sir Hokus for a piece of rope. "It's growing lighter,"Quavered Trot, looking toward the windows. The sky was turning gray with little streaks of pink, and the three girls huddled together on the mattress gave a sigh of relief, for nothing, not even a giant, seems so bad by daylight.

"Perhaps someone has already started to help us, said Ozma hopefully. "But here's the sign board. What shall we write?"

"How shall I begin?" asked the Scarecrow, dipping the brush into a can of green paint. "Dear Ruggedo?"

"I should say not," said Dorothy indignantly, "Then I shall simply say, Sir," said the Scarecrow.

"If you move or turn or shake your head a-gain, ten thou-sand eggs will be hurl-ed from the pal-ace windows," suggested Tik Tok.

As this message met with general approval, the Scarecrow set it down with many flourishes and blotches of paint spilled between. Then Ozma painted her name and the Royal seal of Oz at the end.

Meanwhile, with the help of a pair of field glasses, Sir Hokus had located Ruggedo's nose, sticking out like a huge cliff below the middle window of Dorothy's room. So,. tying a long rope to each corner of the sign, and rolling it up so it would go through the window, the Knight let it down till it dangled directly in front of Ruggedo's nose.

At first Ruggedo did not even see the sign, which was about as large as the tiniest visiting card compared to him. But it blew against his face and tickled his cheek. He tried to brush it away. Then, suddenly noticing it was dangling from above, he seized it in one hand and held it close to his left eye. The words were so small for a giant that Ruggedo had to squint fearfully before he could make them out at all, but when he did he gave a bloodcurdling scream, and began to tremble violently.

Up in the palace the entire company fell over and twenty windows were shaken to bits. Then everything grew quiet and there was perfect silence; for Ruggedo, realizing his danger, grew rigid with fright. Giant drops of perspiration trickled down his forehead. How long could be keep from moving?

"Well," said Dorothy after a few minutes had passed, "I guess that will keep him quiet, but what next? Shall we let ourselves down with ropes?"

"We have none long enough," said Sir Hokus.

"Then I'll fall out and go for help," said the Scarecrow brightly, and started toward the window. When he reached it he paused in astonishment. "Look," he cried, waving excitedly to the others, "here comes someone, walking right over the clouds."

Chapter 15 - The Sand Man Takes a Hand

Someone was coming toward the palace. A little gray-cloaked old gentleman—a surprisingly quick and nimble old gentleman—springing from cloud to cloud and pausing now and then to straighten a huge sack he carried over his left shoulder. He was so busy admiring the lovely sky colors behind him and waving merrily at the fluffy cloud figures above his head, that he did not see Ozma's shining palace until he was almost upon it.

"Stars!" murmured the little old gentleman, balancing perilously on the very edge of a silver cloud. "Another air castle! How delightful! I shall jump right through it!"

Gathering himself together he leaped straight toward the window out of which Dorothy and Ozma and the others were looking. With a soft thud he struck the emerald setting just above the window, and down tumbled his sack. opening as it fell and filling the air with clouds of silver sand. Down tumbled the little old gentleman, turning over and over, and finally landing on a blankety white cloud far below.

All of this Dorothy saw, and was about to ask Ozma what it could mean when an overpowering drowsiness stole over her. Before she could speak her eyes closed, and she sank backward into a big arm chair. Trot and Betsy Bobbin with two little sighs crumpled down to the floor. The head of Sir Hokus dropped heavily on the sill, and not even in Pokes had he snored so lustily. Ozma slipped gently down beside Betsy and Trot, and in a moment there was not a person awake in that whole big palace. Even the little mice in the kitchen were fast asleep, with heads on their paws.

Did I say everyone? Well, not quite everyone had fallen under the strange spell. Tik Tok, Scraps, and the Scarecrow, who had never slept in their lives, were still wide awake, and regarding their companions with astonishment and alarm. The Tin Woodman was taking things calmly, oiling up his joints and polishing his tin jacket with silver polish.

"This is no time to sleep," cried the Scarecrow, shaking Sir Hokus. "I say—wake up!" But all their efforts to arouse their companions were in vain.

"En-chant-ment," said the Copper Man. "Some— With a click and a whirr Tik Tok's machinery ran down, and as Scraps and the Scarecrow were too upset to think of winding him, he stood as silent and dumb as the rest.

"What shall we do?" cried the Scarecrow, seizing Scraps' arm. "Jump out of the window and go for help, or stay here and guard the palace?" Scraps looked out of the window. "Stay here," shuddered the Patch Work Girl, drawing in her head quickly.

"Then," said the Scarecrow, "let us arm ourselves and prepare to withstand any attack." He snatched up a pair of fire tongs and Scraps grasped the poker. Falling into step, the two marched from the top to the bottom of the palace.

Everywhere the same sight met their gaze; rooms turned topsy turvy, and spread over floors and sofas and chairs the sleeping figures of Ozma's once lively Courtiers and servants. The effect was so distressing that Scraps and the Scarecrow found themselves whispering and treading about on tip-toe. After inspecting the whole palace they returned to Dorothy's room and placed themselves disconsolately in the doorway.

"Anyway, Ruggedo is quiet," sighed the Scarecrow, "and that is something." Scraps started to make a verse, but the silence and the ghostlike atmosphere of the sleeping palace had dashed even the spirits of the Patch Work Girl and she subsided with an indistinct mumble.

Ruggedo was silent for a very good reason. Ruggedo was asleep, to—asleep sitting up as stiff as a stone image, for even in his sleep he dreamed of the dreaded bombardment of eggs.

All this had happened because the little man in gray had taken Ozma's palace for an air castle, and who could blame him for that? Even the Sand Man would not expect to find a regular palace set among the clouds. There are plenty of dream castles, to be sure, and one of the Sand Man's chief delights is to jump through them and admire their lovely furniture. But sure—enough castles—the little fellow could not get over it. Sitting cross-legged on the white cloud, which floated close to Ruggedo's head, he stared and stared.

"Well, I never," chuckled the Sand Man, and turned a somersault for very amazement. Then, not knowing what else to do or think, he sensibly decided to hurry home and tell the whole affair to his wife. His empty bag he found on a tall treetop, and without one backward glance he bounded into the air and disappeared. Really, it was quite lucky the little old gentleman spilled his bag of sand where he did, for the only safe giant is a sleeping giant, and while Ozma and her friends lay dreaming they could not worry.

"Will they sleep forever?" sighed Scraps, after she and the Scarecrow had sat silently for an hour.

"Seems likely," said the Scarecrow gloomily. "But even if they do," he plucked three straws from his chest, "we shall stick to our post to the very end."

The Scarecrow regarded the sleeping figures of the little girls affectionately.

"To the end of forever?" gulped Scraps, putting her cotton finger in her mouth. "How long is that?"

"That," said the Scarecrow resignedly and settling himself comfortably, "that is what we shall soon see.

Chapter 16 - Kabumpo Vanquishes the Twigs

D' you think you were alive before?" asked Kabumpo, squinting down his long trunk at Peg Amy. She had begged him to take off his plush robe and, spreading it on the grass, was beating it briskly with the branch of a tree.

"Yes," sighed the Wooden Doll, pausing with uplifted stick and regarding Kabumpo solemnly, "I must have been alive before 'cause I keep remembering things."

"What kind of things?" asked the Elegant Elephant, rubbing himself lazily against a tree.

"Well, this for instance," said Peg, holding up a corner of the purple plush robe. "I once had a dress of it. I'm sure I had a dress of this stuff."

"When you were a little doll?" asked Kabumpo curiously.

"No," said Peg, giving the robe a few little shakes, "before that. And I remember this country, too, and the sun and the wind and the sky. If I'd only been alive one day I wouldn't remember them, would I?"

"Queer things happen in Oz," said Kabumpo comfortably. "But why bother? You are alive and very jolly. You are traveling with the most Elegant Elephant in Oz and in the company of a Prince. Isn't that enough?"

Peg Amy did not reply but kept on beating the plush robe with determined little thumps and staring off through the trees with a very puzzled expression in her painted blue eyes. They had traveled swiftly all morning through the fertile farmlands of the Winkies and had paused for lunch in this little grove. Peg, not needing food, and Kabumpo, finding plenty of tender branches handy, had remained together while Wag and the Prince sought more nourishing fare.

Many a little Winkie farmer had stared in amazement as Peg and Pompa passed that morning but so fast did Kabumpo and Wag travel that before the Winkies were half sure of what they had seen there was nothing but a cloud of dust to wonder over and exclaim about.

"If you had a pair of scissors, I could cut off the burned part of your robe and make it more tidy," said Peg, when she had finished beating the dust out of Kabumpo's gorgeous blanket.

"There might be a pair in my pocket," said the Elegant Elephant. "Here, let me get them," he added hastily. "For suppose she should look into the Magic Mirror," he thought suddenly. "It might tell her something terrible!"

Even in this short time Kabumpo had grown fond of queer wooden Peg and careless as he was somehow he did not want to hurt her feelings again. Sure enough, there was a pair of silver scissors in with the jewels he had tumbled into his pocket before leaving Pumper-dink. So Peg carefully cut away all the scorched part of Kabumpo's robe and pinned under the rough edges with three beautiful pearl pins.

"Now lift me up into that small tree and I'll drop it over you," she laughed gaily. This Kabumpo did quite easily and after Peg Amy had smoothed and adjusted the robe, she crept out on the end of the branch and straightened the Elegant Elephant's pearl head dress and brushed all the dust from his forehead with a handful of damp leaves.

"You're a good girl, Peg," said Kabumpo, sighing with contentment. "I don't care whether you never were alive before or not, you've more sense than some people who've lived for centuries. I'm going to give that gnome something on my own account. Dared to shake you, did he? Well, wait till I get through shaking him!"

"It didn't hurt," said Peg reflectively, "but it ruined all my clothes. Do you think Prince Pompadore minds having me look so shabby?"

Kabumpo shifted about uneasily. "Will this help?" he asked sheepishly, pulling a lovely pearl necklace from his pocket. "Ozma doesn't need everything," he muttered to himself.

"Oh! How perfectly pomiferous!" cried Peg. "Lift me down so I can try it on." In a trice Kabumpo swung her down from the tree and awkwardly Peg Amy clasped the chain about her wooden neck. Then she flung both arms round Kabumpo's trunk. "You're the biggest darling old elephant in Oz!" cried Peg happily.

Kabumpo blinked. He was accustomed to being called elegant and magnificent but no one—not even Pompa—had ever called him an old darling before and he found he liked it immensely.

While Peg ran to look at her reflection in a small pool he resolved to get the Wooden Doll a position at Court, for, in spite of her stiff fingers, Peg was very deft and clever. "And she shall have a purple plush dress too," said Kabumpo grandly.

Just then Pompa and Wag returned in a high good humor. The Prince had tapped on the door of a small farm house and the little Winkie lady had been most hospitable. Not only had she given the Prince all he could eat, but she had allowed Wag to go into the garden and pick two dozen of her best cabbages. His size had greatly astonished her and she had insisted upon measuring him twice with her yellow tape measure but finally, without revealing the purpose of their journey, the two managed to get away. As all were now refreshed and rested, they decided to start on again.

"We ought to reach Ev by evening," puffed Wag, between hops.

"But I wish we could open the Magic Box," sighed Peg, holding on to Wag's ear, "for in that box there's Flying Fluid!"

"We'd make a remarkably nice lot of birds," chuckled Kabumpo, looking over his shoulder, now wouldn't we?"

"You would," laughed Pompa. "What else was in the box, Peg?"

It was hard to talk while they were being jolted along, but Peg, being of wood, did not feel the bumps and Pompa, being a Prince, pretended not to, so that they continued their conversation in jerky sentences.

"There's Vanishing Cream, a little tea kettle and some kind of rays and a Question Box," said Peg, holding up her wooden hand. "A Question Box that answers any question you ask it."

"There is!" exclaimed Kabumpo, stopping short. "Well, I wish we could ask it whether Pumperdink has disappeared."

"And how to rescue Ozma, and who sent the scroll!" cried Pompa. "Oh, do let me try to open it, Peg!"

So Peg handed over Glegg's Magic Box and as they pounded along the Prince tried to pry it open with his pearl pen knife. "It would save us such a lot of trouble," he murmured, holding it up and screwing his eye to the keyhole.

"Better let it alone," advised Wag, wiggling his ears nervously. "Suppose you should grow as big for you as I am for me. Suppose you should explode or vanish!"

"Vanish!" coughed Kabumpo. "Great Grump! Put it away, Pompa. Wait till we reach Ev and make that wicked little Ruggedo open it for us. Who is this Glegg, anyway?"

"A lawless magician, I guess," said Wag, "or he wouldn't have owned a box of Mixed Magic. Ozma doesn't allow anyone to practice magic, you know."

"Why, I'll bet he was the person who sent the scroll!" exclaimed the Prince suddenly. "Don't you remember, Kabumpo, it was signed J.G.?"

"Not a doubt in the world," rumbled Kabumpo. "I'll throw him up a tree when I catch him and Ruggedo, too!"

"Oh, please don't," begged Peg Amy. "Perhaps they are sorry."

"Not half as sorry as they will be," wheezed Kabumpo, plowing ahead through the long grass like a big ferryboat under full steam.

Wag hopped close behind and Peg kept her eyes fixed upon Pompa's back. In spite of his scorched head, he seemed to Peg the most delightful Prince imaginable.

"I'll brush off his cloak and cut his hair all evenly," thought Peg. "Then, perhaps Ozma will say yes when he tells her his story and asks for her hand. But I wonder what will become of me," Peg sighed ever so softly and looked down with distaste at her wooden hands and torn old dress. Nothing very exciting could happen to a shabby Wooden Doll.

"Why, I haven't even any right to be alive," she reflected sadly. "I'm only meant to be funny. Well, never mind! Perhaps I can help Pompa and maybe that's why I was brought to life."

This thought, and the gleam of the lovely pearls Kabumpo had given her, so cheered Peg that she began to hum a queer, squeaky little song. The country was growing rougher and more hilly every minute. The sunny farmlands lay far behind them now and as Peg finished her song they came to the edge of a queer, dead-looking forest. The trees were dry and without leaves and there were quantities of stiff bushes and short stunted little trees standing under the taller ones.

Peg had an odd feeling that hundreds of eyes were staring out at them but the forest was so dim that she couldn't be sure. There was not a sound but the crackling of the dead branches under Wag's and Kabumpo's feet.

"I don't like this," choked Wag. "My wocks and hoop soons! What a pleerful chase!"

96

"It isn't very cheerful," shivered Peg. "Oh, look, Wag! That big tree has eyes!" At Peg's remark the tree doubled up its branches into fists and stepped right out in front of them. At the same instant all the other trees and bushes moved closer, with dry crackling steps.

"Now we have you!" snapped the tallest tree in a dreadful voice.

"Now we have you!" crackled all the other skitter-witchy creatures, crowding closer.

"Pigs, pigs, we're the twigs; We'll tweak your ears and snatch your wigs!"

they shouted all together. One taller than the rest leaned over and seized Wag by the ear with its twisted fingers.

"Help!" screamed Wag, kicking out with his hind legs. Immediately Kabumpo began laying about with his trunk.

"Stand back!" he trumpeted angrily, "or I'll trample you to splinters."

Pompa stood up on Kabumpo's back and began to wave his sword threateningly. At this the ugly creatures grew simply furious. They snatched at the Prince with their long, claw-like branches, tearing at his sadly scorched hair and almost upsetting him.

"Stop! Stop!" cried Peg Amy, waving her wooden arms frantically. "Don't hit him. He's going to be married. Hit me, I'm only made of wood!"

"Don't you dare hit her!" shrilled Pompa, slicing off the branch head of the nearest Twig. "I am a Prince and she is under my protection. Don't touch her!"

By this time Kabumpo had cleared himself a space ahead and Wag a space behind. Every time Kabumpo's trunk flew out, a dozen of the queer crackly Bushmen tumbled over forward and every time Wag's heels flew out a dozen crumpled over backward. Pompa kept his sword whirling and, after several had lost top branches, the whole crowd fell back and began grumbling together.

"Now then!" puffed Kabumpo angrily, "let's make a dash for it, Wag. Come on; we'll smash them to kindling wood!"

"What's all this commotion?" cried a loud voice. The Twigs fell back immediately and a bent and twisted old tree hobbled forward.

"Strangers, your Woodjesty," whispered a tall Twig, waving a branch at Kabumpo.

"Well, have you pinched them?" asked the King in a bored voice.

"A little," admitted the tall Twig nervously, "but they object to it, your Woodjesty."

"Well, what if they do?" rasped the King tartly. "Don't be gormish Faggots. You know I detest gormishness. It seems to me you might allow my people a little innocent diversion," he grumbled, turning to Pompa, "they don't get much pleasure!"

"Pleasure!" gasped the Prince, while Kabumpo and Wag were so astonished that they forgot to fight.

"What does he mean by gormish?" whispered Peg uneasily to Wag. Before he could answer, the Twigs, who evidently had decided not to be gormish, made a rush upon the travelers. But Kabumpo was ready for them with uplifted trunk. With a furious trumpet he charged straight into the middle, Wag at his heels, with the result that the Twigs went crackling and snapping to the ground in heaps.

"All we need is a match," grunted Kabumpo, pounding along unmindful of the scratching and clawing. "They're good for nothing but kindling wood."

"Don't be gormish," he screeched scornfully, as he flung the last Twig out of his way and Wag and he never stopped till they had put a good mile between themselves and the disagreeable pinchers.

"Are you hurt?" asked Kabumpo, stopping at last and looking around at Pompa. "If we keep on this way you won't be fit to be seen—much less to marry. Let's have a look at you." He lifted the Prince down carefully and eyed him with consternation. The Prince had seven long scratches on his cheek and his velvet cloak was torn to ribbons.

"I declare," spluttered the Elegant Elephant explosively, "you're a perfect fright. I declare, it's a grumpy shame!"

"Well, don't be gormish," said the Prince, smiling faintly and wiping his cheek with his handkerchief.

"Let me help," begged Peg Amy, falling off Wag's back. "Ozma won't mind a few scratches and what do clothes matter? Anyone would know he was a Prince," she added, taking Pompa's cloak and regarding it ruefully.

Pompa smiled at Peg's earnestness and made her his best bow but Kabumpo still looked anxious. "Everyone's not so smart as you, Peg," he sighed gloomily. "But come along. The main thing is to rescue Ozma and after that perhaps she won't notice your scratches and torn cloak. She'll think you got them fighting the giant," he finished more hopefully.

With a few more of Kabumpo's jeweled pins Peg repaired Pompa's cloak. Then, after tying up Wag's ear, which was badly torn, they started off again.

"What worries me," said Wag, twitching his nose very fast, "what worries me is crossing the Deadly Desert. We're almost to it, you know."

"Never cross deserts till you come to 'em," grunted Kabumpo, with a wink at Peg Amy.

"Oh, all right," sniffed Wag, "but don't be gormish. You know how I detest gormishness!"

97

While Pompa and Peg were laughing over these last remarks a most terrible rumble sounded behind them.

"Now what?" trumpeted Kabumpo, turning about.

"Sheverything's mixed hup!" gulped Wag, putting back his ears. "Hold on to me, Peg!"

Chapter 17 - Meeting the Runaway Country

Everything was mixed up, indeed. Moving toward the little party of rescuers was a huge jagged piece of land, running along on ten tremendous feet and feeling its way with its long wiggly peninsula. The feet raised it several yards above the ground.

"If we crouch down maybe it will run over us," panted Pompa, sliding down Kabumpo's trunk.

"I don't want to be run over," shrilled Wag, beginning to hop in a frenzied circle.

"Stop!" cried the Land in a loud voice, as Wag and Kabumpo started to run.

"Better stop," puffed Kabumpo, his eyes rolling wildly, "or it'll probably fall on us." Trembling in spite of themselves, they stood still and waited for the Land to approach.

"I've often heard of sailors hailing land with joy," gulped Wag, "but this—well, how did it get this way?"

As the Runaway Country drew nearer, its peninsula fairly quivered with excitement and as it reached them it pulled up its front feet and tilted forward to get a better view. Its eyes were two small blue lakes and its mouth a broad bubbling river.

"I claim you by right of discovery," cried the Land in its loud, river voice and before they could make any objection it scooped them up neatly and tossed them on a little hill.

"This is outrageous," spluttered the Elegant Elephant, picking Peg out of some bushes. "We've been kidnapped!"

"Let's jump off!" cried Wag, beginning to hop toward the edge.

"I wouldn't do that," said the Land calmly, "because I'd only run after you again. You might as well settle down and grow up with me. I'm not such a bad little Country," it added quietly, "just a bit rough and uncultivated."

"Well, what's that got to do with us," demanded Kabumpo, staring the Country right in its lake-eyes. "We're on an important mission and we haven't time for this sort of thing at all."

"It's a matter of saving a Princess," cried Pompa impulsively. "Couldn't you, please—

"Let someone else save her," said the Country indifferently, beginning to move off sideways like a crab. "You're the first savages I've found and I'm going to keep you. Not that you're what I'd pick out," it continued ungraciously. "That wooden girl looks uncommonly odd and you two beasts are even queerer. But I'm liberal, I am, and the boy looks all right so far as I can see.

"But, look here," panted Wag, twitching his nose very fast, "this is all wrong. Land is supposed to stand still, isn't it? You've no right to discover us. We don't want to be discovered. Put us off at once—do you hear?"

"Yes, I hear," said the Runaway country gruffly. "And I've heard about enough. Don't anger me," it shrilled warningly. "Remember, I'm a wild, rough Country."

"You're the wildest Country I ever saw, groaned the Elegant Elephant, falling up against a tree. "And of all ridiculous happenings this is the worst!"

"Never mind," whispered Peg Amy, standing on her tip toes to whisper in Kabumpo's huge ear, it's taking us in the right direction, and maybe, if we were very polite—?"

"Go ahead and try it," wheezed Kabumpo, rolling his eyes. "I'm too upset." He hugged the tree again.

So Peg climbed to the top of the little hill and, waving her wooden arms to attract the Country's attention, called cheerfully:

"Yoho, Mr. Land! Where are you going?"

At first the Land only blinked his blue lake-eyes sulkily but, as Peg paid no attention to his ill temper and began making him pretty compliments on his mountains and trees, he gradually cheered up.

"I'm going to be an island," he announced finally. "That's where I'm going. I'm tired of being a hot, dry old undiscovered plateau and I don't intend to stop till I come to the Nonestic Ocean."

"Oh!" groaned Wag, falling over backwards. "We're going to be cast away on a desert island."

Peg held up a warning finger. "What made you want to run away and be an island?" she asked faintly for, even to Peg, things looked serious.

"Well," began the Land, giving itself a hitch, "I lay patiently for years and years waiting to be discovered. Nobody came—not even one little missionary. I kept getting lonelier and lonelier. You see how broken up I am!"

"Yes, we can see that, all right," sniffed Kabumpo.

"And I'm ambitious," continued the Country huskily. "I want to be cultivated and built up like other Kingdoms. So, one day I made up my mind I wouldn't wait any longer but would run off myself and discover some settlers. As I have ten mountains and each has a foot there seemed to be no reason why I shouldn't run away, so I did—and I have!"

The Country rolled its lakes triumphantly at the little party on the hill. "I have found some settlers and I'm looking to you to develop me into a good, modern, up-to-Oz Kingdom. I'm a progressive Country and I expect you to improve and make something out of me," it continued earnestly. "There's gold to be dug out of my mountains, plenty of good farm land to be planted and cities to be built, and—

"What do you think we are?" exploded Kabumpo indignantly. "Slaves?"

"He'll get used to it in time," said the Runaway Country, paying no attention to Kabumpo, "and he'll be useful for drawing logs. Now you," he turned his watery eyes full on Peg Amy, "you seem to be the most sensible one in the party, so I think I shall bestow myself upon you. Of course you're not at all handsome nor regular, but from now on you may consider yourself a Princess and me as your Kingdom."

"Thank you! Thank you very much!" said Peg Amy, hardly knowing what else to say. cried Wag, standing on his head. "I always knew you were a Princess, Peg my dear."

"Oh, hush!" whispered Pompa. "Can't you see it's getting more reasonable? Maybe Peg can persuade it to stop."

"If it doesn't stop soon I'll tear all its trees out by the roots," grumbled Kabumpo under his breath. "Logging, indeed! Great Grump! Here's the Deadly Desert!"

The air was now so hot and choking that Pompa flung himself face down on the cool grass. The Runaway Country did not seem to notice the burning sands and pattered smoothly along on its ten mountain feet.

"Something has to be done, quick," breathed Peg, clasping her hands, "for soon we'll be in Ev."

Pompa, holding his silk handkerchief before his face, had come up beside her and they both looked anxiously for the first signs of the country that held Ruggedo and the giant who had run off with Ozma's palace.

"Oh, Mr. Land," called Peg suddenly.

"Yes, Princess," answered the Country, without slackening its speed.

"Have you thought about feeding us?" asked the Wooden Doll gently. "I don't see any fruit trees or vegetables or chickens and settlers must eat, you know. We ought to have some seeds to plant and some building materials, oughtn't we, if we're going to make you into an up-to-Oz Country?"

"Pshaw!" said the Runaway Country, stopping with a jolt, "I never thought of that. Can't you eat grass and fish? There's fine fish in my lakes."

"Well, I don't eat at all," explained Peg pleasantly, "but Pompa is a Prince and a Prince has to have meat and vegetables and puddings on Sunday—

"And I have to have lettuce and carrots and cabbages, or I won't work!" cried Wag, thumping with his hind feet and winking at Kabumpo. "I'll not dig a single mountain!"

"And I've got to have my ton of hay a day, too!" trumpeted the Elegant Elephant, "or I'll not lug a single log. Pretty poor sort of a Country you are, expecting us to live on grass as if we were donkeys and goats."

The Runaway Country rolled its lakes helplessly from one to the other. "I thought settlers always managed to get a living off the land," it murmured in a troubled voice.

"Not us!" rumbled Kabumpo. "Not enough pie in pioneer to suit this party!"

"Has your Highness anything to suggest?" asked the Country, looking anxiously at Peg.

"Well," said the Wooden Doll slowly, "suppose we stop at the first country we come to and stock up. We could get a few chickens and seeds and saws and hammers and things."

"You'd run away," said the Runaway Country suspiciously. "Not but what I trust you, Princess," he added hastily, "but them." He scowled darkly at Kabumpo and Wag. "I'll not let them out of my sight."

"How our little floating island loves us, chuckled Wag, nudging the Elegant Elephant.

"They won't run away, said Peg softly. "And if they did you could easily catch them again."

"That's so; I'll stop wherever you say," sighed the Country, starting on again.

"What are you going to do?" whispered Pompa, catching Peg's arm.

"I don't know," said Peg honestly, "but perhaps if we can make it stop something will turn up. We're almost across the desert now and that's a big help."

"You're wonderful!" cried Pompa, eyeing Peg gratefully. "How can I ever thank you?"

"Better get your sword ready," said Peg practically, "for we may run into that giant any minute now." Even Kabumpo and Wag had stopped making jokes and were straining their eyes toward Ev.

"Let's all stand together!" gasped Wag breathlessly. Before Peg or Pompa had time to plan, or Kabumpo to reply, the Runaway Country stepped off the desert and swept over the border and into the Kingdom of Ev, making straight for a tall purple mountain.

"Do you see anything that looks like a giant, or a palace?" asked Peg, leaning forward.

"Oh, help!" screamed Wag just then, while Kabumpo gave an ear-splitting trumpet. Peg grasped Pompa and Pompa clutched Peg and no wonder! Directly in front of them were the legs and feet of the most terrible and tremendous giant they had ever imagined. He was sitting on the mountain itself and only a part of him was visible, for his head and shoulders were lost in the clouds.

"What's the matter? What's the matter?" rumbled the Runaway Country, tilting forward slightly so it could see. One look was enough. With a frightened jump, that sent the four travelers hurtling through the air, it began running backwards and in a moment was out of sight.

Peg was the first to recover her senses. Being wood, bumps didn't bother her. She rose stiffly and gazed around her. Pompa's feet were waving feebly from a small clump of bushes. Kabumpo stood swaying near by, while Wag lay over on his side with closed eyes.

"Oh, you poor dears!" murmured Peg, and running over to the bushes she pulled out the Prince of Pumperdink and settled him with his back against a tree. He was much shaken by his high dive from the island, but pulled himself together and patted Peg's wooden hand kindly. By this time Kabumpo had gotten his bearings and came wobbling over.

"You've got a black eye, I see," wheezed the Elegant Elephant bitterly

"Not so very black," said Peg cheerfully. "Are you hurt, Kabumpo?"

The Elegant Elephant felt himself all over with his trunk. "Well, I'm not used to being flung about like a bean bag," he said irritably. Then he lowered his voice hastily, as he caught another glimpse of those dreadful giant feet. "I'll go help Wag," he whispered, backing away quickly.

It took some time to rouse the giant rabbit, but finally he opened his eyes. "I shought I thaw a giant," he muttered thickly. "Hush!" warned Kabumpo. "He's over there." He waved his trunk in the direction of the mountain and began dragging Wag firmly away.

"C'mon over here," he called in a loud whisper to Peg and Pompa. Leaning heavily on Peg Amy the Prince came. Then he gave a cry of distress. "My sword!" he gasped, staring around a bit wildly.

"I'll find it," said Peg obligingly. "You sit still and rest."

"Where's the Magic Box?" coughed Kabumpo, with an uneasy glance in the giant's direction.

Now that they were actually in Ev, the Elegant Elephant began to doubt the wisdom of his plan for killing the monster.

"Gone!" wailed Pompa, feeling in his pocket. "I dropped it when I fell off the Land. What shall we do, Kabumpo?"

"Don't be a Gooch," gulped the Elegant Elephant, but he said it without spirit.

"It's probably around here somewhere." Moving quietly, Kabumpo began to poke about with his trunk.

Just then Peg Amy came flying toward them, her ragged dress fluttering in the breeze.

"Look!" whispered the Wooden Doll, dropping on her knees before them.

In her hands was Glegg's Box of Mixed Magic and it was open!

Chapter 18 - Prince Pompadore Proposes

While Peg and Pompa and the Elegant Elephant eyed the box, Wag, twitching his nose and mumbling very fast under his breath, backed rapidly away. He was not going to run the risk of any more explosions. So anxious was the big rabbit to put a good distance between himself and Glegg's Mixed Magic, that he never realized that he was backing toward the giant till a sharp thump on the back of the head brought him up short.

Trembling in every hair, Wag looked over his shoulder. Stars! He had run into the terrible, five-toed foot of the giant himself. At first Wag was too terrified to move. But suddenly the hair on the back of his neck bristled erect. He peered at the giant's foot more attentively. His eyes snapped and, seizing a stout stick that lay near by, he brought it down with all his might on the giant's toes.

"It's Ruggedo!" screamed Wag, hopping up and down with rage. "And I'll pound his curly toes off. I don't care if he is a giant! I'll pound his curly toes off!"

The stick whistled through the air and whacked the giant's toes again.

Now of course we have known all along that the giant was Ruggedo, but it was a great surprise for the rescuers. Ruggedo was bad enough to deal with as a gnome—but a giant Ruggedo! Horrors!

"Stop him! Stop him!" cried Peg Amy, throwing up her hands and scattering the contents of the box of magic in every direction.

"What are you trying to do?" roared Kabumpo, plunging forward. "Get us all trampled on?"

A muffled cry came down from the clouds and, as Kabumpo dragged Wag back by the ear, something flashed through the air and bounced upon the Elegant Elephant's head. "It's the Scarecrow!" chattered Wag, wriggling from beneath Kabumpo's trunk. Kabumpo opened his eyes and peered down at the limp bundle at his feet As he looked the bundle began to pull itself together. It sat up awkwardly and began clutching itself into shape.

"Where'd you come from?" gasped the Elegant Elephant. Without speaking, the Scarecrow waved his hand upward and rose unsteadily to his feet. Then, catching sight of Peg Amy and Pompadore, the Straw Man bowed politely. Meanwhile Wag, seeing that Kabumpo's attention was diverted, began to sidle back toward Ruggedo.

"Stop!" cried the Scarecrow, running after him. "Are you crazy? Don't you know Ozma's palace is on his head? Every time he moves everyone in the palace tumbles about. Was it you who stirred him up and made him spill me out of the window?"

"I'll wake him up some more, the wicked old scrabble-scratch," muttered Wag, but Kabumpo jerked him back roughly.

"Great Grump!" choked the Elegant Elephant, shaking Wag in his exasperation. "Here we've come all this way to save Princess Ozma and now you want to upset everything."

"That's the way to do it," said the Scarecrow, rolling his eyes wildly.

"Please stop it, Wag," begged Peg Amy, throwing her wooden arms around the big rabbit's neck, and as Pompa added his voice to Peg's, Wag finally threw down his stick.

"Who is that beautiful girl?" asked the Scarecrow of Kabumpo. The Elegant Elephant looked at the Straw Man sharply, to see that he was not poking fun at the Wooden Doll. Finding he was quite serious, he said proudly, "That's Peg Amy, the best little body in Oz. She's under my protection," he added grandly.

Just then Pompa and Peg came over and Wag, who had often seen the Scarecrow in the Emerald City, introduced them all.

"Did I understand you to say you had come to rescue Ozma?" asked the Scarecrow, who could not keep his eyes off the Elegant Elephant.

"Did I understand you to say Ozma's palace was on Ruggedo's head?" shuddered Kabumpo, glancing fearfully in the direction of the mountain.

The Scarecrow nodded vigorously and told in a few words of their terrible journey to Ev and their present perilous position. How the palace had gotten on Ruggedo's head, he admitted was a puzzle to him. Kabumpo and Pompadore listened with amazement, especially to the part where they had threatened Ruggedo with eggs.

"And he's kept still for two days just on account of eggs?" gasped the Elegant Elephant incredulously.

"Well, no," admitted the Scarecrow, wrinkling up his forehead. "A little man came flying through the air the first morning and bumped into the palace and instantly everyone except Scraps and me fell asleep. Ruggedo was put to sleep, too; we could hear him snoring."

"Why, it must have been the Sand Man," breathed Peg Amy. "I have heard he lived near here."

Are they asleep now?" asked Pompa, clutching the Scarecrow's arm. How romantic—thought the Prince of Pumperdink—to rescue and waken a sleeping Princess! But the Scarecrow shook his head. "A few minutes before I fell out they began to wake up and I'd just gone to the window to look for Glinda when Ruggedo gave a howl and ducked his head and here I fell." The Scarecrow spread his hands eloquently and smiled at Peg.

"Has Glinda been here?" asked Kabumpo jealously.

"Yes," said the Scarecrow. "She came this morning and she's been trying all sorts of magic to reduce Ruggedo without harm to the palace."

"Great Grump! Do you hear that?" Kabumpo rolled his eyes anxiously toward the Prince. "If Glinda's magic takes effect before ours then where'll we be! Peg! Where's the box of Mixed Magic?"

"Would you mind telling me," burst out the Scarecrow, who had been examining one after another in the party with a puzzled expression, "would you mind telling me how you happened to know about the palace disappearing; how you got across the sandy desert; how you expect to help us; how he" (with a jerk at Wag) "came to be too large; how she" (with a jerk of his thumb at Peg) "came to be alive; and—

"All in good time; all in good time!" trumpeted Kabumpo testily. "You sound like the Curious Cottabus! The principal thing to do now is to save Ozma. Will Ruggedo stay quiet a little longer?"

"If he's not disturbed," said the Scarecrow, with a meaning glance at Wag.

"Well, my hocks and woop soons!" cried the rabbit indignantly. "Isn't anyone going to punish him? He shook and shook Peg and he meddled with magic and blew up into a giant. He's run off with the palace. Doesn't he deserve a pounding?"

"Friend," said the Scarecrow, "I admire your spirit but my excellent brains tell me that this is a case where an ounce of prevention is worth a pound of cure. But have we the ounce of prevention?"

"Here's the Question Box," announced Peg, who had run off at Kabumpo's first call. "What shall we ask it first?"

"How to save the lovely Princess of Oz," spoke up Pompa, running his hand over his scorched locks. "Where's my crown, Kabumpo?"

Kabumpo fished the crown from his pocket and Pompa set it gravely upon his head as Peg asked the Question Box: "How shall we save the lovely Princess of Oz?"

These maneuvers so astonished the Scarecrow that he lost his balance and fell flat on his nose. When he recovered Peg was clapping her wooden hands and Kabumpo was dancing on three legs.

"You're as good as married, my boy!" cried Kabumpo, thumping the Prince upon the back.

"What is it? What's happened?" gasped the Scarecrow.

"Why, the Question Box says to pour three drops of Trick Tea on Ruggedo's left foot and two on his right and he will then march back to the Emerald City, descend into his cave and, after the palace has settled firmly on its foundations, he will shrink down to his former size," read Peg Amy, holding the Question Box close to her eyes, for the printing was very small.

"Hurrah!" cried the Scarecrow, throwing up his hat. "Peggy, put the kettle on and we'll all have some tea But where'd you get all this magic stuff?" he asked immediately after.

"Out of a box of Mixed Magic," puffed Kabumpo, his little eyes twinkling with anticipation as he watched Peg. First she filled the tiny kettle at a nearby brook; then she lit the little lamp and dropped some of the Trick Tea into the kettle. Bright pink clouds arose from the kettle, as soon as Peg had set it over the flame, and while they waited for it to boil Pompa put another question.

"Has Pumperdink disappeared?" asked the Prince, in a trembling voice.

"N-o," spelled the Question Box slowly, and Kabumpo settled back with a great sigh of relief.

"I told you everything would be all right if you followed my advice," said the Elegant Elephant. "Stand up now and try to forget your black eye You are the Prince of Pumperdink and I am the Elegant Elephant of Oz."

"But why all the ceremony asked the Scarecrow, looking mystified.

Kabumpo only chuckled to himself and, as the Trick Tea was now ready, Peg took the little kettle and began to tip-toe toward Ruggedo.

"I hope it's red hot," grumbled Wag resent-fully. "He's getting off easy, the old scrabble-scratch! Getting off! Say, look here!" He gestured violently to Kabumpo). "If Ruggedo returns to the Emerald City with the palace on his head, where does Pompa come in?" He pointed a trembling paw at the Prince, his nose twitching so fast it made the Scarecrow blink.

"Stop!" trumpeted the Elegant Elephant, plunging after Peg Amy. He reached her just in time.

"I'm no better than Pumper," grunted Kabumpo, mopping his brow with the tail of his robe. "Suppose, after all our hardship, I had allowed Ozma and the palace to get away without giving Pompa a chance to ask her—"

"But we ought to save her as quick as we can," ventured Peg. "Couldn't we hurry back to the Emerald City again?"

"It might be too late," wheezed Kabumpo. "Let-me-see!"

"Hello!" cried the Scarecrow. "Here comes Glinda." As he spoke the swan chariot of the good Sorceress floated down beside the little party.

"Bother!" groaned Kabumpo, as Glinda stepped out.

"Some strangers," called the Scarecrow, gleefully running toward Glinda, "some strangers with a box of Mixed Magic trying to help."

"If we could have a few words with Ozma," put in the Elegant Elephant hastily, "everything would be all right."

Glinda looked at Kabumpo gravely. "It's unlawful to practice magic. You must know that," said the Sorceress sternly.

"But it's not our magic, your Highness," explained Peg Amy, setting down the little kettle. "We found it, and we're only trying to help Ozma."

"Well, in that case," Glinda could not help smiling at the Wooden Doll's quaint appearance, "I shall be glad to assist you, as all of my magic has proved useless."

"Aren't you the Prince of Pumperdink?" she asked, nodding toward Pompa. The Prince bowed in his most princely fashion and assured her that he was and, after a few hasty explanations, Glinda promised to bring Ozma down in her chariot.

"Tell her," trumpeted Kabumpo impressively, as the chariot rose in the air, "tell her that a young Prince waits below!"

While Pompa was still looking after Glinda's chariot, Peg Amy came up to him and extended both her wooden hands.

"I wish you much happiness, Pompa dear," said the Wooden Doll in a low voice.

Pompa pressed Peg's hands gratefully. "If it hadn't been for you I'd never have succeeded. You shall have everything you wish for now, Peg. Why, where are you going?" "Good-bye!" called Peg Amy, trying to keep her voice as cheerful as her painted face, and before anyone could stop her she began to run toward a little grove of trees.

"Come back!" cried the Prince, starting after her.

"Come back!" trumpeted Kabumpo in alarm.

"I'll get her!" coughed Wag, hopping forward jealously. "I've known her the longest."

Pompa and Kabumpo both started to run, too, but just at that minute down swooped the chariot and out jumped Ozma, the lovely little Ruler of Oz.

"At last!" gasped Kabumpo, pushing Pompa forward.

If Ozma was startled by their singular appearance, she was too polite to say so, and she returned Pompa's deep bow with a still deeper curtsey.

"Glinda tells me you have come a long, long way just to help me," said Ozma anxiously. "Is that so?"

"Princess!" cried Pompa, falling on his knee. "I know you are worried about your palace and your Courtiers and your friends. Two drops of that Triple Trick Tea" (he waved at the small kettle) "upon Ruggedo's right foot and three on his left will set everything right!"

"But where did you get it—and why?" Ozma looked doubtfully at the Scarecrow.

"Might as well try it," advised the Scarecrow.

"We will explain everything later," puffed the Elegant Elephant. "Trust old Kabumpo, your Highness, and everything will turn out happily."

"I believe I will," smiled Ozma. "Will you try the Trick Tea, Glinda?"

Glinda took the kettle and poured it exactly as directed. First Ruggedo gave a gusty sigh that blew the clouds about in every direction.

"Look out!" warned Glinda.

Next instant they all fluttered down like a pack of cards, for Ruggedo had taken a step—a giant step that shook the earth as if it had been a block of jelly—and when they had picked themselves up Ruggedo was out of sight, tramping like a giant in a dream, back toward the Emerald City.

"You wait here!" cried Glinda to Ozma. "And I'll follow him!" She sprang into her chariot.

"How do you know he'll go back?" asked the little Ruler of Oz, staring with straining eyes for a glimpse of the giant.

"Because the Question Box said so," chuckled Kabumpo triumphantly.

"Good magic!" approved the Scarecrow. "But where is that charming Peg? I think I'll run find her."

No sooner had the Scarecrow disappeared than Pompa, swallowing very hard, again approached Ozma. But Ozma, still looking after Glinda's vanishing chariot, was hardly aware of the Prince of Pumperdink.

Poor Pompa dropped on his knee (which had a large hole in it by this time) and began mumbling indistinct sentences. Then, as Kabumpo frowned with disgust, the Prince burst out desperately, "Princess, will you marry me?"

"Marry you?" gasped the little Ruler of Oz. "Good gracious, no!"

Chapter 19 - Ozma Takes Things in Hand

Prince Pompadore jumped up quickly.

"I told you she wouldn't!" he choked, looking reproachfully at Kabumpo. "I'm not half good enough."

"He doesn't always look so scratched up and shabby," wheezed Kabumpo breathlessly. "We've been scorched and pinched and kidnapped. We've been through every kind of hardship to save your Highness—and now!" The Elegant Elephant slouched against a tree, the picture of discouragement. He seemed to have forgotten the jewels that were to have won the Princess for Pompa and his threat of running off with her should ,she refuse him.

"Why, you don't even know me," cried Ozma, dismayed by even the thought of marrying; for though the little Ruler of Oz has lived almost a thousand years she is no older than you are and would no more think of marrying than Dorothy or Betsy Bobbin or Trot. Ruling the Kingdom of Oz takes almost all of Ozma's time and in any that is left she wants to play and enjoy herself like any other sensible little girl. For Ozma is only a little girl fairy after all.

"I'm not going to marry anybody!" she declared stoutly. Then, because she really was touched by Pompa's woebegone appearance, she asked more kindly, "Why did you want to marry me especially?"

"Because you are the properest Princess in Oz," groaned the Prince, leaning disconsolately against Kabumpo. "Because if we don't Pumperdink will disappear and my poor old father and my mother and everyone.

"Not to speak of us," gulped the Elegant Elephant.

"But where is Pumperdink, and who said it would disappear?" asked Ozma in amazement.

"And how did you happen to have this Trick Tea and come to rescue me?"

"The Prince always rescues the Princess he intends to marry," said Kabumpo wearily. "I should think you'd know that."

"Well, I'm very grateful, and I'll do anything I can except marry you," exclaimed Ozma, who was beginning to feel very much interested in this strange pair.

"Thank you," said Kabumpo stiffly, for he was deeply offended. "Thank you, but We must be going. Come along, Pompa."

"Don't be a Gooch!" This time it was Pompa who spoke. "I'm going to tell her everything!"

And Pompa, being as I have told you before the most charming Prince in the world, made Ozma a comfortable throne of green boughs and, throwing himself at her feet, poured out the whole story of their adventures, beginning with the birthday party and the mysterious scroll. He told of their meeting with Peg Amy and Wag and ended up with the ride upon the Runaway Country.

Kabumpo stood by, swaying sulkily. He was very much disappointed in the Princess of Oz. He felt that she had no proper appreciation of his Pompa's importance. "I'm going to find Peg," he called finally. "She's got more sense than any of you," he wheezed under his breath as he swept grandly out of sight.

Ozma put both hands to her head as Pompa finished his recital and really it was enough to puzzle any fairy. Scrolls, live Wooden Dolls, a giant rabbit, a mysterious magician threatening disappearances and Ruggedo's wicked use of the box of Mixed Magic.

"Goodness!" cried the little Ruler of Oz. "I wish the Scarecrow would come back. He's so clever I'm sure he could help us; but first you had better bring me the magic box."

Pompa rose slowly and, picking up all the little flasks and boxes that had spilled out when Wag pounded Ruggedo, he put them back into the casket and handed it to Ozma. She examined the contents as curiously as the others had done. The Expanding Extract was the only thing missing, for Ruggedo had poured the whole bottle over his head. The Question Box seemed to Ozma the most wonderful of all of Glegg's magic.

"Why, all we have to do is to ask this box questions," she cried in excitement. "Has my palace reached the Emerald City?" she asked breathlessly.

"Shake it three times," said Pompa, as Ozma looked in vain for her answer.

"Yes," stated the box after the third shake, and Ozma sighed with relief.

"I suppose you asked it if I were the Proper Princess mentioned in the scroll," she said, a bit shyly.

The Prince shook his head. "Knew without asking," said Pompa heavily.

"Do you mean to say you never asked it that?" gasped Ozma in disbelief. "Why, I am surprised at you." And before Pompa could object she shook the little box briskly. "Who is the Princess that Pompa must marry?" she demanded anxiously.

"The Princess of Sun Top Mountain," flashed the Question Box promptly. Then, as an afterthought, it added, "Trust the mirror and golden door knob!"

"Now, you see!" cried Ozma, jumping up in delight. "I wasn't the Proper Princess at all!"

Pompa smiled faintly, but without enthusiasm. The thought of hunting another Princess was almost too much. "I wish I could just take Peg Amy and Wag and go back to Pumperdink without marrying anybody," he choked bitterly.

"Now, don't give up," advised Ozma kindly. "It was very wrong of Glegg to cause you all this trouble. I'm going to keep his box of Mixed Magic and take away all his powers when I find him, but until I do, you'll have to follow directions. Oh mercy! What's that?"

They both ducked and turned around in a hurry, as a terrific thumping sounded behind them.

"It's the Runaway Country again," cried Pompa, seizing Ozma's hands in distress, "and it's caught all the others."

The Scarecrow had climbed a tree, and was waving to them wildly as the Country galloped nearer. "Might as well come aboard," he called genially. "This is a fast Country—no arguing with it at all."

Ozma looked helplessly at Pompa, and the Prince had only time to grasp her more firmly when the Country scooped them neatly into the air. Down they tumbled, beside Peg Amy and Wag and the Elegant Elephant.

"What do you mean by this?" demanded Ozma, as soon as she regained her breath.

"Don't you know this lady is the Ruler of all Oz?" cried Pompa warningly.

"Peg's the Ruler of me," replied the Country calmly. "I nearly lost her once, but now I've caught her and all the rest, and I am not going to stop until I've reached the Nonestic Ocean—giants or no giants."

Ozma had been somewhat prepared for the Runaway Country by Pompa's description, but she had never dreamed it would dare to run off with her. While Peg Amy began to coax it to stop, she took out Glegg's little Question Box.

"How shall I stop this Country?" she whispered anxiously.

"Spin around six times and cross your fingers," directed the Question Box.

This Ozma proceeded to do, much to the agitation of the Scarecrow, who thought she had taken leave of her senses. But next instant the Country came to a jolting halt.

"Peg, Princess Peg!" shrieked the Island. "I am bewitched, I can't move a step!"

"Then everybody off," shouted the Scarecrow, jerking a branch of a tree as if he were a conductor. "End of the line everybody off!" And they lost no time tumbling off the wild little Country.

"It seems too bad to leave it," said Peg Amy regretfully, picking herself up.

"It threw us off without any feeling or consideration when it saw Ruggedo," sniffed Kabumpo. "Therefore it has no claims on us whatsoever."

"But couldn't you do something for it?" asked Peg, approaching Ozma timidly. "It's so tired of being a plateau. Couldn't you let it be an island, and find someone to settle on it? I wouldn't mind going," she added generously.

"You shall do nothing of the sort," cried Kabumpo angrily. "You're going back to Pumperdink with Pompa and me."

"She's going with me," cried Wag. "Aren't you, Peg?"

"You seem to be a very popular person, smiled Ozma. "While a Country has no right to run away, and while I never heard of one doing it before, I've no objections to its being an island. It's running off with people I object to." She looked the Country sternly in its lake-eyes.

"But I can't move," screamed the Country, tears streaming down its hill, "and I've got to have somebody to settle me."

"Oh! Here's Glinda," shouted the Scarecrow, tossing up his hat. "Now we shall know what's happened to Ruggedo."

Leaving the Country for a moment, they all ran to welcome the good Sorceress of Oz. Glinda's reports were most satisfactory. Ruggedo had walked straight back to the Emerald City, stepped into the yawning cavern, and immediately the palace had settled firmly upon its old foundations. Then had come a muffled explosion, and when Glinda and Dorothy ran through the secret passage, which had been discovered meanwhile by the Soldier with the Green Whiskers, they saw Ruggedo, shrunken to his former size, sitting angrily on his sixth rock of history.

"I have locked him up in the palace," finished Glinda, "and I strongly advise your Highness to punish him severely."

Ozma sighed. "What would you do?" she asked, appealing to the Scarecrow. So many things had come up for her attention and advice in the last few hours that the little fairy ruler felt positively dizzy.

"Let's all sit down in a circle and think," proposed the Scarecrow cheerfully. This they all did except Kabumpo, who stood off glumly by himself. Peg was looking anxiously at Pompadore, for the Elegant Elephant had told her of Ozma's refusal, and wondering sadly what she could do to help, when the Scarecrow bounced up impulsively.

"I have it," chuckled the Straw Man. "Let's send Ruggedo off on the Runaway Country. He deserves to be banished and, if Ozma makes the Country an Island, he can do no harm."

Here Ozma had to stop and explain to Glinda about the Country that wanted to be an Island, and after a short consultation they decided to take the Scarecrow's advice.

"Just as soon as I reach the Emerald City I'll put on my Magic Belt and wish him onto the Island," declared Ozma. "And I think we'd better go right straight back," she added thoughtfully, "for it's growing darker every minute and Dorothy will be anxious to hear everything that's happened."

"Now you—Ozma tapped Pompadore gently on the arm—You must start at once for Sun Top Mountain. I'm going to ask the Question Box just where it is.

Pompa sighed deeply, and when Ozma consulted the Question Box as to the location of Sun Top Mountain, it stated that this Kingdom was in the very centre of the North Winkie Country. "That's fine," said Ozma, clapping her hands. "I'll have the Runaway Country carry you over the Deadly Desert, and as soon as you have married the Princess you must bring her to see me in the Emerald City."

"What's all this?" demanded Kabumpo, pricking up his ears.

"The Question Box says I must marry the Princess of Sun Top Mountain," said Pompa, getting up wearily.

"Well, Great Grump, why couldn't it have said so before?" asked Kabumpo shrilly.

"You never asked it," snapped Wag, twitching his nose. "I told you Ozma wasn't the Princess mentioned in the scroll!"

"Now don't quarrel," begged Peg Amy, jumping up hastily. "There's still plenty of time to save Pumperdink. Come along, Pompa."

"That's right," said Ozma, smiling approvingly at Peg. "And when Pompa finds his Princess you must come and live with me in the Emerald City, for as Ruggedo was responsible for bringing you to life, I want to take care of you always."

Peg Amy dropped a curtsey and promised to come, but she didn't feel very cheerful about it. Then as Ozma was anxious to get back to the Emerald City, they all hurried to Runaway Country.

"You are to take these travelers across the Deadly Desert," said Ozma, addressing the Runaway Country quite sternly, "and you are to set them down in the Winkie Country. If you do this I will restore your moving power again and give you a little gnome for King. Then you may run off to the Nonestic Ocean as soon as ever you wish."

"I want Peg," pouted the Country, "but if that's the best you can do I suppose I'll have to stand it." After a little more grumbling it agreed to Ozma's terms. Wearily, Kabumpo, Wag, Peg and Pompa climbed aboard and then Ozma spun around six times in the opposite direction and immediately the Country found itself able to move again.

"Good-bye!" called Ozma, as she and the Scarecrow jumped into Glinda's chariot. "Good-bye and good luck!"

"Good-bye!" called Peg, waving her old torn bonnet.

"Good riddance," grumbled the Country gruffly and, turning sideways, began running toward the Deadly Desert.

Chapter 20 - The Proper Princess is Found!

Is the mirror safe, and have you still got the gold door knob?" asked Pompa, as the Country swung out onto the Deadly Desert. "The Question Box said I was to trust them, you know."

"And by what right did Ozma take that box?" wheezed Kabumpo irritably, as he felt in his pocket to see whether the magic articles were still there. "That's gratitude for you! We find Glegg's box of Mixed Magic and rescue her, and off she goes with all our magic, leaving us to the tender mercies of a Runaway Country!"

"You find the box!" shrilled Wag. "Well, I like that!"

"Oh, what difference does it make?" groaned Pompa, stretching out upon the ground. They were all completely exhausted by the day's adventures and as cross as three sticks—all except Peg Amy, who never was cross.

"I shall marry this Princess and save my country, but I'm going away as soon as the wedding is over and spend the rest of my life in travel," announced Pompa gloomily.

"Don't blame you," rubbled the Elegant Elephant with a sniff.

"Ah, now!" laughed Peg. "That doesn't sound like you, Pompa. Why, maybe this Princess will be so lovely you'll want to carry her straight back to Pumperdink."

"I think Princesses are a great bore," said Wag with a terrific yawn. "I prefer plain folks like Peg and the Scarecrow."

"You're all hungry, that's what's the matter," chuckled the Wooden Doll. "When you've had some supper you'll be just as anxious to find the Princess of Sun Top Mountain as you were to find Ozma. Here's the Winkie Country now, and there's a star for good luck."

Peg waved toward the green fields with one hand and toward the clouds with the other. It was dusk now and just one star twinkled cheerily in the sky.

"I'll set you down, but I'm not going away, said the Runaway Country determinedly, "for if that little old gnome doesn't turn up I'm going to catch you all again."

"Ozma never forgets. She'll keep her promise," said Peg. "And you must do just as she told you to do for she has some powerful magic and can send you right back to where you came from."

"Can she?" gulped the Country anxiously.

"You might wait a while, though," suggested Pompa darkly. "After I've seen this new Princess a Runaway Country might be very good thing."

"Well, you can't expect her to marry you if you talk that way, said Peg warningly, as the Country came to a stop in a huge field of daisies.

"I'll wait," it said hopefully, as the four travelers swung themselves down.

"I wonder if we are in the North Central part," murmured Peg Amy, looking around anxiously. Now it happened the Country had crossed the Deadly Desert slantwise and although none of the party knew it they were scarcely a mile from Sun Top Mountain.

"I see a garden!" cried Wag, twitching his nose hungrily. "Come on, Prince, let's find some supper." With head down and dragging his feet, Pompa followed Wag. Kabumpo began jerking snappishly at some tree tops and Peg Amy sat down to think.

"I wish," thought the Wooden Doll, looking up at the bright star, "I wish I might have asked the box one little question." Peg Amy looked so solemn that Kabumpo stopped eating and regarded her anxiously.

"What's the matter?" asked the Elegant Elephant gruffly; for he quite counted on Peg's cheerfulness.

"I was thinking about it again," admitted Peg apologetically. "About being alive before. I'm sure I was alive before I was a doll, Kabumpo. I think I was a person, like Pompa," she continued softly.

"You're much better as you are," said the Elegant Elephant uneasily, for it had just occurred to him that the Magic Mirror would tell Peg who she was as well as the Question Box. But should he let her look in it? That was the question. Poor, tired old Kabumpo shifted from one foot to the other as he tried to make up his mind. Two huge drops of perspiration ran down his trunk. What good would it do? he reasoned finally. Suppose it told something awful! It couldn't change her and it might make her unhappy. No, he would not let Peg look in the mirror.

"How would you like to have this pearl bracelet?" he asked in an embarrassed voice.

"Why, Kabumpo, I'd just adore it!" cried Peg, springing up in a hurry. "And I'm not going to worry about being alive any more, for everyone is so lovely to me I ought to be the happiest person in Oz."

"You are," puffed Kabumpo, clumsily slipping the bracelet on Peg's wooden arm, "and if we ever get back to Pumperdink you shall have as many silk dresses as you want and— The rest of the sentence was smothered in a hug.

Peg Amy was growing fonder and fonder of pompous old Kabumpo and by the time he had recovered his breath Wag and the Prince came ambling back together. They had found an orchard and a kitchen garden and as they were no longer hungry, both were more cheerful.

"Let's play scop hotch," suggested Wag amiably. "I'm tired of hunting Princesses." There was a smooth patch of sand under the trees and Wag hopped over and began marking out the squares with his paw.

"Scop hotch!" laughed Pompa, while Peg gave a skip of delight.

"Play if you want to," wheezed Kabumpo, shaking himself wearily, "I feel about as playful as a stone lion. Besides, hop scotch isn't an elephant game."

Peg, Wag and Pompa began to hop scotch for dear life. Peg often tumbled over, for it is hard to keep your balance on wooden legs, but it was Peg who won in the end and Wag crowned her with daisies. "I wish we could go on just as we are, gasped Pompa, mopping his face with his silk handkerchief. "We're all good chums and, if it weren't for Pumperdink's disappearing, we might travel all over Oz and have no end of adventures together."

"Speaking of disappearing," said Kabumpo, opening one eye, for he had dozed off during the game, "I suppose we'd better be starting if we're to save the Kingdom at all."

"Good-bye to pleasure," sighed Pompa, as Kabumpo lifted him to his back. "Good-bye to everything!"

"Oh, cheer up," begged Peg, settling herself on Wag's back.

"Hurrah! Hurrah! Hurrah!" A large yellow bird rose suddenly from a near-by bush and flapped its wings over Pompa's head. "Hurrah! Hurrah!"

"Shoo! Get away!" grumbled Kabumpo crossly. "What are you cheering about?"

"She said to," cawed the bird, darting over Peg Amy's head. "Hurrah! Hurrah! Hurrah! Let me teach you how to be cheerful in three chirps. First, think of what you might have been; next, think of what you are; then think of what you are going to be. Do you get it?" The bird put its head on one side and regarded them anxiously.

"He might have been King of Oz, instead of which he is only a lost Prince, and he's going to be married to a mountain top Princess. Do you see anything cheerful about that?" demanded Kabumpo angrily. "Clear out! We'll do our own cheering."

"Shall I go?" asked the Hurrah Bird, looking very crestfallen and pointing its claw at Peg Amy.

"Maybe you can tell us the way to Sun Top Mountain," said Peg politely.

"You can see it from the other side of the hill," replied the Hurrah Bird. "I'll give you a few hurrahs for luck. Hurrah! Hurrah! Hur-rah!"

"Oh, go away," grumbled Kabumpo.

"Not till you look at my nest. Did you ever see a Hurrah Bird's nest?" he chirped brightly.

"Let's look at it," said Pompa, smiling in spite of himself. The Hurrah Bird preened itself proudly as they peered through the bushes. Surely it had the gayest nest ever built, for it was woven of straw of many colors, and hung all over the near-by branches were small Oz flags. In the nest three little yellow chicks were growing up into Hurrahs and they chirped faintly at the visitors.

"Remember," called the Father Hurrah, as they bade him good-bye, "you can always be cheerful in three chirps if you think of what you might have been, what you are, and what you are going to be. Hurrah! Hurrah! Hurrah!"

107

"There's something in what you've said," chuckled Wag. "Good-bye!"

The moon had come up brightly and even Kabumpo began to feel more like himself. "There's a lot to be learned by traveling, eh, Wag?" He winked at the rabbit, who was just behind him. "Let's see—somersaults for sums—never be gormish—and now, how to be cheerful in three chirps. Hurrah! Hurrah! Hurrah!" The Elegant Elephant began to plow swiftly through the daisy field, so that in almost no time they reached the top of the little hill and as they did so Peg gave a little scream of delight. As for the others, they were simply speechless.

A purple mountain rose steeply ahead, and set like a crown upon its summit was a glittering gold castle, the loveliest, laciest gold castle you could imagine, with a hundred fluttering pennants. All down the mountain side spread its lovely gardens, its golden arbors and flower bordered paths.

"I've seen it before!" cried the Wooden Doll softly, but no one heard her. Pompa drew a deep breath, for the castle, shimmering in the moonlight, seemed almost too beautiful to believe.

"Whe-ew!" whistled Wag, breaking the silence, "The Princess of Tun Sop Wountain must be wonderful."

"Shall we start up now?" gasped Kabumpo, swinging his trunk nervously.

"I don't believe she'll ever marry me. Let's don't go at all," muttered the Prince of Pumperdink in a shaky voice.

"Oh, come on!" called Wag, who was curious to see the owner of so grand a castle.

"But we mustn't go, Wag," gasped Peg Amy. "How would it look to have a shabby old doll tagging along when he's trying to talk to the Princess!" "

If Peg doesn't go, I'm not going," declared Pompa stubbornly.

"You're just as good as any Princess," said Kabumpo, "and I'm not going without you, either."

As the Elegant Elephant refused to budge and there seemed no other way out of it, Peg Amy finally consented and the four adventurers started fearfully up the winding path, almost expecting the castle to disappear before they reached the top, so unreal did it seem in the moonlight. There was no one in the garden but there were lights in the castle windows. "Just as if they expected us," said the Elegant Elephant, as they reached the tall gates. Pompa opened the gates and next instant they were standing before the great castle door.

"Shall we knock?" chattered Wag, his eyes sticking out with excitement.

"No! Wait a minute," begged the Prince, who was becoming more agitated every minute.

"Here's the mirror and the door knob," quavered Kabumpo. "Didn't the Question Box say to trust them? Why, look here, Pompa, my boy, it fits!" Clumsily, Kabumpo held up the glittering door knob he had brought all the way from Pumperdink; then he slipped it easily on the small gold bar projecting from the door.

But instead of looking joyful Pompa groaned dismally. He started to protest but Kabumpo had already turned the knob and they found themselves in a glittering gold court room.

"Now for the Princess," puffed Kabumpo, looking around with his twinkling little eyes. "Here, take the mirror, Pompa." The room was empty, although brilliantly lighted, and the Prince stood uncertainly in the very center. Suddenly, with a determined little cry, Pompa rushed over to Peg Amy, who stood leaning against a tall gold chair.

"Peg," choked Pompa, dropping on his knees beside the Wooden Doll, "I'll have to find some other way to save Pumperdink. I'm not going to marry this Princess and have you taken away from me. You're a proper enough Princess for me and we'll just go back to Pumperdink and be—

"The mirror! Look in the mirror!" screamed Wag, who was sitting beside Peg Amy.

Unconsciously, Pompa had held out the gold mirror and Peg, leaning over to listen, had looked directly into it. Above Peg's pleasant reflection in the mirror they read these startling and important words:

This is Peg Amy, Princess of Sun Top Mountain.

While Pompa stared with round eyes the words faded out and this new legend formed in the glass:

The Proper Princess is Found! This is the Proper Princess.

"I always knew you were a Princess," cried Wag, turning a somersault.

The big rabbit had just come right-side-up, when a still more amazing thing happened. The wooden body of Peg melted before their eyes and in its place stood the loveliest little Princess in the world. And yet, with all her beauty, she was strangely like the old Peg. Her eyes had the same merry twinkle and her mouth the same pleasant curve.

"Oh!" cried Princess Peg, holding her arms out to her friends. "Now I am the happiest person in Oz!"

Chapter 21 - How it All came About

Before Pompa had time to rise, a tall, richly clad old nobleman rushed into the room.

"Peg!" cried the old gentleman, clasping the Princess in his arms. "You are back! At last the enchantment is broken!"

For moment the two forgot all about Pompa and the others. Then, gently disengaging herself, Peg seized the Prince's hands and drew him to his feet.

"Uncle," she said breathlessly, holding to Pompa with one hand and waving with the other at Kabumpo and Wag, "here are the friends responsible for my release. This is my Uncle Tozzyfog," she explained quickly, and impulsively Uncle Tozzyfog sprang to his feet and embraced each in turn—even Kabumpo.

"Sit down," begged the old nobleman, sinking into a golden chair and mopping his head with a flowered silk kerchief.

Pompa, who could not take his eyes from his new and wonderful Peg Amy, dropped into another chair. Kabumpo leaned limply against a pillar and Wag sat where he was, his nose twitching faster than ever and his ears stuck out straight behind him.

"You are probably wondering about the change in Peg," began Uncle Tozzyfog, as the Princess perched on the arm of his chair, "so I'll try to tell my part of the story. Three years ago an ugly old peddler climbed the path to Sun Top Mountain. He said his name was Glegg and, forcing his way into the castle, he demanded the hand of my niece in marriage."

Peg shuddered and Uncle Tozzyfog blew his nose violently at the distressing memory. Then, speaking rapidly and pausing every few minutes to appeal to the Princess, he continued the story of Peg's enchantment. Naturally the old peddler had been refused and thrown out of the castle. That night as Uncle Tozzyfog prepared to carve the royal roast, there came an explosion, and when the courtiers had picked themselves up Peg Amy was nowhere to be seen, and only a threatening scroll remained to explain the mystery. Glegg, who was really a powerful magician, infuriated by Uncle Tozzyfog's treatment, had changed the little Princess into a tree.

"Know ye," began the scroll quite like the one that had spoiled Pompa's birthday, "know ye that unless ye Princess of Sun Top Mountain consents to wed J. Glegg she shall remain a tree forever, or until two shall call and believe her to be a Princess.

The whole castle had been plunged into utmost gloom by this terrible happening, for Peg was the kindliest, best loved little Princess any Kingdom could wish for. Lord Tozzyfog and nearly all the Courtiers set out at once to search for the little tree and for two years they wandered over Oz, addressing every hopeful tree as Princess, but never happening on the right one. Finally they returned in despair and Sun Top Mountain, once the most cheerful Kingdom in all Oz, had become the gloomiest. There was no singing, nor dancing—no happiness of any kind. Even the flowers had drooped in the absence of their little Mistress.

"Why didn't you appeal to Ozma?" demanded Pompa at this point in the story.

"Because in another scroll Glegg warned us that the day we told Ozma, Peg Amy would cease to even be a tree," explained Uncle Tozzyfog hoarsely.

"Then how did she become a doll? Tell me that, Uncle Fozzytog," gulped Wag, raising one paw.

"She'll have to tell you that herself," confessed Peg's uncle, "for that's all of the story I know."

So here Peg took up the story herself. The morning after her transformation into a tree Glegg had appeared and asked her again to marry him. "I was a little yellow tree, in the Winkie Country, not far from the Emerald City," explained Peg, "and every day for two months Glegg appeared and gave me the power of speech long enough to answer his question. And each time he asked me to marry him but I always said 'No!' " The Princess shook her yellow curls briskly.

"One afternoon there came a one-legged sailor man and a little girl." Even Kabumpo shuddered as Peg Amy told how Cap'n Bill had cut down the little tree, pared off all the branches and carved from the trunk a small wooden doll for Trot.

"It didn't hurt," Princess Peg hastened to explain as she caught Pompa's sorrowful expression, "and being a doll was a lot better than being a tree. I could not move or speak but I knew what was going on and life in Ozma's palace was cheerful and interesting. Only, of course, I longed to tell Ozma or Trot of my enchantment. I missed dear Uncle Tozzyfog and all the people of Sun Top Mountain. Then, as you all know, I was stolen by the old gnome and after Ruggedo carried me underground I forgot all about being a Princess and remembered nothing of this." Peg glanced lovingly around the room. "I only felt that I had been alive before. So you!" Peg jumped up and flung one arm around Wag, "and you," she flung the other around Pompa, "saved me by calling me a Princess and really believing I was one. And you!" Peg hastened over to Kabumpo, who was rolling his eyes sadly. "You are the darlingest old elephant in Oz! See, I still have the necklace and bracelet!" And sure enough on Peg's round arm and white neck gleamed the jewels the Elegant Elephant had generously given when he thought her only a funny Wooden Doll.

109

"Oh!" groaned Kabumpo. "Why didn't I let you look in the mirror before? No wonder you kept remembering things."

"But why did Glegg send the threatening scroll to Pumperdink three years after he'd enchanted Peg?" asked Wag, scratching his head.

"Because!" shrilled a piercing voice, and in through the window bounded a perfectly dreadful old man. It was Glegg himself!

"Because!" screeched the wicked magician, advancing toward the little party with crooked finger, "when that meddling old sailor touched Peg with his knife I lost all power over her; because my Question Box told me that Pompadore of Pumperdink could bring about her disenchantment and he has. I made it interesting for you, didn't I? There isn't another magician in Oz can put scrolls up in cakes and roasts like I can nor mix magic like mine. Ha! Ha!" Glegg threw back his head and rocked with enjoyment. "You have had all the trouble and I shall have all the reward!"

Everyone was so stunned by this terrible interruption that no one made a move as Glegg sprang toward Peg Amy. But before he had reached the Princess there was a queer sulphurous explosion and the magician disappeared in a cloud of green smoke. They rubbed their eyes and as the smoke cleared they saw Trot, the little girl who had played with Peg Amy when she was a Wooden Doll.

"Ozma," explained Trot breathlessly, for she had come on a fast wish.

After following the adventures of Pompa and Peg in the Magic Mirror, and as the magician had tried to snatch the Princess, Ozma had transported him by means of her Magic Belt to the Emerald City, and sent Trot to bring her best wishes the whole party.

"I'm sorry I didn't make you a prettier dress when you were my doll," said Trot, seizing Peg Amy's hand impulsively, "but you see I didn't know you were a Princess."

"But you guessed my name," said Peg softly.

There were so many explanations to be made and so many things to wonder over and exclaim about, that it seemed as if they could never stop talking.

Uncle Tozzyfog rang all the bells in the castle tower and stepping out on a balcony told the people of Sun Top Mountain of the return of Princess Peg Amy. Then the servants were summoned and such a feast as only an Oz cook can prepare was started in the castle kitchen. The Courtiers came hurrying back, for during Peg's absence Uncle Tozzyfog had lived alone in the castle. Yes, the Courtiers came back and the people of Sun Top Mountain poured into the castle in throngs and nearly overwhelmed the rescuers by the enthusiasm of their thanks.

Kabumpo had never been so admired and complimented in his whole elegant life. As for Wag, his speech grew more mixed up every minute. At last, when the Courtiers and Uncle Tozzyfog had run off to dress for the grand banquet, and after Trot had been magically recalled by Ozma to the Emerald City, the four who had gone through so many adventures together were left alone.

"Well, how about Pumperdink, my boy?" chuckled Kabumpo, with a wave of his trunk. "Are we going to let the old Kingdom disappear or not?"

"It is my duty to save my country," said Pompa loftily. Then, with a mischievous smile at Peg Amy, "Don't you think so, Princess?" Peg Amy looked merrily at the Elegant Elephant and then took Pompa's hand.

"Yes, I do," said the Princess of Sun Top Mountain.

"Then, you will marry me?" asked Pompa, looking every inch a Prince in spite of his singed head and torn clothes.

"We must save Pumperdink, you know," sighed Peg softly.

"Three cheers for the Princess of Pumperdink! May she be as happy as the day is short!" cried Wag in his impulsive way.

Uncle Tozzyfog was as pleased as Wag when he heard the news, and Pompa, attired in a royal gold embroidered robe, was married to Peg Amy upon the spot, with much pomp and magnificence.

Never before was there such rejoicing—a merrier company or a happier bride. Kabumpo, arrayed in two gold curtains borrowed for the happy occasion, had never appeared more elegant and Wag was everywhere at once and simply overwhelmed with attention.

That same night a messenger was dispatched to Pumperdink to carry the good news and the next morning Pompa and Peg set out for the Emerald City, the Princess riding proudly on Wag and Pompadore on Kabumpo. Knowing the whole four as you now do, you will believe me when I say that their journey was the merriest and most delightful ever recorded in the merry Kingdom of Oz.

After a short visit with Ozma and another to the King and Queen of Pumperdink they all returned to Sun Top Mountain, where they are living happily at this very minute.

Chapter 22 - Ruggedo's Last Rock

There are only a few more mysteries to clear up before we leave for a time the jolly Kingdom of Oz. Ruggedo, much shaken by his terrible experiences with Glegg's magic, confessed everything to Ozma on her return to the Emerald City You can imagine the surprise of the little Fairy Ruler on learning how her palace had come to be impaled upon the spikes of the wicked old gnome's gray head.

"He will never re-form," said Tik Tok mournfully, as Ruggedo finished his recital. The bad little gnome assured Ozma that he had reformed and begged for another chance, but this time Ozma knew better, and putting on her Magic Belt she whispered a few secret words. Then they all hurried over to the Magic Picture, for they knew that Ruggedo had been transported to a safe place at last. The picture showed the Runaway Country rushing along faster than an express train and dancing up and down on its highest hill was the furious old King of the Gnomes. They watched until the Country plunged joyfully into the Nonestic Ocean and, when it was almost in the middle, Ozma stopped it by the magic spinning process and it became Ruggedo's Island.

"Well," sighed Dorothy as they turned from the picture, "I guess that will be Ruggedo's last rock!"

"He's rocked in the cradle of the deep now, chuckled the Scarecrow. "And I hope it quiets him down. They ought to make a good pair—that bad little Island and that bad little King," he added reflectively.

Then Ozma proposed that they follow the adventures of Peg and Pompa, having so satisfactorily disposed of Ruggedo. How she transported Glegg just in time to save the Princess you already know. But what happened to Glegg himself is interesting. When the old magician had asked his Question Box how to regain control over Peg again it had directed him to bury his Mixed Magic under the Emerald City and in two years to send the scroll to Pumperdink. So Glegg had tunneled out the cave under Ozma's palace and left his magic in what he supposed was a very safe place. It had been a great hardship to do without it for two years, but he wanted Peg so badly that he actually did this, never dreaming that Ruggedo had moved in and discovered his treasures. The Question Box had told the exact day Peg would be disenchanted and all that long two years Glegg had waited, hidden in a forest near Sun Top Mountain.

As he knew nothing of the discovery of his magic box, no one was more surprised than he to find himself, just as he was on the point of seizing Peg, transported to the Emerald City.

While Sir Hokus of Pokes held the struggling Glegg, Ozma asked the Question Box how to deal with him. Everybody crowded around the little Fairy Ruler to hear what the wicked old magician's fate was to be.

"Give him a taste of his own magic," directed the Question Box. "Make him drink a cup of his Triple Trick Tea." This Ozma did, although it took fourteen people to get Glegg to drink it. But, stars! No sooner had the liquid touched his lips than the miserable old magician went off with a loud explosion!

The box of Mixed Magic was carefully put away in Ozma's gold safe and then the whole company—Ozma, Dorothy, Sir Hokus, the Scarecrow and all the celebrities devoted themselves to setting the topsy turvy palace to rights, for they knew by the Magic picture that Pompa and Peg Amy were coming to visit them.

"Glegg, Glegg, shake a leg And never more, Sir, bother Peg!"

shouted Scraps, as she swept up the black soot Glegg had left when he exploded. And he never did.

The End

The Wishing Horse of Oz

by Ruth Plumly Thompson

Chapter 1 - The King of Skampavia

"Is this all?" The King of Skampavia frowned at the great stack of bags, bales, crates and carriers heaped around his throne. Leaning forward, he gingerly extracted a fig from one of the baskets and popped it into his enormous mouth. "Pah, dry as a blotter," spluttered the red-faced ruler, gritting his teeth with disgust, "and look at those cocoanuts, no bigger round than a baby's rattle!" Leaping off his throne, he began kicking at the baskets of vegetables and bales of cotton and other merchandise. "What dusty junk is this?" he raged, glaring furiously at Pinny Penny, his patient Prime Minister. "How dare they send me such stuff?" Clasping and unclasping his hands nervously, Pinny Penny nevertheless spoke up boldly.

"Because they have nothing better, your Majesty. What can our poor subjects do with land so unprofitable and barren? Then, not only must they produce enough for their own needs, but are required by the law to give one-third of all they raise to the crown."

"And why not?" blustered Skamperoo, settling back argumentatively on his throne. "I am the KING! You can't get around that, you know."

"No," sighed Pinny Penny, and drawing aside one of the shabby curtains, he looked sorrowfully out into the courtyard.

"What's all that racket?" demanded his Master as a medley of shouts, roars, and dull thuds came rolling up to them. Forgetting his anger for a moment, he bounded to his feet and came across the room to look over Pinny Penny's shoulder.

"A slight argument seems to have arisen among the Supervisors," murmured Pinny Penny resignedly.

Now Skampavia, I must tell you, is roughly divided into seven counties, and over each county Skamperoo had set a Supervisor whose duty it was to govern the province and to turn over to him one-third of all produce and merchandise in that county. To save time and easily identify them, the supervisors were known by the size of the counties they governed. For instance, the Supervisor of the First County, which was one mile wide and ten miles long, was called Onebyten; the Supervisor of the Second County Twobyfour; and the others were variously known as Threebysix, Ninebyfive, Eightby-eight, Fivebynine, and Fourbyseven. Twice a year the Supervisors rode into the capital with their tribute, and now, down in the courtyard, the seven tremendous Skampavians were in a perfect pitched battle, helped out by all the guards and palace servants.

"Argument!" roared the King, slapping Pinny Penny rudely on the shoulder. "It's a fight, and you know it! Ho, ho! Just look at the good-for-nothing rascals. I tell you, old Two Pins, however poorly they serve us as farmers and merchants, our Skampavians can certainly fight. And who says I'm too hard on them? Have I not given every man Jack a dress uniform and gun and made them learn military drilling and marching at the Royal College?"

"And what use is all this drilling and marching?" inquired Pinny Penny wearily. Letting the curtain fall, he hurried away, for well he knew, if he did not put a stop to the conflict in the courtyard, every window in the palace would be broken.

"Now what did he mean by that?" muttered Skamperoo peevishly as his little Prime Minister whisked out of sight. Pursing his lips, he seated himself heavily on his throne. After all, Pinny Penny had only spoken the truth. Why had his father or his father's father ever picked out this pesky little country in the first place? Located in the southern part of the desert of Noland, between the Kingdoms of Ix and Merryland, Skampavia, he was forced to admit, had neither riches,

112

beauty, nor interest. His castle, though poor and shabby, was comfortable enough, and having lived in it all his life, he was used to it. He had put up with the hot, dry climate and the poor quality of the food, but after all, why should he continue to do so? In those long-ago days in the schoolroom he had studied of energetic rulers who had taken their armies and gone forth to conquer richer and more desirable lands from their neighbors. Well, then, why should not he take his men, push over the border into a more fertile and kindly land? The idea pleased but at the same time annoyed him. Skamperoo was fat and lazy. He loved quiet and ease, and the thought of a hard military campaign made him shudder with distaste. Still, he reflected, remembering Pinny Penny's reproachful face, a King should do something for his subjects, and the more he did for them — Ho, ho! — the more he could make them do for him. A rich and prosperous country meant a rich and prosperous ruler. Discontentedly fingering the rough cloth from which his royal robes were fashioned, he began to picture himself decked out in splendid satins and velvets heavily encrusted with jewels. Jewels. Pah! All the jewels he had were his plain gold scepter, badly dented and bent from hurling at Pinny Penny. Taking off the crown, he scowled at it critically and began considering the realms on either side of his own dominions.

To the north there was nothing but a sandy strip of desert and the tossing waters of the Nonestic Ocean. East lay the Kingdom of Ix, and Zixie (sic) the little Queen he considered too pleasant and friendly to conquer. Besides, the climate of Ix was not much better than that of his own country. To the west of Skampavia was Merryland, and at one time a band of his roistering Skampavians had crossed over into that country bent on theft and mischief. Recalling the way they had been welcomed and entertained by the cheerful King of Merryland and sent home simply laden with presents, he hastily dismissed that country too. How could he fight a monarch like that? To the south lay the burning sands of the Deadly Desert, which no man in his own Kingdom had ever succeeded in crossing.

So having exhausted all the possibilities in the immediate neighborhood, Skamperoo tapped his foot in vexation and began casting about in his mind for some fair and faraway country to conquer. He closed his eyes in order to think better and was just on the point of falling into a pleasant doze of riches and conquest when Pinny Penny came noisily into the room. He was preceded by two of the King's Supervisors, who, urged forward by the fearless little Prime Minister, stood sulkily and defiantly before the throne.

"Well, what now?" demanded Skamperoo, blinking his eyes sleepily. "Can you not handle these arguments yourself, Pinny Penny? Is a King to have no rest or privacy at all?"

Instead of answering, Pinny Penny took a small cotton bag from the tallest of the Supervisors and handed it silently to the King. Still half asleep, Skamperoo untied the drawstring of the small bag and emptied the contents into his fat hand. What he saw there made his eyes fly open — wide open. Jewels! The very thing for which he had been wishing. "Emeralds!" gasped the King, rubbing the glittering necklace between his fingers. "Where did you get this, Twobyfour?"

"They were sent to your Majesty by a merchant in the Second County, who got them from a traveling peddler. The peddler had got them from a Gilliken, who had got them from a Quadling, who had got them from a Munchkin, who had once lived in the Emerald City of Oz."

"OZ!" snapped the King, sitting up very straight. "Where is Oz?"

"Oz is a great and powerful Kingdom on the other side of the Deadly Desert," answered Twobyfour, looking uneasily over his shoulder at Pinny Penny.

"Then how did this peddler cross the desert?" demanded Skamperoo, holding the necklace up to the light and feasting his eyes greedily on its gleaming emeralds.

"That I cannot say." Twobyfour cast a longing glance at the door, heartily wishing himself on the other side.

"Then perhaps you will tell us why you did not turn this necklace over to the king," suggested Pinny Penny mournfully.

"Yes, how dared you keep it?" panted Skamperoo indignantly. "And what are you gaping at, Threebysix? I'll wager you were in this, too."

"He was," shouted Twobyfour hoarsely. "He tried to steal the jewels from me. That's how he got the black eye."

"But you tried to steal them from me, and what about that, my fine fellow?" Twobyfour turned a painful and uncomfortable scarlet under the King's accusing eye.

"In Skampavia we have so little, your Majesty," he stuttered miserably. "With these emeralds I thought I might buy a bit of land in some cooler and more comfortable country where my wife and boys could be happy — a country where flowers would grow in a garden, and where a man would not have to spend his whole life wrestling with rocks and weeds and drilling for hours in the hot sun for no reason whatsoever."

"Hah!" exclaimed Pinny Penny, looking meaningly at the King.

"Hah, yourself!" grunted Skamperoo wrathfully. Then, as the emeralds continued to sparkle and glitter in his hand, his anger subsided. "You did very wrong to keep the necklace, Twobyfour," he stated mildly. "But I have decided to

113

forgive you. Return now to the Second County and explain to the merchant who gave you this necklace that I must have all three."

"All three!" exclaimed Twobyfour. "But he's entitled by law to two of them."

"My word is the law here, and you can choose between a broken law or a broken head," Skamperoo told him calmly.

"He is the KING," murmured Pinny Penny in a quiet voice. There was nothing sarcastic in the manner of his speech, but something in the Prime Minister's expression made the King prickle with discomfort.

"Yes, I am the King," he shouted explosively, "and moreover I have spoken. Begone, both of you, and YOU, Twobyfour, have two days to return with those two necklaces. The necklaces or your HEAD, do you understand? And — er — er — you may tell that merchant in your county that he need send no more of his wares to the capital; the three necklaces will suffice," he bellowed as the two Supervisors went bolting through the door.

"Now nice, they will suffice. You are the King," sniffed Pinny Penny with a sour smile.

"Are you a parrot or a Prime Minister? Stop repeating that silly stuff and tell me about Oz," commanded Skamperoo, clasping the emerald necklace around his fat throat. "Have you ever heard of this place, Pinny Penny? It must be a rich and marvelous country if peddlers can trade emerald necklaces as carelessly as we trade wooden beads."

"It is a marvelous country," answered Pinny Penny thoughtfully. "I remember my father telling me about the capital of Oz, an Emerald City where even the streets were inlaid with jewels, and every tower and wall was studded with emeralds."

"Well, why have I never been told about this?" wheezed the King peevishly. "A country like that just a precious stone's throw away, so to speak."

"Your Majesty has never cared for reading or study," Pinny Penny reminded him a bit maliciously. "In our library there is a whole history of Oz."

"Fetch it! Fetch it, bring it to me at once!" panted the King, bouncing up and down on his throne like a big, bad baby (which in truth he was). "I must discover why Oz is so rich and prosperous while we are so poor and unfortunate."

"Not so unfortunate and poor as we are unwise and greedy," stated Pinny Penny, stalking calmly across the room. "If your Majesty would study ways to improve Skampavia and allow your own subjects to keep a fair share of their crops and merchandise, we might be a powerful country, too."

"Nonsense! What can we do with a rocky little desert like this?" blustered Skamperoo contemptuously. "Skampavia is a dull little Kingdom, a dumb little Kingdom — a KingDUMB, that's a good name for it."

"And you?" murmured Pinny Penny under his breath as he hastened away to fetch the book on Oz. Returning, he plumped the fat volume down on the King's knees and stood back with folded arms.

"Well? Well? Do you expect me to read all this?" wailed Skamperoo in dismay. "Why, it would take a year or more. Explain it to me, Pinny Penny. Just give me the gist of the matter. Jist give me the gist — there, I've made a joke. Ha! Ha! Ha! I've made a joke."

"But Oz is no joke," said the Prime Minister shortly. "Your Majesty had better get that through your head at once. Now attend closely, and I will endeavor to give you the most important facts about this rich and enchanting country across the desert. In the first place," Pinny Penny looked severely over his specs, "Oz is about fifty times as large as Skampavia, a great, oblong, undulating country divided into four triangular Kingdoms. Each of these Kingdoms has its own ruler, but all four are subject to the rule of Ozma of Oz, whose capital, the Emerald City, is in the exact center of Oz.

"A girl?" exclaimed Skamperoo, leaning forward excitedly. "How can a mere girl rule over an important country like that?"

"By using her heart as well as her head, by encouraging thrift and rewarding industry," announced Pinny Penny in a tone that made the King wince. "Your Majesty would do well to read of her wise laws and plans for the betterment of her country."

"You may just skip all that," sniffed Skamperoo, closing his mouth stubbornly. "Tell me, who are the rulers of these four Kingdoms and the general customs and characteristics of the people."

Closing his eyes and putting his fingertips together, Pinny Penny began solemnly: "The Northernmost country of Oz is the Land of the Gillikens, famed for its luscious grapes, plums, wisteria, and heather. It is a purple country and is ruled over by Joe King and Queen Hyacinth, who live in an amethyst-trimmed castle high in the Gilliken Mountains. The Eastern Empire of Oz is a yellow country, known for its wheat, corn, butter, pumpkins, daffodils, and gold mines. Nick Chopper is Emperor of the Winkies, and this singular ruler is entirely made of tin plate and celebrated in song and story as `The Tin Woodman of Oz.' " Pinny Penny paused a moment to catch his breath and then continued quietly:

"The Southland is red and noted for its strawberries, tomatoes, beets, red birds, red wood, and red heads. Glinda, the Good Sorceress, governs the Quadlings, who make up its inhabitants, and she knows as much magic as Ozma herself —"

"Oh, it's one of those magic places where one just snaps the fingers to get what he wants," sighed the King discontentedly. "Well — Well, go on —"

"The Western Country of Oz is blue," continued Pinny Penny obligingly, "and everyone has heard of its famous Blue Ridge Mountains, its blue birds, its violets, its blue skies, and its capital, the Sapphire City. Cheeriobed is King and Orin is Queen of the Munchkins, and they live in the Sapphire City in almost as much magnificence as Ozma in the Emerald City. Is that all you wish to know?"

"About the army," muttered Skamperoo, wrinkling up his forehead. "Has this girl ruler a great army stationed at her capital?"

Pinny Penny grinned in spite of himself. "The young fairy ruler of Oz is opposed to all wars and fighting and has at her court an army consisting of one tall soldier with green whiskers," he explained hurriedly.

"One soldier with green whiskers!" shouted the King, nearly tumbling off his throne. "I never heard anything more ridiculous in my life. I thought you said Oz wasn't a joke, and yet you stand there and tell me about an army with one soldier. Why, that's the funniest thing I ever heard. Ha, haw, haw!"

"Laugh if you wish," said Pinny Penny resignedly, "but don't forget that Ozma has more magic at her fingertips than we have pebbles on our desert. In her palace lives the famous Wizard of Oz, who can work every sort of transformation and enchantment, but does so only for the good of the country."

"Humph!" exclaimed the King. "Well, how many fighting men have we?"

"Seven hundred Skampavian soldiers in each of the seven counties," answered Pinny Penny reluctantly, "but let me warn your Majesty that the idea you have in your head is sheer madness and will lead to nothing but ruin. Take off your crown, put on your nightcap and dream away this foolishness."

"And a fine-looking crown it is," snapped the King, snatching off his crown and looking at it angrily. "But these emeralds will brighten it up a bit, eh Pinny Penny?"

"It is not the sparkle of gems in a King's crown that count, it is the jewels of wisdom in the head under the crown that make him happy and well beloved —"

"Stop! Enough!" yelled the King, hurling the crown with all his might at Pinny Penny. "When will you stop this infernal lecturing and scolding?"

"When your Majesty stops talking nonsense," sighed Pinny, catching the crown with one hand and pulling a long bell cord with the other. "Come now, let us have our tea and forget about Oz," he proposed calmly. "Lemon or cream, your Highness?"

"Lemon!" growled the King sourly, and slapping open the book of history on his knees, he stared long and enviously at a picture of the Emerald City of Oz.

Chapter 2 - The King and the Merchant

Two days had passed since Skamperoo had come into possession of the emerald necklace. He had never taken it off for a moment. He even wore it to bed, and spent most of the daytime admiring himself and it in the palace mirrors. Now, as the afternoon of the second day drew to a close, he kept bouncing over to the windows that commanded a view of the Highway.

"If that rascal does not turn up soon, I'll — I'll —"

"Explode, probably," predicted Pinny Penny, who was playing solitaire with the only pack of cards the castle afforded. "Calm yourself, Skamper, what good are these emeralds when you come right down to it?"

"Good? Good? They are worth more than this whole miserable castle," answered the King indignantly. "I can sell them and buy — no, no, I'll never part with them," he corrected himself hastily. "They give me a feeling of importance and power. Our star has risen, Pinny Penny. Great days are ahead. Hark! Listen! Is that a footstep in the courtyard?" Darting back to the window, the portly monarch flattened his nose against the pane. "It's Tooby! It's Twobyfour!" he shouted, hopping up and down like a schoolboy. "And there's a tall, bearded stranger with him."

"If your Majesty will quietly seat yourself, I'll endeavor to announce them," reproved Pinny Penny, gathering up his cards. "Remember, you are a King and not a jumping jack."

"Oh — all right." Skamperoo flung himself heavily down among his cushions, and presently the tramp of feet along the corridor proclaimed the arrival of the long-awaited Supervisor. Pinny Penny advanced stiffly to meet him and after a whispered conversation, he called out in a bored voice: "Twobyfour, Governor of our Second Province, and Matiah the Merchant, your Majesty!"

"Yes! Yes? But where are the emeralds?" panted Skamperoo, leaning forward eagerly as the two travelers advanced respectfully to the throne. Drawing a small bag from his leather jerkin, Twobyfour held it sullenly out to the King.

"Here, your Majesty, and here also is the merchant who goes with the necklace." Twobyfour haughtily indicated the turbaned Skampavian beside him.

"Yes! Yes, the merchant." The King, intent upon the jewels, did not even look up. "He goes with the necklaces, you say? Well, ha! Ha! Now he may go without them. That is all I require of you, my good fellow. Your presence here is not necessary or desirable. You may go. GO, do you understand?"

"Go?" Matiah drew himself up to his fullest height, which was pretty high, I can tell you. "Perhaps your Majesty will suggest where? For these three necklaces I traded my house, my shops, and all my other possessions. You say that is all, and it is indeed. Since you have taken all I own and possess, your Majesty must take me also. You owe me a living, and I am here to say so."

"Say no more," put in Pinny Penny soothingly. "Matiah is right, Skamperoo, and well within his rights as well. We must make a place for him in the palace. What can you do?" he inquired practically.

"Do?" The merchant opened his eyes very wide. "Do? I am a merchant accustomed to dealing in jewels, china, cloth, and basketwear (sic)."

"Then you'll be the very one to help out in the kitchen and laundry," proposed Pinny Penny brightly. "There are no jewels, but we have onions and potatoes aplenty, and with the dirty dishes and hampers of soiled linens you will be right at home."

"What?" screamed Matiah as Twobyfour snickered behind his hand. "You require this mean-ial toil of me — Matiah, son of Metorah, son of Metanic, merchants for these thousands of years? This is preposterous! An outrage! I will go! I will go indeed. I will start a war, an uprising, a revolution! Help! Help! Help!" yelled the merchant shrilly. "The King has stolen my emeralds."

"Stop! Stop! Not so loud," begged Skamperoo, leaping agilely off his throne and pattering anxiously after Matiah. "You may leave us, Pinny Penny, I think I can find something better than kitchen work for this honest citizen."

"Humph!" snorted Pinny Penny, and motioning for Twobyfour to follow him, he marched disapprovingly from the royal presence.

"You musn't mind old Pinny," puffed the King, dropping a bit breathlessly on his throne. "There, there, now, sit down and make yourself comfortable. As I was saying, Pinny Penny has very odd notions at times."

"Very odd," agreed Matiah, and seating himself on a chair opposite the King, he fastened his eyes greedily on the sparkling chains now clasped firmly about the monarch's fat throat.

"Now, then, we must find something easy and pleasant for you," went on the King, scratching one ear reflectively. "You might, er — you might spend your time entertaining me. I'll wager you are just full of good stories, songs, and amusing tricks."

"Tricks?" exclaimed the merchant, elevating his nose disdainfully. Then a sudden gleam came into his small, black eyes. "Tricks!" he repeated more pleasantly. "Ah, your Majesty is right. How well you have guessed my secret." Leaning forward, he held his hand up to his mouth, and looking furtively over his shoulder whispered hoarsely, "I am a magician, King, and well versed in the arts of sorcery."

"Sorcery!" cried Skamperoo, clasping himself delightedly about his middle. "How perfectly panormick! Magic is the very thing we need around here. Tell me quickly, what can you do? How much magic do you know?"

"Is there some place where we can be quite alone?" Matiah held up his hand mysteriously. "NO one must know I am a magician. It must be a secret between us."

"Of course! Of course!" agreed the King, rolling off his throne with more speed than dignity. "Come to my private walled garden. No one can hear us there."

"No one?" asked Matiah sharply. "Are there then no guards upon the wall?"

"No guards, no servants, no one at all is allowed in my garden," the King assured him proudly.

"And is there a door in the garden's wall?" Matiah, stroking his long beard, stood regarding the King thoughtfully. "My first trick requires a door."

"Of course there's a door, or how should I get out and in myself? Come along, come along!" Waddling into the corridor, Skamperoo started off at a quick trot for his private garden. Matiah, grinning wickedly to himself, stepped softly after the King. Once in the garden, he meant to have his necklaces, even if he had to take off the King's head to get them.

116

"One sweep of my scimitar," murmured the merchant to himself, "Ho, ho! this is too easy!" The King's garden when they reached it was no more than a small, sandy square with some cactus plants in the center and a rickety bench against the wall. Seating himself heavily on the bench, Skamperoo made room for the merchant beside him.

"Now, then," he grunted hurriedly. "Begin. Show me what you can do. Prove that you are a magician."

"First I must have the necklaces," stated Matiah calmly. "Without the necklaces I cannot do a single trick."

"But — but if the magic is in the emeralds, I can be my own magician," answered Skamperoo, clutching the chains with both hands.

"But your Majesty is not a magician," Matiah told him reasonably. "You do not know the proper words or incantations. No, I myself must wear these magic jewels. And what harm is there in that? As soon as your wish is granted, I will hand them straight back to you."

"What's that? Can you really grant wishes?" Skamperoo's eyes began to snap and dance with greed and interest.

"Certainly," promised Matiah, blinking shrewdly across the square and estimating with his eye the distance he should have to run to reach the door in the garden wall. "All you have to do is to think of something you want, close your eyes, count slowly to a hundred, and I, wearing the three necklaces, will easily grant your wish. I thought you trusted me and that we were going to be friends," he finished reproachfully.

"We were. Er, that is — HERE, take them!" Unclasping the heavy chains, Skamperoo, who already had a wish in mind, thrust them into the merchant's hands. Closing his eyes, he made his wish and then began to count hysterically, "One, two, three, four, five, six." At six, Matiah was halfway across the garden, when horrors! A great white horse with a golden tail and mane dropped like a plummet from the sky. Pawing up the sand in Matiah's path, he flashed his yellow eyes so wickedly, the merchant fell back into the cactus bushes, where he lay screaming with shock, pain and amazement. But Skamperoo, thinking all the noises he heard were but magic incantations, went calmly on with his counting. He had reached sixty before Matiah had recovered himself enough to crawl out of the cactus and make his way cautiously back to the bench. The immense white horse continued to stare at him threateningly, but as it made no attempt to spring forward, he began to regain a little of his usual assurance and courage.

"Great Garoo! Then there was magic in the emeralds. This horse was undoubtedly the King's wish come true, a beastly wish!" shuddered the merchant as he stared in fascination at the pawing monster and wondered what to do next. He was afraid to run past the white horse and escape with the jewels, but HAH! he could make a wish for himself, a wish that would carry him and the emeralds far from Skampavia, the farther the better. Closing his eyes, he muttered a hurried sentence and waited tensely to be transported to Ev, a country he had once visited in his youth. But nothing at all happened, and gritting his teeth with vexation, Matiah opened his eyes just as Skamperoo finished counting a hundred.

"So!" beamed the delighted monarch heartily. "You have done it. You really are a magician. Behold my horse, a horse in a thousand. A golden-maned charger fit for a King, for a Conqueror —"

"Of all the dumb things," fumed Matiah, wriggling fiercely away from Skamperoo, "of all the dumb things to wish for, a horse is about the dumbest of all!"

"Dumb?" whinnied the white steed with an indignant snort.

"I'm not a dumb beast, I can laugh, I can talk,
That's becoz I'm from Oz, and my full name is Chalk."

"Cha-lk?" quavered Skamperoo, who had never heard an animal speak a word in his life. "He — he says his name's Chalk." The King looked appealingly at the merchant, and seeing he would have to live up to the role of magician, Matiah assumed an air of careless superiority.

"Well, he doubtless knows his own name, your Majesty. If he says his name is Chalk, it probably is Chalk, and the reason he can talk is because he comes from Oz, land of the magic necklaces, where all animals speak as well as we do."

"Better," sniffed Chalk. Then, taking a experimental nibble at the cactus, he gave a terrific squeal of pain and displeasure — flung up his heels and began to race around the garden at such a furious pace, Matiah and the King jumped behind the bench and cowered miserably against the wall.

"Well, there you are!" panted the merchant angrily. "You have your horse, and what now? He's yours, you know, and you'll have to control him." Matiah ducked behind the King as Chalk thundered past, covering them both with dust and sand. "If you ask me, you simply wasted a wish. Why, you might have wished yourself a ton of emeralds, or a Kingdom ten times as large and prosperous as Skampavia, or —"

"But there's plenty of time for that," sputtered Skamperoo, holding desperately to the bench, "since you are a magician, you can grant all of my wishes."

"Oh no, no indeed!" Matiah spoke hastily, remembering the way the emeralds had failed to grant his wish. "I can grant only one wish a week," he explained breathlessly, "and I trust next time you will think before you wish. Whoa, there, you Ozian brute! You silly monster. Stop that! Whoa! Ho! Whoa, I tell you!"

"Are you my master?" Leaping lightly over the cactus, Chalk came to a sudden halt before the bench.

117

"No, this King is your master," answered Matiah thankfully enough. "Speak to him, Skamper," he urged in a lower voice as Chalk reared curiously up on his hind legs to have a good look at the King.

"Be — behave yourself," commanded Skamperoo tearfully. "How do you expect me to ride on your back if you act like this?"

"Ah, so you expect to ride me?" Chalk came down with a thud and grinned broadly at his new master. If you have never seen a horse grin, you have no idea how upsetting it can be. "Well, I suppose I shall have to put up with you," he neighed finally. "Just call a groom or servant, old Rub-atub, and see that I'm served my evening oats, three apples, and a measure of corn."

"Certainly, certainly," agreed the King, starting off on trembling legs.

"Well, I must say this is splendid, splendid!" protested Matiah, hurrying nervously after the King. (He was afraid to stay in the garden with Chalk.) "Where do you expect to get taking orders from a horse?"

"I suppose you'd prefer me to take them from you!" puffed Skamperoo, beginning to grow a little angry himself. "Here, GIVE me my necklaces." Snatching the emeralds from the merchant's neck, he went charging into the palace hardly knowing whether to be glad or sorry for the sudden change in his fortunes.

But by the time he reached the throne room, he had calmed down considerably. Seating himself hurriedly on his throne, he pondered how he could keep all these strange occurrences from Pinny Penny. He felt sure Pinny Penny would never approve of magic necklaces or a talking horse. Well now, he'd just tell his meddlesome Prime Minister that the stamping, snorting steed in the garden belonged to Matiah and must be fed and stabled. When he made another wish — and he had a whole week to think about that — when he made another wish he would be careful to wish for everything he needed. As for this whiskery wizard, he would flatter him along until he discovered the right magic to use with the emeralds. Then he would wish him away like that. Like THAT! Snapping his fingers spitefully, Skamperoo pulled the long bell cord that summoned Pinny Penny. His Royal Charger should be fed. Not many monarchs had a talking horse with a golden mane. Aho, but he was coming on! He'd show Pinny Penny yet what a smart ruler he was!

Now Matiah, following the King slowly into the palace, had done some reflecting, too. He resolved not to lose his temper again with this provoking simpleton of a sovereign. He would simply humor him along, and before the week was out he would have another chance to steal the necklaces and escape to some far country. There at his leisure he would experiment until he discovered the right way to use them. He could not understand why the King had got his wish and his own wish had gone for nothing. What was the secret of the magic emeralds? With his forehead still wrinkled in thought, Matiah entered the throne room and quietly seated himself in a chair opposite Skamperoo. Much to his relief, the King neither reproached nor upbraided him.

"As, so there you are!" he cried in his best meant-to-be-cheerful voice. "I have just sent Pinny Penny to feed your horse."

"My horse?" barked Matiah, starting up in dismay. Then, catching a meaning wink from the King, he quickly winked back.

"It seemed wisest," murmured Skamperoo, "to say nothing of your magic powers for the present. All this will be OUR secret," he finished playfully.

"Oh, yes, yes, indubitably!" While Skamperoo was still wondering what "indubitably" meant, Matiah hurried out of the room and took a long drink of water from the old-fashioned fountain in the hall. "OUR secret!" he repeated bitterly to himself. "Our secret, indeed!"

Chapter 3 - More about the Emeralds

Skamperoo had not slept a wink. He tossed from side to side of the royal bed, his head simply buzzing with enchanting plans for the future. With the magic emeralds he could have everything he desired, and his desires and wishes were multiplying so rapidly he scarcely knew where to begin or what to wish for first. The necklaces pressed uncomfortably against his throat, but he would not take them off. He was so weary he ached in every bone, but still he could not stop thinking, and just as the castle clock tolled seven, the very thing he should wish for first came suddenly to him.

Ah, that was it. Too bad he had to wait a whole week, but a week would pass, and perhaps during that time he would discover for himself the magic secret of his sparkling new treasures. Then he could be his own magician and put that meddlesome merchant in his place. As he was running over in his mind possible places to send Matiah, the door of his room opened cautiously, and Pinny Penny stuck in his head.

118

"Well! Well? And did I ring?" grunted Skamperoo fretfully. "This is a fine time to awaken an Emperor."

"Emperor?" exclaimed Pinny Penny, coming all the way into the room and closing the door. "Since when has Skampavia's King become an Emperor?"

"Oh, go away and don't bother me." Turning his back on Pinny Penny, the King thumped his pillow and closed his eyes as tightly as he could.

"It's all about the horse," whispered Pinny Penny, coming around to the other side of the bed. "A strange and magnificent animal for a mere merchant, if I may be permitted to say so. Not only that, it TALKS. It's ordering the stable boys around in a shocking manner, and it even told ME to mind my own business."

"Well, why don't you?" suggested Skamperoo, rolling over on his back. "Of course he talks, Pinny; he's an Oz horse, and all animals from Oz talk. I thought you knew that."

"Well, if this merchant has a talking horse, he is not so poor as he pretends," persisted Pinny Penny, shaking his finger under the King's nose. "My advice is to set the fellow on his horse and send him about his business as quickly as possible. I don't like his looks, Skamper. He's mean and mischievous, and mark my words, no good will come of him or his necklaces."

"I don't like his looks any better than you," agreed the King, clasping his fat hands on his stomach. "But if I keep the emeralds, I must keep the merchant, and besides, I've a notion I could ride that talking horse myself."

"Oh, good goats and gravy! Then I'd best go and lay in a supply of splints and liniment." Pushing his specs up on his forehead, Pinny Penny cast a disgusted glance at his huge reclining master and rushed hurriedly from the royal presence.

Now Matiah, as you can well imagine, had slept no better than the King. In the small room to which Pinny Penny had taken him, he paced restlessly up and down. After all, he knew only two facts about the magic emeralds, the first that they really could, under certain conditions, grant wishes; the second, that they must not be worn by the person making the wish. This much the merchant had reasoned out for himself.

As the King had got his wish while he, Matiah, was wearing the necklaces, and he himself had not got the wish he made with the emeralds around his own throat, that much seemed certain. Snapping his fingers joyfully and feeling sure the King was now wearing the jeweled chains, Matiah made a second wish, counting slowly to a hundred. But the hearty supper he had ordered as a test failed to appear, and flinging himself down on the bed, he began to rack his brains for some other solution to the mystery. Perhaps the magic power rested in a single stone which he had luckily touched as the King made his wish.

Holding his head with both hands, he tried to remember exactly what he had done as Skamperoo began to count. But it was no use. He could not recall a single thing after he had started to run across the garden. And how, concluded the infuriated fellow, was he ever to discover the way to use the emeralds without arousing the King's suspicions or revealing the fact that he knew no more about them than Skamperoo himself? Muttering with vexation, he kicked a footstool all the way across the room and sat staring morosely at the worn carpet. The short, uneasy nap he finally got before morning did him no good, and cross and jumpy as a cougar, he made his way to the dingy dining hall of the palace.

The King had already breakfasted, and looking out of the window, Matiah saw a terrified servant leading the Talking Horse around the courtyard, Skamperoo following at a safe distance. The sight of the stamping white charger made Matiah shudder anew. What a waste! he reflected bitterly, and if the King grew fond of the saucy monster, it would make his own task even more difficult, for until he succeeded in stealing the necklaces Matiah did not intend to let Skamperoo out of his sight. Gulping down the weak coffee and cold eggs a shabby servant grudgingly placed before him, he hastened outside. "Good morning, your Majesty!" he called out heartily. "And may I have a word with your Royal Highness?"

"What kind of a word?" snickered Chalk, rolling his yellow eyes roguishly round at the merchant. "Give him a word, old Rub-atub, if that's all he wants. The right word for him, I should way, would be `GO!' or `NO!' and then we all could be happy."

"It is about the necklaces," confided Matiah, ignoring the horse utterly and falling uneasily into step with the King. "They must be cleaned every day to keep them in good wishing condition."

"But I was just going for a ride," objected Skamperoo with a little frown. "Won't this afternoon do?"

"No, NOW is the proper time," answered Matiah impressively, thinking how clever he was to have invented this ruse to get hold of the emeralds. "If your Majesty will just give them to me, I'll polish them up while you are — er — exercising."

"No, no, er — That is, I'd better come and help you," Skamperoo spoke quickly. "I can ride this afternoon."

"You think so?" With an exuberant prance, Chalk rose on his hind legs and spun around like a pinwheel. "Well, see you later, old Sos!" And with the terrified stable boy hanging onto his bridle, he went galloping off to the stable.

"If you take my advice, you'll have that creature knocked on the head," said Matiah savagely. "Surely you won't endanger our lives by riding on his back."

"OUR lives!" exclaimed Skamperoo, looking at Matiah in surprise. "You do not have to ride him; in fact, he's really my horse," he stated jealously.

"So long as your Majesty wears the magic necklaces I must go wherever you go and do whatever you do!" explained the merchant loftily.

"How — How very awkward!" In spite of himself, Skamperoo groaned as he thought how tiresome it would be with Matiah trailing after him from morning to night. "I should think a magician like yourself could arrange things more sensibly."

"But consider what is at stake," Matiah reminded him earnestly. "Together we can have and do anything we wish. Is that not worth a little inconvenience?"

"Yes, yes, I suppose so. But if we are to do everything together, I think I should know the magic wishing formula as well as you." Skamperoo looked defiantly up at his newest advisor.

"That is impossible." Striding stiffly along, Matiah shook his head. "The incantation once revealed becomes powerless. Only one versed in magic is permitted to use the emeralds. Have you thought at all about your next wish?" he asked, anxious to direct the King's mind into more cheerful channels. "We should plan and consult about it together, you know. But wait until we are in your Majesty's throne room," he added quickly as Skamperoo began to open and shut his mouth like a fish without saying anything. "While I am cleaning the necklaces, we can talk it over, yes?" Matiah's fingers fairly itched for the sparkling jewels, but restraining a mad impulse to snatch them from the King's throat, he walked along quietly beside Skamperoo talking so calmly and convincingly that he soon had the Skampavian monarch not only willing but anxious to reveal the wish that had kept him awake most of the night.

First assuring himself that they were alone and locking the door so they would not be disturbed, the King seated himself at a small table. Matiah drew up a chair opposite and held out his hand for the necklaces. Reluctantly, Skamperoo handed them over, keeping a jealous eye on the jewels as the merchant began polishing them with a small square of silk he had taken from his pocket.

As he rubbed the silk over the emeralds, Matiah carefully examined each one for some mark or sign that would give him a clue to their magic power. Intent as he was upon this task, a few low-spoken words of Skamperoo made him sit suddenly erect and regard the King with new respect and attention. How in thunderation, thought Matiah wonderingly, has this fat, silly monarch ever managed to hit upon such a magnificent and breathtaking wish, and as Skamperoo explained and elaborated upon his plan and schemes for the future, the merchant's interest grew apace. Quicker and cleverer than the King, he saw not only the possibilities of this splendid wish, but all the difficulties and problems that must be met and disposed of before it could reasonably be granted.

Leaning forward, the emeralds for the moment forgotten, he put his mouth close to Skamperoo's ear. "There are three things that must be done before your wish can be realized." Matiah spoke tensely. "First . . . second . . . third . . ." After each short, whispered direction, Skamperoo nodded to show that he understood.

"Then it will take four wishes to do it," he sighed, resting his elbows heavily on the table. "That will be four weeks, won't it?"

"No, perhaps if we are careful we can work it all into one," answered Matiah thoughtfully, and taking up his bit of silk, he began polishing the emeralds with renewed vigor. The King, watching him, forgot his former dislike and distrust. Matiah's enthusiastic approval of his plans made him feel that perhaps he had misjudged this long-faced, whiskered stranger. Perhaps he would not wish him away, after all. He might prove very useful in the strange and magnificent future that stretched ahead.

Matiah, on his part, had no such kindly intentions toward the King. He merely meant to make Skamperoo's wish his own, and so grand and daring was the prospect that he grew more impatient than ever to discover the way to accomplish it. Holding all three necklaces up to the light, he squinted at them anxiously. The chains seemed identical in every respect, but no — what was this? One had a diamond clasp, while the clasps on the other two were of flattened emeralds. This, then, was the solution. The magic wishing power undoubtedly rested in the diamond clasp. Revealing in no way his satisfaction and elation over this important discovery, Matiah handed the necklaces back to the King.

Somehow, decided the merchant, he must make Skamperoo touch the diamond clasp while he silently repeated the King's wish, but before that he needed a little time to prepare himself for the grand and glorious years that were to be his. As Skamperoo, exhausted by so much thinking early in the morning, waddled wearily over to his throne, Matiah strode to the bookshelves located in an adjoining room.

"While your Majesty rests, I will have a look at this interesting library," he murmured ingratiatingly, "and at the same time store up some useful information for the future." Skamperoo sleepily returned the merchant's broad wink, then, sinking back among his cushions, closed his eyes.

120

>From his chair in the alcove, Matiah could keep the King in view, and satisfied that Skamperoo was really asleep, he began hurriedly turning over the pages of the large volume Pinny Penny had but that morning returned to the shelves. Soon he became so absorbed that he forgot all about the King. And that was a pity, for had he taken the trouble to look, he would have discovered that the King was no longer there..

Chapter 4 - The King and his Talking Horse

Now it is true that the King had closed his eyes as Matiah settled himself in the alcove to read, but he was very far from asleep. In fact, no more than five minutes had been ticked away by the old-fashioned clock in the corner before Skamperoo straightened up as if suddenly struck by lightning. Casting a cautious look at the quiet merchant, he began to slide rapidly toward the door. Opening it without a sound, he slipped out into the corridor and, closing it just as softly, went puffing away to the quarters of the White Wishing Horse at the back of the courtyard. Though usually unenterprising and dull, we must credit Skamperoo with one brilliant idea. As Chalk had been brought to Skampavia by the magic emeralds, why should he not know the trick of using them? Fairly panting with eagerness and impatience, Skamperoo jerked open the door of the stable and stepped recklessly into Chalk's stall.

"Ah, the little Kingaling!" whinnied Chalk, tossing his mane gaily. For some reason or other, he found his fat master tremendously amusing, and while he had an immediate desire to trample on Matiah and frighten off the stable boys, he felt only an affectionate tolerance for the tubby little ruler of Skampavia. "Have you come for your ride?" he inquired, giving the King a playful poke with his soft nose.

"No, I've come to talk to you," wheezed Skamperoo, seating himself carefully on an overturned water bucket. "Quick, tell me all you know about these magic emeralds." Touching his three necklaces with a trembling forefinger, the King looked imploringly into the face of his new and powerful steed.

"Humph!" Chalk shifted a mouthful of hay to his other cheek. "Well, as to that, or rather them, all that I know is nothing. You forget that I only came into existence yesterday afternoon."

"Of course, of course! I was the one who wished you here," explained the King impatiently.

"You wished me here?" mused Chalk, staring meditatively at the comical figure on the water bucket. "Well, I hardly know whether to thank you or to jump on you with all four feet. Even without any experience at all, I can see that this is no place for me."

"You're right," sighed Skamperoo, clasping his knees dejectedly. "It's no place for me, either. That is why I must know about the emeralds. They can satisfy our every wish, and if we just knew how to use them, we could go away together."

"You think you could manage that!" sniffed Chalk, who had his own opinion as to what would happen once the King mounted on his back.

"Yes, together!" insisted Skamperoo. "Try to think," he begged earnestly. "You say you know nothing, then how did you know you came from Oz and your name and all that?"

"That's right, how did I?" Putting one ear forward and one ear backward, Chalk swallowed his hay with a quick gulp. "There must be a lot of stuff in my head that I practically know nothing about," he reasoned thoughtfully. "Suppose you tell me exactly what happened, and then I'll tell you what I think of it." So, hunching forward, Skamperoo recounted the whole story of the merchant and the necklaces, how he and Matiah had retired to his private garden, how there, with the merchant wearing the emeralds, his first wish had been granted.

"And a splendid wish it was, too," sighed Skamperoo, looking fondly up at his white horse. "Never forget that you were my first wish, fellow."

"I'm hardly likely to forget myself," snickered Chalk loftily, "but attend closely, old Crown and Scepter, when I dropped down into that garden, yon whiskered merchant was running for the gate as if his life depended on it. He only stopped because he was afraid to pass me, and from the way he fell into those cactus bushes, I'll wager he was as astonished as you were that the emeralds had granted your wish." Chalk wrinkled his forehead shrewdly. "I don't believe he knows any more about the necklaces than we do. If he did, he would never have sent you one in the first place, and he would have granted all of his own wishes and been in some splendid other place. Matiah's a fraud!" finished the King's horse vehemently, "And he means to steal back the emeralds."

"Of course! Of course! Oh! Oh! Why didn't I think of that myself? What shall we do now?" wailed Skamperoo, jumping up so quickly he overturned the bucket, for Chalk's frankly spoken opinion confirmed his own suspicions of the merchant.

121

"Sit down," advised the white horse not unkindly. "I may not be a magician, but I have a little sense, and horse sense is what your Majesty needs more than anything else." As Skamperoo righted the bucket and meekly sat down again, Chalk closed his eyes, standing silent and motionless for so long the King though he had fallen into a trance. But just as he began to fidget nervously about on the uncomfortable edge of the bucket, the white horse opened his eyes and, flashing a triumphant smile at Skamperoo, began calling in a loud, lordly voice, "Boy! BOY! BOY!"

While the King regarded him with mingled misgivings and admiration, Chalk snapped out directions to the clumsy little groom who came running in answer to his summons. When his mane and tail had been thoroughly brushed and he was decked out once more in the splendid saddle and trappings he had worn on his first appearance in Skampavia, he dismissed the groom with a haughty toss of his head.

"Come!" he breathed mysteriously. "Climb up, Skamperoo, and we'll Skamperoodle before that rascally merchant even misses us. Have you decided upon the place we are to go?" he questioned curiously as the King made seven frantic efforts to put his foot in the golden stirrup. "Heh! Heh! Heh! The other foot, Master. How do you ever expect to mount that way? Stand on the bucket, Kingaling, catch hold of the saddle, and pull. It's easy as oats once you get the hang of it."

"Is it?" Lying mournfully on his back where he had fallen after his last effort, Skamperoo gazed mournfully upward, and Chalk himself began to champ, snort and switch his tail with irritation.

"You wished me on yourself and now it looks as if you would have to wish yourself on me," he muttered savagely. "Here, give me those necklaces — hang them over my ear, and let's have done with this shameful exhibition."

"You mean, if I wish myself upon your back I will really be there?" panted Skamperoo, bouncing up like a rubber ball. "You mean you have discovered the secret of the emeralds?"

"Certainly!" The white horse regarded him scornfully through half-closed eyes, and the king, all too willing to be convinced, unclasped his three necklaces and, standing on tiptoe, hung them over Chalk's right ear.

"I — I wish to be upon this creature's back," puffed Skamperoo, his cheeks swelling out with suspense and importance. "One, two, three, four, five, six —" and scarcely had he begun to count before he found himself firmly seated in the saddle.

"Now, now, not another word," commanded Chalk sternly. "Before you dare to speak, take those emeralds off my ear." With shaking hands the King did as he was told, his heart pounding so violently it almost kicked a hole in his shirt.

"That's right," directed the white horse more mildly. "Now suppose you tell me where you intend to wish us and what we do after that. Wishes are pretty quick, you know, and it is best to be prepared."

"But — but I cannot understand how you make them work," spluttered Skamperoo. "It's wonderful, it's marvelous. Do you understand what this means?"

"Perfectly." Chalk rolled his eyes triumphantly round at his greedy little Master. "My head seems to be full of magic, which is not strange, seeing that I was magically brought into existence, and the trick of the necklaces, once I got to thinking about it, is quite simple. Now I am what I am — a horse, and quite satisfied, but you with these emeralds may easily make a jackass of yourself, so you had better tell me what you wish before you wish it. For instance," he went on reprovingly, "if instead of wishing yourself upon my back you had wished yourself a good horseman, how much wiser that would have been. There's a lot more to riding than getting into the saddle, you know. But never mind that now. What was this great big wish you and Matiah were planning together?" Leaning so far forward he almost lost his balance, Skamperoo hurriedly whispered into Chalk's left ear his grand and glorious wish for the future, being careful to add to his own wish the three crafty suggestions made by the clever merchant.

"You are sure this is what you desire?" Chalk looked sharply and a little sadly at the rotund and royal figure on his back. "You mean to go away and leave your own people without a thought or care? Isn't there anyone here you would like to take along or give a share of your good fortune?" The King shook his head violently.

"I might make a wish for Pinny Penny," he added rather sheepishly.

"Good idea," sniffed Chalk. "What are you going to give old Skinny Pins? You know, I rather like that old codger." Without delay and a bit spitefully, the King told him, and as this time Chalk found no fault with the wish, Skamperoo again placed the emeralds over Chalk's ear and quickly spoke nine words. Then, without waiting to see whether Pinny Penny got his wish, Chalk again took command.

"If you do exactly as I say, we'll get off before Matiah discovers you are gone and comes down here to slice off your head to get his necklaces," said the white horse severely. Lowering his voice to a whisper, he slowly enunciated four brief sentences. Tingling partly with fright and partly with anticipation, Skamperoo repeated the four sentences after Chalk and began his counting. But stars! Scarcely had he reached ten before he felt a great lift and lurch, had just time to snatch back his emeralds and seize the reins before he and the huge white wishing horse, without leaving even a rustle in the quiet air, had gone, vanished and completely disappeared from Skampavia.

Chapter 5 - A Great Celebration in Oz

"Why all the crown jewels, old Toz?" Resting his chin on the window ledge, Highboy
looked inquiringly into the dressing room of Joe King, ruler of the Gillikens and all of the purple countries of Oz. The King's apartment was on the tenth floor of the royal palace, but this made no difference to Highboy, for Highboy was a giant horse whose telescope legs could be raised or lowered to any level, making him one of the most amazing and amusing animals in Oz. "I say, are we going anywhere in particular?" he drawled curiously as the King, decked out in his best braided traveling coat and amethyst crown, surveyed himself cheerfully in the long mirror.

"WE!" chuckled the merry monarch, turning round with a hearty roar. "Ho, Ho, HO! And how do you know YOU are going?"

"Well, I see you are wearing your best purple boots, and when the King of all the Gillikens wears his best purple boots, he usually rides his best purple horse, does he not?"

"Right," admitted the King good naturedly, "and I might as well tell you at once that we are going to the capital at the express invitation of her Imperial Highness, Queen Ozma of Oz!" The King cleared his throat importantly. "There is to be an immense festival to celebrate the discovery of Oz by mortals, the honors to be equally divided between the famous Wizard who arrived here in a balloon from Omaha many years ago and little Dorothy, who came by way of a Kansas cyclone somewhat later. Not only will the rulers of all four Oz Kingdoms be present, but many other important and Royal personages as well."

"Well? Well, indeed!" trumpeted the giant horse shrilly. "There you stand all shined up like a doorknob and never a word to me. How'll I look? Why wasn't I told before? When do we start?"

"Just as soon as her Majesty decides what to wear and what to take with her," answered the King with a solemn wink.

"Oh, then I'll have bushels of time." Highboy sighed heavily with relief. "So we're invited to the Emerald City, eh? How perfectly perf, how simply magnif. Billy! Tommy! JIM!" As he called the name of each little groom, Highboy let himself down a couple of stories, and by the time he reached a usual horse height and level on the ground, he had ordered himself a bath, a mane wave, an oil shampoo and a hooficure. Indeed, Highboy's plans for the party went on apace and with the three grooms pattering after him with buckets, brushes and sponges, he trotted anxiously up and down his great, airy stable picking out his most splendid saddle and bridle and silver-braided blanket for the journey. The giant horse wished to make an impression that would uphold if not enhance the honor and reputation of the Gillikens. He was eager to renew his friendship with Trot, a little mortal girl who lived in the palace and with Herby, the Medicine Man, and the many other interesting characters he had met on a former visit to the capital.

In the Munchkin, Quadling, and Winkie Kingdoms there was also a lively bustle and stir of preparation, and in many of the lesser Kingdoms the Kings, Queens and Potentates made ready for the great spring festival in the Emerald City. And you can imagine the fun and excitement in the capital itself. Everyone had some special part in the program; even the dogs and cats ran importantly about on countless errands like small messengers, their ears and tails quivering with interest and expectancy. After the visitors had been officially welcomed at the gates of the city, there was to be an imperial procession with bands, floats and favors for everybody. Then there were to be games, races, and other exciting athletic events and a grand banquet in the Royal Palace. A magic-lantern ball in Ozma's garden would complete the festivities for the first day. For the second, pageants and tableaux depicting the important and historical events of Ozian history had been arranged for the morning. Notta Bit More, a circus clown who had come to Oz from Philadelphia, was putting on an outdoor circus in the afternoon, helped by Bob Up, the orphan who had come with him, and all the famous animals in the Emerald City. From the squeals, shouts, and hilarious chuckles issuing from the huge white tent set just beyond the city wall, it promised to be an unqualified success.

After the circus, Ozma had planned a picnic supper on the banks of the Winkie River, to be followed by demonstrations in magic by the Wizard of Oz and Glinda, the Good Sorceress of the South, and last, but not least, a lavish display of fireworks sent especially for the grand occasion by Happy Toko, Emperor of the Silver Isles. No wonder the children in the Emerald City could think of nothing but the coming celebration. No wonder Dorothy, Trot, and Bettsy (sic) Bobbin, the little mortals who lived in the great palace and were Princesses in their own right, were too busy to think of their titles or bother with their crowns. Dorothy, the first of the three to reach the capital, was Ozma's favorite companion, and Dorothy was perhaps the busiest of all. Not only had she planned all the tableaux and pageants, but had entire charge of decorating the palace and the Emerald City as well. The Scarecrow, whom Dorothy had discovered on her earliest trip to Oz, was her most willing and tireless assistant. This lively straw-stuffed gentleman had brains given him by the Wizard and was in high favor and constant demand because of his natural cheerfulness and amiable disposition.

At the moment, he and Dorothy were superintending the erection of a floral arch over the great jeweled gates of the City. This arch, grown and tended by the Wizard, was so magically compounded that as each visitor rode through the gateway, a ribbon-tied bouquet of fragrant spring flowers dropped lightly into his or her lap. Dorothy and the Scarecrow had tried it out to their complete delight and satisfaction, and now, clasping their large bouquets, watched three energetic little gardeners tie up the last tendrils of the magic vine to the gaily painted arbor.

"You know," said Dorothy, peering over the flower tops at the Scarecrow, "I can hardly wait till tomorrow. To think we'll be seeing Sir Hokus and Ojo and Unk Nunkie and Urtha and Prince Tatters and all the others —"

"And they'll be seeing us, too, remember that," beamed the Scarecrow, closing one cotton eye. "And now, if you can manage for a few minutes without me, I had better go and study up on my speech of welcome."

"Oh, are YOU making the speech of welcome? How grand! How thrilling!" Dorothy gazed admiringly up at her oldest friend in Oz.

"Yes, and I'm also making the speech awarding medals to the Discoverers of our country," confided the Scarecrow, thrusting out his chin and striking an attitude. "How will you feel when I pin that medal on your chest, my girl?"

"Well," sighed Dorothy, looking dreamily over her bouquet, "I couldn't feel any happier than I do now, but it certainly will be a great honor, Scarecrow."

"A great honor! Well, I should snickerty wicker. But what if I forget my speech right in the middle of a word?" The Scarecrow pushed back his old blue hat and puckered up his forehead anxiously. "How will I feel with all those Kings and Queens staring right at me? Really, I think Ozma had better have someone else make the speeches."

"Oh, go along with you," laughed Dorothy, giving him a little push. "Haven't you magic brains? You'll be a splendid speechmaker."

"Do you think so? Well, I'll do my best." Somewhat reassured, the Scarecrow patted Dorothy on the shoulder and started off through the park. Dorothy could tell from the way he flung his arms about that he was rehearsing, and with an amused little smile she hurried back to the palace to put the finishing touches to the decorations for Ozma's throne room. Halfway there, she met the Hungry Tiger carrying a large basket in his teeth and followed by ten little kitchen boys, also bearing enormous baskets.

"Good gracious, Tige, what's this?" Dorothy stared at the little procession in surprise. The Hungry Tiger and Cowardly Lion have lived in the Emerald City almost as long as Dorothy, and though the tiger's appetite is tremendous and he is always threatening to eat a fat baby, he has never yet done it and is tame as Dorothy's pet kitten Eureka.

"Oh, hadn't you heard?" The Hungry Tiger set down his basket and smoothed back his whiskers complacently. "I'm the head of the reception committee for all visiting animals and am on my way now to buy refreshments for the great banquet and picnic. And trust me," he gave Dorothy a broad wink, "to do it right. Just let me see that list, Kapo." Taking a long slip from the first Kitchen boy, he began to drone off the names of the capital's famous four-footed citizens and then the list of visitors.

"Of course there must be meat for the Cowardly Lion and myself," mused the Tiger, blinking his eyes sleepily. "Then there's Hank, Bettsy Bobbin's Mule, and Doubty, that dromedary you and Sir Hokus brought back from one of those strange journeys, and we musn't forget Peter's Iffin, though he doesn't eat much. Put down a box of violets and geraniums for the Iffin, Kapo, my lad. Ozma's Saw Horse and the Woozy, being of wood, don't care for food, but that fine pink pig Pigasus eats enough for a dozen horses, and Toto, your little dog, and Billina must be taken care of, too, and Scraps' bear Grumpy."

"Of course," agreed Dorothy, leaning her elbow on the Tiger's back so she could read the list over his shoulder. "But they all live here. Who's coming from foreign parts, Tiger?"

"Well," confided the Tiger, "you'll be glad to know our old friend the Comfortable Camel is making the trip with Hokus — I mean the Yellow Knight — and Marygolden, the Princess he married, is riding a warhorse named Stampedro. The King and Queen of the Gillikens will make the trip on the Giant Horse (quite a lot of horses, aren't there?), and I hope Highboy keeps his legs in bounds. It makes me nervous to see a creature one height one minute and another height the next. You knew the Prince of Pumperdink was bringing Kabumpo, the Elegant Elephant?"

"Don't you mean that Kabumpo is bringing him?" put in Dorothy mischievously. "And won't you be glad to see him again?"

"Yes, I'll be glad enough to see him," murmured the Tiger, "but feeding him is quite a big problem."

"Well, you're just the one to do it," said Dorothy, smoothing away the wrinkle between the Tiger's pointed ears. "You have such a big appetite yourself, you'd know just how hungry an elephant would feel. I see you've got Roger down, too."

"I'm pretty sure King Ato will bring his Read Bird, so I'm ordering a dozen boxes of animal crackers for Roger and a barrel of apples for Snufferbux."

"I wonder if he'll dance for us." Dorothy's eyes brightened, for she had taken a great fancy to the faithful bear with whom Ojo had traveled all over Oz. "He's bound to be jolly and full of fun."

"And hungry as a bear," sighed the Tiger with a worried frown. "But that is easy compared to a dragon. King Cheeriobed is bringing a dragon, and this dragon's on a diet of mustard and sulphur — think of that, my child — and SAY, I'd best get along, or I'll never get my marketing done."

"And I must go, too," said Dorothy, reminded of her many responsibilities. So, giving the Tiger's ear an affectionate pull, she ran all the way back to the palace. In the throne room she found Ozma and Tik Tok in a quiet conference.

"I've made Tik Tok Master of Ceremonies," said Ozma, looking up with a smile of welcome, "because he never forgets what he's wound up to remember."

"And I'll be sure to keep him wound up," promised Dorothy, patting the machine man on his copper shoulder. Tik Tok was another of Dorothy's discoveries and had been manufactured by a magician to be a slave of the King of Ev, but here he was, thanks to Dorothy, enjoying a life of interest and ease in the capital. Tik Tok could talk, think, and move about as well as anyone when he was wound, and was much more reliable and tireless than a real person.

"I am to an-nounce the vis-i-tors as they en-ter the pal-ace and per-son-al-ly con-duct them to their roy-al quar-ters," Tik Tok told Dorothy in his slow and precise manner. "Oz-ma can de-pend on me ab-so-lute-ly, and ev-e-ry-thing will go like clock-work." With two stiff bows and ticking with importance, the metal man marched proudly from the room.

"Like clockwork. Ha, ha! Did you hear that, and why not, with a clockwork man in charge? Oh, Ozma, doesn't it all look grand and gorgeous?" Clasping the little Queen around her slender waist, Dorothy gazed around the beautiful throne room. Every window and doorway was garlanded with flowers, while hundreds of palms, ferns, and fluttering silk pennants gave it an unwonted look of pomp and ceremony. "Let me see," mused Dorothy, straightening the folds of a white satin curtain. "I'm to stand on your right, Bettsy Bobbin and Trot on your left, and the Patchwork Girl is to hold your train at the grand reception. Do you think you can trust her, Ozma? She'll probably try to jump rope or wave it like a handkerchief."

"Oh, Scraps is pretty good, considering her giddy make-up," observed Ozma with a little smile, "and she would be so disappointed not to be with us. I'm sure I can trust her — at least for a little while."

"Trust me? Trust me? You disgust me," shouted a merry voice, and Scraps, who had been peeking through the curtains at the back of the room, took a long, running slide, landing in an unladylike heap at the foot of the dais leading to the throne. Scraps, made from an old crazy quilt and stuffed with cotton, had been brought to life by a magician to serve his wife, but the Patch Work Girl had come to the Emerald City with Ojo and never returned to her creators, scorning the humble career of a maid servant. She was so gay and amusing, Ozma had allowed her to remain at the palace.

"Must I go in training to hold a train?" she demanded, springing to her feet and striking so comical an attitude both Dorothy and Ozma had to laugh.

"Of course not," said Ozma kindly, "just be careful and do not do any gymnastics during the reception."

"Oh, I'll be careful and so dignified I'll probably split a seam, but wait till you see the grand-aerial-balance-defying stunt I'm to put on for the big show," puffed Scraps, snapping her button eyes boastfully. "I'm to walk the tightrope in Notta's circus, so SO long, girls, I must go and practice."

"Well, even if she falls, it won't matter," remarked Dorothy with a slight shudder as the Patch Work Girl jumped recklessly out of the window and picking herself up set off for the circus grounds on the edge of the park.

"Oh, Ozma, with all the interesting people here already and with all the grand and exciting ones who are coming, I believe we'll have the best time we've ever had since Oz was discovered."

"Are you glad you discovered us?" Giving her an affectionate squeeze, Ozma linked her arm through Dorothy's. "Let's see how the Wizard is getting on with his tricks for the picnic."

Dorothy nodded eagerly, and hand in hand the two girls hurried across the corridor to the laboratory of the wonderful Wizard of Oz.

Chapter 6 - A Strange Warning

The first day of the grand celebration dawned clear and bright. The Emerald City had never seemed more sparkling or fair. Flags fluttered from every tower and turret of the palace; each house wore a garland of flowers and flaunted a dozen silken banners in the fresh spring breeze. The streets were alive with Ozma's subjects suitable costumed for the big parade, and when, shortly after noon, the Royal Visitors began to arrive, the castle bells broke into a joyous tolling, the hundred bands struck up the Oz National Anthem, and the magnificent and beautiful floats began to swing into line.

The Scarecrow's address of welcome at the City Gates had been greeted with wild enthusiasm and applause, and now, happy but somewhat breathless, the indefatigable Straw Man mounted on the Saw Horse was leading the illustrious Guests into the City, where they were to join the Royal Procession and proceed in triumph to the West Gardens of the park. What shouts and cheers went up from the happy throngs as that impressive company in their glittering coaches or riding their favorite steeds moved majestically through the emerald-studded streets of the capital. Directly following the Scarecrow, all in red and wearing her tallest ruby crown, was Glinda the Good Sorceress of the South, her swan-drawn chariot seeming to float by itself. Marching cheerfully after the Ruler of the Quadlings came Nick Chopper, the Nickel-Plated Emperor of the Winkies, polished to the highest degree but democratically afoot, marching in the center of his ten splendid uniformed Winkie Guards. A few steps behind the Tin Woodman and prancing along in hardly restrained exuberance was the Giant Horse, proudly bearing Joe King and Queen Hyacinth, King and Queen of the Gillikens. And Highboy not only carried his own head high, but he had elevated his sovereigns above everyone else in the procession so that none could miss the happily smiling rulers of the North.

A dazzling blue dragon had pulled the coach of King Cheeriobed, Queen Orin and Prince Philador all the way from Sapphire City, and an eye-filling sight was the Royal Family of the Munchkins. Kabumpo, the Elegant Elephant, resplendent in his jeweled robe, swayed haughtily along after Cheeriobed's blue coach, waving his trunk in a dignified way to this friends in the crowd. In the canopied seat on his back rode Prince Pompadore and Peg Amy of Pumperdink, easily the handsomest young couple in Oz.

Peering mischievously out the side of his gaily painted jinrickisha was the merry Red Jinn himself, and no one could view the rotund little Wizard of Ev without feeling happier. Jinnicky's body was a great red jar. He wore the lid for a hat, and when he grew bored or sleepy he would simply retire into himself like a turtle. But now he did not feel at all like retiring and was showering ginger cookies right and left and simply beaming with interest and jollity. The King and Queen of Ragbad rolled briskly along in their shabby but comfortable open coach. With them were Prince Tatters, Urtha, his flowery little Princess, and Grandpa, an old Soldier with a wooden leg, who had gone through many wars and hardships for the sake of his country.

But the shout that greeted the Yellow Knight was loudest and longest of all. The Prince of Corumbia had lived in the Emerald City for many years as Sir Hokus of Pokes before he was disenchanted and became the young and charming husband of Princess Marygolden of Corabia. Sir Hokus rode the Comfortable Camel, and Camy, who had also spent part of his life in the capital, came in for his full share of the cheering. Princess Marygolden was mounted on Stampedro, the Knight's great, stamping warhorse, and Stampedro was a sight to make any little boy's heart beat faster.

Ato, King of the Octagon Isles, and Samuel Salt, a reformed Pirate now Royal Discoverer and Explorer for the Crown, traveled together in Ato's Octogon (sic) Chariot drawn by eight prancing black horses with eight footmen in eight-sided hats on the high seat behind his merry little Majesty. Roger, the Read Bird, perched proudly on the King's shoulder, reading out the signs and street names as they bowled merrily over the gold paving stones, and chuckling to himself in eight different languages.

Last, but by no means least, came the King and Queen of Seebania, the King's uncle — better known in the Emerald City as Unc Nunkie — and the King's son, Ojo. The King and Queen were seated sedately in the Silver Coach of Seebania, but Ojo and his pet bear Snufferbux were proudly mounted on the back of Roganda, Queen of the Unicorns. This handsome, snow-white beast, who had happened to be visiting Ojo at the time, could not only send her horn darting out like a lance, but could blow it as well. The sound of its clear, bell-like notes made many a trumpeter in Ozma's band turn round with surprise and envy. Drawn up to meet her impressive visitors was Ozma herself. The Royal Float of Her Imperial Highness was formed like a seashell. On an uncut emerald in the center sat the little Ruler of all the Ozians dressed in a shimmering white robe, wearing her flashing emerald crown, and never in all the thousand years of her young life had this lovely young fairy looked more beautiful. Also in white were her attendants, Dorothy, Bettsy, and Trot, each wearing an emerald circlet and carrying a long wand draped with spring flowers.

As the Scarecrow brought his bright cavalcade to a triumphant halt, Ozma's float, drawn by the Hungry Tiger and the Cowardly Lion, swung into place at the head of the line. The other Emerald City Floats, first waiting for the Royal Equipages and mounts of the visitors to pass, swept after them in a burst of music and color. The Wizard of Oz had chosen a huge, revolving, green ball on which the nimble little necromancer ably kept his balance as he propelled himself along. After him came Jack Pumpkinhead, riding the Iffin. Herby, the Medicine Man, clinging precariously to the Doubtful Dromedary's hump, the pills and boxes in his medicine chest rattling like castanets, was another figure of interest. The float of Notta Bit More represented a circus ring, and the antics of the clown, Pigasus, Bob Up, Scraps, Hank and Grumpy, the Patch Work Girl's bear, kept the onlookers in a gale of hilarity.

Tik Tok had rigged up a mechanical handcar, which he operated himself. Benny, the live statue of a public Benefactor, who had come to Oz from Boston, strode solidly along, an expression of pride and deep satisfaction on his well-carved features. Beside Benny marched the Soldier with Green Whiskers, looking neither to the left nor right, as became a man who represented in his own person the whole and entire army of Oz. I have only mentioned the most outstanding of the Emerald City paraders. Besides these, there were countless marchers and hundreds of miniature castles, ships, huge make-believe sea serpents and dragons, and in a blaze of color and harmony they wound through the streets of the capital, ending up in the West Gardens of the palace, where the boys and girls from Professor Wogglebug's Athletic College distinguished themselves in a series of gymnastic displays, and the Scarecrow established an all-time record for pole vaulting.

By the time Ozma had awarded the cups and trophies, the sun had begun to slip down behind the treetops, and in high spirits and with splendid appetites the Royal Party and the Royal Guests turned toward the castle. Here Tik Tok, who had hurried on ahead, nobly discharged his duties as Master of Ceremonies. The Cowardly Lion did the honors for the Four-Footed visitors, leading each to an airy, shower-equipped stall in the Royal Stable so they could rest and refresh themselves before the Grand Banquet. And how shall I do justice to that dazzling affair?

For the first time in its history the magnificent Dining Hall was filled to capacity. Easily as large as a city park, there was just room for the two long, sparkling, flower-laden banquet tables, the first for Ozma's courtiers and guests, the second for the palace pets and visiting animals. The Scarecrow caused a roar of hilarity as the diners took their places by donning a pair of dark spectacles to prevent eyestrain from the flashing of so many jewels and crowns. With each course of the long, delicious dinner, Ozma had a different King, Queen or Celebrity at her side, and so cleverly had it all been arranged, each guest had the honor of sitting for a time beside the Kingdom's Little Fairy Ruler. Soft music floated down from the balcony where the Royal orchestra was concealed behind a bower of palms. The bright robes and jewels of the banqueters and the emerald and silver dinner service twinkled and sparkled in the magic glow of a thousand candles. The hundred footmen were swift and skillful, the speeches were short and merry, "And never," thought Dorothy, looking around with a little thrill of satisfaction, "never has there been so grand and yet delightful a party!"

The Hungry Tiger had remembered the tastes and appetites of each of his guests, and not only were they served with the same dainties enjoyed by the Two-Footed visitors, but every one had a special dish of his own. Even the Dragon seemed to enjoy immensely his matches and mustard, then called in a hoarse voice for three pails of hot coals, after which he blew a whole series of smoke rings and went comfortably to sleep.

Dorothy and the Wizard had with due modesty accepted their medals for their discovery of Oz, and the whole company on its feet for this impressive ceremony were suddenly startled by a shrill scream from the Patch Work Girl. "His beard! His beard! Look at his beard!" yodeled Scraps. (Yes, I think "yodel" best describes the excited noise made by this irrepressible maiden.) "His beard, I said, it's turning RED!" At the word "beard," every eye turned to the Soldier with Green Whiskers, for his beard was the longest and most celebrated in Oz.

"Why, so it is!" exclaimed Dorothy in astonishment.

"Red?" choked the Soldier, desperately clutching his famous whiskers. "Oh! Oh! My beautiful green beard, it's red as fire. Oh! Oh! How can I ever be the Soldier with Green Whiskers if my beard stays red? Who did this? Wizard! Wizard, are you playing a trick on me?"

"Certainly not, Soldier. I'd be the last person to tamper with your sacred beard. Quiet, please! Quiet! This is extremely odd and disturbing." Jumping on his chair, the Little Wizard of Oz looked anxiously around the room.

"Do they hurt? Are red whiskers painful?" asked Scraps while the Royal guests, hardly knowing whether to laugh or sympathize, gazed curiously at the blazing beard of the Army of Oz.

"They — they hurt my feelings," blubbered the poor Soldier, holding out his bristling red whiskers in disgust. "I'll never get used to a red beard. Never! Never!"

"Why not cut it off?" inquired Prince Pompadore with some difficulty controlling his chuckles.

"What? Cut off my beautiful whiskers? Why, why, I'd rather lose my head," moaned the Soldier with a horrified shudder. "How would I look? How would I fight? Oh! Oh! This is ridiculous!" Burying his face in his napkin, Ozma's distracted army rushed violently from the room.

"Red-iculous, if you ask me," observed the Scarecrow in his droll voice.

"No, no, it's MAGIC!" muttered the Wizard, stepping briskly down from his chair. "Wait, I must consult my book of red magic and portents."

"And I'll go with you," offered Jinnicky, rolling quickly out of his cushioned seat. "You know RED magic is my specialty." So, arm in arm, the Wizard of Oz and the Wizard of Ev bustled away together.

"Well, I can tell you what it means without consulting any books," said the Scarecrow as Ozma, looking rather troubled, again took her place and motioned for the others to do the same. "It is a warning," declared the Scarecrow, raising his arm stiffly. "Someone is coming to beard us in our den (pardon such an informal reference to your castle, my dear)." He made an apologetic little bow to Ozma and then continued seriously, "A danger from without threatens the Kingdom of Oz."

"Who would dare threaten the sovereignty of our country?" demanded the Yellow Knight, brandishing his sword.

"What's up? What's up?" neighed Highboy, elevating himself so suddenly he cracked his head against the ceiling.

"You should know, being so high," chuckled the Scarecrow, who could not resist a joke even when he was most serious. "But calm yourself, my good horse, you are not in danger yet." Danger! The short, ugly word dropped like a bomb into that gay and carefree assemblage. Dorothy, with a little pang of dismay, saw the Cowardly Lion creeping under the table, and feeling in her pocket for her handkerchief, drew out instead one of the Wizard's wishing pills. He had given it to her so she could visit the corn-ear palace of the Scarecrow the following week and do it by simply wishing herself there instead of making the journey. Dorothy fingered the pill thoughtfully for a minute or two, then with a sudden quick motion popped the small tablet into her mouth.

"Whatever happens, help me to save Ozma and Oz," murmured Dorothy, and swallowing the pill, she looked sharply around the room for further signs of warning or disaster.

Chapter 7 - What Wizard?

At first, everything seemed as usual. Then, turning to ask the Tin Woodman a question, Dorothy was annoyed to discover that his chair was pushed back and he was nowhere in sight.

"Oh, he's probably helping the Wizard," decided Dorothy, and had no sooner come to this comforting conclusion before she gave a second start of alarm. Glinda, the Good Sorceress, was no longer in her seat at the foot of the table, and running her eye hurriedly down the glittering board, Dorothy saw five more empty places. Pressing a finger to her forehead, Dorothy tried to remember who had been sitting in the five deserted chairs. Surely Joe King and Queen Hyacinth had been there between Bettsy Bobbin and Trot, while Prince Philador, Queen Orin and King Cheeriobed had been directly opposite.

"Good Gillikens!" gasped the little girl, jumping quickly to her feet. "The rulers of all four Oz countries are gone, and Highboy's gone, too." And strangely enough, nobody seemed to have missed them. Instead, they were listening with broad smiles and appreciatively tapping toes to the loud and hilarious singing of the Patch Work Girl. Scraps, thinking it a shame to let a mere change of whiskers spoil a good party, was enlivening the company with her newest and most comical rhymes. So loud was her voice and the applause of the banqueters, Dorothy found it impossible to make herself heard, so running around to the back of the Scarecrow's chair, she tugged him anxiously by the arm. "Scarecrow! Scarecrow!" whispered Dorothy hoarsely. "Where are the Four Rulers of Oz, and whatever can be keeping the Wizard so long?" Tearing his gaze reluctantly from the Patch Work Girl, the Scarecrow looked dreamily over his shoulder.

"WHAT WIZARD?" he inquired blankly.

"THE Wizard, OUR Wizard, the wonderful Wizard of Oz." Dorothy stamped her foot and almost shouted with surprise and vexation.

"Never heard of him," declared the Scarecrow, smiling blandly down at her. "Now, why not sit quietly down and listen to Scraps? She's never been funnier. Ha! Ha! Ha! Never funnier!" Dorothy was so stunned and dumbfounded by the Scarecrow's statement about the Wizard, she opened and closed her mouth several times without saying anything.

"Mercy, I'd better tell Ozma about this," she thought distractedly, and swinging round abruptly, she scurried along back of the diners till she came to the head of the table. "Oh, Ozma!" panted the little girl breathlessly — then stopped short. There was no one in Ozma's great dragon-armed chair of state. The Yellow Knight and Prince Pompadore, who for the last course were in the seats of honor beside the little Queen, leaned unconcernedly across her empty place engaged in a long, earnest argument about horses. They looked up in surprise as Dorothy, her crown by this time very much on the side, bounced suddenly between them. "Where's Ozma?" demanded the little girl, thumping her fist sharply on the table.

"Ozma?" The Yellow Knight and Prince Pompa exchanged an uneasy glance. "Who is Ozma?" asked Prince Pompadore curiously.

"Oh! Oh, I think you are all perfectly horrid. Stop joking! Stop teasing me!" cried Dorothy, and as both Princes in frank amazement jumped up to try to comfort her, she rushed angrily from the room. As she fled along the green corridor she could still hear Scraps singing and the shouts and cheers of her listeners. "This is terrible, terrible!" wailed Dorothy, and running blindly down the long hall, she burst through the swinging doors of the Wizard's laboratory. What she had expected to find, Dorothy hardly knew. Really, she was hoping to see Ozma and the four other rulers grouped around the Wizard's green table.

But only a blank, suffocating silence answered her frantic calls for the Wizard. Frightened into silence herself, Dorothy tiptoed from one end of the other of the long, curiously appointed apartment, peering into cupboards, under sofas and back of screens. Where was the Red Jinn? Where was the Little Wizard of Oz? Not here, certainly. Not in the Banquet Hall. But the THRONE ROOM! THERE she would find all of her missing friends conferring with Ozma over the threatened danger to the realm. With a little gasp of relief, she darted across the corridor into the vast and magnificent Hall of Justice where Ozma received visitors, settled disputes, and carried on all the important business of governing.

They were not in the sumptuous presence chamber, but at least the throne was not empty. No, no indeed! Dorothy looked once, rubbed her eyes, looked again, and then, giving a shrill scream of terror, flung both arms round one of the emerald-studded pillars. An immense white horse was sitting on the throne of Oz. A great, fat King was sitting on the horse, or rather clinging desperately to his neck. Dorothy knew he was a King by the crown perched ridiculously on the side of his head. That crown seemed oddly familiar, and after another horrified glance, Dorothy screamed again, for it was the splendid emerald circlet belonging to Ozma of Oz.

Her screams seemed to rouse the two occupants of the throne, who, to be perfectly frank, looked as dazed and stupefied as Dorothy herself. "Go away!" sputtered the fat King, waving his arms irritably. "Go away, little girl, and don't bother me."

"And kindly bow as you leave," directed the White Horse, lifting one foot sternly. "You are looking at the Emperor of Oz and his Imperial Charger." Bowing more from astonishment than intention, Dorothy backed a few steps, then turned round and ran madly toward the Royal Banquet Hall.

Chapter 8 - Way for the Emperor!

"Here, give her water! Give her air! Stand back, everybody. Now, then, what's the matter, child?" The Scarecrow bent solicitously over the little girl who had rushed into the banquet hall screaming hysterically about disappearances and white horses and fallen breathlessly into the chair beside him. "Come, tell uncle all about it," begged the Scarecrow, patting Dorothy clumsily on the head.

"Tell you!" choked poor Dorothy, twisting her best handkerchief into a hard knot. "Do I have to tell you? Can't you see for yourselves that Ozma is missing, that the Wizard and Jinnicky are gone, that Glinda and the Tin Woodman, that the King and Queen of the Gillikens and the King and Queen of the Munchkins have vanished entirely? And yet here you sit, singing and laughing as if nothing at all had happened. Can't you understand that something dreadful has happened to Ozma and that a big, fat, funny-looking man and a white horse are sitting on the throne of Oz?"

"Ozma, Ozma — who's she?" murmured the banqueters, looking vaguely at Dorothy and then at each other.

"She's feverish, that's what." Herby, the Medicine Man, leaned over to touch Dorothy expertly on the forehead. "I'd advise you to go upstairs and lie down, my dear."

"Yes, who don't you?" urged Bettsy Bobbin, coming over to put her arm around Dorothy's waist. "I'll go up with you and lend you my very best smelling salts."

"Lie down, with that big, fat interloper on the throne of Oz?" wailed Dorothy. Squirming out of Bettsy's embrace, she started indignantly to her feet. "You must be crazy! Camy! Kabumpo! Snufferbux! Toto! You — you'll believe me, won't you?" Hurrying over to the second table, Dorothy looked pleadingly down the long board from the Hungry Tiger at the head to the Cowardly Lion at the foot.

"There, there," mumbled Kabumpo, lifting Dorothy up in his trunk. "don't go on so, my dear, we all have these little funny spells. Here, sit up on my back so you'll have a good view of the Emperor when he arrives. Hi, there he comes now! Ray! Ray! Way for Skamperoo, Emperor of Oz!" Waving Dorothy in his trunk as if she had been a flag, Kabumpo plopped down on his knees and banged his big head three times on the polished floor. From her precarious

129

position Dorothy saw the same fat imposter who had been in the throne room riding his white charger pompously into the Banquet Hall, the horse nodding to the left and right and grinning like a Cheshire Cat.

Cheers, bows and a loud burst of applause and music made his entry so noisy Dorothy's angry protests and cries were entirely drowned out. Disgusted, confused and completely bewildered by the behavior of Ozma's subjects and her own best friends, Dorothy jerked away from Kabumpo and darted through a long French window into the garden. What could it mean? What could have happened? Had all her former memories of Oz been a dream? No, no! Violently, Dorothy decided against such an idea. Rather was this fat emperor a dream, a maddening nightmare from which she would presently awaken. Leaning dizzily against a golden fawn set near a crystal garden pool, Dorothy tried to find some reasonable explanation of the whole dreadful mixup. And here, several minutes later, Pigasus, the winged Pig, found her.

"Thought a little fly over the treetops might help your head," grunted Pigasus, looking unhappily down his pink snout. "Nothing like a little fly for a headache, my girl!"

"My head's all right," answered Dorothy sullenly. "It's the rest of you who have lost your heads or your senses. How in Oz you could stand in there cheering that big, fat fraud I'll never, never understand. Piggins, Piggins dear —" Dorothy bent coaxingly over him " — surely you remember Ozma and the Wizard and Glinda." Instead of answering at once, Pigasus stared thoughtfully at his reflection in the pool.

"Suppose you sit on my back, and then we can talk without being heard," he suggested brightly. "Up in the air we can air our views in safety, as it were."

"To tell the truth, I don't much care where I go now," sighed Dorothy, seating herself disconsolately on the pig's broad back.

"Hey, Hey, we're bewitched and enchanted, I knew it! With you on my back, I can think and see through it!" squealed Pigasus, and flapping his huge wings, he soared high over the flowering plum trees in Ozma's garden.

"Of course Ozma's Queen, not this big Skamperoo. The Ruler of Oz and the whole royal crew

Have been kidnapped, bewitched or put out of the way — We'll fly off for help, and we'll start right away."

"Oh, Piggins!" Dorothy threw both arms round the pig's neck and almost wept for joy:

"Oh Pigasus, to think you remember them, too, But where have they gone? What in Oz shall we do?"

"We'll find them, wherever they are they'll be found, But we'd best make our plans with our feet on the ground," muttered Pigasus, looking below for a likely spot to land.

There was one disadvantage about Pigasus, though some did not regard it as such. Like the winged horse Pegasus, whoever caught him and rode on his back at once became a poet and unable to speak anything but rhymes. The poetic pig could not only tell what they were thinking, but he often spoke his own mind in verse as well. At times this grew terribly tiresome, but except for his jingles, a more cheerful, loyal, little fellow could not be found in the length or breadth of the country. Raised and bred by the Red Jinn, he had been given to the Duke of Dork. The Duke had given him to the Philadelphia boy Peter, who in the course of a voyage with Samuel Salt, the Pirate, had captured the Duke's splendid castle boat. The capture had been quite a social and friendly affair, and the Duke had traded Pigasus for a Bananny Goat. Peter had later brought the flying pig to the Emerald City, where he was petted and admired by the whole court. Now, slanting down into a quiet grove, Pigasus came to a gentle stop, and Dorothy tumbled off his back.

"Oh, Pigasus, isn't it lucky you were in the Emerald City? Nobody else can remember Ozma or the others at all."

"And I only remembered them because you sat on my back," confessed the pig, twitching his nose thoughtfully. "It was my thought-reading gift that did the trick, and I am more than ever convinced that we are under some mischievous spell or enchantment. What I don't understand, my dear, is how you yourself escaped or chanced to remember things as they were. You know, before I came out here, it seemed perfectly right and natural for that roly poly pudding of an Emperor to be sitting at the head of the table. I knew no more about Ozma or Glinda or my former master Jinnicky than a newborn baby. By the way, Jinnicky's gone too, isn't he?"

"Yes," Dorothy shook her head sorrowfully, "and without him or the Wizard to help, we'll have a hard time, I guess. What shall we do first, Piggins?"

"How about having a try at some of the Wizard's magic?" proposed the pink pig daringly. "Then we might look in Ozma's magic picture and ask it to show us where all of our missing friends are now."

"Now why didn't I think of that myself?" cried Dorothy, and springing up she started off on a run.

"Wait! Wait!" grunted Pigasus, pattering breathlessly after her. "Remember, we must be very careful, my dear. No questions about Ozma, no remarks that will arouse the anger of this scalawag Emperor, or we'll both be clapped in a dungeon. We must pretend that we have forgotten, too, and get away quietly later tonight."

This seemed so sensible a plan, Dorothy readily agreed to it, and without attracting any attention at all they re-entered the palace and hurried immediately to Ozma's small sitting room. But if they expected the magic picture to solve their problem, they were soon doomed to disappointment. The picture was gone from its accustomed place, and the safe where Ozma kept her magic treasures and other valuables was wide open and quite empty. A quick search of the

130

Wizard's laboratory proved equally discouraging. The Wizard's famous black bag was nowhere in sight, the little hanging closet where he stored his transformation powders and wishing pills was bare as the cupboard of old Mother Hubbard.

"Whoever planned this thought of everything," wheezed Pigasus, sitting heavily back on his haunches. "There is nothing here for us, Dorothy. If I were you, I'd get a few things together, and we'll leave right away before anyone misses you." From the cheers, shouts and hilarious singing coming from the banquet hall it seemed probably that the celebration would go on for hours. No one in that gay and foolish company even thought of or missed the little girl and the pink pig stealing so quietly through the dim halls of the palace.

"Ozma's palace," reflected Dorothy, looking resentfully over her shoulder; but now it seemed strange, alien and completely unfriendly. With a little shiver, Dorothy drew her cloak more closely about her and stepped resolutely out into the night. Pigasus pattered on ahead, snorting a bit from sheer nervousness.

"Maybe we'd better fly," he grunted uneasily as Dorothy caught up with him. "It's safer, and it's faster, and the faster we get away from here, the better, I'm thinking."

"I've been thinking, too," answered Dorothy in a low voice, "perhaps only the people in the Emerald City are under this forgetting spell, Pigasus; perhaps if we fly to the Winkie Country, the Winkies will remember their Emperor, the Tin Woodman, and will help us raise an army so we can come back, conquer this old Skamperoo, and make him tell where he has hidden all the proper rulers of Oz and the other celebrities."

"That's the talk! That's the talk!" approved the pig, twinkling his little blue eyes joyfully. "Up with you, up with you, my girl, but remember, if you grow sleepy, let me know at once, so I can descend. If you fall asleep, you might fall off my back, and think how I'd feel then."

"Think how I'd feel!" laughed Dorothy, her spirits lifting a little at the pink pig's comical conversation and enthusiastic seconding of her plans. Seating herself carefully on his plump back, she quickly gave the signal to start. Then up soared Pigasus, over the palace gardens, over the City Walls and away toward the East and the Yellow Lands of the Winkies.

"Oh, I believe everything is going to be all right," thought Dorothy, settling herself cozily between his wings.

"So do I," sniffed the pink pig, peering mischievously over his shoulder.

"I forgot you could read all the thoughts, Goodness Gracious!

Of those on your back, Do you mind it, Pigasus?"

"Now when they're nice thoughts like yours," puffed the little pig in answer to Dorothy's surprised rhyme, and winking his eye jovially, he zoomed like a pink Zeppelin through the sky.

Chapter 9 - The Journey Begins

For several hours Pigasus flew without slackening his pace. Then, as several suspicious little yawns and sighs floated past his keen, upstanding ears, he solemnly slanted downward. If he had chosen it on purpose, he could not have found a more comfortable place for Dorothy to spend the night. They had already crossed the border and penetrated far into the Land of the Winkies and were now landing in the quiet garden of a prosperous Winkie farmer. Set in the center of a dancing bed of yellow daffodils and tulips stood a small summerhouse, and with Dorothy rubbing her eyes sleepily, Pigasus trotted briskly into the rustic cottage. The door was invitingly open, and the moon lit up its cozy one-roomed interior. Snorting with satisfaction, Pigasus pattered over to a broad couch piled high with yellow cushions, and rolling drowsily from his back, Dorothy burrowed contentedly into the center of them, falling asleep before the pig reached his own bed, a soft, woolly rug on the hearth.

Pigasus slept lightly but well, and waking around six began to gaze rather anxiously at the round yellow farm buildings just visible from the door. The pink pig had had several unfortunate experiences with farmers. They had a way of looking at his plump body that seemed to reduce him at once to slices of bacon and sides of ham. One enterprising fellow had actually caught him and shut him up in an untidy pen. From this foolish prison Pigasus had escaped by spreading his wings and flying away, but the mere mention of farmer gave him the shivers.

So now, moving impatiently about the little room, he waited for Dorothy to awaken, and as she continued to slumber on, he flew up over the mantel and swept a large yellow jug to the floor with his wing. The crash of the falling jar aroused Dorothy at once, and without stopping to explain, Pigasus suggested that they start off, and Dorothy, not even noticing the broken jug, readily consented.

"We'll probably find a much better place to have breakfast as we fly along," murmured Pigasus as Dorothy seated herself between his wings, holding her small basket of supplies in her lap.

131

"Would it do any harm to stop at the farm And enquire about Ozma and spread the alarm?" asked Dorothy, who had rather counted on a cheerful breakfast at the farmhouse.

"No, it wouldn't do any harm," answered Pigasus, rising in a straight line from the tulip bed and winging rapidly over the yellow fields and fences, "but neither would it do any good. Farmers never know what's happening or going to happen. I tell you, though, we'll ask the first person we meet."

"Who would we meet in the air but a bird? Now really, Pigasus, that's simply absurd."

"Some of the smartest people I know are birds," insisted the pig stoutly. "Take Roger, for instance. He knows more than most of have forgotten. But look! A brook, a quiet wood! Stop! Listen! Look! For I crave food!" Making a swift downward curve, Pigasus landed cleverly by a rippling stream edged by some tall butternut trees. There were yellow raspberries along the bank, and the berries, with some of the sandwiches Dorothy had brought with her, washed down by cool water from the brook, made a splendid breakfast.

"I wonder whether they'll have the tableaux and pageant without me," sighed Dorothy, biting slowly into a sardine sandwich, "and how they manage the circus without you, Piggins, or the picnic supper without Ozma, or the magic and fireworks without the Wizard."

"They've probably forgotten all about today's doings," mumbled Pigasus, nosing busily among the leaves for ripe butternuts. They'll probably spend the time bumping their noses on the floor when that fat Emperor comes waddling through the palace and bending the right knee every time his white horse sneezes or coughs. Pah!" Choking with indignation, Pigasus began gobbling up so many butternuts, Dorothy feared he would never be able to fly or walk again.

"Let's stay on the ground for a while," she proposed, eyeing him rather nervously as she packed the remaining sandwiches neatly back in the basket. "I believe there's a path beyond those trees. Maybe it leads to a town or village where we may meet someone who can tell us what we want to know."

"You don't expect to find out where Ozma and the others are hidden straight off, do you?" Rubbing his back lazily against one of the butternut trees, Pigasus looked quizzically at his earnest little companion.

"No, I don't really expect that," said Dorothy, slipping the basket over her arm, "but it would be pretty nice if we met somebody who even remembered them after all we've been through."

"I can hardly remember them myself unless you are sitting on my back," admitted the pink pig, trotting soberly along at her side. "This Emperor's magic must be strong medicine. Hello! Here comes a fisherman." Pigasus pricked up both ears and his wings. "Shall I question him, or will you?"

Without bothering to answer, Dorothy ran eagerly toward the tall Winkie who was coming leisurely along the path. He carried a basket and had a fishing rod over his shoulder, and though his clothes were rough, Dorothy could tell by his manner and bearing that he was a person of some importance.

"Oh, please, Mr. Winkie," cried the little girl as he nodded politely and would have passed them without stopping, "could you tell us who is King here?"

"King?" answered the fisherman, taking his pipe out of his mouth and looking kindly down at his small questioner. "Why, no one in particular, my dear, but of course we Winkies and the inhabitants of the three other countries of Oz are governed from the capital by Emperor Skamperoo, a great fellow, our Emp, and have you seen his white horse?"

"Yes, I've seen it," said Dorothy, shutting her mouth rather grimly.

"But I thought Ozma was Queen," wheezed Pigasus, out of breath from running after Dorothy and too many butternuts.

"Ozma? What a curious name," mused the fisherman, looking pensively at the winged pig. "What gave you the idea that Ozma was our ruler? Perhaps you are strangers here."

"Well, it would seem so," puffed Pigasus, sitting down and panting a little from sheer discouragement.

"Oh, you'll get used to us," laughed the fisherman with a breezy wave. "Fine country, this; sorry I can't show you 'round, but as I've promised my wife some fish for dinner, I'll have to be moving along. Good day to you. Good day, little girl!"

"Good day," echoed Dorothy in a rather flat voice as the fisherman, lifting his hat, strode briskly into the wood. "You see!" she groaned. "Even here everyone is bewitched. Oh, Piggins, what'll we do? No one in Oz will help or believe us."

"Goose-tea and turnips! What if they don't!" Pigasus shook his head impatiently. "There are other countries, aren't there? Take Ev, for instance, or Rinkitink, or the Rose Kingdom. Why, there are lots of places whose rulers will remember Ozma, my poor old friend Jinnicky, and the others. Come along, my girl, we've only just started.

"While people roar for the Emperor We'll seek our rightful ruler

>From coast to coast, from door to door Though foes grow cruel and crueller!"

"What we need is some magic," finished Pigasus shrewdly. "Know a good place to look for some?"

132

"The Gnome King has plenty of magic," reflected Dorothy, leaning thoughtfully against a tree, and Ozma and I really helped put him on the throne, so surely he'll help us."

"Well, maybe, but I don't set great store by gnomes. They're tricky; nevertheless, we'll go to Ev and everywhere else till we restore this country to its proper rulers." Pigasus looked so impressive with his chest and cheeks puffed out with purpose, Dorothy gave him a quick hug. "Down with the Emperor!" snorted Pigasus, though almost suffocated by Dorothy's embrace. "And up with you, my patriotic young Princess."

"Now you make me feel like a real one. I'd almost forgotten I was a Princess," smiled Dorothy, climbing obediently on his back. "I believe everything will be better from now on."

"Well, it could be a lot worse," chuckled Pigasus, and flapping his wings in a businesslike manner, he rose gracefully into the air and headed for the east. Rolling hills dotted with castles, villages and towns, valleys, farmlands and forests flashed in an ever-changing, pleasant panorama below. At noon they came down beside the Winkie River, finished up the rest of the sandwiches for lunch, and then looked eagerly around for someone else to question. But the yellow-bearded ferryman who presently came into sight poling his old-fashioned raft across the turbulent river knew no more of Ozma and the other rulers of Oz than the fisherman. But he told them many long and boring stories of Skamperoo and his white horse, Chalk. Dorothy and Pigasus had to make such an effort to listen politely, they were relieved when he finally shoved off and began poling himself back to the other side.

"Have you any idea how far we've come?" asked Pigasus, rolling over and over in the cool grass as Dorothy made a face at the ferryman's back.

"Yes," said Dorothy, dropping full length beside him. "This river is in about the center of the Winkie Kingdom, so we are easily half way. We could reach the Deadly Desert by night, fly over tomorrow morning, and either go North to Ev or stop at the underground castle of the Gnome King. Even if he won't lend us his army, he might lend us some magic."

"Speaking of armies, they must have whisked the soldier with the green whiskers off with the others. I don't remember seeing him after he left the banquet hall, do you? Which just goes to show this Skamperoo must be a stranger to Oz, for who else would have been afraid of our precious old army? Why, he wouldn't even tread on a caterpillar. By the way, has Kaliko any magic that might tell us where to look for our vanished friends and rulers?"

"I'm not sure of that," Dorothy told him dubiously, "but he was a wizard, and Ruggedo, who was King before Kaliko, had many magic treasures and powers. He could make floors and walls spin round and round, open yawning caverns at your feet, or drop rocks down on your head without even moving."

"Sounds lovely," sniffed Pigasus, coming to his feet with a short grunt. "Say, haven't we trouble enough at home without going to look for it? Do you really propose to visit this tricky little metal monarch?"

"But Kaliko is not nearly so bad as Ruggedo." Dorothy sat up and smoothed her dress earnestly.

"Well, just as you wish." Pigasus shrugged his wings. "With me, people are like eggs, either good or bad. There's no such thing as a nearly good egg; it's got to be completely good, or it's just as bad as a bad egg. D'ye see? And if this Gnome King is only as good as a nearly fresh egg, I wouldn't trust him with my second-best toothbrush. My idea would be to go to the ruler of Ev."

"That's Evardo, a boy King. Ozma helped him, too," Dorothy explained importantly. "But I tell you, Piggins, let's not decide till we cross the Deadly Desert. Something might turn up before then. You never can tell."

"No," agreed the pig, shaking his head sagely. "In Oz, you never can. Suppose we continue a ways on foot? My wings are a bit stiff, and we really should be on the lookout for a friendly house or castle where we could have supper and spend the night. I could eat a peck of spinach or a bushel of apples right now, so hop up, my dear, and I'll stretch a leg for the good of the coz and Oz!" Chattering away like the good fellow he was, Pigasus trotted briskly across the fields and presently came to a deep, rustling forest. "Shall we fly over or walk through?" questioned the pig, sniffing appreciatively the cool air drifting out to them.

"Let's go through it, in a wood There might be witches, some are good.
A good witch with her magic powers Could solve this mystery of ours!"

"But suppose we meet a bad one," muttered Pigasus, stepping gingerly into the forest and picking his way with great care between the giant trees.

"Then we'll say goodbye and simply fly," laughed Dorothy, snapping her fingers joyfully.

"Yes, but flying would not be so easy in here," objected Pigasus with a troubled glance aloft. "These branches are interlocked so closely I'd stick in a tree like a kite."

"Oh, we probably won't meet anyone," said Dorothy. Slipping off his back, she walked along beside him, one arm flung cozily around his neck. She was rather tired of making verses and thought she could think better if her head were not continually buzzing with rhymes. After the hot, sunny meadows, the cool shade of the forest was very welcome, but as they advanced farther and farther into the shadows, it grew so dark and grim the two began to look at each other in real alarm.

"Must be a squall or thundershower brewing," observed Pigasus in a faint voice.

"Yes, it couldn't be nighttime so soon," agreed Dorothy, looking fearfully over her shoulder. The crackling of twigs as some large animal made its way through the brush sounded like gunfire, and while they were trying to make up their minds whether to run back or push forward, a long, hollow roar sent them skittering forward practically as one. Missing trees by mere inches, they pelted at breakneck speed into the dense and even gloomier stretch of woodland ahead.

"B-b-b-better climb on my back," directed Pigasus, halting at last from lack of breath rather than inclination.

"But where are you? I can't even see you!" wailed Dorothy, feeling about wildly.

"Here, here," grunted the frantic pig, making short dashes in four or five directions and finally bumping violently into the groping little girl.

Snatching at a wing, Dorothy pulled herself thankfully up and clasped both arms round his neck. In a tense and breathless silence they waited for it to grow lighter. They could not see even an inch before their noses now, and the darkness and silence grew more oppressive and unbearable every minute.

"J-j-j-just a cloud passing over," croaked Pigasus, trying to keep his teeth from chattering. "J-j-j-j — Say, what's that? Dorothy, do you hear anything? F-f-footsteps — not four, TWO. Someone's coming. Hello, there. Who are you? Watch out now, we're here."

"I see you," answered a flat, matter-of-fact voice.

"Oh! He sees us, yet we can't see him, I'm frightened deaf and dumb,

Oh, try to fly, Pigasus, why Oh why'd we ever come?"

"That's what I'd like to know," went on the voice sternly. "Now, then, will you come quietly, or must I drag you along?"

Chapter 10 - The Witch of the Black Forest

Dorothy and her companion were too stunned to answer, and in two thumping steps the owner of the voice was upon them. "Do you dare to defy a member of the Invincible Black Watch?" breathed the stranger, grasping Pigasus roughly by the right wing.

"No! No! We don't exactly defy you," squealed the pig, flapping his other wing frantically, "but how can we follow a blackguard whom we cannot even see?"

"Then how do you know I am a blackguard?" demanded their captor suspiciously.

"From your voice," screamed Pigasus, jerking this way and that way in an effort to free himself. "I'd know you for a blackguard anywhere. Unhand me, you surly black monster."

"You talk a lot for a fellow who cannot see," scoffed the Guard, tightening his grip on the pig's wing. "Is the girl blind, too?"

"We're not blind at all, and why should we be, In this horrid black forest how could we see?" cried Dorothy, her indignation getting the better of her fright.

"Well, what color are your eyes?" Dorothy felt the hot breath of the Guardsman on her neck as he leaned over to find out for himself. "Blue!" he murmured in evident puzzlement. "And the pig's eyes are blue, too. So that's the reason."

"What has the color to do with it?" grunted Pigasus, growing a little calmer as the conversation progressed without either of them coming to actual harm.

"Everything," explained the Guard impressively. "In the Black Forest one must have black eyes to see. See? Even a pig should know that."

"Well, I suppose I could run into a tree and black my eyes," sniffed Pigasus bitterly. "But thank you, no. I prefer blue eyes, and now, if you will kindly conduct us to the edge of this deep, dark, dangerous and disgusting domain, we'll be delighted to go, leave, depart, and bid you farewell forever."

"Oh, keep all that for Gloma," drawled the Guard indifferently. "I'm a plain man and prefer plain language. Furthermore, no one leaves this forest unless they break the black laws. If you break the law, you are cast out into the utter and awful light of eternal day. Now then, come along!" and giving the pig's wing a cruel tweak, he tramped doggedly forward. Pigasus, to save his precious feathers, was obliged to come, suiting his gait to the guard's strides.

"The best thing for us to do is to break the law at once," he whispered mournfully to Dorothy as he blinked about in a desperate effort to penetrate the gloom. Dorothy was too depressed to answer, and after clearing his throat several times, the Blackguard began to question Pigasus.

"Why the wings?" he asked inquiringly. "I've seen many a farmyard creature in my day, but never a pig with wings. Are you a pig or a kind of balcony bird? What right has a pig to wings?"

"Let go and I'll show you," puffed Pigasus, hoping the fellow's curiosity would cause him to loosen his hold. But the Guard only laughed at such an idea.

"Let you go? I should say not," he exclaimed with a little chuckle. "You can show all your little tricks to Gloma, and she can decide whether to ride or roast you. This girl on your back will make a splendid slave."

"Slave!" shrilled Pigasus, stumbling angrily along in the dark. "I'll have you know that she is a Princess of Oz and lives in the palace of Ozma of Oz."

"Then why did she not stay there?" observed the Guard reasonably enough. "Anyone coming into this forest comes under the rule of Gloma, Witch of the Black Forest."

"Witch?" coughed the pig as Dorothy, tightening her clutch on his neck, almost choked him.

"Yes, witch," repeated the forester calmly. "Now then, hold up your heads, you pale and pinky skins, for you are in for a good blacking." And before Pigasus knew just what WAS happening, the ground slipped away from under him and he and Dorothy were plunged into the rough, chilly waters of a tumbling forest stream. Striking out with all four feet, Pigasus managed to breast the flood, when he felt himself and Dorothy being forced completely under. As a matter of fact, the Guard swimming beside him had simply put his hand on Dorothy's head and pushed her and the squealing pig beneath the surface. As they rose, gasping and sputtering, he again seized Pigasus by the wing and pulled him quickly to shore.

"There, now you're all right," he boomed heartily as Dorothy rolled off the pig's back and began shaking the water from her eyes and hair and wringing out her dripping skirts. "Just blot yourselves on the bank!"

"Bl-blot ourselves?" gurgled Pigasus, giving himself a violent shake. "Do you take us for letters? You — you'll be sorry for this!" But right in the middle of his angry sputters, he gave a loud and astonished squall. "Dorothy, Dorothy, I can see!" panted the pink pig exultantly.

"So can I," cried Dorothy, running excitedly toward him. "But everything looks black. Everything IS black, even you. Oh, Oh! You're perfectly coal black, Piggins. Am I black, too?"

"Of course," answered the Guard in a bored voice, "and much better so. Since you are black yourselves, you can see in the dark like the rest of us, and what do you think of our forest now?" But Dorothy, instead of telling him, held up her shiny black hands, touched a few strands of her perfectly black hair, and then, dropping her head on the pig's shoulder, began to weep bitterly. Like drops of ink, the tears coursed down her ebony cheeks, and though Pigasus did what he could to comfort her, she continued to sob as if her heart would break.

"Well, I must say I call this ungrateful," the Guard shifted from one foot to the other. "What's the matter with you, anyway? Black is a splendid color, doesn't show dirt, doesn't fade or streak. Besides, it's against the law to be any other color in this forest."

"How dare you blacken us against our will?" burst out Pigasus furiously. "Wait till I get loose, I'll — Why, I'll tear you to pieces and pitch you into a tar barrel."

"Oh, don't make me snort!" The huge Black Forester stared contemptuously down at the winged pig, and now that Pigasus had a better look at him, he saw the folly of his threats, for the Black Guard was well over six feet and lean and tough as black leather. Evidently feeling he had wasted enough time on the pair, he gave them a very black look, and jerking the pig's wing roughly, started walking stolidly through the forest. Never had Dorothy felt so blue — or rather so black and blue — so wet, so discouraged, so thoroughly miserable! And when, sticking out her tongue to see if it was still pink she discovered that it, too, was black, she began sobbing softly to herself.

"No one will know us anymore," she decided dejectedly. "We're as badly off now as Ozma and the others. Why, oh why, did we ever come into this terrible forest?" She could feel Pigasus sniffing with sympathy, and suddenly realizing that she was not behaving very well, she straightened up. After all, she was still a Princess, even though she was black. Princesses did not cry even when they were captured and enchanted. Ozma was probably in a worse fix than this, and if Ozma was being brave, she would be brave too. So with a great effort, Dorothy stifled her sobs and began to look around her. To her surprise and astonishment, she discovered that the Black Forest was not dark and gloomy as it had seemed before, but really quite beautiful. There were many shades and degrees of blackness in the trees and flowers that thickly carpeted the ground.

Black birds twittered musically in the branches overhead, and every now and then a deer peered timidly out at her from the woodsy depths between the tree trunks. The Guard, glancing over his shoulder and catching her interested expression, ventured a smile.

135

"Why, he is not bad looking at all," thought Dorothy with a pleased start. "And maybe this witch may be a good witch — her name sounds rather pretty." Quite comforted by these reflections, Dorothy whispered a few rhymed remarks in the pig's ear. Pigasus, it must be confessed, was as interested in what he saw as Dorothy, and when a sudden break between the trees revealed a great, black, circular wall with a hundred black flags floating from its many turrets, he gave an involuntary grunt of admiration.

"You are about to enter the Royal Circle of Gloma, Witch of the Black Forest," announced the Guard, raising his hand solemnly. "I trust you will conduct yourselves in a fitting manner."

"Don't worry about OUR manners," shrilled Pigasus, tossing his head airily. "We are accustomed to Royalty and move in exclusive circles at home."

"And talk in circles, too," muttered the Guard impatiently. "Well, well, do the best you can and bow three times as you approach the throne."

"Throne?" queried Dorothy, slipping off the pig's back so she would not have to talk in rhyme, for what she had to say to the black witch was very serious indeed. "Is Gloma a Queen?"

"Certainly our witch is a Queen, a bewitching Queen," retorted the Guard, taking Dorothy firmly by the hand and tightening his hold on Pigasus. "Now then, smile and look pleasant, and perhaps she'll allow you to be her slave."

"She wouldn't dare make me a slave," cried Dorothy, trying her best to pull away from her captor.

"Just let her try it!" blustered Pigasus, scuffling unwillingly along on the other side. But paying no attention to their struggles, the Guard lifted his foot and kicked three times on a black ebony door in the wall, and a tall Watchman dressed in a black leather suit admitted them to the Royal Circle. It was all so different from what Dorothy had been expecting, she almost forgot her anger. Enclosed by the black marble wall was a strange and enchanting garden. Now Dorothy had never seen a black garden or dreamed one could be so beautiful. Here sable willows mirrored their feathery branches in long, shining pools; here black plum and cherry trees flaunted their fragile black blossoms, and jet-black fountains sent their smoking waters high into the quiet air. Vast satiny expanses of lawn were dotted with a hundred beds of dusky roses, tulips, velvety pansies and daffodils.

Built all round the circular wall was a low but sumptuous black castle, and seated on an ebony throne in the center of her stately black garden was the Black Queen herself, looking, Dorothy was thankful to discover, much more like a Queen than a witch. Gloma's face was sweet and serious, her hair fine and glossy as a raven's wing. She was dressed in a trailing robe black chiffon that billowed in lacy clouds round her feet. A sparkling crown of jet and long jet earrings were her only ornaments. On each side of the Black Queen crouched a sleek black leopard, and behind the ebony throne stood ten tall foresters with gleaming axes. "Like headsmen in a medieval history book," thought Dorothy as she and Pigasus were dragged rapidly forward. Gloma, gazing dreamily into a black crystal set on a marble stand before the throne, seemed entirely unaware of their presence till the harsh voice of the Black Guard announced them.

"Hail! Black and Imperial Majesty!" called the Guard deferentially, approaching the throne. "Two prisoners, a pig and a Princess, whom I found wandering unlawfully in our forest and whom I took the liberty of blacking."

Dorothy, jerking away from the Guard, was about to explain how she and Pigasus had lost their way when Gloma jumped to her feet with a sharp, agonized scream. "Blotz, General Blotz, what have you done?" panted the Black Queen, beating her hands wildly together. "Your stupidity has ruined us all! You have blackened and insulted my most dangerous and mortal enemy! Leave! Go! Begone and never darken my doors again! Oh why, why did you do it? Why have you brought her here? After all these years must I too be destroyed and obliterated?" Sinking back on her throne, Gloma covered her face with her hair and began rocking backward and forward in agitation and sorrow.

"Why, why — I believe she's afraid of you!" puffed Pigasus, twitching his tail with excitement and interest as General Blotz, looking quite dazed, began to move unhappily toward the gate in the wall.

"Quick!" he grunted as the ten foresters back of the throne rushed forward to surround them. "Do something, Dorothy, while she is still afraid of you. Make her unblacken us. Tell her to set us free. Hurry! Hurry, before she discovers you are only a harmless little girl." But Dorothy, only half listening to the pig, boldly thrust aside the foresters and ran over to the Black Queen.

"Why are you afraid of ME?" asked Dorothy, speaking rapidly but distinctly. "I did not come here on purpose. Pigasus and I are lost and need your help."

"Help?" shivered Gloma, shrinking as far away from Dorothy as possible. "Why should I help you? Are you not Dorothy, the mortal girl who destroyed the powerful Witches of the East and West?"

"But that was long ago," explained Dorothy breathlessly as two of the Queen's henchmen seized her roughly by the arms. "And they were bad and wicked witches. Why should I wish to destroy such a good and beautiful witch like you?"

"Do not listen to her. Do not let her touch you. She means to destroy and ensnare you," hissed the foresters as they dragged Dorothy away from the throne. "Down with all mortals! Away to the dungeons with her! Wing that pig! Chop

136

off their heads!" At these loud, savage cries, startled faces appeared at the windows of the black palace, and struggling in the midst of the foresters Dorothy heartily wished she had taken the pig's advice.

"Shall we take off her head now or later?" puffed the fellow who had hold of her left arm.

"Now!" roared the axman who had hold of her right.

"Stop!" commanded the Queen, rising suddenly. "You cannot harm this girl. Do you not see the star of protection on her forehead?" At these words the woodsmen stared fearfully down at Dorothy, and sure enough, shining in the center of her black forehead was a pure white star. Pigasus, who had not noticed it before himself, gave a grunt of relief and began kicking out in every direction.

"How about the pig?" yelled a forester, leaning down to rub his shins. "Shall we take off his head?"

"If you dare touch Pigasus," screamed Dorothy, resolved to use all the powers she was supposed to have, "I'll turn you all to bats and beetles and horrid black ants." A breathless silence followed Dorothy's threat. The foresters still kept their hold on the prisoner, but at as great a distance as they could manage.

"Do as you wish, comrades," the tallest of the axmen solemnly broke the silence, "but I'm for letting them alone. I've never been an ant before and don't intend to begin now. Come, away to the dungeons with them. This is not for us to settle with axes, it is a case for witch work."

"You are right." The Queen, who had been standing motionless as a statue, took a decisive step forward. "Take them away, but not to the dungeons! Take them to the darkroom in my imperial palace. They shall see what happens to those who defy Gloma, Witch of the Black Forest."

"Aye! Aye! They shall see," muttered the foresters, pushing Dorothy and Pigasus roughly along ahead of them.

Chapter 11 - Black Magic

Dorothy and Pigasus were hustled into the Black Castle, rushed down its shiny black corridors and thrust into a great, dark, dome-shaped room so quickly they had no opportunity to exchange a word.

"Well, anyway, even if it is a darkroom, we can still see," whispered Dorothy as the foresters in their haste to get away from such dangerous prisoners fairly tumbled over each other to get through the door.

"Yes," puffed Pigasus glumly as the key rasped in the lock, "and the first thing I see is that there are no windows. If there was a window we could fly off. As it is, this witch will make short work of us."

"I wonder how much magic she really knows," sighed Dorothy, seating herself wearily on a black velvet stool.

"I wonder!" said Pigasus, flinging himself crossly on the floor beside her. "And what's all this stuff about your being her worst enemy? Did you really destroy two witches, and could you destroy her?" Although Pigasus had lived in the Emerald City for several years, he was not familiar with all of the history that had taken place before his arrival.

"Oh, all that happened when I first came here," explained Dorothy, clasping her knees with both hands. "You see, when the cyclone blew me from Kansas to Oz, my house fell on the wicked witch who ruled the Munchkins and killed her. The Munchkins, supposing I had done it on purpose, came out and thanked me and gave me the witch's silver shoes. Then, when I reached the Emerald City and begged the Wizard, who was ruler of Oz at that time, to send me back to Kansas, he promised to do so if I killed the wicked witch who ruled the Winkies."

"And did you?" asked Pigasus, rolling over and looking up at Dorothy with real admiration.

"Well, that was sort of an accident, too," admitted the little girl honestly. "When the Tin Woodman, the Scarecrow and the Cowardly Lion and I reached the witch's yellow castle, the witch captured us all and made me work hard from morning till night. But one day," Dorothy with an anxious eye on the door hurriedly continued, "one day when she tried to steal my silver shoes, I got SO mad I picked up a bucket of water I'd been using for scrubbing and flung it right over her head."

"And did that destroy her?" Pigasus demanded incredulously.

"Yes," said Dorothy, "it melted her down to nothing at all."

"But what about the star? I never noticed that before."

"That's where the Good Witch of the North comes in," answered Dorothy proudly. "Right after my house fell on the Wicked Witch of the West, she appeared, and when she discovered I was a mortal, she kissed me on the forehead to keep me from harm all the time I was in Oz. It only shows now because I'm black, I suppose."

"Well, why didn't it keep you from turning black, if it's so wonderful?" Pigasus switched his curly tail resentfully.

"I don't know." Dorothy looked thoughtfully around Gloma's strange laboratory. "Maybe the spell has worn off; maybe there's no harm in being black."

"Humph! There may not be any harm in it, but it's pretty sad and mournful, if you ask me," grunted Pigasus, glaring savagely at his satiny black sides. "I prefer myself pink and you pink and white the way you were. Tea and turnips, first thing I know you'll be powdering your nose with ashes and soot! But, after all —" Pigasus swung himself energetically to his feet " — that is the least of our troubles. What do you suppose this witch will do to us now? And what can we do to her? Sa-hay!" Spreading his wings, Pigasus spun round in a triumphant circle. "All we have to do is to find some water. Why, it's simple as soup. Quick, Dorothy, look and see whether there is any water around here, then as soon as Gloma pops her nose in the door, we'll put her out as neatly as you did that other witch."

"But those other witches were bad, and Gloma seems really good and beautiful," objected Dorothy, looking around without much enthusiasm.

"Beautiful or not, she's a dark and dangerous lady," insisted the pig, beginning his search in a methodical way, "and it's her beauty or ours, remember; this Black Queen is quite determined to destroy us if we don't destroy her first."

"Yes, I suppose so," agreed Dorothy. Slowly following Pigasus, she pulled aside black velvet curtains, peered behind cupboards and screens, and looked under sofas and chairs. There were many ebony cabinets standing against the wall, but each one was securely locked, and except for a great black crystal ball on a table in the center of the room there seemed to be no magic apparatus at all. A dark lantern swinging from the domed ceiling cast its curious luminous black rays into every corner of the witch's laboratory. After circling the room three times, Pigasus and Dorothy were forced to admit there was no water of any kind or even a pail available.

"We'll have to think of something else," grumbled the pig as Dorothy again sat down on her stool.

"Are you thinking?" he demanded sharply as the little girl stared absently at the tips of her boots.

"No," confessed Dorothy frankly, "I was just wondering why Gloma calls this a darkroom. She must know since General Blotz ducked us under the Black River we can see in here as well as in the forest."

"I wouldn't be too sure of that," muttered the pig, coming over and crowding as close to Dorothy as he could. It almost seemed as if someone had heard him, for scarcely were the words out of his mouth before the dark lantern over their heads sputtered ominously and went out, leaving them in a perfectly pitch-black darkness.

"I — I — I felt something like this would happen," faltered Pigasus, throwing his left wing protectingly around Dorothy. "Listen! Someone is coming."

A light, sure footstep sounded in the passage, came closer, then a sudden puff of air told them that someone had opened the door.

"Remember, Piggins dear, no matter what happens, we must be brave," whispered Dorothy, trembling a little in spite of herself.

"It's hard to be brave in the dark, but I'll do my best. Here, lean on me." And though the happenings of the next ten minutes were enough to try the courage of a dozen lions, Pigasus kept his word and never uttered a sound. As the two prisoners clung desperately together, the crystal on the center table received a sudden, shattering blow. Up spurted a perfect fountain of fire, coming down over Dorothy and Pigasus in a shower of red-hot sparks. But the sparks fell harmlessly as raindrops on the winged pig and the little girl, and after a great hiss and sputter went out, leaving the laboratory in darkness again.

Scarcely had they recovered from this shock before a second blow was struck, and this time a hundred huge, hideous, black snakes came writhing out of the crystal, their green, glittering eyes lighting up the room with a terrifying, sulphurous light. The great twisting mass grew more and more menacing, sending out its long, curving bodies like arms to encircle them. This, thought Dorothy, burying her head in Pigasus' wing, was black magic at its worst. Now she could feel the clammy coils all around her and waited breathlessly to be crushed and broken. But the cold, heavy bodies seemed powerless and without weight, and presently they, too, slipped away and vanished.

A shower of silver arrows followed the snakes and a cloud of choking green smoke the arrows. But each blow on the crystal only seemed to prove further the potency of the kiss set on Dorothy's forehead so long ago by the Good Witch of the North. And because she clung so tightly to Pigasus, he, too, came unharmed through the hair-raising ordeal. As they both, almost afraid to breathe, waited for the next blow on the dark crystal, a long, tremulous sigh came mournfully through the darkness. "It is no use," murmured a discouraged voice, "my black magic is of no avail. Come, then, destroy me if you must, but do it quickly, and I pray you will spare my people, who have never harmed or hurt a living soul in Oz."

With a little thrill, Dorothy recognized the voice of the Black Queen, and as the dark lantern again shed its twinkling black rays over the circular apartment, Gloma rose and came calmly and rapidly toward them. Dorothy and Pigasus, who had just had their own bravery so severely tested, could not but admire the spirit and bravery of the Witch of the Black Forest. Even though she was sure she faced certain destruction, she walked proudly erect, her head flung back, her great mass of dusky hair billowing behind her.

"Stop!" cried Dorothy, on whom the Queen's dark beauty had made a deep and lasting impression. "Why should we wish to destroy you? We came through the Yellow Wood and from there into the Black Forest, but we only wished to go through as quickly as possible. We are in trouble ourselves. Did you know that Ozma of Oz, the Wizard of Oz, the four rulers of Oz, and many others have vanished? There is a false Emperor on the throne in the Emerald City, and under the magic of his enchantment all the people have forgotten Ozma ever was their Queen. Pigasus and I, escaping this enchantment, are trying to find Ozma and someone to help us restore her to power." Dorothy spoke with such earnestness and feeling, Gloma could not help believing her.

"Then — then you did not come here to destroy me at all?" she exclaimed with an unhappy and embarrassed glance at her two prisoners. "Forgive me for using my magic powers, I only wanted to save myself and my foresters from obliteration."

"Oh, that's all right." Dorothy dismissed with a careless shrug the danger and discomfort of the last hour. "You thought we were going to destroy you, so, of course, you tried to destroy us first. That was fair enough, and I don't blame you, but now that we understand each other better, perhaps you will help us. Do you, yourself, remember Ozma, and is your magic powerful enough to tell us where she is?"

Seating herself in a chair near Dorothy's footstool, Gloma stared thoughtfully at the velvet carpet. "I know or remember nothing of the present history of Oz," she told them after a short silence. "At the time the Wizard of Oz ruled Oz, I ruled by royal right and inheritance the entire southern part of the Winkie Empire. Although the Wicked Witch of the East claimed dominion over the whole country, she only succeeded in bringing the central and northern parts under her control. We in the South were free, but when word came that a mortal girl had destroyed both the Witch of the East and the Witch of the West, I, being a witch, naturally supposed I would be the next one to suffer destruction. So, calling together the strongest and most faithful of my subjects, I begged them to retire with me to a safe and hidden spot where we could live in safety and tranquility far from the wars, dangers, and changing fortunes of the times. Many of my Southern Winkies cast their lot with the new order, marching off to the North, but many came with me, and retiring to this hidden forest, we cut ourselves off from all intercourse with the other Kingdoms of Oz, living the free and happy life of foresters and enjoying all the beauty and benefits of outdoor sport and activity. Of the rulers in Oz since the Wizard, I know nothing whatever."

"And were you always black?" inquired Pigasus, peering inquisitively up into Gloma's face and wondering whether the two small, black wings on each side of her forehead were as useful as his own.

"No," admitted the Queen, smiling graciously down at her plump questioner. "That was part of our disappearing plan; in a dark forest we were so much less likely to be found or discovered, so with my knowledge of the black arts I turned myself and my subjects as black as you now see us."

"What a shame! What a pity!" Dorothy jumped up and perched cozily on the arm of the Black Queen's chair. "If you had just come to the Emerald City, we could have been friends all this while."

"Why not begin now?" smiled the Queen, putting her arm affectionately round Dorothy's waist. "And you must not be sorry for us, for here we have been perfectly happy and content, and I have grown so fond of my black forest and castle I would not change their lovely sable for all the other colors in the rainbow. But tell me quickly again all that has happened in Oz, and perhaps I can make amends for the shabby treatment you have received at our hands."

Contritely the Black Queen leaned down to pat Pigasus, and as Dorothy sketched in most of the important happenings in Oz since the reign of the Wizard, the little pig pressed closely against her side. With many interested nods and exclamations, Gloma listened, and when Dorothy described the great festival that had been planned to celebrate the discovery of Oz by mortals, how Ozma and all her most important visitors and advisers had vanished at the banquet, and a false Emperor taken possession of the palace, the Queen rose and walked solemnly over to the black crystal. But after a long look into its inky depths, Gloma turned sadly away.

"My black magic cannot help you," she told them regretfully. "The rulers of Oz and your other friends have been enchanted by green magic, and only by green magic can they be released and restored to power. But I can assist you in other ways," added the Queen, noting the disappointed expressions on the faces of her two new friends. "One tap of my scepter will transport you to any country and here —" from a drawer in the ebony table the Queen drew a small, black, round box " — in this container you will find a most powerful powder of darkness. One pinch of this powder tossed into the air will cause a black cloud a mile square to envelop and totally darken a city or country. While no one in this darkened area will be able to see you, it will be perfectly possible for you to see them as clearly as in the usual daylight. In case of danger it affords a safe way of escape from the enemy. To dispel the cloud, you merely close the box."

"That ought to be just the thing to use if we ever get back to the Emerald City," observed Pigasus, scratching his left ear with his right hind paw. "Why, we could swoop down on this Emperor, bind him fast, and tweak him by the nose before he even knew what was happening."

"Why, so we could!" beamed Dorothy, brightening up at once. "And now, though of course black is a perfectly beautiful color, could you change us back to the colors we were when we came?" Dorothy spoke timidly, for she did not want to hurt Gloma's feelings.

"As soon as you leave the forest, you will resume your natural coloring," the witch assured them with a little smile. "And where, may I ask, were you planning to go first?"

"Well," said Dorothy slowly, "I thought perhaps the countries outside of Oz might not be under this forgetting spell and that we might find in one of them a King who would lend us his army and help us to chase Skamperoo out of the Emerald City. Could you transport us as far as Ev, your Majesty?"

"As easily as I could invite you to dinner," Gloma assured them with an energetic little nod, "and I hope you will not only have dinner but rest yourselves before you start again on your dangerous journey."

"Pigasus — Pigasus, did you hear that? She can transport us all the way to Ev! Didn't I tell you we might find a good witch in this forest? Now everything will be all right!"

"So glad we met and got acquainted, You're not so black as you are painted!" chuckled Pigasus, breaking into rhyme from sheer good humor and relief. "And did I hear your Majesty invite us to dinner?"

"You certainly did," said Gloma, and dropping them a little bow, she swept gaily through the door.

"D'ye suppose it will be a black dinner?" whispered Pigasus, trotting briskly along beside Dorothy. "I've heard of light repasts, but never of dark ones. But I don't care. I'm hungry enough to eat tar pudding with cinder sauce."

"Sh-hh!" warned Dorothy with a little laugh. "She'll hear you."

Chapter 12 - Farewell to the Black Forest

Although the dinner in the Black Castle was as dark a repast as Pigasus had predicted, never had he or Dorothy dined more royally or partaken of more delicate fare. The black bean soup was followed by a black fish course, then came the dark meat of some superbly cooked fowl, "probably cinder-roosters," as Pigasus remarked in one of his humorous asides. The licorice was the most delicious of the vegetables, though the black asparagus and potatoes were appetizing, too. Black bread was served with the black grape salad and plum cake with black frosting with the black ices and blackberryade. The members of Gloma's household, now that their fear of Dorothy had been explained away, proved so interesting and merry, the time simply flew. The black lace frocks of the women and children and the soft leather suits of the black foresters were simple but elegant, and the Black Queen herself so lovely just to look at her gave one a curious thrill.

General Blotz, recalled from banishment by Blackjack, the Queen's pet Jackdaw, proved a singer of no mean ability and regaled the company with many famous black ballads and hunting songs. Pigasus, too, contributed to the general fun and gaiety with some of his best songs and verses and ate so many slices of the black plum cake, Dorothy began to feel positively uneasy.

Interesting and delightful as it all was, the little girl could not help thinking of Ozma and her other unfortunate and captive friends, and as the black banjo clock in the corner of the hall struck a musical ten, she lightly touched the arm of Gloma. The Black Queen had graciously placed Dorothy beside her.

"I think we had better go now," whispered Dorothy earnestly. "If Pigasus eats any more, he'll fall asleep and we'll have to wait till morning." Gloma smiled and nodded understandingly then, pressing Dorothy's hand for "goodbye," stole quietly off to her workshop. Dorothy tried to signal Pigasus across the gleaming black table, but before she could catch his eye he had vanished, and she herself was whirling dizzily through space.

"Maybe it would have been better to have spent the night in the castle," mused Dorothy, spreading her arms like wings as she sailed through the air. "I don't suppose we'll be able to see in the dark now that we are out of the Black Forest, and goodness knows where we'll come down." There was no moon, and peer about as she would, Dorothy could not even catch a glimpse of the flying pig. "Of course," Dorothy went on conversationally to herself, "we could have flown all this distance on Piggins' back, but this is quicker and less trouble, but oh, dear, I do hope he's all right." Her worry about the pink pig ended rather abruptly, for at that very moment she began to somersault over and over in a headlong drop to the ground. A painful grunt as she landed assured her of the pig's presence.

"What are you trying to do? Puncture me?" puffed Pigasus as Dorothy with an embarrassed little gasp of apology rolled off his back. "Such rudeness!" grunted her companion, scrambling to his feet with an angry snort. "Flinging us out of her castle as if we'd been garbage. Yes, garbage," he repeated, winking rapidly.

"It was my fault," cried Dorothy, moving over to smooth out his ruffled wing feathers. "I asked her to transport us to Ev, and OH, PIGGINS!" By the light of a crooked lamp set in a crevice of the rocky path on which they found themselves, Dorothy regarded him rapturously. "You're pink again!"

"Am I? Well, that's something." Waddling closer to the lamp, Pigasus examined himself with careful attention. "You're pink, too," he said a little more pleasantly, "but these magic transportations are a bit sudden, if you ask me, and I'm not at all sure I like this spot. Where are we, anyway?"

"Oh, it's all right, and now we don't have to travel at all. We're here," announced Dorothy, who had hurried on a few steps ahead.

"And where is here?" grumbled Pigasus, following pompously, more from too much plum cake than from a desire to be disagreeable.

"Why, at Kalico's Mountain!" exclaimed Dorothy, pointing excitedly to a small door in the rocky surface before them. "Now we don't have to decide between the Gnome King and the King of Ev. Since we are here, we'll try Kalico first."

"Trying him is all very well, but I hope he does not try any magic on us," yawned Pigasus, squinting sleepily up at the brass sign hung on the stout wooden door. "What does it say there?" A green lantern hung over the door, and by its flickering light Dorothy read slowly:

"Back door of the Gnome King's Underground Castle. No dogs, babies or chickens allowed. No gold fish wanted. No peddlers or snailsmen need apply. Keep out and stay out. This means YOU."

"Oh, that's all right, laughed Dorothy as Pigasus looked rather alarmed at the sternly worded notice. "We're not babies or chickens or goldfish, and Kalico's a friend of mine. Come on!" Lifting the knocker and smiling confidently, Dorothy knocked three times on the Gnome King's back door.

Chapter 13 - In Kalico's Castle

"What is it, Shoofenwaller?" Kalico, the thin and gray little King of the Gnomes, peered impatiently down from the great carved gem-studded rock that served him for a throne. "Shoo, go away. You know this is my hour for retiring! Go away, I tell you! And if you never come back, it will still be too soon."

"Yes, but your MAJESTY!" While obediently backing toward the door, the King's Royal Chamberlain extended his arms imploringly. "Something has come up; the Long-Eared Hearer reports footsteps on the South Mountain. Two visitors are about to enter the back door of our castle."

"Visitors!" exclaimed Kalico, getting up with an impatient flounce. "At this hour! Well, tell them to go away and come back tomorrow. Here, wait a moment." As Shoofenwaller, shrugging his narrow shoulders, turned to carry out his orders, Kalico changed his mind. "Just hand me my expectacles," commanded the King crossly, "I may as well have a look at the prowling pests."

With another shrug, Shoofenwaller stepped to a small cabinet, and taking a pair of smoked glasses from the top drawer, handed them up to the King. Now Kalico's expectacles were very useful, enabling him to see who was coming before they arrived, and clapping them hurriedly on his thin nose, he stared intently off into space. At what he saw, the King's expression changed from irritation to vague uneasiness. "Botheration!" he muttered morosely. "It's one of those mortals from the Emerald City. Why can't those girls stay home? Always poking their noses into other people's affairs and trying to save somebody from something."

"Which one is it?" asked Shoofenwaller, blinking.

"It's Dorothy," sighed Kalico, taking off his expectacles and putting them absently into his pocket, "and there's a queer kind of winged pig with her. A pig with wings, mind you. Rooks and rockets! Wonder what they want."

"Why not find out?" suggested Shoofenwaller reasonably.

"No! No, not tonight," Kalico waved his hands determinedly. "Just conduct them to the red guest cave, Shoofenwaller, and bring them to me in the morning." With a stiff bow, the Royal Chamberlain backed out the door and pattered away to admit the visitors.

"And about time, too," thought Dorothy as the rock door opened cautiously and the little crooked Gnome thrust out his head.

"In the name of King Kalico the First, I hereby welcome you to Gnome Man's Land," began Shoofenwaller pompously.

"Oh, that's all right," yawned Pigasus wearily, "what we want is a place to sleep, and remember — no trickery!" he added sharply as the Gnome stood aside so that they could enter the narrow rock passageway.

"I suppose your Highness comes on a matter of state?" remarked Shoofenwaller, turning from Pigasus with an involuntary grimace. Pigs reminded him of ham; ham reminded him of eggs; and eggs were immediate death and destruction to gnomes.

"Well, yes," admitted Dorothy, adjusting her step to the short, crooked legs of the King's little Counselor. "What I really need is an army!"

"An army?" groaned Shoofenwaller, realizing what bad news this would be for his master. "Our army?"

"Oh, let's talk about all that in the morning," wheezed Pigasus as Dorothy briskly nodded her head in answer to Shoofenwaller's question. The pink pig was taking sleepy sidelong squints at the elegantly excavated and gem-encrusted corridors of the Gnome King's underground dwelling.

"Just what his Majesty suggested," muttered the Chamberlain, sweeping open a red iron door with a ruby knob. "I trust you will be comfortable here and rest well. If your Highness wishes a cup of Kalicocoa, or your friend a mud pie or pudding, just ring the bell. Goodnight, Princess! Goodnight, er, er — PIG!"

"Sa-hay, I resent that!" Pigasus cocked his ears belligerently as the King's crooked little messenger bowed himself out the door. "Did you notice the way he said `pig,' Dorothy?"

"Yes," said Dorothy with a little yawn, "I did, but then all gnomes are sassy, and you'll have to get used to them. If Kalico helps us, that's all we care about."

Pigasus nodded rather grimly. "I suppose this is what you call getting down to bed rock," he murmured, looking around the red-rock apartment with his amused blue stare. "Hope the beds aren't rock, too." Punching a red sofa experimentally and finding it surprisingly soft, the pink pig jumped up and settled himself cozily among the cushions. Pigasus had lived in castles and palaces all his life and was so accustomed to comfort and luxury that without bothering to look around Kalico's richly appointed guest cavern he closed his eyes and fell asleep. Dorothy, tiptoeing through a curtain into an adjoining red-rock cavern that served as a bedroom, undressed quickly and putting out the ruby lamps slid thankfully between the red silk sheets and was soon as soundly asleep as Pigasus.

They were just having breakfast, served by two small gnomen in their red sitting-cave, when Shoofenwaller came hurrying in to announce that Kalico was ready and waiting to see them. Earlier the Gnome King and his Chamberlain had discussed the possible purposes of Dorothy's visit, and Kalico had been extremely annoyed to learn that she wanted to borrow his army.

"And you will lend it to her, all our hundred thousand trained Gnomen Yoemen?" questioned Shoofenwaller anxiously.

"What else can I do?" Kalico snapped his little gray eyes unhappily. "Remember, it was Dorothy who stole the former Gnome King's magic belt and really was the means of my becoming King."

"That's so," muttered Shoofenwaller, pulling his ear reflectively. "But why not use a little strategy in this conference, King? Why not pretend to help her and at the same time safeguard your own interests? Lending our army is a dangerous experiment. Suppose an enemy threatened us while our fighting forces were in the Emerald City? Anything could happen. Put her off, make excuses," urged Shoofenwaller craftily. This suggestion fell in exactly with the Gnome King's wishes, and curious to know what really had brought Dorothy to his castle, he sent his little Chamberlain hurrying off to bring her to the throne room.

"And now for a little Kalicoaxing," sniffed Pigasus, waddling unconcernedly along beside Dorothy under magnificent arches, over artificial terraces and rock gardens, gazing down long vistas of yet-unmined shafts where hundreds of gnomes worked busily with picks and shovels to further enrich the already enormously rich and powerful little Metal Monarch. Kalico, as they entered the beautifully furnished and lavishly carved cave that he used for a throne room, came hurrying to meet them.

"So charming of you to come all this way just to see me," murmured the Gnome King, taking both of Dorothy's hands in his own and bowing graciously as she introduced Pigasus. "Always delighted to entertain a Princess from the Court of her Royal Highness, Ozma of Oz!"

"Oh, Kalico, then you DO remember her! Oh, please, dear Kalico, will you help us to find her?"

"Find her? Why, what under the earth do you mean? Is Ozma lost?" Kalico's long face at Dorothy's excited greeting grew visibly longer, and after the little girl had explained the disappearance of Ozma and the others, the enchantment of all the people in Oz, and the coming of Skamperoo to the Emerald City, Kalico climbed wearily back on his throne and sat down.

"This — this is shocking!" faltered Kalico, mopping his forehead with a long, gray cobweb, "And just what do you and this — this — pig intend to do about it?"

"What do YOU intend to do about it?" Rather tired of being called a pig, Pigasus planted all four feet and stared defiantly up at the perturbed Metal Monarch.

"Well — er — that is — er — I don't see that it is MY affair at all!" mumbled Kalico with a rueful nod of his head. "Anyone powerful enough to conquer Ozma and Oz would pay small attention to opinions of mine."

"But we don't want your opinions," stated Pigasus bluntly. "What we want is your army and any magic you can conveniently spare!"

"Please, Kalico, do help us," begged Dorothy, running up the carved rock steps of the throne and seating herself coaxingly on the arm. "With all your thousands of gnomes and many magic powers, we can certainly drive Skamperoo out of the Emerald City."

"Well, of course," sighed Kalico, flattered by Dorothy's reference to his magic powers, "I'll do what I can, but if what you say is true, it will take more than one army to reconquer Oz." As he said this, Kalico looked across at Shoofenwaller, and the little Chamberlain, well pleased with his master's strategy, gave him an encouraging wink. "I tell you what I'll do." Kalico crossed his legs and regarded Dorothy through half-closed eyes. "If you find another King willing to send his army into Oz, I will also send mine. Remember, even Ozma's closest friends and retainers have forgotten her, and the entire population, now fully convinced Skamperoo is their rightful ruler, will rise to oppose us."

"Yes, yes, but have you no magic that will dispel this wicked enchantment or help us to locate our friends and sovereigns?" demanded Pigasus, not wholly satisfied with the Gnome King's offer.

"Gnome magic may be of no use in this case; nevertheless, I will send for my wizard and see what can be done." Remembering their last experience with magic, Dorothy stepped down from Kalico's throne and seated herself quietly on the pink pig's back, and Pigasus, grunting with relief, squinted suspiciously at the small, ugly Wizard of the Underworld who presently came shuffling into the royal presence chamber. As quickly as possible, Kalico explained to the Wizard all the dire happenings in Oz.

"Do you think our magic spyglass could locate Ozma and her missing friends and associates or tell us whether they have been utterly and completely destroyed?" demanded the Gnome King gravely.

Potaroo, the King's magician, stood pulling his straggly whiskers for several moments after Kalico had finished speaking, then he stamped four times on the flagged floor with his right foot. Almost instantly four gnome wise men in peaked hats came into the throne room wheeling a huge telescope before them. Dorothy and Pigasus, prickling with suspense and terror, watched the Wizard screw his eye to the end of the twisting spyglass. After several snorts and surprised exclamations, Potaroo straightened up. "The missing Ozians and the Wizard of Ev are hidden away in Thunder Mountain," he stated in a hoarse whisper. An electric little silence followed Potaroo's disclosure, and as no one uttered a sound, the wizard continued, "As the spyglass is now pointing north, I believe you will find Thunder Mountain in that direction, but I must warn you that it will be a long and exceedingly dangerous journey."

"Danger? Well, what do we care for that? Quick somebody, fetch me my coat — my hat —"

"This hardly seems a time for jokes and verses," murmured Kalico, looking at Dorothy in mild disapproval.

"She has to make verses and rhymes when she rides me. I'm a poetry pig, and a lucky star guides me!" grunted Pigasus, too overcome by the wizard's awful news to realize he was speaking in verse himself.

"Oh, what difference does it make?" cried Dorothy, jumping quickly off his back. "We must go to Thunder Mountain at once. Pigasus can fly there."

"Here, here, not in such a hurry," exclaimed Kalico, secretly delighted at the prospect of being so easily rid of his troubles. "We must pack you a lunch basket, and tell me, Potaroo, have you any magic that will make the journey less dangerous for these brave young adventurers?"

"M-magic?" stuttered Potaroo, his eyes growing glassy at the mere thought of parting with any of his magic treasures. "Well, er, I could lend them a box of my famous triple-action stumbling blocks. They will overthrow any enemy, no matter how numerous."

"Splendid!" beamed Kalico, rubbing his hands briskly together, "And don't forget, in the course of your journey north, if you find a King willing to lend his army, my army also will be ready and at your service."

"Oh, Kalico, how kind you are!" Running up the steps of the throne again, Dorothy gave the Gnome King an impulsive hug.

"Come on, COME on!" squealed Pigasus, who had seen the various winks between Kalico and Shoofenwaller and was convinced that the little Gnome King was doing as little as he possibly could. "Give us our lunch and our stumbling blocks and we'll be off, and I must say they'll be an enormous help when we reach Thunder Mountain." Spreading his wings, Pigasus began to fly in angry circles round the Gnome King's head.

"Humph, pork's going up!" sniffed Shoofenwaller as he hurried away to see about packing the lunch basket.

"He ought to be dried, smoked and salted," muttered Potaroo, going sulkily off to fetch the blocks. Dorothy, in earnest consultation with Kalico, heard neither of these remarks, and when a few moments later the two returned with

143

two boxes and Dorothy's hat and coat, she thanked them politely, called Pigasus down from a rocky ledge where he had flown, and climbed happily on his back. Then Pigasus, not giving her time for any lengthy farewells, zipped through the tunneled caverns and corridors of the Gnome King's Underground Dominions and burst thankfully out the back door of South Mountain.

"Now let's see, which way is north?" mused Pigasus, twirling his curly tail around like a propeller. "All we have to do is to fly north to Thunder Mountain, unlock its thunder bolts, restore the rulers of Oz, toss tumbling blocks at all enemies, raise a grand army, and then, THEN King Kalico will help us. Isn't it just too magniferous!"

"Why, Piggins, how mean of you, surely you know The Gnome King's our friend, don't you like Kalico?"

"No!" said Pigasus fiercely, hurling himself into the air.

"Well, anyway, we're better off than we were before," thought Dorothy after several rhymed attempts to draw Pigasus into a conversation. "At least we now know where Ozma is and have two kinds of magic and the promise of an army. Really, we're getting on quite fast." But perhaps had she seen the King and his Chamberlain nodding their heads like two little China mandarins as she and Pigasus left the throne room, she would not have felt so cheerful.

"That's the last we'll ever see of her," chuckled Shoofenwaller, dropping a dried lizard instead of a lump of sugar into his tea. (Gnomes always flavor their tea with lizards.) "No one yet has ever come safely back from Thunder Mountain. But what about this new Emperor of Oz?"

"Oh, that will be all right!" Kalico waved one hand airily. "I would much rather have a man on the throne of Oz. Ozma is always involving me in wars or demanding the rights of smaller Kingdoms, so long may she stay in Thunder Mountain and long Skamperoo rule in Oz!"

"Long live the Emperor!" echoed Shoofenwaller, and clicking their teacups gaily together, the two bad little Gnomes drained to the last drop their black and bitter tea. And we should not be too hard on Kalico, I suppose, for like all the dwellers under the earth, his heart is gray and flinty as the rock that forms his cavern, the blood in his veins cold and sluggish as the leaden waters of the underground rivers that wind sullenly through his dark domain.

Chapter 14 - The Emperor of Oz

The same morning Dorothy wakened in the rustic summer house of the Winkie farmer, Skamperoo opened his eyes upon the unaccustomed grandeur of Ozma's Royal Palace. The banquet had lasted till long after three o'clock, then still chuckling and yawning, he had waved goodnight to his hilarious and amiable subjects and led Chalk off to bed. Twenty footmen with twenty lighted tapers preceded him to Ozma's own apartment, but dismissing this as too plain and simple, he had taken the immense green guest suite across the hall.

Chalk would have much preferred a stall in the Royal Stable with the other four-footed members of the castle party, but Skamperoo would not hear of such a separation. He wanted his white wishing horse close at hand, not only because through him and the magic emeralds he could satisfy every wish, but because for the first time in his long, lazy, selfish life he had found someone he liked better than himself. In Skamperoo's eyes Chalk was absolutely perfect, and as his own wish had brought the golden-maned charger into being, he felt proud and important as a parent with his first child.

After a few regretful sniffs out of the window, a few short turns up and down their immense and elegant sleeping apartment, Chalk leaped lightly on one of the large, green beds and settled himself gracefully for the night. Covering Chalk tenderly with a green satin quilt, Skamperoo hastily disrobed, and clutching his precious necklaces, climbed wearily into the other bed. There, without even stopping to wish himself goodnight, he fell into a deep and tranquil slumber. Indeed, both, in spite of the strangeness of their surroundings, slept soundly till morning.

About eight o'clock, Chalk, lifting his head from the embroidered pillow, looked indulgently across at the new Emperor of Oz. Sitting up in bed, Skamperoo was busily counting the gems in his three magic chains.

"Ho, throw those silly beads away!" advised the white horse, jumping out of bed with a gay toss of his golden mane. "You have nothing else to wish for, Kingaling, nothing more at all! M-mmm, this green carpet looks good enough to eat, but I've a fancy to nibble the clover in Your Majesty's garden while it is still fresh with dew."

"Say it again," begged Skamperoo, closing his eyes and clasping himself blissfully around the middle.

"Your Majesty's garden! Your Majesty's Palace, Your Majesty's Kingdom of Oz!" whinnied the white horse, rising on his hind legs and pirouetting round with mischievous little prances. "But come, Emp! What are your wishes for today? I think we will have to use the necklaces after all. You must certainly have some new clothes. It would never do to appear this morning in the suit you wore last night. You had better have some sleeping garments, too. I've a notion that Emperors do not sleep in their raw hides like horses." Skamperoo, giggling self-consciously, dragged the satin sheets up to his chin, for to tell the truth, he had arrived in the Emerald City with only one suit to his back, and an extremely shabby one at that.

"Maybe I'd better change my face, too," he murmured, "to go with all this, you know." Dreamily Skamperoo waved his hands about, and then, leaning forward, slipped the chains over Chalk's ear.

"What's the matter with the face you have?" demanded Chalk, gazing fondly at the red, rotund countenance of his Master. "I like you just as you are, and if you change I wouldn't even know you, but I'll tell you what you can wish after you've ordered yourself some new clothes — wish yourself a seasoned rider, and then we can go far and wide, Kingaling, far and wide at a furious gallop and none shall say us nay — hey, hey!"

"And none shall say us nay," trilled Skamperoo, rolling out of bed, covers and all. To wish himself fifty jewel-encrusted robes with boots, crowns, and all the undergarments to go with them, fifty splendid sleeping robes, and fifty suits of riding clothes took but a moment. He and Chalk could hear them landing with little thuds on the hangars in the many closets as Skamperoo finished speaking. Then, being naturally lazy, the new Emperor wished that he had already had his bath and was dressed in his green riding clothes. So immediately he was, and winking at his clever assistant adviser, he next wished himself the best rider in Oz. Then, taking back his necklaces, he buttoned them carefully in a little pocket over his heart and went over to the mirror to have a look at himself.

"How about this governing stuff?" puffed the self-made Emperor, turning this way and that to get a good view of his new clothes.

"Oh, I shouldn't bother about governing," answered Chalk carelessly. "A well-governed country like this should be able to run itself for a few weeks. By that time we'll be ready for more serious matters, but right now I'm all for enjoying myself. A splendid idea, that, of putting all the rulers and the Wizard and his magic out of the way. The rest of your court and subjects are exceedingly sensible and jolly, and if we are pleasant and sensible too, everything will be `What ho and so cozy!' So let's go below and start our first day of emperoaring!" Impatiently Chalk pranced away toward the door.

"You're sure I look all right?" asked Skamperoo with another anxious squint at his reflection. "Seems to me I'm a bit fat."

"Oh, don't worry about that," said Chalk, rolling his eyes wickedly. "Come along, come along, and I'll soon shake some of that fat off you. Up with you, Kingaling, and let's to our oats!" To his delight and pleasure, Skamperoo had not the slightest trouble mounting, and once in the saddle he felt perfectly at home, even when Chalk bounded through the door, took the long, circular steps between a canter and a gallop, and ran madly three times round the Royal gardens.

On fine days Ozma always had breakfast in her private garden, and it being an especially fine day, the palace servants without thought or question had placed the royal table under the trees. It was still fairly early, and none of the guests or members of the household were down, but this did not spoil Skamperoo's excellent appetite at all. Ordering Chalk a breakfast of oats, bran and quartered apples, he seated himself gaily at the head of the table. The green riding hat, set well over one ear, became him vastly well, and Chalk, regarding him proudly from the foot of the table, thought him every inch an Emperor, even if round the waist there were a good many too many inches.

"I wish Pinny Penny could see you now," sighed the horse, sinking contentedly back on his haunches, "and how I should have enjoyed seeing Matiah's face when he finally discovered you and the necklaces were gone. By the way, perhaps we should do something about Matiah."

"Pinny Penny will attend to him," said Skamperoo, popping a huge cherry into his mouth and nodding his head reassuringly. "I'll wager Pinny Penny sent the fellow packing the moment he found himself King. Wonder how Pinny is making out, anyway?"

"But suppose Matiah should follow us here?" went on Chalk. Having been in existence only two days, he knew little of Oz or geozophy.

"He can't come here," Skamperoo told him triumphantly. "There's a deadly desert between Skampavia and Oz that no one in my father's lifetime or in mine has ever crossed, that is with the exception of ourselves, and we were wished across, which doesn't count." Then, as four footmen with heaping trays appeared, he winked at Chalk, and the white horse lapsed into a thoughtful silence.

And Skamperoo had been perfectly correct in his conjectures about Pinny Penny. When, with a resounding clunk, the King's gold crown had fallen upon the astonished Prime Minister, his head had gone entirely through so he was forced to wear it much as a dog wears a collar. But even so, he was not slow to realize the significance of this odd happening or the power it brought with it. Gripping the scepter, which had forced itself into his hand, he rushed into the throne room to find out what strange whim of his Master had made him acting King of the Realm. A glance around the throne room was enough to show him that Skamperoo was not there, and when he saw Matiah sitting so unconcernedly in the book alcove, a sudden rage and conviction seized him. Whatever had happened, Matiah was to blame.

"Leave this palace at once!" shouted Pinny Penny, stamping first one foot and then the other. "At once, do you hear, or I'll call out the guard!" Matiah, still deep in the History of Oz, looked up in astonishment, and when he saw the

145

little Prime Minister wearing Skamperoo's crown round his neck and brandishing his scepter, he gave a perfect bellow of anger and dismay.

"Where's the King?" he roared, looking wildly around the throne room, "And why are you wearing his crown? Where's Skamperoo — where're the necklaces?"

"Ask yourself!" raged Pinny Penny, shaking the scepter threateningly. "Everything was quiet and peaceful till you and your necklaces arrived at this palace; there's some magic trickery about them and about you. Don't think I was fooled by that horse story, a horse does not appear out of the air. Well, now the King's gone, the horse is gone, and unless you are gone in ten seconds I'll have you thrown out of the window. Ten seconds, do you hear? This crown and scepter came to me through no wish or choice of my own, but since they did come to me, I AM THE KING! And I intend to rule this country. My first official act will be to rid myself of your filthy presence. Now then, start walking, merchant, and don't stop till you reach the border. Twenty guards will follow to see you safely out of the country."

"You wait till Skamperoo hears about this!" blustered Matiah, backing away in alarm from the determined little Prime Minister. "I'm more important to him than anyone else."

"Then why aren't you with him?" inquired Pinny Penny shrewdly. "No, wherever he's gone, he has gone without you. I am the King, and I do not need you, so be off!" Clapping his hands, Pinny gave a sharp command to the guards who came hurrying in answer to his summons. Retiring rapidly to escape the tips of their sharp spikes, Matiah sullenly began his long march. It was nightfall by the time the little company reached the edge of Skampavia. Here, in a wilderness of rock and rubble, the guardsmen left him with food enough for a couple of days and stern warnings never to return to Skampavia. Far to the west the miserable merchant could see the comforting lights of Merryland, but he had no desire to go there or east to the Kingdom of Ix. Instead, he stared hopelessly across the wilderness to where the heaving sands of the Deadly Desert gleamed like molten silver in the moonlight.

How had that rascally monarch ever escaped without his seeing him? How could he ever safely cross the Deadly Desert and hope to reach Oz? How had Skamperoo, who seemed so dumb and foolish, ever discovered the secret of using the magic emeralds when he himself had failed to do so? How? How? How? Crouched on a flat rock, munching one of the sandwiches left by the guards, Matiah scowled evilly across the grim desert, his thoughts as treacherous and shifting as its deadly sands.

Chapter 15 - The Dooners!

All day, with only a short pause for lunch, Pigasus had flown north, Dorothy keeping a sharp lookout for Thunder Mountain or mountains of any sort, but the wild, desolate country through which they were flying was flat, desert-like and apparently perfectly uninhabited.

"A fine, healthy chance we have of finding an army here!" snorted Pigasus as the afternoon drew to a hot, weary close. "And what we'll do when we find Thunder Mountain I haven't the faintest notion, have you? Even if I butt my nose black, blue and blunt, and you break both knuckles beating on its rocky exterior, how can we ever hope to enter such a place, much less release our unfortunate sovereigns? I told you Kalico was a scoundrel; I'll wager he's sent us on a wild-goose chase just to get us out of the way."

"Ah, don't say I told you so, There's always some way, you know," said Dorothy, almost as downhearted as Pigasus, though she would not admit it. The pink pig, rather ashamed of himself, flew for several miles without saying anything, then, in rather a gruff voice, he called Dorothy's attention to the changing nature of the scenery below.

"Notice the hills?" he snorted more hopefully. "Maybe there is a mountain, after all, but the sun's going down, and I'm ready to sink myself, so let's descend and see whether we can find a soft rock on which to lay our heads."

"Not hills, dunes!" cried Dorothy, bouncing off as soon as Pigasus touched the earth. "Sand dunes; we must be near the coast and the Nonestic Ocean."

"It does smell salty," agreed Pigasus, sniffing the air eagerly, "but suppose we save the ocean for tomorrow; my feet ache, my wings ache, and I'm hollow as a drum."

"Then we'll have supper," decided Dorothy sensibly. So seating themselves comfortably with their backs against a dune, the two weary explorers finished up all the cold meat, fruit, pie and sandwiches Shoofenwaller had packed up for them. After a long, wistful sniff into the box convinced him there was not another crumb, Pigasus folded his wings and lay down in the soft sand at the foot of the dune, giving only indistinct grunts and snorts to Dorothy's questions and observations. Finally, getting no answer at all, Dorothy discovered he was asleep. The regular rise and fall of the pink pig's sides, the soft, drowsy singing of the west wind lulled Dorothy into a pleasant state of dreaminess, and presently, with her head comfortably pillowed on the pig's plump shoulder, she fell asleep, too.

It must have been hours later when terrified squeals from Pigasus and the patter of a hundred hurrying feet made her start up in alarm. Still only half awake, she was startled to find herself and Pigasus surrounded by a horde of savage-looking sandmen. In the pale and watery moonlight they looked like creatures out of some very bad dream. Their bodies were roughly moulded of sand, their eyes strangely green and phosphorescent, while their hair, rising like beach grass from their pointed heads, waved about their lumpy faces.

Clutching the basket that contained her small store of clothing, the Black Witch's powder of darkness, and Potaroo's box of stumbling blocks, Dorothy pressed back against the dune. Her first idea of leaping on the pig's back and bidding him fly was useless. Pigasus lay helplessly on his side, his wings and legs bound tightly with long strands of tough, strong seaweed. Thankful to find that she at least was free, Dorothy went a step closer to her struggling, squealing, furious little comrade. As she did so, a perfect shower of sand balls came flying toward her. The sharp sting of the sandmen's missiles not only awoke her completely, but goaded her into instant and angry action.

"Stop that! Stop that at once!" she cried, stamping her foot indignantly, but her words only brought another shower of sand balls down on their heads.

"You have dared to invade the sacred domain of the Dooners," yelled the rasping voice of the leader, rattling a long string of seashells he wore round his neck. "And therefore you shall be sand balled, sand bagged and made into sandwiches for the sand crabs!"

If the Dooner had not looked so wild and dangerous, his foolish threat might have been amusing, but as he and his bandy-legged sandmen came leaping forward, Pigasus gave a squeal of sheer terror, and Dorothy, raising the basket over her head, hurled it with all her might into the midst of the advancing army. The effect was immediate and astonishing. Cowering down beside Pigasus and expecting to be seized or trampled on, Dorothy saw the first line of Dooners going down like a row of tenpins, then all the others began tumbling and tripping and falling in heaps. No sooner would a sandman rise than he would instantly tumble down again, and their squalls and screeches of rage were so piercing Dorothy put both hands over her ears.

"It's the blocks," wheezed Pigasus, managing to lift his head a few inches. "Kalico's stumbling blocks are flying like fur and fury. Now if they just keep 'em down for a while longer, we might get away."

Dorothy, peering sharply into the midst of the tumbling Dooners, saw the fifty magic squares released from their box when she flung her basket, fairly exploding with activity, and scramble up as they would after each tumble, the sandmen could not advance an inch, or even manage to stand erect. The leader, attempting to crawl forward on his hands and knees, was caught by a dozen of the whirling missiles and rolled back like a log among his churning comrades.

"Hurray! Three cheers for Kalico!" puffed Pigasus. "Quick, my girl, see if you can untie these wretched seaweeds, and we'll be flying and be off in a pigwhistle."

"I had a pair of scissors in my basket, if it hasn't fallen out, and anyway I'm not going without my things," declared Dorothy, now quite bold since the enemy had been overcome by magic. And in spite of the pig's anxious squeals of warning, she rushed forward, grabbed her basket and began picking up her scattered belongings, noting with a sigh of relief that the box containing the powder of darkness was still closed. With the scissors, still safe in the little pocket in the side of the basket, she soon clipped the seaweed trusses from Pigasus, and clasping the basket in her arms climbed swiftly on his back. Pigasus, without one backward glance, rose straight into the air and again headed north. Dorothy, peering fearfully over his left wing, saw the Dooners spring suddenly to their feet and then, like frightened prairie dogs, disappear into many holes in the sand.

Funny, mused Dorothy, that they had not noticed these openings before. Funny that the Dooners had stopped stumbling as soon as she and Pigasus had taken to the air. Funny — but then, everything was funny. Right in the middle of her conjectures, the box of stumbling blocks, now closed and tied with a red ribbon, dropped "plink" into the middle of her basket.

"Someone's throwing things," gasped Pigasus, flapping his wings a bit faster and looking rather wildly over his shoulder.

"No, just our box of stumbling blocks," yawned Dorothy. Now that the excitement was over, she felt dreadfully tired, and even the sight of the Nonestic Ocean rippling and gleaming a few yards ahead did not arouse or interest her.

It did not interest Pigasus either. He was far from pleased to find himself so near the coast. "I don't like this, I don't like this at all," muttered the pig, perking up his ears and wiggling his nose rapidly. "We've flown straight north, and instead of striking Thunder Mountain, we strike the sea, and how could a mountain be in the middle of the sea?"

"There are mountains on islands, and I have a notion There are plenty of islands out there in the ocean," said Dorothy sleepily, recalling the days she had studied geography in the United States.

"Take Japan, for instance, over there Mountains are simply everywhere!"

147

"I don't care if they are," answered Pigasus fiercely. "I won't go to Japan, and I'll not go a wing's breadth over this ocean tonight, islands or no islands. Sa-hay! There's the North Star to our left, so we're not going north at all. We're off our course, that's what we are!"

"North Star? North Star, of course we are!" murmured Dorothy with a drowsy nod.

"You're asleep," scolded Pigasus in a worried voice. "I'd better land."

"If you land too soon, you'll strike a dune," warned Dorothy with another yawn. And after a quick glance below and convinced they were still over the Dooners' domain, Pigasus spread his wings a bit wider and swung along the coast looking carefully for a safe place to land and spend the rest of the night. He was so busy squinting downward that he never saw the long, curious, tube-like shadow shooting after him with incredible accuracy and speed. A terrific blast of air as it rushed by them on the right was his first warning of danger. Dorothy, too, caught unaware, gave a faint shriek as an immense, snake-like body curved back and began to coil round and round them like some gigantic air serpent.

"It is a snake!" thought poor Dorothy as Pigasus clung helplessly in the little circle of air left in the center of its coils. Neither spoke, for truly there was nothing to say or do. Then just as the suspense grew too awful to be endured, the monster opened its mouth, and Dorothy, backing as far along the pig's back as she possibly could, almost lost her balance. Instead of a tongue or long tusks, out popped the head and shoulders of a little old man no larger than Dorothy herself.

"Pardon me," he murmured politely, "I was looking for a sea serpent."

"Do I look like a sea serpent?" snorted Pigasus in a quivering voice, for he was still half choked from shock and fright. "If you and that monster you're riding are looking for a sea serpent, go ahead — look for one, but leave honest travelers alone!"

"Monster?" exclaimed the little man in a hurt voice. "Oh, I say now, you have us all wrong. This is no monster, this is the long, strong, flexible, stretchable, SHOOTING TOWER of my private castle, and I myself am Bitty Bit, the Seer of Some Summit."

In the short silence that followed Bitty Bit's astonishing announcement, Dorothy, examining more closely the tube-like coils encircling herself and Pigasus, saw that they really were of stone with rubber-like sections between. What she had taken for a mouth was really a window. With his elbow resting on the ledge, Bitty Bit was regarding them fixedly.

"Well, even if you are a seer and have a shooting tower," grunted Pigasus, gathering courage as he went along, "there is no reason for you to come towering over us this way!"

"But a seer must be constantly looking for things," explained Bitty Bit, spreading his hands expansively. "That, you know, is his business. I am always looking for something, and tonight it happens to be sea serpents."

"Sorry to disappoint you," said Pigasus more mildly, "but since we are not sea serpents, perhaps you'll be good enough to unwind your tower. As it happens, I have a little looking to do myself. As a matter of fact, when you and your tower overtook us, I was searching for a safe place for this young Princess and myself to spend the night."

"Look no more!" begged Bitty Bit, leaning so far over the sill Dorothy involuntarily put out her hand to save him from falling. "You shall both spend the night in my castle. COME!" Grasping Dorothy by one hand and Pigasus by one wing, the little seer with superhuman strength for one so small and wrinkled dragged them both through the open window of his shooting tower.

Chapter 16 - The Seer of Some Summit

Since coming to Oz, Dorothy had traveled in many strange ways, but to find herself shooting through the midnight sky in Bitty Bit's tower was surely the oddest of all. Both she and Pigasus stared from the window in wide-eyed wonder as the tower uncoiled and started shrinking rapidly backward.

"We may as well go home at once," observed Bitty Bit, rubbing his little hands briskly together. "You are so much more interesting than sea serpents, and I can easily look for sea serpents some other night. Now don't be alarmed when we bump."

"Bump?" repeated Dorothy rather nervously.

"Of course," the sage told her calmly. "As I go forward, the tower stretches out in any direction I wish to go; when I return, it shrinks, contracts, and retires within itself like a telescope, and by the time we reach the castle it is no larger than an ordinary tower. Mm — better hold on to something, we're almost there!"

Running around the circular room a few feet from the wall was a gold railing. Pigasus had just time to seize it with one hand (sic — hand?) when Bitty Bit's tower with a resounding crash snapped back, but up to a vertical position, so that what had been the floor of the little room became the east wall and the window a skylight. Dorothy and Pigasus, describing a complete circle on the bar, landed in a more-or-less upside-down position on what had been the back wall. "That's why I have it cushioned," explained the seer, who also had executed a neat somersault. Hopping up as if landing on his head was a perfectly usual and ordinary occurrence, Bitty Bit opened a trap door and motioned for Dorothy and Pigasus to follow him down a long, winding stair.

"These magic contraptions will be the death of me," wheezed Pigasus, picking himself up with a groan. The cushioned floor had made his fall painless, but he was considerably jolted and upset from the shock, or rather the series of shocks that had so far punctuated their evening.

"But if he's a seer," whispered Dorothy, recovering her basket and trotting eagerly after Bitty Bit, "he ought to be able to help us a —"

"Bitty Bit," sniffed the pink pig. "Well, if he'll just help me to a bed, I'll be satisfied!" And grunting and grumbling, he clumped sleepily down the stairs behind Dorothy. The room into which the stone stairway led them was evidently the cozy and comfortable study of the comical little seer. Its walls were of oak, lined from floor to ceiling with books, and all its furnishings were tan or brown. Dorothy considered this extremely suitable, as Bitty Bit himself looked like a very wise and merry Brownie. On his little round head was a round cap with a yellow quill, and he wore a brown, wrinkled robe rather like a monk's, tied tightly round the waist with a yellow cord. His bright, black, sharp little eyes danced with good humor and interest in his suntanned, honest, little face.

While Pigasus stood sleepily and somewhat disapprovingly on the hearth rug, Dorothy sank into a snug brown armchair and looked expectantly up at their singular host.

"No, no, not a word," begged Bitty Bit, raising his hand pleadingly. "Remember, I am the Seer of Some Summit, a seer who can see and foresee; a seer who can tell and foretell. Just by closing my eyes I can tell who you are, whence you came, and whither you are going."

"Fancy that, now," observed Pigasus in a mocking voice.

"You," retorted Bitty Bit, pointing a skinny brown finger at the pig, "you are a creation of my friend, the Red Jinn, whose taste for low verse I always knew would lead him into some mischief."

"Low verses?" retorted Pigasus indignantly, while even Dorothy looked a little shocked.

"Yes, low verses," insisted Bitty Bit solemnly. "You are so constructed that he who rides must rhyme and break into foolish jingles. Is this not so?"

"They may be jingles, but they are NOT low verse," protested Pigasus, flapping his ears angrily.

"Well, then, let us call them simple verses," amended Bitty Bit with a generous wave of the hand, "at least they are verses that anyone can understand, which, of course, makes them of no value whatever. People never appreciate what they can understand."

"Dorothy does," declared Pigasus, now mad enough to fly right out the window.

"Dorothy? Ah, yes, I was coming to her." Swinging around, Bitty Bit, his eyes still tightly shut, wagged his finger at the astonished little girl. "You are the mortal girl who came to Oz by cyclone. You live in the Emerald City of Oz and are —"

"Oh, tell us something we don't already know," interrupted Pigasus with a bored yawn. "Where is Ozma of Oz now; how could a scalawag Emperor steal her throne?"

"Wait! Wait! Give me time! Not a word more — not a word!" panted Bitty Bit, advancing with short, dancing steps toward Dorothy. "I — I see a necklace," he muttered mysteriously. "One, two, three necklaces! I see a white horse and a fat, red-faced fellow wearing a small emerald crown. Great sea bass and sassafrass! Oz has been conquered, its inhabitants enchanted, its rulers banished, and the King of Skampavia sits on the throne."

"So that's where he comes from!" breathed Dorothy, forgetting Bitty Bit's request for silence. "Oh, quick, tell us more — tell us more, and help us to restore Ozma and the other lost sovereigns to power!"

"I am only a seer," answered the sage, opening his eyes wide and suddenly. "I can see and foresee, tell and foretell, but I cannot change that which has happened or is about to happen."

"But where is Ozma?" demanded Pigasus, edging closer. "If you are a seer and can see 'er, at least you can tell us where she is." In this way Pigasus hoped to check up the information given them by Potaroo, the Gnome King's Wizard.

So again Bitty Bit closed his eyes and, pressing his fingers to his forehead, spoke: "Ozma, my old friend Jinnicky, the Wizard of Oz, a soldier with green whiskers, a purple horse, two Queens, two Kings, a Prince, the Tin Woodman, and Glinda the Good Sorceress are lying at the bottom of Lightning Lake, which is on the top of Thunder Mountain," Bitty Bit told them solemnly.

"Lightning Lake?" cried Dorothy, seizing the little seer frantically by the shoulders. "Why, then, they must be drowned, burned and destroyed altogether!"

"No, no, they are quite calm and as usual," Bitty Bit assured her hastily. "In fact, they are, I should say, in a trance of some kind."

"But what'll we do, how'll we disenchant them or find Thunder Mountain?" Loosing her hold on Bitty Bit, Dorothy spun round three times and then started firmly for the door.

"My shooting tower will take you to Thunder Mountain or any other place you decide you must go," promised Bitty Bit, hurrying anxiously after the little girl, "but not tonight, Dorothy, not tonight. We are all tired, and I must have time to think. The conquering of Oz is a great shock to me. I would like time to look into the matter more fully and consider all of these strange events in their proper order. This problem shall be my pillow. I'll sleep on it, my dear, and in the morning will doubtless have something helpful to suggest."

"Well, then, where're the beds?" yawned Pigasus, who heartily approved of Bitty Bit's suggestion. "Or are we to sleep on our problems, too?" At this, Bitty Bit, who seemed to find Pigasus terribly amusing, laughed right out loud, then taking Dorothy's arm he led the way to a snug little bedroom all done in yellow. Pigasus had a gentlemanly apartment in tan next door, and both were so weary they spent little time examining their new quarters, but instead went directly to bed and to sleep.

When Dorothy wakened next morning, she looked out the window and saw Pigasus flying in slow circles round the tidy castle. Bitty Bit's brown stone palace, though small and unpretentious, perched right on top of Some Summit, and the view was so fine and the mountain air so fresh and invigorating, Dorothy, in spite of all her anxiety and worry, began to feel happy and reckless and ready for anything. With cheerful little glances round her cozy yellow room, she dressed, brushed her hair till it shone, then skipped merrily down the brown marble steps and out into the garden. The garden, really a series of sloping terraces, was bright with hardy mountain posies, with spicy sage bushes and gnarled old trees which clung like acrobats to the steep rocks and dangerous crevices. Pigasus, catching a glimpse of Dorothy seated on a smooth rock near a little waterfall, came swooping down to wish her a merry morning.

"Not a bad little palace," remarked the pig considerately. "Not a bad little palace at all, though so far as I can see there's not a manservant or a woman servant or even a ladybug about. I imagine this fellow is a hermit and from the looks of him probably lives on tobacco and snuff. What do you suppose are the chances for breakfast?"

"I don't know," said Dorothy, refusing to allow such a small matter as breakfast to dash her spirits. "Have you seen Bitty Bit this morning?"

"Yes," sniffed Pigasus, beginning to poke his nose hungrily round the roots of a dwarf oak, "before I flew out my window I saw him going into his brown study. Seer goes into brown study. How's that for the first announcement of the day?"

"You're awful," laughed Dorothy, giving Pigasus a little push.

"No, just awfully hungry," grinned Pigasus. "Now I've been thinking —"

"NO?" Stepping out from behind a sizable bush, Bitty Bit regarded the pig with an air of assumed amazement. "He says he's been thinking," he repeated, turning solemnly to Dorothy. "Must be the air up here."

"That's about all I've had," retorted Pigasus, savagely crunching an acorn between his teeth, "that and a nibble from one of your sage bushes."

"Sage bush, eh?" chuckled Bitty Bit, winking at Dorothy. "That's good, and we'll make a sage of you yet, a sausage!" he whispered in an undertone that Pigasus heard quite distinctly. "And speaking of sausage, how about breakfast?"

Though Bitty Bit's remark about the sausage still rankled, Pigasus was too hungry to let it keep him from following the seer into a small, walled garden that opened out from the larger dining hall of his castle. Here, on a small table covered with a gay yellow cloth, was assembled the most appetizing breakfast Dorothy ever had tasted. Ripe melon and apricots, cereal and eggs, tiny meat pies, pancakes and honey, hot rolls and steaming brown cocoa. There was a huge bowl of mush and cream for Pigasus and another of buttermilk, and under the soothing influence of his favorite foods, Pigasus completely forgot his annoyance, and they were soon chattering away like old friends at a Sunday School Picnic.

Bitty Bit's chef, whom the pig had overlooked in his grand tour of the palace, served them with skill and speed. No wonder Pigasus had not seen him, for he was even smaller than his wrinkled little Master and almost completely enveloped in a great brown linen apron and tall brown cap. Dorothy could not possibly eat all the dainties pressed upon her by the kind little seer and his chef, but she nibbled at each course, and when Bitty Bit saw that neither she nor Pigasus could down another bite, he swallowed the rest of his cocoa and bounced briskly to his feet.

"Now," he cried, tossing away his gay napkin with a flourish. "Now for the Emerald City and Oz!"

"But I thought we were going to Thunder Mountain," exclaimed Dorothy, pushing back her chair so hurriedly she bumped her head on the wall.

"That," exclaimed Bitty Bit, looking over his shoulder, for he was already halfway through the door, "that will not be necessary. All we need to save the celebrities of Oz is the long-lost wishing emeralds of Lorna the Wood Nymph."

"Lorna?" coughed Pigasus, rolling out of his seat and falling a bit sideways. "For pretty sake, who's she?"

"Oh, come along!" urged Dorothy, and without wasting another second she pelted into the brown palace after Bitty Bit. With a groan Pigasus followed, and groaned again when he realized he would have to climb three flights of marble steps and a flight of stone to reach the famous shooting tower. Then, suddenly and joyfully remembering his wings, he spread them wide.

"Wings, hold me up," mumbled the pink pig stuffily, "we're carrying entirely too mush mush!" Rising rather uncertainly, he breathlessly flapped his way up to the tower room where Dorothy and Bitty Bit impatiently awaited him.

Chapter 17 - Skamperoo in Oz

In the company of Scraps, the Scarecrow, the Royal Visitors, and all the amusing members of Ozma's court, the Emperor of Oz and Chalk passed a gay and hilarious morning. The tableaux and pageants proceeded without a single hitch, and no one seemed to miss Dorothy or Pigasus at all, nor did anyone notice the omission of the carefully planned groups showing the Wizard's arrival in Oz, Dorothy's first visit to the Emerald City, or the victory of Nick Chopper over the wolves. These interesting and historical events might just as well never have happened. Notta's circus later in the afternoon went off with a bang, even without Pigasus to jump through hoops and fly round the ring waving flags while Scraps did her balance-defying acts on the trapeze and tightrope. The picnic supper was even more fun than the circus, and the fireworks, set off by Tik Tok, who was in no danger of scorching himself, the best of all. Indeed, Skamperoo's first day in the Emerald City had been so full and so interesting he had not made a single wish or once thought of his magic emeralds.

"Funny we never had jolly times like this at home," mused Skamperoo, putting out the emerald stars in the ceiling that pleasantly lighted his green apartment and burrowing happily down into his splendid green bed. "Oh, Chalk! Are you asleep there, old horse?" As no answer came from the other bed, Skamperoo let himself sink a bit deeper into the luxurious nest of silken covers and soon was asleep himself, puffing and whistling like a steamboat.

But the strange and frightful snoring of the Emperor did not seem to stop or scare away the shadowy figure that presently came stealing into the Royal Chamber. Once, twice, three times, long skinny fingers reached out toward the thick neck of the snoring ruler of Oz. The fourth time there were three distinct little clips, and when the curving, talon-like claw withdrew, it had in its clutching grasp the three powerful wishing chains. Then, without waking the occupant of either bed, the thief stole quietly into the shadows.

Now the Scarecrow, delighted with the success of the celebration so far, had suggested a series of athletic contests and obstacle races for next day, and Skamperoo had heartily agreed to his plans. His first thought on waking was the race to be run by the straw man and himself, the Scarecrow on the wooden sawhorse, he on his splendid white charger.

"I'll wear the white leather breeches and shirt," puffed Skamperoo, bounding out of bed like a schoolboy. He had taken a shower and donned his showy riding clothes before he missed his magic emeralds. Then, all at once, as he stood before the mirror to comb his hair, he gave a loud squall of anguish. "Chalk! Chalk!" roared the distracted Emperor, racing over to the balcony and leaning so far out over the railing he nearly fell on his crown. "They're gone! They're gone! My emeralds! My necklaces! My necklaces! My emeralds!"

Now Chalk, who had risen early to nibble the clover while it was still fresh with morning dew, looked up in alarm, then as his Master's voice grew louder and louder and his gestures more spectacular and desperate, the white horse rose up on his hind legs and shook his head in violent warning and displeasure. "Hush!" he directed in a low voice. "I'll be right up." Making his way quickly but cautiously so as not to arouse the curiosity of any of the palace servants already at work in the lower hallways, Chalk hurried up to the agitated Emperor.

"They're g-g-gone!" blubbered Skamperoo, sitting on the edge of the bed and crying like a baby. "G-g-g-gone! Now everything is ruined, and I'll have nothing left at all!"

"Well, you still have me," murmured Chalk, resting his head affectionately on Skamperoo's shoulder. "Brace up, Kingaling, and for oats sake be quiet! No one here knows about the necklaces, and until the rascal who has stolen them learns how to use them wee are as safe as soap. That rascal, of course, is Matiah. Somehow he has managed to cross the Deadly Desert. Yes," Chalk shook his mane wrathfully, "I am convinced that Matiah has the necklaces, but what good are they to him when we alone know the secret that makes them work? He'll have to come to us in the end, and when he does! Hah!" Chalk expelled the air from his nose in a terrific snort. "Just let me take care of him."

"But shouldn't we give the alarm, have a search made for him, and try to recover the emeralds?"

"Let him alone," counseled the wishing horse firmly. "The thing for you to do is to sit tight on the throne of Oz. Remember, you are still the Emperor!"

"But how can I be, without those emeralds?" Skamperoo dabbed at his eyes with the satin bedsheet.

151

"We got along all right yesterday," said Chalk calmly. "Come, cheer up, Skamper, everything will be ALL right."

"I rather counted on beating the Scarecrow in that race this morning," muttered Skamperoo wistfully. "How can you run as fast as that tireless wooden creature who was magically brought to life?"

"Well, wasn't I magically brought to life?" The white horse shook his mane roguishly. "Come along, Kingaling, we'll not only win that race, but we'll have back our necklaces and chase Matiah out of Oz before we are through."

"I — I really believe you can do anything," sighed Skamperoo, getting almost cheerfully to his feet. "But just the same, I shall keep a sharp outlook for Matiah. He might start a revolution."

"He'll revolute pretty rapidly if I once get my heels on him," promised Chalk with a wicked grin. "Come on. Heads up, and who's afraid?" However, in spite of the white horse's valiant attempts to comfort him, Skamperoo spent a troubled and uneasy day, casting fearful glances behind him when no one was looking, searching the happy holiday crowds with haggard glances for a glimpse of the long, thin face of Matiah the merchant. Even when Chalk beat the Sawhorse in their long, exciting race through the park and the crowds cheered themselves hoarse with delight and approval, the victory was spoiled by the knowledge that somewhere in the Emerald City lurked his most dangerous and relentless foe.

Chalk, too, though he pretended to regard the matter lightly, was almost as worried as his Master and spent every free moment poking his head into doorways and peering down side streets and rearing up over walls. And while Skamperoo was having his afternoon nap, the white horse systematically searched the palace from top to bottom, even the cellar.

But in the cellar Chalk did not go quite far enough, for it was in a hollowed-out chamber under the cellar that the merchant of Skampavia was really hidden. Here, with a goodly supply of food stolen from the pantry, Matiah had seriously settled down to work out the problem of the emerald necklace. He had meant to conceal himself in the cellar itself, but when his foot brushed against an iron ring in the floor, he had lifted it up and discovered to his delight and satisfaction this still-more-secluded and safe retreat.

The tunnels and rocky chambers below the Palace had been constructed and used by Ruggedo, the old Gnome King, when he was plotting to capture the Emerald City. Ruggedo himself had been captured, but the underground caves and passageways had been left pretty much as they were. There were a number of chairs, a rough bed and table, and numerous candles and lamps. Altogether it made an ideal workshop for the merchant to try out his experiments. In the cellar he might easily have been discovered by any of the kitchen boys sent down for supplies, but in Ruggedo's old hideout he could be sure of complete privacy. Lighting the largest of the lamps that hung on its rusty chain over the table, Matiah seated himself on a rickety old chair and prepared to concentrate with all his will power on the glittering emeralds. In the sickly green light he made a strange and sinister figure as he bent over the table, mumbling and chattering to himself. But after a whole day, during which he tried every known formula and combination, touching each gem in succession as he made his wish and counted to a hundred, he was still no nearer the solution of the mystery than he had been in Skampavia.

First he had tried the diamond clasp of the third necklace, sure that that was the key to their power. But nothing at all had happened, and the trick of the magic emeralds continued to elude him. To have in his fingers the means to immense power and good fortune and still be unable to benefit was so infuriating, Matiah began to stamp, splutter, and beat his chest with rage and disappointment. Was it for this he had bribed a red eagle with the promise of three wishes to carry him across the Deadly Desert? Even now the mammoth bird was waiting impatiently on the edge of a little wood near the City ready to tear him to pieces if he failed to fulfill his part of the bargain.

No daylight penetrated into the tunneled chamber, and hardly realizing that it was now midnight, Matiah from sheer weariness and exasperation finally gave up and fell asleep, his head on the table, his hands still clutching the provoking chains. Footsteps pattering overhead wakened him at last, and also told him someone had come to the cellar for supplies. Stretching wearily, he rose and, going over to the stone steps, cautiously ascended and lifted the trapdoor. Now thoroughly convinced that the necklaces would not work unless worn by someone else, he determined to seize the first person entering the cellar and compel him to help.

The merchant did not have long to wait. All unconscious of the part he was to play in Matiah's dark schemes, a young Kitchen Boy came whistling his way toward a great, golden bin of potatoes. The bin was just beyond the trapdoor, and lowering it to a mere crack, Matiah let the boy pass. Then, as he leaned down to fill his basket, the wily merchant flung up the trapdoor, fell upon the boy, and carried him kicking and screaming down the stairs. Here with threats, promises and innumerable shakings, he finally reduced the poor lad to a state of frightened submission. With the sparkling necklaces round his neck, he touched one and then another of the emeralds as Matiah wished and counted and counted and wished. After each unsuccessful trial the merchant would rage and stamp and shake his fists till the boy was quite convinced he was in the presence and power of a madman and frantically waited for someone to overhear Matiah's ravings and come down to rescue him. But nobody did!

152

While the unfortunate Kitchen Boy was spending a miserable morning in the underground chamber, Skamperoo and Chalk were going through the motions of enjoying themselves above stairs, but without any real zest or pleasure. Only half-heartedly Skamperoo laughed at the jokes of the Scarecrow, and Chalk, for all his bright interest in the long recital of Kabumpo's adventures, was really in a fidget of uneasiness, trying to keep an eye on all the doors and windows in the Throne Room at once.

Something was going to happen. The white horse felt it in every bone. And just as the soft musical gong sounded the call for luncheon, his worst fears were realized. Suddenly, without reason or warning, the castle was plunged into total darkness. Thumps, bumps, hysterical shouts and screams followed closely on the heels of this disconcerting event. Chalk, who had been standing back of Skamperoo, immediately leaned forward and grasped his impetuous little Master by the seat of his Royal Breeches.

"Be still!" commanded the white horse through his teeth and the white leather of Skamperoo's riding pants, and he held on for dear life as the Emperor, like all the rest of the court and guests, tried to rush in every direction.

"He's done it! He's done it, and everything is ruined," wailed Skamperoo, struggling in vain to pull away from Chalk. "Matiah has discovered the secret of the necklaces, and now we are ruined. Do you hear? Ruined!"

"I hear," hissed Chalk, giving Skamperoo a little shake, "and so will everyone else unless you shut your mouth. Be quiet, I tell you; do nothing till the right moment, unless you want to dash out your brains against a pillar in the dark." Too frightened to argue or struggle further, Skamperoo at last subsided. All about, courtiers, servants, and guests were screaming and bumping into each other or the furniture, and when a stern hand suddenly seized his bridle, Chalk trembled violently in spite of himself.

"Follow me," directed a firm, stern little voice, "and no harm will come to you..." Now Chalk had been expecting to see or hear Matiah, and the sound of this small, strange voice was a welcome relief and surprise. Taking a firmer hold on Skamperoo, he thrust out his head in an endeavor to touch or feel the newcomer. As he did so, the hand on his bridle began to tug him gently but firmly forward.

"Look out there, mind what you are about, the Emperor of Oz is just ahead!" whinnied Chalk, now thoroughly alarmed. "We are not used to taking orders from strangers."

"Oh, we won't be strangers long," promised the strange voice pleasantly. "So THIS is the Emperor of Oz, and is this the way you usually carry him?"

"Come ON, Bitty Bit, what's the use of all this arguing?" put in another voice impatiently. "Let's get out of this confusion. The Wizard's laboratory is right across the hall. Tell him to come there."

"A girl!" decided Chalk with another gulp of relief. "Maybe we are not so badly off, after all!" And lifting his head in spite of Skamperoo's great weight, he spoke proudly and confidently, "Whoever you are, we welcome you to Oz, and if you can explain this unearthly and unexpected darkness, we will gladly follow you and do as you say."

"Good!" chuckled Bitty Bit, tugging manfully at his bridle. "This way, please." There was still so much screaming and confusion in the Throne Room, no one had overheard the conversation between the newcomers and the Emperor's horse, and guided by the invisible hand Chalk crossed the room without bumping into anything or anybody. A moment later they were in the dark, quiet laboratory that had once belonged to the Wizard of Oz.

Chapter 18 - The Emperor's Horse Makes a Bargain

Bitty Bit's shooting tower had made a record trip to the Emerald City, and guided by the little Seer of Some Summit had come to a deft and dexterous stop right outside the windows of the great Throne Room. After a short, anxious look inside and before anyone was aware of their arrival, Dorothy removed the lid from the box of the powder of darkness and threw a generous pinch into the air, plunging the Emerald City into an instant and thunderous dark. Under cover of this magic darkness, Dorothy, Pigasus and Bitty Bit boldly entered the palace and singled out the white horse and his terrified Master. They had fully expected some resistance — Dorothy had brought a long piece of rope, and Pigasus carried a stout club under his wing — but they were delighted to find the Emperor too frightened and his white horse too clever to resist an invisible foe.

Being able to see in the dark themselves, they had Chalk and Skamperoo at a decided advantage. Dorothy's plans, now that they had actually returned to the Emerald City, were rather vague, but Bitty Bit knew just what he hoped and intended to do. His seerish powers had enabled him to discover that all the changes in Oz had been brought about by the magic emeralds which in some way had fallen into Skamperoo's hands, and these emeralds Bitty Bit meant to have at the earliest possible moment. So first he ordered all the windows and doors to the laboratory closed, then, annoyed by the screams and crashes still issuing from every room in the castle, he advised Dorothy to put the lid back on the powder of darkness.

"But supposing someone disturbs us before we finish," objected Pigasus, looking doubtfully at the tremendous warhorse who stood with feet braced and ears back ready to listen or defy them. Somehow Chalk had managed to toss Skamperoo back into the saddle, and with both hands fixed grimly in the horse's mane the Emperor was blinking his eyes in a vain attempt to see them or catch a glimpse of Matiah, for he was convinced that the merchant was at the bottom of the whole procedure.

"If we agree to lift this pall of darkness, will you agree to grant us an uninterrupted hour of your time?" asked Bitty Bit, turning toward the Emperor, but really addressing the horse, whom he considered the better man of the two.

"I think we can, without undue danger, promise that," answered Chalk guardedly, while Skamperoo hemmed and hawed with indecision. "Of course, you must promise to use no more magic against us."

"Well, the same goes for you, too, remember," put in Pigasus quickly. "An hour's time and conversation and no trickery."

"But who — who are you?" muttered Skamperoo, finding his voice at last. "I seem to hear three different voices."

"You'll soon see," answered Dorothy, clapping the lid on her powder of darkness. With a suddenness that made them all gasp, the laboratory was again flooded with the bright noon sunshine, and in a determined row before him Skamperoo saw a pretty little girl in green, a fat pink pig with white wings, and a small, wrinkled old gentleman in brown.

"W-why," whinnied Chalk, drawing in a deep breath of relief, "at first I thought you were enemies, but now I see that you are merely visitors and friends."

"That depends," observed Bitty Bit, seating himself on a tall stool that brought him on a level with Chalk's nose. "I am the Seer of Some Summit, but these others are Princess Dorothy and Pigasus, the Winged Pig. They really belong in this palace and are close friends of the rightful ruler of this country, Ozma of Oz!"

"I am the rightful ruler of Oz!" shouted Skamperoo, growing red in the face and thrusting out his three chins belligerently.

"Oh, don't bother putting on a show for me," exclaimed Bitty Bit, waving his arms impatiently. "Remember, I am a Seer, I know all, I see all, and what is more, I TELL ALL! You, my pretty fellow, are really the King of Skampavia, a small, no-count country on the other side of the Deadly Desert. In some way the long-lost necklaces of Lorna the Wood Nymph have come into your possession. With these necklaces you have enchanted the people of Oz into believing you are their ruler. You have wickedly banished Ozma and her allies and counselors and unlawfully made yourself Emperor of Oz."

"That seems to cover everything," drawled Chalk as Skamperoo turned from red to purple.

"Not everything!" went on Bitty Bit, shaking his finger sternly under Chalk's nose. "Kingdoms are not won and held by trickery, my friends, and we are here to see that those necklaces are returned and the Kingdom of Oz restored to its proper rulers."

"And suppose we refuse!" suggested the white horse in a bored voice. "What then?"

"Why then," Bitty Bit threw back his shoulders and spun round several times on his shiny stool, "why then, it means WAR!" Bitty Bit did not say who were his friends or allies or where he should get his armies, but he spoke with such firm confidence, both Skamperoo and Chalk were taken aback and completely dismayed. Matiah had been bad enough, but this strange and determined little Seer was worse.

"Perhaps we can make a bargain or come to some agreement," suggested Chalk, resolved to save what he could for himself and his Master. "Suppose King Skamperoo and I agree to return the emerald necklaces, which undoubtedly belong in Oz, will you grant us the privilege of using them twice for ourselves?"

"But — but —" Skamperoo was about to blurt out the fact that they no longer had the necklaces when Chalk gave him a savage nip on the leg which silenced him effectively.

"Why should we do that?" inquired Pigasus, fluttering his wings nervously. "After all the grief and worry you have caused us, you are lucky to get off with your skins."

"Where are the necklaces now?" asked Dorothy, stepping close to Chalk and looking eagerly up into the face of the discomfited Emperor. Skamperoo's face grew long as a balloon suddenly punctured, but remembering Chalk's last bite, he managed to keep silent.

"When you have answered OUR question, we will answer yours," stated Chalk, firmly but pleasantly. "You can, of course, appeal to the Court and members of the household, but I think you will find them entirely satisfied with their present Emperor and ready to stand by him to the last man." At Chalk's words, Bitty Bit looked rather crestfallen. As the white horse had so quietly stated, they were perfectly powerless to take the necklaces by force, and quick inspection of

154

the Emperor when he first reached the palace had convinced him Skamperoo was not wearing the precious emeralds. At this rather embarrassing moment a series of thumps, kicks, and knocks on the door made not only the rescuers but the Emperor and Chalk turn rather pale.

"Oh! Oh! It's Matiah!" quavered Skamperoo, whose nerves were completely shaken by the shocking disclosures of the last few moments. "Oh! Oh! What'll we do now?"

"Hold your tongue," advised Chalk, and swinging round he trotted briskly over to the door.

"Who's there?" he demanded in a dignified voice.

" 'Tis I — Iva the Kitchen Boy!" stuttered a frightened treble. "I must see the Emperor at once."

"Well, shall we let him in?" Bitty Bit looked uneasily at Pigasus and Dorothy and then rather thoughtfully at Chalk.

"Suit yourselves," yawned the white horse indifferently. "It's probably a messenger telling us the pudding is cold with all this delay and darkness. You asked for an hour's time and conversation and we agreed to that demand, so it is for you to decide what to do, not us."

"Oh, let him in," fumed Pigasus, "and tell him to stop this hammering and yammering. What harm is there in a Kitchen Boy?"

So Bitty Bit, taking the key from the lock and squinting through the keyhole to assure himself there was only a small boy outside, quickly admitted him. Now in darted Iva, screaming loudly of a madman in the cellar and bursting into tearful and incoherent recital of his woes. Scarcely had he got out two sentences before Skamperoo fell bodily off his horse and made a desperate snatch at the Kitchen Boy's throat. But Bitty Bit was too quick for him. His eyes, too, had caught the glimmer of emeralds, and jerking the three chains from the lad's neck as Chalk made a savage lunge forward, he tossed them to Pigasus. Catching them on his nose as cleverly as a trained seal, the pink pig spread his wings and flew up to the top of a tall cabinet, where he sat panting and puffing with satisfaction and defiance.

"Come down, you fat scoundrel!" roared Skamperoo, dancing up and down like a dervish, while the poor Kitchen Boy, outraged by the way both Skamperoo and Bitty Bit had rushed upon him, burst into loud sobs and, rushing out the still open door, ran crying down the corridor. Slamming the door and locking it after him, Bitty Bit rather anxiously waited for Chalk's next move, and as usual Chalk was quite prepared and ready to make it.

"Well," he observed with a jaunty flick of his tail, "now that you have the famous wishing emeralds, I suppose you are satisfied, and we may as well go. Come along, Skamperoo, you will get nowhere in an argument with a pig. Just casting pearls before swine, you know, and he already has our emeralds!"

"You mean your wishing necklaces!" shrieked Pigasus furiously. "And I'll tell you what I wish. I wish that you and your silly Master were clams at the bottom of the Nonestic Ocean!" Thoroughly shocked and startled by the pink pig's unexpected wish, Bitty Bit and Dorothy rushed toward the cabinet, hoping in some way to prevent the wish from taking effect. But they need not have worried, for of course nothing happened at all. Then Skamperoo, urged by Chalk, hastily climbed into the saddle.

"Well," whinnied the white horse, twitching his ears provokingly, "goodbye to you. Goodbye! We'll just be trotting along."

"Wait! Look here, hold on a bit." The little Seer of Some Summit stepped angrily in front of the white horse. "How do these emeralds work, how are we to disenchant the rulers of Oz and restore Ozma to the throne unless we know the proper way to use these magic chains?"

"I'm afraid that's YOUR problem," sighed Chalk, rolling his eyes round at Skamperoo. "Come now, my little mannikin, open up the door. We kept our promise, and you must keep yours. After all, my Master has done no real harm here. There has been no war or bloodshed. In fact, everything has been decidedly gay and jolly. If his laudable ambition to better himself brought Ozma and her counselors a little well-earned rest, at least they have suffered no pain or unpleasantness and are perfectly unaware of what has happened to them. Open the door, I tell you, or I'll call for help, and there are many in this palace who would gladly come to our assistance."

"Oh! Oh! What shall we do?" wailed Dorothy as Bitty Bit stood uncertainly with his back to the door. "You're the horridest horse I've ever known!"

"Well, that's all in the way you look at me," answered Chalk, staring steadily into Dorothy's eyes. "You, my dear, are fond of your Mistress, Queen Ozma of Oz, and are trying to help her. I, on my part, am exceedingly fond of my Master, the King of Skampavia, and am trying to help him. You can't blame me for that, you know."

"The creature is right," sighed Bitty Bit, "and we'll have to agree to his plans, preposterous though they are."

"That would, of course, be the sensible thing to do," murmured Chalk, lowering his eyes modestly. "You grant me two wishes, and I will tell you the proper way to use the magic wishing chains."

"But suppose they are bad wishes — I mean," Bitty Bit corrected himself hastily, "good for you, but bad for us, what then? With the necklaces in your possession, you could wish yourselves away in an instant."

"That," admitted Chalk, "is perfectly true, but I am afraid you will have to take that chance — and trust me."

"Never do it! Never do it!" squealed Pigasus, who now had the necklaces tucked tightly under his wing. "We might as well throw ourselves out of the window."

But Bitty Bit, closing his eyes and pressing his fingers close to his forehead, made no reply. "I'll trust you," he said after a short silence, and opening his eyes, he looked cheerfully up at the white horse. "Hand down those necklaces, Pigasus, and be quick about it, too; I hear footsteps in the passageway."

"Well, don't blame me if we're turned to pretzels and pumpernickel," grunted the pig, dropping the necklaces into the seer's outstretched hand. "Goodbye, all." Turning his back in disgust and covering his ears with his wings, Pigasus waited in fear and trembling for the end. But Bitty Bit quite calmly handed the emeralds to Skamperoo, and Skamperoo immediately draped them over Chalk's left ear.

"Now, then," murmured Chalk, looking firmly back at the unhappy Emperor, "repeat exactly what I say, and all will yet be well. I wish," began Chalk, while Skamperoo listened with bulging eyes, "I wish that the five wishes I make when we return to Skampavia shall be instantly granted." As Skamperoo repeated the wish and slowly started to count to a hundred, Dorothy fidgeted with uneasiness, and Pigasus fairly groaned with alarm, for it seemed to them both that their danger had only been postponed and not averted.

"My second wish I will keep for our return," decided Chalk. "Now, my dear, attend closely. Since you are the avowed friend of Ozma and live with her in this palace, it seems to me you are the one to keep safely the secret of the magic emeralds." Moving close to Dorothy, Chalk put his soft, pink nose close to her ear and whispered several very hoarse sentences. "Get it? Get it?" he demanded, backing away exuberantly.

"Oh — is THAT all?" Dorothy pushed back her hair in surprise and bewilderment. "Why, anyone could do that!"

"Then prove it by sending us back to Skampavia," beamed Chalk, shaking his mane approvingly. "It would be embarrassing for us to be here when Ozma and her friends return. Here, my child, take the necklaces, and I'll do the wishing." Pigasus, now more interested than frightened, tried his best to see what Dorothy did after she clasped the emeralds around her neck, and the white horse solemnly wished himself and Skamperoo back in Skampavia, but before Chalk reached ten in his counting, there was a whiff and puff, and except for a slight rustle in the air, no sign at all of the splendid white steed and his red-faced Master.

"It works! It works!" exulted Bitty Bit, hopping about like a Brownie. "Can you do it again, my dear? All we need to do is to wish that the people of Oz shall be released from this wicked spell of forgetting and then wish Ozma and all the others safely back to this palace."

"Don't forget Highboy!" cried Pigasus, switching his little tail violently. "He's gone, too, you know, and don't forget Jinnicky and old Willy Green Whiskers!"

"I'll remember!" promised Bitty Bit. "All ready, Dorothy?" The little girl nodded, and Bitty Bit, looking and feeling more serious and important than he had ever felt in his whole little life, slowly made the wish that was to restore peace and happiness to Oz.

"I wish," said the little sage sternly, "that the wicked enchantment cast by Skamperoo upon the inhabitants of Oz be instantly dispelled. I wish that Ozma herself, the Wizard of Oz, the Red Jinn of Ev, the King and Queen of the Munchkins and their son Prince Philador, the King and Queen of the Gillikens and their giant horse, Glinda the Good Sorceress of the South, Nick Chopper the Tin Emperor of the East, and the Soldier with the Green Whiskers be immediately released from Thunder Mountain and restored to this palace. One, two, three, four, five, six, seven."

At seven Pigasus with a loud squall of astonishment fell from the top of the cabinet, and Dorothy rushed joyfully forward. For now every chair around the Wizard's table was occupied. At the head sat Ozma, calm and gracious as ever; at the foot the spry little Wizard; and between, all the others who had so recently lain at the bottom of Lightning Lake. Highboy stood over by the window looking dreamily out across the garden, and none of them seemed in the least surprised or excited to find themselves in the Wizard's laboratory.

"Let me see —" mused Ozma, raising her hand gravely, "Ah, yes, we are here to discuss a threatened danger to ourselves and the Kingdom of Oz."

"But it's all over now," cried Dorothy, running over to Ozma and flinging both arms round her waist. "It's all over, and we're safe and you're safe and my, how glad we are to have you back here again!"

"Here!" exclaimed the Wizard, popping up like a startled Jack-in-the-Box. "Where else would we be?"

"Only at the bottom of Lightning Lake in Thunder Mountain," murmured Bitty Bit, coming modestly forward to meet the Fairy Ruler of Oz and winking merrily at Jinnicky, whom he already knew.

Chapter 19 - The Story of the Necklaces

Ozma's surprise and the astonishment of all the rest of that company around the Wizard's table can well be imagined.

"I didn't hear any thunder," snorted Highboy, lowering himself down to Bitty Bit's level. "Not a clap! And if we were at the bottom of Lightning Lake, what did we eat?"

"We didn't!" announced Jinnicky in a hollow voice, "What COULD we have eaten in such a place, you old fire-eater, you?" To have been enchanted and put out of existence for three whole days was an amazing experience, and as Dorothy and Bitty Bit, helped out now and then by Pigasus, explained all that had happened to the victims of Skamperoo's ambition and to themselves in the course of their journey of rescue, Ozma's face grew both grave and serious. It was disturbing to realize how easily Oz had been captured and the powerful Wizards and Glinda the Sorceress pushed aside. The Wizard of Oz himself seemed to feel the most discouraged and downcast of all to think he had been so easily overcome, and that his magic had not been strong enough to withstand the wicked spell of the invaders.

"I should have foreseen something like this and been prepared," mourned the little man, mopping his head with a map of Oz which he happened to have in his pocket.

"Yes," sighed the Tin Woodman, feeling his joints anxiously to see whether they had been rusted by his three-day immersion in Lightning Lake, "we might have been prisoners in Thunder Mountain forever had it not been for Dorothy and Pigasus and this sagacious little Seer. But tell me, Dorothy, how is it that you alone of all the people in the palace remembered and missed us?"

"Well," confessed Dorothy, seating herself cautiously on Nick Chopper's tin knees, "it must have been the Wizard's wishing pill. You see, just as the Soldier's beard turned red, I found one in my pocket and popping it into my mouth wished that I might save Oz from any danger that threatened. It kept me from forgetting Ozma and all of you, and when I sat on Pigasus' back, he remembered, too, and we —"

"Did save Oz!" finished the little Wizard, bounding triumphantly to his feet and restored to instant cheerfulness by Dorothy's generous statement. "I tell you, I'll match my wishing powers with any wishing powers in the country!"

"But you won't have to now," smiled Bitty Bit with an envious glance at the sparkling necklaces Dorothy had placed on the table before Ozma. "With these emeralds and your own magic powers, nothing like this could ever happen in Oz again."

"Thank you, Bitty Bit," smiled the little Queen, nodding graciously. "Thank you a hundred times for all you have done for us and for Oz, and perhaps, if we coaxed, you might remain as our Royal Seer."

"Hear, here, our Royal Seer!" cried Pigasus, clapping his wings. "Will you be it, Sir Bitty Bit?"

"Well," acknowledged Bitty Bit with a low bow toward Ozma, "I'm tempted to accept, but on the other hand, I am so foolishly fond of my own castle I just could not be content in any other place. But if Your Majesty ever needs me for serious business, you can always command my services by using either the wishing necklaces or your magic belt."

"And he'll come like a shot in his shooting tower," Dorothy smiled as she slid carefully from Nick Chopper's knee. "But say, what's that?" A hundred footsteps sounded in the corridor, accompanied by confused voices, questioning calls and finally loud thumps on the door. "It must be all the rest of the courtiers and visitors remembering they have a Queen!"

"I hear Scraps and the Scarecrow," squealed Pigasus, "I hear Bettsy Bobb and Trot. Quick, Dorothy, open the door."

"No, no, not yet," said Ozma gently but firmly. "There is more, much more for us to hear and settle. But you go out, Pigasus, and tell them all about our enchantment, Skamperoo's reign, and our rescue."

"Be glad to! Charmed! And trust me to do it right." Swelling up with importance and pride, Pigasus flew out the window before Dorothy had time to open the door. A few moments later the company in the Wizard's laboratory heard him calling everyone to follow him to the Throne Room and hear the most startling news since Dorothy killed the Wicked Witches of the East and West.

"And how he'll love telling it," said Bitty Bit, smiling across at the Wizard of Ev. "A great idea of yours, this pig, Jinny. Even if his verses are low, I like him."

"Oh, everyone likes Pigasus," declared Dorothy, coming over to sit on the arm of Glinda's chair. "But what I'd like to know is how that Kitchen Boy happened to have the emeralds, how Skamperoo got them, and where they came from in the first place."

"Yes," murmured Glinda, who, like the Wizard, felt very much annoyed to have been overpowered by a fat, unimportant monarch like Skamperoo. "Now that we have these wishing chains, we must guard them carefully to keep them from falling into such mischievous hands again."

"I believe Bitty Bit can tell us the story of the emeralds," said Ozma, who had been much impressed by the cheerful little seer of Some Summit. "With his gift of foreseeing and foretelling he probably knows the whole story."

"Can he look backward as well as forward?" inquired the Wizard challengingly.

"Just as well," confessed Bitty Bit with an embarrassed little cough, and as every head turned expectantly toward him, the sage closed his eyes and quietly told them the interesting story of Matiah's three necklaces.

"These magic emeralds," began Bitty Bit, waving his hands rhythmically backward and forward, "were first collected and strung into necklaces by a wizard named Wam for the King of the Green Mountain as a gift for the wood nymph Lorna. But the King of the Green Mountain was an ugly little dwarf, and though she had promised to marry him, no sooner did Lorna have the necklaces than she turned the King into a frog and hid herself away in her own forest.

"In the giant hollow tree where Lorna lived there was a mischievous family of squirrels. That night as Lorna lay sleeping with the emeralds on a little golden plate beside her, one of the squirrels, thinking the gems some new and delicious kind of nuts, stole and buried them away for the winter. Next morning, though Lorna ran crying and searching all through the forest, she was unable to find her wishing necklaces."

"Then what became of them?" gasped Dorothy as Bitty Bit, opening his eyes for a moment, blinked cheerfully over their heads.

"Wait, I'll tell you!" Closing his eyes, the sage went hurriedly on with the story. "Ah, so this is it! A woodcutter's boy, poking about among the leaves, found the emeralds, and as emeralds in themselves are not uncommon in Oz, he traded them to a peddler for a new ax. The peddler, arriving after a long while in Skampavia, had no trouble in disposing of the jewels. In Skampavia, you must know, emeralds, pearls, or jewels of any kind are practically unknown, and a merchant gave the peddler not only his house and shop, but all of his merchandise for the three sparkling chains.

"By a law in Skampavia, every subject must render to the King one-third of all he owns or raises, and in due course one of the necklaces was sent to Skamperoo. The King, delighted with the sparkling gems, insisted on having all three necklaces, and Matiah himself brought them to the castle, determined if possible to steal them back at the first opportunity. In order to do so without arousing the suspicions of the King, he pretends to be a Wizard and tells him if he, Matiah, wears the three necklaces, he can grant any wish the King may make, but that as he makes the wish he must close his eyes and count to a hundred.

"As soon as Skamperoo began to count, Matiah started to run off with the emeralds, and that accounts for the white horse, for you see, Skamperoo's first wish was for a splendid white charger with a golden mane and tail. Frightened almost out of his senses by the sudden appearance of the horse and the knowledge that the chains really did have some magic power, Matiah steals back beside the King, resolved to wait for another opportunity to procure the necklaces.

"Meanwhile, Skamperoo, excited and happy over the granting of his first wish, confides in the merchant his second wish and ambition to be ruler of Oz. Matiah, to gain time in which he can work out the secret of the emeralds' power, approves of the King's idea, but tells him he can only grant one wish a week. He then advises Skamperoo to cause all the people in Oz to forget their former rulers and to remove the Wizard and all his magic, Ozma, and the rulers of the four Oz countries to the inaccessible caverns of Thunder Mountain.

"Now while Matiah is trying his best to discover the trick of the magic emeralds, Skamperoo, growing tired of the tempery fellow, appealed to his horse. The horse, being magically brought to life and being unusually sharp-witted and quick, soon worked out the problem. With his help Skamperoo wished the spell of forgetting upon Ozma's subjects, banished her Highness and all of the others just as Matiah had suggested, and managed to rule Oz for three whole days."

"But what became of Matiah?" asked Glinda, leaning forward eagerly.

"At this moment Matiah is lying in a senseless condition in the underground chamber beneath this castle," Bitty Bit told them solemnly and without opening his eyes. "Soon after Skamperoo left for Oz, the merchant was driven out of Skampavia by Pinny Penny, whom Skamperoo had made King. Matiah, furious to think the apparently stupid sovereign had outwitted him, bribed an eagle to carry him across the desert, arrived at the Emerald City and soon afterward managed to really steal the necklaces from Skamperoo. Discovering beneath the cellar the excavated chambers of the old Gnome King, he retired to this quiet spot to again experiment with the emeralds.

"Needing another person to help, he seized the Kitchen Boy who had come to the cellar for supplies and forced him to assist in his experiments. How soon he might have discovered the real trick of the chains I cannot say, but our own arrival and Gloma's powder of darkness happily interrupted him. The Kitchen Boy, who had kept his eyes glued to the stone steps and trapdoor during the entire morning, made an immediate dash for freedom and managed to escape in spite of the darkness. Matiah, not so fortunate, rushed into a stone pillar and knocked himself senseless. He's still lying there, and I suggest that your Majesty deal with him at once."

"I will," decided Ozma firmly, as Bitty Bit opened his eyes and looked cheerfully around the table. "And I'll do it by means of these very magic emeralds. Put on the emeralds, Dorothy, for you alone know the secret of their magic power." So Dorothy, anxious to have Matiah out of Oz before he recovered his wicked wits, hastily clasped the three chains around her slim throat.

"It is my earnest wish that Matiah shall immediately and henceforth forget the emerald necklaces of Oz, return to his country, and become a good and simple citizen of Skampavia," said Ozma seriously, beginning her count to one hundred.

"He's gone! He's gone!" piped up Bitty Bit, who had closed his eyes as soon as Ozma started to speak. "And if I were you, my dear, I would send off that red eagle, too. I see him lurking on the edge of our city with an exceedingly fierce light in his eye." So Ozma made another wish, turning the eagle to a harmless sparrow.

"And what about Skamperoo?" asked Cheeriobed, King of the Munchkins, who up to this time had not spoken a word. "Should he not be punished in some way?"

"I would not bother with old Skamper," advised Bitty Bit with a small chuckle. "Before I agreed to give his white horse those five wishes, I closed my eyes, looked ahead, and discovered that they would all be good wishes. Not only good but wise, and from now on I think you can trust that clever white horse and a little fellow called Pinny Penny to keep their Master out of mischief and Oz."

"Well, in that case," sighed Ozma rather breathless from so much counting, "everything is happily settled."

"And in that case," boomed Joe King, gallantly helping his little Queen to her feet, "I suggest we start celebrating all over again, not only the discovery of Oz by mortals, but the saving of Oz as well! I for one feel terribly cheated at missing Notta's circus."

"So do I! So do I!" exclaimed the little Prince Philador, climbing boisterously into Highboy's saddle. "I want to see a circus!"

"And so you shall," promised Ozma gaily. "We will start the celebration at exactly the point where we left Oz for Thunder Mountain, and have the tableaux, the pageants, and the picnics all over again."

And that, my dear, is exactly what they did do, and everyone, including Bitty Bit, enjoyed themselves so much there was not an unhappy person in the Emerald City. And not until the end of the second day did Dorothy remember to tell Ozma the magic secret of the wishing emeralds. "On the

sixth count, you wink both eyes," whispered Dorothy, giving Ozma a little hug. "Good night!"

"Good gracious, so THAT'S it!" smiled Ozma, comprehending instantly what Dorothy meant. "I suppose Matiah did it in sheer excitement the first time. Well, I have often heard of doing things in the twinkling of an eye, but now we shall really be able to have them that way. No one knows this secret but you and me and a white horse, and no one must ever know it, for wishes are dangerous and cause more unhappiness than joy, so we'll never tell another soul, will we, Dorothy?"

"Never!" agreed the little girl, looking solemnly over her shoulder at the safe where Ozma had hidden her new treasure.

Chapter 20 - Back in Skampavia!

"So there you are!" Pinny Penny straightened up with a little grimace, for he had been planting flowers in a new rock garden he was planning for the King. With an expression about equally compounded of exasperation and affection, he looked at his former Master and the white horse who had, without sound or warning, dropped down in the path before him. "I thought you'd come back," continued Pinny Penny, calmly rubbing the mud from his fingers and putting out his hand. "So it was your horse after all." His gaze rested speculatively on the splendid white steed and richly jeweled robes of Skamperoo. "And you've made your fortune, I see! Well, welcome home anyway; your crown's hanging on a nail back of the throne, and I think you will find everything in order."

"In order! Why, it looks wonderful!" shouted Skamperoo, leaping exuberantly out of the saddle and honestly surprised and pleased at the pleasure he felt in seeing old Pinny Penny again. "You've had the palace painted, and this garden and that fountain and the flowers. They're all new, aren't they?"

"Yes," agreed Pinny Penny guardedly. "I made a few new laws while you were gone, Skamper, making the tax only one-twentieth of our subjects' earnings. They were so grateful and delighted, they've been sending you presents ever since. Then the guards (having no drill or marching to bother them, I did away with THAT, too), the guards in their odd time agreed to work around the castle, and we've been brightening up the old place quite a bit. I tell you," Pinny Penny exhaled his breath noisily, "we'll make a going and coming country of this yet!"

159

"Of course we will," said Skamperoo, bouncing happily along at his side. "I've had a lot of experience since I saw you, old Skinny Pins. Ho, Pinny, my boy, I've been an Emperor in Oz!"

"OZ? Never!" Closing his lips into a thin line, Pinny Penny looked from his Master to Chalk, who was stepping sedately along on his other side.

"But it's perfectly true," whinnied the white horse, prancing a bit from sheer enjoyment, "and now we are home with five splendid wishes."

"Wishes?" sniffed Pinny Penny, rearing his head suspiciously. "What good are wishes?"

"But these wishes really work and come true," explained Chalk with a toss of his head, "and what's more, they are going to work and come true for Skampavia!"

"Any wish you work hard enough for will come true," insisted Pinny Penny stubbornly. "Wishes — POOH! Wishes — POOH! `If wishes were horses, beggars would ride!' " finished the little Prime Minister half under his breath.

"But don't you see?" Skamperoo grasped Pinny Penny firmly by the shoulders. "This is one time when wishes WERE horses and beggars DID ride. My first wish was for a horse, and here he is, and as true as you are and as wise and clever. Why, even if the magic emeralds give me nothing more, I am still the luckiest fellow on this side of the Deadly Desert!"

"Moons, stars and rainbows! I believe you have gotten some sense," gasped Pinny Penny, staring with wide eyes into Skamperoo's face. "And that's the first good I ever knew to come of magic."

Pulling Pinny Penny down to his old bench, now neatly mended and painted green, the King of Skampavia told his little Prime Minister the whole story I have just been telling you. When he finished and settled back complacently, Pinny Penny, instead of looking glad or pleased, stared mournfully at the ground.

"Now what's the matter?" demanded Skamperoo, clapping him impatiently on the back while Chalk, breaking off a little branch with his teeth, tickled Pinny Penny mischievously under the chin. "Why are you so sad and solemn?"

"Because —" Pinny Penny ground the toe of his boot deeply into the gravel in the path " — if you really have five more magic wishes, you'll probably be going to some grand other place and be spending the rest of your life in travel."

"If that were so, we wouldn't be here at all," puffed Skamperoo. "Now get this through your head, old fellow. We are here by our own wish and from now on my country is good enough for me and, when we've made these five good wishes, good enough for anybody!"

"There you go! There you go!" groaned Pinny Penny, covering his face with his hands. "It's the wishes I'm afraid of."

"Well, you needn't be!" With a great effort, Skamperoo made his first really great and wise decision. "You shall make the wishes yourself, Pinny Penny, and I shall save only one in case of trouble!"

"Bravo! Bravo!" snorted Chalk, prancing three times round the green bench.

"Me? You really mean me?" quavered Pinny Penny, pointing an unbelieving finger at his own midsection. Then, as Skamperoo nodded and before he could change his mind, the old Chancellor fairly leaped into the air. "I wish the King of this country to always be as wise and generous as he has succeeded in being at this moment, as wise as the young Fairy Ruler of Oz," panted Pinny Penny. "I wish that the people of Skampavia, using the powers and abilities they already have, shall make this a rich, happy and prosperous Kingdom. I wish that the climate and soil, the only bad features about which we might complain, shall become mild and fertile! That's all, that's all I can think of!" confessed Pinny Penny, shrinking happily back on the bench.

"Then I'll make a wish," whinnied Chalk, shaking his beautiful golden mane. "I wish that we three may never be separated. Long live the KING AND HIS PRIME MINISTER!"

"And his horse!" cried Skamperoo, bounding up to seize Chalk's bridle.

"And his horse!" echoed Pinny Penny heartily, running round to seize Chalk's bridle on the other side. "We three for Skampavia forever!"

Then, with Chalk stepping proudly in the center, these three strangely assorted comrades made their way into the palace. Knowing the power of the magic emeralds and also the magic power of knowledge and experience, I am sure that Skampavia under its new regime will soon be as happy and prosperous as any Nation in Oz!

The End

160

Captain Salt in Oz

by Ruth Plumly Thompson

Chapter 1 - Sail Ho!

Eight miles east of Pingaree lies the eight-sided island of King Ato the Eighth. While not so large as Pingaree, the Octagon Isle is nevertheless one of the tidiest and most pleasing of the sea realms that dot the great green rolling expanses of the Nonestic Ocean. And Ato himself is as pleasing as his island, enormously fat and jolly with a kind word for everyone. In his eight-sided castle he has every modern convenience and comfort and some of which even an up-to-date country like our own cannot boast. For instance, take Roger, his Royal Read Bird. Roger, besides knowing eight languages, can read aloud for hours at a time without growing hoarse or weary. So Ato never has to strain his eyes poring over his eight hundred huge volumes of adventure and history, or his arms holding a newspaper or court document, or his jaw pronouncing the names of kings and countries in Ev and Oz and other curious places on the mainland west of his own island. And Roger is as handsome as he is handy, his head and bill rather like a duck's, his body shaped and colored like a parrot, but much larger, while his tail opens out into an enormous fan. This is extremely fortunate, for the Octagon Isle is semi-tropical in climate, and on warm, sultry days Roger not only reads to his Majesty, but fans him as well. All in all, Ato's life is decidedly luxurious and lazy.

Sixentwo, Chief Chancellor of the realm, and Four'nfour, its treasurer, attend to all the business of governing, so that Ato and Roger have little to do but enjoy themselves. The Octagon Islanders, one hundred and eighty in number, are a sober and industrious lot, rarely giving any trouble. Once, it is true, they sailed off and deserted the King entirely, but Ato, with Peter, a Philadelphia boy, and Samuel Salt, a pirate who landed on the island at just the right moment, immediately set out after them, using the pirate's stout ship the *Crescent Moon*, for the purpose.

By a strange coincidence, Samuel Salt's men had also mutinied and sailed away, so that there were two sets of deserters to seek out and discover. After a dangerous and lively voyage, the *Crescent Moon* reached the rocky shores of Menankypoo on the Mainland. Here they learned that the Octagon Islanders and Samuel Salt's men had been enslaved by Ruggedo, the former Gnome King, and marched off to conquer the Emerald City of Oz. How Peter and the Pirate, Ato and a poetical Pig outwitted the Gnome King is a long and other story. You have probably read it yourself. But ever since their hair-raising experiences with Ruggedo and their rescue by Ato, the Octagon Islanders have been perfectly satisfied with their own ruler and country. In fact, they were so docile and devoted, so fearfully anxious to please, Ato often wished they would revolt or sass him a little just to relieve the monotony and make life more interesting. To tell the truth, after serving as cook, mate and able-bodied seaman on the *Crescent Moon*, Ato found it quite boring to settle down to a humdrum life of a monarch ashore. Roger, too, missed the gay and carefree life he had led as a pirate and could not even pretend an interest in the books of adventure he still dutifully read to his Master. He and Ato now spent most of their time on the edge of the Island — the King in a comfortable hammock swung between two palm trees, Roger on a tall, golden perch set close beside him. Whenever the Read Bird paused to yawn or turn a page, Ato would pull himself up to a sitting position, raise the telescope he always had with him, and gaze long and wistfully out to sea. Many ships passed Ato's Island, but never a one in the least resembling the splendid three-masted, fast sailing ship belonging to the Pirate.

"You'll give yourself a fine squint there," warned Roger one morning as Ato for about the hundredth time raised his spy glass. "And what is the use of it, pray?" inquired Roger grumpily, ruffling the pages of the Book of Barons. "Samuel Salt has probably forgotten all about us and gone off by himself on a voyage of discovery."

"No! No! Sammy wouldn't do that," said the King, shaking his head positively. "He promised to stop by for us on the very first voyage he made as Royal Discoverer of Oz."

"Ho, one of those seafaring promises!" muttered Roger. "A pirate's promise. Humph! His new honors have gone to his head. Quite a jump from pirating to exploring. I'll wager a wing he's gone back to buccaneering and forgotten us altogether!"

"Now Roger, how can you say that?" Heaving up his huge bulk with great difficulty, Ato looked reproachfully at his Royal Read Bird. "Sammy never cared for pirating in the first place," wheezed the King earnestly, "and he was so soft-hearted about planking the captives and burning the ships, his band sailed off and left him. They only made him Captain because he was clever at navigating, and you know perfectly well he spent more time looking for flora and fauna than for ships and treasures."

"Ah, then I suppose some wild Flora or Fauna has him in its clutches," observed Roger sarcastically, "and a likely thing that is, seeing the poor Captain weighs but two hundred and twenty pounds and stands six feet in his socks."

"What a tremendous fellow he was," sighed Ato, sinking dreamily back in his hammock and half closing his eyes. "I'll never forget how high and handsome he looked when Queen Ozma asked him to give up buccaneering and serve her instead as Royal Discoverer and Explorer for Oz! And a fitting reward it was, too, for capturing Ruggedo and saving the Kingdom. Aha, my lad, THAT was a day! And we had our share of the glory, too! Remember how they cheered us in the Emerald City of Oz?"

"Aye, I remember THAT day and a good many other days since," sniffed the Read Bird disagreeably. "Six months from that day Samuel Salt was to sail into our Harbor. Well, King, it's been six times six months, and nary a sail nor a sign of him have we seen."

"That long?" said Ato, blinking unhappily.

"That long and longer. Three years, eleven months, twenty-six days and twelve hours, to be exact!"

"Dear, dear and dear! Then something's happened to him," murmured Ato. "He's either been shipwrecked, captured or enchanted! I'll never believe Sammy would forget us or break his promise. Never!"

"Well, whatever you believe, the results are the same." Flapping open his book, Roger prepared to go on with his reading. "And depend upon it," he insisted stubbornly, "we'll never see Samuel Salt again, so you may as well put up your telescope and put your mind on something else for a change. Maybe it's your cooking that's keeping him away," finished the Read Bird, who felt cross and fractious and contrary as a goat.

"My cooking?" roared Ato, roused to honest anger at last. "I've a notion to have you plucked and roasted for that. My cooking, indeed! Show me the fellow who can beat up an omelet, a cake, a batch of biscuits, faster than I. Who can brown a fowl, broil a steak or toss out a pan of fried potatoes to compare with mine? I — I, why, I'm surprised at you, Roger!"

Roger, ruffling his feathers uncomfortably, was rather surprised at himself, for the King was speaking the exact truth. A more skillful man with a skillet it would be impossible to find in any kingdom. Ever since his voyage on the *Crescent Moon*, cooking had been Ato's chief pleasure and pastime. The castle chef, though he heartily disapproved of a King in the kitchen, could do nothing to discourage him, so finally stood by in grudging envy and admiration as Ato turned out his delectable puddings, pies, roasts and sauces.

Muttering with hurt pride and indignation, his Majesty continued to frown at the Read Bird, and realizing he had gone too far, Roger started to read as fast as he could from the Book of Barons. As he read on, he could see the King growing calmer, and finally, pausing to turn a page, he let his gaze rove idly over the harbor. "Anchors and animal crackers! What was that?" Stretching up his neck, Roger took another look, then, flinging the Book of Barons high into the air, he spread his wings and started out to sea.

Soothed by the droning voice of the Read Bird, Ato had closed his eyes, and the first warning he had of Roger's departure was a terrific thump as the Book of Barons landed on his stomach. Leaping out of the hammock as if he had been shot, the outraged Monarch looked furiously around for his Read Bird. This really was too much. Not satisfied with insulting him, Roger must now be bombarding him with books, cocoanuts and what not.

Shading his eyes with his hand, Ato glared up and down the beach and finally out over the rippling blue ocean. At what he saw there the King forgot his anger as completely as Roger had forgotten his manners. For swinging jauntily into the Octagon Harbor was the *Crescent Moon* herself! No mistaking the high-prowed, deep-waisted, powerful craft of the Pirate. But a new and gayer pennant fluttered from the mizzenmast today. Instead of the skull and bones, Samuel was flying the green and white banner of Oz, as befitted the Royal Discoverer and Explorer of the most famous Fairyland in History. "He's here! He's come!" shouted Ato, running wildly up and down. "Samuel! SAM-U-EL!" In his delight and excitement, the King forgot the Royal dock and began wading out into the bay. Peering around his wheel, Sammy saw him coming and broke into a loud, cheerful greeting.

"Hi, King! Ho, King! How are you, you son of a Lubber? Wait till I ease her in, and I'll be ashore quicker than quick." Roger had already reached the *Crescent Moon* and perched upon the Captain's shoulder was chattering away at such a rate Samuel could hardly keep his mind on his steering. But he was an old hand at such matters, and before Ato had half recovered from the shock of seeing him, the shining three-masted vessel was made fast and its Master striding exuberantly up the wet planks of the royal dock. "Ahoy! Ahoy!" he boomed boisterously. "What a day for a voyage! Is it really my old cook and shipmate?"

"None other!" puffed Ato, seizing both of the former pirate's hands. "But what have you done to yourself, Sam-u-el? Where's your sash and scimitar? And what's that on your head, may I ask? You don't look natural or seaman-like at all."

"Oh, don't mind these," grinned the Pirate, touching his three-cornered hat and satin coat apologetically. "These are my shore togs for impressing the natives. Can't look like pirates when we go ashore this voyage, Mates. We're explorers and fine gentlemen now, and when we set the flag of Oz on lofty mountains and rocky isles, when we bring savage tribes and strange races under the beneficent rule of Ozma of Oz, we must look like Conquerors. Eh, my lads?"

"Yes, I sup-pose so!" puffed the King, skipping clumsily to keep up with the long strides of Captain Salt. "But I'm sorry this is going to be a dressy affair, Sammy. How'm I to cook in a cocked hat and lace collar and swab down the deck in velvet pants?"

"Ho, ho! You'll not have to," exploded the Pirate, giving the tail feathers of the Read Bird a sly tweak. "On shipboard we'll dress as we please, for the sea is MY country and free as the wind and sun."

"Well, well, I'm glad to hear you say that. Have you still got my old pirate suit and blunderbuss aboard?" inquired the King anxiously.

"Certain for sure, and a couple of new ones, and WAIT till you see your galley all fitted out with copper pots, and provisions enough below to carry us anywhere and back. Wait till you cast your eyes on 'em, Lubber!"

"Don't you call ME a Lubber!" chuckled Ato, giving Samuel a hearty poke in the ribs. "I'm as able-bodied a seaman as you, Sammy, and you know it."

"SIR Samuel, if you please!" roared the former Pirate, striking himself a great blow on the chest with his clenched fist. "Sir Samuel Salt, Explorer and Discoverer Extraordinary to the Crown of Oz."

"So—oooh! You've been knighted?" breathed Roger, peering round into the Captain's face,

"Ho pass the salt and ring the bell And bend the knee to Sir Sam-u-el!"

"Sir Samuel Salt! Well, I'll be peppered!" gasped Ato, sinking down on the lower step of the palace, which they had reached by this time. "Sir Samuel!"

"Yes, SIR" boasted the Pirate, rubbing his hands together. "But come on, step lively, boys. How long'll it take you to pack up and heave your dunnage aboard? Musn't keep a Knight of Oz waiting, you know!"

"Keep you waiting!" Suddenly and determinedly, Ato rose to his feet and shook his finger under Sammy's nose. "Keep YOU waiting? Why, we've been ready and waiting for this voyage three years, eleven months, twenty-six days and twelve hours. Where've you been, you great lazy son of a sea-robber?"

"Four years?" choked the Pirate, falling back in real consternation and dismay. "Never! It's never been four years, Mates. Why, I've scarcely had time to sort out the shells and specimens we picked up on the last voyage, and to fit out the *Crescent Moon* for the next."

"Where have you been?" repeated Ato, wagging his finger sternly.

"Why, home on Elbow Island, of course. Where else should I have been?" muttered Samuel, looking distinctly worried and crestfallen.

"Then you have no clocks or calendars in your cave?" demanded the King accusingly. "And what would the *Crescent Moon* be needing? I thought she was about perfect as she was."

"Ah, but wait till you see her now!" exclaimed Samuel, cheering up immediately at mention of his ship. "The *Crescent Moon*, besides a new coat of paint, has self-hoisting sails and a mechanical steering control in case we wish to take it easy occasionally. The Red Jinn paid me a visit and presented us with these and several other magical contrivances and improvements. I'm minded to make this voyage with no crew but ourselves. It's cozier so, don't you think?"

"Yes, but am I still on bird watch and lookout duty?" demanded Roger jealously.

"Aye, aye!" Samuel Salt assured him heartily.

"I suppose the Red Jinn has supplied you with a mechanical cook in my place as well as a mechanical steering wheel," murmured Ato, tugging uneasily at the cord around his waist.

"In your place!" thundered the Pirate. "Why, shiver my timbers, Mate! Only over my prone and prostrate body shall another man enter my galley to shuffle my rations, sugar my duff or salt my prog!"

163

"Hooray, then let's get going!" squealed Roger, bouncing up and down on Sammy's shoulder. "I was only saying this very morning that you'd never forget your old friends and shipmates or go on a voyage without us!"

"Huh! So THAT'S what you were saying!" grunted Ato, looking fixedly at the Read Bird. "Well, well, let it go. Come along then!"

"Yes, yes, and hurry," screamed Roger, spreading his wings to fly on ahead.

"Sixentwo! Sevenanone! Where are you?" panted the King, plunging up the steps after Roger two at a time. "Where is everybody? Pack a bag, a chest, a couple of trunks. I'm going on a voyage of discovery!"

"And don't forget the cook book!" bawled Samuel Salt, bounding exuberantly after the King.

Chapter 2 - Anchors Aweigh!

With the help of eighteen serving men, eight courtiers, Sixentwo, Sevenanone, and Samuel Salt, who was not above carrying a sea chest or hamper, Ato began stowing his belongings on the *Crescent Moon*. There was little court apparel or finery in the King's boxes. Most of it consisted of bottles of flavoring extract, spiced sauces, cookbooks, minced meats, fruits in jars for pies, numerous frying pans, egg beaters, and rolling pins.

"Are we gypsies, panhandlers, peddlers or what?" panted Samuel Salt as he dumped the last load breathlessly on the main deck. "Goosewing my topsails, Mate, many's the fish we cleaned with a jackknife and potato we pared with a dagger on the last voyage. Mean to say an explorer needs to use all these weapons on his pork and beans?"

Checking off a list as his stuff was placed in the galley, Ato nodded determinedly, then, winking good-humoredly at the perspiring Captain, ducked into the cabin to don his old sea clothes. Samuel was not long following suit, and soon, in short red pants, open shirts and carelessly tied head kerchiefs, the two went below to inspect the stores Samuel had laid in for the voyage. Roger, having nothing to bring aboard but a few books and a bottle of feather oil, was already perched in the crosstrees of the fore topgallant mast looking longingly toward the east and waiting impatiently for the ship to get under way. But the booming voice of the Pirate soon drew him to the lower deck, and from there he swooped down an open hatchway to the hold. This huge space, usually reserved by the pirates for captives and treasure, had been neatly divided into two sections. In one were the tinned, dried and salted meats, the groceries, vegetables and extra supplies of rope, tar and sail. In the other section there were numerous shelves, many iron cages, aquariums and sea chests.

"For any strange animals or wild natives we may encounter and wish to bring home with us," explained Samuel Salt as Roger looked curiously at the cages. "In those chests are the flags of Oz we shall plant here, there and everywhere as we sail onward!"

"And to think a new and mighty Empire may grow from this flag planting," mused Ato, opening one of the sea chests and thoughtfully fingering one of Ozma's green and white silken banners. "But surely you don't expect to plant all these, Samuel!"

"Why not?" demanded the Royal Discoverer of Oz with a wave of the scimitar he had resumed with his old pirate pants. "The sea is broad and wide and no one's to tell us when we may start or sail home again. But Look, Ato, my lad — these will interest you." Turning from the chests, Samuel pointed to a stack of long poles lashed to the side of the ship with leather thongs. "Stilts!" grinned the Pirate as Roger and Ato stared at them in complete mystification. "Fine for keeping the shins dry when we wade ashore and don't feel like lowering the jolly boat. All my own idea." Samuel cleared his throat with pardonable pride. "Of course, it takes a bit of practice, but we'll try 'em on the first island we come to. Eh, boys?"

"Well, thank my lucky star for wings!" breathed Roger after a long, disapproving look at Samuel's stilts. "Two steps and you'll smash yourself to a jellyfish, Ato. Stick to the boats, men. That's MY advice!"

"Too bad he has no confidence in us!" roared Samuel, giving Ato a resounding slap on the back. "Just wait, my saucy bird, and we'll show you how stilting is done. And now, gaze upon this corner I've set aside for my specimens; for rare marine growths, for seaweed, for curious mollusks and other crustacean denizens of the darkest deep." Samuel coughed apologetically as he always did when he mentioned his collecting mania, and Roger and Ato, exchanging an amused grin, swung about to examine the long shelves with iron boxes clamped down to prevent them from shifting with the motion of the vessel, huge aquariums fitted into brass holders, and large trays bedded with dried moss and sand for Samuel's collection of shells.

"You might even bring home a mermaid in this," murmured Ato, touching the side of an enormous aquarium.

"No women!" snapped Samuel Salt, growing red in the face, for he did not like to be teased about his specimen collecting. "I'll — I'll have no women or mermaids switching their tails around my ship and turning things topsy turvy."

"Right," agreed Ato, giving his belt a vigorous tug. "Then how about shoving off, Sammy? Everything's shipshape, there's a good wind, and the best way to begin a voyage is to start."

"I'm for it!" roared the Captain, swinging hand over hand up the wooden ladder. "All hands on deck! Up with your Master's flag, Roger. Cast off the mooring lines, Ato, while I make sail, and we'll be out of here in a pig's jiffy."

"Aye! Aye!" croaked Roger, seizing the cord that would send Ato's octagon banner flying to the masthead, directly under the flag of Oz. "Goodbye, all you lubbers ashore! Goodbye, Sevenanone. Mind you keep the King's Crown polished, and don't forget to feed the silver fish."

"GOODBYE!" called the one hundred and eighty Octagon Islanders drawn up on the beach and dock to see his Majesty sail away. "A fine voyage to your Highness!"

"And neglect not to return!" shouted Sixentwo, using his hands as a megaphone. "You know there is a Crown Council eight days and eight months from yesterday."

"Crown Council be jigged!" sniffed Ato, leaning far over the rail to wave to his cheering subjects. "I'm a cook, an explorer — and a bold, bad, seafaring man out to collect islands and jungles and jillycomewiggles for Samuel's shell box. Crown Council, indeed! Don't care if I never see a castle again."

"Me neither!" squalled Roger, flying up to his post in the foremast. "Seven bells and all's well! Buoy off the beam and no land in sight."

"Unless you look behind you," laughed Samuel, grabbing the wheel with a practiced hand and squinting cheerfully up at the sun. "East by southeast it'll be this voyage, Mates. There's ice in the North Nonestic, and I've a craving for tropical isles and the hidden rivers of some deep and mysterious jungle!"

"Remember Snow Island?" smiled Ato, coming over to stand beside the wheel.

"Shiver my shins! DO I? No more of that, me lads! But Ho! Isn't this like old times?" Stretching up his arms exultingly, Samuel Salt let his hands fall heavily on the wheel, and the great ship, lifting with the wind, plunged her nose eagerly into the southeast swell.

"M—mmm! Like old times, except for the boy," agreed Ato slowly.

"Aye, and we'll surely miss Peter on this trip," sighed the Captain, shaking his head regretfully. "Wonder where the little lubber is now? That's the trouble with these real countries and peoples, there's no getting at them when you need them most. Well, maybe we'll pick up another hand somewhere to serve as cabin boy and keep us lively on the voyage. But take a look at my sail controls, Ato. We can hoist, trim and furl by just touching different buttons nowadays; set this wheel for any course and just let her ride."

"Splendid!" grunted Ato, rising reluctantly from a coil of rope. "But since there are no buttons on my stove, I'd best be thinking about dinner."

"Tar and tarpaulin, why didn't I have the Red Jinn fix you some?" exclaimed the Pirate regretfully. "I'm sorry as a goat, Mate."

"Ho — I'm not," laughed Ato, waddling happily off toward his galley. "That would have spoiled everything. What'll it be, Captain, a fried sole, a broiled steak, or a roaring huge hot peppery meat pasty?"

"All of 'em!" yelled the Royal Explorer of Oz, exhaling his breath in a mighty blast of anticipation. It seemed to Roger, high in the foremast, that the ship gave an extra little skip at its Captain's mighty roar, then, settling easily into her usual graceful pace, she ran smoothly before the wind.

Chapter 3 - The Fire Baby

Morning found the Crescent Moon forging ahead with a stiff breeze, a choppy sea and the last known island far behind her.

"Ahoy, and this is the life, Mates!" bellowed Samuel Salt, bracing his legs against the pitch and roll of the vessel and waving largely to the ship's cook, who sat on an overturned bucket mending his second best sea shirt. "Anything can happen now!" Lovingly Samuel let his gaze rove over the sparkling Nonestic, and Ato, squinting painfully as he pushed his long needle in and out, nodded portentously.

"By the way, Sammy, what are your plans for this flag planting and discovery business?" inquired the portly cook somewhat later. Having finished his mending, he had dragged a canvas chair and a pot of potatoes aft by the wheel. "Do you look for resistance and rebellion when we start taking possession of this land and that land for the crown of Oz?"

"No, no, nothing like that," mused Samuel, removing his pipe and blowing a cloud of smoke into the rigging. "Everything's to be polite and peaceable this voyage. No guns, knives or scimitars. Queen Ozma particularly does not want any country taken by force or against its will."

"And suppose they object to being taken at all?" said Ato, beginning to pare a fat potato. "What then?"

"Well, then — er, then —" Samuel rubbed his chin reflectively, "we'll try persuasion, my lad. We'll explain all the advantages of coming under the flag and protection of a powerful country like Oz. That ought to get them, don't you think?"

"Yes, if they don't get us first," observed Ato, popping a potato dubiously into the pot. "Suppose while we stand there waving flags and persuading, some of these wild fellows have at us with spears, clubs and poison arrows?"

"Well, that would be extremely unfortunate," admitted Samuel, glancing soberly at the compass, "and in that case—"

"I hope you will remember you were once a pirate and act accordingly," Ato blew out his cheeks sternly as he spoke. "The one trouble with you, Sammy, is that you take too long to get mad. So I shall go ashore armed as usual with my kitchen knife and blunderbuss. I don't intend to be sliced into sandwiches while you're talking through your three-cornered hat and waving flags at a lot of ignorant savages. And I'll have Roger carry the books ashore, too."

"No, ho!" roared the Captain of the *Crescent Moon*, giving his knee a great slap. "Just like old times, Ato. Rough, bluff and relentless, Mates, remember?"

"Aye, and I should say I do. And I remember Roger had to drop a good many books on your head before you got mad enough to fight. What makes you so calm and peaceable, Sammy? A big born fighting man like yourself."

"Sea life, I reckon," answered the former Pirate, extending his brawny arms in a huge yawn. "The sea's so much bigger than a man, Mate — it rather makes him realize how small and unimportant he really is. But don't fret, Cook dear, no one shall tread on your toes this voyage. But avast there — it grows warmer, and the air smells a bit thunderish. Had you noticed?"

"'Hoy, 'hoy! Deck ahoy!" bawled a shrill voice from above. "Island astern." Both Samuel and Ato stared up in amazement, for Roger was supposed to be resting in the cabin. But the Read Bird, after snatching an hour's nap, had slipped out an open port and unnoticed taken his position in the foremast. The Read Bird did not trust Ato, who was supposed to be on watch. Besides, he wanted to be the first to report a new island to the Captain.

"Looks like a mountain," mumbled Ato, setting down his potatoes and waddling over to the rail. "Heave to, Skipper, here's our first discovery."

"Now how in sixes did that get by me?" muttered Samuel Salt, hurrying to shorten sail for the zigzag course, back and in, he would have to take to reach the island at all. It showed plainly enough now, a rugged gray and purple mass of rock with apparently no vegetation or dwellings of any kind. As the *Crescent Moon* drew nearer, the sea became smooth and oily and the air sulphurous and hot.

"Think likely this is an island we might well pass by," murmured Ato, peering critically through his telescope. "Positively deserted so far as I can see — but there might be valuable minerals in those rocks."

"Don't doubt it!" Samuel Salt curved himself all the way round the wheel in his interest. Mechanical devices were well enough for the open sea, but Samuel preferred to handle his own ship on occasions like this. As there was no harbor or safe place to put in, he decided to anchor offshore and land in the jolly boat. The anchor had just gone clanking and rattling over the side when a horrid hiss and boom from the center of the island made all hands look up in alarm.

"K-kkk cannons!" quavered Ato, dropping his bread knife with a clatter. "Stand by to man the guns!"

But Samuel Salt, instead of heeding the cook's warning, began to sniff the air. "Volcano, Mates," announced the Captain calmly. "And in that case we may be a bit close for comfort. Still, I've always wanted to observe a volcano in action. I've a theory there may be living creatures in the center."

"Living creatures in the center!" raged Ato, tearing off his white apron and dashing it on the deck. "How long will we be living if that fire pot starts boiling? We mayn't be killed, being of magic birth, but we can be jolly well singed, fried, boiled and melted. And after that, who'd care to be alive? Quick, Roger, heave in on that chain! Anchors aweigh!"

While Samuel stood in rapt contemplation of the volcano and Ato began frantically winding up the anchor, a long tongue of flame leaped out of the crater, and a great jet of bubbling lava shot clear over the *Crescent Moon*. This occurrence soon brought Samuel out of his reverie, and snapping into action and forgetting all about his mechanical devices, he began working like a madman to get the ship in motion, tugging at the sheets, throwing his whole weight against the halyards till the ship, with quivering sail, sped away like a frightened bird, the hot winds from the volcano whistling and rattling through her rigging.

"Where's Roger?" yelled Ato, staggering across the deck with two buckets of water. "Oh, woe! Is he a Read Bird or a just plain Goose? Look yonder, Sammy, he's flown ashore." Outlined against the sky in a sudden flare from the volcano, they could see Roger poised over the center of the smoking island. In his claw was a large rippling banner of Oz, and as they looked he lifted the banner high above his head and flung it straight into the center of the boiling crater.

"We hereby take complete and absolute possession of this island and declare all its inhabitants lawful subjects of her Majesty, Queen Ozma of Oz!" screamed Roger hysterically.

166

"Well, hurray and three cheers for a real Explorer!" shouted Samuel Salt. "He's done it all by himself, the only man among us who remembered his duty under fire. There's a bird for you, Mates. Not even a volcano can turn him from his duty. All we thought of was safety. Pah!" Rubbing the back of his hand across his eyes, which were full of smoke, Samuel looked glumly across at his cook.

"Now, now, don't be too hard on yourself," puffed the King, setting down the fire buckets. "A Captain must think of his ship, even if he is an Explorer. Besides, having wings gives Roger an advantage of us. Still and all, it was a brave and timely act." Ato's further remarks were drowned out in a second tremendous explosion. Sky and sea turned red, whole flaming boulders shot above the ship's spars, while great sullen waves of lava boiled over the crater's edge and rolled smoking and hissing into the sea.

"Missed us again," panted Samuel Salt, hanging desperately to his wheel as the *Crescent Moon* plunged and pitched in the angry sea. "Wonder what started that?"

"The Oz flag, probably," gasped Ato, feeling around in the dense smoke for his fire buckets. "Hope Roger got off safely. Where is that fool bird? Ho, Sammy! Hi, Sammy! Quick, they've hit us amidships."

Hastily setting his mechanical steering gear, the former Pirate rushed forward to where a glowing lump of lava was burning its way slowly but surely through the deck.

"Fire! Fire!" shrilled Roger, who had dropped down on the rail unnoticed in the smoke and confusion. "Water, Ato! Water, you old Slowpoke!"

"Avast," puffed Samuel Salt, staring down in astonishment at the glowing lump at his feet. "It's alive, Mates, and lively as a grig. It's a FIRE baby, that's what! HAH! Didn't I just say there was life on a volcano? Well, this proves it, and I'm taking this young one along for proof."

"Now stop talking like a book and act like a seaman," choked Ato, in his agitation tripping over a rope but still managing to keep his hold on the water buckets. "Fire baby or not, can't you see it's burning a hole in the deck, you seventh son of a seagoing Jackass? Here, put it out! Dash this water over it before it burns up the whole ship!"

"Avast! Avast and belay!" roared Samuel Salt in a terrible voice as Ato raised his bucket. "I'm still Captain here. Do you wish to destroy a rare specimen of volcanic life? Fetch a shovel from the hold, Roger. A shovel, I said, and don't stand there dithering."

"Aye aye, sir!" sputtered the Read Bird, half falling and half flying down the companionway. Now a bird is a quick and handy fellow about a ship, and in half the time it would have taken a seaman, Roger was back with a long-handled shovel. Snatching the shovel, which had often used on former treasure hunts, Samuel scooped up the bawling fire baby and started on a run for the galley.

"It's turning black, it's turning black," wailed the disconsolate collector, crooning to the ugly infant as he ran along as if he were its own mother. "Aye, aye — it's going out!"

"And a good thing, too," panted Ato, who was close behind him. "What in tarry barrels are you fixing to do with it, Sammy?"

Roger, sensible bird that he was, stayed long enough to douse the two buckets of water on the smoking deck, then he too made a bee line for the galley. He was just in time to see Samuel lift the lid of the range and slide the baby down on top of the hot coals. No sooner had the squat infant touched the glowing fire than it stopped yelling at once and began to purr and sing like a teakettle set on to boil. "Well, I'll be swizzled!" gulped Ato, and snatching a wet dish towel from a rack, he wound it round and round his aching head. "Whatever made you think of that?"

"It's my scientific mind," the Pirate told them blandly. "The proper place for any infant that size is bed, and I naturally figured that a fire baby belonged in a fire bed, and a bed of hot coals was the nearest to it, so here it is!" Winking solemnly at Roger, who was regarding the little Lavaland Islander with fear and loathing, Samuel picked up the poker and gave the baby an affectionate poke. "It'll do fine here," he predicted happily, "and prove beyond a quibble that volcanoes are inhabited."

"It'll do nothing of the sort!" exploded Ato, bringing his fat fist down with a resounding thump on the drainboard. "You may be Captain of the ship, Sammy, but I'm the boss of this galley, and that fire baby will have to go. GO! Do you understand? How'm I to cook with the ugly little monster lolling all over the fire bed and like as not falling into the soup when my back is turned?"

"Hark!" interrupted Roger. "More trouble! Something's up, Master Salt, and it's not an eruption, either." And Samuel had to agree with him as groans, moans, shrieks and hisses came whistling after the flying ship.

"Ah, that'll be the rest of them!" exulted the Royal Discoverer, pounding out on deck. "Hah! It's the Lavaland Islanders themselves. Ho — this WILL be interesting!"

"Well, just invite them over, and we'll all burn up happily together," suggested Ato bitterly.

Hanging over the taffrail, Samuel paid no attention to the King's sarcastic suggestion. Indeed, he was much too interested, for showing just above the flaming circle of the volcano's crater was a row of immense and thunderous-

167

looking natives. They were of transparent rock-like structure and burned and glowed from the molten lava that coursed through their veins. With upraised arms and furious faces, they were yelling over and over some strange and indistinguishable threats and phrases. One, shaking the blackened stick of the Oz flag, danced and screamed louder than all the rest put together. "They do not wish to become subjects of Oz, I take it," sighed Samuel, undecided whether to sail back and argue the matter or sail away and save his ship from possible destruction.

"That's not it! That's not it!" cried Roger, flapping his wings triumphantly. "I know what's the matter. They want that baby back. You're probably making off with the Crown Prince of the Volcano. See that woman yelling louder than the others and holding out both arms? Well, look, she has a crown on her head and is likely the Queen. She wants her baby back."

"And she should have it, too," stated Ato, blinking his eyes at the frightful racket the Lavaland Islanders were making. "You can't steal people's children like this, Sammy, unless you're going back to buccaneering. It's just plain piracy."

"She threw it at us, didn't she?" muttered the Captain, who was unwilling to part with so valuable a specimen.

"It probably blew out of its cradle when the volcano erupted. Give it back to her, Sammy," begged Ato, who was determined to get rid of the terrible infant at any cost. "After all, she's its mother."

"But do you expect me to sail back there and endanger all of our lives?" Samuel jerked his head angrily. "And how else can it be done?"

"Er, er, let Roger carry it back in that old wire basket we use for clams," proposed the cook eagerly.

"Not on your life," protested Roger in a surly voice. "The basket would grow red hot and burn my bill. Besides, I'm no stork. Tell you what we could do, though, and we'd better be quick before they start throwing things."

"What?" inquired the Captain, gazing uneasily at the infuriated Islanders.

"Why, simply shoot it back," Roger said calmly. "Stuff it in the port cannon and blaze away. You never miss your mark, Master Salt, and if you can't shoot that baby back into its mother's arms, I'll walk on my wings and be done with it."

"Why, Roger, how clever! The very thing!" rejoiced Ato. "I'll go fetch it with the fire tongs, and you'll have to hurry, Sammy, or we'll be out of range."

"But it might injure the young one," objected the Captain of the *Crescent Moon*, shifting his feet uncomfortably.

"Nonsense. It'll be just like a ride in a baby carriage for that little rascal. Prime your gun, Sammy, while I get the child."

By this time the clamor from the Island had become so alarming that even Samuel realized something would have to be decided. So, somewhat mollified by Roger's compliment on his aim, he made ready to fire the port cannon. The baby, hissing lustily, was brought without accident from the galley. Ato held it gingerly before him, using the fire tongs, Roger following along to hold a lighted candle under the little fellow to keep him from going out before he was shot. The baby fitted nicely into the cannon's mouth and stopped crying instantly. At the last moment Samuel almost lost his courage, but urged on to action by both Ato and Roger, he carefully made his calculations, and then shutting both eyes, pulled the cord that set off the gun. The terrible explosion shocked the Lavalanders into silence, and almost afraid to look, Samuel opened his eyes.

"Yo, ho, ho! Three cheers for the Skipper!" squealed Ato, snatching the towel from his head and waving it like a banner. "The neatest shot you ever made, Mate, and a lucky shot, too." The baby and the cannonball, which would have shattered a less durable lady, struck the Lava Queen amidships. Dropping the cannonball carelessly into the crater, the giantess clasped her child in her arms, smiling and screaming her thanks across the tumbling waters.

"Well, was I right or was I right?" chuckled Roger, teetering backward and forward on the rail and preening his feathers self-consciously. "And I've another idea just as good in case you should be interested."

"Oh, keep it till tomorrow," grumbled Samuel Salt, who felt terribly depressed at the loss of his rare specimen.

"But tomorrow will be too late," persisted Roger, settling on the Captain's shoulder. "Now, while these savages are in a good humor, let me fly over and drop another Oz flag on the Island. Maybe this time they'll let it stand, and once it flies over the crater the Island is Ozma's."

"By the tooth of a harpooned whale, you're right! I'm forgetting my duty to Oz," breathed Samuel, straightening up purposefully. "But our kind of flag won't stand the climate yonder."

The Read Bird, however, had thought even of that. Taking a sheet of iron from the hold, the resourceful fellow stopped in the galley long enough to burn in the word Oz with the red hot poker. Then, thrusting the poker itself through two slits in his iron banner, he flew jauntily back to the Island. "Ahoy, and there's a standard bearer for you!" Rubbing his hands together, Samuel strode to the rail. "Bless my buttons, the boy deserves a medal for this, and shall have one, too."

This time the Lavaland Islanders watched Roger's approach with quiet interest, and as he hovered uncertainly over their heads held up their hands for the iron flag. But Roger, made daring by their friendliness, swooped down suddenly to the crater's edge, and jamming his banner between two smoking boulders, soared aloft. "Lavaland Islanders!" screamed the Read Bird hoarsely. "You are now under the protection and rule of Queen Ozma of Oz. Lavaland Islanders, you are hereby abjured to keep the peace and the law and LAV one another!" His voice cracked from fright and excitement, but finishing triumphantly, he spread his wings and skimmed back to the *Crescent Moon*.

"Hung wung wah HEEE!" yelled the Islanders all together, nodding their heads and waving their arms cheerfully. "Hung wung wah HEEE!"

Chapter 4 - Samuel's First Specimen

"What do you make of that?" puffed Samuel Salt as Roger dropped breathlessly down on his shoulder. "Well, `Hung wung wah HEEE!' it is. Let's give them a cheer for luck." Lifting his great voice, the Royal Discoverer for Oz, helped out by his two shipmates, sent the weird call booming back across the water.

An answering call came from the Island, and then, with a hiss and thud, a small glowing object fell on the deck. Fortunately, the fire tongs were still handy, and picking up the offending object before it could do any damage, Ato marched sternly off to the galley. Stopping long enough for another wave to the island, which was growing smaller and smaller as the *Crescent Moon* sped away, Samuel hastened after his cook, jotting down hurried notes in his journal as to latitude and longitude as he ran along.

"There's something written on this piece of lava," announced Ato, who had dropped the smoking souvenir from Lavaland on the stove. Peering over his shoulder, Samuel could see queer raised symbols and signs on the sulphurous surface of the rock.

"There's something crawling on it, too," volunteered Roger, who was perched on the towel rack above the stove and had a better view, "a golden frog or a lizard."

"Merciful mustard! What next?" groaned Ato.

"Why, this — this—" Samuel's voice quivered with excitement and disbelief, "this, Mates, is as fine a specimen of a Preoztoric Monster as a scientist could hope for; a real, live salamander, a fire lizard, straight from the burning depths of yonder crater. Stars! Tar and Tarrybarrels! This is even better than the baby and will prove my point just as well."

"Does it have to live on my stove?" asked Ato ominously as the Salamander slid merrily backward and forward over the red-hot plates of the range.

"Home on the range!" snickered Roger, winking at the Pirate.

"Just till I can fix up a hotbox for it," apologized Samuel, "but don't fret, old Toff, it doesn't bite, and if it falls on the floor, all you have to do is scoop it up and put it back before it goes out."

"Not only cook, mate and swab, but now I'm nursemaid to a fire lizard." Ato shuddered, and reaching for his tall cook's cap, jammed it down hard on his shiny bald head.

"You can keep it in an iron pot while you cook," suggested Roger practically, "and after all, King dear, it's the only Salamander in captivity. Here, Sally, here Sal — this way, my little crater critter." Tilting the pot on the back of the stove, Roger was delighted to find the Salamander quite willing to answer to her new name. As she slid adventurously into the small cooking vessel, the Read Bird quickly righted the pot and clapped on the cover. "There," he exclaimed with a satisfied nod at his Master, "how's that?"

"Well, I suppose I'll have to put up with it," sighed Ato resignedly. "But in some ways, pirating was easier than discovering, Sammy. At least we never kept the captives on the stove. And NOW—" Ato waved his arms determinedly "—clear out, both of you. It's three bells and time to stir up the food. And just take that pesky rock along with you. I've meat to broil!"

"When this cools, maybe I'll be able to figure out the language," exulted Samuel, removing the offending piece of lava with a cake turner. "All in all, a most interesting and profitable day, eh Roger? An island, a visit from a fire baby, and a real live Preoztoric monster."

"Not bad," agreed the Read Bird, transferring himself to the Captain's shoulder. Depositing the piece of lava on an iron hatchway to cool, Samuel strode happily along the deck, stopping to light the red lamps on the port and the green lights on the starboard. Roger himself had just hung a white light in the rigging when a lusty call from the galley sent him flying off to help Ato serve the dinner. "What could be cozier than a life at sea?" he reflected, winging jauntily into the main cabin with a dish of roast potatoes. Ato puffed cheerfully behind, bearing a huge tray. On the tray a steaming

169

tureen of soup, a pot of coffee, seven dishes of vegetables and two of smoking meats sent up tantalizing whiffs and fragrances. Later, when the Read Bird brought in the pudding, he and Sammy soberly agreed it was the tastiest feast Ato had served on the voyage.

The main cabin of the *Crescent Moon*, with its red leather couches under the ports, its easy chairs and tables clamped to the floor to keep them from shifting, with its ship's clock and ship's lanterns, was a cheery place to be when the day's work was ended. There was a huge fireplace for foggy evenings, and every visible space on the wall was covered with pictures of pirate ships, ancient sailing vessels, and rough maps and charts of strange and curious islands. While Samuel and Ato sat at their ease to finish off the pudding, Roger took his upon the wing, darting in and out between bites to assure himself that all was well on deck. There was a tiny *Crescent Moon* sliding down the sky, and the slap of waves against the side of the ship and the wind creaking in the cordage made as pleasant a tune as the heart of a seaman could wish for.

"Now what could be better than this?" said Samuel Salt, exhaling a cloud of smoke from his pipe and stretching his legs luxuriously under the long table. "A tidy ship, a good wind, and the whole wide sea to sail on."

"Suits me!" grinned Ato, scraping up the last of the hard sauce and settling back with a grunt of sheer content. "Did you mark up our volcano on the chart, Sammy, and what are we calling it, Mates? An island must have a name, you know."

"I know." Samuel blew another cloud of smoke upward and cleared his throat. "If it's agreeable to all hands and Roger, I'd like to call it Salamander Island after Sally."

"Why not? There's a Sally in our galley and a real nice gal is Sally," warbled Roger, settling on the back of Samuel's chair and wagging his head in time to the music.

"Sing like a bird, don't ye?" muttered Samuel, striding over to the map of Oz and surrounding countries and oceans that covered the west wall.

"I AM a bird," screamed Roger, fluttering up to his shoulder. "'Bout here she would lie, Master Salt, sixty leagues from Octagon Island."

As Roger talked on, making numerous suggestions, the Captain of the *Crescent Moon* drew with red chalk a small but effective picture of Salamander Island showing the volcano in action and the Lavaland Islanders grouped around the crater's top. "Taken this day without a shot or the loss of a single man," printed Samuel in neat letters under his sketch.

"Don't forget, you shot the baby," twittered Roger, raising a claw argumentatively.

"Oh, we can't put in small details like that," sniffed the Captain, stepping back to admire his drawing.

"Seems odd for us to be discovering and taking possession of islands for a country we know so little about," mused Ato, looking thoughtfully at the map on the west wall. "Why, we've only been to Oz once ourselves."

"Yes, but everybody knows about Oz," Samuel said, putting the red chalk back in the table drawer. "Our business is with wild new countries that have never been seen or heard of. Besides, anyone can see that Oz is overpopulated and needs new territories and seaports. And since Ozma is so clever at governing and her subjects all so happy and prosperous, the more people who come under her rule the better!"

"Aye! Aye!" agreed Roger, peering with deep interest at the map. Small wonder the Read Bird was interested, for Oz is one of the most exciting and enchanting countries ever discovered. There are four large Kingdoms in Ozma's realm, the Northern Land of the Gillikens, the Eastern Empire of the Winkies, the Southern Country of the Quadlings, and the Western domain of the Munchkins. Each forms a triangle in the oblong of Oz. The Emerald City, which is the capital, is in the exact center where all these triangles meet. Each of these Kingdoms has its own ruler, but all four are under the sovereign rule and control of Ozma, the small but powerful fairy who lives in the Emerald City.

On all sides, Oz is surrounded by a deadly desert, and beyond the desert lie the independent Kingdoms of No-Land, Low Land, Ix, Play, Ev, the Dominions of the Gnome King, and many other strange and important Principalities. These countries form a narrow rim around the desert, and beyond this rim lies the Nonestic Ocean itself, stretching in all directions and to no one knows what far and undiscovered shores.

Each of the four Kingdoms in Oz shown on Samuel's map was so dotted with smaller Kingdoms, cities, towns, villages and the holdings of ancient Knights and Barons, there was scarcely room for another castle. With young Princes growing up on every hand, Roger could well sympathize with the need of Ozma for more territory.

"Won't the Ozians have too long a way to come before they reach these new islands and countries we discover?" inquired the Read Bird after staring at the map for some moments in silence.

"Not a bit of it!" Samuel dismissed Roger's objection with a snap of his fingers. "I hear the Wizard of Oz is working on a new fleet of airships that will make crossing the desert and Nonestic a real lark and enable new settlers to reach these outlying islands in a day or less. So all we have to do is to proceed with our discovering. Ozma will attend to the rest. This volcanic island may not be as useful as some of the others, but one can never tell. How about picking up a few islands for you, Ato, as we ride along?" The former pirate dropped his arm affectionately round the shoulders of his Royal Cook.

"No, thanks," grunted Ato, rolling cheerfully to his feet. "One's enough. What would I want with any more islands? Why, I'd never get off on a voyage. But pick yourself a couple, Sammy, why don't you?"

"Who, ME?" Samuel Salt shook his head emphatically. "A ship's all I can handle, and I wouldn't trade you two buckets of sea water for all the islands in the Nonestic. One ship and one crew's enough for me, and since you're my crew, you'd better turn in— we've had a hard day and another one coming. I'll take first watch; Cooky, here, shall have middle; and you, Roger, can be the early bird on morning watch."

"Ho hum! I'm right sleepy at that," admitted Ato, starting to heap up plates. "Give me a lift with the dishes, Roger, will you?"

"Oh, throw 'em overboard," directed Samuel Salt recklessly. "There's plenty more in the hold, and I'm agin all extry labor."

"Hurray!" screamed Roger, seizing the coffee pot and winging merrily through an open port.

"Avast! Avast there! Not my coffee pot!" pleaded Ato, making after the Read Bird with surprising speed considering his tonnage. "Stop, you great Gossoon! How many times must I tell you I'm boss of the galley?" Catching Roger by the leg just as he reached the rail, Ato snatched back his precious coffee pot and hugged it protectively to his bosom. "Why, I've just got this contraption broken in proper," he panted indignantly. "A coffee pot's like a pipe: it's got to be sweetened and seasoned. Heave over the plates and cups if you like," he went on, relenting a bit as he noted the keen disappointment on Roger's face, "but save the soup tureen. I'll wager there's not another that size on the ship, and the Captain must have his soup. What a splendid pot of soup THIS would make," murmured Ato, looking dreamily down at the sea. "A bit salty, perhaps, but full of snapper and porgy and tender young sea shoots. Why, that foam's as near to whipping cream as anything I've ever gazed on."

Tearing himself reluctantly from the appetizing sight, the Royal Cook padded off to put the galley in order for the night, while Roger with loud squalls of glee dropped the plates and saucers one by one over the side. In this way the dishes were soon done, the cabin tidy and shipshape, and by eight bells the King and the Read Bird were sleeping soundly and Samuel Salt had the ship all to himself. First he made a complete round of all decks, glanced at the barometer and compass, and furled the fore and mizzen topsails. Then he took the cooled piece of lava down to the hold. The strange signs and symbols had hardened, and labeling it carefully with the date and name of Salamander Island, Samuel placed it on his shelves for further study. Then, returning to the main deck, he set a portable ship's lantern on a coil of rope and settled down to fix a hotbox for the Salamander.

Selecting from the material he had brought from the hold an iron box with a glass lid, he covered the bottom with sand and pebbles. Knowing salamanders require hot water as well as hot air, he placed a tiny, flat pan of water in the corner of the box to serve as a swimming pool. A burning glass in the daytime and an alcohol lamp under the box at night would supply the necessary heat, and setting the whole contrivance on an iron tray in the cabin, Samuel went joyfully off to fetch the fire lizard.

The Salamander was still in the pot on the back of the stove, and giving her an experimental poke with his finger, Samuel was astonished to find her quite cool to the touch. This was surprising considering she could only live in the most intense heat. But without stopping to figure it out, the Captain picked her up between thumb and forefinger, carried her to the cabin, and popped her into the iron box. He had already lighted the lamp under the box so that everything was red-hot and cozy for her. The small captive seemed to appreciate her new quarters, wriggling over the hot pebbles and sand, then splashing gaily in her swimming pool.

"Quite a girl," sighed the pirate, resting his elbows on the table and gazing happily down at the first prize of the voyage. "You're going to be great company for me, Sally." As if she really understood, the lizard gave a squeak and tapped loudly on the glass lid with her tail. The pipe almost dropped from Samuel's mouth at Sally's strange behavior, and lifting the lid he peered inquisitively down at her. Before he had a chance to clap it shut, the Salamander hurled herself upward, landing smartly on the bridge of the Pirate's nose, from where she slid cleverly into the pipe itself. "Well, I'll be scuppered!" gasped the Royal Explorer, looking slightly cross-eyed down the bridge of his nose as Sally coiled up comfortably in the bowl of the pipe. "The little rascal wants to keep me company, and so she shall, bless my boots, so she shall! Why, this is plumb cute and cozy and something to write in my journal." Puffing away delightedly, Samuel stepped out of the cabin, and all during his watch, the little Salamander rested contentedly in his pipe. Sometimes she peered up inquisitively over the edge, but mostly she lay quietly on the smoking tobacco, looking with calm interest up at the sky and the rippling sails over her head. Not only did she keep his pipe from going out, but never had it drawn so well. So filled with a vast wonder and content, Samuel strode up and down the deck. Not till midnight when he roused Ato could he bear to put Sally back in her box, and only then after he had promised her another ride in the morning. But when morning came, Samuel had no time to keep his promise, for while Ato was cooking breakfast and the Captain himself catching forty winks in the cabin, the raucous voice of the Read Bird came whistling down from the foremast.

"Land Ho! Land! More Land. Island tuluward Captain!"

Chapter 5 - Patrippany Island

"All hands on deck! Come on! Come on!" yelled Samuel Salt, running past Ato's galley, dragging on his clothes as he ran. "There's an island tuluward, you lubber."

"Well, 'tain't a flying island, is it?" Ato stuck a very red face out the door. "I guess it'll stay there till I turn the bacon, won't it? No cause to burn the biscuits just 'cause an island's sighted, is there?" But in spite of his pretended indifference, the ship's cook shoved all his pans on the back of the stove and hurried out on deck. "Rich and jungly, this one," he observed, resting his arms comfortably on the rail, "and from what I can see, a good place to grow bananas and whiskers. Look, Sammy, even the trees have beards."

"Moss," muttered Samuel Salt, striding over to the wheel. "Fly ashore, Roger, and see whether there's a good place to put in." Twittering with importance and curiosity, the Read Bird flung himself into the air. In ten minutes he was back to report a wide river cutting through the center of the island from end to end. The foliage was so dense that Roger had not been able to discover any signs of habitation, but after viewing the mouth of the river through his glasses, the Captain decided to take a chance and sail through.

"Now Sammy, let's not do anything hasty," begged the ship's cook, lifting his floury hands in warning, "or try to conquer a country on an empty stomach. This may be an important island, so after we eat, let us put on our proper clothes and plant the Oz flags with dignity and decorum."

"Spoken like a King and a seaman," approved Samuel Salt, "and if my eye does not deceive me, I'll have the ship in the river as soon as you have the coffee in the pot. Then we'll ride in with the tide, put on our discovering togs, and proceed with the business of the day." So while Ato returned to his galley and the Read Bird to his post in the foremast, Samuel swung the *Crescent Moon* in toward the island. Each felt a slight twinge of uneasiness as the ship left the open sea and began to slip rapidly up the broad new and unnavigated jungle stream. Vine-covered trees pressed close to the banks, and birds and monkeys in the branches kept up an incessant screech and chattering. A flock of greedy pelicans flopped comically after the ship, and as they penetrated deeper and deeper into the jungle, it almost seemed as if they were entering some dim, green land of goblins.

"A fine target we make for anyone who cares to shoot at us," moaned Ato as he waddled backward and forward between the cabin and galley with cups and covered dishes. "Ugh!"

"Yes, I wouldn't be surprised to feel an arrow in my back any minute now," assented Samuel Salt brightly, "though I must say I'd much prefer a fried mackerel in my stomach."

"Come on, then," shuddered Ato, in no wise cheered by Samuel's remarks, "breakfast's ready, and we may as well eat before we die."

"Now never say die!" roared the Royal Explorer of Oz, touching the buttons to furl sail and yelling to Roger to let go the anchor. "Never say die. Say dee — dee-scovery is our aim and purpose, mates. Dee-scovery with a hi de di dide di dough!" sang Samuel vociferously to keep up his own spirits. Finally, with the ship motionless amidstream, the three shipmates sat down to breakfast. Their nerves were tense and their ears cocked for signs of approaching natives, but except for the noise of the birds and monkeys and the occasional splash of some river creature, there was no sound to indicate the ship had been sighted by the islanders.

"Nobody's home," concluded Samuel, finishing off his third cup of coffee at one toss and hurrying off to his cabin. Roger, having only Oz flags and no shore togs to bother him, generously offered to clear away the dishes and amused himself by throwing scraps and the rest of the biscuits to the pelicans. He had just tossed over the last biscuit when Ato appeared in a grand satin coat and breeches, long cape, and three-cornered hat. The elegance of his apparel was somewhat marred by the breadboard he had belted round his middle and the bread knife and blunderbuss he had stuck through his sash.

"Ha, hah!" roared Samuel Salt, giving the breadboard a resounding whack. "Something to stay your stomach, EH!" Samuel himself was as stylishly attired as the King, his three-cornered hat at a dashing angle. Under his arm he had two pairs of tremendously long stilts. "No need for us to get all grubby lowering the boat. We'll wade ashore this time," explained Samuel as Ato's eyes grew round and questioning. "Easy as walking on crutches. Just watch me, mate."

Now Samuel, it must be confessed, had been practicing stilting on Elbow Island, so naturally it came easy to him. First he put his stilts over the side, then, vaulting the rail, he seized the tops and settled his feet in the crosspieces at one jump and started walking calmly up and down, gleefully calling for Ato to follow. It all looked so simple, Ato handed the basket of lunch he had packed to Roger and, seizing his stilts, began anxiously feeling around for the river bottom. Satisfied that it was solid, he climbed boldly up on the rail.

"That's it! That's it!" applauded Samuel. "Now grab the tops, mate, and start coming."

"Chee tree — tee — hee!" screeched the monkeys derisively as Ato clung precariously to the rail with one hand and maneuvered his stilts with the other. By some miracle of balance, the fat King actually managed to mount and hold on to his perilous walking sticks. Then, with a long, quivering breath, he heaved one forward. He was about to take another step when a desperate scream from Roger almost caused him to topple over backwards.

"'Gators!" croaked the Read Bird, beating his wings together violently. "Watch out! for those 'gators."

"Why bother him with gaiters at a time like this? They look perfectly all right to me." Samuel Salt frowned up at Roger.

"Not his gaiters, river 'gators, alligators, CROCODILES!" wailed Roger, beginning to fly in agonized circles. "Crocodiles and WORSE."

Samuel, eyeing what he had supposed to be a pile of rotten logs on the riverbank, saw dozens of the slimy saurians slide into the water and come savagely toward them.

"Back to the ship! Back to the ship!" babbled the Read Bird, clutching Ato's collar with a frantic claw. But the King was too frightened to move. The sight of the bleary-eyed river monsters made him tremble so violently, his stilts twittered and swayed like trees in a hurricane. He could not for the life of him take a step in either direction. With a loud cry, Samuel started to help him, but a crocodile reached Ato first. Its jaws closed with a vicious snap on the King's left stilt, and with a heart-rending shriek, Ato plunged into the slimy river.

"There, there! Now you've done it!" sobbed Roger. "Fed the kindest soul who ever served a ship's company to a parcel of crocodiles!" Dropping the Oz flags and lunch basket, he made an unsuccessful grab for his Master's arm. But even if he had caught it, Ato's great weight would have pulled them both under; and now only a circle of bubbles showed where the luckless explorer had disappeared. Firing his blunderbuss to frighten off the rest of the crocodiles, Samuel, striking left and right with his stilts, propelled himself forward while Roger pecked futilely at the monster that had felled his Master. But just as Samuel, after boldly driving off the dragon-like creature, prepared to dive in and save Ato or perish with him, a dripping head appeared above the water.

"Thank you. Thank you very much!" murmured a mild voice. "I haven't had as nice a present as this since I was an itty bitty baby. Now what can I do for YOU?" Neither Samuel nor Roger could speak a word, for where the King had gone down, a tremendous hippopotamus was coming up, the lunch basket hanging carelessly out of a corner of its mouth. For a wild moment, Samuel thought his enormous friend and shipmate had been transformed by some witchcraft into this ponderous beast. He even imagined he caught an expression of Ato's in the monster's moist eye. But this gloomy idea was soon dispelled, for, as the creature rose higher out of the water, they could see a desperate and bedraggled figure sprawled across its slippery back.

"Ahoy, mate!" choked Samuel, his heart thumping like a triphammer. "Is it really you? Are you safe, then?"

"Safe!" quavered the half-drowned and mud-covered King of the Octagon Isle. "SAFE?" He peered dizzily at the churning crocodiles just a boat's length away, and his voice cracked and broke. "I never felt safer in my life. What am I riding, a whale or an elephant?"

"A river horse," explained the hippopotamus, looking kindly over her shoulder. Then, as the crocodiles began to hiss and roar and come rolling toward them, she gave a ferocious bellow and snort. "Away with you! Be off, you river scum!" she squealed viciously. "These travelers are MINE. Shoot your firestick, Master Long Legs. That will fix them." For a moment, the crocodiles held their post, then, as Samuel fired his gun repeatedly, they began to slide sullenly across the river to the opposite bank. "Hold fast, Master Short Legs, and I'll soon have you ashore," wheezed the hippopotamus, speaking out of the corner of her mouth so as not to drop the picnic basket.

"Yes, yes, but what then?" shuddered Ato, trying to get a fingerhold on the monster's slippery neck.

"Why, then, we'll both tell our stories, and after that I'll eat," snorted the river horse, paddling joyously toward the bank.

"You'll EAT!" groaned Ato, ready to roll back into the river. "Oh, my father and mother and maiden aunts!"

"Did you hear that?" Dropping to Samuel's shoulder, Roger whispered fiercely. "Quick now, a shot behind the ear before it gets any farther. Are you going to do nothing while this ravenous monster carries off my poor Master?"

"Sh-hh!" warned Samuel, holding up his finger. "These creatures do not eat meat or men. They're herbivorous, my lad, and this one seems uncommonly kind and friendly. But what puzzles me—" the Royal Explorer looked intently into the face of the Read Bird "—what puzzles me is to find this one talking our language. To my knowledge, only animals in Oz, a few in Ev, and you on the Octagon Isle have the gift of speech. And I tell you, mate, this is a valuable discovery, and a simply splendid specimen of a pachydermatous talking aquatic." Whether the last few words in this sentence or a

173

stone in the river bottom tripped up the Captain, Roger never knew, but without any warning Samuel turned a sudden back-somersault into the river, going under as completely as Ato had done. "Ugh-gr-ugh!" he gurgled, coming up full of mud and disgust. "How did that happen?"

"Stilts!" sniffed Roger, whose wings had saved him from going down with Samuel. "A splendid way to get ashore, Master Salt, so neat and tidy. And a fine Discoverer you look now."

Sighing deeply, Samuel watched his stilts floating out of reach, then, shaking his head violently to get the water out of his eyes, he swam thoughtfully after the hippopotamus. As he dragged himself up on the bank, a monkey swinging by its tail from the lower branches of a tree snatched his three-cornered hat and skittered all the way to the treetop, at which all the other monkeys let out shrill hoots of mocking merriment.

"Ah! The welcoming committee!" sniffed Ato, rolling off the hippopotamus. "Well, Sammy, wherever it is, here we are, and a nice mess you've made of the landing. Clothes ruined, weapons gone—" Ato felt his middle dejectedly for his bread knife and blunderbuss, then, hitching up the breadboard at his waist, looked long and accusingly at the Leader of the Expedition.

"Now you musn't mind a little mud," said the hippopotamus, setting down the picnic basket and gazing from one to the other with frank interest and curiosity. "Mud is beautiful, and SO healthy."

"Not for me," frowned Samuel Salt, endeavoring to remove the thick green slime from his hair and ears with his damp silk handkerchief. "But I suppose we'll dry off in time and—"

"Proceed with the business of the day," finished Ato sarcastically as he squeezed the water out of his silk pantaloons and coattails. "But I hope you don't mind my saying that a seaman should stick to his boats, Samuel. If I had not fallen in with this kind and obliging hippopotamus, I'd have been a crocodile's lunch by this time."

"Oh, I'd have got you out somehow," muttered Samuel, smoothing back his hair sulkily. "And those stilts really saved your life. Suppose that animal had bitten your leg instead of your stilt? By the way, what's the name of this island, mate?" Anxious to change the subject, Samuel turned to Ato's tremendous rescueress.

"Mate?" repeated the hippopotamus, wiggling her ears inquiringly. "What may that mean?"

"It is what a seaman calls his crew and his friends," explained Samuel, grinning in spite of himself.

"Seaman? Mate?" mused the hippopotamus in a rapt voice. "How cozy, how beautiful." Overcome with emotion, the mighty monster leaned forward and lapped up the picnic basket, Oz flags, lunch and everything. "I shall remember this as long as I live," she assured them with a gulp as one of the flags went sideways down her throat. "Nikobo, Little Daughter of the Biggenlittle River People, bids you welcome to Patrippany Island."

"Little daughter!" exclaimed Ato in a smothered voice. "Ha, ha! Patrippany Island. Ho, ho! This is interesting. I knew there was a trip in it somewhere. A wet trip for us, eh Samuel?"

"But what I don't understand," said the Royal Explorer of Oz, briskly massaging his beard with his handkerchief, "is how you happen to speak our language. Do all the creatures on this Island talk? I don't mean that monkey chatter above."

"No, none of the other creatures speak the language of man," answered Nikobo solemnly. "I never knew I could speak it myself till five moons ago last Herb Day."

"Herb Day? Dear, dear and dear! How confusing it all grows," sighed Ato, emptying the water out of his hat, which had somehow survived his river ducking. "Do you suppose she means Thursday? Roger! ROGER! Keep away from those monkeys. Do you wish to lose all your tail feathers?"

"Oh, it's all very simple." Nikobo rolled her eyes from side to side. "One day I eat herbs and that is Herb Day. One day I eat twigs and that is Twig Day, and one day I eat grass and that is Grass Day, and—"

"And one day you eat lunch baskets and Oz flags, and I suppose that makes it Flag Day," chuckled Roger, coming down from a little excursion in the treetops. "She's swallowed the Oz flags, Skipper, and if that doesn't make her a citizen of Oz, I'll eat my feathers."

"Go ahead, if it will keep you any quieter," said Samuel Salt, who did not want this interesting conversation interrupted by Roger's nonsense. "So you only began to speak our language five moons ago last Herb Day? What made you do that?"

"A boy," confided Nikobo with a ponderous wag of her head.

"Ah, now we're getting somewhere." Feeling in his pocket, Samuel pulled out a small notebook and pencil, still damp but usable. "Was it a native boy?" he asked eagerly.

"No, no, certainly NOT." The hippopotamus panted a little at the very idea of such a thing. "The Leopard Men speak a strange roaring language I have never been able to make head or tail of. Besides, to speak to them would not be safe or desirable. The Leopard Men have long tusks and spears and—"

174

"Leopard Men!" yelled Ato, flinging both arms round the trunk of a tree. "Oh! Oh! and OH! I wish we were safely back at pirating, Sammy. Here we are marooned on this miserable monkey island, inhabited by Leopard Men, surrounded by crocodiles, and no way of getting back to the ship."

"You forget me," murmured the hippopotamus. Lumbering over to Ato, she gave him a gentle nudge with her moist pink snout. "Nikobo, Little Daughter of the Biggenlittle River People, will carry you anywhere you wish to go."

Chapter 6 - A Little Wild Man

"Not yet, not yet," protested Samuel Salt as Ato made a clumsy attempt to mount the hippopotamus. "Why, we've only just come, mate. We can't go without seeing these Leopard Men and this strange boy who speaks our language."

"Oh, CAN'T we?" Drawing in his breath, Ato made a flying leap at Nikobo, and this time managing an earhold, pulled himself determinedly up on her moist, slippery back. "Goodbye, Samuel," said the King with a firm wave of his hand. "If you bring any Leopard Men back to the *Crescent Moon*, you can discover yourself another cook. No Leopard Men. Mind, now!"

"Oh, you needn't worry about that." The hippopotamus closed one eye and smiled knowingly to herself. Thoroughly annoyed by the desertion of Ato and the superior grin of the river horse, Samuel snatched a long rapier from his belt and glowered belligerently around him.

"Shiver my timbers! You think I'm not strong enough or smart enough to fight these savages? HUWHERE are these Leopard Men?" roared the former Pirate in such a reverberating voice the monkeys fled silently to the treetops, and even Roger put his head under his wing.

"Gone, all gone!" explained Nikobo as she started calmly down toward the riverbank.

"You mean there are no Leopard Men on this Island now?" Looking with horror and aversion at the crocodile-infested river, Ato began tugging at Nikobo's ear. "Not so fast, my good creature! Wait a moment, my buxom lass! Perhaps I'll stay with Sammy after all."

"Well, just as you say." With scarcely a pause in her stride, the hippopotamus turned round and waddled amiably back to the strip of sand where Samuel Salt stood staring sternly into the jungle beyond.

"This is a great disappointment to me, mates," sighed the Captain of the *Crescent Moon*, mournfully wringing out the lace ruffles of his cuffs. "To have taken a Leopard Man back to the Court of Oz would have been an achievement worth the whole voyage."

"Now there's where we're different," murmured Ato, settling into a more comfortable position on the back of the river horse. "I myself would rather be disappointed than speared by a savage, and I don't care how many Leopard Men I miss seeing. Rather be spared than speared, ha, ha! Tee, HEE, HEE!" Ato chuckled from sheer relief.

"Shall I fly back to the ship for some more Oz flags?" Roger flapped his wings inquiringly. "If the Leopard Men are really gone, then Patrippany Island is ours without a spear thrown."

"That's so," mused Samuel Salt, thrusting his rapier back into its sheath and beginning to show a little interest in the island itself. "Fly ahead, my Hearty."

"And bring back some ship's biscuit," called Ato. "All this diving and mud turtling has left me weak as a fish. And while we're waiting for Roger, perhaps Nikobo will tell us a little about these Islanders. Were they little or big, black or brown?"

"Yellow," answered the hippopotamus gravely. "Big and yellow with brown spots all over their hides. They had brown hair, mane and eyes, and rough, snarling voices. They used neither huts nor shelter, but roamed like the animals through the jungle, hunting, fishing and fighting. They had hollowed-out logs for use in the water, and last Twig Day every Leopard man, woman and child climbed into the long boats and paddled out to sea. Shortly afterward—" Nikobo's eyes grew round and shiny at the mere memory "—shortly afterward a great hurricane arose and my family and I, watching from the mouth of the Biggenlittle River, saw the boats and men swept under the waves. Some of the logs floated back to the islands, but the Leopard Men and women we never saw again."

"Not even ONE?" exclaimed Samuel peevishly.

"Not even one," Nikobo assured him solemnly. "And to tell the truth," the hippopotamus flashed a sudden and expansive sigh, "it is much better and safer without them. The one problem is the boy, and I've been feeding him myself."

"Oh, yes, the boy who speaks our language," mused Samuel, still lost in bitter reflections of the Leopard Men he should never see face to face.

"What've you been feeding him?" asked Ato suspiciously. "How would a hippopotamus know what to feed a boy?"

"I do the best I can," said Nikobo in a hurt voice. "Every day I collect fresh roots, herbs and grasses for him."

"Roots, herbs, grasses! Merciful Mustard! A boy's being fed on roots, herbs and grasses, Sammy. Did you ever hear of anything more ridiculous in your life?"

"No worse than spinach," mumbled Samuel Salt. "But SAY, look here—" The Royal Explorer of Oz raised his arm imperiously. "What is a small boy doing on this island? How'd he get here in the first place, and where is he now?"

"Follow me," directed Nikobo in a dignified voice. "Follow me, and you shall know all." As Roger appeared at that moment with the Oz flags and biscuits, the little procession immediately got under way, Ato calmly riding behind.

On her many visits to the strange boy, Nikobo had worn a path through the tangled growth of vines and bush. Tenuous trees dropped their branches over this path and stretched out their gnarled roots to trip the unwary traveler. Several times Roger let out hoarse squeals as a huge snake coiled along the limb of a tree thrust out its ugly head. Gaudy flowers from the vines that closely entwined every tree filled the air with a damp, sleepy fragrance, and Samuel Salt, darting his eyes left and right, held his blunderbuss ready for any savage beast that might spring upon them. But the jungle creatures, thinking the Leopard Men had returned, slunk further and further into the green shadows, and without any mishaps or encounters Nikobo brought the explorers to a small clearing in the whispering tangle of green. Here they were suddenly confronted by a stoutly built cage, its bars constructed of saplings set scarcely an inch apart. On a heap of grass in a corner of the cage crouched the lonely figure of a little boy clothed in a single leopard skin.

"Well, goosewing my topsails!" panted Samuel Salt, deceived at first by the leopard skin. "A little wild man, a Leopard boy, as I'm a salt-sea sailor!"

"It's nothing of the kind," Nikobo contradicted him sharply. "Can't you see he is white and has teeth as straight as your own instead of tusks? He's not like the Leopard Men at all."

"But who put him in this cage? What's he done, and what's he doing here?" Slipping off Nikobo's back, Ato pressed his face close to the bars of the strange prison.

"I am waiting for my people to come and rescue me," stated the boy, rising with great dignity from his bed of grass. Folding his arms, he looked haughtily out at the explorers. "Who are these men, Nikobo?" he inquired sternly. "Why have you brought them here?"

"Because they seemed friendly and speak your language," puffed the hippopotamus, beaming lovingly at her small charge. "Because I thought they might break these bars and set you free. They have a hollow log seventy times as large as the hollowed logs of the Leopard Men. In this they could easily carry you over the waters and back to your own people. I've tried to break this miserable hutch dozens of times," explained Nikobo, turning to Samuel Salt. "But the saplings are sunk so deep I've been afraid I'd crush Tandy as well as the cage if I pushed too hard."

"Quite likely," said Samuel Salt, rapping the bars with his knuckles. "We'll have to fetch an ax from the ship. But who shut you up here, little Lubber, and how long have you been a prisoner on this island?"

"Five months and a half," answered the boy after consulting one of the bars in the corner of his cage. "I've made a nick in this bar with my teeth for every day I have been here."

"Well, that's all over now, you poor child, you!" Ato's voice shook with indignation as he looked in at the little boy whose every rib showed plainly under the skin. In fact, a heap of grass and dried roots in the cage made the kind-hearted monarch shudder with distaste and sympathy. "You shall come with us and eat like a King," he promised, nodding his head cheerfully, "and learn to be an able-bodied seaman to boot." Instead of looking grateful or pleased, the boy whom the hippopotamus had called "Tandy" merely stood looking between the bars of his cage.

"Why should I go with you?" he said finally and wearily. "You look wild and dangerous to me, and far worse than the Leopard Men. Here at least I have Kobo to take care of me, and who knows what further perils and hardships I should suffer at sea?"

"Ho! HO! And how do you like that, my lads?" Roger rocked backward and forward on Samuel Salt's shoulder. "The young one speaks truly. If you could but see yourselves, my Hearties." Now both Ato and Samuel had forgotten their plunge in the river, but with their hair and clothing still covered with mud and slime they looked like the veriest rogues and rascals. And while Ato regarded himself with embarrassment and discomfiture, Samuel took a quick step forward.

"SO!" roared the great seaman angrily. "So, you don't trust us, eh? Well, stay here if you wish and grow up like a monkey. You look like a little wild man already."

"STOP!" Nikobo quivered all over with resentment. "You must not call Tandy a wild man."

"Don't mind." The boy drew the leopard skin around him with quiet dignity. "I can bear it. I have borne far worse. I can bear anything. I am a KING and the son of a King's son! Tell them to go away, Kobo."

176

"Now, now, NOW! This is nothing but nonsense." Ato clapped his hands sharply. "However we look, my young squab, you are in good and royal company. My mate here, Captain Salt, is Captain of the *Crescent Moon*, Royal Explorer of Oz, and a Knight, besides. I, though at present a ship's cook, am King of the Octagon Isle, and Roger here is as Royal a Read Bird as ever wagged a bill and wing. If you say you are a King, we will have to believe you, though 'tis hardly credible." Ato stared with round eyes at the matted hair and dirty body of the little prisoner. "If you say you are a King, we must believe you, but in return you must believe us and stop all this hoity toity talk and clishmaclatter."

"He speaks the plain truth." Nikobo pressed her huge snout close to the bars. "Even I can detect the signs of royalty in this fat and goodly person whom I just this morning helped out of the river. You must go with them, Tandy, and they will carry you back to your own Kingdom."

"But I tell you, I'd rather stay here with YOU," wailed the little boy, relaxing a moment from his kingly and overbearing attitude.

"Roger, fetch the AX." Samuel Salt spoke so loudly and sternly, Nikobo lapsed into a shocked silence and Tandy hastily withdrew back into a far corner of his cage.

"Never argue with a seagoing man," whispered Ato, winking solemnly as Roger flew off to obey Samuel's order. Having settled the matter in his own mind, Samuel turned his back on Tandy and began to examine with deep interest the fungus growth on one of the gnarled old trees. "So you really are a King?" Leaning against the huge body of Nikobo, Ato folded his hands comfortably on his stomach and regarded the boy in the leopard skin earnestly. "Now what country do you hail from, and what do they call you at home?"

"I am Tazander Tazah of Ozamaland," announced the boy proudly, "the land of the creeping bird and flying reptile. Ozamaland on the long continent of Tarara is my home."

"OZAMALAND!" shouted Samuel Salt, swinging round like a teetotum. "So there really IS such a place. I have always said so, Ato, but no one would believe me. Lies to the east of here, doesn't it, sonny, and is twice as large as any known land bordering on the Nonestic?" Somewhat impressed to find that Samuel Salt knew something of his homeland, the little boy nodded. "And do you suppose we could snare one of those creeping birds and flying reptiles if we managed to reach Ozamaland?" Grasping the bars of the cage, Samuel peered anxiously into the young King's face.

"Do you suppose you could ever reach Ozamaland?" sighed Tazander, returning Samuel's eager look with gloomy aloofness. "Do you know that a ship has never touched our shores?"

"Then the *Crescent Moon* shall be the first!" cried Samuel Salt, snapping his fingers joyfully. "Why, this will be tremendous and the most momentous discovery in a thousand years! But how do you happen to be so far from Ozamaland yourself?" asked Samuel Salt immediately afterward. "Did you come by air or sea?"

"That I cannot tell." Tazander seated himself soberly on a log before he continued. "One night I was sleeping soundly in my tower in the White City, next thing I remember I was here in this jungle. The Leopard Men, wild and savage as they were, fed me when they remembered on raw fish and chunks of hard, bitter bread they made from the roots of the Brima Tree. But I could not understand their talk, nor they mine, and till Kobo found me a month after my imprisonment I had no one to talk to at all. But she has come every day to keep me company and try to set me free, and since the Leopard Men were drowned she has fed me, too. See, through this little door." Tazander opened a small door in the bars and stuck both hands through.

"But how did you learn the language?" asked Ato, turning round to gaze up into Nikobo's huge face.

"I don't know," said Nikobo with an excited gulp. "I just started to say `Hello!', and instead of saying it in hippopotamy there I was talking a strange language which I could understand as well as my own. And in this language Tandy answered me, much to my delight and pleasure."

"Strange, very strange." Ato shook his head in a puzzled manner. "Well, all I say is, it was lucky for this small fellow that you happened along, and once we have him aboard he'll soon forget all these hardships and unpleasant experiences."

"I'll never forget Kobo," said the young King, backing stiffly away from the outstretched arms of Ato.

"And Kobo'll never forget YOU," sniffed the hippopotamus. "The talk of the river people seems dull and stupid since I've talked to Tandy. None of the herd really need me, and I don't know what I'm going to do whoo Hoo HOO WHOOO!" Rocking from side to side, Nikobo began to sob as if her heart would break, so violently in fact that Samuel Salt covered both ears, and Ato, alarmed at the enormous grief of the gigantic beast, tried to put his arms around her.

"Here, here!" begged the ship's cook, thumping her hard upon the back. Opening the bag of biscuits Roger had brought from the ship, Ato handed two to Tandy and began shoving the rest as fast as he could down the vast throat of the grief-stricken hippopotamus. After each biscuit, Nikobo choked and sobbed to herself, but on the whole they seemed to comfort her, and when the Read Bird finally returned with the ax, she watched almost cheerfully as Samuel Salt, with well-aimed blows, demolished Tandy's jungle cage. As the last side crashed down and without giving Tandy time to argue any further, Samuel Salt seized the boy firmly in both arms and set him down on the back of the hippopotamus.

Then, giving Ato a hand up behind him, the Captain of the *Crescent Moon* sternly led the way to the edge of the island. Roger, waving an Oz flag, flew ahead screaming defiantly to the monkeys and parrots that infested the island. "WAY, WAY! Way for the Royal Discoverer of Oz! Way for the King of the Octagon Isle! Way for Nikobo, Little Daughter of the Biggenlittle River People. Way for Tazander Tazoo, King and son of a King's son! WAY-ay-ayyy!"

Chapter 7 - Strange Specimens for Samuel Salt

With no one to challenge their going but the birds and monkeys, the little band made its

way back to the sandy beach. Tandy, perhaps because he had been so long pent up in the silent jungle and because he was by nature a naturally sober and solemn little boy, said nothing. Not even the *Crescent Moon*, riding so proudly at her anchor, seemed to arouse any interest or enthusiasm in this strange young Ozamalander.

"Well, here we are!" exclaimed Ato, heartily thankful to be in sight of the ship again. "And I hope you'll not mind ferrying us out to the boat, Nikobo. Those crocodiles still look hungry, and I've no notion of being crocked for the rest of my life."

"Any time you say," grunted the hippopotamus, squeaking a listless greeting to a company of her own relatives who were rolling lazily about in the muddy river water.

"Avast and belay and what's the hurry?" Leaning his ax against a tree, Samuel moistened a finger and held it up. "The wind's against us, mate, so we'll have to wait for the tide. Not only that, but Roger and I must survey the island and dig up some more interesting specimens to take back to the ship." After a long and rather quizzical look at Tandy, Samuel turned and swung along the beach, the Read Bird flapping joyously behind him.

"Run up and down a bit," advised Ato, sliding down from Nikobo's back. "Your legs must need stretching. Wonder if there's anything to eat around here or hereabouts? Aha, those look like oranges, a wild orange grove as I'm a cook and a seaman. Come along, young one, and help me gather a few."

"A King and son of a King's son does not come and go at another's bidding," announced Tandy, stiffly alighting from the hippopotamus.

"Merciful mothers! What's this?" gasped Ato, blinking his eyes rapidly. "As complete a case of ingrowing Royalitis as I've ever had the misfortune to encounter. Well, since it's every King for himself, then I'll be leaving you, sonny and son of a King's sonny. Watch out for him, Kobo, he's probably real important to himself."

"You should not speak like that," reproved the hippopotamus as Ato disappeared into the orange grove. "After all, the big and fat one is himself a King."

"Pooh, King of some potty little island," sniffed Tandy, leaning wearily against a palm. "Break me a cocoanut, Kobo, I'm thirsty." With a discouraged sigh, Nikobo trod on one of the cocoanuts, cracking it from end to end, and then, because she was a generous and kindly creature, she cracked several more for Ato when he should return. Sitting back on her haunches, she anxiously watched while Tandy downed the cocoanut milk, then, stretching out in the sand, fell unconcernedly asleep. Thus Ato found them when he emerged from the orange grove an hour later. His elegant explorer's cape was knotted to form a sack and bursting full of the small, sweet fruit of the wild orange trees.

"These will make us a fine mess of marmalade when I get back to the ship," panted the perspiring monarch, settling down with his back cozily to Nikobo's. "How's young Saucebox?"

"All right." The hippopotamus nodded in Tandy's direction. "He is so small and tired," she murmured worriedly, "and you must know he has been exposed in an open cage in the jungle for five long months with only a miserable hippopotamus for company."

"Miserable hippopotamus," snorted Ato indignantly. "You're a very superior animal, my girl. I'd consider it an honor to converse with you any day. Did you crack these cocoanuts for me?" As Nikobo, trying bashfully to conceal her pleasure at Ato's praise, admitted she had, the King took several long, satisfying draughts from the shells. "Now don't you worry about that young sprout," he advised kindly as Nikobo continued to gaze mournfully at the sleeping boy. "We'll make allowances for his High and Mighty Littleness and set him down in his own country. That is, if we ever manage to find it, though I must say he'll not be much use nor company for us. Ahoy! Here comes Sammy. Wonder what he's found?" As a matter of fact, the Royal Explorer of Oz looked more like a walking window box than a seaman. Long vines hung from his neck and trailed from his pockets. His arms were crammed with spiked and prickly plants, and on his head he balanced a package of seashells tied up in his shoregoing coat. "What are you trying to do, start a conservatory?" roared Ato as Roger helped the Captain set his treasures on the ground.

"Rare and unusual, all of 'em," said Samuel, dropping down beside Ato and looking with complete satisfaction at his curious collection.

178

"Mind those yellow creepers," warned Nikobo, wiggling her vast snout warningly. "Those purple flowered plants in the middle are treacherous, too. They are tumbleweeds, Master Long Legs, and 'tis from them Patrippany Island gets its name. When the Leopard Men fought, they would fling these weeds at one another, and I've seen them falling about for hours, neither side being able to advance a step or even stand up."

"Tumbleweeds!" breathed Samuel ecstatically. "You don't SAY! Why, these might come in real handy if we ever get in a tight place. I'll give a few to the Wizard of Oz and to the Red Jinn when we get back from this voyage. And what about the yellow creepers, mate? Are they fighting plants, too?"

"The creepers, if uprooted and thrown at an animal or man, will creep rapidly after him, catching him no matter how fast he runs and tying him up so tight he will not be able to move until the vine withers," explained Nikobo solemnly. "I happen to know from an experience I had with one of these vines in my early youth."

"Creeping vines," shivered Ato, moving as far away from Samuel's collection as possible. "Just keep them away from me, Sammy. What right have such things on a ship?"

"Oh, they'll be harmless enough when they're potted," answered Samuel easily. "And a splendid weapon they'll make for some up-and-coming country."

"Better keep them for ourselves," advised Roger, fluttering down to Samuel's shoulder. "Exploring's a dangerous business, if you ask me, Master Salt."

"Well, you'll have to admit that it's been pretty safe and successful so far," said Samuel, clasping his hands behind his head and gazing contentedly up at the waving fronds of the palm trees.

"SAFE!" The ship's cook began to shake and quiver all over. "Ho, ho! Safe? Especially sailing round that volcano and going swimming with the crocodiles! Safe! You'll be the death of me yet, Sam-u-el. Have you planted your Oz flags and told the wild creatures in the jungle about their new sovereign?"

Roger nodded his head importantly. "We've raised Oz flags on the tallest trees on the East, South, West and North sides of the Island. I flew across and got a bird's eye view while the Captain walked clear 'round. We've discovered it's bean-shaped, King dear, the exact shape of a kidney bean and a fine, fertile place for settlers and prospectors from Oz."

"Yes, all they have to do is cut down a million trees, drain the swamps, and train the wild beasts in the jungle to be as polite and considerate as Nikobo here."

"Well, what of it? That's their problem." Samuel stretched himself, luxuriously snapping each finger to see that it was still working. "And now, since our part is done, what do you say to waking this son of a King's son and getting aboard the ship? The tide'll run out in a couple of hours and carry us along." Tazander had been awake for some time listening to the conversation with closed eyes. Now sitting up, he calmly spoke his mind.

"I'm not going with you," he stated grandly. "I'm going to stay here with Kobo till my own people come for me."

"Hah! Mutiny!" Leaping to his feet, Samuel glared down at the puny youngster with real anger and exasperation. "If you think I'm going to leave you on this island to be devoured by wild animals when Nikobo's back is turned, you don't know your pirates. CLIMB up on that animal. Lively, now!" Samuel looked so fierce and threatening that Ato felt rather sorry for the stubborn little King, but he was wasting his sympathy.

"I'm not going," said Tandy, settling more determinedly down into the sand. "And no one can make me."

"Don't say that! Don't say that!" Blubbering with grief at the thought of losing her small charge and shivering with anxiety lest he arouse to further anger this tall sea captain, Nikobo lumbered to her feet and began to whisper eagerly in Tandy's ear. During this short conference Samuel gathered up his specimens and Ato his oranges, and when both had finished, the hippopotamus edged nervously forward. "I've decided to go with you," she announced in a slightly shaken voice. "If I go, Tandy'll go, so I'll just GO!"

"WHAT?" roared Samuel Salt, dropping his shells and clapping his hand to his forehead. "Well, that practically solves everything!" Looking wildly from the hippopotamus to the *Crescent Moon*, Samuel had a dreadful vision of Nikobo rolling dangerously from side to side of his cherished vessel.

"What'll you eat?" demanded Roger, who was ever more practical than polite. "How'll we ever feed this enormous lady, Cook dear? Besides, she'll sink the ship."

"I'll be very quiet and stay wherever you put me," murmured Nikobo in a meek voice. "I'll go on a diet and eat whatever is left."

"Well, why couldn't she go?" proposed Ato, who already had formed a great liking for Tandy's devoted guardian. "Why couldn't she? Nice, kind, motherly creature that she is!"

"But a hippopotamus needs fresh water and tons of food and—" Then suddenly Samuel brought his hands together with a resounding smack.

"Have you thought of something?" asked Ato hopefully, shifting his oranges from one shoulder to the other.

"Yes," stated the former Pirate solemnly, "I have." Samuel was secretly delighted to have found a way to carry this superb herbivorous specimen back to Oz. "I'll build her a raft and tow her along after the ship. We'll stop at all the

179

islands we come to for fresh water and grass, and meanwhile she'll have to do with salt baths and such food as we have in the hold."

"Oh, KOBO! Did you hear that?" Springing up with the first signs of life or feeling he had yet shown, Tandy flung himself on his huge companion and friend. "So you're really going. Then I'll go too."

"Can't be all bad, if he's as fond of her as all that," whispered Ato in Samuel's ear.

"Not bad, just a pest," wheezed Samuel, reaching for his ax. "Needs a taste of the rope, if you ask me." Then, while Nikobo went for a last swim in the Biggenlittle River and bade goodbye to her numerous and wondering relatives, Samuel felled trees, split wood, and with nails Roger fetched from the ship fashioned a splendid, strong raft for their new pet. Round the edge he built a sturdy railing to keep Nikobo from sliding off in a rough sea. Ato and Roger, taking thought for the evening meal, heaped one end of the raft with grass and twigs and all the jungle roots they could gather. Without moving or offering to help, Tandy sat watching, and just as the sun sank down behind the palms, a strange procession started out for the *Crescent Moon*. Ahead with the keg of nails soared Roger. Then came the hippopotamus moving like a small dreadnaught through the water. On her back sat Ato, the haughty young King of Ozamaland, and Samuel Salt. Samuel rode last, holding in his hand the long cable he had attached to the raft and with which he meant to fasten it to the *Crescent Moon*.

Following his orders, Nikobo swam close to the side of the ship so Tandy and Ato could climb the rope ladder, then she paddled round to the stern where Samuel drew his cable through an iron ring in the ship's hull and made the raft fast. There was a runway at the back of the raft, and the rails on that side let down so that Nikobo had no trouble clambering aboard. By pulling a rope with her teeth, she could raise or lower the back of her pen and take a swim whenever she felt the need of one. After giving her a bit of advice about voyaging and seeing her comfortably settled, Samuel climbed the cable and nimbly pulled himself aboard his ship. Roger had already stowed their precious specimens in the hold, and rubbing his hands with brisk satisfaction the Captain of the *Crescent Moon* weighed anchor and dropped with the tide down the Biggenlittle River to the sea. Then, touching the automatic controls, he set his sails to catch the evening breeze, adjusted his steering gear for a course east by sou'east and strode happily into his cabin. The Salamander chirped cheerfully as he passed her hotbox, and after tapping a cheerful greeting on the lid the weary explorer stripped off his ruined and muddy shoregoing outfit, took a shower, and climbed thankfully back into his old sea clothes. "Where's the pest?" he called out as Roger flew past the open port.

"Well, since he was so small and important," sniffed the Read Bird, waving a claw, "I gave him a large cabin to himself. I didn't think you and Ato would want him in here."

"Shiver my timbers, NO." Samuel looked ruefully across at the small berth the Philadelphia boy occupied on their last voyage. "He'll never be the seaman Peter was, or the company either. He'd better keep out of my way — HAH! — or I'll give him a taste of my belt." Snatching up his spyglass and looking as stern as a kindhearted pirate well can, Samuel hurried out on deck.

Meanwhile, in the cabin next to the Captain's, Tandy stood regarding himself mournfully in the small glass over his sea chest. He, too, had taken a shower and at Roger's suggestion had donned one of Peter's old pirate suits. "I am a King and the son of a King's son," muttered Tandy, staring sadly at the sallow reflection in the mirror. To tell the truth, the suit was not in the least becoming to the skinny and sullen young monarch. "I am a King and son of a King's son and can bear anything," he repeated dismally.

"Then bear a hand with the dinner," yelled Roger, who had been peeking at him through the porthole. "All who eat must work, and under the hatches with lubbers!"

Pretending not to hear, Tandy sat resignedly on the side of his bunk, though he really was curious to look around the ship and see what Kobo was doing. From the galley came the cheerful rattle of pots and pans and the huge voice of Ato singing as he prepared the dinner. Gulls flew in excited circles all round the *Crescent Moon*, calling out their hoarse challenge and farewell, and Samuel Salt, leaning on the taffrail, gazed dreamily back at Patrippany Island. The Oz flags fluttering from the tall palms gave it quite a gay and festive appearance, and in spite of not seeing the Leopard Men Samuel felt he had done a good day's discovering.

"Ahoy below! How you coming?" called Samuel, leaning down to look at Nikobo. The hippopotamus wagged her huge head.

"Fine! Just fine, mate," she wheezed pleasantly.

"Hah! Good for you!" Samuel's face broke into a broad grin as Kobo remembered to call him "Mate." "We'll make an able-bodied seawoman of you yet, my lass!"

Chapter 8 - Maxims for Monarchs

When Ato, banging boisterously on an iron frying pan with a wooden spoon, summoned all hands to dinner, Samuel and Roger responded with a rush. But Tandy remained sitting gloomily on his bunk. "Now what's the matter?" demanded Samuel Salt as Roger, sent to call the young voyager, came flying back to the table.

"He says I may serve his dinner in the cabin," snickered Roger, popping a biscuit into his mouth and swallowing it whole.

"Well, don't you do it!" roared the Captain, bringing his fist down with an angry thump. "No use to start such nonsense!"

"But he's so thin and feeble. The poor child's just full of raw roots and jungle grass," murmured Ato, beginning to heap a platter with meat and vegetables. "Wait till he folds himself round some of these seafarin' rations. He'll be a different person."

"And he'd better be!" rumbled the Captain of the *Crescent Moon*, pulling in his chair. "And if you and Roger want to spoil the little pest, go ahead, but he'd better keep out of MY way. HAH!"

"I could drop the dinner on his head," suggested Roger helpfully as Ato handed him an appetizing tray for Tandy. "How would that be?"

"Utterly reprehensible, and conduct unbecoming in a Royal Read Bird and able-bodied seaman," chuckled the ship's cook, shaking his finger at Roger. "Why don't you try to help the little beggar and set him a good example?"

Now Roger, in spite of his sharp tongue, was really a sociable and kind-hearted bird, and the sight of Tandy sitting so forlornly on his bunk made him regret his teasing speeches. After all, the little fellow was far from home and had had a hard time in the jungle. "Here!" he puffed, setting down the tray and lighting the lantern. "This'll put feathers on your chest, young one, and mind you eat every scrap."

"Thank you," answered Tandy so drearily that Roger with a shudder of distaste fled back to the cheerful company of Samuel and Ato. But later, when Samuel had gone below to pot the precious plants from Patrippany Island and the ship's cook was leaning over the rail conversing cozily with the hippopotamus, Roger flew back to Tandy's cabin resolved to help him if he could. With calm satisfaction he noted that Tandy had eaten everything on the tray. Lying on his back, the young King of Ozamaland was staring solemnly up at the beams over his bunk.

"Ahoy! And what goes on here?" cried Roger, settling down on the old sea chest. "How about a turn on deck, my lad, and a bit of chatter with the crew?"

"It is not seemly for a King and son of a King's son to talk with his inferiors," observed Tandy coldly.

"In-feer-iors!" screeched Roger, forgetting all his good intentions and mad enough to nip the youngster's nose right off. "Are you by any chance referring to me?"

"Ozamaland is a great and powerful country, and I am its King," stated Tandy, turning his back on the Read Bird. At this, Roger let out another screech and then, suddenly remembering the purpose of his visit, took a long breath to steady himself. When he spoke again, his voice was both calm and reasonable. "Ozamaland may be a great and powerful country, and you may also be its King, but remember that you are no longer in Ozamaland," explained Roger firmly. "You are on this ship by the express wish and kindness of the Captain and in the company of Kings and BETTER. WAIT!" Shaking a claw at Tandy's back, Roger flew off to fetch one of Ato's books from the shelf above the stove. Tandy was in the same position when he returned, but paying him no further attention, Roger pulled the lamp nearer and opened his volume. "When a King is in the company of Kings," began the Read Bird impressively, "he is no longer a special or royal being, but merely a man among men, and as such must maintain his honor and standing by sheer worth and ability alone."

"Who says that? What are you reading?" Tandy sat up with sudden interest, for his whole life had been spent in study and reflection, and the voice of the Read Bird was not unlike the voice of Woodjabegoodja, his royal instructor at home.

"I am reading *Maxims for Monarchs*," answered Roger calmly, "a book of great authority and antiquity that has been used by the Rulers of Oz and Ev and the Nonestic Islands these many thousand years. No great and important country would think of being without a copy of this book," he continued severely.

"Strange, then, that I should not have heard of it," mused Tandy, looking not quite so sure of himself. "We have no *Maxims for Monarchs* in Ozamaland."

"Pooh, Ozamaland!" Roger dismissed the whole country with a shrug of his wing. "A country as young and unimportant as that would probably know nothing about such matters."

"You mean my country is not so old or important as Oz and this two-penny island of your fat Master?" shouted Tandy angrily.

"Of course not. Why, it's not even been discovered, and whoever has been there?" demanded Roger disdainfully. "Take you, as its King, acting in this small upcountry fashion. What CAN a fellow think? Here—" Shoving the book toward the disagreeable young monarch, the Read Bird urged him to look for himself. With a puzzled frown, Tandy reread the passage Roger had just quoted.

"Well, even though your Master is a King, you're not a King and neither is Samuel Salt," said Tandy, looking at Roger with some of his former arrogance.

"Oh, isn't he? Well, just lay to this, young fellow," Roger shook his claw under Tandy's upturned nose. "Samuel Salt is Captain of this ship, a Knight and the Royal Discoverer of Oz, which makes him seventy times as important as you, King Pins. He not only is boss of the *Crescent Moon*, but he ruled the sea, discovering countries for other Kings to govern, and if it were not for Samuel Salt and people like him, there wouldn't be any Kingdoms or people like you to run them. See? As for me, I'm a Royal Read Bird and wouldn't be a King for a minute. I can live my own life and go and come as I please."

"Then while I'm on this ship, I'm not a King at all," said Tandy wonderingly. "Then what am I? What am I supposed to do?" The little boy looked puzzled and positively frightened.

"Why, you're supposed to act like a person, that is, if possible," sniffed Roger, reaching over for his book and looking at Tandy sideways down his bill. "What are you besides a King? What can you do that is useful or interesting?"

"Do, DO?" Tandy's voice rose shrilly. "Why, er, why, I can draw pictures and ride an elephant."

"Good!" Roger put up his claw to hide the grin that, in spite of his best efforts, began to spread round his bill. "Well, there isn't much call for drawing or elephant-riding on a ship, but you can draw water to swab the decks, and I'll teach you to ride the yards and follow the crosstree to the main topgallant mast in the blowingest blow that ever blowed. And depend upon it, young man, you'll have more fun as a person than you ever had as a King. There's no place for having fun like a ship!"

"Fun!" said Tandy flatly and inquiringly. "What's that?"

"Tar and tobaccy jack! What are you tellin' me?" Roger almost toppled off the sea chest. "Do you mean to sit there like a dumb image and tell me you've never had any fun? Never felt so bursting full of ginger and happiness you could sing or do a sailor's hornpipe?"

"It is not seemly—" began the boy in a staid voice, "It is—"

"Seemly! Great goosefeathers, are you alive or aren't you?" gasped Roger. "What in paint did you do in that cussed country of yours before you got carried off and penned up like a pig in the jungle?"

Considering Roger's question, Tandy clasped and unclasped his hands nervously. "Well, you must know," he began in a very grown-up voice, "the King of Ozamaland is not allowed to mingle with the common people. In all things he is alone and set apart. So it was with my father and mother before they disappeared. So it is with me. Furthermore, it being prophesied that I would be carried off by an aunt in the middle years of my youth, it was deemed expedient and necessary to keep me locked away from danger in the White Tower of the Wise Men."

"Hurumph!" grunted the Read Bird, who had not heard so many long words since the voyage began. "And what did you do in this precious tower?"

"I studied," sighed Tandy, reclining wearily back on his pillows, "for there are many things a King must learn. But one hour of every evening I was permitted to walk about the garden on top of the tower and look down upon my Kingdom. On very great occasions I was allowed to come out and ride the white elephant in the grand processions of state."

"Humph!" grunted Roger again, looking at Tandy with round, dismayed eyes. "And with whom did you play?" he asked after a little silence.

"Play?" Again Tandy's voice was politely inquiring.

"The word was play," insisted the Read Bird doggedly. "With whom did you run about, play tag, checkers, pirates or go fishing?"

Tandy looked confused, and Roger shook his head sorrowfully. "Never heard of such things!" he exclaimed indignantly. "Well, all I can say is, whoever carried you off and shut you up in that jungle cave did you a real service. If you had not been there, we never would have found you, and I'm here to tell you that from now on things are going to be different. You're discovered now and aboard the grandest ship afloat. You can forget all about being a King and start right in being a person and an able-bodied seaman. I for my part mean to see you have some fun or break a wing in the attempt."

"But would a King—"

"King! Never let me hear that terrible word again," shuddered Roger, sticking his head under his wing and then popping it out again. "From now on you're just plain Tandy and can do as you please so long as it does no harm to yourself or the ship. Understand? And tomorrow we'll start having fun, so be ready." Roger's promise sounded almost like a threat, but there was such a merry twinkle in his eye, Tandy began to feel interested. "You might even begin tonight," sniffed Roger, taking up the tray. "Just begin by thinking of something you want to do. Think about it hard and then DO it." Winking cheerfully over the empty plates, the Read Bird spread his wings and sailed through the port. For several minutes, Tandy lay where he was, turning Roger's last injunction over and over in his stiff, precise little mind. What DID he really want to do? At first he could think of nothing. Then suddenly he knew. Why, of course — he wanted to talk to Kobo and he just plain WOULD. There was a frosted cake left from his supper, and slipping it into his blouse, Tandy stepped quietly out on deck. The ship, with only a slight roll, was moving briskly through the water, white foam falling in lacy spray from her sides, the moon-white sails spread like giant wings above his head. There was no one in sight, and almost holding his breath, Tandy tiptoed aft and leaned adventurously over the taffrail.

"Kobo, Yo KOBO!" he called huskily.

"Hello! I thought you'd be out soon." Swinging round and turning her vast smile upward, the hippopotamus gazed fondly at her young charge. "Are you comfortable? Did you have a good dinner?" she asked anxiously.

"Yes, and look what I saved for you!" As he spoke, Tandy glanced over his shoulder as if he were almost afraid to have anyone see him enjoying himself. "Open your mouth, Kobo!" he whispered eagerly. Without hesitation or question the hippopotamus stretched her jaws wide, and Tandy, with the first real thrill of his life, flung the frosted cake into that immense pink cavern. As Kobo neatly caught and snapped her lips on the tempting morsel, Tandy let out a faint cheer and began to think there might be something in Roger's suggestions after all. "I'll throw you lots of things tomorrow," he promised gaily. "Good night, Kobo. Good night, Kobo dear."

Humming a tuneless little song, the young King hurried almost cheerfully back to his cabin. Pausing in the doorway of his tidy quarters, he looked about complacently. What did he want to do next? There was no one to tell him to go to bed, so he just plain wouldn't. He'd sit up as late as he plain pleased. Rummaging through Peter's sea chest, which Ato had placed near his bunk, Tandy found a large tablet of stiff paper, a box of paints and some crayons. Settling himself cross-legged on his bunk, he began drawing, not pictures of the castles and courtiers of Ozamaland, but pictures of the queer beasts and Leopard Men he had seen on Patrippany Island. When Roger, on first watch, called out eight bells, he saw Tandy's light still burning, and flying down to investigate found his new pupil fast asleep in the middle of his masterpieces. The whole bunk was covered with bright drawings and pictures, and even to Roger's inexperienced eye they seemed excellently done. So carefully the Read Bird stowed them in the sea chest, then, without bothering to waken or undress the little King, he covered him with a light blanket and went quietly from the cabin.

Chapter 9 - Sea Legs for Tandy

"If what Roger tells us is so, little Sauce Box yonder has had a pretty dull life," said Ato as he and the Captain sat finishing their breakfast next morning. "Lucky for him we happened along, and anyway, the hippopotamus will be good company, eh Samuel? She seems downright sensible and jolly. Reminds me of Pigasus, and I suppose she does belong to the pig family when you come to think of it."

"Well, she's a pretty big pig if she does," laughed Samuel Salt, swallowing his coffee with gusty relish. "Pretty big any way you take her. Personally, I like the animal, but the King and son of a King's son! PAH! Reminds me of Peter, he's so different, and the sooner we reach Ozamaland and set him ashore, the better. Meals in his own cabin. Hoh!"

"Oh, give him time," drawled Ato, helping himself a second time to fried potatoes. "If there's any good in the lad, a sea voyage will bring it out, and what chance has he had shut up in a tower for ten years and in a cage for five months? Though how an aunt managed to have him carried so far and why she left him with those savages in the jungle I can't get through my head at all."

"Maybe it was a gi-ant," whistled Roger, swooping down on Ato's plump shoulder and flapping his wings cheerfully. "How far do you figure it is to Ozamaland, Master Salt?"

"Well, that I couldn't just say," answered Samuel in a milder voice. Pushing back his chair, he stepped over to the map on the west wall. "Maybe a thousand leagues or so from Patrippany Island, maybe more, in a line east by sou'east from Ev. If that is so, we're bound to bump into it sometime, as I've set my course east by sou'east, and anyway it's all in the year's sailing." Samuel bent over with pride to examine the newest island discovery he had marked on the chart the evening before. "And when we do come to it," he announced firmly, "we'll trade this useless young one for some of those flying snakes and creeping birds, eh Mates?"

183

"If we bring any more animals aboard, we might as well set up an ark and be done with it," warned Ato, shaking his fork at the Captain. "By the way, how's Sally this morning?"

"Tiptopsails!" grinned Samuel. "She eats nothing but hot air and water and is no more trouble than a hair in a flea's whisker. I can carry her round in my pipe when I want company. Now there's a lass for you!"

"Well, I'll just see to Nikobo, for she's the girl for me," retorted Ato, rolling briskly out of his seat. "I saved all the potato peelings from last night, and that, with a dozen cans of peas, corn, carrots and beets, should stay her appetite till lunch time."

"Forty cans at one swallow," groaned Roger, clapping a claw to his head in mock dismay. "She'll eat us out of ship and home at this rate. Can't you think of something else, King dear? A nice wind pudding or a tub of sea soup sprinkled with faggots."

"Oh, go along with you," roared Ato, and picking up his precious coffee pot he waddled cheerfully off to his storeroom. The day was bright and breezy and the *Crescent Moon*, going free, breasted the waves like a white-winged sea witch. It was SUCH a morning that even Tandy, peering inquiringly from his cabin, felt an uncontrollable impulse to slide down the deck. So he did, coming up smartly by Roger, who was perched on the rail.

"That's it! That's it! Now you're catching on," approved the Read Bird, hopping cheerfully from one foot to the other. "Now match your step to the sea's roll, sonny, get into her rhythm. You've got to breathe with the ship to carry your rations on a voyage. Watch the Captain, there, and do as he does," finished Roger as Samuel Salt left his cabin and came striding aft.

"Rather watch you!" exclaimed Tandy, who sensed the Captain's dislike. Uneasily, he moved a little nearer the Read Bird.

"All right, come on then!" shouted Roger, heading recklessly for the foremast. "Ever climb a tree?" Tandy shook his head, looking with deep misgivings into the maze of sail and rigging above. But Roger was already aloft and beckoning for him to follow. "Not that way, Brainless!" scolded Roger anxiously as Tandy, gritting his teeth, made a desperate leap upward. "See those rope ladders by the rail? Put your feet in the ratlins, boy, and come along hand over hand. It's easy as flying once you get the swing of it. There, that's better! Come on! Come on! Don't stop! Don't look down." So up, up and up the narrow rope ladders toiled Tandy, till Roger, growing impatient, seized his collar and helped him straddle the crosstree of the fore t'gallant mast. "Ahoy! And isn't this better than riding an elephant?" beamed Roger, winking a knowing eye. "Ahoy, this is fun and NO fooling." Seeing Tandy was too dizzy and breathless to talk for a moment, Roger cheerfully set himself to teach the young Ozamalander a bit about ships and sailing. Soon Tandy was so interested he forgot the leap and plunge of the ship, the rattle and creak of the cordage, and his own precarious perch in the foremast.

"The *Crescent Moon*," began Roger with an impressive jerk of his head, "is a square-rigged three-masted sailing vessel. Normally 'twould take from sixty to eighty men in a crew to set and make sail and bring her about in a blow. But Samuel Salt has magic sail controls, so we three manage quite easily, and now that YOU are here and the handy hippopotamus below, 'twill be easier still. The mast we're riding is the foremast. The mast second from the bow, as we call the front of the ship, is the mainmast, and the mast at the back, or as we salt-water birds say, the stern of the boat, is the mizzenmast. And now for the sails." Roger took a deep breath. "Those below, beginning from the bottom up, are the course, the topsail, the topgallant sail, the royal and the sky sail. And don't forget!" Roger wagged his claw sternly. "Before each sail you must put the name of the mast to which it is attached. As, for instance, this ahead of us is the fore-topgallant sail. SEE? And everything to the left of the ship's center we say is on the port side and anything to the right is on the starboard."

"Then tell me why is the water on the port side bluer than the water on the starboard?" asked Tandy, who had been listening very solemnly as he tried to fix all of these strange terms in his head.

"Bravo!" cried Roger. "Right the first time, Mate. And the water is bluer on the port side of the vessel because it is saltier. The bluer, the saltier," declared Roger, who besides his first voyage with the *Crescent Moon* had read all the sea books in Ato's library and was simply crammed with deep-sea facts and information. "And what is more," he continued, pursing his bill mysteriously, "we're sailing in a magic circle, never knowing what may pop up over the edge. A ship? An island? A hurricane? Or even a fabulous monster! That's what makes sea voyaging so glorious, and sailing so much fun!"

Tandy, staring at the empty circle of blue falling away from the ship on all sides, nodded dreamily. The White City, Patrippany Island, all his former life and existence seemed unreal and far away, and he hoped in his heart of hearts the *Crescent Moon* would not reach his native shores for many a long, gay day. As Roger said, being a person was fun.

"M-mm!" Roger sniffed suddenly. "Wonder what Ato's cooking? Smells like taffy. I'll bet a ship's biscuit we're going to have a candy pull."

184

"A candy pull!" exclaimed Tandy, taking a furious sniff himself. "What is that?" As Roger started in to explain about candy pulls, a large green column shot up on the skyline, a column so surprising and shocking in appearance that Tandy felt positively stunned. "Oh, look! LOOK!" he screamed, grabbing Roger's wing. "There's something now. Oh, Roger, what fun! What terrible fun!"

"Fun?" Roger spun round like a weathercock in a gale. "Fun?" he repeated, stretching out his neck as far as it would go and a few inches besides. "Oh, my best bill and feathers. That's not fun — that's a SEA-Serpent. Help! Help! Deck ahoy! 'Hoy! 'Hoy! Below! King! Captain! Ato! SAMMY! SAM-U-EL!" As if calling them not only by their titles but by their names would increase the number of the ship's officers and crew, Roger tugged wildly at Tandy's arm. "Below! Below! All hands below," shrilled the Read Bird. "Cover all ports and batten the hatches!"

Urged on by Roger, Tandy, still more interested than frightened, descended rapidly to the main deck. At Roger's cries, Ato had run out with a pan of bubbling molasses in one hand and his trusty bread knife in the other. Right behind him stood Samuel Salt, his eye pressed to his largest spyglass. "Well, tar and tarry barrels!" exclaimed the Captain exultantly. "Why, this is a sea serpent second to none, the finest example of a marine ophidian I've ever met in all my voyages!"

"Oh, fiddlesticks!" blustered Ato, shaking him angrily by the arm. "Are you a Captain or a Collector? Quick, now, make up your mind before your ship is crunched down like a cracker and we're all swallowed up with the crumbs! Quick, Sammy! For the love of salt mackerel, DO something!" Squeezing himself between the cook and the Captain, Tandy saw that there were now three immense shiny curves showing above the water, and with scarcely a splash the tremendous monster was moving toward the ship. Then suddenly it was upon them, and its huge, horrid, unbelievable head came curling far over the bow of the *Crescent Moon*.

"Avast and belay! Avast and belay, you villain!" yelled Samuel Salt, dropping his spyglass and grasping his blunderbuss while Roger beat his wings together like castanets and screamed like a fire siren. Tandy, rather frightened himself and not knowing what else to do, fell flat on his stomach, and pulling a pad from his blouse began making a quick and frantic sketch of the dreadful sea beast. Its body was leagues long and yards through, the head was large as a whole elephant with a long, curling, silver tongue and darting green fangs. But it was the teeth that made even the stout heart of Ato hammer against his ribs. Each tooth of this singular sea serpent was a live white goblin brandishing a long spear. Leaning far out of the yawning mouth, they screamed, hissed and yelled at the defenseless company below.

The next forward thrust of the monster brought its head curling right down among them. This so startled Tandy, he could neither move nor scream. Samuel fired his blunderbuss so fast and furiously it sounded like a dozen guns, but it was Ato who really saved the day and his shipmates. With calm and deadly precision, the ship's cook flung the pan of still bubbling molasses straight into the cavernous mouth. Screaming with surprise, pain, and fury, the monster clamped its jaws together, and finding them stuck fast on the taffy, fell writhing back into the sea, dashing and slashing its head under water to ease the burn and setting the *Crescent Moon* to dancing like a cocklebur. But the taffy, hardened by contact with the cold water, stuck faster than ever, and unable to bite and scarcely able to breathe, the discomfited sea monster backed away from the ship and went slithering and thrashing away toward the skyline.

"Well, there goes our candy pull!" sighed Roger, falling in a limp heap to Ato's shoulder. "Nice work! Nice work, King dear. There's a certain touch about your fighting that is well nigh irresistible."

"Mains'ls and tops'ls! You certainly pulled a trick THAT time!" puffed Samuel Salt, picking up his spyglass to have a last look at his lovely specimen. "You saved us and the ship that time, Mate. My bullets rattled off its hide like hailstones off a roof."

"Pooh! Just happened to have the taffy handy," answered Ato, looking rather regretfully into the empty pot. "Here, child, run back and tell Kobo everything's all right." The ship's cook pulled Tandy quickly to his feet. "Just listen to her squealing. The poor lass is probably frightened out of her skin." As Tandy started aft on a run, Ato picked up the sketch he had made of the monster. "Ahoy, and what's this?" he panted. "What did I tell you, Sammy? Look, the boy's drawn as lively a picture of that varmint as you'd ever hope to paste in a scrapbook. Here it is, tail, teeth and everything!"

"Mean to say he drew that while we were all standing here ready to perish and go down with the ship? Hah! That's what I call bravery in action!" exclaimed Samuel. "And goosewing my topsails! If the young lubber can draw like this, he'll be a monstrous help to us, Mates. Why, I'll make him cabin boy and Royal Artist of the Expedition with extra rations and pay."

"Hurray! And I'll tell him," puffed Roger, spreading his wings gleefully. "Hi, King! Hi, Tandy! Ho, Tandy! You've been promoted from King to cabin boy and Royal Drawer of Animals and Islands and extry rations and pay!"

Nikobo was as pleased as Tandy at her little charge's rise to favor, and after they had both listened in rapt silence to Roger's news, Tandy told her how Ato had routed the sea serpent. Meanwhile, Roger had carried all the sketches Tandy had made of the Leopard Men and Patrippany Island to the main cabin. Samuel's delight and enthusiasm at having such spirited and authentic records of the lost tribe and strange animals on Patrippany Island knew no bounds. He beamed on

185

Tandy so kindly and approvingly the next time they met, the little boy felt warm and jolly all the way down to his heels. Roger had already exclaimed his new duties to him, and when Ato sounded the gong for dinner, Tandy was the first to answer. But when he started to pass the vegetables and wait on the table, the Captain gruffly pushed him into a chair.

"All equals here," roared Samuel, slapping him affectionately on the shoulder. "You've earned your place and your salt, sonny, and we'll all help ourselves and each other." Tilting back his chair and keeping time with his teacup, Samuel began to sing lustily:

"Blow high, blow low, "Tis a sea life for me—
With a good ship's crew I'll sail the blue With a good ship going free-eeeh-eeeh!
With a good ship going free!"

Almost before he knew it, Tandy was singing, too.

Chapter 10 - The City of Bridges

The days that followed always seemed to Tandy the happiest he had known. He wondered how he had ever endured his long, tedious, pent-up life in Ozamaland. There was so much to see and do on a ship that the hours were not half long enough. Being a full-fledged member of the crew, he took his turn on watch, his trick at the wheel, and had besides other duties on deck. After a bit of practice, he could scramble aloft like a monkey and liked nothing so much as perching in the rigging looking far out to sea. The Read Bird has fastened a special rope to the mizzenmast so that Tandy could swing out and drop down on Nikobo's raft, and much of his free time was spent with the faithful hippopotamus. Sea life agreed enormously with Nikobo, especially since Ato had solved the largest item of her diet. Noting the tangled mass of seaweed often floating by on the surface of the sea, the clever cook let down the ship's nets daily. The seaweed, crisp, tender and green, was dragged on deck, where Roger and Tandy went carefully through it, removing all crabs, small fish and seashells which seriously disagreed with the hippopotamus. A huge hamperfull was lowered to her every evening, and with this plentiful supply of green food and with the bread and delicious vegetable scraps Ato saved from the table Nikobo fared better than she had on the island. The largest tub on the boat served as a drinking cup, and this Tandy kept full by playing down the hose from the deck, giving her a daily shower of fresh water at the same time. So, lacking nothing in interest or comfort, Nikobo enjoyed herself hugely and to the fullest extent.

On calm mornings, with the *Crescent Moon* hove to, all hands would go swimming. Nikobo loved to swim and to roll over and over like a mighty porpoise, even though the salt water made her eyes sting. Since Tandy had given Samuel the drawings of the Leopard Men, the ship's Captain could not do enough for his young cabin boy, and among other things had made a rope harness for Nikobo so Tandy could hang on when he perched upon her slippery back. At first he had been satisfied to ride Nikobo, but after several days he was splashing recklessly with the others and Samuel had taught him all the swimming strokes he knew and had Tandy diving over and under the hippopotamus in a way to make Roger scream with envy and approval. Swimming was the only part of a sea voyage the Read Bird could not really enjoy, but he was always on hand to give advice, roosting on Nikobo's head so long as she stayed above water and taking hurriedly to his wings when she mischievously tried to duck him.

The hippopotamus made a really splendid raft when they tired of swimming, and Ato, who did not care for water sports so much as Samuel or Tandy, fished for hours from her back, his feet hooked through the ropes of her harness to keep him from falling into the sea. The only thing Tandy regretted was Nikobo's great size and that she could not come aboard ship and join them in the cabin. On cool evenings he and Ato and the Captain (Roger preferring to take first watch) would sit cozily round the fire listening to the stories Samuel told them of the days when he had been a pirate and roamed up and down the Nonestic, capturing the ships and treasure of all the powerful island monarchs. Tandy never tired of these thrilling sea battles or of watching Samuel Salt's pet fire lizard.

Sally was now so tame she would allow any one of them to pick her up. They had to be careful not to hold her against their clothing, however, for though Sally did not burn the fingers, she set fire to whatever she touched. Indeed, whenever they wanted a fire in the grate, they had only to place the Salamander on the kindling beneath the logs, and a cheery flame would blaze up instantly. It was in the fireplace that Sally took most of her exercise, racing and skittering over the glowing logs or rolling happily in the red-hot embers. But most of her time she spent curled up in Samuel Salt's pipe, and it was always a surprise to Tandy to see her comical head pop up over the edge of the bowl or hear her chirping and purring to herself from her cozy bed of tobacco leaves.

Some evenings, when Ato was trying out new recipes in the galley, Tandy and Samuel would descend to the hold to look over the plants from Patrippany Island, try to figure out the script on the piece of lava, and sort and arrange

Samuel's shell collection. Every day after the nets were drawn up there were new specimens to classify and label. The drawing Tandy had made of the Sea Lion and all the pictures of the Leopard Men and beasts on Patrippany Island Samuel had framed and hung above his shelves so that the hold was looking more and more like a scientific laboratory every day.

"Do you suppose we'll ever find anything large enough to put in those big cages and aquariums?" asked Tandy one night as he pasted a pink label on a fluted conch shell.

"Sure's eight bells!" murmured Samuel Salt comfortably. "No telling what'll turn up on a voyage like this. Personally, I've set my heart on a roc's egg, but setting the heart on a roc's egg won't hatch one out, Ho, Ho! No, No! But on the other hand, one never can tell, and we've had a week of such fine and pleasant days I look for something to happen any moment now, so you'd better put up your paste pot and turn in, my lad, so we'll all be ready for the morning."

"Well, what would you do with a roc's egg?" inquired Tandy, reluctantly clapping the top on his bottle of glue. "Aren't they terribly big and terribly scarce, Captain Salt?"

"Terribly!" admitted Samuel Salt, placing his tray of lamp shells back on their stand. "But a newly laid roc's egg is as rare as a mermaid's foot, and no larger than one tar barrel. Now if we could just get a newly laid roc's egg aboard and find some way to preserve it, well and good; if we didn't find a way and it hatched before we landed, it could easily fly off with us and the ship, for THAT'S how big a bird a roc is. But I'll take a chance if I ever find a roc's egg, and there's an island somewhere in these waters where rocs are known to nest. Rock Island it's called, and a roc's nest would be something to see, eh, Kinglet?"

"Please don't call me that," begged Tandy earnestly. "Roger says I don't have to be a King on this ship, and I like not being a King."

"Ha! Ha! And I like you that way myself," roared Samuel, tossing Tandy suddenly to his shoulder. "Why, since you've stopped this King and son of a Kinging, you're a seaman after my own heart, and so long as the *Crescent Moon*'s afloat you've a berth on her! Up with you! Up with you! Tomorrow's another day." Swinging gaily to the main deck, Samuel tumbled Tandy into his bunk and went striding aft to take in his main and mizzen topsails.

Next morning, while he and Ato were cutting up potatoes for Nikobo, Tandy was not surprised to hear a loud hail from above. Something had happened, just as Samuel had predicted. Running out with a paring knife still in his hand, he saw a strange, glittering, mountainous island abaft the beam. It was still a goodish sea mile away, but with the glasses Ato generously pressed upon him, Tandy made out the most curious bit of geography the eyes of a voyager had yet gazed on. There was not a piece of level ground on the island anywhere. Its high, glittering, needle-like peaks rose straight out of the sea with apparently no way of ascending or descending. Of clear crystal, reflecting every color of the rainbow, the beautiful island was almost too dazzling to look at as it lay shimmering and sparkling in the bright sunshine. As they sailed nearer, Tandy saw that a perfect maze of high and airy bridges ran like a gigantic spider web between the peaks. On these bridges all the island's life and activities seemed to take place. Quaint fluted cottages were built in the center, and along the perilous catwalks on either side raced the Mountaineers themselves, brandishing glittering poles and spears and halberds.

"Pikes on the peak! Pikes on the peak! Port your helm, Sammy," roared Ato. "Not too close! Not too near, Sam-u-el. How'd you like to be pinned to the mast with a spear or flattened on the deck with a boulder?"

"Ah, now, they're just excited!" answered Samuel Salt, squinting curiously up at the Bridgemen, but Nikobo, with her short legs resting on the top rail of her raft, squealed out a dolorous warning.

"Fighters! Fighters! These Pikers look savager than the Leopard Men. Best back away, Master Captain, while there's still time."

"Oh, look! LOOK! There's a ship on the mountain," cried Tandy, jerking Samuel's sleeve, "right there where that torrent comes down between the bridges, a three-master, larger than the *Crescent Moon*."

"Then it's a battle!" boomed Samuel, bringing his helm hard around. "Stand by to man the guns. 'Hoy, all hands, 'hoy!" While his shipmates sprang to attention, Samuel darted from mast to mast, touching the buttons on his sail controls.

"AYE DE AYE OH LAY!" The shrill, unexpected cry came from the highest bridge on the island and was immediately taken up and repeated by all the Pikemen on the lower bridges. It resulted in such a mad medley of yodels that Ato clapped both hands to his ears, and Nikobo plunged her head in her drinking tub.

"Not only fighters, but singers!" grunted Ato, swinging the port gun into an upright position. "Beef beans and barley bread! What a rumpus!" Tandy, who with Roger had charge of the other gun, could not help but admire the calm way Samuel Salt ignored the dreadful outcry from the bridges. Whether the pikes of the islanders could be flung down upon them was still a question, but as Tandy looked anxiously aloft, he saw the great white-sailed ship of the Mountain Men sweeping toward the torrent. It paused for a breathless instant on the top and then came rushing down upon them.

187

They were right in the path of the descending vessel, which would strike them with such force both ships would surely be demolished.

"I am a King's son and the son of a King's son," shuddered Tandy, gritting his teeth and waiting desperately for the order to fire. "I can bear anything."

"Not this! Not this!" chattered Roger, sliding wildly up and down the shiny cannon. "It will shiver your timbers — it will shiver all of our timbers. What in salt ails the Captain? Why doesn't he give the order to fire and pepper these rascals before they reach us? Oh, oh! Oh-hh!" But the only orders that came from the Captain were for Nikobo.

"Overboard, Lassie! Dive off! Quick, now, and swim for your life," bawled Samuel Salt, waving both arms frantically at the hippopotamus. As Nikobo with a frightened squeal let down the back rail of her pen and slid into the sea, Tandy felt a quiver and jerk through the whole length of the *Crescent Moon*. Glancing aloft, he saw a strange change in the sails. Where before they had been sturdy single stretches of canvas, they were now great, swelling balloon sails, each a perfect air-filled sphere. As the ship from the mountain with an angry swish catapulted down from the torrent into the sea, the *Crescent Moon* rose buoyantly into the air, allowing the enemy craft to shoot harmlessly beneath her bow.

"What in Monday!" gasped Ato, flinging both arms round the cannon. "What in Monday are you up to now? How'd we do this? Stop! Stop! I'm no flier. No higher! No higher! Do you intend to impale us on yonder Peaks?" Samuel Salt, hanging desperately to the wheel, made no reply, and as the ship, dipping and swaying, soared higher and higher, the deafening yodels of the Bridgemen ceased abruptly.

"Wha-wha-where are you heading?" demanded Roger, spreading his wings in order to keep his balance on the sloping deck. "You never told us you had balloon sails, Master Salt."

"Ahoy, but we never needed them before!" panted Samuel. "Look sharp below, Roger. Tell me whether I'm over that lake or basin. Look sharp, mind you, or we'll come to grief yet."

"Aye, aye!" quavered the Read Bird, dropping obediently over the side. "It all looks sharp to me."

"Mean to say you're coming down in the middle of these pikes, peaks and bridges?" moaned Ato, holding his head with both hands. "Avast and belay, Mate, I signed up for a sea voyage and not a balloon ride. The altitude's got you, Sammy, that's what. You've air holes in your head. How do you expect the four of us to conquer this whole pesky, peaky island? How could we even take half of them?"

"By surprise," announced Samuel Salt grimly. "We'll take them by surprise. Look, they're too surprised to even yodel. Fetch up the Oz flags, Tandy, and all hands aft for further orders."

"Aft and daft!" choked Ato, hanging on to the rail as he made his way toward the wheel. When Tandy came hurrying up from the hold, his arms full of Oz flags, the *Crescent Moon* hung directly over the glittering Island. Roger fluttered anxiously just below, calling up hoarse information as to the size, possible depth and shape of the sparkling blue lake between the peaks.

Listening carefully to Roger's directions, Samuel deflated his balloon sails so skillfully the *Crescent Moon* came down lightly as a swan in the exact center of the Lake. Above and around the ship on all sides hung the glittering spans of a beautiful Bridge City, and in stunned silence and dismay the Bridgemen looked down on the flying ship and its curious crew.

"Ahoy and hail, Men of the Mountain!" challenged Samuel in a ringing voice. "You are now part and parcel of the great Kingdom of Oz, free as before to govern yourselves, but from this day and henceforth on, an island possession and colony under the protection and puissant rule of her Majesty Queen Ozma of Oz!"

"OZ! Ozay Oz Oh Lay?" The cry came from the tallest and most splendid of the Islanders, who was standing with folded arms on the lacy span connecting the two highest peaks on the Mountain.

Chapter 11 - The Prince of the Peaks

The cry, though loud, was no longer defiant, and Tandy with a little gasp of relief saw the Mountaineers on all the bridges bring their pikes to rest beside them and gaze aloft for further orders.

"I am Alberif, Prince of the Peaks," stated the Man on the Highest Bridge, looking coolly down at Samuel Salt. "But YOU— you who come in this flying ship to conquer the Island of Peakenspire, who are YOU?"

"Ato the Eighth, King of the Octagon Isles, Sir Samuel Salt, Captain of the *Crescent Moon* and Royal Explorer of Oz, Tazander Tazah, King of Ozamaland, and myself, a Royal Read Bird," shouted Roger before any of the others had time to speak for themselves. The Prince of the Peaks, tall and splendid in his shining coat and breeches of silver cloth, his broad-brimmed hat with its quill and rosette of wildflowers, looked so much more impressive than anyone aboard the

Crescent Moon, Tandy half expected him to laugh at Roger's boastful announcements. But instead, Alberif, leaning far out over his royal bridge, looked down at them long and seriously.

"Two Kings, a Royal Discoverer, a Flying Ship and a Read Bird! Hi de Aye de Oh!" whistled the handsome monarch, shaking his head ruefully. "No wonder we were captured. What then are your terms, Kings, Captain, Bird and Conquerors?"

"Not conquerors, COMRADE," called up Samuel Salt in his hearty voice. "Only by your own wish, agreement and consent shall ye come under the rule of Oz. If your Highness could but descend from yon Royal Bridge to this ship, everything can be arranged both peaceably and pleasantly."

"'Ware, Alberif! 'Ware, Alberif!" yodeled the Pikemen on the lower bridges. "Once aboard that ship eeee-ip! We may never see you again eeeee-yen!"

"Oh, nonsense!" blustered Samuel Salt impatiently. "I give you my word as a Pirate and a seaman no harm shall come to you on the *Crescent Moon*."

The Prince stood lost in thought for a moment. Then, tapping his long alpenstock sharply, he issued a high, yodeled command. From the bridgehead an immense basket swooped down. The Prince seated himself gravely in the basket and with three men manipulating the ropes made a swift and dizzy descent to the deck of the *Crescent Moon*. While Samuel and Roger welcomed the tall and lordly Ruler of the Mountain Isle, Ato hurried off to the galley to prepare some suitable refreshments for his entertainment. Tandy, after Samuel had introduced him, began making careful sketches of the handsome Prince, of the lovely city of bridges, and of the Pikemen, who still looked with suspicion and distrust upon the ship that had taken the place of their own.

"How about that basket?" whispered Roger, who had come out to help Ato in the galley. "How'd you like to be hoisted and lowered like a sail? And for salt's sake, King dear, dust the flour off your nose and put on your crown, or this fellow will think you're King of the Cookies and Doughnuts."

"Ha, ha! When he's tasted my plum cake, he'll not think it, he'll know it!" puffed Ato, bustling happily from cupboard to cupboard. "Bring out the best tumblers and silver plates, fetch up a dozen bottles of my famous Sea-pop from the hold, and we'll have this island in our pocket before you can say Oz Robinson!"

When Ato with one tray and Roger with another came out, they found the Captain and the Prince of the Peaks striding up and down the deck in the friendliest conversation imaginable. Matched in height and handsomeness, the two were discussing with lively interest everything from ships and governments to the strange limestone that formed the crystalline rocks of Alberif's island. Later, seated around the table with Tandy and Roger passing plum cake and Sea-pop, the Prince grew friendlier and more confidential still. "We've never been conquered before," admitted his Majesty with a puzzled smile, "but really I find it both interesting and enjoyable."

"Just a matter of chance and luck," said Samuel Salt with a modest wave of his hand. "Had I not had balloon sails on the *Crescent Moon*, your ship would have cut us clean in two before we had time to put about."

"That is what I always planned would happen to an enemy craft," sighed Alberif. "Naturally, our own ship, the Mountain Lass, would have been destroyed too, but we could easily have built another. That is what we'll have to do anyway, as we'll never be able to haul her up the torrent."

"Don't you do it," begged Samuel Salt, looking earnestly at the Mountain Monarch. "I'll send you a set of balloon sails as soon as I reach Elbow Island. The Red Jinn presented me with two sets, and I'll be delighted to send you one. Once they're set, you can fly up as easily as we did and be ready for all and sundry, even US if we come again."

"Come and welcome!" beamed Alberif, looking in some surprise at Sally, who had just lifted her head above the rim of Samuel's pipe bowl. "But tell me, what am I to do now that I am conquered? Surely something is required of us?"

"Nothing! Nothing at all!" Samuel spoke earnestly and admiringly. "This island and your men are in fine shape and a great credit to you, so just go on as you are, but from this time forth you'll be in contact with the famous and most modern Fairyland in History, and if you are ever beset by enemies, you can call upon Oz for assistance or help. In time, fruit, foodstuffs, books and merchandise will arrive from Oz, and in return you may send back some of the sparkling crystals composing these mountains. You might even invite a band of settlers from Oz to come and live as your loyal subjects here."

"Gladly! Gladly!" agreed the Prince, his eyes sparkling at the prospect. "We have many uninhabited peaks and spires and could easily accommodate a thousand new bridge builders. Come with me, all of you, to Skytop Tower, and we'll run up the flag of Oz and sign a pledge of allegiance to her Majesty Queen Ozma. AYE DE AYE OH LAY!" Running out on deck, Alberif joyously beckoned to the men who operated the traveling basket, inviting them all to enter. Ato, who had no intention of trusting his two hundred and fifty pounds to this strange conveyance, shook the Prince regretfully by the hand.

"I'll just watch it all from here," said the ship's cook firmly. "I've pie to cook, potatoes to peel, and dinner to stir up for all hands and a hippopotamus, so if you'll kindly excuse me—"

The Prince looked a little disappointed, but cheered up as Samuel, Roger and Tandy followed him into the basket.

"Haul away!" yelled Samuel Salt, winking at Ato, and to the shrill tune of a ringing round of yodels, their curious elevator rose from the deck, spun merrily up to the Twin Peaks and highest bridge of Alberif's Mountain. Used as he was to the tall masts and lofty rigging of the *Crescent Moon*, Tandy felt sick and giddy as the basket swooped and swung upward. But it came down safely at last, and at sight of the shining spans of the lacy city spread out below and the glittering castle rising from the royal bridge, Tandy forgot all his uneasiness. With a little whistle of surprise and interest, he followed Samuel and Alberif into the royal dwelling, while Roger flew off on a little exploring expedition of his own. Roger knew all about castles and was much more interested in the many windowed, fluted cottages of the yodelers. Ato, watching from the deck of the *Crescent Moon*, presently saw the flag of Oz fluttering from the top turret of the Castle Tower, and with a little sigh of relief and pride he gathered up the empty pop bottles and padded off to his galley. Soon Oz flags floated from the posts on all the bridgeheads, adding much to the gaiety and beauty of Alberif's city.

>From the Royal Bridge Tandy and Samuel had a splendid view, and of his many experiences, Tandy always remembered best the afternoon spent on Peakenspire. Alberif was a merry as well as an interesting host, explaining everything from the strange traveling baskets to the age-old customs and treasures of the Islanders. In the baskets the Islanders could travel from bridge to bridge and down to the sea itself when they wished to go fishing. There was little soil between the rocks, but such soil as there was was so amazingly fertile that each family could raise all the fruits and vegetables required in one small window box. After long experimentation and culture, Alberif's ancestors had perfected two curious vines. On one, vegetables grew in rapid rotation, potatoes following peas, corn following potatoes, carrots following corn, beets following carrots, cabbages, lima beans and spinach after the beets. The vine never withered or died, and by cutting off the top every day, the Islanders were assured of a continuous supply of fresh vegetables. The fruit vine was of the same variety, furnishing every known berry, fruit and melon. Each family was given two of these vines and thus had very little worry about food supplies. Birds, something of a cross between wild ducks and chickens, made their nests in the craggy peaks, and with their eggs and a plentiful supply of fish and other sea food, the Islanders fared splendidly.

The Bridgemen were tall, blue-eyed, handsome and happy. Men and women alike wore short trousers and blouses of silver cloth and carried pikes that served both as weapons and alpenstocks. The bridges, while delicate as fine lace in construction, were supple and strong as steel. The material mined from the mountains themselves was like silver and crystal combined, a new, strong and glittering metal, samples of which Samuel happily thrust into his pocket.

"Sounds like magic," said Tandy, who had been listening closely to Alberif's description of life on Peakenspire.

"It is a magic of a kind," answered the Prince with a pleased little nod. "And the air here is so light and sparkling we never tire, grow old or have illness of any kind, so that my people are always light hearted and happy, spending most of their time in dancing and singing."

"I see," murmured Samuel Salt, "er— and hear," he added quickly as the wild, joyous cries of Alberif's yodelers made every window in the palace rattle. "I'll certainly make a note of all this and report Peakenspire Island to Queen Ozma as the most interesting discovery of the voyage."

"I am highly honored!" Alberif bowed stiffly. "Highly honored! HI dee Aye de OH-hhhh!" Jumping into the air, the Prince of the Peaks kicked his heels together from sheer exuberance. "Wait," he told them cheerfully, "and I'll get you some fruit and vegetable vines to take back with you." Tandy and Samuel could not help grinning as Alberif rushed off. To tell the truth, there was something so light and exhilarating about the mountain air they found it difficult to walk calmly themselves. As the Prince returned, Samuel felt a loud and uncontrollable yodel rising in his own throat, and seizing Tandy's arm, he bade Alberif a hasty and hearty adieu. Bidding him keep a sharp lookout for the airships from Oz and loaded down with crystals and vines, the two explorers climbed into the basket and were swung swiftly down to the deck of the *Crescent Moon*. Roger, flying under his own power and yodeling like a native, arrived soon after. With Oz flags flying from all bridges and the Mountaineers calling out rousing and melodious farewells, Samuel inflated his balloon sails, and the ship soared gracefully aloft, circled the island three times, and then dropped lightly down upon the surface of the sea. The Mountain Lass in charge of Alberif's husky crew lay just off shore, and there she would have to stay till Samuel sent a set of balloon sails to lift her back to the Lake among the peaks.

Nikobo, who'd been swimming anxiously round and round, gave a bellow of relief as she spied the *Crescent Moon*. "I thought you'd been captured and destroyed!" wheezed the hippopotamus, scrambling hastily aboard her raft. "Next time you fly off, take me aboard or give me a balloon sail, too. I'm so full of salt water, I'm perfectly pickled and somebody'll have to scrape the barnacles off my hide."

"But we've brought you a present," called Tandy, leaning far over the taffrail, "a vegetable vine that will keep you supplied with fresh vegetables as long as we're at sea. SEE! DEEEE Aye DEE OH!"

"Avast and balaydeeaye!" barked Samuel Salt grimly. "Let's get away from here. This is no way for able-bodied seamen to talk." Rushing from wheel to mast, he quickly set his sail. "Ahoy! Ahoy Dee Oy Dee OH!" he yodeled, then, very red in the face, he blew three shrill blasts on his foghorn, swung his ship about, and the *Crescent Moon*, with a spanking breeze on her quarter, went skimming away toward the southern skyline.

Chapter 12 - Fog

The evening had blown up raw and cold, and after carrying an old tarpaulin down to cover Nikobo, Tandy had come shivering back to the main cabin. Samuel Salt had close-reefed his topsails and double-reefed his courses, adjusted his mechanical steering gear, and now sat beside the fire examining a heap of the glittering crystals from Alberif's island.

"Just sketch Peakenspire Island on the chart, there where I've made the cross," he directed, looking up with an absent smile as the little boy came over to warm himself at the cheerful blaze. "You're such a hand with a brush, even in so small a place you can give a good idea of the City of Bridges."

"And a good idea they are," murmured Ato, who was busy mending his fishing nets on the other side of the fireplace. "In every port we learn something new, eh Mate? All mountains, no matter how high and peaked, could be lived on if they were properly bridged."

"True, quite true," agreed Samuel, squinting contentedly through his magnifying glass while Tandy began sketching in the latest discovery on the sea chart. "I've written it all up in my journal and put down Peakenspire Island as able to accommodate a thousand settlers from Oz and as an especially good place for poets."

"Provided they are deaf," put in Ato, looking comically over his specs. "AYE DEE AYE DEE OH! While you fellows were aloft, I got to yodeling so fast and furious I blew all the saucepans off their hooks."

"Yes, that is one disadvantage," admitted Samuel, glancing approvingly at Tandy's picture of Alberif's Island, "but never mind, we don't have to live there, and think of the splendid specimens we've brought away, Mates!" Samuel ran his fingers lovingly through the heap of crystals and strands of metal Alberif had given him. "And those fruit and vegetable vines will provision us for the whole voyage."

"They're a great comfort to me, I assure you," muttered Ato, holding up his net to the light to see whether there were any more holes. "Now I know Kobo will never starve. I put a vegetable vine in a box on her raft, and that leaves two for us, two for Ozma, and maybe Tandy would like to take the other two home with him?"

"Home?" Tandy swung round in positive dismay. "Oh, we're not near Ozamaland yet, are we Captain?" His voice sounded so dismal, Samuel Salt threw down his magnifying glass with a roar of merriment.

"Shiver my timbers, lad, one would think you did not wish to reach Ozamaland at all," he blustered teasingly. "What's the matter with that country of yours? You wouldn't keep an honest explorer from adding a creeping bird and a flying reptile to his collection, now would ye?"

"No! No! Of course not," answered Tandy quickly. "But perhaps it is farther away than you think, Master Salt, and perhaps the Greys have conquered the Whites, and then I won't be King any more."

"What's this? What's this?" Ato lifted his nose like an old hound that has just finished a fox, for he loved a good story even better than he loved a good meal. "Who are the Greys and Whites, my lad? You never told us anything about this."

"There's really not much to tell," sighed Tandy, seating himself on a small stool before the fire. "In the first place, I suppose you know that the great continent of Tarara is divided into two large, long countries. Ozamaland is on the east coast, and Amaland on the west coast."

"Now, I'll just make a note of that," said Samuel Salt, leaning over to pull his journal toward him.

"My country," went on Tandy slowly, "is made up largely of desert and jungle, best known for its white elephants and camels and the famous White City of Om, first King and ruler of the Kingdom. The Zamas are fierce and still wild tribesmen living in tents on the desert and in huts in the jungle. Only the thousand Nobles and their families who live in the White City have been taught to read and write and live under roofs. That is why the Kings of Ozamaland are so well guarded and never allowed out of the capital."

"Then I'd rather be a tribesman," sniffed Ato, letting his nets drop in a heap around his feet.

"But there's no choice," said Tandy thoughtfully. "The nine Ozamandarins who make the laws have decreed that the King shall remain in the White City."

"Well, what about those Whites and Greys?" asked Samuel Salt, pulling out his pipe and leaning down close to the fire so Sally could light it for him.

"My people, because they dress in white robes and turbans, are known as the Whites, and the Amas, the rough plainsmen who rove the long ranges of Amaland, are the Greys. The Amas care for nothing but their swift grey horses and often charge over the border to make war on my countrymen. Then the Whites, mounted on their white elephants and camels, have all they can do to hold their own."

"Aha, that's what I'd call a REAL battle!" exclaimed Ato, his eyes snapping with enthusiasm and interest. Then, noting Samuel's disapproving frown, he pursed up his lips, shook his head, and added quickly, "All very wild and disorderly, Tandy, my lad. Seems as if the Whites and Greys should manage their affairs more peaceably."

"Yes," said Tandy solemnly, "and I've often thought when I was grown, I'd ride over on my white elephant to visit the Greys and see why they are so unfriendly."

"A good idea, and if I were you, I wouldn't wait till I was grown. I'd do it as soon as I got back," advised Samuel Salt, taking a long pull at his pipe.

"And very probably get himself cut up and captured," shuddered Ato, shaking his head.

"Well, he's been both shut up and captured anyway, hasn't he?" said Samuel mildly. "Now which one of your aunts do you think had you carried off, Matey, and how many aunts do you have, anyway?"

"Three," Tandy answered, counting them off solemnly on his fingers. "And they were all pretty and pleasant enough; but after the prophecy of the Old Man of the Jungle that I would be carried off by an aunt, they were all locked up in the castle dungeon, and I was locked up in the Tower." And resting his elbows on his knees, Tandy gazed soberly into the fire as if he might discover there the reason for his cruel abduction and imprisonment in the jungle. "If I'd only been awake when I was carried away," he exclaimed impatiently.

"They probably gave you a sleeping potion," decided Ato, nodding his head portentously, "but it's such a longish distance, unless this aunt had wings or a flying eagle, I'll never understand how she shipped you so far and so fast."

"Well, whoever it was did us a real service!" boomed Samuel Salt, twinkling his blue eyes affectionately at Tandy. "Even Peter was no better aboard a ship, eh Mate?"

"A real artist and a seaman," agreed Ato, rolling cheerfully back to his feet, "and when we reach Ozamaland, I'll talk to these aunts like an Octagon uncle, and the Ozamalanders had better hold on to their turbans, too."

"But they wear square hats!" roared Tandy, laughing so hard he almost fell off the stool, for he just could not picture the fat King of the Octagon Isle berating the haughty judges of Ozamaland.

"What's the joke?" demanded Roger, flying in through the open port and making a straight line for the fire. "Brrr-rah! Wet weather, boys! Wet weather! Oh, what a coldth and dampth and gloomth. Why, I'm moister than an oyster and clammier than a clam. How about a cup of hot chocolate for the Watch, Cook dear? Better see to your sail, Master Salt. Fog's thicker than bean soup out there."

"We'll all have some chocolate," said Ato as Samuel hurried out to see how dense the fog really was. Later, sitting by the stove sipping Ato's delicious hot chocolate, Tandy could not help comparing this cozy life aboard the *Crescent Moon* with his dull and lonely existence in the Royal City of his Fathers.

"I wish the Greys would capture the Whites," he thought vindictively as he followed Roger across the slippery deck. "Then I'd never have to leave this ship." The kind-hearted Read Bird was carrying a pail of hot chocolate down to Nikobo on the raft. She could not get her great snout into the bucket, but she opened her enormous mouth, and with one toss Roger poured the whole pail down her throat.

"That'll keep her warm till morning," chuckled Roger, flying back to join Tandy, "and now you'd better turn in, little fellow, for you're on morning watch, and eight bells will be sounding before you know it!" All through his dreams about the Whites and Greys, Tandy heard the raucous voice of the fog horn, and when he rolled sleepily out of his bunk to relieve Ato, the ship seemed to be hardly moving at all.

"Ahoy, Captain! Isn't a fog dangerous?" Tandy's voice seemed more hopeful than worried, and Samuel Salt, peering down at the little boy buttoned to his chin in Peter's old sou'easter, grinned approvingly.

"Just about as dangerous as a man-eating tiger," he answered cheerfully. "We're liable to ram a ship, run on the rocks, or scrape our bottom on a hidden reef or sand bar. These waters, as you know, being all unnavigated. But I've brought Sally along to keep my nose warm and throw a bit more light on the subject, and we'll have to take our chance, eh Matey? Just step aft and see if you can make out anything astern, will you, Tandy?"

Four o'clock, or rather eight bells, was always pretty dark, and one had to depend more or less on the ship's lanterns, but this morning was the darkest Tandy had ever experienced. Clinging to the rail, he moved cautiously to the stern and gazed intently down into the gloom. Nothing an inch beyond his nose was visible, and as for the raft and Nikobo, they might just as well not have been there. "Kobo, Kobo, are you all right?" There was no answer to Tandy's call, but presently a huge and resounding snore rolled upward, and greatly comforted, Tandy hurried back to the Captain. Samuel Salt was busy lighting extra lanterns, and as he straightened up, a hollow boom, followed by a splintering crash, sent them both sprawling to the deck. Leaping to his feet and unmindful of the glass from the shattered lanterns, Samuel seized an unbroken one and ran furiously to the rail.

192

"Ship ahoy! Heave to, you blasted son of a cuttlefish lubber! You've rammed us amidships, you blasted Billygoat. Where are your lights? Why didn't ye sound the horn?" His lantern, held far over the rail, made no impression at all on the choking fog. Jumping up and running after Samuel, Tandy strained his eyes for a glimpse of the ship that had hit them, for unmistakably to his ears came the scrape and rasp of wood on wood. Yes, surely it was a ship. But no answer to Samuel's hail came out of the fog, only the swish and murmur of the sea and the rattle of wind in the rigging. But all this creaking could not come from the *Crescent Moon* alone. There was a ship beyond them in the fog, but where, as Samuel had demanded, were her lights and crew? Wildly, Tandy, hardly knowing what to think or do, continued to blink into the maddening darkness. Ato and Roger, wakened by the horrible jolt, now came hurrying out, each waving a lantern. "Let go the anchor, Mates," ordered Samuel in a stern voice, "we're to grips with an enemy ship, so stand by for trouble." Further shortening his sail, Samuel waited tensely for the first move from their invisible foe. "Might be pirates," he whispered out of the corner of his mouth to Tandy, who stood close beside him grasping the scimitar that had once been Peter's. "Jump the first man aboard."

"How about a long shot in their general direction?" wheezed Ato, who found the silence and suspense well nigh unbearable.

"No, it is not for us to start a fight," stated Samuel grimly. "But hah! Just let them start one! Fetch me my stilts, Roger, and be quick about it, too!"

"Stilts?" choked the Read Bird, dropping the blunderbuss with which he had armed, or rather winged, himself. "You'll never be trying these things again; they nearly shivered our timbers last time. Why take another chance?"

"My stilts!" repeated Samuel savagely, and Roger, who knew his duty as a sailor, flew without further argument to the hold. When Roger returned with a stilt in each claw, the Captain grasped one and, moving silently as a cat over to the port rail, he thrust the long pole experimentally out into the fog. There was an instant thud, and Samuel himself got a severe jolt as the stilt struck against some firm and immovable object beyond. Convinced that it was an enemy ship, Samuel returned to the others, and drawn up in an anxious row the four shipmates waited for the fog to lift or the first enemy seaman to leap aboard.

"I'll wager it's a derelict or an abandoned vessel with no crew," breathed Ato, seating himself on a fire bucket to somewhat ease the long wait. The first hour Tandy stood fairly well, but the second seemed interminable. The flickering lanterns, the tense quiet, the choking fog and gentle roll of the ship all made him desperately drowsy, and much to his later disgust, he must have finally fallen asleep. The next thing he remembered was the shrill squall of the Read Bird and the pleasant feel of the sun on his eyelids.

"The ship! The pirates! The fog!" thought Tandy, springing up wildly. But neither ship nor pirates met his astonished gaze. Abaft the beam lay a great, whispering, deep-sea forest, its trees higher than the masts of the ship, springing directly out of the water and stretching their leafy branches to the sky. It was into one of these giant greenwoods the *Crescent Moon* had crashed in the fog. Samuel was staring at the sea forest with the rapt look of a scientist who has just made an unbelievable discovery, and Ato, with his elbows resting on the rail, was gazing dreamily in the same direction.

"'Hoy! Ahoy! Why, I never knew there were forests in the sea," exclaimed Tandy, running over to insinuate himself between the cook and the Captain.

"There aren't! It's just plain impossible!" breathed Ato, moving over to make room for Tandy. "But impossible or not, there she lies. And isn't it pretty?" he mused, resting more than half of his great weight on the rail. "I suppose Sammy'll want to dig up a sea tree and bring it along," he leaned over to whisper mischievously in Tandy's ear. "And anyway, it's better than pirates."

"Look, look, there's fish in those trees," screamed Roger, bouncing up and down on Ato's plump shoulder. "How about some flying fish for breakfast, Cook dear?"

"Breakfast? Breakfast? Can it really be time for breakfast? Ho, hum! I thought I was still asleep and dreaming," grunted Ato, giving himself a little shake. "Well, forests or no forests, a man must eat, I suppose!" And still gazing delightedly over his shoulder, the ship's cook trod reluctantly toward the galley while Tandy hurried into the cabin for his paints.

Chapter 13 - The Sea Forest

Tandy had to call Samuel twice before he would come to breakfast, and when he finally did sit down, he was so busy preparing to explore the sea forest he ate scarcely a bite.

"We'll take the jolly boat," he decided, making long notes in his journal between his sips of coffee, "the small nets and knives and baskets for cuttings and any specimens we may pick up and—"

"Why the jolly boat when we have a jolly seagoing hippopotamus?" inquired Roger, elevating one eyebrow. "A jolly hippopotamus, I might add, who runs under her own power and saves us the trouble of rowing!" Roger was much annoyed because he had failed to catch a flying fish before breakfast, and instead of eating his hard-boiled eggs, kept winging over to the open port to glare at his finny rivals. Tandy, like the Captain, was too excited to eat, and even Ato downed his omelet and fresh strawberries from the Peakenspire fruit vine with rare speed and indifference.

"It's a lucky thing you're so enormous, Kobo," puffed the ship's cabin boy, dropping down on the raft a few minutes later. "Ato's got his crab nets and fishing lines, Samuel's bringing an aquarium, a couple of baskets, and a box. And I have this pail, my paints, and a cage in case Roger does manage to catch one of those flying fish." Kobo was staring fixedly at her vegetable vine as Tandy dropped down beside her, and now snapping off a whole bushel of beans, she turned round and, munching contentedly, surveyed the excited boy at her side.

"Whatever you have can be hung to my harness," she assured him, speaking a bit thickly through the beans. "But turn the point of that scimitar up instead of down. You wouldn't want to carve old Kobo, now would you? It will seem funny swimming through a forest, won't it, little King? The further we go on this voyage the queerer everything grows."

"But I like it queer," stated Tandy, climbing with a satisfied little sigh on Nikobo's broad back.

"I, too, find it most interesting and jolly," agreed the hippopotamus, fastening her eyes dreamily on the vegetable vine to see what was coming on next. "I thought I might be on short rations when I came on this voyage, Tandy, but I declare to goodness I've never had such a rich and varied diet in my life. You, too, look fine and strong and much happier than when we met in the jungle. But to get back to the fare— why, today I've had a basket of biscuits, a bushel of beans—"

"And that makes it Bean and Biscuit Day, I suppose," giggled Tandy, remembering Kobo's strange way of dividing up her week. "But look! Listen! Here they come!"

"Ahoy below, Hip Hip OPOTOMUS, AHOY!" roared Samuel Salt jovially from above. "All ready to cast off, my lass?"

"Aye, aye, sir!" grinned Kobo as Samuel and Ato came panting down the rope ladders to the raft. "Move over, Tandy, and make room for the Cook and the Captain!" It took nearly ten minutes to get all the gear and crew aboard, and Nikobo looked like some curious deep-sea monster when she finally shoved off. Two large baskets were slung from ropes across her back. The pail and bird cage slapped up and down on one hip, the aquarium on the other, and through her collar various fishing rods, nets and poles were stuck like quills on a porcupine.

"Now whatever you do, don't submerge," warned Samuel, holding his tin box for especially fragile specimens high above his chest to keep it dry. "Just slow and steady, m'lass, so we'll have time to observe and admire and make notes of any strange growths and creatures as we ride along."

"Creatures!" exclaimed Tandy, twisting round. He was perched on Nikobo's head, his paints held carefully in his lap. "Would there be any wild animals in a sea forest, Master Salt?"

"Sea Lions, likely," predicted Samuel, peering round eagerly as Nikobo paddled between two slippery-barked sea trees into the murmuring forest itself. Except for the fact that the floor of this curious sea wood was the blue and restless sea, it might almost have been a forest ashore. The trees, tall, straight, and stately, towered up toward the sky. Staring down into the clear green water, Tandy saw their trunks going down, down, down as far as he could see. "Rooted in the very ocean bed," marveled Samuel Salt, touching one lovingly as they passed. "What splendid masts these would make, Mates! Avast and belay, Nikobo, I believe I'll just take a cutting or two."

"Ha, ha!" roared Ato, peering over Samuel's shoulder. "So now we're going to grow our own masts."

Samuel himself, leaning far out over Nikobo's back, severed three young shoots from the sea tree and popped them happily into the aquarium. Vines that were really of coral ringed the gigantic trunks like bracelets, and the leaves of the trees were long ribbons of green and silver that whipped and fluttered like banners in the morning breeze.

"What's that?" puzzled Ato as the hippopotamus made her way leisurely between the trees. "Looks like mushrooms, Sammy! Wait, I'll just pick me a few and see." Hooking his heels in Nikobo's harness, Ato began vigorously cutting from the trunk of one of the trees the colored fungus growths which sprouted in great profusion just above the water line. Nikobo bravely offered to sample some, and after waiting anxiously to see whether they would have any ill effects, the ship's cook decided they were harmless and joyfully filled one of the baskets. The only specimens that really interested Ato were of the edible variety.

While he was thus employed, Tandy, an experienced climber by now, scurried up to the top of one of the sea trees, breaking off several branches so Samuel could press the curious leaves in his album. High above his head, Tandy could see Roger chasing angrily after a flying fish, muttering with anger at his unsuccessful efforts to overtake the nimble little sea bird. In our own southern waters there are large flying fish that leap out of the water of the gulf stream, but the flying

194

fish in this Nonestic Sea Forest were small, and where most fish have gills wore strong, transparent wings. Their claws, somewhat like a crab's, made it possible for them to perch jauntily in the branches of the sea trees, and these strange little fellows could swim and dive as well as fly. Pulling out his pad, Tandy made a lively sketch of one in the tree opposite, for it did look as if Roger would never succeed in catching one.

All morning Nikobo paddled calmly through the dreamy sea forest, Samuel making notes, Tandy sketches, and Ato catching in his long-handled nets plump little fish and crabs, and filling another basket with the small, delicious clams that clung like barnacles to the slippery bark of the sea trees. In the shadowy center of the forest where the trees pressed closer together and great flat rocks stuck their heads out of the water, the explorers came upon several fierce sea lions. They were not smooth and shiny like the seals of our own oceans, but yellow and tawny with long yellow tusks, tufted tails, and scaly manes. Their front legs ended in sharp claws, their back legs were shorter, and their feet were webbed for swimming. Only the fact that Nikobo was larger and more frightening to the sea lions than they were to her saved the party from a savage attack by these malicious-looking monsters. As it was, they retired sullenly into the deeper shadows, snarling and roaring defiance as they backed away, but not before Tandy had made an effective sketch of the whole group.

"'Tis a lucky thing for us that you're along!" grunted Ato, drawing his feet up out of the water and looking with grim disfavor after the snarling sea lions. "Likely as not, if you had not made that picture, Samuel would have tried to drag one along by its tail, regardless of our feelings or safety."

"A wild maned sea lion would be a valuable addition to any collection," sighed Samuel Salt, shaking his head regretfully. "But then—" He grinned in his sudden pleasant way. "Not much of a mascot at that."

The only other happening of note was Roger's capture of a monkey fish. Unable to overtake a flying fish, the Read Bird had pounced on this small combination of a land and water beast as it sat quietly sunning itself on the limb of a tree. Screaming and chattering, he bore it proudly down to the Captain, and Samuel was so pleased with the curious little creature that when Nikobo suggested going back, he made no serious objection. And as the hippopotamus, rather weary from her long swim, headed thankfully back for the ship, Tandy and Samuel made ambitious plans for the monkey fish's care and comfort. Thrusting it into Tandy's bird cage, Samuel regarded it with increasing enthusiasm and interest. "I'll rig up a wooden tree in one of the aquariums, set the aquarium in one of the large cages so it'll have both air and water, and call it `Roger' after its discoverer," beamed the former Pirate with a wink at Tandy.

"Don't you dare call that monkey fish after me," screeched the Read Bird, flying round to have another look at his strange prize. "Why, it's uglier than a blue monkey. Looks like a regular goblin, if you ask me." And to tell the truth, the monkey fish was even uglier than a goblin, shaped like a monkey but scaled all over and with unpleasant goggly eyes and three short spikes sticking out of its forehead.

"It does look like a goblin," agreed Tandy with an amused sniff. "But let's call it Mo-fi, which is short for fish and monkey."

"Tip tops'ls!" approved Samuel Salt, taking out his notebook. "Wonder what it eats?"

"Great grandmothers, what would it eat?" moaned Ato, looking blankly at Samuel. "Another mouth to feed and listen to! Dear, Dear and DEAR!"

"Oh, give it a box of animal crackers," put in Roger carelessly.

"No, I brought along some goldfish food for just such an emergency as this," declared Samuel, making a little flourish with his pencil as he wrote busily in his journal. "Goldfish food will be splendid for a monkey fish."

"Well, don't forget the bananas, for remember, it's a monkey, too," chirped Roger, settling on the Captain's shoulder to read what he had written. So, laughing and joking and in the highest good humor, the exploring party returned to the *Crescent Moon*. What with planting the slips from the sea tree, settling Mo-fi in his aquarium cage, pressing the leaves from the marine forest, and making copies and further notes about the sea lions in his journal, Samuel did not get his ship under way till late afternoon. Ramming into the sea tree, beyond scraping off some paint, had done little damage, so singing boisterously, Samuel finally heaved up his anchor. And soon, with Ato stirring up a huge clam chowder, Tandy painting the sea forest on the chart, and Roger scouring the hold for Mo-fi's fish food, the *Crescent Moon* again dipped adventurously into the southeast swell.

Chapter 14 - The Sea Unicorn!

"Ahoy! And how goes it with the able-bodied seaman?" called *Roger*, swooping down from the foremast. Tandy, polishing the brass trim on the binnacle, looked up with a welcoming grin.

"Tip topsails!" he answered, pausing a minute to stare off toward the skyline to see whether any islands or sea serpents were visible.

"And look at that muscle, now," marveled Roger, touching Tandy's arm admiringly with his claw. "You're twice the lad you were, Mate, and I'll wager my last feather you can lay any lubber by the heels. If anyone gets fresh-water ashore, remember you're a salt seagoing sailor and you just take a poke at him. That's my advice without any charge or obligation. But then again, a chap that's a King, the Royal Artist of an exploring expedition, with a sea forest named after him, might not need to take any advice at all," added Roger with a long and knowing wink.

"But I like you to tell me things," said Tandy, looking earnestly up at the Read Bird. "You make everything seem so interesting and jolly." With a secret smile, for Tandy was thinking how much he would enjoy taking a poke at Didjabo, the Chief Ozamandarin, the little boy went on with his polishing. If Didjabo said anything further about shutting him up in the Tower, he just plain would take a poke at him. But saying nothing of all this to Roger, he called up cheerfully, "How's Mo-fi? Has he stopped scolding and begun to eat?"

Roger, who was running races with himself up and down the taffrail, stopped short and held up his claw. "Everything I give him," he told Tandy solemnly. "And I declare to badness he's getting to know me, Mate. He only pulled out three feathers instead of a fistful when I gave him breakfast just now. Before long he'll be so tame he'll be riding around on your shoulder."

"Not MY shoulder," laughed Tandy, waving his bottle of polish at the Read Bird. "Goodness, I believe you're growing fond of that monkey fish, Roger."

"Well, why not?" retorted the Read Bird, puffing up his chest. "Ato has me, the Captain has Sally, you have Kobo, so why shouldn't I have a little pet if I want one?"

The monkey fish seemed such a strange, prickly sort of pet that Tandy could hardly keep his face straight, but seeing Roger was quite in earnest, he tactfully changed the subject. "Do you suppose we'll make any new discoveries today?" he asked, screwing the cap on the bottle of polish. "Any as important as the sea forest, I mean?"

"Why not call it by its proper name?" teased Roger, scratching his head with his left claw. "And I think it most unlikely we'll strike anything as curious and important as Tazander Forest. Two discoveries like that just couldn't happen two days running. Still, I'll just fly up to the main truck and have a look around."

"Main truck?" Tandy wrinkled up his brows. "I thought I knew all the parts of this ship by now. You never told me about the main truck, Roger."

"Just the top of the main mast, Brainless." Giving Tandy an affectionate little shove, Roger soared into the rigging, and Tandy went joyfully off to have another look at the forest Samuel had insisted on naming after him. He had taken great pains with the painting and printing when he sketched it on the map, and now with a sigh of complete satisfaction he stood regarding the sea chart. Then, suddenly remembering he had promised to water Samuel Salt's plants, he jog-trotted contentedly down to the hold. The tumbleweeds in their small red pots grew so rapidly, Samuel had to cut them back every day. These Tandy watered very sparingly, snapping his fingers at Mo-fi, who was gravely chinning himself on a branch of his artificial tree. The slips of the sea trees in their covered aquarium required no attention at all. Ato had planted all the vegetable and fruit vines from Peakenspire on the rail outside the galley, so that left only the creeping vines from Patrippany Island to care for. He had just picked up one of the small potted creepers when a sharp rap tap under his toes made Tandy leap straight up in the air. Someone was knocking on the bottom of the boat.

"Ato! Captain! ROGER!" shrilled the little boy, scurrying up from the hold faster than he had ever done before. "Su-su-SOMEBODY'S knocking on the bottom of the boat." Before he could explain or tell them anything further, a perfectly terrific knock from below made the *Crescent Moon* shiver from end to end. Samuel and Ato, leaning over the port rail, turned round so suddenly, they bumped their heads smartly together. Next, with a scrape, screech and splintering of timber, a giant white horn came tearing up through the decks.

"Whale! Whale!" croaked Roger, falling off the main truck and coasting crazily down to the deck. "Wha-what ever 'n ever's that?" he quavered, pointing a trembling claw at the rigid white column between the main and mizzen masts. Samuel did not even try to explain, for at that instant the ship began to rise, to fall, to lash and plunge both up and down and east and west. Hooking his arms through the rail, Tandy blinked, gasped and shudderingly waited for the *Crescent Moon* to fly asunder.

"Narwhal, Mates!" panted Samuel Salt, throwing himself bodily upon the wheel. "Horn like a—unicorn—branch of the Odontocetes and—"

"Oh — you — don't — say — it — is!" chattered Ato, who was lying on his stomach bouncing up and down like a ball at each frightful lunge of the monstrous fish. "Well, it's spiked us. Is that a horn or a ship's mast? Oh woe, oh! What'n salt'll we do now?"

Samuel had not the heart to answer, for he had all he could do to hang on to the wheel as the ship, like a wounded animal, reared and plunged, thrashing the sea to a fury of foam and spray. Nikobo, diving precipitously off her raft, began to squeal in high and low hippopotamy, making brave but ineffective lunges at the lashing giant beneath the ship.

"Su-suppose it su-submerges?" wailed Ato, who had managed at last to seize a rope from the end of which he banged and slammed continuously up and down against the deck. "Oh, my stars! Oh, my spars! Oh, my beams and—" Tandy never heard Ato's last anguished cry, for at that moment a savage shake of the Narwhal's head sent him flying into the sea. Coming up coughing and choking, Tandy instinctively began to swim and for the first time became aware of the creeping vine he still had clutched in one hand. And in that instant and in that whirl of danger, disaster and destruction, the little boy suddenly grew calm and purposeful. This vine — Well, why would this powerful vine from Patrippany Island not work as well under water as on land? The chances were that it would. Swimming boldly back to the ship, Tandy took a quick dive, hurling the vine, pot and all, in the general direction of the Narwhal. No sooner had the vine touched the water than it began to open, creep and grow, and spraying out a hundred strong tentacles, it seized and bound the plunging monster in a secure and inescap

able cradle of leafy wood.

Gasping and sputtering but with his heart pounding with joy to think he had really saved Samuel's beautiful ship, Tandy rose to the surface. Nikobo, letting off shrill blasts of anger and fright, came paddling anxiously toward him. But giving the hippopotamus a reassuring wave, Tandy seized the end of a rope ladder and pulled himself up to the deck. Samuel, though battered and bruised, still clung to the wheel, and Ato, almost pounded to a jelly, had rolled into the scuppers where Roger was fanning him vigorously with a butter paddle. The Read Bird, having wings, could have left the ship at any time, but had clung bravely to his post, preferring to go down with the ship and his shipmates. Now all three of them stared in dazed silence at Tandy as he climbed back over the rail, for in the terrible confusion and excitement, no one had seen him go overboard.

"Tandy! Tandy! Where've you been?" With outstretched arms, Samuel Salt rushed groggily forward. "Shiver my liver! Why's everything so quiet? Could it be that you single-handedly have destroyed that ship-shaking menace?"

"I don't think he's destroyed, Master Salt," answered Tandy, limping happily to meet the Captain, "but he's caught fast as a lobster in a lobster pot and can't move at all."

"Caught?" rasped Samuel, running across the deck to peer over the rail.

"By the creeping vine," explained Tandy, and in short, breathless sentences he told them all that had happened after he was flung into the sea.

"Well, bagpipe my mizzenmain sails!" gasped Samuel Salt, staring at Tandy with round eyes. "This is the strangest and happiest day of my life. You've saved the ship and the whole expedition, my boy, and all we have to do now is cut loose from this cavorting unicorn of the sea and sail off with the largest ivory horn in captivity. An ivory mast, blast my buckles! Wait till the Ozites see us sailing up the Winkie River with four masts instead of three! Ahoy, below! Ahoy, Kobo! Can you dive with me beneath this ship?"

"Dive and stay under as long as you can," vowed the hippopotamus, shaking the water out of her eyes and looking cheerily up at the Captain. "You see, I was right about those creeping vines, now wasn't I?" Nikobo, having done a little investigating on her own account, was well nigh ready to burst with pride at Tandy's quick action and the way in which the vines had overcome their gigantic foe.

"RIGHT!" boomed Samuel Salt, hurrying off for his oxygen helmet and powerful diamond-toothed saw. Ato was too bruised and exhausted to rise, but Tandy and Roger, perching on the ship's rail, watched Samuel in his queer diver's helmet climb down the rope ladder and clamber up on the hippopotamus. Next minute Nikobo had disappeared under the surface, and presently from the slight shiver and shake of the boat they knew that Samuel was determinedly at work cutting them loose. Fortunately, there was room between the ship's bottom and the whale's head for Nikobo to swim about, and so splintering sharp was Samuel's saw that in less than five minutes he had cut off the great column of ivory level with the ship's bottom, carefully caulking the edges with material he had brought down.

In its tight and live wood crate, the Narwhal could not stir an inch, and while the cutting of its horn was not painful, it blubbered and spouted so terrifically that Samuel and Nikobo heaved tremendous sighs of relief when the dangerous operation was accomplished. Backing off a few paces, Nikobo began butting the crated sea beast with her head till she had driven it out from beneath the boat. Roger and Tandy, with little shrieks of wonder and excitement, saw the crated fish, like some queer and monstrous mummy, rise to the surface and go floating sullenly away toward the east. Now that they had a full view of the Narwhal, they saw that it was three times the length of the *Crescent Moon*.

"A great wonder Sammy didn't tie it to the ship and tow it along," sighed Ato, who had at last got to his feet and draped himself weakly over the rail. "Some fishin', eh Mates?"

"But look at the beautiful mast we have!" cried Tandy, waving to Nikobo and the Captain as they came cheerfully alongside.

197

"Huh! You're as bad as Sammy," grunted Ato, rubbing his bruises sorrowfully. "And of course a mast was just what we were needing! Whale of a mast! Mast of a whal! HUH!"

Chapter 15 - The Collector is Collected

"What are you going to call this one?" inquired Tandy next morning as he and Samuel squinted thoughtfully up at the gleaming ivory column between the main and mizzenmasts.

"Might call it the whalemast," said Samuel, rubbing his chin reflectively. "And it's a lucky thing for us the point was sharp enough to cut through the decks without damaging the ship. At any rate, it's given us the biggest fish story a voyager ever had to relate. Tossed on the horns of a Narwhal! And the best part of the whole story is that we have the proof right along with us. Hah! Right here!" Samuel in his glee and exuberance gave the whalemast a hearty slap.

"Kobo says that vine won't unwind for a couple of days, but anyway it'll be a fine rest for the whale floating around without having to swim. And I expect it can grow another horn."

"I expect so," agreed Samuel, winking down at Sally, who was standing on her head in the bowl of his pipe. "If this little Lady would just talk, she could give us a heap of valuable information about life in Lavaland, Mate."

"Roger's taught Mo-fi to say `Ship ahoy!'" observed Tandy, strolling over to the rail to watch the white foam sweep past the ship's side. "And your sea tree sprays have grown an inch since yesterday, Captain."

"They have?" Samuel blew three rings from his pipe, then walked aft to glance at the compass. "Well, my boy, if the rest of the voyage is as good as the beginning, we'll sail home loaded to the gun'ls." The mention of home always made Tandy wince, for the *Crescent Moon* was the first real home he had known. To think that he would be put ashore in Ozamaland while Samuel's ship would continue its adventurous voyage of discovery without him was a fact almost too terrible to consider.

"Maybe we'll never come to Ozamaland at all," mused Tandy as he climbed into the rigging to join Roger. "Maybe the Captain's reckoning is wrong and Ozamaland is to the north instead of the south." Vastly comforted by this idea, Tandy swung nimbly to the crosstree on the fore t'gallant mast. Roger was staring intently through Ato's telescope, and as Tandy squirmed along to a position beside him, the Read Bird let out a shrill squall, all his head feathers standing straight on end.

"What do you see? What is it?" cried the little King, shading his eyes with his hands and staring in all directions. "I can't see a thing."

"Take the glasses," urged Roger, handing them over with a frightened gulp. "Take the glasses and then tell me it isn't so." Tandy, scarcely knowing what to expect, screwed his eye close to the telescope, then he, too, gave a shriek of consternation.

"Why, it's a big HOLE, a HOLE in the sea!" he stuttered, lowering the glasses and staring at the Read Bird in blank dismay.

"Exactly!" croaked the Read Bird, "and whoever heard of such a thing? A hole in the ground, certainly, but a hole in the sea? Why, that's just plain past believing. Ahoy, DECK AHOY!" Wagging his head, Roger lifted his voice in a long warning wail. "Heave to, Master Salt! Heave to! Danger on the bow!"

Somewhat surprised, but without stopping to question Roger, in whom he had the utmost confidence, Samuel hove his vessel to. And not a moment too soon, for barely a ship's length away yawned an immense and unexplainable hole in the sea. Round its edges the waves frothed, tossed and bubbled, making no impression on that quiet, curious vacuum of air. Crowding into the bow, the ship's company stared down in complete wonder and mystification. "Now, goosewing my topsails, this'll bear looking into!" puffed Samuel, breaking the silence at last.

"Now, now, NOW!" Ato snatched wildly at Samuel's coattails as he raced aft, bellowing loudly for Kobo to come alongside. "You'll not go a step off this boat. We can sail round this air hole and no damage is done, but as for looking into it! Help, HELP! Avast and belay and I'll knock eight bells out of anyone who leaves this ship!" Seizing an iron belaying pin, Ato made a desperate rush after Samuel Salt, and failing to catch him before he slid down the cable to Kobo's raft, he grabbed Tandy firmly and angrily by the seat of the pants. "Not a step!" panted the ship's cook savagely. "Not a step! Roger! Roger! Come back here this instant."

But Roger, with a screech of defiance, had already flown down after Samuel. Tandy, pinned against the rail by Ato's two hundred and fifty pounds, was forced to watch Nikobo, with Roger and Samuel on her back, moving cautiously toward the edge of the air hole. Over his shoulder, Samuel had a huge coil of rope, the end of which he had attached to the capstan of the boat before he dropped over the side. "Oh! Oh! And OH!" wheezed the ship's cook. "If

Sammy goes down that cavern we're as good as lost. No one to navigate, to up sail or down sail or lay to in a storm. My, my and MY land!"

"Well, there he goes!" cried Tandy as Samuel flung the rope down in to the sea hole. "Don't worry, Ato, he's always come back before, hasn't he? Let me go! Let me go, I tell you!" With a sudden jerk, Tandy tore out of Ato's grasp, climbed up on the rail, and dove into the sea. Swimming rapidly toward the hippopotamus, he climbed on her back, and with Roger fluttering in excited circles overhead Nikobo swam as close to the edge of the sea hole as she dared, watching in terrified fascination as Samuel calmly lowered himself into the clouded blue depths. With mingled feelings of interest and alarm, Tandy saw the Royal Explorer of Oz go down lower and lower and finally disappear altogether into the deep blue air below. Now not a glimpse of Samuel was visible and not a sound came up to reassure them that he was still there.

"I'll just fly down and see what's up," quavered Roger, and in spite of the loud shouts and threats of Ato on the *Crescent Moon*, the Read Bird spread his wings and coasted slowly and bravely into the immense air shaft. Nikobo, now as alarmed as the ship's cook, began swimming frantically round the edge of the misty chasm, letting out piercing blasts that sounded like nothing so much as a ferryboat whistle. Tandy himself felt uneasy and frightened, and Ato, unable to bear the suspense any longer, climbed over the side and came swimming out to join them. After an endless fifteen minutes during which dreadful fear and premonition gripped the watchers, the head of the Read Bird popped mournfully into view.

"Is he all right? Where's Sammy? What in soup's he doing? What'd you find out?" gasped Ato, reaching out to clutch Roger by the wing. Roger, limp and bedraggled, with all the stiffness out of his feathers, said nothing for a whole minute.

Then, beating his wings together, he began to scream out hoarsely, "The Captain's caught! The Collector's collected. They have Master Salt forty fathoms below. They've got him shut up, I mean down at the bottom of the sea like a goldfish in a bowl, only he's in a big bowl of air. They're poking little fish and crabs through a trap door in the air shaft, and I cannot break or even make a dent in the transparent slide they've shot across the air hole to shut him off from us. And oh, my bill and feathers! Every time they open the trap door to shove things in to him, water rushes into the vacuum. He's standing in water to his knees now, and unless we can break a hole in that lid, the Captain's done for — done for, do you hear?"

"They?" asked Tandy, while Nikobo's eyes almost popped out of her head. "Who do you mean?"

"Oh, oh, don't ASK me!" choked the poor Read Bird. "They're not fish and they're not men. They're about the size of Tandy, here, sort of stiff and jellied and perfectly transparent. On a shell hanging outside of one of their caves it said `Seeweegia.'"

"Seeweegia!" moaned Ato, clutching his head in both hands. "Let me see! Let me see! What's to be done, boys? Now quick! What's to be done?"

"Have Roger fetch the saw we used on the whale's horn," gurgled Nikobo.

"And I'll climb down and saw a hole in that slide," cried Tandy eagerly.

"No, I'll climb down," said Ato firmly. "I've known Sammy the longest, and if he's going to come to a watery end I might as well end with him." Leaving the two arguing, Roger flashed back to the ship, returning in almost no time with the scintillating and powerful saw. Tandy had meanwhile convinced Ato that he could climb down the rope faster, being so much lighter, and now, with tears in their eyes, Nikobo and the ship's cook saw Tandy and Roger disappear into the air shaft.

Tandy let himself down carefully hand over hand, Roger keeping abreast of him with the saw. To slide rapidly to the bottom would have been quicker, but the resulting blisters would make it difficult to use the saw. Forty fathoms, nearly two hundred and forty feet, is a long way to go hand over hand on a rope, and before he reached the glass-like slide, Tandy's palms stung and his shoulders ached and burned from the strain.

But at last he was down, and dropping to his hands and knees with Roger mourning and muttering beside him, Tandy peered fearfully through the glassy substance. For a moment everything was a green and misty blur, but gradually the figure of Samuel Salt standing sturdily in the middle of the air bowl became visible. Although waist high in sea water and surrounded by loathsome sea creatures and crabs the Seeweegians had tossed in for him to eat, Samuel was making slow and interested entries in his journal.

Pressed against the sides of his strange aquarium, Tandy could see the round, square and triangular faces of the jellyfish men and women. Brilliantly colored vines and seaweed waved and tossed in the current. The floor of the ocean was covered with bright shells, polished stones and all manner of sparkling deep-sea jewels. Had Tandy not been so worried about Samuel Salt, he would have liked nothing better than sketching this strange and beautiful undersea Kingdom with the Seeweegians flopping and swimming busily in and out of their grottoes and caves, or disporting themselves in the seaweed forests. But as it was, his only thought was of quickly freeing the Captain of the *Crescent Moon* from his curious prison.

"Look, they've put up a sign," hissed Roger, handing over the saw. Looking in the direction indicated by Roger, Tandy saw an immense shell on which long wisps of seaweed had been arranged to form the words:

COME SEE THE CURIOUS HIGH AIR MANSTER
ADMISSION 1 PEARL 5 CORALS AND A CLAM.

The sight of this sign swinging from a small sea tree close to Samuel's air bowl sent a wave of rage up Tandy's back. Rubbing his palms briskly together, the little boy seized the saw and struck it with all his might against the unyielding surface of the slide. The noise attracted Samuel's attention, and looking up he began waving his arms, yelling out wild orders and commands. Not being able to hear any of them and being quite sure Samuel was telling them to leave the air shaft before the Seeweegians shot another slide over their heads and caught them, too, Tandy proceeded grimly with his task.

Roger helped, scraping away with both claws and bill. For five desperate minutes they worked without success, then a tiny crack split the slide from edge to edge. Wedging the saw into the narrow opening, Tandy began sawing away like a little wild man, for a fresh batch of snails and crabs tossed into Samuel had let in another rush of sea water. Immersed to his chin, Samuel started to swim round and round, dodging the end of the saw as it flashed up and down above his head.

"Oh!" gasped Tandy, stopping a moment to blow on his fingers. "I'll never be able to make this opening large enough. Look, look, Roger, they're opening that trap door again. Oh, oh! I can't bear it!"

"Help! Help!" yelled the Read Bird, looking despairingly up the empty air shaft. "Help, for the love of sea salt and sailor men!" His cry, increased by the curious nature of the compressed air in the air shaft, increased a hundredfold and fell with a hideous roar upon the anguished ears of Ato and Nikobo. Almost instinctively and without thought of her own safety or Ato's or the dire consequences, the hippopotamus jumped bodily into the sea hole. Roger, still glaring upward, had a quick flash of an immense falling object.

Realizing at once what had happened, the Read Bird had just time to snatch Tandy and drag him to the opposite side of the slide before Nikobo landed, broke through the thick glass, plunged into Samuel's aquarium and shot out through the side into a group of horrified Seeweegians. Now do not suppose for an instant that Tandy, Roger or Samuel himself saw all this happen. Indeed, after Nikobo struck the slide, none of them remembered a thing, for the ocean, rushing in through the puncture the hippopotamus had made in the vacuum, rose like a tidal wave, carrying them tumultuously along.

Nikobo came up at a little distance from the others, with Ato, completely wrapped and entangled in seaweed, clinging tenaciously to her harness and looking like some queer marine specimen himself. Too shocked and stunned to swim, the five shipmates bobbed up and down like corks on the surface of the sea. Then Roger, spreading his wet and bedraggled wings and coughing violently from all the salt water he had swallowed, started dizzily back to the *Crescent Moon*. Nikobo had several long gashes in her tough hide, but still managed to grin at Tandy. "I — I must have lost the saw," panted the little boy, pulling himself wearily up on her back.

"Never mind the saw. I still have my journal, and look what I caught!" puffed Samuel Salt, dragging himself up on the other side of the hippopotamus. "Ship ahoy, Mates, a live and perfect specimen of a jellyfish boy." Holding up his prize, Samuel smiled blandly, all his danger and discomfort apparently forgotten.

"Oh, my eyes, ears and whiskers!" quavered Ato, peering out of his net of seaweed. "Is it for this we've been scraping our noses on the sea bottom?" Nodding cheerfully, Samuel plunged the squirming and transparent little water boy under the surface, holding him there as Nikobo swam slowly and painfully back to the ship.

Chapter 16 - The Storm!

Tandy was so exhausted from his dreadful experiences at the bottom of the sea hole he spent the rest of the morning flat on his stomach on deck making lively sketches from memory of the City of Seeweegia. Of the sea hole itself not a sign nor vestige remained. The sea, tumbling through the breach made by Nikobo, had closed it up forever and ever. Ato had Roger fetch bandages and witch hazel down to the raft, and it took him two hours to bind up the cuts and hurts of the faithful hippopotamus. Then, climbing wearily up the rope ladder to the deck, he spent another hour rubbing himself with oil and liniment, muttering darkly about reckless collectors who got themselves and their shipmates collected.

"What would WE have done if you'd never got out of that air bowl?" scolded Ato, waving the bottle of liniment at the Captain, who was cheerfully changing into dry clothes. "You know I know nothing about navigation, nor one sail from t'other."

"Ah, but what you know about sauces!" retorted Samuel, rolling his eyes rapturously. "Of course, I'll grant a ship cannot sail on its stomach, but if the worst had come to the worst, you could have left a note for the sails on the binnacle. `If it comes up a blow, tie yourselves up.' Ha, ha! Tie yourselves UP!" Jamming his feet into his boots, Samuel blew a kiss to his still muttering shipmate and tramped down to the hold to settle his jel

lyfish boy in one of the large aquariums.

The water boy, about half the size of Tandy, was a jolly enough looking specimen, but kept opening and shutting his mouth like a fish and staring anxiously from his captor to Mo-fi in the cage opposite. Whistling happily and unmindful of the cuts and bruises he had suffered, Samuel filled the bottom of the aquarium with pebbles and shells, put in several seaweed plants he'd fished up in the nets, and soon had the little stranger as happy and cozy as a clam. Giving him and Mo-fi a wafer of fish food, the Royal Explorer of Oz went above to have a look at the weather, for he did not like the way the ship was pitching.

In spite of the desperately fatiguing morning they had had, it seemed the voyagers were in for some further excitement. The sky had grown dark and threatening. Dark clouds in ever-increasing numbers scudded along from the east; the sea, rough and angry, was full of racing little whitecaps. Nikobo's raft plunged and rocketed up and down like a bucking bronco, flinging the hippopotamus from side to side and bringing her with squealing protests up against the rail first on one side and then on the other.

Fearing for her safety, Samuel with Tandy's help rigged a temporary derrick to the mizzenmast, hove his vessel to, and bidding Nikobo swim round to the side, cleverly hoisted her to the main deck by a hook caught through her harness. Nikobo took it all quite calmly, coming down with a thankful little grunt, glad to be with her shipmates in the gale that was lashing the sea into a rolling, tossing fury of mounting gray water and foam.

The wind had risen now almost to hurricane proportions, and taking in all sail and with only a tarpaulin lashed in the main rigging, Samuel prepared with bared poles to ride out the storm. Ato, always ready and helpful in a crisis, trudged up and down the heaving decks with pails of hot soup and coffee, and after a hasty lunch, all hands fell to closing ports, battening hatches and removing from the decks all loose gear and equipment. As it was impossible to shove Nikobo through the door of the main cabin, Samuel lashed her tightly to the mizzenmast, and with an old sail round her shoulders the hippopotamus anxiously watched the mountainous waves breaking over the bow and running down into the scuppers.

It was all so wild and new, so dangerous and exciting, Tandy begged Samuel to let him stay on deck. Much against his better judgment, Samuel finally gave his consent, tying Tandy fast to Nikobo and the mizzenmast. If anything happened to the ship, reflected Samuel, fighting his way back to the wheel, the hippopotamus could keep Tandy afloat and take care of him besides.

Ato and Roger, not being needed on deck and not caring for storms, shut themselves up in the main cabin for a game of checkers. But checkers and board soon flew through the air, and the two had all they could do to hang on to their chairs as the *Crescent Moon* pitched headlong into the cavernous hollows and struggled up the mountainous ridges of the great running seas.

Chapter 17 - The Old Man of The Jungle!

In the splendid white marble Palace in the splendid White City of Ozamaland, the nine Ozamandarins sat in solemn conference.

"This time we have succeeded," stated Didjabo, chief of the nine Judges of the realm. "This time we have succeeded, and our plans may now be accomplished. Last time, we merely destroyed the King and Queen, neglecting to do away with the Royal Offspring, Tazander Tazah, and for that reason we failed utterly. So long as this boy survived, the natives insisted on considering him their rightful King and Ruler. But, hah! That prophecy we invented about an aunt carrying him off was a clever and useful idea, eh my fellow Zamians? Now as the child, with a little help on our part it must be confessed, has really been carried off and destroyed, we can blame these same silly females, and they and all the royal family can be tossed into the sea to pay for this heinous crime. Ha, ha! Quite an idea, a famous idea!" murmured

Didjabo, and the eight Ozamandarins nodded their narrow heads in complete and satisfied agreement. "Leaving the throne clear for us, the Nine Faithful Servants of the People!" Again the Ozamandarins nodded, but Didjabo, slanting his cruel little eyes up and down the long table, was already making plans to destroy the lot of them and have the whole great country for himself.

"But how can we be sure the boy is destroyed and out of the way?" questioned Lotho, the second Ozamandarin in point of rank and power.

"Because," Didjabo curled up his lip in a hard little smile, "the Old Man of the Jungle has brought us proof. Boglodore! BOGLODORE! It is our wish that you appear before us."

At Didjabo's call there was a slight rustle and stir behind the curtains in the doorway, and an immense, wrinkled old native clad only in a turban and loin cloth stepped noiselessly into the Chamber of Justice. Without waiting for further orders, Boglodore began in a high, dismal, droning voice: "Following the commands of the highest among you, I, Boglodore the Magician, did carry off on my famous, never-known or seen flying umbrellaphant, the heir and small King of this country, coming down after two days on Patrippany Island.

"Not wishing to destroy the boy with my own hands, I left him to the wild beasts and savage Leopard Men known to inhabit this island. That, as you know, was five months and two weeks ago. Having just returned from a second flight to the Island, where I found no trace or sign of the boy, I can safely assure you that he is no more, that he has undoubtedly been killed by the savages or the wild beasts of the jungle." There was not a trace of pity or remorse on the cruel, flat faces of his listeners as Boglodore finished this shameful recital.

"In that case, there is nothing left to do but punish the royal aunts and family, issue a proclamation of our accession to power, and divide up the Kingdom," mused Lotho, drumming thoughtfully on the table with his long, skinny fingers.

"But do not forget my reward," wheezed Boglodore firmly. "For this cruel and infamous deed I was promised one tenth of Ozamaland, and I am here to claim as my share the entire jungle reach of this country." Extending his arms, the old man of the jungle advanced threateningly toward the long table.

"Ha, ha! Just listen to him now," sneered Didjabo, gathering up his papers and looking insolently across at the angry native. "Have a care what you say, fellow. Too much of this and you'll go over the cliff with the royal relatives. Now then, clear out! Your work is done! If you ever set foot in this city again, you shall be trampled beneath the feet of the royal elephants!"

"Ah-hhh!" Boglodore recoiled as if he had been confronted by a poisonous reptile. "So that's to be the way of it? Aha! Very good! I will go. But do not think this is the end! It is but the beginning!" Snapping his fingers under the long noses of the Ozamandarins, the old man, not bothering with the door, leapt out the window and vanished into the garden.

"Do you think that was quite wise?" questioned Teebo, third in rank of the Ozamandarins. "This fellow and his flying elephant are dangerous and may do us a world of harm."

"Do not forget, anything he says will involve himself, and he'll have a hard time proving to the people that it was on my orders the young King was carried off."

"Oh, hush!" warned Lotho, glancing nervously over his shoulder. "Not another word!" Shrugging his shoulders and rising to indicate that the meeting was over, Didjabo started pompously for the door. "I will go now to prepare a Royal Proclamation explaining that as the young King has not after exhaustive search been found or located, the authority and governing power of the state shall pass to us, the Nine Faithful Ozamandarins of the Realm! We can then meet again and here in this star-and-barred Chamber of Justice divide the Kingdom among us."

"Very well, but see that you remember it is to be divided!" Staring fixedly at Didjabo, Lotho strode away, colliding violently at the door with a small, breathless page who was entering on a veritable gallop.

"Your Honors! Your Ozamandarin Majesties!" shrilled the boy, wildly waving his trumpet instead of blowing upon it. "A ship. There is a ship with four masts beneath the chalk cliffs, a strange ship with full sail is riding into our harbor."

"There, there, don't shout!" snapped Didjabo, seizing the boy roughly by the shoulders. "Go back at once and discover what flag this ship flies from her masthead. Quickly now. RUN!"

"What could it mean? Where could it be from? Such a thing has never happened before!" muttered the others, hastening over to the long windows.

"Confoundation!" raged Didjabo as the page with frightened stutters turned and ran out of the Hall of Justice. "This ruins everything. Who are these meddling foreigners? And why do they have to arrive now of all times? NOW! Lotho! Teebo! Call out the camel corps and the white elephant guard. Have them drawn up in war formation on the chalk cliffs. You others!" Impatiently, Didjabo waved his arms at the six remaining Ozamandarins. "See to the defense of the palace! If these meddlers set foot upon our territory, they are to be trampled upon, trampled upon — do you understand?"

Nodding with fierce and cruel determination, the eight tall Keepers of the White City set about carrying out Didjabo's orders. Didjabo, hurrying up to the highest tower in the castle, looked through his telescope to see what manner of ship had come sailing out of the west to spoil or postpone his well-laid plans.

Chapter 18 - A New Country

Driven by the pitiless wind, pounded by the merciless seas, the Crescent Moon rode before the gale, coming toward morning into quiet waters at last. The sky, now pale grey instead of black, showed a small, single star in the east, and with a huge sigh of weariness and relief, Samuel let go the anchor and bade his crew turn in all standing. This they were only too glad to do, sleeping heavily and thankfully in their clothes, Nikobo still wrapped in her sail snoring like a whole band of music beneath the mizzenmast.

Tandy, to whom the storm had been a thrilling adventure, was the first to waken. Still stiff and bruised from the pounding he had taken as the *Crescent Moon* tossed and pitched in the terrible seas, he sprang eagerly out of his bunk, curious to know where the storm had carried them. The morning mists, lifting like a shimmering veil or the curtain of a stage on some new and strange scene, showed a long, white line of chalk cliffs to the east, and beyond the cliffs the dim outline of a great and splendid city.

With joy and lively expectations Tandy had run out on deck, but now, after a long look over the port rail, he crept silently and soberly back to his cabin, closing the door softly behind him. Later, as the sun rose higher and his shipmates awoke, the excited screams of Nikobo and Roger and the eager voices of Samuel and Ato told him that they too had seen the bright land beyond the cliffs. Already Samuel was clewing up his sail, and above the rattle in the rigging Tandy could hear the rasp of the anchor cable as it came winding over the side. But he only bent lower over the fat book in his lap, and when the Read Bird, loudly calling his name, came hurtling through the porthole, he did not even look up.

"Land! Land and MORELAND!" croaked Roger, dancing up and down on the foot of the bunk. "None of your pesky islands this time, but a whole, long, new continent. What in salt's the matter, youngster; this is no time to be a-reading! Come on, come on, the Captain's looking for you!" As Roger peered sharply down at the book in Tandy's lap, two tears splashed on the open page. Quickly brushing two more off his nose, the ship's cabin boy unwillingly met the puzzled gaze of the Read Bird.

"Roger," demanded Tandy in a smothered and unsteady voice, "which is most important, being a King or being a person?" Roger, his head on one side, considered this for a moment, and then spoke quickly.

"Well, you can't be a good King without being a good person, so I should say being a good person is most important."

"But it says here," with a furious sniff Tandy put his finger on the middle paragraph of the page, "'In no circumstances and for no reason may a King forsake his country nor desert his countrymen.'"

"What's that? What's this? Humph! *Maxims for Monarchs.* Well, what in topsails do we care for that musty volume?" Giving the book a vicious shove, Roger, forgetting how much he had formerly praised Ato's fat volume, fluttered down on Tandy's shoulder. "So THAT'S it!" he burst out explosively. "This pernicious country yonder is Ozamaland. Well, we can't spare you, and that's final. They didn't know how to treat a good King when they had one, now let 'em practice on somebody else. Say the word, m'lad, and we'll put about and sail away as fast as a good ship can take us! CAPTAIN! Master Salt! Deck ahoy! All hands 'HOY!" Without waiting for Tandy's answer, Roger skimmed through the port and winged over to the Captain.

"Wait! Wait!" sputtered Tandy, hurrying aft where the officers and crew of the *Crescent Moon* were now engaged in earnest conversation. "Don't you remember you wanted some of those creeping birds and flying reptiles, Captain? Well, this is the place!" puffed the little boy, waving his arm toward the cliffs. "This is Ozamaland, and I've got to go ashore. It's really all right," he continued earnestly as Samuel began unhappily rubbing his chin. "It's been a grand voyage, and I've learned a lot, but a King has to stick to his post, hasn't he?"

"Not all the time," snapped Ato, giving his belt an indignant jerk. "You stuck to your post, and they stuck you in a tower and then in a pigpen in the jungle. So what do you owe them? Nothing, say I, absolutely nothing!"

But Samuel Salt, regretful as he was to lose this handy young artist and cabin boy, felt that Tandy must decide the matter for himself. "If you're as good a King as you are a seaman, I'm not the one to hold you back," he sighed sorrowfully. "But just let these lubbers start any more nonsense, and I'll give them a taste of the rope. HAH! And we'll not be leaving you till everything's shipshape, and you can lay to that!"

"I'm not leaving you at all," snorted Nikobo, lumbering hugely over to Tandy and almost flattening him against the port rail. "I'll miss this ship worse'n the river, and Ato's cooking and the Captain's stories and Roger's jokes, but wherever Tandy goes I go, and that's flat!"

"Just plain noddling nonsense, putting him ashore," fumed Ato angrily. "He's not old enough to manage these wild tribesmen and scheming aristocrats. Besides, we need him on this expedition, and you know it." Samuel, sighing deeply, smiled at Tandy, and Tandy, sighing just as deeply, smiled back.

"Never you mind," promised the former Pirate with a wink that somehow lacked conviction, "there'll be other voyages!" And seizing the wheel, he began tacking in toward Tandy's homeland. But he had lost all pleasure and interest in charting for the first time on any map the long continent of Tazara and adding strange animals and plants to his ever-growing collection. Losing Tandy spoiled the whole expedition for him, and by taking longer and wider tacks he delayed their landing to the latest possible moment.

But at last they were in the very shadow of the chalk cliffs and with no further excuse for not going ashore. Nikobo had agreed to carry them and had abruptly heaved herself overboard, sending up a fountain of spray as high as the ship itself when she struck the water, thus astonishing no end the watchers on the bank. Tandy, after running down to the hold to say goodbye to Mo-fi and have a last look at the jellyfish boy, regretfully joined the others at the port rail.

Having brought nothing aboard the *Crescent Moon*, he insisted on leaving in the same way, soberly waving aside all the gifts and presents Ato and Samuel sought to press upon him. Clad only in the leopard skin he had worn on Patrippany Island, he swung nimbly down the rope ladder. The Captain and the cook, in honor of Tandy's homecoming, had donned their finest shore-going togs, and Samuel, with a scimitar in his teeth, and Ato, armed as usual with his bread knife and a package he refused to explain, followed him more slowly down the ladder. Then they all climbed aboard the hippopotamus.

Roger, flying ahead with some Oz flags just for luck, could not help comparing the brown, hard-muscled young seaman with the skinny, fretful boy they had taken on at Patrippany Island. Trying to comfort himself with Tandy's improved health and spirits, he looked curiously at the great company assembled on the cliffs. All of the Nobles and their families in flowing white robes were present, and many of the turbanned tribesmen who happened to be in the capital had gathered to see for themselves the first ship that had ever touched the shore of Ozamaland. Beyond the Nobles and natives, Roger could see row on row of white guards mounted on enormous white elephants and snow-white camels.

"Trouble, trouble, nothing but trouble!" snorted the Read Bird drearily to himself. Tandy, familiar with the whole coast, guided Nikobo to the only possible spot for landing, and grunting and mumbling the hippopotamus hauled herself up on the rocks, glancing sharply and suspiciously at the little boy's subjects. A narrow path wound and curved up through the cliffs, and puffing and panting Nikobo finally made her way to the top, where she stood uncertainly facing the milling multitude.

"Hail and greetings!" called Samuel Salt, raising his arm to attract their attention, for the crowd looked both dangerous and unfriendly. "We are here to return to you safe and sound your lost King, Tazander Tazah, rescued by us from the wild jungle of Patrippany Island."

"King? King?" shrilled a dozen shrill and unbelieving voices. "Where? Where?" And everyone craned his neck to get a better view of Nikobo and her three curious riders. "Is it really our lost and stolen Kinglet?"

"Yes!" cried Tandy, springing erect. "I am Tazander Tazah, King's son and son of a King's son. You are my lawful subjects, and Ozamaland is my Kingdom!" A little shiver of excitement ran through the crowd at these words.

"He does in truth resemble our young ruler," murmured one Noble to another, "though much stronger and more bold." Drawing a long sword, he waved it imperiously above his head. "Summon the Ozamandarins," he called loudly. "They will decide whether this be our King or some small Imposter, and DEATH to all strangers and enemies who come in ships to lay waste our realm."

"Oh, hold your tongue!" advised Ato, settling himself more comfortably between Nikobo's shoulders. "Who are you to challenge the Royal Explorer of Oz, the King of the Octagon Isle—"

"And his Royal Read Bird," piped Roger, flying savagely round and round the head of the speaker.

"Yes, who are you to challenge the rightful ruler of Ozamaland?" cried Tandy, folding his arms and gazing calmly out over the curious throng.

"Hi, is this the young slip they kept locked in the tower? Hoo, hoo!" yelled an old tribesman, brandishing his long lance. "He's the salt of the sea and the sand of the desert. Shame on you, Zamon, not to recognize and welcome your young King. I'm for you, young one, down to my last breath!"

In spite of these brave words, the nobles, natives and guards made no move or motion to let Nikobo pass through. Then suddenly there was a break in the crowd, and the nine square-hatted Ozamandarins stepped rigidly forward. And nine taller, thinner, meaner-visaged rogues, decided Samuel, lovingly fingering his scimitar, it had never been his misfortune to encounter. Didjabo, recognizing Tandy at once in spite of his new and seamanlike beari

ng, was the first to speak.

"The blessing of the stars, moon and sun upon you!" cried the wily chief, bowing rapidly ten times in succession. "And upon these strangers who have brought you safely back to these shores! Welcome, most welcome, small King and ruler of the Ozamanders!" Speaking calmly but with black fury in his heart to have his plans so unexpectedly thwarted, Didjabo advanced rapidly toward Nikobo. "And now that you are here and really safe, we must see that you are locked securely in the White Tower of the Wise Man away from all future hurt and harm!" Reaching the side of the hippopotamus, he put up his hand to help Tandy dismount.

"I'm not going back to the Tower!" said Tandy, looking the Chief Ozamandarin straight in the eye. "Ever! I'm riding on to the castle, so kindly order some refreshments for my friends and shipmates."

"Hi, yi, yi!" approved the old tribesman, pounding the cliff with his lance. "Here's a King for us. What good did your Tower do before, old Square-Hat? He was carried off in spite of it, wasn't he? Well, trot along now and do as he says; he's the King, and I'm here to see he gets his rights!" Shocked by the determination in Tandy's voice and the evident delight of the crowd at his defiance, Didjabo put up his hand for silence.

"It is the law of the land that the nine Ozamandarins shall guard the life and preserve the health of the country's sovereign," stated Didjabo in his cold and impressive voice. "Until this boy becomes of age he must be cared for and protected from his enemies. Forward, guards! On to the Tower! You OTHERS!" Didjabo nodded disagreeably at Samuel Salt, Ato, Roger and Nikobo. "You others may return to your ship, where a suitable reward will be sent out to you. We are deeply indebted to you for finding our King, but the law of Ozamaland says that all foreigners landing on our shores shall be instantly and without delay be flung over the cliffs. In your case we graciously permit you to leave. Come, Tazander!"

While Samuel Salt could not help admiring the way the old Ozamandarin was trying to keep the upper hand, he had no intention of leaving till he had assured himself that Tandy was in safe and proper hands. "But surely you will wish to hear the story of how we found this boy and explain how he happened to be on that jungle island!" observed Samuel mildly. "Step back, my good fellow, Nikobo has large feet, and she just might happen to tread on you."

"Yes," wheezed Nikobo sullenly, "I must might happen to do that very thing." Slipping round to the other side of the hippopotamus, Didjabo, paying no attention to either remark, tried to pull Tandy to the ground. But the little boy, remembering Roger's advice about lubbers, gave him a fast and sudden poke in the nose that sent his hat flying off and the Ozamandarin himself rolling head over heels.

"Hurray, hurray! Avast and belay! And down with old Square-Hats forever!" shrilled the Read Bird, while Ato and Samuel exchanged a proud and pleased glance. While the other Ozamandarins stood uncertainly, the crowd, long weary of the rigid rule of the nine judges, began to laugh and cheer.

"The King is King! Long live the King!" shouted the old tribesman vociferously.

But Didjabo, pulling himself furiously to his feet, flung up his arm. "Guards! Guards!" he screeched venomously. "Do your work! Save this poor, misguided child from these unspeakable foreigners, or we are all lost. Can you not see they are savages, sorcerers and enemies? Seize the King and over the cliff with these hippopotamic invaders!"

Chapter 19 - Boglodore's Revenge

The word "hippopotamic" seemed to rouse the undecided guards to action, and Samuel, as the crowd moved uneasily aside to let the elephant- and

camel-mounted guardsmen through, heartily wished himself back on the ship. Nikobo, squealing with rage and defiance, began moving cautiously back toward the path down the cliffs. But Ato, who had been merely biding his time, tore open his package and began tossing right and left the tumbleweeds and creeping vines which fortunately it had contained.

The first creeper caught Didjabo, bound him up and laid him by the heels before he could issue another order. Taking careful aim, Ato threw a creeping vine at each of the other Ozamandarins. The tumbleweeds, whirling beneath the feet of the elephants and camels, caused them to fall to their knees, tossing their riders over their heads, and between the yells of the guards, the squeals of the camels, and trumpeting of the elephants, confusion was terrific. The natives and Nobles and all who could still move or run set off at top speed for the city without once looking behind them. Muttering angrily under his breath, Ato continued to hurl vines and tumbleweeds till none was left. Unable to advance an inch, the white guards and their mounts rolled and groveled together in the deep sand.

"Now we can go on to the palace!" cried Tandy, a bit breathless by the suddenness of it all. "Oh, Ato, how did you ever happen to bring those plants along?"

"I suspected some of these subjects of yours were villains," answered Ato grimly, "and the only way to meet villains is with villainy. Forward, march, my Lass! On to the King's castle!"

Picking her way around the fallen men and beasts, Nikobo, snorting at each step to show her superiority and contempt, set out for the Royal Palace. Of all the people who had run out on the cliffs, besides the securely bound Ozamandarins and the guard, only the old tribesman who had first cheered Tandy remained. "Oh, please do come with us," invited Tandy earnestly as the old man stepped smilingly out of Nikobo's way. "You could tell me all about the tent dwellers and help me so much if you would."

"I am Chunum, the Sheik, head of a thousand tribes and speaking for them. I can say they all will proudly and gladly serve your brave young Majesty. Too long have the city dwellers ruled this great liberty-loving land."

"Then over the side and under the hatches with 'em," cried Roger, beside himself with joy and exuberance at the neat way Ato had handled Tandy's subjects. "This boy's an able-bodied seaman and explorer and will stand no nonsense!"

"My sea is the desert," said Chunum, striding jauntily along beside Nikobo, "and my ship is a camel, but I'll wager we'll understand each other well enough for all that."

To Tandy, conversing eagerly with Chunum, the splendor of the White city of Om was an old story, but to the others it seemed, with its flashing marble walks, great waving palms, and towering dwellings and castle, one of the loveliest capitals they had yet visited.

Word of the happenings on the cliff had traveled fast. Longing to welcome the young King, but fearing the strange magicians who had come with him, the Nobles had barred themselves in their fine houses, and the natives had fled to the hills beyond the city gates. The many-domed marble palace was absolutely deserted when Nikobo pushed her way through the wide doors. Not a footman, page or courtier was in sight. Seeing no attention or service was to be had for some time, Ato hurried away to the kitchen and was soon happily at work preparing a splendid feast to celebrate Tandy's homecoming.

Tandy himself felt quiet and sad, examining with scant interest and enthusiasm the splendid rooms which he had never yet been allowed to live in. To tell the truth, he would have traded the whole castle for his small cabin aboard Samuel's ship. Samuel himself, never really happy or comfortable ashore, wandered about aimlessly, opening books on the long tables, peering out windows, and finally settling with a sigh of resignation in a huge chair beside the throne. Nikobo had found a long pool and fountain in the same room, and lying at full length in this luxuriant marble bath, tranquilly waited for events to shape themselves.

"Why not sit on your throne?" asked Roger as Tandy seated himself on a small stool beside Samuel Salt.

"Oh, it's much too big for me," sighed Tandy, thinking how very big and lonely the palace would seem when all his shipmates had gone.

"Aho, and methinks you are right! Ahoy, the beginning of a beautiful idea doth at this moment start to seep through the head feathers. Of which, more anon!" Chunum, who had never before heard a bird talk, stared at Roger in amazed interest and surprise, but giving him no more satisfaction than a mischievous wink, the Read Bird flew off to help Ato with the dinner. And now Samuel proceeded to tell the old tribesman how he had found Tandy in the jungle imprisoned in the wooden cage. As he finished, Chunum shook his head in stern displeasure.

"It has long been my conviction and belief," he stated solemnly, "that the Ozamandarins are at the bottom of this. Every year they usurp more and more power, and keeping the young King shut up in the Tower was but an excuse to give them their own will and way. Nor can I believe that the royal parents of this boy accidentally fell into the sea as they were reported to have done, or that the young aunts mentioned in the prophecy had anything at all to do with Tandy's abduction. Tell me, how long will the vines hold those villains prisoner, for only that long is Tazander safe. We must think and act quickly," said Chunum, tapping his staff thoughtfully on the floor.

"The vines will not unwind for two days, and before THEN — HAH!" Samuel expelled his breath in a mighty blast and sprang purposefully to his feet. "Before then we shall put those fellows in a very safe place for Tandy and for them, too, shiver my timbers!" Taking Chunum by the shoulder, Samuel started toward the door, and seeing the two intended to leave the castle, Nikobo climbed out of the fountain and offered to carry them. Tandy nodded absently as the two left the castle, his thoughts still far away on the *Crescent Moon*, and considering the work they had to do, Samuel and Chunum were well pleased to leave him behind.

With surprising speed the hippopotamus made the return trip to the cliffs. The effects of the tumbleweed had evidently worn off, and the guards and their mounts had fled with the rest of the inhabitants of White City to the hills. But the nine Ozamandarins still lay in their curious cradles in the deep, coarse sand. As Samuel and Chunum, in absolute agreement as to what should be done, rolled off Nikobo's back, a furious bellow and screech brought them up short. Nikobo, startled out of her usual calm, fell back on her haunches and after one horrified look upward, buried her head in the sand.

"It can't be!" cried Samuel, clutching Chunum's sleeve. "It can't be, but it is!"

"An elephant, a flying elephant!" panted Chunum, dragging Samuel from under the immense shadow. "Flatten yourself in the sand, seaman, and we may yet be spared." As Samuel, more amazed than scared at so strange and curious a specimen, and even vaguely hopeful of capturing the unwieldy creature, made no move, Chunum dragged him down by main force. The elephant meanwhile lighted like some gigantic butterfly on the edge of the cliff. Fairly bleating with fright and terror, the nine Ozamandarins watched him swooping toward them with a sinister and soundless speed. Just behind his ear perched Boglodore, the Old Man of the Jungle, looking cruel and ugly as the genie of all evil.

"Revenge! Revenge!" shrilled the turbanned native, clenching his fists. "Now shall Boglodore have his reward!" Addressing himself to Chunum and Samuel Salt, the Old Man of the Jungle began screaming out the story of his wrongs. "For those scheming rascals I carried away on Umbo, my great and useful umbrellaphant, the young King of this country. For this I was to receive one-tenth of the Kingdom, the Ozamandarins themselves to divide the rest of the country among them. But hah! What happened?"

Dancing up and down on the elephant's head, Boglodore again clenched his fists, his face distorted with rage and fury. "What happened? Why, these miserable cheats refused to pay me, intending to keep the whole country for themselves. But hearken well, you and YOU!" Jerking his thumb contemptuously toward his rigid and helpless enemies, the Old Man continued his story.

"All along I have suspected these thieving Zamans; all along I intended to fool them and return the little King to his castle, keeping only the jungle for my own. That is why I built the boy his cage in the jungle and set Nikobo, the great hippopotamus, to watch over him, giving her the power of speech and the desire to seek out and protect this unfortunate child of an unfortunate country. I am a magician and could well bring about these things. You, whoever you are, who found and brought him back to Ozamaland did no more than I myself intended to do and intend to do now. After restoring Tandy to his throne, I meant to deal with his enemies, and now as they are so neatly bound up and ready, I shall reward them well for their pains and treachery."

"Stop! Stop! Avast there and belay!" shouted Samuel Salt as the umbrellaphant, obeying an order from the terrible Old Man, picked up Didjabo in his trunk and flew swiftly toward the cliff's edge. But Chunum, again dragging Samuel down, whispered fiercely in his ear.

"It is justice, seaman, and only what we ourselves planned to do. The vines will keep these rogues afloat for two days, then haply they will sink — not to die, as death comes not to the people of my country, but to lie for long, forgotten ages at the bottom of the sea, harmless and sodden and unable to do any more harm to the country they have so dishonorably served and betrayed!"

Shuddering and in a tense silence, Samuel and the Sheik watched the umbrellaphant toss the wretched Ozamandarins one after the other into the sea. The immense zooming monster fascinated the Captain of the *Crescent Moon*. Not wings, but a balloon-like structure of its own tough skin billowing over its back like a howdah enabled Umbo to navigate in the air. Samuel was anxious for further talk with the Old Man of the Jungle, but as the last Ozamandarin fell over the cliff, the umbrellaphant, with a trumpet of defiance, headed rapidly for the open sea.

"Look! Look! It's getting away!" cried Samuel, rushing to the cliff's edge and almost tumbling over. "Do you realize that there goes the only umbrellaphant in captivity?"

"Well, well, and what if it is?" muttered Chunum, again pulling Samuel back to safety. "I expect Boglodore does not find this country healthy after the pretty story he has just told us, and come, COME, Master Seaman, what would you do with a flying elephant aboard your ship?"

"I'd tie it to the mast and carry it back to Oz," explained Samuel, staring gloomily after the disappearing prize. "Why, it would be the most rare and amazing specimen ever brought back from anywhere, and now — now — I've lost it—"

Samuel's arms dropped heavily to his sides, and turning away from the cliff, he began walking slowly back toward Nikobo, who had at last ventured to lift her head from the sand. Surprised enough was the hippopotamus to learn that she had been given her power of speech by the ugly little magician on the umbrellaphant, and frightened lest she forget Tandy's language, she began talking rapidly to herself.

"But you forget what all this means!" panted Chunum, catching up with the Explorer and shaking him energetically by the shoulder. "Why, this clears up the whole mystery. Not an AUNT, but an ELEPHant carried Tazander to Patrippany Island. We must return quickly to the castle and release his innocent relatives. I myself will call back Tandy's frightened subjects and tell them of the great good fortune that has befallen, that we are rid of nine rogues and have a brave young King to rule Ozamaland. Come, come, do not stand here dreaming about lost elephants; there is much to be accomplished and done."

"Goosewing my topsails, you're right!" breathed Samuel Salt, coming completely out of his reverie. "Round up the citizens, comrade, and I'll carry the good news to the castle."

Chapter 20 - King Tandy

When Samuel reached the castle, he found Ato and Roger had set a small, cozy table in the Throne Room, and Tandy was anxiously looking out of one of the gold-framed windows for his return. The whiffs from the covered dishes were so appetizing the Royal Explorer of Oz was almost inclined to let his news wait till afterward. But thinking better of it, he blurted out the whole story of what had happened to the Ozamandarins.

"Then they're all gone and done for," sniffed Ato, seating himself at the head of the table. "Well, a couple of hundred years at the bottom of the sea should soak all the sin and wickedness out of 'em! And you say it was an unbrellaphant that carried Tandy off? My! and MY! Dear, dear and DEAR! Just pour me a cup of coffee, Roger. I'm feeling weaker than soup!"

"Well, how do you suppose I feel," grumbled Samuel Salt, throwing his hat up on a bronze figure, "to lose an elegant specimen like that? Why, I'll wager we'll never see another creature like it!"

"There! There! Always talking about the elephant that got away instead of appreciating your good fortune!" scolded Ato, throwing a corn muffin down to Nikobo and lifting the gold cover off the roast fowl.

"Yes, and you'd better listen to OUR news, Master Salt!" Roger said, pouring a cup of coffee for all hands.

"News? NEWS? Has anything happened here?" Samuel looked more anxious than interested.

"Oh, YES!" cried Tandy, running round to his side of the table and pressing eagerly against Samuel's knee. "Roger has a wonderful plan, and I as King of Ozamaland have agreed to it, and oh, Samuel, SAMUEL!" Forgetting he usually called the tremendous seaman "Captain," Tandy flung both arms round his neck and almost squeezed the breath out of him. "I'm going straight back on the *Crescent Moon*, and I'm not coming ashore for years and years. I'm going with you to Ev, Oz, Elbow Island, and everywhere!"

"What?" spluttered Samuel Salt, disentangling himself with great difficulty and holding Tandy off at arm's length. "Are you joking? Are you crazy? Have you abdicated or what? Why, this is too good to be true!"

"But it is true!" insisted Roger, strutting up and down the table and illy concealing his pride and satisfaction.

"Oh, tell him, tell him," begged Tandy, too happy to speak for himself.

"Well," said Roger, spreading his wings self-consciously, for the plan was his, and he felt prouder of it every minute, "we are placing Ozamaland under the general rule and protection of Oz and leaving as Ruler in Tandy's place that long-legged son of the desert, Chunum. Now there's a fellow who can handle these scary Nobles and natives and wild elephant and camel riders. A King must complete his education before he starts ruling, you know." Roger paused to scratch his head and wink gaily at Samuel Salt. "And if this King chooses to finish his education on our ship, that is his own affair."

"Oh, quite! Quite!" Samuel began to rock backward and forward and roar with merriment. "Roger, you rascal, you've done as good a job of reasoning as a whole flock of Wise Men! Fall to, Mates, now we can enjoy our victuals, and I give you a toast to King Tandy, Cabin Boy, Explorer and Artist Extraordinary to this Expedition!"

"Tandy! Tandy!" echoed Ato and Roger, lifting their coffee cups.

"Tandy! Tandy!" mumbled Nikobo, who was lunching largely and luxuriantly on the flowers in a low window box. "When do we sail?"

Chapter 21 - A Voyage Resumed

Anxious as Tandy was to return to the Crescent Moon and continue the voyage, it was a whole week before they finally shoved off. Chunum, true to his word, had rounded up the frightened citizens of the capital and explained to them the wicked plots of the Ozamandarins and their punishment by Boglodore, the Old Man of the Jungle. Then Tandy, addressing them from the castle balcony, called upon them to consider Chunum as their King until he himself should have completed his education in foreign parts and aboard the *Crescent Moon*, during which time he promised to keep them always in mind and have their welfare always at heart. Next, Tandy explained how Ozamaland was now a province and under the general rule and protection of Ozma of Oz, how settlers from that famous fairyland would soon arrive to help them build new cities and towns, tame the wild jungles of the interior, and repel the dangerous invasions of the Greys.

Here Chunum rose to declare he himself would be responsible for peace along the border between Amaland and Ozamaland, that the Greys had long desired to be friends with the Whites, but trouble had been stirred up by the Ozamandarins so they might have the credit of protecting the country. Then Tandy spoke again of all the advantages that would be enjoyed from their association with the Kingdom of Oz. It was a long and splendid speech, Roger and Tandy having spent the whole morning in its preparation, and delighted and surprised by the energy and ambition of their young Ruler, Tandy's subjects cheered him long and vociferously, greeting each new plan and proposal with loud acclaim and enthusiasm. The royal aunts and relatives, already released from the castle dungeons and restored to their royal dwellings, could not speak highly enough of their young relative's bravery and cleverness and the bravery and cleverness of all of his new friends. They quite wore Nikobo out with their questions and petting, and the hippopotamus sighed hugely for the time when they would all be at sea.

"Was I right or was I wrong?" questioned Roger on the third afternoon as Tandy, resplendent in his court suit of white velvet, reviewed the vast parade of Loyal Nobles and Natives, and the long lines of elephants and camels went sweeping by the palace. "They love you just as much for going away as they would if you stayed. And Chunum is a Man in a Million."

"Right!" Tandy nodded, waving happily to the crowds that in a high holiday mood thronged the walks and parks of the beautiful White City. Chunum had taken Samuel Salt and Ato on an expedition into the jungle so that the Royal Explorer of Oz could procure a creeping bird and flying reptile for his collection. Nikobo, old jungaleer that she was, had gone along to see that no harm came to them.

To Tandy, a snake with feathers and a bird with scales and fangs was no novelty, but Samuel, returning with a pair of each, considered them the most peculiar and precious of his queer specimens. He carried their cages everywhere he went and spent long, rapt hours watching the snakes fly and the birds creep about their new cages. Ato had discovered a new and rare fruit and had brought along several slips to plant in the rail boxes he had outside the galley. Nikobo had swum to her heart's content in a green and muddy jungle stream, and all three were now quite ready and anxious to continue the voyage. Aboard the *Crescent Moon* one of the Guards had been established to feed the monkey fish and water boy and tend to the plants in the hold and serve as watchman. And early one bright morning, just a week after they had landed, the members of the Royal Exploration Party of Oz set forth from the palace.

Oz flags fluttered and snapped in the fresh morning breeze, mingling with the white banners of Ozamaland, and the streets and avenues were lined with Tandy's cheering and now quite cheerful subjects. Riding Nikobo, accompanied by Chunum on a white elephant and the entire camel corps and elephant guard, the party made their way down to the water's edge, feeling exactly, as Ato whispered in a laughing undertone to Roger, like a whole circus and a zoo. Besides Roger, Tandy, Samuel Salt and Ato, Nikobo carried two large cages and two small cages. In the small cages were the flying reptiles and creeping birds. In the large cages a baby white camel and a baby white elephant. "You'll sink, my Lass," worried Samuel Salt as Nikobo, having safely made her way down the rocky cliff road, waded confidently out into the sea.

"Not me," murmured the hippopotamus comfortably. "You may get wet, but I'll get you safely out to the ship. Trust me."

"Goodbye! Goodbye, all!" cried Tandy, standing up on her back to wave to the crowds collected on the cliffs. Now that he was leaving, he felt a strange fondness for them. "Goodbye, Chunum! I'll be back, never fear!"

"Goodbye, Little Fellow! Goodbye, Little King! A fair and faraway voyage to you," called the tall old desert chief, standing up in his stirrups to wave his long lance. "To the sun, the moon, the stars I commend you! Go in happiness and return in health and live long to rule over Ozamaland."

"You take care of the country, and we'll take care of the King," shouted Samuel. "Goodbye! Goodbye! Be watching, all of you, for the ships from Oz!"

"Goodbye! Goodbye!" called the Nobles, the natives, the guards; even the elephants and camels raised their shrill voices in farewell as Nikobo swam strongly away from the shore and toward the *Crescent Moon*.

The guard left in charge of the ship thankfully turned the vessel over to its rightful owners, and shaking Tandy feelingly by the hand, climbed down the ladder and dropped nervously on the back of the hippopotamus, who was to carry him to shore.

"Here, Brainless, lend a hand with the freight," yelled Roger as Tandy stood gazing rather thoughtfully toward the cliffs. "The King's ashore! Long live his cabin boy! I'll carry these pesky reptiles if you take the camel." Roger winked at Tandy as Samuel Salt, bent double under the baby elephant's cage, started carefully down to the hold. The baby camel and its cage were so small, Tandy could manage them quite easily, and with a little laugh he hurried after Samuel and Roger. By the time they had finished, Nikobo had returned from her shore trip and climbed thankfully back on her raft.

"All hands stand by to heave up the anchor," bellowed Samuel, stepping cheerfully over to his sail controls. "Anchors aweigh! And away we go, boys, and the hippopotamus take the hindmost!"

"Ho, ho! Well, she's built for it," roared Ato, bending his weight to the cable as sail after sail rattled up the masts and bellied out from the yards. "Where to now, Sam-u-el? Oz?"

"OZ, I should say not! We've a lot of geography to discover before we go back to Oz. We'll need a roc's egg before we go there, eh Tandy? A roc's egg and sixty more islands for Ozma's Christmas stocking."

"Oh! Will we really spend Christmas in Oz?" cried Tandy, skipping up and down the deck and forgetting all about his subjects waving from the cliffs.

"Why not?" demanded Samuel Salt, letting his hands fall happily upon the wheel. "Oz is as merry a place as any to spend Christmas, eh Roger?"

"Merry as eight bells!" cried Roger, flying joyfully into the rigging. "Ahoy! Ahoy! Nothing but sea t'seaward!"

And when the *Crescent Moon* flies over Ev and drops down the Winkie River on Christmas morning with its chart full of islands and curious continents and its hold full of strange beasts, plants and treasure, I for one should like to be there, shouldn't you?

The End

Handy Mandy in Oz

by Ruth Plumly Thompson

Chapter 1 - Mandy leaves the Mountain

"What-a-Butter! What-a-Butter!" High and clear above the peaks of Mt. Mern floated the voice of the Goat Girl calling the finest, fattest, but most troublesome of her flock. All the other goats were winding obediently down toward the village that perched precariously on the edge of the mountain. But of What-a-Butter there was not a single sign or whisker.

"Serves me right for spoiling the contrary creature," panted Mandy, pushing back her thick, yellow braids with her second-best hand. "Always wants her own way, that goat, so she does. What-a-Butter, I say WHAT-A-BUTTER, come down here this instant." But only the tantalizing tinkle of the goat's silver bell came to answer her, for What-a-Butter was climbing up, not down, and there was nothing for Mandy to do but go after her.

Muttering dire threats which she was much too soft-hearted ever to carry out, the rosy-cheeked mountain lass scrambled over crags and stones, pulling herself up steep precipices, the goat always managing to keep a few jumps ahead, till soon they were almost at the top of the mountain!

Here, stepping on a jutting rock to catch her breath and remove the burrs from her stockings, Mandy heard a dreadful roar and felt an ominous rumbling beneath her feet. What-a-Butter, on a narrow ledge just above, heard it too and cocked her head anxiously on one side. Perhaps she had best jump down to Mandy. After all, the great silly girl did feed and pet her, and from the sound of things a storm was brewing. If there was one thing the goat feared more than another, it was a thunderstorm, so, rolling her eyes as innocently as if she had not dragged Mandy all over the mountain, she stretched her nose down toward her weary mistress.

"Bah—ah-ah-ahhhhhhhhhh!" bleated What-a-Butter affectionately.

"Oh, `Bah' yourself!" fumed Mandy, making an angry snatch for the Nanny Goat's beard. "Pets and children are all alike, never appreciate a body till they have a stomach ache or a thunderstorm is coming. Now then, m'lass, be quick with you!"

Holding out her strong arms, Mandy made ready to catch the goat as it jumped off the ledge. But before What-a-Butter could stir, there was a perfectly awful crash and explosion and up shot the slab of rock on which Mandy was standing, up, UP, and out of sight entirely. Where the mountain girl had been a crystal column of water spurted viciously into the air, so high the bulging eyes of the goat could see no end to it. Rearing up on her hind legs, What-a-Butter turned round and round in a frantic effort to catch a glimpse of her vanishing Mistress. Then, thinking suddenly what would happen should the torrent turn and fall upon her, the goat sprang off the ledge and ran madly down the mountain, bleating like a whole herd of Banshees.

And Mandy, as you can well believe, was as frightened as What-a-Butter and with twice as much reason. The first upheaval, as the rock left the earth, flung her flat on her nose. Grasping the edges of the slab with all hands, Mandy hung on for dear life and, as a stinging shower of icy water sprayed her from head to foot, wondered what under the earth was happening to her. Thorns and thistles! Could the thunderstorm really have come UP instead of down? Certainly it was raining up, and whatever was carrying her aloft with such terrible force and relentlessness?

How could the Goat Girl know that a turbulent spring pent up for thousands of years in the center of Mt. Mern had suddenly burst its way to freedom? And you have no idea of the tremendous power in a mountain spring once it uncoils and lets itself go. Mandy's rock might just as well have been shot into the air by a magic cannon. First it tore upward as if it meant to knock a hole in the sky, then, still traveling at incalculable speed, began to arch and take a horizontal course over the mountains, hills and valleys west of Mern. All poor Mandy knew was that she was hurtling through space at breakneck speed with nothing to save or stop her. The long, yellow braids of the Goat Girl streamed out like pennants, while her striped skirt and voluminous petticoats snapped and fluttered like banners in the wind.

"What-a-Butter! Oh, What-a-Butter!" moaned Mandy, gazing wildly over the edge of the rock. But pshaw, what was the use of calling? What-a-Butter, even if she heard, could not fly after her through the air, and when she herself came down, not even her own goat would recognize her. At this depressing thought Mandy dropped her head on her arms and began to weep bitterly, for she was quite sure she would never see her friends, her home, or her goats again.

But the strength and frugal life on Mt. Mern had made the Goat Girl both brave and resourceful, so she soon dried her tears, and as the rock still showed no signs of slowing up or dashing down, she began to take heart and even a desperate sort of interest in her experience. Slowly and cautiously, she pulled herself to a sitting position and, still clutching the edges of the rock, dared to look down at the countries and towns flashing away below.

"After all," sniffed the reckless maiden, "nothing very dreadful has happened yet. I've always wanted to travel, and now I AM traveling. Not many people have flown through the air on a rock — why, it's really a rocket!" decided Mandy with a nervous giggle. "And that, I suppose, makes me the first rocket-rider in the country, and the LAST, too," she finished soberly as she measured with her eye the distance she would plunge when her rock started earthward. "Now if we'd just come down in that blue lake below, I might have a chance. Perhaps I should jump." But by the time Mandy made up her mind to jump, the lake was far behind, and nothing but a great desert of smoking sand stretched beneath her.

Chapter 2 - The End of the Ride

The sky, from the rosy pink of late afternoon had faded to a depressing grey, and Mandy could not help thinking longingly of the appetizing little supper she had set out for herself before going up to call the goats. Who would eat it now or even know she was flying through the air like a comet? No one, she concluded drearily, for Mandy was an orphan and lived all by herself in a small cottage on Mt. Mern, high above the village of Fistikins. In a day or two some of her friends in the village might search the cottage and find her gone, but NOW, now there was nothing to do but sit tight and hope for the best.

Mandy's next glance down was more encouraging. Instead of the dangerous-looking desert, she was sailing over misty blue hills and valleys dotted with many small towns and villages. High as she was, she could even hear the church bells tolling the hour, and this made Mandy feel more lost and lonely than ever. All these people below were safely at home and about to eat their suppers, while she was flying high and far from everything she knew and loved best.

Hungrily, the Goat Girl cast her eyes over the rock she was riding, thinking to find a small sprig of mountain berries or even a blade of grass to nibble. At first glance, the rock seemed bare and barren, then, sticking up out of a narrow crevice, Mandy spied a tiny blue flower. "Poor little posy, it's as far from home as I am," murmured the Goat Girl, and carefully breaking the stem she lifted the blue flower to her nose. Its faint fragrance was vaguely comforting, and Mandy had just begun to count the petals when the rock gave a sickening lurch and started to pitch down so fast Mandy's braids snapped like jumping ropes and her skirts bellied out like a parachute in a gale.

"NOW for it," gasped the Goat Girl, closing her eyes and clenching her teeth. "OH! My poor little shins!" Mandy's shins were both stout and sturdy, but even so we cannot blame Mandy for pitying them. Stouter shins than hers would have splintered at such a fall. Hardly knowing what she was doing, Mandy began to pull the petals from the blue flower, calling in an agonized voice as she pulled each one the names of her goats and friends. She had just come to Speckle, the smallest member of her flock, when the end came.

Kimmeny Jimmeny! Was this ALL? Opening one eye, the Goat Girl looked fearfully about her. She was sitting on top of a haystack; no, not a haystack, but a heap of soft blue flower petals as soft as down. Opening the other eye, she saw the rock on which she had traveled so far bump over a golden fence and fall with a satisfied splash into a shimmering lake. But what lay beyond the lake made Mandy forget all her troubles and fairly moan with surprise and pleasure.

"A CASTLE!" exulted the Goat Girl, putting one hand above her heart. "Oh! I've always wanted to see a castle, and now I AM." And this castle, let me tell you, was well worth anyone's seeing, a castle of lacy blue marble carved, and decorated with precious stones in a way to astonish the eyes of a simple mountain lass. From the tallest tower a silken pennant floated lazily in the evening breeze.

"K-E-R-E-T-A-R-I-A," Mandy spelled out slowly. Sliding off the heap of flower petals, she stood for a long, delicious moment lost in admiration. Then, giving herself a businesslike shake to be sure she was not broken or bent by her amazing flight and tumble, Mandy turned to examine the rest of her surroundings. When she looked at the spot on which she had fallen, the stack of blue petals had disappeared, but there, twinkling up cheerfully, was the blue flower as much at home as if it had grown there in the first place. Thoroughly puzzled, Mandy picked the little flower a second time and slipped it into the pocket of her apron.

Even without the mystery of the blue flower, it was astonishing enough to find herself in the stately park of this gorgeous blue castle. There was a tree-lined avenue, and velvety lawns splashed with star-shaped flower beds stretched in every direction. Only the small patch of land on which she was standing was bare and uncultivated. And evidently someone was at work here, for a great white ox with golden horns, yoked to a gold plow, stood with his back to Mandy, dozing cozily in the pleasant dusk. At sight of the ox, Mandy gave a little sigh of relief and content. Long ago an old mountain woman had given her this sensible piece of advice. "When you do not know what to do next, do the first useful piece of work that comes to hand." Now here, right at hand, was a useful piece of work, and while she was trying to figure out the whole puzzle of the flying rock and strange blue flower, she might just as well be plowing. Then when the owner of the castle saw her working so industriously, he might invite her to supper. So, grasping the tail of the ancient plow, Mandy clicked her tongue in a cheerful signal for the ox to start.

The white ox, who had not seen or heard the Goat Girl till this minute, turned his head in a lordly fashion and gave her a long, haughty look. Not really believing what he saw, he took another look, and then, with a bellow of fright and outrage, went charging across the park, pulling the startled Goat Girl behind him. Mandy might have let go, but she just did not think of it, and with pounding heart and flying braids held fast to the pitching plow as it tore through flower beds, ripped up lawns, and cut fearful furrows in the pebbled paths. Clouds of earth, stones and whole plants uprooted ruthlessly from their beds showered round her ears, and as they reached the palace, a hard metal object hit her squarely between the eyes. Putting up a hand, Mandy caught the flying missile and mechanically slipped it into her pocket, and the next instant the ox, lunging through an open French window, dragged her into the magnificently furnished throne room of the castle. Not only into the throne room, mind you, but into the lap of royalty itself!

Chapter 3 - The King of Kereteria

The white ox in his mad dash across the throne room had run violently into a marble pillar, hurling Mandy straight into the arms of a very tall, very stern, and very blue-looking monarch. Pages and courtiers tripped and fell left and right in a scramble to get out of the way, while the ox, snorting and trembling, looked balefully over his shoulder at the Goat Girl.

"Whu-what is the meaning of this outrageous intrusion?" panted the King. "Unhand me, woman! Remove your finger from my eye and your arms — your ARMS! Hi! Hi! Hi!" The King's sentence ended in three frightened squeaks. "Is it a girl or an octopus?" he puffed, heaving up his chest in an endeavor to dislodge Mandy. "Hi! Hi! Hi! Are you going to allow this clumping savage to insult my Majesty in this — er — high-handed manner?"

As the Goat Girl, by this time scarlet from anger and mortification, jumped off the King's lap, three very high officials of the Court of Keretaria darted forward. "The High Qui-questioner! The Imperial Persuader! And the Lord High Upper Dupper of the Realm!" bawled a page. Having delivered himself of this impressive announcement, the page bolted back of a curtain and from there peered with astonished eyes at the visitor. Everyone in the grand blue throne room looked frightened and ready to run at a moment's notice. Wondering what could be the matter with them all, Mandy with many misgivings watched the counselors of Keretaria advance in a threatening row.

"Now then, not a move!" thundered the High Qui-questioner, tapping her sharply on the shoulder with a golden staff shaped like a huge interrogation point. "It is my duty to question all strangers who ride, fall, fly or break into our Kingdom, and you," the Haughty Nobleman gave Mandy a cold blue stare, "YOU are stranger than any stranger who has ever come to Keretaria."

"It is my duty to persuade you to do as his Majesty commands," stated the Imperial Persuader, raising his gold spiked club.

"And it is MY duty to put you in your place," sniffed the Lord High Upper Dupper, rattling a bunch of keys that hung from his belt.

"Well, if you ask me," puffed the Ox, rolling his eyes wildly round at the Goat Girl, "her place is in a museum, and the sooner you lock her upper dupper, the better." Now Mandy was so astonished to hear the Ox actually speaking, she gave a loud cry and flung up her hands, every single seven of them.

"Help! Help!" yelped the Courtiers, scurrying like mice into corners and corridors. Only the white Ox, the King and his Counselors kept their places.

"How DARE you come into a King's presence armed in this barbarous fashion!" gasped the High Qui-questioner, taking a step toward the Goat Girl, but too frightened to touch her.

"PIGS!" cried Mandy, suddenly losing her temper. "Can I help my seven arms? All of us on Mt. Mern have seven arms and hands, and you with your skinny two seem far funnier than I. I am Mandy, the Goat Girl, as anyone in his senses can see."

"The girl is right," observed the Ox, gazing more attentively at Mandy and now speaking quite calmly. "She can no more help those seven arms than you can help those seven warts on your nose, Questo. I tell you this maiden is a real curiosity, and if you three Hi-boys will cease rattling your teeth and your clubs, perhaps she will explain why she has come to Keretaria. I myself shall call her Handy Mandy."

"Why, the beast has more sense than its masters," thought the Goat Girl in surprise.

"Well," rumbled the King ungraciously, "if you have anything to say before we lock you up, SAY IT, but do not wave your arms about, PLEASE."

Swallowing nervously, clasping four of her hands behind her back and stuffing the other three into convenient pockets in her apron, Mandy began to speak. "I was driving my goats home from the mountain, Your Majesty, when the rock on which I was standing exploded suddenly into the air, flew like a bird over hill, valley, and desert, and dropped me into your garden—"

"And not a bruise or a bump to show for it," grunted the Imperial Persuader, elevating his nose to show he was not taken in by such a tale. In spite of his suspicious glance, Mandy decided to say nothing of the blue flower that had so miraculously softened her fall.

"And since when have rocks flown through the air?" inquired the Lord High Upper Dupper sarcastically.

"Ahem — in the garden," continued Mandy, undaunted by the two interruptions, "I saw this great white ox, and thinking to do a bit of honest work for my supper grasped the plow, but—"

"That was a little oxident," murmured the great beast in a jovial voice, "for, catching sight of a seven-armed maiden all at once and without warning, I took to my heels and landed her in her present unpleasant predicament. Is that not so, m'lass?"

Looking at the Ox with round eyes, Mandy nodded.

"But she still has not explained all these arms," complained the Imperial Persuader. "Whoever heard of a seven-handed maiden?"

"I have!" asserted Mandy stoutly. "And what, pray, is there to explain? This iron hand —" the Goat Girl raised it slowly and thoughtfully as she spoke "— I use for ironing, lifting hot pots from the stove, and all horrid sort of hard work; this leather hand I keep for beating rugs, dusting, sweeping, and so on; this wooden hand I use for churning and digging in the garden; these two red rubber hands for dishwashing and scrubbing; and my two fine white hands I keep for holding and braiding my hair." With all seven hands extended before her, Mandy smiled engagingly up at the King.

"Undoubtedly a witch," whispered the Imperial Persuader darkly as the King, in spite of himself, gazed curiously down at his seven-armed visitor.

"A dangerous character, Your Majesty," hissed the High Qui-questioner, shaking his head disapprovingly.

"To the dungeons with her!" rasped the Lord High Upper Dupper, rattling his keys like castanets.

"WHAT?" bawled the white Ox, stamping all of his gold-shod feet in rapid succession. "You mean to consign this marvel of skill and efficiency to a dungeon? What a set of dunces you are! Come, Handy, I myself will take you for a

213

slave. Out of my way, DOLTS!" Swaggering a bit and with the golden plow still clanking and bumping behind him, the Ox ambled at a dignified pace toward the door. Mandy, though she did not relish the idea of becoming his slave, was greatly relieved at the interest the Ox was taking in her case, but before following him she looked inquiringly up at the King.

"Yes, GO!" commanded His Majesty harshly. "I hereby give you into the care and service of Nox, the Royal Ox of Keretaria. Harm one hair of his head and you will pay for it with your life and perish, I promise you, most ignominiously."

"Mercy—ercy," muttered Mandy, tiptoeing nervously after her new master, "doesn't the fellow know any short words? How queer everything is on this side of the mountain: people with only two arms, animals talking and giving orders to Kings. Suppose the goats at home started bossing the villagers?" And what would the villagers think of her strange flight and reception in Keretaria? Well, from what she herself had seen of Royalty, decided the Goat Girl, she much preferred her goats or even the company of this haughty white Ox. Stepping briskly beside him, Mandy resolved to humor the creature till she saw a bit more of the country or found some safe way back to her mountain. Nox, swinging along at his own indolent gait, paid no further attention to the Goat Girl, but when they reached his royal quarters, which to Mandy looked more like a castle than a stable, he began bawling so fiercely for the stable boys she decided uncomfortably that being his slave might prove both unpleasant and dangerous. However, when six little boys dressed in blue overalls and aprons ran out, the royal Ox addressed them quite kindly. The first, without waiting for instructions, unhitched the plow and lifted the yoke from the royal shoulders.

"Prepare Kerry's quarters for my new slave," directed Nox, turning to the second and third. "You others, bring dinner for two, and mind you fetch Handy Mandy everything they have at the King's table." With a playful lunge, Nox started them smartly on their way, then moved grandly into the huge stone stable and along to his own luxurious gold-paved stall.

"My—y!" exclaimed the Goat Girl, sinking breathlessly to a three-legged stool, "How grand and elegant you are here! My—y, I wish What-a-Butter could see this!"

"One of your goats?" murmured Nox, burying his nose in the huge marble bowl he used for a drinking trough.

Mandy nodded. "I wish she were here now!" she added with a rapturous little sigh.

"Well, I don't." Deliberately, the Royal Ox licked the water from his lips. "Do you suppose I'd allow a miserable goat in my sapphire-trimmed stall?"

"Miserable!" squealed Mandy, springing off the stool. "What-a-Butter's the smartest goat on the mountain; she wouldn't give two bleats and a BAH for an old Hoopadoop like YOU!"

"Hoopadoop!" repeated the Ox in a dazed whisper. "Do you mean to stand there and call the Royal Ox of Keretaria a Hoopadoop?"

"Yes," said Mandy firmly, but backing off a bit as she spoke. "What makes you think you're so much better than a goat, even if you do talk, put on airs, and have golden horns?"

"Well," and to Mandy's surprise and relief, Nox cleared his throat and grinned quite amiably, "after all, I AM the Royal Ox, you know, more precious to the King than all his court and subjects. Everyone jumps at my least command, so why shouldn't I put on a few airs? Besides, do you think it's polite to call me an old Hoopadoop when I've just saved you from a dungeon?"

"No," admitted Mandy, resuming her seat thoughtfully, "I don't suppose it is. Maybe you *are* as good as a goat," she added with a little burst of generosity.

"Oh, thank you! Thank you very much!" Through half-closed eyes, the Royal Ox looked quizzically at the Goat Girl. "I believe we shall get on famously, m'lass, famously. The truth is, you amuse me no end, and so long as you amuse me, everything will be smooth as silk. But of course, if you bore me, I will bore you. Oh, positively!" Lowering his head, Nox shook his horns playfully.

"Now, I shouldn't try that, if I were you," advised Mandy, raising her iron hand and cracking the fingers warningly. "For if you do, I might throw things!"

"Ha ha! I believe you would." The enormous beast, charmed by so much spirit and independence, fairly beamed upon his new slave. "I take it you are pretty good at throwing things."

"Yes, and at catching them, too." Reaching up, Mandy took seven of the dozen brushes off the shelf above her head. Tossing them all into the air with three of her hands, she caught them easily with the other four. Then, dragging her stool closer, she began brushing the coat of her royal charge so hard and vigorously he blinked with pleasure and astonishment. "Will you have your tail plain, curled, or plaited?" asked Mandy in a businesslike voice.

"Er—er—plain, thank you." With admiration and some alarm, Nox regarded the whirling arms of the Goat Girl, but the four little stable boys, appearing at that moment, stared at her in glassy-eyed fright and consternation. For Nox they had brought a tray heaped high with corn and oats and another with fresh sliced apples. For Mandy there were two trays of gold dishes containing a sample of everything from the royal table. Dropping her brushes, Mandy seized all the trays at once in her various hands, which so frightened the stable boys they took to their heels yelling at the tops of their voices.

Winking at the Royal Ox, Mandy set his supper on the gold stand meant for that purpose, then, dropping to the floor before her own two trays, began her first dinner in a strange land. And WHAT a strange land, mused Mandy, helping herself from the gold dishes with first one hand and then another.

"Well, m'lass?" inquired Nox, daintily nibbling his oats and apples. "Is this not better than bread and water in a dungeon cell?" Too full for utterance, Mandy rapturously nodded.

Chapter 4 - The Message in the Horn

After the Goat Girl had finished her supper and the stable boys had hurried off with the trays, Nox showed his new slave to her quarters. Handy Mandy, who had expected nothing better than a heap of straw in the corner of an empty stall, decided that for a slave she was faring pretty well. A small but complete apartment had been built in the wing next to Nox's stall, with not only a comfortable bedroom and bath, but a small sitting room as well. The bed was a huge, gold four-poster with blue silk sheets and comforters. Never in her hard and simple life had Handy dreamed of such elegance!

"Here, try the chairs," urged Nox, trotting almost briskly into the sitting room. This Mandy was only too willing to do, and the pretty little room with its bookshelves, lamps and pictures seemed to the honest Goat Girl much more desirable than the palace.

"All belonged to Kerry," mumbled the royal Ox, settling himself largely on a white rug beside her.

"Was Kerry one of your slaves?" asked Mandy, rocking herself cheerfully to and fro with all her hands resting quietly in her lap.

"SLAVE!" The Ox spoke sharply. "I should say not. Kerry was a King! Our own little King up to a few years ago, and what a lad he was — what a lad!"

"Was?" exclaimed Mandy. "Why, what happened to him?"

"He disappeared," Nox told her sadly. "Nobody knows how or where; just disappeared, my girl, on a hunting trip, and this blue-nosed scoundrel who claims to be his uncle came to rule over Keretaria. Since then," Nox lowered his voice cautiously, "everything is different — and changed. The people are treated no better than dogs. DOGS!" repeated the Royal Ox bitterly. "Of course, this fellow cannot interfere with me or take any chances, for there is a prophecy on the west wall of the castle that has stood for a thousand years."

"What does it say?" asked Mandy, leaning forward and clasping the arms of the rocker with all hands.

Impressively, Nox repeated the prophecy: "So long as the Royal Ox of Keretaria is in good health and spirits, so long and no longer shall the present King rule over the Land."

"But who wrote it?" Mandy's rocker stopped with a surprised squeak.

"Nobody knows," answered Nox soberly, "but it has come true dozens and dozens of times. Each time a new King is crowned in Keretaria, a new Ox appears mysteriously at the Royal coronation. If anything happens to the Royal Ox, the King also is destroyed!"

"My—y!" The Goat Girl now rocked very fast indeed. "So that's the reason they take such good care of you, old Toggins. But tell me, where do all of you Royal Oxen come from in the first place? And how is it you can speak? None of the beasts on Mount Mern can say a word."

"Oh, that—" the Royal Ox lifted his head lazily. "Keretaria is in the wonderful Land of Oz, my dear Handy, and all Oz creatures can talk, even the mice and squirrels. But what part of Oz we white oxen really come from I myself cannot say. I seem to remember a great blue forest and many happy days there. Then one evening a silver cloth was thrown over my head, and I fell into a deep and immediate slumber. When I awakened, I was here in Keretaria, and on that same day little King Kerry was crowned King of the Realm. From the attendants and courtiers I learned of the strange prophecy, but the young boy King was so devoted to me — and I to him — I did not miss the forest or my former freedom. To be near me, Kerry had this apartment built in the stable and spent more than half of his time in my company. My life being easy and pleasant, I gave little thought to the past or to the future, but spent all my energies enjoying the present. Once in a while, just for the looks of the thing, I appeared in Royal Processions, and each day at sundown I was yoked for an hour to the golden plow and required to stand for an hour in the royal garden. But I never did any real work or plowing till you, my reckless Handy, came along today."

"But what about the little King?" begged the Goat Girl as Nox lapsed into a thoughtful silence and seemed to have forgotten all about her.

"He disappeared, just as I told you." The Royal Ox rolled his big eyes mournfully upward. "On this day, as on many others, I carried him on my back to the edge of the wood. There, mounting his favorite steed, he rode away with the Royal Huntsmen for an hour's sport. As I was returning to the castle, someone struck me a terrific blow that felled me to the earth, where I lay for several hours in complete unconsciousness. Whoever struck me down evidently thought I was finished, for when I finally did regain my senses, I was buried beneath a heap of loose earth and leaves. Still dazed and hardly knowing what I was about, I struggled out and staggered back to the courtyard. One of my horns had been bent during the encounter, and my expression was so wild and distracted that no one recognized me as BOZ, the Royal Ox of little King Kerry. The whole castle was in an uproar, for a new King had taken possession of the throne, and thinking, of course, I was the next and new Royal Ox, this rascally imposter named me NOX. The Keretarians, without daring to inquire what had become of their former ruler, crowned me with daisies and laurel and hurried to do the bidding of their new ruler."

"WHY — the big *cowards!*" said Handy Mandy, clenching all of her fists. "And do you mean to tell me nothing has been heard of the little King since then?"

"Nothing." The Royal Ox moved his head drearily from side to side. "The people think the Royal Prophecy has been fulfilled again, and what can they DO? A farmer's boy brought word that Boz, the Royal Ox, had been struck down and spirited away, so naturally they felt sure that Kerry also had been destroyed or taken prisoner."

"Then no one suspects you are really Boz and not NOX?" questioned the Goat Girl, now on the very edge of her chair. "Oh, my—y, but don't you see, if you are still the same Ox who came to Keretaria with King Kerry and you are still all right, he must be all right, too. That is, if the prophecy means *anything*."

"Sh—hh!" warned Nox, looking about nervously. "Someone might hear you. That is what keeps me here," he went on seriously. "I felt if I stayed quietly in my place, Kerry would some day return, claim his own throne, and drive this miserable tyrant out of the country."

"Stay quietly here when the little fellow may be needing you!" cried Handy aghast. "Oh, why don't you go look for him, you great big OX, you? Come on, what are we waiting for? Why, I'll drag that old rascal off the throne with my own hands," promised the Goat Girl, indignantly waving her arms.

"Wait! Stop!" Nox sprang up with surprising lightness for one usually so ponderous and slow. "Do you realize that I am treasured and watched more closely than the crown jewels? At this very moment, twenty guardsmen stalk round and round the stable. I have as much chance of leaving Keretaria as a goldfish has of flying through a forest."

As if to prove his words, a tall soldier in a blue shako thrust his head suddenly through the window from the outside. "Is everything in order and as you wish, your Highness?" puffed the Guard, looking suspiciously at the Goat Girl's revolving arms.

"Everything is lovely," murmured the Ox in a sleepy voice. "My slave here is doing her exercises, and when she finishes she will polish my horns." At his warning wink, Handy Mandy dropped all her arms at her side.

"Well! Well! A pleasant evening to you," mumbled the soldier, withdrawing his head after another disapproving look at the Goat Girl. For a moment after he had disappeared, neither spoke, then Handy Mandy, snatching a silk cover from one of the pillows, fell to polishing Nox's left horn for very dear life.

"I can always think faster when I'm working," she observed earnestly.

"Think away," replied the Ox, closing his eyes so as not to see the numerous hands flashing past his nose. "But be careful what you say and do. If you rouse the suspicions of old King Kerr, you'll be flung into a dungeon in spite of all my influence."

"Now don't you be worrying about me," chortled Handy with a little wink and nod. "I've been taking care of myself and a flock of goats for ten years! Say, this *is* a bend, for sure." The Goat Girl ran her rubber fingers curiously along the curve in the Ox's left horn, and then, with one of her sudden and kind-hearted impulses, tried to straighten the quirk with a quick twist of her wrist. Imagine, then, if you can, her horror and surprise when the golden horn came off in her hand. "Oh, my goats and my goodness!" shuddered Handy, hopping from one foot to the other. "What'll I do? Where's some glue? Oh My—igh—igh! I'm mighty sorry!"

"Sorry!" gulped the Royal Ox, glaring at the Goat Girl with rolling eyes and lashing tail. But before he could lunge forward, as he certainly intended to do, Handy gave a little scream of excitement. "Oh look," she panted, pointing all thirty-five fingers at the base of Nox's horn. "Oh, my dear—ear, it screws on. There are regular grooves. Wait, I'll have it back in a jiffy."

Nox, who couldn't possibly see the top of his own head, merely gave a grunt, but Handy Mandy, lifting the horn in her wooden hand, screamed again and then began to shake the horn violently. At her second shake, two silver balls tumbled out and rolled away into a corner. Scrambling after them, with Nox now as interested as she, the Goat Girl

216

recovered them both and dropped breathlessly on a sofa. On closer examination, Handy discovered the balls would open as easily as cardboard Easter eggs, and with Nox's head resting heavily on her shoulder, she gave the first a quick turn. It came apart at once, and in the hollow center lay a small folded paper. Spreading it out on her knees, Handy read in a hoarse whisper: "Go to the Silver Mountain of OZ."

"Silver Mountain? Do you know where that is?" exclaimed the Goat Girl, looking wildly round at Nox.

"No, but I'll wager my head it has something to do with Kerry! Quick, m'lass, open the other ball."

With the trembling fingers of her good white hand, the Goat Girl obeyed. Inside the second sphere lay a small silver key. After they had examined this and read the message all over again, Handy carefully tucked the two articles back in the silver balls and returned the balls to the golden horn. Then, hastily screwing the horn back on its base, the two began whispering earnestly together. "Mean to say you never knew your horn came off?" questioned Handy, clasping and unclasping her hands. "Mean to say you never heard of this Silver Mountain?"

"No, to both questions," answered the Ox with an anxious little sigh. "But now that we *do* know, we must start off at once to search for it and see for ourselves whether Kerry is imprisoned there by his enemies. Though how we'll escape these guards or ever get away with half the Kingdom watching I cannot imagine!"

"Never fear, we'll manage," promised Handy easily. "Why, with your horns and my hands it will take an army to stop us. Now get your rest, Ox dear, and in the morn's morning we'll be journeying."

"You're right," breathed the Ox, starting obediently toward his stall. "I more than half believe you."

"Good night, then," called the Goat Girl softly. "Don't talk in your sleep and give our plans away!"

Chapter 5 - Out of Keretaria!

Nox was asleep on a heap of white flower petals in the corner of his stall, asleep and dreaming of the Silver Mountain of Oz, when a sharp tap on the shoulder rudely awakened him.

"Come!" whispered an urgent voice. "Time to start! Come, I've managed everything." Lurching to his feet and still in a daze, the Royal Ox looked askance and with no great favor at the Goat Girl.

"Why, it's not even light!" he moaned feebly.

"Of course not," admitted Handy Mandy guardedly, "but I poked my nose out the door a moment ago and saw all the guards were a bit drowsyish, so I tapped them on the head with this." Handy Mandy raised her iron hand and with a little grimace beckoned Nox to hurry. "Come along now, and we can be out of here before they know what's what or who."

So Nox, with a regretful look round his comfortable stall and a sigh for his morning bath and breakfast, moved quietly after her. While the Royal Creature had spent most of his time during the past two years thinking of ways to rescue his young Master, now that he was actually starting out, he was filled with doubt and dismay. How could they ever find this Silver Mountain and overcome the enemies that most certainly would beset them? The sight of the twenty guards lying in a stiff row somewhat reassured the downhearted beast, and in the dim light of early morning he looked thoughtfully up at the sturdy mountain lass stepping so resolutely beside him. In each hand Handy carried a different weapon, and resting on her broad shoulders were a rake, an axe, one guard's gun, another guard's sword, a spade, and a long-handled broom. Noting his astonished glance, the Goat Girl grinned and with her one free hand touched her fingers to her lips. So silently and without exchanging a word the two crossed the stable yard, the Royal Park, hurried through a little wood, and came out on a dusty blue Highway.

"NOW!" said Handy, looking up and down the road to make sure no one was coming, "Now we can talk and decide which direction to take."

"How can we do that," objected Nox, panting a little from the unaccustomed exertion before breakfast, "when neither of us knows where this Silver Mountain is?"

"Well, we have tongues, haven't we? And can ask, can't we?" Handy Mandy rattled her weapons impatiently. "But before we worry about the Silver Mountain, we must get out of Keretaria. Which is the quickest way to the border?"

"Oh, North," answered Nox promptly. "Keretaria is in the upper part of the Munchkin Country of Oz, and once we cross the Northern branch of the Munchkin River, we'll be entirely out of the country."

"Fine! Then we'll go North. And what lies beyond the Munchkin River?" inquired the Goat Girl, shifting the axe to her left shoulder.

"I've never crossed, myself," admitted Nox, moving along in his slow and dignified manner, "but I have heard there many purple mountains, and if we go far enough the Purple Land of the Gillikens."

"Sounds interesting," decided Handy Mandy, "and who knows, among all those mountains we may find the one we are looking for! By the way, am I to call you Boz, Nox, or Goldie Horns? But I believe I'll call you Nox, for somehow I like Nox the Ox best."

"Anything you say," yawned her companion, switching his tail negligently, "but I shall always call YOU Handy Mandy. It suits you, m'lass, and you need no longer consider yourself a slave."

"Ho, ho, I never did," roared the Goat Girl, glancing cheerfully down at her lordly companion. "That was just a joke, wasn't it? You know, everything in this Land of Oz is extremely funny and peculiar. Two-armed natives, animals talking, Kings disappearing, and mysterious messages and prophecies."

"People always think a new country is strange!" observed the ox philosophically. "To us it seems quite right and natural. But I daresay if I were to find myself on Mt. Mern I'd consider everything there very odd and upsetting; rocks flying through the air, for instance, and landing one soft and light as a daisy in a strange King's garden."

"But all of our rocks don't fly. In fact, I never knew one to do such a thing before. And no wonder I landed as soft as a daisy — there was a blue daisy under me, or I'd have been splintered to smithereens!"

"Daisy?" Nox licked his lips hungrily. "You never said anything about a daisy."

"Oh, I never tell all I know," confided Handy, "especially to Hi-qui-cockadoodlums like the King and his Counselors. But there was a daisy — growing on the rock, and I picked it. As I started to fall, I began pulling off the petals, and when I landed I came down on a high, huge pile of them, a heap as high as a haystack," continued Handy Mandy dreamily. "So I slid off the stack and turned to look at the castle, and when I looked again, the petals were gone, but there was the daisy itself growing up as pert as you please in this strange garden. So what did I do but pick it again, and here it is!" Triumphantly, Handy pulled the blue flower from her pocket.

"My, what a dear little daisy!" murmured the Ox. "How delicious it would taste."

"No! NO!" cried Handy as Nox rolled his long tongue out toward the flower. "It's too pretty to eat."

"Nothing's too pretty to eat," replied the ox plaintively. "Funny it hasn't wilted, though."

"Well, I believe it's magic," stated the Goat Girl with a positive little shake of her head. As she returned the daisy to her pocket, Handy felt the hard metal object that had hit her in the forehead when she and Nox plowed through the King's garden. "Look! What do you suppose this is?" she queried, tapping the Ox sharply on the shoulder, for he was walking sleepily along with his eyes closed. "This is what we dug up when we rushed through the garden, you know."

"How should I know?" grunted the Ox indifferently, opening one eye. "Just a silver hammer, isn't it? Maybe we can trade it for a good breakfast when we cross the river."

"My—y how you talk!" scolded Handy. "We're not going to trade it at all. See, there's an initial on it. A big W. Now what would W stand for?"

"Who, what, which, where, oh why worry?" mumbled the Ox, plodding resignedly along beside her.

"Well, anyway, it will make a splendid potato masher," concluded the Goat Girl, returning the hammer to her pocket.

"Yes, if we had any potatoes." The Ox sighed heavily as he spoke, looking off into the distance with such a mournful eye Handy Mandy laughed a little all to herself.

"Oh, cheer up," sniffed the Goat Girl, "you're not starved yet. And hurry up, too, the sun's going higher every moment, and we'd better pass those farms before the people waken."

It was against Nox's nature to hurry, but realizing the wisdom of the Goat Girl's advice, he broke into an awkward gallop. In spite of his great weight, the Royal creature was light as a daisy on his feet, and except for the faint rattle of Handy's weapons they made little noise as they ran past the dome-shaped blue houses and barns of the Munchkin farmers. "Couldn't we stop for a few greens?" puffed Nox, looking longingly over the fence at a field of cabbages.

"Not here, dear—ear!" Red-faced and breathless, the Goat Girl ran on. "Wait till we cross this river—iver."

"But I'm not used to this sort of thing," complained Nox peevishly. "Running races before breakfast on an empty stomach. No bath, no brush, no rubdown!"

"Well, here's your brush," gasped Handy, picking her way through a dense thicket as the highway ended in a small wood, "and yonder's your bath, Mister. My—y, what a blue river!"

"Everything's blue in the Munchkin Country of Oz," Nox told her sulkily as sharp briars and thorns reached out to scratch his satiny hide.

"Even the Royal Ox of Keretaria," hinted Mandy with a sly wink. "Oh, the river's blue and the houses are blue and even the wind blew — Hoo Hoo! Come on."

"Don't try to be funny," with heaving sides, the Ox stepped on the edge of the gleaming blue stream. "Don't try to be funny, I beg."

"Oh, I don't have to try, I am!" laughed Handy, flinging the axe, the rake, the spade, the sword, the gun and the broomstick across the river.

"Wait!" snorted the Ox as Handy, having got rid of her load, raised all of her hands above her head and prepared to dive in. "Wait, can you swim?"

"I don't know, but I'll soon find out," cried Handy, and before Nox could prevent it, the Goat Girl leapt off the bank and disappeared beneath the blue waters of the Munchkin River. For once, Nox forgot his dignity and Royal station and plunged frantically after his reckless companion. Swimming around with his head under water, he finally located Handy Mandy, and gripping her yellow plaits firmly in his teeth dragged her to the opposite bank. The Goat Girl was so full of water she had little say and lay soggily on the grass while Nox looked down at her with mingled admiration and concern.

"Never do such a thing again," he wheezed severely as Handy finally sat up and began wringing the water from her voluminous skirts. "Swimming is an art and must be learned and practiced. But for oat's sake, why didn't you flap all those arms when you hit the water?" he finished irritably.

"Oh, is that what you're supposed to do? This way?" Before Nox could step a step, the Goat Girl had jumped into the river again. This time, instead of going down, she splashed and whirled her seven arms so fast and furiously she just managed to keep her head above water. But Nox, now thoroughly annoyed and without giving her a chance to get far from shore, waded in and determinedly dragged her back to dry land.

"What in sky-blue onions are you trying to do?" he sputtered angrily, "Drown yourself?"

"No, I'm trying to swim," coughed the Goat Girl, struggling to get away from the angry Ox. "Do you suppose I'm going to let this Munchkin River get the best of me?"

"Yes, and while you are swimming, or rather practicing your swimming, some of these Keretarians will come and capture us," gurgled Nox. "Are we escaping or are we swimming? Quick now, make up your mind."

Nox's earnest words brought Handy quickly to her senses, and as the Royal Ox let go her skirts she snatched up her weapons and, without waiting to wring out her clothes, started briskly across the meadows.

"Never mind, you'll be a fine swimmer some day," said Nox, trotting more amiably beside her. The cool river water had refreshed the Royal creature, and Handy Mandy's determination and courage made him a little ashamed of his own complaints. "Takes a little practice, that's all."

"Practice!" repeated Handy, dripping water from every plait and pore. "Well, just wait till we come to the next river; I'll show you! But LOOK, here are more blue houses, so we must still be in the Munchkin Country."

"Yes, but we're out of Keretaria," Nox reminded her cheerfully. "What's that signpost say, my girl?"

Hurrying forward, Handy squinted up at the rough board nailed to a blue spruce, and then began to clench and unclench her one free fist.

"TURN HERE!" directed the sign. "Turn here and go straight back where you came from."

"Well, I'll be buttered!" cried the Goat Girl, throwing down every one of her weapons. "I'll be churned and buttered."

"But what had we butter do?" muttered the Royal Ox, so taken aback by the saucy message that even his tongue was twisted.

"Why, we'll go straight on, of course," declared Handy Mandy, tossing her yellow plaits defiantly. "Who are whoever they are to tell us our business?" And recovering her weapons one by one, the Goat Girl tramped down the crooked lane directly ahead of them, the Royal Ox with lifted nose and horns, stepping warily behind her.

Chapter 6 - Turn Town!

Determined as she was, Handy found it impossible to go straight on, for the lane curved and twisted this way and that, ending finally in a perfect corkscrew turn. The trees on both sides were now so dense Handy and the Royal Ox could not have left the road even had they wished to do so. "We're going round and round and getting nowhere," said Nox in an abused voice. "Of all the roads in Oz, why did we have to pick this one?"

"Because it dared us, I suppose. Hi—Yi!" exclaimed Handy, leaning against a tree to rest. "I'm dizzy as a bat and hungry as a goat."

"Too bad you're not a goat," murmured Nox, who had stopped to nibble the lower branches of a maple. "These leaves are quite tender."

"Well, I may come to them," sighed Handy, looking at him enviously. "But shall we go on? I think one more turn will bring us out of here."

Handy was right, for one more round brought them to the end of corkscrew lane, but only to find themselves facing a high, forbidding wall. There were a gate and turnstile in the wall, and beyond the Goat Girl caught a glimpse of a confused, whirling village where everything seemed to be turning round or over. "It's just because I'm so dizzy," thought Handy, clutching her head with her one free hand. But Nox, peering over her shoulder, gave a loud and indignant bellow as a house on the corner of the street nearest them turned completely over and began spinning merrily on its chimney, while the fence running around the bakery shop next door started really to run around, kicking up its posts with great glee and abandon.

"Hu—what kind of silly place is this?" rumbled the Ox, backing hastily away. But Handy Mandy had seen a whole row of little pies in the bakeshop window, and motioning vigorously for Nox to follow, stepped over the stile and through the movable gate. It was too much of a squeeze for Nox, but determined not to be left behind, he jumped neatly over. A revolving sign on one of the large public buildings caught their attention at once, but as the building was going one way and the sign another, it was several minutes before they could discover what it said.

"TURN TOWN!" read the Goat Girl in some surprise. "So that's where we are! And would you loo—ook, every house on every street is going round or over. Mercy—ercy on us, and where do you suppose the people are?"

"Turning over and over in their beds, I take it. It is still quite early, you know," whispered the Royal Ox, speaking cautiously out of the corner of his mouth. "But come on, the streets are not turning, and perhaps if we hurry we can go through before they waken and turn on us. Hurry, hurry. What are you waiting for?"

"Food," sighed Handy wistfully. "I thought I might catch us a few pies, Old Toggins. Here, watch my stuff, and I'll bring us each some."

Nox looked sharply up and down the street, as the Goat Girl set down her axe, rake, spade, gun, broom and sword and started off toward the bakery. Not only the fence, but the shop itself was turning now. Handy quite cleverly waited till the gate came opposite her and dashed through, but the open door of the shop kept going by so rapidly she was knocked down several times before she finally darted inside. As she disappeared, Nox gave an uneasy snort, but cheered up as the shop window came past and he saw Handy with a pie in every hand smile at him reassuringly. But alas, the whirling floor of the shop was too much for the Goat Girl, and as she started out, there was a clatter of broken china and falling furniture.

"Great Gazoo, what's she done now?" moaned Nox as Handy leaped through the door and fell sprawling in the little garden. She still had six of the pies clutched in her various hands, but as she jumped up and raced through the garden gate, windows all up and down the street were flung open. From the rightside-up ones and the downside-down ones kinky little black heads came popping out by the hundred.

"Turn out! Turn out! Topsies turn out!" yelled the excited citizens, their voices going higher and higher. "Thieves, robbers, tramps and Stand-Stillians!"

"Here," gasped the Goat Girl, reaching Nox in one bound. "Eat these quick and destroy the evidence." Stuffing one of the tarts into her own mouth, Handy made a wry face. "Ugh, TURNIPS!" choked the Goat Girl, dropping the other five in huge disgust. "Whoever heard of turnip turnovers?"

"I'll eat them," offered Nox, lapping up the little pies in his stride. "But run! Hurry, here come the natives!" But before Handy could snatch up her weapons, the Topsies, hurling out of windows and doors, came whirling down upon them. Startled though she was, the Goat Girl could not disguise her interest and curiosity. With one arm around Nox's neck and the other six stretched stiffly before her to keep back the screeching crowd, she stared with round and fascinated eyes. And no wonder! The Topsies were about as tall as children, but where their feet should have been they had sharp, horny pegs. Another peg of the same description sprung from each kinky head. With their plump hands the small black-and-blue men and women spun themselves along by cords attached to their round little middles, and they kept reversing themselves, spinning first on one end and then another in a manner very upsetting and confusing to their visitors. The hum made by the Topsies' spinning and their loud, raucous cries filled the early morning air, and as Handy tried to push her way through the crowd several butted her with their sharp pegs.

"Ouch! Stop that!" bellowed Nox, who had been butted too. "Keep still, m'lass, and sooner or later these little pests will run down."

"Turn them out! Turn them in! Turn them round! Turn them over!" shrieked the Topsies hysterically. In the midst of the dreadful confusion, a Topsy taller than all the rest came zooming down the middle of the street. "Look! STAND-STILLIANS!" shouted a round little spinster waving both arms. "Travelers with legs instead of pegs. Robbers! Thieves! And tramps, your Topjesty."

"Yes, and they have broken into my shop and stolen all my turnip turnovers," screamed the Topsy Baker, spinning round in indignant circles. "Aha, you wait, here comes the Tip-Topper. Now you'll catch it, you — you Turnover snatchers, you!"

"Now you'll catch it!" shrilled all the rest of the Topsies, spinning faster and faster till Handy and Nox were dizzy just from looking at them.

220

Except for his size and a flag fluttering from the peg on his head, Tip-Topper looked just like his subjects. "Spin! Spin!" he whistled angrily. "What do you mean standing still in the middle of Turn Town? Don't you realize you are breaking every one of our rotary laws? Why are you here? Did you come to do us a good turn or a bad?"

"Turn 'em down! Turn 'em out! Turn 'em over! Turn 'em round!" insisted the townsmen shrilly. Between the revolving houses and the spinning Topsies, Handy Mandy scarcely knew which foot she was standing on. As for Nox, he gave a great groan, and closing his eyes left everything to his companion. Handy put two hands over her ears, and raising all the others addressed Tip-Topper in a firm and reasonable manner.

"Tell your people to stand back," directed the Goat Girl calmly. "All we wish is to pass quietly through your city and never return. NEVER!" she repeated emphatically. It was hard to speak to a person who kept going round and round, but at every third turn Handy managed to catch Tip-Topper's eye, and at last he seemed to catch her idea.

"Very well, then, GO!" he commanded haughtily. "And at once!" But when Handy, without stopping to pick up her weapons, started forward, perfect shrieks of anger rose on all sides.

"Not that way! Not what way. Turn! Turn! Turn!" yelled the Topsies. And getting back of Handy and the Royal Ox, they tried to push them round by main force.

"Stop! Stop! It's no use," panted Tip-Topper as Nox, letting out a frightful bellow, laid seven Topsies by the pegs with his left hind foot and Handy with a sweep of her arms swept down ten more. "They're all made wrong. Fetch the Turn Coat, drive them to the turning point, and we'll turn them to Topsies in two shakes of a tent pole."

"M—mmmmmmm! M—mmmmmmm! Did you hear what I heard?" Nox peered desperately around at Handy, who was now spinning dizzily herself as she was flung and pushed from one group to another. "Could they really turn us to Topsies?"

"I don't know! I don't know! Oh, my head, my HEAD!" moaned the Goat Girl, clutching it with all hands. "It's going round and round—"

"Fine! Fine! That's the way!" cheered the Topsies heartily. "You'll be spinning circles before you know it and have beautiful wool like the rest of us."

"Wool!" gasped Handy, who was extremely fond of her shining yellow braids. "Oh, I wool not. That's just too much! Stand back, you little buzzards, and I'll show you a turn or two myself."

"Go ahead," said Turn Uppins, who seemed next in importance to Tip-Topper himself. "It's your turn anyway. Stand back, Topsies, and let this waddling whangus show us what she can do."

At a signal from their leader, the Turn Towners fell back a pace and, spinning in a loud, agitated circle, impatiently waited for the Goat Girl to take her turn. First Handy shook her head to dispel the dizziness, then with a loud screech she flung her arms and heels into the air in such a succession of handsprings that even the Topsies were impressed. The seventh brought her back to the Royal Ox, and in the center of a now cheering and admiring circle, she turned fifty more so fast that she looked like an animated cartwheel with arms and legs for spokes. A loud buzz of applause went up as Handy finally fell over from sheer exhaustion, but then they began pointing accusing fingers at Nox. "Look! Look at the stupid Gumflumox, why he hasn't turned a single hair."

"How about turning on them," raged Nox, "and tossing a few dozen on my horns? Hop on my back, m'lass, and we'll make a run for it."

"No! No! There are too many. We'll be perfectly punctured," worried Handy as seven Topsies prodded the Royal Ox sharply in the flank. "We might run right into that turning point, too. Wait! Wait! I'll think of something. We don't want to spin on here forever, what*ever* happens! Whew—hewey, what a dust the little pests kick up. I'd give my best hand for a drink; I'm choking with thirst. Oh! Oh! I wish I were in a river right this minute." Steadying herself by holding to Nox's right horn, Handy faced the angry multitude.

"Turn! Turn! Take your turn!" shouted the Topsies incessantly. "Can't you even turn your head, old four-leg?"

"Of course he can," shouted Handy Mandy, clapping six of her hands for silence. "Not only his head, but his horns. Watch this, my friends!" The Goat Girl gave the horn she was leaning on a sharp twist.

"Not that one. Not that one!" fumed the Ox anxiously. "Quick, the other. It's the other one, I tell you! Oh, my hide, hair, and Heavens! Ulp! Gurgle Ooooop!"

And "Oooop gurgle ULP!" it was with everyone, for at Handy Mandy's second turn, Nox's horn came completely off, and as the Goat Girl held it up for the Topsies to see, out spurted a perfect torrent of water that flooded the whole city till every Turner and Topsy-turvy house in it was awash or afloat. In wild and astonished voices, the kinky-headed little citizens called out to each other as they bobbed up and down like corks on the raging tide. And just as wet and surprised as the Topsies, the Goat Girl and Nox were swept along by the impetuous flood.

Chapter 7 - A Horn of Plenty

After the first awful ducking, Handy, without losing a second began to practice her swimming. Striking out with strength and purpose and her seven good arms, she managed to keep abreast of Nox, who was moving easily along in the center of the torrent. Bothersome as the Topsies had been, the Goat Girl could not help feeling sorry for the little Turn Towners. At first, she feared they would all go down. But they just spun like water bugs on the surface, and while they made no progress, they seemed in little danger of drowning. In fact, they could no more sink than corks or kindling. So busy with her own struggles, Handy dismissed them from her mind and tried to figure out the reason for the sudden and overwhelming rush of water that had deluged the city.

At any rate, it was fine to be rid of the Topsies, she reflected philosophically, and when the flood did recede Turn Town would be good as new and twice as clean. The current was racing along so swiftly now that the last Topsy had long since disappeared, leaving only herself and Nox in the broad, tumbling expanse of water. Nox had not uttered a word since his first outcry when the flood had overtaken them, but he looked so glum and disagreeable that Handy, thrashing along beside him, wondered what would be the best way to start a conversation. As it happened, the Royal beast saved her the trouble by starting one himself.

"Well," he snorted bitterly. "I see you still have it."

"WHAT?" gulped the Goat Girl, forgetting to use her arms for a moment and in consequence shipping about a bucket of water. "Ulp — gulp — have what?"

"My horn. HORN!" gurgled Nox, glaring at her angrily over a wave. "And if in the future you will keep your hands, all of them, off my horns, it will be the better for us." This seemed to Handy a very unjust and unreasonable attitude for Nox to take, but she was too occupied keeping afloat to stop and argue the matter.

"Swim closer and I'll screw it back," she offered, obligingly holding up the wooden hand in which she still clutched the right half of the royal headgear. But at this, poor Nox was deluged by a robust stream that still poured from the golden horn. Hastily plunging it under the surface again, Handy watched her fellow adventurer emerge sputtering and furious from the depths.

"Well of all the stupid tricks!" gasped the Ox, swimming rapidly away from her. "Stop. Keep off. Don't you dare come near me."

"But see here," panted Handy, going after him in real exasperation, "after all, it is your horn, and am I to blame if there is a river inside? What do you want me to do, throw it away?"

"No! No!" bellowed the Ox, stopping short and looking frantically over his shoulder. "If you throw it away, I'll look like a fool. If you keep holding it, we'll spend the rest of our lives swimming round in this torrent. If you screw it back on my head, it will probably give me water on the brain. Oh, blub glub! What shall we do? THINK of something, can't you, before we both drown in your stupid old river?"

"My river!" Handy Mandy was so indignant that for a moment she was perfectly speechless.

"Yes, your river!" roared Nox, treading water angrily. "Didn't you wish for a river just before you jerked off my horn? Well, this is it, and I hope you like it."

"Why Nox, how clever of you to guess," bubbled the Goat Girl, a great light breaking over her wet head. "I remember now. I was thirsty and wished for a drink, then a whole river. And lo! a river was here."

"You mean HIGH it was here," raged Nox, beginning to swim again.

"But look," cried Handy, beating and slapping the water exultantly with her many hands. "If that is so, all we have to do is to wish it away again. I'm still holding the magic horn, and there's magic in it, old Toddywax — MAGIC! I here and now wish this river AWAY."

Handy yelled her wish in a booming voice that almost split the Ox's eardrums, and both were so sure the wish would be granted they stopped swimming, so both had a fine ducking as the river continued to rush merrily and unconcernedly over their heads.

"Bosh! It wasn't magic, after all. My—y, if I ever get out of here, I'll never go swimming again as long as I live," sobbed Handy, pushing her arms and legs wearily through the water.

"Oh, I think I'll just sink and be done with it," moaned the Ox, churning breathlessly along beside her.

"You think you'll sink!" exclaimed Handy, popping her head up indignantly. "Don't you dare sink and leave me here all alone. Besides, we set out to find that little King, and we're going to find him! Where's your sporting blood?"

"Watered!" gurgled the Royal Ox in a faint voice. "Goodbye, m'lass, you probably did it all for the best!" It seemed to the Goat Girl that Nox was really sinking, so flinging out her leather hand she grasped him firmly by his left horn. Then, acting quickly and before he could object, Handy pushed his head under water and quickly screwed his right horn in place.

"I wish this dumb river would go straight back where it came from," quavered Handy as Nox, bellowing and bubbling, backed indignantly away. And THIS TIME the river went. So suddenly and completely the Goat Girl and the Ox were dropped forty feet to the bottom of a rocky gorge through which the torrent had been tumbling. For a long moment, they lay where they had fallen, then stiffly they arose and peered anxiously around them. Handy, thanks to her voluminous petticoats, was saved from serious injury, and Nox, who had landed in a patch of brush, was not dangerously hurt either. But they both were so shocked, shaken and worn out from their long swim, they were perfectly content to stay where they were.

"You see," sighed Handy, wringing out her skirts with four hands and smoothing back her hair with the other three, "the magic is in the horn and only works when you are wearing it. As soon as I screwed it back and made the wish, everything was all right."

"Oh, was it?" Scowling round at his scratched flanks and skinned shins, the Royal Ox shook his head dubiously.

"And just think," continued the Goat Girl brightly, "if your horn really is a wishing horn, as soon as we decide where we want to go, all we have to do is wish ourselves there."

"No! No! Absolutely no more of that," squealed Nox, lashing his tail and flashing his eyes dangerously. "Your last wish nearly killed me, and if any more wishing is to be done, I'll attend to it myself."

"But how can you unscrew or even touch your own horn all by yourself?" inquired Handy reasonably. "You see, you need my hands, and I need your horns." Throwing back her head, Handy burst into a loud chuckle, thinking how comical she would look if she actually wore Nox's golden headgear.

"Oh, why not go on the way we started?" said the Ox querulously. "I'd rather travel on my feet than my horns any day, and had you noticed, Handy, that these rocks are purple? Your river has carried us clear into the Gillikin Country where there are mountains galore, and even a silver one for all we know."

"Yes, but is there anything to eat?" asked the Goat Girl in a hollow voice. "If those rude little Topsies had just given us some breakfast."

"I expect all they eat is spinach or turnips," sniffed Nox, "and you would not have cared for either. Well, at any rate we're even. You certainly turned the tide on them, m'lass." Nox, who was beginning to feel more cheerful, began to shake all over. "I'll wager my tail they'll be more polite to travelers in the future."

"Well, as it all turned out so well, let's make another wish," proposed Handy Mandy practically. "Let's wish ourselves out of here. No use scrambling over all these rocks when all we have to do is wish yourselves to the spot where your little King happens to be."

"M-m-mm, M-m-m!" mused Nox, half closing his eyes. "Nothing is as easy as that, and I cannot help feeling—"

"Neither can I," said Handy, and stepping briskly up to the royal Ox, she gave his right horn a determined twist, at the same time saying softly: "I wish myself and Nox with Kerry, the rightful ruler of Keretaria." Nox twitched his ears nervously as his horn came off in the Goat Girl's best white hand, and Handy herself, with all her arms outspread as if she were a bird about to take flight, waited in rapturous expectation for her wish to take effect. But this time nothing at all happened. Neither she nor the Ox moved an inch.

"There you are. I told you it wouldn't work," grumbled Nox, looking at her crossly. "It's probably not magic at all."

"Oh yes it is," insisted Handy, screwing up her eye and peering down into the hollow interior. "It gave us a river when we asked for it, and you can't get away from that."

"We certainly had a hard enough time getting away from it," agreed her companion. "Come now, be a good girl, screw back that horn, and let's be starting on."

"But I just cannot understand why it grants some wishes and not others," muttered Handy discontentedly. "When I was thirsty and wished for a river, I got a river— AHA! I have it. This horn gives you things but does not take you places. Now let's see, what do we need the most?"

"Breakfast," suggested the Ox in an interested voice. "Oats and apples for me, eggs, rolls and coffee for you. But for GOAT'S sake be careful how you wish, m'lass. We don't want too much even of a good thing, and one can drown in coffee or smother in oats. Remember the river and be exact as to size and quantity."

"My—y, this wishing is dreadfully complicated." Rubbing her forehead with one hand after the other, Handy Mandy prepared to order breakfast. First she screwed the right horn back on the head of the Ox, then, pursing her lips firmly, she spoke: "I wish for Nox two measures of oats and apples; for myself two plates of eggs and rolls and one cup of coffee." Turning the horn round till it came off once more, the Goat Girl almost held her breath as the two breakfasts were set promptly and noiselessly down on the rock at her feet.

223

"Now you're getting the idea!" Happily Nox advanced upon his breakfast.

"Say, isn't this simply manubious?" cried Handy, snapping her thirty-five fingers for sheer joy. "Why, Nox, your horn is a real horn of plenty!"

"And plenty of trouble if you don't watch your wishes," mumbled her partner, already up to his ears in oats.

"Oh, I'll be careful, never fear," promised Handy, screwing the horn back on its base and falling upon her breakfast with a right good will and appetite. "Won't the eyes of the villagers back home stick out when I tell them about this?"

"Yes, provided you ever GET home," observed the Ox, who seemed always to take a dark view of the future. But Handy Mandy, popping the last of the biscuits into her mouth, scarcely heard him. Now that they need no longer worry about provisions for the journey, she felt that they would safely reach the Silver Mountain wherever it might be, rescue the little King from his enemies, and restore him to his throne. Then after seeing all she wished of the marvelous country of Oz, she would return to Mt. Mern and startle the country folk with the amazing story of her travels.

"Come along," she called gaily. "Let's climb out of here." With some astonishment, they watched the empty containers and dishes vanish away, and then, saying very little but thinking a great deal, the two adventurers began to scramble up the rocky sides of the gorge.

Chapter 8 - Handy Mandy learns about Oz!

Handy, who had climbed up and down mountains all her life, reached the top of the gorge first, and with her various hands tugged Nox up the last steep incline.

"So this is the Gillikin Country!" panted the Goat Girl, staring away over the heather-covered Highlands. "Now about the natives: do they spin, bounce, or tumble?"

"That I really couldn't say," gasped Nox, leaning against a tree to regain his wind. "But as you can see, my girl, all the hills, trees and vegetation shade from violet to purple. Lovely color, purple!"

"I suppose purple would appeal to a Royal Ox like you." Resting her hands on her hips, Handy Mandy squinted critically about her. "Now as for me, I prefer the more cheerful colors, red, yellow or green, for instance."

"Then you'd like the Quadling and Winkie Countries," murmured Nox, nibbling languidly at the tops of the heather, "or the Emerald City. We have all color countries in Oz, and a body can take his choice."

"Oh, we'll just take them as they come," decided the Goat Girl sensibly, "or at least till we find your young Master and this Silver Mountain. But tell me, Nox, is each country in Oz a different color, and is there really an Emerald City?" Moving slowly through the heather, the Royal Ox nodded his lordly head.

"Take that stick," he directed, coming to a ponderous stop, "and I'll show you how Oz looks. See, on that level bit of sand there, just draw an oblong." Quite interested, Handy marked out an oblong with the point of the stick. "Connect the corners," breathed the Ox, lifting his forefoot complacently, "and what have you?"

"Four triangles," answered the Goat Girl promptly.

"Put a circle in the center where all the triangles meet." Nox fairly radiated pride and importance as he geozophy lesson progressed.

"Then what?" demanded Handy, the stick upraised in her rubber hand.

"That's all!" Tossing back his horns, the Ox surveyed his pupil triumphantly. "Simple, isn't it? That triangle on the west is the blue Munchkin Country we have just left, the triangle to the north is the purple Gillikin Country we are just entering. Over there on the east we have the Yellow empire of the Winkies, and to the south the red lands of the Quadlings. In the circle is the Emerald City of Oz, and surrounding the whole Kingdom is a deadly desert of burning sand."

"My—y!" marveled the Goat Girl, clasping all her hands but one behind her back. "The desert I crossed when I fell in Keretaria?"

"Of course," answered Nox, snapping lazily at a purple dragonfly. "Mt. Mern must lie to the west of Oz on the other side of the deadly desert. There are many countries beyond the desert, but I know very little about them, as there are only Oz maps in the castle at home."

"Then I suppose the King of Keretaria is King of the Munchkins?" said Handy, looking thoughtfully down at her map.

"Oh, my, no!" The Royal Ox positively chuckled at such an idea. "Keretaria is just one of the small countries of the West. Cheeriobed is King of the Munchkins, and he lives in the Sapphire City seventy leagues below our southernmost borderline. Glinda, the Good Sorceress, rules all the small Kingdoms in the Quadling Country, the Tin Woodman of Oz is Emperor of the Winkies, and Jo King governs the Gillikins. Besides these, there are Kings, Queens and Princes galore, but most important of all is Ozma, the young Fairy who lives in the Emerald City, for Ozma is supreme sovereign of the entire Kingdom of Oz."

"Dear—ear, what a lot to remember," groaned the Goat Girl. "And all these other Kings and Queens have to do what Ozma says? However does she keep track of them all? I'll bet they're worse than a flock of goats."

"Oh, she manages," said the Ox, beginning to move slowly forward. "Being a fairy and having a wizard right in her own castle, Ozma knows what is going on without even turning her head."

"Even where we are going?" exclaimed Handy Mandy indignantly. "Hi—yi, what a little busybody. I just know I won't like her."

"Well, in that case she will just have to give up her throne and throw her crown out of the window, I suppose! Better have a care, m'lass, you're speaking of a powerful fairy, you know." Nox looked so stern as he went plowing through the heather that Handy began to feel a little uneasy herself.

"But how could a fairy in the center of Oz see way off here?" she demanded scornfully.

"Magic, that's how!" explained Nox, looking very calm and superior. "In her castle, Ozma has a magic picture that shows her everything she wishes to see."

"I don't believe it," scoffed the Goat Girl, swinging all her arms recklessly, "and besides, why would she wish to see us and this particular piece of country at this particular minute?"

"I'm sure I don't know," said the Royal Ox haughtily. "But I do say, be careful. There, what did I tell you?" Framed in the woodwork of a small summerhouse they were approaching was a large poster.

"You are now in the Land of Oz," stated the poster pleasantly enough. "Be good to us, and we'll be good to you. Keep our laws and practice no magic, either for good or evil. By order of Her Imperial Highness, Queen Ozma of Oz." Below was the bright green seal of Oz and a picture of its pretty dark-haired ruler.

"Why, she's nothing but a little girl!" cried Handy, positively aghast at such a state of affairs. "How could a little mite like that rule a whole country and be so bossy?"

"Oh, hush!" begged Nox, rolling his eyes anxiously. "Mite or not, Ozma is a mighty powerful and important fairy."

"Well, we're pretty important ourselves," sniffed the Goat Girl, squinting at the poster with all her arms akimbo. "And besides," Handy lifted her chin defiantly, "we've broken the law already when we used your gold horn of plenty. `Practice no magic.' Hoh! What does she expect us to do with good magic right at hand — starve? But, ho ho! We can get around that, old Toggins. After all, we are not practicing magic, we don't have to practice it — our magic is perfect, so put that in your pipe and smoke it, Miss Ozma to Bozma." Snatching up a rock in each of her seven hands, Handy flung them hilariously over a clump of prune trees. (Yes, prunes already wrinkled grow in the Land of Oz.) There was an uncomfortable little silence after Handy's rash outburst, then a perfect tempest of shrieks and screeches.

"Now see what you've done," gulped the Ox, switching his tail nervously. "Quick, quick, jump on my back and we'll rush by. These chaps look dangerous."

"Why, they have HOOK noses!" sputtered Handy, too startled to move as a band of kilted Highlanders came racing down toward them. The noses of these singular Hillmen were long and thin, curving out and up far above their foreheads. On these hooks hung dangerous-looking rings almost as large as barrel hoops. While Handy was wondering what they could be for, the nearest Hooker pulled a ring from his nose and flung it with all his might at her head.

"Up, UP!" bellowed Nox, pawing the ground in his agitation. "Are you going to stand there till you are pegged like a top?" The iron ring missed Handy by mere inches, and grasping Nox's horn, she pulled herself to his back. There were about sixty of the hooknoses, and swinging to the left Nox tried to skirt the warlike tribe, but they were too quick for him, and spreading out in a long line, they began hurling their wicked, whizzing weapons. One caught neatly on the horn of the Royal Ox, another hit Handy a horrid blow on the knee, and as Nox, snorting and furious, turned to run, a dozen more came whanging down about their ears. Dodging left and right, Handy Mandy leaned forward and began to unscrew Nox's right horn.

" `Be good to us and we'll be good to you!' HOH! Like fun you will!" muttered the Goat Girl, catching six of the flying missiles in her clever hands and tossing them back with all her might. "Take that and these and them and THOSE!" Pulling off the Ox's horn with the only hand she had left, she added desperately, "I wish a barrel of molasses over the head of each Hooknose in this band. Cats, Bats and Billy Goats! They've GOT me!" And they had, too, for just as Handy finished her wish, down flashed an iron ring, pinioning her arms tightly to her sides. Still grasping the precious horn, Handy dug her heels into Nox.

"Hurt?" grunted the Ox, leaping forward.

"Not hurt, just hooked and humiliated, can't move a muscle," raged the Goat Girl. "But ha ha! Neither can they! LOOK!" Nox, who had been bellowing too hard to hear Handy's wish or miss his horn, glanced back hurriedly.

"Why, what's come over them?" he wheezed in astonishment. "Who snuffed them out with barrels, and what's that sticky fluid running all around?"

225

"Molasses," Handy told him with extreme satisfaction as she tried vainly to wriggle out of her ring. "I wished barrels of molasses on their heads, and we'd better dash on while they're stopped and stuck with it."

"Then you've been breaking the law again," reproached Nox, dodging in and out and around their frantic enemies.

"Well, as between broken heads and broken laws, I choose the laws. Besides, look what they did to me!" exclaimed the Goat Girl indignantly. "I may never get this hoop off or be able to lift a hand again. Nice people you have in Oz, I must say."

"If you hadn't hit them with stones, they wouldn't have hit us with hoops," Nox reminded her sternly, at the same time breaking into a gallop to put as much distance as possible between himself and the troublesome Gillikins. A few had managed to lift the barrels from their heads, but most of them were rolling over and over on the ground, half choked with rage and molasses.

"When we stop, I think I can help you," promised Nox, looking anxiously at Handy, who was now quite purple in the face from her struggles with the hoop. "Just forget it, can't you, and think of the interesting people we are meeting. I'll wager you have no hooknoses on Mt. Mern!"

"I should say NOT!" sputtered the Goat Girl in disgust, and then, realizing she was making no progress with the ring, sensibly gave up the attempt to free herself. Somewhat comforted by the thought that the Hook Noses were probably as uncomfortable as she was, Handy kept a sharp lookout for natives. If they ran into any more, she wanted to be sure of seeing them first.

But the rocky hills and glades were entirely deserted, and at every step the way became more mountainous and lonely. Nox, panting and wheezing from the long pull, slackened his pace to a walk. Handy Mandy with some difficulty managed to dismount, and the Ox, slipping his horn under the offending ring, gently forced it upward till the Goat Girl was able to wriggle free. Then together they climbed up the flinty inclines — up and up till they came to a wide ledge and a sparkling waterfall. Here they had a drink without having to wish for one, Nox sticking his head right into the water and Handy cupping three pairs of her hands to hold enough to satisfy her thirst.

"Ho hum," sighed the Ox. "I wonder how much farther we'll have to go before we can find anyone who can direct us to this Silver Mountain? I'm sure I saw some castles when we were below."

"So did I," said Handy, screwing his right horn back with a businesslike flourish. "My—y, seems a long time since we started from Keretaria. Do you suppose they have missed us yet?"

"Probably," yawned the Ox, scratching his back against a rock while Handy, suddenly deciding she needed another drink, stepped close to the waterfall. But instead of quenching her thirst, the Goat Girl spilled water all over her feet.

"Nox! Nox!" she screamed, jerking all her thumbs in his direction. "Come! Look here! There's a big hollow behind this waterfall — a high wall of rock with a door in it! I can see it!"

"Well," sniffed the Ox, rubbing his back luxuriously, "does it say `come in'? Must we try every door we come to?"

"Yes," Handy Mandy told him firmly, "we must! Where there's a door there's bound to be a doorkeeper or at least someone who might tell us where we are. Now then, I'll jump through the waterfall first and knock on the door. There wouldn't be room for you on the ledge until the door is open."

"Sounds risky!" objected the Royal Ox, putting back his ears. "What kind of people would live behind a waterfall? Ask yourself that." But the Goat Girl, without stopping to ask herself anything, had already plunged through the misty sheet of water and, gasping and spluttering, was hammering on the door with all seven of her fists.

Chapter 9 - The Magic Hammer

There was no answer to Handy's loud knocks, and pausing to catch her breath and blow on her fingers, the Goat Girl wondered what to try next. Then, in spite of Nox's warning bellow, she began to shove and push the wet planks with her shoulder. But that did no good either, so she felt in her pocket for something to use as a wedge. Almost at once her fingers closed on the silver hammer they had plowed up in Keretaria. While the hammer would not do for a wedge, it would at least save her knuckles, so, lifting it high above her head, Handy Mandy brought it down with a resounding whack. A shower of silver sparks followed the hammer blow, and Nox, peering through the waterfall, saw a gnarled and crooked elf with a purple beard dancing madly round the startled girl.

"I am the elf of the hammer, who Must do whatever you ask me to," sang the elf between his high leaps and prances.

"Then open this door," directed Handy, spinning round in a circle herself to get a good look at the little fellow. "My—y, how funny Oz is! Magic horns, Topsies, Hook Noses, and now *you!* Don't tell me a little body like you can really open this great, heavy door?"

"Pick up the hammer and doubt no more — Himself, the elf, will now open the door."

In a daze, Handy Mandy picked up the hammer and put it back in her pocket, and Nox, thunderstruck by the whole proceedings, thrust his head through the waterfall just in time to see the knobby little gnome push the door open with one thump of his brown fist. Quick as a flash, Handy was on the other side.

"Come on! Come on!" she called hoarsely to Nox. "Can't you see it's closing? Oh mercy—ercy, do you want to leave me here all alone?"

"Yes!" snorted Nox in an exasperated voice, but jumping as he snorted. "I'd like nothing better." As he came to "better," he landed on the other side of the waterfall and skidded through the open door into the mountain. He had just time to tuck in his tail when the door with an ominous creak slammed shut.

"*Now* see what you've done!" gasped Nox, eyeing the gloomy interior with distaste and foreboding. "I—thought—you—were going to be a help to me and all—puff—splutter—you do is get me into trouble! What sort of place is this, anyway?"

"A c-c-ave," quavered Handy, wrapping all her arms tightly round herself. "My—y, it's so high—igh, I can hardly see the top. Where's that elf?"

"Gone!" sighed the Ox, taking a cautious step forward. "But I expect he'll come back at the first tap of that hammer. All very puzzling, if you ask me."

"Well, shall I call him back?" asked Handy uneasily. "It's kinda lonely in here, and maybe Himself could tell us where we are."

"Better wait till we need him," advised the Ox. "After all, we know we are in a cave, seems to be of silver rock, too. Just cast your eye at those stalactites, m'lass."

"So that's what you call 'em," the Goat Girl glanced curiously up at the silver icicles hanging in jagged points from the ceiling. "We have caves on Mt. Mern, but nothing like this." She looked apprehensively round the silent cavern, from which a perfect honeycomb of passageways branched off in all directions. "A fine place to get lost, I'd call it," she shivered, moving as close as she could to her companion. "What makes this lavender light? I see no lamps."

"Jewels!" confided the Ox in a hushed voice. "See, there are hundreds of amethysts embedded in those rocks, each glowing like—"

"An eye!" finished Handy nervously. "And all watching us, I dare say. My—y
, do you suppose anyone lives here? But they must—" Unwinding her arms, Handy suddenly began snapping all thirty-five of her fingers. "Nox, Nox!" she cried excitedly, "I've just thought of something!"

"Can't you think without shouting?" asked the Ox, flashing his eyes suspiciously from left to right.

"No," said Handy triumphantly, "for this is something to shout about. Look, old Toggins, if this is a silver cave, why wouldn't a Silver Mountain be on top? All we have to do is open that door and start climbing again."

"As I remember, there was a sheer precipice back of the waterfall. How could we climb that? No, no! The best thing for us to do is to travel down one of the passageways and hope it will bring us out on the side of the mountain itself."

"Yes, but which one?" demanded the Goat Girl. "There are about a hundred, it seems to me."

"Let's try that first one to the right," proposed the Ox judiciously. Their voices echoed and reverberated back and forth so uncannily in the big, hollow cavern that almost without realizing it they began to talk in whispers and tread as softly as thieves in the night. Halfway to their destination they stopped, rigid with horror and consternation. Thumping footsteps were coming toward them from the labyrinth on the left.

"Some one does live here, after all," said the Goat Girl. "Someone who weighs a ton. Hark to that!"

"Watch yourself!" warned Nox, planting all four feet and making ready to charge if the cave dweller proved unfriendly.

"Oh, my aunt — a GIANT!" With a shrill scream, Handy flung all her arms round Nox's neck and buried her face in his shoulder. Poor Nox, nearly strangled by the Goat Girl's embrace, could neither move nor speak and could scarcely breathe. With rolling eyes and quaking legs, he watched the monster approach. The Giant's body, almost ten times the size of a grizzly bear, was encased in a tight purple uniform with bells instead of buttons that jingled whenever he moved. He wore a huge silver helmet, and his neck, almost a foot long, kept darting up and down as he shot his head in this direction and that.

"Ho! THERE you are!" he roared, suddenly catching sight of the two travelers trembling together in the center of the cavern. "How dare you enter the cave of the King of the Silver Mountain without invitation or permission?"

"This this really *IS* the Silver Mountain!" marveled Handy, twisting her apron nervously in her wooden fingers.

"Of course!" yelled the giant, thumping the floor with an enormous silver club. "And I, Snorpus the Mighty, am Keeper of the Hidden Door. I am OUTKEEPER for this whole mountain," he boasted, truculently expanding his chest

227

and looking complacently down at the two midgets at his feet. But something in his manner began to reassure the Goat Girl.

"I'll bet he's as dumb as he's big," she confided hurriedly to Nox. Then, raising her voice and all of her arms, she called up loudly, "Then you must indeed be strong and sturdy!"

"Oh, I AM!" bawled the Giant, twirling his silver moustache and fixing Handy for a moment with his glittering eye. "Snorpus the Door Keeper is strong as an OX!" There was something very peculiar about the eye of the Giant. It seemed to revolve on a moving belt, peering out as it passed through the four wide-open lids set at intervals round the top of his head, so that half the time he was looking the other way.

"Did you ever see an ox?" inquired Handy politely as the eye of Snorpus again flashed by.

"No, but I'd like to," admitted the Giant, shooting his head out to the side.

"Well, this is an ox," cried Handy, tapping the anxious beast at her side with a rubber hand. "And if you are as strong as an ox, you are strong as Nox, and nothing much can stop you."

"How strong is he?" asked Snorpus, lowering himself stiffly to one knee in order to get a look at what he had first supposed to be a small and insignificant animal.

"So strong," explained the Goat Girl impressively as she pointed with all hands to the side of the cave, "that if he so much as bumped into that wall yonder, this whole cavern would collapse like a pack of cards."

"Then I hope he'll be very careful," faltered Snorpus, taking out a huge silk handkerchief to mop his forehead. "It would annoy the King frightfully if you destroyed his cavern, and I might even lose my head and position here."

"Oh, he'll be careful," promised Handy Mandy generously. "He, being an ox, and you being strong as an ox makes us all friends, doesn't it?"

"I — I suppose so," muttered Snorpus, tapping his knee uncertainly with his club. "But just the same, I am still the outkeeper and must do my duty at all hazards. AT ALL HAZARDS!" he shouted, standing up to give himself courage and puffing out his cheeks like a porpoise.

"But you have done your duty," bellowed Nox in a voice even louder than the doorkeeper's. "If we were outside the mountain, it would be your plain duty to keep us there, but since we are already inside, you have nothing more to do with us. Isn't that so?" Lowering his head, Nox made a little lunge at the Giant's shins. And backing away, Snorpus gave the pair several long, puzzled looks.

"Well, then," he decided finally, "if I have nothing more to do with you, you had best come along to the King."

"That is exactly what we wish to do," answered the Goat Girl promptly.

"My, you *are* brave, aren't you?" The Giant's eye flashed for a moment in real admiration upon Handy Mandy; then, picking up his club, he began clumping away to the left.

"Now I wonder what he meant by that?" puffed Nox, for they both had to run to even keep the Giant in sight.

"I don't know," gasped Handy, "but never mind what he means. We still have your golden horn and the silver hammer and will manage somehow. But imagine getting right inside the Silver Mountain and never knowing it!"

"Yes, and we may go out the same way," predicted the Royal Ox gloomily, following the Giant down the wide, glittering corridor. "I never did like these tunnely places or people."

Chapter 10 - The King of the Silver Mountain

"I hear water," worried *Handy* as *Snorpus* suddenly vanished round a bend in the corridor. "Oh, dear—ear, I do hope we won't have to go swimming again."

"Then mind your manners!" warned the Royal Ox, giving his horns a little shake. "Remember, it is safer to keep on the right side of Kings and Giants, and if we are to learn anything about Kerry, we must be extremely patient and polite." A loud gasp interrupted Nox's speech, for Handy Mandy, well in the lead, had also stepped round the bend. Hastening to catch up with her, the Ox, too, gave an involuntary exclamation of wonder and astonishment.

The silver corridor had brought them into a second cavern, smaller than the entrance cave but so light and lacy, so bright and beautiful, for once Handy Mandy stood perfectly speechless. The silver sides of the dome-shaped grotto had been carved to show all the historical figures and characters of ancient Oz. Wizards, giants, knights, witches, huntsmen, robbers, kings, queens and their patient subjects marched in a splendid procession round the walls. Sparkling lavender sand covered the floor, and a lake of shimmering quicksilver took up the entire center, lapping the shore with its swift soundless waves. On a small island of purest amethyst in the middle of this lake, the King of the Silver Mountain reclined at ease. His back was toward the newcomers, and he seemed lost in some deep and entirely satisfactory contemplation.

228

"A king if I ever saw one," breathed Nox moistly in Handy's ear. With a wordless nod, the Goat Girl agreed, for in this long, indolent yet majestic figure Handy felt she was seeing royalty for the first time. The unusual height of the silver monarch was at once apparent, and his tight-fitting suit of deepest purple, without ornament save for his jeweled belt and sword, set off his handsome figure to the best advantage. His hair, of an astonishing thickness, was as silver as his cavern.

When he turned his head, as he presently did at a little cough from Snorpus, Handy saw that his eyes were of a clear and piercing violet. Quietly and without hurry, the Silver King rose and, picking up his filigreed crown, set it firmly on his head. Then, retrieving a long-stemmed pipe from a crevice in the rock, he established himself in a seat carved from the amethyst and looked inquiringly across at his visitors.

"So," he whistled, his eyes sparkling with lively interest as they rested for a long moment on the Goat Girl, "two very, VERY clever travelers."

"Why do you say that?" blurted out Handy, and was instantly overcome at her own boldness in speaking to so grand a person.

"The fact that you are here in this cavern proves you are clever," answered the King, leaning over to fill his pipe in the quicksilver lake. "You have opened the door in the mountain that does not open; passed the impassable guardian and keeper of that door — SNORPUS!" The King's pleasant voice changed so quickly and cruelly, Handy almost lost her balance. "What have you to say for yourself, you lazy Bozwokel?" roared His Majesty, his eyes flashing flinty sparks of purple. "I'll have you potted for this, potted and reduced to a smithering smith, do you hear?"

Poor Snorpus, who could not have helped hearing the King's booming sentence, dropped to his knees and began pleading, explaining and blubbering all in the same breath. Even Nox, startled as he was, tried to put in a good word for him. But the muttering monarch, paying no attention to any of them, had lifted his silver pipe to his lips, and an enormous bubble was rising from the bowl. Handy, with chattering teeth, watched the bubble grow larger and larger, float off the pipe, and hover over the unlucky head of the Giant. As Snorpus tried in vain to dodge, the bubble broke with the sound like a doomsday bell, enveloping him in a cloudy mist. When it cleared away, the Giant was indeed reduced, coming now scarcely to Handy's shoulder. "How about it, shall we run?" whispered the Goat Girl as the King began to blow another bubble. "Boy, do *I* feel a draft!"

"But he's not mad at us!" answered the Ox, ducking nervously as the second bubble soared over their heads. "Wait! Be patient; remember the little King." As Nox finished speaking, the bubble sailed off and away down one of the silver corridors leading away from the royal cavern. Presently they heard a bell ringing in the distance as the bubble broke, and before you could say Pop Robinson, seventy silver-jacketed little bellboys came trotting into the cave.

"Take this poor failure to Nifflepok and see that he is potted," directed the King sternly, setting down his bubble pipe. "Have Timano guard the mountain door and see that I am not disturbed. Important matters have come up this morning, important matters!"

"Yes! Yes! Your Highness! It shall be done, Your Excellency!" mumbled the bellboys, pushing poor Snorpus ahead of them.

"Watch yourselves! Watch yourselves!" warned the little Giant as he was rudely hustled out of the royal presence.

"Now," smiled the Silver King, positively beaming upon his visitors, "now we can proceed with our conversation. Sorry to trouble you with this small matter, but discipline, as the old army officers will tell you, discipline must be maintained."

"Humph!" sniffed Handy Mandy under her breath, looking with dislike and disillusion at the royal figure on the rocks. "The Giant was right, you're a fellow who'll bear watching." Fortunately, her words did not carry, and lazily glancing at them through his long purple lashes, the Silver King continued his speech.

"Since you have so easily entered my mountain," he observed blandly, "I assume you have some powerful magic treasure or appliance in your possession. Am I right?" At the sudden forward lurch of the Royal Ox and Handy Mandy's surprised expression, the King gave a satisfied little nod. "Fine!" he chuckled, rubbing his hands together briskly. "And now, let us waste no more time. WHO sent you? WHAT have you to offer? As you doubtless know, the Wizard of Wutz pays well for magic treasures and formulas."

"Wizard!" choked Handy Mandy, carelessly clapping her iron hand to her forehead and knocking herself over backward. "Wizard!" she repeated, dazedly picking herself up. "I thought you were a King!"

"I am both!" stated the owner of the cavern proudly. "I am King of the Silver Mountain and also the Wizard of Wutz, second in importance only to Glinda and the Wizard of Oz. And, ha! ha! it won't be long before I am the ONLY wizard, the sole, supreme and only Wizard of Oz! Not long! Not long!" Again the Silver King rubbed his hands exultantly together. "I have my secret agents in every Kingdom in this country and even in the Emerald City of Oz," he told them impressively. "I already have the Record Book of Glinda, the Good Sorceress, and many more of the magic treasures of Oz, and soon I will have them all — ALL! My agents are clever, and I have trained them well."

"But I thought magic was against the law!" cried Nox with an outraged snort. "I understood no one was allowed to practice magic but Ozma, Glinda and the Wizard of Oz!"

"Then why are you here?" demanded Wutz sternly. "YOU have been practicing magic, or you could not have entered this mountain. Come, now, let us stop all this nonsense and get down to silver tacks and business. What have you to offer? Who sent you: Three, Six, Nine, Five, or Eleven?"

As you can imagine, this was perfect jargon to Nox and the Goat Girl, but Handy Mandy, convinced by this time that the Silver King was both sly and dangerous, resolved to fall in with his little supposition and see what would come of it.

"Nine sent us," she answered boldly, while Nox looked across at her in perfect stupefaction.

"You don't say! I rather thought you came from the Munchkin Country," mused the Wizard. "Something in the way the Ox talked, though you, yourself, are not a native Ozian?"

"No!" Handy said noncommitally, rather pleased she had chosen Nine, since this number had something to do with the Munchkins.

"Did Nine say anything about the silver hammer?" asked the King, twinkling his eyes at the Goat Girl.

"He told us nothing," stated Handy, quite truthfully this time.

"That's Nine for you," fumed the King discontentedly. "He's the slowest and most unsatisfactory agent I have. Two years searching for that hammer and no report yet. I've a good notion to kick him out and put little King Kerry back on the throne. A bargain's a bargain, and I've kept my part. Besides, I've got to have that hammer before I can make myself supreme ruler in Oz. Why, it's the second most important magic in the four Kingdoms!" At this surprising statement, Handy pricked up her ears.

"What did you say about Kerry?" panted Nox, almost stepping into the quicksilver lake at mention of the little King.

"Nothing. I was talking about Nine," scowled the Wizard. "If that fellow does not show some action soon, I'll — I'll—" The King clenched his fists and looked so terribly angry that Handy was afraid he was going to blow bubbles again. But instead, he glared across the lake and demanded impatiently, "Well, if you didn't bring the silver hammer, what did you bring?"

"A magic flower," explained the Goat Girl hurriedly, and before Nox could give away the fact that they did have the silver hammer. She could guess from the expression in his eye that he was about to offer the hammer in exchange for Kerry.

"A flower!" bawled Wutz, his face turning from red to purple. "My caves are full of flowers, frosted silver lilies, long-stemmed sterling roses, daisies and violets with jeweled centers. I can grow any kind of flower I wish. How dare you take up my time with a flower! PAH! Go back and tell Nine he had better look out — he's flirting with dismissal and destruction."

"But this flower saves you from injury when you fall," stammered Handy, heartily wishing she had never got herself into such a controversy.

"Fall!" sneered the Silver King, simply bounding off his throne. "I NEVER fall!" and had hardly finished speaking before he caught his toe on a jutting amethyst and pitched headlong to the rocks. Horrified, and without waiting for the irate monarch to regain his feet, Handy and Nox began to run toward one of the outgoing corridors, the Goat Girl colliding as she ran with a plump little dignitary in a jeweled robe and high hat.

"Your Highness! Your Highness!" puffed the little fat man, stopping long enough to glare at Handy Mandy. "At last our efforts are to be crowned with success! Five has but this moment arrived with — with—"

"With what?" demanded the King, springing lightly as a cat to his feet. "With a jug," exulted the little fat man, tossing his high hat into the air. "With a jug that was Rug and the magic picture of Queen Ozma herself."

"Ah, SPLENDID!" beamed the monarch, who could turn his smiles and rages on and off like electric lights. "That will be a lesson to those Emerald Cityites!" Then, suddenly remembering Handy and Nox and his undignified fall, he shouted shrilly: "Stop those impostors! Stop them, Nifflepok, and lock them up in the prison pits till I have time to demolish them. Hah! We'll pot the Ox's tongue, make soup of his tail, saddles and boots of his hide, and use his head for a hat rack. As for that seven-armed monstrosity, she shall work in the polishing caves for the rest of her stupid life."

"I'll polish your nose first!" promised Handy, shaking all her fists at the King.

"Better come quietly," warned Nifflepok, looking so worried Handy felt a little sorry for him. "Wutz'll blow bubbles if you make him too mad, and that'll be much worse than being locked up, you know."

"Oh, let's go with the Little High-Hat," groaned Nox, blinking his eyes at Handy to remind her they still had his horns and the silver hammer. "For my part, I'd like a little peace and quiet."

"Take 'em away! Take 'em away!" ordered the King, stamping up and down his rocky island. "Send in Five! Send in Five at once!"

"Come along, then," said Nifflepok, being careful to keep out of the way of Nox's horns. "Come, give me your hand, maiden. Not that one! Not THAT one!" he howled dismally as the Goat Girl clasped his outstretched fingers in her iron hand. "Let go! Let go!"

"Let's go! Let's go!" chuckled Handy Mandy mischievously. And squealing with pain, the little Minister hurried them down a long, dim passageway.

Chapter 11 - Down to the Prisoners' Pit!

"Oh! Oh! Give me another hand, and I'll do my best to help you," sputtered Nifflepok as Handy Mandy ruthlessly continued to squeeze his fingers.

"We'll help ourselves, thank you," retorted the Goat Girl tartly. Then, relenting a little, she relaxed her hold, for she could not help pitying Nifflepok and all the subjects of this cruel King. "Where are these prison pits?" she asked impatiently, for she was anxious to be alone with Nox. "If you are going to lock us up, do hurry along with it."

"Yes, yes, absolutely yes!" moaned Nifflepok, glancing nervously over his shoulder to be sure the white Ox was not going to tread on his heels. "You'll be there in no time, no time at all," he assured them earnestly. "Step over here, please." Moving a sliding door in the wall of the corridor, the King's assistant waved them toward a smooth, wheelless silver carriage. It looked to Handy a lot like an old-fashioned sleigh, and as there were seats in front and a space in back large enough for the Ox, she let go Nifflepok's hand and quite willingly climbed aboard. Nox, grunting a little, stepped over the side and settled himself behind her.

"Well, goodbye," sniffed Nifflepok, rubbing his bruised fingers tenderly. "You'll find everything you need below, not that you'll be needing anything," he added mournfully as he pulled out a silver switch. "Goodbye. I'm sorry for you!" he shouted as the car with a lurch that almost loosened Handy's teeth shot down a sliding runway to the deep pits of darkness below.

Now you and I, who are used to scenic railways and have enjoyed the thrills of chute the chutes for years, would have been less startled by the wild, dizzy leaps, the swoops, curves and climbs, and the sickening drops of the Silver King's chariot. But neither the Goat Girl nor the Royal Ox had ever heard of a scenic railway, much less ridden in one, and the underground car of the Silver Monarch was more like a chute the chutes than anything else. Sometimes the two travelers were in complete darkness, at other times they whirled by the narrow, well-lighted ledges of a queer cave city where the subjects of the Mountain King lived in cell-like apertures in the silver rock like the cliff dwellers of old. Then without warning the car would plunge to the work caverns below, past the gloomy shafts of the silver mines, or dart up to the living quarters and grottoes of the King himself, caves so lavishly furnished and glowing with jewels Handy let out little shrieks of astonishment. In the King's subterranean gardens, silver swallows bathed in the silver fountains, silver maples rustled their lacy branches in the lavender-scented breezes, silver-petalled flowers with jeweled centers grew as riotously as daisies and buttercups in the upstairs world.

The mountaineers themselves, working listlessly with pick and shovel in the mines or walking soberly along the ledges beside their little cliff dwellings, seemed undersized and unhappy to the Goat Girl. Not that she caught more than a flying glimpse of them as the silver car tore by. In fact, she was so frantically busy holding on to the front rail of the car with all her various hands and catching her breath after each dizzy swoop that her mind was in a perfect whirl. The groans and snorts of Nox were far from reassuring, but afraid to look back lest she herself be flung out, Handy clung desperately to the rail wondering when the wild ride would end and where under the mountain the silver car was taking them. The last words of Nifflepok rang unpleasantly in her ears, and as they raced by a cave marked "Potters Den," the Goat Girl positively shuddered. Here, set out in vast silver pots and buried to their chins in the silver earth, were scores of the King's pale-faced prisoners. A grim-looking gardener was watering them from a milk can, and from the hungry way they lapped up the few drops that fell to them, Handy concluded that this was probably their only food.

"First I shot over a mountain, and now I'm shooting through one!" moaned the distracted Goat Girl, trying to collect her spinning thoughts and faculties. "Oh, my—y, we're going to pot for sure. Oh, this time we are really done for!"

Then all at once Handy's good common sense began to assert itself. And as their strange chariot with a sudden increase of speed and power again dashed down into the darkness, she snatched the precious blue flower from her pocket and at the exact moment the silver car turned over and flung them into space, Handy began pulling the petals from the flower and letting them drift down ahead of her own rapidly falling body. It was just light enough for her to see Nox, with bristling horns and quivering nostrils, fall past, when she herself started to turn so many and such dizzy somersaults she lost all count of time and distance.

Chapter 12 - Prisoners of the Wizard

What seemed to be hours later, though in reality it was only a few moments, the two luckless
prisoners found themselves side by side on a heap of soft blue flower petals. They were in a small circular pit with one amethyst burning dimly in the grating that covered the top. The Goat Girl had no recollection of her final landing and gazing up at the grilled ceiling wondered dully how they had come through without being cut to pieces.

"It tilted," wheezed the Royal Ox, answering the unspoken question in Handy's eyes, "just tilted and slid us down. A fortunate thing you kept that magic flower, m'lass. Ha—rumph!" Weakly and still trembling in every limb, Nox tried to rise, but his legs gave way beneath him, and for a good fifteen minutes he and the Goat Girl rested on the flower petals saying never a word. The tapping of footsteps in the corridor brought Handy quickly to her feet, and as Nox managed to heave himself upright the blue petals vanished, leaving only a tiny flower on the floor. Handy had just time to stuff it into her pocket when an invisible door in the side of the pit opened and twelve depressed workmen in silver cloth caps and overalls stepped inside. They carried brooms, mops and dust pans and stood staring in dismay at the seven-armed Goat Girl and angry-looking Ox.

"We were sent to brush up!" stuttered the first workman, touching his cap uneasily. "But — there — seems—"

"To be nothing to brush!" finished Handy sarcastically. "Sorry to disappoint you. Now get OUT!" ordered the Goat Girl furiously, and seizing buckets, brooms and mops from their nerveless fingers, Handy pummeled them left and right with her seven hands. "Get out and don't come back till Christmas," she panted as the workmen, tumbling over one another, clawed open the door and banged it to behind them. The knob was on the other side of the door, and not even the edges of the door were now visible. "What a place!" groaned Handy Mandy, leaning dejectedly against the side of their prison. "What a King! And he looked so nice!" grieved the Goat Girl, sliding down to a sitting position and holding her head in all of her hands.

"Never mind," said the Ox, settling on the floor beside her. "He hasn't gotten the best of us yet. It was pretty clever of you to remember that flower, but what I can't understand is why you did not tell him at once that we *did* have this silver hammer he is so anxious to possess. Then we could have traded the hammer for the release of Kerry."

"I don't trust him," answered the Goat Girl somberly. "Why, I wouldn't trust that Wizard as far as a goat can butt. Didn't you hear him say the hammer was the second most important magic in Oz? Didn't you hear him say he was stealing and planning to steal the best magic from all the four Kingdoms to make himself supreme ruler of Oz? Well, now that Five has brought him this jug-a-rug or whatever it is and Ozma's own magic picture, he's probably well on the way to realizing his ambitions. But he's not going to get our silver hammer. I found it, and I'm going to keep it, for it's far safer with me than with him. Do you suppose we're going to help an old Bozzywog like that? What good would it do to put Kerry back on his throne if Wutz is to be Ruler of Oz? He'd probably pot all the Kings and keep everything for himself."

"Very probably," agreed Nox, wagging his head mournfully. "But what are we to do? Are we an army to fight a mountain full of silver moles and minions, are we magicians to risk our necks with this wizard? Besides," Nox's face grew thin and anxious, "if Wutz has treated Kerry the way he has treated us, the boy needs us right now and this very minute."

"But didn't you hear him say he'd put Kerry back on the throne if Nine did not soon find the hammer?" put in Handy patiently. "That proves the little King is still here, and safe. Of course we must find him and get him out of this miserable mountain, but we're not going to give Wutz our hammer or any help at all, and he can put that in his silver pipe and blow bubbles till he bursts," said Handy vindictively. "Now the thing to do is to rest and eat, and then set ourselves to find the way out of this pit and this mountain. Wutz and Nifflepok think we're all swept away by this time. Besides, they'll be too busy talking with Five to bother us. So first to eat and then to think!" proposed Handy in a businesslike manner.

"Perhaps you're right," sighed the Ox, "but I'll not have an easy moment till we're out of this magic mountain. That ride!" Nox lashed his tail and rolled his eyes at the mere thought of their dash down the underground railway. "Did you ever experience anything like it in your life?"

"Well," grinned Handy, "it's one way of seeing the country, I suppose. But let's not look back, old Toggins, let's look ahead. Remember, we still have the Dwarf of the Hammer on our side, and when we are ready to leave, he'll
surely show us the way."

"Not before I put a few gores in that Wizard's pants and plans," rumbled Nox belligerently. "I'll teach him to take liberties with the Royal Ox of Keretaria."

"Hi—yigh! That's the old Oz spirit!" cheered Handy, reaching out to touch his golden horn. "Horn, dear, just serve two dinners, and no fooling." Unscrewing Nox's horn of plenty as she spoke, the Goat Girl held it quietly in her wooden hand. And there was certainly no fooling about the two splendid dinners the horn delivered in answer to Handy's wish. Never had she eaten a more appetizing repast, and half of the prison pit was taken up by the fresh hay, fruit and grains brought to satisfy the hunger of the Royal Ox. So, forgetting for a time their awful danger and their disagreeable imprisonment, the two adventurers refreshed themselves and, after the dishes and containers had disappeared, settled down to evolve some plan to outwit the Wizard of Wutz.

Chapter 13 - In the Emerald City of Oz

Ten days before the Goat Girl left Mt. Mern, a weary and footsore pilgrim arrived in the Emerald City. At least, he gave that impression to all who saw him shuffling with his long staff and beggar's cup along the shining streets of the capital. The man's head was clean shaven, and his small cap, coarse belted robe, and sandals marked him as a monk of some old and ancient order. He nodded gently to each person he passed and seemed, in spite of his many years and wrinkles, innocent and harmless as a child. The splendor and magnificence of the capital astonished and bewildered the old gentleman, and in a sort of stupefied disbelief he stared at the emerald-studded streets and houses and gazed up at the lofty peaks and spires of the royal palace.

And this was not strange, for of all the fairy cities out of the world, the Emerald City of Oz is the most dazzling and beautiful. But its citizens are kindly and simple, for all that, and many stopped to drop emeralds in the pilgrim's cup and ask him if there was anything else that he needed. To all he mumbled in a strange and indistinguishable tongue, and seeing that he was bound for the palace and sure that Ozma herself would know best how to deal with him, the Emerald Cityites let him go his way unmolested.

The afternoon was warm and pleasant, and Ozma and some of her favorites were having a lazy game of croquet in the royal garden. The click of the gold mallets as they tapped the gold balls presently attracted the attention of the old wayfarer, who paused to peer curiously over the hedge. The simple summer dresses of the girls in the garden seemed out of all keeping with their majestic surroundings. Except for Ozma's frock, which was longer, the emerald crown on her dark curls, and the golden circlets worn by her three companions, they might have been any four little girls playing croquet in a garden. But all around were the unmistakable signs of rank and royalty.

At ease under a lime tree stood a tall soldier with green whiskers leaning on his gun. Three footmen in satin uniforms stood stiffly beside an emerald-topped tea table, ready at a moment's notice to serve Ozade and frosted cake. On a gold bench nearby a straw-stuffed scarecrow was quietly reading the paper, and walking arm in arm down a little path talking composedly together were an energetic little man with a bald head and a curious fellow who seemed to be constructed entirely of copper. To all who are familiar with the quaint and merry folk at Ozma's court, there would be nothing odd about a live scarecrow or a mechanical man, and most of us would have recognized Ozma's companions at once as Dorothy, Betsy and Trot, three mortal girls who long ago came to live in the royal palace.

It was Dorothy who had discovered the Scarecrow on her first visit to Oz, lifting him down from his pole and traveling in his gay and carefree company all the way to the Emerald City. In those days, the Wizard of Oz had been ruler of the country, he himself having flown in a balloon from Omaha. Astonished by the circus tricks of this little fellow, the Ozians, believing him to be a real wizard, made him their sovereign, and under his wise rule and direction built the now famous City of Emeralds. The sight of Dorothy had made the humbug wizard homesick, and after presenting the Scarecrow with a fine set of brains, he flew off to America in a balloon of his own construction, leaving the straw man to rule in his place.

Afterward, when Ozma was disenchanted and proved to be the rightful ruler of Oz, the Scarecrow had cheerfully resigned. But he still spends most of his time in the palace and is one of Ozma's most trusted friends and counselors. Later, the Wizard himself returned to Oz and this time took up the study of magic with such zeal and earnestness he was soon famous from one end of the country to the other. This made him exceedingly valuable to the young fairy ruler, and he, like the Scarecrow, is an old and honored member of Ozma's cabinet.

It was the Wizard who was now talking so earnestly to Tik Tok. The Metal Man was another of Dorothy's discoveries. She met Tik Tok on her second visit to Oz and brought him to the Emerald City for safekeeping. Tik Tok, made by the firm of Smith and Tinker, is a completely mechanical man and a loyal and dependable citizen when he is properly wound up and oiled. Betsy and Trot, like Dorothy, arrived more or less by wind, wave and accident in the Land of Oz. They liked it so well and proved so gay and amusing that Ozma begged them to stay with her and Dorothy in the green castle and help rule the many merry Kingdoms that make up her wonderful empire. This they were only too happy to do, so here they are, Princesses in their own right and living in the most gorgeous City out of the world.

Besides the celebrities in the garden, there are numerous other important people at Ozma's court. For instance, there is Herby, the Medicine Man, whose chest is really a medicine chest full of pills, cures and ointments. Then there is Scraps, a lively girl made from a patchwork quilt by a wizard's wife and brought to life by the wizard; and there's Pigasus, a flying pig. There's a doubtful dromedary, a cowardly lion, a hungry tiger, and Dorothy's little dog Toto; a glass cat belonging to Scraps, a wooden sawhorse belonging to Ozma, an Iffin whom Jack Pumpkinhead discovered near the Land of Barons, and a dozen more unique and unusual characters. The old pilgrim seemed to find the group in the garden surprising enough, for he watched them closely and silently for almost ten minutes, cupping his hand behind his ear in an endeavor to catch what the Wizard was saying.

"It is just as I have told you," the little Wizard was remarking earnestly to Tik Tok. "The great record book of Glinda has vanished from her castle without trace or reason, and even with my powerful searchlight and looking glasses I have been unable to discover any signs of it. Word of the theft came yesterday by pigeon post."

"Some-one has sto-len it for no good pur-pose," answered the Metal Man solemnly. But the old man leaning over the hedge heard none of this, for the two were conversing in low and guarded tones. So after a long, puzzled look at the Scarecrow, the pilgrim took up his staff and shuffled along the gold-pebbled path to the palace itself. A pompous footman in gold and green came to answer his timid knock at the door.

"What name, please, what business, and why in the wood (sic) does a fellow like you come begging at the door of a castle?" inquired the footman in a loud, displeased voice.

"There, there, Puffup," admonished a rosy-cheeked maid in a ribboned cap and apron, peering around the wide shoulders of the footman. "Don't be so shouting proud. You've frightened the old gentleman half out of his wits. Can't you see he is tired and hungry and probably in need of a lunch?" At the little maid's kind speech, the pilgrim bowed at least a dozen times, nodding his head energetically to show that she was perfectly right in her conjecture. "Come along with you," urged Jellia Jamb, giving him a friendly wink.

Edging nervously past the muttering footman, the old beggar followed Jellia into the castle's spacious and splendid dining hall. "Wait right here, and I'll bring you some cake and applesauce, an omelette and a pot of tea," promised the obliging girl. "How will that be?" Jellia Jamb, who was Ozma's own personal maid and a privileged character around the castle, grinned cheerfully at her ancient visitor, and though the old monk pretended not to understand a word that she said, he nevertheless seated himself at the table and with round eyes watched her skip through the swinging door into the pantry.

No sooner had Jellia disappeared than the old rascal sprang nimbly to his feet and began to peer eagerly all around him. Passing hurriedly over a rich gold service on the sideboard, he pounced upon an earthen jug on a crystal stand and, tucking it under his robe, slipped silently as a shadow out of the dining hall, up the green carpeted stairs and straight into the private sitting room of Ozma of Oz. Once there and without losing a moment, he walked to the west wall, took down a large gold-framed picture, blew upon it with a small glass tube till it was no larger than a cake of chocolate, and thrust it into an inner pocket. Then, holding his robe high above his skinny shins and with the jug clasped tightly in his arms, he galloped down the stairs and out an open window into the garden, reaching a large clump of snowball bushes without encountering anyone.

Hiding himself well in the bushes, he tore off the monk's robe, turned it inside out, dragged a white wig from his sock, and presently emerged as dignified and plausible an old grandmother as anyone would wish to see. The other side of his monk's robe was green and made up in a style much affected by old ladies in the capital, so that now he attracted no attention whatever. The jug in a large string bag dangled carelessly from his wrist, and smiling and nodding amiably, he hurried through the garden, passed rapidly down one street and another, through the city gates on and on, till he was far out in the country, walking faster and faster and less like a monk or an old lady at every step.

Chapter 14 - The Robbery is Discovered

"Prunes and peppermints!" ejaculated the Scarecrow, springing up from his bench as Jellia Jamb, with streaming eyes and cap ribbons, came flying across the garden.

"Peanuts and pretzels!" Dorothy, about to hit the pole and win the game, dropped her mallet at Jellia's fire-siren screeches, while Ozma and the others swung round in amazement as the little waiting maid, sobbing and panting, rushed into their midst.

"Oh, that beggar! Oh, that pilgrim! That old Monk, or whatever he was!" wailed Jellia, wiping her eyes on the corner of her apron. "He's gone and stolen the jug, I mean Rug, and Oz knows what will become of us!"

"There, there, my girl. Stop crying! Begin at the beginning and tell us just what happened," begged the Scarecrow, patting Jellia clumsily on the shoulder.

"But this is serious, very serious," muttered the Wizard, who had at once realized the importance of the little maid's news. "If Ruggedo is released from that jug and enchantment, he'll be up to his old tricks in no time and doing anything in his power to hurt and destroy us."

"But who could have known we turned Ruggedo into a jug, or where the jug was kept? And why would anyone steal an old earthenware pitcher when there are so many other rare and beautiful objects in the palace?" Ozma, looking anxious and troubled, seated herself on the bench beside the Scarecrow.

"The same person who knew the value of Glinda's record book and stole that," answered the Wizard gloomily. "Dark forces are at work in Oz, my dear, dark forces. Just how did this rascal look, Jellia?"

"Like an old monk with a beggar's cup," said the little maid with a sorrowful sniff. "He seemed so poor and hungry I went off to get him something to eat, and no sooner was my back turned than he grabbed the jug and ran off — though he shuffled slowly enough when he came into the palace."

"Disguised, of course," observed the Scarecrow, raising one eyebrow, "and no more a monk than I am. But what was he monkeying around here for? And what could he want with that jug, even if he knew it was the old Gnome King? Really, you know, you shouldn't let perfect strangers into the palace, Jellia."

"Just what I was telling her," wheezed Puffup, breathlessly adding himself to the group on the lawn, "and I hopes this will be a lesson to you, Miss."

"If we just knew where the old villain came from," worried the Wizard, tapping his fingers absently on Tik Tok's copper arm.

"Or where he was going," finished Dorothy, pushing back her crown.

"Why not look in the ma-gic pic-ture?" proposed the Machine Man calmly. "The pic-ture would show us where he is now."

"Of course it would!" Ozma rewarded Tik Tok with a bright smile, and jumping up, the little Fairy hurried across the garden and into the palace with the others just a few steps behind here. But when they reached the small sitting room where the magic picture was hung, of course it was not there, and now in real distress and consternation they all sat down to discuss the mysterious forces working against them.

"I thought Ruggedo was the only enemy I had left," sighed Ozma, leaning wearily back in her satin tufted armchair. "I thought when we turned the Gnome King to a jug all our troubles would be over."

"Who-ev-er stole the jug knows that Rug-ge-do was once the pow-er-ful me-tal mon-arch who tried a-gain and a-gain to con-quer Oz," rasped Tik Tok in his slow and precise fashion.

"Right!" agreed the Wizard, striding up and down with his hands clasped behind his back. "And whoever stole that jug and the magic picture plans to disenchant the Gnome King and learn from him the best way to destroy us. But that will be pretty difficult," asserted the little Wizard, thrusting out his chin. "That transformation was one of the best you ever made, my dear Ozma, one of the best. It will take a pretty smart wizard to turn that jug back to Rug again."

"Whoever stole the jug and Ozma's magic picture WAS pretty smart," Betsy Bobbin reminded him seriously. "And without the picture, how're we going to find out who it is? Can't you do something, Wiz dear, or do we just have to sit around and wait to be conquered?"

"I shall go to my laboratory at once," decided the Wizard importantly, "and there by some magic means I'll try to discover who is at the bottom of all this wretched plotting and thievery. Lock up the magic treasures in your safe, Ozma, especially the Gnome King's magic belt, and have them guarded day and night." Briskly, the little Wizard rushed out of the room, returning in a moment to repeat gloomily, "DAY and NIGHT!"

"And I'll go and drill the army," declared the Scarecrow, stepping recklessly out an open French window and falling flat, but undaunted, in a flower bed below.

"And I'd better call Tige and the Cowardly Lion," said Dorothy, who had always found the lion a splendid fighter in spite of his cowardice, and the Hungry Tiger, ready at the drop of a handkerchief to protect his royal patrons with tooth and claw. "They can sit right here beside the safe, and I'd just like to see anyone get by them!"

"Maybe it will be someone they cannot see," shivered Betsy, peering out into the darkening garden.

"Oh, my, isn't it too exciting!" Trot, bouncing up and down on a small sofa, leaned over to touch Ozma on the knee. "It reminds me of the time Ugu the Shoemaker stole all the magic treasures in Oz. Remember?"

Ozma, looking at the space where her magic picture had hung, nodded her head sorrowfully, saddened and sobered by the thought that she still had dangerous and unscrupulous enemies in Oz.

Chapter 15 - The Pilgrim Returns to the Mountain

Traveling northward by foot and as quickly as he could, Number Five had come to the Silver King's Mountain just a few moments after Nox and Handy Mandy. Now dressed in the silver armor and helmet worn by all the Wizard's M-Men, he waited in great agitation for the wizard to appear. Nifflepok had at once taken Five to the den where Wutz carried on all his magic experiments and kept his valuable treasures, and quite sure none of the other agents had been as successful as he, Five paced impatiently up and down, fancying himself already co-ruler with the wizard in Oz.

"So, there you are at last!" Entering from an invisible door in the back of his workshop, Wutz stared coldly at Five. "Well, what trash is that you have stolen?" he asked finally. The wizard always pretended the discoveries of his agents were of little use and importance. And when Five, completely taken aback and crestfallen, began to explain the wonderful properties of the magic picture and the fact that the old jug had once been the powerful King of the Gnomes, the Silver Monarch cut him short. "Yes, yes, but just see what Seven has brought," he told him gloatingly. "Seven, by a trick known only to himself, has stolen and transported to our mountain the great record book of Glinda the Good Sorceress!" Following the direction of the King's imperious finger, Five gazed jealously at a huge volume chained with golden chains to its marble stand. "In that book," went on the wizard quickly, "everything that ever happened in Oz is recorded, not only everything that has happened, but everything that is happening. You can see the entries appearing at this very minute on the open page."

"I see, I see!" Five scarcely glanced at the record book. "But this magic picture shows you any person you desire to look at. With this picture and the help of the powerful Gnome King, now disguised as a jug, we can soon make ourselves rulers of Oz. All we need to do is release Ruggedo from his enchantment. I have been told by people in the Emerald City that Ruggedo is familiar with all the magic secrets of Ozma and the Wizard of Oz, and is, besides, a skillful magician himself. Once we have disenchanted him, everything will be easy."

"We? We?" sneered Wutz, who secretly agreed with Five, but would not give him the satisfaction of knowing it. "Well, put the picture there on that stand so I can examine it. Show us this silly ruler of Oz who sets herself above all other rulers," he ordered sharply. "Where is she now, and what is she doing?" Then, though the wizard and Five and Nifflepok, who had come noiselessly into the workshop, gazed into the canvas till their eyes stung and watered, not a single figure appeared to enlighten them. "HAH! A hoax!" raged the Silver King, rushing at Five and shaking him till his armor rattled. "How dare you fool me in this dangerous manner?"

"But it's not a hoax," screamed Five as soon as he could speak. "It worked perfectly well in the castle."

"Perhaps it was hurt when you reduced it to carry it here," put in Nifflepok nervously. He was always trying to keep peace between the cruel King and his subjects. "Perhaps it only obeys the commands of Ozma, its rightful owner. And remember, you still have the jug and the magic record book. The record book might explain about the picture," he suggested hopefully. "I thought so. It says here: `The magic picture and Rug, the jug, have been stolen from the castle of Ozma of Oz by an agent of the Silver King.' "

"There!" exclaimed Five, brushing himself off indignantly. "I told you it was the one and only picture."

"Yes, but what good is it to me if it doesn't work?" scoffed the wizard. "I'll not have you potted this time, Five, but next time don't bring me damaged goods and old jugs. Bring something of real value." As Five, red-faced and furious, jerked himself out of the King's presence, Wutz turned joyfully to Nifflepok. "Getting on, old Tubbykins, we're getting on! Without that magic picture, Ozma will not be able to trace her stolen property, and without the record book, Glinda will not be able to help her. So who's to stop us from stealing everything? Everything!" exulted Wutz, picking up the earthen jug and waving it over his head.

"But do you think it wise to treat our agents so shabbily?" sighed Nifflepok. "They might betray us, you know."

"Oh, no, they won't," sniffed the wizard, grinning broadly at his anxious little assistant. "The way I treat them is perfectly all right, keeps them on their toes, and with each trying to outdo the other we get the best results."

"Well, I hope you're right," Nifflepok still looked unconvinced. "But I cannot help thinking—"

"Out of your line, Niffy; just leave the thinking to me. Now fetch me my magic blower, there's a good fellow, till I see what can be done with this jug. It may take some time and doing to release this ugly little gnome. By the way, did you pulverize those meddling Munchkins?"

"Oh, yes!" Nifflepok nodded his head with a little shudder of distaste. "I shot them down into the prisoner's pit just as your Majesty commanded."

"That's strange." The wizard in crossing the den to fetch a glass test tube had paused for a moment beside the book of records. "It says here, `The Goat Girl from Mern and the Royal Ox are in the Silver King's Mountain planning to release the little King of Kereteria.' So that's what brought them here," mused the wizard softly. "Now then, Nifflepok, something must have slipped up instead of down. If your prisoners were powdered or pulverized, how could they be planning and plotting?"

"They must have some powerful magic to help them," muttered Nifflepok, "or how could they have survived that fall?"

"Better find out, my dear fellow. Go spy on those Munchkins, and if their magic is important or worthwhile, come back and tell me. And in the future be more careful how you carry out my orders and instructions!" The wizard's voice was still low and pleasant, but his eyes flashed so threateningly that Nifflepok rushed out of the royal work den, flung himself in the silver car, and went speeding down to the prison pits at the bottom of the mountain.

Chapter 16 - The Wizard's Bargain!

While Nifflepok had been interviewing Five, Handy and Nox had been having a troublesome conference of their own. Each plan they devised for finding the little King and escaping from the Silver King's Mountain proved impractical. To summon the hammer elf to release them from the prison pit would probably rouse the underground guards and minions of the wizard and give Wutz himself an opportunity to steal the hammer. To tap the hammer lightly and ask the advice of Himself had next seemed a good idea, but as Nox quickly pointed out, that, too, was dangerous. "In a wizard's den like this, anything can happen," groaned the Ox, looking around with a gloomy eye. "How do we know we are not being watched at this very moment? If you so much as show that hammer, somebody may pounce in here and snatch it away, which will leave us with nothing to protect ourselves with in a last emergency — except that blue flower, my horns, and your hands."

Handy did not like the sound of "last emergency," but even Handy realized they would not escape from the mountain without some sort of battle. To the free and sun-loving mountain girl, every minute underground was sheer torture. She longed for a breath of the pure upper air, and the unreal light and pale faces of Wutz's underground citizens and workers filled her with pity and loathing. "Of course, no matter how long they leave us here, your horn of plenty will keep us from starving, but if we don't soon find some way out, I believe I'll explode!" she choked in a desperate voice.

"Let's look at the message in that silver ball again," suggested Nox unexpectedly. "Are you sure you read it all, m'lass? There might have been directions on the other side."

"I don't think so," said Handy, shaking her head. Then, because action of any sort was a relief, she deftly twisted off Nox's left horn and tilted the silver balls into one of her always handy palms. The first ball when she opened it contained nothing further than the silver key. In the center of the second lay the same folded paper, but this time when Handy unfolded the paper there was a new message inside.

"Wait!" cautioned the little slip of paper in small blue letters. "Do nothing until the wizard appears."

"Oh," breathed the Royal Ox, touching the paper gently with his nose. "Someone is helping us."

"Then I'd better keep this silver ball in my pocket," decided the Goat Girl, "where I can easily get it. In a tight corner I might not have a chance to unscrew your horn. Dear—ear, how puzzling it all grows! So we're to hear from the wizard again. Whist! What was that?" As Handy, with her wooden hand, slipped the first ball back into the horn, with her leather hand screwed the horn back on Nox's head, and with one of her best white hands stuffed the second ball and message into her pocket, they heard agitated footsteps pattering along the outside corridor. After a tense moment, however, they died away, and exchanging a relieved glance, Nox and Handy settled down to wait for the wizard.

The footsteps, as you have already guessed, belonged to Nifflepok. Peering in at them through an invisible window, the King's messenger had been just in time to see Handy shaking the silver balls from the golden horn. Without waiting to see what use they would make of this curious magic, Nifflepok rushed back to inform his master. "They are wizards!" he panted, bursting unceremoniously into the Silver King's den. "The magic is in the ox's horn. With my own eyes I saw the seven-armed maiden shaking silver balls from his horn."

"What do *I* care about silver balls?" snarled Wutz, who was in a terrible temper. "If I had them here, I'd bounce you over the head with them." The den was full of sulphurous smoke, but the earthenware jug still stood unchanged on the table before him. "The magic in the Emerald City is still better than mine," hissed the Silver Monarch, his voice quivering with anger and disappointment. "I've tried every single formula in my book of incantations, every straight and crooked pass in the magician's manual, every powder and potion on my shelves, and this ugly jug is still a jug and nothing but a jug! What are we going to do?" he yelled furiously. "Think of something, you noddle-headed pig! I must have the help of this little Gnome King, but how'm I going to get him out of the jug?"

"Perhaps, with a little more time," faltered Nifflepok, twisting his high hat nervously in his hands.

"Time! TIME!" exploded the wizard. "When did time ever break an enchantment?" Snatching up a pair of silver pliers, he flung them wrathfully at his assistant. Nifflepok, fortunately for his head, caught the dangerous missile in his hat and, darting behind a tall cabinet, looked pleadingly out at his unreasonable Master.

"Wait! Wait!" he begged earnestly as Wutz, with a menacing frown, took up his silver bubble pipe. "I HAVE thought of something. Make these Munchkins break the Gnome King's enchantment. They have passed all the hazards of our mountain unharmed. Undoubtedly the girl is a sorceress and the Ox a powerful magician in disguise. Let them do this trifling service for your Majesty in return for the useless captive we are holding for Number Nine."

"Hm—mmmm!" Deliberately, the Silver Monarch put down his pipe. "That's not a bad idea, Niffle, not a bad idea at all." Picking up the jug, Wutz brushed rudely by his trembling little Minister and hurried out of his workshop. A few minutes later, he stood bowing and smiling before the two travelers in the prisoner's pit. But warned by the message in the silver ball, his entrance through the invisible door neither frightened nor impressed Handy Mandy or the Royal Ox.

"So here you are at last," exclaimed the Goat Girl, looking the Silver Monarch sternly in the eye. "And about time, too. How dare you imprison us in this miserable pit for no reason at all?"

"Oh, yes, there is a reason," stated Wutz, a little surprised at Handy's defiance. "You broke into my mountain without invitation or permission, and as you are nothing but a pair of trespassers, you certainly deserve imprisonment and even destruction."

"Nonsense," snorted the Royal Ox, lurching forward heavily. "We came here seeking a lost boy whom you are unlawfully holding captive. As soon as you release the little King of Keretaria, we will take him and leave this mountain!"

"And the sooner you tell us where he is, the better!" added Handy, snapping her thirty-five fingers under the Silver King's nose.

"Ah, you think so?" sneered Wutz. "Well, nothing is ever given for nothing in this mountain, but I may give you a chance to earn the boy's release. Here in my hand is a jug, an ordinary enough looking jug. With the magic you have in your possession, you must transform this jug to its proper shape. If you succeed, you and the Ox and the Boy King of Keretaria may leave my mountain unharmed. If you fail, ha ha!" The heartless wizard threw back his head and laughed uproariously. "If you fail, the walls of this pit will contract until you are — well, shall we say obliterated? To keep your part of the bargain and perform this slight service, I will give you *one half hour*. Here is the jug, and in case you fail, GOODBYE!"

"Good Gillikins!" whistled Nox as the wizard strode through the invisible door and left them alone. "What does that fool think we are, wizards, magicians, necromancers?" Groaning and snorting, he began to gallop round and round the hot little pit.

"Look out! Look out! You'll break the jug," warned Handy, snatching it up in her arms. "And for goat's sake stop that galloping! I'm dizzy enough as it is."

"But you heard what he said?" lowed the Ox, coming to a trembling stop beside her. "What are we to do? We know nothing of magic or magic transformations!" In their distress and excitement, they both forgot there might be a message to help them in the silver ball, and Handy, taking the jug in one of her white hands, surveyed it with horror and curiosity.

"It's so old and ugly now," said the Goat Girl slowly, "I'll bet it was something old and ugly to begin with. Didn't Nifflepok mention something about a jug that was a rug? Maybe it's a rug, though more likely a rogue. Say, I wonder if I broke the jug whether that would not break the enchantment?"

"Oh, no, no, no! Don't do that!" begged Nox, rolling his eyes in terror. "If you break the jug, the wizard will be furious, and how do you know what will break the spell? Here, let me look at it." Passing the jug rapidly from one hand to another, Handy started to place it on the floor under Nox's nose with her seventh and last hand when a sudden and unexpected scream from the interior made her drop it with a loud crash to the silver stones.

"Ouch! Oh, stop! How dare you bang me around in this hateful manner?" Up from the flying fragments of earthenware at Handy's feet sprang a fierce little gnome with a long, ragged beard, shaking his fists and howling like a child.

"Oh, my—y! I've actually done it!" quavered the Goat Girl, falling over Nox. "Look! Look! Didn't I tell you it would be old and ugly?" The gnome, at Handy's words, suddenly stopped howling.

"Where am I? Where am I? WHO am I?" he mumbled in a frightened voice.

"Well, I don't know who you are, but I'm afraid you're in a pretty bad place," said Handy, straightening up to have a better look at her handiwork. "You're in the underground caverns of the King of the Silver Mountain, if you must know."

238

"Caverns!" beamed the gnome, his face breaking into a wide smile. "What's the matter with caverns? I LOVE caverns. Why, I used to live in one myself. And who did you say I was?"

"We don't know who you are," explained Nox in a cautious voice. "A moment ago and before Handy took you in hand, you were nothing but a jug."

"A jug?" pondered the gnome, pulling his beard thoughtfully. "You mean to say I was a JUG?"

"Maybe `Was-a-jug' is your name," volunteered the Goat Girl, now quite interested in her transformation.

"No, not `Was-a-jug,' but something like a jug. Let me think: bug, hug, chug, mug, pug, rug. RUG? That's it, THAT'S my name, *Ruggedo!*" shrieked the little gnome joyfully, "And now I know who I am!"

"Well, who are you?" inquired the Ox, stretching his royal nose down toward the whirling gnome.

"I, why, *I* am the most important King on the other side of the desert!" shouted Ruggedo exultantly. "I am the one and only Metal Monarch and Ruler of all the Gnomes! My caves and caverns under the mountains of Ev sparkle with jewels and precious stones, mined by my faithful workers, and my grand army of gnomes outnumbers any army in Oz." Proudly, the ragged little King thumped himself upon the chest.

"Oh, my! Oh, me! Oh, mercy—ercy! If you're as powerful as all that, maybe you'll help us!" cried the Goat Girl, clasping her hands eagerly.

"Help you? Why should I help you?" The little Gnome stared scornfully at the two occupants of the cave.

"Because she broke your jug and enchantment, you ungrateful little wretch!" snorted Nox, lowering his horns. "And you don't look like a king to me, you just look like a plain, ordinary, wicked little ragamuffin, a RUGAMUFFIN!" he bellowed angrily.

Chapter 17 - Out of the Prison Pit

Nox's angry words had a strange effect on the boastful Gnome King. Leaning dejectedly against the side of the pit, he drew his hand wearily across his forehead. "I remember now," he told them hoarsely. "I once was the powerful Metal Monarch, but that was before I fell into the hands of Ozma and that wicked Wizard of Oz."

"So it was Ozma who turned you to a jug!" exclaimed Handy with all her hands on her hips.

"Yes, and before that she deprived me of my Kingdom, ducked me in a Truth Pond, marooned me for years on a desert island, struck me dumb, and then, when she could think of nothing worse, turned me to this jug!" screamed Ruggedo, kicking at the fragments of broken china at his feet.

"You and Ozma must have been enemies for a long time, then?" observed the Ox, looking at the Gnome with great disfavor.

"Yes, yes, ever since that girl Dorothy stole my magic belt and gave it to Ozma," raged Ruggedo, stamping furiously up and down. "And every time I try to recover my own property, or capture those wretched girls and the Emerald City, something goes wrong, and they conquer ME! The last time, Ozma turned me to a jug!" cried Ruggedo, his voice rising to a shrill whistle.

"Well, what did you expect?" inquired Handy Mandy sharply. "That Ozma would sit calmly on her throne and allow you to conquer her? My—y, such goings on!"

"Oh, then you are friends of Ozma?" said the Gnome King suspiciously. "But no, you could not be her friends or you would not have broken the jug. Who ARE you? The Ox is usual enough, except for his golden horns, but you" — Ruggedo's eyes grew round and anxious as he looked at the seven-armed Goat Girl —"*YOU* are odd, aren't you?"

"No, she's not odd!" snapped the Royal Ox severely. He had been through so much with the sturdy mountain lass, he felt almost as if they were related. "Handy is just seven times as smart and seven times as handy as most people, that's all. And since her seven hands have served you pretty well, try to keep a civil tongue in your head, will you?"

"Oh, all right!" Ruggedo, scuffing his foot, looked sulkily from one to the other. "Much obliged, I'm sure. But what in rockets are we doing in this miserable hole, and what are we waiting for?"

"For a fellow Metal Monarch and Wizard," answered a smooth voice, and appearing as quietly as he had vanished, Wutz stood calmly before them. "Come with me, Ruggedo. I have surprising news for you, comrade!" And without so much as a nod or "thank you" to Nox and Handy Mandy, he linked his arm through the Gnome's and drew him through the invisible door, slamming it viciously behind him.

"Hi—yi!" yelled Handy Mandy indignantly. "Come back here! Come back here! A bargain's a bargain, you old cheat and villain! We've kept our part, and you shall keep yours. Where have you hidden the little King of Kereteria? Let us out! Let us out, you false-faced rascal!"

239

Nox, as angry as Handy, charged forward, butting his head against the exact spot where the wizard had disappeared. To his astonishment and joy, the whole section of wall swung outward, and he and the Goat Girl, rushing through, found themselves in a narrow, dimly lit silver tunnel. "To think, to think we could have got out any time!" gulped the Royal Ox in a vexed voice. "The door was invisible but not locked. Imagine that, m'lass!"

"Oh, I've other things to do," puffed Handy, peering down the long passageway to see whether she could catch a glimpse of the two Kings. "No use trying to imagine anything about this mountain, it's just plain bewitched and goblinish. But that wizard made us a promise, and I'm going to see that he keeps it. Come on!"

"No! No!" said the Royal Ox, leaning weakly against the side of the tunnel. "I couldn't bear to look at him again, at least not just yet. Wait! I may think of something else! WAIT!" bellowed Nox as Handy, in spite of his pleas, started off on a run. "There now, you've dropped something out of your pocket."

"That silver ball," muttered Handy, scooping it up without slackening her pace.

"The ball! The *BALL?*" exclaimed Nox, galloping breathlessly to catch up with her. "Oh, what muddleheads, *WHAT* muddleheads! It told us to wait for the wizard. Quick, see what it says now!"

"Well, a lot of good it did waiting for that wizard," grumbled the Goat Girl; but nevertheless, she stopped and opened the silver ball. Taking out the folded paper, she held it up toward an amethyst gleaming dully in the side of the tunnel.

"Follow me," directed the paper rather mysteriously.

"But who does `me' mean?" asked Handy as Nox, still breathing heavily, read the message over her shoulder. "I don't see any me, do you? Beans and butternuts! If you hadn't stopped me, I'd have caught those villains by this time!"

"And what good would that have done?" sniffed the Ox impatiently. "Remember, there are two of them now, and that little gnome is worse than Wutz and twice as dangerous." Closing his eyes in an effort to concentrate, Nox repeated over the message, "Follow me! Follow me! Follow ME! Why, of course, it's as plain as oats!" he snorted joyfully. "`Me' means that ball. Put the message back in the ball, set the ball down, and then see what happens." And what happened was amazing enough, for the silver ball, once it was on the floor of the tunnel, began to roll rapidly along ahead of them, faster and faster and faster, till Handy and Nox had all they could do to keep it in sight.

"Where do you suppose it's taking us?" gasped the Goat Girl, thankful that so far the tunnel had been more or less straight and fairly well lighted.

"To Kerry," said the Royal ox positively. "Now watch that turn, m'lass. What's ahead? It's growing so dark I can't even see my own shadow!"

"It's a flight of steps," whispered Handy, gazing fearfully into the deep well of a circular stairway winding down into the darkness. They could hear the chink of the silver ball as it rolled from step to step, so, taking her courage in all hands, the Goat Girl herself began to descend. Nox, grunting and muttering lugubriously, came just behind her. Steps were difficult enough for the Ox at any time, but negotiating a flight of circular steps in pitch darkness was terrifying and dangerous in the extreme. "Be careful!" warned Handy, looking up anxiously. "Don't slip, or you'll break my heart."

"More than that, I'm afraid," quavered the Royal Ox, setting his front feet cautiously on the step below while he balanced his hindquarters perilously on the one above.

Chapter 18 - Wutz and the Gnome King leave for the Capital!

Meanwhile, Wutz and Ruggedo had shot up in the wizard's silver car and were now in earnest conversation together. "How in suds did that girl break your enchantment?" asked Wutz, dropping irritably to his silver workbench. "I was watching her every minute through an invisible window, and I didn't see her do a thing but break the jug. Now why couldn't I have thought of that?"

"Oh, what does it matter?" Ruggedo settled himself with a joyful little wriggle beside the Silver Monarch. "What does it matter so long as I am free and able to help you? So you really think you can make yourself Ruler of Oz?" he went on, glancing enviously round the wizard's well-stocked den with its tables full of magic apparatus and its shelves and shelves of dusty volumes of wizard and witch works. Wutz had confided his plans and intentions to Ruggedo on the ride up. "Say!" exclaimed the Gnome King suddenly, "How did you get Glinda's record book? That's the most important treasure in her castle!"

"Of course!" Lazily, the wizard reached for his silver pipe. "Well, it's a long story, Rug, but I don't mind telling you that I have agents working in every Kingdom of the country. Seven, who was assigned to the Quadling Country, brought in the record book, smallifying it in order to steal and carry it here and restoring it to proper size when it arrived. Six and Eleven have brought me useful magic from the Winkies and Gillikins, but Five managed to steal Ozma's own magic picture, and — ha ha! — since he couldn't find the Gnome King's belt, he brought me the Gnome King himself! Pretty clever of him to discover you were a jug, eh?"

"Remarkable!" sighed Ruggedo as Wutz paused to blow a silver bubble which floated out of the work den, breaking somewhere outside with a tinkling, bell-like explosion.

"Two glasses of melted silver," snapped the wizard to a smart-looking bellboy who came in answer to this singular summons. "Now," continued Wutz, looking at the Gnome King through half-closed eyes, "before I attempt to capture the Emerald City, I must have one of two things: either the silver hammer belonging to a witch of the West, or the magic belt that once belonged to you. So far, none of my agents has been able to find the witch, locate the hammer, or discover where Ozma now keeps your magic belt. But you, its rightful owner, must know exactly where it is hidden."

Ruggedo, without saying anything, nodded briefly. "Well then," said Wutz, "if you will help me steal the magic belt, which I understand is the most potent and powerful magic in Ev or Oz, I will kick Kaliko off your throne, restore your own Kingdom, and give you besides any one of the four Oz Kingdoms you may fancy."

"Oh, don't bother me with any of the Oz Kingdoms. I'm sick of the place!" frowned the Gnome, wagging his beard vindictively. "All I want is my own old Kingdom and my own magic belt! But I tell you what I will do. I'll help you steal this belt, for I know exactly where it is hidden, show you how it works so you can transform Ozma and all her friends and counselors to rocks and rubble. BUT, when you are safely established as supreme Wizard of Oz, you must return the belt to me."

"Oh, naturally!" promised the wizard, chuckling to himself as he thought how quickly he would turn Ruggedo to a rock once he was wearing the famous belt. Taking a glass of melted silver from the tray the boy had just set down, Wutz lifted it to his lips, and Ruggedo, his eyes glittering with all their old spitefulness, raised his own glass to drink to the wicked bargain.

"Come," he sputtered, wiping his mouth on the back of his hand. "When do we start? What magic have you to carry us to the capital and open the emerald safe where the magic belt and other important treasures of Ozma are hidden? But wait, perhaps we had better look in the magic picture and see where Ozma and the Wizard of Oz are now."

"I am afraid we cannot do that," Wutz explained regretfully. "Seven spoiled the canvas in some way when he reduced it to carry it here. It doesn't show anything now, and I've not had time to repair the damage."

"Pshaw, that's too bad," said Ruggedo, going over to touch the picture, now hanging on the wizard's wall. "But the record book is still working, I suppose."

"Oh, yes," said the wizard, stepping up to the marble table and glancing down at the open page. "And listen to this. It says," roared the Silver King, holding his sides and simply rocking with wicked merriment, "it says: `The two metal monarchs are plotting the downfall of the present ruler of Oz.'"

"What else does it say?" inquired the Gnome King, who had more experience than his companion in dealing with the magicians of the Emerald City.

"It says, `Ozma and her counselors have gone to the castle of Glinda the Good,' " Wutz told him, complacently closing and padlocking the big volume.

"Then we'd better start at once and before they return," declared Ruggedo. "For as soon as we have my belt, we can change them to rocks wherever they are. The most important thing is to get that belt before they know we are after it. But how are we going to get to the Emerald City, and how're we going to open that safe?"

"My silver blowpipe will reduce the safe to a heap of ashes without injuring the contents," answered the wizard, "and reaching the capital will be the simplest part of all!" Taking a silver tube from a high shelf, Wutz put it in his pocket and, reaching for his bubble pipe, he began to blow an enormous quicksilver bubble round himself and the Gnome King. Slowly and with both Kings inside, the bubble rose, passed in a silver mist out of the wizard's den, up through the honeycomb of caves, caverns, and grottos, on up and up till it floated right out of the top of the Silver King's Mountain.

Chapter 19 - At the Bottom of the Mountain!

At the same moment the silver bubble carrying Wutz *and* Ruggedo *burst out of the top of* the mountain, Handy Mandy and Nox reached the bottom, arriving at last at the end of the winding stair. One amethyst burned dimly on the small landing, and crowded uncomfortably together the two prisoners found themselves facing a heavily barred door.

Private Lower of the Wizard of Wutz.
Keep Out!

announced a surly sign. But Handy and Nox, their legs still quivering from the long downward climb, were in no humor to be stopped by a sign.

"Lower!" sniffed Handy Mandy disgustedly. "I should think it was. We must be at the very bottom of this miserable mountain. Lower indeed! Well, I expect a lower is the opposite of a tower. Come on!" Picking up the silver ball, Handy squinted sharply at the door, giving it a quick shove to see whether it was locked or fitted with an invisible moving panel. But there was nothing remarkable about this door and nothing on it except a very small silver keyhole, which at once recalled to the Goat Girl the key she had been carrying around ever since she left Keretaria.

"Oh, Nox, I believe the key in your horn will fit!" she cried excitedly, and deftly removing the left prong of Nox's headgear, she shook out the ball. Then, while Nox, fairly panting with impatience, looked on, Handy took the key from the ball and inserted it in the silver lock. When it turned easily and smoothly, she was almost afraid to open the door. What would they find on the other side? What had the wizard done to his helpless young captive? As Handy hesitated, Nox rushed forward, banging the door open with his great shoulder.

"Kerry! Kerry!" wailed the faithful Ox, and falling to his knees, Nox began to snort and blubber in real earnest. Handy, hurrying after him into the small, stuffy cell, saw a handsome boy in hunting costume standing motionless and silent as a statue in the center of a great, shimmering, violet bubble. Without thinking or reasoning or even stopping to consult the Ox, the Goat Girl flung out all of her arms toward the solitary figure, her iron hand puncturing the bubble with a deafening pop.

"Why, hello Nox!" The Little King stepped calmly out of the misty vapor, all that was left of the wizard's bubble. "Where's your other horn? And who is this jolly-looking girl?"

WHO indeed? There was so much to be told and explained, even with Handy and Nox talking as fast as they could and taking turns, it took almost an hour to tell the story of their journey from Keretaria to the Silver Mountain and their awful experiences with the Wizard of Wutz. Kerry himself remembered nothing since he had started out on the hunting expedition. He listened with angry exclamations and bounces as Nox related the tale of King Kerr's treachery and the sad state of affairs in Keretaria. "And I've been shut up in this bubble for two years!" mourned the little King, looking round the dismal cell with a shudder. "Why, it makes my head ache just to think of it!"

"Mine, too," agreed Handy, clapping Nox's left horn in place. "But it's almost over now, my lad. If we can just find some way out of this mountain, I'll settle old King Kerr and his High Boys, not to speak of this woozling wizard!"

Placing Kerry on Nox's back, Handy looked nervously out the door of the Lower. At sight of the winding stair, Nox gave a great groan and shudder. "I'll never climb those steps again!" he declared, planting his feet stubbornly. "Never! Where's that silver hammer, m'lass? Give it a tap and see what the dwarf can do for us. Wutz and Ruggedo are too busy with their wicked plans to bother us now."

"I wouldn't be too sure of that," muttered the Goat Girl. Nevertheless, she pulled out the hammer and tapped it lightly on the floor.

"Well, what's wanted?" yawned Himself, appearing instantly and in the exact spot the hammer had struck.

"We want to get out of here!" cried Kerry, so excited and delighted with the purple-bearded dwarf he instantly forgot all his troubles. With a crooked smile at the little King, Himself looked questioningly at Handy, and at the Goat Girl's quick nod rapped his knuckles on the north wall of the Lower. At once, a small panel slipped aside, revealing an elevator, its door invitingly open. Waving all her hands to thank Himself, who was already beginning to disappear, Handy stepped inside. Nox, with Kerry still perched on his back, just managed to squeeze in when the door snapped shut and the elevator sped upward carrying its three passengers in double-quicksilver time to the work den of the wizard. Handy, a bit disappointed not to find herself on top of the mountain, stepped out first. As Nox, with an awkward jump, followed her, the door slammed sharply and the elevator dropped like a plummet to the bottom of the mountain.

"Oh, this must be where Wutz works all his magic transformations," breathed Kerry, sliding off Nox's back and gazing around with deep interest and curiosity. "I'll bet he blew a bubble round me right in this very den. Wonder where he is now?" There was a slight cough at Kerry's question, and turning, they saw Nifflepok standing uncertainly in the doorway.

"Ah, so we meet again!" cried Handy, doubling up all her fists and walking grimly toward the Silver King's fat Minister. "Where is that rascally Master of yours? As you probably know by this time, we kept our part of the bargain, but he still has to keep his."

"Indeed, you are fortunate to have escaped with your lives," muttered Wutz, taking off his hat and looking anxiously inside. "And I'm sorry to tell you the Wizard of Wutz NEVER keeps his bargains. No matter how hard we work or try to please him, sooner or later we are all shelved or potted!"

"Then why work for such a villain?" snorted the Royal Ox gruffly. "Where is he now?"

"Yes, where is he now?" asked Kerry, who in spite of the terrible stories he had heard, hoped to get a look at the wonderful wizard who had enchanted him.

"Gone!" answered Nifflepok, putting on his high hat and giving it a couple of taps. "He's bubbled off with the Gnome King to conquer Oz, and I expect by this time they've bewitched about half the inhabitants of the Emerald City."

"Oh, what a shame!" burst out Kerry.

"Bubbled off? What do you mean by that?" The Goat Girl reached out all her arms to pull the Silver King's little Minister closer.

"I mean bubbled off," repeated Nifflepok, struggling to release himself from Handy's clutches. "He blew a quicksilver bubble, and he and Ruggedo sailed away in it, if that's any plainer."

"Oh, then we had better go right after them," snorted the Ox in an anxious voice. "Show us out of this mountain, you little pudding, or I'll toss you higher than a kite."

"Oh, do let's do something!" begged Kerry, who, being young, was quite daring and absolutely foolhardy. "We aren't going to let those dreadful Kings conquer the country, are we, and not lift a hand?"

"Well, I'm sure I'd lift all seven if it would do any good," mused Handy Mandy in a depressed voice. "But how can we stop them? Wutz and Rug have probably stolen all the magic in Ozma's palace by this time, the thieving rascals!"

"But surely YOU have some magic," ventured Nifflepok, who had finally jerked himself free, "or you could never have disenchanted that gnome or found the wizard's Lower and rescued this boy; and if you have—" he warned, backing rapidly away, "—if you have, you'd better use it QUICK. When Wutz finishes conquering Oz, he's sure to remember you and turn you to rocks and rubble. He's going to turn everyone to rocks and rubble!" wailed Nifflepok, dashing out of the workshop.

"Great Gazoo, what shall we do? I don't want to be a rock," snorted Nox.

"And I won't be a rock!" stormed the little King. "It was bad enough being shut up in a bubble and missing two whole years. Oh, you won't let him turn us to rocks, will you Handy? And do let's help poor Ozma before it's too late!"

Kerry looked up at her so pleadingly that Handy, against all her inclinations and better judgment, pulled out the silver hammer again. "The hammer will be better than the ball," she reasoned quickly, "for the ball only seems to help Keretarians. Now then!" Lifting the hammer in her iron hand, the Goat Girl brought it down sharply on the wizard's marble table. Silver sparks flew up in every direction, and out of the very middle of the shower stepped the yawning dwarf.

"Say, I'm trying to take a nap," grumbled Himself, stretching his arms up sleepily. "What do you fellows want now?"

"We want to go to the Emerald City of Oz and save Ozma from Wutz and the Gnome King!" explained Handy in one breathless sentence.

"My! All that?" Stifling another yawn, Himself grinned mischievously at the Goat Girl. "Then stand in line, please." So Handy placed herself in front of the Royal Ox and Kerry stepped behind him, and the dwarf, seizing the hammer, brought it down with a terrible blow just behind the little King. And what a blow it was you can readily understand when I tell you that its force carried the three travelers clear out of the Silver King's Mountain and all the way to the Emerald City itself. Flying along for a moment beside them, Himself slipped the hammer back in the Goat Girl's hand, and then with another tremendous yawn disappeared.

Chapter 20 - Just in Time!

In Ozma's palace in the Emerald City, everything was very quiet and still. Not surprising when you consider that the Wizard of Wutz had blown his patent stupefying powder down all the chimneys before he and Ruggedo dared to enter. Then, mooring the silver bubble to one of the castle spires, the two conspirators had slipped through an open window and proceeded without delay or interference to the private sitting room of the absent ruler. There Ruggedo with a spiteful laugh thrust his head right into the mouths of the Hungry Tiger and Cowardly Lion. Rigid and helpless they sat before Ozma's safe, motionless and completely stupefied, as were all of Ozma's other faithful servants and retainers. Reducing the safe to a heap of green ashes was the work of but a moment, then, pulling the Gnome King's belt from the sparkling heap of treasures, Wutz sprang to his feet. "Quick! How does it work?" he cried, clasping the belt round his thin waist. "We'll not have a second's safety till Ozma, Glinda, the Wizard of Oz and all those girl Princesses are out of the way."

"But first you must restore my Kingdom!" insisted Ruggedo, dancing up and down. "Here, give it to me. I'm used to it and can work faster. First I'll wish Kaliko off my throne and myself back in my underground castle, then—"

"Oh, no, you won't!" declared Wutz, holding the bouncing Gnome King off with one hand. "How do I know what you will do once you reach your own Kingdom? Why, I might never see this belt again."

"But I promise to send it back to you," hissed Ruggedo, his eyes snapping real sparks.

"I'd rather have the belt than the promise," said Wutz, shaking his head stubbornly.

"Give it to me, I say, GIVE it to me!" yelled Ruggedo, now in a perfect rage. "How do I know what *you* will do when you know the trick of using it? Why, you might even turn me to a rock to be rid of me."

"What? Change my dearest friend and most powerful ally to a rock?" exclaimed the Wizard with pretended horror. "By the left horn of my silver cow, I promise to return this belt as soon as I am Ruler of Oz!" Ruggedo longed to snatch his belt away from the scheming Silver Monarch, but as he was neither big or strong enough to do this, there was nothing for him to do but agree to the wizard's terms.

"All right," he groaned dismally. "Listen, then—" But as Wutz bent his head and the little gnome began to whisper hoarse directions in his ear, there was a dreadful thump and clatter behind them.

"STOP!" commanded the Goat Girl, the first to recover from the shock of the landing, and dear knows Handy should have been used to sudden landings by this time. "STOP!" Whirling round with a howl of fury, Wutz sprang straight at her, but Handy, who still clutched the silver hammer in her iron hand, was too quick for him and brought it down with a resounding crack on the top of his head. "Take 'em away! Take 'em away!" cried Handy hysterically as Wutz fell over backwards and Himself, appearing exactly where the hammer had struck, leaped off the wizard's head to save himself from a fall.

"But first we must have that magic belt," chuckled the hammer elf. Giving Ruggedo, who was struggling frantically to get his belt from around the Silver King's waist, a push, Himself unbuckled the clasps and tossed the magic girdle to the Goat Girl. Then, grabbing the howling gnome and senseless wizard each by the neck, the efficient dwarf vanished in a flash of lightning and a crash of thunder that shook the castle to its foundations. Nox dropped to his knees. Kerry, still stunned by the hammer blow that had carried them to the Emerald City, and Handy herself with her arms still upraised, stared in dumb astonishment at the quivering vacuum where the two Kings and Himself, the elf, had been whirling a moment before.

"Oh, Handy, HANDY, you've really done it!" shouted Kerry, finding his voice at last. "Why, you've saved the whole of Ozma's Kingdom and struck only one blow! But watch out, are those beasts alive or just statues?"

"Statues, I hope," grunted the Royal Ox, lurching dizzily to his feet. "Well, here we are in the capital, m'lass, and I must say you have handled everything beautifully, beautifully!"

"Halt! Who goes there? Whoa! HO! Halt and Surrender!" piped a frightened voice. "Here they are, your Majesty, the robbers themselves, caught red-handed in the act of robbing our royal safe!"

"Red-, white- and blue-handed, if you ask me!" cried the Patchwork Girl, blinking her shoe-button eyes at the red rubber hand with which Handy grasped the Gnome King's belt, the white hand she had reached out to hold on to Kerry, the iron hand still clutching the silver hammer. All the rest of her hands the Goat Girl held stiffly before her. Brushing aside the Soldier with the Green Whiskers, who promptly dived behind a sofa, Scraps jerked the Gnome King's belt out of Handy's rubber hand and gave her a shove that sent her flying over backwards. "Take that, you Monster!" yelled Scraps.

"Well," sputtered the Goat Girl, sprawling flat on her back, "here's gratitude for you!"

"How dare you call Handy a Monster?" bellowed Nox, charging angrily after the Patchwork Girl.

"Oh! Do be careful!" called Ozma with a little scream as Nox almost caught up with Scraps and Kerry began to belabor the Soldier with Green Whiskers over the head with a candlestick. "Oh! Oh! My poor Lion! My poor Tiger! My SAFE! Why, I just can't believe it!" wailed the little Fairy Ruler, staring sorrowfully down at the Goat Girl, who had made no attempt to rise or explain her embarrassing position.

"Then don't believe it!" cried Kerry breathlessly, "For it isn't true! This brave girl and Nox have got the best of Wutz and the Gnome King and saved your whole bally Kingdom, and here you've gone and had her knocked down. Shame on you! Get away from me, you cotton-stuffed horror!" screamed the little King as Scraps, eluding the Ox, made a determined jump in his direction.

"Quiet! QUIET!" The Scarecrow, who with Glinda, the Wizard, Dorothy, Betsy and Trot now came hurrying into the room, raised both arms and looked around pleadingly. The whole royal party, traveling in Glinda's swan chariot, had just arrived on the balcony outside, but Ozma, Scraps and the Soldier with Green Whiskers had been first on the scene of action.

"The boy is right," declared Glinda, crossing slowly to a green sofa. "I can see by her face and hands—" Glinda smiled faintly, "—that this girl is both honest and industrious."

"Thanks!" murmured Handy as the Scarecrow, ever a gentleman, bounded forward to assist her to her feet. The flimsy straw fellow lost his balance in the attempt, but his little act of gallantry did much to relieve an awkward moment.

"You see," puffed the Scarecrow, seating Handy with a flourish, "for the last ten days we've all been pretty much upset around here, and you'll have to excuse Scraps for jumping at conclusions."

244

"Please do!" Ozma spoke pleasantly and seriously as she seated herself in her small armchair, leaning over to take the Gnome King's belt from Scraps. "But if some of you kind people will just explain..." The Little Fairy looked anxiously from the stupefied Tiger and Lion to her pulverized safe, her eyes coming back to rest on the Goat Girl, the great White Ox, and the handsome young Munchkin.

Chapter 21 - The Hammer Elf Explains

"Go ahead and explain," said Handy, closing her eyes and leaning back in her chair with all her hands hanging limply at her side. So Nox, a bit haughtily and tossing his head proudly from time to time, began at the beginning and told all that had happened since Handy Mandy had flown from Mt. Mern: how the Goat Girl had found the magic in his horn, how they had traveled together from Keretaria to the Silver Mountain and there, in their search for the little King, discovered Wutz's plot to make himself Supreme Wizard of Oz. And last of all, he explained how Handy, with the help of the silver hammer, had subdued the two wicked Kings.

"Well, it certainly was very kind of you to take all this trouble for us after you had already had so many worries of your own," sighed Ozma as Nox, finishing his story, gazed round the room with lordly condescension.

"Yes, wasn't it?" Handy opened her eyes and thoughtfully regarded the little Ruler of Oz. "Still, I'm glad now that we did save you." The Goat Girl's round pleasant face was suddenly wreathed in smiles. "I didn't think I was going to like you, but I do," she admitted cheerfully. "I believe you're about the best ruler Oz could have, and besides, you're pretty as a goat."

"As a goat!" gasped the Wizard of Oz while Dorothy and all the other girls had all they could do to keep from laughing right out loud. But Ozma, who was a very understanding little person, smiled kindly back at Handy Mandy.

"Goats *are* pretty," she agreed, nodding her head politely. "And since you miss your own goats very much, perhaps you would like me to send you back to Mt. Mern after you've seen a bit of the capital."

"Oh, Handy wouldn't leave us!" snorted the royal Ox, moving as close to the Goat Girl as he could get. "We couldn't get along without Handy Mandy, your Majesty."

"Oh, please let her stay in Keretaria," begged the little King, adding his voice to that of his Royal Ox. "You will live with us in the palace, won't you, Handy?"

"Well, if I just had my goats—" considered the seven-armed maiden. "Mt. Mern would seem rather dull after Oz," she acknowledged pensively. "But what about that old King who's still on Kerry's throne, and what am I to do with this silver hammer, and what do you suppose Himself has done with Wutz and Ruggedo?"

"Yes, what's to be done with Wutz?" echoed the Scarecrow, wrinkling up his cotton forehead. And now the little sitting room began fairly to buzz with excited questions and suggestions, for there was still a lot to be explained and settled. The Ozites could hardly keep their eyes off the seven-armed Goat Girl, the handsome young ruler of Keretaria, and his Royal Ox. Dorothy longed to unscrew his horn and test its magic power for herself, but Ozma, anxious to repair all the damage done by the wicked wizard, now raised her scepter for silence.

Clasping on the Gnome King's belt, Ozma first brought back her magic picture and with a quick wish returned Glinda's book of records to her castle in the South. Next, though she knew neither the extent nor the nature of the wizard's other thefts, she caused to be restored to their rightful owners all the magic appliances in the Silver King's den. The Scarecrow had already reported the stupefied condition of the other occupants of the palace, so Ozma's next thought was to restore them to their accustomed selves. No sooner was the Cowardly Lion released than he crawled under a table, but the Hungry Tiger rushed out on the balcony, growling and lashing his tail as he thought of the indignity he had suffered.

After a short conference with Handy Mandy, Ozma freed all the potted prisoners of the wicked wizard and made Nifflepok King of the Silver Mountain. She moved the cliff dwellings of the people to the outside of the mountain so Wutz's pale subjects could enjoy with the rest of the Gillikins the bright sunshine and beneficent climate of Oz. The Magic Mountain itself, with all its dark pits and jeweled caverns, Ozma sealed up tightly and forever. The wizard's agents were turned to moles, for they were already more like these boring little animals than men.

After each magic wish or transformation, the little group in the royal sitting room would look in the magic picture, which Ozma had immediately repaired. And in each case Handy felt that the ruler of Oz had used both wisdom and good judgment. Nox, as they were watching the wizard's agents turn to moles, gave a snort of surprise, for the first figure shown was old King Kerr, who was really Number Nine. As the wicked imposter changed quickly from a man to a mole and scurried off the throne and away to bury himself in the blue forest, Nox and Handy both heaved a sigh of relief and satisfaction.

While Ozma was working on the magic safe, Handy, deciding to try a little of her own magic, softly tapped the silver hammer on the arm of her chair. At once, to the delight and interest of everyone, Himself, the elf, appeared astride the arm, holding a small cactus plant in each hand. "I wish you in the future to obey the summons of her Majesty Ozma of Oz," smiled the Goat Girl, placing the silver hammer as she spoke in Ozma's lap. "This young fairy is more experienced in magic than I and will know to use the hammer to best advantage."

"Oh, all right! But I rather liked working for you," grinned Himself. "And say, I tried to turn these rascals to plants, but this was the best I could do." Setting the two pots of cactus down on a small writing desk, the hammer elf bowed first to Handy and then to Ozma. "Wait! Don't go!" begged the little Fairy as Himself showed unmistakable signs of disappearing. "Do tell us about this silver hammer and who owned it first."

"It belonged to Wunchie, a witch of the West who's lived in the Munchkin Mountains for about a thousand years and used it to control as many of the Munchkin Kings as she could," explained the dwarf, balancing himself cleverly on an inkwell.

"Then I suppose Wunchie was responsible for the prophecy in Keretaria," surmised Nox, blinking his eyes at the hammer elf. The dwarf nodded cheerfully.

"Yes, Wunchie invented that prophecy," he told them, "and placed her own white oxen in the country. Each time she had trouble forcing the King to do as she wished, she tapped him and the ox on the head with her hammer. But I took rather a fancy to you," admitted Himself, looking fondly at Nox. "So when she ordered me to tap you off and traded the little King Kerry to Wutz for a basket of jumping beans and put Wutz's agent on the throne of Keretaria, I decided to take a hand myself. So I gave you only a light tap and at the same time I stored enough magic in your horns to help you find Kerry — and with the help of this handy Goat Girl, you DID find him!" beamed the hammer elf. "I knew my magic was good. You can't work for a witch without learning good magic. But now, since everything is turning out so splendidly, I'll just go back to my tree stump. One, two, three, back to my tree!"

"But what became of the witch?" cried Ozma, catching hold of the dwarf's purple beard (for his head had already vanished).

"Ha, ha! She exploded and popped off!" roared a voice from the place where the elf's head had been. "I told her not to eat those jumping beans! And after that, I buried her hammer in the garden of Keretaria, and there it stayed till Handy plowed it up. Goodbye, all!" And the body of the hammer elf melted into nothing and was gone.

"My—y, what a clever fellow!" chuckled Handy. "So now Wutz and Ruggedo are a couple of cactuses! Mm—mmm! Mmmm—mm! Unpleasant to the last! Do you suppose anyone can ever disenchant them? For goatness sake, be careful!" begged Handy as Jellia, in answer to her Mistress' ring, came to carry the plants to the conservatory. "Whatever you do, don't drop 'em. And to think that the Wizard is potted himself! Well, I'll never have a hand in breaking *his* enchantment!"

"I never thought anyone could ever break Ruggedo's enchantment," confessed Ozma. "When I changed him to a jug, I commanded him to keep that shape till he was broken by the seventh hand of a traveling Mernite. And at that time I did not even know there was such a place as Mt. Mern or a clever Goat Girl like Handy."

"But aren't you glad there was?" shouted the little Wizard of Oz, tossing up his hat and catching it on his nose. "Aren't we all glad to know Handy Mandy, Nox and this jolly young King?"

"Long live the Royal Ox and the Little King of Keretaria!" cried the cheering Ozites. "Long live Handy Mandy, the seven-armed wonder of the world and OZ!"\

And, of course, they will live long; everyone lives long in Oz. But even if Handy lives to be a hundred, she will never forget the grand banquet given that evening in her honor. Besides the famous people she already knew, the Goat Girl was presented to all the other celebrities at Ozma's court, and shaking hands with them heartily and seven at a time she had never been so flattered and fussed over in her life. Nox and Kerry came in for their share of honors, too. There was nothing the Ozians would not have done for their three new friends and rescuers.

Ozma, overwhelmed by Handy's generosity in giving her the silver hammer and already indebted to her for saving the Kingdom, racked her brains for some wonderful gift to reward the brave mountain lass. But it was Nox who solved the difficulty by confiding to Ozma that Handy desired more than anything else a set of gloves for her hands. It seemed she had never had enough gloves for more than two at a time. So, smiling secretly to herself, Ozma gave the Goat Girl seven sets of fine kid gloves and an emerald necklace that wound three times round her sturdy neck. With the necklace, a complete new outfit, and her forty-nine gloves, Handy Mandy felt herself quite ready for high life and royal society.

"Though you really should wear a boxing glove on that iron hand," whispered the Scarecrow as Handy blushingly resumed her seat after Ozma's speech of presentation. "Stay in the Emerald City, and we will make you a general in the army," promised the straw man earnestly. But Handy shook her head with tears of merriment in her eyes. Though she never quite forgave Scraps for pushing her over, she and the Scarecrow were already as friendly and easy as an old pair of shoes. "Handy Monday, Tuesday, Wednesday, Thursday, Friday, Saturday and Sunday," the straw man had nicknamed her because she had a hand for every day in the week.

Nox had insisted on Himself being invited to the banquet, and the clever elf added much to the pleasure and hilarity of that memorable occasion. Indeed, many times afterward when she felt bored or lonely, Ozma would summon Himself just to amuse and cheer her up. The silver hammer was stored away with the other important magic treasures and is regarded by many as the most powerful magic in the castle. Handy Mandy kept the blue flower to help her on future journeys, and after she and her two friends had spent a happy week in the Emerald City, Ozma reluctantly wished Kerry and Nox to Keretaria and the Goat Girl back to Mt. Mern.

There for a month Handy Mandy astonished the villagers with the story of her travels, then, gathering up her goats, she took herself and them by a fast wishing pill the Wizard had given her to the Kingdom of Keretaria. As the Goat Girl's hands retained all of their strength and willingness and Nox's horns all their magic — even to giving wise and useful messages — these two and little Kerry ruled the Kingdom between them with such skill and cleverness that everyone was enormously happy and prosperous!

<h1 style="text-align:center">The End</h1>

The Silver Princess in Oz

by Ruth Plumly Thompson

Chapter 1 - The King Rebels

In a faraway northwestern corner of the Gilliken Country of Oz lies the rugged little Kingdom of Regalia, and in an airy and elegant castle set high on the tallest mountain lives Randy, its brave young King. When the Regalians are not busy celebrating one of their seventy-seven national holidays, they are busy tending their flocks of goats or looking after the vines that cover every mountain and hill, producing the largest and most luscious grapes in Oz. These proud and independent mountain folk have much to recommend them, and if they consider themselves superior to any and all of the other natives in Oz, we must not blame them too much. Perhaps the sharp, clear air and high altitude in which they live is responsible for their top-lofty attitude. Randy, it must be confessed, found the stiff and unbending manner of his subjects and their correct and formal behavior on all occasions stuffy in the extreme; and of all the stuffy occasions he had to endure, the weekly court reception was the stuffiest. Just as I started this story, he was winding up another of these royal and boring affairs.

"Hail! Hail! Give Majesty its proper due,
Hail Randywell, King Handywell of Brandenburg and Bompadoo!
Boom! BOOM! BOOM!"

At each crash of the drums, the young King winced and shuddered, then, pulling himself together, he nodded resignedly to his richly attired courtiers and subjects who were retiring backwards from the royal presence. As the last bowing figure swished through the double doors, Randy gave a huge sigh and groan. This was his three hundred and tenth reception since ascending the throne. Ahead stretched hundreds more, besides the daily courts where he acted as presiding Judge to settle all disputes of the realm; countless reviewings of troops; inspections of model goat farms; and attendance at numerous celebrations for national heroes of Regalia.

"Oh, being a King is awful," choked the youthful monarch, loosening his regal cape and letting it fall unheeded to the floor. "AWFUL! Will it always be like this, Uncle?"

"Like what?" His uncle, the Grand Duke Hoochafoo, who was still inclining his head mechanically in the direction of the door, caught himself abruptly in the middle of a bow.

"Oh, all this silly standing round and being bowed at, this `Hail! Hail! and Way for His Majesty!' stuff. Galloping Collopers, Uncle, I'd like to step out by myself occasionally without twenty footmen springing to open doors and fifty pages tooting on their blasted trumpets. Why, I cannot even cross the courtyard that a dozen guardsmen do not fall in behind me!" Flouncing over to the window, Randy stared out over the royal terrace. "Even the goats on the mountain have more fun than I do," he observed bitterly. "They can run, jump, climb and even butt one another, while—" Randy let his arms fall heavily at his sides. "I have not even anyone to fight with. If just ONCE somebody would punch me in the nose instead of bowing." Randy clenched and unclenched his fists.

"Hm-mm!! So that's what you want!" Looking quizzically at his young nephew, Uncle Hoochafoo crossed to the bell rope and gave it a savage ring. As Randy's personal servant and valet appeared to answer the ring, he spoke sharply, "Dawkins, kindly hit His Majesty on the nose!"

"The nose? Oh, but Your Lordship, I couldn't do a thing like that. 'Tisn't right, nor fitting — nor —"

"I said hit him in the nose," commanded Uncle Hoochafoo, advancing grimly upon the terrified valet.

"Yes, yes, like this!" Bringing up his fist, Randy made such a splendid connection with the valet's nose, Dawkins toppled over backwards. Dancing from one foot to the other as the outraged servant sprang to his feet, Randy prepared to defend himself. But with his hand clapped to his nose, Dawkins was retiring rapidly. "Thank you!" he muttered in a strangled voice, "thank you very much!"

"Did you hear that? He said `Thank you,'" screamed Randy as Dawkins disappeared with an agitated bow. "Oh, this is too much; I wish I were back with Nandywog in Tripedalia — or anywhere but here, doing nothing but this."

"Now, now! Don't take things so hard," begged his uncle, patting him kindly on the shoulder.

"Hard?" Randy glared at the old nobleman. "I can take things hard, Uncle, but I cannot take them soft. I'll never forgive my father for getting me into this — NEVER!" Randy's father, former King of Regalia, tiring of a royal life and routine, had retired to a distant cave to live the life of a hermit, and Randy, after traveling all over Oz to fulfill the seven difficult tests required of a Regalian ruler, had succeeded to the throne.

"You should not speak like that of your royal parent," chided Uncle Hoochafoo, tapping his spectacles absently against his teeth, "for you are very much like him, my boy, very much like him. Hmm! Hmm! Harumph!" Uncle Hoochafoo cleared his throat thoughtfully. "What you need is a change, a new interest. Ah, I have it! You must marry, my lad, you must marry! Some pretty little Princess or rich young Queen, and then everything will be punjanoobious!"

"Is being married anything like being a King?" inquired Randy suspiciously.

"Oh, no. No, indeed, quite the reverse." The eyes of the old Duke, who had once been married, grew glazed and pensive. "Once you are married, you will feel less like a King every day," he promised solemnly. "And the arguments alone will keep you occupied for hours." Uncle Hoochafoo raised both shoulders and eyebrows. "Wait, I'll just go consult the wise men about a proper Princess for you."

"No! No! I do not wish to be married," announced Randy, stamping his foot. "I'll not marry for years," he declared stubbornly. Then, as loud outcries and tremendous thumps interrupted them, he hurried over to an open window just in time to meet a large rock that came crashing through the amethyst pane.

"Look out!" blustered Uncle Hoochafoo, jerking Randy to his feet, for the rock had completely bowled him over. "Well, I see you have your wish. How's that for a knock in the nose, my lad? Not only the nose, but also the beginning of a beautiful black eye!"

"Have I really?" Racing over to a mirror, Randy proudly examined his injured orb. "Oh, Uncle, isn't this fun? Who did it? What's up, d'ye s'pose — a revolution?" Hurrying back to the window, Randy recklessly thrust out his head to stare down into the courtyard. Kayub, the Gatekeeper, had his shoulder braced against the gold-studded doors in the castle wall, but even so the doors were bulging and creaking from the thunderous blows struck from the other side.

"Open in the name of the LAW!" boomed a tremendous voice. Thump! Thump! Kerbang! "OPEN in the name of a Prince of the Realm! Open this door, you unmannerly Scuppernong!"

"No, no, stay where you are!" panted Kayub, waving desperately with one arm for the guards to come help him. "Stay where you are, or go to the rear entrance! Who do you think you are, hammering on the doors of His Majesty's castle?"

"I don't think, I know!" raged the voice from the other side of the wall. "I am a Prince of Pumperdink, you unspeakable clod. Open up this door before I break it down!" And after even more furious thumps, another shower of rocks came flying over the wall.

248

"Great Gillikens! I think — I believe — why, it IS! Kayub, Kayub, open the door! It is a Prince!" shouted Randy, using both hands as a megaphone.

"'Tis nothing of the sort," grunted the Gatekeeper obstinately. "I looked through me little grill but a moment ago, and it's no Prince at all, but a parade! A parade of one elephant, if you please, and when I orders him to the rear entrance, he ups with his trunk and flings rocks over our wall!"

"But this elephant IS a Prince," insisted Randy, banging on the window ledge. "Besides, he's a great friend of mine."

"Open the door, fool!" directed Uncle Hoochafoo, leaning so far out the window his crown fell to the paving stones. "The King has spoken. Admit this elephant at once! At once!"

"And about time," fumed an indignant voice as Kayub reluctantly drew the bolts and swinging wide the doors stepped back to let a magnificently caparisoned elephant swing through. "A fine welcome this is, I must say, for the Elegant Elephant of Oz! Out of my way, wart!" Picking Kayub up in his trunk, the visitor jammed him down hard into a golden trash barrel, trumpeted fiercely at the double line of guards who had instantly sprung to attention, and went swaying across the courtyard.

Now nowhere but in Oz could an elephant talk, much less come hammering on the doors of a royal castle, but in Oz, as we very well know, animals talk and act as sensibly as people, which makes Oz about ten times as exciting as any other country on the map. But while I've been explaining all this, Randy had run down the steps and was halfway across the courtyard.

"Kabumpo, KABUMPO, is it really you? Oh, at last — AT LAST you are here!" Impatiently waving aside the guards, Randy led his mammoth and still muttering guest into the palace.

"Kabumpo, is it?" sniffed Kayub, jerking himself with great difficulty out of the trash barrel. "Such goings on. Well, all I say—" The Gatekeeper peered carefully over his shoulder to see that the elephant was safely inside the castle, then, raising his arm for the benefit of the staring guards, he cried fiercely, "All I can say is — just let him show his snoot around here again, and I'll kabumpo him down the mountain!"

Chapter 2 - The Elegant Elephant of Oz

Fortunately, the doors of Randy's castle were high and wide, and the rooms so large and spacious, even a guest as large as this elephant could quite easily be accommodated. Still irritated by the Gatekeeper's insolence, Kabumpo followed the young ruler to the throne room, where he sank stiffly to his haunches and waited in outraged silence for Randy to speak. Randy, h

owever, was so surprised and happy to see his old friend and comrade that he could not utter a word. But the Elegant Elephant could not long withstand the honest delight and affection beaming from the young King's eyes, and under that kindly glow his wrath melted away like fog in the sunshine. "Well! Well!" he rumbled testily. "How do I look?"

"Elegant!" breathed Randy, stepping back to have a better view. "Elegant as ever. You've worn your best robe and jewels, haven't you?"

"Always wear your best when I call on a King," said Kabumpo, smoothing down his embroidered collar complacently with his trunk.

"And I believe you've grown a foot," went on Randy, standing on tiptoe to pat Kabumpo on the shoulder.

"A foot," roared the Elegant Elephant, throwing back his head. "Oh, come now. I couldn't have grown a foot without noticing it, and I still have but four — here, count 'em! Say, who in hay bales gave you that black eye?"

"YOU did," Randy fairly spluttered with mirth at Kabumpo's discomfited expression. "I was just wishing someone would hit me in the nose, when along came that rock, and NOW look at me!"

"Yes," put in Uncle Hoochafoo, regarding Kabumpo severely through his monocle. "Now look at him!"

"Well, why didn't you tell that wart of a doorkeeper I was expected?" demanded Kabumpo explosively.

"The King of Regalia does not hold conversation with his doorkeeper," explained Randy's uncle, giving the Elegant Elephant a very sour look.

"Oh, he doesn't!" Kabumpo lurched grandly to his feet. "Well, it's time somebody told him about the Elegant Elephant of Oz and how he should be received and welcomed. Let me tell you, sirrah — trumpets blow when I come and go in Pumperdink!"

"Then why did you ever leave there?" inquired the Duke coldly.

"Oh, Uncle, don't you remember, we were to review the Purple Guard at five? YOU go," urged Randy, fearful lest the tempery old Duke would still further insult the even more tempery old elephant. "Honestly, I feel a cold coming on." Randy coughed plaintively, at the same time winking at Kabumpo.

"Very well, I'll go," agreed his uncle stiffly. "But do not forget there is a dinner for the Grape Growers at seven, a concert of the Goat Herdsmen at eight, maneuvers of our Highland Guards in the Royal Barracks at nine, and—"

"Yes, yes! All right!" Randy fairly pushed his royal relative toward the door.

"An ancient pest if I ever saw one," grumbled Kabumpo as the Grand Duke disappeared with a very grim expression. "Great gooselberries! Do we have to do all those dumb things? Why, it's six years since I've seen you, Randy, and I kinda thought we'd have a cozy time all to ourselves."

"I never have any time to myself," sighed the young monarch wistfully. "I do nothing but lay cornerstones and raise flags and stand around at Royal Courts and Receptions. Everybody bows and bows. Why, it's got so I even bow to myself when I look in the glass, and NOW—" Randy raised his arms indignantly. "Now Uncle Hoochafoo says I must marry."

"Marry!" trumpeted Kabumpo, twinkling his eyes angrily. "What nonsense! Why, you are nowhere near old enough to marry. You were only about ten when I met you, and that makes you sixteen now, though I must say you don't look it!"

"Oh, no one in Oz looks his age," grinned Randy, "and you know I'd been ten for about four years before I knew you, Kabumpo, so that makes me twenty or so, doesn't it?"

"I don't care what it makes you," rumbled Kabumpo, "it makes me mad. And to think I actually helped get you into all this boring business. My ears and trunk, Kingling, it's up to me to get you out of it."

"How?" demanded Randy, folding his arms and leaning despondently against the mantel. "How does one stop being a King, Kabumpo?"

"Why, by stopping," announced the Elegant Elephant, spreading his ears to their fullest extent. "By taking a vacation, my fine young sprig. By departing and going hence for a suitable season. Do you suppose I came all the way from Pumperdink to hear Goatherds tootling on bells and Highlanders tramping round a barracks? I came to see you, my boy, and nobody else." Kabumpo paused to blow his trunk explosively on a violet silk handkerchief. "And after that, I thought we'd go and visit the Red Jinn."

"Oh, Kabumpo, could we?" Randy's face brightened and then as quickly fell. "I don't believe Uncle Hoochafoo will let me go," he finished dolefully.

"A King does not ask whether or not he may go, he GOES," stated the Elegant Elephant, beginning to sway like a ship under full sail. "But to avoid all arguments, we'll not start till later. Could you be ready by midnight, young one?"

"Oh, I'm ready now," declared Randy, picking up his cloak from the floor and snatching a sword from its bracket on the wall. "Why ever did you wait so long, Kabumpo? You promised to visit me six months after I was crowned."

"Well, you know how it is at a court." The Elegant Elephant sighed and settled back on his haunches again. "If it isn't one thing, it's another, but here I am at last. So — order up your dinner and a few bales of hay and a barrel of cider for me. I crave rest and refreshment."

"And what about the Grape Growers, the Goatherds and Highlanders?" worried Randy.

"Oh, them!" exclaimed Kabumpo inelegantly. "Here!" Seizing a pen from the royal desk, he scribbled a defiant message on a handy piece of parchment: "No admittance under extreme penalty of the Law. Do not disturb! By special order of His Majesty, King Randywell Handywell of Brandenburg and Bompadoo."

"See, I remembered all your names, and I've used them all!" Opening the door with his trunk, Kabumpo impaled the notice on the knob, then quietly closed the door and turned the key in the lock. And only once did they open it, and then to admit ten flustered footmen with Randy's dinner and Kabumpo's cider and hay. To imperious raps, taps and numerous notes thrust under the door by the young King's agitated uncle they paid no attention whatever. They were too busy talking over old times and the exciting days when they had journeyed all over Oz and with the help of Jinnicky, the little Red Jinn, saved the Royal Family of Pumperdink from the Witch of Follensby Forest.

Pumperdink, as most of you know, is in the north central part of the Gilliken Country of Oz, and ruled by King Pompus and Queen Posy. Their son, Prince Pompadore, has much to say about affairs in that Kingdom, but it is to Kabumpo, his Elegant Elephant, that Pompus turned oftenest for counsel and comfort. Given to the King by a celebrated Blue Emperor, Kabumpo has proved himself so wise and sagacious, Pompus depends on him for almost everything. It is Kabumpo who advises His Majesty when to have his hair cut and put aside his woolen underwear, when to go to the dentist, when to turn in his old four-horse chariot for a twelve-horse model, when to save money, when to spend it, how to get on with neighboring Kings, and how to get on without them. In fact, so heavy are the duties and responsibilities of this remarkable elephant, 'tis a wonder, even after six years, he managed this visit to Randy.

Randy's first meeting with Kabumpo had been more or less by chance. Sent out disguised as a poor mountain boy to pass the seven severe tests of Kingship required of Regalian Rulers, Randy had happened to come first to the Kingdom of Pumperdink and had been hailed before the King as a vagrant. The Elegant Elephant, taking an instant fancy to the boy, had insisted that he be allowed to stay on as his own royal attendant, and in this comical capacity Randy's adventures had begun. For scarcely had he been in the palace of Pumperdink a week before Kettywig, the King's brother, and the Witch of Follensby Forest, plotting to steal the crown, caused the whole royal family to disappear by some strange and fiery magic. Barely missing the same fate, Randy and Kabumpo managed to escape. On their way through the forest, they met a Soothsayer who told them to seek out the Red Jinn. Now no one in Oz had ever heard of this singular personage, but after many delays and hair-raising experiences, Randy and Kabumpo finally arrived at his splendid red glass castle. Jinnicky, it turned out, was the Wizard of Ev, and a merry and strange person he was. Jinnicky's whole body is encased in a shiny red jar into which he can retire like a turtle at will, and the little Wizard's disposition is so gay and jolly, everyone around him feels the same way. Not only did he welcome his visitors, but set off immediately to help the Royal Family of Pumperdink out of their misfortunes and enchantment. Once in Pumperdink, Randy, with the help of the Red Jinn's magic looking-glasses, was able to trace the lost King and his family and release them from the witch's spell. But before that, and while he was traveling here and there with Kabumpo and Jinnicky, the little Prince was fulfilling all the tests and conditions required by the ancient laws of Regalia of their Kings. In other words, he had made three true friends, served a strange King, saved a Queen, showed bravery in battle, overcome a fabulous monster, disenchanted a Princess, and received from a Wizard an important magic treasure. And now, looking back on those brave, bright days, he could not help thinking that earning his crown had been more fun than wearing it.

"I wish we could do it all over again," he mused as Kabumpo, after recalling their visit to Nandywog, the little giant, tossed off the last of the cider.

"But think where we're going now," gurgled Kabumpo, setting down the barrel with a resounding thud. "If something strange or exciting does not happen on the way there or back, or in Jinnicky's castle itself, I do not know my Oz and Evistery. Can't you just see Jinnicky's face when we arrive? I wonder if Alibabble is still Grand Advizier and if the magic dinner bell is still working. Yes! Yes? Who's there?" Kabumpo raised his voice irritably as a persistent whistling came through the keyhole.

"It's Dawkins," explained an anxious voice from the other side of the door. "The Duke says as it's high time His Highness was in bed, Your Highness!"

"Oh, be off with you. Go dive in the feathers yourself. His Highness is going to sleep in here on the floor." Kabumpo stood so close and spoke so violently through the keyhole, Dawkins was blown back against the opposite wall. For a time, footsteps pattered up and down the corridor, then finally deciding the young King was to have his own way at last, the footmen and courtiers and even Uncle Hoochafoo took themselves off. But not till everything was absolutely quiet and still and everyone in the castle asleep did Kabumpo and Randy venture forth. Then, stepping softly as his own tremendous shadow, the Elegant Elephant with the young King on his back slipped through the silent halls and deserted courtyard, past the snoring sentries and keeper of the gate, and on out into the foresty Highlands beyond the palace wall. Here in the bright white light of a smiling moon they took the highway to the north, for the castle of the Red Jinn lies to the north by northeast of Regalia and Oz.

"How'll we cross the Deadly Desert?" murmured Randy, drowsily clutching the few belongings he had tied up in an old silver tablecloth. In it he had his oldest suit, some clean underwear, his toothbrush, and his trusty sword.

"Never cross a desert till you come to it," advised Kabumpo. "And we've crossed it before, you know."

"Yes, I know." Smiling to himself, Randy dropped his head on his bundle, and lulled by the agreeable motion of his gigantic bearer, soon fell asleep, to dream pleasantly of Alibabble and of Ginger, slave of the Red Jinn's dinner bell.

Chapter 3 - Gaper's Gulch

Kabumpo, as happy to escape from Court life as Randy, moved rhythmically as a ship through the soft spring night. Humming to himself and busy with his own thoughts, he scarcely noticed that the highway was growing steeper and narrower until he was brought up sharp by an impassable barrier of rock.

"Now, Bosh and Botherskites! I was sure this road ran straight to the Deadly Desert," he muttered, reaching back with his trunk to see that Randy was still safely aboard and asleep. "Beets and butternuts! Do I have to turn back, or plough through all this rubble?" The Elegant Elephant's small eyes twinkled with irritation, and easing himself to the right off the highway, he peered crossly up at the offending mass of stone. Finding no way round here, he swung over to the left and examined it closely from that side, and was just about to start resignedly through the brush when he discovered that what he had taken for an especially dark shadow was really a cleft in the rock. It was barely wide enough for him to squeeze through without scraping the jewels from his robe. "Now then, shall I risk it or wait till morning?" mused Kabumpo, swaying undecidedly to and fro. "It might take us straight through to the other side of the highway. On the other trunk, it might lead into a robber's cave or plunge us suddenly over a precipice!"

Edging closer, the Elegant Elephant thrust his trunk in to the crevice. It seemed smooth and solid, and resolved to try it even though little of the moonlight penetrated into the narrow opening, Kabumpo stepped inside and proceeded to pick his way cautiously along the rocky corridor. For about the length of a city street it ran straight ahead, then curved sharply to the right. Here Kabumpo was heartened to see a lantern hanging from an iron spike, while carved on the smooth rock below was a blunt message: "This is the entrance to Gaper's Gulch. Pause here and give three yawns and a stretch for Sleeperoo, Great, Grand and Most Snorious Gaper!"

"Snorious Gaper! Ho! Ho! Kerumph! Who ever heard of such nonsense?" snorted Kabumpo, squinting impatiently down at the notice. "Ah, Hah! HOH, HUM!" At this point, and without seeming able to help it, the Elegant Elephant yawned so terrifically his headpiece fell over one ear, and his jaw was almost dislocated. To recover his dignity and with tears starting from his eyes, he gave himself a quick shake, then stretched up his trunk to straighten his headgear.

"Splen-did!" drawled a sleepy voice. "You may now proceed as before." Blinking angrily about to see who had addressed him, the Elegant Elephant spied a round-faced and widely gaping guard standing in a little niche in the rock. Strapped to his shoulders, instead of a knapsack, was a fat feather pillow, and as Kabumpo came opposite, the guard's eyes closed and, falling back against his cushion, he began gently to snore. As Kabumpo stopped in some astonishment, the guard's nap was rudely interrupted by a pailful of pebbles that cascaded merrily down over his ears. There were twenty pails operating on a moving belt above his head, and at three-minute intervals they pelted him awake, as Kabumpo presently discovered. The buttons on the guard's uniform were illuminated and spelled out his name, "WINKS."

"Well, do I surprise you?" inquired Winks, shaking the pebbles from his shoulders and rubbing his eyes with his yellow-gloved hands. Kabumpo, too amused to speak, nodded.

"And you surprise me," admitted the guard, gaping three times just to prove it, "you big, enormous, impossible whatever you are — you! Why, you should have been underground months ago! But that'll all be taken care of," he added smoothly. "Just follow the arrows, and you cannot miss — just follow the arrows — just fol—"

As Kabumpo, fuming from what he considered a mortal insult, lunged forward, the little soldier's eyes fell shut again. Held more by curiosity than by a desire to continue the conversation, Kabumpo waited for the next bucket of pebbles to shower over the guard.

"'Low the arrows," went on Winks as calmly as if he had not been interrupted at all. "There are forty guards to point the way. Forty Winks," he repeated, closing one eye. "Ha, Ha! To point the way. Ha, Ha! HOH, HUM! Do you get the point?"

As Kabumpo started off with a little snort of disgust, he felt a slight prick in his left hind leg, for Winks, just as he fell asleep, let fly an arrow from his old-fashioned bow. Before Kabumpo had reached the end of the passageway, he had passed forty of the Gaper Guards. After his experience with the first, he did not stop for further talk, but made the best speed possible, resolved to rush through Gaper's Gulch when he came to it without even pausing to express his contempt. The pebble awakeners were so neatly timed, each guard had a chance to speed an arrow after the flying elephant, and by the time Kabumpo reached the opening at the other end of the rocky pass, he had forty arrows pricking through his robe or stuck here and there in his ears and ankles. With his tough hide, they hurt no more than pin pricks, but vastly indignant at such treatment, the Elegant Elephant began jerking them out with his trunk.

"What do they think I am, a pincushion? Hoh!" he snorted, pulling out the last one and relieved to note that Randy had escaped the missiles entirely. Indeed, the young King of Regalia was sleeping as placidly as if he were home in his own castle. Kabumpo, too, felt unaccountably drowsy, and as he pushed his way down into the rocky little glen, his steps grew slower and slower. So far as he could see by the light of the fast-waning moon, there were neither houses nor people in Gaper's Gulch. In the center of the valley the rough stones and brush had been cleared away, and a series of flat rocks were spaced out almost like a gigantic checkerboard. Pausing beside the largest rock, Kabumpo spelled out the name of Sleeperoo the Great and Snorious.

"What is this, a cemetery?" gulped the Elegant Elephant. "But that could not be, for no one in Oz ever dies. Ho, Hum!" Leaning up against a dead pine and blinking furiously to keep awake, he pondered the unpleasant situation. Then, deciding that, cemetery or not, he must have some sleep, he lifted Randy down from his back and rolled him in a blanket he had thoughtfully brought along. Then, divesting himself of his jeweled robe and headpiece, Kabumpo stretched out carefully beside his young comrade, and in twenty minutes was fast asleep. How long he slumbered Kabumpo never knew, but from a nightmare in which he was struggling in a bank of treacherous quicksand, he awoke with a frightful sinking feeling to find he was surrounded by forty more of the Gaper Guards. Their buttons were also lit up, and on each

252

plump chest he could read the word "Wake." The Wakes were busily at work with pick and spade, and unlike the Winks, did not seem the least bit drowsy. Half convinced he was still asleep and dreaming, Kabumpo peered out at them through half-closed lids, then gave a tremendous grunt. Great Gillikens! He was sinking! The busy little Wakes had dug a trench at least twenty feet deep all around him, and now, careless of their own safety, were shoveling away at the mound on which he was still precariously resting.

"Quick, a few more to the right," directed a crisp little voice. "Watch yourself there, Torpy. Ah, here he comes! Heads up, lads!"

As the chief Wake spoke, Kabumpo felt the mound give way, and down he rolled into the pit, while the Wakes scrambled frantically up the sides. "Did you hear that fierce TOOT?" puffed the little Guard addressed as Torpy. "It's awake, fellows! What's wrong with those sleeping arrows, don't they work anymore? I myself saw forty sticking in the big Whatisit when he came pounding out of the pass. Hurry, hurry! Let's get him underground!" And seizing their picks and spades again, the Gaper Guards began shoveling dirt into the pit, paying no attention to Kabumpo's furious blasts and bellows, which grew wilder and more anguished as he suddenly realized that Randy was no longer beside him.

"What have you done with the boy? Halt! Stop! How dare you cast dirt on an Imperial Prince of Pumperdink or try to bury the Elegant Elephant of Oz?" Shaking the mud from his head and raising his trunk, Kabumpo let out such an ear-splitting trumpet, twenty Wakes fell to their knees and the others dropped pick and shovel and stared at him in positive dismay.

"But sir, it is quite customary to bury all visitors," quavered Torpy as soon as he could make himself heard. "We'll dig you up in six months, and you'll be good as new. Our dormitories are so very comfortable, and all Gapers lie dormant for six months!"

"But I'm not a GAPER," screamed Kabumpo, interrupting himself with a yawn both wide and gusty.

"Oh, but you soon will be," asserted Torpy, squinting down at him earnestly. "Why, you're gaping already. Now lie down like a good beast. Sleeping underground is lovely."

"LOVELY!" repeated all the rest of the Wakes, beginning to croon as they shoveled. Kabumpo, opening his mouth to protest again, caught a bushel of earth between his tusks, and half choked and blind with rage, the Elegant Elephant hurled himself at the side of the pit. He could almost reach the top with his trunk, and as the Wakes, squealing with alarm, shoveled faster and faster, he wound his trunk round an old tree stump and by main strength hauled himself up over the edge.

"NOW!" he bellowed, spreading his ears like sails, "Where have you buried the boy? Quick, speak up or I'll pound you to splinters." Snatching a log in his trunk, Kabumpo surged forward. But the terrified Wakes, instead of answering, fled for their lives, leaving Kabumpo all alone in the ghostly little valley.

"Randy! Randy, where are you? Oh, my poor boy, are you suffocated?" Galloping this way and that, Kabumpo peered desperately about for a patch of newly turned earth. But only the wind whistling drearily through the dead branches of the pine trees came to answer him. Frantic with worry, the Elegant Elephant began pounding with his log on the headstones of the dormant Gapers, trumpeting at the same time in a way to wake the dead.

Chapter 4 - Out of Gaper's Gulch

Now the Gapers were not dead, but only sleeping, and soon the dormant natives of this strange Hiber-nation lifted up their headstones and began blinking out indignantly to see what and who had got loose in their quiet valley.

"Silence! Cease! Desist!" shuddered Sleeperoo the Great and Snorious, holding up his headstone with one hand and waving his other arm feebly at Kabumpo. "A bit more of that racket and we'll be roused for months. Who are you? And what is the meaning of all this Hah Hoh Humbuggery?"

Gaping ten times in quick succession, Sleeperoo stuck out his lip at the Elegant Elephant. Kabumpo, startled by the spectacle of a hundred lifted headstones and the round, dirty, moonlike faces gaping up at him, said nothing for a whole minute. Then, stepping over to the Chief Gaper, he burst out angrily: "I am a traveler whom your guards stuck full of arrows and then tried to bury. The young King who was with me has disappeared. I, the Elegant Elephant of Oz and Pumperdink, DEMAND his release. What have you done with the King of Regalia? Produce him at once, or I'll stand here and trumpet till doomsday!" To show he meant what he said, Kabumpo let out such a terrific blast the headstones of his listeners rocked and shivered.

"Oh, my head! My ears! My ears, my dears! Give him what he's yelling for," sobbed Sleeperoo, crouching under his headstone as Kabumpo lifted his trunk for another trumpet.

"Is this — a — king?" called a fretful voice, and lurching 'round Kabumpo saw a fat old Gaper now halfway above ground. Balancing his stone on his fat head, he held Randy out at arm's length. "Instead of digging him a proper bed, they stuck him in with me," he complained. "Here, take him. He kicks like a mule, and I can't abide a kicker." With a relieved grunt, Kabumpo snatched Randy from the Gaper's damp clutches, thankful the boy still had strength enough to kick. Randy's face was quite pale and covered with dirt, but after a few anxious shakes he opened his eyes and looked confusedly 'round him.

"It's nothing," sniffed Kabumpo. "It's quite all right, my boy. You've just been buried to the ears and sleeping with a groundhog."

"Buried?" shivered Randy as Kabumpo set him gently on his back.

"Not buried at all, just lying dormant as a sensible body should," corrected the old Gaper, dropping out of sight with a slam of his headstone.

"Go away! Please go away!" begged Sleeperoo as Kabumpo began stepping gingerly between the stones. "You're ruining our rest, you big bullying Behemoth!"

"I'll not stir a step till you send a guide to lead me out of this gulch," declared Kabumpo. "Call a guard, or I'll call one myself."

"No. No! Please NOT! Torpy Snorpy — I say, Torpy," wheezed Sleeperoo, stretching up his thin neck. "Come, come all of you at once. At ONCE!" As quickly as they had vanished, the Wakes slid from behind boulders and trees and up out of rocky crevices, their buttons twinkling cheerfully in the dark. "Conduct these travelers to the head of the valley," ordered Sleeperoo with a weak wave at the Gaper Guards.

"I thought this was a gulch," yawned Kabumpo, while Randy began to shake the dirt from his hair and ears.

"A gulch is a valley," sniffed Sleeperoo, lowering himself crossly. "Look it up in any pictionary. A gulch is a valley or chasm."

"And Gaper's Gulch is a yawning chasm," mumbled Kabumpo as the Chief Gaper and all the others began ducking back into their holes like rabbits into warrens. "Good night to you," he added as the last stone slammed down. "Now, then, you boys fetch my headpiece and robe from that pit, and let's start on."

Kabumpo spoke so sharply ten Wakes sprang to obey, and after they had brought them and both had been adjusted to Kabumpo's liking, he signaled imperiously for Torpy and Snorpy to lead the way, and their companions took thankfully to their heels. For a while the two little Wakes marched ahead in a subdued silence as the Elegant Elephant picked his way around rocks and tree stumps.

"Not mad, I hope." Torpy, most talkative of the two, looked anxiously over his shoulder.

"No, no, certainly not. I don't know when I've spent a more delightful evening," Kabumpo said. "Being stuck full of arrows and then buried alive is such splendid entertainment."

"Oh, I say now, we cannot all be alike," put in Snorpy, coming to the rescue of his embarrassed companion. "If those arrows had taken effect, you'd have been dead asleep before we buried you, and known nothing for six months. That's a lot of sleep to miss, Mister — er — Mister?"

"Kabumpo," chuckled Randy, who was now wide awake and quite recovered from his harrowing experience. "But you see, Kabumpo and I sleep every night and not all in one stretch as you do."

"More trouble that way," murmured Snorpy, shaking his head disapprovingly. "Keeps you hopping up and down all the time. In the Gulch we sleep half the year, and then we are done with it."

"And what do you do when you are not sleeping?" inquired Kabumpo, stifling a yawn with his trunk.

"We eat," grinned Snorpy, his eyes twinkling brighter than his buttons. "Breakfast from July to August thirty-first; lunch from September first till October thirty-first; and dinner from November first till New Year's."

"You mean you eat straight through without stopping?" gasped Randy, raising himself on one elbow. "All the time you're awake? Don't you ever work, play or go on journeys?"

"I do not know what you mean by 'work, play and going on journeys,' but whatever they are, we don't. We eat and sleep, sleep and eat, and everything is perfectly gorgeous," confided the Wake with a satisfied skip.

"Gorging is gorgeous to some people, I suppose." Kabumpo tossed his head to show it was not his way. "Then how is it you fellows are not sleeping along with the other Gapers?"

"Oh, we're trained to sleep in summer and fall and to eat in winter and spring. The Winks are not so clever at staying awake as we are, but they'll learn, and meanwhile the pebbles keep them fairly active."

"Yes, active enough to shoot at visitors," grunted Kabumpo, winking back at Randy. "Do you shoot one another asleep, or is that a special treat you reserve for travelers?"

"We just shoot at travelers," admitted Snorpy quite cheerfully. "Otherwise they would interfere with our customs, interrupt our sleeping and eating, and wake us up out of season."

"Just as we did," chuckled Randy. "I suppose we interrupted your dinner, this being one of the dinner months?" Both Guards nodded, exchanging pleased little smiles.

"Come on back and have a bite with us," invited Snorpy generously. "We've weak fish for the first week, chops for the second—"

Randy, tugging at Kabumpo's collar, begged him to stop, for Randy was hungry as a brace of bears, but the Elegant Elephant, shaking his head till all his jewels rattled, declined the invitation with great firmness. "No knowing what will come of it," he whispered to his disappointed young comrade. "Might put us to sleep for a century, and it's about all I can do to keep my eyes open now. Wait till we're out of this goopy gulch, my lad, and we'll eat and sleep like gentlemen. After all, we are gentlemen and not groundhogs."

Urging his guides to greater speed, the weary beast pushed doggedly on through the brush and stubble. Snorpy and Torpy, insulted by the shortness with which the Elegant Elephant had refused their invitation, had little more to say and in less than an hour had brought the travelers to the end of the rocky little valley. From where they stood, a crooked path wound crazily upward, and with a silent wave aloft the two Wakes turned and ran.

"Back to their dinner," sighed Randy, looking hungrily after them. But Kabumpo, charmed to see the last of the ghostly gulch and its inhabitants, began to ascend the path, not even stopping for breath till he had come to the top. Even after this, he traveled on for about five miles to make sure no sleepy vapors or Gapers would trouble them again. The moon had waned and the stars grown faint as he stopped at last in a small patch of woodland. Here, without removing his headpiece or robe, Kabumpo braced his back against a mighty oak and fell asleep on his feet, and Randy, soothed and rocked by his tremendous snores, soon closed his eyes and slept also.

Chapter 5 · Headway

When Randy wakened, Kabumpo had already started on, grumbling under his breath, because nowhere in sight was there a green bush, a tree or anything at all that an elephant or little boy might eat. "Where are we?" yawned Randy, sitting up and rubbing his eyes with his knuckles. "Great Gillikens, this is as bad as Gaper's Gulch!"

"All the countries bordering on the Deadly Desert are queer, no-count little places," sniffed the Elegant Elephant, angrily jerking his robe off a cactus. "And from the feel of the air, we must be near the desert now."

At mention of the Deadly Desert, Randy lapsed into an uneasy silence, for how could they ever cross this tract of burning sand, and how could they reach Ev or Jinnicky's castles unless they did cross it? While this vast belt of destroying sand effectively kept enemies out of Oz, it also kept the Ozians in. "If we only had some of Jinnicky's magic or even his silver dinner bell to bring us a good breakfast!" sighed Randy, glancing around hungrily. "Pretty stupid of me not to have brought along a lunch, and there's not even a brook or stream in this miserable little patch of woods where a body could quench his thirst. Maybe it will rain, and that would help a little."

"Maybe," admitted Kabumpo, squinting up at the leaden sky. "Anyway, here we are out of the woods, but take a look at those rocks!"

"And those heads behind the rocks," whispered Randy, clutching Kabumpo's collar.

"There's something pretty odd about those heads, if you ask me," wheezed the Elegant Elephant, curling up his trunk. "Odd, or I'm losing my eye- and earsight."

"Odd!" hissed Randy, tightening his hold on Kabumpo's collar. "Good goats and gravy! They're flying 'round loose like birds. Why, they've got no bodies on 'em, no bodies at all!"

"Read the sign," directed Kabumpo, uncurling his trunk and pointing to a crude warning scratched on a flat slab at the edge of the road leading to the rocky promontory above.

"Heads up! This road leads to Headland, nobody's allowed."

"Humph! Well, we won't make much headway without our bodies," grunted Kabumpo as Randy read the message slowly to himself. "Such impudence! Why should we pay any attention to such stuff? Bodies or not, we're going on, and how can fellows minus feet and arms hope to stop us?"

"They might crash down on us with their heads," worried Randy as an angry flock of Headmen circled round and round at the top of the road, "and those heads look hard."

"Not any harder than mine. Keep your crown on, Randy," advised Kabumpo grimly. "The spikes will dent 'em good, and if you reach down in my left-hand pocket, you'll find a short club. The club will be better than your sword; you can't cut a head off no neck, and besides, we don't really want to injure the pests. All ready? Then here we go!"

Randy did not answer, for hooking his heels through Kabumpo's harness, he was already delving into the capacious pockets on the left side of the Elegant Elephant's robe, discovering not only a club, but a quiver full of darts. Jerking himself upright, the club in one hand and the darts in the other, he peered aloft with growing anxiety as, foot over foot, Kabumpo climbed up the granite slope. The faces of the Headmen were round and deeply wrinkled from the hot winds blowing off the desert; their ears, huge and fan-shaped, flapped like wings and like wings propelled them through the air. Before Kabumpo reached the top, a whole bevy came whizzing toward them, screaming out indignant threats and warnings.

"Off, be off!" they shouted hysterically. "Off with their arms, off with their legs, off with their bodies! Halt! Stop! Begone, you miserable, creepy-crawly creatures. You dare not set a foot on our beautiful Headland."

"Oh, daren't we?" Kabumpo shook his trunk belligerently. "And who is to stop us, pray?"

"I am," rasped the ugliest of the Headmen. Snatching a coil of wire from a niche in the rocks with his teeth, the ugly little Mugly came flapping toward them. Another of the Headmen hastened to seize the opposite end of the wire in his teeth, and stretching it between them they came rushing on.

"Watch out!" warned Randy, dropping flat between Kabumpo's ears. "They're going to trip you up."

"Wrong, how wrong," chattered all the Headmen, bobbing up and down like balloons let off their strings. "They're going to cut off his body," confided one of the long-nosed tribesmen, zooming down to whisper this information in Randy's ear. "The creature's head is welcome enough, and with those enormous ears he'll have no trouble at all flying, but his body — oh, his body is awful and must stay behind. And your body, too, you little monster, we'll cut that off, too," promised the Headman in his oily voice. "What use is a body, anyway? I see you have very small ears, but they can be stretched. And just wait till you've been debodicated. You'll feel so right and light and flighty."

"Help! Stop! Help! Help!" screamed Randy as the ugly Mugly gave him a playful nip on the ear. "Back up, Kabumpo, back down. They're going to catch you in that wire and choke you."

"Oah! Nonsense," panted the Elegant Elephant. And heaving himself up over the last barrier, he stepped confidently out on the rocky plateau.

"Heads up! Heads up!" shrilled the Headmen, while the two with the wire, deftly encircling Kabumpo's great neck, began to fly apart in order to draw the noose tighter. Kabumpo ducked but much too late, and though his ferocious trumpeting sent swarms of Headmen fluttering aloft, the two holding the wire stuck to their task, pulling and jerking with all their might till Kabumpo's jeweled collar was pressing uncomfortably into his throat.

"Don't worry," he grunted gamely, "their teeth will give way before my neck goes. Calm yourself, my boy, ca-alm yourself."

But how could Randy feel calm with his best friend in such a predicament and already beginning to gasp for breath? Jumping up and down on Kabumpo's back, he rattled his club valiantly, but the Headmen were too high for him to reach, and when at last he flung the club with all his strength at the one on the left, it seemed to make no impression at all on the hard head of the enemy. Redoubling his efforts, he drew the wire tighter and tighter in his yellow teeth. In desperation, Randy suddenly remembered the darts, and drawing one from the quiver, sent it speeding upward. The first missed, but as the Elegant Elephant began to sway and quiver beneath him, the second found its mark, striking the Headman squarely in the middle of the forehead. An expression of surprise and dismay overspread his wrinkled features, and next instant, with a terrific yawn, he dropped the wire and fell headlong to the rocks, where he rolled over and over and over.

"Great Goopers!" exclaimed Randy, hardly able to believe his luck. "Why, he's not hurt at all, but has fallen asleep."

"Watch the others, the — others!" gulped Kabumpo, shaking his head in an effort to free it from the wire. Already another had flown to take his fallen comrade's place, but before he could snatch the wire, Randy brought him to earth with one of his sharply pointed darts. The next who ventured he shot down, too, and as the rest of the band came swarming down to see what was happening, Randy sent arrow after arrow winging into their midst till the flat, smooth rock was dotted with sleepy heads, for each one hit promptly fell asleep. Though his arm ached and his heart thumped uncomfortably, Randy did not even pause for breath till he had sent the last arrow into the air, and then quite suddenly he realized he had won this strange and ridiculous battle. More than half of the ear-men, as he could not help calling them to himself, lay snoring on the ground; the rest with terrified shrieks and whistles were flapping off as fast as their ears could carry then. Now entirely free of the wire, but still trembling and gasping, Kabumpo stared angrily after them.

"What I cannot understand," puffed Randy, sliding down to the ground to examine a group of the enemy, "is what put them to sleep? I thought your darts might hurt or head them off or puncture them like balloons, but instead — here they are asleep, and HOW asleep! Shall I pull out the arrows? I might need them later."

"They're not MY arrows," Kabumpo said, wrinkling his forehead in a puzzled frown. "I didn't have any arrows, but Ha, Ha, Kerumph!" The Elegant Elephant began to shake all over. "They must be Gaper Arrows — the Wakes must

256

have stuck them in my pocket when they fetched my robe and headpiece. Pretty cute of the little rascals, at that. Why, these must be the same arrows the Winks shot at me, Randy, but my hide was too tough for them, and they didn't work."

"Well, they certainly made short work of the Headmen," said Randy, turning one over gently with his foot. "Goodness! I thought you'd be choked and done for, old fellow!"

"Who, ME? Nonsense! My neck would have broken their teeth in another minute or two."

"Well, then, shall I pull out the arrows?" asked Randy, who had his own opinion about Kabumpo's narrow escape. "We could use them again some time."

"No, NO! Leave them in! So long as those arrows stick fast, the little villains will sleep fast, and that's the only way I can stand 'em."

"But suppose the others fly back?" Randy still hesitated.

"Pooh! Don't you worry about that." Kabumpo raised his trunk scornfully. "They're frightened out of their wits and probably half way to the Sapphire City by this time. And when they do come back, we won't be here."

"Won't we?" Dubiously, Randy began to pace across the bare and arid plateau. "I certainly don't think much of Headland, do you?"

"I wouldn't have it for a gift, even if they threw in a tusk brush and diamond earrings besides!" snorted Kabumpo. "Why, it's nothing but a humpy, bumpy acre of rock without a tree, a house, a bird or even a blade of grass. I'd give the whole country for a mouthful of hay or a bucketful of water!"

"We might find a spring among the rocks," proposed Randy, hurrying along hopefully.

"More likely a fall," predicted Kabumpo, trudging gloomily behind him. But just then, Randy, who had vanished behind a sizeable boulder, gave an excited whoop.

"Hi, yi, Kabumpo! We're here! We're here, right on the edge of it!" he shouted vociferously. "LOOK!" The Elegant Elephant, pushing round the rock, did look, then, mopping his forehead with the tip of his robe, sank heavily to his haunches, and for a moment neither said a word. For, truly enough, the jagged point of Headland projected over the desert as a high cliff hangs over the sea. Below, the seething sand smoked, churned and tumbled, sending up sulphurous waves of heat that made both travelers cough and splutter.

"So all we have to do is cross," gasped Randy, dashing the tears brought by the smoke out of his eyes.

"And a simple thing that will be," grunted the Elegant Elephant sarcastically, "seeing that one foot on the sand spells instant destruction. If we could just flap our ears like the Headmen, we could fly across."

"But as we can't," sighed Randy, seating himself despondently on a boulder, "what are we to do?"

"Well, that remains to be seen," muttered Kabumpo, who had not the faintest notion. "'Never cross a Deadly Desert on an empty stomach,' is my motto, and I'm going to stick to it."

"Sticking to mottoes won't get us anywhere," Randy said, skimming a stone off the edge and watching with a little shudder as it was sucked down into the whirling sand. "Doesn't that desert make you thirsty? Goopers, if I had a dipperful of water, I'd gladly do without the breakfast."

"Humph! Looks as if you might have that wish." Feeling hurriedly in the right pocket of his robe, Kabumpo dragged out a waterproof as large as a tent. "Just spread this over me, will you?" he puffed anxiously. "Storm coming. Hear that thunder? Storm coming."

"Coming?" cried Randy, springing up to help Kabumpo with the buckles. "Why, it's here!" He had to raise his voice to a scream to make himself heard above the gale that, arising apparently from nowhere, struck them furiously from behind. He had just fastened the last strap of the waterproof to Kabumpo's left ankle when the rain swept down in perfect torrents: rain accompanied by hailstones as big as Easter eggs. There was ample room for Randy beneath the Elegant Elephant, and standing between his front legs the young monarch lifted the waterproof, and reaching out caught a huge hailstone in his hand. Touching it against his parched lips, Randy gave a sigh of content, then, crunching it up rapturously, stuck out his head and let the pelting downpour cool his hot and dusty face. "Wonder if this will put out the desert?" he mused, ducking back as a terrible clap of thunder boomed like a cannonshot overhead. "SAY, it's a lucky thing you're so big, Kabumpo," he called up cheerily, "or we'd be blown away. Whee, listen to that wind, would you?"

"Have to do more than listen," howled the Elegant Elephant, bracing his feet and lowering his head. "Ahoy below! Catch hold of something, Randy! Help! Hi! Hold on! HOLD ON! For the love of blue — mountains! Here we GO! Here we blow! Oooomph! Blooomph! Ker-AHHHH!"

"Oh, no, Kabumpo! NO!" Leaping up, Randy caught the Elegant Elephant's broad belt. "Put on — the brakes! Quick!" And Kabumpo did try making a futile stand against the tearing wind. But the mighty gale, whistling under his waterproof, filled it up and out like a balloon, and with a regular ferryboat blast, Kabumpo rose into the air and zoomed like a Zeppelin over the Deadly Desert, while Randy, hanging grimly to the strap of his belt, banged to and fro like the clapper on a bell.

Chapter 6 - The Other Side of the Desert

Remembering the deadly and destroying nature of the sands below, Randy did not dare to
look down. Besides, holding on took all his strength and attention, for Kabumpo was borne like a leaf before the howling gale, faster and faster and faster, till he and Randy were too dazed and dizzy to know or care how far they had gone or where they were blowing to. Which was perhaps just as well, for, as suddenly as it had risen, the gale abated, and coasting down the last high hill of the wind, saved from a serious crash only by his faithful tarpaulin, which now acted as a parachute, Kabumpo came jolting to earth. With closed eyes and trunk held stiffly before him, the Elegant Elephant remained perfectly motionless awaiting destruction and wondering vaguely how it would feel. He was convinced that they had come down on the desert itself. Then, as no fierce blasts of heat assailed him, he ventured to open one eye. Randy, shaken loose by the force of the landing, had rolled to the ground a few feet away, and now, jumping to his feet, cried joyously: "Why, it's over, Kabumpo. Over, and so are we! Ho! I never knew you could fly, old Push-the-Foot."

"Neither did I," shuddered the Elegant Elephant, and jerking off the waterproof, he flung it as hard and as far as he could.

"Oh, don't do that!" Randy dashed away to pick it up. "That good old coat saved our bacon and ballooned us across the desert as light as a couple of daisies."

"But we're no better off on this side than on the other," grumbled Kabumpo, surveying the barren countryside with positive hatred. "Not a house, a field, a farm or a castle in sight."

"The idea was to get away from castles, wasn't it?" Randy grinned up at his huge friend, and folding the waterproof into a neat packet, tucked it back in its place.

"Well, there's one thing about castles," observed the Elegant Elephant, giving his robe a quick tug here and there. "At least, the food's regular. I could eat a royal dinner from soup to napkins."

"Give me a boost up that tree, and I'll have a look around," proposed Randy.

"Need a spy glass to find anything worth looking at in this country," complained Kabumpo, lifting Randy into the fork of a gnarled old tree. Shinning expertly up the rough trunk, Randy looked carefully in all directions.

"We certainly cleared the desert by a nice margin," he called down gaily. "It's at least a mile behind us, and toward the east I see a cluster of white towers that might be a castle."

"And nothing between," mourned Kabumpo with a hungry swallow, "no fields, orchards, or melon patches?"

"There are fields, but they're too far away for me to see what's growing, and there's a forest, too. What country is this, Kabumpo? Do you know?"

"Depends on how we blew," answered the Elegant Elephant, lifting Randy out of the tree and tossing him lightly over his shoulder. "If we blew straight from Headland, which is certainly the northwestern tip of the Gilliken Country of Oz, we should be in No Land. If we blew slantwise, this would be Ix."

"Then I hope we blew slantwise," Randy spread himself out luxuriously behind Kabumpo's ears. "For if we are in Ix, we have only one country to cross before we reach Ev and Jinnicky's castle."

"And the sooner we start, the sooner we'll arrive," agreed Kabumpo, swinging into motion. "But if I drop in my tracks, boy, don't be too surprised. I'm hollow as a drum and weak as a violet."

"Too bad we're not like the Headmen," said Randy, who felt dreadfully hollow himself. "Without a body, I suppose one does not feel hungry. Wonder what became of them, anyway?"

"Who cares?" sniffed Kabumpo, picking his way crossly through the rocks and brambles. "They probably blew about for a while, but with ears like sails, what's a gale of wind or weather? Ho! What's that I see yonder, a farmer?"

"No, just a hat stuck on a pole to scare away the crows," Randy told him after a careful squint. "But nothing grows in the field but rocks, so why do they bother?"

"Did you say a 'hat'?" Kabumpo's small eyes began to burn and twinkle, and breaking into a run he was across the field like a flash.

"Kabumpo!" gasped Randy as the Elegant Elephant snatched the hat from the pole and took a huge bite from the brim. "Surely, surely you're not going to eat that old hat?"

"Why not?" demanded the Elegant Elephant, cramming the rest of the hat into his mouth and crunching it up with great gusto. "It's straw, isn't it? A little old and tough, to be sure, but nourishing, and anyway better than nothing!" Almost strangling on the crown, Kabumpo glanced sharply across the field, then looked apologetically back at his young rider. "Great Gooseberries," he muttered contritely, "I'm sorry as a goat. Why, I never saved you even an edge!"

258

"Oh, never mind," choked Randy, holding his sides at the very idea of such a thing. "Even if I were starving, I couldn't eat a hat. But look, old Push-the-Foot, isn't that a barn showing over the top of that hill?"

"Barn!" wheezed Kabumpo, lifting his trunk joyfully. "Why, so it is! Ho! This is something like!" And hiccoughing excitedly — from the effects of the hat, no doubt — Kabumpo went galloping over the brow of the little hill.

A pleasant valley dotted with small farms stretched out below. Randy was relieved to note that its inhabitants were usual-looking beings like himself. Children rode gleefully on wagons piled high with hay. Farmers in wide-brimmed yellow hats, rather like those worn by the Winkies in Oz, worked placidly in the fields. Everyone seemed contented, calm and happy; that is, until Kabumpo, delighted to find himself again in a land of plenty, came charging down the hill trumpeting like a whole band of music.

"Oh, too bad, you've frightened them nearly out of their wits," mourned Randy, hanging on to Kabumpo's collar to keep his balance as the Elegant Elephant, forgetting his elegance, made a dash for the nearest hayrick. "Help Hi — stop! Now see what you've done!"

To tell the truth, the havoc ensuing was not all Kabumpo's fault. No one in this tranquil valley of Ix had ever seen an elephant before, and the sight of one rushing down upon them was so unnerving and strange they fled in every direction, leaping into barns and houses, and barring and double-barring the doors against this terrifying monster. Horses hitched to their hay wagons cantered madly east and west, and the air was filled with loud shrieks, neighs and the bellows of stampeding cattle.

"Such dummies!" panted Kabumpo, coming to a complete standstill. "Well," he gave a tremendous sniff, "if they don't want to meet a King, a Prince, and the most elegant elephant in Oz, what do we care? I've invited myself to breakfast anyhow, and they can like it or Kabump it. Just wait till I load away one stack of this hay, my boy, and I'll find you a breakfast fit for a King and Traveler." And the Elegant Elephant was as good as his word. After tossing down a great mound of new-mown hay, he swaggered over to the nearest farmhouse. Pushing in the kitchen window with his trunk, he handed up to Randy everything the little farmer's wife had on her kitchen table
— a bowl of milk, a pat of butter, a loaf of bread, a cold half chicken, and three hard-boiled eggs. "Do control yourself, madam," he advised as the palpitating little lady flattened herself against the opposite wall. "These pearls will more than pay for your provisions."

Afraid to touch the lovely chain Kabumpo placed on the table, the little lady watched with round eyes as Kabumpo backed away.

"Ho, I guess that will give her something to tell her grandchildren!" snorted the Elegant Elephant. Randy was too busy taking rapturous bites, first of bread and then of chicken, to answer.

"Why is it that everything tastes so much better when you are traveling?" he remarked a bit later as he finished off the rest of the chicken and put the bread, butter and eggs away for his lunch.

"'Cause we're hungrier, I suppose," smiled Kabumpo, crossing another field, "and then, there's the novelty."

Recalling the straw hat with a little chuckle, Kabumpo winked back at his young rider. "But now that we've breakfasted, I think we'd better be moving. I see some of these farmers gathering up their courage and their pitchforks, and I'm too full to fight."

"Pooh! They couldn't hurt us," boasted Randy, stretching out comfortably. "I rather wish they hadn't run off, though; I'd like to ask them something about the country, and you know, Kabumpo — I've never ridden on a hay wagon in all my life, and I'd sorta like to try it."

"That's the worst of being a King," observed Kabumpo, walking carefully around a brown calf. "You miss a lot of the common and ordinary pleasures. Hmm-mmn, let's see, now, all the horses have run off, but there's still a heap of hay about, so why shouldn't you have a ride?"

"Without any wagon?" inquired Randy, looking wistfully at the largest of the haystacks.

"Why not?" puffed Kabumpo, and lifting Randy hurriedly down from his back, he rushed at the hayrick, burrowing into it with tusk, feet and trunk till he was in the exact center. Then, heaving up with his back and forward with his trunk, he pushed till his head stuck out the other side. "Come ON!" he grunted triumphantly. "You'll not only have your hay ride, but I'll have my lunch!"

Throwing Randy to the top of the load, the Elegant Elephant, looking far from elegant, set off at a lumbersome gallop, carrying the haystack right along with him. At sight of his prize haystack apparently running away by itself, the outraged owner stuck his head out of the window and screamed. But that did not bother Kabumpo. The load was but a feather's weight to him, and with the young King of Regalia dancing and yelling on the top, he swept merrily through the startled valley. Those at the lower end who had not seen Kabumpo arrive, now catching sight of a load of hay moving off by itself, simply fell against fences and barn doors, blinking and gulping with astonishment, too stunned and shocked to return the gay greetings of the nonchalant young Gilliken riding the load. Kabumpo, sampling stray wisps as he ran and peering out comically from under the hay, enjoyed to the utmost the sensation he was causing.

"Make a wish, my boy," he shouted exuberantly. "It's awfully lucky to wish on the first load of hay."

"Then I wish we would reach the Red Jinn's castle before night," decided Randy. "And wouldn't Jinnicky laugh if he could see us now? Did you leave a pearl for the hay, Kabumpo?"

"Certainly," retorted the elephant, speaking rather stuffily through the haystack. "We're travelers, not thieves. Hi! What's ahead, my lad? This load has shifted a bit over my left eye, and I can scarcely see out of my right."

"A dry river bed," called Randy, bouncing up and down with the keenest enjoyment. "Go slow, old Push-the-Foot, or you'll lose your lunch."

"Not on your life!" puffed the Elegant Elephant. "I'll stop and eat it first. Ho—"

"Hay foot, straw foot, any foot will do,
Down the bank and up the bank, and now, how is the view?"

"Elegant," breathed Randy, grinning to himself at Kabumpo's verses. "More fields, meadows, forests, everything!"

"But even so, I smell sulphur!" Kabumpo moved his trunk slowly from side to side. "Something's burning, my lad, and close at hand, too."

"Why, it's a HORSE!" Randy's voice cracked from the sheer shock of the thing. "And coming straight for us, too. Wait! Stop! Hold on! No, maybe you'd better run. Great Gillikens, it's smoking!"

"A pipe?" inquired Kabumpo, trying to see through the fringe of hay that was obscuring his vision. "And what if it is? Am I, the Elegant Elephant of Oz, to run from a mere and miserable equine?"

"But this horse," squealed Randy, sliding head first off the haystack, "this horse is different. Oh, really, REALLY, Kabumpo, I think we'd better run."

"Never!" Pushing the hay off his forehead with his trunk, Kabumpo looked fiercely out, then, with a start that dislodged half the load, he began running off as rapidly as he could, dragging Randy along by the tail of his coat.

Chapter 7 - The Princess of Anuther Planet

Even so, Kabumpo was not fast enough, and as the immense black charger with its tail and mane curling like smoke, its fiery nostrils flashing flames a foot long, came galloping upon them, Randy flung himself face down on the ground to escape its burning breath. The most terrifying thing about the black steed was the complete silence of its coming. Its metal-shod feet struck the earth without making a sound, giving Kabumpo such a sense of unreality he could not believe it was true, or move another step. In consequence, as the enormous animal swirled to a halt before them, a dozen darting flames from its nostrils set fire to the load of hay on his back, enveloping him in a hot and exceedingly dangerous bonfire.

Now thoroughly aroused, Kabumpo leapt this way and that, and Randy, unmindful of his own danger, jumped up and tried to beat out the fire with his cloak. But the hay blazed and crackled, and the Elegant Elephant would certainly have been roasted like a potato had he not reared up on his hind legs and let the whole burning burden slide from his back. Scorched and infuriated, his royal robes burned and blackened, Kabumpo backed into a handy brook and sat down, from which position he glared with positive hatred at his prancing adversary. But a complete change had come over this strange and unbelievable steed; his nostrils no longer spurted flames, and as Randy plumped down beside Kabumpo, deciding this was the safest spot for both of them, the lordly creature dropped to its knees and touched its forehead three times to the earth.

"Away, away! You big meddlesome menace!" panted the Elegant Elephant, throwing up his trunk. "Begone, you good-for-nothing hay burner!"

"But, Kabumpo," pleaded Randy as the horse, paying no attention to the Elegant Elephant's angry screeches, began throwing little puffs of red smoke into the air, "he's trying to give us a message. LOOK!"

"Hail and salutations!" The words floated out smoothly and ranged themselves in a neat line. "I hereby acknowledge you as my master! I can flash fire from the eye, the nose, and the mouth; but you — you flash fire from the whole body! Yonder rests my Mistress Planetty, Princess of Anuther Planet! Who are you, great-and-much-to-be-envied spurter of fire?"

"Sky writing!" gasped Randy. "Oh, Kabumpo, how're we going to answer? He did not hear your scolding. I don't believe he can hear at all. Fire spurter! Ho, ho! And HOW are you going to keep up that reputation?"

"I'm not!" grunted Kabumpo, but in a much less savage voice, for he was almost completely won over by the Thunder Colt's flattery. "Hmmm-hhh, let me see, now, couldn't we signal to the silly brute? There he stands looking up in the air for an answer."

"Well," Randy said, "with your trunk and my arms we could form any number of letters, so—"

"This is Kabumpo, Elegant Elephant of Oz. I am Randy, King of Regalia." With infinite pains and patience, the two spelled out the message. Puzzled at first, then seeming to understand, Thun's clear yellow eyes snapped and twinkled with interest. Tossing his smoky mane, he puffed a single word into the air. "Come!" Then away he flashed at his noiseless gallop.

"Shall we?" cried Randy, jumping out of the creek, for he was curious to know more about the Thunder Colt and to meet the Princess of Anuther Planet. "Are you cooled off? Did the water put you out?"

"Oh, I'm put out, all right," grumbled Kabumpo, lurching up the bank. "Very put out and in splendid shape to meet a Princess, I must say."

"Come on, you don't look so bad," urged Randy, tugging impatiently at his tusk while Kabumpo himself endeavored to wring the water out of his robe with his trunk. "Even without any trappings or jewels at all, you'd stand out in any company. There's nobody bigger or handsomer than you, Kabumpo! Know it?"

"HAH!" The Elegant Elephant let go his robe and gave Randy a quick embrace. "Then what are we waiting for, little Braggerwagger?" Tossing the young monarch over his shoulder, the Elegant Elephant started after the Thunder Colt, moving almost as smoothly and silently as Thun himself. Without one look behind, Thun had disappeared into a green forest, and how cool and delicious it seemed to Randy and Kabumpo after the dry desert lands they had been traversing. Flashing in and out between the tall trees, the Thunder Colt led them to an ancient oak, set by itself in a little clearing. Here, leaning thoughtfully against the bole of the tree, stood the little Princess of Anuther Planet.

Kabumpo, recognizing royalty at once when he saw it, lifted his trunk in a grave and dignified salute. Randy bowed, but in such a daze of surprise and admiration he scarcely knew he was bowing. The small figure under the oak was strange and beautiful beyond description, giving an impression both of strength and delicacy. Planetty was fashioned of tiny meshed links, fine as the chain mail worn by medieval knights, of a metal that resembled silver but which at the same time was iridescent and sparkling as glass. Yet the Princess of Anuther Planet was live and soft as Randy's own flesh-and-bone self. Her eyes were clear and yellow like Thun's; her hair, a cascade of gossamer net, sprayed out over her shoulders and fell halfway to her feet. Planetty's garments, trim and shaped to her figure, were of some veil-like net, and floating from her shoulders was a cloak of larger meshed metal thread almost like a fisherman's net.

"Highnesses, Highness! Oh, very high Highnesses!" Prancing lightly before her, Thun puffed his announcement importantly into the air. "Here you see Kabumpty, Nelegant Nelephant of Noz, and Sandy, Kind of Segalia."

"Oh, my goodness! He has us all mixed up," worried Randy in a whispered aside to Kabumpo, whose ears had gone straight back at the dreadful name Thun had fastened upon him.

"Never mind, I too am mixed up. Everything down here is too perfectly lettling."

"Oh, you can speak?" Leaning forward, Randy gazed delightedly down at the little metal maiden. He had been afraid at first she would use the same skywriting talk as Thun.

"But surely," smiled Planetty, each word striking the air with the distinctness of a silver bell, so that Randy was almost as interested in the tune as in the sense. "Only the creature folk on Anuther Planet are without power of speech or sound making. They must go softly and silently. That is the lenith law."

"And a good law, too," observed Kabumpo, looking resentfully up at the Thunder Colt's fading message. "Permit me to introduce myself again. Your Highness, I am Kabumpo, Elegant Elephant of Oz, and this is Randy, King of Regalia, which is also in Oz."

"Oz?" marveled Planetty, lifting her spear like silver staff, whose tip — ending in three metal links — fascinated Randy. "Is this, then, the Planet of Oz? And what are those, and these, and this?" In rapid succession the little Princess touched a cluster of violets growing round the base of the oak, a moss-covered rock, and the tall tree itself.

"Why, flowers, rocks and a tree," laughed Randy. "Surely you must have flowers, trees, and rocks on Anuther Planet."

"No, no, nothing like this — all these colors and shapes. Everything on my planet is flat and greyling." The metal maiden raised her hands as she searched for the right words to explain Anuther Planet. "It is all so different with us," she confessed, dropping her arms to her side. "Yonder we have zonitors; not trees, but tall shafts of metal to which we fasten our nets when we sleep or rest. Underfoot we have network of various sizes and thicknesses with here and there sprays of vanadium. In our vanadium springs we freshen and renew ourselves, and without them we stiffen and cease to move."

With one finger pressed to his forehead, Randy tried to visualize Planetty's strange greyling world, but Kabumpo, ever more practical, inquired sharply: "And how often must you refresh and renew yourselves, Princess?"

261

"Every sonestor in the earling," answered the Princess with a bright nod. Thun, tiring of a conversation he could not hear, had cantered off to investigate a rabbit, and Randy, sliding to the ground, came over to stand nearer to this strange little Princess.

"Kabumpo and I do not understand all those words," he told her gently. "'Sonestor — earling' — what do they mean?"

"Why, a sonester," trilled Planetty, throwing back her head and showing all of her tiny silver teeth, "is one dark, one light, one dark, one light, one dark, one light, one dark, one light, one dark, one light, one dark, one light, and earling is when you waken from ret."

"Help!" shuddered Kabumpo, shaking his ears as if he had a bee in them.

"I know what she means," crowed Randy, snapping his fingers gleefully. "A sonester on Anuther Planet is the same as a week here; all those lights and darks are days, and earling is the morning and ret is rest!"

"Then, do you realize," worried Kabumpo, as Planetty looked questioningly from one to the other, "that if this little lady and her colt are separated from their vanadium springs for a week, they will become stiff, motionless statues? And that—" the Elegant Elephant looked the pretty Princess first up and then down "—that would be a great pity! We must help them back to Anuther Planet as soon as we can, my boy."

"Yes, yes, that is what you must do," Planetty clapped her small silvery hands and blew a kiss to the elephant. "If Thun had just not jumped on that thunderbolt!"

"Jumped on a thunderbolt, did he?" A reluctant admiration crept into Kabumpo's voice. The Princess nodded so emphatically her long, lovely hair danced and shimmered round her face like a cloud shot with starlight.

"You see," she went on gravely, "we were on our way to a zorodell." Kabumpo and Randy exchanged startled glances, but realizing there would be many odd words in Planetty's language, did not interrupt her. "And halfway there," continued Planetty calmly, "a dreadful storm overtook us. A bright flash of lightning frightened Thun, and though I signalled for him to stop, he sprang right up on a huge glowing thunderbolt that had fallen across the netway, and it fell and fell and fell, bringing us to where we are now."

"Well, that's one way of going places," commented Kabumpo, swinging his trunk from side to side.

"But how can we find Anuther Planet when none of us fly?" demanded Randy anxiously. "It must be miles above this country, for think how fast and far thunderbolts fall when they fall."

"Now you've forgotten the Red Jinn," boomed Kabumpo, winking meaningfully at the young King, for at Randy's words the little Princess had covered her face with her hands and three yellow jewels had trickled through her fingers. "Jinnicky can help Planetty and Thun go anyplace they wish," insisted Kabumpo in his loud, challenging bass. "Come, Princess, summon your fire-breathing steed, and we will travel on to the most powerful wizard in Ev."

"Ev? Wizard? Oh, how gay it all sounds." Planetty's voice rang out merrily as Christmas bells. With a lively skip she tapped her staff three times on the ground, and Thun, though out of sight, came instantly bounding back to his little mistress. Vaulting easily upon his back, the Princess of Anuther Planet lifted her staff, and Kabumpo, picking up Randy, started away like a whole conquering army.

Chapter 8 - On to Ev

Is there any way you can signal to your mount to trot ahead?" inquired *Kabumpo, looking* down sideways at the Thunder Colt, whose breath was blowing hot and uncomfortable against his side. "Let Thun be the vanguard," he suggested craftily. "When I trumpet once, turn him left; at two, turn right; at three, he must halt."

"Oh, fine," approved Planetty, tapping out the message with her heel on the Thunder Colt's flank. "That will be simply delishicus." Thun evidently agreed with her, for, tossing his smoky mane, he cantered to a position just ahead of the Elegant Elephant, at which Kabumpo heaved a huge sigh of relief. He did not wish to hurt Thun's feelings; neither did he wish to catch fire again.

"Here travel Thun, the Thunder Colt; Planetty, Princess of Anuther Planet; Kabumpty of Noz; and Slandy, King of Seegalia! Give way, all ye comers and goers, and arouse me not, for I am a seething mass of molten metal!"

"Is he really?" marveled Randy, gazing up at the fiery message floating like a banner over their heads. Planetty nodded absently, her interest so taken up with the wildflowers below, the blue sky above, and the wide-armed, lacy-leafed trees of this ancient forest she could not bear to turn her head for fear of missing something. On her own far-away metal planet, skies were grey and leaden, and the various states of slate and silver strata arranged in stiff and net-like patterns. The gay colors of this bright new world simply delighted her, and Randy and Kabumpo she considered beings of rare and singular beauty. The word she used to herself when she thought of them was "netiful," which is Anuther way of saying beautiful.

"A wonder that high-talking Thomas couldn't get a name straight once in a while!" complained Kabumpo out of one corner of his mouth as Thun's sentence spiraled away in thin pink smoke.

"Oh, what difference does it make?" laughed Randy. "I think `Kabumpty' is real cute."

"CUTE!" raged the Elegant Elephant with such a fierce blast Planetty promptly turned Thun to the left.

"Now see what you've done," snickered Randy, giving Kabumpo's ear a mischievous tweak. "They think you want them to go left."

"As a matter of fact, I do," snapped Kabumpo grumpily. "We must go east through Ix and then north to Ev."

"Puzzling and more puzzling," murmured Planetty, looking round at the Elegant Elephant. "Where are all these curious places, Bumpo dear? I thought all the time we were in Noz. Did you not tell us you were the Big Bumpo of Noz?"

Randy peered rather anxiously over Kabumpo's ear to see how he was taking this second nickname, but he need not have worried. The "dear Bumpo," spoken in the metal maid's ringing tones, fell like a charm on Kabumpo's ruffled feelings. And fairly oozing complacency and importance, he began to explain his own and Randy's real names and countries, hoping Planetty would straighten them out in her own head, if not in Thun's.

"You are right," he started off sonorously. "Randy and I both live in the Land of Oz, a great oblong country surrounded by a desert of burning sand. But in Oz there are many, many Kingdoms: first of all, the four large realms — the Gilliken Country of the North, the Quadling Country of the South, the Empire of the Winkies in the East, and the Land of the Munchkins in the West. Each of these Kingdoms has its own sovereign; but all are under the supreme rule of Ozma, a fairy Princess as lovely as your own small self, and Ozma lives in an Emerald City in the exact center of Oz."

Kabumpo paused impressively while Planetty's eyes twinkled merrily at his delicate flattery. "Now Randy and I hail from the north Gilliken Country of Oz," proceeded the Elegant Elephant, moving along as he spoke in a grand and leisurely manner. "I come from the Kingdom of Pumperdink, and Randy from the Regal little realm of Regalia. Only yesterday I arrived in Regalia to visit Randy, and we are now on our way to the castle of the Red Jinn, as I think I told you before. If we were in Oz, my dear—" Kabumpo lingered over the "dear" "—Ozma and her clever assistant, the Wizard of Oz, would quickly transport you to Anuther Planet with the magic belt. But, you see, we are not in Oz, for the same storm that overtook you and Thun overtook us and hurled us across the Deadly Desert to this Kingdom of Ix, where we all now find ourselves. Fortunately, too, for otherwise we might never have met a Princess from Anuther Planet."

The little Princess nodded in bright agreement.

"So," continued Kabumpo, picking up a huge tiger lily and holding it out to her, "as it is too difficult to travel back to the Emerald City of Oz, we will take you with us to the Wizard of Ev, whose castle is on the Nonestic Ocean in the country adjoining Ix."

"And a wizard is what?" Planetty turned almost completely round on her black charger, smiling teasingly over the tiger lily at Kabumpo.

"Why, a wizard, er, a wizard—" The Elegant Elephant fumbled a bit trying to find the right words to explain.

"A wizard is a person who can do by magic what other people cannot do at all," finished Randy neatly.

"Magic?" Planetty still looked puzzled.

"Oh, never mind all the words," comforted Kabumpo, flapping his ears good-naturedly, "you'll soon see for yourself what they all mean, and I'm sure Jinnicky will be charmed to do his best tricks for you and send you back in fine and proper style to your own planet."

"Yes, Jinnicky can do almost anything," boasted Randy, taking off his crown and setting it back very much atilt, "and he's good fun, too. You'll like Jinnicky."

"As much as big Bumpo?" Planetty rolled her soft eyes fondly back at the Elegant Elephant, and Randy, feeling an unaccountable twinge of jealousy, wished she would look at him that way.

"Oh, maybe not so much as Kabumpo. Of course, there's nobody like HIM — but pretty much as much," declared the young King loyally.

"But I like everything down here," decided Planetty, leaning forward to tickle Thun's ear with the lily. "It's all so nite and netiful."

"So now we know what we are," whispered Randy under his breath to Kabumpo. "And wait till Jinnicky sees us traveling with a fire-breathing Thunder Colt and the Princess of Anuther Planet. Oh, don't we meet important people on our journeys, Kabumpo?"

"Well, don't they meet US?" murmured the Elegant Elephant, increasing his speed a little to keep up with Thun. "Though I wouldn't call this colt important myself. How is he any better than an ordinary horse? His breath is hot and dangerous, and it's not much fun traveling with a deaf and dumb brute who burns everything he breathes on."

"Oh, he's not so dumb," observed Randy. "Look at the way he leaped over that fallen log just now, and think how useful he'll be at night to blaze a trail and light the campfires."

"Hadn't thought of that," admitted Kabumpo grudgingly. "I guess he would show up pretty well in the dark, and I suppose that does make him trail blazer and lighter of fires for this particular expedition. Ho, HO! KERUMPH! And between you and me and the desert, this expedition had better move pretty fast and not stop for sightseeing. Suppose those two Nuthers had that vanadium shower at the beginning of the week instead of the middle. That would give them only about two more days to go. Great Goosefeathers! I'd hate to have 'em stiffen up on us halfway to Jinnicky's. I might carry the Princess, but what would we do with the colt?"

"Let's not even think of it," begged Randy with a little shudder. "Great Goopers! Kabumpo, I hope Jinnicky will be at home and his magic is in good working order and powerful enough to send them back or keep them here if they decide to stay."

"If they decide to stay?" Kabumpo looked sharply back at his young rider. "Why should they?"

"Well, Planetty said she liked it down here, you heard her yourself a moment ago, and I thought maybe—" Randy's face grew rosy with embarrassment.

"Ha, Ha! So that's the way the wind lies!" Kabumpo chuckled soundlessly. "Well, I wouldn't count on it, my lad," he called up softly. "She probably has some nite Planetty Prince waiting for her up yonder, and will fly away without so much as a backward glance. And as for Jinnicky being at home, why shouldn't he be at home? And as for his magic not being powerful enough, why shouldn't it be powerful enough? He was in fine shape and form when I saw him in the Emerald City three years ago. By the way, why weren't you at that grand celebration? I understood Ozma invited all the Rulers of the Realm."

"Uncle Hoochafoo did not want me to leave," sighed Randy. "He thinks a King's place is in his castle."

"I wonder what he thinks now?" said Kabumpo, trumpeting three times, for Thun was racing along too far ahead of them.

"Probably has all the wise men and guards running in circles to find me," giggled Randy, immediately restored to good humor. "And say, when I do get back, old Push-the-Foot, I'M going to be KING, and everything will be very different and gay. Yes, there'll be a lot of changes in Regalia," he decided, shaking his head positively. "Why, all those dull receptions and reviewings would tire a visitor to tears."

"Ho, Ho! So you're still expecting her to visit you?" Waving his trunk, Kabumpo called out in a louder voice. "Not so fast there, Princess; hold Thun back a bit. We might run into danger, and we should all keep together on a journey. Besides," Kabumpo cleared his throat apologetically, "Randy and I must stop for a bite to eat."

Planetty's eyes widened, as they always did at strange words and customs, but she tugged obediently at Thun's mane, and the Thunder Colt came to an instant halt. Randy himself tried to coax the little Princess to eat something, but she was so upset and puzzled by the idea that he finally desisted and tried to share his bread and eggs with Kabumpo. But the Elegant Elephant generously refused a morsel, knowing Randy had little enough for himself, and lunched as best he could from the shoots of young trees and saplings. Thun was so interested when Kabumpo quenched his thirst at a small spring that he, too, thrust his head into the bubbling waters, but withdrew it instantly and with such an expression of pain and distress, Randy concluded that water hurt the Thunder Colt as much as fire hurt them. He was quite worried till the flames began to spurt from Thun's nostrils, for he was afraid the water might have put out Thun's fire and hastened the time when he should lose all power of life and motion.

"Do you do this often?" inquired Planetty as Randy tucked what was left into one of Kabumpo's small pockets.

"Eat?" Randy laughed in spite of himself. "Oh, about three times a day — or light," he corrected himself hastily, remembering Planetty had so designated the daytime. "I suppose that vanadium spray or shower keeps you and Thun going the way food does Kabumpo and me."

Planetty nodded dreamily, then, seeing Kabumpo was ready to start, she tapped Thun with her silver heels, and away streaked the Thunder Colt, Kabumpo swinging along at a grand gallop behind him.

"Strange we have not passed any woodsmen's huts or seen any wild animals," called Randy, jamming his crown down a little tighter to keep it from sailing off. "Hi! Watch out, there old Push-the-Foot! There's a wall ahead stretching away on all sides and going up higher than higher. What's a wall doing in a forest? Perhaps it shuts in the private shooting preserve of Queen Zixi herself. Say-ay, I'd like to meet the Queen of this country, wouldn't you?"

"No time, no time," puffed the Elegant Elephant, giving three short trumpets to warn Planetty to halt Thun. "Great Grump! Whoever built this wall wanted to shut out everything, even the sky. Can't even get a squint of the top, can you?"

264

"Is this the great Kingdom of Ev?" asked Planetty, who had pulled Thun up short and was looking at the wooden wall with lively interest.

"No, no, we're not nearly to Ev." The Elegant Elephant shook his head impatiently. "Back of this wall lives someone who dotes on privacy, I take it, or why should he shut himself in and everyone else out? Now then, shall we cruise round or knock a hole in the wood? I don't see any door, do you, Randy?"

"No, I don't." Standing on the elephant's back, Randy examined the wall with great care. "Why, it goes for miles," he groaned dolefully. "Miles!"

"Then we'll just bump though." Backing off, Kabumpo lowered his head and was about to lunge forward when Randy gave his ear a sharp tweak.

"Look!" he directed breathlessly. "Look!" While they had been talking, Thun had been sniffing curiously at the wooden wall, and now a whole round section of it was blazing merrily. "Hurray! He's burned a hole big enough for us all to go through," yelled the young King gleefully. "Come ON!"

Vexed to think the Thunder Colt had solved the difficulty so easily, and worried lest the whole wall should catch fire, Kabumpo signaled for Planetty to precede him. But he need not have worried about Thun's firing the wall. The Thunder Colt had burned as neat a hole in the boards as a cigarette burns in paper, and while the edges glowed a bit, they soon smouldered out, leaving a huge circular opening. So without further delay, Kabumpo stepped through, only to find himself facing the most curious company he had seen in the whole course of his travels.

Chapter 9 - The Box Wood

"Why! Why, they're all in boxes!" breathed Randy as a group with upraised and boxed fists advanced upon the newcomers.

"Chillywalla! Chillywalla!" yelled the Boxers, their voices coming muffled and strange through the hatboxes they wore on their heads.

"Chillywalla! Chillywalla, Chillywalla!" echoed Planetty, waving cheerfully at the oncoming host.

"Shh-hh, pss-st, Princess, that may be a war cry," warned Randy, drawing his sword and swinging it so swiftly round his head it whistled. Thun, too astonished to move a step, stood with lowered head, his flaming breath darting harmlessly into the moist floor of the forest.

"Chillywalla! Chillywalla! Chillywalla!" roared the Boxers, keeping a safe distance from Kabumpo's lashing trunk. "Chillywalla! CHILLYWALLA!" Their voices rose loud and imploring. As Randy slid off the Elegant Elephant's back to place himself beside Planetty, a perfectly enormous Boxer came clumping out of the Box Wood to the left.

"Yes! Yes?" he grunted, holding on to his hatbox as he ran. When he caught sight of the travelers, he stopped short, and not satisfied with peering through the eyeholes in his hatbox, took it off altogether and stood staring at them, his square eyes almost popping from his square head. "Box their ears, box their ears! Box their heads and arms and rears! Box their legs, their hands and chests, box that fire plug 'fore all the rest! An IRON box!" screamed Chillywalla as Thun, with a soundless snort, sent a shower of sparks into a candy box bush, toasting all the marshmallows in the boxes. "Oh, aren't you afraid to go about in this barebacked, barefaced, unboxed condition," he panted, "exposed to the awful dangers of the raw outer air?"

Chillywalla hastily clapped on his hatbox, but not before Randy noticed that his ears were nicely boxed, too. Without waiting for an answer to his question, the Boxer, with one shove of his enormous boxed fist, pushed Thun under a Box Tree. Planetty had just time to leap from his back when Chillywalla shook a huge iron box loose, and it came clanking down over the Thunder Colt. It was open at the bottom, and Thun, kicking and rearing underneath, jerked it east and west.

"He'll soon grow used to it," muttered Chillywalla, jabbing a dozen holes in the metal with a sharp pick he had drawn from a pocket in his box coat. "Now then, who's next? Ah! What a lovely lady!" Chillywalla gazed rapturously at the Princess from Anuther Planet, then, clapping his hands, called sharply, "Bring the jewel boxes for her ears, flower boxes for herself, a bonnet box for her head, candy boxes for her hands, slipper boxes for those tiny silver feet. Bring stocking boxes, glove boxes, and hurry! HURRY!"

"Oh, PLEASE!" Randy put himself firmly between Planetty and the determined Chillywalla. "The outer air does not hurt us at all, Mister Chillywalla. In fact, we like it!"

"Just try to find a box big enough for me!" invited Kabumpo, snatching up the little Princess and setting her high on his shoulder.

"I think I have a packing box that would just fit," mused the Chief Boxer, folding his arms and looking sideways at the Elegant Elephant. "Pack him up, pack him off, send him packing!" chattered the other Boxers, who had never seen anything like Kabumpo in their lives and distrusted him highly. But Chillywalla himself was quite interested in his singular visitors and inclined to be more than friendly.

"Better try our boxes," he urged seriously as he took the pile of bright cardboard containers an assistant had brought him. "Without bragging, I can say that they are the best boxes grown — stylish, nicely fitting and decidedly comfortable to wear."

"Ha, ha!" rumbled Kabumpo, rocking backward and forward at the very idea. "Mean to tell me you wear boxes over your other clothes and everywhere you go?"

"Certainly." Chillywalla nodded vigorously. "Do you suppose we want to stand around and disintegrate? What happens to articles after they are taken out of their boxes?" he demanded argumentatively. "Tell me that."

"Why," said Randy thoughtfully, "they're worn, or sold, or eaten, or spoiled—"

"Exactly." Chillywalla snapped him up quickly. "They are worn out; they lose their freshness and their newness. Well, we intend to save ourselves from such a fate, and we do," he added complacently.

"You're certainly fresh enough," chuckled Kabumpo with a wink at Randy.

"But might not these boxes be fun to wear?" inquired Planetty, looking rather wistfully at the bright heap the Boxer Chief had intended for her.

"No, No and NO!" rumbled Kabumpo positively. "No boxes!"

"As you wish." Chillywalla shrugged his shoulders under his cardboard clothes box. "Shall I unbox the horse?"

"Better not," decided Randy, looking anxiously at the sparks issuing from the punctures in Thun's box. "But perhaps you would show us the way through this, this—"

"Box Wood," finished Chillywalla. "Yes, I will be most honored to conduct you through our forest. And you may pick as many boxes as you wish, too," he added generously. "I'd like to do something for people who are so soon to spoil and wither."

"Ha, ha! Now, I'm sure that's very kind of you," roared Kabumpo, wiping his eyes on the fringe of his robe. "And I think it best we hurry along, my good fellow. Ho, whither away? It would never do to have a spoiled King and Princess and a bad horse and elephant on your hands."

"Oh, if you'd ONLY wear our boxes!" begged Chillywalla, almost ready to cry at the prospect of his visitors spoiling on the premises. Then as Kabumpo shook his head again, the Big Boxer started off at a rapid shuffle, anxious to have them out of the woods as soon as possible. Thun, during all this conversation, had been kicking and bucking under his iron box, but now Planetty tapped out a reassuring message with her staff and the Thunder Colt quieted down. On the whole, he behaved rather well, following the signals his little mistress tapped out, and pushing the iron box along without too much discomfort or complaint, though occasional indignant and fiery protests came puffing out of his iron container.

Randy considered the journey through the Box Wood one of their gayest and most entertaining adventures. The woodmen, in their brightly decorated boxes, shuffled cheerfully along beside them, stopping now and then to point with pride to their square box-like dwellings set at regular intervals under the spreading boxwood trees. The whole forest was covered by an enormous wooden box that shut out the sky and gave everything an artificial and unreal look. It was in one side of this monster box that Thun had burned the hole to admit them. Randy and Planetty, riding sociably together on Kabumpo's back, picked boxes from branches of all the trees they could reach, and it was such fun and so exciting they paid scarcely any attention to the remarks of Chillywalla. Even the Elegant Elephant snapped off a box or two and handed them back to his royal riders.

"Oh, look!" exulted Randy, opening a bright blue cardboard box. "This is just full of chocolate candy."

"Oh, throw that trash away," advised Chillywalla contemptuously. "We think nothing of the stuff that grows inside; it's the boxes themselves we are after."

"But this candy is good," objected Randy after sampling several pieces. "And mind you, Kabumpo, Planetty has just picked a jewel box full of real chains, rings and bracelets."

"Oh, they are netiful, netiful," crooned the Princess of Anuther Planet, hugging the velvet jewel box to her breast.

"Keep them if you wish," sniffed Chillywalla, "but they're just rubbish to us. When we pick boxes, we toss the contents away."

"Now, that's just plain foolishness," snorted Kabumpo, aghast at such a waste, as Randy picked a pencil box full of neatly sharpened pencils and Planetty a tidy sewing kit fitted out with scissors, needles and spools of thread. The thimble was not quite ripe, but as Planetty had never stitched a stitch in her royal life, she did not notice or care about that. Indeed, before they came to the other side of the Box Wood, she and Randy were sitting in the midst of a high heap of their treasures, and Kabumpo looked as if he were making a lengthy safari, loaded up and down for the journey.

Randy had stuffed most of the boxes into big net bags Kabumpo always brought along for emergencies, and these he tied to the Elegant Elephant's harness. There were bread boxes packed with tiny loaves and biscuits, cake boxes stuffed with sugar buns and cookies, stamp boxes, flower boxes, glove boxes, coat and suit boxes. Last of all, Randy picked a Band Box and it played such gay tunes when he lifted the lid, Planetty clapped her silver hands, and even Kabumpo began to hum under his breath. Traveling through the Box Wood with kind-hearted Chillywalla was more like a surprise party than anything else. To Planetty it was all so delightful, she began to wonder how she had ever been satisfied with her life on Anuther Planet.

"Are all the countries down here as different and happy as this?" she asked, fingering the necklace she had taken from the jewel box. "All our countries are greyling and sad. No birds sing, no flowers grow, and people are all the same."

"Oh, just wait till you've been to OZ," exclaimed Randy, shutting the band box so he could talk better. "Oz countries are even more surprising than this, and wait till you've seen Ev and Jinnicky's Red Glass Castle!"

"You'll never reach it," predicted Chillywalla, shaking his hatbox gloomily. "You'll spoil in a few hours now, especially the big one, loaded down with all that stuff and rubbish. Throw it away," he begged again, looking so sorrowful Randy was afraid he was going to burst out crying. "Toss out that rubbish and wear our boxes before it is too late!"

"Rubbish!" Randy shook his fingers reprovingly at the Boxer. "Why, all these things are terribly nice and useful. If we go through enemy countries, we can placate the natives with cakes and cigars, and if we go through friendly countries, we'll use the suits and flowers and candy for gifts. Really, you've been a great help to us, Mr. Chillywalla, and if you ever come to Regalia, you may have anything in my castle you wish!"

"Are there any boxes in your castle?" Chillywalla peered up at Randy through the slits in his hat box.

"Not many," admitted Randy truthfully. "You see, in my country we keep the contents and throw the boxes away."

"Throw the boxes away!" gasped Chillywalla, jumping three times into the air. "Oh, you rogues! You rascals! You, YOU BOXIBALS! Lefters! Righters! Boxers all! Here! Here at once! Have at these Box-destroying savages!"

"Now see what you've done," mourned Kabumpo as hundreds of the Boxers, heeding Chillywalla's call, darted out of their dwellings and came leaping from behind the box bushes and trees. "You've started a war! That's what!"

"Box them! Box them good!" shrieked Chillywalla, raining harmless blows on Kabumpo's trunk with his boxed fists. A hundred more boxed both Thun and the Elegant Elephant from the rear, and so loud and angry were their cries Planetty covered her ears.

"Too bad we have to leave when everything was so pleasant," wheezed Kabumpo. "But never mind, here's the other side of the Box Wood. Flatten out, youngsters, and I'll bump through."

And bump through he did, with such a splintering of boards it sounded like an explosion of cannoncrackers. Thun, at three taps from Planetty, bumped after him, and before the Boxers realized what was happening, they were far away from there. "I'll soon have that box off you!" panted Kabumpo. And putting his trunk under Thun's iron box, he heaved it up in short order, screaming shrilly as he did, for the Thunder Colt's breath had made the metal uncomfortably hot.

"I thank you, great and mighty Master!" Thun sent the words up in a perfect shower of sparks. "Let us begone from these notorious boxers."

"Oh, they're not so bad," mused Randy as Planetty signaled for Thun to go left. "Just peculiar. Imagine keeping the boxes and throwing away all the lovely things inside. And imagine a country where everything grows in boxes!" he added, standing up to wave at Chillywalla and his square-headed comrades, who were looking angrily through the break in the side of their wall.

"Goodbye!" he called clearly. "Goodbye, Chillywalla, and thanks for the presents!"

"Boxibals!" hissed the Boxer Chief and his men, shaking their fists furiously at the departing visitors.

"And that makes us no better than cannibals, I suppose," grunted Kabumpo, looking rather wearily at the stretch of forest ahead. He had rather hoped to find himself in open country.

Chapter 10 - Night in the Forest

All afternoon the four travelers moved through the Ixian forest, Planetty exclaiming over the flowers, ferns and bright birds that flitted from tree to tree, Thun sending up frequent high-flown sentences, Kabumpo and Randy looking rather anxiously for some landmark that would prove they were on the road to Ev. As it grew darker, the Elegant Elephant wisely decided to make camp, stopping in a small, tidy clearing for that purpose. As Kabumpo swung to an impressive halt, Randy slid to the ground, pulling the net bags with him, and began to sort out boxes containing food. Then he quickly gathered some faggots for a fire, as the night was raw and chilly, and had Planetty signal Thun to breathe on the wood. Thun, only too happy to be of some use, quickly lighted the campfire, and he and the little Princess watched curiously while Randy prepared his own and Kabumpo's supper, making coffee in a tin box with some water Kabumpo had fetched in his collapsible canvas bucket. The Elegant Elephant did rather well with the contents of seven cake boxes and four bread and cereal containers, and Randy found so many good things to eat among Chillywalla's presents he felt sorry not to be able to share them with Planetty or Thun.

"It would be more fun if you ate, too," he observed, looking down sideways at the little Princess, who was sitting on a boulder, hands clasped about her knees, while she gazed contentedly up at the stars.

"Would it?" Planetty smiled faintly, tapping her silver heels against the rock. "This seems nite enough," she sighed, stretching up her arms luxuriantly, "but now it is time to ret." Slipping off her metal cape, the Princess of Anuther Planet tossed one end against a white birch and the other to a tall pine. To Randy's surprise, the ends of the cape instantly attached themselves to the trees, making a soft, flexible hammock. Into this Planetty climbed with utmost ease and satisfaction. "Good net, Randy and Big Bumpo, dear," she called softly. "Take care of Thun. I've told him to stay where he is till the earling, and he will, he will."

With a smile, Planetty closed her bright eyes, and the wind swaying her silver hammock soon rocked her to sleep. It had been a long day, and Randy felt very drowsy himself. Walking over to the Thunder Colt, he turned his head so that his fiery breath would fall harmlessly on a cluster of damp rocks. He was pleased to find this steed from another planet so obedient and gentle. Though formed of some live and lively black metal, Thun was soft and satiny to the touch and seemed to enjoy having his back rubbed as much as an ordinary horse.

"Tap me twice on the shoulder if aught occurs, Slandy," he signalled, blowing the words out lazily between Randy's pats. "And good net to you, my Nozzies! Good net!"

"That language is just full of foolishness," sniffed Kabumpo, spreading a blanket on the ground for Randy and then stretching himself full length beneath a beech tree. "Put out the fire, Nozzy, my lad, the creature's breath makes light enough to frighten off any wild men or monsters."

"Oh, I don't believe there are any wild beasts or savages in this forest," Randy said, stamping out the embers of the campfire. "It's too quiet and peaceful. I have an idea we're almost across Ix and will reach Ev by morning. What do you think, Kabumpo?"

Kabumpo made no answer, for the Elegant Elephant had stopped thinking and was already comfortably asnore. So, with a terrific yawn, Randy wrapped himself in the blanket, and curling up close to his big and faithful comrade, fell into an instant and pleasant slumber. Morning came all too soon, and Randy was rudely awakened by Kabumpo, who was shaking him violently by the shoulders. "Come on! Come on!" blustered the Elegant Elephant impatiently. "Stir out of it, my boy, we've all been up for hours. Is it proper to lie abed and let a Princess light the fire?"

"She didn't!" Sitting bolt upright, Randy saw that Planetty, with Thun's help, actually had lighted a fire and set water to boil in the tin box just as he had done the evening before. "Oh my goodness, Planetty! You musn't do that rough work," he exclaimed, hurrying over to take the big cake box from Planetty's hands.

"Why not?" beamed the little Princess, hugging the box close. "See, I have found the great choconut cake for Big Bumpo to eat — I mean neat."

"Ha, ha! Choconut cake!" Kabumpo swayed merrily from side to side. "Very neat, my dear. If there's one thing I love for breakfast, it's choconut cake." Laughing so he could hardly keep his balance, Kabumpo held out his trunk for the cake box. "What a splendid little castle keeper you'll make for some young King, Netty, my child!"

"Netty? Is that now my name?" Planetty pushed back her flying cloud of hair with an interested sniff.

"If you like it," said Randy, his ears turning quite red at Kabumpo's teasing remarks. Leading the little Princess to a flat rock, he sat her down with great ceremony and then began opening up boxes of crackers and fruit.

"Netty's a nite name," decided the Princess, her head thoughtfully on one side. "I must tell Thun." Skipping over to the Thunder Colt, who with drooping head and tail was enjoying a little colt nap, she tapped out her new nickname in the strange code she used when talking to him.

"No longer Planetty of Anuther Planet!" flashed Thun, awake in a twinkling and sending up his message in a shower of sparks. "But Anetty of Oz!"

"At least he's left off the N," mumbled Kabumpo, speaking thickly through the cocoanut cake which he had tossed whole into his capacious mouth. "Sounds rather well, don't you think?"

"Wonderful!" agreed Randy, who could scarcely keep his eyes off the sparkling little Princess. "It's too bad she's not like us, Kabumpo, then she could go back to Oz and stay there always."

"If she were like us, she wouldn't be so interesting," said Kabumpo, shaking his head judiciously. "Besides, down here the poor child is completely out of her element and liable to disintegrate or suffocate or Ev knows what—" he went on, discarding a box of prunes for a carton of tea.

"How was the cake?" Randy changed the subject, for he could not bear to think of Planetty in danger of any sort.

"Stale," announced Kabumpo, making a wry face as he swallowed some tea leaves. "I'll certainly be glad to catch up with some regular elephant food. This eating bits out of boxes is diabolical — simply diabolical! Here, give me those crackers and eat some of that other stuff. And look at little Netty Ann, would you, shaking out that blanket as if she'd been traveling with us for years. Why, the lass is a born housewife!"

"And isn't she pretty?" smiled Randy, waving to Planetty as he began packing the boxes in the net bags again and stamping out the fire. "I wonder what it's like up where she lives, Kabumpo?"

"Why not ask her?" Swinging up his saddle sacks, Kabumpo called gaily to the little Princess, who came running over, the blanket neatly folded on her arm.

"Thank you, Netty. You are certainly a great help to us!" Taking the blanket and giving her an approving pat on the shoulder, Randy caught hold of Kabumpo's belt strap and pulled himself easily aloft. "All ready to go?"

Planetty nodded cheerfully as she mounted the Thunder Colt. "Will this lightling be as nite as the last?" she demanded, tapping Thun gently with her staff.

"Nicer," promised Randy as Thun pranced merrily ahead, Planetty's long cape billowing like a silver cloud behind them.

"What do you do when you are at home?" called Randy as Kabumpo, giving two short trumpets, followed close on the heels of the Thunder Colt.

"Home?" Planetty turned a frankly puzzled face.

"I mean, do you have a house or a castle?" persisted Randy, determined to have the matter settled in his mind once for all. "Do you have brothers and sisters, and is your father a King?"

"No house, no castle, no those other words," answered Planetty in even greater bewilderment. "On Anuther Planet each is to herself or himself alone. One floats, rides, skips or drifts through the leadling heights and lowlands, hanging the cape where one happens to be."

"Regular gypsies," murmured Kabumpo under his breath. "So nobody belongs to nobody, and nobody has anybody? Sounds crazy to me."

"Yes, if you have no families, no fathers or mothers—" Randy was plainly distressed by such a country and existence "—I don't see how you came to be at all."

"We rise full grown from our Vanadium springs, and naturally I have my own spring. Is that, then, my father?"

"Tell her 'yes,'" hissed Kabumpo between his tusks. "Why mix her all up with our way of doing things? If she wants a spring for a father, let her have it!" Kabumpo waved his trunk largely. "Ho, ho, kerumph! I've always thought of springs as a cure for rheumatism, but live and learn — eh, Randy — live and learn."

Randy paid small attention to the Elegant Elephant's asides; he was too busy explaining life as it was lived in Oz to Planetty, making it all so bright and fascinating, the eyes of the little Princess fairly sparkled with interest and envy. "I think I will not go with you to this Wizard of Ev," she announced in a small voice as the young King paused for breath. "I do not believe I shall like that old wizard or his castle." Touching Thun with her staff, Planetty turned the Thunder Colt sideways and went zigzagging so rapidly through the trees they almost lost sight of her entirely.

"Now what?" stormed the Elegant Elephant, charging recklessly after her through the forest. "What's come over the little netwit? Come back! Come back, you foolish girl!" he trumpeted anxiously. "We'll take you to Oz after you've been to Ev," he added with a sudden burst of comprehension.

At Kabumpo's promise, Planetty half turned on her charger. "But this Wizard of Ev will send us back to Anuther Planet. It is yourself that has said so."

"No, no! We just said he would help you!" shouted Randy, leaning forward and waving both arms for Planetty to turn back. "Oh, you really must see Jinnicky," he begged earnestly. "Without his magic, you cannot live away from that Vanadium spring. Do you want to be stiff and still as a statue for the rest of your days?"

"I'd rather be a statue down here with you and Bumpo, where the birds sing and the flowers grow and the woods are green and wonderful, than to be a live Princess of Anuther Planet!" sighed the metal maiden, hiding her face in Thun's mane.

"You WOULD?" cried Randy, almost falling off the elephant in his extreme joy and excitement. "Then you just SHALL, and Jinnicky will change everything so you can live down here always and come back to Oz with Kabumpo and me! Would you like that, Planetty?"

"Oh, that would be netiful!" Clasping Thun with both arms, the little Princess laid her soft cheek against his neck. "NETIFUL!"

"Then ride on, Princess! Ride on!" Kabumpo spoke gruffly, for his feeling had quite overcome him. "Toss me a 'kerchief, will you, Randy?" he gulped desperately. "Oh, boo hoo, kerSNIFF! To think she really likes us that much! Do you think she'd hear if I blew my trunk?"

269

"No, no, she's way ahead of us now," whispered Randy, handing an enormous handkerchief down to Kabumpo after taking a sly wipe on it himself. "Oh, isn't this a gorgeous day, Kabumpo, and isn't everything turning out splendidly? And see there — we've actually come to the end of the forest."

Chapter 11 - The Field of Feathers

"Good Gapers, everything's pink!" marveled Randy as Kabumpo, still muttering and snuffling, pushed his way through the last fringe of the forest.

"So now we're in the pink, eh?" With a last convulsive snort, Kabumpo stuffed the handkerchief into a lower pocket and trumpeted three times for Thun to halt. "Are those flowers, d'ye 'spose? May I see one of them, my dear?"

Catching up with the little Princess, who was already on the edge of the field, Kabumpo took the long spray she had picked and passed it back to Randy. "My gooseness, it's a feather! The largest and finest I've ever seen," Randy said in surprise. "Hey, I always thought feathers grew on birds, yet here's a whole field of feathers, Kabumpo — imagine that! And taller than I am, too."

"Well, there's no harm in feathers," observed Kabumpo jocularly. "Pick a plume for your bonnet, my child. The girls in our countries adorn themselves with these pretty fripperies. I've even worn them myself at court functions," he admitted self-consciously. "But do you think you can hold the colt's head up as we go through? Burnt feathers smell rather awful, and we don't wish to anger the owner or spoil his crop."

A bit confused by the words "owner" and "crop," Planetty nevertheless caught the idea and explained it so cleverly to Thun, the Thunder Colt started through the field holding his head high and handsome so that the flames spurted upward and not down.

"It was rather like plowing through a wheat field," decided Randy as Kabumpo, treading lightly as he could, stepped after Thun. It was, though, more like a sea of waving plumes, endlessly bending, nodding and rippling in the wind. Planetty gathered armfuls of these bright and newest treasures, liking them almost as much as the flowers in the forest. Thun, for his part, found the whole experience irksome in the extreme.

"These pink feathers give me the big pain in the neck," he puffed up indignantly as he trotted along with his head in the air. Planetty, reading his message with a little smile, was astonished to hear a series of roars and explosions behind her. Surely Thun's remarks were not as funny as all that! Turning round, she was shocked to see Kabumpo swaying and stumbling in his tracks, coughing and spluttering, and torn by such gigantic guffaws he had already shaken Randy from his back. The young King himself rolled and twisted on the ground, fairly gasping for breath.

"It's the feathers!" he gasped weakly as Planetty, leaping off the Thunder Colt, ran back to investigate. "They're tickling us to death. Get away quickly, Netty dear, before they get you — Oh, ha, ha, HAH! Oh, ho, ho! Quick! Before it is too late. Oh, hi, hi, hi! I shall die laughing!" To the startled little Princess, he appeared to be dying already.

"No, no! Please not!" she cried, dropping her armful of feathers. With surprising strength she jerked Randy upright, and in spite of his continued roars and wild writhings, managed to fling him across Thun's back. Now Kabumpo was down, kicking and rolling hysterically. It seemed to Planetty that the feathers were wickedly alive and tickling them on purpose. They tossed, swayed and brushed against her and Thun, too, but having no effect on the metallic skin of the Nuthers, curled away in distaste.

"Stop! Stop! I hate you!" screamed Planetty, stamping on the bunch she had picked a moment before, then struggling in vain to pull Kabumpo up by his trunk. "Thun! Thun! What shall we do?" Racing back to the Thunder Colt, Planetty tapped out all that was happening to their best and only friends, holding the convulsed and still laughing Randy in place with one hand as she did so. Thun, from anxious glances over his shoulder, had guessed more than half the difficulty.

"Search in the Kabumpty's pocket for something to tie round him so I may pull him out of the feathers," flashed the Thunder Colt, swinging in a circle to prance and stamp on the plumes still curling down to tickle the helpless boy on his back.

Feeling in Kabumpo's pockets as he tossed and lashed about was hard enough, but Planetty, who was quick and clever, soon found a long, stout, heavily linked gold chain Kabumpo twisted round and round his neck on important occasions. Slipping the chain through his belt, the little Princess clasped the other ends round the Thunder Colt's chest, making a strong and splendid harness. Then, mounting quickly and holding desperately to Randy, Planetty gave the signal for Thun to start. And away through the deadly field charged the night-black steed, burning feathers left and right with his flashing breath and dragging Kabumpo along as easily as if he had been a sack of potatoes instead of a two-ton elephant. The feathers bending beneath made the going soft so that the Elegant Elephant did not suffer so much as a scratch, and Thun galloped so swiftly that in less than ten minutes they had reached the other side of the beautiful but treacherous field. Going half a mile beyond, Thun came to an anxious halt, the golden chain falling slack around his ankles, while Planetty jumped down to see how Kabumpo was doing.

The Elegant Elephant had stopped laughing, but his eyes still rolled and his muscles still twitched and rippled from the terrible tickling he had endured. Randy, exhausted and weak, hung like a dummy stuffed with straw over the Thunder Colt's back. "Oh, we were too late, too long!" mourned Planetty, wringing her hands and running distractedly between the Elegant Elephant and the insensible King. "Oh, my netness, they will become stiff and still as Nuthers deprived of their springs," she tapped out dolefully to Thun.

"Do not be too sure." The Thunder Colt puffed out his message slowly. "See, already the big Kabumpty is trying to rise." And such, indeed, was the case. Astonished and mortified to find himself stretched on the ground in broad daylight and still too confused to realize what had happened, the Elegant Elephant lurched to his feet and stood blinking uncertainly around. Then, his eyes suddenly coming into proper focus, he caught sight of Randy lying limply across the Thunder Colt.

"What in Oz? What in Ix? What in Ev is the matter here?" he panted, wobbling dizzily over to Thun.

"Feathers!" sighed Planetty, clasping both arms round Kabumpo's trunk and beginning to pat and smooth its wrinkled surface. "The feathers tickled you and you fell down, my poor Bumpo. Randy too was almost laughed to the death. What does death mean?" Planetty looked up anxiously into his eyes.

"Great Grump! So that was it! Great Gillikens! I remember now, we were both nearly tickled to death, and it was awful, AWFUL! Not that Ozians ever do die," he explained hastily, "but, after all, we are not in Oz, and anything might have happened. And what I'd like to know is how in Ev we ever got out of those feathers."

"Thun pulled you out," Planetty told him proudly. "And look, LOOK, Bumpo dear, Randy is going to waken, too."

"Randy! Randy, do you hear that?" Kabumpo lifted the young King down and shook him gently backward and forward. "This colt of Planetty's, this Thunder Colt, all by himself, mind you, pulled us out of that infernal feather field! You and me, but mostly me. Now tell me, how did he manage to pull an elephant all that way?"

Randy, only half comprehending what Kabumpo was saying, said nothing, but Thun, guessing Kabumpo's question, threw back his head and puffed quickly: "We Nuthers are strong as iron, Master. Strong for ourselves, strong for our friends. Thun, the Thunder Colt, will always be strong for Kabumpty!"

"Strong! Strong? Why, you're marvelous," gasped the Elegant Elephant. Placing Randy on the ground, he fished jewels from his pocket with a reckless trunk till he found a band of pearls to fit Thun. Then carelessly risking the sparks from the Thunder Colt's nostrils, he fastened the pearls in place. "Tell him, tell him THANKS!" he blurted out breathlessly. "Tell him from now on we are friends and equals, friends and warriors together!"

With a pleased nod, Planetty translated for Thun, and the delighted colt, tossing his flying mane, raced round and round his three comrades, filling the air with high-flown and flaming sentences. "Friends and warriors!" he heralded, rearing joyously. "Friends and warriors!"

By this time Randy had recovered his breath and his memory and felt not only able but impatient to continue the journey. The field of feathers could still be seen waving pink and provokingly in the distance, but without one backward glance the four travelers set their faces to the north. A few of Chillywalla's boxes had been crushed while Kabumpo rolled in the feathers, and he and Randy still felt weak and worn from their dreadful experience, but these were small matters when they considered the dreadful fate they had escaped through the quick action of Planetty and Thun. "I always thought of Ix as a pleasant country," sighed Randy as Kabumpo moved slowly along a shady bypath.

"I don't believe this is Ix," stated the Elegant Elephant bluntly. "The air's different, smells salty, and this sandy road looks as if we might be near the sea. I think myself that we've come north by east through Ix into Ev and will reach the Nonestic Ocean by evening." Kabumpo paused to peer up at a rough board nailed to a pine.

"So! You got through the feathers, did you?" sneered the notice in threatening red letters. "Then so much the worse for you! Beware! Watch out! Gludwig the Glubrious has his eye on you."

"Glubrious!" sniffed Kabumpo, elevating his trunk scornfully as Randy read and re-read the impertinent message. "I don't recall anyone named Gludwig, do you?"

"Sounds rather awful, doesn't it?" whispered Randy, sliding to the ground to examine the billboard from all sides. "Say, look here, Kabumpo, there's something on the back. It's been scratched out with red chalk, but I can still read it."

"Then read it," advised Kabumpo briefly.

"This is the Land of Ev! Everybody welcome! Take this road to the Castle of the Red Jinn."

"Oh, that means we're almost there!" exulted the young King, but his joy evaporated quickly as he re-read the other side of the board. "Looks as if someone had switched signs on Jinnicky," he muttered, pushing back his crown with a little whistle. "Do you think anything has happened to him?"

"Probably some mischievous country boy trying out his chalk," answered the Elegant Elephant, not believing one of his own words. "Straight on, my dear," he called cheerfully to Planetty, who had pulled in the colt and was looking questioningly back at them. "At last we are in the Land of Ev, and just ahead lies the castle of our wizard."

"Oh, Bumpo, how nite!" Planetty hugged herself from pure joy. "I've never seen a castle, I've never seen a wizard!"

"But Kabumpo," worried Randy as the little Princess of Anuther Planet galloped gaily ahead of them, "suppose this Gludwig really has his eye on us? Suppose he rushes out before we can reach Jinnicky's castle?"

"Well, that will not be very 'nite,' will it?" The Elegant Elephant spoke ruefully. "But what can we do? Are we going to stop for a mere sign?"

"No!" declared Randy, feeling about for his sword. "Of course not. But I'll wager a Willikin he was the fellow who planted those feathers."

"Very likely," agreed Kabumpo, pushing grimly along through the sand.

Chapter 12 - Arrival at the Castle of the Red Jinn

The further they traveled into Ev, the more interesting the country became to Planetty and Thun. Now wild orange and lemon trees added their spicy tang to the salty air; waving palms edged the sandy roadway; and after traversing a grove of lordly cocoanut trees, the four suddenly found themselves facing the great, green, rolling Nonestic.

"A spring!" caroled Planetty, galloping Thun down to the water's edge. "Oh, never have I seen so netiful a spring!"

"Not a spring, Princess, an ocean," corrected Kabumpo, ambling good naturedly after Thun. "This is a salt, salt sea, full of ships, sailors, shells, crabs, islands, fish and fishermen."

"And will I see all of them?" Slipping from Thun's back, Planetty waded out a little way, hopping gleefully over the edges of the smaller waves.

"Sometime," promised Randy, dismounting hastily to keep her from venturing too far. "Look over your shoulder, Netty," he urged, drawing her back toward shore, "and then tell me what you think!"

Explaining this gay, wide and wonderful world to the little Princess of Anuther Planet Randy found more fun than anything he had ever done or imagined. Tense with expectation, he and Kabumpo watched as Planetty gazed off to the right. "Why — 'tis a high, high hill of red that glitters! Or what? What is it?" Planetty whirled Thun round so he could see, too.

"It's a castle, m'lass." Kabumpo swaggered down the beach, as if he alone were responsible for all its splendor and magnificence. "There you see the imperial palace of the Wizard of Ev, built from turret to cellar of the finest red glass studded with rubies, and there this night we will be suitably entertained by Jinnicky himself."

"The inside's even better than the outside," Randy whispered in Planetty's ear as she tapped out this astonishing news to the Thunder Colt. "Come on, come on, it's not more than a mile, and we can go straight along the edge of the seashore. Say, weren't we lucky not to run into Gludwig?" Pulling himself up on Kabumpo's back, Randy spoke the words softly. "It would have been too bad to have the first person outside of ourselves that Planetty met turn out a villain. I believe that sign WAS a joke."

"Well, everything seems all right so far," admitted the Elegant Elephant guardedly. "But keep your eyes open, my boy, keep your eyes open. Is that a welcome committee marching along the beach, or is it an army?"

"They're still too far away to tell," answered Randy. "Looks to me like all Jinnicky's blacks; I can see their baggy red trousers and turbans."

"Yes, but what's that gleaming in the sunlight?" demanded Kabumpo, curling up his trunk uneasily.

"Only their scimitars," Randy said, standing up to have a better view. "Each man is carrying a scimitar over his shoulder, but that's perfectly all right, they're probably parading for our benefit."

"Mm-mm! Sometimes things are not what they scim-itar!" sniffed Kabumpo, snapping his eyes suspiciously. But Randy, paying no attention to the Elegant Elephant's remark, was feeling round in the net bags for Chillywalla's band box, and next moment the lively strains of a military march filled the air.

Swinging along in time to the music, Kabumpo peered sharply at the oncoming host for signs of Alibabble or Ginger, the slave of the bell, or some of Jinnicky's other old and trusted counselors. But in all that great throng there was not one familiar face, and because he was beginning to feel more than a bit worried, Kabumpo lifted his feet higher and higher. "Everything looks black, very black," he muttered dubiously.

"Why not?" cried Randy, waving his arms like a bandmaster. "They're all black as the ace of spades. Mind you, Planetty, it takes all these black men to take care of Jinnicky and his castle."

"And will they take care of us?" Planetty eyed the marchers with positive amazement and alarm. "So many," she murmured in a hushed voice, "so black. I thought everyone down here would be like you and Bumpo."

"My, no," Randy told her complacently. "Everyone is liable to be different. I believe I'll toss out some of Chillywalla's boxes. Visitors should come bearing presents, you know!"

Hastily, Randy began pulling out boxes of candy, boxes of cigarettes, beads, cigars and whole suits of clothing to dazzle Jinnicky's subjects. But when the leader of the procession came within ten feet of the travelers, he threw back his head and emitted such a blood-curdling howl, Randy's hair rose on his head, and as the rest of the blacks, brandishing scimitars and yelling threats and imprecations, came leaping toward them, the desperate young King began hurling down boxes as if they were bombs. He caught the Headman on the chin with the bandbox, but while it stopped the music, it did not stop the gigantic Evian from slashing at Thun. As his scimitar fell, Kabumpo gave a trumpet that felled the whole front rank of the enemy, and snatching up the villain in his trunk, he hurled him back among his men.

"Is this — is this taking care of us?" shuddered Planetty, clasping her arms round the neck of the plunging Thunder Colt.

"No, no! My goodness, NO! Is Thun hurt? Quick, Kabumpo!" screamed Randy as a second scimitar slashed down on Thun's flank. Then he managed to breathe again, for the razor-sharp weapon glanced harmlessly off the metal coat of Planetty's coal black charger. The wielder of the scimitar, however, did not escape so easily, for a hot blast from Thun's nostrils sent him reeling backward.

"That's it! Give it to them! Give it to them!" shouted Randy, forgetting in his excitement that Thun could not hear, and he himself hurled Chillywalla's boxes hard and viciously and one after the other. As for Kabumpo, every time he raised his trunk there was a black man in it, and as fast as they came he slung them over his shoulder.

But it was Planetty who really turned the tide of battle. While Randy, who had exhausted his supply of boxes, was digging desperately for some more missiles, he heard a perfect chorus of terrified screeches. Popping up with an umbrella and an alarm clock, he saw the Princess of Anuther Planet standing erect on the galloping colt's back, calmly and precisely casting her staff at the foe. Each time the staff struck, the victim, in whatever attitude he happened to be, was frozen into a motionless metal figure. And after each stroke, the staff returned to Planetty's hand.

"Yah, yah, mah-MASTER!" wailed the frantic blacks who were still able to move, and tumbling over one another in their effort to escape, they fled wildly back to the Red Castle, leaving behind sixty of their vanquished brethren. "You — you — YOU'LL be sorry for this!" shouted the Headman, tearing off his turban and waving it as he ran.

"So will you!" bellowed Kabumpo fiercely. "Just wait till Jinnicky hears about this! How dare you treat his visitors in this violent wicked fashion?"

"Jinnicky! Jinnicky!" jeered the Headman as Planetty aimed her staff threateningly at his back. "Jinnicky is at the bottom of the sea!"

"Mm-Mnnn! Mnmph! I knew it, I knew it!" groaned the Elegant Elephant as the Headman reached the palace and scittered wildly up the glass steps. "I knew something was wrong the moment I saw those scimitars."

"Jinnicky gone! Jinnicky at the bottom of the sea? Why, I just can't believe it!" Randy, glancing over his shoulder at the tumbling Nonestic, looked almost ready to cry. Then, putting back his shoulders, he declared fiercely, "Well, I'M not going off and leave this old pirate in Jinnicky's castle, are you? It must be Gludwig's doing — all this! Let's go inside and throw him out of there! We have lots of help now. Thun's a regular flame thrower, and Planetty's worth a whole army, and best of all, nothing can hurt them. Why didn't you tell me you had a magic staff?" Randy looked admiringly down at the resolute little Princess at his side. "Why, with that staff we can conquer anybody."

"Is that what you call magic?" Planetty regarded her staff with new interest.

"It certainly is!" panted Kabumpo, fanning himself with a handy palm leaf. "And we're mighty sorry to have gotten you into all this danger and trouble, my dear. Looks as if we had a war on our hands instead of a pleasant vacation."

"Oh, that! It is nothing, nothing!" Planetty shrugged her shoulders eloquently. "On our planet we too have the bad beasts and Nuthers, and when they try to hit or bite us, we just subdue them with our voral staffs."

"Mmmn-mn! So I see." Kabumpo, still fanning himself, looked thoughtfully at Gludwig's petrified warriors. "There must be a goodly bit of statuary on your planet, m'lass?"

"Very many," answered Planetty soberly, polishing her staff on the end of her cape. With a slight shudder, the Elegant Elephant turned from the fallen slaves, resolving then and there never to offend this pretty but powerful little metal maiden.

"Well, have the scoundrels dispersed and gone for good?" inquired Thun, sending up his question in a cloud of black smoke. Restively pawing the ground, the Thunder Colt looked from one to the other, waiting for someone to enlighten him.

"Tell him they've gone, but for nobody's good," wheezed Kabumpo, who was still out of breath from the violence of the combat. "Tell him Gludwig the Glubrious has destroyed the Wizard of Ev and that we are now going into the castle to continue the battle."

"But where shall we start?" sighed Randy, staring despondently up at the gay red palace where he and Kabumpo had been so royally entertained on their last visit.

"We'll start at the bottom of these steps," announced Kabumpo grimly, "and mount on up to the top. Then we'll burst into the presence of this wretched wart and fling him out of the window."

"But that won't help Jinnicky if he's at the bottom of the sea," mourned Randy, trying to smile at Planetty, who was busily tapping off instructions to Thun.

"Hah! But don't forget, Jinnicky's a wizard," sniffed Kabumpo, pulling in his belt a few inches, "and nobody can keep a good wizard down. Besides," Kabumpo dragged his robe a bit to the left and straightened his headpiece, "once inside that castle, we can use some of the Red Jinn's own magic to help him."

"Magic? Why, of course, I'd forgotten about that." Randy's face cleared and brightened, and seeing Planetty and Thun so eager and unafraid beside him, he girded on his sword and, standing upright on Kabumpo's back, gave the signal to start. As they trod up the hundred red glass steps, they could hear windows and doors slamming, the patter of running feet and the tinkle of the hundred glass chimes in the tower. But step by step and without a pause, Thun and Kabumpo mounted to the top.

"Beware! Beware, Gludwig the Glubrious! Here march Kabumpty and Thun, Slandy and Planetty, Princess of Anuther Planet. Friends, equals and warriors!" The Thunder Colt's flaming message, floating like a battle emblem in the air, alarmed the wicked occupant of Jinnicky's castle even more than the invaders themselves. But still confident of his power to vanquish all comers, he waited in evil anticipation for the moment when they would force their way into his presence. Did they imagine because they had frightened a company of foolish slaves, they could frighten him?

"Ha, ha!" Crouched on the Red Jinn's throne and laughing mirthlessly, Gludwig rubbed his long hands up and down his skinny knees.

Chapter 13 - Gludwig the Glubrious

"Pss-sst! Wait! Hold on a minute!" As they reached the huge double doors of the red castle, Randy tugged violently at Kabumpo's left ear, for the Elegant Elephant, all humped together, was preparing to bump through. "Let Thun break down the door," directed the young King firmly. "Thun is of metal, and the glass will not cut him; then as soon as there is an opening, we can follow. Will you tell him, Planetty?" Randy looked fondly down at the earnest little Princess. "And as soon as we are inside," he went on hurriedly, "fling your staff at the first person I point out to you."

"That I will," promised Planetty with a brief nod, and giving Thun his orders, she galloped the Thunder colt straight at the glass doors. With a crash like the fall of a hundred trays of dishes, the glass doors shivered into bits. Rushing through the flying splinters, Kabumpo and Thun raced together into the palace.

How well Randy remembered this cozy throne room, its transparent, red, glass pillars and floors, its gay, red, lacquered furniture, its tinkling curtains of strung rubies, and the long line of enormous red vases leading up to the throne. But instead of the jolly little Jinn, encased in his own shining jar, a long, lank, black man in a red wig lounged on the seat of state. He was smoking a tenuous red pipe, and as Kabumpo and Thun came to an abrupt halt before him, he blinked wickedly out from under his bushy red lashes. Besides the red-wigged imposter, Randy noted with some relief, there was not another soul in sight.

"Well," demanded Gludwig insolently, "what do you hope to accomplish by this unwarranted intrusion?" Taking his pipe out of his mouth, he blew a cloud of villainous black smoke into the faces of his visitors. So thick and sulphurous were the fumes, Randy and Kabumpo were rendered speechless. While they choked and spluttered, Planetty, who did not seem aware of the smoke at all, gazed in wide-eyed delight around her. So THIS was a castle!

"How nite, how netiful!" Lost in wonder and admiration, the little Princess forgot all about the stern purpose of their visit.

"Off that throne! Off that throne, you wart!" rasped Kabumpo, clearing his throat with an ear-splitting trumpet. "What have you done with Jinnicky? You're no more a wizard than I am! You're as false and crooked as your wig! Down with him! Down with him, Randy! Let him repent of his wickedness in uttermost disgrace and debasement!"

"So my downfall is the little plan?" Speaking calmly but trembling with fury at Kabumpo's taunting speech, Gludwig rose. At the same instant, Randy, recovering his breath, called desperately.

"Now, Planetty, your staff! Throw it straight at him. Oh, quickly!"

Thun's hot breath was already singing Gludwig's ankles, and leaping over the throne, he crouched down like a great black panther behind it. "Ha, ha!" he shouted again. "My downfall and debasement, is it? Well, try a bit of downfalling and debasement yourselves." Just as Planetty, taking careful aim, hurled her gleaming staff, Gludwig pulled a tremendous lever in the wall beside him. Instantly, the floor on the other side of the throne dropped down, slanting Kabumpo, Thun and both riders into the dark, damp and long-unused cellar of the castle.

"A trap door," raged the Elegant Elephant, coming down like a carload of bricks.

"A trap floor, you mean," gasped Randy, picking himself up with a painful grimace, for the jolt had sent him flying off the elephant. Thun had retained his balance, and neither he nor Planetty seemed to mind the force of their landing. As they gazed angrily upward, the floor of the throne room swung noiselessly back into place, leaving the four prisoners to contemplate the heavy glass beams and panels of its underside.

"So that was the downfall, and this is debasement," grunted Kabumpo, sitting down furiously on an overturned washtub. "Great Grump, I've never been so humiliated in my life. Don't cry, Planetty," he begged gruffly, "we'll have you out of here in a pig's whistle."

"It's not that, Bumpo dear." Planetty buried her face in Thun's cloudy mane and sobbed bitterly. "It's my staff! It did not return after I flung it at the red-wigged one, and without it I have nothing, NOTHING!"

"Good Gollopers!" Randy clapped his hand to his forehead as he realized the awful significance of Planetty's disclosure. "The floor tilted too quickly for it to return, and OH, KABUMPO!" he wailed, almost forgetting he was a King and Warrior. "If Gludwig has that staff, what can we do? He can come down here and petrify us any time he wants."

"We'll hide!" gulped Kabumpo, bounding off the washtub. With furious concentration his small eyes roved round and round their gloomy prison.

"But you're so big," declared Randy, running over to comfort Planetty.

"I'll hide anyway!" said Kabumpo, who had no intention of spending the rest of his life as an iron elephant, or of adorning the palace of Gludwig the Glubrious as the mere image of himself.

Chapter 14 - The Slave of the Magic Dinner Bell

How thankful Randy and Kabumpo were now for the Thunder colt's fiery breath. Otherwise they would have been in almost complete darkness, as scarcely any light at all trickled down through the dark red glass of the cellar windows. And there was small danger of his setting Jinnicky's castle on fire, for the basement, like the rest of the palace, was constructed of thick plates and solid glass. But here below, the glass was not bright and sparkling as it was above stairs. Cobwebs clung to the glass beams, dust powdered the floors, and round the walls in boxes and barrels stood the old or worn-out magic appliances of the Red Jinn. There was no furnace in the cellar, for the castle was warmed in winter by a magic process of Jinnicky's own invention; and there were no doors, not even a closet or cupboard where any of them could hide. With Thun stepping ahead to act as a torch, the others marched anxiously round the great, gloomy, vault-like apartment.

"No place to hide, no provisions, nothing to eat or drink. NOTHING!" exclaimed the Elegant Elephant, sinking down on the washtub. "That is, nothing to do but wait for destruction," he concluded bitterly.

"Well, we're not destroyed yet!" declared Randy, sticking out his chin. "Everything seems quiet above. Maybe Gludwig is not going to use Planetty's staff till morning."

With a discouraged sniff, Kabumpo began poking in the boxes behind him. Finding one full of excelsior, he started to stuff the choking material into his mouth with his trunk. Randy was sure the excelsior would disagree with him, but when Kabumpo was in such a mood, it was quite useless to argue with him; so, beckoning for Thun to light the way, he and Planetty set out on a second tour of investigation.

Randy paused dubiously before a collection of squat bottles and jugs. He was convinced they contained liquids or vapors powerful enough to help them, but the directions on the labels were all in some strange magician's code, and Randy hesitated to open even one of the magic bottles. Experience had taught him that a wizard's wares were dangerous, and he himself had seen the Red Jinn subdue whole armies by releasing incense from a blue jug. So selecting two pocket-size jars to use only in case everything else failed, Randy moved on to the other side of the cellar. Here on top of a chest, he discovered a small red handbag. Instead of the usual fastenings, two real hands formed the clasp, and when

Randy opened the bag, it quickly jerked out of his grasp and began springing all over the cellar on its hands, pouncing gleefully on papers and bottles and stuffing them into its side pockets. It did look so comical, Planetty burst into a peal of merriment. Even Randy could not keep back a grin. It was a relief to see the little Princess more like herself again, for since the loss of her voral staff she had been unnaturally quiet and sad.

"Wait, I'll catch it for you," offered Randy, dismissing for a moment all thought of the dreadful danger they were in. "It must be one of Jinnicky's inventions. Look, Kabumpo, a bag that really packs itself."

"Watch out it doesn't pinch you!" warned Kabumpo morosely. He had already begun to regret the excelsior and was rumbling with indigestion. "I was never one to hold with hand luggage, myself."

"Oh, yes you were!" crowed Randy, falling on the bag as if it had been a football and coming up triumphantly with it clutched to his middle. "You use your trunk for a hand, Kabumpo, and doesn't that make it hand luggage? Hey, hey, hurray! Never thought I'd make a joke in this dismal place!"

"It's a pretty dismal joke, if you ask me." The Elegant Elephant heaved himself stiffly off the washtub. "Keep it away from me!" he warned crossly as Randy, paying no attention to the thumps of the handbag, managed to get it shut again. As soon as it was closed, the bag subsided and seemed absolutely unalive. "Here!" puffed Randy, holding it out to Planetty. "This bag will pack itself, madam, and you can use it every time you go on a journey."

"Can I? How nite!" Planetty beamed at her young companion.

"Well, who's going on a journey?" inquired Kabumpo sarcastically, walking up and down to relieve his indigestion. "We'll probably spend the rest of our unnatural lives in this abominable basement. Say something, can't you?" he shouted, glaring at poor Thun. "I can hardly see where I'm going." As fast as Planetty translated this rude speech, the Thunder Colt sent up his answer.

"If I said all the words I am thinking," puffed Thun temperishly, "this room would be very red bright, Mister Kabumpty, very red bright indeed." The Thunder Colt's speech and his further remarks made Randy and Planetty laugh again.

"Let's see what else we can find," proposed the young King. In spite of Kabumpo's gloomy predictions, he was feeling more hopeful. "Maybe this time we'll turn up something we can really use."

"Oh, maybe yes, maybe yes!" trilled Planetty, slipping swiftly as quicksilver after Randy. Passing by some dusty apparatus and an old spinning wheel, they discovered a huge red drum behind a pile of old trunks. The sticks were struck through a cord in the side, and it was so heavy that the two between them could hardly carry it. But giggling and puffing, they dragged it down into the center of the cellar and dropped it down before Kabumpo.

"See what we have now!" Dusting off his clothes, Randy surveyed it proudly.

"Humph! A DRUM!" The Elegant Elephant moved his ears forward and then back. "Well, what grumpy use is a drum? Am I in a parade? Do you expect me to beat it?"

"Beat the drum?" Planetty looked surprised and shocked. "Is that for what a drum is for, Bumpty, dear?"

"Well, yes, in a way." A bit ashamed of himself, Kabumpo drew out one of the sticks. "It goes like this," he said, raising the drumstick high in his trunk.

"Oh no! Kabumpo, NO! Don't do that or you'll have Gludwig down here! It would make too much noise."

"What if it does?" Kabumpo shrugged his great shoulders. "We may as well perish now as tomorrow. I'm perishing of hunger, anyway." Before Randy could interfere, he brought the drumstick down with a thump that split the taut surface of the drum from edge to edge. The loud rip and BONG made the rafters ring, and scarcely had they recovered from that shock before a small black boy in an enormous turban sprang out of the drum itself and began sobbing and spluttering and hugging Kabumpo as if he never would let him go.

"Good Gillikens! It's Ginger!" panted Randy as Planetty caught him anxiously by the sleeve. "It's the slave of the magic dinner bell. He can bring us dinners and whatever one wants when Jinnicky rings for him. Hi — who shut you up in that drum, boy?"

"That big old Red Wig," sniffed Ginger, drying his tears on Kabumpo's robe. "Oh, how can I ever thank you, Mister Elephant so Elegant! I remember you! I remember him!" The bell boy jerked his thumb delightedly at Randy. "And many times I thank you — fifty times eleven, I thank you. You see, if I am shut up in a drum, it is impossible for me to answer the Master's ring if he needs me. And he needs me now, I know it, I know it!"

"But how can he call you unless he has the dinner bell?" asked Randy, edging closer. "Did Jinnicky take the bell with him when — when —" To save himself, Randy could not finish the dismal sentence.

"When Gludwig pushed him into the sea, you mean?" Ginger's brown face puckered up again, but controlling his sobs with a great effort, he sat down on the edge of the drum and told them the whole story of Jinnicky's mischance and misfortunes. "The Master, as you know," explained Ginger, his eyes rolling sideways as he caught sight of Planetty and Thun, whose like he had never seen in his entire magic existence, "the Master is always kind and jolly and unsuspecting. This Gludwig was the manager of our ruby mines and one of Jinnicky's most trusted officers. But all the time this viper, this snake, this villainous black snake —" Ginger clenched his fists and kicked his heels angrily against the drum "— was planning to steal our Red Jinn's throne and magic, in addition to his own splendid mansion and fortune. One evening, seven moons ago, having trained his miners into an army of rebellion, Gludwig marched upon our castle and drove everybody out."

"Everybody?" The Elegant Elephant, picking Ginger up in his trunk, looked earnestly into his face.

"Every EV body!" repeated the little bell boy, wagging his turban sorrowfully. "Alibabble, the Grand Advizier, all the members of the court and household were sent to the mines under the cruel rule of Glubdo, Gludwig's brother, and they are there now, working without rest, hope or reward. He marched the Master to the head of the highest cliff and pushed him violently into the sea with his OWN hands!" Ginger began to tremble with grief and anger at the memory of it all. "He ordered the bandsmen to seal me up in this drum, knowing a drum is the only place from which I cannot escape, and hoping I would shrivel up and perish. But I —" asserted the little black triumphantly "— I am the best part of Jinnicky's magic, so he couldn't destroy me." A quick grin overspread Ginger's face. "And he could not destroy my Master, either. Of that I am sure, and now that the elephant so elegant has let me out — NOW —"

"Now what?" breathed Randy, almost afraid Ginger was not going to tell him. "You see, Ginger, we came to visit the Red Jinn and were immediately captured and dumped down here ourselves. So how can we get out? And what can we do?"

"I will think of something," promised the bell boy. Wriggling out of Kabumpo's trunk, he scurried across the cellar and disappeared beneath an overturned wheelbarrow.

"So! He will think of something," sniffed Kabumpo, trying not to make it sound too sarcastic. "Well, of course, that settles it. And while he is thinking, I intend to take a nap. I'm completely worn out with all these vile plots and villainies."

"I too will ret," decided Planetty, reaching over to pat the Thunder Colt. The strange excitements of the day had wearied the little Princess, and this last story of Ginger's had still further puzzled and distressed her.

"I never thought when I brought you here you'd have to sleep in a place like this," groaned Randy, glancing ruefully round the dingy basement.

"Oh, it's not so bad," smiled the little Princess. Slipping off her cape, she swung it casually between two grimy pillars, and with the handbag tucked under her arm, climbed contentedly into her silver bed. "Good net, Randy and Bumpo, dear!" she called softly. "I believe I shall ret for a long, long time."

"Now what does she mean by that?" worried the young King as the Princess blew them each a wistful kiss. "Something's wrong, Kabumpo, I feel it! And look there at Thun! Why is he acting so strangely? Almost as if he could not see."

"Look at him! Look at him!" wailed the Elegant Elephant. "Where is he? How can I? It's dark as thunder in here now! Great Grump, Randy, I can't see you, him, or anything at all." Stumbling and tripping, he somehow crossed the cellar to the spot where he remembered Thun had been. Then, as his trunk struck against hard, cold metal, he recoiled in horror. "He's OUT!" moaned the Elegant Elephant hoarsely. "He's not even breathing. Why, he's cold and stiff as a stone. Oh, Good Grump, the colt saved my life, and now what can I do for him? What'll we do, Randy? I say, what'll we DO?"

Randy had no answer at all, for, moved by a dreadful foreboding, he leaned down to touch the face of the little Princess of Anuther Planet only to find it still and cold. No sparkling light radiated from Planetty now as, quiet and motionless as a statue, she lay wrapped in her silver nets. "Ginger, where are you? Ginger, come help us!" Randy screamed desperately. Scrambling out from under the 'barrow, the startled bell boy reached Randy's side in a split second, for Ginger could see as well in the dark as in the daytime.

"Did — Gludwig — do — this?" he panted, his eyes rolling wildly from Planetty to the frozen Thunder Colt.

"No, no, they are far from their own country and need the powerful Vanadium springs," groaned Kabumpo, putting out his trunk to touch the little Princess. "They cannot exist down here. And with Jinnicky gone, who's to help them?" His tears fell thick and fast on Planetty's silver tresses.

"Then why do we stay here?" shuddered Ginger, tugging at Randy's cloak and Kabumpo's robe. "Why do we stay?"

As if to answer Ginger's mournful cry, there was a long whistling rustle in the air, and next moment Randy, Ginger, Kabumpo and the Princess of Anuther Planet were wafted like feathers through the night, passing easily as mist through the narrow glass windows, up over the castle itself, and out over the silvery moonlit sea.

Chapter 13 - Nonagon Island

The same afternoon the four travelers arrived at the Red Jinn's castle, a lonely fisherman in an odd nine-sided dory pulled out from Nonagon Isle. This strange, small, nine-sided island lies about ninety leagues from the mainland of Ev. Flat, barren and rocky, it affords but a meager living to the nine fishermen who are its sole inhabitants. Each keeps strictly to his own side of the island, subsisting frugally on fish and the few poor vegetables he can grow in his rocky little garden. Hard and unfriendly as their island itself, the nine Nonagons go their own ways, exchanging brief nods on the rare occasions when they meet one another.

The habit of silence had so grown upon Bloff, the fisherman in the nine-sided dory, he did not even talk to the cat who shared his rough dwelling and accompanied him on all of his fishing trips. And so accustomed was poor Nina to her gruff and taciturn master that she expected nothing from him but an occasional kick or fish head. Never sure which would be forthcoming, she kept her green eyes watchfully upon him at all times. This afternoon she was certain it would be a fish head, and as Bloff reached the spot where he had set his nets, her tail began to wave gently in pleasant anticipation.

Bloff himself seemed a little less grim, for the net seemed quite heavy, and sure he had made a good haul, he began pulling on the lines. But when his net came wet and dripping over the side of the boat, he gave a grunt of anger. In it were only three small fish and an immense red jug. His first impulse was to toss the jug back into the sea, but reflecting grumpily that he could use it to salt down fish for the winter, he rolled it into the bottom of the boat and, kicking the disappointed cat out of the way, rowed rapidly back to the island.

Stamping into his nine-sided shack with the net over his shoulder, Bloff banged the jug down on the hearth, cleaned and cut up the fish and popped them into a pot hung on a crane over the fire. Then, lighting his one poor lamp, he sat sullenly down to wait for his supper. The fish heads he flung cruelly into the hot ashes, and whenever he dozed for a moment, Nina tried to pull one out with her paw, for she knew full well she would get nothing else to eat.

For perhaps an hour there was not a sound in the fisherman's hut except the crackling of the driftwood in the grate and the hoarse breathing of the fisherman himself. Then suddenly Nina, who had almost succeeded in dragging her supper from the flames, gave a frightened backward leap.

"Oh, my, mercy me! Mercy me!" came a muffled but merry voice. "Where, but where am I now?" As Nina and her master turned startled eyes toward the red jug — for the voice was undoubtedly coming from the jug — the lid slowly lifted, and a round jolly face peered out at them. What he saw was so discouraging, Jinnicky — for of course it was Jinnicky — dropped back out of sight. The magic fluid with which he had sealed himself in the jug before Gludwig hurled him into the sea had been melted by the warmth of the fisherman's fire, and the same warmth had restored the little Red Jinn to his usual vigor and liveliness. In a sort of protective stupor he had managed to survive the long months at the bottom of the ocean. A quick thinker at all times, Jinnicky rapidly regained his senses and realized at once what had happened. A fortunate tide had carried him into this fisherman's net, and at last he was on dry land again; and NOW to find and face the villain who had usurped his throne and castle. "But why, why—" groaned the little Jinn dolefully — "with all the fishermen in the Nonestic Ocean, did I have to be pulled out by this long-jawed fellow?"

Venturing another look and at the same time thrusting his arms and legs out of their proper apertures in the jug, he saw that Bloff had seized an oar and seemed about ready to whack it down on his head. "Non, non, NON! My good fellow!" puffed Jinnicky, fixing his rescuer with his bright glassy eye. "Put up your oar. This is no battle, and I have much to say that will interest you, but first of all I want to thank you for pulling me out of the ocean. Heartily! Heartily! A suitable reward will be sent you as soon as I get back — er — get back my castle."

To this polite speech Bloff paid no attention whatsoever, but Nina, liking the pleasant voice of this curious visitor, began rubbing herself against his ankles. "I am the Red Jinn of Ev!" announced the little Wizard, keeping a wary eye on the oar. "At present banished from my castle by the treachery of a trusted officer. In fact," Jinnicky tapped himself smartly on the jar, "this villain actually took everything I had and tossed me into the sea."

"What's wrong with the sea?" inquired the fisherman hoarsely. Never having seen anyone in his whole life but the eight other Nonagon Islanders, Bloff did not really believe what he saw now. "I'm asleep and having a nightmare," he concluded, grasping the oar more determinedly still. And we can hardly blame him, for a fellow whose body is a huge red vase into which he can draw his arms, legs and head at will is pretty hard for anyone to believe. Realizing he was getting nowhere and that his grim and dour rescuer cared nothing about his troubles, past or present, Jinnicky decided to try another line.

"Perhaps you could tell me the name of this place and your own name," he murmured politely.

"I am Bloff, my cat is Nina, and this is the Nonagon Island," announced the fisherman, frowning at the little Wizard.

"Ah, a nine-sided island!" The Red Jinn stretched his arms and hopped up and down to get the kinks out of his legs. "And I see you have a nine-sided cottage and a cat with nine lives."

Picking up poor skinny Nina, who was purring for the first time in her life, Jinnicky stroked her back thoughtfully as he counted the nine pieces of furniture in the rude hut, noted that it was nine o'clock and the ninth of May. "But is NINE my lucky number?" he pondered wearily. Could this churlish fisherman ever be persuaded to sail him back to the mainland? Looking at Bloff out of the side of his eye, he very much doubted it. Though Bloff had put down the oar, his manner was anything but cordial.

"Are there any other people on the island?" asked Jinnicky, more to keep up the conversation that because he really wanted to know.

At his question Bloff put back his head and in a long, singsong voice drawled, "Bluff, Bliff, Bleef, Blaff, Bloof, Blaaf, Bleof and Bluof!"

"Oh, my! Mercy me!" At each name Jinnicky gave a little jump, and as Bloff came to the end of the list he seated himself gingerly on the edge of the bench and stared into the fire. What could he hope from such people? Then suddenly in the midst of his worries he became aware of the fish chowder bubbling cozily on the crane and realized at the same instant his enormous and devouring hunger. After all, you know he had not eaten for seven months.

"Ah!" he beamed, extending both arms toward his host, "DINNER!"

"MY dinner." The two words were spoken so gruffly, Jinnicky's heart fell with a loud clunk into his boots. Why, this was unbelievable! He, Jinnicky, the one and only Wizard of Ev, to be flouted and insulted by a miserable fisherman. Well, at least he could leave the fellow's miserable hut and try his luck with the other Islanders. Reflecting sadly that a wizard without his magic is no better off than any other man, the Red Jinn slid off the bench and started for the door, trying to walk in a calm and dignified manner. But halfway there, a sharp grunt brought him up short.

"Aho, no you don't," rasped Bloff, catching up with him in two strides. "Where do you think you're going? STOP! I need that jug to salt my fish. Here, give it to me."

"Why, you, you miserable mollusk, don't you dare touch me!" panted the Red Jinn, trying to beat off the fisherman with his puny hands. "This jug is an important part of me. Without my jug I cannot live at all."

"And do you think I care for that?" sneered Bloff. "You're just an old lobster in a pot to me. Here, give me that jug!"

Seizing Jinnicky by both arms, Bloff tried to shake him out of the jug. Nina, enraged at such barbarous treatment of the only one who had ever been kind to her, proved an unexpected ally. Flying at the fisherman, she began to scratch and claw his face and hands so successfully that Bloff had to drop Jinnicky to grab the cat. The force of the drop sent the Red Jinn rolling over and over, dislodging a small silver bell from a hidden pocket in his sleeve. As the bell fell tinkling to the flagstones, Jinnicky gave a bounce of relief. His magic dinner bell, and up his sleeve all the time! How had he ever forgotten it? Oh, now, now, if Ginger had not been destroyed by Gludwig and just answered the bell, everything would be different. And Ginger DID answer the bell, and everything WAS different! My, yes. So different that Bloff threw the cat at Jinnicky and simply raced for the door. No wonder, in his small, nine-sided shack were now an elephant carrying a silvery Princess in his trunk, a black boy in a tall turban, and a white boy in a sparkling crown. With one more terrified glance, Bloff took to his heels and never stopped running till he was waist high in the Nonestic Ocean.

Chapter 16 - All Together at Last

"Kabumpo! Kabumpo! Randy! Oh, my mercy me!" Rolling to his feet, Jinnicky tottered over to the hearth, and encountering Ginger halfway there, clasped his faithful Bell Boy to his shiny glass bosom. "As soon as that bell rang I knew everything was going to be better," he puffed. "And I rather expected Ginger, but YOU! Why, my dear old Gagoscis, fancy meeting YOU here!"

"But I don't fancy it at all," grunted Kabumpo, placing the sleeping Princess gently down on the fisherman's bench and glancing disgustedly round the mean little hut. "How in Ev did you ever happen to be in such a place, how did you get here, and where in Oz are we, anyway?"

"Oh, Jinnicky, are you really all right?" Grasping the little Wizard by both arms, Randy examined him carefully from top to toe. "Kabumpo and I came to see you, and instead of you there was Gludwig in your castle. He told us you were at the bottom of the sea, and after first trying to destroy us with his army, he flung us into the castle basement.

There we found Ginger sealed up in a big drum, and we let him out, and after a while, in a way I cannot figure out at all, we find ourselves here. How did it happen?"

"Why, Ginger brought you, of course." Releasing the little black boy from his tight embrace, Jinnicky planted a huge kiss on his ebony forehead, and with a flashing grin the slave of the bell vanished into space. "Don't worry! He's always going, but he'll come back any time I ring the bell. You must all have been touching Ginger when the bell rang, so naturally when Ginger answered the bell he brought you right along."

"Nothing natural about it," fumed Kabumpo, drawing his trunk wearily across his forehead.

"But you haven't told us how YOU got here," said Randy, bending over Planetty to see that she had made the trip without coming to any harm.

"And what is that, pray?" demanded the little Jinn, eyeing the sleeping Princess with round, astonished eyes. "Something you brought me for a present? A pretty little idol you've stolen from some heathen temple? My, mercy me! What a beauty it is! I'll mount it on a ruby pedestal and worship it all the rest of my days!"

"Oh, no, Jinnicky, no!" Randy's voice broke, and he could not utter another word, try as he would. In puzzled concern the Red Jinn turned to Kabumpo.

"She's not a present, but she's an idol, all right — Randy's idol — and he intends to spend the rest of his life worshiping her, if I read the signals aright," said Kabumpo dryly. "There you see the Princess of Anuther Planet, old boy, and up to an hour ago she was as live and bright and happy as any of us."

"But what happened to her? Oh, my, mercy me, another mystery!" Jinnicky clasped his hands in genuine distress.

"Well, you tell us what happened to you, and then we'll tell you what happened to her and us," offered Kabumpo. "That is, if we don't die of hunger first."

"Hunger?" Jinnicky swallowed four times in rapid succession. "Oh, my, mercy me and us! You do not even know the meaning of the word! I have not eaten a bite for seven months! But, har, har, har! That is all over now. With my magic dinner bell right at hand, why should anyone be hungry? Four dinners and at once," beamed the Red Jinn, ringing it smartly. "See, my dear, I've not even forgotten you." Jinnicky leaned down to stroke Nina, who had hidden behind the hearth brush when so many strangers came dropping into the hut. "This valiant Nonagon Puss fought bravely in my defense and has thereby earned herself a place in my heart and castle for all the rest of her nine natural lives."

"But first you must get back to your castle," said Kabumpo as Jinnicky began dancing up and down the room, the miserable cat hugged tightly in his arms. Even Randy had to smile at that. No one could be around the little Jinn and stay sorrowful, and worried as he was over Planetty and Thun, the young King could not help feeling that now they were together everything was going to turn out right. Some how and way, Jinnicky would help them.

"Isn't this like old times?" he beamed, bustling around like a busy host as Ginger, with four enormous trays balanced on his head, flashed down, set an appetizing dinner before each of the company, and melted away like smoke up the chimney. For Nina he had brought nine saucers of cream and some minced chicken. For Kabumpo, a huge bowl of assorted nuts and another bowl of cut raw vegetables, each bowl capable of replenishing itself so that there was enough for even an elephant. For Randy and Jinnicky there were the finest of roast duck dinners. So forgetting their mean surrounding and Gludwig's wickedness, the three Royal Wayfarers fell to and ate with an abandon and gusto that would have astonished their own castleholds and footmen. Nina, lapping up her rich and plenteous viands, seemed to grow fat and content before their very eyes. And while they dined, Jinnicky explained how he had been tricked by Gludwig, pulled out of the sea by Bloff, and then nearly shaken out of his jar by the surly fisherman, who at the same time had shaken out the bell and brought him assistance.

"Where is he? Wait till I get my trunk on him," raged Kabumpo, glancing sharply round the nine-sided shack. Jinnicky, on his part, when he discovered how Gludwig had treated his friends and visitors, was no less enraged and indignant.

"Used my very own patented trap floor on you, did he? Hah! Wait — I'll fix him!" Beating his small hands angrily together, Jinnicky's eyes burned with a bright red hatred.

"Yes, we were floored, all right," admitted the Elegant Elephant, pushing away his two bowls, for at last he had had enough, and while Randy and the Red Jinn were finishing their suppers he told the whole story of their journey through Oz and Ev and Ix, of their meeting with Planetty and Thun and the sad fate that had overtaken these loyal comrades in the Red Castle when they could no longer avail themselves of their own Vanadium Springs.

"Vanadium?" murmured the Red Jinn, resting his head in his chubby hands. "I believe I could make a substitute for that. Why, in my laboratory—"

"Yes, but this isn't your laboratory," sighed Randy, "and how ever are we to get off this nine-sided island if all the fishermen are as hateful as Bloff?"

"Har! Har! Har! Now that is the least of our troubles." Jinnicky waved airily to the owner of the cottage whose glum face had just appeared in the window. "Ginger shall carry us back, as easily as he carries the trays! First I shall ring the dinner bell, then when Ginger appears I shall hang on to his coat; you, Randy, must hang on to me, and Kabumpo, bless his big heart, shall hang on to you, being careful to hold the Princess of this Other Planet in his trunk. Oh, my, mercy me! I'd almost forgotten the cat."

Scooping up Nina, Jinnicky waited till the Elegant Elephant had lifted Planetty in his trunk. Then, taking the silver bell from his sleeve, he gave it a cheerful tinkle. "Ho, this!" puffed the little Jinn, blowing a kiss to the glowering fisherman, "This is the finest place to leave I've ever left in my whole life. Oh, my, mercy me! You and us! Here's Ginger! Hold on, everybody! We're OFF!"

And they were, sailing along as smoothly behind the little slave of the bell as if they weighed nothing at all, and leaving Bloff running in frantic circles round his hut, for he was now more convinced than ever that this was a nightmare or that, worse still, he had taken entire leave of his wits and senses.

Chapter 17 - In the Red Jinn's Castle

While Jinnicky and his friends had been having all these ups and downs and hair-raising experiences, Gludwig had passed an exceedingly pleasant and profitable evening. As his enemies had dropped into the cellar of the castle, the silver staff of Planetty missing him by a wide margin had fallen harmlessly at his feet. Gludwig's army had had much to say about this terrible weapon, and picking it up he turned it gloatingly over and over in his hands. It is true that he had all of Jinnicky's treasures and possessions, but in his whole seven months in the castle he had not discovered a way to use any of the Red Jinn's magic or able to cast a single spell or transformation. This had taken half the zest out of his victory. But here he had a simple and easily managed magic weapon — or had he?

Frowning suddenly, Gludwig wondered whether it only worked for the silver war maiden who had used it so disastrously against his men. Well, he would quickly find that out. Stepping to the door, he whistled for the huge hound that guarded the outer passageway. As it came bounding to his side, he hurled the silver staff at its head. As the staff struck, the hound's progress was instantly arrested, and instead of a live dog he had a life-sized bronze with a look in the eyes that made even Gludwig turn away. But the staff did work! As it returned to his black hand, Gludwig hurried out of the throne room, rushing here and there about the castle to cast the staff again and again at his unsuspecting aids and servants.

"Are you mad?" hissed Glubdo, coming upon his brother in the act of petrifying a small boot boy. "If you continue in this reckless fashion, who will do the work or wait upon us?"

"Oh, I've only tried it on a dozen or so," said Gludwig, holding the staff jealously behind his back. "Mind you don't overstep your authority, brother, or I might be tempted to use it on you." Chuckling wickedly at Glubdo's shocked expression, Gludwig mounted to his own quarters and hastily throwing off his clothes, curled up in Jinnicky's sumptuous ruby-trimmed four-poster. He was too weary to descend to the cellar and deal with his enemies, and resolving to finish them off the first thing in the morning, the miserable imposter fell asleep, Planetty's magic staff clutched tightly in his hands.

While he slumbered, strange things were happening below stairs, for just as the clock in the tower tolled two, Ginger noiselessly set his royal passengers down in the deserted throne room and vanished away with a flashing smile.

Snapping on a ruby lamp, the Red Jinn looked around him with a long sigh of content. Motioning for Kabumpo to place the sleeping Princess on his comfortable cushioned throne, he tiptoed about, touching one after another of his possessions.

"Where do you suppose he is?" whispered Randy, treading close behind him.

"I don't suppose, I know," Jinnicky whispered back. "Where would he be but in my own royal bed? Come along, we'll take him by surprise and the ears and throw him out of the window. Careful now, boys, step softly! Confound the black-hearted scoundrel! He's been using the silver staff." Sorrowfully, the little Jinn paused before the statue of his favorite dog.

"Never mind," comforted Randy. "When you find a way to restore Planetty, she'll find a way to undo this mischief, and you know you still have Nina."

"Yes," said Jinnicky, placing the Nonagon cat tenderly on a red cushion. "Come on, then, we'll creep up on him. Nobody's around, nobody's on guard, this should be easy." Stepping softly up the broad stair, Kabumpo as lightly as any of them, the three made their way to Jinnicky's vast bedroom.

"Leave him to me," begged the Elegant Elephant in a fierce whisper. "I'll wring his neck with my own trunk."

"No, wait. I'll ring my dinner bell," puffed Jinnicky, "and have Ginger carry him to the other side of the Nonestic Ocean."

"Even that wouldn't be far enough," muttered Randy, tiptoeing over to the bed. "If we just knew where he had hidden Planetty's staff, we could turn him into a big brass monkey, for that's just what he looks like."

"Ho! I do, do I?" The unexpected interruption made them all jump. Gludwig, wakened by Kabumpo's first whisper, had lain silently watching from beneath his long lashes. Now, tossing back the silk covers, he sprang up, throwing the staff straight at Randy's heart.

"Now let's see what you'll turn to," he panted savagely.

Too startled to move or act, Kabumpo and Jinnicky watched in fascinated horror as the staff struck. And strike it did, but instead of petrifying Randy, the rod passed like a flash of lightning through the young King's body and returned to Gludwig's hand, leaving Randy live and lively as ever he was, lively enough in fact to leap forward, snatch the dangerous weapon, and bring it down hard on his red-wigged head. With a thud that splintered Jinnicky's best bed, Gludwig fell back.

"Hah! What did I tell you?" exclaimed Randy, and indeed the former holder of the castle in his petrified condition looks as much like a brass monkey as Randy had said he would.

"Oh, my, mercy me! Oh, my! Oh, me!" With trembling fingers, the Red Jinn began to feel Randy all over. "With my own eyes I saw that staff go through you, lad, yet here you are — no mark, no statue. I declare, I'm —" With tears running down his nose, Jinnicky embraced Randy over and over.

"Out of that bed with you!" screamed Kabumpo, "OUT!" And winding his trunk round the rigid Gludwig, he flung him violently out of the window. As the image fell with a resounding clunk into the vegetable garden below, the Elegant Elephant sank on his haunches and mopped his brow with one of the red silk bed sheets. "Never, never do I hope to live through such a moment again," he groaned, blowing his trunk explosively. "I thought you were frozen and done for, my boy — done for!" Rocking to and fro, Kabumpo blinked the tears out of his eyes.

"I don't understand yet why I wasn't," admitted Randy, wriggling out of Jinnicky's grasp and touching the spot where the staff had struck him.

"Someone or something was protecting you," declared the little Jinn, nodding his head like a mandarin. "Do you carry any charms or talismans against evil, my boy?"

"Not a one." Turning out his pockets, Randy displayed a collection of knives, rubber bands, coins, and the other odds and ends that a man usually stores in his pockets. Among the strange assortment were two small, squat jars, and on these Jinnicky pounced with a triumphant little crow.

"Why, Randy Spandy Jack a Dandy, you have two bottles of my best weapon-turning elixir! How did you happen to have them?"

"Those?" Randy squinted down at the bottles in positive mystification. "Oh, I must have picked them up in the cellar. Of course I did, I remember distinctly now."

"Oh, glory be! Glory me! Har, har, har! Am I a good wizard or am I a good wizard? And to think you should have happened on the very thing you'd be needing." Jinnicky danced in exuberant circles.

"Sh-hush! Somebody's coming." Crowding all his belongings back into his pocket, Randy turned in alarm. Half the courtiers and servants were crowded into the doorway. And when they saw Jinnicky and his friends instead of Gludwig in the Royal Apartment, they began to back away in chagrin and embarrassment.

"Oh, it's all right." Jinnicky waved airily. "You threw in your fortunes with the wrong man, that's all! You'll find Gludwig below in the cabbages. But I forgive you! I forgive you!" he added impulsively as his former mine workers began to stammer apologies and excuses. "Go back to your beds now, but see that breakfast is on time and hot and appetizing." With an impatient nod of his head, Jinnicky dismissed them, and looking very downcast and crestfallen they hurried away.

It was a long time before the Red Jinn and his rescuers could bring themselves to retire. There was so much to talk of, to wonder over and to plan. But finally, even Randy acknowledged that he was sleepy, and confident that Jinnicky would find some way to help Planetty and Thun in the morning, he curled up on a small red sofa and fell into a peaceful slumber. As for Kabumpo, he stretched out on the floor, and Jinnicky, not caring to occupy a bed so recently slept in by Gludwig, made himself comfortable on a bear rug beside the Elegant Elephant, enjoying the first real rest he had had in seven long months.

Chapter 18 - The Red Jinn Restored

Word of his return had quickly spread through the Red Jinn's vast dominions, and when Jinnicky and his guests descended next morning, a whole loyal black legion were cheering from the courtyard and lined up along the shore. After Gludwig had seized the castle and enslaved the household, the rest of the natives had fled for their lives, refusing to stay or acknowledge the red-wigged imposter as their ruler. Now that Jinnicky was restored and safely at home again, their joy knew no bounds. Appearing briefly on one of the castle balconies, the Red Jinn made one of his best and merriest speeches, telling of his experiences and assuring his faithful flock that Gludwig was gone and would trouble them no more. To prove his statement, he pointed to the fallen figure in the cabbage patch. Glubdo, fearing Jinnicky's anger, had already left for an unknown destination, and now there was nothing to be done but restore the Kingdom to its former cheerful status and prosperity.

While the Red Jinn, Kabumpo, Randy and Nina breakfasted happily on the terrace, a willing delegation marched off to the ruby mines to release Alibabble, the courtiers and servants from their long servitude. The miners who had taken their place in the castle and army were only too willing to return to the mines, for with Jinnicky back in power their hours were short, their wages high, and each miner had his own cozy cottage and garden. The petrified miners who had served in the army that issued out to capture Randy and Kabumpo were stood along the highways to act as signposts and also as warning to all of the hard fate awaiting those who lent their ears to treachery and their arms to rebellion. Randy could hardly contain himself while all these necessary matters were attended to. The young monarch spent nearly all his time arranging and rearranging the cushions on Jinnicky's throne, where Planetty still lay in complete beauty and insensibility. Kabumpo was almost as bad, pacing anxiously between the throne and the terrace where Thun had been carried by fifty interested blacks.

"Even if I cannot bring them back to life and activity, they are a handsome addition to any castle," puffed Jinnicky, sinking down at last on one of his red lacquer sofas and fanning himself rapidly with his lid. "Oh, my mercy me! Don't look at me that way, my boy! Of course I'll do my best and double best. But suppose my best is not good enough?"

"Oh, it will be," declared Kabumpo, giving the Red Jinn a pat on the back with his trunk. "I'll bet on your red magic any day in the year. Look at the way that elixir saved Randy from the magic staff. Where is Planetty's staff, by the way? Sort of dangerous to leave it about!"

"It's locked up safely in my iron cabinet," said Jinnicky, closing one eye. "So you really think I'm good, old Gaboscis — better even than the Wizard of Oz, eh?"

"Oh, much," asserted the Elegant Elephant, wagging his head positively.

"All right, then, leave me — leave me," begged the Red Jinn, fairly pushing them out of the throne room. "I've ordered all my magic brought to me here, and here I'll stay till this pretty little Princess and her charger come out of this metal trance. My, mercy me! Trance — entrance

— entrancing. Oh, har, har, har! I've an idea there, my boys!" Bouncing off the sofa, Jinnicky skipped over to the Princess of Anuther Planet.

"Oh, Kabumpo! Do you think he really has?" whispered Randy as he and the Elegant Elephant hurried through the door of the throne room and closed it safely behind them.

Chapter 19 - Red Magic

The hours Randy and Kabumpo spent waiting for Jinnicky to summon them to his throne room were the longest and most anxious they had ever endured.

"Even if he does restore them," groaned Randy, pacing feverishly up and down one of the garden paths, "he'll have to send them straight back to Anuther Planet." Rumpling up his hair, he looked wildly back at the Elegant Elephant, who was just behind him. "And if they go," declared the young King in a desperate voice, "I warn you, Kabumpo, I shall jump on Thun's back and go with them."

"What? And leave ME?" gasped the Elegant Elephant, putting back his ears, "And your Kingdom and friends and all your responsibilities? No, no, Randy, this won't do. Besides, you'd probably perish in that outlandish metal wilderness with nothing to eat and no place to rest your head. You can't do it, my boy, and furthermore, I won't let you."

Snatching Randy up in his trunk, he held him as tightly as if he were already running away instead of threatening to do so. In the course of this bitter argument and as the young monarch began pummeling Kabumpo futilely with his fists, they were both lifted bodily into the air and set swiftly down in the Red Throne Room.

"The Master has good news for you," explained Ginger. "LOOK!" With his flashing white grin, the little bell boy pointed to the throne itself and then, as was his wont, inexplicably vanished. What he saw made Randy rush forward and fling both arms round the Red Jinn's neck.

"Oh, you did it! You really did it!" he cried, embracing Jinnicky all over again. "How can I ever thank you enough?"

"Where am I?" murmured the clear, silvery voice that Kabumpo and Randy knew so well. "Oh, what a netiful, netiful castle. Randy! Randy! And there you are, Big Bumpo, and Thun! But how did we come out of that debasement?"

Without bothering to answer, Randy seized Planetty's hands and looked and looked at her as if he were never going to stop. "You're the same, and yet different," he mused, scarcely able to believe what he saw. "And Thun is the same, yet different, too."

"I am Thun the Thunder Colt, now, then, and always!" announced Thun, and gave a frightened jump, for he had actually spoken the words at the same time they went spiraling up into a sparkling sentence over his head. "Oh, Princess, Princess!" he whinnied joyously. "Do you hear? Do you see? I can talk, I can hear, I can see and hear myself talking!" At each word Thun gave an ecstatic bound and then began racing madly round and round the throne room, in and out between the red pillars, leaping over chairs and tables in a positively hair-raising fashion.

"Oh, my! Oh, my mercy me!" faltered Jinnicky, and scooping up the Nonagon Cat, he jumped up on a red tabouret. "Stop him, somebody! Stop him!"

"Whoa, there! Come back here, Thun, come back; we want to look at you!" Running after the Thunder Colt, Randy caught him by his plumy tail and hung on till he actually did stop.

"And he doesn't make a sound when he gallops — not a sound," marveled Jinnicky, edging nervously over to his throne and taking a seat beside Planetty. "A sound but soundless steed! Har, har, har! And do not mind his breath, Randy, it cannot burn you now; it's cold fire and will not singe a thing!"

"But how did you do it?" demanded Kabumpo, touching Planetty lightly with his trunk.

"Oh, partly by my red incense, partly by my red reanimating rays, and partly by an old incantation against entrancery," explained Jinnicky as Randy brought Thun back and handed him over to Planetty. "Do you feel all right now, my dear, and as beautiful as you look?"

"Oh, yes! Oh, very yes!" answered Planetty, smiling shyly round at the Red Jinn. "And you, I know it now, you must be the Wizard so wonderful of Ev?"

"Wonderful! Wonderful? Well, I should say hay hurray!" Randy threw his crown up in the air and caught it. "Wonderful enough to save himself and us too. Oh, SO many things have happened, Planetty, since you and Thun turned to cold metal in that awful cellar!"

"I must make a note," muttered Jinnicky, patting Thun rather cautiously on the neck. "I must make a note to clean and cheer up that cellar. My! Mercy! Me! I haven't been down there for years!"

"And if I never see it again, it will still be too soon," grunted Kabumpo, leaning up against a red pillar. "Look, Jinnicky," he muttered out of a corner of his mouth as Randy and Planetty moved over to one of the windows and Randy began to tell the little Princess all that had happened on Nonagon Isle and Thun began kicking up his heels and talking to himself just for the fun of the thing. "Look, will those two have to go straight back to their own planet?"

"That is what is worrying me," Jinnicky said, speaking behind one hand and patting his hound, also released from its enchantment, with the other. "I managed to reawaken and reanimate them, but as you've probably noticed, they are changed. Most certainly they are alive, but no longer of living metal, see? The girl's hair is no longer of fine spun metal strands, but it is real hair, still silvery in color as her skin retains its iridescent sheen, but I'm very much afraid, as things are, that the Princess and her colt are unfitted for life on that far and rigorous planet of theirs. Yes," Jinnicky nodded his head emphatically, "I'm very much afraid they'll have to content themselves down here and live, eat and behave generally as natives of Oz or Ev."

"WHAT?" trumpeted Kabumpo so fiercely Nina jumped out of Jinnicky's arms and hid under the red throne. "Oh, say it again!" he begged, swallowing convulsively. "Great Grump, why, this is the best news I've heard since you've come up out of the sea."

"You mean they won't care?" exclaimed the Red Jinn, rubbing his palms nervously together.

"Care!" spluttered Kabumpo, waving his trunk toward the small red sofa where Randy and Planetty sat in rapt and earnest conversation. "They care for nothing but each other, old fellow. Right there, my dear Wizard, sits the future Queen of Regalia, or I'm a blue-bearded Nannygoat!"

"Oh, my, mercy me! You don't say! Oh, har, har, har! How delightful! Why, this calls for a celebration, a feast, and a fiesta." Beaming with interest and benevolence, Jinnicky banged on the side of his throne with both fists and his elbows. "Prepare a feast," he ordered breathlessly as Alibabble, his Grand Advizier, entered in a calm and dignified manner, showing no ill effects from his long months of servitude in the ruby mines. "Prepare a feast, Old Tollywog, there's to be a wedding, with rings, bells, palms, presents and all the fruity fixings."

"A wedding?" Alibabble looked sternly at his master, whom he instantly suspected of being the groom, then as the Red Jinn, grinning wickedly, waved to the engrossed pair on the red sofa, he nodded briefly. "In that event," he remarked, backing rapidly away as he spoke, "I earnestly advise your Majesty to have a haircut."

"Oh, my mercy me! Did you hear that?" screamed the Jinn as he turned to Kabumpo, his face very red and angry.

"I certainly did," roared the Elegant Elephant, giving Jinnicky a playful little push. "Hasn't changed a bit, has he? And neither have you. The last time I was in this castle he was advising the very same thing."

"That's all he ever thinks of," fumed Jinnicky, fingering his long locks lovingly. Then as his eye rested again on the happy little Princess and the prancing Thunder Colt, his expression grew milder. "Randy! RANDY!" he called, jerking his thumb imperiously at his royal guest. "See here, my boy," he explained, puffing out his cheeks importantly as Randy came to stand beside the throne, "I have done MY part to save your little Princess, and now you must do yours! Unfortunately," Jinnicky's face grew long and dolorous, "unfortunately, Planetty and Thun, from this time on, will be unable to exist on Anuther Planet, so now, without a home or country, what will become of them?" In mock distress, the Red Jinn stared down at his young friend.

"Oh, Jinnicky! How wonderful! Oh, Jinnicky, do you mean it? Thank you! Thank you! THANK YOU!" Pressing the little Jinn's hands, Randy went racing across the throne room. "Planetty," he whispered breathlessly in the little Princess's ear, "how would you like to be Queen of Regalia, to go back to Oz with Thun, Kabumpo and me and live in my castle for always?"

"Oh, I think —" Planetty's soft yellow eyes fairly danced with surprise and happiness "— I think that would be very nite. Oh, Randy, that would be netiful, netiful!"

Chapter 20 - King and Queen of Regalia

The feast to celebrate Randy's and Planetty's wedding was the grandest and merriest in all the merry annals of Oz and Ev. It was, in fact, a double celebration. The Red Jinn's return and his victory over Gludwig was enough to keep his subjects cheering for days, and to honor his rescuers and especially the little Princess of Anuther Planet and her royal consort, the Evians outdid themselves, putting on one show after another. There were parades and pageants, fireworks and speeches, and so many presents and parties it makes me jealous just to think of them. Over and over again Planetty and Thun rejoiced in their new life and way of living, and eating the delicacies prepared by Jinnicky's chef was not the least of its privileges. In the Red Jinn's castle, eating was a pleasure as well as a necessity. But after a month's merry stay, during which every point of interest in Jinnicky's vast realm was visited, the travelers bade the little Jinn a hearty and affectionate adieu.

Mounting Kabumpo and Thun and laden with gifts and good wishes, the young King and Queen set out for the Land of Oz and their own royal castle. Uncle Hoochafoo had already received his instructions, and as Randy had predicted, things were very gay, very different, and very cozy in that regal and mountainous little Kingdom. Planetty's staff, powerful as ever, was a great help and protection to the young rulers, and the small red handbag that packed itself went on many journeys with the little Queen of the country.

If this story were the beginning instead of ending, I could tell you a whole book of adventures they had traveling with Kabumpo and Thun through the great Land of Oz, for these days the Elegant Elephant spends almost as much time with Randy and Planetty as he does with the Royal Family of Pumperdink, and most of it in travel. And in Oz, what a gay way one travels! The other morning as I lay dreaming of them all, I got to thinking how nite it would be if the horses on milk wagons here were all soundless gallopers like Thun!

The End

Ozoplaning with the Wizard

of  Oz

by Ruth Plumly Thompson

Chapter 1 - At Home with the Wizard of Oz

In his big, brightly lighted laboratory back of the throne room, the Wizard of Oz paced impatiently forth and back, his hands clasped tightly behind him. Every minute or two he would glance at the clock or dart over to peer out to the already-darkening garden.

"Are you sure you told them all, Jellia? Are you sure you told them tonight?" he asked, turning to the pretty little serving maid who was setting a table near the fire, for the fall evening was quite cool and frosty.

"Four, five, six, seven—" Jellia, counting places, nodded her head firmly to answer the Wizard's question, then stepped back to regard her handiwork with complete satisfaction. "Oh, doesn't that tiny house in the center look too cute and cunningish? Real smoke coming out of the chimney, too. How ever did you manage it, Wiz? And having those silver slippers at each place for nuts and candies is just plain beautiful."

"Do you really think so?" The little Wizard positively blushed with pleasure. "Well, ye see, Jellia, this party is to celebrate Dorothy's first trip to the Emerald City. That is an exact model of the house in which she blew from Kansas to Oz in a cyclone, the house that fell on the Wicked Witch of the West and destroyed her, all but her silver slippers. Remember?"

"Ho, everybody remembers that," said Jellia with a toss of her head that set all her green cap ribbons fluttering. "If I live to be a million, I'll never forget the day she came to this castle with the Cowardly Lion, the Scarecrow and the Tin Woodman. Not if I live to be a million! Will I light the candles now, Wiz dear, or wait until they arrive?"

"Oh, wait till they arrive, by all means. But see here," the Wizard, taking a last look at the party table, was plainly distressed. "You've only seven places, Jellia, and there are eight of us. My idea was to have everyone immediately associated with Dorothy's first visit, and that would be: one, Dorothy herself; two, myself; three, yourself; four, the Cowardly Lion; five, the Scarecrow; six, the Tin Woodman; seven, the Soldier with the Green Whiskers; and eight, the Guardian of the Gate. Quick, my dear! Another plate for the Guardian of the Gate."

"He's not coming," announced Jellia primly. "He says he has not deserted his post for forty years and does not intend to desert it now. But if you'll send his refreshments to the Guard House, he'll take it very kindly. I've already fixed him a basket," said Jellia, smoothing her apron.

"Good old Guardy!" The Wizard absently brushed back the hair he no longer had, then, hearing voices and steps in the corridor, bounced over to open the door while Jellia tripped joyously about, lighting the candles set everywhere in the big workshop. Candle and fire light are so much cozier for parties, and it all looked so cheery and gay that Dorothy, who was first, stopped short in the doorway with an exclamation of delight.

"Oh, Wizard! How beautiful! Oh, how I do wish Ozma could see it all!"

"Tut tut!" chuckled the Wizard, leading her into the room. "Ozma is having a fine time in Glinda's palace by now. To tell the truth, Dorothy, this party is just for YOU and to remind us all of the old Oz days when—"

"You were nothing but a humbug," snorted the Scarecrow, laughing so hard he had to lean against the door jamb.

"Don't forget he gave you your famous brains, friend." The Tin Woodman spoke reprovingly, for Nick Chopper did not like anyone's feelings to be hurt, even in fun. "And don't forget he gave me my splendid heart!"

"And me my grade A, double-distilled, instant-acting courage," purred the Cowardly Lion. Moving over to the fire, the big beast stretched himself luxuriously on the hearth rug.

"And don't forget our little Wiz was once Supreme Ruler of Oz!" boomed the Soldier with the Green Whiskers. Marching three times round the party table, the thin, immensely tall soldier brought up with a smart salute before their embarrassed little host.

"Three cheers for the Wizard of Oz!" cried Jellia Jam. Seizing a silver bell with an emerald clapper, she rang it so hard the Cowardly Lion's mane blew straight back, and even the candles flickered.

"Thank you! Thank you very much!" The Wizard bowed and rubbed his ear, which still tingled from the cheers and bell-ringing. "But where is Toto, Dorothy? I thought of course you'd bring your little dog."

"Oh, Toto's with Ozma," explained Dorothy, drawn in spite of herself to the brightly decorated party table. "You know how he dotes on traveling, so Ozma took him along for company."

"Then of course he cannot be here," sighed the Wizard regretfully. "Now Jellia, off with that cap and apron. Tonight you are my guest and not a maid-in-waiting to Ozma or anyone else. Dorothy, suppose you sit at the head. I'll sit at the foot, and the others may find their own places."

"My place will always be next to little Dorothy," rumbled the Cowardly Lion, hoisting himself sleepily to the chair beside the little girl.

"Mine will be next to the pickles. MM-mmmm! I LOVE pickles," said the Soldier, slipping into the seat next to the lion, while Jellia, with a purposeful bounce, settled near a plate of green cookies. There was no doubt where the Tin Woodman and Scarecrow would sit, for at one plate the Wizard had put a silver box of metal polish and an emerald bottle containing purest oil. Then, instead of a chair, he had provided a bale of freshly packed straw for the Scarecrow.

"Well, well, here we all are!" Rubbing his hands briskly, the Wizard beamed on his guests as Fredjon, wearing his best suit of green and silver, bustled in with the first course.

"And isn't it fun to be here?" Dorothy took a long, satisfying sip of her Ozade. "I'm awfully glad I came back to live in the Land of Oz. Aren't you, Wizard?"

"A country where a body grows no older, where animals talk as easily as men and where the practice of magic is not only possible but practical, a country like that has many advantages," admitted the Wizard, winking at the Cowardly Lion, who was drinking his fruit juice in a refined way from a huge, green aquarium. "I myself never have regretted the years spent in this marvelous fairyland. Sometimes I hardly can believe I ever did live in Omaha, or travel through the West with a circus."

"I know," agreed Dorothy, nodding her head slowly. "Kansas, when I think of it, seems very far away, as much like a dream, I suppose, as Oz seems like a dream to boys and girls in Kansas who read Oz history."

"Oh, why think of Kansas?" Jellia spoke scornfully. "In Kansas you were only an ordinary little girl, while here you are a Princess and second in importance to our Ruler, Ozma, herself."

"And in Kansas," observed the Scarecrow as Dorothy rather self-consciously straightened her crown, "I'll bet you never had as much fun or as many adventures as we have here." The Scarecrow, being well stuffed with straw, never indulged in any refreshments. In fact, he just came to parties for the conversation, and to be sure of a good time, he tried to do all the talking himself.

"That's right," said Dorothy thoughtfully, "that cyclone was about the only thing that ever happened in Kansas."

"A great blow to you, my dear, but a fortunate thing for Nick and me." The Scarecrow patted the Tin Woodman affectionately on the funnel he wore for a hat. "If you had not blown to Oz, I'd probably still be hanging on a pole in that cornfield, and Nick would be rusting away his life in the greenwood."

"And in some ways," mused Dorothy, looking dreamily at the model of her small Kansas house, "in some ways that first adventure always will seem best. Just imagine how surprised I was to blow all those miles and find myself in a strange, wonderful country like Oz. The Munchkins thought I was a sorceress because my house had killed the Wicked Witch of the East. Then the Good Witch of the North told me to put on her silver shoes and go to the Emerald City to ask the great OZ to send me home. And on the way I discovered you, and do you remember how astonished I was when I lifted you down from your pole and found you really were alive and could talk?"

The Scarecrow nodded cheerfully.

"And remember how we traveled on together till we found the Tin Woodman?" went on Dorothy. "And Nick told us about the witch who had enchanted his axe so that it chopped off a leg here and an arm there, and finally his head and body, too. And after each accident he'd go to a tinsmith who made him new tin arms and legs and finally even a body and a head. You didn't mind being Tin at all, did you, Nick? Except that day you went out to chop wood and left your oil

287

can at home. Then that storm came up, your joints rusted, and you couldn't move, and there you had been, rusting and helpless for months!"

"But we hustled back to your hut, fetched the oil can and fixed you up in fine shape, didn't we, old fellow?" The Scarecrow flung his flimsy arm around Nick Chopper's shoulder, and the Tin Woodman, at the mere mention of rust, uncorked the emerald bottle and let three drops of oil slide down his neck.

"I never shall forget your kindness," he told them earnestly, turning his head first to look at Dorothy and then at the Scarecrow.

"And after that you came along so the Wizard could give you a new heart," Dorothy reminded him gaily. "And right afterwards, we met the Cowardly Lion."

"And he was more afraid of us than we were of him," teased the Scarecrow, leaning across the table to give the lion a poke.

"Yes, I was just a big coward in those days," admitted the lion, blinking approvingly at the rare roast Fredjon had brought him instead of the chicken he was serving the others. "Just a great big coward! Ho, hum!"

"But not too cowardly to fight for us," said Dorothy, taking quick little bites of her biscuit, "and to come with us to the Emerald City."

"Oh, that was because I wanted the Wizard to give me some courage," roared the lion. "And weren't we surprised when we did reach the Emerald City to find it all built of green marble, studded with real emeralds! And remember how the Guardian of the Gate gave us all green specs, even me, and then led us up to the palace?"

"You looked awfully funny in those specs!" laughed Dorothy. "I'll never forget how funny!"

"But remember, it was I who carried your messages to Oz," put in the Soldier with Green Whiskers.

"Of course it was," said Dorothy, nodding her head quickly. "You gave us some splendid advice, Soldier, and Jellia showed us to the grandest rooms in the castle and loaned me the loveliest dresses to wear."

"I liked you from the very first!" declared Jellia, choking a bit on her seventh cooky.

"But Old Man Wizzy wouldn't give us a thing!" said the Scarecrow, waving his napkin toward the head of the table. "He told us we'd have to kill the Witch of the West before he'd send Dorothy home or grant any of our requests."

"But you see, I didn't know any real magic then." The Wizard looked quite unhappy, for he did not like to remember the time before he was a real Wizard. "And besides, I needed more time."

"Ho ho! You were doing very well for yourself!" chuckled the Scarecrow. "Living in a splendid castle and having the whole country eating out of your hand. As it happened, we did kill the witch of the West, or at least Dorothy melted her with a bucket of water, and the Winkies were so tickled they gave us all presents and made Nick their Emperor. So when we got back at last, you did give me some brand-new brains, and Nick a red plush heart—"

"And me some real red, true-blue courage," grinned the Cowardly Lion, wiping his mouth delicately with the tip of his tail.

"And you made me Ruler of OZ! Ah! My Majesty the Scarecrow, Hah, those were the days!" The Scarecrow thumped his pudgy chest and fairly glowed at the memory.

"You would have taken me back to Kansas, too, only your balloon flew away too fast, didn't it?" Dorothy leaned all the way across the table to pat the Wizard's arm.

"But don't forget it was I who told you to go to the palace of Glinda, the Good Sorceress of the South," interrupted the Soldier with Green Whiskers again.

"So we all went to Glinda's," rumbled the Cowardly Lion, half closing his eyes. "And Glinda told Dorothy the Witch's silver shoes would carry her home. And they did!" There was a little silence following the lion's last sentence, as if all of Dorothy's friends were recalling their sorrow at that first parting from their cheerful little comrade.

"But you came back," declared the Scarecrow, balancing a fork on the edge of his tumbler. "And so did our little Wizard."

"Well, to tell the truth, Omaha seemed rather dull after the Emerald City," admitted the Wizard, motioning for Fredjon to bring on the dessert. This caused many admiring "Oh's" and "Ah's" when it arrived, for it was ice cream moulded into small Tin Woodmen, Scarecrows, Lions, and all the other guests. Then, out of a huge, frosted cake the footman set down before Dorothy, flew four little witches riding green broomsticks, straight into the fire.

"I tell you, it takes a real Wizard to perform a trick like that." Nick Chopper wagged his head solemnly. "You certainly have made progress since Ozma made you Chief Magician of the Realm."

"Well—" drawled the Wizard, pushing the pickle dish away from the Soldier with Green Whiskers, who already had eaten twenty-seven and was looking rather dill. "Magic is like any other science: it takes practice. Of course, if you are a born fairy like Ozma and the former rulers of Oz, working spells and charms just comes natural, like playing the piano by ear. But if you are not a Fairy, you must study witchcraft and sorcery as I have done with Glinda the Good. It only has been by continuous study and research that I have managed to perfect myself in the arts of wizardry."

"Well, how is wizness lately?" inquired the Scarecrow, wrinkling his cotton forehead at all the big words.

"Fine, just fine!" The Wizard assured him brightly. Marching over to his desk, he returned with a long, tube-like object resembling a seaman's spyglass. "This is one of my latest inventions," he confessed modestly. "Here, take a look." Beaming with anticipation, he pressed the spyglass into Dorothy's hands.

Chapter 2 - The Wizard's Spy Glass

With the Wizard's latest invention clapped to one eye and pointed straight at the Wizard himself, Dorothy peered through the green glass hardly knowing what to expect. Certainly not what happened, for from the other end of the instrument a composed voice began making announcements proudly and impressively as a radio speaker.

"You are now looking at Oscar Zoroaster Phadrig Isaac Norman Henkle Emmanuel Ambroise Diggs," it informed them crisply. "Calls himself Oz after the first letters of his first two names, as his other initials spell Pinhead. Born in Omaha, Diggs ran away as a young man to join a circus, where he made balloon ascensions to amuse the crowds, his balloon bearing his initials, O.Z.

"One day in a storm, Oscar's balloon was carried to our wonderful Land of Oz. At that time, the rightful King of the Country and his son had been destroyed by Mombi the Witch, who also had enchanted and hidden away Ozma, the little Granddaughter of this unfortunate monarch. And four witches had divided the country between them. When the balloon bearing the name OZ on its side sailed out of the clouds, the inhabitants instantly hailed the traveler from America as their ruler, supposing him to be another member of the famous fairy family of Oz. Unable to return to America, Oz accepted the people's decision with good grace and ruled the realm for many years. Under his wise direction the people built this castle and the famous City of Emeralds; and the four witches, thinking Oz more powerful than they, did not question his rule or authority.

"Later, when little Dorothy from Kansas arrived in Oz, the Wizard decided to return with her to the United States, leaving the Scarecrow to rule in his place. The Scarecrow was deposed by Jinjur and her Army of Girls. Jinjur in turn was conquered by Glinda, the Good Witch of the South, who also forced Mombi to disenchant Ozma, the young and rightful girl ruler of the realm. Ozma has ruled over Oz ever since. Not long after Ozma was restored to her throne, the Wizard returned to Oz and our clever girl ruler made him Chief Magician of the realm. In this ancient and honorable capacity he has served ever since, PERIOD — STOP — DROP OR POINT ELSEWHERE!" These last words were uttered so rudely, Dorothy almost did drop the spyglass.

"My! MY GOODNESS!" gasped the little girl.

"It always says that when it has told all it knows. You see, it is a `tell-all-escope.'" explained the Wizard, reaching out for his spyglass with an embarrassed cough.

"And it certainly tells ALL, all right!" roared the Scarecrow, pushing back his chair. "Congratulations, my dear Mr. Diggs!"

"Look out! Be careful! Don't you point that thing at me! Please don't!" The big lion simply cowered in his chair, and no wonder he felt nervous. There had been some pretty savage incidents in that old lion's life before he met Dorothy and came to live in the Emerald City as a civilized citizen of Oz. And the thought of the tell-all-escope telling all it knew about him made the Cowardly Lion positively shudder. But the others were so busy examining the Wizard's spyglass, they did not even notice the lion's terrific agitation.

"You know, a thing like that would be of great value to a traveler," remarked Nick Chopper, tapping the tell-all-escope thoughtfully with his tin fingers.

"That's just what I figured," grinned the Wizard, thrusting the instrument into his pocket. "And speaking of traveling, I have something else to show you!" Clapping on his high hat, Ozma's Chief Magician hastened over to the door that opened on the garden, signaling for the others to come along.

Having had experience with inventors before, Dorothy and Jellia snatched up coats, Dorothy her own, and Jellia one of the Wizard's. Then, followed by the rest of the party, they stepped out into the sparkling, starlit evening. The Soldier with Green Whiskers, who had stopped to eat the last pickle in the dish and stuff an extra piece of cake in his pocket, came last of all. At each step he gave a little groan, for all by himself the soldier had eaten enough for a whole army. But then, he was a whole army; he was every single man, private, corporal, captain, major, colonel and general in the entire fighting force of Oz.

Anxious to exhibit his latest treasure, the Wizard walked rapidly along leading the little party across the park, through the Emerald City, out of the Gates and into the thick woodland beyond.

"Where do you suppose he is taking us?" shivered Jellia, thinking longingly of the cozy fire back in the laboratory.

"No knowing," giggled the Scarecrow. "But a-hunting we shall go! A-hunting we shall go! Ta-Ta-Ta-Ta-Ta-Ta-Ta-TAH!" Blowing an imaginary horn, the Scarecrow pretended to gallop and fell flat on his face, his legs never being what you really could call reliable.

"Sh-hh!" whispered the Wizard, looking back warningly as the Tin Woodman jerked the straw man to his feet. "What I am about to show you has been seen by no one in Oz except my faithful assistants! So please be more quiet!"

"You mean it's a secret?" whispered Dorothy, skipping forward to catch up with the Wizard and linking her arm through his.

"Two secrets!" confided Ozma's Chief Magician mysteriously. Pushing impatiently through the last fringe of trees, the group stepped into a moonlit clearing.

Chapter 3 - Latest Invention of the Wizard of Oz

"Ooooh! A conservatory!" murmured Jellia, blinking at the shining glass structure that occupied the entire treeless space.

"A barn, if you ask me!" guessed the Scarecrow. "But why build it of glass, Mr. Wiz?"

"Because glass is the latest and lightest building material known. But this is no barn, as you'll soon discover." Handing his flashlight to Dorothy, the Wizard slid back the vast doors, switched on the lights and stood back, his hands in his pockets, as the little group in silence and astonishment viewed the two shining planes housed as snugly as giant butterflies in a glass cocoon.

"Airplanes!" exclaimed Dorothy when she found her voice at last.

"No, Ozoplanes," corrected the Wizard, trying to keep the excitement out of his voice. "Somewhat like the planes in America, but more powerful, for remember, my dear, I had not only the scientific knowledge of aeronautics available to mortals, but the scientific knowledge of magic to help me as well!"

"Well," echoed the Tin Woodman, gazing approvingly at the Wizard's planes, which, except for their silver wings, might have been huge silver-and-glass torpedoes.

"Not for the army, I hope," exclaimed the Soldier, clutching his whiskers nervously. Being the entire army himself and quite old-fashioned and set in his ways, the Soldier felt sure he never could pilot these gleaming airplanes.

"On, No! No! NO!" The Wizard frowned at the mere thought of war. "These are pleasure planes for traveling and exploring the unknown regions of the upper air. As soon as Ozma returns from the South, I plan to present them both to our illustrious young Ruler and arrange for her to make the first triumphant flight."

"But there are two," said Dorothy a little wistfully. She had hoped to make the first flight with the Wizard herself.

"Of course, of course!" he answered in a matter-of-fact way. "Most experimental flights fail because they depend on one ship. We shall have two!"

"We?" Dorothy brightened up considerably at the Wizard's plural.

"Yes, we," repeated the Wizard, turning round to smile at the little girl. "Counting Ozma and those of us here, there will be eight passengers — four for each plane."

"Now please don't bother about me!" begged the Cowardly Lion, his tail dragging on the ground at the very thought of flying. "I'd not think of troubling you. Besides, I'm much too heavy for flying."

"Not at all, not at all," the Wizard reassured him with a wink. "I have made exact calculations about weight, old fellow, and you and the Scarecrow balance each other nicely. So don't worry about that."

"Oh, I'm not worrying about that!" rumbled the lion, rearing up on his hind legs to read the names outlined in emeralds on the luminous sides of the Wizard's ships.

"Ozpril and Oztober!" The lion spoke in a slightly trembling roar. "Mmmn! Mmmnnmn! Kerumph!"

"Why, those are beautiful names," exclaimed Dorothy, tilting back her head to spell them out for herself.

"I thought they were rather neat," said the Wizard complacently. "Suitable, too, one to rise and one to fall!" Expressively, he lifted an arm and let it fall limply to his side.

"To — to fall?" quavered the lion, dropping to all fours.

"Oh, just in a figurative way, of course." The Wizard shrugged his shoulders. "You will observe," he went on enthusiastically, "that these planes need no runway or special track to take off. They really are balloonaplanes. Note those round packets on the top of the fuselage." The lion blinked rapidly, for he had no idea that fuselage meant the body of the plane, but the others nodded quite knowingly. "Well, those," declared the inventor proudly, "are my own patented balloon attachments. At the touch of a button, the wings are depressed and the balloon inflated with a magic gas, lighter than helium, that carries the ship as high and as far as desired. Then the balloon can be deflated, and the Ozoplane can continue under its own power. But you will readily see how my ship, with its balloon attachment, has twice the altitude possibilities of an ordinary airplane. Hah! We shall fly higher than higher!" boasted the little Wizard happily.

"Oh, quite!" agreed the Tin Woodman, mounting the ladder of the Oztober, the Soldier with Green Whiskers pressing nervously at his heels.

"But how will you move them out of here?" inquired the Scarecrow, taking off his hat and scratching his cotton head.

"Oh, as to that—" The Wizard pulled a switch just behind him, whereupon the top of the glass airdrome lifted like the lid of an enormous jewel box.

"Hmmmn! I see!" The Scarecrow slapped his knee and grinned with appreciation. "Off with the roof! Up with the planes!"

"Exactly!" Seizing the Straw Man's arm, the Wizard urged him toward the ladder of the Ozpril, Dorothy skipping cheerfully behind them. After Dorothy plodded the Cowardly Lion, talking to himself in anxious whispers and growls.

"Be sure not to touch anything over there," called the Wizard as Nick and the Soldier with Green Whiskers disappeared into the cabin of the other plane.

"I'll keep an eye on them," promised Jellia, tripping up the ladder as lightly as a feather. "Don't give us a thought, Wiz dear."

"Jellia's so funny!" laughed Dorothy.

"Sensible, too," added the Wizard, helping the little girl over the high door sill and into the plane. While he and the Scarecrow went forward to examine the steering gear, Dorothy looked delightedly 'round the snug little cabin. There were four seats upholstered in pale green leather along one side. The whole top was of thick glass, through which she could distinctly see the moon and stars winking down at her. The side walls of the Ozpril were of a silvery grey, with all trimmings in green. At the back was a small dinette with chairs and table locked to the floors as they are on seagoing vessels. A cabinet full of china, a wall full of charts, a bookcase full of books, and a tiny kitchen and dressing room completed the equipment.

"It's just as cozy as a little house," sighed Dorothy contentedly as the Cowardly Lion, having glanced round in a discouraged way, seated himself in one of the green chairs and pressed his nose against the round window pane. "Won't we have fun, Liony, when we really get off?"

"Getting off will be the best fun of all," sniffed the lion, glancing briefly at the door. The Lion, as you probably have guessed, felt no enthusiasm for the trip. Once, much against his will, he had been carried to an island in the sky, and that experience had been more than enough. In his own mind he already had decided not to accompany the Wizard on his proposed flight. Yessir, when the party assembled for the trip he would just turn up missing and manage to stay behind. Immensely relieved by this secret decision, he ambled forward.

"You will notice," the Wizard was pointing out briskly, "that I have done away with all controls and levers. On this board are all the buttons necessary to operate the ship."

"Looks like an organ," observed Dorothy, squinting at the bright array of buttons set in the top of the table within easy reach of the first seat. "Must you play all those stops and starters to guide the plane?"

"Not quite all," smiled the Wizard, "but if we wished to start, first I'd press this green button to depress the wings and inflate our balloon. Next I'd push the button marked `up' and, if I decided to go North, this `North' button as well. Then I'd use the wheel to hold her steady, and if I preferred to go up in a gradual way, I'd push this button marked `zig.'FF2

0"

"And I suppose if you saw something interesting or wished to dodge a mountain, you'd `zag,'" suggested the Scarecrow, indicating the "zag" button with his pudgy finger. "Or you could `spin,' `spiral' or `level off'—"

"Stop! Stop!" panted the Cowardly Lion, clapping his paw to one eye. "All this up-zig and down-zig makes me positively giddy!"

"It does seem a little complicated," said Dorothy, looking dubiously at the Wizard's button-board.

"Why, it's perfectly simple!" the Wizard assured her brightly. "All you have to do is touch the right buttons at the right time!"

"But—"

The Scarecrow, who had been about to ask another question, whirled round on one heel and flopped on his back in the aisle. The Cowardly Lion skidded rapidly past to wedge under the little dining table, while Dorothy and the Wizard clung to the steering board to keep from falling. For a terrific roar like the tearing of a gigantic sheet had made the Ozpril tremble like a leaf. There came a sudden flash of silver smoke, and the gradual dying away of all sound. Then a complete and ominous silence.

"WHAT? WHAT! Why, it's gone!" shouted the Wizard, racing over to the door and staring amazedly at the empty space occupied a moment before by the Oztober. Then he glanced up into the starlit expanse of sky.

"Gone?" Creeping on hands and knees, the Scarecrow peered out to see for himself. "Why, what right have they to go off like that?" he demanded, pulling himself up by the door jam. "April comes before October and goes before October, too. Fall before spring — Why, that's ridiculous! The Ozpril should have led off!"

"Oh, what will become of them?" cried Dorothy in distress, clasping her hands anxiously. "I'm sure it was a dreadful mistake."

"Mistake!" moaned the Wizard, pushing back his high hat. "Worse than that, Dorothy! Why, everything is ruined! Here they've gone off before I even had a chance to show the plane to Ozma. They have no directions, no supplies; they'll crash, smash or wreck themselves. I intended to teach Nick Chopper to navigate the plane before we started!"

"But can't we stop them? Can't we go after them?" exclaimed Dorothy, clutching the Wizard's coattails.

"Go after them? Yes! That's the idea, go after them! Of course!" panted the Wizard, falling over the Cowardly Lion, who was making a stream-lion for the door.

"I was just going back for my overshoes," wheezed the lion, slinking rather guiltily into his seat at the Wizard's reproachful glance.

"Stay where you are!" the Wizard directed sharply. "Now then, steady, everybody steady! Shut that door, Scarecrow, we are about to ascend." The Wizard bent over the steering board to touch the green button that would inflate the Ozpril's balloon. "But I never expected to go without my black bag of magic, an extra vest, or even my bottle of hair tonic."

"Haven't you any magic at all"" called Dorothy as the Ozpril began to vibrate and tremble from the rush of gas into its balloon.

"A little, a little," confessed the Wizard, pressing the buttons marked "Up" and "South." "Here, Dorothy, take the tell-all-escope and see if you can catch a glimpse of the Oztober when we are aloft." Grasping the wheel, the Wizard settled grimly into the pilot's seat. Dorothy had just time to clutch the tell-all-escope before the Ozpril rose straight into the air. Lifted and borne by its buoyant gasbag, the graceful ship pointed toward the stars.

Chapter 4 - First Flight of the Oztober

Now the start of the Oztober had been nothing like the orderly takeoff of the Ozpril. The first hint Jellia had of their departure was when a china coffee pot from the open china closet into which she was looking with great interest hit her a sharp clip on the chin. Next moment she was rolling round on the floor of the cabin, dodging all the rest of the green dishes.

"Oh! Oh! Dishes awful!" choked poor Jellia Jam, not even realizing she was making a pun.

"Stop!" yelled the Tin Woodman, turning a complete somersault and coming down on his funnel with one leg hooked through the luggage rack. "Stop! Who did that?"

"Pickles!" moaned a faint voice from the forward end of the cabin. "Oh, those pickles!" And that was probably as correct an answer as any to Nick's indignant question. Even upside down as he was and subject to the fierce rocketing of the plane, the Tin Woodman could see a tall, green figure sprawled across the navigator's table. As he had bent over to examine the Oztober's steering apparatus, the Soldier with Green Whiskers had been taken with a violent cramp from the twenty-nine pickles he had eaten at the party. Falling heavily on the board, he had pushed down ten of the Wizard's bright-colored buttons. Following the directions of all ten, one after the other, the Oztober had exploded into the air and now, whistling and whirling like a comet bound for Mars, was charging into the Heavens.

Jellia Jam was too bruised and shaken to do anything but cling to the side of one of the seats. The Soldier, after his head had been whacked down three times on the board, had lapsed into complete and utter silence. Only Nick managed to preserve a semblance of his usual calm and composure. Though severely dented by the plane's takeoff, the Tin Woodman, being of metal, felt no pain. Nor was he subject to the giddiness that assailed ordinary flesh and bone bodies under such trying conditions. Even standing on his head did not greatly inconvenience him, and after the first dreadful shock he began to perceive a certain order and rhythm in their flight. This was not strange.

The Soldier's fall had pressed down the button to inflate the Oztober's balloon, the "Up" and the "South" buttons, the "fast," "spin," "spiral," "zig," "zag," "slow" and "circle" buttons as well. So first the Oztober would shoot straight up, then it would go into a fast spin, and spiral. The zigs and zags were a little less terrible, and on one of the slow circles the Tin Woodman managed to extricate his foot from the luggage rack. Clattering full length in the aisle, he lay still till the next slow circle. Then, leaping to his feet, he rushed forward and pulled the Soldier off the steering board. He had just time to prop the unconscious army into the third chair and fall into the pilot's seat himself when the Oztober went into another fast spin and spiral. This rather upset Nick.

He had taken a hasty look at the navigator's table when he entered the ship and then, more interested in the metal of which the plane was constructed, had gone tapping about, testing it with his tin knuckles, intending to return to the steering gear later. He naturally had supposed that when he pulled the soldier off the board the plane would slow down or change its course. But nothing of the kind happened. All the buttons the soldier had fallen on stayed down.

Grasping the wheel, Nick was relieved to find he could steady the Oztober a bit in this way. Holding to it with one hand, he tried to pull out the "spin" and "spiral" buttons with the other. But even his strong tin fingers could not budge them. Next he glanced frantically over the board for a "stop" or "down" button, but the "down" button when he found it filled him with apprehension. If they shot downward at the speed they were hurling upward, the plane most certainly would be wrecked. No, decided Nick, drawing his fingers hastily back from the "down" button, they were much safer in the air until he learned a little more about flying, and he'd just have to hang on till he discovered how the Ozoplane worked.

Grasping the wheel resignedly in both hands, he glanced back to see how Jellia was faring. Jellia was sitting dizzily in the middle of the aisle. But she was so encouraged to see Nick actually at the wheel that she made her way to him and hung firmly to the arm of his chair. Just then the Oztober whirled into its twentieth spin and spiral, and Jellia — dislodged from the chair — caught at the steering table to save herself from falling.

"Oh, now you've done it!" gasped Nick as the Oztober gave a wicked lurch. "Oh, now—" His voice trailed off into a hoarse squeak, for as abruptly as it had started the plane stopped, and held aloft by its still-buoyant balloon, swung easily to and fro in the faint wind that stirred above the clouds. "Say! How did you do it?" Letting go the wheel, the Tin Woodman seized Jellia by the shoulders.

"What?" panted Jellia. "What did I do?"

"Why, you saved the ship. You stopped her. See, all the buttons are up again!" Removing Jellia's clutching fingers gently from the table top, Nick discovered a flat bar on the underside of the board. As soon as Jellia pressed the bar, all the buttons had popped back to their normal position. "So THAT'S it!" exclaimed Nick, rubbing his tin forehead anxiously. "Each time you want to change the course, you press this bar and then begin all over again."

"But now we're sinking," groaned Jellia. And sinking herself into the seat back of Nick, she stared at him with round, desperate eyes.

"Sinking, are we? Well, I'll soon put a stop to that!" Pouncing on the green button to inflate the Oztober's gas bag, Nick pressed it quickly, for of course as soon as Jellia had touched the bar, the buttons had all sprung up and the magic gas had begun to seep out of the plane's balloon attachment. As it again filled and became taut, the slow downward drift of the ship ceased, and again it hung motionless between a cloud and a star. "Now!" breathed the Tin Woodman, eyeing the button board with grim purpose and determination, "Now we can take our time and start off right."

"Oh, Nick, must we go through all that again?" Jellia began to cry softly, drying her eyes on the sash of her party dress. "Oh, Nick, I never thought flying would be like this. Please, can't we just stay as we are?"

"Certainly not," said the Tin Woodman briskly. "Hanging 'round the sky is dangerous. We might be hit by a shooting star or even by a meteor. Now just trust yourself to me, my dear Jellia. Remember, I am the Emperor of the East!" Nick smote his tin chest a resounding blow. "And after ruling the Winkies all these years, I surely can handle one small plane!"

Reassuring himself if not Jellia, the Tin Woodman searched the array of buttons for one marked "slow." After he had found it, he slowly began to map his course. He would continue to fly up for a time. Next he would take a horizontal direction until he grew more accustomed to piloting the Ozoplane. Then, as night passed and the sun rose, he would zig and zag slowly downward and make a safe landing near the Emerald City.

The Soldier with Green Whiskers had regained consciousness only to fall at once into a heavy slumber. His snores blended nicely with Jellia's sobs as Nick Chopper pushed the "up," the "South" and the "slow" buttons. Braced for a new shock, Jellia grasped the arms of her seat. But this time the Oztober soared gently and gracefully aloft, the motion of the plane so smooth and pleasant Ozma's little Maid in Waiting soon forgot all her fears. Relaxing against the soft green cushions, she too fell asleep. This left only Nick awake and alert.

But if the Wizard had searched all over Oz, he could not have found a better pilot than the Tin Woodman. Being practically tireless and requiring neither food nor rest, he could keep his place at the wheel for days if necessary. Delighted at the way the Oztober responded to his clever manipulation of the wheel and buttons, he flew up and up and on and on, scarcely realizing the distance he was putting between himself and Oz. Glancing out the round window beside him, Nick viewed the starry expanse of the upper air with growing interest and enthusiasm. Sometimes he was almost tempted to waken Jellia to point out the splendid cloud mountains and cities they were passing. As he swept along, the sky turned from deep blue grey and was now suffused with the rainbow tints of early morning. Switching off the lights, the Tin Woodman slightly changed his course.

"I really need a lot more practice before I go back or try to make a safe landing," he observed softly to himself. "It never would do to crack up a valuable ship like this." But the truth of the matter was, the Tin Woodman did not wish to turn back. And after all, who was to insist? The Soldier and Jellia still slept on, and far ahead, between a bank of fog and an arch of platinum sun rays, loomed a long, lavender crescent. Nick even fancied he could see people moving about its glittering surface.

"A new world!" gloated the Tin Woodman, setting his funnel at a more daring angle. If this were so, he would be its discoverer. Not only that, but he could claim it for Ozma and win for himself as much honor and renown as Samuel Salt, the Royal Explorer of Oz. "Even if it's not inhabited, it would be a good place to practice landing," reflected Nick happily. So again he pressed the black bar, touched the button to deflate the Oztober's balloon and raise the wings. For now he wished to fly horizontally, and the wings would be faster than the gas bag. Next, touching the "straight-on" and "faster" buttons and twirling the wheel expertly, he headed the ship straight for the tip of the lavender island.

Chapter 5 - The Spikers

Nick waited until he was well over the crescent before he attempted to land. As he flew along, he planned exactly how he would go about it, and everything worked out as planned except for one thing. The "slow," the "zig" and the "down" buttons brought the Oztober within a foot of the glittering air Isle, but the "stop" button functioned a bit late. Instead of stopping on the surface, the plane dropped clear through with a crash like the smashing of a thousand thin tumblers. Peering up through a spray of splinters, the Tin Woodman found he had knocked a jagged hole in the Crescent.

"Attention! Shoulder arms! Company, fall in!" yelled the Soldier with Green Whiskers. Jolted completely awake, he sprang up in the aisle, aiming his gun at the ceiling.

"Yes? Yes! Coming, your Majesty!" Jellia, mistaking the musical crash for the ringing of Ozma's morning bell, rolled sleepily out of her seat and started down the aisle after the Soldier.

"Now, now, don't be alarmed," remarked Nick Chopper. "I was just trying to land."

"Land? Where is it? Quick! Let me out of here!" panted Jellia Jam, remembering all in a rush where she was and the dreadful experiences of the night before.

"I see no land," said the Soldier, pressing his nose against one of the windows.

"Well, it certainly looked like land!" The Tin Woodman spoke in a slightly exasperated voice. The Oztober, still quivering from its impact with the island, was hanging motionless about ten feet below the Crescent. "Can't tell about these Sky Countries till you try them."

"I'll bet it's nothing but a cake of ice," shivered Jellia, hugging herself to keep warm. "Being of tin, I don't suppose you'd notice that it was freezing! I wonder if that stove lights."

"Ice?" meditated Nick as Jellia hurried toward the back of the cabin. "Why, I do believe you are right, my dear. In the upper stratas the air does become colder. We probably cracked through a frozen cloud!"

Jellia, turning all the switches on the stove, paid little attention to Nick's scientific discourse. She was too busy warming herself over the glowing burners. "If we just had something to cook," sighed the little Oz maid, staring wistfully into the cupboard beside the stove. But the shelves were perfectly empty. Reflecting that the Wizard had not yet had time to stock up for the flight, Jellia, who was an orderly little soul, began picking up the china that had broken when it fell from the cabinet the night before. Rather pompously, the Soldier with Green Whiskers began to help her.

"Will someone kindly explain what we are doing flying around in this dangerous and haphazard manner?" he inquired loftily. "I understood we were to wait for Ozma's return before we made a trial flight! And really, you know, I'm needed at home to guard the castle."

"Oh, indeed!" sniffed Jellia. "And who do you suppose started us off, Mr. Whiskers? Nobody but yourself. A fine pickle you put us in when you fell on that steering board."

"I?" The Solder straightened up, aghast.

"Yes, YOU!" declared Jellia. "You and your pickles." Sweeping the rest of the broken plates into her skirt, she marched to the end of the cabin and dumped them into the big basket beside the water cooler. "Goodness knows whether we shall ever get back," she sighed, sinking despondently into the last seat and staring out the window.

"But we're backing now," muttered the Soldier. This was quite true, for Nick, to avoid hitting the crescent of ice again, was maneuvering the plane from beneath; then, feeling it might be dangerous to go any higher, he began slowly and cautiously to descend. Neither he nor Jellia paid any more attention to the Soldier with Green Whiskers, who glanced uncomfortably from one to the other. After a little silence, he remarked in a hollow voice, "I shall consider myself under arrest. I shall walk guard for two hours without a pause for rest or rations!"

"Oh, don't be a goose!" giggled Jellia. "You'll probably go without rations because there aren't any. But what good will walking guard do?"

"As Commander-in-Chief, I have sentenced myself to walk guard. As a first-class Private in the Army of Oz, I shall carry out this sentence," insisted the Soldier. "Discipline must be maintained!" Hoisting his old-fashioned blunderbuss to his shoulder, he began tramping stiffly up and down the short aisle of the cabin.

Born in a small Munchkin village to a family named Battles who had promptly christened him Wantowin, he had applied as soon as he was grown for a position in the army of Oz. The Wizard, then Supreme Ruler of the Kingdom, impressed by the Soldier's height and long green whiskers, had immediately hired him. Later he had been promoted by Ozma to fill the position of the entire staff and army of Oz. Wantowin had never been much of a fighter, but as war in Oz is practically outlawed and victories usually won by magic, he had got on very well. At his tenth about-face, Wantowin suddenly recalled the piece of cake he had stuffed into his pocket the night before, and generously offered it to Jellia.

"Oh, Wanny, how wonderful!" To the famished girl, the cake tasted even better than it had at the Wizard's party. Breaking it in half, she tried to force the soldier to eat a piece, but raising his hand sternly, Wantowin continued his self-imposed sentence. Seeing argument was useless, Jellia ate her own share and put the other half in the cupboard for the soldier's supper.

The plane was still slanting smoothly downward. After oiling all of Nick's joints and thinking how fortunate it was they had brought along the oil can, Jellia began marching up and down behind the Soldier, examining the pictures and charts on the wall as she went along. The cake and a long drink of water from the cooler had done much to restore her courage and cheerfulness, and an occasional glance out the window was both pleasant and reassuring. The Oztober was dropping through fluffs and puffs of creamy cloud. "Just like whipped cream on strawberries — if we had any strawberries!" mused Jellia, withdrawing her gaze reluctantly from the window and resuming her march. "Oh, Nick, here are some directions!" she cried suddenly, stepping before a finely printed notice beside the water cooler.

"Directions?" The Tin Woodman looked round rather annoyed. He felt he had almost mastered the mechanism of the Ozoplane and did not care to start a new system. But the directions that Jellia read off had nothing to do with the navigation of the plane. They were rules for the behavior of passengers in the strat. "The air in this cabin has been magically treated," stated the notice. "So long as the windows and doors are closed, riders may safely pass through the highest strata. On debarking, however, it would be well to don my patent protective air helmets, see chest beneath second seat, or to take one, for each mile up, of my elutherated altitude pills from the recess in the table leg."

Jellia, whose bump of curiosity was larger than most, lost no time hunting for the helmets. Dragging the chest from beneath the second seat and paying no attention to the marching soldier, who stepped over her each time he passed, she impatiently lifted the lid. The four helmets in the chest were of some pliant, glassy material resembling cellophane. They belted in at the waist, and after holding one up for Nick's inspection, Jellia put them back and returned the chest to its place.

"Now which leg of which table?" pondered the little Maid in Waiting, her mind turning to the altitude pills.

"Oh, what does it matter?" grinned the Tin Woodman as Jellia crawled under the navigator's table and began tapping its legs one after the other. "You'll soon be on solid earth and won't need altitude pills." Nick had made up his mind to bring the Oztober down to a landing wherever they happened to be. But Jellia scarcely heard him, for at that moment she had discovered a small hook on one of the front legs of the table. Pulling it down, she disclosed a tall, triangular bottle in the hollow center. The pills were triangular too, and of every color in the rainbow.

"Take one after each mile," read Jellia, uncorking the bottle and taking a good sniff. The pills smelled as good as they looked, and she was about to sample one when the Soldier with Green Whiskers gave a hoarse scream and such a leap that his head hit the ceiling.

"Now what's the matter?" demanded Nick Chopper, turning around stiffly, while Jellia hastily corked the bottle, shoved it back into the table leg and crawled into the aisle.

"NICK!" shrieked poor Jellia. "What is it? What are they? Oh, Ozma! Oh, Wizard! Oh, help! HELP!"

And well might Jellia scream, for swarming round the tail of the Oztober came a perfect horde of iridescent monsters. In shape each resembled an octopus, but instead of arms they had long, horny spikes and spines. Pressing close to the plane, they ogled at the shivering passengers as if they were fish in some strange aquarium. Then, evidently angered at what they saw, they began hurling and banging themselves against the sides of the Oztober till it sounded like the rattle of machine guns. At this juncture, I am sorry to report, Wantowin Battles, after sounding a shrill retreat on the bugle attached to his belt, rushed into the dressing room and wrapped himself in the shower curtain.

Nick Chopper, who already loved the Wizard's ship as if it were his own, shuddered as each spike struck the shining metal. Then, deciding that flight was the better part of valor, he hastily changed course, zooming up and up, faster and faster and FASTER! For perhaps a thousand feet the goggle-eyed monsters pursued them, but at last the air grew too thin and rare for the spikers, and one by one they fell away. Their horrid squeals and screeches still came faintly to the three voyagers, and Jellia ran quickly to the back window to stare down after them.

"Why, I never knew there were wild animals in the air," stuttered Jellia, blinking her eyes rapidly.

"Now, I wouldn't exactly call them wild animals," said Nick argumentatively, twisting his neck from side to side to be sure he was not rusting.

"Well, they certainly weren't birds!" declared Jellia indignantly. "And how did they fly without wings? Come on out, Soldier, they're gone."

"Ah, so we have won?" Jauntily, the Soldier stepped out of the dressing room and resumed his marching. "Give me credit for sounding the retreat, comrades," he observed cheerfully. Jellia sniffed, and Nick Chopper said nothing.

"What are we going to do now?" inquired the little Oz Maid, going over to stand by the wheel. "How can we ever fly down with those awful creatures below?"

"We'll just travel horizontally till we are out of their area," Nick told her complacently. "But for a while, anyway, we'll go up. After all, one has to go up to come down, you know. And when we do come down—" Nick gave a satisfied little nod "—it will be in a safe spot and far from those spiky airimals."

"So that's what they are! But how did you know?" Jellia looked admiringly at the Tin Woodman.

"Oh, it just came to me," admitted Nick with a modest cough. "Beasts of the air must have names, I suppose. Make a note of those monsters, will you, Wantowin?"

"I'm writing them up in my little green book now," mumbled the Soldier, who was in fact scribbling away hastily as he tramped up and down. "I've made a sketch of one, too."

"Good! Although I didn't suppose you'd looked at them long enough for that!" said Nick, a bit sarcastically. He glanced hastily at the page the soldier had before his nose. Then, deciding they had flown high enough, he pointed the Oztober toward the east, and after an hour's leisurely flying again began a slow and cautious descent.

"I do wonder where we'll land," mused Jellia, trying to pierce with her bright eyes the bank of fog that lay beneath.

"Somewhere in the Quadling Country, I should judge," answered Nick, twirling the wheel deftly to the right. "And when we do—" At that moment, the Soldier with Green Whiskers let out another panicky squawk.

"Climb! Climb!" he panted, running up and down the aisle so fast he almost ran himself down on the about-faces. "We're ambushed, comrades! Fire in the fog! Land on the stern!"

"Oh, tin cups and canyons!" rasped Nick Chopper, losing his temper at last. "If this keeps up, how are we ever to get down? Hammer and tong it! Something's always getting in the way. WILL you stop that silly marching?" he yelled, snatching at the Soldier's sleeve as he raced by.

"HALT!" quavered Wantowin. Instantly obeying his own command, he stood trembling beside the navigator's table as Nick peered desperately down through the fog.

Chapter 6 - Strut of the Strat

"What is it, Hippenscop?" Strutoovious the Seventh looked up impatiently as his first and fastest messenger came to a panting halt under the Imperial Canopy. Instead of answering, Hippenscop, his chest heaving and his eyes bulging, made a wordless gesture over his shoulder. Then, catching his foot in the royal bootscraper, he fell violently up the steps of the dais. This was not unusual, for anyone who falls in Stratovania falls up instead of down. Rather relieved to find himself before the throne at last, Hippenscop scrambled to his feet. Sucking in his breath, he announced hoarsely:

"I beg to report a strange and sonorbious monster falling through the fog over Half Moon Lake."

"Are you sure it is not a Zoomer?" Throwing down the morning star which he had been reading, Strutoovious stared coldly at the messenger.

"Ho, no! Ho, NO!" Hippenscop shook his head positively. "It has wings and a tail, your Stratjesty. Wings, a tail, and seven eyes! But HARK!" The menacing whirr and sputter following the messenger's speech made even the Ruler of all the Stratovanians leap off his throne. Striding rapidly after the terrified servitor, Strut, followed by half the inhabitants of his irradiant Tip-toposphere, reached the shores of Half Moon Lake.

"Skydragon!" he announced after a brief glance at the gleaming shape drifting down through the fog. "Quick, Hippen! Summon the Royal Blowmen! Back, stand back, you witless woffs! Do you wish to be crushed and eaten? Yon monster will alight on the North shore any moonite now!" At Strut's loud warning, half of his subjects took to their heels, while the rest scurried round to the South side of the lake, every head turned up toward the mysterious dragon.

Only of course it was not a dragon. It was the silver-bodied Oztober, inside of which the agitation was almost as great as the alarm of the Airlanders below.

"How long have we? How long'll it be before we land?" gulped Jellia. Remembering the Wizard's instructions, she jerked out the box of air helmets and next made a dive under the navigator's table. "Here, take one

— two— three— Oh, how many shall we take?" groaned the little Oz Maid, holding up the bottle of altitude pills. "'One, after each mile up,' but how many miles have we come?"

"One hundred and one thousand, eight hundred and sixty-seven feet!" mumbled the Soldier with Green Whiskers, reading the figures from a shining metal hypsometer clamped to the navigator's table. "All we have to do is figure how many feet in a mile."

"Fifty-two hundred and some," puffed Nick, working away desperately at his wheel and buttons to bring the Oztober down without crashing. "Oh, take twenty!" he directed sharply as Jellia and the Soldier stood regarding him with open mouths. It was no time, as Jellia later told Ozma, to be doing long division. With trembling fingers she counted out twenty pills for the Soldier with Green Whiskers. Then, popping twenty into her own mouth and crunching them desperately between her teeth, she handed the bottle to Nick Chopper.

"No, No! None for me!" The Tin Woodman waved the bottle impatiently aside. "High altitude won't injure my metal, but keep this oil can handy, Jellia, and whatever happens, don't let me rust!" Choking on the pills, which were dry and rather bitter, Jellia nodded earnestly. Tucking the oil can into the little bag that hung from her wrist, she began nervously dragging on her air helmet. Wantowin Battles already had adjusted his and swallowed his pills. Now, peering out one of the round windows, he trembled so violently all his weapons rattled and clanked to the dismal tune of his fright.

"Th-thousands of them!" quavered the Soldier. "What kind of place is this, anyway? It's so bright it hurts my eyes. Oh, I just know there'll be fighting! Look, I'd far better stay in the cabin, as someone must guard the plane!"

"But not YOU!" Nick Chopper spoke with great firmness. Then, spinning the wheel rapidly and gauging to a nicety the distance between the ship and the sparkling airosphere, he touched the "down" and "stop" buttons simultaneously. Coating down the last little hill of wind, the Oztober came to a gentle and complete stop on the shore of a rainbow-hued body of water.

"Now, now! Take your time," cautioned the Tin Woodman as Jellia started impulsively toward the door. Pulling off one of the cushion covers, Nick began polishing himself vigorously. As the discoverer of this new and astonishing airland, he wished to make a good impression. From what he had seen, it was a country well worth claiming for Ozma of Oz. "Here, let me go first," he said, tossing aside the cushion cover. "Keep close to me, Jellia and Soldier. Under no circumstances are you to retreat unless I give the signal. Great Tinhoppers, what was that?" A long wail rather like the squall of a cat suddenly had rent the quiet air of the cabin.

"Stowaway!" cried Jellia as another unmistakable meough followed the first. "Sounds like Dorothy's cat." But it was not Eureka that Jellia pulled from behind the second seat cushion. It was a small black kit-bag. The green eyes turned off and on like electric lights, and the tail curved over the back to form a handle. Round its neck hung a green placard:

"This Kit-Bag of Magic to be used

Only in cases of extreme emergency.

To open, pull the tail. — WIZ."

"Well, Gee Whiz, is this an emergency?" Jellia held the bag out nervously.

"Er— YES!" declared Nick Chopper after a second glance out of the window. "Bring it along! And remember, you have nothing to fear! I, the Emperor of all the Winkies, am with you. With kind words and courteous gestures we will win the friendship and allegiance of these strange airlanders for Ozma of Oz."

Jellia knew Nick's red plush heart, given him by the Wizard, was the kindest in all Oz. Nevertheless, she took a firmer hold on the kit bag, and only after assuring herself that Wantowin had his saber and blunderbuss did she follow the Tin Woodman down the Oztober's ladder.

There was a complete and astonished silence as the three Ozians stepped from the plane. And it must be confessed, Jellia and the Soldier in their transparent helmets and the Tin Woodman without a helmet were strange enough to startle any airbody. So it's no wonder the Stratovanians were as amazed at the appearance of the travelers as the travelers were amazed at the Stratovanians. Separated only by the waters of Half Moon Lake, they confronted each other with growing alarm. Strut, who had expected this dragon to roar, spurt flames and then rush forward to attack them, hardly knew what to do when these three curious beings stepped from the monster's interior. Noting with alarm that his Blowmen had not yet arrived, he determined to hold the invaders in conversation, if possible.

So with his head and chest high and walking with the queer, strutting gait that characterized all of the dwellers in Stratovania, he advanced slowly around the edge of Half Moon Lake. A few paces behind strutted the rest of his retainers. Just as slowly, Nick Chopper and his two companions advanced to meet them.

The Airlanders were a head taller than even the Tin Woodman. Their hair grew straight up on end, sparkling and crackling with electricity in a really terrifying manner. Their eyes were star-shaped and shaded by long, silver lashes; the noses and mouths were straight and firm, the foreheads transparent. Some shone as from a hidden sun, while across the brows of others tiny black clouds chased one another in rapid succession. Watching their foreheads would be a good way, decided Jellia Jam, to find out whether they were pleased or angry. Strut and his subjects wore belted tunics of some iridescent, rainbow-hued material, and silver sandals laced to the knee.

>From the ears of the men hung huge, crescent pendants, while from those of the women star earrings danced and dangled. Each Stratovanian carried a tall staff tipped with wings. Beyond, Jellia saw a country of such dazzling beauty, she was almost afraid to breathe lest it vanish before her eyes. The trees were tall and numerous, with gleaming, prism-shaped trunks and a mass of cloudlike foliage. Some bore fruit that actually seemed to be illuminated — oranges, pears, and peaches glowing like decorated electric light bulbs! Moon and star flowers grew in great profusion, and in the distance caves and grottoes of purest crystal scintillated in the high noon sun. So far as Jellia could see, there were no houses or castles, but there were hundreds of gay canopies held up by crystal poles. Jellia was just standing on tiptoe to glimpse the furnishings of the nearest Canopy when Nick Chopper, feeling that time had come to speak, raised his tin arm and called out imperiously:

"I, Emperor of the East and the Winkies, hereby claim this new and beautiful airosphere for Ozma of Oz, and bid you, its illustrious inhabitants, pledge to her your allegiance! At the same time, I bestow upon all of you Upper Airians free citizenship in the glorious Land of Oz!"

At this bold speech Strut stopped and stood as if rooted to the spot. Not only was he dumbfounded to discover he could understand the language of these curious beings, but if what he heard were correct, they actually were claiming his Kingdom for their own.

"Well, how was that?" whispered Nick, looking down sideways at Jellia.

"Terrible! Terrible!" moaned the little Oz Maid. "Oh, my! We'd better look out!" Catching hold of Wantowin's hand, for he already showed signs of retreating, she looked anxiously at the approaching Airman. Black clouds were simply racing across his imperial brow; his eyes flashed red and blue lights, and his hair positively crackled with indignation and fury.

"Oh, my, I do hope you are feeling well," ventured Jellia as Strut took an enormous stride toward them. "If you have a headache or anything, we could easily come back tomorrow."

"Stand where you are!" sneered Strut. Looking over his shoulder, he made sure his twenty tall Bowmen had arrived and were pushing their way through the crowd. "Stand where you are, or I'll have you blown to atoms!"

"Now, now, let us not come to blows!" begged Nick Chopper. "We have much to learn from you, and you from us, and I assure you we have come in the spirit of highest friendship!"

"Humph! So that's what it is, a friend ship! Looks like a dragon to me!" Folding his arms, Strut scowled past the three travelers to where the Oztober rested like some giant butterfly on the shore of Half Moon Lake. Then, making a secret signal to the Blowmen who had lined up before him, he shouted fiercely, "I am Strut of the Strat and Supreme Ruler of all the Upper Areas. In daring to claim Stratovania for your foolish countrywoman, you indeed aim high and will go, I promise you, still higher! Three blasts and a toot, men!" As Strut issued this cruel command, his twenty stern-looking warriors lifted their curved horns and puffed out their cheeks for a tremendous blow.

Jellia Jam, feeling that if they ever needed help it was right here and now, frantically sought with her one free hand to open the Wizard's Kit-Bag. As she fumbled with the curved handle, Strut raised his long arm. "Wait!" he cried tensely. "Not yet!" Lowering their horns and exhaling their breaths in loud whistles, the Blowmen stared at him in surprise. Strut had been examining the strangers from Oz more attentively. Now he strode over to Jellia, jerked off her helmet and ran his hand slowly over her smooth brown hair. Jellia, expecting to faint or expire without the helmet, let out a piteous groan. But the altitude pills were evidently powerful enough to protect her, and feeling no ill effects she glanced up timidly at the towering Stratovanian. Dark clouds no longer flitted across his brow. Indeed, he looked almost pleasant. "Ve-ry pret-ty!" he mused, stroking Jellia's hair softly. "Not wiry or stand-uppish like ours. Hippenscop!

298

Summon her Majesty the Queen. She'll be delighted with this beautiful little creature! But it is my intention to blow away these other insolent invaders from Oz, keeping only this smooth-haired lassie for our Starina."

"Oh, No! Oh, NO!" begged Jellia, pulling back with all her strength.

"Stop! You can't have Jellia," yelled Nick Chopper, flinging out his arms.

"Ready — aim — fire!" quavered the Soldier with Green Whiskers. And pointing his ancient gun at Strut, he valiantly pulled the trigger. But Wantowin's aim was very bad. The twenty marbles with which the gun was loaded sipped harmlessly past the Airman's ears, stinging quite a few of his subjects and frightening at least fifty into full flight. Strut himself was not impressed. Giving Nick a push that sent him sprawling and the Soldier a shove, he drew Jellia firmly away from her friends. Terrified as she was, the little Oz Maid could not help a small thrill of satisfaction to have been chosen by a monarch as High and Mighty as Strut of the Strat to be Starina to him and his Queen.

"As for you two," said Strut to Nick and the Soldier, "blowing up is quite painless, I assure you, and if you ever do come down, you'll doubtless have many interesting things to tell."

The Blowmen placed a guard around Nick and the Soldier, and stepped back to their posts. Nick Chopper and Wantowin, stunned by the swiftness of events, stared sadly at their little Jellia as the Blowmen for a second time raised their horns. But Strut, intent on his Warriors, had dropped Jellia's hand. Quick as a flash, she pulled the kit-bag's tail and pulled out the first object her fingers closed on. It was a small, green trumpet. Without stopping to think or reason, Jellia placed it to her lips and blew three frantic toots. Instantly a light-green vapor flowed from the mouth of the horn, spreading like a fast-moving cloud over the entire assemblage — a light-green vapor accompanied by three musical notes.

Chapter 7 - A Most Reluctant Starina

As the last note died away in a sweet, reluctant echo, Strut's Bowmen threw down their horns. With wild shouts and cheers, they began to embrace as if each were the other's long-lost brother. The behavior of the rest of the Stratovanians was equally puzzling. They sang, they whistled, they laughed and stamped their feet from sheer gaiety. Strut, hurrying over to Nick Chopper, shook him heartily by the hand.

"Say, Hay-Hurray! How ARE you?" he demanded exuberantly. "How are you and all of your aunts, uncles and infant nieces?"

"Wha — what's that?" sputtered Nick Chopper, completely taken aback by this sudden show of friendliness. Kabebe the Queen, tears of joy streaming down her moon-shaped face, seized the hands of the Soldier with Green Whiskers and was dancing him 'round and 'round. Unnoticed in the general hubbub and hilarity, Jellia managed to steal another glance at the green trumpet. Printed in white letters on the handle was this surprising sentence: "This trumpet contains cheer gas." Cheer Gas! With a tremulous sigh, for the last few moments had been a great strain, Jellia slipped the Wizard's instruments back into the kit bag and zipped it shut. Strangely enough, the gas had not affected any of the people from Oz. In fact, Jellia had never felt less like cheering in her whole life.

"This way! Ray, Ray, hurray!" shouted Strut, who now had Nick by one arm and the Soldier by the other. "Quickly! Go and prepare the Guest Canopies, Queen Kabebe! These travelers are doubtless weary and need rest and refreshment. Have you any preference as to canopies?" he inquired, leaning down to look in Nick Chopper's face.

"Do you have any tin canopies?" asked Nick hoarsely. He was still dazed by Strut's unaccountable change of manner. "I always feel safer under a tin roof. It is such a beautiful and dependable metal."

"Tin? Oh, Ha-Ha-HA!" Strut blinked his star eyes rapidly. "I'm afraid we have no tin, but any other kind, my dear—"

"Nick Chopper, Tin Woodman of Oz," put in Jellia, who felt it was high time they were properly introduced. "And there—" she hastily indicated the Soldier with Green Whiskers "—there is Wantowin Battles, the Grand Army of Oz!" At Jellia's introduction, Wantowin dropped Strut's arm to shake hands.

"And who are you, my lively little Skylark?" he questioned.

"Oh, I'm just Jellia Jam, Ozma's Chief Maid-in-Waiting," Jellia said as she trotted uneasily along at his side. The rest of the Stratovanians, still cheering and singing, but in a more subdued way, came streaming after them. Rather anxiously, Jellia wondered how long the effects of the cheer gas would last and how soon Strut would remember about blowing Nick and the Soldier away again. It seemed unlikely that she would have another chance to open the kit bag without detection.

The Queen, who had not been as cheered by the gas as the others, seemed somewhat unfriendly as she walked along behind her Royal Husband. Every few minutes, in fact, she would lean forward and give Jellia a spiteful pinch.

Jellia bore this rude treatment with extreme patience, making no complaint or outcry and merely walking a little faster to keep out of the creature's way. Jellia wanted to see all she could of this wonderful, sparkling airland so she could tell Ozma and Dorothy all about it when she returned to Oz.

The Soldier with Green Whiskers had fallen back to a place beside Queen Kabebe and was gazing about him with contemptuous snorts. Any country that was not green like the land surrounding the Emerald City held no interest for him. Noticing that Jellia was faring quite well without her helmet and finding his rather stuffy, he took it off and slung it over one shoulder. As he did so, he caught the Queen in the very act of pinching Jellia. Disgusted by such conduct, he sternly took her arm, and each time Kababe pinched Jellia, the Soldier would slap her fingers. After the fifth slap, the Queen peered at him with astonished admiration, for on this whole Tip-toposphere there was no man bold enough to strike a member of the reigning family. Soon Kababe was so fascinated by Wantowin's flowing green whiskers, she forgot all about pinching Jellia. By this time the strange and still faintly cheering procession had reached Strut's Royal Canopy. Waving away his giggling Bowmen, Strut lifted Jellia to one of the splendid Star Thrones.

To Kabebe King Strut spoke impatiently. "Don't you remember you were to see about the Guest Canopies?" Kababe dared not object, but looked quite displeased. "Just tell Bittsywittle to bring us a tray of air-ades and a wind pudding," ordered Strut, giving the Queen a jovial shove to help her on her way. "You'd like an air-ade, wouldn't you, little lady?" Poor Jellia shook her head no and then quickly changed it to yes. The furnishings of the Royal Pavilion were so rich and dazzling and the Star Throne so high and grand that she felt completely bewildered. As Kabebe shuffled away, Jellia smiled nervously at Nick and the Soldier. At Strut's invitation they had seated themselves cross-legged on bright-blue air cushions and looked as uncomfortable as they felt.

"Well, what do you think of Stratovania by now?" inquired Strut, settling back complacently. "I believe you will all enjoy high life as much as we do once you are used to it."

Nick Chopper was on the point of saying they had no intention of getting used to it or of staying one single moment longer than was positively necessary when he caught Jellia's worried expression and muttered instead, "Beautiful, very beautiful."

"But where are the houses?" asked the Soldier with Green Whiskers bluntly. "These tent tops are all right for a war or for field sports, but I should think you'd find them rather chilly for all year 'round living."

"Stratovania," explained Strut as he crossed his long legs, "is never chilly. It is surrounded by a rim of warm air that keeps the temperature just as you find it today. No wind, no rain, no storms of any kind," he concluded proudly.

"And it's all so bright and shiny," sighed Jellia Jam, blinking down at the floor of the pavilion, which was an inlay of sparkling glass, and then off to the countless bright canopies that dotted the airscape beyond. The surface of Strut's curious Skyland was of gleaming crystal, sometimes smooth as ice, sometimes rough and rocky, but always flashing with the brilliance of diamonds. "Everything sparkles so," finished Jellia, rather wishing she had brought her dark glasses.

"That's because Stratovania is formed of solid air," smiled Strut, tapping one of the iridescent posts that supported the silken canopy over their heads. "And I am its High and Mighty Sovereign, ruler of the Spikers who inhabit the strata below and of the Zoomers who inhabit the strata above, and of all the other spheres and half-spheres in this particular area. Strut of the Strat! Consider THAT, Little One, and be proud that you have been chosen to be our Starina!"

"But Jellia can't stay here!" cried the Soldier with Green Whiskers, springing indignantly to his feet. "Jellia's—"

"Tut! Tut! Now do not excite yourself! Here comes Bittsywittle, and we'll all have a glass of liquid air." As Strut leaned forward to speak to his small, electric-haired page, Jellia shook her head sharply at Nick and the Soldier, for both seemed on the point of dragging her off the throne.

"Wait!" Jellia formed the word soundlessly, and with puzzled frowns her two friends sank back on their air cushions, accepting rather glumly the sparkling goblets of air-ade from the light-footed servitor. With the air-ade Bittsywittle passed heaping saucers of wind pudding, a fluffy, cloud-like confection that made Jellia's mouth positively water.

"You will find the diet here light but nourishing," Strut informed them blandly. "Our atmosphere is so rare and exhilarating, we need little but sun and starlight to keep us going. But now, friends, I propose a toast to Jellia, our new Starina!" As Nick and Wantowin rose unwillingly to their feet, for the whole affair struck them as perfectly preposterous, Strut lifted his glass and downed his air-ade. Then the Soldier rather sulkily drank his. Nick, who never partook of food or drink of any kind, set his goblet on a small tabouret and stared sadly at Jellia Jam. The Tin Woodman feared she was seriously considering Strut's proposal. Jellia surmised what Nick was thinking, but as there was no way of explaining that she was just trying to gain time till they could find some way to escape, she smiled wanly back at him and swallowed her own air-ade.

Suddenly Jellia felt herself rising into the air. Before she could utter a sound, her head was pressed tightly against the top of the canopy. Then, dizzily, she began to float 'round and 'round like a pretty balloon just let off its string.

"Ho, Ho!" roared Strut. "Our air-ade has made you light-headed, m'lass! But wait, I'll fetch you down!" He tapped the winged staff he held in his right hand sharply on the floor. Instantly, it spread its wings, carrying him up beside Jellia. Grasping her hand, he drew her down to the throne.

"There," he chuckled, handing her a heavy glass globe to hold, "that will weigh you down!" Reflecting that one of these winged sticks might be a handy thing to have, Jellia clutched the glass globe. Still weak and giddy from her flight, she could not bring herself to touch the wind pudding Bittsywittle had placed on the arm of the throne. The Soldier with Green Whiskers, on account of his heavy weapons and boots, had not gone so high as Jellia, but even he, instead of sitting on his air cushion, was now seated on nothing — three feet above Nick Chopper's head. He looked extremely unhappy, as indeed he was.

"Don't worry," grinned Strut, who seemed highly amused by the whole affair, "you'll come down presently." He tapped his winged staff on the head as he spoke, and the staff immediately folded its wings. "Tell me," he urged, turning to Nick Chopper, who was looking anxiously from the Soldier to Jellia. "Do you come from below or be-high?"

"Be-oth," answered the Tin Woodman, too confused by this time to know what he was saying. "Taking off from the Emerald City of Oz, we first flew up, then over, then up and next down!"

"Hmmm-mmmn, OZ?" Two very black clouds floated across Strut's transparent brow. "I seem to remember your mentioning Oz before! I seem to remember—" Strut's voice was no longer pleasant, and watching his brow growing blacker and blacker, Jellia frantically sought to open the Wizard's kit bag. Unless she could release some more of the cheer gas, almost anything might happen.

Out of the third point of his left star eye, Strut saw what she was doing. "Don't fidget, my dear," he snapped crossly. "It is unbecoming for our new Starina of Stratovania to fidget or to unpack her own bag. Here—" Taking the kit bag from her, he tossed it carelessly beneath his throne. Jellia's heart sank. She hoped Nick would say no more about claiming Stratovania for Ozma. But the Tin Woodman, already launched upon a glowing description of their famous Fairy Land, was working up to that very point.

"One hundred and one thousand, eight hundred and sixty-seven feet below this airosphere," began Nick, taking a long breath, "lies the grand, grand and incomparable Fairyland of Oz. Oblong in shape, it is divided into four triangular Kingdoms. The Northern and Purple Land of the Gillikens is ruled by Jo King; the Blue, Western Land of the Munchkins by his Majesty King Cheeriobed; the Eastern, Yellow Land of the Winkies is governed by myself; the Southern Red Land of the Quadlings by Glinda, the Good Sorceress.

"But all of us are subject to the benign rule of Ozma, the young Fairy Ruler of the whole Kingdom. Her capitol, the Emerald City, in the exact center of Oz, is one of the most beautiful cities out of the world! Surrounding Oz and protecting it from invasions is a deadly desert, and in Ozma's possession are more jewels and treasure than you doubtless have seen in the whole of your air existence."

"Humph!" growled Strut, looking fiercer than ever. But paying no heed to the ominous storm clouds forming on his brow, Nick loftily proceeded. "Not only is Ozma possessed of more jewels than any other sovereign known, but in her castle are magic appliances that make her the most powerful of rulers. For instance, Ozma has a magic belt with which she can transport anyone anywhere. On her wall hangs a magic picture in which she can see what is happening to her friends or foes, right while it is happening. In her safe is a magic fan to blow away her enemies, and so many other strange instruments of magic I have not time to describe them. Among her advisors is the famous Wizard of Oz, who spends all his time studying magic and perfecting new inventions. The Ozoplane in which we made this perilous flight is his latest masterpiece. And now that you know a bit more of Ozma and her famous country, I am sure you will be delighted to become a part of our happy realm and acknowledge Ozma as the Supreme Sovereign of Stratovania."

"What?" screamed Strut, bounding off his throne and furiously confronting the Tin Woodman. "How DARE you suggest such a thing? This is the second time you have done so! Why should I, Strut of the Strat, acknowledge this miserable earthlander as my supreme anything? I am a thousand times richer and more important than any Belowlander below. Oz! OZ! Indeed!"

As Nick backed off in alarm, Strut shook his long staff over the Tin Woodman's head. "Why, you can't even pronounce the name of your own country!" he sneered. "It is not Oz, as you say it, but OHS — the Zone of Ohs, to be more correct. And if Ohs is in the zone of Ohs, it is Ozone, which means AIR — and that makes it belong to ME! So I, Strut of the Strat, hereby do claim OZONIA for myself and my people, and you, my fine Mr. Funnel Top, shall take me there!"

Chapter 8 - Strut of the Strat Sets off for Oz

"Don't you do it! Don't you do it!" Plumping down on his air cushion, for the effects of the air-ade had worn off at last, the Soldier with Green Whiskers wildly sounded retreat on his green bugle. Jellia, knowing he would run as fast as he could and perhaps wreck the Ozoplane before she and Nick could reach it, jumped off her throne and seized him by the coattails. As she did so, Strut gave the glass gong beside him a resounding whack. Before any of the three travelers could take another step, the twenty Blowmen tramped back into the Royal Pavilion. The cheer engendered by the cheer gas had entirely evaporated by now, and they looked very grim indeed. At a signal from Strut, one seized Nick, a second the Soldier. A third was taking hold of Jellia when Strut sternly waved his aside.

"No, No! Not that one! She is our new Starina!" he told the Blowmen roughly. "Now, you are to stay right here, Jellia, my dear, and help rule over Stratovania while I descend to Ohs and take possession of that rich and prosperous country. And sooner than soon I will return, bringing you the magic treasure and jewels and the crown and scepter of this Ohsma!"

"Oh, but you musn't!" wailed Jellia, clasping her hands desperately. "Ozma is a real Princess and much more beautiful than I!"

"In that case, I shall bring Ohsma back and make her a Starina also!" promised Strut.

"Now Hippenscop," he directed, shaking his finger at the odd-looking page, "you and Junnenrump are to obey Jellia in everything. I'll leave three Blowmen here to protect our Starina. The others, and all of my able-bodied fighters, shall fly with me to Ohs."

"The Ozoplane holds only four!" cried Jellia, looking desperately over at Nick, who was struggling angrily to free himself from the Blowmen. But they had his arms pinioned behind his back, and the poor Tin Woodman was unable to help himself.

"Oh, that's all right!" answered Strut. "I and this Tin Emperor will ride in the Friend-ship, and the others will follow on their flying sticks, and soon I will return with all the treasures of Ohs!" As the Blowmen started away, shoving Nick and the Soldier with Green Whiskers ahead of them, Jellia felt so frightened and alone that she burst into tears.

"Oh, please, please, couldn't you leave the Soldier to keep me company?" she sobbed, wiping her streaming eyes on her sash.

"Of course, if you wish!" Motioning to the Blowmen, they picked up Wantowin as if he had been a sack of potatoes and tossed him roughly back into the Royal Pavilion. He landed with a clatter at Jellia's feet.

"But see here! I am not sure I can find the way back to Oz!" protested Nick Chopper as Strut fell into step at his side. "I happened upon this airosphere by the merest chance and have no idea in which direction Oz now lies."

"Just the same, I think you will take me there!" Strut grinned wickedly, tapping Nick on the shoulder with his staff. He already had sent Junnenrump to summon the army, and, glancing over his shoulder, Nick saw a thousand young airmen strutting along behind them. As they came to the shores of Half Moon Lake, Hippenscop came panting and gasping into view.

"Her Skyness the new Starina bade me give you this," he puffed, handing the Tin Woodman the small oil can the Wizard had given him at the party. Nick had forgotten all about his oil can, and without it he was likely to rust and become perfectly helpless. Taking it thankfully from the messenger, he hung it on a hook beneath his arm and headed reluctantly for the Oztober. Nick had no intention of flying Strut to the Emerald City. Even if he had to wreck the plane, he would find some way to keep the greedy airman and his legions from conquering Oz. Then he would return and rescue Jellia and the soldier.

But without a word to Strut, for argument at this point would have been useless, he mounted the ladder, walked through the cozy cabin, and seated himself in the pilot's chair. Strut paused on the top rung of the ladder before he entered. "Follow us closely, men," he commanded gruffly, "no matter how far or fast we fly." Strut's young warriors raised their flying staffs to show that they understood, and with a few final directions, the Stratovanian stepped over the sill, slammed the door of the Oztober and walked rapidly forward, examining everything with lively interest.

"So this dragon-body really flies?" he said, bending curiously over the navigator's table. "Ho, what's this? I thought you told me you had no way of finding the route back." Nick Chopper, much more surprised than Strut, picked up the tidy map that lay on top of the buttons. It certainly had not been there when he left the plane, but here it was now, showing the complete course they had taken since leaving the Emerald City. Concluding this was some of the Wizard's magic, Nick examined the map attentively. Each turn up or down, each mile east or west, was charted accurately.

"All you have to do is follow this in reverse," exclaimed Strut. Unaccustomed as he was to flying except by staff, he was nevertheless sharp enough to realize the value of a good map when he saw one. "And remember now, no tricks!" he warned sternly. "Land me safely in Ohs and you will be suitably rewarded. But land me anywhere else and you will be completely obliterated!"

Nick said nothing. Weary of Strut's threats and boasts, the Woodman touched the button to inflate the Oztober's balloon, and the "up," "south" and "fast" buttons. In the whirr and splutter of their takeoff, the Airlander's further remarks and directions were completely drowned out.

Chapter 9 - Jellia In a Frightful Jam

For a long time after the departure of the Tin Woodman and of Strut and his legions, Jellia sat forlornly on the Star Throne trying to stem the tears that coursed slowly down her cheeks. To be stranded on this high and dangerous airosphere was bad enough, but the thought of Strut flying off to destroy Ozma and steal all her treasures was more frightening still.

"What on airth shall we do?" questioned Jellia with a rueful smile of the Soldier with Green Whiskers, who was tramping morosely up and down the pavilion. Halting in his march, Wantowin shook his head dubiously.

"That I cannot say!" he murmured, taking off his cap and staring gloomily inside. "I have no standing in this country at all! But you, Jellia, are a Starina. Therefore you must decide what is to be done. And whatever your Majesty's orders may be, I will carry them out to the letter. To the letter!" declared Wantowin, standing up very straight and tall.

"Oh, bother `my Majesty'!" scolded Jellia. "You know perfectly well I didn't ask to be a Starina of this terrible place!"

"It is not what you want, but what you are that counts!" insisted the Soldier, stubbornly. "And there's no getting around it, Jellia, you are a Starina! So while you are deciding what is to be done, I'll just do a bit of reconnoitering. It might be well to know the lay of the air!"

"Wait!" cried Jellia as Wantowin started smartly down the steps. "Whatever you do, Wanny, don't run!" she implored earnestly. "You might easily run off the edge, and then where'd you be? So do please be careful, and if anything frightens you, run straight back here! Do you promise?"

"Nothing ever frightens me!" said the Soldier in an offended voice. Marching sternly down the steps, he was off at a double-quick, without even a glance over his shoulder. Feeling more alone than ever, Jellia sighed and folded her hands in her lap. But Wantowin's words, foolish as they were, had done her good. After all, she was a Starina, for the time being anyway. So, straightening her crown and drying her tears, Jellia tried to think how she should act under such bewildering circumstances.

How would Ozma act, for instance, if she were sitting on the throne of this singular airtry? Even thinking of the gentle and dignified little Girl Ruler of Oz steadied Jellia. Holding her head very high, she stepped down from the dais and began pacing slowly up and down the pavilion, switching her green skirts in such a regal manner that the two messengers who had returned quietly to their posts stared at her with new interest and admiration.

"Is there anything we might bring your Stratjesty?" asked Junnenrump, bowing from the waist and clicking his heels smartly together. At his question Jellia paused and eyed the two speculatively.

"Why, yes," she decided after a moment's thought. "You, Junnenrump, may send someone to amuse me, and you, Hippenscop, may bring me two of those winged staffs. It is neither safe nor proper for a Starina and her Army to be without them!"

"But your Skyness!" Hippenscop leaped into the air and spun round and round in an agony of embarrassment. "There are no extra staffs!" he blurted, finally coming to a stop before her. The little fellow looked so distressed, Jellia was on the point of letting him off. Then, remembering just in time that she was bound to be obeyed, she raised her arm.

"Go!" she commanded haughtily. "And do not return without two winged staffs!" Junnenrump already had started, and at Jellia's stern command Hippenscop backed dejectedly down the steps, his eyes bulging with dismay and consternation.

"If Wanny and I had flying sticks, we'd at least be as well off as the rest of these Airlanders," reasoned Jellia, resuming her walk. "But what funny names," she mused as the messengers disappeared in two different directions and at two different speeds. "They make me think of—" Here Jellia took a little run and jump, following it with a skip and a hop. "I suppose," she continued, talking conversationally to herself, "that is what their names really mean, everything is so mixed up here." Regaining her throne in one long slide, Jellia brought up with a slight start. This, she decided, was no way for a Starina to act. Smoothing down her dress, she walked sedately to Strut's throne and reached underneath.

The real reason she had got rid of the messengers, of course, was so she could recover the kit-bag and have a chance to examine its contents without being observed. The cheer gas had saved them on one occasion, and perhaps there was magic powerful enough to enable her and the Soldier to escape from the airosphere before Strut returned. The bag was still there, and snatching it up in her arms, Jellia climbed back on the throne. But just as she was about to zip it open, Junnenrump bounded up the steps of the pavilion, dragging a lean old Skylander by the hand.

"His Majesty's Piper!" announced Junnenrump, giving the Piper a shove forward and seating himself expectantly on the messenger's bench. Jellia was annoyed to have Junnenrump return so soon. But since she had sent for someone to amuse her, she could not very well object. So, resting her chin in her hand, she looked curiously at the Royal Piper. The old Skylander was tremendously tall and thin. His tunic was short and plaited, and under his arms he carried a pair of enormous bagpipes. Jellia had not cared for bagpipes, but on an airosphere she supposed wind instruments such as this naturally would be popular. The Piper, however, did not immediately play on his pipes. Instead, he struck a few light and pleasant chords on the top buttons of his tunic.

"Shall I do a buck and wing, or a little Skyland fling?

Shall I sing a little sing, for you, Dear?"

bawled the Piper cheerfully. He looked so funny that Jellia burst out laughing. Thus encouraged, the Piper proceeded to sing, punctuating his song with extraordinary leaps and toe tappings.

"When we Skylanders feel low, we just Dance the stratispho;

"Step it high, kick and fly, toss the Partner up ski-high. High HO!

"Would you care to try it?" he asked politely, holding out his hand to Jellia.

"No, No! Not today!" gasped the Oz maid, backing as far as the star throne would allow. "But I've really enjoyed watching you very much, and your singing is lovely," she added generously.

"Ah, but wait until you hear me play," puffed the Piper. Raising his pipes, he blew forth such a hurricane of whistles, squeals and fierce thunderings that poor Jellia clapped both hands to her ears. "Tell him to go away," she screamed above the awful din, wildly motioning to Junnenrump, who was tapping his foot in time to the pipes and looking highly diverted. "Tell him to come back tomorrow."

The fierce music of the bagpipes had brought airlanders running from every direction. Crowding round the pavilion, they waved and bowed to the new Starina. Realizing she never would have any privacy under the Imperial Canopy, Jellia slipped off her throne. The messenger had the Piper by the tunic tails and was easing him gently down the steps. Jellia waited till they reached the bottom, then, as all the airlanders began to run after the still furiously pumping piper, Jellia started in the opposite direction. Surely somewhere, she thought, clutching the kit-bag close to her, somewhere she could find a quiet corner or cave or clump of bushes where she could examine the contents of the Wizard's bag without interruption.

So anxious was Jellia to be by herself, she broke into a run. Failing to notice a crystal bar stretched across the path, she tripped and fell violently up a tune tree. Falling down is bad enough, but falling up is worse still. Jellia not only had barked her shins on the crystal bar, but had bounced into the air so high she lost her breath and plunged down so abruptly among the top branches of the tune tree that she was somewhat scratched and shaken. She knew it must be a tune tree because plump black notes grew in clusters like cherries between the leaves. Several, dislodged by her fall, broke into gay little arias and chords. At any other time Jellia would have been quite interested, but now she was too agitated and upset to care.

"Such a country — or airtry!" groaned the Oz maid, rubbing her left ankle and her right knee. "One can't even fall down in their own way!" Parting the branches, the ruffled little girl looked crossly out. It was quite a long way to the ground, but nevertheless Jellia decided to climb down. But suddenly it occurred to her that the top of the tune tree was as good a place as any to open the kit-bag. Easing herself to a larger limb, she balanced the bag carefully in her lap and stretched out her hand to pull the tail. Then a piercing scream and the thump of a hundred footsteps made her draw it back in a hurry. Parting the branches of the tree for a second time, she saw Wantowin Battles running toward her like the wind.

"Help! Help! Save me!" yelled the Soldier with Green Whiskers. And he had reason to yell, for just two leaps behind him panted Kabebe, waving an enormous crystal rolling pin. After the Queen pounded the three big Blowmen, and after the Blowmen came nearly a hundred men, women and children. Before Jellia had time even to guess why they were chasing the Army, Wantowin tripped over the same crystal bar that had caused her upfall and landed with a terrific grunt in the branches beside her, scattering half- and quarter-notes in every direction. The Airlanders stopped short and watched with breathless interest as the Soldier disappeared into the thick foliage of the tune tree.

"What's the matter? What happened?" whispered Jellia, reaching out to steady the soldier, who was bouncing wildly up and down on a nearby limb.

"YOU?" gasped Wantowin, almost losing his balance at the shock of seeing her. "Oh, Jellia! We must leave at once! AT ONCE! As I was passing the cooking caves, Kabebe rushed out and grabbed me. She has decided to blow us away most any minute now. She has persuaded the Airlanders that Strut is lost and never will return. Oh why, WHY, did we ever fly to this terrible place?"

"Be quiet!" hissed Jellia, frightened almost out of her wits at this new turn of affairs. "How can I think with you making all that noise?"

"Come down! Come down!" bawled Kabebe. "Come down before I shake you down!" Grasping the trunk of the tune tree, she gave it a playful shake.

"You might as well go down," she whispered resignedly as the Queen gave the tree a tremendous shake that nearly dislodged them both.

"Not without you," shivered Wantowin, hugging his branch for dear life.

"Oh, well, let's get it over with," said Jellia despairingly. "Blowing away may not be so bad, and I'd rather do anything than stay up here." Tucking the kit-bag under one arm, Jellia swung herself down by the other and dropped lightly to the ground.

"What is the meaning of this outrageous behavior?" she demanded as Wantowin dropped fearfully beside her. "His Majesty shall hear of this, I promise you."

Kabebe, astonished to see Jellia as well as the Soldier with Green Whiskers drop out of the tree, took a hasty step backward. Jellia quickly followed up her advantage. "I'm amazed!" she said sternly. "I thought you knew that I was to help you rule while King Strut is away!" At this bold speech, Wantowin looked at Jellia in round-eyed admiration. Though her cheeks were scratched and her crown slightly askew, the little Waiting Maid looked every inch a ruler's helper, if not a ruler. Even the Blowmen began to shift uneasily from one foot to the other, their mouths falling open at Jellia's indignation. But Kabebe raised both arms and fairly screeched at the little Oz Maid.

"How dare you speak to me like that?" she shrieked. "King Strut is lost and never will return! I am Queen here, and I don't need your help! Blowmen! Seize this impudent pair, march them to the edge of the cliffs, and blow them away." The crowd of Stratovanians looked uncertainly from Kabebe to Jellia.

"His Highness left you here to protect me!" Jellia reminded them sternly. But even as she spoke, she knew they had decided to obey Kabebe. She was flashing her star eyes so threateningly and waving her winged stick to close to their heads that the Blowmen were afraid to defy her.

"Come along now," grumbled the first Blowman, taking Jellia roughly by the arm. "You've caused enough trouble here!"

The other two Blowmen seized the trembling Soldier and began marching sternly toward the edge of Strut's Skyland. Jellia pulled back with all her strength, as also did Wantowin, but hustled along by the huge Skylanders they could do little to help themselves. Relentlessly, with the jeering citizens of Stratovania running along after them, the unfortunate Oz pair was dragged on.

"Just wait till your Master hears about this," sobbed Jellia as the Blowmen shoved them as near to the edge of the cliffs as they dared go themselves. Then they stepped back to lift their horns. Jellia had managed to retain her hold on the Wizard's kit-bag, but even so she felt that their last moment had come.

Jellia gave a final sad little wave to the Soldier, who really was quite brave now that his doom had arrived. The Blowmen pointed their horns straight at them, but before they even could inflate their cheeks, a fierce roar and splutter from the clouds caused every head to turn upwards.

"The ship, the ship! The flying ship!" cried the First Blowman, letting his horn fall disregarded to the ground.

"It's Strut!" screamed the Stratovanians, treading on one another's toes in their sudden frenzy to be out of sight of their Master when he landed.

"'Tis the Master himself!" cried the first Blowman, yanking Jellia and the Soldier back from the edge of the Skyland. Pulling Kabebe along with them, the Blowmen ran as never before, closely followed by Strut's scurrying subjects. One moment later there was not a single airbody in sight. Convinced that their cruel and brilliant ruler had returned, they ran like rabbits. Some even flew, helping themselves along with their winged staffs, while Jellia, sinking on a large crystal boulder, stared dazedly at the silver-bodied plane dropping rapidly toward them.

"It can't be the Oztober!" cried Jellia delightedly. "It couldn't have come back so soon!"

"It's not!" cried Wantowin Battles, tossing up his cap and waving his arms exuberantly. "It's the other one, the Ozpril, and that means—" In his extreme excitement, the Soldier tripped over a balloon bush and fell seven feet into the air. "It means the Wizard himself has come to help us," sputtered Wantowin, blinking rapidly as he landed hard on the rock beside the young Oz maid. "Three cheers, Jellia! The Wizard of Oz has saved us!"

Chapter 10 - The Wizard in Stratovania!

It was indeed the Ozpril, just as the Soldier with Green Whiskers had said. Even at a distance, Jellia could spell out the name on the gleaming body, and as the silvery plane came swooping toward them she could not repress a shout of joy.

Too exhausted by the dreadful ordeal she had just been through to run to meet the ship, she jerked off her scarf and waved it wildly over her head. About ten feet from the crystal boulder on which she had been sitting, the Ozpril came to a gentle and perfect landing. Scarcely had the whirr and sputter of its engine died away before the door of the cabin burst open, and down climbed the little Wizard of Oz, followed by Dorothy and the Scarecrow. The Cowardly Lion, last of all, had difficulty fitting his paws on the rungs and after a trembling descent rolled over on his back, his four feet straight up in the air. The trip had not agreed with the Cowardly Lion at all. Weak and dizzy, he made no attempt to rise.

"Here you are at last!" cried the Wizard happily, rushing over to Jellia and seizing both of her hands. "So THIS is where you've been! Well, I must say it's a fine place. Why, it's beautiful, beautiful!" Swinging round so he could look in all directions, the Wizard positively glowed with interest and enthusiasm.

"What's so beautiful about it?" growled the lion without turning over. "Is there any grass? Are there any trees? Is there anything to eat?" Dorothy, on the point of embracing Jellia, gave a little scream, for the Tell-all-escope, which she had picked up just before leaving the plane, was making terse announcements. At this point it happened to be pointed at Jellia. Clearing its throat, it remarked in a superior way:

"You are now looking at Miss Jellia Jam, formerly of Oz, at present new Starina of the Strat, by edict of Strutoovious the Seventh. Miss Jellia Jam, Starina of Stratovania! Period! Stop, drop or point elsewhere!"

"Why, Jellia!" gasped Dorothy, letting the Tell-all-escope fall with a crash. "Are you really? Oh my! I don't suppose you'll ever want to return to Oz now. Why, you must be having a wonderful time!"

"Humph!" sniffed Jellia with a slightly wan smile. "If being pinched, chased and nearly blown to atoms is having a wonderful time, then I guess I've been having it, all right!"

"Tell me," requested the Scarecrow, who had been walking in a slow circle around Jellia. "Does one prostrate oneself before a Starina, or does one merely kiss her hand?"

"Neither," laughed Jellia. Jumping up, she gave the Scarecrow such a hug he was out of shape for hours. "But quick! Let's all hop in the Ozpril and fly away before something terrible happens."

"Fly away?" cried the Wizard, shoving back his high hat. "But, my dear, we've only just come! I've been flying all night and need a little rest and refreshment before we start off again. Besides, I would like to see more of this interesting airland and its people and add to my data on the Strata."

"That's what Nick thought," observed Jellia, putting both her hands on her hips. "And look what happened to him!"

"What did happen to him?" demanded the Wizard, realizing for the first time that Nick was not among those present.

"You tell him," sighed Jellia to the Soldier. Sinking back on the boulder, she held her aching head in both hands. All eyes turned toward the Soldier with Green Whiskers, who opened and closed his mouth several times without saying a word. The Wizard, now thoroughly alarmed, began shaking him on one side and the Scarecrow on the other, until finally Wantowin took a tremendous swallow and gave them the whole story.

When the narrator reached the part where Strut had ordered Nick and him blown away, the Scarecrow hurried over to the balloon bush and began picking the almost-ripe balloons as fast as his clumsy cotton fingers would permit. Not till he had about twenty did he even pause. So light and flimsy was the straw man that the bunch of balloons on their long stems kept jerking him into the air. After each jerk he would give a little grunt of satisfaction.

"These are just to keep me aloft— in case of accidents," he explained hastily to Dorothy, who was watching him intently.

"But what of us?" asked the little girl, looking anxiously toward the Canopied City, which at present seemed absolutely deserted.

"You say that this wretched Strut, after naming Jellia Starina, forced Nick to fly him to Oz?" exclaimed the Wizard, grasping Wantowin Battles by both arms and gazing into his face.

"Not only that," Wantowin told him hoarsely, "but he's taken his Blowmen and a thousand fighting men to conquer the country! He intends to bring back Ozma's crown, scepter, jewels and all the treasures in our castle!" finished the Soldier dolefully.

"Oh, can't we do something, Wizard?" cried Jellia determinedly. "I simply won't be Starina! I won't! I WON'T!"

"Just the same, you make a very pretty one," murmured the Scarecrow, patting the little Oz Maid consolingly on the shoulder. "But of course, we cannot allow this bounding airlander to take Oz!"

"If Nick had not `taken possession' of Stratovania for Ozma, he'd never have thought of it," groaned Jellia. Rising stiffly, she picked up the kit-bag from the crystal rock beside her.

"Ah, so you still have my magic kitty!" In spite of his anxiety, the Wizard smiled.

"Indeed I have," said Jellia firmly. "It saved us from being blown away. I used some of your cheer gas, Wiz, but I didn't have time to try out any of the other magic. Here, you'd better take it now, and do let's be starting. No telling when Kabebe and those three Blowmen will be coming back."

"Forward march! Forward march!" Wantowin Battles started off all by himself for the Ozpril. "Hurry, hurry!" he called over his shoulder. "If those fearful people return, they'll surely make trouble!" yelled the Soldier, his voice growing more emphatic.

"Well, it's certainly a mix-up," said Dorothy, moving closer to the Wizard.

"What do these people look like, Jellia?" she asked curiously. "Really, I'd enjoy seeing a few."

"They look like nothing you have ever imagined!" Jellia told her with a slight shudder. "Goochers! Here come some now! And oh, it's those Blowmen, and all the others! Look, Wizard! Could we reach the Ozpril before they reach us?"

"Let's not try," decided the Wizard as the Blowmen broke into a run. "Even if we made the plane, they might blow us to bits before I could get her started. Let's stay here and reason with them till I find something in this bag to help us."

"Oh, woe is we! Oh, woe is we!" gulped the Scarecrow, taking little runs and leaps into the air, hopeful that his balloons would lift him out of the danger zone as the threatening company drew closer. The Queen was marching grimly ahead of her subjects. In some way, decided Jellia, she had discovered Strut had not been in the silver plane. As the Wizard opened his kit bag, the little Oz Maid rushed over to the Cowardly Lion.

"Get up!" directed Jellia, giving him a desperate prod with her toe. "Get up! We need your growl — and LISTEN!" she begged as the big beast rolled over and blinked sleepily at the approaching airlanders. "Do everything I tell you, or we are lost, LOST!"

Dorothy concluded Jellia had been quite right about the inhabitants of Stratovania. They certainly were like no one she ever had seen, and she could not help admiring the bold way Jellia stepped out to meet her dangerous adversary.

"Just what are you doing here?" demanded Jellia, folding her arms and tilting up her chin. "Did I not order you to leave us strictly alone? Blowmen, take this Kabebe woman away!"

"Kabebe's our Queen," muttered one of the Blowmen, scowling at Jellia. "At least," he corrected, glancing at his comrades, "she is our Queen until Strut returns."

"What makes you think Strut has NOT returned?" questioned Jellia grandly. "Do you not recognize your Master?" With a regal wave, Jellia pointed to the Cowardly Lion. "Do you not believe that this is Strut — changed to this great beast by Ozma of Oz? But he is as powerful and able as ever to rule this Kingdom! Strut!" Imperiously, Jellia appealed to the Cowardly Lion. "Am I the Starina of Stratovania?"

The poor lion was as startled at Jellia's question as the Stratovanians. From sheer shock, he rose on his hind legs and let out a perfectly awful roar — which was perhaps as convincing an answer as he could have given.

"There! You see?" Jellia shrugged her shoulders as Queen Kabebe and the Blowmen turned white as ghosts and began to move away.

"It does sound like the Master," stuttered the Blowman as the Cowardly Lion followed up his roar with a reverberating growl.

"What are your Majesty's wishes?" inquired Jellia, inclining her head graciously toward the trembling lion.

"Take that woman away and have our supper prepared and served at once in the Royal Pavilion!" directed the lion in his most commanding roar.

Chapter 11 - King, King — Double King!

The effect of the Cowardly Lion's speech was astonishing indeed. The Stratovanians behind the Queen turned and ran for their lives. They started backing away so fast they fell up at every step, so that their progress was curious enough to watch. There were few animals on the airosphere, and certainly none that talked. Thoroughly convinced that the Cowardly Lion was Strut and Strut was the lion, his terrified subjects fled in all directions.

"Whew!" exclaimed the Wizard, snatching out his green handkerchief and mopping his moist forehead. "That was quick thinking, my dear. Good acting, too," he puffed, leaning down to give the lion an approving pat.

"Oh, wasn't he WONDERFUL?" Jellia hugged the lion so energetically he fairly gasped for breath.

"Not so hard for ME to play King," he wheezed when he managed to escape from Jellia's embrace. "After all, I AM the King of the Forest!"

"Well, however that may be, Jellia is certainly Starina of the Strat!" declared the Scarecrow. "I'm beginning to think Strut was right in choosing her! You've been wasting your talents in Oz, my dear, and you surely have earned a crown today!"

"But I don't want a crown!" asserted Jellia with spirit. Nevertheless, she was quite pleased at such high praise. "Now, look! Since the Cowardly Lion ordered supper in the Royal Pavilion, perhaps we'd better go. It will be as good a place as any to rest while we plan our next move."

"Hi there, is everything all right?" Wantowin Battles, who had hidden himself behind a crystal rock at the Blowmen's approach, now peered out nervously.

"For the present," called the Wizard, waving his kerchief, "for the present. Come along, Soldier, we're going to have supper in the Royal Pavilion!"

"Not I," said the Soldier, falling in step with the Scarecrow. "Count me out of that!"

"I'm sure I'll not be able to eat a bite," sighed Dorothy, picking up the Tell-all-escope. "How can you even think of supper with those awful airmen flying to the Emerald City? Oh, why don't we go after them now?"

"Because I do not believe Nick will take them to the Emerald City," said Jellia, straightening her crown. "He'll lose them somehow and then come back here for Wanny and me."

"My own deduction exactly," agreed the Wizard, walking briskly along beside Jellia. "But wherever Nick is, we'll find him same as we have found you."

"How did you find us?" asked Jellia, stopping short and staring up into the Wizard's face. "I've been wondering about that."

"Well, you see," explained the little magician impressively, "on the Ozpril there is a magnetic compass that shows the exact course taken by the Oztober, provided that both planes are in flight. By following the compass, I followed your exact route. The delay in our arrival was caused by the difference in speed!"

"Why, them, you saw the very same things we did," cried Jellia, nodding distantly to several airlanders who were bowing to the ground as the little procession passed.

"The very same," said the Wizard. Then, as a little afterthought, "By the way, what did you see?"

"Oh, nothing much but clouds, fog, an icecloud, and some flying airimals with spikes," Jellia told him briefly as she started up the long steps to the Royal Pavilion.

"The same with us," said the Wizard, taking out a little book and squinting hastily at the precisely written entries. "`Clouds, fogs, spiked monsters.' AH!" He closed the book with a little exclamation of admiration. "So this is the seat of Government?"

"I must say I prefer a castle," observed the Scarecrow, jumping up the steps three at a time. "Still, all these columns are very pretty. Very pretty indeed!"

"Is my throne comfortable?" inquired the Cowardly Lion with a lordly sniff.

"That's right," giggled Jellia, "you will have to sit on the throne — that is, if Wanny doesn't mind." The little maid turned mischievously to the Soldier with Green Whiskers. "After all, you are a kind of King, too!"

"Not on your life!" declared Wantowin violently. "I wouldn't trade one button on my uniform for all the jewels in Strut's crown, nor one blade of Oz grass for all the rocks in Stratovania!"

"Bravo! Bravo!" applauded the Scarecrow. Having tied his balloons to one of the pillars, he was bouncing up and down on a blue air cushion. "Try one," he invited, shoving a couple toward the Wizard. Instead of one, the Wizard put three of the air cushions together and stretched out at full length.

"You can't imagine how tired a fellow grows after sixteen hours of flying," he murmured drowsily. "Hah, hoh, HUM! I hope you girls will excuse me if I take a little nap."

"I wouldn't mind a nap myself," yawned Dorothy. Though she had dozed part of the night before, she felt extremely sleepy. Without much urging from Jellia, she curled up on a couch at the back of the pavilion and was asleep almost before her head touched the pillows.

"The best thing in the world for them," grinned the Scarecrow as Jellia looked rather nervously from one sleeper to the other. "We'll probably have to fly all night — if we get away from here at all! The Wiz needs a good rest before he does any more piloting."

"Yes," agreed Jellia with a sigh, "I suppose he does. But I hope the lion's not going to sleep, too." Climbing to her throne, Jellia gave him a good poke in the ribs. The lion, who was leaning back against the cushions with both eyes closed, shook his head.

"I never sleep on an empty stomach," he declared firmly. "Besides, a lion can go for days — if necessary — without rest or refreshment."

"Didn't you bring anything to eat at all?" inquired Jellia. Being terribly hungry herself, she could sympathize with the hungry beast.

"Oh," answered the lion without opening his eyes, "we did have a few square meal tablets the Wizard happened to have in his pocket. But while they fill you up, they don't seem to satisfy."

"Same with the food here," said Jellia.

"Food!" The Cowardly Lion's nose began to twitch with eagerness. "Where is any?"

"If I am not mistaken, supper is approaching now!" announced the Scarecrow, peering out through the side draperies of the Canopy. "Is this one of your many servants, my dear?"

"Oh, I suppose so," said Jellia as Bittsywittle trudged up the crystal steps balancing a huge tray on his head. He had been warned of the change in Strut, but the sight of the huge monster on the throne unnerved the little fellow, and he began to tremble so violently, the dishes on the tray danced a regular jig.

"Just put the tray on the table," directed Jellia patiently. "And don't jump, Bittsywittle! Strut won't bite you."

"How do you know I won't?" roared the Cowardly Lion, opening his eyes so wide Bittsywittle set down the tray and scuttled off like a hare. Without much enthusiasm, Jellia noted Kabebe had sent them six saucers of wind pudding and six glasses of air-ade."

"Don't touch it!" warned the Soldier with Green Whiskers as the lion slithered off the throne and ambled to the table. "It will make you feel very funny."

"Well, I'd rather feel funny than sad," said the lion, sniffing the pudding delicately, "and I'd rather feel funny than starve. Aren't you having any, Jellia?"

"No, thank you!" Jellia shook her head sharply and exchanged a quiet wink with Wantowin. But the Cowardly Lion did not notice the wink. Or at least he pretended not to and hurriedly lapped up all six saucers.

"Why, it's delicious!" he murmured rapturously. "Deli—"

"Hey, where are you going?" The Scarecrow had been watching him enviously, for the pink pudding looked so good he almost wished he found it necessary to eat. But now he spun round in alarm, for without any warning at all the lion had swelled and puffed up like a carnival balloon and gone wafting upward to soar in dizzy circles over their heads.

"Oh, he's just putting on airs because he's King," teased Jellia, wishing Dorothy were awake to enjoy the fun.

"But he might easily float off," worried the Scarecrow, pursuing the luckless lion with outstretched arms. "Wait, I'll save you!" he puffed, and snatching the cord from a long bell pull, he leaped on Strut's throne. After several unsuccessful attempts, he managed to lasso the lion and tie him fast to the arm of the throne. "How do you feel?" he called solicitously, for the lion, with closed eyes and a desperate expression, was paddling his legs like a drowning dog.

"Oh, take it easy!" advised Jellia, relenting a little. "You'll float around all by yourself and come down presently as light as a feather. I know, 'cause I've tried it. Hello, here's Hippenscop! Now I wonder what he wants. Oh! My goodness! He's actually brought me two of those flying sticks!"

"Flying sticks?" exclaimed the Scarecrow, sliding off Strut's throne. "You don't tell me!" The messenger by this time had reached the top step of the Pavilion. After a fearful look at the people from Oz, he advanced timidly toward Jellia.

"I have brought the flying sticks, your Majesty!" explained Hippenscop, holding them out with great pride and satisfaction. "I stole them from two sleeping watchmen and managed to bring them here without Kabebe seeing me."

"KABEBE?" said Jellia with an uncomfortable start. "Why, where is Kabebe?"

"In Star Park," whispered the Messenger hoarsely. "She's got all the people worked up and excited! They're coming here presently to blow you away!"

"What?" gasped Jellia in an exasperated voice. "Again? Why, she knows Strut will never allow that."

"But Kabebe says HE isn't Strut!" said the messenger with an apologetic bow toward the Cowardly Lion, who, paying no attention to the conversation, was floating in distracted circles above the throne. "Now Junnenrump and I believe your Majesty, and consider you the best and prettiest Starina Stratovania ever had! But no one else does, so first they are going to blow away the Friend Ship, and then they are coming here to blow you all away! So while I do not presume to give orders, if I were in your Majesty's place, I'd fly this very instant and while there still is time!"

"The boy is right," declared the Soldier, grabbing up his blunderbuss. "Company! Fall in! Forward, march!"

"Wake up! Wake up!" cried the Scarecrow, pummeling the Wizard with both hands. "The Airlanders are destroying our Ozoplane!" While Jellia, really touched by the messenger's loyalty, gave him one of her emerald rings, Wantowin Battles lifted Dorothy off the soft sofa and set her hastily on her feet.

"Forward! Forward!" he urged, pushing her ahead of him. "Kabebe's coming to blow us away!" Dorothy, blinking her eyes after a look at the Cowardly Lion floating over the throne, concluded she still was dreaming. But the Soldier kept shaking her till she finally realized she was awake and in danger.

"This way!" cried Jellia as the Wizard bounced off his cushions. "This way! The thing for us to do is to run to the other side of the airosphere. Then, while those villains are blowing the Ozpril away, we can be reaching the edge and—"

"And WHAT?" queried Dorothy, looking at Jellia with round, scared eyes. Jellia, for reasons of her own, did not answer. The Scarecrow already had retrieved his balloons. Now he pressed the cord, still attached to the Cowardly Lion, into Wantowin's hand.

"You must pull him along with you," directed the Scarecrow earnestly. "I am too light. And DO let's be starting!" The angry buzz of the crowd on its way to Half Moon Lake already could be heard. So without stopping to plan or reason the travelers from Oz slipped through the back curtains of the Royal Pavilion and began running as fast as they could toward the other side of Strut's curious air realm.

The Wizard, grasping his kit-bag in one hand and Dorothy by the other, went first. Next came Jellia, carrying the two flying sticks; the Scarecrow clutched his bunch of balloons. Last of all ran Wantowin, dragging the growling and disgusted lion after him through the air. Fortunately, Stratovania is long and narrow. In less time than they had dared hope, the little cavalcade came to the edge. Forbidding cliffs stretched along the whole coast, and the moist, blue air seemed actually to be breaking in great waves against the rocks. As they all gazed unhappily outward, a terrific "BOOM" made them all shudder.

"Well, there goes the Ozpril," mourned Jellia, patting the Wizard compassionately on the shoulder. The Wizard, looking very angry and grim, nodded his head. "Come on," puffed Jellia, stepping closer to the cliffs, "unless we want to go up with the ship, we've got to jump! And really, it's not so bad as it sounds! I've seen the airlanders fly with these winged staffs, and these two will have to do for us all."

"How do they work?" asked Dorothy in a faint voice.

"Why, you tap them once on the ground to start, and once on the handle to stop," explained Jellia breathlessly. "Now, suppose Dot and I and the Scarecrow ride one and Wiz and the Soldier the other. And for cake's sake, don't let go our lion!" added Jellia.

"But suppose he deflates and pulls us all down with his weight," groaned the Soldier. "Why can't he float along by himself?"

"Because I'm not going to have it!" said Jellia determinedly. "You must hold on to him and risk whatever happens! And if anything does happen, the Wizard will think of something!"

"I have thought of something!" said the Wizard composedly. "But first we must do as Jellia says. HARK! Isn't that Kabebe calling you?" As a matter of fact, it was. The Stratovanians, after witnessing the blow-off of the Ozpril, had rushed back to the Royal Pavilion. Furious at the disappearance of their victims, they now were rushing toward the crystal cliffs, the screams of Kabebe rising above all the rest.

"What do we do, ride 'em like broomsticks?" jabbered the Scarecrow as Jellia with shaking hands held out one of the sticks to the Wizard.

"A good idea!" approved the little magician, watching with deep interest as the wings on the tip of his staff opened and spread. "Come along, Soldier, or the mob will get you yet!" With wildly beating hearts, Dorothy and Jellia watched the Wizard and the Soldier mount the flying stick and boldly leap from the cliff's edge. The Cowardly Lion let out a terrified howl as he was dragged after them, but Jellia, Dorothy and the Scarecrow without further hesitation mounted their own staff and hurled themselves into space just as the Queen and her cohorts came panting into view.

Chapter 12 - The Flight to Oz

Keeping the flying sticks in a more-or-less level position so they would not slip off and at the same time pointing them downward required no little skill. The Wizard, being used to magic appliances, mastered his in double-quick time. But Jellia, who sat in front on the other staff, soared up for seventy feet and across for fifty before she learned the trick of flying it. During the first twenty minutes of their flight not a word was spoken. Each had enough to do to hold on, and the Cowardly Lion, hurtling through the air beside the Soldier with Green Whiskers, looked the picture of despair and discouragement. A dozen times Dorothy, after a glance downward, gave herself up for lost. But gradually the strangeness of their situation wore off. Passing out of the moist, clammy strata just below Strut's Kingdom into a drier and less-clouded area, the spirits of the little band of adventurers rose. The wings of each flying staff, though not large, were powerful as airplane propellers, and they flapped as rhythmically as the wings of a bird.

"Not exactly like riding in an Ozoplane!" called the Wizard, waving cheerfully to Jellia. "Still, it's better than falling, eh?" Jellia, who had maneuvered her staff to a position close to his, nodded emphatically.

"What worries me is the altitude!" she called back presently. "Somewhere or other we lost our air helmets. Will the effects of those altitude pills wear off before we're out of the strat?"

"No, we'll be all right," promised the Wizard. "My altitude pills condition one for the upper areas for several days at a time!"

"Oh! Then everything's splendid!" sighed Jellia, pushing back her curly locks and smiling at Dorothy.

"Unless we meet a meteor, and then our flight will soon be o'er," quavered the Scarecrow, waving his arm in a doleful circle.

"Now, now, don't anticipate!" advised the Wizard, guiding the staff with one hand and opening his kit bag with the other. For several moments he had been anxiously regarding the Cowardly Lion. The buoyancy resulting from the wind pudding was at last subsiding, and the swelled and bloated appearance of the unfortunate beast was fast disappearing. At almost any time now, the lion would become a dead weight. His poundage, added to the Wizard's and the Soldier's, would be too much for the flying staff, and they all would plunge like plummets to the earth. Feeling hurriedly around in the kit-bag, the Wizard pulled out a small black bottle. Uncorking it with his teeth, he turned it upside down and held it out at arm's length until not a drop of its oily contents remained.

"Now, don't be alarmed at a sudden bump!" he warned as his companions watched him with surprise and curiosity. "Whatever happens, hold on to your staff!" Scarcely had the Wizard issued his warning when the air directly beneath them froze into a solid block of blue ice on which they landed with a series of bumps and began sliding around in great confusion. "Nothing to worry about! Nothing to worry about!" panted the Wizard, keeping a firm hold on his flying stick and at the same time managing to extract a large envelope from the kit-bag. "Hold on to that stick, Jellia, and keep it down!"

The Cowardly Lion, completely deflated by his smack against the ice, was sprawled flat as an animal skin in the center of the berg. Dismounting from his own staff, the Wizard scurried perilously round the edges of the rapidly falling block of ice, scattering seeds from his envelope with a lavish hand. Instantly, or so it seemed to Dorothy, a thick, green hedge sprang up, enclosing them snugly inside.

"To keep us from tumbling off," explained the Wizard, sliding anxiously after Wantowin Battles, who was galloping round and round on his flying stick like a child on a merry-go-round. "Whoa, whoa!" cried Ozma's chief magician, grabbing the Soldier's coattails. "We need these sticks to act as brakes to stop our fall!" Unseating the Soldier, the Wizard lifted the flying stick and stuck it through the top branches of the hedge. Bidding the others dismount from their staff, he thrust it through the hedge on the opposite side. The wings of both staffs kept up their steady beating and, as the Wizard had predicted, acted as strong brakes on the plunging cake of ice.

"I was afraid we'd lose our lion," explained the Wizard as the little company of adventurers gathered breathlessly round him.

"I'd just as lief be lost as frozen!" Sneezing plaintively, the lion pulled himself to his feet and slid over to the hedge, bracing his back against its stouter branches.

"It won't be long before we strike solid earth now, old fellow," the Wizard observed brightly.

"Strike the earth!" roared the lion. "Well, goodbye, friends! I'll say it now, before I'm squashed and scattered to the four points of the compass!"

"Never mind, you'll make a lovely splatter!" teased the Scarecrow. "Better stamp your feet, girls, to keep from freezing!"

"Here, stand on my coat," offered the Wizard gallantly. "Not YOU!" Indignantly he pushed the Soldier with Green Whiskers aside. "You can stand on your own coat!"

"But it's against regulations for a soldier to appear without his jacket," shivered Wantowin piteously. "The manual of arms says—"

"How about the manual of feet?" snorted the Scarecrow, thankful he was stuffed with cotton and incapable of feeling the cold. "Say, Wiz, I guess this is about the oddest flying trip a band of explorers ever had."

"Did those magic drops freeze the air into ice?" called Dorothy. "And how'd you grow the hedge so fast?"

"Yes, the drops froze the air," the Wizard bawled back, for the rush of air as they shot downward made it difficult to hold polite conversation. "And I just happened to have some of my instant sprouting saplings in that kit-bag."

To keep up their spirits, they continued to shout back and forth as they fell. "I don't suppose we'll ever catch up with Strut and Nick Chopper now," screamed Jellia, hooking her arms securely through the hedge.

"Why not?" cried the Wizard. "As soon as we land, we can fly these flying sticks straight to the Emerald City and be there before the Oztober arrives. Remember now, the first one up after we hit the earth is to snatch a winged staff."

"And how do you suppose we will be able to rise after striking the earth at one hundred and forty miles an hour?" roared the lion a trifle sarcastically.

"Well, it won't hurt me!" boasted the Scarecrow, holding to his hat with both hands. He had lost the balloons long ago. "And I promise to pick up the rest of you as soon as possible. Is there anything in that kit-bag for breaks, sprains and bruises, Wiz?"

"Oh, hold your tongue!" snapped Jellia, trying to peer over the hedge. "We're not going to crash at all! We'll probably get stuck on a steeple or tower!"

"How'd Nick manage with his flying?" shrieked the Wizard, who was anxious to change the subject. The less said about their landing the better. Of course, they could take to the flying sticks and abandon the Cowardly Lion, but that did not seem exactly sporting. So he resolutely put the thought of it out of his mind."Grand, just grand!" answered Jellia, making a megaphone of her hands. "Nick had the Oztober going smoothly as a swallow!"

"That's good!" boomed the Wizard, beating his arms against his breast to keep warm. "Maybe we'll get the best of Strut yet and bring the Oztober safely down. I'd certainly like to have one ship left to present to Ozma!"

"How long'll it be before we do get down?" called Dorothy as the Wizard paused for breath. "Seems to me we're falling faster. FASTER AND FASTER!"

"Any minute now," predicted the Wizard, popping his head over the top of the hedge. "Oh! It's going to be all right! he shouted joyfully. "We're coming down right in the middle of a great big—"

SPLASH!

Before the Wizard could finish his sentence, the block of ice struck the smooth surface of a large mountain lake and went completely under. As it came bobbing to the top, its drenched and shivering passengers looked at one another with mingled dismay and relief. Dorothy, picking up the Wizard's coat, handed it back and then went slipping and sliding over to help the Scarecrow, who was too water-soaked and sodden even to move.

"Wring me out! Hang me up to dry, somebody!" gurgled the straw man dismally.

"Grrr-rah!" The Cowardly Lion, outraged at the cold plunge after all the other shocks and indignities of the day, jumped over the hedge and began to swim grimly for the shore. The Soldier with Green Whiskers, better at carrying out orders than the others, already was pulling one of the flying sticks from the hedge. As it came loose, he took a brief glance over the top, gave an agonized shriek, and fell backward, stepping all over the Wizard, who was just behind him.

"An army!" shivered Wantowin, clutching his dripping beard. "Thousands of them!"

"It is an army, too!" echoed Jellia, who had parted the hedge to have a look for herself.

"What do they look like?" demanded the Wizard, shoving past the soldier and grabbing the winged staff, which was on the point of flying off by itself.

"Like trouble!" said Jellia, reaching for Dorothy's hand. "They have long bows and pointed red beards and — my goodyness — their beards are pointed straight at us!"

"Bearded Bowmen, eh?" grunted the Wizard. "Well, that doesn't prove they're unfriendly." The Wizard stuck his head over the hedge, barely avoiding the arrow that sped past his ear.

"I suppose you'd call THAT unfriendly," sniffed Jellia, flopping on her stomach and pulling Dorothy down with her. The Wizard had no time to answer, for Wantowin Battles had one of the winged staffs and was preparing to ride by himself.

"Drop it! Drop it at once!" commanded the Wizard sharply. "How dare you fly off without us? Why, it's plain desertion, that's what!"

"I was just going to do a bit of reconnoitering," mumbled the Soldier, looking terribly abashed and then diving to a place beside Jellia as three more arrows came hissing over the hedge. Quickly recovering the staff, the wet little Wizard crouched down.

"Now girls!" he directed, panting from the exertion of holding down both sticks. "When I give the signal, you and the Scarecrow mount one staff, and Wantowin and I will mount the other, and fly high over the enemy lines!"

"The higher the better," said Jellia as a perfect shower of arrows whizzed over their heads.

Chapter 13 - The King of the Kudgers

The Wizard's plan worked very well at first. He and the Soldier astride one stick,
Dorothy and Jellia holding the poor, sodden Scarecrow between them on the other, shot high into the air, across the lake

and over the amazed ranks of Bowmen drawn up on the bank. Before the Red Beards had recovered from their surprise, the travelers were winging strongly toward the turreted red castle that crowned the mountaintop. The Cowardly Lion, to escape the flying arrows, had swum under water. Now, scrambling up the bank, he neatly skirted the enemy and ran swiftly beneath the two flying staffs.

"As soon as we're safely past this castle, we'll descend, rest, dry our clothes and then proceed to the Emerald City," called the Wizard, turning to wave encouragingly at the two girls.

But at that moment a dreadful thing happened. Sprawled on a huge camp chair on the sloping terrace before the castle, its huge, red-bearded owner suddenly sighted the flying sticks and their riders. Seizing the long bow that lay beside him, he sent two arrows speeding upward, one right after the other. Each arrow found its mark and splintered a flying stick. With spine-shattering suddenness, the travelers crashed to earth. Dorothy, describing it to Ozma later, explained that although she never had been in a battle, she knew exactly how a warrior felt when his horse was shot from under him. Except, of course, that a horseman would not have had so far to fall. The Scarecrow, tumbling off first, softened the bump for both girls. The Wizard and Soldier plunged headlong into a red-pepper bush. While not seriously injured, they were grievously scratched and shaken. But the worst was not the blow to their pride and persons; the worst was to see the upper and winged halves of their precious sticks flying away without them.

"Oh! Oh!" groaned the Wizard, leaping out of the pepper bush and running for an anguished yard or two after the vanishing staffs. "This is awful, AWFUL! Come back! Come down!" he implored, realizing even as he shouted that the sticks could neither hear nor obey.

"Noo then, whew are yew?" The startled Red Beard hoisted himself out of his camp chair. "W-itches riding on br-hoom sticks? Noo then, call off yewer dog!" The Cowardly Lion, noting the mischief already done by the Red King's bow, had seized it in his teeth and backed rapidly into the bushes. The Wizard, reluctantly withdrawing his gaze from the sky, now stamped over to the astonished owner of the castle.

"Just see what you've done," he cried angrily. "Destroyed the only winged staffs in Oz. We flew them all the way from the Strat, and now how are we to reach the Emerald City in time to stop the airlanders? Don't you realize — but how could you?" In sudden discouragement, the Wizard broke off and stared despondently around the rugged mountaintop. "I must tell you," he began in a hoarse and desperate voice, "that Ozma and the Emerald City are in great danger. Strut of the Strat and a host of his flying Stratovanians are descending to conquer Oz and carry off Ozma's treasure. If we fail to warn her, the city is lost, doomed, I tell you! Since you have shattered our flying sticks, you must quickly supply us with some other means of travel. We must reach the capital before morning!"

"MUST!" roared the Bearded Bowman. "Are yew shouting `must' at ME?"

"Be careful!" cried Dorothy. For the Wizard in his earnestness had stepped closer and closer to the red King. But her cry was too late. Without any warning, the King's pointed beard, rising with his wrath, pointed straight out and struck the valiant Wizard to the earth. For a whole minute he lay perfectly still, staring up at this curious phenomenon. Though he had seen many a beard in his day, he had never been knocked down by one before.

"Whew are yew?" demanded the burly mountain monarch again. "How dare yew fly over my castle and swim in my lake without permission?" Stroking his beard, which gradually resumed a vertical position on his chest, he stared from one to the other of the adventurers. "No use to run," he sneered as Wantowin Battles began to back toward the bushes. "My bowmen will be here any moment now! But WHEW are YEW?"

"Wheww!" groaned Jellia, propping the bedraggled Scarecrow against a rock. "A body'd hardly know after such a welcome. Whew are hew yewerself, yew old Redbeard?"

"I?" roared the Bowman, taken completely by surprise. "Why, don't yew know? I am Bustabo, King of the Kudgers and Red Top Mountain."

"I don't believe it," said the Wizard, leaping agilely to his feet and shaking his fist under Bustabo's long nose. "A real King would not treat travelers as you have done, shoot away valuable flying sticks and keep two lovely girls standing out here in the wind."

"How dew yew know what a King would dew?" demanded Bustabo, puckering his forehead in an uneasy frown.

"Because," stated the Wizard, folding his arms disdainfully, "I personally know all the most important rulers in Oz, and none of them would behave as you have done. If you are a King, act like a King!"

"Whew are yew?" repeated the Ruler of Red Top, walking around the little group with hands clasped behind his back.

"Oh, for Oz sake, tell him!" snarled the Cowardly Lion, poking his head out of the bushes. "If he asks that question again, I might eat him up, pointed beard and all!"

"Well, this is the Wizard of Oz," explained Dorothy as the Lion stalked grimly out of the bushes. "Chief Magician for Ozma of Oz. This—" Dorothy, with a wave of her hand, indicated the trembling soldier "—

this is Wantowin Battles, the Grand Army of Oz. Beside him is our famous live Scarecrow. I am Princess Dorothy of Oz, and this is Jellia Jam, First Lady in Waiting to Ozma. Coming toward you is the Cowardly Lion of Oz."

"He doesn't look very cowardly to me," muttered Bustabo, putting the camp chair between himself and the approaching beast.

"Oh, but I am cowardly," growled the lion growlishly, "and when I'm frightened I never know what I'll do. I might even chew up the King of this Mountain! Whoever heard of a King pointing his beard at harmless travelers? Whoever heard of a King with a beard as hard and red as yours, anyway? It's hard as iron from the looks of it."

"Harder!" agreed the King, evidently considering the lion's remark a compliment. "All we Kudgers have red beards, not of soft hair like his

—" The Red King gazed contemplatively at the Soldier with Green Whiskers "—but of hard hair like mine. I don't suppose yew've ever seen a beard like this before. The point's sharp as a dagger, too," he warned as the lion sprang a pace closer.

"Oh, I'm sure it is," said Dorothy nervously. "And it's dreadfully handsome, too. But could your Majesty please let us dry out in your castles, and then could you show us the quickest route to the Emerald City? If you don't," finished Dorothy, clasping her hands anxiously, "the ruler of this whole country of Oz may be captured and carried to the Strat."

"What do I care about the Ruler of Oz?" sniffed Bustabo, scratching his head in a most unkingly manner. "Ozma never does anything for me! Even if she were conquered, I'd still have my Mountain. Why should I help yew or her or them?" His scornful wave included the whole little group. "What can yew dew for me?" he asked sullenly. "Can yew sing?" His dull eye brightened momentarily as it rested inquiringly on Dorothy.

"Well, a little," confessed Dorothy, smoothing down her damp dress. Clearing her throat and fixing her eye on the top of a red pine, she started in rather a choked voice:

"Oh, Bright and gay is the Land of Oz. We love its lakes and hills becoz—"

"There, there! That will dew!" Bustabo snapped his fingers impatiently, and taking out a little book scribbled hastily, "Can't sing."

"Can yew dance?" he demanded, addressing himself to Jellia. "We are short of good dancers on this mountain." Jellia by this time was in such a state of cold and temper, she stamped her foot and turned her back on the unmannerly monarch. "Can't dance," wrote Bustabo under the first entry.

"Well, then, what dew yew dew?" he asked, turning in exasperation to the Wizard.

"I?" said the Wizard, twirling his water-soaked topper, "I am a Wizard. Naturally, I supposed a King like yourself would have everything he desired. But if that is not the case, tell me what you wish and perhaps I can help you. Only be quick!" he added earnestly. "For we have no time to lose."

"Sooo, yew really are a Wizard!" Bustabo's expression became almost agreeable. "Well, then," he drew himself up pompously. "The Princess whom I wish to wed has unaccountably disappeared. Find and return her to this castle, and I will speed yew and yewer friends to the Emerald City by the safest and swiftest route!"

"But that would take too much time," objected the Wizard, rubbing his chin anxiously. "Who is this Princess? Why has she gone? What is her name and what does she look like?"

"If yew were a real Wizard, yew would know all these things without my telling yew," answered Bustabo, looking suspiciously at Ozma's Chief Magician. "I'll tell you this much, though. The Princess whom I would marry is called Azarine, the Red. Not three days ago she was in this castle, but on the morning of our wedding day she ran off into the forest, and though all my Bowmen have been searching ever since, not a trace of her have they found!"

"Humph, the girl showed very good sense, if you ask me," sniffed the Cowardly Lion, shaking his mane. "What did you do? Point your beard at her? Come on, Wiz! Let's go. We're just wasting time here."

"Aha, but yew cannot leave! Look behind yew!" Bustabo, with an enormous laugh, pointed over his shoulder. Silently as Indians, the Bearded Bowmen had crept up and entirely surrounded the little company on the green. Standing in a circle with bows raised and beards pointed, they fairly dared anyone to take a step. "Soo, then, it's all settled!" The Red King clapped the Wizard heartily on the back. "Don't think I have not heard of yewer skill, Mister Weezard. Even here on Red Top we've heard rumors of the wonderful Weezard of Oz. Now all yew have to dew is walk into that forest, find the Princess and bring her back to me. Meanwhile, I shall treat these others as my guests. They shall rest and warm themselves and have all they wish to eat. If by morning yew have failed to return, I shall regretfully be forced to throw them off the mountain. If yew dew return, yew will find that Bustabo will keep his word and bargain."

The Wizard hardly knew what to say.

"If he knows so much, why does he not help himself?" demanded one of the Red Beards, stepping insolently out of the circle. "People who can fly through the air on icebergs and sticks do not need help from ordinary folk like us. Why doesn't he fly to the Emerald City if he's so smart? I'll tell you why: because he's not the Wizard of Oz! He's a fraud, that's what!"

"If he's a fraud, then you're a rascal!" cried Jellia Jam, remembering suddenly that she recently had been a Starina. "Your Princess is as good as found, Mister King! Isn't that so, Wizard?"

Meeting Jellia's firm gaze, the Wizard nodded quickly. "This young Oz girl is right, your Majesty! Before the sun rises, Azarine will return to this castle!"

"Yes, and now bid your vassals lead us into the castle!" ordered Jellia sharply. "Bring us soup, meat, bread, vegetables and plenty of fruit and cake!"

Bustabo, after a long look both at Jellia and the Wizard, motioned for the Bowmen to lead the visitors into the castle. The Cowardly Lion trailed suspiciously along in the rear, keeping a sharp watch to see that no beards were pointed at his friends. The Wizard accompanied them part way, conversing in earnest whispers with Jellia and Dorothy. Wantowin Battles supported the dripping and still-helpless Scarecrow, and each tried not to show the anxiety he felt when the Wizard finally turned to leave them.

"Goodbye, all!" he said, lifting his dripping hat. "Goodbye, Jellia, here is your bag!" Tapping the kit-bag significantly, he pressed it into Jellia's cold hands. Then, without a word to Bustabo or his Henchmen, he strode resolutely toward the dark forest that covered the sides and more than half of the top of the mountain. Relenting a little, the Red King sent a Bowman running after him with a basket of provisions. Taking the basket with a brief nod of thanks, the Wizard waved again to his friends and marched straight into the gloomy and forbidding woods.

Chapter 14 - Azarine the Red

The late afternoon shadows made the forest seem even gloomier. The little Wizard, trudging along under the rustling red trees, hands thrust deep into his pockets, never had felt more depressed or unhappy. He had hated to leave his friends with a Monarch as cruel and untrustworthy as Bustabo. Still, he had the utmost confidence in Jellia Jam. The Young Oz Miss doubtless had some plan in her clever little head and had chosen this way for him to escape, meaning to follow with the others at the first opportunity. Anyway, he reflected, dropping down on a heap of fallen leaves and resting his back against a tree, they had the kit-bag to help them if worst came to worst. Perhaps if he had concentrated and thought very hard, he could recall the powerful incantation for locating missing persons and articles.

But a wizard without his books and equipment is almost as helpless as a doctor without his pills and medicine bag. Try as he could, the Wizard could not remember the proper combination of words to bring back the missing Princess. His short nap in Stratovania had rested him a little, but he still was dreadfully weary from his grueling flight and the recent shocks and mischances. The loss of the Ozpril had been the worst blow of all, and now his tired brain simply refused to work. So, sitting sadly under the tree, he munched the sandwiches from the basket, drank from the bottle of cold tea, and wished fervently for a fire to warm himself, for his clothes were still damp and clammy from the dive in Bustabo's lake. It comforted him a little to know that the others were drying out and enjoying a good supper in the castle. But it was no comfort at all to realize that Strut and his legions were winging their way toward the Emerald City, the city he had built and lived in so long it seemed more like home than any place he had known in America.

The Wizard crammed the rest of the sandwiches into the basket and started recklessly through the forest, tripping over tough vines and rocks, bumping into trees and peering desperately about for traces of a Princess or for any sign that might tell him in which direction the Emerald City lay. From the slant of the ground he knew he was traveling down the mountain, and the deep red foliage told him he was somewhere in the Quadling country of Oz. But with night coming on and the shadows growing deeper and darker, he probably would lose his way entirely and never get out of the forest at all. He felt uneasy at leaving his comrades behind in the Red King's Castle. Was it better to try to save Ozma and the Emerald City or to stay in this forest and help Dorothy and Jellia and the devoted friends who had embarked on this unexpected adventure with him?

Stopping short, the Wizard pressed both hands to his forehead in an effort to make up his mind. Night already had overtaken him, and it was now so dark, it was impossible to see more than a foot or so in any direction. Occasional roars, the snapping of twigs and the gleam of yellow eyes from the thicket caused him no little anxiety. At an especially savage roar he suddenly stopped worrying about Ozma and the others and began to do considerable worrying about himself.

How humbling for a Wizard to be devoured by a hungry beast! Backing softly away from the approaching monster, he began looking sharply about for a hollow tree, a cave, or even a clump of bushes where he might conceal himself. On the tip of his tongue and ready for instant use was the magic word that would render him invisible. Fortunately, he did remember that. But the Wizard never wasted words, magic or otherwise. Resolving to wait till the last possible moment, he continued to back rapidly and cautiously. Then, unexpectedly from behind him came another distraction: the clear ringing of a silver bell. At the same time the gloom was pierced by a dancing ray of light. Swinging round, the Wizard flung up both arms, and not knowing whether to dash into the teeth of the monster in front of him or risk the lowered horns of the huge beast behind him, the startled magician uttered the word that rendered him invisible.

"Brr-rah!" raged the burly, bear-like creature, rearing up on his hind legs. "Where is that pesky man-creature? I saw him a moment ago, but now, though I still catch his scent, he has hidden from me. And why must you, Shagomar, come horning in to spoil my supper? Why cannot you mind your own business, Br-rrah!"

"I am minding my own business," roared the creature addressed as Shagomar. "AWAY, you Entomophagus monster! Haven't I told you time and again to keep away from the cave of the Princess? The very next bug-bear that comes prowling 'round shall have a taste of my antlers! Get on with you now, and after this leave harmless travelers alone!"

The great red stag made a short rush at the ugly beast blocking his path. Large as a Grizzly, half insect and half bear, it held its ground uncertainly for a moment, then shuffled off into the darkness, grunting angrily. The Wizard, who had jumped hastily from between the two beasts, had listened to the stag's words with lively interest and astonishment. Huge and sandy, with antlers of tremendous breadth, the huge creature now stood quiet as a statue. From one antler prong hung a flashing silver lantern. From another dangled the bell which had so startled the Wizard.

"Well, friend! Are you still there?" whispered the Stag softly. Instead of answering, the Wizard uttered the word that would make him visible. "Come with me!" directed the Stag, showing neither surprise nor curiosity at the Wizard's sudden reappearance. "You will be safer with us in the cave. Surely you are a stranger, or you would know it is dangerous to wander in this forest at night."

"Oh, I don't mind danger," said the Wizard, striding sturdily beside the Stag. "I am used to danger, and I must reach the Emerald City before morning! Ozma and her whole capitol are threatened by a band of ruthless Airlanders, and unless I can give them some warning, the Emerald City certainly will be captured by Strut of the Strat. I am Ozma's Chief Magician, fallen by great misfortune into this forest."

"I thought you might be a Wizard," murmured Shagomar, pausing to nibble at a few tender leaves. "And you say the Ruler of the whole Land of Oz is in danger? Hah, well, we all have our troubles." Exhaling his breath noisily, Shagomar looked off between the trees with a troubled frown. "I cannot direct you to the Emerald City, but I'm sure the Princess can help you."

"What Princess do you mean?" asked the Wizard, curious to hear what Shagomar would say.

"Azarine!" whispered the Stag, looking around carefully to see that no one was listening. "Azarine the Red, Ruler of Red Top Mountain!"

"But I thought Bustabo was ruler of the mountain! I just came from his castle!" sputtered the Wizard. "He certainly told me he was King of the Kudgers."

"King of the Kudgers, pfui!" The stag shook his head as if a bee were in his ear, while his bell played a regular roundelay. "Bustabo was, till a week ago, Chief Bowman in Her Majesty's Guard. Using his position and his men to help him, he has wickedly seized Azarine's throne, insisting that Azarine permit him to be the King of all the Kudgers. When our little Princess refused, she was locked up in the tower. But with the assistance of a faithful servant, she managed to escape and has been hiding in this forest ever since. I, being an old and trusted friend, have been looking out for her and will protect her with horn and hoof until her own loyal subjects unseat this miserable imposter!"

"Whew, so that's the way it is!" The Wizard thrust his hands more deeply into his pockets. "Well, that settles that! I won't do it, no matter what happens!"

"Won't do what?" questioned the Stag, looking down sideways at the little man.

"Oh — nothing!" Kicking at a stone, the Wizard walked along in a depressed silence. Surely no one ever had been in a worse dilemma. If he managed by a trick or by force to carry Azarine back to the Red Castle, Dorothy and his friends would be released instantly and all of them speeded on their way to the Capitol. If he did not return the Princess to the castle, his brave and faithful companions would be flung off the mountain, Strut would conquer the Emerald City, and everything would be lost. LOST!

But when, a few minutes later, the Stag pushed through a cluster of bushes that concealed the entrance to the cave and the Wizard stepped into the presence of Azarine herself, he knew he never would force her to surrender to the infamous Bustabo.

Seated pensively on a rough boulder beside a small fire was the prettiest little Princess the Wizard had almost ever seen. Her hair, long and red as Glinda's, fell in satiny waves to her feet. She wore a little mesh cap of pearls and a white satin Princess dress. A long, red velvet cloak hung loosely from her shoulders. Not exactly the costume for a cave, but vastly becoming. Azarine's pale and flower-like face was sweet and gentle, and when she saw the wet and weary traveler with Shagomar, she jumped up to welcome him as graciously as though she still were mistress of her castle.

316

"Why, it's the Wizard of Oz!" she cried joyfully after a second look at the guest. "Oh, we all know the Wizard of Oz! I have a picture of you right over the grand piano in my castle. Wherever did you find him, Shaggy, dear? Has he come all this way to help us?"

"It will be a great pleasure and privilege, if I may," said the Wizard, sitting on a rock opposite the Princess and placing his high hat between his knees. "Just now, I happen to be in as much trouble as your Highness. But perhaps—" The Wizard looked thoughtfully at the Stag standing motionless at the entrance of the cave. "Can Shagomar run?"

"Oh, yes! Terribly fast!" Azarine assured him eagerly. "Faster than eagles can fly, than water can fall down the mountain, faster than any creature on Red Top. Shaggy can do anything!" Jumping up, the Princess ran over to lean her head against the Red Stag's shoulder. "He goes to the village each day and returns with food. He has brought me blankets for my bed, pillows for my head, and has kept away the fierce Bug-bears and all other wild beasts that roam the Red Wood. I don't know what I should have done without him!" The Princess added softly, "Shaggy's such a dear!"

"You're both dears!" agreed the Wizard.

"Are we?" Azarine twinkled her eyes at the Wizard. "But Shaggy's the biggest, and we've always been friends, haven't we?" The Stag, looking down at Azarine with his bright, steadfast eyes, nodded so vigorously that the bell on his antlers rang a veritable medley, and the rays from the silver lantern danced into every corner of the dreary cavern.

"Well, then," the Wizard rubbed his hands briskly together, "Shaggy shall carry us straight to the Palace of Glinda the Good Sorceress of the South. As Red Top Mountain is in the Quadling Country, her palace must be somewhere quite near."

"Oh, it is! It is!" beamed Azarine. "I've often seen her lights from the towers on Red Top. It's just a mile or two from the base of this mountain. I never have seen Glinda, but I have heard she is very good and a Powerful Sorceress. Do you think she can force Bustabo to give me back my castle and my Kingdom?"

"I know it!" declared the Wizard, picking up his hat and clapping it on the back of his head. "But before we start for Glinda's, I must go back and rescue my friends from that thieving Red Beard."

Marching forth and back before the fire, the Wizard related all that had happened since he and his party had started off in the two Ozoplanes. Hearing the strange tale, Azarine almost forgot her own troubles. When the Wizard told how Bustabo had broken the winged staffs on which they hoped to ride to the Emerald City and of the wicked bargain he had driven, the little Princess generously offered to return to the Red Castle so that Ozma and Oz might be saved. But the Wizard would not hear of such a thing. "No!" he decided. "Shaggy and I will go back and manage, somehow, to release my comrades from the castle. Then we all can start for Glinda's together."

"Wait," whistled the Stag, who had been listening to the Wizard's story with distended eyes and nostrils. "Wait, first I will fetch Dear Deer."

"Who in Oz is Dear Deer?" inquired the Wizard as Shagomar melted like a shadow through the dark opening of the cavern.

"His wife," explained Azarine with an excited skip. "And that will be just splendid, for Dear Deer shall carry all of your friends, and we can ride Shaggy!"

Chapter 15 - In the Red Castle

And now let us peek in to the doings of Jellia, Dorothy and the others after they mournfully watched the Wizard stalk off into the forest.

With Bowmen ahead of them and Bowmen closely following, the prisoners marched slowly into the castle. Afraid not to hurry on account of the sharp-pointed beards of the Guards, the little party progressed almost at a run.

Hurrying them through the beautiful throne room and other cheerful apartments on the first floor, the Bowmen led them to a covered stone stairway curving up from the back courtyard. Up, up, and up tramped the Bowmen, and up, up and up trudged the weary travelers. It seemed to Dorothy they had climbed a thousand steps before they reached the top. Both girls were frightened, but holding their backs straight and their chins high, they stepped haughtily along without even a glance at their red-bearded captors. Unlocking an iron door at the head of the stair, the Guards gruffly ushered them into a round, stone-walled room at the very top of the tower. Relocking the door just as gruffly, they took their departure.

"Thank gooseness there's a fire!" shivered Jellia, running across the room to hold out her hands to the crackling blaze. "As soon as we're warm and dry, we can decide what to do. Pull up a couple of those benches, Wantowin, and for cake's sake don't look so glum! Nobody's been hurt yet!"

"Ah, but what of the morning?" The Soldier with Green Whiskers wagged his head dismally. "That rogue of a Red Beard will pitch us off this mountain quick as that!" Wantowin snapped his cold fingers. "One toss from this tower and we're done!" groaned the Army, turning away from one of the barred windows with a positive shudder. Glancing out the window nearest her, Dorothy saw that the tower had been built at the very edge of the mountain. Jagged rocks far below and long-dead trees jutting out from the sides of the sheer precipice made it even more formidable.

"I'm going to sleep," mumbled the lion, settling himself near the fire. "What I don't see won't make me feel more cowardly."

"How true," thought Dorothy. Backing away from the window and resolutely keeping her mind off the precipice, she began to help Jellia drape the Scarecrow over a bench close to the fire.

"Not too close, girls," begged the Straw Man nervously. "Fire's almost as bad for me as water. One little spark and pouff! Nothing but a bonfire of your old friend and comrade!"

At this point a sharp tap on the door made them all jump, but it was only a servant carrying a large tray. At least, Bustabo was keeping his promise about supper. The servant was round and jolly. He looked sympathetically at the little company, but evidently was afraid to speak to them. Placing his tray on a table in the center of the room, he bowed stiffly and withdrew, locking the door carefully after him.

"Not bad," said Jellia, lifting cover after cover from the silver serving dishes. "Not bad at all! Give us a hand, Wanny, and we'll pull the table over to the fire. My gooseness, this is almost as good as a party!"

Seating herself next to Dorothy, who already was busy, Jellia bit rapturously into a crisp roll. "Mmmm, mmm! This is the first food I've tasted since we left the Emerald City. Draw up, Liony! This roast lamb will make you forget that wind pudding. You may have all the roast, and we'll manage with the vegetables, the soup, salad and dessert!"

Dusk was falling, and the tower room was hardly cheerful, but sitting on their hard benches close to the fire, the prisoners dined almost as well as though they had been in the Emerald City. Now that his hunger was satisfied, even the Soldier with Green Whiskers began to look less desperate. The Scarecrow, now completely dry though a little wrinkled, was his old, witty self again.

As it grew darker, Jellia lit the rusty lantern on the stone mantel, and Wantowin placed another log on the fire. There was a heap of blankets on one of the benches. No other beds being visible, the girls spread several on the hearth. Resting their backs comfortably against the sleeping lion, they conversed in low and guarded whispers. Wantowin, considering it his duty to stand guard, dragged a bench across the doorway. Wrapping himself up in a blanket, he was soon snoring louder than the Cowardly Lion. The servant had removed the tray, and sounds from below had long since ceased. They knew it must be way past midnight, but Dorothy and Jellia were unable to relax.

"I wonder how the Wizard's getting along!" mused Dorothy, pulling the blanket a little closer. "It must be awfully dark in that forest."

"Oh, Wiz'll be all right, depend on that!" Jellia spoke with a heartiness she was far from feeling. "He'll have that Princess here before sun-up. If he doesn't, we'll just light out and find him!"

"Light out?" inquired the Scarecrow, drawing back still further from the fire. "How do you mean?"

"Yes," echoed Dorothy, moving closer to Jellia as a board creaked somewhere below. "How do you mean?"

"Oh, I don't just know," admitted Jellia frankly. "But there might be something in this kit-bag to help! Let's have a look, anyway." Dragging it from under a bench where she had stowed it on their arrival, Jellia zipped it open and began feeling inside, curiously. "I never have had a chance to examine it properly," Jellia said. "But that cheer gas certainly came in handy, and the freezing fluid and sapling seeds were pretty neat, too! My, whatever are these, now?" Folded neatly on the very top were four suits of blue pajamas with hoods and feet attached like those in an infant's sleeping garment.

Holding one near to the blaze so she could read the pink placard on the pocket, Jellia gave a little gasp. "Oh, listen!" she whispered, catching Dorothy's sleeve. "It says: `These falling-out suits have not been tested, but I believe they will work and prove safe and practical in case of accident. — WIZ."

"I suppose the Wizard meant them for his Ozoplane passengers to use instead of parachutes," decided Dorothy, fingering one rather doubtfully. "Well, I should hate to be the first to try one!"

"Oh, I don't know," Jellia, her head on one side, pensively considered the blue pajamas. "I think they're real cute. I think — HARK! What was that?" Dropping the pajamas, she clutched Dorothy as the unmistakable tread of a heavy boot came stamping up the stair.

"Bustabo!" shivered Dorothy. "Oh, he's not going to wait till morning! He's coming for us now! Oh, Jellia, JELLIA, what shall we DO?" Dorothy's voice, rising almost to a shriek, roused the Cowardly Lion. Cocking one ear and arriving at exactly the same conclusion as the little girl, the lion sprang over to waken the Soldier with Green Whiskers. The Scarecrow already was hurrying from window to window, trying the bars with his flimsy cotton fingers. At the window nearest the fireplace he gave a joyful little grunt, for some former prisoner had managed to saw through three of the iron bars. As the Scarecrow pushed, they moved creakily outward.

"Quick! Come help me!" urged the Scarecrow, dragging the terrified and only half-awake Soldier to the window. "On with those parachute suits, girls! We'll jump before we're tossed out!" Dorothy and Jellia exchanged desperate glances and then — as the steps on the stair thumped louder and nearer

— each grabbed a falling-out suit and zipped herself tidily inside.

"Here!" panted Jellia, down on her hands and knees beside the Cowardly Lion. "You can put your front feet in anyway, and anything will be better than nothing when you fall!" To her relief and surprise, she discovered that the pajamas would stretch! Even the lion could wear them without too much discomfort. Except for a cramp in his tail, which was coiled tightly on his back, the lion fitted into his pajamas nicely.

As the Soldier with Green Whiskers was trembling too violently to help himself or anyone else, Jellia jerked and pushed him into one of the falling-out suits. Then, picking up the Wizard's kit-bag and looking solemnly back at her anxious comrades, Jellia climbed to the window sill. "I'll go first," she announced, closing her mouth to keep her teeth from chattering.

"No! Let me! I insist on going first," cried the Scarecrow, springing nimbly up beside Jellia. "Falling does not hurt me at all."

"Oh, hurry! Hurry!" begged Dorothy, glancing fearfully over her shoulder. The footsteps were now so loud and near, she expected the door to burst right open and Bustabo's red face to appear.

"Goodbye! I'm off!" Before the Scarecrow could stop her, Jellia was off indeed! Clutching the kit-bag to her bosom, she squeezed through the opening between the bars and dove headlong into space! Next, the Scarecrow, with a sad little wave to Dorothy, dropped out of sight. "Help me push this so-called Soldier out!" puffed Dorothy as the Cowardly Lion signalled for her to go next. "If we leave him till last, he'll never jump at all!"

"Halt! About face! Help! Mama! Papa! Help! Help! HELP!" wailed Wantowin Battles. But Dorothy relentlessly forced him to the sill and through the op

ening. As his wildly thrashing legs disappeared over the edge, whoever was coming up the stairs broke into a run. Thump, thump, THUMPETY-THUMP! Trembling in every muscle, Dorothy climbed to the sill. Spreading both arms, she launched herself into the air.

She heard the grunt of the Cowardly Lion as he forced his way through the opening. Then the fierce rush of wind past her ears as she pitched downward drowned out all other sounds. At first she was sure the Wizard's falling-out suits were failures, for the lion plunged past her, falling like a plummet. She, too, was whirling downward so fast she felt sure she would be crushed on the rocks below. Closing her eyes, she tried to resign herself to whatever was coming. Then, suddenly, the pajamas filled with air, ballooning out till she floated lightly as a feather. The question now was, would she ever come down?

There was no moon, and in the faint starlight she could make out three other bulky shapes spinning through the air just beneath her. By kicking her legs and flapping her arms, Dorothy managed to miss several jutting rocks and tree limbs. As she floated lower, the suit began gradually to deflate, finally letting her down as softly as could be, on a strip of sand at the base of the mountain. A little distance away she could see Jellia, already stepping out of her falling-out suit, and the Cowardly Lion, waiting impatiently for someone to help him out of his. Wantowin Battles, very brave now that the danger was past, already had stripped off his flying suit and was shaking and patting the Scarecrow into shape, for the poor straw man had been completely flattened out by his fall.

"Well, how did you like it?" called Jellia, hurrying over to help the lion untangle himself. "After the first swoop, it wasn't bad at all. Really, I quite enjoyed it!"

"Enjoyed it!" choked the Lion, looking indignantly from Dorothy to Jellia. "I'll never set foot in a plane again as long as I live. Brrrah! Ever since we left the Emerald City we've been falling, flying and blowing about like yesterday's papers. Now that I'm on solid ground at last, I intend to stay there! The rest of you may do as you please, but I shall walk home if it takes a year!"

"I don't blame you," said Jellia, patting the lion soothingly on the nose. "But we can't start without the Wizard. We'll have to hide here till morning and then try to find him."

"Let him find us," growled the Lion, lashing his tail experimentally to see whether there was any wag left in it after the shameful way it had been cramped in the suit. "The whole trip was his idea, not mine!"

"Oh, hush," warned Dorothy. "Someone will hear you! Ooooh! Someone has!" And sure enough, the faint tinkle of a bell came mysteriously through the gloom.

"Mercy, do you suppose those Red Beards have started after us already?" cried Jellia, looking around for the kit-bag. "But how could they have come down the mountain as fast as we fell?"

"They couldn't," whispered the Scarecrow, picking up the bag and handing it to Jellia. "But don't worry, my dears! It's probably a herd of goats or cattle. These mountaineers often put bells on their animals. Just keep still and don't move, and they won't notice us at all." Flattening themselves against the rocks at the foot of the mountain, the five adventurers waited tensely. But when a huge, shaggy shape loomed out of the darkness and came charging straight toward them, all five screamed and started to slither sideways.

"Wait! Don't run! Don't be frightened!" begged an agitated voice. "Don't you know me? It's I! It's me! THE WIZARD!"

Chapter 16 - Escape From Red Top

As the great stag came to a sliding halt, the rays from his silver lantern cast a wavering light over the little group crouched against the rocks.

"Hello! How ever did you escape from the castle?" demanded Ozma's little Magician, sliding recklessly off the high back of his steed and embracing them jubilantly. "We were just coming to help you. Girls, Scarecrow, Soldier, Lion, may I present Azarine, the real Princess of this Mountain, and Shagomar and Dear Deer, her friends!"

Dorothy and Jellia were so stunned by the unexpected appearance of the Wizard, they were able only to manage a couple of breathless bows. And indeed, the lovely picture Azarine made seated demurely on the huge red stag was enough to render anyone speechless. Shaggy himself was breathtaking, too. Not only the lantern and bell hung from his antlers now, but perched unconcernedly on the tallest prong was a lovely white pigeon with a key in his bill.

"This pigeon was going to fly up to the tower with the key to the door," explained the Wizard as his five comrades continued to gaze at him in stupefied silence. "Fortunately, Azarine, who was imprisoned there before you, had an extra key. She said Bustabo would lock you up in the tower!" exclaimed the Wizard with a nod at the Princess. "But since you already are out and down, we'll not need the key. Tell me, how did you manage to escape? What did you do? Break down the door?"

"No, we just stepped out the window," the Scarecrow told him with a nonchalant wave upward.

"You mean you jumped all this distance?" gasped Azarine, leaning forward to peer between Shaggy's branching antlers while Dear Deer trotted closer to nudge Dorothy with her soft, moist nose.

"Well, sort of," explained Jellia, putting an arm around the Cowardly Lion, who still was looking extremely sulky. "But first we put on those falling-out suits, Wiz, and you'll be glad to know they really worked."

"Splendid! Splendid!" beamed the Wizard with a satisfied shake of his head. "You know, I'd completely forgotten them, but I felt sure you'd find some useful magic in the kit. Did Bustabo keep his promises?"

"Well, he locked us up in the tower, and he gave us a pretty good supper," answered Dorothy. "But we didn't like being prisoners, and we didn't feel safe in that castle. Then a little while ago when we heard him thumping up the stair, we just decided to leave! And so — we left!"

"So we see! So we see!" The Wizard grinned appreciatively, delighted by the spirit of the two girls. "But perhaps we'd better be off! No knowing when Bustabo and his Bowmen will be coming to look for you. Shagomar and Dear Deer have kindly agreed to carry us to the castle of Glinda the Good. Once there, with Glinda's magic to help me I'll find some way to deal with Strut and to force Bustabo to give up Azarine's throne. Now suppose you two girls and the Scarecrow mount Dear Deer, and the Soldier and I will ride with the Princess."

Dear Deer, at the Wizard's words, moved over to a flat rock. Without any trouble at all, Jellia and Dorothy climbed to places on her back. Then the Scarecrow vaulted up behind, clasping his arms 'round Jellia to keep from slipping off. When Wantowin and the Wizard had mounted behind Azarine, the two Deer swung away from the mountain. With the Cowardly Lion loping easily between, they ran swiftly toward the Southlands.

Their gait was so smooth it seemed to Jellia they were flying like figures in a dream through the shadowy forest, with only the twinkle of the silver lantern to light their way. As they raced along, Azarine again told the story of Bustabo's treachery and how Shagomar had brought the Wizard to her hidden cave. Then the two girls amused the little Princess with the story of their experiences in the Strat. They told her all about their life at home in the Emerald City, and of the curious celebrities who lived in the palace with Ozma. Azarine already was charmed with the Scarecrow and the Cowardly Lion, and kept leaning down to have a better look at the tawny beast trotting so unconcernedly between the two deer.

"I tell you," she proposed generously. "I tell you, if Strut destroys the Emerald City you all can come back and live with me. That is, if Glinda and the Wizard can make Bustabo give my castle and Kingdom back."

"But I do hope we'll find some way to stop Strut! How long will it take him to reach the capitol?" Dorothy called across to the Wizard.

"Well, it took us a night and half a day to fly to Stratovania," calculated the little Magician, wrinkling his forehead. "So I'm afraid if Strut and the Tin Woodman left yesterday, they'll be in the Emerald City tomorrow. That is, today."

"And it's almost morning now," shivered Jellia, glancing off toward the East, where the sky already showed the first streaks of lavender and rose.

"Now don't you worry," begged the Wizard, holding fast to his high hat. "As soon as we reach Glinda's castle and I have some proper magic to work with, I'll find a way to make both Strut and Bustabo behave. The few trifles in this kit-bag are a help, but not nearly so powerful enough for rascals like those. Look, girls, isn't that Glinda's castle now?"

"Oh, it is! It is!" cried Dorothy, clasping Dear Deer around the neck, she was so relieved and happy. And the silver-trimmed towers and spires of Glinda's lovely red castle shimmering through the early-morning mists were enough to make anyone happy. Flashing through the beautiful gardens and parks, leaping hedges and flower beds as lightly as swallows, the stag and his mate brought the little band of adventurers to the very door of the castle.

"Goodbye now," breathed the stag as the Wizard and Soldier slipped off his back and the Wizard lifted Azarine down. "Take care of my little Princess!"

"Oh, don't go!" cried Dorothy, for Dear Deer seemed on the point of vanishing, too. "Do stay and see how it all turns out. Later on, wouldn't you like to go to the Emerald City and meet the famous animals who live in the capitol?" Shagomar looked questioningly at Dear Deer, and as his pretty little wife seemed interested, he allowed himself to be persuaded.

"We'll wait in the garden," he whistled softly. "Houses and castles are too stuffy and shut in for Deer people. If you need me, Princess, just ring the silver bell." Lowering his head so the Princess could slip the bell from his antlers, the stag stood looking at her solemnly.

"I will," promised Azarine, waving her little red handkerchief as the two deer sprang away. They actually seemed to float off above the flowers, so lightly and easily did they run.

Chapter 17 - The Wizard gets to Work

"Please announce us to your Mistress at once!" directed the Wizard to the sleepy little castle-maid who presently came in answer to his loud knock.

"But Her Highness and Princess Ozma are not here!" stuttered the maid, her eyes popping at sight of visitors so early in the morning. "They left yesterday to visit Prince Tatters and Grampa in Ragbad!"

"Ha, well," the Wizard turned to the others with a little shrug. "Looks as if I shall have to manage alone. A fortunate thing Ozma did not start back to the Emerald City. At least she will not fall into Strut's hands. Here, HERE! Don't shut the door!" The Wizard quickly pushed past the little serving maid. "Glinda will wish us to make ourselves comfortable in her absence. Now then, Miss, Miss—?"

"Greta," mumbled the girl, looking bashfully at her feet.

"Oho, a Greta to greet, eh?" chuckled the Scarecrow, taking off his hat and bowing to the ground. "Well, now, my dear Miss Greta, will you kindly show these young ladies to suitable apartments, and tell the cook to prepare breakfast for six."

"Make it twelve!" growled the Cowardly Lion with a little bounce toward the maid. "I could eat six all by myself!"

"Yes Sirs! Yes Sirs!" quavered Greta, running off so fast she lost one of her red slippers.

"Never mind," laughed Dorothy. "Jellia and I know this castle as well as our own. We'll show Azarine about and have time for a short nap before breakfast." The hundred pretty girls who acted as Glinda's Maids-in-Waiting were still asleep. In fact, no one was stirring in the castle except a few servants. Waving briskly to the girls as they started up the marble stairway, the Wizard went striding toward the red study where the Sorceress kept all her books on witchcraft, her magic potions, her phials and appliances.

The exquisite palace of Glinda, over which Azarine was exclaiming at every step, was an old story to the Cowardly Lion. Throwing himself down on a huge bearskin, he soon was in a doze and making up the sleep he had lost on the two previous nights. Wantowin Battles had at once gone off to waken an old Soldier Crony of his who drilled Glinda's Girl Guard, and the Scarecrow, about to follow the Wizard into the study, paused to look at the great record book.

This book, fastened with golden chains to a marble table in the reception room of the castle, records each event as it happens in the Land of Oz. When Glinda goes on a journey, she usually locks the Record book and takes the key with her. But this time she had neglected to do so, and sentences were popping up, row after row on the open pages. As he bent over to peruse the latest entry, the Scarecrow's painted blue eyes almost popped from his cotton head.

"Fierce Airlanders from the Upper Strat are descending on the Emerald City of Oz," read the Straw Man, nearly losing his balance. "If measures of defense are not taken at once, the capitol will fall under the fierce attack of the invaders!"

"Wiz! YO, WIZ!" yelled the Scarecrow, taking a furious slide into the study. "Hurry! HURRY! For the love of Oz, hurry, or Strut will blow Ozma's castle into the Strat! The Record Book says so!" he panted, grabbing the Wizard's arm to steady himself. The Wizard, working over the delicate apparatus on a long table, looked up with an anxious frown.

"Now, now, you must be a little patient," he told the Scarecrow earnestly. "I'm hurrying just as fast as ever I can."

"But what do you propose to do?" demanded the Scarecrow, puckering his forehead into almost forty deep wrinkles. "Can't you whiz these Stratovanians away or send them back where they came from?"

"Not without Ozma's magic belt," sighed the Wizard. "And you know perfectly well that the belt is back in the Emerald City safe in the castle!"

"Then can't you transport the safe here?" asked the Scarecrow, playing a frantic little tune on the edge of the table.

"Just what I'm trying to do!" admitted the Wizard, turning a lever here and a wheel there. "But this triple-edged, zentomatic transporter of Glinda's does not seem to be working as it should. I'll probably be able to fix it in a little while, but meantime I tell you what you can do. Post yourself beside the record book, and the minute it announces Strut's arrival in the Emerald City, rush straight back here to me!"

Before he had finished his sentence, the Scarecrow was gone, and for the next two hours the faithful Straw Man, without once lifting his eyes, bent over the great book of records, reading with tense interest and lively appreciation of the progress of the Oztober and the Airlanders toward the Capitol of Oz.

Chapter 18 - Strut of the Strat arrives in Oz!

For several hours after leaving Stratovania, Nick followed the Wizard's map implicitly.
With Strut leaning over the back of his seat, eyes glued to both map and board, there was nothing else he could do. If he deviated from the course so much as a hair's breadth, the Airlander would tap him on his tin head with his staff. The Tin Woodman had not expected Strut to be so clever about navigating, and as time passed he grew less and less hopeful of outwitting the wily Airman.

If he increased the speed of the Oztober in an effort to outdistance Strut's flying warriors, they also increased their speed. Try as he would, it seemed quite impossible to lose them. But Nick Chopper did not despair. He was counting on the night to help him. Never tiring or needing sleep, he would have the advantage of Strut then. As soon as the Airlander relaxed in his seat, the Tin Woodman meant to fall upon him, hurl him from a window, put all the plane's lights out, and speed off in the dark so swiftly the Stratovanians would be unable to follow. That failing, he depended on the difference in altitude to subdue the enemy. Perhaps when they reached the lower areas, Strut and his Airmen would faint, wilt, and become harmless.

So, bolstering his spirits with these heartening hopes, Nick bore as patiently as he could the long afternoon and the unpleasant taunts and company of his captor. Repassing the ice crescent without meeting any Spikers, the Tin Woodman zoomed along, not even bothering to answer Strut's many questions about Oz and its inhabitants.

Night, when it did come, was especially dark and murky. No moon and only a few stars dotted the arching Skyway. The darker the better, rejoiced the Tin Woodman, taking quick little glances over his shoulder to see whether Strut was falling asleep or showing any signs of drowsiness. If it were just dark enough, he'd rid himself of these flying pests in a hurry. But all his plans proved futile. As the Oztober rushed on and on and the hours dragged slowly by, Strut grew even more alert and watchful. His star-shaped eyes twinkled and glowed with sulphurous lights, and he showed no more signs of weariness than the Tin Woodman himself.

The endurance of the Airlander and his warriors was positively uncanny, and Nick, maneuvering the buttons and wheel of the plane, grew increasingly discouraged and gloomy. Flying at this rate, they would arrive in the Emerald City early in the morning, and to think that he was leading this band of savages upon the defenseless City almost broke Nick Chopper's heart. As it was a red plush heart, it could not really break, but it fluttered up and down in his tin bosom like a bird beating against the bars of a cage. To Nick's suggestion that he rest, Strut gave a contemptuous glance.

"I'll rest in Ohsma's palace," he sneered maliciously. "D'ye think I trust you enough to sleep? Ho no! Just attend to your flying, Mr. Funnel Top, and I'll take care of the rest of this little adventure." After this, Nick made no further remarks, and morning found the Oztober sailing high above the Hammerhead Mountains in the Quadling Country of Oz. All too soon the Tin Woodman made out the glittering green turrets and spires of the Emerald City itself.

"Quite a pretty little town," observed Strut condescendingly as Nick, his thoughts in a perfect tumult, tried to think of some excuse for not landing.

"Why are you not flying over the castle?" demanded Strut sharply. "It's the castle I am most anxious to reach. There, you can come down right inside the walls. My, My! So this is the wonderful Land of OHS. Well, it owes me its crown jewels and treasure to pay for your insolent invasion of the Strat. Collecting them should prove pleasant! Very pleasant indeed!"

"I wouldn't be too sure of that," snapped Nick, turning his head stiffly. "I suppose you realize you are in great danger. If Ozma sees you before you have time to storm the castle, you and your silly flock of flyers are likely to be turned to crows and sparrows! The chances are, she HAS seen you," concluded Nick, slanting the Oztober sharply downward. At Nick's warning, the few clouds flitting across the Airman's forehead became positively thunderous.

"Pouf!" he sniffed, snapping his fingers scornfully. "Do you suppose a mere girl like this Ohsma of Ohs can frighten me? My Blowmen will soon attend to her and anyone else who stands in our way!"

"That," shouted Nick, raising his voice above the roar of the engine, "remains to be seen!" As a matter of fact, the Oztober and the swarm of flying warriors had been sighted almost as soon as they appeared above the green lands edging the capitol. Long before they reached the Emerald City itself, terrified messengers had brought word of the approaching airmen. Ozma being absent, Bettsy and Trot, the two little mortal girls who lived with Dorothy and the Supreme Ruler in the Emerald Palace, were in charge.

After one glance at the flying army, they had called all the celebrities, servants and courtiers together and bade them flee for their lives. Then Bettsy, Trot, and the Patchwork Girl climbed into the Red Wagon. With the Saw Horse to pull them, they set off at a gallop to hide in the Blue Forests of the Munchkin Country till the invasion was over. Tik Tok, the Machine Man, carrying all of Ozma's loose jewels and valuables, marched rapidly after them. The Medicine Man rode the Hungry Tiger, and the rest of the palace inmates ran helter-skelter down the yellow brick highway from the Capitol.

The inhabitants of the Emerald City itself, never having seen the Wizard's Ozoplanes and having no way of knowing that Nick Chopper was inside this one, were almost as afraid of the Oztober as of the Stratovanians. Pelting into their houses and shops, they bolted windows and doors and waited in terror-stricken silence for whatever was to come. Only the Guardian of the Gate stayed bravely at his post, waving his bunch of keys defiantly as the Ozoplane and the Airlanders swooped over the castle wall.

"Ho! No you don't!" cried Strut as Nick, having brought the plane to a landing, started to run for the door. "You'll stay with me as a hostage!" he rasped, gripping the Tin Woodman's arm. Furious but helpless in the iron grasp of the Stratovanian, Nick was forced to lead him into Ozma's beautiful castle.

Strut's warriors, after fluttering like curious birds from tree to tree and alighting in chattering groups on the wall, finally furled the wings of their staffs, formed ranks and marched, singing and shouting, up the steps after their jubilant leader.

In vain Nick sought for any signs of weakening among them. The Airmen seemed as comfortable and carefree in this lower altitude as they had been on their own airosphere. The Tin Woodman's only consolation was that he had brought back the Wizard's Ozoplane in as good order as when it had started away so unexpectedly. It was also a great relief to him to find the castle deserted. Not a courtier, servant or celebrity was in sight — not even the Glass Cat or Dorothy's little kitten, Eureka. Strut and his rude army stamped through the first floor from end to end without encountering a single soul.

"Very good," sniffed the Ruler of all the Stratovanians, shooting his eyes sharply to left and right, "so this powerful fairy Ohsma of Ohs has run off and left us her castle, and we win the war without blowing a blow! Ho, Ho! I shall spend my summers in this enchanting palace," he added with a malicious wink at the Tin Woodman. "But now," his grasp on Nick's arm tightened, "where are these famous magic treasures and jewels you were boasting of, this belt and fan and all the other foolishments and fripperies?"

"In a safe in Ozma's own apartment," Nick told him reluctantly. Now that Strut was in complete possession of the castle, little was to be gained by concealing the location of the treasures.

"Take me there at once," commanded Strut, and because the thousand Airlanders were a bit too numerous for comfort, Strut ordered them out to the garden, bidding them man the walls, guard the gates and all entrances, and give the alarm should any of the Ozlanders approach. Then, with lowered head and dragging feet, the Tin Woodman led the way to Ozma's private sitting room. The safe, sparkling with emeralds embedded in metal more valuable than platinum,

323

stood in an alcove behind a pair of silk curtains. Giving little heed to the elegant appointments of the apartment itself, Strut knelt before the safe, fairly panting with impatience and curiosity.

"How does it open?" he asked, spinning the little knob on the door round and round without any results whatsoever.

"I am sure I cannot say." Resting one elbow on the golden mantel, the Tin Woodman looked indifferently at the kneeling Airman. "Only Ozma and our Wizard ever open that safe."

"Oh, is that so!" Strut straightened up angrily. "We shall see about that. All I have to do is call one of my Blowmen and BLOW it open."

"Suit yourself," said Nick with a shrug of his shoulders. "Only if you do, the safe probably will blow away, and all the treasures with it!"

"Then how in the Dix shall I open it?" screamed Strut, giving it a spiteful kick with his silver-shod toe. Worn out by his long vigil of the night and the excitement of taking possession of the castle, he lost his temper completely and stamped and raged up and down before Ozma's jeweled strongbox. But thump and bang at the door as he would, it still remained shut. "Ha!" he puffed at last. "I'll call my swordsmith! He can hammer it open!" Racing over to the window, he yelled for the Swordsmith to come up.

But Strut's Swordsmith had no more success than his Master. Kindling a fire in the grate, he heated a poker red hot and tried to burn a hole in the door, but the poker did not leave even a scratch on the glittering surface. "Stop! Stop! You witless Woff. I'll do it myself," raged Strut. "I'll blow it open with star powder!"

"Surely you wouldn't do that," protested Nick, who up to this time had been watching the effort of the two airmen with quiet amusement. "If you blow up the safe, you might set fire to the castle and destroy all the treasures you have won."

"Oh, hold your tongue!" advised Strut. Dragging two smouldering logs from the grate, he shoved them under the safe. Then, unscrewing the end of his flying stick, he sprinkled a fine, black powder that smelled and looked like gunpowder, over the logs. Lighting a twisted paper, he stuck it beneath the logs and jumped back, waiting impatiently for the safe to fly apart.

Nick Chopper waited not a moment longer. Darting into the dressing room, he hastily filled a pitcher with water. But before he could return, an ear-splitting explosion rocked the castle and flung him and the pitcher through the doorway of the sitting room.

Without stopping to recover his breath, the Tin Woodman jumped up and hurried across the room. The two airmen, with blackened clothes and faces, stared dazedly at the spot where the safe had been. Where it had been

— because the safe was no longer there! Not a sign, emerald or single splinter of it! There was no hole in the ceiling, so it could not have blown up; there was no hole in the floor, so it could not have blown down. The windows were unbroken, the walls intact. Only the two logs, smoking sullenly on Ozma's priceless rug, remained of the Airlander's bonfire — unless we count the expression on Strut's face, which simply blazed with wrath, bafflement and unadulterated fury.

Chapter 19 - The Travelers Return!

"I told you not to do that," said Nick, running over to Strut and the Swordsmith. *"I warned* you! Now see what you've done!"

"But where is it? Where did it go? Where did it BLOW?" screamed the Airlander, his electric hair standing more on end than ever and crackling like summer lightning.

"Ask Ozma! Ask the Wizard!" suggested Nick, folding his arms and surveying the two quite calmly. "But if you take my advice, you'll hustle right out of this castle before the same thing happens to YOU!"

"Who asked for your advice?" cried Strut, streaking over to the window to see whether the safe had blown into the garden, though how it could have done so without knocking a hole in the wall or ceiling he could neither imagine nor understand. Drawing aside the curtain, he gave a great gasp. Nick, who had hurried after him, uttered a loud shout of joy.

"See! I told you!" cried Nick, and unhooking his oil can, the Tin Woodman let four drops of oil slide down his neck. "I told you!" Strut made no reply. He just hung on to the curtain as if he were drowning and the flimsy portiere a life preserver. "See!" shouted Nick again.

But it was Strut didn't see that upset the Airman! What he didn't see was his entire army of nine hundred and ninety-nine splendid fighters! The garden below was as empty and quiet as a park on a rainy Sunday. "Calm yourself, Man! Calm yourself!" advised Nick as Strut, turning from the window and noting the disappearance of his Swordsmith, began running in frenzied circles, overturning chairs and tables and tripping over rugs and footstools.

"Quick," he hissed, making a dive for the Tin Woodman. "Fly me back to the Strat. At once! At ONCE! Do you hear?"

"Oh, yes! I hear you quite well!" said Nick, eluding Strut easily. "But I'll never fly you anywhere again! Besides, don't you realize you cannot fly from magic? You'll have to stay, my good man, and face the music!"

Nick's words seemed to bring the Airlander to his senses. Remembering, even in defeat, that he was a powerful King and Ruler, he straightened up proudly and, with one hand resting on an emerald-topped table, stood looking tensely from Nick Chopper to the door. He did not have long to wait, for in less time than it takes to count ten, nine excited Ozians burst into the Royal Sitting room.

"Oh, Nick! Are you really safe? Is everything all right?" Jellia Jam rushed over to the Tin Woodman and took both of his hands in her own.

"So that's the fellow I was supposed to impersonate!" roared the Cowardly Lion, thrusting his head between Dorothy and the Soldier. "Well, Goosengravy, girls, I'm insulted!"

"And is this really Strut, the high and mighty Stratovanian who has come to conquer us?" Ozma, who was just behind the Soldier, gazed so steadily and sorrowfully at the Airman that he uncomfortably averted his gaze. He was, to tell the truth, astonished at the youth, beauty and regal manner of the young Fairy. He cast a questioning look at the others crowding through the doorway. He already knew the Soldier with Green Whiskers, but the Scarecrow, the Cowardly Lion, the small, High-Hatted gentleman talking earnestly to a cheerful little girl, the little, red-cloaked Princess and the tall, imposing red-haired Glinda were all new and bewildering strangers. For the first time since they had met, Nick felt sorry for his discomfited foe, and as each of the celebrities approached, he called out the names.

"Our famous live Scarecrow, His Majesty the Cowardly Lion, Glinda the Good Sorceress, the Wonderful Wizard of Oz, Princess Dorothy of Kansas and the Emerald City and—"

"Azarine the Red," finished Dorothy, helping him out. For Nick, completely at sea, looked inquiringly at the pretty little Princess in the red cloak. At each introduction Strut bowed stiffly. If he could have reached his flying stick, which he had left standing beside the mantel, he would have flown out of the window, regardless of the fact that he might never find his way back to the Strat. But as he could not reach the staff, he stood stonily waiting for whatever was to befall.

"How'd you find Jellia and the Soldier? What became of the Ozpril? Where's the Emerald safe?" questioned Nick, leaving Strut's side and hurrying to seize the little Wizard by both lapels, for he could restrain his curiosity no longer.

"Quite a story, quite a story," puffed the Wizard, closing one eye. "Ask me again some long winter evening." Jerking away from Nick, he ran off to fetch his black bag of magic, from which he had been separated far too long.

"I suppose you are quite anxious to return to your own country," said Ozma, addressing herself to the Ruler of the Strat as she seated herself on a small satin sofa.

"Not without my army," blustered Strat defiantly. "It is neither fair nor honest for one ruler to destroy by magic the fighting forces of another!"

"Your army is not destroyed," Ozma told him evenly. "It already is in Stratovania, transported there by this magic belt." Lightly, the dark-haired fairy touched the gem-studded girdle she was wearing. "And speaking of honesty and fairness," she went on seriously, "did you think it honest or fair to come here, take possession of my castle and try to steal all my treasure and jewels?" Strut had the grace to blush, and as there was no good answer to Ozma's question, he looked haughtily over the heads of the company regarding him so accusingly.

"Well, have you anything to say?" inquired Ozma sternly. "Whether or not you return to your Kingdom depends entirely upon yourself and how you treat Kabebe." At mention of his Queen, Strut started involuntarily.

"By the way, here's that silly crown you made me wear!" said Jellia, handing over the star-tipped circlet she had been wearing since her visit to the Strat. "Remember me to the Piper when you see him, and to Junnenrump and Hippenscop."

"Are you sure you'd rather not live in the Strat as a Starina than stay here with us?" asked Ozma, smiling mischievously as Jellia backed away from the frowning airman.

"Never! Never! NEVER!" cried Jellia, taking a long step backward at each word. "I've had enough of Kings to last me the rest of my life!"

A little ripple of laughter followed Jellia's blunt refusal, and taking pity on the mortified Airlander, Ozma touched her belt and whispered the magic word that would transport him to his own country.

"But can you trust him?" worried Nick Chopper as the Stratovanian vanished before their eyes. "How do you know he won't blow things up as soon as he returns?"

"Because I've removed all power from his Blowmen's horns," Ozma told him quietly. "He'll be all right, and for the kind of people he rules Strut probably is the best sort of ruler they could have."

"If you ask me," observed the Cowardly Lion, shaking his mane vigorously, "the worst punishment anyone could have would be to live on wind pudding and air-ade. Wooof!"

"Oh, what a shame!" Dorothy ran over to the mantel where the flying stick had been standing. "The winged staff's gone! I rather had hoped we could keep it for Hallowe'en or New Year's or something!"

"Haven't you had enough flying?" grinned the Scarecrow, settling on the green sofa beside Ozma. "By the way, where's the tell-all-escope?"

"Oh, I'm so sorry," Dorothy felt ruefully in the pocket of her coat. "I must have left it in Strut's Royal Pavilion!"

"Never mind! I'll bring it back with the magic belt," smiled Ozma, "and I presume it's all right to bring the safe back, too." As Glinda nodded in agreement, the Ruler of Oz touched her belt twice, and with two thumps — one louder than the other — the safe and tell-all-escope thumped down on the floor beside the sofa. The tell-all-escope was pointing directly at Ozma, and it immediately began broadcasting her whole history. So the little Fairy, with a chuckle of amusement, locked it up in her desk drawer.

While Ozma had been meting out her gentle justice, Jellia had been telling Nick all that had happened since he was forced to fly Strut to Oz. She told him of the arrival of the Ozpril, the escape of the whole party from the angry Kabebe, their fall to Red Top Mountain, their rude treatment by Bustabo, their meeting with Azarine and the red Deer, and their final journey to Glinda's castle.

Spellbound, Nick learned how the Wizard finally had mastered the intricacies of Glinda's zentomatic transporter and brought the safe to her red castle just as Strut was on the point of taking violent measures. With the safe in his possession, it had been an easy matter for the Wizard to transport both Glinda and Ozma from Ragbad. After listening to the whole exciting story, Glinda, Ozma and the Wizard had sent the Stratovanian army back to the Strat and returned to the Emerald City to deal with Strut personally.

"It's certainly handy to have a Fairy around," sighed Dorothy, slipping an arm around Ozma's slim waist. "One little wave of Ozma's wand and we soared right into this castle! Isn't it grand to be home again? Not that I didn't enjoy the trip," she added hastily as the Wizard came briskly into the room with his black bag. "Oh, Ozma! Just wait till you see the beautiful Ozoplanes our Wizard has built for you!"

"She'll need pretty strong glasses to see the Ozpril," observed the Wizard, looking rather sadly at the ceiling. "I expect it's hanging to the tip of a star by this time! And I suppose Strut made hash of the Oztober!"

"Hash!" sputtered Nick Chopper indignantly. "I should say NOT. I've taken splendid care of your ship, Wiz, and you'll find the Oztober below in the garden as bright and beautiful as the night she was launched!"

"Hurray for Nick," shouted Jellia, waving the duster she already was flipping briskly over pictures and books. "He should have a medal, your Majesty! No one could have flown that Plane better than the Tin Woodman!"

"He shall have a medal!" promised Ozma with a special smile for Nick Chopper, who was one of her special favorites. "And when he needs a vacation from the Winkies, he can come here and be our official Pilot answerable only to me and to the Wizard!"

"And I hereby present your Majesty with my two splendid Ozoplanes — for exploring, for pleasure, or for warfare!" announced the little Wizard, extending both arms dramatically. "But now you will have to excuse me, as the Tin Woodman and I are leaving at once!"

"Leaving!" wailed Jellia, plumping down on a footstool. "But you've only just returned!"

"Can't help it," panted the Wizard, who seemed in a perfect phiz to be off. "I'll show you the Ozoplanes later, Ozma, but now Goodbye! Goodbye, Dorothy! Goodbye, Jellia! Take good care of Azarine till I return!"

"But look, where are we going?" demanded Nick Chopper as the Wizard seized his arm and marched him rapidly toward the door.

"To find the Ozpril, of course!" explained the Wizard impatiently, as if that should have been clear to everybody! "To find the Ozpril and bring her back to the Emerald City!"

"But think how high those Blowmen may have blown it," worried Dorothy. "They may even have blown it to Bitz!"

"Then we'll bring back the pieces," declared the Wizard firmly. "How about coming along?" With a wink at Jellia Jam, he paused beside the Lion, who was busy licking his front paws.

"WHAT?" roared the Lion, springing up as if someone had shot him. With a thoroughly indignant glance at Ozma's little magician, he bolted through the curtains and was gone.

"Just not a flyer!" mused the Wizard, shaking his head in amusement. "Well, goodbye, Friends! Farewell, all!" With an energetic nod, he stepped through the door, pulling Nick along with him.

"Couldn't you bring the Ozpril back with your magic belt?" questioned Dorothy, hurrying over to the window to watch the plane's takeoff.

"I suppose so," answered Ozma thoughtfully. "But they both are so fond of flying, they'd much rather bring it back themselves! I'm sure of it!"

326

Chapter 20 - Azarine is Restored to Red Top

From the castle window, the whole party cheered wildly as the Ozoplane, roaring with power, soared over the wall, over the treetops and up, up, and up, till it vanished into the cloudless blue sky.

"My pie! I do hope Nick doesn't start claiming any more countries," sighed Jellia, drawing in her head reluctantly. "And for cake's sake, why couldn't they have waited a few days? Of course, the Tin Woodman is never tired, but Wiz certainly needed a rest after all we've been through!"

"Never you mind about that!" Glinda patted the kind-hearted little Jellia on the shoulder. "The Wizard has his black bag along this time, and in that bag there is a cure for almost everything — even lack of sleep!"

"Look!" called Dorothy, pulling Jellia back to the window. "Shaggy and Dear Deer are running races round the pond, and here come all our servants and celebrities! Hiah, Tik Tok! Hello, Scraps! See, Azarine! That's the Patch Work Girl! You'll simply love her! We all do! Someone must have sent word that Strut had been defeated!"

"I did. I dispatched one of my doves," explained Glinda. "And now, my dear," the tall and lovely Sorceress motioned significantly to Ozma, "is it not time to deal with Bustabo and restore this Little Lady to her Castle?"

"Oh, not yet! Please, not yet!" begged Dorothy as Azarine looked expectantly from Glinda to Ozma. "We want Azarine to stay here a long time, don't we, Jellia? Come on, Azzy dear, I'll lend you an old dress, and we'll all go for a ride before lunch! You on Shaggy, Jellia and I on Dear Deer, Bettsy and Trot on the Cowardly Lion, and the Scarecrow on the Hungry Tiger!"

"It's all right, go ahead," Ozma nodded indulgently as the little Princess hung back. She did want so much to stay and meet all the interesting people in the garden, but she felt it her real duty to return to her subjects, now suffering under the cruel rule and temper of Bustabo.

Then: "I've already turned Bustabo into a red Squirrel!" Ozma told the Princess gravely. "In that form he still can enjoy himself, but do no harm to others. I've also sent a message saying you will be home in a few days and placed Archibald the Archer in charge till you return!"

"Oh, how did you know Archy is the one I trust most?" marveled Azarine, her eyes shining with happiness and astonishment. "Bustabo threw Archy into a dungeon a week ago because he tried to help me!"

"Ozma knows everything," confided Dorothy with an adoring glance toward the little Ruler of all Oz. "And everything's going to be lovely! Come on, Azzy! I'll beat you to the fountain in the garden!"

So now, with her last worry removed, the little Princess of Red Top skipped off with Dorothy to meet all the exciting celebrities in the garden. The two deer, alarmed by the strange appearance of some of the Ozlanders, had hidden themselves in a snowball bush. But Azarine soon coaxed them out, and in no time at all they were chatting like old friends with the Hungry Tiger and the Saw Horse.

Jellia stayed in the garden only a short while, for Jellia had other things to do. The little Oz Maid was determined to have a party to celebrate their homecoming, and soon, in deep conference with the castle chef, she was planning the most gorgeous feast the Green Castle ever had known.

It began at noon and lasted till nightfall. Even long after the tall candles had burned low, the cheery company sat around the royal table while Dorothy, Jellia and the Scarecrow told and retold their amazing adventures in the Strat and on Red Top Mountain.

So delightful did Azarine and the two Deer find life in the capitol, they stayed on and on. Each evening, the girls and Ozma and her most important counselor would gather in her private sitting room. There, looking at the magic screen, they followed the progress of Nick and the Wizard as they flew on and on through the strange Highways and Byways of the Stratosphere.

What a story they will have to tell us when they return. WHAT a story!

The End

The Magical Mimics in

by Jack Snow

To the Children

As long as I can remember, I have been reading Oz books, and now I am very proud and happy to have been permitted to write a book about the latest happenings in the Land of Oz.

Mr. Kramer has made may delightful illustrations for this book, and I know you will enjoy the fun and life that he has so skillfully put into his pictures.

As for the Magical Mimics, I think you will agree with me that these surprising creatures made things pretty exciting for our Oz friends while they were in the Emerald City. Nevertheless, now that the Mimics are powerless, I am inclined to forgive them; since, had it not been for them, Dorothy and the Wizard would not have discovered winsome little Ozana and her Story Blossom Garden.

I hope this story pleases you and that you will write me many letters — all of which I promise to answer as soon as possible. I am sure that your suggestions and ideas will be of great help to me in writing future Oz books, and I am looking forward with much pleasure to receiving them.

JACK SNOW
January 10, 1946.

This Book Is Dedicated to My Mother Roselyn Hyde Snow

"....to please a child is a sweet and lovely thing that warms one's heart and brings its own reward."
—L. FRANK BAUM

Chapter 1 - Toto Carries a Message

"Toto," called Princess Ozma of Oz as a small, black dog trotted down the corridor past the open door of her study in the Royal Palace of the Emerald City. "Toto, will you do me a favor?"

"Certainly," answered the little dog, his bright eyes regarding the Princess questioningly. "What can I do for your Majesty?"

Ozma smiled. "I wonder if you would go to Dorothy's rooms and ask her to join me here as soon as possible."

"That'll be easy, Ozma," said Toto. "I was just on my way to see Dorothy. It's time for our morning romp in the garden."

"Well," laughed Ozma, "I shall keep Dorothy for only a few minutes, then she can join you in the garden for your play."

"Thank you, Ozma," replied Toto as he turned and trotted down the corridor leading to Dorothy's suite of rooms.

As the little dog disappeared, the smile slowly faded from Ozma's face, and the lovely little ruler of the world's most beautiful fairyland looked unusually serious.

The truth was that Ozma was thinking of events that had happened many years before in the history of the Land of Oz. Not always had Oz been a fairy realm. In those olden times Oz had been nothing more than a remarkably beautiful country of rolling plains, wooded hills and rich farmlands. Indeed, Oz had not been so much different from our own United States, except that it was surrounded on all sides by a Deadly Desert.

It was this desert which prevented curious men from the great outside world from finding their way to Oz. For the fumes and gasses that rose from the shifting sands of the desert were deadly poison to all living things, and for a human to have set foot on the desert would have meant instant and terrible death. Consequently, all living things avoided the Deadly Desert, and it is no wonder that Oz was so entirely secluded and went unnoticed by the rest of the world for so many long years.

Meanwhile, the Oz people were happy and contented, living their simple, carefree lives without worries or troubles. The soil of Oz was fertile and the people naturally industrious, so there was always an abundance of everything for everyone. Hence destructive and terrible wars were unknown in Oz, even in the olden days.

One fine day Queen Lurline, Ruler of all the fairies in the world, chanced to be flying over the Land of Oz with her fairy band. She was greatly impressed with the beauty of the hidden country. The Fairy Queen paused, flying in wide circles over the peaceful land. Here was a country so entirely beautiful and charming that it deserved to be a fairy realm.

Queen Lurline sought out the King of this favored land and found him to be an old man with no son or daughter to whom he could pass on his crown. With great joy the old King accepted the tiny baby fairy whom Queen Lurline placed in his care. When the baby fairy attained her full age of girlhood (no fairy ever appears to be older than a young girl of fourteen or fifteen), she was to be crowned Princess Ozma of Oz.

>From the time of Lurline's visit, Oz became a fairyland, abounding in enchantments and strange happenings. Indeed, several of the inhabitants of Oz fell to studying the magic arts and became witches and magicians, very nearly preventing Ozma from becoming the rightful ruler of the fairyland.

Ozma was fully aware that she was a member of Queen Lurline's fairy band, and she was justly proud of her immortal heritage. She knew, too, that she owed allegiance to the powerful Fairy Queen, and that was the reason she appeared so thoughtful this morning as she awaited Princess Dorothy.

Ozma's reverie was broken by a gentle rap on the open door. Looking up, she saw Dorothy standing in the doorway.

"Come in, my dear," said Ozma. "There is something I must discuss with you."

Chapter 2 - Ozma and Glinda go Away

"What is it, Ozma?" Dorothy asked as she sat down beside her friend.

"Dorothy," Ozma began, thoughtfully, "you have heard me tell the story of how the good Queen Lurline left me here as a baby to become the Ruler of the Land of Oz."

"Of course, Ozma, and how you were stolen by old Mombi, the witch, and—"

"Yes," interrupted Ozma, smiling, "all that is true, but the important fact is that now the day has arrived when I must answer the summons of the great Fairy Queen. You see," continued the girlish ruler seriously, "every 200 years all the members of Queen Lurline's fairy band gather for a Grand Council in the beautiful Forest of Burzee, which lies just across the Deadly Desert to the South of Oz."

"Isn't that the forest where Santa Claus was found as an infant and adopted by the Forest Nymphs?" asked Dorothy eagerly.

"Yes," replied Ozma, "Burzee is indeed a famous forest. For untold centuries its cool groves have been the meeting place of Queen Lurline and her subjects. They gather to discuss and plan the work they will do during the next two centuries. In the old days," Ozma's voice was musing and thoughtful as she continued, "when mankind was simpler and gentler of nature, it was easier for the fairies to do their good works and to aid the helpless humans. But today few humans believe in fairies."

"The children do," Dorothy suggested.

"Yes," said Ozma, "but unfortunately as the children grow older and become men and women, they forget all they ever knew about fairies. I wish," she added wistfully, "that the men and women of the world would keep a bit of their childhood with them. They would find it a valuable thing."

"When will you be going, Ozma?" Dorothy asked softly.

"Tomorrow morning," Ozma replied. "and so important is this meeting that I have asked Glinda the Good to accompany me, although she is not a member of Queen Lurline's fairy band."

"Ozma," said Dorothy seriously, her chin cupped in her hand, "there is one thing I have often wondered about. What did Queen Lurline do after she left you here to become the Ruler of Oz?"

"There is a story," Ozma began with a faraway look in her eyes, "that after she made Oz a fairyland, Queen Lurline flew away to the Land of the Phanfasms, that strange realm lying southeast of Oz across the Deadly Desert and bordering the Kingdom of the Nomes."

"I remember the Phanfasms," Dorothy nodded. "They are the wicked creatures who came with the Nome King through his tunnel under the Deadly Desert to conquer Oz."

"Yes, and thanks to the wisdom of our famous Scarecrow, we were able to render them harmless," Ozma recalled with a smile.

"Did Queen Lurline go to see the Phanfasms after she left Oz?" asked Dorothy.

"No," replied Ozma. "It seems that instead of going to Mount Phantastico, where the Phanfasms dwell, Queen Lurline flew to the second of the twin peaks — to Mount Illuso, home of the dread Mimics."

"I don't remember hearing about the Mimics before. Just who are they, Ozma?" asked Dorothy with interest.

"Not a great deal is known about them," replied Ozma seriously, "and what we do know is so unpleasant that the Mimics are avoided as a subject of conversation. They are not humans, nor are they immortals. Like the Phanfasms, to whom they are closely related, they belong to the ancient race of Erbs — creatures who inhabited the Earth long before the coming of mankind. Both the Mimics and the Phanfasms hate all humans and immortals, for they feel that mankind, aided by the immortals, has stolen the world from them."

"They don't sound very nice to me," said Dorothy with a shudder. "Why did Queen Lurline go to see such dreadful creatures?"

Ozma's voice was grave as she answered. "Queen Lurline knew that the Mimics bitterly hated all that was good and happy and just in the world. The wise Queen fully realized that now that Oz was so beautiful and favored and its people so happy and contented a fairy folk, the Mimics would lose no time in seeking to bring unhappiness to Oz. It was to prevent this that Queen Lurline paid her visit to Mount Illuso."

"And did she succeed?" asked Dorothy.

"Yes, my dear," replied Ozma. "Queen Lurline placed a fairy spell on the Mimics to make it impossible for them to attack the inhabitants of Oz. But let's not discuss the unpleasant Mimics any further," Ozma concluded. "Thanks to good Queen Lurline we don't even have to think about the creatures. Let us return to our conversation about you."

"About me?" asked Dorothy.

"Yes," replied Ozma. "Can't you guess why I asked you to see me this particular morning?"

"Why, to tell me about the trip you and Glinda are planning," said Dorothy.

"And something more, too," continued Ozma. "Who do you think will rule the Emerald City and the Land of Oz while both Glinda and I are absent?"

"I suppose either the Little Wizard or the Scarecrow," ventured Dorothy, remembering that in the past both the Wizard and the Scarecrow had ruled the Land of Oz.

"No," replied Ozma calmly. "You, Dorothy, will be the ruler of the Emerald City and the Land of Oz in my absence."

"I?" cried Dorothy. "Oh, Ozma, I'm only a little girl! I don't know the first thing about ruling!"

"You are a Princess of Oz," stated Ozma with dignity. "I shall appoint the Wizard as your Counselor and Advisor. With his wisdom and your honesty of heart and sweetness of nature, I am confident the Land of Oz will be well ruled."

Dorothy was silent, considering.

"Come, my dear," said Ozma with a smile. "I shall be gone only three short days. I am sure once you have become accustomed to the idea, you will enjoy the novel experience of being a real ruler, so do not worry."

Rising from the divan, Ozma concluded, "I must go now to inform the Courtiers and Lords and Ladies of my journey. I will instruct them in the regular affairs of state to be carried on in my absence, so that you will not be annoyed with these routine matters."

Ozma kissed Dorothy on the cheek, and the two girls left the room arm in arm, parting a few minutes later as Ozma went about making preparations for her journey. Dorothy joined Toto, who was waiting patiently for her in the lovely gardens of the Royal Palace.

The little dog quickly noticed that his mistress was not nearly so carefree in her play as usual, but seemed more serious and thoughtful. He wondered if this had anything to do with her conversation with Ozma, but since Dorothy didn't mention the subject to him and seemed to be so busy with her own thoughts, Toto, being a wise little dog, refrained from troubling her with questions.

Dorothy had a long talk with the Wizard later in the day. The little man pointed out that Dorothy's duties as ruler would be very slight, so well governed was Oz and so well behaved were the Oz people. Nevertheless, Dorothy was greatly cheered and relieved when the Wizard promised to help her should any problem arise that she found troubling.

Ozma's time was so entirely taken up with affairs of state and the many preparations for her absence from her beloved country that Dorothy saw nothing of the girlish ruler during the remainder of the day.

The morning of Ozma and Glinda's departure dawned bright and clear, with the sunlight shining brilliantly on the beautiful City of Emeralds. Breakfast had been over for several hours when Glinda the Good Sorceress arrived from her castle far to the South in the Quadling Country of the Land of Oz. Glinda and Ozma went immediately to the Royal Throne Room, where the famous Oz personages waited to witness their departure.

At exactly 10 o'clock, Princess Ozma seated herself in her Emerald Throne, while the stately Glinda stood at her right. Before them was as strange and impressive an assemblage of Nobles, Courtiers and old friends as ever gathered together in any fairy realm.

Among those present were: the famous Scarecrow of Oz with his highly polished companion Nick Chopper, the nickel-plated Tin Woodman; comical Jack Pumpkinhead astride the wooden Sawhorse, who was Ozma's personal steed and earliest companion; Scraps, the jolly Patchwork Girl; sweet little Trot and her faithful sailor friend, grizzled old Cap'n Bill; Betsy Bobbin and her mule Hank; the cheerful Shaggy Man, looking shaggier than ever; the Highly Magnified and Thoroughly Educated Woggle Bug wearing his wisest expression for this important occasion; the stately Cowardly Lion, who was one of Dorothy's oldest friends, and his companion, the Hungry Tiger, who longed to devour fat babies but never did because his conscience wouldn't permit him to; that strange creature the Woozy, whose eyes flashed real fire when he became angry; Button Bright, the boy from Philadelphia, who had been Dorothy's companion on several wonderful adventures; Ojo the Lucky and his Unc Nunkie; Dorothy's beloved Aunt Em and Uncle Henry; and of course the Little Wizard and many more.

Ozma stood before her throne and raised her hand. Immediately silence settled over the assemblage in the vast Throne Room.

"As you all know," the Princess said, "Glinda and I are about to attend an important Fairy Conference in the distant Forest of Burzee. We shall be gone from Oz for a period of three days. During that time, Princess Dorothy will be your sovereign and ruler."

Ozma removed her dainty fairy wand from the folds of her gown and lifted it into the air. For a moment she smiled on all, then, with a graceful wave of the wand and before the onlookers realized what was happening, both she and Glinda had vanished.

But Dorothy knew that even at that moment Queen Lurline was greeting the lovely Ozma and the stately Glinda in the depths of the enchanted Forest of Burzee.

Chapter 3 - Mount Illuso

On that faraway day those many years ago, when Queen Lurline had left the baby Ozma to become the ruler of Oz, Queen Lurline did not pause, for she knew the most important part of her work was still to be done. If the Land of Oz was to be the happy fairyland she hoped it would be, she must protect it from the evil of the Mimics.

With this thought in mind, the good Queen left Oz and flew straight to the bleak land of the Phanfasms. Signalling to one of her Fairy Maidens to accompany her, Queen Lurline flew down to grim Mount Illuso, home of the dread Mimics.

Pausing at the entrance to the great hollow mountain, Queen Lurline bade her fairy companion await her return. Then, taking the precaution to make herself invisible to the eyes of the Mimics, the Fairy Queen stepped into the enchanted Mountain.

The sight that met her eyes caused even the good Queen Lurline to chill and falter momentarily on the rocky ledge on which she stood. Above her rose the vast, cavernous walls of the hollow mountain. Spread out below were the corridors burrowed into the rock by the Mimics. In dark caverns deep below these corridors the monsters made their homes.

All of this scene was lighted by flaming torches set at intervals in the walls of the cavern. The torches flared red, casting lurid, flickering shadows and adding to the weird unreality of the scene. As Queen Lurline gazed, the Mimics were moving through the rough-hewn corridors or flying through the air. The most unusual thing about the creatures was their strange habit of constantly changing their shapes. They shifted restlessly from one form to another. Since they were creatures of evil, the shapes they assumed were all forms of the blackest evil and dread.

Even as Queen Lurline watched, fascinated by the strange spectacle, the Mimics shifted and changed and flitted from one loathsome shape to another. A monster bird with leathery wings and a horned head dropped to the ground, and in another second assumed the squat body of a huge toad with the head of a hyena, snarling with laughter. A crawling red lizard all of ten feet in length turned into a giant butterfly with black wings and the body of a serpent. A great, green bat with wicked talons alighted on a ledge not far from Queen Lurline and in an instant changed to a mammoth, hairy creature with the body of a huge ape and the head of an alligator.

The good Queen shuddered in spite of herself. What she had seen had only served to strengthen her resolution to protect the Oz people for all time against the Mimics. Immediately she began weaving a powerful incantation. In a few minutes the enchantment was complete. Queen Lurline breathed a sigh of relief, for she knew that the Mimics were now powerless to harm any of the fairy inhabitants of the Land of Oz.

Queen Lurline was well aware that the Mimics' strange habit of changing their shapes was the least of their evil characteristics. Much more dreadful was the power possessed by these creatures to steal the shapes of both mortals and immortals. A Mimic accomplished this simply by casting himself on the shadow of his victim. Instantly the Mimic arose, a perfect double in outward appearance of the person whose shadow he had stolen. As for the unfortunate victim, he fell into a spell of enchantment, unable to move or speak but conscious of all that was taking place about him.

No wonder Queen Lurline sighed with relief when she thought that her powerful magic had made the Oz people secure against the dread evil of the Mimics! Queen Lurline slipped from the cavern through the stone portal of Mount Illuso. For a moment she paused, breathing deeply and gratefully of the fresh air. But she must not tarry now. She still had other important work to do here. When she returned to her fairy companion, Queen Lurline gave her brief instructions concerning the important part she was to play at Mount Illuso in the coming years. Then they both spread their fairy wings and flew straight to the very summit of the hollow mount.

Chapter 4 - The Mimics mean Mischief

On the same morning that Ozma and Glinda left the Land of Oz for the Forest of Burzee, events of equal importance were happening in Mount Illuso, home of the Mimics. The Mimics were ruled over by two sovereigns — King Umb and Queen Ra. It is a question which was the more wicked and dangerous of this pair. King Umb was bold and brutal, while his wife, Queen Ra, was clever and cunning. Together they made a fitting combination to rule so wicked a horde as the Mimics.

On this particular morning King Umb and Queen Ra secluded themselves in a hidden cavern, deep in the underground caves that honeycombed the depths of hollow Mount Illuso. Roughly hewn from the grey rock, this cavern was circular in shape and was filled with ancient books and strange and weird implements of sorcery and enchantment. King Umb possessed little skill in magic arts, but Queen Ra was powerful in the practice of conjuring and evil incantation.

After the visit of Queen Lurline to Mount Illuso and the casting of the powerful enchantment that prevented King Umb and Queen Ra from leading their Mimic subjects in the destruction of Oz, Queen Ra had at first raged and fumed and wildly vowed vengeance on Queen Lurline and Princess Ozma. Then, as the years passed by, the evil Queen spent more and more time lurking in the secret cavern studying the ancient sorcery of the Erbs, employing her black arts to follow events in the history of Oz, and plotting the destruction of the fairyland.

Of course the Mimic King and Queen were free to lead their hordes in attacks on people of other lands, and you may wonder why they didn't forget all about Oz and content themselves with bringing misery to other countries. The reason was that the wicked King and Queen of the Mimics despised all that was good, and they could not endure the thought of the Oz people living in peace and contentment, safe from their evil-doing. So long as the Oz inhabitants remained the happiest people in all the world, King Umb and Queen Ra could derive no satisfaction in bringing misery to other less happy lands.

Queen Ra was well aware that Princess Ozma was one of the most powerful fairy rulers in existence, and that her loyal friend, Glinda the Good, was the mightiest and wisest of all sorceresses. Nevertheless, through her own dark magic, Queen Ra had recently made two important discoveries that raised her hopes so high that she believed she might be able soon to defy both Ozma and Glinda.

First, she had discovered that Ozma and Glinda were about to depart on a journey that would take them away from the Land of Oz. Second, she had learned that in one of Ozma's books of magic records in the Royal Palace of the Emerald City was written the charm that would break the spell Queen Lurline had cast on the Mimics to protect Oz!

This morning Queen Ra had assumed the shape of a huge woman — almost a giantess — with the head of a grey wolf. King Umb wore the form of a black bear with an owl head. The Queen held in her hands a circlet of dully gleaming metal. The red eyes of her wolf head gazed at it steadily, while she muttered an incantation. As the wolf-headed woman spoke, a wisp of grey mist appeared in the center of the metal ring. The mist expanded into a ball, growing denser in appearance. Next it became milky in hue, then opalescent, finally glowing as with an inner light. Slowly a scene appeared in the metal-bound ball of shimmering opal mist.

While King Umb and Queen Ra watched, the Throne Room of the Royal Palace in the Emerald City grew distinct in the milky depths of the captive ball. Princess Ozma stood by her throne with Glinda the Good at her side. The lips of the little ruler were moving, forming words, although the Mimic Monarchs could distinguish no sound. Ozma was addressing her subjects. Then the girl Ruler smiled and raised her wand. In an instant both Ozma and Glinda had vanished. The ball of glowing mist disappeared. With a clatter, Queen Ra threw the metal circlet to the stone floor of the cave and triumphantly faced the owl-headed bear.

"They have gone!" she cried.

"You are positive that now is the time for us to act?" asked King Umb.

"Absolutely," said the wolf-headed woman. "We know that one of Ozma's magic record books holds the secret of the enchantment cast on us. We know that Ozma and Glinda will be absent from Oz for three days, leaving the country and the Emerald City unprotected by their magic arts. We know that those people who have in recent years come from the great outside world to live in Oz were not inhabitants of Oz when Lurline made it a fairyland. Thus they are not protected by the enchantment she cast on us. It will be simple for us to assume the shapes of these people — of course they are mere mortals," the Queen added with a sneer, "but even so they will serve our purpose."

"You have a plan, then?" asked the owl-headed King.

"A plan that will result in the utter destruction of Oz and the enslavement of the Oz people," asserted the Queen with grim relish. "Listen!" the wolf-headed woman commanded. "Tonight you and I, with Styg and Ebo, will fly swiftly across the Deadly Desert to the Land of Oz. We will go directly to the Emerald City. There we will seek out the two mortals from the great outside world whose shapes will admit us to every part of the Royal Palace. My magic arts have told me that at a certain hour tomorrow morning these two mortals will be together with no one else about to witness or interfere with our deed. After we have stolen their shapes, the helpless mortals will be seized by Styg and Ebo and returned here, where they will be our prisoners. Then we will be free to search through Ozma's magic record books. As soon as we locate the magical antidote to Lurline's enchantment, we will break the spell binding our subjects. By the time Ozma and Glinda return, Oz will be overrun by Mimics, and we shall be ready to give their royal highnesses a proper reception!" Queen Ra smiled wickedly as she finished this recital.

The owl eyes of King Umb had been regarding Queen Ra intently as she revealed her plan. When she had finished, an evil leer spread over the King's furry features.

"Ra," said King Umb, "you are the most wicked Queen who ever ruled the Mimics!" And that, by Mimic standards, was the highest compliment King Umb could pay his Queen.

Several hours after midnight, King Umb and Queen Ra, followed by the two Mimics Styg and Ebo, slipped outside the entrance of the hollow mountain. Immediately all four assumed the shapes of giant birds, black of plumage and with powerful wings. During the creatures' long flight over the Deadly Desert to Oz, they changed shapes a number of times, but always to another form of powerful bird.

As they mounted into the air and soared through the dark night over the peak of Mount Illuso, King Umb cast a backward glance toward the summit of the mountain. "What about the Guardian?" he asked Queen Ra uneasily.

"Bah!" the giant bird that was Queen Ra croaked derisively. "Who cares about her? Let her go on dreaming over her foolish flowers and sticks of wood — that's all she has done all these years!"

Chapter 5 - Prisoners of the Mimics

High in the top of the tallest tower of the Royal Palace was the Wizard's apartment. In this secluded spot the little man kept his magical tools and apparatus and could work undisturbed for long hours over difficult feats of magic. The morning after Ozma and Glinda had left, Dorothy had climbed the stair to the Wizard's quarters, and she and the Wizard were deep in a discussion of matters of state.

Two sides of the room they occupied were composed of tall French windows, rising from the floor to the ceiling and opening onto a spacious veranda. The windows were flung wide open to admit the refreshing breeze and the welcome sunlight.

Suddenly the air was filled with the flutter of powerful wings, and four large, black-plumed birds settled on the veranda and stepped into the room. Glancing up in surprise at this sudden interruption, the Wizard exclaimed with annoyance, "Here, what's the meaning of this intrusion?" (Since all birds and animals in the Land of Oz possess the power of human speech, the Wizard naturally addressed the birds as he would have spoken to human beings.)

But the birds made no reply. Instead, two of them stepped swiftly toward Dorothy and the Wizard, who had risen in surprise and were standing beside their chairs. The two birds flung themselves on the shadows cast by the girl and the man. Instantly the birds vanished, and Dorothy and the Wizard found themselves staring in amazement at exact duplicates of themselves!

Sensing that he was confronted by some sort of evil magic, the Wizard made an effort to reach his black bag of magic tools, which rested on a nearby table, but it was too late. Caught in the Mimic spell, the little man was powerless to move. Dorothy's plight was the same; she could not so much as lift her little finger. All this had happened in much less time than I have taken to tell it, and it was so sudden and unexpected that our friends had not even had time to cry out.

Now the Mimic form of Dorothy, speaking in Dorothy's own voice, said to the two remaining birds, "Seize them, Ebo and Styg, and see that my commands are fulfilled!"

One black bird grasped the form of the helpless Wizard, the other that of Dorothy. Then, flapping their powerful wings, the two birds passed through the windows and soared aloft, bearing their captives high into the heavens. Swiftly they left the Emerald City. In a few minutes it was no more than a lovely jewel set in the farmlands around it. The birds headed southeast in the direction of the Deadly Desert.

At times in their flight, when the captives were able to exchange glances, Dorothy read in the Wizard's kindly eyes a mute expression of concern for his little comrade. The girl tried to reassure him, but it was difficult to look brave when she was unable to move even an eyelash — and besides, Dorothy had to admit to herself, she didn't feel at all brave just now.

In another minute when Dorothy was gazing at the bird that was carrying her so swiftly through the air, she was startled to see the form of the creature shift and change. From a huge, eagle-like bird it changed to an enormous condor. Strange birds these were, Dorothy thought, which went about changing their shapes and stealing little girls and Wizards.

As they flew over the yellow land of the Winkies, the motion of the bird's body occasionally permitted Dorothy to look downward. Once she glimpsed, sparkling in the sunlight, the highly polished towers and minarets of a handsome tin castle. This, she knew, was the home of her old friend Nick Chopper the Tin Woodman, Emperor of the Winkies. Dorothy found herself wondering what the kind-hearted Nick Chopper would say if he could know that at this moment his dear friends were being carried high in the air over his castle, prisoners of two giant black birds! But there was no use speculating in this fashion. The Tin Woodman was powerless to aid them even if he had known their plight.

With a start, Dorothy realized that the birds had crossed the border of Oz and were now flying over the Deadly Desert. The fact that they had left the Land of Oz behind them disturbed Dorothy greatly. Yet the little girl did not give way to fright. She had experienced so many strange and sometimes dangerous adventures in her lifetime that she had wisely learned never to despair.

The journey over the desert seemed endless. Despite the great height at which the birds flew, Dorothy was beginning to feel faint and ill from the evil fumes of the sands by the time they reached the border of the Land of the Phanfasms. However, once past the desert, she was revived by the fresh air.

Where were these great birds taking them? And why? As Dorothy pondered, she noted a sharp mountain peak jutting suddenly out of the grey, grim land of desolate waste and stone that lay below. Straight for the mountain flew the birds. In a few more minutes they descended with their victims to the entrance of the mountain. Passing through the stone portal, the Mimics retained their bird shapes, circling through the vast cavern of the hollow mountain. The cavern and corridors were deserted now that the sun was in the heavens, and the Mimics had returned to their underground caverns to rest after the night of revelry.

Styg and Ebo flew to a ledge of rock that jutted out from the mountain wall. Ebo muttered a magic word, and a rude stone door swung open revealing a lightless cavern. Dorothy was thrust into the cave, and a moment later the Wizard was deposited beside her in the darkness.

Until now Dorothy had entertained a vague hope that in some way the Wizard's magic powers would come to their rescue. But since the little man had none of his magic tools with him and could not speak to utter an incantation or move to make the motions of a charm, Dorothy realized that he was quite as powerless as she.

Chapter 6 - Dorothy and the Wizard speak Strangely

"Oomph!" puffed the Scarecrow.

"Whooosh!" gasped the Patchwork Girl.

Colliding suddenly as they met headlong at a sharp turn in the garden path, both the Scarecrow and the Patchwork Girl tumbled in a heap on the garden walk. A moment later they had risen to sitting positions and were regarding each other comically.

The Patchwork Girl was a sorry sight. The high-grade cotton in her patchwork or "crazy-quilt" body was bunched together in all the wrong places. After running and dancing a great deal that morning — as she always did — the Patchwork Girl's body had sagged, and she had grown dumpy in appearance. When this happened, she always lay down and rolled about until she had resumed her original plump shape. Now, after her abrupt meeting with the Scarecrow, her figure was in bad need of attention.

The pointed toes of the red leather shoes sewn on her feet stood straight up. Her fingers, carefully formed and fitted with gold plates for fingernails, dug into the path on which she sat. Her shock of brown yarn hair hung down over her suspender-button eyes and over her ears, which were made of thin plates of gold. Between the two rows of pearls sewn in her mouth for teeth, her scarlet plush tongue stuck out impudently at the Scarecrow.

The Patchwork Girl's brains were slightly mixed, containing among other qualities a dash of poesy, which accounted for her habit of breaking into rhymes and jingles when it was least expected. Now she was too surprised to speak. She had been brought to life in the first place by a magic powder, and since she was always jolly and good-natured, the Patchwork Girl was a prime favorite among the Oz folks. Nicknamed Scraps, the queer girl laughed at dignity and liked nothing better than to dance and sing. It was impossible to be downcast for long in the company of this merry, carefree creature.

"Why don't you look where you're going, Scraps?" said the Scarecrow ruefully as he brushed his blue Munchkin farmer trousers.

"Now that you mention it," replied the Patchwork Girl reprovingly, "I don't have X-ray eyes, so I couldn't see through to the other side of the hedge where I was going."

"All right," said the Scarecrow as he rose to his feet. "Please accept my humble apologies." The straw man gallantly assisted the Patchwork Girl to stand. "There's no harm done. The spill was as much my fault as it was yours. I was thinking so deeply that I didn't see you."

"What were you thinking about?" asked Scraps.

"Dorothy," replied the Scarecrow with a sigh. "Tell me, Scraps, have you seen her today?"

"Not once," answered the Patchwork Girl, combing her yarn hair with her fingers. "Until a few minutes ago, I've spent the entire day with Aunt Em, who sewed tight some of my stitches that were coming loose, sewed on my eyes with new thread so I wouldn't lose 'em, and sewed on a new pair of red shoes, as I'd worn holes in my old ones. Now I'm as good as new!"

"Well," replied the Scarecrow, with his broad smile, "that may be true, but I'd say no matter in how good condition you are, you're always just sew-sew." The smile quickly faded from the straw man's painted face as he continued seriously, "Scraps, I'm worried about Dorothy."

"Don't worry about Dorothy; she's able to take care of herself," said practical Scraps.

"You don't understand," explained the Scarecrow. "You see, yesterday after Ozma and Glinda left for the Forest of Burzee, Dorothy asked me to help her plan a banquet to celebrate their return. Dorothy wanted me to think up some ideas for the entertainment to accompany the dinner. I agreed to set my famous brains to work on the problem and spent all last night in deep thought. This morning, bright and early, I rushed to Dorothy and started to tell her the ideas I had. You can imagine my surprise when Dorothy stared at me as though she hadn't the faintest idea what I was talking about, and then turned and walked away from me."

The Scarecrow paused, his brow wrinkled with perplexity. "I don't understand it," he continued. "It isn't like our sweet little Dorothy to be rude or absent-minded. She and the Wizard have been in Ozma's Chamber of Magic all day, and I tried twice to see her, but each time she said she couldn't be disturbed."

"Come to think of it," replied Scraps quickly, "Aunt Em remarked that she couldn't understand why Dorothy hadn't been in to see her. Dorothy always visits her Aunt Em and Uncle Henry at least once a day. But maybe she's busy ruling while Ozma's away."

This explanation failed to satisfy the Scarecrow. He was gazing into the distance down the garden path. "Isn't that Trot and Cap'n Bill sitting on that bench over there?"

"Whoop ti doodle who? Cap'n Bill and Trot It is as like as not!"

sang the Patchwork Girl, turning a handspring and dancing toward the bench.

The Scarecrow followed, and he and Scraps were warmly greeted by little Trot and old Cap'n Bill. The Scarecrow repeated his story of the strange manner in which Dorothy had been acting, but neither Trot nor Cap'n Bill had seen

Dorothy that day. The old sailor was silent for a moment, considering. Then he said: "You know, it's funny; but I was tellin' Trot only a minute ago that the Wizard had me puzzled by the curious way he was behavin'."

"What do you mean?" asked the Scarecrow.

"Well," went on Cap'n Bill, "fer some time past I've been workin' on a boat fer Ozma an' her friends, so they could go sailin' on that lake jest outside the Emerald City. I had everythin' I needed 'cept fer some tools, so the Wizard lent me some o' his thet get the work done extra fast, 'cause they're magic tools. The boat's nearly finished — a handsome craft, if I do say so myself. All she needs to make 'er trim is a coat o' paint. I thought it would be nice to have 'er finished as a sort of surprise fer Ozma when she returns from this here fairy conclave, so I asked the Wizard to lend me his magic paint bucket and brush — the bucket always stays full, no matter how much paint you use from it, an' the brush paints any color you want from the same bucket o' paint. Well, the Wizard jest give me a funny sort o' look and walked away, mumblin' somethin' about bein' busy and havin' somethin' important to do. 'Tain't like the Wizard at all. Somethin' ailin' him," concluded Cap'n Bill, wagging his grizzled head.

"Then it's the same thing that's ailing Dorothy," remarked the Scarecrow sagely.

The four old friends were silent, each turning over the problem in his own mind. The bench on which Trot and Cap'n Bill were sitting was in front of a high hedge — so high that none of them could see over it. On the other side of the thick hedge ran another garden path. Suddenly, they heard footsteps as if several people were hurrying down the garden path which was hidden from their view. While they listened, wondering who it could be, the footsteps halted just opposite them on the other side of the hedge. Before they could call out a greeting, they recognized the voice of the Wizard saying: "We can talk here. There's no one about. Now tell me, why are we wasting time in the garden?"

"Because," it was the voice of Dorothy replying, "it would look suspicious if we did not leave the Chamber of Magic occasionally."

"Have you found the spell yet?" asked the Wizard's voice.

"Not yet," replied Dorothy's voice. "I've been through only half of Ozma's magic record books. Give me time — it's there. And I'll find it!"

"Time!" replied the Wizard's voice, raised in excitement. "We have no time to lose! Do you realize that Ozma and Glinda will be back in a day and a half? We must find the spell before then if we don't want Ozma to wreck our plans and rob us of the chance we have waited for!"

"Never fear," asserted Dorothy's voice. "I'll find the spell long before Ozma and Glinda return. We'll be ready for those two when they do come back!"

Gradually the voices subsided as the two walked slowly down the garden path toward the Royal Palace. On the other side of the hedge, Trot, Cap'n Bill, Scraps and the Scarecrow stared at one another in bewilderment. What could this mean? It was incredible that Dorothy and the Wizard could be plotting against their dearest friends, Ozma and Glinda.

Chapter 7 - In the Cavern of the Doomed

Neither Dorothy nor the Wizard could tell how long they lay in their cavern prison deep in hollow Mount Illuso, but it is certain that minutes seemed like hours to them.

While the Wizard had recognized the country to which he and Dorothy had been carried as the Land of the Phanfasms, he was not aware of the existence of Mount Illuso and its Mimic dwellers. He was sure, however, that the creatures who had captured Dorothy and him were not Phanfasms. He had seen the Phanfasms when those evil creatures had once attempted to invade Oz, and they bore no resemblance to the beings who had made Dorothy and him captives.

Dorothy found some comfort in telling herself that as soon as Ozma and Glinda returned to the Emerald City the imposters would be detected and she and the Wizard speedily rescued. But what if Ozma and Glinda were deceived? How long would she and the Wizard be kept in the cave? What wicked plot was behind all this? And just how powerful and clever were the creatures who had captured her and the Wizard?

Suddenly something happened that banished all these puzzling questions. There was a light in the cavern! The two prisoners could see each other! True, the light was feeble, but it was increasing steadily in strength. As the light grew more brilliant, Dorothy felt pleasantly warm and glowing, as though she were lying in bright sunlight. And then to her intense joy the little girl realized that the spell cast on her was broken. The light had released her. She was free to move about as she pleased.

Dorothy jumped happily to her feet. The Wizard, too, was freed from the spell, and a moment later was standing, smiling broadly with satisfaction.

"Was the light your magic, Wizard?" asked Dorothy eagerly.

"No, my dear, I had nothing to do with the light," replied the Wizard.

"But I wonder who or what turned it on," said Dorothy. "Could it be a trick, do you think?" she asked after a moment's hesitation.

"No, I believe not," replied the Wizard. "There would be no point in our captors' troubling themselves to enchant us and make us prisoners and then releasing us from the enchantment. I believe we will find this light is a part of a greater mystery than we know anything about."

"Well, seems to me there's plenty of mystery about everything that's happened today," said Dorothy. "What are we going to do now, Wizard?"

"Explore our prison," answered the little man promptly.

Dorothy looked about her. They were entirely surrounded by the solid stone walls of the cavern, which was about one hundred feet square. She could detect no sign of the door by which they had entered. "Look, Wizard," Dorothy exclaimed. "See how the light shines from one small point in the far end of the cavern?"

"Yes," agreed the Wizard. "It's almost as if someone had built a powerful flashlight into the stone wall. Come, let's examine the light more closely."

The two walked to the opposite side of the cavern and found that, as Dorothy had observed, the flood of light originated from one small point. This point was a circular bit of stone, round and polished, and no larger than a small button. "Why," exclaimed Dorothy, "it looks 'zactly like the button of an electric light switch! Wonder what would happen if I pressed it?"

Impulsively, Dorothy reached out and pressed the button of rock with her finger. In the deep silence that filled the cave, the two adventurers detected a faraway humming sound like the whirring of wheels in motion. As Dorothy and the Wizard listened, the sound grew louder. "What do you suppose it is?" whispered Dorothy.

"I haven't the faintest idea," said the Wizard, "but I don't think we'll have to wait long to find out."

At last the whirring noise seemed to be just opposite them on the other side of the stone wall. It stopped completely, and there was silence. A second later a section of the stone wall swung outward, and Dorothy and the Wizard found themselves staring into a small room — much like the car of an elevator. The car was painted bright blue, trimmed with red and gold, and sitting on a small stool was a curious little man.

Chapter 8 - Toto Makes a Discovery

"Where's Dorothy?" Toto asked pretty little Jellia Jamb, Ozma's maid, as he paused outside the door of Dorothy's apartment early in the morning of the day after Ozma and Glinda departed.

"She's gone up to the Wizard's rooms in the tower," replied Jellia Jamb.

"Thanks," said Toto. "I imagine Dorothy will have her hands full while Ozma is gone."

With this the little dog trotted down the corridor, philosophically seeking some other amusement. He hadn't gone very far before he was hailed by Betsy Bobbin, who appeared with a small wicker basket on her arm.

"Hello, Toto!" Betsy called. "Want to go on a picnic with Hank and me? I'm going to pick wildflowers in the green fields outside the Emerald City, and Hank's coming along. I have a nice picnic lunch packed," the girl added, indicating the basket she carried.

Now there were few things Toto liked better than to get out in the country and frolic in the fields, so the little dog accepted the invitation gratefully. A short time later, Betsy, her devoted companion Hank the Mule, and Toto arrived at the gates of the Emerald City and were greeted by Omby Amby, the Soldier with the Green Whiskers. He was very tall and wore a handsome green and gold uniform with a tall, plumed hat. His long, green beard fell below his waist, making him look even taller. In addition to being the Keeper of the Gates, Omby Amby was also the Royal Army of Oz, Princess Ozma's Bodyguard, and the Police Force of the Emerald City. You might suppose that, holding all these offices, Omby Amby was a very busy man. To the contrary, so seldom was there ever any breaking of the Oz laws — which were all just and reasonable — that it had been many years since the Soldier with the Green Whiskers had acted in any of his official capacities other than that of Keeper of the Gates.

As Omby Amby unlocked the gates for them, Betsy promised to bring him a bouquet of flowers for his wife, Tollydiggle.

Outside the Emerald City lay pleasant, gently rolling fields in which buttercups and daisies grew in profusion. Sniffing the fresh country air, Toto ran happily across the field. Hank hee-hawed loudly and fell to munching the tall field grass. Betsy was delighted with the hundreds of pretty flowers and gathered several large bouquets.

Shortly after noon the happy trio sought the shade of a large tree. Nearby, a spring of cool, crystal-clear water bubbled from a mossy bank and flowed across the field as a tiny brook. Betsy opened her basket and took out sandwiches, hard-boiled eggs, potato salad and other picnic delicacies, which she and Toto shared. Betsy offered Hank a peanut-butter sandwich, but the Mule refused disdainfully, saying, "No, thank you, Betsy, I much prefer this fresh, green grass."

"Well, don't eat too much of it," advised the girl, "or you'll get the colic."

The mule winked one eye at Toto and replied, "I'd be much more likely to get the colic if I ate your strange human foods."

After they had eaten and refreshed themselves with the water of the spring, they rested for a time in the cool shade of the tree, and then leisurely made their way back to the Emerald City. At the city's gates, Omby Amby welcomed them back and gratefully accepted the bouquet Betsy gave him for Tollydiggle.

Arriving at the palace, the three friends said goodbye, Betsy going to her apartment, while Hank made his way to the Royal Stables to talk with his cronies, the Cowardly Lion and the Hungry Tiger. Jellia Jamb tripped down the palace steps on an errand, and Toto called to her, "Is Dorothy still busy?"

"Yes," answered Jellia Jamb, "she and the Wizard have been in Ozma's Chamber of Magic all afternoon."

This did not strike the little dog as strange. He knew Ozma might have left instructions for Dorothy and the Wizard to carry out in the Chamber of Magic. As it was now nearly mid-afternoon, Toto decided to have a nap in the garden. Curling up in the cool earth under a large rosebush, he fell asleep, telling himself that he would awaken in time for dinner, when he would surely see Dorothy. Toto knew that however busy Dorothy and the Wizard might be, they would leave the Chamber of Magic and appear for dinner, always a festive occasion in the Grand Dining Room of the Royal Palace.

Promptly at seven o'clock, the inhabitants of the Royal Palace began to gather in the Grand Dining Room. Cap'n Bill and Trot took their accustomed places at the table, as did Betsy Bobbin, Button Bright, the Shaggy Man, Aunt Em and Uncle Henry. While the Scarecrow, the Patchwork Girl and Tik-Tok the Machine Man were non-flesh and could not partake of the food, nevertheless they had their places at the table. For these dinners were as much occasions for the enjoyment of merry conversation as they were for satisfying hunger and thirst.

At the far end of the room was a separate table shared by the animal companions of the Oz people. At this table were set places with the proper foods for Hank the Mule, the Cowardly Lion, the Hungry Tiger, Billina the Yellow Hen, Eureka the Pink Kitten, the Woozy, Toto and the Sawhorse. Although the Sawhorse was made of wood and required no food and seldom took part in the conversation, nevertheless the odd steed enjoyed listening to the table talk of the others.

Everyone was in his place except Dorothy, the Wizard and Toto — and of course Ozma's chair at the head of the table was vacant. Dorothy's place was at Ozma's right, while the Wizard sat at her left. A few minutes later, King Umb and Queen Ra, having decided that it would arouse too much comment if they were absent from the dinner, entered the sumptuous dining room and took their places on either side of Ozma's vacant chair. Now only Toto remained absent. The truth was that the little dog had overslept and had awakened from his nap to find the shadows lengthening across the garden. Realizing he was late for dinner, Toto hurried to the nearest palace entrance and ran as quickly as he could to the Grand Dining Room.

As he entered, the first course of the meal was being served, and a ripple of conversation rose from the two tables. The Scarecrow and Scraps were chatting together, Betsy was telling Trot about the lovely wildflowers she had found, and the Cowardly Lion and the Hungry Tiger were discussing a visit they planned to their old jungle home in the forest far to the south in the Quadling Country.

In spite of the apparent atmosphere of gaiety, this gathering was not at all like the merry company that usually assembled in the dining room for the evening meal. First of all, the absence of the radiant Ozma was keenly felt by the entire gathering, and this automatically subdued the spirit of the occasion. Next, no one at the table had failed to note and wonder at the fact that Dorothy and the Wizard — usually so cheerful and cordial — had merely nodded unsmilingly to their assembled friends as they had taken their places at the head of the table. Finally, Scraps, the Scarecrow, Trot and Cap'n Bill, unable to forget the strange conversation they had overheard in the garden earlier in the day, stole curious glances at Dorothy and the Wizard seeking some clue to their unusual behavior.

As Toto trotted into the dining room, his bright little eyes immediately sought out his mistress. Toto stopped short; his body became tense with excitement. He barked loudly and then growled, "Where's Dorothy?"

In the silence that fell over the dining room at the dog's unusual actions, Toto repeated his question. "Where's Dorothy?" he demanded.

The Scarecrow was staring earnestly at Toto. "Why, here's Dorothy," the straw man answered. "Right here, where she always sits."

338

"You're wrong — all of you are wrong," growled Toto ominously. The little dog was quivering with excitement. "Whoever that is sitting there might fool the rest of you, but she can't deceive me. She's not Dorothy at all. Something's happened to Dorothy!"

Chapter 9 - Mr. and Mrs. Hi-Lo

"Step right in, folks! Watch your step, Miss. We're on our way up — next stop the top! Only two stops — bottom and top. Next stop's the top!"

The little man spoke with an air of importance as he smiled at Dorothy and the Wizard from the stool on which he was perched in the car which the opening in the stone wall had revealed. They peered at him curiously. "Shall we go in?" asked Dorothy, drawing a deep breath.

"To be sure," said the Wizard. "Anything is better than this stone prison."

"Ah, a philosopher, and a wise one, too," remarked the little man.

As soon as Dorothy and the Wizard were in the elevator — for such it proved to be — the stone door swung shut. At once the little man pressed one of several buttons on the side of the car, and again they heard the whirring sound which had puzzled them in the cavern. Dorothy concluded it was caused by the machinery that operated the elevator. The little car was shooting upward with a speed that caused her ears to ring.

"Just swallow several times," advised the Wizard, sensing Dorothy's discomfort. "That will make equal the air pressure inside and outside your body. It's a trick I learned when I went up in my balloon to draw crowds to the circus back in Omaha."

Dorothy did as the Wizard suggested and found the ringing sensation disappeared.

"Who are you?" asked the Wizard, gazing curiously at the little man. "And where are you taking us?"

"You don't know who I am?" exclaimed the little man with surprise. "After all, you know, you did ring for the elevator, and since I am the elevator operator, naturally I answered. Allow me to introduce myself. My name is Hi-Lo, and I am taking you to the only other place the elevator goes except for the bottom — and that's to the top of Mount Illuso. I assure you it's a far better place than the bottom!"

While he spoke, Dorothy had been regarding the little man who called himself Hi-Lo. He was very short, his head coming only to Dorothy's waist. He was dressed in a bright-blue uniform with big, gold buttons. A red cap was perched at a jaunty angle on his head. His face was round, and his cheeks as rosy as two apples. His blue eyes were very bright and friendly. But the oddest thing about him was that his clothes appeared to be a part of his body, as though they were painted on. And Dorothy concluded he was most certainly made of some substance other than flesh and blood.

"Ah, I see I've aroused your interest," remarked the little man with satisfaction. "Well, I'm proud to tell you that I am made of the finest white pine and painted with quick-drying four-hour enamel that flows easily from the brush and is guaranteed not to chip, crack, craze or peel. I'm easily washable, too; spots and stains wipe off in a jiffy with a damp cloth or sponge — no rubbing or scrubbing for me! And I suppose," Hi-Lo concluded vainly, "you've already admired my rich, glossy finish and beautiful rainbow colors."

Dorothy smiled at this speech, and the Wizard asked, "Tell me, Hi-Lo, do people live on top of Mount Illuso?"

"Of course," Hi-Lo replied in his cheerful voice. "We have a thriving community of folks — Pineville, it's called. But we're all very happy and contented," he went on hastily. "There's not a lonesome pine among us, although are several trails on the mountaintop."

"But are there no flesh and blood folks like us?" queried the Wizard.

Before Hi-Lo could answer, the elevator came to an abrupt stop. "Well, here we are!" announced Hi-Lo cheerily. He pressed another button. The door of the elevator swung open and Hi-Lo called, "All out! All out! Top floor — all kinds of wooden goods, the best pine to be had — pine tables, pine chairs, pine houses and pine people!"

Dorothy and the Wizard stepped from the elevator and surveyed the scene before them. Yes, this was certainly the top of Mount Illuso. The elevator exit was in a large stone wall at least ten feet in height that appeared to circle the edge of the mountaintop. Before them spread a dense pine forest, while a small path led from the elevator to a tiny cottage that stood nearby. The cottage was painted bright blue with trim white shutters, and smoke was rising cheerily from its red brick chimney.

"Right this way! Just follow me, folks," said Hi-Lo, trotting along the path to the cottage, his little wooden legs moving with surprising speed. "Mrs. Hi-Lo will certainly be surprised to see you. You are a real event — the very first visitors we have ever had from down below."

As they approached the tiny cottage, the front door swung open, and a little woman stood in the doorway. She was even smaller than Hi-Lo, and like him was made of wood and painted with the same bright enamels. She wore a blue-and-white apron over a red polka-dot dress. On her head was a trim little lace cap. "My goodness!" she beamed. "Visitors at last! Do come in and make yourselves comfortable."

The Wizard found it necessary to bend over to get in the doorway, so small was the cottage. Once inside, his head nearly touched the ceiling. The cottage was neatly and attractively furnished with comfortable pine chairs, tables and a large davenport drawn before a fireplace on which a log fire crackled cheerfully. The air was sharp on the mountaintop, so the bright fire was a welcome sight to the two wanderers. All the furniture glowed with the cheerful, gaudy hues of glassy enamel. Dorothy thought that the wholesome aroma of pine scent that filled the cottage was especially delightful.

"Great pine cones!" exclaimed Mrs. Hi-Lo. "You must be half starved. I'll get you something to eat in no time at all. Tell me, would you like a delicious cross-cut of pine steak with pine-dust pudding, fresh, crisp pine-needle salad with turpentine dressing and a strawberry pine cone for dessert?"

Dorothy almost laughed aloud at this strange food, but the little Wizard answered courteously, "You are most kind, Madame, but I fear our systems would not be able to digest the delicacies you suggest. Perhaps you have something that meat folks like us could eat."

"Of course!" cried Mrs. Hi-Lo. "How stupid of me! You are meat folks. Too bad," she added critically, "it must be a terrible bother to take off and put on all those clothes and to keep your hair trimmed and your nails pared."

"Now, Mother, let's not draw unkind comparisons," cautioned Hi-Lo diplomatically as he settled himself into a comfortable chair. "None of us is perfect, you know. Remember that spring when you sprouted a green twig on your right shoulder?"

"You are right," said Mrs. Hi-Lo with a laugh. "We all have our weak points." And with that the little lady bustled off into the kitchen.

Dorothy and the Wizard sat down gingerly on two of the largest chairs the room contained. But small as the chairs were, they proved quite sturdy and readily supported their weight. "Is there any way," asked the Wizard, "that we can leave this mountaintop?"

Hi-Lo sat bolt upright in his chair and stared at the Wizard in amazement. "Leave the mountaintop?" he repeated as if he couldn't believe his own ears. "Do I understand you to say that you want to leave this delightful place, this most favored spot in the universe?"

"We do," said the Wizard emphatically. "Our home is in the Land of Oz, and we desire to return there as quickly as possible."

"But why?" asked Hi-Lo. "No place could be as delightful as this mountaintop. Just wait until you have become acquainted with it — our healthful, refreshing climate, our beautiful pine forest, our handsome village of Pineville and its delightful people."

"Have you ever been anywhere else?" asked the Wizard quietly.

"No, never, but—"

"Then permit me to say," replied the Wizard, "that you are not qualified to judge. Little Dorothy and I have traveled in many strange lands all over the world, and we prefer the Land of Oz for our home."

"Well, everyone to his own taste, of course," muttered Hi-Lo, unconvinced and a trifle crestfallen.

Just then Mrs. Hi-Lo re-entered the room bearing a tray laden with steaming hot foods. At her invitation Dorothy and the Wizard pulled their chairs up to a table, and Mrs. Hi-Lo served the food on gleaming white enameled pine platters and dishes. There was savory vegetable soup, scrambled eggs, cheese, lettuce and tomato salad, chocolate layer cake and lemonade. The food was delicious, and as Dorothy and the Wizard had not eaten since breakfast and it was now nearly evening, they did full justice to the meal. Mr. and Mrs. Hi-Lo looked on with polite curiosity, marveling that the strangers could enjoy such odd food.

When they had finished, the Wizard sighed with satisfaction and sat back in his chair. "Where did you get this excellent food, if there are no human beings on the mountaintop?" he asked.

"Oh, but there is one meat person like yourselves on Mount Illuso," said Mrs. Hi-Lo. "She is our ruler, and many years ago she gave me the magic recipe for the preparation of human food. As you are the first human visitors we have ever had, this is the first time I have had occasion to use the recipe."

"Who is this ruler of yours?" inquired Dorothy.

"She is a beautiful Fairy Princess named Ozana," Hi-Lo replied.

"Ozana!" exclaimed Dorothy. "Wizard, did you hear that? Ozana — doesn't that sound an awful lot like an Oz name?"

"It certainly does," agreed the little man. "May we see this Princess Ozana of yours?" he asked Hi-Lo.

340

"I was about to mention," replied Hi-Lo, "that it was Ozana's orders when she appointed me Keeper of the Elevator that I was to instruct any passengers I might have to seek her out at her home in Pineville."

"Oh, let's go see her right away!" exclaimed Dorothy.

"Not tonight," objected Hi-Lo. "You would never find your way through the Pine Forest in the dark. You may stay with us tonight and be on your way to see Princess Ozana early in the morning."

Dorothy and the Wizard could offer no objection to this sensible and kindly offer of hospitality. Since it was now quite dark outside and the little cottage was cheerful and cozy with the log fire casting dancing reflections in the brightly enameled furniture, they were quite content to spend the night there. After several more questions about the ruler who called herself Ozana, Dorothy and the Wizard decided that Hi-Lo and his wife knew nothing more beyond the facts that Princess Ozana had created the pine folks and built the village for them to live in.

"Have you and Hi-Lo always lived here alone?" Dorothy asked Mrs. Hi-Lo.

The little woman's expression was sad as she answered, "No. Once we had a son. He was not a very good boy and was continually getting into mischief. He was the only one of our wooden folks who ever was discontented with life here on Mount Illuso. He wanted to travel and see the world. We could do nothing at all with him." Mrs. Hi-Lo sighed and continued, "One day a friendly stork paused in a long flight to rest on Mount Illuso, and the naughty boy persuaded the stork to carry him into the great outside world. From that time on we have never heard anything more of him. I often wonder what happened to our poor son," the little woman concluded in a sorrowful tone.

"How big was your boy?" asked the Wizard. "Was he just a little shaver?"

"Oh, no," replied Mrs. Hi-Lo. "He was almost fully grown — a young stripling, I should call him."

"And was his name Charlie?" inquired the Wizard thoughtfully.

"Yes! Yes, it was! Oh, tell me, Sir," implored Mrs. Hi-Lo, "do you perchance know my son?"

"Not personally," replied the Wizard. "But I can assure you, Madame, that you have nothing to worry about where your son Charlie is concerned. That friendly stork knew his business and left Charlie on the right doorstep." The Wizard had a small radio in his apartment in the Royal Palace in the Emerald City which he sometimes turned on and listened to with much curiosity. But he never listened for long, as he was subject to headaches when listening to anything but good music.

"Oh, thank you!" exclaimed Mrs. Hi-Lo. "It is such a relief to know that our Charlie turned out all right after all. There were times," the woman confessed, "when I had a horrible suspicion that he was made from a bad grade of pine — knotty pine, you know."

"There are those who share that opinion," murmured the Wizard. But Mrs. Hi-Lo was so overjoyed to hear of her son that she paid no attention to the Wizard's words.

Hi-Lo, who seemed totally uninterested in this conversation concerning his wayward son, merely muttered, "A bad one, that youngster," and then yawned somewhat pointedly and remarked that since their beds were far too small for their guests to occupy, he and his wife would retire to their bedrooms and Dorothy and the Wizard could pass the night in the living room. Mrs. Hi-Lo supplied them with warm blankets and soft pillows, and then she and Hi-Lo bid them a happy goodnight. Dorothy made a snug bed on the davenport, while the Wizard curled up cozily before the fire.

Just before she dropped off to sleep, she asked, "Do you suppose this Princess Ozana has any connection with Oz, Wizard?"

"It is possible, and then again, the name may be merely a coincidence, my dear," the little man answered sleepily, "so don't build you hopes too high."

A moment later Dorothy's eyes closed, and she was sound asleep dreaming that Toto, in a bright-blue uniform with big gold buttons and a little red cap was operating the elevator and saying, "Right this way, Dorothy! Step lively, please. Going up — next stop, Princess Ozana!"

Chapter 10 - The Village of Pineville

Dorothy and the Wizard awakened bright and early the next morning, eager to pursue their adventures. Mrs. Hi-Lo prepared a hearty breakfast for them from her magic recipe, and as they made ready to leave the pretty little cottage, Hi-Lo advised them, "Just follow the trail that leads through the Pine Forest and you will come to the Village of Pineville where Princess Ozana lives. You can't miss it, and if you walk steadily you should be there by noon."

Stepping from the cottage, Dorothy and the Wizard found the morning sun bright and warm and the air filled with the pungent aroma of pine from the forest. "Goodbye!" called Mrs. Hi-Lo from the door of the cottage.

"Goodbye!" called Mr. Hi-Lo. "Don't forget to remember us to the Princess!"

"We won't," promised Dorothy. "We'll tell her how kind you've been to us."

In a short time the cottage was lost to their view, and the two travelers were deep in the cool shade of the Pine Forest. The trail over which they walked was carpeted with pine needles, making a soft and pleasant path for their feet.

Once when they paused to rest for a few moments, a red squirrel frisked down a nearby tree and, sitting on a stump before Dorothy, asked saucily, "Where to, strangers?"

"We're on our way to see Princess Ozana," said Dorothy.

"Oh, are you indeed!" exclaimed the squirrel with a flirt of his whiskers. "Well, you are just halfway there. If you walk briskly, you'll find yourselves out of the forest in another two hours."

"How do you know we are just halfway there?" asked Dorothy.

"Because I've measured the distance many times," replied the squirrel.

"I should think you would prefer to live nearer the village of Pineville," remarked Dorothy. "It must be very lonesome here in this deep pine forest."

"Oho! That shows how unobserving you mortals are!" exclaimed the red squirrel. "My family and I wouldn't think of living anywhere but here, no matter how lonely it is. Know why?"

"No, I must say I don't," confessed the girl."

"Look at my tree, look at my tree!" chattered the squirrel, flirting his big, bushy tail in the direction of the tree from which he had appeared.

"Of course!" chuckled the Wizard. "It's a hickory tree!"

"But I don't see—" began Dorothy in perplexity.

"What do squirrels like best of all, my dear?" asked the Wizard, smiling with amusement.

"Oh, Wizard, why didn't I think of that? They like nuts, of course!"

"Exactly!" snapped the little red squirrel. "And since pine trees do not bear nuts and hickory trees do — well, city life and fine company may be all right for some folks, but I prefer to remain here in comfort where I know my family will be well provided for." And with that the wise little creature gave a leap and a bound and darted up the trunk of the one and only nut tree in all the Pine Forest.

Dorothy and the Wizard followed the pine-needle trail on through the Pine Forest until finally the trees thinned and they stepped out into an open meadow bright with yellow buttercups. The sun was almost directly overhead by this time.

Below the two travelers, in a pretty green valley that formed the center of the mountaintop, lay a small village of several hundred cottages, all similar to Hi-Lo's. The buildings were painted with glossy blue enamel and shone brilliantly in the sun. They were grouped in a circle about one large central cottage that differed from the others in that it was considerably larger and, from where Dorothy and the Wizard stood, appeared to be surrounded by rather extensive gardens and grounds.

Dorothy and the Wizard followed the trail over the meadow to a point where it broadened into a street that led among the houses. The two travelers set out on this street, which was wide and pleasant and paved with blocks of white pine. As Dorothy and the Wizard walked through the village, they saw that the cottages were occupied by wooden folks much like Hi-Lo and his wife. A wooden woman was washing the windows of her cottage. A wooden man with wooden shears was trimming the hedge around his house. Another was repairing the white picket fence around his cottage. Tiny wooden children, almost doll-like they were so small, played in the yards. From one cottage a spotted wooden dog ran into the road and barked at the strangers.

"I suppose he's made of dogwood," observed Dorothy with a smile.

Dorothy and the Wizard aroused much curiosity among the little wooden folk, most of whom paused in their work to stare at the strangers as they passed. But none of them seemed to fear the meat people. A wooden lady approached them, walking down the street with quick, lively steps. On her arm was a market basket full of green pine cones. Pausing, the Wizard removed his hat and in his most polite manner addressed her. "Pardon me, Madame. Can you tell me if this street leads to the palace of Princess Ozana?"

"Palace? What's that?" asked the woman with a puzzled expression on her face. "I don't know what a palace is, Sir, but if you follow this street you will come to the cottage where our Princess Ozana dwells."

"Thank you, Madame," said the Wizard, and the little woman trotted busily down the street. In a few minutes more, Dorothy and the Wizard had reached the central part of Pineville. Here a trim, white picket fence encircled a large area that seemed to be one huge flower garden with every sort of flower imaginable growing in it. In the exact center of this enclosure stood an attractive blue cottage, large enough to accommodate comfortably full-sized human beings. Just in front of the cottage was a pond of placid blue water. In the pond grew water lilies and all sorts of flowering plants that one finds in lakes and ponds.

The path that led from the entrance of the cottage divided at the pond's edge and encircled the water, meeting on the opposite side of the pond and running again as a single path to a gate in the fence before which Dorothy and the Wizard stood. Forming a bower over the gate was a white wooden trellis covered with roses. From the center of the pretty trellis hung a blue sign with these words in white enameled letters:

WELCOME
COTTAGE OF PRINCESS OZANA
WALK IN

"Well, I guess that means us," said the Wizard with a smile as he read the sign and pushed open the gate.

Chapter 11 - Princess Ozana

Dorothy exclaimed with delight as they stepped through the garden gate. She had no idea any garden could be so beautiful. Flowers of every known variety grew in profusion. Save for the mossy paths that wound through the garden, there was not a spot of ground that was without blossoming plants. As for the pond, it was like a small sea of lovely blossoming water plants. At the far edge of the pond Dorothy noted three graceful white swans sleeping in the shade of a large flowering bush that grew at the edge of the pond and trailed its blossoms into the water. The air was sweet with the perfume of thousands and thousands of flowers.

"Oh, Wizard," gasped Dorothy, "did you ever see anything so lovely?"

"It is indeed a beautiful sight," replied the little man admiringly.

Here and there throughout the garden, a score or more of little wooden men were busily at work. Some were watering plants from blue wooden pails, others were trimming blossoming bushes and hedges, some were digging out weeds, and others were building trellises for climbing vines. None of them took the slightest notice of Dorothy and the Wizard, so absorbed were they in their work.

Not far from where Dorothy and the Wizard stood was a little maid on her knees digging with a trowel in the soft earth about a beautiful rambling rose bush that climbed above her in a blue trellis. "Let's ask her where we can find Princess Ozana," suggested Dorothy.

A few steps brought them to the side of the maiden, who wore a pretty blue apron with a pink petal design. On her hands were gardening gloves, and her golden hair fell loosely down her back. "I wonder," began the Wizard, "if you can tell us if the Princess Ozana is in."

The little maid looked up, regarding the strangers with friendly curiosity. Dorothy saw that she was very lovely. Her eyes were as soft as shy woodland violets, and of the same purple hue; her skin as delicately colored as fragile petals, and her lips were like rosebuds. "No," the maid replied with a suspicion of a smile in her voice, "Princess Ozana is not in her cottage at the moment."

"Perhaps you know where we can find her," suggested the Wizard.

At this the little maid gave a silvery laugh and exclaimed, "You have found her — I am Princess Ozana!"

"Of course, Wizard," said Dorothy, "Princess Ozana is the only flesh and blood person on Mount Illuso 'cept for us, so this just must be she. Besides," she added, "no one else could be so beautiful."

"Thank you, my dear," said Ozana graciously as she rose to her feet. "And you, Sir," she continued, turning to the Wizard and sweetly easing the little man's embarrassment, "could scarcely be blamed for failing to recognize a princess garbed so simply and digging in a garden."

"I most humbly ask your pardon," murmured the Wizard.

"Come," said Ozana, "let us go into my cottage, where we can talk at ease. I must know all about you."

As they started for the cottage, a small voice called after them, "Wait! Wait for me! Don't leave me here! It's time for my milk!"

Dorothy glanced behind her and saw, scrambling from under a bush, a tiny kitten with pure white fur and china-blue eyes. "Oh, what a darling!" she cried.

"This is Felina, my pet kitten," announced Ozana as she knelt and gathered the small bundle of fur into her arms.

Ozana led her guests to the living room of the cottage, an attractive room fragrant with pine scent and comfortably furnished with pine chairs, divans and tables. Pressing a button set in the pine-paneled wall, Ozana bid her guests make themselves comfortable while she ordered lunch. A moment later a little wooden maid in a blue dress and spotless white pinafore, followed closely by a small wooden boy in a page's livery, appeared smiling in the doorway. The maid curtsied gracefully, and the boy bobbed his head as Ozana said, "This is Dolly and Poppet, my maid and page. Dolly, will you and Poppet please prepare sandwiches and refreshments for us? My guests have traveled far and must be quite hungry."

"We are happy to serve your Highness," answered the wooden girl and boy in unison. With another curtsy and bow, the maid and page disappeared from the room.

Ozana seated herself beside Dorothy and, taking the little girl's hand in her own while she smiled warmly at the Wizard, the Fairy Princess said, "Now, let us become acquainted."

"Well," began Dorothy, "this is the famous Wizard of Oz, and I am—"

"Princess Dorothy of Oz," Ozana finished for her.

"You know us?" asked Dorothy eagerly.

"To be sure I know you," replied Ozana. "By my fairy arts I keep myself informed of all that goes on in the Emerald City. I recall when our Wizard first visited the Land of Oz in his balloon, and when the cyclone lifted your house into the air and carried you, Dorothy, all the way from Kansas to Oz."

"Why do you say `our' Wizard?" asked the Wizard.

"Because I consider myself very close to the Land of Oz. I have a great fondness for all its inhabitants, and especially for the Wizard, who built the Emerald City and united the four countries of Oz," replied Ozana earnestly.

The Wizard blushed modestly. "As for building the Emerald City," he remarked, "I have said many times before that I only bossed the job. The Oz people themselves did all the work."

Dorothy nodded. "When I first heard your name, Ozana, I suspected it was connected in some way with Oz."

"I am called Ozana," stated the violet-eyed maid simply, "because I am a member of Queen Lurline's Fairy Band and first cousin of Princess Ozma of Oz."

"Wizard, did you hear that? Princess Ozana is Ozma's cousin!"

At this moment Dolly and Poppet reappeared bearing trays heaped with sandwiches and glasses of cool, fresh milk. Dorothy was so excited over the revelation Ozana had just made that she could scarcely eat.

While they enjoyed their food, Ozana and her guests exchanged stories. First Dorothy and the Wizard related their adventures. "I have no doubt at all," said Ozana, "that the two strange birds who took your forms were none other than King Umb and Queen Ra, the Mimic Monarchs."

"Did you say Mimics?" exclaimed Dorothy.

"Yes, my dear. Mount Illuso is the home of the dread Mimics."

"Oh," said Dorothy thoughtfully. "That explains a lot of things. Why, only the day before she left the Land of Oz, Ozma and I were discussing the Mimics."

The Wizard, who knew nothing of the Mimics, listened with interest as Ozana described the creatures. "I don't understand," said the Wizard when Ozana had finished, "why you should be living alone on the top of this mountain in which such evil creatures as the Mimics dwell."

"That question is easily answered," replied Ozana. "Immediately after Queen Lurline enchanted the Mimics so that they could not attack the Oz inhabitants, she flew with me, her fairy companion, to the top of Mount Illuso. Here she left me, giving me certain fairy powers over the Mimics and instructing me that I was to remain here at all times as the Guardian of Oz to prevent the Mimics from doing any harm to the Oz people should the evil creatures ever succeed in lifting Queen Lurline's spell. I was not even permitted to leave the mountain to attend Queen Lurline's fairy councils in the Forest of Burzee."

"Then it must have been your fairy light that freed us from the Mimic enchantment in the cavern prison," surmised Dorothy.

"Yes, it was," Ozana admitted. "You see, after Queen Lurline departed from Mount Illuso and I was left alone, the first thing I did was to place the button of light in that cavern which the Mimics call their Cavern of the Doomed. I enchanted the light so that it would appear soon after prisoners were placed in the cave. I gave the light power to overcome the spell cast by the Mimics on their victims."

"Then you are responsible for the elevator and Hi-Lo, too," said the Wizard.

"Yes," replied Ozana. "I placed the elevator in the mountain and stationed Hi-Lo there to operate it. I did all this by my fairy arts. Of course, the Mimics have no knowledge of my arrangements to bring about the release of their victims. I knew the escaped prisoners would find their way to me, and I could aid them if I judged them worthy. But I never expected to find inhabitants of the Land of Oz in the Mimic Cavern of the Doomed!"

"How is it," asked the Wizard, "that the Mimics were able to capture Dorothy and me despite the fact that we are inhabitants of the Land of Oz?"

"You must remember," said Ozana, "that both you and Dorothy came to Oz from the great outside world, and neither of you was an inhabitant of Oz when Queen Lurline cast her spell over the Mimics. Hence you were not protected by that spell. It was for just such an unlooked-for development as this that the wise Queen Lurline left me on this mountaintop."

"May I ask, then," said the Wizard, "why you knew nothing of the flight of the Mimic King and Queen to the Emerald City?"

Ozana's face flushed slightly at this question, and she replied hesitatingly, "I must admit that I am fully responsible for all your troubles. But I plead with you to consider my side of the story. I have dwelt on this forsaken mountaintop with no human companions for more than two hundred years. At first I amused myself by creating the little wooden people and building their pine village for them. But it was too much like playing with dolls, and I soon tired. Then I busied myself with my garden, growing in it every variety of flower that exists. This occupied me for many long years.

"Please remember that I have taken many precautions against the Mimics. I believed I could rely on my fairy light to free any prisoners in the Cavern of the Doomed, but apparently the Mimics took no captives they thought important enough to occupy the Cavern of the Doomed until they made you prisoners. And then my fairy light served me well. Can you find it in your hearts to forgive me that I did not spend all my time keeping guard over the Mimics through all those long years?"

"Of course. We understand, Ozana," said Dorothy, pressing the fairy maid's hand affectionately.

"And I must confess," continued Ozana with a grateful smile at Dorothy, "that had I not been so completely absorbed in my garden during the last few days, I would surely have known of Ozma and Glinda's departure from the Emerald City and your own plight."

The Wizard had been very thoughtful while Ozana was speaking. Now he asked, "Just what do you believe to be the plans of the two Mimics who are now masquerading as Dorothy and me in the Emerald City?"

Ozana was grave at this question. "It is evident," she replied, "that King Umb and Queen Ra hope to take advantage of the absence of Ozma and Glinda to search for the counter-charm that would release the Mimics from Queen Lurline's enchantment and permit them to overrun Oz. Queen Ra must have discovered by her black arts that Queen Lurline had given the secret of the magical antidote into Ozma's keeping, knowing it would be safest with Ozma. It may be," added Ozana thoughtfully, "that if King Umb and Queen Ra have not discovered the spell by the time Ozma and Glinda return, they would even be so bold as to remain in the Emerald City, hoping they could deceive Ozma and Glinda as they have the rest of the Oz folks."

"What do you think they will do if they find the magic spell?" asked Dorothy fearfully.

The violet depths of Ozana's eyes darkened as she considered. "I don't like to think about that, my dear," she answered slowly.

After a moment's silence, Princess Ozana brightened. "Come now, let's not borrow trouble. The Mimic Monarchs have had so little time that I am sure they could not have succeeded in their search! We have nothing to fear now. However I will spend the entire afternoon and evening in study, and by use of my fairy arts I will be able to discover just what King Umb and Queen Ra's plot is. With that knowledge we can act wisely and quickly to defeat the Mimic Monarchs."

"Do you think we should wait that long?" asked the Wizard.

"It is necessary," replied Ozana firmly. "I must have time to study Ra and Umb's actions during the past few days and to prepare myself to fight them. Remember, they are powerful enemies. Unless I am mistaken, we shall be on our way to the Emerald City in the morning, and I shall be fully armed with whatever knowledge is necessary to defeat the Mimic Monarchs completely. Do not worry, my friends. I am confident I can bring about the downfall of King Umb and Queen Ra before Ozma and Glinda return to the Emerald City tomorrow."

"Of course you are right," assented the Wizard slowly.

"Now," said Ozana, rising, "let me show you my garden, of which I am quite proud. I am sure you will find it so interesting that you will regret you have only one short afternoon to spend in it. I have passed countless days in it and found it ever more fascinating."

The White Kitten, Felina, had finished lapping up the milk from the bowl placed on the floor for her by the little wooden maid. Dorothy knelt, cuddling the tiny creature in her arms. "May I take Felina in the garden with us?" Dorothy asked.

"To be sure," replied Ozana. "I shall be far too occupied this afternoon to give her my attention."

As they stepped from Ozana's cottage into the garden, the Fairy Princess said, "I believe you will find my garden different from any you have ever seen. I call it my Story Blossom Garden."

Chapter 12 - Story Blossom Garden

"Now I will show you why I call my garden Story Blossom Garden," began Ozana as she advanced toward a rose tree laden with lovely blooms. "You see, these are not ordinary flowers. They are fairy flowers that I created with my fairy arts. And the soil in which they grow is magic soil. Take this rose, for instance." Here Ozana cupped a large, red rose in her hand. "Look into its petals, Dorothy, and tell me what you see."

"Why, the petals form a lovely girl's face!" Dorothy exclaimed in delight.

"And so it is with all the blossoms in my garden," said Ozana. "If you look closely into them, you will see a human face. Now, Dorothy, put your ear close to the rose and listen."

Dorothy did as she was bid and quite clearly she heard a small but melodious voice say pleadingly, "Pick me, pick me, little girl, and I will tell you the sweetest story ever told — a love story."

Dorothy looked at the rose in awe. "What does it mean?" she asked Ozana.

"Simply that all the flowers in my garden are Story Blossom Flowers. Pick a blossom and hold it to your ear, and it will tell you its story. When the story is done, the blossom will fade and wither."

"Oh, but I shouldn't like any of the beautiful flowers to die," protested Dorothy, "even to hear their lovely stories."

"They do not die," replied Ozana. "As I said, these are no ordinary flowers. They do not grow from seeds or bulbs. Instead, as soon as a blossom has told its story, it fades and withers. Then one of my gardeners plants it, and in a few days it blooms afresh with a new story to tell. The flowers are all eager to be picked so that they may tell their stories. Just as ordinary flowers give off their perfumes freely and graciously, so my flowers love to breathe forth the fragrance of their stories. A poet once said that perfumes are the souls of flowers. I have succeeded in distilling those perfumes into words."

"Can't the flowers tell their stories while they are still growing?" asked Dorothy.

"No," replied Ozana. "Only when they are separated from their plants can they tell their stories."

"Do all the roses tell the same love story?" Dorothy asked.

"No indeed," said Ozana. "While it is true that all the roses tell love stories — for the rose is the flower of love — all roses do not tell the same love story. Since no two rose blossoms are identical, no two blossoms tell the same story. It was my purpose in creating the garden to supply myself with a never-ending source of amusement as an escape from the boredom of living alone on this desolate mountaintop. I was reminded of the Princess in the Arabian Nights tales. You will recall that she told her stories for a thousand-and-one nights. My story blossoms," Ozana concluded with a smile, "can tell many, many more than a thousand and one stories. There are many thousands of blossoms in my garden, and each blossom has a different story."

"You are certainly to be congratulated on your marvelous garden," said the Wizard. "It is a miraculous feat of magic," he added admiringly.

"Thank you," replied Ozana graciously. "And now I will leave you, as I must form our plans for tomorrow. I must ask you to excuse me from the evening meal. Dolly and Poppet will serve you, and when you are ready they will show you to your sleeping rooms. Goodbye for the present, my friends."

Dorothy and the Wizard bid their lovely hostess goodbye and then turned to the wonderful garden of Story Blossoms. Putting Felina on the ground to romp beside her, Dorothy dropped to her knees before a cluster of pansies. As she bent her ear over one of the little flower faces, it murmured, "Pick me, little girl, pick me! I'll tell you an old-fashioned story of once-upon-a-time about a wicked witch and a beautiful princess."

The Wizard found himself admiring the flaming beauty of a stately tiger lily. Placing his ear close to the blossom, he listened and heard the flower say in a throaty voice, "Pick me, O Man, and hear a thrilling story of splendid silken beasts in their sultry jungle lairs."

Now Dorothy was listening to a purple thistle that spoke with a rich Scotch burr, "Pick me, little girl, an' ye'll make naw mistake, for I'll tell ye a tale of a Highland lassie for Auld Lang Syne."

Noticing a tawny blossom with gay purple spots, Dorothy placed her ear close to it. This was a harlequin flower, and it said, "Pick me, child, and I'll tell you a wonder tale about Merryland and its Valley of Clowns, where dwell the happy, fun-loving clowns who delight in making children laugh." Dorothy remembered reading in a story book about Merryland and the Valley of Clowns.

Next was a Black-Eyed Susan that murmured to Dorothy, "Pick me, and I will tell you the story of three things that men love best — black eyes and brown and blue. Men love them all, but oh, black eyes — men love and die for you!"

Dorothy smiled and moved on to a daisy, which whispered to her in halting, doubtful tones, "Does he really love her? I shouldn't tell, but I know, I know — and I will tell, if only you'll pick me, little girl."

"And I thought daisies didn't tell," Dorothy said to herself. She stopped before a rambling rose that spoke in a rapid, excited voice and wanted to relate a story of vagabond adventure in faraway places. Then a bright red tulip whispered about a tale of windmills and Holland canals and pretty Dutch girls. At last the little girl came to a sunflower so tall that she had to stand on tiptoe to hear its words. "Pick me," the sunflower urged, "and hear my story of sun-baked prairies and western farm homes and great winds that sweep across the plains."

"I wonder," thought Dorothy, "if the sunflower would tell me a story about my old home in Kansas. There used to be a great many sunflowers on Uncle Henry's farm back there."

A tiny violet growing in a mossy bed caught the girl's eye, and as she knelt to hear its words, a shrill, unpleasant voice exclaimed, "Pick me! Pick me! Pick me immediately! I'll tell you a story that will burn your ears off! All about Dick Superguy — greatest detective in the world! He can't be killed — he's all-powerful!" Dorothy was sure the shy little violet hadn't uttered these words. While she looked about to see where the rude voice was coming from, one of the little wooden gardeners stepped up and said apologetically, "Beg your pardon, Miss, it's just a weed. They're always loud and noisy, and while we don't care much for their stories, we feel they have as much right to grow as any other plants. Even a magic fairy garden has its weeds."

The Wizard had strolled over to the pond of placid blue water, and placing his ear close to a green pad on which nestled an exquisite water lily, he heard these words, "Pick me, O Man, and I'll tell you a tale of a magic white ship that sails the jeweled seas and of the strange creatures that dwell in the blue depths."

Turning to a lotus blossom, the Wizard heard a sleepy voice murmur, "Pick me, pick me. I'll carry you afar to the secret islands of the never-ending nights, where the winds are music in the palm trees and the hours are woven of delights."

Now that they had listened to the pleading voices of so many of the blossoms, Dorothy and the Wizard decided to pick some of them and hear their stories. Dorothy's first selection was a Jack-in-the-Pulpit, which proved to be an unfortunate choice, as the story the blossom told was preachy and sermon-like. She decided the blossom was a trifle green. Next she tried a daffodil. The story this blossom whispered to her in silver tones was about a lovely Spring Maiden who went dancing around the earth, and at her approach all ugliness and coldness and bitterness vanished. In the Spring Maiden's wake appeared a trail of anemones and violets and daffodils and tulips, and gentle winds that caused new hopes to arise in the hearts of the winter-weary people.

The Wizard selected a pink carnation. This spicily scented blossom told him an exciting story of intrigue and adventure in high places. It was a romantic, dashing story, full of cleverness and surprises. Then the Wizard plucked a cluster of purple lilacs. Each of the tiny blossoms growing on the stem joined in a chorus to sing him a story of home and love, of patience and virtue and all the common things of life in which the poorest may find riches and happiness.

Almost before Dorothy and the Wizard realized it, the shadows of evening were lengthening over the garden, and Dolly and Poppet appeared to inform them the evening meal was awaiting them. Dorothy picked up the White Kitten, which had fallen asleep in the shadow of a nearby hedge, and she and the Wizard followed the maid and the page back to the cheery comfort of Ozana's cottage. They chatted happily over the good food served them by Dolly and Poppet. Felina had her bowl of milk on the floor near Dorothy's chair.

Then, since they realized the next day was likely to be a busy and exciting one, they followed Dolly and Poppet to the rooms Ozana had prepared for them and said goodnight at their doors. The rooms were delightfully furnished with deep, soft beds and everything to make them comfortable for the night.

As Dorothy pulled the covers over her and Felina snuggled into a small, furry ball at the girl's feet, Dolly reappeared with a poppy blossom in her hand. "Here, Princess Dorothy," the thoughtful little maid said. "Listen to the story of the poppy blossom, and you'll be sure to sleep."

So Dorothy listened to the soft, slumbrous voice of the poppy and was asleep almost before the tale was finished. What kind of a story did the sweet poppy tell? Why, a bedtime story, of course.

Chapter 13 - The Three Swans

Dorothy was awakened by the sunlight streaming through the windows of her bedroom.
Refreshed and eager for the adventures that lay ahead, she bathed and dressed and, with Felina in her arms, knocked on the door of the Wizard's room. The man was already awake and in excellent spirits as he greeted Dorothy. A moment later Dolly and Poppet came to lead them to the living room, where Ozana was awaiting them for breakfast.

The Fairy Princess, radiant with loveliness, was dressed in a simple blue dress with a circlet of roses set in her golden hair. Dorothy thought this an excellent crown for the Princess of Story Blossom Garden.

When the meal was finished, Ozana said, "It will please you to learn that my studies which I completed late last night revealed that the Mimic King and Queen have accomplished no real harm in the Emerald City. However, Queen Ra has succeeded in doing something that has surprised me. She has thrown up a magic screen about her activities which has made it impossible for me to discover whether she has found the spell that would release the Mimics form Queen Lurline's enchantment. It is logical to believe Ra has failed, since if she had discovered the spell, she would surely have used it to permit the Mimic hordes to overrun Oz."

"But you cannot be sure, is that it, Ma'am?" asked the Wizard.

"Yes, I am afraid so," Ozana admitted, frowning slightly. "This magic screen that Queen Ra has devised baffles me and resists all my efforts to penetrate it. For this reason I think it would be wise for us to go as quickly as possible to the Emerald City. As you know, Ozma and Glinda will return from the Forest of Burzee this morning at ten o'clock. I would like to be present to greet them and to explain what has happened. There is no use causing them undue alarm. After all, I am responsible for the Mimics in regard to the Land of Oz," Ozana concluded thoughtfully.

"Well," said Dorothy, "I'm ready to go. How about you, Wizard?"

The little man's expression was grave as he answered. "The quicker we get back to Oz, the better. I have an uneasy feeling that we are not finished with the Mimics, by any means."

"Then it is settled," announced Ozana. "Come, my friends, let us make all possible haste. We have no time to lose."

"May I take Felina to Oz with us?" asked Dorothy.

Ozana smiled. "Certainly, my dear. Only let us hurry."

Dorothy and the Wizard followed Ozana to the cottage door and down the path that led to the edge of the pond. The garden was fresh and lovely in the early morning. The side of the cottage that faced the morning sun was covered with blue morning glories. Dorothy regretted that there was no time for her to pick one of the delicate blossoms and listen to its story.

Standing at the edge of the pond, Ozana uttered a soft, musical whistle. From under the low-hanging branches of a large bush that trailed into the water on the far shore of the pond emerged the three graceful swans which Dorothy and the Wizard had admired the day before. The snow-white birds moved swiftly across the water in answer to Ozana's summons. "These are my swans, which will carry us over the Deadly Desert to the Emerald City," said Ozana.

"They don't look big enough to carry even you or me, let alone the Wizard," said Dorothy doubtfully.

Ozana laughed. "Of course they are not large enough now, Dorothy, but soon they will be."

The three swans were now at the pond's edge just at Ozana's feet. The Fairy Princess bent, touching the head of each of the birds gently with a slender wand which she drew from the folds of her blue dress. While Dorothy and the Wizard watched, the birds grew steadily before their wondering eyes. In a few seconds they were nearly five times the size of ordinary swans.

The Fairy Princess placed a dainty foot on the back of one of the swans, and then settled herself on the bird's downy back, motioning to Dorothy and the Wizard to do likewise.

Dorothy stepped gingerly to the back of the swan nearest her. She found the great bird supported her easily. Holding Felina in her lap, the little girl nestled comfortable among the feathers. The Wizard had already mounted the third swan. Seeing that the passengers were all aboard, Ozana signaled the swans, and with mighty strokes of their great wings, the birds soared into the air. Dorothy looked behind her and saw Ozana's cottage growing smaller as the birds climbed higher and higher into the heavens. In a short time, they had left Mount Illuso so far in the distance that it was no longer visible.

The soft feathers of the bird that carried her and the gentle motion with which it sped through the air made Dorothy think of riding through the sky on a downy feather-bed. "Isn't it grand, Wizard?" Dorothy called.

"It certainly beats any traveling I ever did," admitted the Wizard. "It's even better than my balloon back in Omaha."

Ozana's bird flew in advance, with the swans bearing Dorothy and the Wizard slightly to her rear on either side of her. They crossed the border of the Land of the Phanfasms and soared high over the Deadly Desert. The swans flew even higher over the desert that had the Mimic birds. For this reason none of the travelers suffered from the poisonous fumes that rose from the shifting sands of the desert. As they approached the yellow Land of the Winkies, Dorothy noticed that Ozana cast several anxious glances at the sun, which was rising higher and higher in the heavens. It seemed to the little girl that the Fairy Princess was disturbed and anxious.

"Is anything wrong, Ozana?" called Dorothy.

"I cannot say for sure," replied Ozana. "Something has taken place in Oz of which I was not aware. I can feel the change now that we are actually over the Land of Oz. I am trying to discover what has happened by means of my fairy powers. I am afraid, too, that the journey is taking longer than I expected, and we shall not be able to arrive before Ozma and Glinda."

At a signal from their mistress the three swans quickened their already swift flight. Again and again Ozana consulted the sun, and her appearance became more grave and worried as they approached the Emerald City. Suddenly the Fairy Princess's expression changed. A look of anger and dismay clouded her face, and the next instant she cried out beseechingly, "Forgive me, my friends! I now understand all that has happened. The Mimics have cunningly outwitted me!"

Chapter 14 - The Mimic Monarchs lock Themselves in

Back in the Emerald City a great deal had been happening while Dorothy and the Wizard were adventuring on Mount Illuso. You will recall that Toto had startled the Oz people by trotting into the Grand Dining Room and declaring that it was not Dorothy who sat at the head of the table. You see, in some ways animals are wiser than human beings. King Umb and Queen Ra were able to fool the Oz people just by looking like Dorothy and the Wizard, but they couldn't deceive the keen senses of the little dog so easily. Toto's animal instinct warned him that this was not his beloved mistress Dorothy or his old friend the Wizard. When Toto made his astonishing assertion, every eye in the dining room turned questioningly upon the Mimic King and Queen.

Suddenly Queen Ra leaped to her feet. Grasping King Umb by the arm and hissing, "Hurry, you fool!" she pulled the Mimic King after her, and the two dashed from the dining room. For a moment everyone was too startled to move — except Toto. He sped like an arrow after the fleeing monarchs.

The quick-witted Scarecrow broke the spell by leaping to his feet and following with awkward haste after the dog. Instantly there rose a clamor of startled exclamations and bewildered questions from the Oz people, who were thrown into confusion by these strange happenings.

By the time the Scarecrow had reached the corridor, King Umb, Queen Ra and Toto were nowhere in sight. But the straw man could hear Toto's excited barking. Following in the direction of the sound, down one corridor and up another, the Scarecrow arrived in the wing of the palace usually occupied by Ozma and found Toto barking before a closed door. The little dog's eyes flashed angrily.

When Toto saw the Scarecrow, he stopped barking and said, "I was just too late. They slammed the door in my face, and now I suppose it is locked." The Scarecrow attempted to turn the knob with his stuffed hand and found that, as Toto suspected, the door was locked. "Do you know what room this is?" Toto asked.

"Of course," replied the Scarecrow. "It's Ozma's Chamber of Magic."

"Yes," went on the little dog, "the same room where the imitation Dorothy and Wizard have shut themselves in all day. Why? I want to know! I tell you, Scarecrow, there's something awfully funny going on here."

The straw man was thoughtful. "I agree with you, Toto. Something is happening that we don't understand. We must find out what it is. I believe the wisest thing we can do is to return to the dining room and have a council to talk this thing over. Maybe we will be able to find an explanation."

Silently the little dog agreed, and a short time later a group of the best-loved companions of Dorothy and the Wizard was gathered in a living room adjoining the Grand Dining Room. The Scarecrow presided over the meeting. "All we really know," he began, "is that Dorothy and the Wizard have been acting very strangely today — the second day of the absence of Ozma and Glinda. Toto insists that they are not Dorothy and the Wizard at all."

"Lan' sakes!" exclaimed Dorothy's Aunt Em, "I'll admit the child ain't been herself today, but it's downright silly to say that our Dorothy's someone else. I ought to know my own niece!"

"Em, you're a-gittin' all mixed up," cautioned Uncle Henry. "You jest now said Dorothy ain't been herself today; that means she must be somebody else."

"But who could look so much like Dorothy and the Wizard?" queried Betsy Bobbin with a frown.

"And why should anyone wish to deceive us?" asked tiny Trot.

Now Cap'n Bill spoke up. "S'posin'," began the old sailor gruffly, "that we admit fer the moment that this ain't the real Dorothy and the Wizard. Then the most important thing is — where are the real Dorothy and the Wizard?"

"That's the smartest thing that's been said yet," declared Toto earnestly with an admiring glance at Cap'n Bill. "Here we are wasting time in talk when something dreadful may be happening to Dorothy and the Wizard. Let's get busy and find them quickly."

"Maybe they're lost," suggested Button Bright. "If that's the case, there's nothing to worry about, 'cause I've been lost lots of times, and I always got found again." But no one paid any attention to the boy.

With her yarn hair dangling before her eyes, the Patchwork Girl danced to the front of the gathering. "The trouble with you people," she asserted, "is that you don't know how to add two and two and get four."

"What do you mean by that, Scraps?" asked the Scarecrow.

"Just this," retorted the stuffed girl, saucily making a face at the Scarecrow. "What did we overhear Dorothy and the Wizard discussing today in the garden? Magic! They were talking about a magic spell which they hoped to find before Ozma and Glinda returned. All right. Now where did Dorothy and the Wizard spend most of the day, and where have they fled just now to lock themselves in? To Ozma's Chamber of Magic!" the Patchwork Girl concluded triumphantly. "Mark my words, there's magic behind all this, and the secret is hidden in Ozma's Chamber of Magic."

With his chin in his hand, the Scarecrow was regarding Scraps in silent admiration. "Sometimes," he said, "I almost believe your head is stuffed with the same quality of brains the Wizard put in mine."

"Nope!" denied Scraps emphatically. "It's not brains — just a little common sense." And with that the irrepressible creature leaped to the chandelier suspended from the ceiling and began chinning herself.

"Yes," agreed the Scarecrow with a sigh as he regarded her antics, "I guess I was wrong about your brains."

"But what are we going to do? That's what I want to know," demanded Toto impatiently.

"I believe," declared the Scarecrow finally, "there is only one thing we can do. We must go to Ozma's Chamber of Magic and try to persuade this strange Dorothy and the Wizard to admit us. If they refuse, then we shall be obliged to break open the door and demand an explanation of their mysterious behavior."

"Good!" exclaimed Toto. "Let us go at once."

They all filed out of the room and made their way to Ozma's Chamber of Magic. The door was still locked. Several times the Scarecrow called to Dorothy and the Wizard to open the door and admit them, but there was no response. Then Cap'n Bill stepped forward. He knew what was expected of him as the biggest and strongest of the group. He placed a shoulder against the door and pushed. The door creaked and yielded. Again Cap'n Bill pushed. This time the door yielded more noticeably. Upon the third trial the door suddenly gave way before the old sailor man's weight, and the Scarecrow, followed by Scraps, Trot, Betsy Bobbin, Button Bright and the rest, crowded into Ozma's Chamber of Magic.

Chapter 15 - In the Chamber of Magic

When Queen Ra seized King Umb by the arm and fled with him from the dining room, the Mimic Queen was alarmed. She realized it was useless to attempt to deceive Toto, and she greatly feared the little dog would succeed in convincing the Scarecrow and the others that something had happened to Dorothy and the Wizard. Fear lent speed to the Queen's feet as she ran down the corridor, dragging King Umb after her, with Toto in close pursuit. She slammed the door of the Chamber of Magic and locked it just in time to prevent Toto's entry. Then she flung herself in a chair, gasping for breath.

When King Umb, who was even more frightened than his Queen, had got his breath and could speak, he said raspingly, "So this is the way your plan works — a miserable dog robs us of success!"

"Silence!" commanded Queen Ra angrily. "We are far from defeated. We still have time to find the magic spell. And we will! We were fools to give up the search and go to that silly dinner," she concluded bitterly.

She turned to Ozma's magic books and began feverishly leafing through them. For perhaps ten minutes she continued her search fruitlessly. Flung carelessly on the floor was a great pile of books through which she had previously looked in vain for the magic spell. Only four books remained to be searched through.

While King Umb watched nervously, the Queen continued her frantic quest. Now only two books remained. The magic spell must be in one of these two volumes. Suddenly Queen Ra leaped to her feet with a cry of triumph. "I have found it!" she announced with exultation. She tore a page from the book and cast the volume to the floor.

"Come," she urged, "let us return to Mount Illuso as speedily as possible. Soon we will come again to Oz. But we will not be alone!" Both Ra and Umb laughed with wicked satisfaction. Just then the Scarecrow called to Dorothy and the Wizard to open the door and admit them. "Fools!" muttered Queen Ra. "In a short time you will all be my slaves."

Pausing to pick up Dorothy's Magic Belt, Queen Ra walked to a large French window that looked down on the palace courtyard. Turning to King Umb, she said, "These hateful shapes can serve us no longer, so let us discard them and be on our way." Instantly the figures of Dorothy and the Wizard vanished, and in their places appeared two great, black birds with huge, powerful wings. Just as Cap'n Bill burst open the door and the Scarecrow and the rest crowded into the room, the birds flew from the window.

The little group hurried to the window and looked out. High above the palace and swiftly disappearing in the night flew two enormous, bat-like birds. The night was too dark and the birds too far away for any of the Oz people to see that one of the creatures clutched Dorothy's Magic Belt. While Queen Ra had not yet learned how to command the many wonderful powers of the Magic Belt (or she would most certainly have used the belt to transport herself and Umb to the Mimic Land in the twinkling of an eye), nevertheless she had no intention of leaving the valuable talisman behind to be used by the Oz people.

More bewildered than ever, the Scarecrow and his companions turned from the window. "I told you so!" declared Toto excitedly. "You see, those creatures were not Dorothy and the Wizard at all."

"You are right," said the Scarecrow. "Those great birds must be the same beings that we thought were Dorothy and the Wizard."

"Certainly," replied Toto. "You can see for yourself that Dorothy and the Wizard are not here."

It was true enough. There was no trace of Dorothy or the Wizard in the Chamber of Magic. "But who were those creatures? And why did they want us to believe they were Dorothy and the Wizard? And what has happened to the real Dorothy and the Wizard?" the Scarecrow asked helplessly.

"Why not look in the Magic Picture and find out?" asked the Patchwork Girl as she danced about the room.

"Of course, the very thing!" exclaimed the Scarecrow. "Why didn't I think of that myself?"

"Because your brains are of an extraordinary quality," retorted Scraps, "and you can't be expected to think common-sense thoughts."

The Magic Picture which hung on a wall in Ozma's boudoir was one of the rarest treasures in all Oz. Ordinarily the picture presented merely an attractive view of a pleasant countryside with rolling fields and a forest in the background. But when anyone stood in front of the picture and asked to see a certain person anywhere in the world, the painted picture faded and was replaced by the moving image of the person named and his or her surroundings at that exact time.

The Scarecrow and his companions gathered about the Magic Picture, and the straw man said solemnly, "I want to see Dorothy and the Wizard." Instantly the painted scene faded, and in its place appeared the interior of Hi-Lo's little cottage. Dorothy and the Wizard were just about to sit down to the food Mrs. Hi-Lo had prepared for them.

"I wonder who those two funny little people are?" murmured Trot, fascinated by the quaint appearance of Mr. and Mrs. Hi-Lo.

"They are not familiar to me," observed the Scarecrow reflectively, "nor have I ever seen a cottage quite like that one in the Land of Oz."

For a time the group watched in silence while Dorothy and the Wizard ate their food and conversed with Mr. and Mrs. Hi-Lo. But at length, as nothing of importance occurred, the Scarecrow said, "Even though we don't know where Dorothy and the Wizard are, at least the Magic Picture has shown us they are safe for the moment, and we don't need to worry about them."

"Why not use Dorothy's Magic Belt to wish Dorothy and the Wizard back here in the palace?" Trot asked suddenly as she stared at the images in the Magic Picture.

"An excellent suggestion!" agreed the Scarecrow, his face beaming. "Trot, I believe you have solved our problem," he said admiringly. The Scarecrow knew that when Dorothy was not wearing her Magic Belt on a journey, it was always kept in Ozma's Chamber of Magic. So the straw man went there himself to get the belt. A few minutes later he returned and announced gloomily, "It's gone. The Magic Belt is nowhere in the Chamber of Magic. Either Ozma took it with her, or it has been stolen. The magic Picture has shown us that Dorothy is not wearing the belt."

Disappointment was reflected on everyone's face, and for a moment no one spoke. Then the Scarecrow declared, "My friends, there remains only one more thing to do."

"What is that?" asked Cap'n Bill.

"One of us must leave immediately for Glinda's castle in the Quadling Country to consult Glinda's Great Book of Records. The book will provide us with a complete account of all that has happened to Dorothy and the Wizard."

"A wise suggestion," agreed Cap'n Bill. "Who will go?"

"I will," volunteered Dorothy's Uncle Henry quickly. "I want to do everything possible to bring Dorothy back to us, and it 'pears to me we can't do much of anything until we know what has happened to her."

"Good!" exclaimed the Scarecrow. "You can leave at once. I will order Ozma's wooden Sawhorse to carry you to Glinda's Castle and back. But even though the Sawhorse is swift and tireless, you will not be able to make the journey, consult the Great Book of Records and return to the Emerald City before Ozma and Glinda come back day after tomorrow. That is too bad. The disappearance of Dorothy and the Wizard and all this mystery will not provide a very cheerful homecoming for Ozma and Glinda. But at least we shall have the information contained in the Great Book of Records, and then Ozma and Glinda will know best what to do."

Uncle Henry kissed Aunt Em goodbye and hurried to the Royal Stable where the Sawhorse was waiting for him. "I understand," said the queer steed, whose body and head were made from a tree trunk, "that we're going to Glinda's castle in the Quadling Country."

"That's right," nodded Uncle Henry, "and this is no pleasure trip, so go as fast as you can."

Glancing at Uncle Henry for a moment from one of his eyes — which were knots in the wood — the Sawhorse turned as soon as Uncle Henry was mounted and dashed down the stable driveway into the street leading to the gates of the Emerald City. Once outside the city, the Sawhorse ran so swiftly that its legs, which were merely sticks of wood which Ozma had caused to be shod with gold, fairly twinkled. It sped with a rolling, cradle-like motion over fields and hills, and Uncle Henry had to hold on for dear life.

Perhaps I should explain that Glinda's Great Book of Records is a marvelous book in which everything that happens, from the slightest detail to the most important event taking place anywhere in the world, is recorded the same instant it happens. No occurrence is too trivial to appear in the book. If a naughty child stamps its foot in anger or if a powerful ruler plunges his country into war, both events are noted in the book as of equal importance.

The huge book lies open on a great table occupying the center of Glinda's study and is bound to the table by large chains of gold. Next to Ozma's Magic Picture, Glinda's Great Book of Records is the most valuable treasure in Oz. The Scarecrow knew that by consulting this wonderful book Uncle Henry would be able to discover exactly what had happened to Dorothy and the Wizard.

The Scarecrow and Scraps, having no need for sleep, sat before the Magic Picture all night long, conversing quietly and occasionally glancing at the images of Dorothy and the Wizard as the picture showed them sleeping in Hi-Lo's cottage. The rest of the Oz people retired to their bedrooms, but none of them slept well that night. They were far too worried over the plight of Dorothy and the Wizard to rest easily.

Chapter 16 - A Web is Woven

Arriving at Mount Illuso early the following morning, King Umb and Queen Ra passed the day secluded in the secret cavern where the Queen was accustomed to study the dark sorcery of the Erbs and practice her evil magic. This cavern was so well hidden far in the depths of Mount Illuso and its location was so closely guarded, that only a few of the most faithful subjects of the Mimic King and Queen were aware of its existence.

While Queen Ra's shape was that of a woman, her body was covered with a heavy fur of a reddish-brown color, and her head was that of a fox with a long snout and sharply pointed ears. Two green eyes blazed with a fierce light from her furry face. In her hand the fox-woman held a brass whistle on which she blew a shrill blast. In answer to this summons came the Mimic known as Ebo. Ebo wore the body of a jackal with the head of a serpent.

"Go to the Cave of the doomed and bring the two prisoners to me at once," the Queen commanded.

"Yes, your Highness," hissed Ebo as he swayed his serpent head in obeisance and left the cavern.

"We might as well have a little fun while we wait for midnight," grinned the fox head of the woman evilly.

King Umb appeared as a great, gray ape with cloven hoofs and the head of a man. From the center of his forehead projected a single horn. The man-face was covered with a shaggy, black beard which fell to the hairy chest of the ape-body.

"What do you intend doing with the girl and the man?" asked the gray ape.

"I shall practice transformations on the man, giving him a number of unusual shapes and then perhaps combine them all into one interesting creature. It is amazingly easy to change the shapes of humans, so it will not be much of a feat of magic. Then, just before we leave for the Emerald City, I shall change him into a salamander — a green salamander instead of the ordinary red kind, of course, since he is from the Emerald City — and then when we are over the Deadly Desert I shall drop him into the sands. Salamanders are the only creatures that can exist in the desert, so it will really be a merciful fate, since it will not stop him from living."

"And the girl?" prompted King Umb.

"I think I shall keep the girl chained in my cavern to amuse me when the excitement of conquering and devastating Oz is over and I am in need of diversion," said Queen Ra.

While the Queen was relating her wicked plans, Ebo made his way to the Cave of the Doomed and was amazed and terrified to find it empty. How could there be an escape from the cave from which there was no exit save the single stone door which was always closely guarded? The jackal body of Ebo trembled with fear of the punishment he knew Queen Ra would be quick to inflict on him. But there was nothing else for him to do but to report the mysterious disappearance of the prisoners to the Mimic King and Queen.

Queen Ra received the news with a scream of rage. Blowing on her brass whistle, she summoned two other Mimics. Pointing to Ebo, who cringed with fear, she cried, "Carry him away and cast him into the Pit of Forked Flames."

King Umb was uneasy. "I don't like this," he said. "How do we know that the two mortals will not interfere with our plans to conquer Oz?"

"Bah! What can two weak mortals do in the face of our might?" demanded the Queen derisively.

Knowing his wife's temper, King Umb refrained from reminding Ra that the mortals had somehow miraculously succeeded in escaping from the Cave of the Doomed. Instead, he merely shrugged his ape shoulders and said, "Just the same, I wish we were on our way to Oz now instead of waiting until midnight."

Queen Ra glared at her husband. "I have told you that Lurline's enchantment can be broken only at midnight. Tonight at twelve, I will cast the spell which Lurline foolishly left in Ozma's possession. Since it is the antidote to the enchantment which protects Oz from the Mimics, Lurline knew Ozma would guard it most carefully. But we succeeded in stealing it. Once the spell is cast, the Mimics will be free in all their power to attack Oz and enslave its people. I tell you, Umb, the famous Land of Oz is doomed. In a few short hours it will be a shambles. Nothing can save it!"

A few minutes before the hour of midnight, the Mimic hordes assembled in the vast domed cavern which forms that portion of hollow Mount Illuso that towers above the earth. In the center of the cavern on a stone dais stood King Umb and Queen Ra. The Mimic Queen lifted her arms, and immediately silence fell over the shifting mass of evil beings.

The Queen held in her hand a small box of black enameled wood. Placing the box on the stone dais before her, she raised the lid and muttered an incantation. Immediately there crawled from the box a scarlet spider as large as the Queen's hand. At the first word of the incantation the spider began to grow. In a few seconds its body was four feet in thickness, and its hairy legs sprawled to a distance of fifteen feet from its body, which was covered with a crimson fur.

"Now go," Queen Ra commanded the spider, "and weave the web that will enmesh the fairy enchantment that hangs over us!"

The Mimic hordes parted to make a path through their midst for the spider. The loathsome creature scuttled first to the wall of the cavern, and then climbed up the side of the wall. In a few seconds it had reached the top of the cavern. Then, moving with incredible speed, it wove a monster spider web of crimson strands as thick and tough as heavy rope cables.

Queen Ra watched silently until the fashioning of the scarlet web was completed. At that moment she cried aloud for all to hear: "So long as this web remains unbroken, the Mimics are freed from the enchantment cast on them by Lurline! The web is a snare and a net for Lurline's fairy enchantment and holds every remnant of it caught fast in its coils."

The Queen spoke triumphantly, and well she might, for the magic spell she had stolen from Ozma had worked perfectly. "Come!" shouted Queen Ra. "Let us tarry no longer. We have waited too many years for this hour!"

With this, the Mimic King and Queen assumed the shapes of giant birds and soared through the cavern to the stone portal. The throngs of their Mimic subjects followed, beating the air with great, leathery wings as they passed from the cavern into the night. Soon the sky above Mount Illuso was darkened with the great numbers of the Mimic horde, and the light of the moon was blotted from the earth by the flapping wings. Following the lead of King Umb and Queen Ra, they headed straight for the Deadly Desert and the Land of Oz.

Chapter 17 - The Mimics in the Emerald City

On the morning when the Mimic hordes swept over the border of the Deadly Desert and the Winkie Country and on to the Emerald City, Button Bright and the Patchwork Girl were playing leapfrog in the garden of the Royal Palace. Cap'n Bill was sitting nearby on a bench in the sun, carving on a block of wood with his big jackknife. The old sailor man worked slowly and painstakingly, but when he finished he knew he would have a good likeness of Princess Ozma's lovely features carved in the wood. This he planned to mount as a figurehead on the prow of the boat he was building as a surprise for Ozma.

Suddenly Button Bright, who had tumbled flat on his back, cried out, "Look! Look at those birds!"

Scraps swept her yarn hair out of her button eyes and tilted her head back. The sky was darkening with a great cloud of birds. And what beautiful creatures those birds were!

"Birds of a feather Flock together. Red, blue, green and gold Match my patches bold. Not a grey topknot In the whole lot! See the popinjay Flirt its colors gay..."

cried the Patchwork Girl, dancing about in wild excitement.

"Stop it, Scraps!" commanded Button Bright, who was nearly as excited as the stuffed girl.

"Trot, Betsy, Ojo, Scarecrow!" the boy called. "Come out and see the pretty birds!"

Of course, this taking the forms of gorgeous, plumed birds was a clever part of Queen Ra's cunning scheme. She knew the beauty of the birds, instead of alarming the Oz people, would fascinate them. The Queen hoped by this wily stratagem to take the Oz inhabitants completely by surprise with no thought of danger in their minds. The scheme worked even better than Queen Ra dared dream.

Ojo the Lucky, Aunt Em, the Scarecrow, Betsy Bobbin, Trot, Jellia Jamb, and all the others came hurrying from the Royal Palace, while from the Royal Stable came the Cowardly Lion, the Hungry Tiger, Hank the Mule, the Woozy, and others of the animal friends of the palace residents. Gathering in the gardens and courtyard, they all stared up in wonder at the beautiful birds.

Outside the grounds of the Royal Palace much the same thing was happening throughout the Emerald City. Those people who were out of doors witnessing the spectacle called to those who were indoors, urging them to hurry out and see the lovely visitors. It was no time at all until every building in the city was emptied of its curious inhabitants.

This was just what the Mimics wanted. With the people of the Emerald City standing in the daylight, plainly casting their shadows, Queen Ra gave a signal, and the Mimic birds ceased their slow circling in the sky for the enjoyment of the Oz people and dropped down to the city. King Umb and Queen Ra led those birds which settled in the palace courtyard and gardens.

A bird with brilliant scarlet and royal purple feathers and a topknot of gleaming gold alighted close to Trot. The little girl stepped forward with delight to stroke the bird's lovely plumage. Instantly the creature vanished, and in its place stood a perfect duplicate of Trot, while the real Trot was frozen in her tracks, unable to move. Mystified at suddenly seeing two Trots before him, Cap'n Bill rose from his bench and started toward them. But he was confronted by one of the giant birds, and an instant later the old sailor man was unable to move. He could only stare with amazement at an exact double of himself — wooden leg and all. Button Bright was about to leap playfully on the back of another bird when he fell to the ground powerless to move. At the same moment the bird vanished, and the boy's double appeared in its place.

And so it went throughout the Emerald City. The friendly Oz people were delighted that the lovely birds should approach so near that they might be treated to a closer view of their gorgeous plumage, which, it must be admitted, was exceedingly beautiful. Only the eyes of the birds betrayed their true natures. They flamed a fierce red. One or two of the Oz people, upon meeting the glare of those piercing eyes, were alarmed and would have turned and fled. But it was too late. In a few minutes, all the human inhabitants of the Emerald City were made captives.

However, the Mimics were able to steal the shapes only of human beings. The Scarecrow, the Patchwork Girl, Tik-Tok, the Glass Cat, Billina the Yellow Hen, the Woozy, Toto, Hank the Mule, the Cowardly Lion and the Hungry Tiger remained unchanged. Fearing the mule, the lion and the tiger might prove dangerous because of their size, Queen Ra quickly placed a magic spell on the three beasts that caused them to fall on the courtyard lawn in a deep sleep.

The Scarecrow, Scraps, Tik-Tok and the others who had escaped the magic of the Mimics were completely confused by these sudden and baffling events. The stuffed girl rubbed her suspender-button eyes and gazed with disbelief at two Button Brights — which one was it she had been playing with only a few minutes before? And there were two Aunt Ems and two Jellia Jamb! Wondering if the world had somehow suddenly become double, the bewildered Patchwork Girl looked about for her own twin.

Of all the horde of beautiful birds that had settled on the Emerald City, only two remained in the Royal Gardens. These were King Umb and Queen Ra. At this point the Mimic King and Queen cast off their bird forms. A strange man and woman suddenly appeared in the midst of the Oz people and the Mimic Oz People. The woman was big, raw-boned and red-skinned. Her hair was twisted on her head in a hard black knot, on which was set a small, golden crown. The Scarecrow started with surprise when he saw that the strange woman was wearing Dorothy's Magic Belt. (Until now the belt had been concealed by the plumage of Ra's bird form.) Queen Ra had brought the Magic Belt with her because of its wonderful powers, which she had been studying and which she felt would be useful in carrying out the conquest of Oz. Beside the woman stood a giant man with a flowing black beard and tangled black hair. His eyes were fierce and hawklike.

Quickly Queen Ra uttered a command, at which a number of the Mimic Oz people leaped forward and proceeded to bind the non-human Ozites with strong ropes, which the magic of Queen Ra placed in their hands. To his amazement, the Scarecrow found himself being made captive by Cap'n Bill and Ojo the Lucky. The straw man was wise enough to know that these twin likenesses were not really his old friends Cap'n Bill and Ojo, so he resisted with all his might. But the poor Scarecrow's body was so light that the Mimics had no difficulty in fastening the ropes about him and pinning his arms to his sides.

Scraps was more of a problem. It required the combined efforts of the Mimic Jellia Jamb, Aunt Em, Betsy Bobbin and Button Bright to bind her. But even with these odds none of the Mimics escaped without scratches on his face from

Scraps' gold-plated fingernails. Tik-Tok, the Woozy, the Glass Cat and the rest were all securely bound in a few more seconds.

While our friends were being made prisoners, King Umb and Queen Ra hastened away to the Throne Room of the Royal Palace. There the prisoners of the Mimics were carried into the presence of the Mimic King and queen. The Scarecrow and the others were shocked and outraged at the spectacle of the harsh-looking woman brazenly occupying Ozma's throne, while at her side stood the fierce-visaged man.

The Mimic Ojo and Button Bright lined up the captives before the throne, while Queen Ra regarded them scornfully. "A pair of stuffed dummies, an animated washing machine, and a menagerie," she commented derisively.

"I demand," shouted the Scarecrow boldly, "that you release us immediately!"

"Ah! The famous Scarecrow of Oz!" gloatingly exclaimed Queen Ra. "And as brave as ever! I believe I will have your body destroyed by fire, first removing your head so that you will be able to entertain me with your thoughts. It would be a shame," she added with sarcasm, "if such great brains were lost to the world." Now the one thing in the world the Scarecrow feared was a lighted match, so it is no wonder that, brave as he was, he shrank before so terrible a fate as that proposed by the wicked Queen.

"And you are Tik-Tok the Machine Man," said Queen Ra. "As useless a pile of rubbish as was ever assembled. I shall have you carefully taken apart, piece by piece, and amuse myself in my spare time by trying to put you back together again like a jigsaw puzzle."

"My ma-chin-er-y does not per-mit me to fear," replied Tik-Tok calmly, "e-ven when I am thor-ough-ly wound up, so you are wast-ing your threats on me."

The evil Queen went down the line of captives, plotting terrible fates for each of them. Billina, she predicted, would soon be roasted for dinner. The Patchwork Girl would become a combination pincushion and personal slave. The Glass Cat would be melted down into marbles. Finally she came to the last of the prisoners — the square-shaped Woozy — whom Ra promised to have chopped into cubes for building blocks.

It was at this moment that the Scarecrow became aware that with the exception of Hank the Mule and the Cowardly Lion and the Hungry Tiger, who lay sleeping in the courtyard, all the animals of the Royal Stable were present save the Sawhorse, who was at that moment swiftly bearing Uncle Henry back to the Emerald City from Glinda's Castle in the Quadling Country — and one other.

That other was — Toto!

Chapter 18 - The Return of Ozma And Glinda

After his first sense of joy at finding that Toto had somehow escaped capture, the Scarecrow reflected more soberly that even though the little dog was free, there was nothing he could do to rescue his friends from their desperate plight.

But the Scarecrow had been in dangerous situations before, so he did not give up hope, by any means. While Queen Ra was gloating over her prisoners, the Scarecrow's famous brains were hard at work. Suddenly, it occurred to the straw man that Ozma and Glinda were to return to the Emerald City at ten o'clock this morning. It was almost that time now. If only he could engage the wicked Queen in conversation until Ozma and Glinda appeared, then the Royal Ruler and the Good Sorceress might take their enemies by surprise. The Scarecrow was confident that Ozma would be able to deal with these usurpers to her throne.

With this plan in mind, the Scarecrow cried out in a bold voice, "I demand to know what you have done with Dorothy and the Wizard!" When he had witnessed the peculiar manner in which the gaudily plumed birds had assumed the shapes of his human friends in the garden, the Scarecrow had first suspected that these creatures were responsible for the disappearance of Dorothy and the Wizard. Then the sight of Dorothy's Magic Belt about the waist of the big woman had convinced him of the truth of his suspicions.

Queen Ra answered the Scarecrow with a scornful laugh. "You are quite brave, my blustering, straw-stuffed dummy, but your braveness will do you no good. As for your Princess Dorothy and the man who calls himself a wizard, you will never see them again. Furthermore," the Queen went on, "as soon as I have suitable disposed of you and the rest of these animated creatures and beasts, I will use the Magic Belt to transport the helpless bodies of all the Oz people in the Emerald City to Mount Illuso, where they will share the same fate as your Dorothy and her wizard friend."

In spite of the assurance with which she spoke, the evil Queen was uneasy when she recalled the disappearance of Dorothy and the Wizard from the Cave of the Doomed. Had she underestimated the Wizard's powers of magic? Queen

Ra shrugged this thought from her mind. What had she to fear from two mere mortals? What had she to fear from anyone now? The Emerald City was hers, and Oz was as good as conquered!

"Do not heed the threats of this wicked woman!" the Scarecrow called to his captive companions. "She is boasting too soon!"

At these words Queen Ra turned angrily upon the Scarecrow. "Enough of your insolence, miserable wretch!" she cried. "I will show you who is boasting. Since you dare challenge me, I will destroy you immediately!" Her eyes flashing with rage, Queen Ra leaped from the throne and moved toward the Scarecrow. When she was about six feet from him, Ra paused and muttered an incantation. Instantly dancing flames of fire leaped from the marble floor of the throne room, making a circle around the Scarecrow. With a smile of satisfaction, Queen Ra resumed her place on Ozma's throne to enjoy the spectacle in comfort.

The dancing circle of fire moved swiftly inward. As the blazing circle grew smaller in circumference, the flames leaped ever higher and closer to the helpless Scarecrow, who stood in the circle's exact center. The leaping fire had moved so close to the Scarecrow that it almost scorched his stuffed clothing. The friends of the Scarecrow watched in horror. Prisoners themselves, there was nothing they could do to save their old comrade from this terrible fate.

Whish! There was a sudden rush of air, and in the center of the throne room stood Princess Ozma and Glinda the Good on the exact spot from which they had vanished three days before. Ozma swept the throne room with a glance that instantly comprehended the Scarecrow's great danger. In another moment her old friend would be reduced to a pile of smoldering ashes. Quick as a flash, the little Princess pointed her fairy wand at the flames that were licking the straw man's boots. While the onlookers blinked, the flames vanished. A long sigh of relief went up from the Scarecrow's friends.

Queen Ra was glaring with terrible rage at the Royal Ozma, who advanced calmly toward the wicked Queen with an expression of stern dignity on her girlish features. "Who are you, and what are you doing on my throne?" Ozma asked.

"Your throne no longer!" replied Ra harshly. "For you are no longer ruler of the Land of Oz. Instead you are my prisoner, and soon I will make it impossible for you to interfere with my plans as you have just done."

The stately Glinda spoke now, her voice grave and thoughtful. "I believe I know who you are," she said. "You must be the Queen of the evil Mimics. I have read about you in my Great Book of Records."

"If this is true," said Ozma sorrowfully, "then your Mimic hordes are these creatures who so closely resemble my own beloved subjects, while the true Oz people are robbed of the power of motion by your evil spell."

"Good!" sneered Ra. "I am glad you understand everything so well. You have not a friend in the Emerald City to aid you. Every one of your subjects in the city is a victim of the Mimic magic. Soon this will be true of all the Land of Oz. I am sure you will agree with me," Queen Ra went on mockingly, "that it is only fair and just that you should share your subjects' fate. Indeed, I know you are so foolishly loyal that you would not escape and leave your people to suffer, even if you could. So King Umb and I, ourselves, will oblige you by making it possible for you to join your beloved subjects. Owing to your high rank as the two most powerful persons in the Land of Oz, we will do you the honor of taking your shapes."

Concluding this triumphant speech, Queen Ra grinned with malicious satisfaction and said gloatingly, "At last the Royal Ozma and the Great Glinda bow to a power greater than their own! Come," she called to King Umb, "you take the form of Glinda, I will take that of Ozma." With this, the Mimic Monarchs advanced on Ozma and Glinda. The little Ruler and Glinda the Good were silent. Both realized that Queen Ra had spoken the truth when she had declared their powers to be useless against the Mimics. Therefore the girl Ruler and the Sorceress made no effort to combat their enemies, but stood bravely and proudly awaiting their fate.

At that very moment when King Umb and Queen Ra were about to seize the shadows of Ozma and Glinda, a small, black form streaked with the speed of light from underneath Ozma's throne straight to the menacing figures of the Mimic King and Queen. It was Toto! With fierce growls and barks, he began worrying and snapping at the ankles of the Mimic Monarchs. The sudden attack of the little dog and his desperate attack took Ra and Umb completely by surprise. For a moment they entirely forgot Ozma and Glinda and devoted all their efforts to freeing themselves from the snapping jaws of the furiously snarling little dog.

This respite which Toto had so bravely won saved Ozma and Glinda from sharing the fate of their subjects. A few seconds after Toto's attack, there suddenly appeared in the entrance of the throne room three figures, two of whom the Scarecrow joyfully recognized as Dorothy and the Little Wizard. They were accompanied by a maiden who was unknown to the Scarecrow, but whose beauty was quite evident. For an instant the trio stood in the doorway surveying the strange scene that met their eyes in Ozma's Royal Throne Room.

Chapter 19 ~ Ozana's Fairy Arts

Swiftly Princess Ozana — for the maiden was she — advanced to the center of the throne room. She was followed closely by the Wizard and Dorothy, who bore in her arms the sleeping form of a tiny white kitten. At the appearance of Dorothy, Toto stopped worrying the ankles of King Umb and Queen Ra and ran to meet the little girl. So happy was the excited little dog to see his beloved mistress that he even ignored the presence of the sleeping kitten. Dorothy knelt and caressed him.

Meanwhile, Queen Ra, recognizing Ozana, paled and gasped, "The Guardian of Oz!"

"Yes," admitted Ozana calmly, "it is I, Princess Ozana."

King Umb was so terrified at the appearance of the little maiden that the big fellow's knees knocked together, and his face turned a sickly, green hue. But it cannot be said that Queen Ra lacked courage. After the first shock of Ozana's appearance, the Queen summoned her spirits and faced the fairy maid defiantly. Ra had determined not to give up her triumph without a struggle. Clasping her palms to Dorothy's Magic Belt, the Mimic Queen whispered a command to it. But nothing happened. Ozana divined what the Queen was about, but she only smiled. In a rage, Queen Ra tore the useless belt from her waist and flung it to the throne room floor.

"You should know better," Ozana gently chided the infuriated Queen, "than to attempt to work such simple magic on me. Even if you had succeeded in transforming me into a wooden doll, I would still have retained my fairy powers and been able to defeat you."

Fright and realization that she was defeated mingled in Queen Ra's eyes as she stared at Ozana. The unhappy Queen said not a word. She sat spellbound, gazing with fearful fascination at the serene features of her girlish opponent.

Ozana was speaking with an air of calm justice. "Because I appeared absorbed in my own occupations," she addressed Queen Ra, "you counted me harmless. You believed I would be unaware of your evil-doing. You thought you could attack Oz without my knowing it. But you were wrong. And now the time has come for me to fulfill the trust placed in me by Queen Lurline when she made me Guardian of Oz. At that time she imparted to me the same powers over the race of Mimics that only she, of all fairies, possesses. I shall use those powers as Queen Lurline would wish me to. I shall place her enchantment once more on the Mimics so that they will be powerless to steal the shapes of all who dwell in the Land of Oz. At the same time, the re-weaving of this fairy enchantment will release all those Oz people whose shapes are now held by the Mimics."

As Ozana completed this speech, she described a large circle in the air before her with her fairy wand. Immediately that space was filled with a silvery, cloud-like radiance that glowed and shimmered. Then, while Ozma and the rest watched, a scene appeared in the cloud of silver mist. Dorothy and the Wizard recognized it as the interior of the Mimic cavern inside hollow Mount Illuso. Far in the top of the cavern they saw a scarlet spider web, in the center of which squatted a huge crimson spider. While those in the throne room watched with fascinated interest, the spider, seeming to sense that it was being observed, scuttled with a sudden, crablike motion to the outer edge of the web. There it squatted, its eyes glowing like dull red coals.

With the tip of her wand, Ozana touched the head of the image of the spider. Instantly the creature leaped into the air and trembled convulsively as though it had received an electric shock. Then it began slowly to dissolve before their eyes. First its legs wilted, grew shapeless and melted away. Next, its body collapsed inwardly, like an over-ripe melon, finally shriveling and disappearing altogether.

Now the spellbound spectators in the throne room saw a spot of silver light appear on the outermost strand of the crimson web. The light raced over every coil of the immense web, progressing swiftly to the web's center. As fast as the silver light flashed along the scarlet coils, they vanished. In a few seconds more not a trace remained of the vast web or its loathsome occupant. The point of cleansing silver light winked out; the image of the Mimic cavern faded; and the silver mist vanished from the throne room.

At this same instant, shouts of joy and exchanges of affectionate greetings rang through the Royal Palace and were echoed throughout the Emerald City. The sound of these happy voices told Princess Ozma that her beloved subjects were no longer under the spell of the Mimics. In the throne room itself, the Mimic Oz people who had bound the Scarecrow and his companions and brought them before King Umb and Queen Ra vanished. In their places stood Mimics in their variety of repulsive animal and bird shapes. While the startled Oz people watched, the Mimics flitted and shifted about the Royal Throne Room, changing their forms in the manner peculiar to these creatures.

But for the moment the Mimics were forgotten as all eyes were fastened with admiration and gratitude on Princess Ozana. Ozana smiled happily. "Queen Ra," she said, "you are now quite powerless to harm the people of Oz."

Queen Ra, who had watched Ozana's fairy magic with fascinated interest, knew she was utterly defeated. All her old arrogance and overbearing manner vanished. With bowed head she refrained from meeting the eyes of Ozana or those of any of her former victims.

Chapter 20 - In the Mirrored Ballroom

Now Ozma stepped forward. With happy tears of gratitude sparkling in her eyes, she grasped the hands of Princess Ozana. "How can I ever thank you for what you have done?"

Ozana seemed embarrassed. "The truth is," she admitted, "had I done my duty as Queen Lurline instructed and watched the Mimics more closely, the creatures would never have dared to invade Oz. I owe all of you my humblest apology for this neglect of duty. The least I could do," she added soberly, "was to right the wrongs already committed."

"Well," said Dorothy happily, "all's well that ends well, an' we think you're fine, Ozana."

"Thank you, my dear," smiled Ozana, affectionately stroking the little girl's hair.

"I think we owe Toto a great debt of gratitude," observed the wise Glinda. "Had it not been for the little dog's bravery, you and I, Ozma, would have undergone the unpleasant experience of becoming Mimic victims."

"You are right," agreed Ozma, turning to the dog. "I had not forgotten your brave action, Toto. Nothing Glinda and I can say or do will properly reward you. Nevertheless, I shall have made for you a handsome new collar studded with emeralds and bearing your name in gold letters as a slight token of our gratitude."

"Thank you, your Highness," said Toto shyly. "It was nothing, really. When I saw the big birds stealing the shapes of Trot and Betsy and Button Bright and all the others out in the garden, I was frightened, so I ran and hid under your throne. I could peep out and see everything that was going on, and when the Mimic King and Queen threatened you and Glinda I became so angry that I just forgot about everything else."

"Good dog!" said the Wizard, patting Toto's head. Dorothy beamed proudly at her little pet.

"Dear me!" exclaimed Ozma, gazing at the Mimics in the throne room. "How are we ever to transport all these creatures to their cavern home? We can't have them here to overrun Oz, even though they are now harmless," she added, shuddering with revulsion at the shifting shapes of evil assumed by the Mimics.

"That is simple," said Ozana. "Is there a room in the palace with a great many mirrors?"

"Yes," replied Ozma, "the Grand Ballroom which adjoins the throne room — its walls and ceiling are composed entirely of mirrors."

"Then let us go to the ballroom," said Ozana.

Ozma and Glinda led Ozana to the entrance of the Grand Ballroom. Dorothy and the Wizard and Toto followed. Ozana paused before the great door which was flung wide open. In her bell-like voice she murmured the words of a powerful fairy spell. Immediately King Umb and Queen Ra, followed by the other Mimics in the throne room, advanced as though they were in a trance to the portal of the mirrored ballroom. Then they passed into the room itself. Ozana continued to chant her fairy spell. Now came a whole procession of the Mimic creatures, first from all over the Royal Palace and finally from every part of the Emerald City. They came trooping in by the hundreds, wearing a myriad of fantastic shapes and forms. At length the very last Mimic had entered the ballroom, and huge though the room was, it seemed to the onlookers that it must surely be filled to overflowing with the Mimic horde.

By this time, the Scarecrow, Scraps, Tik-Tok and the rest who had been bound with ropes by the Mimics were freed, and they with Trot, Cap'n Bill, Betsy Bobbin, Button Bright and the others all crowded about the entrance to look curiously into the ballroom. Even the Cowardly Lion, the Hungry Tiger and Hank the Mule crowded into the throne room. The three beasts had awakened from the sleep cast on them by Queen Ra when Ozana had re-woven the spell that protected the Oz inhabitants.

"Why," rumbled the Cowardly Lion, "the room's empty!"

In a sense the lion was right. There was no one in the Grand Ballroom, it was true. But Dorothy and the others could plainly see the flitting, shifting shadow shapes of the Mimics in the mirrors that paneled the walls and ceiling of the great room — shadow creatures caught and confined in the depths of the mirrors!

"I wonder," Dorothy whispered, "what will become of them."

Chapter 21 - The Shattering of the Mirrors

"Now we can send the Mimics back to Mount Illuso at will," said Ozana in answer to Dorothy's question. "All we need to do is shatter the mirrors, and the Mimics will return to their gloomy realm, banished forever from Oz."

It was Ozma who followed Ozana's suggestion and brought about the breaking of the mirrors. The dainty ruler lifted her wand and murmured a fairy charm. Instantly every mirror in the Grand Ballroom shivered and shattered with a vast, tinkling sound. Not one of the scores of mirrors in the great chamber was left whole.

"It would be too bad," Ozana remarked, "to mar permanently the beauty of your lovely ballroom." She lifted her wand, and while the onlookers blinked the mirrors were whole again. In their gleaming depths there was no trace of the Mimic horde. The Grand Ballroom was as splendid as ever.

As it was now nearing noon, Ozma graciously invited Ozana to join her and Glinda with Dorothy and the Wizard, Aunt Em, Trot, Cap'n Bill, Betsy Bobbin, Button Bright, the Scarecrow, Scraps and others of her friends for luncheon in the dining room of her own Royal Suite.

Dorothy and the Wizard related their adventures on Mount Illuso, and then the Scarecrow tried to make clear to Ozma, Glinda and Dorothy and the Wizard everything that had happened in the Emerald City during their absence. Scraps helped him out, and Betsy Bobbin reminded him of things he had forgotten, while Trot chimed in and Button Bright wanted to tell the story his way. There was such a chatter it was a wonder Ozma and the rest understood anything.

Just as the meal was about to end, there was a knock on the door and Uncle Henry breathlessly entered the room. After Aunt Em and Dorothy had hugged and kissed Uncle Henry, Dorothy told him how she had got back to the Emerald City. (He had read an account of the rest of her adventures in Glinda's Great Book of Records the night before.) Scraps, helped out by Aunt Em, filled in the details of what had happened in the Palace since he and the Sawhorse had left.

When they had finished, Uncle Henry exhibited several sheets of paper closely filled with writing. "Here's the whole story of the Mimics. I copied everything the Great Book of Records had to say about 'em, and then I left Glinda's Castle last night, travelin' all night long so as to get here as early today as possible. But I guess," he concluded, gazing ruefully at the papers he carried, "these ain't much use anymore."

"Not one of us could have done better than you did, Uncle Henry," Ozma consoled him. "Instead of regretting your trip," she added wisely, "let us instead be grateful that there is no longer any need for us to concern ourselves with what the Great Book of Records has to say about the Mimics."

Glinda announced that she must return to her Castle in the Quadling Country, from which she had been absent too long. Bidding goodbye to all her friends, the Great Sorceress was transported in the twinkling of an eye by her magic art to her faraway Castle.

With Glinda's departure, the rest of Ozma's guests began to take their leave, until finally the Girl Ruler was alone with only Dorothy and Ozana. Ozma had noticed that throughout the merry luncheon, Ozana had appeared quiet and subdued, as though she were deeply occupied with thoughts of her own. "Tell me," Ozma said gently, taking Princess Ozana's hand in her own, "is there something troubling you, my dear?"

With a smile, Ozana replied, "Yes, Ozma, there is. Truthfully, I dread returning to lonely Mount Illuso. In the short time I have been privileged to enjoy the companionship of Dorothy and the Wizard, and the society of the Oz people here in the Emerald City, I have come to realize more than ever what a terribly lonely life I lead on Mount Illuso. And," she added, gazing affectionately at Dorothy, "I have become very fond of little Dorothy. I shall be very sorry indeed to leave her and all the rest of you for that forsaken mountaintop."

Ozma laughed softly. "Everyone loves our Princess Dorothy. But," and the Little Ruler's expression grew serious as she continued, "I sympathize with you, Ozana. Perhaps there is a way out of your predicament. Is there any real reason why you should return to Mount Illuso? The Mimics are harmless enough now. We can follow their actions in the Magic Picture and the Great Book of Records. And you can use your fairy powers to control the Mimics from the Land of Oz as easily as you could from the top of Mount Illuso."

"You mean—?" exclaimed Ozana eagerly.

"That we would like nothing better than to have you make your home here in the Land of Oz," said Ozma warmly. "Furthermore, it is my belief that through your long years of lonely vigil on Mount Illuso and your courageous rescue of the people of Oz from the Mimics, you have more than earned a home in Oz."

"Oh, Ozma, thank you!" exclaimed Ozana. And then she added doubtfully, "Do you think Queen Lurline will give her consent?"

"I see no reason why she should not," answered Ozma. "It so happens that I am to speak with Queen Lurline within the hour. We made arrangements to confer this afternoon on some important happenings in the great outside world. During our conversation I will ask her about your remaining in Oz."

"Thank you, Ozma," murmured Ozana. "I can't begin to tell you how grateful I am."

"Now, if you will excuse me," said Ozma, "I must prepare to establish communication with Queen Lurline."

Arm in arm, Dorothy and Ozana made their way to Dorothy's rooms, where they spent the next hour in conversation. Dorothy was well pleased with the prospect of Ozana's making her home in Oz, for she believed the Princess would be a delightful companion. At last there came a gentle rap on the door, and Princess Ozma entered Dorothy's room. Ozana and Dorothy rose to their feet and looked questioningly at Ozma.

"It is all settled," the Girl Ruler announced with her brightest smile. "Queen Lurline readily gave her consent. From this moment on, dear cousin, you are no longer Ozana of Mount Illuso, but Ozana, Princess of Oz."

Chapter 22 - What the Magic Picture Revealed

After the first happy excitement over Ozma's news had subsided, Ozana grew serious, and Dorothy thought she detected a note of sadness in the Fairy Maid's voice as she said, "There is one duty I must perform, Ozma, before I can begin my new existence as an inhabitant of your lovely fairyland."

"What is that?" asked Ozma.

"I must restore the pine folk and their village to their original forms as part of the Pine Forest that covers the top of Mount Illuso. Likewise, Story Blossom Garden must be returned to its original state, that is, ordinary wildflowers blossoming in the forest."

"Why must you do that?" asked Dorothy.

"Since I am not to return to Mount Illuso, the pine folk and the garden are left entirely to the mercy of the Mimics and other wicked creatures who dwell in the Land of the Phanfasms. Quick transformation of the mountaintop to its original state is far better than destruction of the village and the garden by creatures of evil."

Ozana's voice was tinged with real regret. "Ozma, may I look into your Magic Picture to see the garden and the village just once more before I cause them to vanish forever?"

Ozma made no reply other than to nod and lead the way to her boudoir, where hung the Magic Picture. Dorothy was mystified by the expression on the Little Ruler's face. She was sure Ozma was repressing a smile and was secretly amused at something.

On the way to Ozma's boudoir, Dorothy, who had grown fond of Felina the White Kitten, asked, "What about Felina, Ozana? Did you find her on Mount Illuso?"

"No, indeed," Ozana explained. "Felina accompanied me when I first went to Mount Illuso. She is my own pet. She is a fairy kitten and is as old as I am — and that is many hundreds of years."

Standing before the Magic Picture, Ozana said quietly, "I wish to see the Story Blossom Garden on Mount Illuso."

Instantly the Magic Picture's familiar country scene faded. In its place appeared not the lovely Story Blossom Garden, but a barren, desert waste. Even the blue pond had disappeared. There was no sign of any living thing in the dreary desert scene. "What can it mean?" Dorothy cried. "Ozma, do you think something's gone wrong with the Magic Picture?"

Ozana paled slightly, and her eyes were troubled as she spoke again, "I wish to see the Village of Pineville on Mount Illuso."

This time the Magic Picture shifted only slightly to show a second expanse of grey wasteland as gloomy and forbidding as the first. "They are gone," cried Ozana in dismay. "The garden and the village are gone!"

To the amazement of Ozana and Dorothy, Ozma met their consternation by laughing merrily. "Of course they are gone," the Little Ruler said, "because they are here!"

"What do you mean?" asked Ozana.

"First of all," began Ozma, "you didn't think, did you, Ozana, that no matter how much we wanted you to make your home with us, we would ask you to sacrifice your lovely Story Blossom Garden and the quaint people of your Village of Pineville? Queen Lurline and I discussed this matter seriously and agreed we could not permit the garden and the village to be destroyed. So after I finished my conversation with Queen Lurline, I consulted a map of the Land of Oz prepared by Professor Woggle Bug and found just what I was looking for — a small mountain in the Quadling Country only a short distance to the south from the Emerald City and not far from Miss Cuttenclip's interesting village. The top of this mountain was about the same in area as the top of Mount Illuso, and it was an uninhabited, sandy waste. While you and Dorothy talked, I worked a powerful fairy spell that transported the Pine Forest, the Village of Pineville and the Story Blossom Garden to the Oz mountaintop. Hereafter that mountain will be known as Story Blossom Mountain. That is why my Magic Picture showed only a desert waste when you asked to see the pine village and the Story Blossom Garden on Mount Illuso. The Magic Picture couldn't show them to you on Mount Illuso, for they are no longer there! Instead," Ozma concluded, "they are here in the Land of Oz." Turning to the Magic Picture, she said, "I wish to see Story Blossom Garden on Story Blossom Mountain."

The image of the desert waste faded, and in the frame of the Magic Picture appeared the beautiful fairy garden. The vision was so real that Dorothy could almost hear the blossoms whispering among themselves. Bright tears of joy and gratitude sparkled in Ozana's violet eyes.

"What happened to Hi-Lo and his elevator?" Dorothy asked.

"They were transported, too," replied Ozma quickly. "I imagine," the Girl Ruler went on, "that Hi-Lo will be a very busy little man carrying visitors up and down in his elevator. And you, Ozana, will be able to live in your pretty cottage and work in your wonderful garden without fear of ever becoming lonely. Every day will bring you visitors from the Emerald City and all parts of the Land of Oz who will be eager to see the pine folk and their village and to enjoy Story Blossom Garden. Really, Ozana, it is we who are indebted to you," Ozma concluded.

Dorothy beamed lovingly at Ozma. Then, turning to Ozana, the little girl said, "Now I guess you understand, Ozana, why you're just about the luckiest person in the whole world to be invited to live in the Land of Oz."

Chapter 23 - The Grand Banquet

The next day was given over entirely to welcoming Ozana to Oz. Early in the morning, the Sawhorse was hitched to the Red Wagon, and a merry company of travelers rode out of the Emerald City to be the first visitors to Story Blossom Mountain. In the front seat of the Red Wagon rode Ozma, Ozana, Dorothy and Trot. In the rear seat were Betsy Bobbin, Cap'n Bill, the Wizard and the Scarecrow.

The Sawhorse needed no reins to guide him, as this intelligent horse responded to spoken commands. Being tireless and having no need for oats or water, he was in many ways superior to ordinary horses. As the Red Wagon pulled up near the entrance to Hi-Lo's elevator, the party was met by flaxen-haired Miss Cuttenclip. Not far distant was a pretty little paper village of paper people ruled over by Miss Cuttenclip, who had skillfully cut out the entire village and all its inhabitants from "live" paper furnished her by Glinda the Good. Ozma had communicated with Miss Cuttenclip before the journey, inviting her to meet them and visit Story Blossom Mountain and afterwards to accompany them to the Emerald City for the Grand Banquet to be given that evening in Ozana's honor. Ozana and Miss Cuttenclip became friends at once.

Hi-Lo greeted Ozana and the rest joyfully, but it was necessary for him to make two trips to carry this large party to the mountaintop. Ozana showed the visitors around the Village of Pineville and Story Blossom Garden. On the surface of the blue pond floated the three swans. Knowing that Ozana would no longer need them to carry her back to Mount Illuso, Ozma had thoughtfully transported the swans from the courtyard of her palace to their pond when she had worked the fairy spell that had brought the Story Blossom Garden to Oz.

After pausing several happy hours in the Story Blossom Garden, Ozana and her guests returned to the bottom of the mountain, where the Sawhorse and the Red Wagon waited to carry them back to the Emerald City. The rest of the day was devoted to preparing for the Grand Banquet to be given in Ozana's honor that evening in the Grand Dining Room of the Royal Palace. All of Ozma's old friends and companions were invited.

Late in the afternoon the guests began arriving. The Tin Woodman journeyed from his glittering Tin Castle in the Winkie Country. Jack Pumpkinhead left his house — a huge, hollowed-out pumpkin in the middle of a pumpkin field. The Highly Magnified and Thoroughly Educated Woggle Bug traveled from the Royal Athletic College of Oz, of which he was Principal. Among other guests who came from great distances were Glinda the Good, the Giant Frogman, Cayke the Cookie Cook, Dr. Pipt — the Crooked Magician who was no longer crooked or a magician — his wife, Margolotte, the Good Witch of the North, and Lady Aurex, Queen of the Skeezers.

Dorothy transported all of these visitors to the Emerald City by means of her Magic Belt, except Glinda, who arrived by her own magic. The Grand Banquet proved to be one of the most brilliant and delightful occasions ever to be enjoyed in the Emerald City and was long remembered by all who were present. In addition to the delicious food, there was music and special entertainment for the guests. The Scarecrow made a gallant speech of welcome to which Ozana charmingly replied.

The Woggle Bug could not be restrained from reading an "Ode to Ozana," which he claimed he had composed on the spur of the moment, writing it on the cuff of his shirt sleeve. A number of the guests thought the composition sounded suspiciously like an "Ode to Ozma," which the Woggle Bug had written some years before, but they were all too kind-hearted to mention this. The Tin Woodman sang a love song, which he had written especially for the occasion and which he had titled "You're My Tin Type." While the song was only moderately good, the Tin Woodman sang in a metallic tenor with great feeling, and the company applauded politely.

Then the Little Wizard made them all gasp with a truly wonderful display of magic. The Wizard opened his show by causing a fountain of many-colored flames of fire to appear in the center of the banquet table. At his command, streamers of fire of different colors — red, green, blue, rose, orange, violet — leaped out from the burning fountain to touch the unlighted candles that stood at the place of each guest. After this the fountain of fire vanished, while the now-lighted candles continued to burn throughout the banquet, each shedding the light imparted to it by the colored fire.

The Wizard concluded his entertainment by tossing a napkin into the air above the banquet table. Instantly the napkin disappeared, and a storm of confetti showered down on the guests, while band after band of what appeared to be brightly colored paper ribbon fell over the party. But it didn't take Button Bright long to discover and announce with shouts of glee to the rest of the guests that the confetti and the many-colored paper ribbons were really the most delicious of spearmint, peppermint, clove, licorice, lime, lemon, orange and chocolate candies and mints. This, of course, provided the perfect ending for the dinner.

At the table occupied by the animals, there was a great deal of talking and merrymaking. Toto received many compliments on his handsome new red leather collar, embellished with clusters of emeralds and his own name in solid gold letters. Princess Ozma herself had fitted the collar about the proud little dog's neck that very afternoon as a tribute to Toto's loyalty and bravery.

Just as the happy banquet was about to end, Toto, who had been so absorbed in all the excitement and the Wizard's marvelous tricks that he had scarcely tasted his food, turned to his bowl of milk. He found the tiny White Kitten Felina daintily lapping the last of the milk from the bowl with her little pink tongue. Toto sniffed. "I never could understand," he growled, "what it is that witches and fairies and little girls see in cats!"

The End

The Shaggy Man of

by Jack Snow

Chapter 1 - The Twins Look In

"It just isn't fair," declared Tom, staring unhappily through the window at the heavy rain pelting the lawn and garden about the house.

"Well, there's nothing we can do about it, so we might as well make the best of it," replied Twink philosophically.

"But I wanted to go outdoors and play this afternoon. You know we have only a few more weeks until school starts. Besides, I'm sick and tired of this old house and of every single thing we have to play with."

Almost as if he understood Tom's words, Twoffle, the children's wooden clown, tumbled over on his head in the corner where he had been standing neglected. "Now look what you've done! You've hurt Twoffle's feelings," accused Twink reprovingly as she hastened to stand the funny little clown erect again in his corner of the room.

Twink was especially fond of Twoffle. The little wooden clown with his hinged joints and gaudily painted features and clothing had been a part of their lives almost as long as Twink could remember. He had taken part in many of their games, and being constructed of a fine grade of durable wood he had outlasted many other more fragile toys that had come and gone.

Twink and Tom were twins. They lived in a large, comfortable house in the city of Buffalo, New York, with their Mother and Father and Rosie the cook. This afternoon the house was very quiet. Twink's and Tom's father, Professor Jones, was at work at the University, where he taught young people all about electrons, atoms, molecules, and other mysterious matters. Mrs. Jones was attending a meeting of her Club of Lady Voters. Rosie, the cook, dozed in her warm kitchen, nodding over the latest issue of a fashion magazine.

So it was no wonder the twins were a bit lonesome. The rain streamed down the window monotonously, and it seemed the afternoon would drag on forever. Twink glanced at the clock on the mantel. It was a little Dutch cottage clock, and the hands indicated it was almost three o'clock. Twink was struck with a sudden idea. "Come on, Tom!" she called. "Look at the time. If we don't hurry, we'll miss Chapter Four of Buffalo Bill Rides Again!"

Tom came to life immediately, and in an instant both children were dashing down the broad stairway and into the library. Here was the solution to their dull afternoon: a television set that Professor Jones had built himself and installed in the library. It was a very special set with a large "projection screen." The glass tube of the television set enlarged the picture on the screen. At three o'clock each afternoon Twink and Tom could see another chapter in the exciting moving picture serial of the wild west. The children were sure, of course, that Buffalo Bill had been named after their own city, and this made the picture all the more interesting.

Tom was busily turning knobs and dials and making adjustments. In a few seconds the big screen lighted up with a bluish-green glare, and a moment later the pictures appeared. Buffalo Bill was ambushed by a wildly howling mob of Redskins who were on the warpath. There was no doubt in Twink's and Tom's minds that the famous scout would emerge unharmed, while the Indians would take to noisy flight.

But just as Buffalo Bill brought his rifle to his shoulder and was sighting the nearest Redskin, something happened. The flickering motion picture vanished from the television screen, and in its place appeared a picture that made the children gasp. It was one of the most beautiful scenes they could imagine: a peaceful, rolling meadowland bright with all kinds of wildflowers on which the sun shown down from a blue sky dotted with white, baby clouds. In the distance rose the spires and minarets of a great castle, glittering and glistening in the sun. But it was not the castle or the sunny meadowland that held the children's attention. Twink and Tom stared unbelievingly at a figure that stood in the center of the television picture looking out at them with the most familiar of smiles. It was Twoffle, their wooden clown.

Chapter 2 - On the Isle of Conjo

"Good afternoon, children," said the clown quite clearly and calmly.

"G-g-g-good afternoon!" stammered Twink and Tom.

The little clown suddenly doubled up with merriment and then gasped, "If you could only see yourselves! You're all eyes, positively bug-eyed if I ever saw anyone who was!"

"But what are you doing in the television picture?" asked Twink, regaining a little of her composure.

The clown disregarded her question and was suddenly serious. "Come on," he ordered. "Conjo can hold this picture only a few minutes, and you just have time to walk through."

"Walk through?" echoed Tom. "What do you mean?"

"Start walking toward the television screen and you'll find out," answered the clown. "Or perhaps," he added, "you would rather stay there where it is raining and you can't go outdoors."

"But you're only a picture," objected Twink.

"Will you please do as I tell you and start walking toward the television screen?" asked the clown sternly.

Twink and Tom looked at each other questioningly. Tom smiled and shrugged. "Might as well try it. Can't do any harm," he said.

"That's the spirit!" exclaimed the little clown, smiling again. "Just join hands and walk straight toward me." Tom took Twink's hand, and the two children slowly advanced toward the television screen. The screen was nearly five feet high — several inches taller than the children — and almost six feet wide. So vivid and real was the picture that Twink imagined she could really walk right into it. Just as the children were about to take the last step that would bring them directly in front of the television screen, a sudden powerful gust of wind hit their backs and sent them tumbling forward.

"This is where we'll catch it," thought Tom, sure that the wind must have blown them into the screen. He sat up, fully expecting to see the expensive screen torn to shreds. Instead he saw an expanse of rolling meadowland, and he felt the warm sun beating down on his head. Twink was sitting beside him on the green grass, staring about in utter bewilderment. Before them stood the clown, smiling broadly.

"It's magic," breathed Twink, "pure magic."

"Well, it's magic, all right," answered the clown, "but I wouldn't say how pure it is."

"But what has become of our library, and how did we get here, and how can this be real, and why is it you're not upstairs in my room?" The questions tumbled out almost faster than Twink could ask them.

"One question at a time, please," said the clown, "and I'll try to answer. Your library is right where it always is. This can be real because it is real. And I am not in your room because I belong here."

"But Twoffle," protested Tom, "we left you in Twink's room not fifteen minutes ago."

"You didn't leave me there, and don't call me Twoffle," objected the clown.

By this time Twink and Tom were standing up and brushing off their clothes. "But you are our Twoffle, you know," stated the girl. "We have had you for years and years."

"I am not your Twoffle — of all the silly names," said the clown with some irritation. "I am my own Twiffle."

"Then how is it you look so much like our Twoffle?" asked Tom, who noted the clown was the same size as Twoffle and looked like his double.

"I was about to tell you," exclaimed the clown, "that my name is Twiffle, and Twoffle is my third cousin."

"Oh, so then you know Twoffle?" asked Twink curiously.

"Know him?" replied Twiffle. "Of course I know him. And I also know you two very well. Many nights Twoffle and I have sat in your rooms with the moonlight streaming through the window and talked by the hour while you children slept."

Twink and Tom said nothing. They were busy thinking. All this was so strange and had happened so unexpectedly and suddenly that they were still bewildered. Tom's eyes were puzzled as he asked, "Just before we came through the screen, you said something about Conjo being able to `hold the picture for only a few minutes.' Who is Conjo?"

Twiffle was suddenly alert. "That reminds me," he said, "that we must be on our way at once. Conjo is expecting you, and we musn't keep him waiting." Without another word, Twiffle started walking across the grass. The children followed.

"But who is this Conjo, and where does he live?" asked Twink.

"And what does he want with us?" added Tom.

Without pausing to look at the children, Twiffle answered, "Conjo is a Wizard, the sole ruler of this island, the Isle of Conjo. He lives in the castle you can see in the distance. What he wants with you, he will undoubtedly tell you himself." With this, the little clown flashed Twink and Tom a bright smile and then walked steadily on toward the glittering castle.

Twink found that she had no trouble at all in keeping up with Twiffle, because his legs were so short and his stride so small. She had plenty of time to pause occasionally and gather the colorful wildflowers that dotted the green meadowland.

Chapter 3 - Omby Amby bears Bad News

"Ozma! Where is Ozma? I must see her at once — immediately!" The Soldier with the Green Whiskers had run all the way from the gates of the Emerald City of Oz to the Royal Palace with his whiskers streaming at least six feet behind him. Now that he had arrived at the palace, he was panting and wild-eyed with excitement.

"Whatever is the matter with you, Omby Amby?" asked Jellia Jamb, Ozma's dainty little maid, eyeing the distraught Guardian of the Gates with undisguised curiosity.

Omby Amby groaned. "Something terrible has happened. I must report it to Ozma at once."

"Can't you give me just an inkling of what it is?" coaxed Jellia.

"No," replied Omby Amby firmly. The Soldier, who was Ozma's Royal Army, was rapidly regaining his composure — and his breath — after his wild dash through the emerald-studded streets of the city.

"Well, then come along," replied Jellia Jamb with a sigh. "I suppose I shall have to wait for Ozma to tell me what has upset you so terribly." The little maid led the way down the corridors of the Royal Palace until she came to a large double door. Here she knocked, and a moment later Ozma's voice answered, "Come in."

Jellia Jamb opened the door, and the Soldier with the Green Whiskers followed her into the room. This was Ozma's library, where the shelves that rose from the floor to the ceiling were filled with Magic Books of Records. The little ruler of Oz was seated at a table, deep in the study of one of the books. She looked up questioningly as Omby Amby stood before her. Jellia Jamb silently departed, closing the door behind her.

"Your Highness," began Omby Amby, "it is my painful duty to report a most regrettable misfortune."

"What is it, Omby Amby," asked Ozma with a kindly smile. "What has happened?"

"It's the Love Magnet, your Highness," gulped the Soldier. "It's been broken!"

"Broken!" exclaimed Ozma, rising from her chair. "How could that ever have happened?"

"It was the nail," exclaimed Omby Amby miserably. "If your Highness will recall, the Love Magnet has been hanging from a nail over the Gates of the Emerald City for many years — in fact, ever since the Shaggy Man came to live in the Land of Oz."

"Yes, I know," said Ozma.

"Well," went on the Soldier, "the nail must have rusted, and this morning it snapped. The Love Magnet fell to the bricks of the Yellow Road and broke into two pieces."

Ozma's face was grave. "You brought the pieces with you?" she asked.

"Yes, your Highness, I did," replied Omby Amby. Delving into one of his pockets, he handed Ozma the two pieces of the Love Magnet, a small bit of metal shaped like a horseshoe when it was whole.

Ozma held the broken Love Magnet in her hand, regarding it sadly. "It is too bad," she said, "that so wonderful a charm should be broken."

"Do you mean it can't be repaired, your Highness?" asked Omby Amby.

"Of that I am not sure," replied Ozma. "Perhaps the first thing we should do is ask the Shaggy Man to come here and explain to him how the Love Magnet came to be broken, since it does, after all, really belong to him."

"I will go for him immediately," said the Soldier, turning to the door.

"You will find him in the garden with Dorothy and Jack Pumpkinhead, who is trying on a new head," said Ozma as Omby Amby made a low bow and closed the door behind him.

By luck, Ozma reflected, the Shaggy Man was in the Emerald City. She knew that Shaggy was fond of making long trips about the Land of Oz, exploring the little-known corners and regions of this most famous of all Fairylands. Now he had just returned from a visit with his brother, who was in the Gillikin Country. While she waited, Ozma recalled how the Shaggy Man had befriended Dorothy in the Great Outside World and had found his way to the Land of Oz in the company of little Dorothy. With him he had brought the Love Magnet, a curious magical talisman which caused whoever carried it to be loved by all he met. Shaggy had gratefully accepted Ozma's invitation to make his home in the Land of Oz, and since he had no further need for the Love Magnet, Ozma had caused it to be hung over the Gates of the Emerald City so that all who entered might be loving and loved.

Before she had done this, however, Ozma had wisely altered the powers of the Love Magnet so that the talisman did not automatically cause the person who carried it to be loved by all he met, but must be displayed by its carrier before the eyes of the person or persons whose love he wished to win. Thus, control of the powers of the Magnet were given to its owner. All this had happened so long ago that it was now duly written down in Professor Wogglebug's Chronicles of the Land of Oz.

Ozma's reflections were ended by the appearance of Omby Amby and the Shaggy Man, who had no idea that anything was the matter. "Dorothy said to tell you, your Highness, that it's one of the best heads Jack ever had," the Shaggy Man announced with satisfaction as he entered the room. "Dorothy's fitting it on Jack's body now."

"Won't you sit down, please, Shaggy Man?" invited Ozma.

The little Ruler's expression was so serious that the Shaggy Man asked with concern, "What is it, Ozma? What's wrong?"

Ozma answered silently by extending her palm in which lay the halves of the broken Love Magnet. The Shaggy Man's eyes clouded. "Oh, that is too bad. I was very fond of the Love Magnet. It always made me feel happy whenever I entered or left the Emerald City. How did it come to be broken?"

Ozma explained in a few words what had happened. "But can't the Love Magnet be repaired?" asked the Shaggy Man. "I should think it would be an easy matter for you or the Wizard or Glinda to put it together again as good as new."

"No," Ozma shook her head. "It isn't as simple as that. A long time ago I looked up the history of the Love Magnet in my Magic Record Books, and I found that, if broken, it could be made whole only by one person — the person who created it."

"And who," asked the Shaggy Man with deep interest, "is that?"

"It has been so long ago," admitted Ozma, "that I have forgotten who it was. But I can look it up in a few seconds."

Ozma moved to the far side of the library, where she selected one of the Magic Record Books and opened it on a table. After turning the pages until she found the one containing the Love Magnet's history, Ozma ran her finger down the finely printed column. "Here it is," she announced. "The man who made the Love Magnet and the only person who can repair it is a Wizard named Conjo, who lives on a tiny island in the middle of the Nonestic Ocean."

Chapter 4 - Ozma uses the Magic Belt

Omby Amby had returned to his post at the Gates of the Emerald City, and Ozma and the Shaggy Man had retired to the Chamber of Magic. Here were kept many of the most valuable magical instruments in all the Land of Oz. "There is only one thing to be done," the Shaggy Man was saying. "I must take the broken Love Magnet to this Conjo and ask him to repair it."

"I am not sure at all that Conjo will agree to repair the Love Magnet for you," Ozma replied with a troubled expression. "You see, we know very little about this Conjo. He lives alone on this tiny island in the middle of the Nonestic Ocean and practices magic. There is no record of his actually misusing his magical powers. Nor, so far as we know, has he caused trouble for anyone. However, we have reason to believe he is rather selfish and thoughtless and that he might cause harm without really meaning to, just to satisfy his vanity. Also, it might not suit his whim to mend the Love Magnet."

"What is the name of the island on which Conjo lives?" asked the Shaggy Man musingly.

"It is called the Isle of Conjo, and since it is many miles from the Land of Oz, I have no power over the Wizard at all. In fact," concluded Ozma, "that is the reason we here in the Land of Oz know so little about Conjo."

"Nevertheless," maintained the Shaggy Man, "I think I should go as soon as possible to this island and do everything I can to persuade Conjo to make the Love Magnet whole."

"Even after you crossed the Deadly Desert, you would have several days' journey through the Land of Ev, and then you would only be on the shores of the Nonestic Ocean. So I think it would be best, since you are determined to make the journey, for me to use the Magic Belt to transport you directly to the Isle of Conjo."

The Shaggy Man willingly agreed to this plan, stating that he was ready to leave at once. "First," said Ozma, "let us have a look at the Isle of Conjo in the Magic Picture. The girl Ruler swept aside the velvet curtain that hung over the Magic Picture when it was not in use. The picture appeared to be a peaceful country farmland scene with purple hills rising in the distance. "Show us the Isle of Conjo in the Nonestic Ocean," said Ozma.

Immediately the picture shifted and changed. It now reflected a gently rolling meadowland with a great castle in the distance. Approaching the castle were a young girl and a boy, accompanied by the figure of a wooden clown.

Ozma gasped in surprise. "Those are human children, Shaggy Man! What can they be doing there when my Magic Record Books state that Conjo is the only human being on the island? We can see that the clown accompanying them is a puppet, evidently brought to life by Conjo."

"Perhaps they are lost," ventured the Shaggy Man.

"But how would they get to the island? It is surrounded by miles and miles of ocean."

"I don't know," admitted the Shaggy Man, "but it is one more good reason for me to go there as quickly as possible — those children may be in need of help."

"I agree with you," said Ozma quickly. "You must find out what the children are doing on the island and see that they are returned to their homes. If you cannot do that, then you must bring them with you to the Land of Oz."

"Will you use the Magic Belt to transport us back to the Land of Oz?" asked the Shaggy Man.

"That will be impossible," stated Ozma, "since I must leave this afternoon to visit Glinda the Good. We are working on some extremely important magic charms in which the powers of the Magic Belt are needed. I am not sure how long I will be gone — perhaps for several weeks. However," Ozma went on as she stepped to a heavy wooden chest, opened one of its drawers and withdrew a small object, "I want you to take this with you. It will enable you to return to the Land of Oz anytime you wish."

"What is it?" asked the Shaggy Man curiously.

"It is a Magic Compass," explained Ozma. "You will notice that it is not round in shape like ordinary compasses, but is formed like a rectangle, as is the Land of Oz."

Shaggy looked at the Magic Compass and found that instead of being marked North, South, East and West as is the usual compass, it bore the words Gilliken, Quadling, Winkie and Munchkin, which are the four countries makin
g up the Land of Oz.

"Should you wish to return to any one of the four countries," Ozma went on, "just set the compass needle to the one to which you wish to journey. If you want to come directly to the Emerald City, you have only to spin the needle of the compass and you will be here as quickly as the Magic Belt could bring you."

The Shaggy Man inspected the Magic Compass more closely and found that the pivot on which the needle rested rose from a spot of green in the very center of the compass. This green spot he knew represented the Emerald City. "But what about the children?" the Shaggy Man asked. "If I can find no way to send them home, I cannot simply leave them on the island."

"Of course not," replied Ozma. "If you think it necessary to bring them to Oz with you, just have them put their arms in yours; then spin the compass needle, and all three of you will be transported to the Emerald City."

The Shaggy Man placed the Magic Compass carefully in his pocket and said, "Perhaps it would be well for me to be on my way. There's no way of telling what will happen on that island, and those two children may need help."

Ozma slipped on the Magic Belt. "Goodbye, dear friend," she said, smiling fondly at the Shaggy Man. "Return as quickly as you can." Then she made the magic signal, and the Shaggy Man was no longer in the Chamber of Magic.

Chapter 5 - The Castle of Conjo

"Hello!" Twink, Tom and Twiffle stopped in their tracks. From out of nowhere had suddenly appeared a man of medium height with rosy cheeks, twinkling blue eyes, shaggy hair and clothing that, while it was composed of the finest silks and satins, was nevertheless a mass of shags and bobtails.

Twiffle was so surprised he found it impossible to speak. Twink was regarding the stranger seriously. Suddenly, recognition lighted up her eyes. "Oh, it can't be!" the little girl cried. "You just can't be the famous Shaggy Man of Oz!"

The Shaggy Man smiled. "Don't know about the famous part, but I am known as the Shaggy Man, and until a few seconds ago I was in the Land of Oz."

"Oh! Seeing you here made me think maybe this was a part of the Land of Oz," said Twink, who had begun to hope since the moment she had recognized the Shaggy Man.

Tom was regarding the new arrival curiously. "Yes," he said, "you certainly do look just like your pictures in the books. How did you get here so fast? Magic? I suppose the Land of Oz is quite a distance."

"Right both times!" replied the Shaggy Man. "Ozma sent me here with her Magic Belt, and the Land of Oz is many miles away from here."

"Why did Ozma send you?" asked Twink.

"Oh, I have a little business with this Conjo fellow," answered the Shaggy Man.

"You have business with Conjo?" Twiffle had recovered from his astonishment. "Then you must forgive me for not greeting you more properly. It is so seldom that we have visitors on the island."

"Looks like you already have two visitors," observed the Shaggy Man, staring at Twink and Tom.

"Yes, but they were expected — and invited," pointed out Twiffle primly. "However, since you have business with Conjo and we are on our way to see him, there is no reason you should not accompany us."

"No reason whatsoever," agreed the Shaggy Man. "I hope this Conjo has plenty of big, red apples."

"Why?" asked Tom.

"They happen to be my favorite food, that's all," explained the Shaggy Man.

Led by Twiffle, the Shaggy Man and the two children were advancing over the meadow toward the Castle of Conjo. The sun was now setting, burnishing the spires and turrets of the castle with rich hues of gold and copper. The Shaggy Man judged they had less than a mile to travel to the castle doors. "Don't you children think introductions are in order," asked the Shaggy Man, "since you seem to know me already?"

"Well," Twink began, "this is Twiffle, who is a third cousin of Twoffle." Twiffle bowed briefly, and the Shaggy Man nodded. "And this is Tom, and I am Twink. We live in Buffalo."

"Wait a minute," interrupted the Shaggy Man. "How did you happen to get a name like Twink?"

"Twink and Tom are not our real names," explained Tom. "Our parents named us Abbadiah and Zebbidiah."

"Why did they do that?" asked the Shaggy Man indignantly.

"Well," Tom went on, "they didn't expect twins — we are twins, you know

— and they couldn't make up their minds what to name us. So they just picked names at the beginning and end of the alphabet. That's how we came to be named from A to Z."

The Shaggy Man sighed. "And then," Twink went on, "I began to toddle when I was supposed to be still crawling, and everyone called me Twink, because I got from one place to another in a twinkle. Tom got his nickname in a funny way, too."

"I have always been interested in everything mechanical and electrical," explained Tom, "so when I was only two years old and took my toy phonograph apart to see where the little men and women who made the talking and music were, my Father said, `Why, you're a regular Tom Edison.' And so ever since then I have been Tom."

"At least they are better than those other names," said the Shaggy Man.

Conjo's castle loomed even larger, casting lengthening shadows as the sun lowered behind it. In a few more minutes Twiffle had led them to a large door that was evidently the entrance of the castle. Hanging on the door was a sign which Twink, Tom and the Shaggy Man read.

CASTLE OF CONJO
WORKING WIZARD

"This way, please," said Twiffle. The door opened at his touch, and they entered. All they could see was a vast corridor with doors on each side. At the end of the corridor was a handsome marble staircase that wound up to the upper floors. Twiffle's little wooden feet pattered busily down the polished marble floor of the corridor until he came to an arch-shaped doorway upon which hung the sign:

QUIET!
Wizard at Work

As they passed before this door with its strange admonition, the Shaggy Man and his friends heard a sound that reminded them of a buzz-saw. "I wonder," ventured Twink, "if Conjo is building some new magical machine."

Twiffle disregarded the little girl's question and proceeded to push the door, which opened as easily as had the door of the castle.

Inside they found a vast, domed room. All around the sides of the room was a series of tables, workbenches, and tall cabinets. The tables and benches were filled with every kind of chemical instrument imaginable — beakers, retorts, test tubes, hundreds of bottles of different kinds of colored liquids, crucibles, and a series of burners over which simmered vials and pots of chemical mixtures. From these rose vari-colored vapors, filling the room with a pungent haze. The cabinet shelves were crowded and jumbled with thousands of containers of various powders, ointments, and mixtures used by wizards in working their magic spells. One cabinet contained nothing but books of magic recipes and formulas — everything from changing people into doorknobs to curing headaches.

The Shaggy Man and the children had scarcely glanced at all this array of tools and materials for working magic when their attention was drawn to a huge divan that rested in the very middle of the marble floor of the great chamber. This luxurious divan was covered with the softest and most expensive of rich velvet robes and comforts. Curled up in a ball in the midst of the blankets and downy, satin-covered cushions was a little man. He was snoring.

Twink almost laughed aloud. So this was Conjo, the working Wizard! She realized now it was Conjo's snoring they had mistaken for the sound of a buzz-saw. Twiffle seemed neither surprised nor disturbed to find his master sound asleep. The little clown trotted over to the handsome divan and, seizing Conjo by the shoulders, shook him vigorously. The Shaggy Man was grinning broadly, and Tom was holding a hand over his mouth to suppress his laughter.

Sputtering and yawning, Conjo sat up on the divan. Since he was rubbing the sleep out of his eyes with his knuckles, he did not see his guests for several seconds. Then he blinked, yawned widely, and smiling a little foolishly said, "Well, wiz my wand if it isn't Twink and Tom."

"You already know us?" asked Twink.

"Oh, goodness yes," replied Conjo, stretching lazily. "Twiffle has been telling me about you for years — ever since you were mere babies. I let Twiffle visit your friend Twoffle in your home, you know. Send him there by my magic," explained Conjo proudly.

Conjo was coming more awake every minute. "Jumping June Bugs!" he exclaimed as his eyes fell on the Shaggy Man. "I didn't tell Twiffle to bring your Father along — or is this person your Grandfather?"

"Neither one," said the Shaggy Man with an amused smile. "Your magic had nothing to do with my coming here, Conjo. I came of my own accord."

"Came from where?" demanded Conjo, and then went on before the Shaggy Man had a chance to answer, "You were shipwrecked — that must be it, of course — you are a poor, forlorn castaway, a helpless victim of the deep and mighty ocean."

"No," contradicted the Shaggy Man, "I was not shipwrecked. I came here from the Land of Oz."

Conjo started. "The Land of Oz!" he exclaimed incredulously. "You mean the Emerald City, Ozma, Dorothy, the Scarecrow, the Tin Woodman, Scraps, Toto—" and then, because he was out of breath, the Wizard concluded weakly, "and all of that?"

"I see you have heard of the Land of Oz," said the Shaggy Man, "so perhaps you will know why I am here."

Conjo, who was a fat, bald little man not much taller than Twink or Tom, with a fringe of white hair about his pink head, closed his little eyes, placed a forefinger on his cherry-like nose, and thought hard. "You will just have to tell me," he said, opening his eyes and staring appealingly at the Shaggy Man. "I don't have a single idea. It usually takes several hours after I wake up before I get any ideas — and it is so seldom that we have shipwrecks."

"I told you," the Shaggy Man reminded Conjo patiently, "that I was not shipwrecked. I came here from the Land of Oz to ask you to do me a favor."

"A favor?" said Conjo, thinking hard. "Why, that is strange indeed! The last shipwrecked person who was here wanted me to do him a favor, too. He stayed several months and then wanted to return to his home. He asked me to make a boat for him. That was an easy trick. And because the fellow wasn't a bad sort at all, I made him a present — I gave him one of my newest creations, the Love Magnet."

"The Love Magnet," gasped the Shaggy Man.

"Don't interrupt, please," went on Conjo. "Not polite, you know. This shipwrecked person tied the Love Magnet onto the mast of his boat and set sail. Last I ever saw of him. Understand he encountered a whale, who upon seeing the man and the Love Magnet, became so fond of the fellow that he ate him." Conjo wiped a tear from his eye.

The Shaggy Man wasn't sure whether the Wizard was serious or was poking fun at him. He decided to pretend, at any rate, that he accepted Conjo's absurd story, saying, "Well, apparently the unfortunate man's boat was blown ashore, and an Eskimo found the Love Magnet, for it was an Eskimo who gave it to me, and I took it to the Land of Oz."

"My Love Magnet in the Land of Oz!" exclaimed Conjo.

"No," replied the Shaggy Man, "not your Love Magnet, since you gave it away. It now belongs to all the people of the Land of Oz. That is why I am here now. The Love Magnet has been broken. The favor I ask you is to repair it, since you, its creator, are the only person who can do that."

Twink and Tom had been listening with deep interest to this conversation. They had read about the Love Magnet, and they were surprised to learn that it had been broken.

"Of course, of course, my dear Shaggy Man, for I perceive that is indeed who you are, a quite famous personage of the Land of Oz." Conjo was wide awake now. "I shall be most happy to mend the Love Magnet if it can be mended. But surely you don't expect me to do so important and difficult a feat of magic without, ah, er, let us say — a reward?"

Chapter 6 - The Magic Airmobile

"Yes, that's it," said Conjo, nodding his round head so violently that his three chins rippled like the steps of an escalator. "You have asked me to do you a favor — a very great favor — so it is only just that I should claim a reward. That's fair, isn't it?" Conjo was regarding the Shaggy Man with eyes from which was gone the somewhat foolish innocence.

The Shaggy Man considered uneasily. He was beginning to remember Ozma's warning that Conjo was not to be trusted entirely. "What kind of a reward could I give you?" the Shaggy Man asked.

Conjo's finger shot out, pointing toward the Shaggy Man. "That," he said. "That in your pocket will be my reward!"

Involuntarily, the Shaggy Man's hand went to the pocket in which rested the Magic Compass Ozma had given him. "You must be joking," said the Shaggy Man incredulously. "The Magic Compass belongs to Ozma. And if I did give it to you, how could I return to the Land of Oz? No, what you ask is impossible."

Conjo's voice was wheedling. "Surely you don't think Ozma expected me to repair the Love Magnet for nothing, do you? I can assure you that Ozma will regard the trading of the Magic Compass for the repair of the Love Magnet an excellent bargain. Actually, the Magic Compass is, by Ozma's standards, a minor bit of magic."

The Shaggy Man was perplexed. Perhaps Conjo was right. "Supposing I do give you the Magic Compass. Then how will I get back to Oz?"

Conjo's eyes glowed. "Nothing to it!" he declared. "You can return to Oz anytime you like. Just as soon as I repair the Love Magnet, if you wish. Of course, I would be happy should you care to remain my guest for a time, but the decision is entirely up to you."

"How do you propose that I return to Oz?" asked the Shaggy Man. "I can't walk across the Deadly Desert, you know."

"Ha, ha, ho, ho, ho!" Conjo laughed. "Walk across the Deadly Desert! Certainly not! He, he he! You shall sail high across it, swiftly and safely! Come with me! I have something to show you." Conjo wriggled about until his fat little body emerged from the cushions and silken coverings of the divan. As he stood up, the Shaggy Man and his friends saw that the little man was dressed in a loose robe of rich purple on which were embroidered stars, crescents, black cats and the signs of the Zodiac. All these designs were in the brightest colors, while the robe flowed about him, secured by a golden cord tied about his middle. On his feet were sandals woven of silver thread, with toes that curled up like question marks. "Come with me," repeated the fat little Wizard as he waddled to the door, "and I will show you how you can sail away in a jiffy."

The Shaggy Man and the two children followed Conjo while Twiffle remained behind busily arranging and straightening the royal cushions and comforters of the regal divan. In the great corridor Conjo paused before a small door that opened at his touch, revealing a cage-like little room. "Step in," the Wizard invited his guests. "This is an elevator that will whisk us to the roof of the tallest tower of the castle — an improvement over the stairway, up which I find it difficult to whisk myself in my present state of, shall we say, stoutness. Ho, ho, ho, ho, he, he, he!"

Conjo beamed good humor and friendliness as the elevator shot noiselessly upward. In a few seconds the door clicked, slid open, and Conjo led his guests to the roof of the great tower. From this height they could see that the Isle of Conjo was small indeed, for the blue waters of the Nonestic Ocean were visible in any direction they looked. The sun was a great red ball of fire in the west, but it would still be several minutes before actual twilight set in.

"And here," said Conjo, leading them across the roof, "is the means by which I propose you return to the Land of Oz." The Shaggy Man and the children saw before them a most curious object. It might have been the body of an automobile, except that it seemed to have neither front nor back. Both ends of it curled up like a gondola. Nor did it have wheels. The flat bottom rested solidly on the roof. To all appearances it had no means of locomotion. Conjo was regarding the strange object proudly. "Behold!" he said. "One of my most ingenious creations, the Airmobile!"

"You mean to say," the Shaggy Man sighed, "that this thing is actually supposed to fly through the air?"

Conjo looked hurt. "You see before you," he said resentfully, "the most perfect means of air travel yet invented."

Tom broke in, "But how can it fly? It has no wings, no propeller, no jets, nothing but places to sit down!"

Conjo regarded the boy pityingly. "Do you suppose I would rely upon such clumsy and inefficient means of flying as propellers, wings and jets? The Airmobile is the perfect flying machine. It repels gravity."

"It does what?" asked the Shaggy Man.

Conjo stepped to the machine and opened one of the doors. "Look," he said. "See these metal plates on the floor of the ship? They are gravity resistor plates. You must know," he went on patiently, "that it's the force of gravity pulling objects to the earth that causes things to have weight. Well, my gravity resistor plates overcome gravity when exposed. Hence the ship has no weight whatever."

"Yes," said Tom, "I can understand that. But what makes it move — backward and forward, I mean?"

"Oh, that," sniffed Conjo. "These are gravity resistor plates. They not only overcome gravity, but resist it. The power of resistance forces the machine upward. The more surface of the plates you expose, the higher you will go. And you will notice," Conjo continued, reaching inside the ship and pressing a button, "that the metal plates are mounted on rods through their middle so that they may be operated like flaps or fins — and they rotate. Thus, if you tilt them in one direction, the resistance to gravity forces you ahead in one way; tilt them in the other direction and you travel in the opposite way. Rotate them, and you can veer to right or left."

"If it works, it is wonderful," said the Shaggy Man doubtfully.

"Oh, it works to perfection," assured Conjo. "If it were not so late in the day, I would propose a little trip. As it is, I suggest that we go downstairs for dinner. Then I will have to leave you to examine the Love Magnet. We will all arise early in the morning, at which time you will have the pleasure of a journey over the island in my Airmobile."

Twink guessed that Conjo's dinner must have been prepared and served by magic, for there were no servants in the grand dining room into which their round little host ushered them. But the food was quite as elaborate and rich as the dining room itself. The Shaggy Man and the children were hungry, and they ate heartily. Even so, they could not help noticing that Conjo ate nearly twice as much as the Shaggy Man. Shaggy was gratified to find a large bowl of rosy-cheeked apples in the center of the table, which made the meal a perfect one for him.

Conjo sighed with content, wiping his lips on a fine damask napkin. "Inhospitable as it may seem," he apologized, "I must leave you now to see if the Love Magnet can be repaired. I will examine it in my laboratory and tell you tomorrow if it can be fixed. Please give me the Love Magnet."

This the Shaggy Man did, and Conjo waddled to the door, pausing to say, "Twiffle will show you to your rooms. I hope you sleep well. I know I shall, after I finish this work." Conjo was already yawning as he left the dining room.

A few seconds later Twiffle appeared in the doorway and invited Shaggy and the children to follow him. The sleeping rooms to which Twiffle led them up the marble stairway were on the second floor and were beautifully furnished with every convenience and comfort. Twink and Tom's room contained two inviting beds, and Twink noticed that pajamas of just the right size had been carefully laid out. Conjo seemed to think of everything.

"See you children in the morning," said the Shaggy Man as he entered his room which adjoined that of Twink and Tom. The Shaggy Man found his bed soft and luxurious, so he slipped off his shaggy clothes, carefully arranging them on a chair so that not one frill or furbelow was out of place, put on the pajamas which Conjo had also provided for him, and slipped into bed. Instantly the light faded from the room. More magic, thought the Shaggy Man a bit uneasily, for it had appeared to him that the light was an ordinary electric one which he might switch on and off at will. But moonlight was beginning to fall through the window, so the Shaggy Man sighed with content and in a minute was sound asleep.

It was several hours later when the Shaggy Man stirred and then sat up, wide awake. What had awakened him? He was sure he had heard a clicking sound, like the door of his bedchamber closing. The moonlight revealed that the door was closed just as he had left it. Shaggy glanced at his clothes on the chair. He leaped from bed and searched through the pockets of his clothing. He gave a gasp of dismay. The Magic Compass was gone!

What was this? In another pocket Shaggy found a hard, metallic object, the Love Magnet, perfectly repaired, with no trace of its ever having been broken. The Shaggy Man sat down on his bed and thought hard. What should he do? For some reason, Conjo had evidently entered the room, slipped the repaired Love Magnet into Shaggy's pocket, removed the Magic Compass, and left the room. It was the clicking of the door that Shaggy had heard. And Conjo had slightly disarranged Shaggy's clothes — that had called his attention to them.

What did all this mean? Shaggy was sure now that Conjo was not the jolly, straightforward person he pretended to be. Perhaps he was not exactly evil, either, but he was so vain and scheming and selfish that he would bear watching. Then a sudden thought struck Shaggy and made him extremely uneasy. He had come to the Isle of Conjo of his own accord to seek out Conjo. But it was Conjo himself who had brought Twink and Tom there. Why? Were the twins in danger? What was Conjo's purpose in taking them from their home? It was up to him, thought the Shaggy Man, to find out and protect them if Conjo meant them harm or had some crazy plan that would endanger them.

Shaggy unhappily concluded there was nothing he could do now. In the morning he would find out if the Airmobile was everything Conjo claimed. Then he would try to discover Conjo's plans for Twink and Tom. Perhaps Twiffle could enlighten him. Shaggy sighed. Well, at least he did have the Love Magnet.

The Shaggy Man lay down on the bed and tried to sleep. After a long time he drifted into a fitful slumber broken by dreams in which Conjo sailed through the air, clutching the Love Magnet, and Twink and Tom were transformed into dolls no larger than Twiffle. In his dream the Shaggy Man seemed to be bound with ropes to his bed, powerless to stop any of Conjo's mischief, while Twiffle tugged at his bonds saying, "Wake up, Shaggy Man, wake up!"

Shaggy opened his eyes and stared. There was Twiffle, at the side of his bed, shaking him and saying, "Wake up, Shaggy Man, wake up!"

Chapter 7 - Into Hightown

The Shaggy Man was awake in an instant. "What is it, Twiffle, what is wrong?"

"There is no time to lose," whispered Twiffle. "Quick, get into your clothes, and I will arouse the children."

Shaggy dressed as speedily as possible, but no sooner had he finished than Twiffle, followed by Twink and Tom, now wide-eyed with excitement and fully dressed, appeared in the doorway. "Come," Twiffle whispered.

Silently, Shaggy and the children followed Twiffle down the marble stairway to the elevator. The castle was not entirely dark, thanks to the bright moonlight flowing through the windows. They stepped into the elevator which had a dim light of its own. Once more it shot up to the roof of the tower. Stepping out on the roof, Twiffle beckoned them after him. The clown made his way straight to the Magic Airmobile. He climbed in, motioning for Shaggy and the children to do likewise. They all squeezed into the contraption after him. Twink noted the cushioned seats in each end of the Airmobile were soft and yielding. Conjo certainly liked comfort. "Where are we going? And why?" demanded the Shaggy Man.

"There is no time to talk now," retorted Twiffle briefly. "Wait until we are well in the air."

"Do you know how to operate this thing?" asked Tom.

"I have watched Conjo run it many times. I am sure I can manage it," replied Twiffle. The little clown was busy with the buttons which exposed the gravity resistor plates, and almost before they realized it, the Airmobile had risen gently from the roof and was moving silently through the night. "Ah, that is a relief," sighed Twiffle as he watched Conjo's castle recede in the distance.

"But where are we going?" asked Twink, who was thoroughly enjoying the ride through the cool night air.

"The main thing," explained Twiffle, "is to get as far away from Conjo as possible."

"Then he is a villain, as I suspected," said Shaggy.

Twiffle nodded. "Conjo is a curious man. He repaired the Love Magnet because he couldn't bear seeing one of his own charms broken. He is very vain. Actually, he doesn't care anything about the Love Magnet, which has no effect on him, since he made it. He doesn't love anyone, and he doesn't want anyone to love him. He came to this island many years ago. He wanted to be alone, since he disliked people and desired only to work on his wizard charms and incantations. He brought me to life merely to amuse himself and to have someone to talk to when he felt like boasting. Recently he has become restless. He has found that, after all, he wants someone before whom he can show off his magic tricks. But he hesitated to bring many people to the island, fearing they would steal some of his precious magic tools."

Twiffle paused and sighed. He went on, "I had made the mistake of telling him about you, Twink and Tom. Those visits he permitted me to your home while you slept were the only kindness Conjo ever showed me, so I don't feel I owe him any allegiance, even though he did bring me to life. Well, yesterday Conjo announced he was going to use his magic to bring you children to his island."

"I see," murmured Twink. "and so you have rescued us."

"I hope so," replied Twiffle. "After what I found out tonight, I couldn't let you stay here. Conjo talks in his sleep a great deal, and tonight he mumbled enough for me to learn completely for the first time what his plans are for you two children."

"What do you mean, `plans'?" asked Tom.

"Why, Conjo was going to make you drink a magic potion that would wipe out all memory of your home, parents and former lives. Then you would be content to stay on the island with him."

"How dreadful!" exclaimed Twink, shuddering.

"And I suppose he never meant for me to return to the Land of Oz," said the Shaggy Man.

"Oh no," replied Twiffle. "Conjo wanted your magic Compass badly, because it possesses a kind of magic that he knows nothing about. I believe he meant to transport you to the Land of Ev, where you could find your way back to Oz as best you could."

"But now," said Twink happily, "the Airmobile will take us all to the Land of Oz."

Twiffle shook his head. "No," he said, "I'm afraid it won't. Conjo is a clever wizard of sorts, but he is not powerful enough to invent a machine that will fly across the Deadly Desert."

"You mean this contraption won't carry us over the desert and back to Oz?" the Shaggy Man asked, greatly disturbed.

"No," said Twiffle. "I have heard of powerful birds managing to fly high enough to cross the Deadly Desert, but I know of no magic that can penetrate the barrier of invisibility that Glinda the Good spread across the deadly waste many years ago — certainly not Conjo's magic!"

"Then what shall we do?" asked the Shaggy Man.

"As I said," reminded Twiffle, "the most important thing was to get out of Conjo's power. The Airmobile will carry us to the edge of the Deadly Desert, but no farther."

The Shaggy Man was silent, considering. Once he had managed to cross the Deadly Desert in a sandboat — that had been before Glinda had laid down the magic barrier. But even since then, others had crossed the desert. So the Shaggy Man didn't give up all hope.

The Airmobile was carrying them swiftly and silently through the night. Below them the waters of the Nonestic Ocean gleamed silver in the moonlight. There was just the faintest rocking motion as the Airmobile sped along. Perhaps it was this and the fact that Shaggy and the two children were deep in their own thoughts that made them all fall asleep before they knew it. Twiffle smiled and applied himself to the operation of the Airmobile. He had no need for sleep.

Twink was the first to awaken. The sun was well up in the sky, and the morning was bright and clear. She shook Tom awake, and at the same time the Shaggy Man aroused himself. They looked over the side of the craft and saw below them a pleasant land of hills and rolling farmlands. "The Land of Ev," announced the Shaggy Man. "We shouldn't be so very far from the Deadly Desert now."

Twiffle had looked up and was staring ahead of him in amazement. The little clown slowed down the Airmobile. Directly ahead of them was a cluster of little houses and buildings — a good-sized village — in the sky. "What in the world can that be?" gasped Twink.

The Airmobile was moving very slowly as they approached the sky village. Directly before them, on what would have been the outskirts of the town had it been on the earth, was a sign reading:

YOU ARE NOW ENTERING HIGHTOWN

Population — 522

Altitude — approximately 15,000 feet (but it varies)

They could see people walking about among the houses just as though they were on solid ground. The Shaggy Man shook his head. Twink and Tom were staring, fascinated. The Airmobile glided silently a few feet past the sign. Then it jerked several times and came to an abrupt halt.

Twiffle looked puzzled. He pushed one button, then another. Nothing happened. Twiffle did it all over again, a bit frantically this time. Still nothing happened. "It's no use," said Twiffle. "The Airmobile won't budge. We're stuck in mid-air!"

Chapter 8 - The Lord High Mayor

While Twiffle fussed with the controls of the Magic Airmobile, a crowd of curious people began to gather about the stalled aircraft. They were men, women, children, and even dogs, and they walked on the air easily and unconcernedly, as if it were the normal thing to do. These people were all very tall and exceedingly thin. The grown-ups were well over eight feet in height, while the older children averaged about six feet tall. Perhaps the fact that they lived so high up had caused them to grow that way, too. Their clothing was what we would consider old-fashioned, but was neat and well cared for. The women wore the brightest of colors, which flashed gaily in the clear sunlight. The people chattered among themselves, pointing toward the Airmobile, and several dogs barked excitedly. A loud voice exclaimed, "What is the meaning of this? What is going on here?"

The crowd made way for the speaker, who proved to be a sour-faced, tall individual wearing a frock coat and a high silk hat — a stovepipe hat, the Shaggy Man would have called it.

"Pardon us," began the Shaggy Man, "but I am afraid we are the cause of all the excitement. You see, our airship has stalled just inside your town."

The tall man stared curiously at the occupants of the Airmobile as he said, "Of course your flying machine won't operate in Hightown. In fact, a flying machine in Hightown is an utter absurdity — against all the town ordinances and rules. I must ask you to remove it immediately."

"Not very friendly, is he?" remarked Tom.

But Twiffle was interested. "What do you mean, sir, that the aircraft is against your laws?"

The tall man sniffed. "It should be apparent to you that the last thing in the sky we need is an airplane. Here in this favored spot we walk on air and are not compelled to crawl across the earth like worms."

"Yes," said the Shaggy Man, "we can see all that. But tell us, your Honor, do you think we would be able to walk on air as you do?"

The top-hatted man was distinctly flattered by the Shaggy Man's mode of address. "Ah," he replied, "I can see that you recognize me as a person of importance. I am the Lord High Mayor of Hightown, and my word here represents the highest law of the land. As for your being able to walk as we do on the air, I see no reason why you shouldn't since in Hightown there is no gravity to pull you to the earth."

"What was that you said? No gravity?" Twiffle was obviously excited.

"Exactly," replied the Lord High Mayor with great dignity. "Within the boundaries of Hightown, the earth does not exert the least bit of gravity

— none whatsoever."

"Then that explains it," said Twiffle. "The Airmobile operates on the principle of gravity, and since there is no gravity here, the craft is useless."

"What are we to do?" asked the Shaggy Man. "I am not sure I want to go walking around on the air, although these folks seem to take to it naturally enough."

"Tell me," said Twiffle, addressing the Lord High Mayor, "is Hightown of very great area?"

"Oh," exclaimed the Lord High Mayor, "it is simply enormous — no less than four square acres of the most delightful air!"

"Have you any idea, your Honor," asked the Shaggy Man, "how we can get our flying machine out of Hightown?"

"Oh, that's very simple," replied the Lord High Mayor. "Since your craft has only just crossed the boundary into Hightown, I would suggest that you get out and push the machine to the edge of the boundary — then push it a few inches more, and it will be in the field of gravity again where it is equipped to operate."

"Of course!" exclaimed Twiffle joyfully. "Why didn't I think of that?"

The Lord High Mayor smiled with smug satisfaction.

"I'll adjust these gravity plates now," continued Twiffle, "so the plane won't fall when it passes the boundary." After he had pressed some buttons, he and the Shaggy Man and Twink and Tom climbed out of the Airmobile. The air seemed as solid under their feet as the earth. Nevertheless, this walking on thin air was a most curious experience, and in spite of themselves they found they were treading gingerly as though they were walking on eggs.

The Lord High Mayor and the crowd of Hightowners that had gathered watched curiously as the Shaggy Man and Tom slowly pushed the Airmobile toward the boundary of Hightown. It was no task at all, since the Airmobile had no weight. They knew the sign that had greeted them as they entered Hightown marked the spot where gravity again exerted its pull, so they pushed the Airmobile slowly over this invisible line.

Zoom! Like an arrow shot from a bow, the Airmobile darted upward. Far above their heads it continued its mad climb into the sky. So fast did it move that within a few seconds it was visible only as a tiny speck far above them.

"What in the sky has happened?" gasped the Shaggy Man.

"It is all my fault," said Twiffle despondently. "I must have exposed the gravity plates too much when I adjusted them. I was so afraid the plane would fall. When the Airmobile passed into the area of gravity, it shot upward. Now it is lost to us forever." Twiffle looked as if he were about to weep.

"Cheer up, Twiffle," said the Shaggy Man. "Maybe we can get the Airmobile back." Shaggy turned to the Lord High Mayor and asked, "Since we can walk on air as well as you, couldn't we just walk up there and climb into the Airmobile?"

"You could if you wanted to stop breathing," said the Lord High Mayor cheerfully.

"Why do you say that?" asked the Shaggy Man.

"Because," exclaimed the Lord High Mayor, "we have discovered that the higher up you go, the thinner the air becomes. At the altitude now attained by your craft, the air would be so thin that it would be unbreathable."

"Anyway," said Twink with a sigh, "the Airmobile isn't there any more."

They all stared upward. The girl was right. The speck that had been the Airmobile had vanished completely. "Wonder where it went," said Twink.

The Lord High Mayor explained pompously, "Apparently your craft attained so great a speed that it shot off into space, beyond the power of gravity. From now on there's no telling where it will go."

"And astronomers will report that folks from earth are about to visit another world, I suppose," grinned the Shaggy Man.

"Too bad old Conjo isn't in it," grumbled Twiffle.

"The question is," said Tom, "what do we do now?"

"Right," agreed the Shaggy Man as he turned to the Lord High Mayor and asked, "Sir, can you tell us how we can leave Hightown and proceed on our journey?"

"You wish to leave Hightown? Where could you possibly wish to go?" inquired the Lord High Mayor.

"Well, eventually we hope to reach the Emerald City in the Land of Oz," replied the Shaggy Man, "so we're heading for the Deadly Desert surrounding the Land of Oz. Then we'll have to figure out some way to cross the desert."

The Lord High Mayor stared at Shaggy in horror. "The Deadly Desert!" he exclaimed. "Do you mean to stand here in the sky and tell me you actually wish to go near that terrible, burning, dry waste of shifting deadly sands when you can stay here and enjoy the delightful perfection of the aerial climate of Hightown?"

"No," began the Shaggy Man patiently, "we don't like the Desert any more than you do, but in order to get to Oz we must cross the Desert. I assure you the Land of Oz has a climate just as delightful as that of Hightown."

"That is impossible!" declared the Lord High Mayor indignantly. "Hightown has the only perfect climate in the world, and now that you are here, you might as well stay and enjoy it."

"Wonder if he ever heard of California?" murmured Tom to Twink.

"We would like very much to stay and enjoy your climate, your Honor," replied the Shaggy Man, "but it is impossible. We must be on our way to the Land of Oz, much as we admire your high airs. So if you will kindly tell us how we may leave your town, we will be much obliged."

The Lord High Mayor seemed to be deep in thought. "Leave our town?" he said incredulously. "I don't believe it. No one could want to leave Hightown. It is the pinnacle of civilization, the highest point in high life ever reached by man. Sir, I conclude that I must have misunderstood you. It is beyond comprehension that you should wish to depart from this exalted community and go crawling about the lowly earth like a worm. I simply must have misunderstood you."

"There's nothing wrong with your ears," replied the Shaggy Man. "I said it, and I'll say it again — we want to leave Hightown! Maybe we haven't advanced to the state where we can fully appreciate your hi-falutin' ways, and if you want to know the truth, we actually like to feel the earth beneath our feet."

The Lord High Mayor stared at the Shaggy Man unbelievingly. There was a suspicion of tears in his eyes. "My poor, dear fellow," he said. "How I grieve for you — to have such low tastes. The earth under one's feet — ugh! But then," he went on, brightening, "you have not been here long enough to appreciate the soaring virtues of life in Hightown. Once you have become accustomed to the lofty plane on which we live and the superiority we enjoy over earth-crawlers, I am sure that all the sod in the world will not tempt you to put foot upon the earth again."

"Please," said the Shaggy Man in exasperation. "Will you stop talking like the Chamber of Commerce and tell us how we can get back to earth?"

The Lord High Mayor eyed Shaggy narrowly. "Well," he said, "if you insist on leaving Hightown, you could walk to the boundary there, where gravity begins again, step over and fall very quickly to the earth. That is the fas
test way I can think of leaving Hightown, but I wouldn't recommend it."

"No, no," the Shaggy Man assured him. "We have no desire to fall to the earth." Shaggy looked below him with a shudder. "We would be in no shape to continue our travels if we did that."

"Well, then, you see, it is all settled," said the Lord High Mayor with a beaming smile. "You will stay with us. Everything is settled and there is not the slightest doubt that you will find Hightown the Garden Spot of the Sky. Now, since I am the Lord High Mayor of Hightown, it is my elevated privilege and honor to welcome you and make you comfortable. You will please follow me on what is the most fortunate journey of your life, for you are on your way to savoring the high and flighty life of Hightown."

There seemed nothing else to do, so Shaggy and his friends followed the Lord High Mayor, stepping gingerly on what seemed to them to be the airiest space. As the Mayor proceeded, the crowd of curious Hightowners made way for him and the little company of adventurers.

"Might I inquire," asked Twiffle, "where you are taking us?"

"Why, to my Air Castle, of course," answered the Lord High Mayor. "Since you are my guests, you must be treated with the greatest courtesy. Later we will find a permanent dwelling for you."

They had now reached the center of the small town, and here the Lord High Mayor paused before a dwelling that was little different from any other of the houses which were scarcely more than bungalows except that they were all quite high and narrow to suit the shapes of the Hightowners.

"This is your Air Castle?" asked the Shaggy Man. "It looks no different from the other houses."

"And why should it be different?" demanded the Lord High Mayor. "Here we all live in Air Castles. You people who crawl around on the earth just dream of them. We are privileged to enjoy them." This last was said with an air of great pride.

One thing did distinguish the Lord High Mayor's dwelling from the others in the town. Directly in front of it there stood a handsome flower pot in which was blossoming a beautiful magnolia. The Lord High Mayor paused to enjoy the delightful aroma of the flower. "Ah, magnolia! That means we shall have a south wind soon. You visitors are indeed fortunate to have arrived in Hightown at this time."

"I'm not so sure we would be fortunate to arrive here any time," grumbled Twiffle.

"You see," the Mayor went on, disregarding Twiffle's remark, "when the magnolia blossoms, that means a south wind is coming. And that means we shall soon have a delightful southern cloud on which to walk. I assure you there is nothing more delightful than walking on a southern cloud."

"Seems to me clouds of any sort would be sort of squiggy for walking purposes, no matter how pretty they are to look at," said the Shaggy Man.

"What happens when there's a north wind coming?" asked Twink curiously.

"Oh, then the plant blossoms with a beautiful wild thyme, and we are privileged to enjoy that delightful scent. When there's an east wind on its way," the Lord High Mayor continued, "then the plant bears chrysanthemums. When the west wind is coming, we enjoy the blossoms and scent of wild roses."

"Doesn't the west wind bring rain clouds?" asked Tom, remembering that it usually did in Buffalo.

"Yes," said the Mayor, "that is right."

"Then it rains here in Hightown where you have a have a perfect climate?" asked the boy, remembering his disgust with the rain at home.

"Not at all," replied the Mayor. "There is no gravity to pull the raindrops earthward, so it can't rain. We just go out wading in the rain cloud."

"That's quite a plant," said the Shaggy Man, staring at the flower pot with its beautiful blossoms.

"It's much more than that," said the Mayor. "Certainly since we have the most perfect weather in the world in Hightown, we would have the most perfect weather forecaster. That's just what the plant is."

While Tom was trying to puzzle out why, if Hightown always had perfect weather, it needed any weather forecaster at all, the door of the Mayor's home opened and they were welcomed by a tall, thin woman in a blue checked bungalow apron. She proved to be the Mayor's wife. The good woman immediately served dinner, hurrying about and doing her best to make the visitors at home. She was particularly pleasant to Twink and Tom and was greatly amazed and a little awed by Twiffle.

Strangely enough, the food consisted entirely of fruits, but they were all fresh and tasty. When the meal was over, the Lord High Mayor announced that it was time for a nap. "A nap!" exclaimed the Shaggy Man. "Why, it is only a little past noon. We can't sleep now."

"It is the custom in Hightown," remarked the Mayor placidly, "and you will soon come to enjoy the siesta as much as we. However, if you cannot sleep, you may sit on the front porch. But don't go off the porch and wander about, as you may come to the edge of the town and fall to the earth."

With this, the Lord High Mayor and his wife retired to their room, and the visitors were left to themselves. There seemed nothing else to do but to follow the Mayor's suggestion and while away the Town's hour of sleep on the front porch. Here they found several chairs and a swing and soon made themselves comfortable.

There was nothing interesting about the scenery, and little to talk about, and they were beginning to be a bit bored when a saucy brown wren flitted out of the sky and perched on the porch railing, regarding Shaggy and his friends with bright little eyes. "Strangers here, aren't you?" asked the bird. "Fine place to live. You'll like it, I'm sure."

"We don't like it, and we don't intend to stay," said the Shaggy Man a bit ill-humoredly.

"Well, if you don't like it, then why don't you leave right away?" asked the bird.

"How?" asked Shaggy. "Walk to the edge of the town and fall to the earth? We can't fly like you, you know."

"You don't need to fly. You can walk down through the air — or rather, swim down — using your arms to push you through the air. There's no gravity, you know." And with a flirt of its saucy trail, the bird was gone.

With a shout, Twiffle leaped to his feet. "What fools we've been! Of course there's no gravity, and we can push ourselves right down to earth! Come on, let's be on our way." Twiffle ran to the edge of the porch and leaped out head first. They could see the little clown below them, moving his arms like a swimmer.

"Should we try it?" asked the Shaggy Man doubtfully.

Tom didn't wait for an answer. He jumped from the porch just as Twiffle had done. He found that by moving his arms he could force himself downward. Indeed, it was no more effort than walking on a level on the air. In a short time he discovered that, since there was no gravity, he could move at will up or down through the air. Now Twink was at his side, thoroughly enjoying the novel experience. The Shaggy Man was following close behind. Twink glanced upward once and saw the spectacle of a whole town suspended in the air above her. She could even make out the Mayor's house and the flower pot in front of it. They were all swimming earthward at about the same level when there was a flirt of small wings, and the wren who had spoken to them on the porch of the Lord High Mayor's house alighted on the Shaggy Man's shoulder. "I see you took my advice," said the wren.

"Yes," said the Shaggy Man, "and we are grateful to you for telling us about this easy way to leave Hightown."

"Think nothing of it," replied the wren airily. "I always feel sorry for anyone who gets stuck in Hightown. There isn't a stupider place in the world. Those Hightowners have never seen anything but their own silly little town, so they just can't imagine there's anything else in the world."

"You get around quite a bit, I suppose," ventured the Shaggy Man.

"Being a bird, naturally," retorted the wren with a saucy flirt of his tail.

"Well, then," said Shaggy, "would you mind doing your own flying and getting off my shoulder?"

"That's gratitude for you," said the wren reproachfully. "I save you from a life of boredom and you refuse to let me hitchhike down to earth." But the bird didn't move from Shaggy's shoulder.

"Where are you going, anywhere in particular?" asked Twink.

"Oh yes, of course," the wren replied. "Just below Hightown there is a lovely orchard of all kinds of fruit trees. That's where the Hightowners get all their food. They live on fruit. They can boast about their silly town all they like, but when they want food, you can bet they hurry down to the orchard on earth for it. That's why they don't like us birds. We enjoy eating the fruit in the orchard, too. We seldom go near Hightown, except when the people are asleep. They are so disagreeable they throw things at us and accuse us of stealing from their orchard. Their orchard, indeed!"

"Tell me," said the Shaggy Man, "was your mother a magpie?"

"Of course not," replied the wren indignantly.

"I thought she must have been," said the Shaggy Man, "because you certainly chatter like a magpie."

"That's enough," declared the wren. "If you can't appreciate intelligent conversation, I shan't waste it upon you. You are far too slow for me anyway. No hard feelings, though. Good luck to all of you." And with that, the wren was off, darting swiftly earthward. Shaggy and his friends all had a good laugh over the gossipy little bird.

Ten minutes more "swimming" brought them within sight of the orchard about which the bird had told them. "The Hightown sign said `altitude 15,000 feet,'" said Tom. "That's almost three miles. I can't believe we've been swimming that far."

"Probably they boosted that figure as high as their opinion of Hightown," said Twiffle, "and anyway, it did say the altitude varied. Varies very much, I'd say."

A few minutes later they were standing on the earth in a grove of apple, plum, and cherry trees. Every branch was filled with ripe, luscious fruit. Twink looked for their friend, the wren, but saw nothing of him. The Shaggy Man began looking about the ground for apples. Suddenly he laughed. "That was really stupid of me," he called to Twink and Tom. "Of course there aren't any apples on the ground. They can't fall off the trees!"

"This must be where the Hightowners get their fruit," said Twink.

"Of course," replied Shaggy. "They thought they would keep us with them by not telling us how easy it is to reach the earth from Hightown."

"But they must have known we would see some of them coming and going to the orchard and find out sooner or later how to escape," said Tom.

"Well, thanks to that bird, we found out sooner," said Twiffle.

Before they left the grove, Shaggy walked in the air to the upper branches of the biggest apple tree in the orchard and filled his pockets with the largest and ruddiest of the fruit. "Can't tell where we'll find our next meal," he explained.

Knowing the area that was freed from the force of gravity was of very small extent, Shaggy and his friends walked steadily in one direction, treading several feet in the air, since that was easier than walking on the earth. As there was no difference in the appearance of the countryside where gravity exerted itself again, they had no way of telling when they would suddenly emerge from the gravityless land.

Shaggy was in the lead when he suddenly experienced that curious sensation that comes when you step unexpectedly into a hole. The result was that Shaggy toppled forward and found himself sprawled on the grass. Following him came Twink, Tom and Twiffle. Only Tom managed to maintain his balance. What he had realized in time was simply that the others had stepped off the air on which they had been walking to the earth a foot or two below them. The Shaggy Man sighed. "Give me the earth to crawl around on any day, as our friend the Lord High Mayor would put it, even though it does mean an occasional tumble."

Chapter 9 - The Valley of Romance

Before the travelers lay one of the most beautiful valleys they had ever seen. Gently sloping hills led down to green fields. Through the middle of the valley flowed a steam that looked like a shimmering blue ribbon stretched out on a green carpet. On the near bank of the stream, in the very center of the valley, stood a castle. Its spires, turrets, and towers were so delicately formed that they glistened like lace-filigree in the sunlight. Twink's eyes glowed. "Isn't it just the most beautiful sight you ever saw?" she exclaimed.

"It certainly is elegant," admitted the Shaggy Man. "But what we want to know is, what kind of folks live in it."

"Oh, I'm sure they must be very happy and contented," said Twink. "They just must be to live in a place like that."

"Then we are going to visit the castle?" asked Twiffle a bit doubtfully.

"It seems the only thing to do," replied the Shaggy Man. "I admit I have no idea where we are, and there is just the possibility that whoever lives in that castle may be able to help us get to Oz, or at least give us directions to the Deadly Desert."

Tom was already on his way, running happily down the green slope toward the stream and the castle. A ten-minute walk in the bright sunlight brought the little group of adventurers to the doors of the castle. So far they had seen no living persons. Birds sang in the trees, and once a white rabbit had bounded across Tom's path, but there were no signs of human beings.

The Shaggy Man stepped forward and knocked boldly on the heavy door. Instantly it swung silently open. As the adventurers stepped inside, Twink gasped, and even the Shaggy Man, accustomed as he was to the splendor of Ozma's Royal Palace, was impressed with the magnificence of his surroundings. The floor and walls of the castle were of the whitest alabaster, polished so that the creamy depths of the stone mirrored the luxurious furnishings, casting a luster that enhanced the woven richness of the deep-hued draperies in the paneled walls.

Who had built such a castle? Each of the travelers tried to picture in his own mind the kind of people who might live here. Would they be friendly or unfriendly, helpful or dangerous? Still there was no sign of people. The only sound that broke the stillness of the foyer in which Shaggy and his friends stood was the tinkling of water as it flowed from a small fountain in the center of the room. This fountain was fashioned like an ordinary drinking fountain, the stream of water that rose from it being not more than three or four inches in height. Around the rim of the alabaster fountain was a metal plate with writing inscribed upon it.

Her curiosity aroused, Twink advanced to the fountain and read:

This is a Phontain.

Any visitors are requested to speak

their messages into it.

Signed: Rex Ticket & Regina Curtain.

"What in the world can it mean?" whispered Twink. Her companions had gathered about her and were reading the metal plate with wonder.

"Rex and Regina," ventured the Shaggy Man, "are King and Queen. That's Latin. So evidently the head folks of this castle are King Ticket and Queen Curtain. Hmmm — certainly odd names for a King and Queen."

"A Phontain, and we're supposed to talk into it!" sniffed Twiffle with disgust. "Whoever heard of such nonsense?"

"Well," observed the Shaggy Man, "I've heard of babbling brooks, so why not a talking fountain that will carry our words?"

"A phoney fountain, I suppose," said Tom, grinning.

Shaggy stooped over the Phontain and spoke clearly and distinctly: "This is the Shaggy Man of Oz speaking. In behalf of my friends, Twink and Tom of the United States of America, Twiffle, late of the Isle of Conjo, and myself, I request an audience with King Ticket and Queen Curtain."

Almost immediately a red neon sign lighted up over two large double doors at the opposite end of the foyer. The sign flashed the single word "Entrance." "I guess this is where we go in," remarked the Shaggy Man as he walked to the door and pushed the large metal handle.

They were in a small, brightly lighted theater containing about one hundred seats. On the stage, seated on two thrones, were a man and a woman — evidently King Ticket and Queen Curtain. All about the King and Queen on the stage there was a bustle of the most frenzied activity. There sounded the clash and clatter of hammers, the ripping of saws and the whirring of drills and bits. Perhaps fifteen or twenty men were hard at work knocking together and erecting a bewildering array of scenery. Calmly seated about the stage on three-cornered stools, their sewing baskets at their sides, were a number of ladies sewing on costumes. Others were apparently sewing together large pieces of canvas. Still other ladies were engaged in painting artistic pictures on the canvas which was then stretched on wooden frameworks to serve as backdrops for the stage.

After Shaggy and his friends had watched this display of industry for several minutes, they advanced down the middle aisle of the theater. The King and queen had been doing no actual work. They merely issued directions to the others, who seemed not to pay them the slightest heed, but continued with their tasks. King Ticket looked up. "Well," he said to the Shaggy Man, "you certainly took your time getting here. It was at least three minutes ago that you announced yourselves on the Phontain."

"Do you mean you really heard us through that water fountain?" asked the Shaggy Man.

"Water hath a limpid tongue with which to lave the naked ear," said King Ticket in a voice which was meant to be impressive. "Of course we heard you through the Phontain. There are Phontains in all the rooms of the Castle — even in the theater, here — which repeat messages when we speak into them."

Twink thought this was much nicer than telephones which (sic — with?) rudely jangling bells, although probably not as private. "You didn't think," commented Queen Curtain as though she had read Twink's thoughts, "that we would use ordinary means of communication such as telephones in the Valley of Romance, did you?"

"Oh," said the Shaggy Man, "is this the Valley of Romance?"

"It is, and since you are from the Land of Oz," said King Ticket, "you must surely have heard of the Valley of Romance."

The Shaggy Man reflected. It seemed he could recall Ozma mentioning something about some such valley, but he couldn't remember anything that she had said about it. "How far are we from the Land of Oz?" asked Twiffle.

"Dear me!" exclaimed King Ticket, staring at Twiffle. "For a moment I thought you were real!"

"I am real," stated Twiffle with dignity. "I just don't happen to be made of flesh and blood and bones, that's all."

"And as for the Land of Oz," remarked Queen Curtain meditatively, "it is indeed very far away — over the stream and over the hill — far, far away to the desert, and then over that, too. In fact, it isn't even in the Valley of Romance, so that means it must be quite some distance off. Too far even to think of," she added as though to say that closed the subject.

The Shaggy Man shrugged. Evidently these two weren't going to be of much help to the travelers in finding their way back to Oz. Well, they would make a lunch of the apples he carried in his pockets and then continue on their journey. Shaggy and his friends made themselves comfortable in the deeply upholstered seats in the front row of the theater. Shaggy divided the apples between Twink, Tom, and himself. He offered several to King Ticket and Queen Curtain, who refused them rather disdainfully.

Shaggy and his friends ate in silence while they watched the activity on the stage. Not one of the busily working men and women seemed even to be aware of the presence of the strangers. Finishing his apples, the Shaggy Man arose and said, "Looks like you folks are getting ready for quite a play. What's the name of it?"

Unexpectedly one of the workers on a ladder stopped his task of hammering together a bit of framework for the scenery and replied to Shaggy's question: "That we won't know until the curtain goes up tonight. Tonight's the First Night of this new play, and I shall be in charge." The fellow added impressively, "For I am the First Knight of the Realm, you know."

"No," replied the Shaggy Man, "I didn't know." Shaggy was a little angry, for he thought the man was making fun of him.

"Oh yes," Queen Curtain went on placidly. "He is the First Knight of the Realm — in fact, all these people are Lords and Ladies of the Royal Theater."

"And do you always build your own scenery and make your own costumes?" asked the Shaggy Man.

King Ticket shifted uneasily on his throne. "Yes, and it always seems to turn out rather badly. I suppose all we were really meant to do was to enjoy the magnificent performances on the stage. And," the King brightened, "that is all we truly have any desire to do. That is a full life for us and quite enough — to sit in the theater and watch great drama unfold. What need have we for any lives of our own when the stage is a world in itself and therein we are content to dwell?" The King's voice gently subsided to a whisper, and his eyes stared dreamily into space.

Queen Curtain took up the story. "During the performances Lord Props and Lady Cue help the actors, although none too well, I must admit. Lord Props seldom gets things right: when a gunshot is called for, there is very likely to be a bell ringing. Once when the scene required a bowl of goldfish, Lord Props actually managed to cram a whole live lobster into a soup tureen. Lady Cues does, however, manage to do a bit better with her cues. She is seldom more than two lines behind the actors."

"How long do your plays run?" asked Shaggy.

"Night after night after glorious night for years and years and years — sometimes as long as we can remember there has been the same wonderful play for us to see on the stage at night," said the King, who had awakened from his dream.

"And what do you do the rest of the time?" queried the Shaggy Man.

"Nothing — nothing but sleep," answered King Ticket. "Why should we? We have the glorious stage for our lives." The King looked about him at the work going on.

"Who are your actors?" asked Tom.

For a moment, King Ticket seemed embarrassed. Then he replied vaguely with a wave of his hand as if to dismiss the matter as of little importance. "Oh, just actors — you know, the usual thing, leading man, leading lady, villain, comedian, and so forth."

"Come," said the Shaggy Man, "we're wasting time here. We should be on our way if we ever hope to reach the Land of Oz."

Queen Curtain looked up. "You won't stay for dinner and the theater?"

"No thank you," replied Shaggy. "We have a long journey ahead of us, and we really must be going on our way now." With this, Shaggy and his friends walked up the aisle toward the door by which they had entered the theater. King Ticket had been staring intently at the Shaggy Man, and now he whispered something in a low voice to Queen Curtain. The Queen considered for a moment and then nodded her head. Twink and Tom, who were directly behind the Shaggy Man, stopped and stared at each other. They were only halfway up the aisle. The Shaggy Man had been only a step ahead of them. Now he was gone — vanished completely!

379

Chapter 10 – Lady Cue

Twink and Tom were utterly bewildered at their friend's disappearance. They didn't know what to do next. Twiffle turned to King Ticket and Queen Curtain on the stage and demanded, "Where is the Shaggy Man?"

King Ticket looked up innocently. "Why, has he gone somewhere?"

"Certainly he has gone somewhere," said Twiffle, who was becoming angry. "And you had better tell us where. Don't forget that the Shaggy Man is an important personage of the Land of Oz. If anything happens to him, you will be sorry."

"Pooh!" sniffed King Ticket. "We know all about the Land of Oz and its silly girl ruler, Ozma. But your famous Shaggy Man had not even heard of the Valley of Romance. What can anyone in Oz do? They don't even know of our existence."

"I wouldn't be too sure of that," declared Twiffle with more courage than he felt.

"Anyway," continued King Ticket musingly, "the Land of Oz is vastly overrated. Why, as far as I know, there isn't a single theater in all the country!"

"And so," began Queen Curtain quietly, "why don't you children just make yourselves comfortable until dinner time? Then you may join us for the meal, and afterwards you shall be our guests in the Royal Box to witness the performance of our new play."

Twiffle was aroused now. He climbed right up on the arm of King Ticket's chair. "We don't want your dinner. We don't want to see your play. All we want is the Shaggy Man, and then we shall continue our journey."

"Tut, tut," admonished King Ticket. "What a violent disposition the little puppet has."

"I am afraid," said Queen Curtain, "that you really have no choice. You must stay here until we are ready for you to depart. After all, you came of your own accord, you know."

Twiffle was silent. He was at a loss to know what to say or do. Twink and Tom felt suddenly alone and a little bit frightened now that the Shaggy Man was gone. Even in the brief time they had known him, they had grown very fond of him and had come to rely upon him. Seeing this, Twiffle returned to stand by the children and said, "Never you mind. We'll find the Shaggy Man all right. Perhaps it would be wise to remain here tonight as these people wish us to do. That will give us a chance to find out what they have done with Shaggy."

This was said in a whisper, to which Tom answered, "Well, I could enjoy a good meal. We haven't had anything to eat but fruit since yesterday." Actually, Tom was as worried about Shaggy as Twink, but being a boy, he didn't want to let the girl know.

Twink was indignant. "I'm surprised at you, Tom! The idea of talking about food when we've just lost our best friend! But I suppose Twiffle is right."

"Good!" said King Ticket. "Then that is settled, and you will be with us for dinner and the theater!"

"Gosh!" exclaimed Tom. "Do you suppose he heard everything we said?"

"I don't have any doubt of it," replied Twiffle calmly. "Therefore we might as well converse in our ordinary voices."

"You were indeed fortunate to have arrived just in time for the opening night of our new play," said Queen Curtain pleasantly. "I am sure you will enjoy it immensely. Tell me, have you children seen many plays?"

"Oh yes," replied Tom, "we have seen lots of our school plays, and last Christmas Twink and I had important parts in the Christmas pageant."

"Well, then, you will certainly enjoy yourselves tonight," said the Queen, smiling happily at the children. "We will work only about an hour more. Then everything will be in readiness. That will give us plenty of time to tidy up, dress in our finest, and enjoy the dinner and the play to the utmost."

The hour passed swiftly. The children apparently were engrossed in the work going on on the stage, but actually their thoughts were busy puzzling over the mystery of what had happened to the Shaggy Man.

"Lady Cue will show you to your rooms, children," announced Queen Curtain, rising from her throne. The Lords and Ladies were putting away their tools and sewing. A tall, thin, worried-looking woman, sewing basket on her arm, stepped down a short flight of stairs from the stage and smiled rather absent-mindedly at Twink and Tom. "You will come with me, I think?" she said hesitantly.

Twink and Tom looked at Twiffle, who nodded, and all three followed the tall lady, who was proceeding uncertainly up the aisle. Outside the theater, Lady Cue led Twiffle and the children up a broad staircase leading to the second floor of the castle. Here there was a long corridor, with smaller corridors leading off of it, each with many doors opening into various suites and rooms. Lady Cue had advanced only a short distance down the main corridor when she stopped uncertainly before a door and turned to her charges. "This is a door," she said, "but do you think it is the right one?"

"I'm sure we wouldn't know, Madame," replied Twiffle. "After all, you live in this castle and should know all about it."

Lady Cue sighed. "Of course, of course. I forgot for the moment that you are the strangers. Well, we shall have to do our best to find the right door."

"Haven't you been in any of these rooms?" asked Tom curiously.

"In them?" asked Lady Cue vaguely. "Oh, I must have, since I live here, you know. Once inside the rooms I am sure I would be able to find my way with no trouble. But outside them it is most confusing. How is one to know what is inside when one is outside?" Lady Cue looked at them beseechingly and wandered down the corridor to another door exactly like the one she had just left. She stared at this one for several minutes, then boldly opened it a crack and peered in. "Oh goodness! I beg your pardon," she said to someone in the room, hastily closing the door. "Well," she said, "that's one that isn't the one. The First Knight of the Realm is in there pressing his breeches for tonight's performance."

"The First Knight of the Realm presses his own clothes?" asked Twink.

"He does, he does," asserted Lady Cue, wagging her head. "I did it for him once, but somehow the creases ran zigzag, and he looked like he was corrugated. It is my opinion, though," Lady Cue added in a confidential whisper, "that he wears a poor quality garment." Lady Cue turned and started off down one of the smaller corridors. Twink, Tom and Twiffle followed her, at which Lady Cue stopped and looked at them with a puzzled expression. "Did you wish to see me?" she asked.

"You were taking us to our rooms," reminded Twiffle.

"I was?" exclaimed Lady Cue, greatly surprised. "Well, then you just show me where your rooms are, and I will be glad to take you to them."

"But you were supposed to show us to our rooms," said Tom.

"I was? Oh dear, this is confusing," said Lady Cue.

"Have you no idea where our rooms are, Madame?" asked Twiffle.

"I wouldn't say that," replied Lady Cue. "I did have a very good idea, but it seems I mislaid it somewhere. There are so very many rooms, you know, and any one of them might be yours, if only there weren't so many other people in the castle. That's what we must be careful about, you know. I don't think you would want to share rooms with someone else, would you, maybe?"

All the time they were wandering from corridor to corridor while Lady Cue became more and more unsure of her bearings. At last she stopped and said hopelessly, "You'll have to pardon me, my friends, but I am afraid I am lost. I haven't the faintest idea where we are."

"What shall we do?" asked Twink.

"I have it," said Lady Cue. "I will pin my handkerchief to this door," and she indicated a door opposite them, "so that we can't get more lost. Whenever we pass this door with the handkerchief on it, we will know exactly where we are."

"And where will that be?" asked Twiffle.

"Why, where the handkerchief is, of course," replied Lady Cue. With that, Lady Cue reached in her pocket and pulled out a large linen napkin that bore traces of food on it. "Oh dear," she exclaimed. "I seem to have picked this up at luncheon. How thoughtless of me." She advanced to the door and, removing a large safety pin from the front of her dress, carefully pinned the napkin to the door.

"Whose rooms are these?" asked Twiffle.

"I haven't the faintest idea," replied Lady Cue.

"Why not open the door and find out?" pursued Twiffle.

"Why not?" echoed Lady Cue as she turned the knob and pushed open the door. They all stepped inside. There was no sign of any occupants of the room. The closets were all empty, and there were no personal articles about. The suite consisted of a large, beautifully furnished living room with doors leading to two comfortable bedrooms with baths.

"Why can't we use these rooms?" asked Twiffle.

"What a wonderful idea," exclaimed Lady Cue. "Then we won't have to hunt any longer for your rooms, because these will be your rooms. But are you sure it's all right? It sounds much too simple." And with a worried look, the poor lady started to take down the napkin from the door.

"No, no," said Twiffle. "Leave the napkin there. Then you will be able to find us again. Remember now, just look for the napkin on the door and you'll know which is our room."

381

Lady Cue nodded and extracted a large, old-fashioned watch from the depths of her sewing basket. She squinted at it, and said, "You have just one half hour to prepare for dinner. I will call for you and take you to the, the

— oh yes, the dining room. That," she confided, "is where they are serving dinner tonight." With that, the befuddled Lady Cue closed the door, only to find she was still in the room. So she opened it, stepped outside, and then carefully closed it again.

Twink, Tom and Twiffle, in spite of their troubles, burst out laughing. If anything went right with the play tonight, they were sure it wouldn't be due to Lady Cue's efforts. While Twiffle waited patiently, the children bathed, scrubbed their faces and hands, and reappeared much refreshed and quite ready for the dinner that had been promised them. Twink was fascinated with the long rows of books on one side of the luxuriously furnished room, but she hardly had time to do more than glance at a few pictures when there came a gentle rapping on their door.

Twiffle opened it. There stood Lady Cue. Her dress was on backwards, and she had forgotten to do her hair. Solemnly she counted Twink, Tom and Twiffle

— one, two, three. "Is that right?" she asked them anxiously. "Were there just three of you? So often when I count I have something left over. This time it seems to come out even. That's very odd."

"Three would be odd," muttered Twiffle. Fortunately, Lady Cue didn't hear him, or she might have become even more confused. She was already on her way through the corridors, so the children and the clown followed her. After several false starts and wandering through a number of corridors, they finally found their way to the great staircase.

Chapter 11 - What Happened to Shaggy

The Grand Dining Room of the castle was brilliantly lighted by three huge crystal chandeliers. Each of the chandeliers flamed with more than a score of tapering lights which were reflected shimmeringly in the alabaster ceiling and walls. As soon as Twink, Tom and Twiffle entered the dining room, they were espied by Queen Curtain, who motioned them to seat themselves at her right. Queen Curtain and King Ticket occupied the head of the table. The Lords and Ladies of the Castle were filing into the dining room, chattering spiritedly, and all handsomely gowned and garbed. In a few minutes all were seated. There were a few curious glances at the three strangers at the table, but for the most part the Lords and Ladies of the Valley of Romance were far too excited over the play they were to witness that evening to give more than a passing glance to the children and the little clown.

The meal passed through many delicious and elaborate courses with no incidents. Queen Curtain played the charming host, occasionally tossing pleasant remarks to the children and Twiffle. Poor Lady Cue put salt in her tea instead of sugar, but she drank the entire cup without seeming to notice her mistake. "Perhaps she really likes it that way," Twink whispered to Tom.

At the end of the meal, King Ticket rose and addressed the assemblage solemnly. "The moment has come for which we have prepared these many days. We will now pass into the theater for the first performance of the new play." No one spoke. This apparently was an important moment. The only sound in the vast dining room was the rustling of the ladies' skirts and the patter of footsteps on the alabaster floor.

Queen Curtain took Twink by the hand, and Tom and Twiffle followed into the theater. It was brilliantly lighted as the Lords and Ladies settled into their seats. A few of them hurried backstage — they were the ones who worked the scenery and otherwise aided in the presentation of the play. Twink, Tom and Twiffle found themselves seated in the Royal Box with King Ticket and Queen Curtain. The houselights dimmed, the curtains went up, and with no preliminaries the play was under way.

Two actors walked woodenly forward on the stage. They were dressed in what Twink and Tom could tell was supposed to be armor, but was obviously kitchen utensils strung together and about to fall off. From the words they were saying, the two knights seemed to be getting very angry with one another. But they looked at the audience instead of looking at each other, and spoke their lines in a dazed, unexcited way as though they were talking in their sleep. Impossible as it seemed from their lack of action, it became apparent that they were so enraged they had decided to fight out in a tournament their quarrel over a lady. Oh yes, there she was at the side of the stage, paying no attention at all to the knights.

The tournament scene came next. The knights in their pots and pans were mounted on extraordinary horses. Each was made up of two men covered with tufted candlewick bedspreads. They too moved about the stage in a slow and sleepy way. The lady who had inspired the fight looked on from her box seat at the side of the stage, waving her handkerchief. But it had slipped her mind apparently that it was the tournament she was watching, and she looked straight at the audience and listlessly waved her handkerchief as if trying to attract the attention of anyone who might care to wave back at her.

When the knights supposedly rushed their horses at each other and aimed their spears, the steeds ambled slowly in opposite directions so far apart that they seemed not to be aware of each other at all. When they did finally get together, the horse of the knight who was to be winner slipped and fell down, and the bedspread slid to the floor. The horse and the knight who was to be victorious had to be re-assembled before he could triumph over his victim, who had been watching him pick himself up off the floor.

Twink and Tom had to clap their hands over their mouths to keep from bursting out with laughter. They did this because it was apparent that King Ticket, Queen Curtain and the Lords and Ladies took the play quite seriously. Indeed, they were wildly enthusiastic. Throughout the entire play the scenery kept toppling over. Lord Props provided the wrong sound effects and stage furniture at every opportunity, and Lady Cue became so interested in a book of poetry that she read from this instead of giving the actors and actresses their proper lines.

Twink and Tom thought it strange that the people on the stage should mumble their lines so badly and behave altogether as though they were only half awake and were moving by clockwork. Act after act continued in this fashion. But the audience saw only the drama as it was intended. The Queen and the Ladies wept openly, applying delicate lace handkerchiefs to their eyes. King Ticket and the Lords, being men, contented themselves with brushing away a furtive tear and repeatedly blowing their noses loudly in their spotless white linen kerchiefs.

"Magnificent!" exclaimed King Ticket.

"Glorious!" proclaimed Queen Curtain through her tears. "This play will run for years. It is one of the greatest romances we have ever staged!"

"Romance!" sighed King Ticket. "Ah, sublime romance. There is nothing in the world so touching and beautiful!"

It was near the end of the last act. Twink and Tom were nodding. Suddenly a new actor appeared upon the stage. Twink's half-shut eyes flew open. She grasped Tom by the arms and shook him awake. Twiffle leaned forward, holding on to the rail of the box. None of them said a word. For a few seconds they merely stared unbelievingly. The new character who had come on the stage and was even then mumbling his lines in a mechanical voice was the Shaggy Man!

Chapter 12 - A Midnight Adventure

At the sight of the Shaggy Man on the stage, Twink couldn't contain herself. She leaned far out of the box and called, "Shaggy Man! Here we are. It's Tom, Twiffle and Twink!"

If the Shaggy Man heard, he gave no indication of it. His eyes stared straight ahead of him, and he mumbled the words of his lines as though he were speaking in a dream in which he was only half awake. But King Ticket and Queen Curtain as well as the audience of Lords and Ladies heard. A wave of annoyed "Sshhhhhs" arose from the audience, while Queen Curtain grabbed Twink by the arm, pulling her back into her seat and saying angrily, "How dare you interrupt the play? For that you shall join your precious Shaggy Man on the stage tomorrow night."

Tom started from his seat indignantly at the Queen's threatening words, but Twiffle, who looked worried, pulled him back. The three unwilling playgoers fell into an uneasy silence. A few moments later the curtain came down with a crash and the play was over. "Dear, dear me," remarked King ticket. "There go the curtain ropes again. We shall have to repair them tomorrow."

Queen Curtain turned to Twiffle and the children. "Go to your rooms immediately," she ordered sternly. "You know where they are. Don't try to escape. That is impossible. All the doors leading out of the castle are securely locked. And as for you," she said, shooting Twink an angry glance, "you will be taken care of tomorrow. Now be gone, all of you!"

Twink shivered. Tom took her hand, and with Twiffle following they made their way out of the theater to their rooms. They passed unnoticed through the Lords and Ladies, who were noisily discussing the play, exclaiming over its excellence and looking forward to the next night's performance — of the same play.

As soon as they were in their rooms, Twiffle quickly closed the door and silently motioned the children to his side. The little clown was plainly excited. "Listen," he whispered to the children. "I believe I have figured out what has happened to the Shaggy Man and all the rest of the actors and actresses, for that matter. They have been enchanted. King Ticket and Queen Curtain have cast some kind of spell upon them so that they are only half awake. The only existence they have is their dreamlike life on the stage as they go through their parts in the play."

"I see," nodded Twink. "I believe you're right. Otherwise Shaggy would surely have answered when I called to him from the box."

"Of course," said Twiffle.

"Then you don't think," surmised Tom, "that any of the actors and actresses are Lords and Ladies of the castle?"

"Not a bit of it," stated Twiffle firmly. "It is my belief that they are people from adjoining countries who, like ourselves, have wandered unwittingly into the castle and have been enchanted for the pleasure of King Ticket, Queen Curtain and the Lords and Ladies who have always lived there."

"You must be right," murmured Twink, recalling how King Ticket had brushed aside their question as to the identity of the actors and actresses.

"Of course I am right," asserted Twiffle. "It is the only solution that answers all the questions. What we must do now is find a way to rescue the Shaggy Man tonight before King Ticket and Queen Curtain have a chance to cast their disgusting old spell on Twink tomorrow."

"Then let's get started," said Tom. "What do we do, Twiffle?"

"Nothing now," replied Twiffle. "We must wait until everyone in the castle is asleep. Only then will it be safe for us to act."

Twink and Tom tried to be calm during the next hour as they discussed with Twiffle their chances of rescuing the Shaggy Man and making an escape from the castle. At last Twiffle went quietly to the door and slowly opened it, peering up and down the hall corridor. The entire castle seemed to be wrapped in deep silence. There was not a sound. "Come," whispered Twiffle. "I believe it is safe to proceed now. Everyone seems to be asleep. You must walk on your tiptoes so your steps won't be heard."

"Where are we going, Twiffle?" whispered Tom.

"To the theater and then backstage. That is where I am almost sure we will find the Shaggy Man and all the rest of the unfortunate actors and actresses." The lights of the castle were dimmed to a soft glow, but this was enough for the adventurers to find their way to the theater with no trouble. Here the same soft light glowed, filling the theater with a thin, ghostly luminescence.

Twiffle quickly led the way down the aisle, then up the small flight of stairs to the stage. Beckoning the children to follow him, Twiffle darted through the wings to the back of the stage. Here an amazing sight greeted them. Lined up in two rows like soldiers on a drill field were about fifty men, women and children. Some of them Twink and Tom recalled having seen on the stage earlier that evening. They ranged in age from small children to elderly men and women. They stood stiffly, as though they were at attention. Their eyes were tight shut. So still were these figures that Twink couldn't tell whether or not they were breathing. In the front row stood the Shaggy Man.

"Every type for every part," muttered Twiffle to himself. Then, turning to the children, he whispered, "Here they are, just as I suspected, the unfortunate victims of King Ticket and Queen Curtain. They have no more life than mere dummies until the curtain goes up and they walk on the stage to play their parts in that absurd drama."

Twiffle approached the Shaggy Man and studied him intently. At last he sighed and shook his head. "I am afraid there is nothing we can do just now," he admitted. "I learned a little magic from Conjo, and I hoped that I might be able to release the Shaggy Man, but the spell that is upon him is a strange one. I have no power to break it."

"There must surely be something we can do," said Tom, thinking of Queen Curtain's threatening speech to Twink.

"I must have time to think," said Twiffle. "At least we have discovered the whereabouts of the Shaggy Man, and we know what has happened to him and all these other poor people. There must be some way to release them, if only I can hit upon it. I suggest we return to our rooms. We certainly don't want to be discovered here."

"But what about Twink?" asked Tom with dismay.

"I am hoping I can prevent Queen Curtain from making good her threat," replied Twiffle grimly.

"Oh, don't worry about me," said Twink bravely. "If worst comes to worst and I don't make a better actress than the rest of these folks, I'll be awfully disappointed in myself."

Chapter 13 - Tom Goes to the Rescue

Despite the late hour at which they had gone to bed, Tom awakened bright and early in the morning, hurried into his clothes and bounded into Twink's room. The bed was empty! Thinking that Twink might have risen before him, Tom dashed into the living room. There he found Twiffle alone, deep in thought.

"Twiffle! Twiffle! Twink is gone!" exclaimed Tom.

Twiffle nodded his head gravely. "I know," he said. "I looked for her about half an hour ago, and she was gone. I was afraid this would happen."

"But this is terrible!" protested Tom. "Think of poor Twink — one of those senseless dummies just for the amusement of these wicked people." The boy was thoroughly incensed as he went on. "They call this the Valley of Romance! Why, they must be heartless. They don't even know what real romance or love is!"

Twiffle let out a shout and leaped to his feet. "My boy, you've done it!" he cried.

"Done what?" gasped the astonished Tom.

"You've just given me the solution of all our problems. I now know how we can save not only Twink and the Shaggy Man, but all the other people enslaved by King Ticket and Queen Curtain!"

"You do?" said Tom wonderingly.

"Yes," responded Twiffle. "You were wrong about only one thing: King Ticket, Queen Curtain and the Lords and Ladies are not heartless. They have hearts, all right. But you were very right when you said they don't know what real romance or love is. They don't. We're going to show them, and in the process we will rescue Twink and Shaggy!" Twiffle excitedly unfolded his plan. As Tom listened, he grew more and more cheerful. When Twiffle finished, Tom picked up the little clown and danced exuberantly about the room with him.

"Twiffle," the boy shouted, "you're a wonder!"

Twiffle grinned from ear to ear. "It was you who gave me the idea," he reminded Tom modestly. "But we must plan very carefully," he went on, becoming serious. "Remember, there is only a slim chance that our plan will work. We must take that chance and hope for the best. As there is nothing we can do until tonight when the play is again presented, we should make use of this time to work out every single detail of our plan."

Twiffle and Tom went over their plan again and again. Nevertheless, the day seemed to Tom one of the longest he had ever spent. The long hours of waiting were broken only three times — when Lady Cue brought in Tom's meals. The food was quite good, but a bit mixed up. For breakfast the befuddled Lady brought Tom a large slice of roast beef with corn flakes and apple pie. Lunch consisted of fried eggs, mashed potatoes and doughnuts, while dinner was made up of broiled apricots, strawberry shortcake and graham crackers. But Tom was hungry and didn't mind the strange assortment of foods too much. He managed to eat everything, even though Lady Cue brought him six spoons with each meal and no knives or forks.

When Lady Cue appeared with the evening meal, Tom was a bit worried because they had not been asked to dine with the Lords and Ladies in the Royal Dining Room. Could this mean they would not be invited to the play? If so, then their plan of rescue would be ruined. Twiffle was not worried. He was sure they would be asked to share the King and Queen's Royal Box, if only as a form of punishment, since they would be compelled to see Twink as one of the puppets on the stage. Twiffle proved to be right. Early in the evening Lady Cue appeared in the doorway and led them again to the theater.

King Ticket and Queen Curtain were already settled in the Royal Box when Tom and Twiffle arrived. Except to give them an icy stare, the monarchs paid no attention to their guests. Twiffle winked at Tom, but both of them were quaking lest Twiffle's plan might not work. If it did not work, they would be worse off than ever. If possible, the play — it was the same one — was even worse than on the previous night. The players went through their parts in a dreamlike fashion, chanting their lines woodenly. Scenery fell apart, the curtain came down at the wrong moments, and everything possible went wrong. But King Ticket and Queen Curtain were enchanted. Along with the Lords and Ladies they applauded vociferously and reacted to the ridiculous performance with even more enthusiasm than they had displayed the night before.

This night, Tom had no trouble in keeping awake. He squirmed about in his seat with impatience, waiting until Twink and the Shaggy Man would appear. This didn't happen until the play was well into the fourth and last act. As on the night before, the Shaggy Man wandered blindly onto the stage, speaking the same lines in an almost indistinguishable voice. A moment later Tom tensed with excitement. A new character had been added. It was Twink. Her eyes stared as she moved mechanically across the stage, murmuring the words of her lines. Tom took a deep breath and glanced at Twiffle. The time had come to act. Twiffle nodded.

In the next moment Tom climbed to the wide rail that encircled the Royal Box. Poised there for a moment, he gave a leap and landed on the stage. Without hesitating a moment he dashed to the Shaggy Man, and to the amazement of everyone in the audience except Twiffle went through the Shaggy Man's pockets. Tom gave an exultant cry. He had found what he wanted. He held the Love Magnet before him, waving it first at the Shaggy Man and then at Twink.

Shaggy and Twink started, then rubbed their eyes and stared about them unbelievingly. Meanwhile, Tom was busy. He didn't hesitate until he had exposed the Love Magnet to the gaze of each of the enchanted actors and actresses. As each one looked at the Love Magnet, he lost his glassy stare and came to life. In a few seconds the stage was filled, not with dummies but with human beings, bewildered but freed from the thralldom of King Ticket and Queen Curtain's evil spell. As they recovered, several of them threw their arms around Tom, while all gazed at the boy with fondness and love in their eyes. Twink suddenly realized how greatly she loved her brother, and the first thing the Shaggy Man said was, "A great boy, that Tom!"

Meanwhile, King Ticket and Queen Curtain, as well as the entire audience of Lords and Ladies, had risen to their feet. None of them spoke. The real drama suddenly being lived on the stage held them fascinated. At this very moment, Tom advanced to the front center of the stage and with all eyes upon him flashed the Love Magnet before the audience. A vast sigh went through the theater. And then there was a confused babel (sic! — babble) as the Lords and Ladies crowded into the aisle, each of them bent upon reaching the stage and embracing Tom, who, they realized suddenly, was quite the most lovable person they had ever beheld.

King Ticket leaped from the Royal Box onto the stage, hurrying toward Tom. "My dear boy," he exclaimed, "how could I have been so blind? Isn't there something I can do for you? Name it, and you shall have it! My Kingdom is yours for the asking!"

Queen Curtain was standing in the box, arms outstretched appealingly to Tom. "You darling boy!" she cried. "How wonderful it is that you have come to visit us!"

Twiffle was sitting quietly in the Royal Box, grinning broadly. "Wouldn't old Conjo be surprised," he thought, "if he knew how well the Love Magnet has done its work? Tom really is quite a boy!"

Chapter 14 - The Valley of Love

That night there was a great feast in the Grand Dining Room of the castle. Tom was the guest of honor, sitting at the head of the table between King Ticket and Queen Curtain. Twink, feeling very proud of her brother, sat at the Queen's right with the Shaggy Man and Twiffle at her side. In addition to the Lords and Ladies of the castle, all the people who had formerly been actors and actresses were seated about the table. There were speeches, merrymaking and much laughter while everyone enjoyed course after course of the delicious food served. King Ticket and Queen Curtain talked together during the feast, seeming to discuss something on which they finally appeared to reach a decision.

King Ticket arose and, banging with a silver fork against a drinking goblet, obtained the attention and silence of the merrymakers. "My dear friends," began the King, beaming on his audience. "Good Queen Curtain and I have been discussing a proposal which we are sure will meet with your approval. You are well aware that although we did not know it, we, the people of the Valley of Romance, have been living in a bondage that was even greater than that which we cast over the poor unfortunates who wandered into the castle. For we lived without knowing the meaning of true romance and love. We found our only pleasure in artificial romance as we saw it on the stage. We had no love for each other, no romance among ourselves. Now all this is changed. Not only do we now appreciate and know the true meaning of real love, but the people whom we enslaved are freed and happy once more. We have one person to thank for this: Tom, who with the Love Magnet brought us our present joy and happiness. Queen Curtain and I propose that we yield our thrones and that Tom become the new King of the Valley of Romance."

The applause was tremendous. Apparently everyone in the Grand Dining Room favored King Ticket's startling plan. But Tom leaped to his feet and exclaimed, "Your Highnesses, Ladies and Gentlemen, thank you for this great honor, but I cannot be your King. Maybe I'll never get the chance to be a king again. But the important thing for Twink and me is to find our way home. The Shaggy Man has promised that Ozma of Oz will send us home if we can only reach Oz. That is the thing we want most. Anyway, I have no right to be your King. I don't know anything about the job, and you should really be grateful to the Love Magnet for making you happy, not me. Now that you folks know the meaning of real love, I'm sure King Ticket will make you a fine King and Queen Curtain will be a real Queen."

Again the applause resounded. At last King Ticket rose again, expressing his regret that Tom could not remain with them to be their King. King Ticket promised that he would do his best to be a kind and loving monarch. His first move, he said, would be to grant complete freedom to the people who had wandered to the castle and had become slaves on the Stage of False Romance. These people, he said, might return to dwell as Lords and Ladies in the Castle of Romance.

Since they would have no further use for the theater, King ticket promised to have the seats removed and the theater remodeled into a real Temple of Learning where each of his subjects might learn some craft or art that would be useful or pleasing to his fellows. Here they would meet each day and study and work at their arts and crafts, enjoying companionship and the satisfaction of real accomplishment and creation.

"If you do manage to get to the Land of Oz," King Ticket said to the Shaggy Man, "I wonder if you would ask Professor Wogglebug if he would like to come to our Temple of Learning as a visiting Professor? I am sure there are many things he could teach us that would be both interesting and useful." Shaggy promised to extend the invitation to the learned Wogglebug, who was head of the Royal College of Oz.

In spite of all the excitement, Twink and Tom were nodding by the time the feasting and speechmaking were ended. Everyone bade them a happy goodnight, and Lady Cue conducted them once more to their rooms. The Love Magnet had wrought its change on Lady Cue, too. Gone was her former befuddled state in which she was not at all sure of anything or anyone. Now she was a charming, gracious lady with the manners of a cordial and perfect hostess.

Shaggy and the children were fast asleep almost as soon as their heads touched the soft pillows. Twiffle passed the night looking at the pictures in the books on the living room shelves. By the middle of the following morning they were ready to begin their adventures again. They found that King Ticket, Queen Curtain, the Lords and Ladies and the former actors and actresses, many of whom had decided to make their homes in the Valley of Romance, were gathered in the courtyard to bid them farewell. King Ticket gave them general directions for traveling to reach the Deadly Desert. That was the nearest he could come to directing them to the Land of Oz.

Just as they were about to leave, Lady Cue arrived breathlessly on the scene. She was so excited that she nearly lapsed into her old bewildered state. "I — I — I have been so busy all morning cooking this for you that I was afraid I would miss you." Lady Cue looked anxiously at Shaggy and his friends as though she couldn't believe they were still there. As she spoke, she handed Shaggy a large lunch basket filled with deliciously prepared good things to eat. Shaggy, Twink, Tom and even Twiffle — who didn't eat — thanked Lady Cue warmly for her thoughtfulness. They were glad she had not changed entirely, for they had grown fond of her. As they turned away from her and started once again on their journey, Lady Cue was staring after them and dabbing at her eyes with a dishcloth.

Waving goodbye, the little band of adventurers followed the stream to the south as it wound through the green and peaceful Valley of Romance. When they were almost out of sight of the Castle of Romance, Twink looked back and saw the delicately fashioned spires shimmering in the sun. "Now," the girl said, "it is truly as beautiful a castle as it looks."

Chapter 15 - The King of the Fairy Beavers

Beyond the valley, the country became rugged and rolling, with outcroppings of grey rock, while the river narrowed, grew deeper, and flowed much more swiftly. It was well into the afternoon when the Shaggy Man suggested that they rest under a gnarled tree near the river bank and enjoy their luncheon. They were all glad for the rest on the grass which grew high and coarse over the countryside, and the food which Lady Cue had packed for them was both satisfying and delicious.

Twink took a long look at the rather forbidding scenery about them. In the distance loomed dark mountain peaks, while trees became fewer and fewer. "Doesn't look like there's a living thing within miles!" said the little girl a bit disconsolately.

"In a way, that's a good sign," replied the Shaggy Man. "For the nearer we come to the Deadly Desert, the more wild and desolate the country is. From the looks of things here, I wouldn't be surprised if we were near the Kingdom of the Nomes."

"Have you any idea how we can get to Oz once we arrive at the Deadly Desert?" asked Twiffle.

"No," said the Shaggy Man, "I haven't. But one can never tell what will happen when traveling in a fairy country, and I figure the closer we re to the Deadly Desert, the closer we are to Oz. Now if I just hadn't lost Ozma's Magic Compass — But there's no use crying over spilt milk."

"Did I understand you to say you are going to the Land of Oz?" The words were spoken in a small, clear voice. At the same time the tall grass just in front of Shaggy and his friends parted, and a beaver stepped out and viewed them fearlessly. Twink was amazed to see that the beaver wore a small golden crown on his head, while in his right paw he carried a slender beech rod.

"Yes," said the Shaggy Man, calmly regarding the beaver while he continued to munch a peanut butter and jelly sandwich. "That is, we hope to get to the Land of Oz. First we must find some way to cross the Deadly Desert."

The beaver was silent for a moment, then he said, "Will you take me to Oz with you?"

"Take you with us!" exclaimed the Shaggy Man. "Why, we aren't at all sure we can get there ourselves. But why do you want to go to Oz? I can tell by your crown that you're a King of some sort and not an ordinary beaver."

"I am the King of the Fairy Beavers," announced the little animal a bit proudly. "None of us are ordinary beavers, since we are fairy creatures. And as for why I want to visit Oz — well, I have heard wonderful tales of that famous fairyland, and I have long dreamed of visiting it."

"Seems to me," observed Tom, "that since you are a Fairy King, your magic powers could take you to Oz."

"No," replied the beaver King, "my magic is mostly water magic, and that would be less than useless on the fiery sands of the Deadly Desert. But that isn't the main reason that keeps me from visiting Oz."

"What is it, then?" asked Shaggy.

"I have not been invited," replied the beaver King simply.

"I am sure that if Ozma knew enough about that, she would fix it," said the Shaggy Man kindly.

"Do you think so?" asked the beaver. "Do you really think Ozma would invite me? I hoped you would say that, for it gives me courage to put forth a suggestion I have in mind."

"What is that?" asked Shaggy.

"If you, the famous Shaggy Man of Oz, were to invite me to visit Oz, then everything would be quite proper, wouldn't it?"

"I suppose it would," admitted the Shaggy Man, smiling. "But how do you propose to get to Oz, since we can't cross the Desert?"

"Then you really invite me to accompany you? That is wonderful! As for the Deadly Desert, I have a plan which might work."

"How did you know who the Shaggy Man was?" asked Twink.

"Oh, everyone knows about the Shaggy Man of Oz, and when I saw you here discussing your journey to Oz, I was almost sure this could be none other than the famous Shaggy Man."

Shaggy looked modestly at the ground.

Twiffle asked, "Just how far are we from this Deadly Desert?"

"Quite a distance," replied the beaver King. "The Desert lies just beyond our own Kingdom, which is in the hills and mountains you see in the distance."

"And what is your plan for crossing it?" asked the Shaggy Man.

"Come to my palace, where you will be comfortable," said the King, "and we will discuss my plan."

"It must be a long walk," sighed Twink. "And the farther we go toward the Desert, the rockier and grayer the country becomes."

"Oh, we shan't walk. It will be much quicker to ride," declared the beaver King. With that, the King of the Fairy Beavers walked to the edge of the stream and uttered a shrill whistle. Shaggy and his friends followed the little animal. A few hundred feet below them, the river curved to the left. Around this bend in the stream they could now see some twenty little heads — beavers swimming swiftly upstream and pulling after them a barge-like boat with a canopy to shut out the rays of the sun. In a few moments the boat was drawing near the shore on which they stood. Twink could see that each of the little beavers wore a harness connected to the boat by a rope of woven reeds. The boat itself was brightly painted and filled with soft, silken cushions.

"You will be my guests on the journey down the river to my Kingdom, where it will give me great pleasure to welcome you to my humble abode."

Twink, Tom, the Shaggy Man and Twiffle stepped into the boat. The Shaggy Man had to stoop a bit to miss the canopy, but once they were seated on the soft cushions there was room for all. The King of the Fairy Beavers hitched himself into the front of the harness with the other beavers. "I hope you'll forgive me for not riding with you," he said, "but when I have guests, I like to do my share of the work — we beavers always enjoy working together, you know, and occasions like this give me an opportunity to forget I'm a King." The boat moved swiftly down the river, pulled easily by the team of strong little animals.

"Well, this certainly beats walking, your Majesty," said the Shaggy Man as he sighed with content and settled back among the cushions.

Chapter 16 - In Beaver Land

Tom, who was especially fond of animals, longed to hold one of the little beavers and fondle it to his heart's content. And what fun it would be, the boy thought, just to jump into the stream and swim along with the busily paddling, happy-looking little animals. But Tom contented himself with marveling at the ease with which the beavers pulled the boat.

Although the journey consumed more than an hour, it did not seem nearly that long to the travelers, who were kept busy watching the changing scenery as the boat sped swiftly downstream. The banks of the river grew much steeper, and they could see scarcely any trees, while grey rocks jutted from the earth and forbidding mountain peaks loomed only a few miles distant.

The beavers swam out of the current of the river and drew the boat into a placid pool among the rocks. At the far end of the pool there was a stairway leading from a wooden landing to a wicket (sic — "wicker"?) door set in the face of a cliff of grey stone that ran steeply down to the pond's edge. The fairy beavers seemed to be full of energy and untired by the journey, as they chattered among themselves, drawing the boat to the landing and making it secure.

The Shaggy Man looked about him and observed to the King, "I always thought, your majesty, that beavers liked to live where there was plenty of wood. I've heard tell of them building whole series of dams from trees they had gnawed down. Even human engineers have taken some lessons in water control from the beavers."

"You're right," replied the King of the Fairy Beavers. "But those beavers you heard about were of the ordinary kind. Not that we fairy beavers don't do a lot of engineering. We do. But we prefer this desolate region for our home since we are less likely to be disturbed here. And any trees we may need we can always fell and float downstream from the more fertile lands." As he spoke, the beaver King ascended the steps to the wicker door and swung it open. The Shaggy Man had to stoop to enter, but once inside he found he could stand with ease.

It took a few minutes for Shaggy and his friends to adjust their eyes from the glare of the sun on the water to the lighting of the cave in which they stood. For that was what it was, a vast cave in the cliff. A fairy light of a silver-white issued from the rock walls and dome of the cave. The cavern proved to be merely the anteroom of the beaver kingdom, which consisted of a labyrinth of large and small tunnels burrowed into the earth at the rear of the cave. Sleek, well-fed beavers hurried in and out of the burrows, bent upon the tasks that made up their daily work.

Indeed, everyone in this underground kingdom seemed to be hard at work and intently busy on one task or another. New tunnels were being constructed and reinforced with carefully hewn beams of wood, new rooms and homes were under construction, and there didn't seem to be an idle moment with all the work that was going on. The beaver King was perhaps even busier than his subjects, and while he was gracious and did everything in his power to make his guests comfortable, they got the impression that even while he was chatting with them his mind was busy with new plans and ideas for the improvement of his kingdom.

The King of the Fairy Beavers hesitated only long enough for Shaggy and his friends to glance about them and then led his guests down one of the burrows, which was really a good-sized tunnel. A short distance down this passage the beaver King paused before a large, granite door set in the tunnel's side. Just above the door was mounted a golden crown. "It is my pleasure," said the beaver King as the heavy door swung open, "to welcome you to my royal suite, where I hope you will accept my humble hospitality."

There was a large reception hall, then a huge throne room that could easily accommodate an assemblage of several thousand beavers, and finally a dining room with mirrored walls and ceiling and a sumptuously laid table. Shaggy and his friends were amazed at the elegance and beauty of their surroundings. The dining room table was set with the finest of china, and the linens were snowy white and hand woven.

The King of the Fairy Beavers still carried the slender beech rod, which Twink had noticed in his right paw when he had first appeared among them that afternoon. After inviting his guests to be seated at the table, the beaver King waved the beech rod — which Twink and Tom had already guessed to be his magic wand — and at once the table was loaded with the most savory dishes imaginable. "I don't ordinarily employ magic unless it is necessary," the beaver King explained. "We beavers prefer to work for what we get, but magic affords the quickest manner of providing the strange foods that you human beings seem to enjoy."

Twiffle and the beaver King conversed while Shaggy, Twink and Tom enjoyed the food. They were much hungrier than they realized; the ride on the river had given them a tremendous appetite. When they had finished eating, the King of the Fairy Beavers said, "Now, my friends, would be a good time to plan our trip to the Land of Oz."

No one said a word, but every eye was fixed with eager attention on the little animal. "We cannot fly over the Deadly Desert," the beaver King went on. "Nor can we cross it. The devouring sands would mean quick death for all of us."

"Then we're just not going to Oz, I guess," said Tom sadly.

"Oh, yes, I think we are," replied the beaver King quickly. "There is one way left to cross the Desert."

A hush fell over the company as they waited for the beaver King's next words. "We can cross under the Desert," he said simply.

"You have burrowed clear under the Deadly Desert to Oz?" asked the Shaggy Man incredulously.

"No," replied the King of the Fairy Beavers, "we have not. But someone else has."

"And who is that?" asked Twink.

"The Nome King," said the beaver King.

Chapter 17 - The Tunnel Under the Desert

The Shaggy Man leaped to his feet and stared at the beaver King. "What?" he exclaimed. "You discovered the Nome King's tunnel under the Deadly Desert?"

"Oh yes," replied the beaver King. "We have known for some time of its existence and location."

"But this is wonderful!" gasped the Shaggy Man. "Our troubles are all over. All we have to do is walk through the tunnel to the Emerald City!"

"No," said the King of the Fairy Beavers. "It isn't as easy as that. You must remember we still have Glinda's Barrier of Invisibility to contend with."

"Hmmmm," said the Shaggy Man, seating himself. "That is true. But there might be some way we could get past that barrier. Tell me, how did you happen to discover the Nome King's tunnel?"

"We stumbled onto it accidentally when one of our burrows led into it," explained the beaver King. "We followed it to the Kingdom of the Nomes, where the tunnel opens into one of the Nome King's mines. There was a company of Nomes working there, and the ill-natured creatures hurled diamonds at us. In fact, the Nomes were so discourteous that we have never since entered that section of the tunnel."

"But if you knew the tunnel led to Oz in the other direction, why didn't you follow it?" asked Twiffle.

"Because we also know Ozma's wishes, and we respect them," replied the beaver King quietly. "But certainly Ozma would not object to the Shaggy Man and his friend using the tunnel. And since the Shaggy Man has so kindly invited me to visit Oz, I feel perfectly free to accompany him."

"Then you know the story of the tunnel the Nome King built under the Deadly Desert to the Emerald City?" asked the Shaggy Man.

"Our fairy powers keep us informed of important happenings not only in Oz but in all other parts of the world," replied the beaver King.

Twink and Tom knew the story, too. They had read how the Nome King, seeking revenge on Ozma and Dorothy because they had once conquered him, set his Nomes to burrowing a tunnel from the Nome Kingdom to the Emerald City. When it was finished, Roquat the Red (as the Nome King was known then) and a horde of evil allies marched through the tunnel intent on conquering and laying waste all of Oz. Ozma refused to fight, but instead gathered all her closest friends about her in the garden near the Fountain of Oblivion, where the invaders were about to break through from the tunnel.

The famous Scarecrow of Oz had given Ozma the idea that had saved her from the necessity of fighting. The tunnel was hot and dry, and Ozma had used her magic powers to scatter dust through the underground passage. As a result, when the Nome King and his allies came bursting through the earth, they were consumed with a terrific thirst. The first thing they saw was the Fountain of Oblivion. Just as the Scarecrow had planned, they all dashed to the fountain and drank. The waters of this fountain cause anyone who drinks of it to lose all memory of his former life. Consequently, the Nome King and all his allies became as harmless as little children, having forgotten their former evil lives. Ozma had sent them back by means of the Magic Belt to their own lands, and then closed the earth over the tunnel's entrance into her garden. Soon after that, Glinda had laid down the Magic Barrier of Invisibility over the Deadly Desert, which Ozma hoped would prevent any other invaders from attacking the Land of Oz.

"Trying to get through the tunnel really seems the only thing to do," said the Shaggy Man thoughtfully. "That will be far better than just sitting and waiting for Ozma to return to the Emerald City — I have no idea how long she plans to visit with Glinda. I suppose the only thing we can do is try to deal with the Barrier of Invisibility when we come to it. Perhaps your Majesty's magic could overcome it."

The Beaver King was thoughtful. "Perhaps," he said. "But you must remember Glinda's magic is very powerful. We may discover that the desert is just as impassable underground as it is above ground. So don't let us raise our hopes too high, my friends. At any rate," he concluded, "we shall undertake the journey in the morning, and then we shall know."

The beaver King led his guests into his throne room, where comfortable seats were provided. Next a troop of beaver acrobats came running into the throne room. They wore brightly colored tights and put on a performance of such skill and daring that Twink and Tom were delighted. The animals were amazingly agile, and some of their tumbling tricks were so droll that even Twiffle laughed aloud. "I never saw anything to beat this at the circus," Tom confided to Twink as the twins loudly applauded.

When the entertainment was over, it was growing late, and saying he had some work to do in his magic workshop in preparation for the journey in the morning, the beaver King led his guests to a suite of beautifully furnished sleeping rooms. Twink and Tom were not a bit surprised that the beaver King should work while they slept. Indeed, they wondered if anyone in this busy little kingdom ever took time off to rest.

"As soon as you lie down on the beds," the beaver King told Twink and Tom, "you will be lulled to sleep by the most beautiful music in the world." With that, he closed the door softly and left them. Twink and Tom were in their beds in no time at all, eager to hear the music the beaver King had promised them. No sooner had their heads touched the pillows than they heard it. It was like the sleepy murmuring of a thousand voices. There were no words, only a soft whisper that seemed to come from a great distance and yet was close by — was everywhere. Twink closed her eyes, and the wordless music sang of green meadows under a golden sun, of mountain rills that tripped from stone to stone down to beautiful valleys, of great rivers that flowed through the hearts of vast lands, and finally of the sea itself, singing eternally of endless wonders.

Just before Tom dropped off to sleep, he said, "Twink, I know what it is. The beaver King said it was the most beautiful music in the world, and it is—"

"I know," said Twink sleepily. "It's the music of running water."

Chapter 18 - The Flame Folk

Early the next morning Shaggy and his friends found a steaming hot breakfast waiting for them in their rooms. No sooner had they finished than the King of the Fairy Beavers appeared to lead them to the Nome King's tunnel. They followed the King through several miles of weaving and twisting beaver burrows until at last they stood at the entrance of the tunnel. Shaggy had noted that the King bore on his back, like a tiny knapsack, a small bundle. Now he saw that the twenty young beavers who were waiting at the tunnel's entrance to undertake the journey with them bore similar though smaller bundles on their backs. In addition, each of the young beavers carried a pine torch to light the way through the dark tunnel. At a signal from the beaver King, the torch-bearing beavers advanced into the tunnel, and the journey was on.

"How far are we from the Deadly Desert?" inquired the Shaggy Man.

"Not more than a mile," answered the beaver King. "We will know when we reach the Desert, because of the heat radiated downward by the sands. The tunnel is not far from the surface — no more than twenty feet, I would judge."

The tunnel was hewn from solid rock, but the floor of it was smooth, so the travelers were able to proceed at a good rate of speed. They all noticed that the heat increased perceptibly the closer they came to the shifting sands above them.

"Whee-ew!" exclaimed the Shaggy Man. "This is no place for a pleasure trip. I can see why the Nome King was thirsty when he got out of here."

They were now directly under the Deadly Desert, and the heat radiated by the shifting sands above them was intense. But Twink and Tom were lightly dressed, so they didn't mind the heat so much. Twiffle naturally paid not the slightest attention to the temperature. The beavers, who were used to underground heat, moved swiftly forward. The pine torches of the young beavers cast flickering shadows on the rough stone walls about the travelers. But suddenly the light of the torches dimmed and faded in a greater brilliance. The torch-bearing beavers stopped in their tracks and were chattering excitedly among themselves, waiting for the beaver King and his party to catch up with them. The travelers hurried forward and found to their amazement that the new light came from a rift in the rock roof. Sunlight was shining down into the tunnel!

But no sooner had they recovered from this surprise than they were overwhelmed by another. Directly ahead of them, blocking their passage through the tunnel, was a group of the strangest people they had ever seen. These beings were human in shape, yet they seemed to be made of flame. The living fire that formed their bodies varied in hue from a deep, glowing red to light orange and yellow, while their fingertips, eyes, and features gave off blue and greenish colored flames.

There were perhaps ten of the creatures, standing side by side so that the beaver King and his friends found their way completely blocked by this wall of living flame. Waves of heat radiated from their flaming bodies, and Twink and Tom had to blink their eyes several times to become accustomed to the glare of flame and light. "Halt! You can go no further. Turn back at once to whence you came." One of the flame folk was speaking. He appeared to be their leader, since he was taller than his companions, and his eyes glowed much more fiercely than the rest.

"Who are you?" asked the beaver King calmly.

"We are Dwellers of the Desert. We live on the shifting sands on the surface. Occasionally we visit the oasis just above, where there is no sand, but blue grass that glows with blue flame," the flame being answered.

"An oasis on the Deadly Desert?" asked the Shaggy Man incredulously.

"Certainly. Did you ever hear of a desert that didn't have an oasis?" replied the fire creature.

"Maybe not," muttered the Shaggy Man. "And I suppose the flame grass keeps the deadly sand from shifting into the tunnel."

"Exactly," replied the fire creature. "But we are not concerned with sand in the tunnel. There are other things much more objectionable — yourselves, for instance."

"How did you find out about the tunnel?" asked the beaver King, ignoring the fire being's insult.

"Not that it is any of your business, but we were aware of the tunnel's existence while the Nome King was building it. After he returned to his own kingdom, we burned our way down through the rocks from the oasis above."

"Why did you do that?" persisted the beaver King.

The leader of the fire creatures hesitated for a moment, then replied in an angry voice, "Because we enjoy the coolness of the tunnel. By contrast it makes the fiery sands of the desert even more pleasant. Now, be on your way back where you came from, or we will advance upon you and blast you to cinders."

"My, what a fiery-tempered fellow," said Shaggy. This seemed to infuriate the fire creature, and he was about to leap toward Shaggy when the beaver King stepped forward holding out his beechwood wand. Instantly from the tip of the wand there came forth a spray of water that showered on the row of fire creatures. As soon as it touched their flaming bodies, the water hissed into steam. The effect on the fire beings was amazing. They uttered loud howls of pain and fright and leaped like flames from a great fire into the air and through the rift in the rock. Their cries resounded as they dashed over the oasis to roll in the flaming sands of the desert.

"Come," urged the beaver King, "let us hurry, although I do not think there is any danger of pursuit."

The young beavers went first, followed by Shaggy and his friends. They hurried until they had passed out of sight of the sunlight that flowed down the rift into the tunnel. "I guess that's the first time those critters ever saw water," said the Shaggy Man, grinning.

"The water didn't hurt them," said the beaver King, "and the burning sands will soon restore whatever heat they lost. Nevertheless, I don't think they will cause us any further annoyance."

They walked ahead rapidly hour after hour with the young beavers lighting the way through the Nome King's tunnel.

Chapter 19 - The Barrier of Invisibility

Suddenly Shaggy stopped and stared about him. He was alone in the tunnel! He had been walking along looking at nothing in particular, when in a flash his companions had vanished. Just ahead of him he could hear the excited chattering of the twenty young beavers. But there was no sign of any living thing. Then Shaggy looked down at himself and cried out in amazement — he wasn't there either! He could see nothing of his body, although he felt as firm as ever.

"You will be kind enough to remove your wand from my eye, please!" It was Twiffle's voice speaking somewhere near Shaggy.

"I beg your pardon, we are both invisible, so my poking my wand in your eye was entirely unintentional, I assure you," the beaver King's voice answered.

"Hey! Stay off my foot!" Tom called out.

"Was that your foot? I'm sure I didn't see it," Twink's voice answered soothingly.

"Neither do I, but it's there just the same," replied Tom's voice ruefully.

All about them the young beavers' voices had risen, and several angry disputes were taking place. Evidently some accidents had occurred among the little animals, too. The Shaggy Man said sadly, "Well, this seems to be the Barrier of Invisibility, and it's most effective, too. I propose we all stay just where we are until we decide what to do, for we all seem to be quite invisible."

"Must we turn back?" asked Twink anxiously.

"Don't you worry, Twink," said Tom. "Even if we can't get to the Land of Oz, we'll find our way home."

"Yes, I think we must turn back," announced the beaver King. "Let us retreat in the tunnel to the point where the Barrier of Invisibility begins. It should be only a few feet from where we are now, since we just entered it."

"But we have turned about and lost all sense of direction since becoming invisible," said the Shaggy Man. "Since we cannot see the tunnel, it looks the same in every direction, so how are we to know which way to turn to go back?"

"Walk ten steps in one direction, and if you are still invisible, then turn about and walk twenty feet in the other direction," instructed the beaver King. This they all did, and after a bit of experimentation and several minor collisions, they were relieved to find themselves visible once more and standing on the edge of the Barrier of Invisibility. At the King's order the young beavers had remained where they were until the others had found their way out of the Barrier. Now the beaver King uttered a series of calls that quickly guided the animals beyond the Barrier of Invisibility.

Shaggy and his friends stood about in the tunnel gazing from one to another almost despairingly, wondering what to do next. "There is still hope that we may not have to go back and may be able to use the tunnel to reach Oz, my friends," began the beaver King quietly. "Last night and far into the morning, while you were sleeping, I was busy in my fairy workshop studying the problem. I believe I have solved it, although of course we cannot be quite sure until we make the test."

With that, the little animal unstrapped from his back the small bundle he had been carrying. Laying it on the tunnel floor, he carefully unfolded it. The bundle seemed to consist of a number of shimmering pieces of silver cloth so light they might have been spun from spiderwebs. The beaver King selected one of the folds of gossamer cloth and handed it to Twink. "Unfold it and put it about you, my dear," he said. "I think you will find it just your size."

Twink did as instructed and found the cloth fitted about her like a fairy cloak. "Oh, it's lovely," she exclaimed.

"It's more than that, I hope," said the beaver King. "It is a Cloak of Visibility."

"A cloak of what?" exclaimed the Shaggy Man.

"You have all heard and read tales of cloaks of invisibility," explained the beaver King. "Cloaks that make the wearer invisible are famous in the fairy tales of all lands. Well, I knew that we would become invisible today against our wishes, so I have attempted to create a Cloak of Visibility — a cloak that would overcome the spell of invisibility."

"Do you think it will work?" asked the Shaggy Man hopefully.

"I do not know," confessed the beaver King. "I am sure it wouldn't work above ground where Glinda's Barrier of Invisibility is full strength. Underground, Glinda's spell is much less intense because the earth and sands absorb and destroy the fairy spell. Glinda is a fairy just as Ozma is, and fairies, you know, are creatures of the light and air, and it is there that their powers are the strongest." The beaver King then handed out Cloaks of the shimmering material to all of them. There was a tiny one that fitted Twiffle perfectly. The twenty young beavers opened their knapsacks and drew from them their own Cloaks of Visibility, which they adjusted about themselves. "We are now ready to test the power of the Cloaks," said the beaver King. "They should not only make us visible, but should enable us to see the invisible." Twink thought she detected the slightest tremor in the King's voice. It was no wonder, she thought, for so much depended on those cloaks he had made.

Once again they proceeded into the tunnel, this time holding their breaths with excitement. Would the Cloaks of Visibility work? One, two, three, four, five steps and they found themselves watching one another to see if they were still visible. Six, seven, eight, nine, ten steps, but no one breathed freely until they had covered twenty steps. They all were still visible! And they could see the tunnel walls. The Cloaks of Visibility worked perfectly. Eagerly, the twenty young beavers took the lead again.

Chapter 20 - At the End of the Tunnel

"Seems to me," remarked the Shaggy Man after they had progressed for some distance, "that by now we may have crossed the Barrier of Invisibility."

"You're right," agreed the beaver King. "And that means we are now journeying underground in the Land of Oz. It also means that the Cloaks of Visibility are no longer necessary for our journey, so I propose that we discard them here, and I will destroy them so that they may never be used by anyone else for reaching the Land of Oz."

Each of the travelers removed his shimmering cloak and placed it on a little pile in the center of the tunnel. When all the cloaks were there, the beaver King waved his beechwood wand over the little heap of silvery material, and in a flash it had vanished.

"Seems a shame," murmured Twink. "They were so beautiful."

But Twink forgot the Cloaks as they journeyed on. She and Tom could scarcely believe it — just over their heads was the marvelous Land of Oz. They began talking of all the famous people who lived in Oz, and the boy and girl would probably have walked all night had not the King of the Fairy Beavers announced after they had been trudging steadily for more than six hours, "My fairy powers tell me it is dark in the land above. That means we have been walking all day. I propose we stop and sleep here and resume our journey in the morning. We should reach the Emerald City shortly after noon."

The Shaggy Man looked a bit ruefully at the hard stone floor of the tunnel. "Well," he sighed, "in my wanderings I have slept in less comfortable places. Twink can have my coat to rest her head on."

The beaver King chuckled softly. "Don't worry, Shaggy Man," he said. "I will provide beds for us. First let us enjoy a good dinner so that we will sleep the more soundly." After the dinner two small beds and a large one magically appeared for Twink, Tom and Shaggy. Although he did not need to sleep, Twiffle was provided with a little bed just his size. The beaver King curled up on a silken cushion. Other cushions were provided for the young beaver torchbearers, who took turns throughout the night sleeping and standing guard. The next morning found them refreshed and eager to be on their way toward the Emerald City. The tunnel was cool now, and they advanced rapidly. They were all weary of the sameness of the rocky tunnel walls and eager to reach the Land of Oz.

At last the young beavers who were leading the way came to a halt. For some distance the travelers had noticed that the tunnel had been gently sloping upward. Now they had arrived at its end. Just before them was a round patch of earth — a sort of "cork" of earth that Ozma had set in the end of the tunnel where it emerged in her garden. The young beavers knew exactly what to do. They set to work digging and burrowing around the rim of this patch of earth. When they had loosened it sufficiently, it would roll back into the tunnel, leaving free the exit for the Shaggy Man and his friends to emerge from the underground passage.

Twink and Tom watched in fascinated silence while the beavers worked. They were amazingly fast and skillful. Their paws fairly flew as they scooped out the earth and then brushed it from behind them with their wide, flat tails. In a few more seconds the beavers would be through the earth. The beaver King warned his comrades to step back in the tunnel, as the earth was about to come tumbling down.

There was a creaking and crashing of earth and stones, and the beavers dashed to safety. Suddenly loud roars of mingled anger and fright filled the tunnel. Sitting on the pile of earth that had crashed down into the tunnel and glaring at them frightfully while he roared was an enormous beast.

Chapter 21 - The Wizard is Excited

The great beast that had plunged into the tunnel suddenly stopped roaring, shook the gravel and dirt from his mane and back and said calmly, "I'm surprised at you, Shaggy Man! What do you mean by digging holes in Ozma's garden and leaving them open for unsuspecting folks to fall into? I might very easily have broken a leg or fractured a paw."

The Shaggy Man was grinning broadly. "Ten to one you were running away from something in an effort to work up your well-known but careful courage to the point of fighting." The huge lion looked down at the ground in embarrassment.

"You seem to know this great beast," said the beaver King, who had been regarding the sudden entrant into the tunnel with intense curiosity.

"Indeed I do!" replied the Shaggy Man. "He's an old friend of mine and quite harmless — if he is your friend. For this, you see, is the famous Cowardly Lion of Oz."

Twink and Tom had been staring with fascination at the huge lion. It was the first time they had ever come face to face with so great a beast, and although they had read so much about the famous Cowardly Lion of Oz that they recognized him, he had looked so fierce when he had fallen into the tunnel that they would surely have been frightened had it not been for Shaggy's reassuring words. "I don't know what this is all about, Shaggy," sighed the lion. "I was told Ozma had sent you out of the country on an errand for her, and now you turn up in a hole in her garden with a group of strange people and animals."

"It can all be explained," soothed the Shaggy Man. "Meanwhile, do you think you can help us out of here?"

"Of course," replied the Cowardly Lion. "Any friends of yours are friends of mine. Just climb on my back and you will have no difficulty in pulling yourselves to level ground. Those little animals don't bite, do they?" The great lion looked anxiously at the beaver's sharp teeth. With a laugh, Shaggy assured him he had nothing to fear.

The beavers and their King went first, followed by Twink and Tom, who found the lion's coat to be delightfully thick and soft, and finally be Twiffle and the Shaggy Man. The Cowardly Lion leaped from the tunnel and surveyed Shaggy and his friends. "Children, animals, a wooden clown — all popping up from what I now perceive is the Nome King's tunnel and not just a hole in the ground as I thought when I first tumbled into it. Tell me, Shaggy, have you had trouble with the Nome King again?"

Shaggy started to relate his adventures, but after a few words the Cowardly Lion interrupted him. "That can wait. You can tell me all about it later. The important thing is that you are here safely and — I almost forgot — there is plenty going on here!"

"What do you mean?" asked the Shaggy Man.

"Well, to tell the truth, I was running because I was frightened. Then the ground gave way beneath me and I fell into the tunnel."

"But why were you frightened?" persisted the Shaggy Man.

"Something is going on in the Royal Palace that I don't understand. The Wizard is very excited. He claims someone has stolen his Black Bag of Magic Tools and locked the door of the tower that leads to his magic workshop so he can't get in. I overheard him telling Dorothy about it, and they both seemed very upset. I decided I had better hide somewhere until I had gathered enough courage to lead an attack on the enemy."

The Shaggy Man smiled to himself. "You come with us," he said to the Lion. "First, I want you to meet my friends, Twink, Tom, Twiffle and the King of the Fairy Beavers. Then we must find the Wizard and Dorothy and see what this is all about."

The Cowardly Lion acknowledged the introduction so cordially that Twink and Tom felt as if they had been friends for years. They all walked through the beautiful gardens of Ozma's Royal Palace until they came to a large French door leading into a study. Here, by a stroke of good luck, they found Princess Dorothy and the Wizard of Oz deep in conversation. Dorothy and the Wizard looked up in amazement as Shaggy and his strangely assorted band of followers trailed into the study. Introductions were made again, and this time Twink and Tom were very nearly tongue-tied as they realized they were actually in the company of a real Princess of the Fairyland of Oz and the one and only Wizard of Oz. But Dorothy was so friendly and sweet that the little boy and girl felt quite at ease almost at once.

Shaggy told his story as briefly as possible and then asked the Wizard for an explanation of what had been happening in the Palace. "I wish I could tell you more definitely," said the Wizard ruefully. "But I am as mystified as anyone. Here is all I know: I had ordered the Royal Stables to have the Sawhorse saddled so that I might ride him to the College of Natural History, where I wished to consult some of the books written by Professor Wogglebug. I had placed on the ground my Black Bag of Magic Tools, which I needed for some experiments I planned to make at the College. I was about to mount the Sawhorse and pick up the bag when suddenly from out of nowhere a wild-eyed little man appeared. He gave me one stare, picked up my Black Bag, and dashed into the Palace. I was so startled that it was several minutes before I called to him to stop. Then I went dashing into the Palace after him. But the little man was nowhere to be seen. I hurried to Dorothy's rooms, and she accompanied me to the throne room. Just as we entered the throne room, the little man whisked past us and was up the tower stairs that lead to my magic workroom."

"Did he have the Black Bag then?" asked Shaggy.

"No, that's the strange part of it. He did not," replied the Wizard. "He locked the tower door securely after him, so Dorothy and I couldn't follow. We have searched everywhere, but there just is not a single trace of the Black Bag."

Twink and Tom listened, spellbound by the Wizard's story. Here they were — not only in the Emerald City of Oz, but in the midst of an adventure that excited even the famous Wizard of Oz!

"I just can't understand it," said the Wizard, rubbing his bald head in perplexity.

"Well, can't we break down the door to the tower?" asked Dorothy.

"Perhaps we could, but there are six other doors after that one before my magic workroom can be reached. And all are protected by my own magic!" groaned the Wizard.

"Are there no other magic tools that can be used?" inquired Shaggy.

"None," said the Wizard despondently. "Ozma took Dorothy's Magic Belt with her when she went to visit Glinda, so we are helpless for the moment.

Twiffle had been listening with great interest. Now he said, "Tell me, was the little man who suddenly appeared quite fat and bald save for a fringe of white hair? And did he have blue eyes and a sort of cherry-like nose?"

"Why, yes, that describes him quite well, from the glimpse I had of him," said the Wizard thoughtfully.

"I think," Twiffle went on calmly, "that if you had had the opportunity to observe him more closely, you would have seen that he wore on his wrist Ozma's Magic Compass!"

Chapter 22 - Conjo in Control

"Conjo!" exclaimed the Shaggy Man. *"Of course that's who it is. He used Ozma's Magic*
Compass to bring him to the Emerald City and then started his mischief!"

"I wonder what he wants, what his purpose is in hiding my Black Bag and then locking himself in the tower," mused the Wizard.

"Perhaps," said Dorothy, "It would be a good thing it Twiffle told us all he knows about this Conjo, since he seems to be better acquainted with him than anyone else is."

"A good idea," agreed the Wizard, and they all turned to Twiffle. The little clown recounted his life with Conjo, telling all he could remember from the time when Conjo brought him to life to his escape with Shaggy and Twink and Tom in the Airmobile. The Wizard considered. "Apparently the only really bad thing Conjo has done is to take these children out of their home and plan to make them prisoners. Outside of that he has been merely selfish, lazy, and foolishly vain. Perhaps if we tried to talk with him we could prove the folly of his latest actions. He must know that as soon as Ozma returns he will be helpless before her fairy powers."

The Wizard led the way to Ozma's Grand Throne Room, on one side of which was the door that led to the tower and Magic Workroom. The young beavers and their King hurried along after the Wizard and Shaggy and the rest. "Perhaps Conjo would listen to you," the Wizard suggested to Twiffle, "If you asked him to come out and talk with us."

Twiffle walked to the tower door, knocked as loudly as he could on it, and said, "Come out, Conjo. It is foolish of you to hide away in there. These people want to talk with you and try to be your friends."

Everyone waited with hushed breath. Had Conjo heard? Would he come out? After a few moments the door opened a crack, then slowly farther and farther, until Conjo stood revealed in the doorway. The little man was quivering with excitement. "Yes," Conjo said with what was meant to be a smile, "I will talk to you. But don't any one of you come one step nearer to this door. If you do, I will transform you all into doormats and jumping jacks."

"What do you want?" asked the Wizard quietly. "Why have you hidden my Black Bag of Magic Tools and shut me off from my Magic Workroom?"

"You should be able to figure that out," replied Conjo. "I had to do that to render you helpless. Without your magic you are powerless to defend yourselves. I now have at my command all of your magic as well as my own. So I rather think you will be glad enough to do as I say."

"And just what is that?" asked the Wizard.

"From now on," said Conjo, "I am the Wizard of Oz, and you," Conjo pointed to the Wizard, "are my assistant."

Dorothy gasped at the audacity of the little man, while the Shaggy Man laughed aloud. The Wizard could only whisper unbelievingly, "You want to be me?"

"No," said Conjo, who seemed relaxed now and enjoying the consternation he had caused, "I want to be the Wizard of Oz — it's only a title, you know, and I deserve it just as much as you. I'm tired of being a wizard nobody knows about. Now I have all your magic, so who is there to say I am not the Wizard of Oz? Ho, ho, ho, ha, ha, he, he, he!" The little man seemed vastly amused.

"Ozma will have something to say about this," said Dorothy indignantly. "If you think she'll let you come in here and steal all the Wizard's magic and then try to steal his name on top of all that, you're very badly mistaken."

"I'll take care of Ozma when the time comes. After all, she's only a girl," said Conjo easily. "And now, if you'll excuse me, I think I'll go up and study the Wizard's magic. Please set a place for me at dinner; I shall be quite hungry. And don't bother to look for the Wizard's Black Bag. You'll never find it. Ha, ha, ha, ho, ho, he, he, he!"

Conjo was about to close the door when the King of the Fairy Beavers raised his beechwood wand. From the tip of it came a stream of water that played directly on Conjo's face. Conjo gasped and sputtered, opened his mouth to cry out, and the stream of water filled his mouth. He choked and swallowed a large amount of the water. Immediately the stream ceased flowing from the beaver King's wand. Conjo stared at them all with innocent wonder in his eyes.

"Where am I?" he said.

Chapter 23 - Twiffle Says Goodbye

Conjo wandered from the doorway of the tower toward the Wizard and his friends. "Do you know who I am?" he asked the Wizard amiably. Then the fat little man saw the young beavers. He immediately seated himself on the floor and called to the animals to play with him.

"I think his Majesty, the King of the Fairy Beavers, can explain what has happened to Conjo," said the Wizard.

"It is very simple," replied the beaver King. "As I have told you, I am proficient in water magic. So when I saw that Conjo could not be talked out of his mischievousness and that he meant further trouble, I directed a stream of water through my Fairy Wand toward Conjo. The water came from Ozma's Fountain of Oblivion."

"Then Conjo has forgotten all his bad ways and all his magic powers?" asked Dorothy.

"Yes," replied the beaver King. "He is now as harmless as a child. The water of the Fountain of Oblivion is truly wonderful. With Ozma's gracious permission I shall take a quantity of it back to my kingdom with me when I return."

"You have the permission now, your Majesty," said a girlish voice.

All eyes turned to the throne from which the voice came. There sat Ozma, regarding them with a quiet smile. "I returned only a moment ago," Ozma said, "just in time to see the outcome of Conjo's ambitious schemes and to grant the request of our good friend the King of the Fairy Beavers. I am sure he will use the water from the Fountain of Oblivion wisely and well."

"Then you know all about our adventures?" asked the Shaggy Man.

"Yes," replied Ozma. "Glinda and I finished our tasks on which we have been working steadily, and only a few minutes ago we hurried to open Glinda's Great Book of Records and brought ourselves up to date on what has happened to you, Shaggy, and your friends, as well as the events transpiring here in the Emerald City during my absence. Now that we are together, I am happy to greet all my friends old and new," Ozma concluded, smiling at Twink and Tom.

The Wizard stepped to the side of Conjo, who was still seated on the throne room floor prattling to the beavers. He reached down and unfastened from Conjo's wrist Ozma's Magic Compass. The Girl Ruler received the magic instrument gravely, her eyes upon Conjo. "I wonder," she said, "what we should do with him. He is quite harmless now, but we don't want him to learn his old, bad ways again."

Here Twiffle stepped forward. "Your Highness," the little clown began, "if I may make a suggestion. I have known Conjo longer than anyone else here. He is not really a bad man. His threats are worse than his deeds. Most of the time he is quite jovial and pleasant. He loves his magic and his wizardry and wants to show off. Now that he has a chance to begin all over again, if he learned everything again except vanity and if he had the right guide, I believe it is possible that he might become a good wizard."

"And you want to be that guide," said Ozma, smiling kindly at Twiffle. "What do you think, Wizard?"

"I believe Twiffle is right," said the Wizard. "Conjo needs someone to help him now, and Twiffle seems the person to do it."

"I am very fond of my old home on the island, and I would like to help Conjo," said Twiffle simply.

"For my part, Twiffle is a brick," put in the Shaggy Man heartily.

"Then it is decided," replied Ozma. "I will use the Magic Belt to send Conjo and Twiffle back to the Isle of Conjo. There Twiffle will help Conjo to become a thoroughly good wizard. Here, Twiffle," Ozma removed a small golden ring from her finger and handed it to Twiffle. "Keep this ring with you always. Should Conjo ever again cause any mischief, or should you need any help, just rub this ring and you will be transported immediately to wherever I may be."

"Thank you, your Majesty," said Twiffle, looking at Ozma gratefully.

Twiffle then bade a fond farewell to Twink and Tom, the Shaggy Man, the King of the Fairy Beavers, and all his other new friends. When he had finished, Ozma placed her hands on the Magic Belt and murmured a command.

Twink and Tom looked about the throne room. Conjo and Twiffle were nowhere to be seen. The children knew they would miss the little toy clown. But perhaps he would come to their home sometimes to visit his third cousin, Twoffle.

Chapter 24 - Twink and Tom in Oz

The remainder of the day was given over to sightseeing for Twink, Tom, the King of the Fairy Beavers, and the young beavers. Dorothy and the Shaggy Man loaded the party into the Red Wagon, which was drawn by the Sawhorse, and conducted their guests on a tour of the beautiful City of Emeralds and the nearby countryside. When they reached the gates of the Emerald City, the Shaggy Man ordered the Sawhorse to stop while he, with the aid of Omby Amby, a bright new nail and a hammer, proudly restored the Love Magnet to its position over the entrance to the city. The company then drove out to call on Miss Cuttenclip and her famous village whose inhabitants were artfully cut out of magic paper and moved about and talked like living people. Next they visited Professor Wogglebug in his College, where the students learned their lessons by swallowing sugar-coated pills.

On the return journey they met the Scarecrow, who had been spending the day with a Munchkin Farmer for the purpose of being restuffed with fresh new straw — all except his head, of course, which was filled with the marvelous brains the Wizard had given him. Twink and Tom were delighted with this droll personage, who took an instant liking to them.

That evening there was a great dinner in honor of Twink, Tom and the King of the Fairy Beavers. Many of the most famous personages of Oz were there. Among these were the Patchwork Girl, the Tin Woodman — who had traveled from his tin castle in the Winkie country for the occasion — Princess Ozana, the Cowardly Lion and the Hungry Tiger, Ojo, Button Bright, Betsy Bobbin, Trot, Cap'n Bill, the Woozy, and many, many others.

It was a wonderful dinner, and Twink and Tom were fascinated by all the curious and unusual personalities. The twins felt as if they were among old friends, since they had read so much about the famous people of Oz and their exciting adventures. On such occasions as this it was always the custom of the Wizard to put on a display of his magic. Tonight he did not. In fact, the Little Wizard seemed silent and worried throughout the dinner. As the guests began to leave the table, the Wizard approached Ozma unhappily. "I can't imagine what Conjo did with my Black Bag of Magic Tools," he said. "We should have questioned him before you sent him back to the Isle of Conjo."

Ozma shook her head. "That would have done no good. Conjo lost all memory of his former actions when he drank of the waters of the Fountain of Oblivion."

The only others remaining around the table now were Dorothy, Shaggy, Twink, Tom and the beaver King. "Did you look in the Magic Picture to see where Conjo might have hidden the Black Bag?" Ozma asked.

"No," said the Wizard. "We were so excited and things happened so swiftly that we never thought of the Magic Picture."

"Then let us consult the picture immediately," said Ozma. The Girl Ruler rose and motioned the rest to follow her as she made her way to her suite of rooms and the Magic Picture.

Chapter 25 - The Black Bag of Magic Tools

Ozma swept the velvet drape from the Magic Picture. There was the familiar scene that appeared when the Picture was not in use: a peaceful Oz countryside with rolling fields and hills and a large tree growing in the foreground. "Show us the Wizard's Black Bag of Magic Tools," Ozma said.

There was no change in the picture. "What can be wrong?" whispered Dorothy soberly.

"Perhaps the Magic Picture can only show people and not things," suggested the Shaggy Man. "I don't recall our ever having asked it to show an object before."

Ozma's face was puzzled. She was staring intently at the familiar picture. "No," she said quietly. "I think the Magic Picture is doing its best to show us the Black Bag right now." Everyone looked at Ozma in astonishment. There was nothing in the Magic Picture that looked anything like the Black Bag. It was merely the old familiar scene that the magic picture showed when it was not in use. "Conjo was very clever in a way," said Ozma. "He hid the Black Bag by means of his wizard powers in a place where few people would think to look. But he forgot that the Magic Picture is my own fairy creation, and I understand its magic better than anyone else."

The Little Ruler paused, saying to those around her. "Watch this closely, now." She murmured a fairy charm so softly that none of the group could distinguish the words. Something was moving in the Magic Picture. From behind the trunk of the tree that arose in the foreground of the picture slipped a small, black object. It grew larger and larger until it filled a quarter of the picture. Then it fell out of the picture frame to the floor. It was the Wizard's Black Bag of Magic Tools!

The Little Wizard leaped forward and gratefully seized his precious Black Bag. "So Conjo hid it behind the tree in the Magic Picture!" he exclaimed.

Chapter 26 - Twink and Tom Home Again

"It is growing quite late," Ozma said, turning to Twink and Tom, "and I am sure you children must be tired after the strenuous adventures of the day." The Little Ruler paused and then added, "I know, too, that you are anxious to return home to your parents."

Twink nodded. "Yes, your Highness," she said. "We have had a wonderful time in Oz, and we love you all very dearly, but we must go home as soon as we can."

"Twink's right," agreed Tom. "We have had a great time, and I wouldn't have missed it for anything, but we belong at home in Buffalo."

Ozma smiled her most charming smile. "Very well," she said. "We will say goodbye now. Then Dorothy and the Shaggy Man will show you to your room, where beds are prepared for you. While you sleep, I will use the Magic Belt to transport you to your beds in your own home." Twink and Tom bade goodnight and goodbye to Ozma and the King of the Fairy Beavers. The little animal had accepted Ozma's invitation to be her guest as long as he felt he could absent himself from his Kingdom. Then Dorothy and the Shaggy Man led Twink and Tom to one of the most beautiful sleeping rooms the children had ever seen. The four talked together for a short time, after which Dorothy and Shaggy said farewell and slipped quietly from the room.

It had been a long, exciting day, and Twink and Tom had no difficulty falling asleep, although they knew that sometime during the night they would travel magically from the Land of Oz to their own beds in their home in far-away Buffalo.

And that was just what happened.

The End